100 PAR

An
Encyclopaedia
of
Philosophy

An
Encyclopaedia
of
Philosophy

GENERAL EDITOR

G.H.R. Parkinson

ASSOCIATE EDITORS

T.E. Burke
J.G. Cottingham
M.A. Proudfoot
J.E. Tiles

ROUTLEDGE

First published in 1988
Reprinted in 1989 and 1993
by Routledge
11 New Fetter Lane
London EC4P 4EE

© 1988 Routledge

Reprinted in 1996

Printed and bound in Great Britain by
Mackays of Chatham PLC, Chatham, Kent
Printed on acid free paper

British Library Cataloguing in Publication Data

An Encyclopaedia of philosophy.
    1. Philosophy
I. Parkinson, G.H.R.   II. Burke, T.E.
100   B72

ISBN 0-415-00323-7

Contents

Contents

Contents

Preface

This encyclopaedia of philosophy is intended for a very wide audience. It is intended for the general reader, who wants to know what philosophy is; for the sixth-former, who may have experienced for the first time the fascination of the problems of philosophy and who may be thinking about studying the subject at a university; and for university students of philosophy who want a general map of the various regions of philosophy that picks out the important features and relates them to each other. Finally, although this encyclopaedia is not a reference work for the specialist, it is hoped that it may be of some use to teachers of philosophy, who may find it helpful from time to time to see how their own special area of interest is related to other areas.

An encyclopaedia, by its nature, should aim at being comprehensive; but comprehensiveness has to be weighed against two other factors – size (which also means expense) and intelligibility. A one-volume encyclopaedia, such as this is, could achieve a fair measure of comprehensiveness, but the material that it contained would have to be compressed. Such an encyclopaedia would be useful only to someone who already has some knowledge of the subject, or who wants to pick up bits of information – the exact title of a book, perhaps, or a date. The present encyclopaedia, however, is meant to give its readers some understanding of philosophy, and this means that limits have had to be placed on its scope. It has been decided that it should be an encyclopaedia of contemporary philosophical thought, an account of the current state of philosophical thinking. This does not mean that the history of the subject will be neglected. It is my belief that current philosophical problems have their roots in the past, and can best be understood by tracing them back to those roots. But there will be no discussion of issues that belong wholly to the past.

There is another restriction on the scope of this encyclopaedia. One of the most striking features of recent Western philosophical thought is the existence within it of two broad traditions, which are commonly called the continental and the Anglo-Saxon traditions. The continental tradition is by no means confined to the continent of Europe, but has many adherents in America; it descends from a method of inquiry known as phenomenology, expounded in the first instance by Brentano and Husserl, and developed by (among others) Heidegger and Merleau-Ponty. More recently, some continental philosophers have found inspiration in 'structuralist' methods of inquiry drawn from linguistics; others have moved on from structuralism, though in what direction is not wholly clear. The Anglo-Saxon tradition goes back to the British empiricists of the seventeenth and eighteenth centuries – to Locke, Berkeley and Hume – but it is not restricted to philosophers of the English-speaking world; it has also taken root in continental Europe, particularly in West Germany and in the Scandinavian countries. Now, there is nothing new in the coexistence of different philosophical traditions; what is new and disturbing is the fact that, in the main, the attitude of these two traditions towards one another is one of mutual incomprehension. Attempts have been made, and are being made, to end this state of affairs, but it cannot be said that they have had much success. Most of the contributors to this book are firmly within the Anglo-Saxon tradition, and it seemed to me that an attempt to deal adequately with the continental tradition would add considerably to the length and difficulty of the encyclopaedia. I have therefore decided, with regret, to omit those parts of the continental tradition that have made little or no impact on the Anglo-Saxon tradition. For similar reasons, no attempt will be made to give an account of oriental philosophy.

I have spoken of the aims and the limits of the encyclopaedia, and of its intended audience. It is now time to say something about the method of presentation, which is unusual for an encyclopaedia. An encyclopaedia is by its nature systematic; the question is, which method of systematisation suits the subject best? The method usually favoured by encyclopaedists is an alphabetical arrangement of a large number of articles of varying length. Some connection is established between these by means of cross-references. There are also usually a number of long articles of some generality, which provide a survey of important topics and point to more specific topics discussed elsewhere in the encyclopaedia. This is a long-established method of procedure, and when an encyclopaedia covers a wide range of disparate topics it is perhaps the best. The method adopted here, however, is different. As already mentioned, the aim of the book is to provide as it were a map of a whole region of thought – a map which will also provide some understanding of what it depicts. For this reason, the book is divided into just 37 chapters. Each of these covers one major area of philosophy, and taken together the chapters make up a survey of recent philosophical thought, within the limits that have just been explained. This is not to say that an alphabetical method of arrangement cannot also provide a survey; however, the connections between the various branches of philosophy are more clearly exhibited if one arranges the subject-matter by topic.

Although the chapters form a connected whole, the links between them are not strong. Each chapter is meant to be self-contained, so nothing prevents readers from turning first to those topics which they find most interesting. But I hope that readers, having picked out some chapters, will be led to read others, until a fairly complete picture of philosophy emerges. Each chapter of the book is followed by a select bibliography, which is meant to help readers to carry their studies further. Since a bare list of titles it not very helpful, the bibliographies also contain some elucidatory comments. Two other helps have been provided, one of which is a glossary of commonly used philosophical terms. The other is a chronological table of philosophy from 1600 to 1960. This encyclopaedia is not a history of philosophy, but, as I have said, it often refers to that history, and the chronological table is meant to relate the major philosophers and their most important works to each other and to the culture of their epoch.

Each chapter of the encyclopaedia is a survey, and a survey is of necessity made from some point of view. Although this encyclopaedia is in the main located within one tradition of philosophy, there are within that tradition many schools of thought, and no attempt has been made to select authors who belong to one and the same school. As general editor, my sole concern was to choose contributors who know their subject and can communicate their knowledge. Some initial planning was necessary to ensure that as far as possible all relevant topics were covered, and contributors were provided with a set of guidelines that had been drawn up by the general editor with the advice of his associates. But the relative weight to be given to the topics listed, and indeed their order and connection, were left to each author.

There remains the pleasant task of acknowledging the help that I have received as general editor of this work. In the first place, my thanks are due to all my fellow contributors. Special thanks are due to my colleagues in the Philosophy Department of the University of Reading – Edmund Burke, John Cottingham, Michael Proudfoot and Jim Tiles – who have not only written chapters and compiled bibliographies, but have also helped me greatly with their advice. Warm thanks are due, too, to the Secretary of the Philosophy Department, Miss Joan Morris, for much efficient work, calmly and cheerfully done. Finally, my thanks are due to Jonathan Price, reference books editor of Croom Helm Ltd, who first suggested to me the idea of this encyclopaedia.

G.H.R. Parkinson

1 | What is Philosophy?

G.H.R. Parkinson

In almost every university, in whatever countries universities are found, a subject called 'philosophy' is studied and taught. Almost every large library, almost every large bookshop has a section devoted to 'philosophy'. But what is this 'philosophy' that is taught and studied in universities? What is contained in books that are devoted to philosophical topics? This chapter will try to provide an answer.

It may already have been gathered that my concern here is with what is sometimes called 'academic' philosophy – the philosophy that is taught and studied in most universities and in some schools. When many people use the word 'philosophy' they do not use it in this sense. A businessman may talk about the philosophy of free enterprise; hairdressers may talk about the philosophy that underlies the way in which they style their customers' hair. What such people mean by 'philosophy' is roughly a general view of a subject; a view which in a way underlies what they do. Academic philosophy, too, involves general views. But it involves much more than these, and it is this 'much more' that earns it a place in institutions of higher education.

Since my concern is with academic philosophy, I will henceforth drop the prefix 'academic' and speak simply of 'philosophy'. What, then, is philosophy? The word has a long history, and in order to understand how it is now used one needs to have some knowledge of how it, and words related to it, have been used. As the word has its roots in the language of the ancient Greeks, it will be worth our while to begin with them. Literally, the Greek word *philosophia* means 'love of' (*philo-*) 'knowledge' (*sophia*). But how did the Greeks view this knowledge, this *sophia*? For many of them, what the philosopher sought was knowledge of almost any kind. For example, the Greek politician Solon once left Greece to travel and,

1

as we should now say, 'broaden his mind'; he is described as 'philosophising'. A Greek statesman of a later generation, Pericles, is represented as saying that the entire citizen body of Athens was engaged in philosophising.[1] But besides this broad sense of 'philosophy' there was also a narrower one, and in this sense relatively few people could be said to be philosophising. This is the sense that concerns us.

To see what this was, let us begin by looking at someone whom many regard as the very model of a philosopher – Socrates. When most people think of Socrates, they probably think of him as a person who combined a total lack of dogmatism with a probing intelligence; a person who went around the city of Athens asking awkward questions of important people and exposing their pretensions by showing that they did not have knowledge. This picture of Socrates is not inaccurate, but it is incomplete. To complete it, one needs to consider the aims that lay behind Socrates' questions. It is not an easy matter to assess these, because Socrates himself wrote nothing; our knowledge of his views depends entirely on the reports of other people. Still, what was written by our informants – and in particular by Plato, who knew Socrates personally, and by Plato's greatest pupil, Aristotle – makes it possible for us to be reasonably sure about Socrates' aims.

Let us begin by asking just what, according to Socrates, the people whom he criticised did not know. Socrates did not question their ability to give correct answers to questions such as 'Is this action impious?', 'Is this man brave?', 'Is this the action of a temperate person?' His objection to them was that if they were asked, 'What *reason* have you for answering as you do? *By virtue of what* is this act impious, or this man brave, or that man temperate?', then they did not know the answer. But it was precisely knowledge of this kind that Socrates thought most important.[2] Two generations later, Aristotle explained Socrates' aims by saying that he was looking for *definitions*;[3] more recent philosophers might say that he was seeking the correct *analysis* of concepts. The notion of analysis will meet us again; it needs refinement if it is to be satisfactory, but as a rough indication of what it means to call Socrates a philosopher – and indeed of what other philosophers have done, and still do – it has its use.

I have spoken about the aim of Socrates' inquiries; it remains to say something about his methods. The term 'Socratic method' has entered modern dictionaries, where it is defined as (for example) 'procedure by question and answer'. But not every series of questions and answers is an example of what Socrates did. The distinctive feature of Socrates' questions was the fact that they were directed at finding out whether the person questioned could give satisfactory reasons for the assertions that he made. In a word, Socrates' method of question and answer was a method of *argument*. The methods of argument that he used are not peculiar to philosophers; for example, Plato sometimes presents him[4] as using the method of argument known as 'reductio ad absurdum', which was also employed by Greek mathematicians. But the point is that he did argue, the aim of his arguments being a satisfactory account of the nature of (say) piety, bravery and temperance. In this respect, Socrates was entirely typical; the provision and examination of arguments are the hallmarks of the philosopher.

I said at the beginning of this chapter that there is more to philosophy than the statement of certain general views, and this account of Socrates' inquiries will, I hope, have shown something of the 'more' that is involved. But although Socrates was a great philosopher, his philosophical interests were restricted. He was concerned primarily with what is now called moral philosophy; more specifically, he was concerned with the problem of giving the right account of what the Greeks called the human virtues, such as piety and courage and temperance. But even before Socrates lived, Greek thinkers were concerning themselves with philosophical problems of another sort. Some of the slender knowledge that we have of these early Greek philosophers is due to Aristotle. The first book of his *Metaphysics* contains a survey of the views of earlier philosophers; in the course of this, Aristotle remarks that the first philosophers were interested (as Socrates was not) in 'the world of nature as a whole'.[5] The phrase 'as a whole' indicates that they were not concerned with this or that particular thing or event; their questions were of a more general character. Some of them asked the question, 'What, in the last analysis, are all things made of? This chair, say, is made of wood; but is wood itself a form of something which is more basic?' Others asked, 'Is there really only *one* thing that exists? That is, is plurality a mere illusion?'

I have said that these are questions for philosophy, but this could be challenged. The question 'What are all things made of?' is, a critic might say, the concern of the natural scientist. In this connection, it may be pointed out that the Greek thinkers in question – people such as Thales, Anaximander and Anaximenes – also appear in books about ancient Greek science.[6] Aristotle, for his part, would not have regarded natural science and philosophy as different in kind; for him, natural science was a branch of a wider discipline, philosophy.[7] However, he would have said that these early philosophers were engaged in inquiries which were not those of the natural scientist; they were engaged in a search for something more fundamental, a search for 'first principles' or 'original causes'.[8] Aristotle's name for this was 'first philosophy'; the term survived until at least the seventeenth century, but it has now been replaced by the term 'metaphysics'.

This is not the place for a more detailed discussion of Aristotle's views about the branches of philosophy; what matters here is what later philosophers made of these views. For the Catholic philosophers of the thirteenth century, Aristotle was *the* philosopher. On the basis of their reading of him, they came to divide philosophy into the three parts that have already been mentioned – metaphysics, moral philosophy and what

3

came to be called 'natural philosophy', i.e. natural science.[9] This view became deeply entrenched; so deeply, indeed, that it survived the attacks on Aristotle that were made in the seventeenth century. Seventeenth-century thinkers might believe that Aristotle's science was worthless, but they agreed with him that there was a place for science within philosophy. They agreed with him, too, that metaphysics is fundamental, in that it studies *first* principles, *first* causes. The scientist who has not thought about metaphysical issues has not pushed his inquiries as far as they can, and should, be pushed. This view of the nature of philosophy was stated forcefully by one of the chief exponents of the new science, Descartes. Philosophy, Descartes said, was like a tree, of which the roots are metaphysics and the trunk and branches are the various sciences.[10]

But although Descartes agreed with Aristotelian views about the main divisions of philosophy and the way in which they are related to each other, he introduced something new into philosophy – so new that modern philosophy is regarded as beginning with him. For Descartes, philosophy was still the search for knowledge; the important difference was that he operated with a standard of knowledge which was very stringent, and which led him to say that the reasons that many people had produced to justify their claims to knowledge were not good enough. Descartes' criterion of knowledge was simply this. For something to be known, it must be something that a rational agent cannot doubt; conversely, what a rational agent can doubt is not known. The exact reasons for which Descartes adopted this criterion are still a matter of controversy among scholars, and a full discussion of them would take us too far from our present inquiry. However, it seems likely that the following considerations may well have influenced him. Let us begin by considering the nature of doubt; more specifically, let us consider what it is to doubt *that* something is, was or will be the case. For convenience, we will abbreviate this to 'What it is to doubt that p'. Now, to say, 'I doubt that p' is in a way an expression of caution, of holding back. One does not go so far as to say that it is false that p, but one does say or imply that the reasons brought in support of the assertion that p are not good enough; they leave open the possibility that p is false. Suppose now that someone – say, X – claims to know that p, and suppose that it is also possible to doubt that p. Descartes would say that in such a case, X does not have the knowledge that he claims to have. His argument may be this. It is agreed that it can be doubted that p, and this implies that it can be false that p. Now, suppose that at some time it is discovered that it *is* false that p. In such a case, all that one can properly say is that X used (wrongly) to believe that p; one cannot properly say, 'X used to know that p, but proved to be mistaken.' So if one is really to know that p, it must not be possible for one at some time to take back one's assertion that p. That is, there must be no possibility of one's being wrong; the very possibility of doubt must be excluded.

4

This view about the condition that knowledge must satisfy may seem to be abstract and barren, but in fact it turned out to be very fruitful – though whether the fruits were altogether good is another matter. Armed with his criterion of knowledge, Descartes set out to discover which of the things that he formerly thought he knew, he really did know. He was especially concerned with the question, 'What do I know about what exists?' and in the course of his inquiries he found that many claims to knowledge were insecurely based. Suppose, for example, that someone claims to know that material things exist, and bases that claim entirely on the evidence of his senses. Such a person, Descartes would say, does not have knowledge. For he can be wrong; human beings are subject to sense-illusions, and human beings have dreams. It is important not to misunderstand Descartes here. He is not implying that the existence of material things cannot be known; what he is saying is that if it is to be known, it must be placed beyond the possibility of doubt.

In fact, although Descartes rejected many claims to knowledge, he believed that there were many things that he did know about what exists. The first of these was that he existed as a thinking being. His reasoning was that his own existence was something that he could not doubt, at any rate for as long as he thought about the matter. For in asking whether or not he cannot be wrong about his own existence, he is thinking, and thought implies the existence of a thinker. This is the force of Descartes' famous assertion, 'Cogito, ergo sum' – 'I am thinking, therefore I exist.' But *what* is this 'I' that the thinker knows to exist? Not, Descartes said, a physical body; for I know that I exist as a thinking being before I know that material things of any kind exist. So we should expand the 'sum' of 'Cogito, ergo sum' into 'Sum res cogitans' – 'I exist as a thinking being.'

Once again, this may seem unexciting; but its implications were far-reaching. In Descartes' view every thinking being, every mind, has what he called 'ideas'. The word 'idea', as a technical term of philosophy, has a history which goes back as far as Plato. However, the history of the word does not concern us here, because Descartes claimed that he used the word 'idea' in a new sense.[11] For him, ideas are thoughts of a certain kind; they are 'as it were the images of things'.[12] Such an idea is private to the person who has it, and it is something that that person cannot be wrong about. To illustrate this, suppose that I look in a certain direction and say, on the basis of what appears to me, 'There is a cat in my chair.' As we have seen, Descartes would say that I cannot claim to know, on the basis of the evidence of my senses alone, that there really is a cat in my chair; I could be wrong. But there can be no doubt that it looks to me as if there is a cat in the chair; this is something that I cannot be wrong about. That is, Descartes would have said, I know that I have an idea of the cat, and furthermore I know what the features of that idea are, in that I know that what appears to me is cat-shaped and cat-coloured. This is only one illustration of what Descartes

5

means by an 'idea'; one should add that it is not only sense-perception that involves ideas. Descartes argued that whenever we think, or whenever we make a decision about something, ideas are present to us, and about these ideas we cannot be wrong.

It can now perhaps be seen why Descartes is thought to have initiated a new era in philosophy. With his insistence that what we know is what we cannot doubt, Descartes was led to view the existence and nature of physical things as a problem, a problem whose solution demands a reference to those 'ideas' of which he spoke. So philosophers after Descartes took the view that they ought to look within themselves at those private entities about whose existence and nature there could be no doubt. They believed, too, that they ought to discover the way in which these ideas are related to the world outside and how, in knowing that world, we operate on our ideas. In other words they were concerned not just with ideas, but also with the operations of the mind. But these operations, like the ideas on which they operated, were internal and private.

This view of the nature of philosophy was shared by many philosophers who came after Descartes; it was shared (to mention only a few important names from the seventeenth and eighteenth centuries) by Locke, Berkeley, Hume and Kant. Philosophy was seen as being, or at any rate as involving, a kind of psychology, a study of the ideas that the mind has and of the ways in which it operates on its ideas. This is not to say that the old questions were neglected. Philosophers still analysed concepts, still discussed the goodness or badness of the reasons that people brought for their assertions. What was distinctive was the fact that such discussions were linked with a kind of philosophical psychology; a psychology in which no experiments were made, but in which people just looked within themselves.

It is perhaps only in the present century that this view of philosophy has been widely rejected. But there were already stirrings of revolt in the first half of the nineteenth century. This revolt was associated with the distinctive kind of metaphysics put forward in Germany by Hegel, whose major works were published between 1807 and his death in 1831. Hegel believed that everything is mind; not minds and matter, as Descartes and Locke had believed, and not a collection of minds, as Berkeley had believed, but mind – *one* mind. Stated baldly, the idea might seem to be wild in the extreme, but in fact it contains a kernel of sound sense. Hegel was trying to get away from the idea that philosophy is a study of private entities and private activities. Instead, he saw philosophy as studying ways of thinking – sometimes the ways of thinking of a whole group of people, and sometimes of an entire society; and there is nothing private about these. These ways of thinking, Hegel argued, do not exist in isolation from one another. Rather, they are connected, in that each of them tries to correct the deficiencies of some other, until one reaches a stage at which all errors have been put right, and human thought forms a single rational whole. The

6

philosopher's job is to bring out the structure that underlies this constant process of the correction of faulty views. Because of philosophy's connection with the structure of thought, Hegel said that philosophy is logic; but he also insisted that it is intimately connected with the way in which thought develops. In short, philosophy is essentially historical.

One may have one's doubts about Hegel's view that thought is developing towards an end-state of total rationality; all the same, there is much that is sound in Hegel's insistence that philosophy is a kind of logic, and that it is also a historical study. Unhappily, Hegel's metaphysical views about the nature of reality blinded his critics to the importance of what he had to say about the nature of philosophy. The result was that the attack on the idea that philosophy is a study of private entities and activities had to be renewed after Hegel's death. The new attack was made early in the twentieth century by philosophers who were hostile to Hegel, and who were associated with a different view of the nature of philosophy – namely, the view that the business of the philosopher is analysis. In Britain, the attack on Hegelianism was led by Bertrand Russell and G.E. Moore. Of the two, it is perhaps Moore who is more closely associated with the view that philosophy is analysis, but even more important in this connection was Ludwig Wittgenstein, who studied for a time under Russell. It was perhaps Wittgenstein, more than anyone else, who made philosophers think about the nature of their activities. His first major work was his *Logisch-philosophische Abhandlung*, published in German in 1921; an English translation, entitled *Tractatus logico-philosophicus*, appeared in the next year. Wittgenstein saw that philosophers were faced with a new problem; one might even say, a crisis. This crisis had to do with the rapid development, and the increasing independence, of the natural sciences. I mentioned earlier that for many centuries science had been regarded as a branch of philosophy, and that it was thought to be the business of the philosopher to provide a basis for what the scientist did. Increasingly, however, scientists felt no need of philosophy; they had their own methods of acquiring knowledge of reality, and they regarded such methods as self-sufficient. What, then, was left for philosophy? In the *Tractatus*, Wittgenstein argued that philosophers must abandon all claims to make pronouncements about the nature of reality; that is, they must abandon metaphysics. Our only way of finding out how things are is by means of the natural sciences; indeed, only the utterances of the natural sciences strictly speaking say anything.[13] It was also necessary to abandon the idea that philosophy is a kind of psychology, an inspection of private entities and processes. Philosophy, Wittgenstein argued, is not one of the natural sciences, and has no more to do with psychology than with any other science.[14]

What, then, is philosophy? Wittgenstein replied that philosophy is an activity, and that this activity is the clarification of thoughts.[15] This clarification of thoughts – commonly called 'analysis' or 'philosophical analysis' – itself stands in need of clarification. The problem is that clarity seems to be a relative matter, in that what may be clear to one person may not be clear to another. For Wittgenstein, however, and for many other analytical philosophers, clarity was something absolute. These philosophers believed that ordinary language often disguises the structure of our thought. Take, for example, what are called 'universal propositions', such as the assertion 'All Greeks are human.' This sentence, Bertrand Russell argued, is misleading, in that it gives the impression that the person making the assertion is committed to the belief that Greeks exist. In fact, Russell argued, one should express the proposition as 'For all x, if x is Greek, then x is human.' We need not stop to ask whether or not Russell was right; it is sufficient to have seen what he was trying to do – namely, to make clear what ordinary language leaves obscure, by translating ordinary language into one which is logically adequate. Wittgenstein, for his part, believed that we are not yet in possession of such a language; nevertheless, a logically adequate language was a possibility, and valuable work had been done on its foundations by logicians such as Frege and Russell. Their logic, or at any rate an improved version of it, would provide the structure of such a language.

From what I have said, it can be seen that language plays an important part in the conception of philosophy contained in the *Tractatus logico-philosophicus*; indeed, Wittgenstein remarked that all philosophy is a critique of language.[16] This view has been dominant in the philosophy of this century; however, it would be wrong to suppose that this has been the only answer to the view that philosophy is concerned with what exists and occurs in the mind. One must not overlook a movement which has had a wide influence in France, Germany and the USA – the movement known as 'phenomenology'. The movement owes its name to Edmund Husserl (1859–1938). Broadly, Husserl thought that it was the philosopher's business to examine 'phenomena', in the sense of acts of consciousness and their immediate objects. Such phenomena could be known, and known infallibly. Superficially, this might seem to resemble what Descartes had said about 'ideas', but Husserl denied that he was turning philosophy into a kind of psychology. What are known, he said, are not ideas in Descartes' sense of the term, but 'essences', and these are accessible to more than one thinker. Critics object that it is not clear what these essences are, or why they should be supposed to exist. But whatever weaknesses it may have, phenomenology was an undoubted influence on the philosophy of the existentialists, and it is perhaps in this that its importance lies (cf. Chapter 28).

I noted above that the view that philosophy is the analysis of language has been dominant in the philosophy of this century. But the question 'Just what is analysis?' has received various answers. The idea that philosophy is essentially analysis was energetically defended in the 1930s by a group of philosophers who called themselves 'the Vienna Circle', but who are more widely known as 'logical positivists'. Though in no sense a Wittgensteinian school, they discussed his ideas among themselves, and their view of the nature of philosophy did not differ radically from that put forward in the *Tractatus logico-philosophicus*. They agreed with Wittgenstein that metaphysics is to be abandoned as meaningless, and that the business of the philosopher is clarification or analysis. They agreed, too, that this analysis consisted in the translation of the sentences of ordinary language into a logically adequate language, and that the structure of this language, broadly speaking, was provided by modern logic. But whereas Wittgenstein was elusive on the subject of the *content* of this logically adequate language, the logical positivists said that the language should consist of sentences which recorded actual or possible observations. They argued that a proposition had factual meaning if, and only if, it could be verified by the senses; this was, indeed, their chief weapon against metaphysics.

However, this view of the nature of philosophy changed, and it changed largely because of the later work of Wittgenstein himself. In his *Philosophical investigations*, published posthumously in 1953, Wittgenstein criticised the views that he had put forward in the *Tractatus*, and in the course of these criticisms he put forward a new view of the nature of philosophy. The new view was connected with a new theory about the nature of meaning. In the *Tractatus* Wittgenstein had said that the meaning of a basic word, i.e. of what he called a 'name', was the object for which it stood. In the *Philosophical investigations*, this view is rejected; to ask about the meaning of a word is not to ask about some entity, but is to ask about the rules in accordance with which the word is used. The meaning of a word, Wittgenstein said, is its use in a language – where by 'language' is meant not, say, English or French or German, but language in the sense in which one might speak of the language of carpentry, or bricklaying, or cookery, as well as of more abstract languages such as those of physics or mathematics. This view is discussed in greater detail in Chapter 2; what makes it important for our purposes is the fact that it was linked with a new view about the nature of philosophy. We have seen that, for the Wittgenstein of the *Tractatus* and for the logical positivists, the task of philosophical analysis was the translation of the utterances of ordinary language into an ideal language. But for the Wittgenstein of the *Philosophical investigations* there was no such thing as an ideal language; every sentence in our language, he said, 'is in order as it is'.[17] What, then, was the business of the philosopher? Early in the eighteenth century, Bishop Berkeley argued that many, and perhaps all, of the problems that have exercised philosophers are self-created: 'We have first raised a dust, and then complain we cannot see.'[18] This sentence might have served as a motto for the view of philosophy propounded in the *Philosophical investigations*. Philosophical problems, Wittgenstein argued, arise when people reflect on the rules that govern the use of words, and are misled by a false picture of the way in which language works. It is this that creates philosophical perplexity, and the business of the philosopher is to remove this perplexity by tracing it back to a false view about language. Our knowledge of other people's sensations may serve as an example. If I reflect on the reasons which I have for describing other people as being (say) in pain, I may be led to wonder whether I can ever know that anyone other than myself is in pain. My line of reasoning might be this: I can never have direct access to another person's sensations, but always have to infer those sensations on the basis of observed behaviour. This need to infer something that is never directly accessible to me is what causes the difficulty; for how can I ever be sure that I have inferred correctly? Wittgenstein would reply that a person who argues in this way has a wrong picture of the way in which the words 'is in pain' function, or, less metaphorically, that he has failed to grasp the rules that govern the use of the words. Briefly,[19] Wittgenstein would say that the person in question believes that the words 'is in pain' refer to a private inner state, which is not in fact the way in which the words function. Once the false picture has been removed and replaced by a correct one, the philosophical perplexity disappears.

Wittgenstein's new way of viewing philosophy has influenced many philosophers. Such philosophers would still say that their business is analysis, but they would say that the analysis is of a different sort from that of the *Tractatus logico-philosophicus* or of the logical positivists. No longer does the philosopher try to make clear a logical structure that is concealed by ordinary language. The philosopher does indeed try to get a clear picture of the rules that govern our use of language, but the obstacles that stand in the way of such a picture do not come from ordinary language itself. Rather, they come from faulty thinking about language; in other words, from bad philosophy. The problems of the philosopher are self-generated: 'We have first raised a dust, and then complain we cannot see.' Someone may object that there is something inward-looking about philosophy of this sort; the sole business of the philosopher, it might seem, is to unravel the tangles made by other philosophers. The answer would be that we are all liable to philosophise badly; the errors about language that the Wittgensteinian philosopher tries to correct can be made by anyone.

One point must be emphasised. I have said that Wittgenstein wants to get a clear view of the workings of language. But this is not sought as an end in itself; it is sought as a means of getting rid of philosophical perplexity, of solving puzzles. So the task of the philosopher came to be compared to that of the psychoanalyst, who solves a patient's problems by getting the patient to bring clearly to mind what has happened in his or her past. There are, of course, important differences. The psychoanalyst is concerned with the patient's personal history; the Wittgensteinian philosopher is concerned not with people in their character as individuals, but with *ways of thinking* that are sources of perplexity. Still, the comparison has its point. But one does not have to accept the propriety of the comparison to accept the name 'analysis' for Wittgenstein's later philosophy. The original sense of the Greek word *analusis* was a loosening or releasing, and Wittgenstein certainly aimed at doing just that.

This new approach to philosophy constituted a radical break, not only with the kinds of philosophical analysis that immediately preceded it, but with most of preceding philosophy as a whole. To put the difference in a sentence: for very many philosophers, philosophy was something systematic, whereas for the later Wittgenstein and those who thought like him it was not. This notion of the systematic character of philosophy needs some clarification. When one speaks or hears of a philosophical system one tends to have in mind the great metaphysical systems, such as Hegel's *Encyclopaedia of the philosophical sciences*, which tried to present in an orderly way both what we now call philosophy and the natural sciences. But philosophical systems are not the work of metaphysicians alone. The logical positivists, too, thought that philosophy should be represented as a system, and some of them tried to compile an 'Encyclopaedia of Unified Science' which (like Hegel's *Encyclopaedia*, but in a very different way) was to present in systematic form both philosophy and the natural sciences. All such systems were rejected by the later Wittgenstein and his followers, on the grounds that they give a false picture of our language. The rules of a system, the argument ran, are rigid and relatively few, whereas the rules that govern ordinary language are so elastic and so numerous that no system can do justice to them.

The view of the nature of philosophy that Wittgenstein presented in the *Philosophical investigations* has been very influential, but it has also been subjected to severe criticism. These criticisms, it should be stressed, do not spring from any general hostility to the ideal of philosophical analysis as such; the objection is specifically to the Wittgensteinian conception of such analysis. One major target of criticism has been Wittgenstein's thesis that philosophy is by its very nature unsystematic. This thesis was attacked by a group of philosophers who were active in the 1950s. They defended what is commonly called 'ordinary language philosophy', and their leader was the Oxford philosopher J.L. Austin. Austin agreed with Wittgenstein in thinking that many of the errors of philosophers are self-induced; in particular, philosophers were at fault in trying to introduce new technical languages which they claimed to be better than ordinary language, but which were in fact inferior to it. Ordinary language, Austin argued, is a complex and delicate instrument that has been fashioned over centuries, and philosophers disregarded it at their peril. But whereas Wittgenstein was opposed to any systematisation, Austin believed that some systematisation, in the shape of a classification of some important ways in which sentences are used, was both possible and useful.

Ordinary language philosophy did not long survive the death of Austin in 1960; however, there were other critics of Wittgenstein whose views are still influential. The history of philosophy does not proceed in a straight line; it sometimes involves loops, when an earlier view is revived. Such a revival took place when the 'use theory' of meaning was followed by what is called the 'truth condition' theory. This theory (which will be discussed in detail in Chapter 3) was initially put forward by Frege; it was defended by Wittgenstein in the *Tractatus*, but was rejected by him in the *Philosophical investigations*. In its modern form, it is particularly associated with the American philosopher Donald Davidson, but many philosophers on both sides of the Atlantic have been involved in its elaboration and defence. The theory can be stated succinctly in the words of the *Tractatus*: 'To understand a proposition is to know what is the case if it is true.'[20] Take, for example, the sentence 'The cat is in the chair.' To grasp the meaning of this sentence is to know that the sentence is true if, and only if, a certain cat is in a certain chair. Put like this, the theory hardly seems earth-shaking, but interesting and difficult problems arise when it is asked whether this view of meaning can cover the whole of our language. The attempts to find the truth-conditions of all meaningful sentences form a highly technical part of recent philosophy, which uses the techniques of formal logic, and to which the name of 'semantics' is given. The question that concerns us is whether the truth-condition theory of meaning involves a change of view about the tasks and methods of the philosopher. The answer is that it does, though the view in question is not so much a new view as an old one revived. The business of the philosopher is still seen as analysis, but analysis in the sense in which it was understood by the Wittgenstein of the *Tractatus* and by the logical positivists: that is, the translation of the sentences of ordinary language into a preferred type of language. Analysis of this kind (unlike the analysis favoured by the later Wittgenstein) is highly systematic, and it gives back to formal logic the important position that it had in the philosophy of the *Tractatus* and of the logical positivists. But one should add that the truth-condition theory of meaning is not without its critics.

The question now to be considered is this. Let it be granted that at least some philosophy is analysis, in one or other of the senses of the word just explained; is it true to say that philosophy is *nothing but* analysis? We have seen that many philosophers thought this to be so; there are also many philosophers who still think it. However, this narrowness of outlook has come under increasing criticism, and it is noteworthy that among its critics are philosophers who have themselves made major contributions to philosophical analysis. One such philosopher is A.J. Ayer, who in his *Language, truth and logic*, published in 1936, made what has become a classical statement of the philosophy of the logical positivists. In that work, Ayer stated that the philosopher should 'confine himself to works of clarification and analysis'.[21] But in his more recent work Ayer has insisted that, although clarification forms part of philosophy, it is not the whole of it. The philosopher is concerned not just to make clear the meaning of what is said, but also to ask questions about its justifiability. Take, for example, the philosophy of science. The philosopher of science is indeed concerned with what it means to talk about a scientific law or a scientific theory. But, Ayer would add, the philosophy of science is not merely descriptive; it is also critical. Philosophers are concerned with the reasons for preferring one theory to another, when both seem to be in accord with the factual evidence. Again, when a theory is not in accordance with the evidence, philosophers are concerned with the question of whether it should be abandoned or merely modified. There are also important philosophical questions about the confirmation of scientific hypotheses by means of observations – questions which are linked with the problem of induction, which asks how it can be legitimate to move from a statement about *some* members of a certain class to a corresponding statement about *all* members of the class. Such inquiries, says Ayer, 'are not limited to the clarification of scientific procedures, but are concerned also with the question how they can be justified'.[22]

Ayer's change of attitude is just one example of a widespread movement in recent philosophy, a shift of interest from questions about meaning to questions about justification. This shift can be seen with particular clarity in recent political philosophy. As its name suggests, political philosophy has to do with questions about the relations between the state and the citizen. Classical political philosophers regarded these as questions about justification. Philosophers such as Plato, Aristotle, Hobbes, Locke, Rousseau and Hegel asked why there should be states – by which they meant, not how it was that political institutions came into being, but what could justify their existence. Some political philosophers were more concerned with the question of whether there are any moral limits on the power of the state; this often took the form of the question of whether there are any human rights which the state is morally obliged to respect. All these were questions of justification; however, under the impact of the analytical philosophy of the 1930s, questions of whether and to what extent political institutions could be justified fell into disrepute. All that the philosopher could do, it was argued, was to make clear the rules that govern the language of politics,[23] and it was seriously wondered whether the operation was of any great importance. Political philosophy, it used to be said, had a great past, but it was by no means certain that it had a future. In the last twenty years, however, political philosophers have returned to questions of justification. Demands for human rights in general, and for the rights of women and of various minorities in particular, are not new; but in recent years they have become insistent, and this has led philosophers to look afresh at the question of whether such demands can be justified. The demand for rights is part of a general demand for justice, and it is significant that one of the most important of recent works in the field of political philosophy, John Rawls' *A theory of justice* (1972), does not simply analyse the way in which people use the word 'justice', but asks what a just society *would be*.

This answer to the question 'What is philosophy?' has been very general; to give a fuller and more satisfactory answer to the question one needs to look more closely both at the questions which

13

philosophers ask, and at the answers which they give to these questions. Such a closer look will be provided by the chapters that follow; it only remains for me to make a few remarks about the present state of philosophy, as I see it. J.L. Austin once suggested, as a motto for a 'sober philosophy', the maxim 'Neither a be-all nor an end-all be.'[24] Austin's philosophy is not as influential as it once was, but there is a case for saying that much current philosophy does display sobriety of the kind that Austin recommended. The age of the philosophical be-all, in the sense of the builder of definitive and all-inclusive metaphysical systems, is past. But so, too, is the age of the end-all, in the sense of those who (like the logical positivists) thought that they were in possession of some general principle which would rule out of court as meaningless whole regions of human discourse, such as the language of the metaphysician or of the religious person. The age is one of philosophical tolerance, in the sense of a readiness to admit that the utterances which philosophers examine do at least make sense. At the same time, the tolerance is not boundless, in that the philosopher asks, 'Granted that this makes sense, what justification is there for asserting it?'

It also seems to me (and here I recognise that my views are more controversial) that the present age is one in which the history of philosophy has come to regain some of the importance that it had for Hegel. In the heyday of philosophical analysis – say, in the 1950s and 1960s – philosophers tended to view the history of their subject as relatively unimportant. The problems of philosophy were seen very much in the way in which scientists and mathematicians see their problems: what matters is what has been written by those working on the subject most recently, and perhaps by a few others who happened to be ahead of their time. This does not mean that the history of philosophy was wholly neglected, nor would it be fair to say that, when the works of past philosophers were discussed, they were seen only as a storehouse of fallacies. But even when the philosophers of the past were credited with correct views, there was no suggestion that the modern philosopher might learn from the past; no suggestion that past philosophers gave support to, or threw light on, the views of their successors. They merely happened to agree with modern views; those views were in no way made more secure, or even more intelligible, by what had been said in the past. Today, however, there is an increasing tendency to believe that we can fully understand the problems that we pose only if we see how we came to pose them, and this involves a serious study of the past. So, in trying to give an account in this chapter of the nature of philosophy, I have found it necessary to consider the ways in which the philosophers of the past have viewed their task. I do not suggest that such an attitude is shared by all contributors to this encyclopaedia, but I believe that its influence can be detected in much of the work.[25]

14

Notes

(An author's name followed by a number in square brackets refers to the book or article which has that number in the bibliography.)

1. Solon: see Herodotus, *History*, I, 30. Pericles: see Thucydides, *History of the Peloponnesian War*, II, 40.

2. Plato, *The apology of Socrates*, 22d.

3. Aristotle, *Metaphysics*, A 6, 987 b1–4. Cf. M 4, 1078 b17ff.

4. E.g. Plato, *Republic*, I, 331–6.

5. Aristotle, *Metaphysics*, A 6, 987 b2 (trans. W.D. Ross).

6. E.g. Benjamin Farrington, *Science in antiquity* (Thornton Butterworth, London, 1936), pp. 33–50.

7. Aristotle, *Metaphysics*, E 1, 1026 a18.

8. 'First principles': *Metaphysics*, A 2, 982 a26. 'Original causes': ibid., A 3, 983 a24.

9. Cf. N. Kretzmann, A. Kenny and J. Pinborg (eds), *The Cambridge history of later medieval philosophy* (Cambridge University Press, Cambridge, 1982), p. 521.

10. Preface to *The principles of philosophy* (French version). See *The philosophical writings of Descartes*, trans. J. Cottingham, R. Stoothoff and D. Murdoch (Cambridge University Press, Cambridge, 1985), vol. I, p. 186.

11. *Replies to third objections*, ibid., vol. II, pp. 127–8.

12. *Meditations*, III, ibid., vol. II, p. 25.

13. *Tractatus logico-philosophicus* (Routledge, London, 1961), 6.53.

14. Ibid., 4.111, 4.1121.

15. Ibid., 4.112.

16. Ibid., 4.0031.

17. *Philosophical investigations* (Blackwell, Oxford, 1953), I, para. 98 (p. 45).

18. Berkeley, *Principles of human knowledge*, Introduction, para. 3.

19. *Philosophical investigations*, I, paras. 243–50 (pp. 88–90).

20. *Tractatus logico-philosophicus*, 4.024.

21. Ayer [16], p. 69.

22. A.J. Ayer, *The central questions of philosophy* (Pelican Books, Harmondsworth, 1976), p. 45; cf. pp. 50, 57.

23. Typical of this trend of thought is a book by T.D. Weldon, *The vocabulary of politics* (Pelican Books, Harmondsworth, 1953).

24. J.L. Austin, 'Pretending' in J.L. Austin, *Philosophical papers*, 2nd edn (Oxford University Press, Oxford, 1970), p. 271n.

25. I am grateful to my colleague Dr J.G. Cottingham for helpful comments on an earlier draft of this chapter, and on the introductions to the six parts of the encyclopaedia.

Bibliography

Socrates

A helpful introduction to Socrates is provided by

[1] W.K.C. Guthrie, *The Greek philosophers from Thales to Aristotle* (Methuen, London, 1950), pp. 71–80.

At a more advanced level, see e.g.

[2] W.K.C. Guthrie, *A history of Greek philosophy*, vol. III: *The fifth century enlightenment* (Cambridge University Press, Cambridge, 1969). Part Two: *Socrates* (published separately as a paperback, Cambridge University Press, Cambridge, 1971). See especially pp. 325–77, 417–49.

[3] G. Vlastos (ed.), *The philosophy of Socrates* (Doubleday, New York, 1971). See especially: (a) G. Vlastos, 'Introduction: the paradox of Socrates' (pp. 1–21); (b) A.R. Lacey, 'Our knowledge of Socrates' (pp. 22–49).

Aristotle

Aristotle's views about philosophy are best studied in the context of his discussions of philosophical problems. Two excellent introductions to his philosophy are

[4] J.L. Ackrill, *Aristotle the philosopher* (Oxford University Press, Oxford, 1981).

[5] Jonathan Barnes, *Aristotle* (Past Masters, Oxford University Press, Oxford, 1982).

Descartes

A short and clear account of Descartes' views, and of their relation to modern philosophy in general, is to be found in

[6] Roger Scruton, *From Descartes to Wittgenstein. A short history of modern philosophy* (Routledge and Kegan Paul, London, 1981), pp. 13–49.

Helpful discussions of Descartes' 'method of doubt' (his critical application of his criteria of knowledge) are provided by

[7] Anthony Kenny, *Descartes: a study of his philosophy* (Random House, New York, 1968), pp. 14–39.

[8] Margaret Dauler Wilson, *Descartes* (Routledge, London, 1978), pp. 1–49.

More advanced students should also consult the subtle and complex account given by

[9] Bernard Williams, *Descartes: the project of pure enquiry* (Penguin Books, Harmondsworth, 1978), pp. 32–71.

Hegel

There are several introductions to the thought of this difficult philosopher. The shortest, and one of the clearest, is

[10] Peter Singer, *Hegel* (Past Masters, Oxford University Press, Oxford, 1983).

What is Philosophy?

Russell and Moore

[11] A.J. Ayer, *Russell and Moore, the analytical heritage* (Macmillan, London, 1971). See especially Chapters 1 and 9.

Phenomenology

Some clear accounts of this movement (the writings of whose members are often difficult) are to be found in

[12] Edo Pivčević (ed.), *Phenomenology and philosophical understanding* (Cambridge University Press, Cambridge, 1975). See especially: (a) Anthony Quinton, 'The concept of a phenomenon' (pp. 1–16); (b) J.N. Findlay, 'Phenomenology and the meaning of realism' (pp. 143–58).

Wittgenstein

[13] G.P. Baker and P.M.S. Hacker, *Wittgenstein: understanding and meaning* (Basil Blackwell, Oxford, 1980). This commentary on the *Philosophical investigations* is a combination of detailed exposition and extended essays. The essay on 'The nature of philosophy' (pp. 457–91) is particularly relevant to the present chapter.

[14] Anthony Kenny, 'Wittgenstein on the nature of philosophy' in Brian McGuiness (ed.), *Wittgenstein and his times* (Basil Blackwell, Oxford, 1982), pp. 1–26. Less advanced than the Baker and Hacker essay, and could with advantage be read before it.

The idea that philosophy is a kind of psychoanalysis was developed by John Wisdom. See especially

[15] John Wisdom, *Philosophy and psycho-analysis* (Basil Blackwell, Oxford, 1953).

Logical positivism

[16] A.J. Ayer, *Language, truth and logic* (Pelican Books, Harmondsworth, 1971). This powerful and lucid polemic, first published in 1936, has proved to be the most influential exposition of logical positivism, and indeed one of the most important philosophical books of the 1930s and 1940s. For its view of the nature of philosophy, see especially (in the Pelican edition) pp. 29–34, 61–5, 68–9, 80–1, 199–202.

For the views of the school in general, see

[17] A.J. Ayer (ed.), *Logical positivism* (Free Press, Glencoe, Illinois, 1959), pp. 3–28. A fuller account is given by

[18] Oswald Hanfling, *Logical positivism* (Basil Blackwell, Oxford, 1981).

Ordinary language philosophy

(Also known as 'linguistic philosophy' and 'Oxford philosophy'.) A clear and sympathetic account is to be found in

[19] Isaiah Berlin, 'Austin and the early beginnings of Oxford philosophy' in I. Berlin (ed.), *Essays on J.L. Austin* (Clarendon Press, Oxford, 1973), pp. 1–16.

What is Philosophy?

Philosophical analysis and the history of philosophy

[20] Michael Ayers, 'Analytical philosophy and the history of philosophy' in J. Rée, M. Ayers and A. Westoby (eds), *Philosophy and its past* (Harvester, Hassocks, 1978), pp. 42–66.

For a more general discussion of the relations between philosophy and its history, including illustrations of the way in which the history of philosophy can throw light on present problems, see

[21] R. Rorty, J.B. Schneewind and Q. Skinner (eds), *Philosophy in history* (Cambridge University Press, Cambridge, 1984).

G.H.R.P.

Part A: Meaning and Truth

Introduction

To speak of philosophy is to speak of a number of inquiries, each of which deals with its own characteristic problems. If one wants to make a systematic survey of philosophy, one must first decide on the parts into which philosophy is to be divided; then one must decide on the best way in which to arrange the parts. It might seem that the first problem, at any rate, has a ready-made solution. For it may be pointed out that there already exist certain recognised ways of dividing philosophy into parts – parts which have names such as 'Theory of knowledge', 'Metaphysics', 'Ethics', and so on. But the matter is not so simple. First, even if those who divide up the territory of philosophy were to agree on its parts, we would still want to know why they settle on just these parts. Second, the fact is that there is no complete agreement about the nature of the parts of philosophy. For example, in some works (of which this encyclopaedia is one) problems of meaning and truth are taken together, and are distinguished from the theory of knowledge. Some philosophers, however, regard the theory of knowledge as including the discussion of problems about meaning and truth; others, again, regard these problems as belonging to what they call the philosophy of language. But even if these difficulties are surmounted, one still has to face the second of the two problems mentioned earlier – the problem of order. For although the parts of philosophy are relatively independent of one another, this independence is not total. For example, a writer on ethics may find it necessary to say something about the philosophy of meaning, whilst the philosophy of religion (as can be seen from the final chapter of this encyclopaedia) involves many other areas of philosophy.

The themes and the arrangement of the 36 chapters which follow provide answers to these problems. The chapters are divided into six groups, each of which forms one part of the encyclopaedia; each of

21

these is closely related to a generally recognised way, or set of ways, of dividing up the field of philosophy. Each part will have its own introduction, provided by the general editor, explaining what the part contains and what its place is in the general scheme.

The first part of the encyclopaedia is concerned with questions about the nature and the criteria of meaning and truth. That is, it is concerned with the questions 'What is the nature of meaning and truth?' and 'What conditions must an utterance satisfy, if it is to be counted as meaningful or as true?' That these are different questions can be seen from two examples. Suppose that one says (as some philosophers have said) that a proposition is meaningful if, and only if, there is some way of verifying it. Here one is offering a *criterion* of meaning – that is, one is putting forward a test that a proposition must pass if it is to be meaningful. But one has said nothing about the *nature* of meaning, i.e. about what meaning *is*. For even if the criterion offered is a correct one, it by no means follows that the meaning of a proposition *is* the method of its verification. Or take truth. Suppose that someone says that if, and only if, a belief is true, it is also useful. Such a person can also use this as a criterion of truth; for if he wants to know if a belief is true, he simply asks, 'Is it useful?' But this is quite different from saying that the truth of a belief is *constituted by* its usefulness.

It may now be asked, 'Why treat meaning and truth together? Why not assign them to separate parts of the encyclopaedia?' This can best be answered in the course of a reply to another question – namely, why meaning and truth should be placed first. To answer this, let us first consider another possible claimant for first place – that is, metaphysics. Much more will be said about metaphysics in Part C; for the moment we may say provisionally, following the hint given in Chapter 1 (p. 3), that metaphysics is concerned with 'first principles' or 'original causes'. These terms suggest that it deals with fundamental issues, and as such ought to be considered first. This, indeed, has been the view of many philosophers. As an example, one may take the *Summa theologica* of the thirteenth-century philosopher and theologian St Thomas Aquinas. This 'compendium of theology', which is also a compendium of philosophy, has as its first major philosophical topic the existence of the first cause, God. However, I mentioned in the first chapter the change in philosophy that took place in the seventeenth century, as questions about knowledge came to the forefront. Should one, then, follow Descartes, and begin by considering knowledge?

Certainly, questions about knowledge are of great importance for the philosopher, and one could go so far as to say that they form the main theme of this encyclopaedia. Despite this, there are good reasons for discussing meaning and truth before knowledge, and for discussing meaning before truth. One of these reasons is logical, and the other is historical. The logical reason may be stated as follows. Let us suppose that someone claims to know that the human mind survives the death of the body.

For this claim to be justified, it must at least be *true that* the mind survives the body's death. Truth, in other words, is a necessary condition of knowledge, and there is therefore a good case for discussing it before one discusses knowledge. Should one, then, discuss truth first of all? The answer is that truth itself has a necessary condition, and that necessary condition is meaningfulness. If one is to say something true, what one says must at least be meaningful. We cannot say of a string of words that makes no sense, 'That's true' or again 'That is false.' As this is so, there is a good case for considering problems of meaning first.

The historical reason of which I spoke earlier involves one of the most challenging philosophical movements of this century, the movement known as 'logical positivism'. This movement, whose views about the nature of philosophy were mentioned in Chapter 1, argued that many sentences which appear to state something which is true or false – the sentences uttered by metaphysicians, for example – are in fact meaningless. This put problems of meaning in the centre of the philosophical stage. Logical positivism flourished some fifty years ago, and one is often told that 'There are no logical positivists nowadays.' Doubtless this is true; but an account of the way in which the logical positivists came to say what they did about meaning and about what is meaningful, and of the views about meaning which superseded theirs, is a good starting point for a survey of contemporary philosophy.

Problems about meaning are discussed in Chapters 2 and 3. In Chapter 2, the dominant figure is Wittgenstein, whilst Chapter 3 is concerned with what may be called post-Wittgensteinian views about meaning. The most influential of these at the present time is the view that meaning is constituted by what are called the 'truth-conditions' of a sentence. This close connection between meaning and truth gives the answer to a question raised earlier – namely, why the two topics are grouped together to form one part of this encyclopaedia. A discussion of truth follows in Chapter 4. The problem of truth is here taken, as it is usually taken by philosophers, to concern true propositions which are such that they could have been false. That is, it is concerned with propositions such as 'Queen Elizabeth II was crowned on 2 June 1953.' This proposition is a true one, but it is not inconceivable that the Queen should have been crowned on some other day; that is, the proposition just happens to be true. But with the truths of logic and of mathematics, the situation is different. Propositions such as 'Either Queen Elizabeth II was crowned on 2 June 1953 or she was not' or again 'If two things are equal to a third, they are equal to each other' are not just true; they are *necessarily* true. This raises the question 'By virtue of what are they necessarily true?', a question which is fundamentally different from those raised in Chapter 4. For this reason, the truths of logic and of mathematics are treated as a separate topic, and are discussed in Chapter 5.

G.H.R.P.

2 | Theories of Meaning: from 'Reference' to 'Use'

O. Hanfling

'When we ask someone what the number one is, or what the symbol 1 means, we get as a rule the answer "Why, a thing".' With this claim Gottlob Frege, one of the pioneers of the philosophy of language in our time, opened his *Foundations of arithmetic*[1] of 1884.

Frege's remark illustrates the liability of philosophers to fall into strange errors regarding the views and sayings of ordinary people. It is hardly likely that one would answer, 'Why, a thing' to this question; most people would simply not know what to say. But behind Frege's question and answer there lies a view of language which many have found plausible. Surely, it may be said, the number one is not *nothing*; if it were, would not the word 'one' be meaningless? But if it is not nothing, what is it? It must be something – some thing; it remains only to say what kind of thing it is.

The idea that meaning is essentially a one-to-one relation between words and corresponding things lies behind much of the philosophy of language of our time (and long before that). It was, however, renounced by Wittgenstein in his 'later' philosophy, as we shall see in the final section.

Frege: sense and 'reference'

In 1892 Frege published the important article 'Sinn und Bedeutung', which appears in the English translation of 1952 as 'On sense and reference'. This pair of terms has become established as part of the philosopher's vocabulary. By 'reference' is meant the thing corresponding to a given word or expression. For example, the planet Venus is the 'reference' of the word 'Venus'. Now the English reader may simply take 'reference' to be a technical term, introduced for this role. But this would be a mistake. The straightforward translation of *Bedeutung* is 'meaning'. Frege was not introducing a technical term; his view, which he assumed without argument, was that the *meaning* (*Bedeutung*) of a name is a corresponding object.

This view leads to a number of problems, one of which was introduced as follows by Frege. We sometimes say that *a* is the same thing as *b*. Is this identity, he asks, 'a relation'?[2] If so, is it 'a relation between objects, or between names or signs of objects'? If the former, then statements of identity must be empty of cognitive content; they would amount to no more than saying that an object is identical with itself. But, as Frege points out, statements of identity have the form '*a*=*b*' and not merely '*a*=*a*'; and they may represent 'valuable extensions of our knowledge', as when it was discovered that 'the rising sun is not new every morning, but always the same'.[3] His solution was to introduce another aspect of meaning, which he called the 'sense' of an expression. The sense 'contains the mode of presentation' of the object.[4] For example, the expressions 'the evening star' and 'the morning star' *mean* the same object (both are, in fact, the planet Venus), but they 'present' the object in different ways. This is why such statements as 'the evening star is the morning star' have cognitive value, unlike the vacuous '*a*=*a*'.

Frege applied his schema of sense and meaning both to proper names and to such expressions as 'the evening star'. But do proper names have 'sense'? According to Frege they do, but 'opinions as to the sense may differ'. One person who uses the name 'Aristotle' might take its sense to be 'pupil of Plato and teacher of Alexander the Great', while for another it might be 'teacher of Alexander the Great who was born in Stagira'. But, he added, so long as the *meaning* remains the same, 'such variations of sense may be tolerated' – though they 'ought not to occur in a perfect language'.[5] He did not, however, explain *how* the 'meaning' (the object designated) can do the work of uniting the uses of 'Aristotle' by people who attach different senses to it.

Frege made a point of denying that sense is *subjective*. The same sense may call up different associations or images in different people, but *they* are not the sense. The sense of an expression 'may be the common property of many and therefore is not a part or a mode of the individual mind'. Hence 'one need have no scruples in speaking simply of *the* sense' of an expression.[6]

A feature of Frege's theory, which it shares with other 'realist' theories of meaning, is that according to it the true or full meanings of our words are hidden from us. 'Comprehensive knowledge of the meaning would require us to be able to say immediately whether any given sense belongs to it. To such knowledge we never attain.'[7] Thus the objectivity of sense and meaning are bought, so to speak, at the price of placing them beyond the reach of finite beings.

Now the view that meaning is a corresponding object may seem plausible in the case of names and name-like expressions. But what about common nouns, such as 'evening' or 'whale'? In this case, according to Frege, the meaning is a corresponding *concept*. Thus the proposition 'All whales are mammals' is really about the concepts 'whale' and 'mammal'.[8] The appearance of a sentence may be misleading. We might think that 'The King's carriage was drawn by four horses' is a statement about the King's carriage, but it is really about a concept: 'I assign the number four to the concept "horse that draws the King's carriage".'[9]

This view may be thought to have unacceptable ontological implications – about the nature of things that may be said to exist. For it now appears that there exists something – a concept – which stands to the word 'whale' as the planet Venus stands to the name 'Venus'. We are not, however, to think of concepts as *mental* entities, for, as Frege points out, this would make meaning (and truth) subjective.

An underlying feature of Frege's thought (which he shares with many others) is the desire to apply the same schema to different parts or aspects of language. This is especially striking in his treatment of sentences. Here again we are to think in terms of sense and meaning. A sentence, he said, 'contains a thought'.[10] But this thought, he argued, cannot be the meaning. The sentences 'The evening star is illuminated by the sun' and 'The morning star is illuminated by the sun' express different *thoughts*, even though the *'meanings'* of 'the evening star' and 'the morning star' are the same. He felt there must be something belonging to these sentences (their 'meaning') which would remain invariant to the changes of 'thought'. The answer was to be found in their *truth*. 'We are therefore driven into accepting the *truth value* of a sentence as constituting its meaning. By the truth value of a sentence I understand the circumstance that it is true or false.'[11] A declarative sentence, he concluded, 'is therefore to be regarded as a proper name, and its meaning . . . is either the True or the False'.[12] It followed that 'on the one hand all true sentences have the same meaning and so, on the other hand, do all false sentences'.[13] These meanings, again, must be regarded as 'objects'.[14]

Russell: logical atomism

Meaning and acquaintance

The word–object assumption was continued in the works of Bertrand Russell, especially with regard to 'universals'. 'When we examine common words', he wrote in *The problems of philosophy* (1911), 'we find that, broadly speaking, proper names stand for particulars, while other substantives, adjectives, propositions and verbs stand for universals'.[15] Even such a word as 'in' must have something – in this case a relation – corresponding to it, failing which it would be meaningless.[16] Again there are ontological implications, and Russell expressed surprise that they were not more widely accepted. 'Seeing that nearly all words ... stand for universals, it is strange that hardly anybody except students of philosophy ever realizes that there are such entities as universals.'[17] For Russell, as for Frege, names and other words have meaning by 'standing for' a corresponding entity. But according to Russell, meaning is dependent on one's 'acquaintance' with the entity concerned. 'The meaning we attach to our words must be something with which we are acquainted.'[18] He took as an example the name 'Bismarck'. Now according to Frege, as we saw, the *meaning* of this would be the person of Bismarck, and there would also be an invariant *sense*, in spite of variations among individual speakers. But Russell (who spoke only of 'meaning') claimed that the meaning of a name would depend on what is 'before one's mind' when one uses it. This would be 'some *description*' of the person concerned, such as 'the first Chancellor of the German Empire'.[19] However, 'the word "German" will, again, have different meanings for different people. To some it will recall travels in Germany, to some the look of Germany on the map, and so on.'[20] Ultimately the meaning of a name or statement 'is composed wholly of particulars and universals with which we are acquainted'.[21]

What did Russell mean by 'acquaintance'? It might be thought that those who *knew* Bismarck would be acquainted with him. But Russell meant something more subjective than this.

> What this person was acquainted with were certain sense-data which he connected (rightly, we will suppose) with Bismarck's body. His body, and still more his mind, were only known as the body and mind connected with these sense-data.[22]

He explained that by 'sense-data' he meant 'the things that are immediately known in sensation: such things as colours, sounds, smells, hardnesses, roughnesses, and so on'.[23]

This usage of 'sensation' and 'sense-data' has been the source of much confusion (cf. Chapter 7). But without going into this matter, it is clear that for Russell meaning is an essentially personal matter. According to Frege, sense and meaning are objective; but this means that we cannot attain full knowledge of them. Russell's view, by contrast, is that meanings are known in the most intimate possible way ('acquaintance'), but are therefore subjective. He claimed that this, so far from being a difficulty, is an essential condition of the use of language.

> The meaning you attach to your words must depend on the nature of the objects you are acquainted with, and since different people are acquainted with different objects, they would not be able to talk to each other unless they attached quite different meanings to their words.[24]

It might be said, contrary to this, that people would not be able to talk to each other if they *did* attach 'quite different meanings' to their words; and this might be taken to show that Russell's account of meaning cannot be correct.

The theory of descriptions

The view that names have meaning by standing for corresponding objects leads to a difficulty about questions of existence. If '*a*' is name, can we ask whether *a* exists? It would seem not, for if the object did not exist, the name (and hence the question) would be meaningless; but if the name is *not* meaningless, then the object *must* exist. Nevertheless we do sometimes question the existence of an object or person referred to by name, for example 'Homer'. This led Russell to deny that such names are really names.[25]

What, then, is 'Homer' if not a name? According to Russell, it is 'an abbreviated description: we may replace it by (say) "the author of the *Iliad* and the *Odyssey*" '.[26] And if someone asserts that Homer existed, he is really saying that some such *description* is true of something. 'It is only of descriptions ... that existence can be significantly asserted.'[27]

Another difficulty concerns the existence of objects corresponding to such descriptions as 'the author of the *Iliad*', when these appear as the subjects of sentences. One of Russell's examples was 'The present King of France is bald.' This, he pointed out, 'implies that the present King of France exists'.[28] We might therefore regard the statement as false. But the contradictory of the statement ('The present King of France is not bald') *also* implies that he exists, and would therefore also be false. Yet it may be thought that if two statements are contradictory, they cannot both be false.

Russell's solution was to remove 'The present King of France' from the subject position. A subject–predicate proposition of this kind, he maintained, really consists of two assertions, one being that *there is* a thing answering to the subject-term, and the other that the predicate is true of that thing. Thus what we are really saying in the case of this example is: 'there is a *c* such that *c* is now King of France and *c* is bald'.[29] And the contradictory of this is not the simple 'is not bald', for there are now *two* ways of contradicting the proposition.

The implication of the definite article ('the') – that there is only one such thing – must also be considered. Thus the full analysis of the proposition would be: (1) at least one thing is now King of France; (2) at most one thing is now King of France; (3) this thing is bald.[30]

Now Frege had maintained that a name without a corresponding object, such as 'Odysseus', was meaningless, and that a sentence about Odysseus must likewise be meaningless (and neither true nor false).[31] Similarly, as Russell pointed out, on Frege's view 'one would suppose that "The King of France is bald" is nonsense'; but, said Russell, 'it is not nonsense, since it is plainly false'.[32]

28

But is it plainly false? If an ordinary person were asked this question, he might well hesitate over the answer. Is there a 'correct' answer? Referring to a subsequent critic, Russell wrote: 'Mr Strawson admits that the sentence is significant and not true, but not that it is false ... For my part, I find it more convenient to define the word "false" so that every significant sentence is either true or false.'[33] But 'convenient to define' is no answer to someone who questions whether Russell's account is *correct*.

Logically proper names

As we have seen, Russell denied that ordinary names like 'Bismarck' or 'Homer' are really names. A real name would be one that has *no* descriptive content. Are there such names? 'That makes it very difficult', concluded Russell,

> to get any instance of a name at all in the proper strict logical sense of the word. The only words one does use [thus] are words like 'this' or 'that'. One can use 'this' as a name to stand for a particular with which one is acquainted at the moment.[34]

Thus 'this' would function as a name in the 'strict logical sense' if it is applied not to a physical object, but to an object of 'acquaintance' – a sense-datum occurring in the speaker at that moment. Hence 'it has a very odd property for a proper name, namely that it seldom means the same thing two moments running and does not mean the same thing to the speaker and the hearer'.[35] The importance of such 'proper names' was, he said, 'in the sense of logic, not of daily life'.[36]

Logical atomism

'In a logically perfect language', said Russell, 'the words in a proposition would correspond one by one with the components of the corresponding fact ... There will be one word and no more for every simple object.'[37] He thought that an analysis of language would show that it consists of 'simple signs' standing in this relation to simple objects. Comparing this analysis to that which occurs in physics and chemistry, he proposed to call his view 'logical atomism', because the atoms in question were logical and not physical. These atoms, again, would be objects of 'acquaintance'. Thus 'all analysis depends ... upon direct acquaintance with the objects which are the meanings of certain symbols'.[38] By such analysis he would 'get down in theory, if not in practice, to ultimate simples, out of which the world is built'.[39] He gave 'this is white' as an example of an atomic fact.[40]

The reader may wonder, however, what the results of such analysis would look like, even 'in theory'. Are all propositions about particular things to be reduced to sentences like 'This is white' – where 'this' has the 'very odd properties' quoted above? And how could universals (such as 'white' or 'man') be treated as 'simple objects' in the required sense?

Knowledge, meaning, ontology

Russell's account of meaning is affected by his epistemology. He takes the empiricist view that our knowledge consists ultimately of items of 'sensation' (sense-data) occurring in the mind or brain. But the limits of knowledge are also the limits of meaning: my words can only *mean* these objects of acquaintance. Moreover, given the one-to-one correspondence between words and objects, an analysis of language will also be an analysis of the structure of the world. And since objects of acquaintance are momentary, we must resist any temptation to 'believe that the real is permanent'.[41] 'The things that are really real last only a very short time.'[42] Yet he vacillated on this point. He would not deny, he said, that there *may* be things that last longer; but these are not 'within our experience'.[43]

Wittgenstein: logical atomism

The picture theory

Russell's most famous pupil was Ludwig Wittgenstein. They collaborated closely in the years before the First World War, and it would be hard to say who learned more from whom. Wittgenstein's ideas were published in the *Tractatus logico-philosophicus* (1921), and the references below (e.g. '4.0311') are to sections of this work.

Like Russell, Wittgenstein held that ordinary words (and ordinary names) could be analysed into logically simple constituents, which he called 'names', and which stand in one-to-one correspondence with equally simple 'objects'. Out of these names can be constructed atomic (or 'elementary') propositions, corresponding to equally atomic 'states of affairs'. Such a proposition is necessarily either true or false. It will be true if the names in it are related in a way corresponding to the relations of the objects named. Wittgenstein found an attractive illustration of this conception in a newspaper report of a road accident. In court a physical model of the situation had been produced. The figures in this model represented ('meant') the corresponding objects, and the model would be 'true' if the objects had really stood in those relations. He thought that atomic propositions have the same character. 'One name stands for one thing, another for another thing, and they are combined with one another. In this way the whole group – like a *tableau vivant* [lebendes Bild] – presents a state of affairs' (4.0311). He was able to claim (4.012) that some sentences are actually experienced as pictures, namely those of the form '*aRb*'. Here an object *a* is said to stand in a certain relation *R* to an object *b* – for example, the knife is to the left of the fork. Now obviously there are not many sentences which correspond in this satisfying way with states of affairs; and objects are related in many different kinds of ways. But Wittgenstein pointed out that, on the face of it, there is a similar disparity between a piece of music and the corresponding notation; and yet there is a one-to-one correspondence between them (4.011).

But what is the meaning of *R* in the above example? Does it stand for a relation (as *a* and *b* stand for objects)? According to Russell, as we saw (p. 26), relations (such as 'in') are among the objects of acquaintance whereby our words have meaning. But Wittgenstein held that relational terms are not really components of language; hence the form '*aRb*' is misleading. In a picture of that situation, *R* would not appear as an object. This relation would be expressed in the *arrangement* of objects in the picture, and the same is true of propositions. Hence *R* is not a name and there is no need to postulate a corresponding object.

Meaning and ontology

We are not to think of language and reality, proposition and fact, as belonging to two separate realms. Consider an arrangement of tables and chairs etc. in a room. Here we have a fact, which may be stated in a corresponding proposition. But the arrangement of tables and chairs can *itself* be regarded as a proposition. We can 'imagine . . . a propositional sign' composed of 'tables, chairs and books instead of written signs'. Then 'the spatial arrangement of these things will express the sense of the proposition' (3.1431).

'Logic', declared Wittgenstein, 'pervades the world' (5.61). 'To give the essence of a proposition means to give . . . the essence of the world' (5.4711). Now Russell, as we saw (p. 30), was inclined to make inferences from language to 'the real'. He also claimed that by a 'study of syntax, we can arrive at considerable knowledge concerning the structure of the world'.[44] But this is not Wittgenstein's position. For him language is part of the world, and propositions are themselves facts. Hence the logic (or essence) of propositions *is* the logic of the world, and there is no *inference* from one to the other. On the other hand, speculations about a reality beyond language must be rejected as nonsensical.

Atomism

'What can be said at all, can be said clearly' (Preface). A proposition must be either true or false; it must not 'leave something undetermined', as would be the case with 'the present King of France'. Wittgenstein was influenced by Russell's Theory of Descriptions.[45] 'A proposition that mentions a complex will not be nonsensical, if the complex does not exist, but simply false' (3.24). When the proposition is 'completely analysed', the complex will be replaced by 'simple signs' ('names') (3.201); and in their case, as we have seen, the

31

object must exist. If there were no such signs, then, he said, 'determinacy of sense' could not be achieved; hence there must be such signs (3.23).

What would these simple signs (and the corresponding objects) be like? Russell, as we saw, held that they had only a momentary duration. Wittgenstein, less concerned about questions of knowledge ('acquaintance'), claimed that 'objects are . . . unalterable and subsistent; their configuration is what is changing and unstable' (2.0271). Such a change would mean that a proposition which is true at one time is false at another. But the objects themselves are not alterable. There are no properties in respect of which an object could change; for if it had properties, it would not be simple. 'In a manner of speaking, objects are colourless' (2.0232). Nor can we suppose that an object changes from existence to non-existence, for its existence is already presupposed in using the corresponding name.

On the question of simplicity (as on others) Wittgenstein was more rigorous than Russell. As we saw (p. 29), Russell regarded 'This is white' as atomic. This, he said, was 'about as simple a fact as you can get hold of'.[46] But, questioned by one of his listeners about simple and complex, he replied: 'No facts are simple.' According to Wittgenstein, by contrast, 'we know, on purely logical grounds, that there must be elementary [atomic, simple] propositions' (5.5562). Moreover, he understood simplicity in a very strict sense. A proposition would be 'elementary' only if 'there can be no elementary proposition contradicting it' (4.211). Atomic facts, likewise, are 'independent of one another'; 'from the existence or non-existence of one . . . it is impossible to infer the existence or non-existence of another' (2.061–2). Now this condition would not be fulfilled in the case of colours, since from 'This is white' we can infer 'This is not red' (6.3571). This shows that colours are not simple, and propositions about them not yet fully analysed.

But what Wittgenstein's account gains in rigour it loses in plausibility. For the reader who expects to find examples of the relevant names and propositions in the *Tractatus* will be disappointed. To Russell, who asked him about the simple constituents of a thought, he replied: 'I don't know *what* the constituents of a thought are, but I know *that* it must have such constituents which correspond to the words of language.'[47] But both Russell and Wittgenstein held that the true logic of language was something beyond the knowledge of ordinary users of language. 'Russell's merit', wrote Wittgenstein, 'is to have shown that the apparent logical form of a proposition need not be its real one' (4.0031; author's translation). Human beings, he claimed, use words 'without having any idea how each word has meaning or what its meaning is' (4.002).

Analysis and the essence of propositions

The analysis of propositions was to be achieved by the 'truth-functional' system of logic; and when Wittgenstein spoke of 'the essence of a proposition' (and hence of the world), he meant the applicability of this system to them. This logic, originally introduced by Frege, is nowadays explained in standard textbooks, and only a brief sketch will be given here.

Consider a proposition p (e.g. 'This is white') and another proposition q (e.g. 'That is red'). Out of these we can build a 'conjunction', 'p and q'. It will be seen that the truth of the latter depends on the truth of the conjuncts, p and q. If one of them is false, then 'p and q' will be false; if both are true, 'p and q' will be true. In this sense the truth of the latter is a 'function' of the truth of its components. Now consider the disjunction 'p or q'. This needs, for its truth, the truth of only one of the components p or q. (If p is false, 'p or q' may still be true, etc.)

There are two other constants, besides 'and' and 'or'. One is the negation 'not': if p is true, not-p is false, and conversely. The other is usually given as 'implies' or 'if ... then' (if p, then q).

Wittgenstein invented the method of 'truth tables' to display the meaning of the four constants. The meaning of 'and', for example, can be displayed by going through the four possible varieties of true (T) and false (F) with regard to propositions p and q.

p	q	p and q
T	T	T
T	F	F
F	T	F
F	F	F

The four constants are interdefinable within the system. Moreover, it was discovered that all of them could be replaced by a single constant, known as the 'Sheffer stroke', which Wittgenstein rendered as 'neither p nor q'. It can be shown that repeated applications of this constant can do the same work as (albeit more clumsily than) the original four. However, the details of the system will not be given here. What is important is that according to Wittgenstein and Russell, all ordinary propositions can be reduced, by means of this single constant, to the required atomic propositions, containing only 'names'. Thus, behind the apparent complexity and variety of propositions there lies the possibility of analysis by a uniform method into simple and uniform constituents. 'One could say', concluded Wittgenstein, 'that the sole logical constant was what *all* propositions, by their very nature, had in common' (5.47). Here lies 'the essence of a proposition' (and hence 'the essence of the world'). This essential logical structure also belongs, according to Wittgenstein, to the final atomic propositions. Such a proposition, he said, 'is a truth-function *of itself*' (5).

What cannot be said

The aim of his book, wrote Wittgenstein in the Preface, 'might be summed up in the following words: What can be said at all can be said clearly, and what we cannot talk about we must pass over in silence' (p. 2). Here we come to the famous paradox of the *Tractatus*. For it turns out that the propositions of that work itself 'cannot be said'. They will have served their purpose if 'anyone who understands me eventually recognises them as nonsensical' (6.54). The account of propositions given in the *Tractatus* cannot be applied to that account itself. In the latter we are told, for example, that propositions have a certain 'logical form', whereby they can depict facts. But this statement cannot itself have meaning in that way. 'Propositions can represent the whole of reality, but they cannot represent what they must have in common with reality in order to be able to represent it' (4.12). The point can also be made in terms of pictures in the ordinary sense. A picture can be used to represent a fact, for example that *a* is to the left of *b*. But the relation between picture and fact, whereby this is achieved, is not itself depicted. 'A picture cannot ... depict its pictorial form' (2.172).

A similar point arises with the existence of simple objects. That *a* exists 'shows itself' in the fact that '*a*' is a name; but we cannot *say* that *a* exists. We cannot do it by giving a description of *a* (if we could, '*a*' would not be simple). Nor, as we have seen (p. 28), can we do it by using '*a*' itself.

The logical constants too must be excluded from 'what can be said'. A word like 'and' does not represent an object. 'There are no "logical objects" ... (in Frege's and Russell's sense)' (5.4). (Russell, in his *Principles of mathematics* of 1903, thought that we were 'acquainted' with logical constants, but had many changes of mind thereafter.) Wittgenstein illustrated his denial by reference to negation ('not'). The meaning of a proposition does not depend on its truth-value. Now the only effect of adding the negation-sign is to reverse the truth-value. Hence this sign cannot be part of the meaning of a proposition (4.0621). Again, there are no negative facts. A fact is 'a combination of objects' (2.01). If a proposition is false, then there is *no* corresponding fact; and in that case the negation of the proposition will be true. But this does not mean that, corresponding to this negative proposition, there must be a negative fact which includes an object called 'not'.

The Vienna Circle: verificationism

The Verification Principle

Wittgenstein, as we have seen, was less concerned than Russell about how we *know* the meaning of a word. He did say that 'to understand a proposition means to know what is the case if it is true' (4.024), but did not explain what this knowing consists in. But when he returned to philosophy in 1929, he came to think that the meaning of a proposition consists in the method of *finding out whether* it is true. He formulated the 'Verification Principle': 'The sense of a proposition is the method of its verification.'[48] This saying (more usually 'The meaning of a proposition ...') became one of the principal ideas of the logical empiricists (or logical positivists) of the Vienna Circle, who flourished at the University of Vienna until the mid-thirties, under the leadership of Moritz Schlick.

That there is a connection between meaning and method of verification will probably be granted at once. But it is not clear what can be meant by *identifying* them. It hardly makes sense to say that the meaning of a piece of language *is* a method, a way of doing something. However, it appears, especially from Schlick's writings, that verification was conflated with certain other ideas, especially that of 'ostensive definition' – 'a pointing gesture combined with the pronouncing of the word, as when we teach a child the [meaning] of "blue" by showing a blue object'.[49]

Another approach was to identify *understanding* the meaning with knowing how to verify. Friedrich Waismann understood the above remark from the *Tractatus* in this way. He continued: 'To become aware of the sense of a proposition one has to be clear about the procedure for establishing its truth.'[50] This is more intelligible than the Verification Principle, but there is a difficulty about the scope of 'the procedure'. Must one be aware of *every* method of verifying the proposition? This would be too strong. On the other hand, it might be said that understanding a proposition means *more* than knowing how to verify it; one must also know how to act in accordance with it, in what contexts to state it, etc.

The Criterion of Verifiability

From the Verification Principle there follows a criterion for deciding *whether* a proposition has meaning: if there is *no* method of verification, then it is without meaning.

The Criterion was sometimes advocated independently of the Principle. It reflected the scientific and anti-metaphysical orientation of the Circle. By means of the Criterion, it was thought, the age-old problems of philosophy could be shown to be meaningless, in contrast to the meaningful problems and statements of science. 'The scientific conception of the world does not acknowledge any insoluble riddles.' Investigation would show that the 'traditional philosophical problems' are either 'pseudo-problems' or can be 'transformed into empirical problems'.[51]

A.J. Ayer, who published these or similar views to the English-speaking world in his *Language, truth and logic* of 1936, began with a chapter called 'The elimination of metaphysics'. 'We say', he declared,

35

'that a sentence is factually significant to any person, if and only if he knows ... what observations would lead him to accept it as true or reject it as false.'[52] Thus a philosopher who questioned whether the physical world might not be an illusion, or who speculated about a non-empirical reality, would be told that his questions are meaningless; and the same would happen to those who assert – or question or deny – the existence of a transcendent God.

An initial difficulty about the Criterion is simply that of acceptance. Why should I, the philosopher or religious believer will ask, accept the Criterion? What proof have you that it is true? It is not as if the Criterion were merely a statement of the actual usage of 'meaningless' and 'meaningful', for it is not normal to conclude that a statement is meaningless merely because it cannot be verified by empirical observation.

Again, it may be asked whether the Criterion can itself be verified by observation. May it not turn out to be self-eliminating? These difficulties were met by describing the Criterion as a 'proposal' or 'methodological principle' (and hence not a statement). But again, it proved difficult to give reasons for accepting such a proposal. Moreover, it is not clear what it would *mean* to accept it. Of course we could agree to *say* 'meaningless' to a given proposition, but – would we mean it? This will depend on whether we *believe* it to be meaningless.

Applications of verificationism

A difficulty about verificationism concerned the meaning of 'verify'. Consider some ordinary statement such as 'Cambridge won the boat race.' One might verify this by reading a newspaper. But clearly there is more to the meaning than this method of verification.[53] But what if I actually saw the event? This observation would still not exhaust the meaning of the statement. Firstly, I would have seen only one aspect of the event and, secondly, the meaning is not confined to one observer. Verificationists accepted that it would not be possible to give a finite list of observations corresponding to a given statement; and from this it was concluded that ordinary empirical statements are not (or not 'conclusively') verifiable. Ayer proposed that a statement would be meaningful if, and only if, some 'observation-statement' could be *deduced* from it. But this condition proved too weak, for it would be satisfied by metaphysical statements which had *some* empirical consequences. That there are fish in the sea is deducible from what we read about God in the first book of Genesis; but clearly the concept of God goes beyond such empirical data. What was needed was to *analyse* a statement so as to arrive at its empirical content (if any); it would be meaningful to this, and only this, extent.

However, certain types of statement, other than metaphysical, proved difficult to accommodate. Statements of science (which the Criterion was especially intended to favour) often go beyond empirical data. A scientific theory says more than the evidence on which it is based; and this 'more' does not consist merely in the prediction of further empirical data.

Again, statements about the past may be verified by *present* observations, but we cannot observe past facts themselves. It would seem to follow that such statements, or what is meaningful in them, are really about the present.

How am I to verify statements about the thoughts and feelings of others? If it is by observing their behaviour, then again, the meaning must be confined to this.

> A proposition cannot say more than what is established by the method of verification. If I say 'My friend is angry' and establish that this is so through his behaving in a certain observable way, then what I *mean* by this proposition is merely that he is showing this behaviour.[54]

This view ('behaviourism') may seem plausible with regard to other people, but what about my own feelings? It was largely this problem that caused Wittgenstein to draw away from verificationism in his 1930–3 lectures. 'Is it correct', he asked, 'to say that his toothache is only his behaviour, whereas when I talk about my toothache I am not talking about my behaviour?' If so, does the word have two different senses?[55] Rudolf Carnap, however, maintained that the difference between the first and third persons is 'only a matter of degree'. The first-person statement too is based on 'a kind of observation'. He took the 'physicalist' view, that all facts and all meaning were about physical entities (including human brain-processes and behaviour), and claimed that in the case of a human feeling the same physical fact is empirically observed by the first and third persons.[56]

Moral statements were another source of difficulty. Schlick took the view that ethics can be regarded as a science, part of the science of psychology. But a more usual approach was to deny that moral statements have any 'factual' or 'cognitive' meaning. Their function was to express 'certain feelings [of approval or disapproval] in the speaker',[57] and to arouse similar feelings in the hearer.

The elimination of experience

As we saw, one of the main aims of verificationism was the 'elimination of metaphysics' in favour of empirical science. But further reflections led, paradoxically, to the view that sense-experience had itself to be excluded from the realm of meaningful statements.

The *Tractatus* idea of 'elementary propositions' had been given a verificationist meaning by Waismann. 'If, in order to verify a proposition, I can no longer appeal to other propositions, then this indicates that the proposition is elementary.'[58] He thought it obvious that propositions about tables and chairs are not elementary, but are based on propositions about 'experiences' which *are* elementary. This led to the characteristic empiricist conclusion that meanings are subjective, depending on the person having these experiences. As we saw (p. 27), such a conclusion was happily embraced by Russell. But it was not acceptable to the scientifically minded members of the Vienna Circle, who insisted that the language of science is (or ought to be) 'intersubjective'. Carnap and Otto Neurath, especially, argued that the analysis of language should not be taken beyond language (to a realm of experiences, sense-data, etc.), but must remain within language. This led to a 'coherence theory' of truth. On this view, the truth of a statement depends on whether it is consistent with other *statements*, and not on any facts outside language. It then becomes an arbitrary matter which set of consistent statements is adopted as 'true'. Schlick, a stout opponent of the theory, pointed out that according to it 'any fabricated tale' would be 'no less true than a historical report'.[59]

Schlick himself made various attempts to cope with the problem of subjectivity. In the lectures on 'Form and Content' (1932) he maintained that there were two kinds of meaning, subjective and intersubjective. The latter was about 'structure' (or 'form'). There was, he said, a 'logical structure' that is shared by propositions and facts; and (echoing the *Tractatus*) that 'we express a fact by another fact'.[60] These structures are not relative to persons, and so intersubjective communication is possible. But there is, in addition, an 'ineffable content' which is 'filled in' by each individual. Here is the element of personal experience, essential to the empiricist view. However, Schlick was aware of the tension in trying to accommodate this. Again echoing the *Tractatus*, he admitted that there can really be 'no proposition about content ... It would be best not to use the word "content" at all.'[61] What he was trying to say could not really be said.

Stevenson: the causal theory

The accounts considered so far have paid little attention to the *effects* of language on the people to whom it is addressed. In his *Analysis of mind* (1921), Russell considered the causal properties of words. He claimed that a word (e.g. 'John') *means* a certain object, if its appearance has the *same effect* as the appearance of the object (the person John). Here, as elsewhere, he adheres to the name–object conception of meaning. However, in the case of most words, it would be difficult to produce an object which is capable of appearing to an observer.

The name–object conception was rejected by C.L. Stevenson in *Ethics and language* (1944). He proposed to define 'meaning' in terms of certain 'psychological reactions'.[62] Stevenson was especially interested in what he called 'emotional meaning'. Human beings express feelings and evoke reactions in natural ways, such as sighs, laughs and groans.[63] There are also certain words, like 'hurrah', which have a similar function, this being acquired through conditioning in a particular language-community. According to Stevenson, the meaning of this word *consists* in its causal properties: the disposition, on the one hand, to arouse certain 'psychological processes in the hearer'[64] and, on the other, 'to be used' by a corresponding speaker.[65] He thought that this account could be extended to words and sentences in general. (Words 'combine to yield sentence-meanings'.[66])

Stevenson was aware that the effects produced by a given word or sentence vary a great deal, whereas their meanings are relatively stable. He dealt with this disparity by pointing out that sameness of disposition does not entail sameness of effect. Coffee may be said to have a disposition to stimulate, but whether and to what extent this disposition is realised in a particular case will depend on who is drinking the coffee, and in what circumstances.[67] Similarly, he thought, the psychological power of a word (which is its meaning) may remain unchanged in spite of varying effects.

But what are these psychological processes that words are disposed to produce? This may seem easy enough with 'emotive' words like 'hurrah'. But Stevenson also turned his attention to descriptive meaning. 'Descriptive meaning', he claimed, 'is the disposition of a sign to affect cognition.'[68] He pointed out that cognition and belief are themselves largely dispositional terms. Someone who believes that it is raining will be disposed to behave in certain ways (though his *actual* behaviour will, again, depend on circumstances).

Now the connection between disposition and belief is a question for the philosophy of mind and will not be discussed here. But the reader may wonder what the dispositional account of *meaning* amounts to, without this addition. It is, after all, obvious that a descriptive sentence, such as 'The cat is on the mat,' is 'disposed to affect cognition', if this means that it is suitable for informing someone that the cat is on the mat. Stevenson's claim was that this disposition *is* the meaning. But what is the point of this claim, and why should it be accepted? It may be thought that there must be some answer to the question 'What *is* meaning?' and that it is up to the philosopher of language to supply it. But it may be doubted whether the question is justified or indeed intelligible.

Stevenson's analysis of moral terms, such as 'wrong', 'good' and 'ought' is of special interest. He claimed (in his initial 'Working Model') that 'This is wrong' can be analysed into two components: 'I disapprove of this' and 'Do so as well.'[69] The first is 'an assertion about the speaker's state of mind', which may be verified like any other.[70] The second, however, is an 'imperative' and therefore cannot be true or false. He tried to show that moral arguments are emotive rather than rational – trying to act on the other person's feelings rather than giving him reasons for belief. It may be questioned, however, whether these types of discourse are really so distinct. A person's feelings *may* be affected by emotive language (in various ways), but they may also result from a consideration of suitable reasons. Again, the imperative 'Do so as well' does not make sense; one cannot be *requested* to approve or disapprove. Approval, like belief, is subject to reason and justification.

It has not been possible here to do justice to the subtlety and resourcefulness of Stevenson's account. But whatever the final verdict, it has the merit of trying to deal with the uses of language in human situations, rather than treating language abstractly as a relation between words and objects.

Wittgenstein: meaning and use

Rejection of 'theory'

One of the first works of Wittgenstein's 'later' philosophy was the *Blue book* of 1933–4. It opens with the question 'What is the meaning of a word?' We have considered a number of answers to this and similar questions, including Wittgenstein's own in the *Tractatus*. But his response now is to question the question. We can of course explain the meanings of particular words, but these explanations will vary according to the type of words; there is no *general* explanation of meaning, of the kind sought by philosophers. Again, the explanation of a particular word will not lead us to an object or process that *is* the meaning of that word. The name–object theory is rejected, and no general theory or explanation is put in its place.

According to the later Wittgenstein, 'the use of the word *in practice* is its meaning'.[71] This view is sometimes described as 'the use theory', but this is misleading. Wittgenstein was not indicating another kind of entity, 'use', which would explain how words have meaning; for the use in question – words used in actual human situations – already presupposes meaning. His point was that there is *no more* to the meaning of a word than its use.

According to Wittgenstein, there is no place in philosophy for explanation and theory. 'We may not advance any kind of theory ... We must do away with all *explanation*, and description alone must take its place.'[72] Faced with the question 'What is meaning?' we can do no better than to describe the use to which words are actually put in various human situations ('language-games'). It is wrong to think that behind this diversity there is some 'deeper', more general principle or explanation. In the *Investigations*, he put the following accusation in the mouth of an imaginary objector: 'You take the easy way out! You talk about all sorts of language-games, but have nowhere said what the essence ... of language is: what is common to all these activities, and what makes them into language.'[73] His reply is: 'And this is true.' He is not now prepared to produce such an 'essence', as he had been in the *Tractatus*.

The rejection of theory and explanation is one of the major issues in the philosophy of our time. Russell, in particular, saw its importance and bitterly attacked his former pupil and friend for having 'grown tired of serious thinking', and abandoning philosophy in favour of mere 'lexicography'.[74]

Wittgenstein's argument for the rejection is twofold. On the one hand, there is no need to postulate an underlying principle, since language can work in its diverse ways without this. On the other hand, 'explanations come to an end'. Whatever explanation is given, something will always be left unexplained; and then we must return to mere 'description', remarking merely that this and this is how human beings in fact behave in regard to language.

'Family resemblance'

In illustration of the first point, we may take Wittgenstein's discussion of the word 'game'. (The second point will be illustrated later.) There are many different kinds of games; but what is the essence of a game? What, essentially, does the word mean? Russell, as we saw, held that there must be 'such entities as universals', which such a word would 'stand for'. Now someone who rejects this assumption may still think that there must be something, some set of conditions that all games have in common, which would *explain* why we use this word as we do. But Wittgenstein challenges this assumption. He gives examples of various games, pointing out that features which appear in one are missing in others, and so on. The result of this examination, he says, is 'that we see a complicated network of similarities overlapping and criss-crossing'.[75] The situation is that of a 'family resemblance'. Among the members of a family, some have the same build, others the same eyes or gait, etc.; but there is no need, in order to recognise the family resemblance, to suppose that all members must have a set of features in common.

Wittgenstein admonishes the reader: 'Don't say: "There *must* be something in common, or they would not be called 'games'" – but *look and see* ...'[76] Here he rejects the 'must be' of the philosopher (notably his earlier self) who insists that there must be some structure *behind* the uses of words, even though this may be hidden from ordinary users of language. 'What is hidden', he now declares, 'is of no interest to us.'[77]

Wittgenstein's challenge regarding the essential meaning of a word may seem at first sight extremely rash. How can he be sure that an essential set of properties will not be discovered, in the case of 'game' and other words? However, if we consider how concepts actually develop in the course of time, we see that this is not as plausible as it may at first seem. Suppose we *begin* with an 'essentialist' definition of a concept '*X*': something is to count as an *X*, if and only if it has features *a*, *b* and *c*. Sooner or later we shall find instances, not previously thought of, which we find it natural to call '*X*' even though they lack one of the features *a*, *b* or *c*; and others that we shall *not* want to include even though they have them (but lack other features which, in the meantime, have come to seem more important). 'And [so] we extend our concept ... as in spinning a thread we twist fibre on fibre. And the strength of the thread ... [lies] in the overlapping of many fibres.'[78]

Ostensive explanation

The issue about explanation arises also at the level of explaining a word *to* someone. If the essentialist view were correct, we should be able to do this, in the case of 'game', by reference to features that games, and only games, have in common. But according to Wittgenstein, this kind of explanation is neither available nor necessary.

> How should we explain to someone what a game is? I imagine that we should describe *games* to him, and we might add: 'This *and similar things* are called "games".' And do we know any more about it ourselves?[79]

This explanation will only work, however, if the learner understands the examples in the right way. Here again 'explanations come to an end'. The learner's use of the examples is not itself explained, or brought about, by the explanation.

A similar point arises about 'ostensive' explanation. As we saw (pp. 35, 38), one of the concerns of the philosophers of the Vienna Circle was about breaking out of the circle of verbal definitions, so as to connect words with 'reality'. It was thought that this was achieved by pointing to suitable objects – 'as when we teach a child the [meaning] of "blue" by pointing to a blue object' (p. 35). But, Wittgenstein now argued, such a procedure can never give the whole meaning of a word; it will work only if the learner already has some knowledge of the meaning. He introduced the word 'tove' and imagined someone pointing to a pencil with the words 'This is tove.'[80] Such an explanation can always be understood in a variety of ways. 'Tove' might be taken to mean 'pencil' or 'round' or 'wood' or 'hard' or even 'one'. The learner would need to know which aspect of the object is meant; and every object (unlike the postulated 'objects' of the *Tractatus*) has indefinitely many aspects. Again, he would need to know whether 'tove' is meant as a proper name or a common noun; whether it is more specific or less specific (e.g. 'number' as opposed to a particular number); etc. He would also need to understand the meaning of the ostensive act itself; such a word as 'this', for example, could not itself be taught by the ostensive method.

There is, if Wittgenstein is right, no way of explaining or justifying language (whether in particular or in general) by reference to an independent 'reality'. In the end we are brought back to describing the actual uses of language in particular kinds of situation (of which the ostensive teaching situation is one).

Implications for philosophy

When philosophers use a word – 'knowledge', 'being', 'object', 'I', 'proposition', 'name' – and try to grasp the *essence* of the thing, one must always ask oneself: is the word ever actually used in this way in the language-game in which it is at home?[81]

Wittgenstein holds that philosophical problems arise because philosophers have given artificial, idealised meanings to such words as these. To the sceptic who maintains that one person can never really know whether another is in pain, he replies, 'If we are using the word "know" as it is normally used (and how else are we to use it?) then other people very often know when I am in pain.'[82] The question 'How else are we to use it?' is important. Of course the sceptical philosopher may say that according to his usage we do *not* know this. But if usage is the criterion of meaning, then it will follow that his denial is not about knowledge in the normal sense, but about 'knowledge' – a word with similar sound but different meaning. And similar distortions occur, if Wittgenstein is right, in the case of the other words mentioned above.

Now it may be thought that in philosophy, as in science, there is a need for technical terms in place of the (alleged) vagueness and imprecision of ordinary usage. But this cannot be so in the case of the above example. When, in ordinary conversation, we have occasion to say, 'I know he is in pain,' this is not vague or imprecise, and no improvement in this respect is brought about by the sceptic's denial.

It is sometimes thought that Wittgenstein regarded ordinary usage as *correct* usage, as opposed to that of the philosophers. But this is a misunderstanding. Ordinary usage is neither correct nor incorrect; there is no exterior standard by reference to which such an evaluation could be made. Ordinary usage is that which we actually have, and it is rooted in (though not justified by) human needs and interests. There may be no harm in introducing new usages, but it should not be thought that they are 'more correct' in any absolute sense. The meaning of 'correct', 'precise', etc. depends on the context in which these words are used.

Necessary truths, logical compulsion

As we have seen, there is, according to Wittgenstein, no hard and fast definition of such natural words as 'game'. To explain this word we can do no better than to give some examples and trust to the learner to catch on to what is meant. Speaking a language is not like 'operating a calculus according to definite rules'.[83] But what if it were? Wittgenstein argues that no calculus or set of rules is self-guaranteeing; it is always possible to interpret them in different ways. A rule does not explain why we interpret the rule as we do. He considers the case of someone who has been trained in the use of '+2' with numbers up to 1,000. One day this person is asked to continue the series '+2' beyond 1,000. To our surprise he writes '1,000, 1,004, 1,008, 1,012'.

> We say to him: 'Look what you've done!' – He doesn't understand. We say: 'You were meant to add *two*: look how you began the series!' – He answers: 'Yes, isn't it right? I thought that was how I was *meant* to do it.'[84]

Wittgenstein shows that ultimately we cannot force this person to accept that his is the wrong way of going on. We can only fall back on the assertion that *our* way is the 'obvious' and 'natural' one; that it is 'the same' as what was done with numbers below 1,000. But to this he may reply that he regards *his* way as obvious, etc.

Similar points are made by Wittgenstein with examples of imaginary tribes in which, for example, prices are calculated in what would seem to us absurd ways. Again there is no independent standard by which we can show that our ways are the right ones. 'If I have exhausted the justification, I have reached bedrock, and my spade is turned. Then I am inclined to say: "This is simply what I do." '[85] Wittgenstein is sometimes described as a 'relativist', 'conventionalist' and the like. But this is not correct if it means that we can choose as we like between one system of concepts and another. 'Then according to you', says Wittgenstein's imaginary objector, 'everybody could continue the series as he likes, and so infer *any*how!' Wittgenstein replies: 'In that case we shan't call it "continuing the series" [or] "inference".'[86] And in an extreme case we would not be able to regard the 'language' of another tribe as a language at all.[87]

Rejection of mentalism

It may be said that what made it wrong for the learner to write '1,004' was that the teacher *meant* him to write '1,002' (etc.). But was this 'meaning' in the teacher's mind when he made the request? He may have thought about this step at the time, but then again he may not. And 'even if you did think of this step, still you did not think of other ones'.[88] The teacher's meaning covered an infinity of steps, but he cannot have been thinking of each of these.

It is sometimes thought that mental processes (thought or images) are essential to meaning, and to such concepts as remembering and recognising. There is also a mental version of the name–object view. According to this, the meaning of a word is a *mental* object, and communication consists in causing such objects to appear in the

44

minds of others, who thereby *understand* what is meant. But Wittgenstein argues that such mental objects are neither necessary nor sufficient for meaning and understanding. Whether someone has understood the request 'Fetch me a red flower' depends on what he does and not on the existence of a mental image.[89]

On the other hand, the explanatory power of mental images is an illusion. For if the recognition of a red flower is to be explained by reference to a mental image, then we must ask how the *image* is recognised. Must we postulate a further image to account for this? Again, every image or picture is capable of different interpretations. Take a picture of a boxer in a particular position. This, says Wittgenstein, might be used to show how one should stand, how one should not stand, how someone did stand, etc.[90] It is also a mistake to think that the *learning* of one's native language can be explained by postulating a pre-existing 'innate' language. For if the former is in need of explanation, then the same will be true of one's understanding of the innate language.

The 'private language' argument

There is, according to Wittgenstein, no independent 'reality', whether physical or mental, which sets the standard of correct usage. This consists only in the agreement of actual speakers about right and wrong ways of going on.

But could there not be a 'private' language, one in which, say, a person records 'his immediate private sensations' – and which no one else can understand? In Wittgenstein's example someone writes 'S' in a diary, intending it to stand for such a sensation, and repeating the entry on subsequent days. He argues that in this case there can be no 'criterion of correctness. One would like to say: Whatever is going to seem right to me is right. And that only means that here we can't talk about "right".'[91] The example of 'sensations' must be compared with the widely held belief that many ordinary words, including 'pain' and 'red', have meaning by standing for 'private' occurrences, so that each person's meaning is different and known only to him. According to Wittgenstein, this is a false view, resulting from 'the model of "object and designation"'.[92] He points out that the word 'pain' (unlike the imaginary 'S') is learned and used in interpersonal situations, including the behaviour associated with pain. This is not to say that 'pain' *means* behaviour (there is nothing that *is* the meaning of the word). It does mean, however, that the use of this word, like that of others, is subject to the constraints of the language-speaking community.

Conclusion

Wittgenstein's account of language has left many readers unsatisfied. His claims, as we have seen, are largely negative. He tells us what meaning is not, and what cannot be achieved by theory and explanation. Many philosophers today, not content to leave matters there, have returned to the approach of Russell and others. They continue to face problems of the kind outlined in the previous sections. For others, however, the arguments of the later Wittgenstein represent a decisive advance in the history of philosophy.

Notes

'An author's name followed by a number in square brackets refers to the book or article which has that number in the bibliography.)

1. Frege [1], p. 1.
2. Frege [2], p. 56.
3. Ibid.
4. Ibid., p. 57.
5. Ibid., p. 58.
6. Ibid., pp. 59–60.
7. Ibid., p. 58.
8. Frege [1], p. 60.
9. Ibid., p. 59.
10. Frege [2], p. 62.
11. Ibid., p. 63.
12. Ibid.
13. Ibid., p. 65.
14. Ibid., pp. 63–4.
15. Russell [5], p. 93.
16. Ibid., p. 90.
17. Ibid., pp. 93–4.
18. Ibid., p. 58.
19. Ibid., pp. 55, 58.
20. Ibid., p. 55.
21. Ibid., p. 59.
22. Ibid., p. 55.
23. Ibid., p. 12.
24. Russell [6], p. 195.
25. Russell [3], p. 179.
26. Ibid., p. 179.
27. Ibid., pp. 178–9.
28. Russell [6], p. 251.
29. Ibid.
30. Russell [3], p. 177.
31. Frege [2], p. 62.
32. Russell [6], p. 46.
33. Russell [4], p. 179.
34. Russell [6], p. 201.
35. Ibid.
36. Ibid.
37. Ibid., p. 197.
38. Ibid., p. 194.
39. Ibid., p. 270.
40. Ibid., p. 198.
41. Ibid., p. 274.
42. Ibid.
43. Ibid.
44. Russell [4], p. 129.
45. Wittgenstein [7], p. 128.
46. Russell [6], p. 198.
47. Wittgenstein [7], p. 130.
48. Wittgenstein [8], pp. 47, 244.
49. Schlick [10], p. 458.
50. Wittgenstein [8], p. 244.
51. 'The scientific conception of the world', *Erkenntnis*, I, p. 15.
52. Ayer [11], p. 48 (Penguin edn).
53. Cf. Moore [9], p. 266.
54. Wittgenstein [8], p. 244.
55. Moore [9], p. 107.
56. Carnap [12], p. 79.
57. Ayer [11], p. 142 (Penguin edn).
58. Wittgenstein [8], p. 249.
59. Schlick [10], p. 376.
60. Ibid., p. 302.
61. Ibid., pp. 306–7.
62. Stevenson [13], p. 60.
63. Ibid., pp. 37–8.
64. Ibid., p. 54.
65. Ibid., p. 57.
66. Ibid., p. 67.
67. Ibid., p. 46.
68. Ibid., p. 67.
69. Ibid., p. 21.
70. Ibid., p. 26.
71. Wittgenstein [16], p. 69.

72. Wittgenstein [14], para. 109.
73. Ibid., para. 65.
74. Russell [4], p. 161.
75. Wittgenstein [14], para. 66.
76. Ibid.
77. Ibid., para. 126.
78. Ibid., para. 67.
79. Ibid., para. 69.
80. Wittgenstein [16], p. 2.
81. Wittgenstein [14], para. 116;
    author's translation.
82. Ibid., para. 246.
83. Ibid., para. 81.
84. Ibid., para. 185.
85. Ibid., para. 217.
86. Wittgenstein [15], Part I, para. 116.
87. Wittgenstein [14], para. 207.
88. Ibid., para. 187.
89. Cf. Wittgenstein [16], p. 3.
90. Wittgenstein [14], p. 11, note.
91. Ibid., para. 258.
92. Ibid., para. 293.

Bibliography

Frege's pioneering work on the philosophy of language was motivated by his work on the foundations of mathematics. One important source for this work is available in an excellent translation by J.L. Austin:

[1] *The foundations of arithmetic* (Basil Blackwell, Oxford, 1959). Frege's subtle defence of the view that numbers are self-subsistent objects will be found in sections 45–69. Frege's most important philosophical articles are translated by Max Black and P.T. Geach and appear as

[2] *Frege, philosophical writings* (Basil Blackwell, Oxford, 1952). This collection includes 'On sense and reference' (or 'On sense and meaning' as the third, 1980, edition translates it) as well as 'On concept and object', where Frege attempts to distinguish that which corresponds to a proper name (an 'object') from that which corresponds to a predicate expression (a 'concept'). An excellent brief introduction to Frege's philosophic achievement is 'Frege's philosophy' in Michael Dummett, *Truth and other enigmas* (Duckworth, London, 1978).

Much of Russell's early work was likewise devoted to the foundations of mathematics. His

[3] *Introduction to mathematical philosophy* (Allen and Unwin, London, 1919) was written for a popular audience. His intellectual autobiography,

[4] *My philosophical development* (Allen and Unwin, London, 1959) is a very accessible account of how his ideas developed from these early concerns, especially under the influence of Wittgenstein. An early (again 'popular') venture by Russell into the wider issues of philosophy is

[5] *The problems of philosophy* (Oxford University Press, Oxford, 1912), while his influential contributions to the new 'logical' empiricism are well represented in

[6] *Logic and knowledge*, ed. R.C. Marsh (Allen and Unwin, London, 1956). David Pears, *Bertrand Russell and the British tradition in philosophy* (Collins, London, 1967) is an extended exposition of Russell's form of logical atomism. The theory of descriptions was central to this set of doctrines; the best-known criticism of this theory is 'On referring' in P.F. Strawson's *Logico-linguistic papers* (Methuen, London, 1971).

The standard translation of Wittgenstein's *Tractatus logico-philosophicus* is by D.F. Pears and B.F. McGuinness (Routledge and Kegan Paul, London, 1961). There are many commentaries on this work. One written by a person who was close both personally and intellectually to Wittgenstein is by G.E.M. Anscombe, *An introduction* to *Wittgenstein's Tractatus* (Hutchinson, London, 1959). The notebooks which Wittgenstein kept while working on the *Tractatus* have been translated by G.E.M. Anscombe as

[7] *Notebooks 1914–1916* (Basil Blackwell, Oxford, 1961). The member of the Vienna Circle with whom Wittgenstein collaborated most closely was Friedrich Waismann. His

[8] *Wittgenstein and the Vienna Circle*, trans. by B.F. McGuinness (Basil Blackwell, Oxford, 1979) is largely a record of conversations between Wittgenstein and members of the Vienna Circle, taken down by Waismann. The final 'Theses' (pp. 233ff) were written by Waismann, but under the influence of Wittgenstein. Wittgenstein's thinking immediately after his return to philosophy in 1929 is also represented in

[9] 'Wittgenstein's lectures in 1930–33' in G.E. Moore, *Philosophical papers* (Routledge, London, 1959).

Good representations of writings by members of the Vienna Circle, and those whom they influenced, are to be found in A.J. Ayer (ed.), *Logical positivism* (Macmillan, New York, 1959) and O. Hanfling (ed.), *Essential readings in logical positivism* (Basil Blackwell, Oxford, 1981). The writings of members of the Circle have been assembled and translated into English in a series of books published in Holland, for example,

[10] Moritz Schlick, *Philosophical papers* (Reidel, Dordrecht, 1979). (All references in the text are to vol. II.) The ideas of the Vienna Circle were first conveyed widely to the English-speaking world through

[11] A.J. Ayer, *Language, truth and logic* (Victor Gollancz, London, 1936) (paperback edn, Penguin Books, Harmondsworth, 1971).

The Vienna Circle scattered in the turmoil of the 1930s. Waismann settled in Oxford; Carnap and others continued their careers in US universities. An influential piece by Carnap from this period is

[12] 'Testability and meaning', which can be found abridged in H. Feigl and M. Brodbeck (eds), *Readings in the philosophy of science* (Appleton, New York, 1953). Russell's response to the issues raised by the Vienna Circle emerged from a series of lectures and seminars (some of them attended by Carnap) in a book, *An inquiry into meaning and truth* (Allen and Unwin, London, 1940), which is still one of the best introductions to the issues of this period.

The doctrines which the members of the Vienna Circle transplanted from Europe to America were not wholly unlike some indigenous varieties already flourishing there. As early as 1878 an American philosopher, C.S. Peirce, advanced a primitive form of verificationism, and in the 1920s P.W. Bridgman, in *The logic of modern physics* (Macmillan, New York, 1927), linked meaning and methods of verification in a doctrine which he called 'operationalism'. Bridgman took the slogan 'meaning is the method of verification' more literally than did members of the Vienna Circle. C.L. Stevenson's

[13] *Ethics and language* (Yale University Press, New Haven, 1944), although positivist in spirit, cannot be seen entirely as the product of the imported European influences.

The development of the doctrines of Wittgenstein's 'later philosophy' can be traced through numerous posthumous edited and published manuscripts. The central text of the later period is

[14] *Philosophical investigations* (Basil Blackwell, Oxford, 1953), much of which was

nearly ready for publication when Wittgenstein died. Wittgenstein's criticism of the idea that meaning is essentially a one-to-one relation between words and corresponding things is to be found in the first paragraphs of this book. An indispensable companion to the *Investigations* is a collection of fragments,

[15] *Remarks on the foundations of mathematics*, trans. G.E.M. Anscombe (Basil Blackwell, Oxford, 1978). Among the earliest and most important of the writings from Wittgenstein's later period is

[16] *The blue and brown books* (Basil Blackwell, Oxford, 1958), which consists of notes dictated to students in 1933–5. (In the case of the *Blue book* Wittgenstein prepared stencilled copies of the notes.) A useful introduction to Wittgenstein's later philosophy is P.M.S. Hacker, *Insight and illusion* (Oxford University Press, Oxford, 1972).

J.E.T.

3 | Theories of Meaning: After the Use Theory

B.J. Copeland and R.H. Stoothoff

Hostility to the concept of meaning

The concept of linguistic meaning has received an enormous amount of attention from philosophers, who have been struggling with the concept for several centuries now. The problem of how language functions, of how it is possible for us to use sounds and symbols to communicate with each other about our complex world, has held a perennial fascination for philosophers; and the concept of meaning has been considered by many to be the key to understanding the whole phenomenon of language. Recently, however, some philosophers have questioned whether this emphasis on the concept of meaning may not be misplaced.

Quine's argument

A forceful participant in this hostility towards the traditional notion of meaning is the American philosopher W.V. Quine. Quine believes that the traditional concept of linguistic meaning should be rooted out of respectable, scientific thinking and inquiry. He has an ingenious argument with which to support this belief, an argument which has been extremely influential in recent years. In outline, the strategy of the argument is to focus on certain very basic characteristics which meaning is traditionally supposed to have, and show that there *is* nothing with those characteristics. Thus, if the argument works, philosophers attempting to analyse and understand the notion of linguistic meaning are shown to be rather like a group of hunters pursuing a unicorn: in each case the object of the quest is mythical. It may surprise you to learn that the basic characteristics which the argument focuses on are such straightforward-sounding ones as these: that a precise, unambiguous sentence has a definite, determinate meaning; that competent speakers of a language know these meanings; that several sentences of the same language may mean the same as one another; and that sentences of different languages, too, often mean exactly the same as one another. Quine's argument is designed to show that these commonplaces are completely mistaken: the whole idea that there are determinate, language-independent sentence meanings is wrong, and so the traditional concept of meaning must be abandoned.

The argument consists of two stages. The first concerns the situation of a lone traveller in distant lands who comes across a tribe of people speaking a language completely unknown to him. Having no interpreter, and finding himself with no knowledge of even a distantly related language to use as a starting point, the traveller must rely entirely on his observations of the people's behaviour in order to fathom their language. Quine dubs this situation *radical translation*. The point he wants to establish is that no matter how diligent the radical translator is in his observations of the use the tribespeople make of sentences of their language, these observations will never narrow down the range of possible translations to just one. Consider, for example, their sentence 'Gavagai.' The translator observes that the tribespeople utter this sentence, or assent to it, only when a rabbit is present. It would thus be natural enough for him to translate the sentence by 'There is a rabbit,' or some such. However, there are other, utterly different, translations just as compatible with the observational evidence. 'It is rabbiting here,' for example, on a parallel with 'It is raining here.' The latter sentence reports the presence of a general *feature* in the local environment, the feature of raininess. No mention is made of individual raindrops. Perhaps the tribespeople are as indifferent to individual rabbits as we are to individual raindrops, and are content merely to register the presence of a feature in a local environment, the feature of rabbitiness. This may seem odd to us, but we cannot assume that the tribespeople entirely share our way of thinking about the world. Nor does this exhaust the alternatives. Perhaps the tribespeople take more of a butcher's-eye view of animals than we do, and 'Gavagai' is to be translated as 'There are some undetached rabbit-parts.' Or perhaps the tribe's metaphysical and scientific views lead them to have a greater interest in brief temporal segments of objects than in (what we see as) the continuing objects themselves. When we say, 'There is a rabbit,' we are affirming the presence of an object which persists through several months or years; but perhaps when the tribespeople say, 'Gavagai,' they are affirming the presence only of what we would call a short phase or stage in the existence of a rabbit. In this case 'Gavagai' is to be translated along the lines of 'There is a rabbit-stage' (there is no natural-sounding English rendition available here). Or again, perhaps the tribespeople's religion leads them to be more concerned with totalities than we are. When the natives see an individual rabbit, as we would put it, they think of themselves as seeing a small part of an organic whole, the aggregate of all rabbits as we would describe it. Here the best translation of 'Gavagai' might be the awkward 'There is a bit of the rabbit-aggregate.'

You may feel that the translator simply needs more data: it is tempting to think that it *must* be possible for him to tell what the tribespeople mean by the word 'gavagai' if only he can accumulate enough information about the use they make of their sentences. But ask yourself what information could possibly settle the issue. For instance, suppose the translator learns the native expressions for assent and dissent, and also learns the right tone of voice to use to turn a sentence into a query. Couldn't he then settle the issue simply by pointing at a whole rabbit and saying 'Gavagai' queryingly to a tribesperson who understands that translation is in progress? No. The answer would be of no help, since in pointing at a whole rabbit the translator will also be pointing at a piece of the rabbit-aggregate, at an assortment of undetached rabbit-parts, and so on through all the other alternatives. Quine urges that no matter *how* much information the translator accumulates he will never be in a position to eliminate all but one of the possible translations of 'gavagai'. Even when the translator is able to formulate his own complex questions in the language, it will still not be possible to finally settle the issue, Quine says. An example will illustrate why Quine thinks this. Suppose after pointing to the tail and the head of the same rabbit, the translator asks, 'Ei gavagai seif-seif ei?', for which his tentative translation is 'Is this one and the same gavagai as that?' Surely an affirmative answer would at least rule out rabbit-parts (and perhaps also rabbit-stages)? No. For although this particular translator fixes on 'is one and the same as' for the translation of 'seif-seif', and allows assent to his question to rule out 'undetached rabbit-part' as the translation of 'gavagai', a second, independent translator could fix on 'undetached rabbit-part' as the translation of 'gavagai' and allow assent to 'Ei gavagai seif-seif ei?' to rule out 'is one and the same as' for 'seif-seif'. (Perhaps he might favour 'is part of the same thing as' for 'seif-seif'.) Conceivably nothing at all in the tribespeople's speech and associated behaviour would ever conflict with either of these different schemes of translation. As Quine puts it, any of the alternative translations of 'gavagai' can be sustained given some 'compensatory juggling' elsewhere in the scheme of translation.

The gavagai example is artificial and rather frivolous. However, the point it is intended to illustrate is serious: in view of the possibility of 'compensatory juggling' there are bound to be alternative schemes of translation for any language, says Quine, schemes which differ in the translations they provide of very many individual sentences but which nevertheless fit equally well with the totality of observable behaviour of speakers of the language (both actual behaviour and possible behaviour). This phenomenon is known as the *indeterminacy of translation*. From it flows Quine's case against the traditional concept of meaning. He maintains that the existence of the phenomenon makes nonsense of the traditional idea that sentences of different languages may have the same meanings as one another: it is nonsense to think of there being language-neutral meanings which, so to speak, attach themselves to sentences of different languages. Let me return to the gavagai example to illustrate what Quine is saying here. If we operate with the traditional concept of meaning we will say that the one-word sentence 'Gavagai' does *have* a determinate meaning: 'Gavagai' means the same as one or other of 'There is a rabbit,' 'There is a rabbit-stage,' and so on – it is just that no matter how much information we accumulate about the use the tribespeople make of their language we can never *tell* which. All this, says Quine, is nonsense. Language is a tool for communication, for social interaction. Anyone who thinks that there can be some crucial property of a sentence which will remain hidden no matter how much the radical translator comes to know about the way the tribespeople use the sentence to communicate with one another has simply lost sight of the basic fact that the be-all and end-all of language *is* communication. In the traditional view meaning is both a crucial property of a sentence, and yet may leave no mark on the use speakers make of the sentence in communication. But you can't have it both those ways.

Someone who wanted to defend the traditional concept of meaning might object at this point that it is not particularly relevant how much the radical translator may or may not come to learn through his observations of the tribespeople. It is the tribespeople who matter, not the translator. *They* know the meaning of 'Gavagai,' and so of course sentence meanings enter crucially into the process of communication between them, irrespective of whether or not the role these meanings play is visible to the radical translator. However, Quine would urge that this objection is ill thought out. The translator may come in the end to participate as fully as any tribesperson in the local daily round, all speech behaviour included, and yet the indeterminacy of translation will remain. Indeed, in Quine's view there is no essential difference between tribesperson and translator: every tribesperson is in a sense a radical translator amongst his or her friends and acquaintances. Whilst learning the language and in making a lifetime's use of it for social intercourse, each tribesperson has no more data to go on than does the alien translator, namely observations of the speech and behaviour of other users of the language. And of course this applies to us and our language just as much as to the tribespeople. This is in fact the second stage of Quine's argument that I mentioned earlier. Emphasis is shifted from an intruding alien to any speaker at all. We are all radical translators. (As Quine puts it, radical translation begins at home.) When you say, 'Look, there is a rabbit,' how am I to translate this sentence of your personal 'dialect' into mine? As 'Look, there is a rabbit' or as 'Look, there is a rabbit-stage', or ...?

No one should feel that there is any practical difficulty here. Indeterminacy does not in the least hinder our interaction with each other, precisely because the various translation schemes are ex hypothesi equally compatible with all possible behaviour on our part, and so it can make no difference to our business together which one I fix on. Doubtless everyone unreflectingly fixes on the first translation I mentioned of a neighbour's utterance of 'Look, there is a rabbit,' but any of them would do equally well, and the question of which one of the equally good alternatives is 'the right' translation seems to have little point. No, the difficulty is not practical but theoretical: it arises for the theoretician who wants to cling to the traditional concept of meaning. Such a person must say that even though you and I manage to communicate without a hitch, neither of us knows the meaning of the other's sentences. What crazy concept of meaning is that? The correct view, says Quine, is not that the facts about what you mean lie forever hidden from me, but rather that there are no facts about meaning at all, for the whole concept of meaning is a nonsense.

This argument of Quine's is liable to produce a feeling of intense intellectual discomfort. For most of us are prone to think in terms of what I have been calling the traditional concept of meaning: it embodies the viewpoint of common sense. Yet the concept has, it seems, been made to crumble before our eyes.

Criticisms of Quine's argument

Quine has not in fact managed to establish the existence of a pervasive and malignant indeterminacy of translation. For one thing, the gavagai example does not work. It is simply false that there could be no features of the tribespeople's behaviour which would enable the translator to choose between the alternatives. Suppose, for example, that a white rabbit and a black rabbit with a white tail are sitting side by side in front of the translator and a tribesman. Pointing to the white rabbit the translator says queryingly, 'Blanco gavagai?' and the tribesman assents. (The translator originally heard 'blanco' on the occasion of his first wash in the river, when the tribespeople scrutinised his pale flesh with giggling interest.) Repeating the process with the black rabbit, however, evokes dissent, even when the translator tries pointing to the white tail. Whatever the details of 'blanco', surely this rules out 'It is rabbiting' for 'Gavagai'? For the tribesman has just demonstrated that the term 'gavagai' is responsive to differences between individual rabbits, whereas this focusing on individuals is precisely what is avoided by 'It is rabbiting.' The fact that the tribesman assents to 'Blanco gavagai?' when the translator points to the white rabbit's white tail but not to the black rabbit's white tail looks bad, too, for the suggestion that 'gavagai' can be rendered 'undetached rabbit part'. Likewise for 'piece of the rabbit-aggregate': the tribesman has just dissented from 'Blanco gavagai?' when presented with a blanco piece of the rabbit aggregate, the tail. Nor is this alternative saved by reconstruing 'gavagai' as 'rabbit-shaped, rabbit-sized piece of the rabbit-aggregate', for it happens that the tribesman dissents from 'Blanco gavagai?' even when the translator patiently arranges a dozen or so white-tailed black rabbits so that the tails combine to form a perfectly rabbit-shaped, rabbit-sized piece of the rabbit-aggregate. Where one translator diagnoses indeterminacy a colleague of greater ingenuity may find none.

The collapse of the gavagai example would not matter if Quine's general argument for the existence of indeterminacy were a success. This, remember, is his point about 'compensatory juggling': there are, he says, bound to be different schemes of translation for a language all equally compatible with all possible behaviour on the part of the speakers, because divergence at one point can so to speak be cancelled out by further divergence at another point (recall 'seif-seif' and its divergent translations 'is one and the same as' and 'is part of the same thing as'). However, Quine does nothing to substantiate this large claim, and thus there is no reason for us to accept it. An analogy (which is due to Simon Blackburn) is helpful here. If you solve the first couple of clues of a crossword puzzle wrongly it may not show because the mistakes cancel out (perhaps both words have the letter 'O' where they cross). Clearly, though, this provides no reason to think there will be a number of different solutions to the *whole* puzzle which are all equally as good as one another. The mutually compensating errors will most likely become exposed as further words are fitted into place. Now, it is certainly true that two independent radical translators may adopt different translations at a number of points, with the differences at first all cancelling out. As in the case of the crossword, though, this provides no reason to think that the two 'solutions' will remain equally tenable as translation proceeds and new contexts are examined. Quine *may* be right that for every language there will be different schemes of translation whose differences cancel out even when all contexts are taken into consideration; but he has done little to establish that this is so.

There is, then, no reason to believe in the existence of the wholesale indeterminacy of translation envisaged by Quine. It may be that indeterminacy will be established to exist not throughout language but in certain regions (the sentences of highly theoretical science are often cited as a possible case in point). If so, then for these regions the traditional concept of meaning must be abandoned. Relinquishing the traditional view that meaning in the case of such sentences is so to speak absolute, perhaps we would settle for a much diluted notion whereby talk about meaning is no more than a way of recording the treatment given to individual sentences relative to a particular way of translating that region of the language. Thus we might say things like: relative to the system of translation T_1 sentence S means that $\cdots$, whereas relative to the equally good system T_2, S means that ---- ($\cdots$ and ---- being substantially different). For the present, though, we have seen little reason not to persist with the traditional concept of meaning, especially in the less exotic regions of language.

Semantics and truth theories

One of the most important characteristics of human language is that messages are produced by fitting the same basic elements together in different combinations. By varying the combinations of a relatively small number of basic elements human speakers are able to produce a seemingly boundless assortment of different messages. To put it somewhat metaphorically, from the basic building blocks of word meanings speakers construct an enormous number of different sentence meanings. Suppose we are studying, with reference to some specific language, how the meaning or content of sentences is built out of basic components. For illustration, say the language is Arabic. Our goal is a systematic theory which describes how the meaning of any Arabic sentence is formed from the meanings of its parts. The idea is that given an Arabic sentence the theory should enable us to derive a statement of what it means, starting from statements about the meanings of the words it contains (plus any basic units of speech other than words), together with statements about its structure (for example that it consists of two words, the first a noun and the second a verb). Thus, given the sentence

Al-Qahirah madinah

it should be possible to derive in the theory the statement

'Al-Qahirah madinah' means that Cairo is a city.

In general, for each Arabic sentence the theory will enable us to compute a statement of the form

'S' means that P

where the letter P is replaced by a sentence of the language in which the theory is stated – in this case English – which gives the meaning of the Arabic sentence that replaces the letter S. Such a theory is called a *semantics* for Arabic, or sometimes a *theory of meaning* for Arabic. (Incidentally, there is no difference between the singular and plural forms of the noun 'semantics' – as with 'sheep', for example.)

Meaning and truth

What form should be taken by the statements of the theory which give the meaning of the words of the language? How is the derivation of sentence meaning from word meaning to proceed in the theory? These have proved to be difficult questions, and much modern research utilises a slightly indirect approach to constructing theories of meaning. The approach involves the concept of truth. In his pioneer work on this concept in the 1930s the logician Alfred Tarski showed how to construct what is called a *theory of truth* for certain rather simple artificial languages. His work has been extended to richer languages, both natural and artificial, by many researchers (but notably by Saul Kripke and Richard Montague). A theory of truth for a language has the same basic structure as a theory of meaning: from statements concerning the parts of a sentence it is possible to derive in the theory a statement which tells you under what conditions the sentence is true. So, for example, in a theory of truth for Arabic it should be possible to derive the statement

'Al-thalj abyad' is true (in Arabic) if and only if snow is white.

(Statements of this form are generally called *T-sentences*.) It has long been appreciated that there is an intimate connection between truth and meaning. It is the meaning of an indicative sentence that fixes what circumstances make the sentence true, and understanding an indicative sentence involves grasping what these circumstances are. (An indicative sentence is one used to make an assertion, as opposed to ask a question, give a command, and so on.) Moreover, it is often possible to explain what an indicative sentence means by describing the circumstances which would make it true. For example, if you ask me what the Arabic sentence 'Al-thalj abyad' means, I can tell you by saying that it is an indicative sentence which is true if and only if snow is white.

There was a cumulative realisation amongst researchers that a theory of truth for a language can serve as a theory of meaning for the language. This idea can be illustrated by considering a Tarski-like theory of truth for a very small fragment of Arabic. This fragment consists of just five words: the names 'al-Qahirah' and 'Misr', the descriptions (or predicates) 'madinah' and 'bilad', and the connective 'wa'. The basic statements (or axioms) of the truth theory are:

(i) 'al-Qahirah' denotes Cairo
(ii) 'Misr' denotes Egypt
(iii) an entity x satisfies the description 'madinah' if and only if (henceforward abbreviated 'iff') x is a city
(iv) an entity x satisfies the description 'bilad' iff x is a country
(v) a sentence consisting of a name followed by a description is true iff the description is satisfied by the entity which the name denotes
(vi) where S_1 and S_2 are sentences (of our little five-word language) the sentence formed by writing 'wa' between them is true iff S_1 and S_2 are themselves both true.

Although this little language contains only five words there are infinitely many sentences in it (because of the presence of 'wa'), and for each one of them the truth theory yields a statement of the form: '*S*' is true iff *P*. For illustration you might check for yourself the derivation of the theorem: 'Al-Qahirah madinah wa Misr bilad' is true iff Cairo is a city and Egypt is a country. This truth theory, then, seems to serve very well as a semantics for the five-word language. The axioms suffice to describe the functions of the component words of the language and to describe the significance of the structure of sentences of the language (granted, of course, an understanding of the concepts of denotation, satisfaction and truth). From the axioms, theorems can be derived which state the meanings of the sentences of the language, and these derivations display how the components of each sentence contribute to its overall meaning. Moreover, the truth theory tells you all you need to know in order to be able to speak and understand the five-word language (barring pronunciation). Thus constructing a truth theory for a language and constructing a theory of meaning for a language have come to be conceived as the same project by many. The enterprise is often described as 'truth-theoretic semantics'.

A theory of meaning is often stated in the very language that the theory is about – a semantics for (some part of) English stated in English, for example. (A semantics so stated is called homophonic.) You should not find this puzzling: after all, our truth theory for the five-word fragment of Arabic will still *say* the same if it is itself translated into Arabic, and the translated theory will no less effectively show how the components of a sentence contribute to its overall meaning. Obviously, it is convenient for researchers to state their theories in their own language even when working on that language.

Possible limitations on truth-theoretic semantics

Researchers have not yet succeeded in constructing even in outline a truth-theoretic semantics for the whole of a natural language (such as English or Arabic), although there is now a large body of results concerning particular categories of expressions (for example adverbs, adjectives, comparatives, tense indicators and other indexical expressions, articles, sentential connectives, quantifiers). However, at the present stage it remains an open question whether the truth-theoretic approach can be applied throughout language, or whether only a subset of constructions is amenable.

One possible limitation lies in the fact that a straightforward truth theory gives only a single brand of information about complete sentences, namely that a sentence is true if and only if something-or-other; and some suspect that a theory which offers a wider variety of information about complete sentences may be required for certain constructions. This can be illustrated by a simple example. The Egyptians have two ways of referring to the River Nile, al-Nil and al-Bahr. A straightforward truth theory can 'see' no distinction between the sentences 'Al-Nil flows into the Mediterranean' and 'Al-Bahr flows into the Mediterranean.' Each is true if and only if the

Nile flows into the Mediterranean, and so there is no significant difference between them as far as a straightforward truth theory is concerned. Thus the truth theory 'sees' no difference between the compound sentences 'Mary is wondering whether al-Nil flows into the Mediterranean' and 'Mary is wondering whether al-Bahr flows into the Mediterranean,' since as far as the theory is concerned these two sentences are built in the same way out of component sentences which do not differ significantly from each other. Yet there *is* a vital difference between these two compound sentences, in that the first may be true but the second false. Mary in her geography exam may be quite certain that al-Nil flows into the Mediterranean, but nonetheless be wondering whether al-Bahr flows into the Mediterranean or the Red Sea, having forgotten that they are in fact the same river. 'Wonder' is a member of an important family of verbs, called the *intentional verbs*, all of which are similarly prima facie resistant to straightforward truth-theoretic semantics. Some other members of the family are: 'intend', 'think', 'feel', 'desire', 'believe', 'perceive', 'hope', 'fear'. There have been a number of ingenious attempts to bring the intentional verbs within the ambit of truth-theoretic semantics, but no approach commanding universal assent has yet emerged.

Another area which is not yet well understood concerns the relationship between indicative and non-indicative sentences. For example, how should a semantics handle the sentence 'Are you on holiday?', which at first sight is neither true nor false? Can it be regarded as a paraphrase of 'I ask you whether you are on holiday,' and thus as either true or false after all? Or does the treatment of mood require a radical departure from the truth-theoretic approach to semantics?

Possible worlds semantics

It is not yet known to what extent truth-theoretic semantics for natural languages must rely on the concept of sentences being true in possible situations, rather than simply on the concept of sentences being true. Semantics which use the former concept are quaintly known as 'possible worlds semantics'. (It is the latter concept, truth pure and simple, which figured in Tarski's original style of truth theory, and in our example.) To get a feel for the need to introduce the concept of truth in a possible situation, think of the word 'might', as in 'Pigs might fly.' For convenience we can rewrite this as 'M Pigs fly.' A natural choice of axiom for M is:

'M Pigs fly' is true iff 'Pigs fly' is true in some possible situation.

(In general, any sentence can replace 'Pigs fly.') It is extremely hard to see how to handle 'might' without resorting to possible situations. Indeed, most of the actual progress in truth-theoretic semantics has in fact utilised the concept of truth in a possible situation. However, a strong philosophical lobby believes that truth theories should keep to Tarski's original form, since the notion of a possible situation is 'unscientific'. It is far from clear what that charge amounts to, though.

Some benefits and uses of semantics

The main reason for undertaking a semantical investigation of natural language is to gain a greater understanding of how language works: a semantics gives a systematic description of how sentence meaning arises from sentence structure and word meaning. Here are some further payoffs.

(1) A traditional philosophical teaser concerns the nature of meanings. What sort of thing is the meaning of a sentence, or the meaning of a word? Philosophical analysis, it appeared, was the only way to discover the nature of these mysterious entities, meanings. Yet, frustratingly, even philosophical analysis seemed incapable of yielding an unequivocal answer. Are meanings ideas? Are they some sort of objectively existing universal? The evidence seemed to point inconclusively in both directions (and more besides). Strikingly, however, a truth-theoretic semantics makes no mention of these murky entities. Despite this there is no large gap in the theory that can be filled only once we finally discover what meanings are really like. The theory for our example five-word language says what each sentence of the language means, and describes how the words in a sentence determine its overall meaning, and all this is achieved without there being any need to think of meanings as being a kind of object. The obvious moral is that meanings are *not* a kind of object. Contemplating a truth-theoretic semantics should have a therapeutic effect on anyone gripped by the fantasy that talk about the meanings of sentences is talk about some elusive species of entity.

(2) A truth-theoretic semantics is an empirically testable theory. The statements that the semantic theory yields as theorems can – like the statements yielded by theories in physics, biology and psychology – be matched against the empirical evidence and pronounced true or false. For example, the evidence overwhelmingly favours the truth of the statement: 'Al-thalj abyad' is true (in Arabic) iff snow is white. The importance of this point is that their empirical character places theories of meaning squarely amongst other scientific theories, whereas not so long ago the study of meaning was often viewed as a dubious enterprise by those with a high regard for scientific methodology. Admittedly the precise details of the relationship between a theory of meaning and the phenomena that constitute evidence for its truth – ultimately the behaviour of members of a linguistic community – have yet to be fully charted out, but there is no reason to suspect the presence of difficulties embarrassingly deeper than those which philosophers are apt to find in connection with the other sciences. Admittedly, too, it could turn out that several different theories of meaning for a language or part of a language

are equally confirmed by the evidence available, or indeed by any possible evidence (recall our discussion of the indeterminacy of translation) – but these two possibilities are no less present in the traditional sciences. (However, it must be stressed that if the second of these possibilities *were* to be realised, then in the light of the foregoing discussion of the consequences of the indeterminacy of translation, a revision would be required in what we have called the traditional way of conceiving meaning.)

(3) Logicians, mathematicians, computer scientists and others design their own languages. A semantics may be used to give a formal and systematic account of what the sentences of a new artificial language are supposed to mean (although the semantics may not always take the form of a truth theory). Equally importantly, a semantics may be used to characterise the logic of an artificial language (that is, tell you which sentences follow from which). For example, suppose an artificial language constructed for some purpose or other contains a sentential connective | whose axiom in the truth theory is: $A \mid B$ is true iff it is not the case that both A and B are true. This axiom yields all the logical principles governing sentences whose only connective is |. For example, it tells you that $A \mid B$ follows from $A \mid A$ (think about it!).

Has the concept of meaning disappeared?

Truth-theoretic semantics makes no explicit use of the concept of meaning at all. Some philosophers hostile to the concept of meaning have taken this to show that there is no need to employ the concept in the study of language. They suggest that instead of speaking in terms of what a sentence *means*, we need speak only in terms of the *truth-condition* of the sentence – that is, the condition under which the sentence is true, as stated by a theorem of the form '*S*' is true iff *P*. (So, for example, the truth-condition of 'Al-Qahirah madinah' is that Cairo is a city.) Other philosophers, not hostile to the concept of meaning but wanting an *analysis* of it, take these same facts to show that the concept of meaning boils down to the concept of truth-conditions. However, the idea that the concept of meaning can be either eliminated or analysed in this way is a mistake, as we shall see.

It is certainly the case that the meaning of 'Al-Qahirah madinah' is given by the T-sentence:

'Al-Qahirah madinah' is true if and only if Cairo is a city.

(The term 'T-sentence' was introduced on page 57.) However, only some true T-sentences are meaning-giving, not all. This is because in standard logical usage (to which all truth theories subscribe) the phrase 'if and only if' asserts nothing more than equivalence of truth-value. That is, '*A* if and only if *B*' says nothing more than that *A* and *B* are either both true, or both false. So, perhaps surprisingly, the following is a true T-sentence:

'Al-Qahirah madinah' is true if and only if Moscow is a city

(since the contained sentences 'Moscow is a city' and ' "Al-Qahirah madinah" is true' are both true). Yet this T-sentence is obviously not meaning-giving, even though it is perfectly true.

This T-sentence can be imported into the truth theory for our five-word language by replacing axiom (i) (see p. 57) by: 'al-Qahirah' denotes Moscow. That would be, of course, a strange choice of axiom, but nonetheless the result of the substitution is a truth theory for the five-word language, and all of its T-sentences are true. However, since many of the T-sentences of this truth theory are clearly not meaning-giving, the theory is not a semantics for the language.

So, then, not every theory of truth all of whose T-sentences are true is a semantics. Once fully appreciated, this fact frustrates the hope that the difficult and slippery concept of the meaning of a sentence can be reduced to, or abolished in favour of, the much more straightforward concept of the condition under which the sentence is true, as stated by a truth theory which generates a true T-sentence for each sentence of the language in question. The 'mutilated' truth theory of the preceding paragraph illustrates the problem nicely: the condition under which 'Al-Qahirah madinah' is true according to that theory clearly has nothing to do with the meaning of the sentence. In fact the concept of meaning stoutly resists abolition, for truth theorists evidently need the concept in order to be able to distinguish between truth theories which are semantics, and those which are not. A truth theory is a semantics for a particular language only if it generates a *meaning-giving* T-sentence for each sentence of the language.

Communication-intention and meaning

Speaker-meaning and semantic meaning

Normally we know what a person means in saying 'Please pass the mustard' because we know the meaning of this English sentence. Nevertheless, what the person means does not depend solely on the meaning of the sentence: it depends primarily on psychological facts about the person – that is, on the intentions, beliefs and desires that underlie the person's uttering the sentence. Normally, of course, English speakers say, 'Please pass the mustard' with the intention of requesting someone to hand them some mustard which they believe to be available and desire to be handed. Any competent speaker of English who knows the meaning of 'Please pass the mustard' knows this fact about the normal or conventional use of the sentence, and someone who did not know it would have, at best, an incomplete grasp of the sentence's role in standard English. That explains why, although what a person means in saying 'Please pass the mustard' depends on psychological facts about the person, we usually know what the person means through our knowledge of the meaning of this sentence.

The distinction between what a person means in uttering a sentence and the meaning of the sentence itself is especially clear in cases where speakers indulge in sarcasm or irony. What Mrs Gladrags means when she says, 'That's a *lovely* dress you're wearing' may well be quite different from the literal meaning of this sentence. But the distinction can be drawn even in cases where language is used literally. That is, even in such cases it appears that two different sorts of meaning can be ascribed to the sentence uttered by a speaker – one the sort of meaning which the sentence bears in virtue of the speaker's intention and state of mind, and the other the sort of meaning which the sentence bears in virtue simply of its being a sentence of a certain language. The first sort of meaning may be called the *speaker-meaning* of the sentence and the second its *semantic meaning*. (Semantic meaning is, of course, the sort of meaning which is studied by truth-theoretic semantics.)

Some sentences, like 'Please pass the mustard,' are conventionally used to perform very specific functions, which are associated with a narrow range of intentions, beliefs, desires, etc. For these sentences, knowledge of semantic meaning provides very direct access to speaker-meaning. But not all sentences of a natural language have a conventional use that is associated with only a few intentions and states of mind: many can be used with various different intentions and to express various states of mind. How does semantic meaning provide access to speaker-meaning in the case of such sentences? For example, the sentence 'The mustard is hot' might be used with the intention of warning someone about some mustard, of commending the mustard, or simply of stating a fact about it, and it may express such diverse states of mind as consternation, delectation, or simple belief. Very often we can tell what intention and state of mind underlies a given utterance of 'The mustard is hot' by combining our knowledge of the semantic meaning of the sentence with knowledge of the circumstances of its utterance. If, for example, we hear a mother say to her son, 'The mustard is hot' in a certain tone of voice as the boy is about to eat a mustard-laden sausage, then we might reasonably take the mother to be issuing a warning and expressing concern, rather than simply expressing an opinion about the mustard. In this way – through acquaintance with the circumstances of utterance – we gain access to speaker-meaning through our knowledge of semantic meaning even in the case of sentences which may be used with various intentions and to express various states of mind. Occasionally, of course, we are stymied, or we get things wrong. Contrary to appearances, the mother may have been simply commenting upon the hotness of the mustard. For the most part, however, we seem to get things right: that is, our knowledge of a sentence's semantic meaning, together with knowledge about the circumstances in which the sentence is uttered (who utters it, in what manner, to which audience, etc.), usually enables us to determine the speaker-meaning of the sentence on that occasion of its utterance.

This distinction between speaker-meaning and semantic meaning raises some interesting philosophical questions. A basic issue is whether one of these sorts of meaning is more fundamental than the other. Some philosophers maintain that speaker-meaning is fundamental, and that semantic meaning can in a sense be reduced to it, or completely explained in terms of it. Other philosophers maintain, on the contrary, that semantic meaning is largely independent of speaker-meaning, and can (or even must) be explained without any reference to the psychological factors that underlie our use of language. Lying behind this difference is a disagreement about the nature of language. On the one hand, those who maintain the priority of speaker-meaning generally think that language functions in essentially the same manner as non-linguistic communication systems, such as drivers' hand-signals. These philosophers adopt what has been called a *communication-intention* approach to meaning. On the other hand, those who maintain the autonomy of semantic meaning – its independence from speaker-meaning – maintain that language differs essentially from other communications systems in that it has a structure which permits the formation of a boundless variety of messages on the basis of a finite stock of basic elements. (As might be expected, some proponents of the truth-theoretic approach to meaning discussed above are among those who maintain this position.) We shall discuss later the extent to which there is a conflict between these views about language and meaning. But first let us examine some of the basic ideas behind the communication–intention approach to meaning.

Grice's analysis of speaker-meaning

One of the foundation-stones of the communication–intention approach was laid by the English philosopher Paul Grice in 1957, when he presented an ingenious analysis of speaker-meaning and sketched a programme for using this analysis to construct a systematic account of semantic meaning. Grice and others have subsequently refined the analysis and developed the programme, but the basic ideas are contained in Grice's 1957 presentation.

There Grice explains speaker-meaning as an instance of a more general sort of meaning which he calls *non-natural meaning* (*meaning-nn*). He chooses this term in order to indicate a contrast with so-called 'natural' meaning, as exemplified by 'Those clouds mean rain.' Meaning-nn, by contrast, always involves one person making a sound or some other signal with the intention of affecting another person's beliefs (or other state of mind) through this person's *recognising* that the sound or signal was produced with that intention. For example, suppose a bus conductor rings a bell twice with the intention of informing people that the bus is full. Here the bus conductor rings the bell twice with the intention of getting the people to believe that the bus is full *through their recognition* that he rang the bell twice with precisely this intention. So, using Grice's terminology, in ringing the bell the bus conductor means-nn that the bus is full, and the two rings themselves have this meaning-nn. (But if the bus conductor had rung the bell with the intention of waking up the passengers, then although he did this with the intention of affecting their state of mind, he did not rely for the fulfilment of this intention on the passengers *recognising* that he had it, and so on that occasion neither the bus conductor nor the two rings mean-nn anything at all.) Again, when the bus conductor says, 'The bus is full,' intending to get people to believe that the bus is carrying as many passengers as it is allowed to carry, and relying for the fulfilment of this intention on the people recognising that he uttered the sentence with it, then the bus conductor means-nn that the bus is carrying as many passengers as it is allowed to carry, and so the sentence has this meaning-nn. Likewise, according to Grice's analysis, when I utter the sentence 'Please pass the mustard' with the intention that the person I am addressing should become aware that I am requesting her to hand me some mustard, and I intend that to happen through her recognition that I am uttering the sentence with precisely this intention, then I mean-nn that I want her to please hand me some mustard, and the sentence has this meaning-nn.

Difficulties with Grice's analysis

Grice's notion of meaning-nn certainly seems to capture an important feature of the use of languages and other communication systems. However, as a foundation for a general account of speaker-meaning, and ultimately of semantic meaning, it runs into several difficulties. First it is not hard to discover or invent counter-examples to Grice's analysis – for instance cases where, according to Grice's definition, a person's utterance would be said to have a certain meaning-nn, but it would be unclear whether this is the speaker-meaning of the utterance. For example, imagine you are a tourist in China, and a smiling shopkeeper speaks to you in Cantonese. Ignorant of the language, you take him to be saying something like 'Please come into my shop and look at my wares.' And suppose he is, indeed, uttering the words with the intention of getting you to believe he is graciously inviting you to enter his shop and look at his wares, and he is relying for the fulfilment of this intention on your recognising that he utters the words with it. So it seems that his utterance has the meaning-nn that he is graciously inviting you to enter his shop. But suppose the sentence he utters has the semantic meaning of 'A curse upon you, O rich fat pig of a tourist'; and suppose, moreover, that he is uttering it with the *intention* of cursing you. So apparently he is producing the sentence with two distinct intentions. Do these intentions endow the sentence with two different speaker-meanings? On Grice's account it has only one (its meaning-nn) but it is not at all clear that this correct. Grice deals with this sort of counter-example, and many others, in the course of refining his original account of meaning-nn. But ingenious critics have been able to produce a seemingly endless barrage of apparent counter-examples to Grice's definition, and this fact gives grounds for scepticism regarding the idea that speaker-meaning can be adequately explained in terms of meaning-nn.

Secondly, a difficulty of principle seems to confront Grice's account when it is applied to standard cases of communication, both non-linguistic and linguistic. Normally, when we do or say something with the intention of communicating some information to an audience, we rely for the fulfilment of our intention upon *conventions* whereby the audience understands our action or utterance to have a certain meaning quite apart from our intentions. Consider a lazy bus conductor, who rings the bell twice with the intention of misinforming people that the bus is full when he knows it is not. Plainly he does not rely for the fulfilment of his intention on people recognising it: what he relies on is a convention whereby people are accustomed to understand two rings to mean that the bus is full. And this is precisely what the diligent bus conductor relies on for the fulfilment of his intention – he too relies on the people recognising his two rings to have the meaning which they conventionally have. The point seems even more obvious in cases of linguistic communication. In saying 'Please pass the mustard' to a person, I would indeed have the intention of making the person aware that I want her to hand me some mustard. But what I rely on for the fulfilment of this intention is the person's understanding the utterance, or grasping its conventional meaning, not her recognising that I am uttering the words with that intention. Of course, given that the person understands the utterance, she will recognise that I have that intention; but I do not rely for the fulfilment of the intention on her recognising that I have it. In this case, as in virtually all linguistic communication, speakers rely on convention-based understanding for the fulfilment of their communicative purposes, not on their audience's divining their intentions. (Grice and his followers have made some interesting attempts to meet this objection, by explaining convention-based communication as a natural outgrowth of communication based on the recognition of intentions.)

Semantic meaning and communication-intention

There is one feature of semantic meaning which many philosophers and linguists regard as quite beyond the scope of a communication-intention approach, and that is its *compositional* character – the fact that the meaning of a complex expression is determined by the meaning of the words that compose it. The sentence 'Please pass the mustard' has the meaning that it has because the component words have the meanings that they have. If the word 'mayonnaise' were substituted for 'mustard' in this sentence then we would have a sentence with a different meaning, and the difference would be due solely to the difference in meaning between 'mustard' and 'mayonnaise'. This fact should be explained by any theoretical account of the meaning of the sentence. Even if the semantic meaning of the whole sentence could be explained, in line with the communication-intention approach, by reference to the intentions and desires that conventionally accompany its utterance, there is considerable difficulty in seeing how this approach can be used to explain how the meaning of the whole sentence depends upon the meanings of the words that compose it. To give a theoretical account of this compositional aspect of semantic meaning, another approach to meaning seems to be required. As we have seen, truth-theoretic semantics is just such an approach.

This brings us back to the question whether there is a conflict between the communication-intention approach to meaning and the approach of truth-theoretic semantics. For each approach there are enthusiasts who claim that all the essential features of linguistic meaning can be explained by their theory, and only by their theory. Such enthusiasm is understandable, but unwarranted. There is, in fact, little incompatibility between the two approaches, provided they are recognised as dealing with different aspects of meaning. An analogy may help to illustrate this point. Biologists typically study bodily organs, such as the heart, both with regard to their structure and with regard to their development. Plainly there is no incompatibility between these two approaches to the study of bodily organs, and it is generally assumed that a full understanding of the function of an organ will require knowledge gained through both approaches. Likewise, it seems reasonable to expect that a full understanding of linguistic meaning will require both a semantic description of language and an account of language as one communication system among others. In so far as the truth-theoretic approach to meaning is intended to provide the former, and a communication-intention approach aims at the latter, there is no incompatibility between these approaches.

Theories of reference

Referring to particular objects

Reference to particular objects is a ubiquitous feature of our use of language. This is true both in everyday discourse, where the objects of reference are typically mundane things such as persons, cities and chairs, and in the abstract discourse of mathematicians and physicists, who refer to such recondite things as transcendental numbers, electrons and quasi-stellar objects. In both sorts of discourse, there are three basic methods of referring to particular things, corresponding to three different types of linguistic expression. One method is to use a *proper name*, like 'Shakespeare' or 'Alpha Centauri'; another is to use a *demonstrative expression*, for example 'this' or 'that'; and the third is to use a descriptive phrase of the form 'the such-and-such', such as 'the Prime

Minister of Britain in 1923' or 'the nearest quasi-stellar object' (phrases of this form are called *definite descriptions*). Sometimes we can choose which method to employ, our choice depending upon our estimate of the most efficient (and perhaps most stylish) way of picking out the object of reference, or of enabling our audience to identify it. But often we have no such choice, for instance because the object has no proper name, or because it is not present before the audience, or we don't know how to describe it, or we reckon that the audience wouldn't understand our description.

The methods of demonstrative and descriptive reference seem relatively easy to explain. The former depends for its success on contextual pointers, which link the demonstrative expression with the object of reference. Thus, if I say, 'That smells awful,' intending 'that' to refer to a particular thing – say, a piece of cheese – then plainly I must depend on the context to provide pointers which will enable my audience to pick out the thing that I describe as smelling awful. These contextual pointers may be partly linguistic or entirely non-linguistic. For example, I may say, 'You see the piece of cheese on my plate? Well, that smells awful': here the linguistic context helps to establish the reference of 'that'. Or I might simply gesture at something and say 'That smells awful.' In either case my audience knows the object of reference – the thing which the demonstrative refers to – through their ability to understand the contextual pointers: if they lack this ability, or misconstrue the pointers, then they will not (correctly) identify the object of reference.

In the case of descriptive reference – that is, reference involving the use of a definite description – the object of reference is specified through the meaning of the description. Thus, in using 'the piece of cheese on my plate' to refer to an object, I depend on my audience's grasping the meaning of this phrase well enough to be able to pick out an object that uniquely satisfies the description 'piece of cheese on my plate'. Of course they must know more than just the meaning of this description in order to be able to identify the object of reference: they must also know, for example, which plate is mine. Nevertheless their ability to pick out the object depends crucially on their grasping the meaning of the description.

So, demonstratives pick out objects of reference through contextual pointers, and definite descriptions refer to objects through the meaning of the description. How, then, do proper names pick out the objects which they are used to refer to? Philosophers have found this question to be fraught with difficulties. This is perhaps surprising: of all the methods for referring to particular things, the use of proper names is the most common and apparently the least problematic. Nothing could be simpler, it might seem, than the use of 'Shakespeare' to refer to Shakespeare. There is no dependence on contextual pointers or linguistic meaning here: reference is secured – the object of reference is specified and understood – simply through a conventional connection that exists between the name and the person who bears it. To put it metaphorically, the name 'Shakespeare' seems to be simply a label conventionally attached to a certain person. (Since there is, of course, more than one person with the name 'Shakespeare', and there are probably things other than persons bearing this name (cats, for instance), we may need to use contextual pointers or descriptive language in order to determine which of these persons or things is the object to which the name refers on any particular occasion of its use. But this difficulty seems to arise simply from imperfections in our method of assigning proper names: it would be eliminated if we ensured that a unique proper name was assigned to each particular object we are capable of mentioning.)

Frege's puzzle

What are the difficulties, then, in explaining how proper names function? First there is a puzzle that was discussed by the German philosopher Gottlob Frege. Suppose you attend a concert in which one of the performers is a singer called Rick Zapp; and later you hear a recording by a singer identified on the record label as Dickey Dingley. You don't realise that Rick and Dickey are one and the same person, but subsequently you do discover this. Thus, what you discover is that the sentence 'Dickey Dingley is Rick Zapp' is true. In that case, you find the sentence to be informative in a way in which the sentence 'Rick Zapp is Rick Zapp' is not: it conveys knowledge which the latter does not convey. But how could this be so if a proper name, like 'Rick Zapp' or 'Dickey Dingley', functions simply as a label of the particular object to which it is conventionally attached? For if these names are simply alternative labels of the same person 'Dickey Dingley is Rick Zapp' tells us no more about that person than 'Rick Zapp is Rick Zapp' tells us about him: the first part of each sentence picks out the same individual, and the second part tells you that this individual is Rick Zapp. Yet the first sentence obviously possesses informative content which the second lacks; indeed, one might say that the second has no informative content at all. Drawing the moral that proper names are not simply labels, Frege attempted to resolve the puzzle by distinguishing between the sense (*Sinn*) and reference (*Bedeutung*) of a proper name. According to this distinction, proper names may have the same reference, or refer to the same object, yet do so through different senses, or different ways of presenting the object. Thus, the difference in informative content between 'Rick Zapp is Dickey Dingley' and 'Rick Zapp is Rick Zapp' results from the fact that in the imagined situation 'Rick Zapp' and 'Dickey Dingley' have the same reference but different senses: these proper names refer to the same person, yet present this person in different ways (as the performer in a certain concert and as the singer on a certain record), and so have different senses. According to Frege this difference in sense accounts for the difference in informative content between the two sentences.

What exactly does Frege mean by the sense of a

proper name? It is not entirely clear. He remarks that one person might take the sense of 'Aristotle' to be: the pupil of Plato who taught Alexander the Great; and another might take it to be: the teacher of Alexander the Great who was born in Stagira; so that these two persons would attach different senses to the sentence 'Aristotle was a philosopher.' This seems to indicate that Frege thought the first person would understand the sentence to mean 'The pupil of Plato who taught Alexander the Great was a philosopher,' while the second would take it to mean 'The teacher of Alexander the Great who was born in Stagira was a philosopher.' Whether this is a correct interpretation of Frege's notion of sense has been debated, but there is no doubt that Frege seems to hold a form of the so-called *description theory* of proper names – the theory that proper names, like definite descriptions, refer to objects through their descriptive or informative content.

Russell's theory of proper names

A very clear statement of the description theory was put forward by the English philosopher Bertrand Russell earlier this century. For various reasons, based chiefly on his views concerning the nature of knowledge, Russell held that ordinary proper names, like 'Shakespeare' and 'Alpha Centauri', have descriptive meaning, and it is through this meaning that they refer to objects. Indeed, Russell held that ordinary proper names are best viewed as being merely disguised definite descriptions – so that, for example, the sentence 'Ramsay MacDonald was born in Scotland' is simply shorthand for a sentence like 'The first Labour Prime Minister of Great Britain was born in Scotland.' One of the advantages of this assimilation of proper names to definite descriptions, Russell thought, was that it enabled him to resolve another puzzle that figures prominently in recent controversies concerning the function of proper names.

This puzzle concerns vacuous proper names – names that appear to refer to a particular object but in fact do not refer to anything at all. The problem is that such a name may be used in asserting that there exists no object to which the name refers. This would be hard to understand if proper names functioned as if they were simply labels conventionally attached to particular objects of reference. How could we make a (true) statement like 'Sherlock Homes never really existed' if the proper name 'Sherlock Holmes' functioned in this way? It seems absurd to suppose that someone who makes this statement refers both directly to an object (in using the proper name 'Sherlock Holmes'), and denies the existence of that very thing. In order to avoid this absurdity Russell argued that we should understand 'Sherlock Holmes' as shorthand for a definite description – e.g. 'the extraordinary detective whose exploits are recounted by A. Conan Doyle' – and take the statement to be shorthand for 'There never existed a person uniquely satisfying the description "extraordinary detective whose exploits are recounted by A. Conan Doyle".' This latter sentence makes no reference to someone bearing the name 'Sherlock Holmes'. In general, Russell argued, all ordinary proper names are to be construed as disguised definite descriptions, since only in this way can we explain the fact that each sentence containing a proper name would have meaning even if the object bearing the name happened not to exist.

Although there are significant differences between Russell's view of proper names and Frege's, there are obvious similarities. They both hold that proper names are linked indirectly with objects, Frege maintaining that they refer to objects through their senses, and Russell claiming that they are related to objects in just the same way as definite descriptions, viz. through the meaning of a descriptive phrase.

Kripke's criticisms of the description theory

In recent years this so-called Frege–Russell description theory of proper names has been subjected to vigorous criticism. Among the most interesting and influential objections to the theory are those put forward by the American philosopher Saul Kripke. Some of his objections involve counter-examples – that is, cases where the reference of a proper name is not determined indirectly by its sense or by the meaning of a descriptive phrase, or where an absurdity seems to result from the supposition that reference is determined in this manner. Consider, for example, the case of a person who knows, or thinks she knows, just one thing about a certain object, although in fact what she believes about the object is not true. Perhaps the only thing she would claim to know about Thomas Edison is that Edison was the inventor of the wireless – although in fact Edison did not invent the wireless (Marconi did). Now, according to the Frege–Russell theory, when this person uses 'Thomas Edison' we *must* take her to be referring to someone who uniquely satisfies the description 'inventor of the wireless'. But this would mean that we must take her to be referring to Guglielmo Marconi when she says, for example, 'Thomas Edison was an inventor,' and that seems absurd: we have no reason to suppose that, despite her mistaken belief, she is referring to Marconi when she makes this statement. Moreover this sentence, 'Thomas Edison was an inventor,' seems to provide another difficulty for the Frege–Russell view. As it happens, the sentence is true: Thomas Edison invented many things. He need not have been an inventor, though: it is not a necessary truth that Thomas Edison was an inventor, but only a contingent fact about Edison – something that might not have been so. Now suppose someone knows of Edison only that he invented the telegraph (which, in fact, he did). Then, according to the description theory, if this person said, 'Thomas Edison was an inventor' we should understand him to be saying, 'The inventor of the telegraph was an inventor.' In that case, however, he would be asserting a necessary truth – and yet we have no reason to suppose that the

71

person would deny the contingency of the fact that Edison was an inventor. Thus we seem to have another counter-example to the Frege–Russell view.

But the existence of counter-examples is not all there is to Kripke's criticism of the Frege–Russell account of proper names. The counter-examples are, for Kripke, symptomatic of a conflict between this account and certain fundamental principles of logic and metaphysics. In order to accommodate these principles Kripke thinks it necessary to reject the idea that proper names refer to objects through their sense or descriptive meaning. He replaces it with the view that a proper name refers to an object through a 'chain of communication' which links a use of the name with an initial baptism (or other name-giving process). Thus, the use of 'Shakespeare' to refer to the famous English playwright has been passed from speaker to speaker through a 'chain' starting at the occasion on which this person was given this name, and stretching to the present day. According to Kripke, proper names need have no Fregean sense or Russellian descriptive meaning: their reference is fixed by the initial baptism and the 'chain', not by any informative content or descriptive meaning which speakers may subsequently assign to them.

One fundamental principle that Kripke finds controverted by the Frege–Russell account of proper names is the principle that whenever we use a proper name in asserting something about a particular object, what makes our assertion true or false is an absolutely rigid condition – a condition which does not vary, for example, according to what we happen to believe about the object. What makes it true or false that Shakespeare was fond of cider is *that* particular person's having been fond or not fond of cider, and this condition determines the truth or falsity of 'Shakespeare was fond of cider' no matter what we may believe, truly or falsely, about Shakespeare. Using Kripke's picturesque terminology, the proper name 'Shakespeare' functions as a *rigid designator* of Shakespeare. How does this count against the Frege–Russell theory? Well, suppose Shakespeare was not in fact the author of *Hamlet*, even though everyone believes that he was. In that case, what would make it true or false that Shakespeare was fond of cider would still be something about the person who, we're supposing, we falsely believe to be the author of *Hamlet* – not something about the person who really was the author of *Hamlet*. On the Frege–Russell theory of proper names, however, the latter is precisely what *would* happen. For on that theory 'Shakespeare was fond of cider' would be shorthand for a sentence like 'The author of *Hamlet* was fond of cider,' and hence true or false depending on whether the person uniquely satisfying the description 'author of *Hamlet*' – who we are supposing was not Shakespeare – was fond of cider. Kripke's theory would not have this consequence, because of the 'rigidity' with which 'Shakespeare' designates or refers to Shakespeare.

Assessing the theories

In weighing the merits of Kripke's account of proper names and the Frege–Russell description theory, it is difficult to escape the conclusion that each gives a satisfactory explanation of some cases whilst neither is adequate to cover all cases. For Kripke's counter-examples to the description theory may be balanced against instances that cannot be handled easily by his own theory. The name 'Madagascar', for example, refers to an island off the coast of Africa, but originally it was applied to a part of the African mainland. How did this change come about? Allegedly it occurred because map-makers, misunderstanding Marco Polo's use of the name, started using it to refer to the island. Since the map-makers *intended* to use the name to refer to whatever Marco Polo had used it to refer to, there is a 'chain of communication' linking their use of 'Madagascar' (and hence ours) with the place on the African mainland to which Marco Polo was referring. Nevertheless they *believed* they were referring to the island which we now call 'Madagascar', and it is their belief, or the corresponding description (whatever it was), that fixes the reference of the name – not the map-makers' intention, or the corresponding 'chain of communication'. In the Shakespeare example, however, just the opposite was true. There it seemed appropriate to ignore the belief (supposed false) that Shakespeare was the author of *Hamlet*, and take the reference of 'Shakespeare' to be fixed by the intention to refer to a certain individual. So we took this example to weigh against the description theory, and in favour of Kripke's account of proper names. But in the Madagascar example it seems appropriate to ignore the intention (or 'chain of communication'), and take the reference to be fixed by the belief (or description). So this example seems to weigh against Kripke's account, and in favour of the description theory.

On balance, then, it seems that a complete theory of proper names must incorporate insights drawn both from the description theory and from the 'chain of communication' approach. This should not be surprising. Proper names are used in a huge variety of circumstances: sometimes we use a name without caring that we know virtually nothing about the object we are referring to; sometimes practically all the beliefs we hold about the object are false; sometimes we already have other names for the object; sometimes, as in the case of fictional names, we believe that the 'object' does not exist. Given this variety, it is to be expected that no single account will adequately explain how all proper names function.

Bibliography

Quine sets out his views on the indeterminacy of translation and its consequences in his books *Word and object* (MIT Press, Cambridge, Massachusetts, 1960), Ch. 2, and *Ontological relativity and other essays* (Columbia University Press, New York, 1969), Ch. 2. Simon Blackburn discusses radical translation in Chs. 2 and 8 of his book

Spreading the word (Oxford University Press, Oxford, 1984) – a book which contains clear and thorough discussions of many of the topics covered in the present chapter. Gareth Evans gives the argument for indeterminacy a hostile reception in his article 'Identity and predication' in the *Journal of Philosophy* (vol. 72 (1975), pp. 343–63), to which our critique of the gavagai example is indebted.

Alfred Tarski's classic paper on truth, 'The concept of truth in formalised languages', appears in his book *Logic, semantics, metamathematics* (Oxford University Press, Oxford, 1956). Much pioneer work on truth-theoretic semantics was done by Rudolf Carnap in the 1940s. A classic reference is his *Meaning and necessity* (University of Chicago Press, Chicago, 1950). Lately Donald Davidson has been influential in his support for the idea that a Tarskian theory of truth is a theory of meaning. His article 'Truth and meaning' generated much interest in truth-theoretic semantics; it is reprinted in Davidson's *Essays in truth and interpretation* (Oxford University Press, Oxford, 1984). The so-called possible worlds semantics for the 'might' construction is due to Saul Kripke, and is discussed in his article 'Semantical considerations on modal logic', which is reprinted in *Reference and modality*, ed. Leonard Linsky (Oxford University Press, Oxford, 1971). Richard Montague has done a large amount of work on the semantics of natural language, using the possible worlds approach. A number of his papers are collected under the title *Formal philosophy*, ed. Richmond Thomason (Yale University Press, New Haven, 1974). Quine urges that possible worlds are unscientific in his article 'On what there is', which appears in his book *From a logical point of view* (Harvard University Press, Cambridge, Massachusetts, 1953). David Lewis discusses the semantics of non-indicative sentences in 'General semantics', which is reprinted in volume I of his *Philosophical papers* (Oxford University Press, Oxford, 1984).

Paul Grice sets forth his account of meaning in 'Meaning', which was first published in *The Philosophical Review*, vol. 66 (1957), and has since been reprinted in a number of anthologies, perhaps the most readily accessible being *Philosophical logic*, ed. Peter Strawson (Oxford University Press, Oxford, 1967). Grice deals with various counter-examples to his theory in 'Utterer's meaning and intentions', *The Philosophical Review*, vol. 78 (1968), and his most recent thoughts about meaning are contained in 'Meaning revisited', published in *Mutual knowledge*, ed. Neilson Smith (Academic Press, London, 1982). The contrast between the communication-intention approach to meaning and the approach of truth-theoretic semantics is sharply drawn by Strawson in his inaugural lecture 'Meaning and truth', which has been reprinted in his collection *Logico-linguistic papers* (Methuen, London, 1971). The communication-intention approach is vigorously criticised by the American linguist Noam Chomsky in his *Reflections on language* (Pantheon, New York, 1975). A lively defence of the approach is offered by Jonathan Bennett in *Linguistic behaviour* (Cambridge University Press, Cambridge, 1976). David Lewis has devised an interesting account of convention-governed behaviour, which he relates to Grice's theory in Ch. 4 of his book *Convention* (Harvard University Press, Cambridge, Massachusetts, 1969). Scepticism regarding the explanatory value of Lewis' theory has been expressed by Donald Davidson in 'Communication and convention', published in *Synthese*, vol. 59 (1984).

Gottlob Frege introduced his distinction between sense and reference in 'Über Sinn und Bedeutung', which is translated in Frege's *Collected papers in mathematics, logic and philosophy*, ed. Brian McGuinness (Basil Blackwell, Oxford, 1984). Bertrand Russell presented his theory of reference in a number of publications during the period 1903–18, but the clearest presentation is probably in his *Lectures on logical atomism*, which are reprinted in *Russell's logical atomism*, ed. David Pears (Fontana/Collins, London, 1972). The Frege–Russell theory of proper names is further developed by John Searle in his article 'Proper names', which has been reprinted in *Philosophical logic,* ed. Peter Strawson (Oxford University Press, Oxford, 1967). Searle defends his theory against the criticisms of Saul Kripke in Ch. 9 of his book *Intentionality* (Cambridge University Press, Cambridge, 1984). Kripke put forward these criticisms in some lectures which have been published under the title *Naming and necessity* (Basil Blackwell, Oxford, 1980). Related criticisms of the Frege–Russell 'description' theory of reference have been advanced by Keith Donnellan: see, for example, his 'Reference and definite descriptions' in *The Philosophical Review*, vol. 75 (1966). Perhaps the most extensive and profound recent discussion of issues connected with the theory of reference is Gareth Evans' *The varieties of reference* (Oxford University Press, Oxford, 1983), but this is not a book for beginners.

B.J.C., R.H.S.

4 | Truth

Brian Carr

Factual truth

The concept of truth is of central importance in philosophy, so much so that rival positions on many other major questions are a reflection of different beliefs about that concept. The grand debate we portray as the burning issue of the seventeenth and eighteenth centuries – the debate between the 'continental rationalists' and the 'British empiricists' – was about the nature of our knowledge of truth, but reflected a fundamental disagreement about truth itself. In the present century the philosophical school of 'logical empiricism' or 'logical positivism' rejected much traditional speculation as barren – as issuing indeed in meaningless utterances – on the basis of a theory of meaningfulness which reflected an austere view on what kinds of truths there are. Moral philosophers, too, find themselves pushed, by their own presuppositions about the nature of truth, into the question of an adequate characterisation of moral judgements; and philosophers of logic and mathematics are centrally occupied with the problem of the peculiar kind of truth which belongs to logic or to mathematics.

Since other chapters in this *Encyclopaedia* are devoted to logic, epistemology and moral philosophy, this chapter will concentrate on the concept of truth and (for the most part) leave aside the details of these connections. What is more, it will be concerned with one kind of truth only, albeit a very central and commonplace one with which we are all familiar. Following established tradition we can call it 'factual truth'.

What is special about *factual* truth? How can factual truths be distinguished as a special subclass of truths in general? A factual truth, we may say, concerns *the way things are*; a proposition states a factual truth if it states *how things are in the world*. Some things we assume to have no intelligible alternatives: for instance, that 2 plus 2 produces 4 and that bachelors are unmarried, we think, are not just a matter of how things are but more a matter of logical necessity. The proposition that 2 plus 2 produces 4 hardly expresses a *factual* truth, for it does not state the way things are as opposed to some alternative way they might have been. It is not a matter of *fact* that 2+2=4, more a matter of logical necessity, and factual truth concerns matters of fact.

But this is as yet an inadequate specification of what philosophers have meant by 'factual truth'. For one thing, there is a case for extending the notion of 'fact' to cover even, say, mathematical truths as well as the 'matters of fact' we have in mind here. The notion of factual truth in that case is seen to reflect a distinction between truths concerning some special kinds of facts – those of mathematics, logic and language (such as 'All bachelors are unmarried') – and all the rest. Let us, then, make explicit this distinction and say that 'factual truths' concern matters of non-mathematical, non-logical and non-linguistic facts.

This distinction seems less arbitrary if we note that it matches the traditional one between analytic and synthetic truths. We can readily agree that there is a difference between a proposition like 'All bachelors are unmarried,' which tells us something about the meaning of the word 'bachelor', and a proposition like 'John is a bachelor,' which tells us something about the man John himself. Other examples of the first class, the analytic propositions, are 'Triangles have three sides,' 'A spinster has never been married' and 'Physical objects can be located in time and space.' Other examples of the second, the synthetic propositions, are 'Peter is taller than Jane,' 'There is nobody in the room next door,' and 'That tree is sixty feet tall.' One way of making this distinction – as well as by saying they are about words or things – is to say that the analytic propositions do not tell us how the world is, they do not tell us something about the way things are in the world. Synthetic propositions on the other hand do just that, and if they are successful at doing so they express synthetic truths. Now it is plausible to suggest that the only analytic truths are mathematical, logical or linguistic ones: it follows that factual truths are synthetic truths and vice versa.

However, our characterisation is still inadequate, since it suggests that factual truths involve only contingent matters, and that is contrary to one strong philosophical tradition. The distinction between necessity and contingency – between necessary truths and contingent truths, or between necessarily true propositions and contingently true propositions – has a long history in philosophy, and there are various ways of marking it. Leibniz did so in terms of his notion of 'possible worlds', that is, worlds other than the actual world which God could have created instead. Necessity concerns what is true in all possible worlds, not just in some; contingency concerns what is true in some, but not all, possible worlds. A necessary truth, then, is true in all possible worlds, and a contingent truth is true only in this world (and possibly some others). It would be wrong for us to assume at the outset, without a careful consideration of the rationalist tradition which explicitly holds that certain synthetic truths may nevertheless be necessary truths for all that, that factual truth concerns only what is contingent. We must be careful, therefore, to characterise factual truths in a way that avoids this assumption. When we say that factual truths concern the way things are as opposed to other ways they might have been, this must be understood as making room for *some* kind of necessary truths in the class of factual truths. What we need to exclude are the *logically* necessary truths of mathematics, logic and language. Equating factual truths with synthetic truths effectively achieves just that.

Let us take as our paradigm cases of factual truths the following, assuming for the sake of argument that they are indeed true:

'There are trees in Russell Square'
'$E=mc^2$'
'God exists.'

In terms of these examples we can make two more preliminary points. One is that we must keep apart the questions of what a factual truth *is* and how a factual truth is *known*, for clearly these three truths will be known to be true in different ways. The first requires us only to go along to Russell Square and have a look. The second requires that we use our faculty of reason as well as our senses. The third, it has often been argued, can be established purely by the use of reason alone, and is therefore an *a priori* rather than an empirical truth. Now it is not obvious that different answers to the question how a truth is known demand different answers to the question what a factual truth is. We know that a candle is lit because we can see that it is, and we know that a bell is ringing because we can hear it: these involve different senses, but must we therefore say they are different *kinds* of facts? Extending this to our three examples, since they too involve different procedures, must we say they are different kinds of facts? We should try to arrive at a general characterisation of factual truth before taking that position.

Finally, we must note that some factual truths are much more difficult to know for certain than others – indeed, some may not be knowable at all. There is no difficulty in knowing whether Russell Square has trees in it and we would normally take this to be a case of certain knowledge. That $E=mc^2$ is much more difficult to know for certain, and would normally be taken to be at best *probably* the case. That God exists might not be knowable at all, if the arguments for His existence are as open to objection as many philosophers claim. So if we accept all three as cases of factual truths we must keep apart the notions of fact and of what is knowable, or knowable with certainty. We should ignore, therefore, locutions like 'That's a fact!', 'It's a fact that ...', and 'The facts are that ...' which might suggest otherwise.

Some traditional theories of truth

What account, then, can be given of factual truth? What conditions does a proposition have to fulfil if it is to be said to have expressed a factual truth? What do we *mean* when we say of such a proposition that it is true? The most plausible answer is simply this: that such a proposition is true if it says how things in fact are. A sophistication of this answer, attempting to spell it out in detail and resolve various areas of unclarity, is the traditional theory of truth known as the Correspondence Theory. Its initial plausibility has encouraged substantial efforts at developing and defending it against its rivals. Amongst those rivals there are two which have themselves numerous champions, the Coherence Theory and the Pragmatic Theory. I will expound these theories in turn, trying to highlight their strengths and weaknesses in relation to each other.

The Correspondence Theory

The Correspondence Theory has had a long history, going back to Plato's *Sophist* and Aristotle's famous statement of the theory: 'To say of what is that it is not, or of what is not that it is, is false; while to say of what is that it is, and of what is not that it is not, is true.'[1] It found numerous adherents in the British empiricist tradition, from Locke in the seventeenth century to Russell and Moore in the twentieth. One very detailed version can be found in Wittgenstein's *Tractatus logico-philosophicus* of 1921, and a more recent version was propounded by J. L. Austin in 1950.

According to Wittgenstein's *Tractatus*, ordinary propositions are constructed, by means of logical connectives, out of elementary propositions. An elementary proposition is composed of simple symbols – 'names' – configured in a particular manner, and it is by means of this configuration that it says how things are in the world. In the world itself are to be found the referents of these names, which Wittgenstein calls 'objects'. Here, therefore, are the ingredients of Wittgenstein's Correspondence Theory: elementary propositions, names, objects and configuration (or structure). The theory now holds that truth consists in the following. If the objects referred to by the names of an elementary proposition have the *same* configuration as those names have in the proposition – if, in other words, there is a 'state of affairs' corresponding in components and structure with that proposition – then the proposition is true. Elementary propositions are in fact attempts to picture reality, they say how things are by picturing or modelling reality.

A picture represents a possible situation in logical space ... A picture agrees with reality or fails to agree; it is correct or incorrect, true or false ... The agreement or disagreement of its sense with reality constitutes its truth or falsity.[2]

Wittgenstein's picture theory is primarily offered in the *Tractatus* as a theory of meaning, and is developed much beyond this simple outline to cover the nature of logical connectives and of analytic truth. It is, however, a particularly explicit version of the Correspondence Theory, serving not just as an account of the truth or falsity of elementary propositions but of ordinary, non-elementary propositions too. The truth or falsity of the latter is explained in terms of that of the former which comprise them and the logical structure of the non-elementary propositions themselves. Ordinary propositions are said to be pictures too, and are said to function like their constituent elementary propositions in picturing or modelling reality. 'A proposition is a picture of reality: for if I understand a proposition, I know the situation that it represents ... A proposition *shows* how things stand *if* it is true. And it *says that* they do so stand.'[3]

Austin's Correspondence Theory is offered without Wittgenstein's accompanying metaphysics of simple 'objects' in configuration, and without the Wittgensteinian analysis of the logical structure of non-elementary propositions. Austin's theory makes use of linguistic convention instead. There are, he says, two sorts of convention relevant to truth, descriptive and demonstrative conventions. Descriptive conventions correlate 'the words (=sentences) with the *types* of situation, thing, event, etc. to be found in the world'; demonstrative conventions correlate 'the words (=statements) with the *historic* situations, etc. to be found in the world'.[4] Austin's definition of truth is this: 'A statement is said to be true when the historic state of affairs to which it is correlated by the demonstrative convention (the one to which it "refers") is of a type with which the sentence used in making it is correlated by the descriptive conventions.'[5] He explicitly disavows Wittgenstein's picture theory. On the nature of the correspondence involved he comments that it is

> absolutely and purely conventional ... There is no need whatsoever for the words used in making a true statement to 'mirror' in any way, however indirect, any feature whatsoever of the situation or event; a statement no more needs, in order to be true, to reproduce the 'multiplicity', say, or the 'structure' or 'form' of the reality, than a word needs to be echoic or writing pictographic.[6]

Different versions of the Correspondence Theory clearly offer different answers to the problem of spelling out the intuitive thesis that factual truth is a matter of saying how things in fact are. Most importantly, they differ in their interpretations of the relationship of correspondence; of the bearer of truth and falsity (that which is said to be true or false); and in their understanding of the nature of what, in the world, makes the bearer true or false. Let us take first the relationship of correspondence.

Wittgenstein and Austin differ fundamentally on this. For Wittgenstein, a proposition corresponds with a state of affairs in a very strong sense, since the one mirrors or pictures the other. They have structure in common, and as a prerequisite of that they have corresponding parts too. On the face of it, Austin is surely right in rejecting this thesis. Why should a proposition and the fact which makes it true have the same structure? Isn't it sufficient simply for there to *be* a fact which the proposition expresses, and which therefore makes it true? Why emphasise the structural identity? We should be careful to distinguish between two kinds of correspondence, 'correspondence-to' and 'correspondence-with'. The latter is the kind of correspondence which involves the matching or mirroring relationship required by Wittgenstein, as for example when we say that one torn edge of a piece of paper corresponds with the torn edge of another. 'Correspondence-to' involves no more than a one-to-one correlation between two sets of things, as for example when we say that the rank of general in the army corresponds to that of admiral in the navy. Austin's position seems the better version of the Correspondence Theory in requiring only that true propositions have facts which they correspond *to*, rather than *with*.

I believe, however, that there is something to be said on the other side. It has been pointed out by D.W. Hamlyn that one reason for empiricists' fondness for the Correspondence Theory is its promise of a recognisable matching between propositions and facts, to provide for the possibility of certain knowledge of truth: if there is that kind of mirroring between 'Here is a blue patch' and the fact which makes it true, at least there can be certain perceptual knowledge. I have already insisted though on the need to keep questions of truth and knowledge separate, and must agree with Hamlyn that the empiricists' search for certainty is doomed in any case. No, the point to be made in favour of a correspondence-with version of the theory is this.

Putting aside Wittgenstein's picture theory of meaning, and allowing with Austin that language can convey sense without picturing the world, we must recognise that propositions and the facts which make them true are identifiable in precisely the same words. What makes the proposition that there are trees in Russell Square true? – the fact that there are trees in Russell Square. What makes the proposition that $E=mc^2$ true? – the fact that $E=mc^2$! A correspondence-with theory can, I believe, ignore the picture theory of meaning, and it need not get involved with the question of how to discern the different parts of a proposition and a fact in order to decide whether the proposition is true. This question of deciding on what is true is, in any case, irrelevant to the nature of truth. Propositions and facts correspond with each other because they both have logical structure; but a theory of truth need not place too much emphasis on their structural identity. Since structure is partially definitive of proposition and fact in any case, the distinction between correspondence-with and correspondence-to seems irrelevant to the truth relation.

One final point, though. P.F. Strawson rejects the

Correspondence Theory on the grounds that proposition and fact correspond too well:

> What could fit more perfectly the fact that it is raining than the statement that it is raining? Of course, statements and facts fit. They were made for each other. If you prize the statements off the world you prize the facts off too.[7]

However, that propositions and facts have the same conceptual structure is itself a conceptual truth and hardly undermines the Correspondence Theory. It would, perhaps, only if true propositions and facts were one and the same thing, but they are not. Facts are what *make* true propositions true.

Let us move on to the second issue dividing proponents of the Correspondence Theory, the question of truth bearers. What is it that is true or false? An inadequate answer clearly undermines a philosopher's version of the theory; and we can see from the above quotations that Wittgenstein and Austin seem to favour different answers.

Firstly, it would not be acceptable to say that truth and falsity belong to *sentences*. Take the sentence 'There are trees in Russell Square.' For one thing, until it is known which Russell Square is being referred to, and until it is known when the sentence is being used, the question of truth cannot arise. Perhaps some Russell Squares have trees and some do not, and perhaps any particular Russell Square can lose its trees even if it has them now. To overcome this objection some will wish to make the distinction between type and token: the 'same sentence' being used on different occasions is the sentence type, and on each occasion a different token of that type is produced. Why not say that the sentence token is the truth bearer? The point is, however, that even the sentence token is not true or false independently of its being *used* to say something about a particular Russell Square at a particular time. Only in this context has the sentence any connection with truth at all, and more accurately it is what the sentence is used to say that is then true or false, not the sentence itself.

Austin's preference was for *statements* as truth bearers, and we might say that what a sentence says constitutes a statement. But we have to make a distinction here too. There is a sense of 'statement' whereby different people can make the same statement at different times – for example that '$E=mc^2$'; but there is also a sense in which these people would be making different statements, as for example when we say that Einstein's statement came before Eddington's. And it is in the first sense that statements can be said to be true or false. Moreover – and perhaps Austin would have agreed with this too – the important thing is *what* is stated rather than the stating of it. It is the *content* of Einstein's statement that is true, not Einstein's stating of it. The distinction is clear enough: many things can be said about the stating which are irrelevant to what is stated, for example that it was in German, that it was in print, and that it occurred in 1905. What is relevant to what is said is that it is true.

Truth bearers are therefore the contents of statements. We must remember, too, that these contents can be true or false even before they have been stated, in other words that contents bear their truth values quite independently of whether anyone ever states them. It was true that $E=mc^2$ before Einstein's statement, of course. Now this notion of content is actually equivalent to what many philosophers have meant by 'proposition', including Wittgenstein in the *Tractatus*.

What of the candidates favoured by such as Russell and Moore for the role of truth bearers – beliefs and judgements? The difference between these two candidates essentially concerns their status as abiding opinions or conscious occurrent acts, but in either case if they have any chance of serving the role of truth bearers it would be in terms of their *contents*. We do have a use for the term 'belief' and the term 'judgement' in which it is *what* is believed or *what* is judged that is referred to, the content of the believing and the judging. Once more, these are equivalent to propositions. In sum, propositions are the contents of statements, beliefs and judgements, and propositions are the bearers of truth and falsity.

Propositions are not only the contents of these 'epistemic acts' as they are called, but also of wishing, hoping, fearing and so forth. Just as I can state that God exists, I can fear that God exists and hope that God exists – the same proposition occurs in all these diverse acts. The proposition is the statement, the hope and the fear, all of which are contents. There is another use of the term 'proposition' such that it refers to the meaning of a sentence, and obviously in that sense a proposition cannot be said to be a truth bearer. But as contents, propositions are good candidates for that role and a Correspondence Theory which adopts that position is at least consistent with our ordinary thought and talk about reality. Of course, the term 'proposition' is being used as a philosophical term of art, but it refers to something which undoubtedly pre-exists that usage. There are objections which some would raise against them which we will look at later, but in the meantime we will turn to the third issue dividing the Correspondence theorists, the question of the nature of the facts which make propositions true.

Both Wittgenstein and Austin preferred 'state of affairs' to 'fact', though the terminology matters little; they were clearly not in agreement over what they were, even though agreed on the term. Wittgenstein at least treated them as complex things, sets of 'objects' in configuration, and Russell tended to do likewise. The fact that there are trees in Russell Square would on that account be a complex of trees, Russell Square and the relationship between them. Now since the relationship is the spatial one of 'being in', it is important to realise that it is actually relating the objects concerned, and raising the complex object above the realm of the spatiotemporal. The fact has a logical structure which ordinary objects lack, and is not itself to be located in space and time. Whether or not Russell or Moore appreciated this, Wittgenstein certainly did. Austin unfortunately did not, since he came to view facts as equivalent to events.

Particulars and events have locations in space and time, but facts do not. Where and when could we possibly locate the fact that being blue is being coloured? Where and when the fact that Napoleon met his Waterloo in 1815 – at Waterloo in 1815? But then it *is* a fact that Napoleon met his Waterloo even today and no matter where I happen to be while putting it down on paper. And where and when could we locate the fact, for example, that if my desk had not been made of wood it would have been made of metal?

The case against facts having spatiotemporal location is perhaps most obvious in terms of facts which are about non-spatiotemporal phenomena or phenomena existing throughout all space and time. Where, for example, could we locate the fact that $2+2=4$? Where would we place the fact that $E=mc^2$? Further evidence, if needed, can be drawn from the existence of facts of more complex kinds, such as the fact that Napoleon did not meet his Waterloo in 1810, that my desk is not made of metal, and the fact that if this desk was made of metal it would not be my desk. However tempted we may be to think that we can locate, in space and time, the fact that there are trees in Russell Square, these logically more complex facts should surely establish that facts have no such location.

One other objection to Austin's equation of facts with events is that the latter lack the formers' logical structure. They can therefore stand only in causal relationships to one another, whereas facts have logical relationships, just like propositions. The fact that there are trees in Russell Square implies that the city is not totally a concrete jungle; the fact that $E=mc^2$ implies the fact that E does not equal mc^3. The fact that God exists implies the fact that atheists hold a false belief.

The Coherence Theory

Stated carefully, the Correspondence Theory has some hope of avoiding many of the standard objections. Nevertheless there are other difficulties which are not so easy to overcome, essentially concerning the ontological status of propositions and facts. In one guise, these lead to its traditional rival, the Coherence Theory.

The argument might be put like this. The Correspondence Theory assumes that discovering the truth or falsity of a proposition simply involves comparing it directly with the facts – with reality. Now the problem with this is that we have no knowledge of reality as such, only of the conceptualised version of it for which our intellect is, at least in part, responsible. When we are aware that there are trees in Russell Square, this awareness, rather than being simply a direct acquaintance with a mind-independent, unconceptualised bit of the world, is on the contrary an imposition on to the world of our own conceptual scheme. The 'facts', in other words, are not 'out there' to be compared with our judgements or propositions, but exist in the same realm as propositions. They are really themselves propositional in nature, and what looks to the Correspondence theorist to be correspondence between proposition and fact is simply correspondence between proposition and proposition. An assessment of the truth of the proposition that there are trees in Russell Square is therefore an assessment of consistency between propositions. And what the Coherence Theory holds truth to be is a systematic coherence between propositions.

The strength of this argument is its claim that facts are concept-involving entities just like propositions: its weakness is that it underplays the role of reality itself in constituting facts. We are responsible only for the conceptualisation of the facts, and the raw data have to come from outside us. We do not create the trees in Russell Square, and are not solely responsible for the fact that there are trees there. No more have we created the proportional relationship between energy and mass, even though we needed to develop the relevant concepts in order to grasp it. The facts are what they are, though conceptual in nature, independently of our believing them to be so.

A further objection to this argument is its rapid jump to the conclusion that truth is systematic coherence. Why systematic? The comparison would appear to be between two propositions only, that there are trees in Russell Square. But there are supporting arguments that can be brought forward. Firstly, the point can be made that the application of concepts is not independent of propositional beliefs. The concept of a tree involves beliefs about physical objects, living things, spatiotemporal continuity and so forth; the concept of a city square involves much more. All these propositions are, therefore, being matched against the new one that there are trees in Russell Square, and the idea of system is vindicated. Secondly, it is clearly false to suppose that any proposition can ever be judged true or false on its own, neither propositions of mathematics and logic nor propositions of a factual nature. To assess whether there are trees in Russell Square involves making assumptions about the truth of many other propositions such as those concerning the proper functioning of the senses. Some, like Quine, would go further and insist that all one's beliefs form a system against which a new proposition's truth can be tested. Coherence theorists take the final step and claim that truth simply *is* coherence with the system.

Correspondence theorists will point out that these arguments involve a confusion between truth and the knowledge of it. Accepting the points behind them, their conclusion should concern no more than the nature of our knowledge of truth, the manner in which we decide that a proposition expresses a fact. Yet Coherence theorists have a reply. In mathematics and in logic, it will readily be agreed, this distinction between the nature of truth and the criterion for deciding truth is inapplicable: they are both a matter of coherence between the individual proposition and the rest of the system. Now reality, the sum total of the facts, we assume to have an inherent intelligibility. We assume that facts do not just coexist in brute independence of one another, but that they relate intelligibly to each other. There is in reality in general – not just in logic and mathematics – a kind of coherence which enables us to find the reason for one fact in others. Coherence in logic and mathematics is at the very least a model for coherence in facts in general; and the conclusion must follow that coherence is the very nature of truth.

The Coherence Theory has long been associated with the rationalist tradition, since philosophers in that tradition subscribe to this notion of the intelligibility of nature. Traditionally this goes under the guise of the 'principle of sufficient reason', and forms a fundamental presupposition of the very practice of the rationalists in their attempt to establish facts by the use of reason unaided by the senses. Prime examples of such attempts are the *Monadology* of Leibniz and the *Ethics* of Spinoza; more recent philosophers such as Hegel and Bradley have followed that tradition too.

Oddly, in the twentieth century the logical positivist philosophers O. Neurath and C. Hempel have also adopted the Coherence Theory. In their philosophy of science they have, of course, not been persuaded by any consideration of the intelligibility of nature, but rather by the argument that brute facts are not available to the scientist. All he can achieve is an uncertain, conceptualised judgement of perception and the test of truth is whether this judgement coheres with the system of other judgements already accepted by the scientific community.

The most obvious and major objection to the Coherence Theory in general is the possibility of more than one system of propositions which cohere in the manner required. The very existence of rival metaphysical systems of the rationalists themselves should have made this obvious to them; and for the positivists, the fact that accepted science changes considerably over time should have brought home the same point. There are even alternative coherent logical systems, suggesting that even in the case of logic and mathematics truth cannot be equated with systematic coherence. The only defence for the Coherentist would be to insist that 'coherence' means more than simply 'logical consistency', and in that case it might be that only one 'coherent' system of propositions is possible. Yet no clear notion of coherence warranting that move has ever been provided. Rationalists instead have tended to justify their own systems in terms of their ability to provide solutions to a variety of philosophical problems.

Often associated with the Coherence Theory are two doctrines which have brought the theory into disrepute, the doctrine of internal relations and the doctrine of degrees of truth. The former holds that the relationships in which things stand to one another are part of the very nature of those things, so that to change any one of those relations is to change the very things themselves. In the words of McTaggart:

> If anything changes, then all other things change with it. For its change must change some of their relations to it, and so their relational qualities. The fall of a sand-castle on the English coast changes the nature of the Great Pyramid.[8]

According to Bradley, 'A relation must at both ends affect, and pass into, the being of its terms.'[9] The model for this thesis is the nature of numbers: the number 7, for example, is what it is because of its relations with the number 6 and the number 8, indeed with all other numbers. Yet a generalisation from numbers to *all* other things appears totally unacceptable both to Aristotelian scholastic philosophy, which distinguished the essential properties of individuals from their accidental properties, and to most twentieth-century philosophy, which treats all the properties of individuals as accidental. From the latter point of view the doctrine of internal relations is simply wrong-headed, and Moore could easily refute it as involving a rather crass confusion over modalities. Yet the doctrine is closely associated with the notion of reality's intelligibility, and the very nature of coherence itself.

The second doctrine, of degrees of truth, maintains that all individual propositions are partly false, that they involve a misrepresentation of the facts. Only the whole system of propositions expresses the truth as such, and anything less must therefore express falsehood. It has often been pointed out that this involves, on the face of it, a confusion between the notions of expressing all the truth and expressing only the truth: clearly the doctrine would be acceptable if it held that anything less than the whole system would express less than the whole truth. But then the doctrine would be unexciting too.

The Pragmatic Theory

The third theory of truth which has established itself as the major rival to Correspondence and Coherence is the Pragmatic Theory, developed in the late nineteenth and early twentieth centuries by the American philosophers Charles S. Peirce, William James and John Dewey. The theory is fundamental to a rich and varied philosophical tradition that counts as other members F. C. S. Schiller, C. I. Lewis, F. P. Ramsey and W. V. Quine. It is not to be expected that all these philosophers agree in their Pragmatism generally, or even share the same version of the Pragmatic Theory of truth.

The simplest statement of the theory is that it equates truth with success: a proposition is true if it 'works in practice', if it has a practical utility or usefulness. This thesis is of course in danger of collapsing into a tautology, if success is equated with successfully conforming to the facts. The Pragmatists certainly did not intend it that way, offering instead the striking and prima facie implausible claim that if a proposition satisfies the needs or wants of the individual it is true. According to James, 'On pragmatic principles, if the hypothesis of God works satisfactorily in the widest sense of the word, it is "true".'[10] He saw the truth of a theory in science, a metaphysical or religious hypothesis, a moral belief and so on as residing in their practical usefulness in satisfying the needs of the believer. There are several obvious objections to this thesis.

Firstly, the position taken by James makes truth a subjective matter. If belief in God satisfies you but not me, then it is true for you but not for me. Truth, however, is the objective matter *par excellence*. What is true is true for everyone – or, rather, since that might be taken to equate truth with universal assent, what is true is true independently of what anyone believes. If it is true that God exists, then it is true just as much for the atheist as for the believer. Secondly, the thesis makes truth a time-dependent attribute, since it is clearly possible for a believer to become dissatisfied with his belief. If John becomes filled with remorse about his past sins, and fears to meet his maker, the belief in God becomes false for him where it had been true before. On the Pragmatic Theory, of course, John need no longer fear the consequences of his sins!

Among other problems for the thesis is the obvious need for a careful handling of the notion of the 'usefulness' of an idea. James subsumes so many different things under the term 'idea' – theories in science, religious beliefs and moral codes, as well as singular beliefs about the physical world – that it is only to be expected that the term 'useful' (or the term 'satisfies') covers a multitude of possibilities. There is a world of difference between believing one's children are grateful for all one has done, and believing in Einstein's equation. The first might give you a warm feeling, the second enables you to send a rocket to Venus. The first offers a most implausible interpretation of 'truth equals usefulness', the second a far more plausible possibility. In the final analysis, however, we must reject even this more plausible case. Different theories can, in various applications to problems of a practical nature, have very much the same 'cash value', but we would obviously not want to call them all true. Working in practice, even in the case of physical science, is not the same as being true.

It would be unfair to pin the Pragmatic Theory as expounded above on all Pragmatists, and even James can be defended a little. In his philosophy the theory of truth is conjoined with a Pragmatic Theory of meaning, and in that context becomes more plausible. If the *meaning* of 'God exists' is equated with the practical difference a belief in God makes to the believer's life, then the truth of the belief is a matter of its practical benefits. If the meaning of '$E=mc^2$' is no more than the difference it makes in experimental circumstances and technical projects, its truth can be its success there. But then, this theory of meaning is itself suspect.

The theory of truth described above would be at best

a parody if ascribed to Peirce or Dewey. These philosophers developed their Pragmatism in the specific context of scientific knowledge, leaving the more general but much more vague application of the principal idea to James. Peirce's theory of meaning is very similar to operationalism and to the logical positivists' verification theory: his theory of truth takes truth in science to be equivalent to 'the opinion which is fated to be ultimately agreed to by all who investigate',[11] making truth at least an objective and time-independent matter. For Dewey, a proposition is true when, as a result of a problem situation being resolved by rational inquiry, it becomes a 'warranted assertion'. Dewey's conception, at least, maintains a connection between truth and objectivity through rationality: the objection stands, though, that a warranted assertion might still be a false one.

It is sometimes suggested that the three theories we have now looked at – the Correspondence, Coherence and Pragmatic Theories of truth – can be reconciled by a simple expedient. If they are treated as theories concerning the *criteria* we use for deciding whether a proposition is true, rather than theories about the *nature* of truth itself, they fit quite nicely to different areas of inquiry. Logic and mathematics offer a good home for the Coherence Theory, since truths there are judged in terms of their consistency with other propositions; the sciences in general use pragmatic tests for truth; and ordinary empirical judgements are judged true by their correspondence to fact. This is unsatisfactory for two reasons. One is that the theories were not offered as accounts of different criteria of truth, nor even of *the* criterion of truth in general, but as accounts of truth itself. The second is that it takes the theories out of their respective philosophical traditions. I have tried to indicate the richness of the philosophical environments in which they have flourished.

Some recent challenges

Traditional theories of truth have met with a number of challenges during this century, and we will look at the four most important.

Quine's eternal sentences

Propositions are the contents of beliefs, judgements, statements and so on, and are expressed by sentences. In one guise or another they have performed the role of bearer of truth and falsity, and (in consequence) have been the terms standing in logical relations to one another. That there are propositions seems uncontentious, since beliefs and so on do have content. It is, on the other hand, a further question what account to give of them. One account has been offered by Frege which, at least, has the merit of simplicity, and has been dubbed 'Platonic' after Plato's account of concepts. According to Frege, propositions are objects, things existing in their own right and not reducible to other things such as sentences. They inhabit a third realm of existence, distinct from the usually accepted first realm of physical objects and events, and the second realm of mental phenomena. Their existence depends not at all on the other two realms, yet we apprehend or contemplate them by our mental activities of belief, judgement and so forth.

Now many philosophers, following the medieval logician William of Occam, would reject this account as offending against Occam's 'razor' principle of parsimony, that 'entities should not be multiplied beyond necessity'. A world of two basic types of entity is theoretically more acceptable than one containing three, unless there is strong reason to multiply them. Moreover, not only are there true propositions in this third realm of being, but we must reckon with an infinity of false propositions too, since for each true proposition there is an unlimited number of false ones. Again this seems to contravene Occam's principle.

In defence of Frege it could be said that the hypothesis of propositional entities is merely an account of the way we think and talk about beliefs, judgements, logic and so forth; it avoids the charge of lack of parsimony by claiming simply to describe that practice. Frege did not see it in this light, though, taking propositions to have a real existence beyond our use of them. It does seem better to treat propositions as abstractions from our cognitive practices.

To these considerations about metaphysical parsimony Quine adds his own objection. The fundamental weakness of the notion of the objective propositional content of a sentence – the meaning expressed by it – is that no adequate philosophical account has ever been given of it, and it remains therefore unconscionably obscure. Consequently we should try to work without it, treating sentences themselves as the truth bearers instead. Quine's attack on propositions unfortunately fails to make a clear distinction between the notion of a proposition as the meaning of a sentence, and our notion of a proposition as the content of statements, beliefs, etc. – that is, *what* is stated, believed and so forth. However, it is in any case true that the second notion itself involves that of meaning, since the best formula stating the criterion of identity for propositions is this: that two sentences express the same proposition if and only if they are used to say the same thing about the same thing, where 'saying the same thing' involves identity of meaning. Quine's attack, therefore, is not easily diverted by a distinction of senses of 'proposition'.

The problem with sentences as truth bearers is, as Quine himself notes, that they usually depend on the individual circumstances of their production for their truth values. The truth or falsity of a sentence like 'You owe me ten dollars' depends on who says it, to whom, and when it is said. The sentence type 'You owe me ten dollars' will be variously true or false depending on the circumstances of the production of the token of it: the token, if we can allow sentence tokens to be truth bearers, may be true where another token of that type is false. Quine sees tokens as allowable candidates, though he tends to favour sentence types over their tokens. One consideration in favour of types is that logical relations hold because of the truth values of the sentences involved: it is clearly a presupposition of logical argument that occurrences of the same sentence type have the same truth value within an argument.

How can sentence types be made truth bearers in general? The above problem does not arise for sentences of arithmetic, for example, since time and place are irrelevant to their truth values. The same applies to the laws of physics, since they hold for all times and places too. Such examples are 'eternal sentences', 'sentences that stay for ever true, or forever false, independently of any special circumstances under which they happen to be uttered or written'. A proposal to treat sentence types as truth bearers is, for Quine, a proposal to fill out any statement of fact 'into an eternal sentence by supplying names and dates and cancelling the tenses of verbs. Corresponding to ... "You owe me ten dollars" we have the eternal sentence ... "Bernard J. Ortcutt owes W.V. Quine ten dollars on July 15, 1968".'[12] Such sentences must, of course, be understood as eternal relative only to a particular language at a particular time – say, our present-day English language habits.

Are the advantages of this proposal sufficient to outweigh the disadvantages? It has been pointed out by D.J. O'Connor that the ontological status of eternal sentences is much the same as that of propositions: they are, as types, abstract entities. Moreover, there are not just the (probably) finite number of true sentences to be reckoned with, there are an infinite number of false ones too. Occam's razor is contravened as much by sentences as by propositions. More directly against Quine's argument, however, we should realise how much goes with the rejection of the notion of meaning. Quine is happy to relinquish such notions as synonymy and analyticity, and what is more the idea of a correct translation from one language into another: 'Il pleut' and 'It's raining' cannot be said to express the same proposition since they do not 'have the same meaning'. There are obviously problems with the notion of a precise translation, but it might reasonably be felt against Quine that these problems are only intelligible given the notion of what a sentence expresses anyway. Finally, it is not clear that eternal sentences could in all cases replace the sentences of ordinary conversation, for it is not obvious that all context-dependent referential terms could be translated in the relevant way. Terms like 'here' and 'now' – the egocentric 'indexicals' of standard usage – have no obvious translation into a non-referential vocabulary.

Ramsey's 'assertive redundancy' thesis

Another challenge to traditional theories of truth comes in the form of a denial that the words 'is true' have any assertive function in any case. Traditional theories have been concerned with spelling out what it means to say of a proposition that it 'is true', yet according to F.P. Ramsey this is fundamentally mistaken. Ramsey's thesis is that 'It is true that it is raining' actually says no more than 'It is raining,' so the extra words have no assertive content, no descriptive meaning, of their own.

It is not clear, however, that all uses of 'is true' can be treated in the same manner. Ramsey recognises two kinds of case, where the proposition concerned is explicitly given and where it is merely described. An example of the first is 'It is true that Caesar was murdered' which can be seen as equivalent to 'Caesar was murdered.' An example of the second is 'What he says is always true,' where we can paraphrase this as 'For all propositions p, if he asserts that p, p is true' and where we can obviously then drop the words 'is true'. But not all cases of the second kind seem so readily paraphrasable in this way. What of 'I do not know whether it is true or false that p'?

Ramsey gives no supporting evidence for his thesis, but it might be thought to follow from the logical equivalence of 'p is true' and 'p'. Yet logical equivalence does not necessarily mean equivalence in meaning: witness 'This is an equilateral triangle' and 'This is an equiangular triangle.' In any case, it is arguable that 'p is true' and 'p' might not have the same truth-values for some propositions. Strawson would say, for instance, that, if John has no children, 'All John's children are asleep' is neither true nor false, so 'It is true that all John's children are asleep' does not share its truth-value.

The main problem with Ramsey's thesis, however, is that it leaves out any substantial account of the *function* which the words 'is true' or 'is false' have. He does allow simply that 'they are phrases which we sometimes use for emphasis or for stylistic reasons, or to indicate the position occupied by the statement in our argument'.[13] Strawson thinks that this is insufficient, and needs supplementation by an account of the 'performative' value of those words.

Strawson's performative theory

Strawson agrees with Ramsey that 'is true' is an 'assertively redundant' phrase, but adds the following. In the most straightforward case, we use it to *endorse* or *confirm* the proposition 'p' when we say 'It is true that p': other expressions Strawson uses are 'agree with', 'admit' and 'underwrite' the proposition. He compares the use of the phrase to the use of 'ditto' or 'Yes.' They all have a point only on particular linguistic occasions, such as, in the case of 'is true', when someone has asked 'Is p true?' or when someone has made the statement 'p'. If this linguistic setting is missing, the phrase lacks a point, and will be met with puzzlement. One other use which Strawson recognises for 'is true' is a *concessive* one, where we might say, 'It is true that *p*, but nevertheless *q*' to concede that *p*. The words are never used to assert something about the proposition, such as correspondence with fact: 'The phrase "is true" plays no part in the making of a meta-statement. The phrase "is true" *never* has a statement-making role,'[14] he insists.

Now even if we agreed with Strawson on the performative aspect of the words, it would not require us to deny them a descriptive role also. A statement-making role is not ruled out by words having a performative aspect: the words 'You are an idiot,' which serve to insult, nevertheless have a descriptive meaning; indeed they perform the insult-making role because of that descriptive meaning.

But should we accept even the performative aspect of 'is true' which Strawson claims? It is apparent that in certain constructions the words cannot be given that function: in particular, in hypothetical statements such as 'If it is true that the timetable is wrong, I'll miss my train,' and in disjunctive statements such as 'Either it is true that I'll miss my train or it isn't.' Moreover, if a performative role can be found for these occurrences of 'is true', the theory ought to be able to explain a systematic connection between the various performative roles discerned. As J.R. Searle has said, the theory must show how their use in these complex cases is derivable from their primary use in open cases to confirm or endorse a proposition. There are, too, questions connected with the effect of a performative use on the validity of logical inferences. If '*p* is true' uses 'is true' in one way, and 'If *p* is true, then *q*' uses the phrase in another, how can there be a valid argument to the conclusion '*q*'? On the face of it, the argument would involve the fallacy of equivocation.

Strawson's theory falls, of course, if Ramsey's thesis is rejected: objections to Ramsey's thesis are therefore equally objections to Strawson's. Both philosophers have put their case, however, in terms which are prima facie attractive. For Ramsey, 'there is really no separate problem of truth' – separate that is from the problem of judgement – 'but merely a linguistic muddle';[15] for Strawson, there is no problem of truth independent of that of assertion, of what it is to make a statement. We can agree that these notions are indeed closely tied. A statement or proposition is, after all, the sort of thing that can be true or false; the problem of what it is to state a fact is, after all, the problem of what it is to say what is the case, what is true. Yet the notion of truth is therefore needed in our account of propositions and of statements, so even though there is no *separate* problem of truth the notion cannot be dispensed with.

Tarski's semantic theory

Tarski's theory of truth constitutes the greatest challenge to traditional theories, having received widespread acclaim as the final word on this philosophical issue. The theory is presented in the context of a puzzle about truth going back to Greek philosophy, which concerns the possibility of constructing paradoxes with that notion. Epimenides the Cretan said that all Cretans were liars. Was he right? If so, he was not to be believed. More formally, take the proposition 'The proposition given here as an example is false.' Is this proposition true or false? If we say it is true, then it follows that it is false; if we say that it is false, it follows that it is true. How can this paradox be resolved?

Tarski's theory offers a solution which makes central use of a distinction between two levels of language. These are an 'object language' in which we make statements about things in the world, and a 'metalanguage' in which (as the name implies) we make statements about the object language. We might say, for instance, using English as our object language, 'There are trees in Russell Square.' We can go on to make statements about that statement, but these will be at a metalanguage level. We might say that 'Russell Square' is a referring term, and has as its referent a certain place in London: the notion of reference is one we use, therefore, not in the object language but in the metalanguage. Similarly, Tarski says, the notion of truth is a metalanguage one. Truth and reference are 'semantic' notions, relating object language to the world.

The proposition 'It is true that there are trees in Russell Square' is, therefore, a metalanguage proposition concerning the object language proposition 'There are trees in Russell Square.' How is this relevant to the truth paradoxes? These paradoxes arise, Tarski thinks, because no distinction is made in natural languages between object language and metalanguage: indeed, our example uses English throughout. Is the proposition 'The proposition given here as an example is false' in the object language or the metalanguage? We suppose that it can refer to itself and hence that it can supply the metalanguage semantic notion of falsehood to itself: but that notion can only be applied in a metalanguage to propositions in an object language. If English made a clear distinction between the two levels of language such paradoxical cases could not arise.

There are two other points which need to be added to this brief exposition. The first is that Tarski takes the metalanguage to be about the object *language*, that is the terms and sentences themselves. Truth and falsity are therefore properties of sentences, not propositions. An improvement on 'It is true that there are trees in Russell Square' would be the following: 'The English sentence "There are trees in Russell Square" is true.' The second point is that Tarski develops his theory to give an account of truth in *formal* languages, languages which can be made to keep strictly to the division between object languages and metalanguages. He offers a recursive definition of truth for formal languages which is logically quite complex, and which we need not go into here.

At one point Tarski says that he is offering a version

of the Correspondence Theory of truth. The impression that this is so is given by a condition he lays down for the formal definition of 'truth in a language *L*': it must imply, for any sentence '*S*' in *L*, that '*S*' is true if and only if things are as '*S*' says they are. Supposing for argument's sake that English were amenable to this kind of definition, then a successful definition of 'truth in English' would imply things like: 'Snow is white' is true if and only if snow is white; 'There are trees in Russell Square' is true if and only if there are trees in Russell Square. But such a definition cannot be given for natural languages and it follows that Tarski's theory is far removed from the problem to which the Correspondence Theory provides a solution. The question of the nature of factual truth concerns the propositions which are expressed in ordinary language, formal languages concerning themselves for the most part with logic and mathematics. Indeed, there are formal languages which do not permit the kind of definition offered by Tarski, since they cannot satisfy the above condition. At best, then, Tarski's account of truth is relevant to a limited range of formal languages only.

There are other reasons for which philosophers have rejected the semantic theory of truth. For one thing, it takes truth and falsity to be properties of sentences instead of propositions. For another, it is arguably circular in its formal definition of truth: it makes use of the formal notion of 'satisfaction', whereby an object is said to satisfy a function if the result of substituting the name of that object in the function produces a true sentence. However, many equally eminent philosophers have found Tarski's theory to resolve the issue of truth. Karl Popper, for instance, subscribes warmly to the theory; and Donald Davidson uses it to build an influential theory of meaning.

Notes

(An author's name followed by a number in square brackets refers to the book or article which has that number in the bibliography.)

1. Aristotle, *Metaphysics*, 1011b.
2. Wittgenstein [5], 2.202–2.222.
3. Ibid., 4.021–4.022.
4. J.L. Austin, 'Truth', *Proceedings of the Aristotelian Society*, supplementary vol. 24 (1950); quoted from reprint in Pitcher [4], p. 22.
5. Ibid.
6. Ibid., p. 24.
7. P.F. Strawson, 'Truth', *Proceedings of the Aristotelian Society*, supplementary vol. 24 (1950); quoted from reprint in Pitcher [4], pp. 38–9.
8. J.M.E. McTaggart, *The nature of existence*, (2 vols, Cambridge University Press, Cambridge, 1921 and 1927), vol. II, Book V, Ch. 33.
9. Bradley [7], p. 392.
10. James [11], p. 299.

11. C.S. Peirce, 'How to make our ideas clear' (1878), reprinted in Buchler [10].
12. Quine [12], p. 13.
13. F.P. Ramsey, 'Facts and propositions', *Proceedings of the Aristotelian Society*, supplementary vol. 7 (1927); quoted from reprint in Pitcher [4], p. 16.
14. P.F. Strawson, 'Truth', *Analysis*, vol. 9, no. 6 (1949).
15. Ramsey, 'Facts and propositions', p. 16.

Bibliography

In Gerd Buchdahl's *Metaphysics and the philosophy of science (the classical origins, Descartes to Kant)* (Basil Blackwell, Oxford, 1969) the central figures in the seventeenth and eighteenth centuries' debate between 'continental rationalists' and 'British empiricists' are examined in the light of their answers to the question 'What is the nature of the relation between the subject and predicate of a proposition (by virtue of which the proposition is either true or false)?' To sample the debate see John Locke, *An essay concerning human understanding* (Dent, London, 1961), Book IV, Chs. 5 and 6, and the commentary by G.W. Leibniz on Locke's *Essay, New essays on human understanding*, trans. and ed. Peter Remnant and Jonathan Bennett (Cambridge University Press, Cambridge, 1981), pp. 396–406. See also Leibniz's essay, 'Necessary and contingent truths' in *Leibniz: philosophical writings*, ed. G.H.R. Parkinson (Everyman, London, 1973), pp. 96–105.

The repudiation by logical positivists (empiricists) of 'metaphysics' on the basis of certain presuppositions about the nature of truth is well represented in

[1] A.J. Ayer (ed.), *Logical positivism* (The Free Press, New York, 1959), Chs. 2, 3 and 4.

Other treatments of the three traditional theories of truth covered in this chapter will be found in B. Carr and D.J. O'Connor, *Introduction to the theory of knowledge* (Harvester, Hassocks, 1982), Ch. 7; D.W. Hamlyn, *Theory of knowledge* (Macmillan, London, 1970), Ch. 5

[2] Alan R. White, *Truth* (Macmillan, London, 1970), Ch. 6, and

[3] Susan Haack, *Philosophy of logics* (Cambridge University Press, Cambridge, 1978), Ch. 7.

[4] George Pitcher (ed.), *Truth* (Prentice-Hall, Englewood Cliffs, New Jersey, 1964) brings together several important articles and selections from books, which are discussed in this chapter.

For example Austin's article, 'Truth' is reprinted in [4], pp. 18–31, as well as appearing in Austin's *Philosophical papers* (Oxford University Press, Oxford, 1961), pp. 117–33.

[5] Ludwig Wittgenstein, *Tractatus logico-philosophicus*, ed. D.F. Pears and B.F. McGuinness (Routledge and Kegan Paul, London, 1961) is a difficult as well as important work. For an introduction which places the *Tractatus* in the context of Wittgenstein's philosophic development see Anthony Kenny, *Wittgenstein* (Penguin Books, Harmondsworth, 1973). D.J. O'Connor, *The correspondence theory of truth* (Hutchinson, London, 1975) examines in detail the approach to truth which Austin and Wittgenstein have in common. In

[6] Simon Blackburn's *Spreading the word* (Clarendon Press, Oxford, 1984), Chs. 5, 6 and 7, there is a sensitive and imaginative confrontation between Correspondence

type theories and the general outlook represented in Coherence and Pragmatic theories.

Philosophic concern with truth developed in the context of a concern with human knowledge and understanding, and was not uncommonly taken to be a name for the goal of belief or judgement if either is to constitute knowledge. As a consequence questions about the notion of truth were not seen as separable from questions about what can be known. Both the coherence and pragmatic theories of truth grew out of this framework of concerns; and because the logical positivists stressed what can be verified or known to be true, it is not surprising that some of them developed a preference for the coherence approach. Those who did faced vigorous criticism from others, who regarded the positivist outlook as requiring a Correspondence Theory. A sample of this debate appears in articles by Otto Neurath and Moritz Schlick in [1], Chs. 9 and 10.

Earlier a coherence approach had found favour among idealist philosophers. F.H. Bradley argued on behalf of such an approach not only in

[7] *Appearance and reality*, 2nd edn (Oxford University Press, Oxford, 1897), Ch. 15, but also in

[8] *Essays on truth and reality* (Clarendon Press, Oxford, 1914), Ch. 7, and H.H. Joachim, *The nature of truth* (Clarendon Press, Oxford, 1906) argued on behalf of a Coherence Theory from an idealist standpoint. Bertrand Russell criticised Joachim in

[9] *Philosophical essays* (Longmans Green, London, 1910), Ch. 6, and Bradley included a critique of Russell in [8].

Pragmatism was not originally formulated as a theory of truth. C.S. Peirce applied the name to a method he had earlier advanced in an article, 'How to make our ideas clear', reprinted in

[10] Justus Buchler (ed.), *Philosophical writings of Peirce* (Dover, New York, 1955), Ch. 3. This was a method for clarifying 'intellectual' concepts, which carried implications about the meanings of such concepts, and the method was illustrated by the claim that by 'truth' we mean 'the opinion which is fated to be ultimately agreed to by all who investigate'. This doctrine had emerged earlier in Peirce's writings in tandem with an avowedly idealist metaphysical theory which did not regard reality as independent of thought. See Philip P. Wiener (ed.), *Charles S. Peirce, selected writings* (Dover, New York, 1958), pp. 80–4. (Wiener's selection also contains the article reprinted as Ch. 3 of [10].)

Peirce did not wholly approve the way his friend William James developed pragmatism (see [10], Ch. 18) and renamed his position 'pragmaticism' to make clear its distance from James. In

[11] *Pragmatism* (McKay, New York, 1907) and in other writings James displayed a gift for vivid turns of phrase which communicated his drift effectively but made it easy for hostile critics to dismiss his theory. For attacks on James from both Correspondence and Coherence quarters see Russell [9], Chs. 4 and 5 and Bradley [8], Chs. 4 and 5. A recent and very valuable attempt by Susan Haack to set straight what became, as a result of James' loose phrases, a very distorted picture of 'The pragmatist theory of truth', appears in *The British Journal for the Philosophy of Science*, vol. 27 (1976), pp. 231–49.

If truth is a concept which must be analysed in isolation from questions of what we can know and what we can do with our knowledge, then Dewey's concept of 'warranted assertibility' represents a movement to abandon the concept of truth for something which does not prejudice the issues involved in such isolation. Dewey introduced the concept in *Logic, the theory of inquiry* (Allen and Unwin, London, 1938) and it was criticised by Russell in P.A. Schilpp (ed.), *The philosophy of John Dewey* (Tudor Publishing, New York, 1939), pp. 135–56. Dewey replied to Russell on pp. 544–9 and again in 'Propositions, warranted assertibility and truth', which appears in S. Morganbesser (ed.), *John Dewey and his critics* (The Journal of Philosophy, New York, 1977).

A more recent approach to truth which does not treat it as something wholly independent of human knowledge is that developed out of the intuitionist philosophy of mathematics and dubbed 'anti-realism' by Michael Dummett. Dummett's key article, 'Truth', is reprinted in [4], pp. 93–111 as well as in Dummett's *Truth and other enigmas* (Duckworth, London, 1978), pp. 1–24, where it appears along with a number of valuable supplementary articles.

The early views of Russell on truth and the question of the bearers of truth appear in [9], Ch. 7. The corresponding views of Moore appear in *Some main problems of philosophy* (Allen and Unwin, London, 1953), Chs. 3, 12, 14 and 15. Quine's doctrine of eternal sentences as the bearers of truth is set out in

[12] *The philosophy of logic* (Prentice-Hall, Englewood Cliffs, 1970), Ch. 1. The issue of the bearers of truth is surveyed in [2], Ch. 1 and [3], Ch. 6.

Ramsey's statement of his thesis is included in [4], pp. 16–17, as well as in his *The foundations of mathematics and other essays* (Routledge and Kegan Paul, London, 1921), pp. 142–3. Strawson's elaboration of Ramsey's position also appears in [4], pp. 32–53 (as does his claim about 'All John's children are asleep,' on pp. 85–7). This elaboration took place in the context of a reply to Austin's article and can also be found with further supplements in Strawson's *Logico-linguistic papers* (Methuen, London, 1971), pp. 190–250.

Ramsey's thesis and the 'semantic theory of truth' are considered in [2], Ch. 5. 'The liar' and related paradoxes are discussed in [3], Ch. 8. Tarski's semantic theory of truth is a moderately advanced piece of mathematical logic, but Tarski offers a layman's introduction to the problems it confronted in 'Truth and proof' which appeared in the *Scientific American* (June 1969), pp. 63–77. His reasons for thinking that his theory amounted to a version of the traditional correspondence theory are not technical either. They appear in 'The semantic conception of truth' in H. Feigl and W. Sellars (eds), *Readings in philosophical analysis* (Appleton-Century-Crofts, New York, 1949), pp. 52–84.

Tarski's basic idea that truth for a given language can be defined by specifying how one would define the set of its true sentences has been regarded as philosophically important by Karl Popper; see *Objective knowledge* (Clarendon Press, Oxford, 1972), Ch. 9. (The book is dedicated to Tarski.) It also forms the basis of a philosophic research programme founded by Donald Davidson in articles collected in *Inquiries into truth and interpretation* (Clarendon Press, Oxford, 1984), especially Chs. 1–5. Tarski's theory and its use in Davidson's programme are considered in [6], Ch. 8.

J.E.T.

5 | The Truths of Logic and of Mathematics

J.E. Tiles

Logic and its place in philosophy

The first men in the history of the West to identify themselves as philosophers, Plato and Aristotle, did so partly to distinguish themselves from contemporaries who offered to teach people rhetoric, the skills of persuasion. Although neither refused to teach such skills, both clearly believed that questions of what *will* as a matter of fact change people's minds should be subordinate to questions of what *should* change people's minds. It seemed to them intellectually dishonest to think only as far as the question of what *will* persuade people, rather than trying to offer people, wherever possible, reasons that *ought* to persuade them.

In other words, philosophy was, from a very early stage in its history, bound up with the idea that there were better and worse arguments or reasons – where 'better' did not just mean 'effective in changing people's minds'. With this came the idea that philosophy's concern was not only to advance the better arguments, but also to try to identify such arguments, and to say what made them superior. In one sense of the word this is what logic is. In this sense logic will naturally be a major concern of philosophy and where the term has this sense it tends to be used in a way which is nearly synonymous with philosophy.

There is, however, a way of exploring the difference between good and bad arguments, which considerably narrows the field of interest; and if logic is thought to consist in following this path, the scope of logic is correspondingly narrowed. Whether an argument should or should not persuade a person, whether the reasons offered are good or bad, depends on whether the *premises* of the argument (the considerations advanced on behalf of some *conclusion*) are true or otherwise worthy of acceptance. But however worthy of acceptance the premises may be, they may also be irrelevant or offer only the feeblest of support for the conclusion. Thus to arrive at what is most commonly regarded as the concern of logic we have to set aside questions of how true or worthy of acceptance the premisses of an argument may be and ask, 'If they were true or worthy of acceptance, should anyone go on to accept the conclusion?'

The strongest reason one could give for an affirmative answer to this question, when it is asked of some particular argument, would be to point out that someone who accepted the premisses *had already in effect* accepted the conclusion. All a person does, when he is prompted by the premisses to accept the conclusion, when he *infers* the conclusion, is to draw out what is contained implicitly in the premisses. (What this means will be illustrated below.) Such *inferences* were called 'explicative' by the nineteenth-century American philosopher and logician C.S. Peirce. Not all the inferences which we make on the basis of arguments, which we wish to classify as rationally (as opposed to rhetorically) compelling, are explicative. In many arguments the conclusion makes a claim which goes well beyond what is contained in the premisses; Peirce classified inferences made on the basis of such arguments as 'ampliative'.

Among ampliative inferences are inductions, such as those which are said to proceed by simple enumeration. For example, we observe n cases of people who have (had) a disease and find that all have a certain antigen in their blood, and we conclude that all persons (including all those whom we have yet to examine) who have (had) that disease will have that antigen in their blood. There are clearly cases covered in our conclusion (the ones we have not yet examined) which are not covered in our premisses. How rationally compelling this sort of inference is depends on how many cases we have examined. More importantly (because this also determines how many cases we ought to have examined before drawing our conclusion), it depends on how likely there is to be some connection between the things which we have observed. If we had found that n people who have (had) a certain disease were all born on the sixth day of one or another month of the year, we would feel uneasy about an inference to the conclusion that all sufferers from this disease were born on the sixth of some month even if n were a very large number. (There is more about this kind of reasoning in Chapter 9.)

The strength of an ampliative inference such as this depends in a crucial way on whatever background knowledge we have, and our assessment of its strength may change as our knowledge changes. Thus although we can compare and classify forms of ampliative inference (different kinds of induction, inferences to the best explanation, probabilistic inferences, etc.), we cannot study their *validity* (the extent to which a person who accepts the premisses is rationally compelled to accept the conclusion) independently of the subject-matter which they involve.

Explicative inferences are different. It is possible to

examine such an inference and, without knowing anything about the subject-matter which it treats, say positively that it is or is not *without qualification valid*, i.e. that a person who accepts the premisses cannot rationally resist the conclusion. This can be done by making it evident that to reject the conclusion will involve contradicting what the premisses say, so that a person who accepts the premisses and rejects the conclusion contradicts him/herself. Thus a person who accepts that some mammals are predators and that all mammals suckle their young cannot without contradicting him/herself deny that some creatures which suckle their young are predators.

An argument which is in this way valid without qualification is said to be *deductively* valid. Peirce recognised only one kind of explicative inference, viz. those which purported to be deductively valid. The study of deductive validity is the starting point of logical theory, partly because it represents the ideal – it studies the arguments which ought rationally to persuade a person wholly on the strength of the acceptability of the premisses – and partly because it can be studied by concentrating entirely on the forms of arguments – whatever the constituent premisses and conclusions say, true or false, all arguments which have one of the correct forms are valid.

Theories of deductive validity

To see an illustration of the sort of form on which deductive validity depends, compare the example two paragraphs above about mammals with the argument 'Some men are prodigal. All men are saints. So, some saints are prodigal.' Both arguments have the same form:

Some M are P.
All M are S.
_____

Some S are P.

Arguments of this form are valid (although the second example has a false second premiss and a doubtfully true conclusion). Clearly their validity does not depend on the fact that the different words involved begin with 'M', 'P' and 'S'; that was a coincidence contrived to make it easier to see that not only does each argument involve two premisses, but also exactly three *terms*. Of these terms, one occurs in each of the premisses (the 'M' for 'middle' term) and the other two each occur in one premiss and the conclusion. Arguments which have these formal features and in addition where the two premisses and conclusion are of one of the four forms, 'All —— are ——,' 'Some —— are ——,' 'No —— are ——,' 'Some —— are not ——,' are known as *syllogisms* (from Aristotle's word meaning, roughly, 'deduction').

Aristotle made the first efforts to explore deductive validity and among his achievements was the identification of the valid forms of syllogisms. Syllogisms proved to be an important class of arguments. They could be combined into chains (the conclusion of one syllogism providing a premiss for another) and much of what people find troublesome in ordinary reasoning can be clarified by means of syllogistic theory. But the validity or otherwise of a syllogism depends on there being sub-sentential fragments (i.e. what have been called 'terms' here) common to several of the sentences used to express the argument. It was not long before it was recognised (particularly by Stoic philosophers who lived a few generations after Aristotle) that the deductive validity of some arguments depends on the recurrence of whole sentences within other sentences.

Thus within the sentence 'Harrison was to arrive either in New York or in Baltimore' are in effect two sentences, 'Harrison was to arrive in New York' and 'Harrison was to arrive in Baltimore,' which are joined by an 'or'. If we add the premiss that Harrison (for some reason) will not land in New York, we may infer with deductive validity that he will arrive in Baltimore. This and other patterns of argument depend not on how terms (which cannot by themselves stand as sentences) are joined within sentences, but on how sentences may be combined to form further (complex) sentences. For example, this argument has the form 'From P or Q, and not P, we may conclude Q.' These patterns cannot be accounted for in syllogistic theory, and for a long time they were overlooked, or given *ad hoc* treatment by logicians who believed that syllogistic theory could not be improved.

Syllogistic theory is also unable to handle arguments involving relations, such as the relation of ownership. From 'Every villager owns a mule' and 'All mules are barren' we may validly infer that 'Every villager owns a barren animal.' But from 'Every sheep has hooves' and 'No hoof is a horn' we cannot validly infer that 'No sheep has horns.' Logicians found themselves unable to account for the difference in validity using Aristotle's theory, but arguments of this form came to be increasingly important in mathematics from the seventeenth century onward. Finally, in the nineteenth century, the German logician and philosopher Gottlob Frege produced a theory which united the treatment of both Aristotelian syllogisms and Stoic sententially structured arguments and which was powerful enough to handle arguments involving relations as well. Modern logic takes Frege's work as its point of departure.

Different logicians have taken, and continue to take, different approaches to the question of what makes a form deductively valid. If pressed to explain why the particular syllogistic form which was used above as an example was valid, Aristotle would have set out to demonstrate its validity by appealing to other syllogistic forms, which he regarded as *obviously* valid, such as the form 'All S are M, some M are P, therefore some S are P.' He would also have appealed to 'immediate inferences' such as from 'Some P are M' we may infer 'Some M are P,' again which he regarded as *obviously* valid. This way of showing how the validity of many forms rests on that of a few forms taken to be obviously valid has evident affinities with the axiomatic method of mathematics, where the acceptability of many theorems is shown to rest on that of a few axioms taken to be obviously true (or at any rate mathematically acceptable). This approach would now be termed a 'natural deduction' approach to logic and validity.

Another way to explain the validity of a syllogism was developed in the nineteenth century by, among others, John Venn. Many people have been taught to test the validity of syllogisms by means of Venn diagrams. This is a way of providing a spatial representation of all possible classes created by the terms involved in a syllogistic argument. It enables one to decide by visual inspection whether it is possible for the premisses of a syllogism to be true and its conclusion false. If it is *not* possible, the argument is valid. Venn diagrams constitute what is called a *'semantic'* approach to the validity of arguments, which can be put in syllogistic form. Such an approach studies validity by considering all the ways in which it is possible to interpret an argument schema, i.e. an argument considered as a purely formal arrangement of linguistic items of some kind.

Another commonly encountered semantic tech-nique is 'truth tables'. (Some logic books make use of an elegant variant on the truth table idea which is known as 'semantic tableaux'.) Unlike Venn dia-grams truth tables apply to arguments whose validity depends on sentential structure, rather than on the structure based on sub-sentential 'terms'. Like Venn diagrams truth tables present an exhaustive account of a certain range of possibilities. The possibilities represented on a Venn diagram are all the combinations of things which could be said about an individual using just the three terms which occur in the argument being tested. The possibilities represented on a truth table are all the ways in which the truth or falsity of the premisses and conclusion could vary with the truth or falsity of their smallest constituent sentences. As in the case of the Venn diagram test, this enables one to determine conclusively whether it is possible for the premisses to be true and the conclusion false. If it is not possible for this to occur, then, as with the case of the Venn diagram test, the argument is valid. An extension of the truth table idea discovered by the twentieth-century Polish logician Alfred Tarski provides logicians with a semantic account of validity for the very powerful logical framework which Frege devised.

Although logicians differ as to whether a natural deduction approach or a semantic approach to validity is primary, few are prepared wholly to ignore the other. A natural deduction approach is an excellent vehicle for organising an account of what are the valid forms; but what leads a logician to treat a form as valid is that it 'preserves' some property of sentences, such as truth or mathematical provability. (Saying that it 'preserves' such a property means that the form guarantees that, if the premisses all have the property, so does the conclusion.) When exploring what are regarded as the frontiers of logical theory such as modal logic (treating the concepts of possibility and necessity) and tense logic (treating temporal concepts), logicians regard it as desirable to have both a semantic and a natural deduction account of validity. The aim then is to provide a 'completeness proof', i.e. to show that whatever comes out valid under one account will also be valid under the other. The different approaches also provide logicians with different ways of focusing dissatisfaction with existing accounts.

The truths of logic

Investigations concerning the deductive validity of arguments yield statements to the effect that a conclusion, C, follows deductively from premises, $P_1, P_2, \ldots P_n$. This is now commonly expressed by means of the sign '$\vdash$', thus:

$$P_1, P_2, \ldots, P_n \vdash C.$$

If it is thought that the primary aim of any respectable theoretical enterprise is to state the truth and that logic is such an enterprise, then these would be the truths of logic.

Talk of logical truths, however, invites questions concerning what kind of truths these are. The approach taken so far, via the validity of certain patterns of inference or forms of argument, suggests that the truths of logic are normative principles, which determine what constitutes good or sound reasoning. Whoever accepts certain premises and rejects a conclusion which follows validly from them is guilty of a form of bad practice.

This way of looking at logic makes some philosophers distinctly uneasy. These are philosophers who want to distinguish sharply between facts and norms, descriptions and prescriptions (Chapter 27). Logic is not, such philosophers insist, about what human beings do or ought to do, but about relations of *implication* which exist between the sentences of whatever language people happen to speak or between the propositions which constitute elements of their thoughts. Whether a person, in moving from proposition to proposition or sentence to sentence, follows or fails to follow relations of implication, it is of no concern to logic.

Seeing the 'truths of logic' as norms of the practice of making inferences will incline one to regard a natural deduction approach to validity as having priority over a semantic approach. Seeing them as reports of relations of implication obtaining between sentences or propositions will incline one to take the semantic approach as primary. The attempt to find a semantic account equivalent to some existing natural deduction account, or vice versa, is therefore sometimes motivated by the desire to restate, in one's own terms, claims arising from a view of logic to which one is unsympathetic.

Talk of 'truth' also invites the question 'In virtue of what are the truths of logic true?' In answer to this question both parties to the above debate can at least agree that such truths are true in virtue of the deductive validity of argument forms, and that our assessment of the truth or falsity of a logical statement will be relative to our account of validity. As long as one approaches the question via the validity of arguments, a good deal of needless puzzlement can be avoided.

If we consider the truth of quite ordinary statements, such as 'Some conifers are deciduous,' 'Many of Britain's sewers will soon need to be replaced' or 'Last summer was uncommonly dry,' we can readily imagine what would be involved in determining whether they are true or false, and we could readily identify those aspects of the natural world in virtue of which such statements are either true or false. The truths of logic, however, do not seem to answer directly to any readily identifiable aspects of the natural world. For this reason it is tempting to start speaking of logical features of the world or possibly of a separate logical world in virtue of which logical truths are true, and of special intellectual faculties which we possess for apprehending these truths.

The temptation to think of the truths of logic in this way is reinforced by several factors. One is the way many of the statements which a logician makes about the validity of individual arguments can be cast into a form superficially similar to ordinary factual statements. All statements to the effect that a certain conclusion follows from given premises can be cast in a conditional form. Thus one of the examples used above could be expressed, 'If Harrison is landing either in New York or in Baltimore, and he is not landing in New York, then he must be landing in Baltimore.' This has a superficial similarity to the statement 'If a pan of fat is very hot and drops of water fall into the pan, the mixture will hiss and splatter.' But clearly the truth (or falsity) of the former does not answer to the world in the way the latter does.

Some of the truths of logic, moreover, seem neither to state that a certain conclusion can be deduced from given premises nor even to have a conditional form. Some of these arise because to deny them would be self-contradictory, for example, any statement having the form 'a thing which is F and G is F' (a female fox is female). Others may not seem at first glance any more informative than this example, but may nevertheless be thought to embody important principles. The most famous of these are the Principle of Non-Contradiction, 'It is not the case that P is true and that not-P is also true,' and the Law of (the) Excluded Middle, 'Either P is true or not-P is true,' where in each case P may be filled by any (assertoric) sentence. These statements are unconditionally true (valid). It is (setting aside for the moment the controversy surrounding the last of these) a criterion of having understood them that a person sees that they cannot fail to be true. Yet we do not seem to come to appreciate these truths by experience in the same way as those about trees, sewers and the behaviour of water when it comes into contact with hot fat.

Rather than yield at once to the temptation to talk about logical facts and rational faculties for apprehending them, it is worth reflecting on how in general a logician goes about establishing the validity of an argument. We have seen that in the case of a logician taking a 'semantic approach' to validity this involves giving an exhaustive account of some range of possibilities, an account which enables us to examine an argument and see whether it is possible for its premises to be true and its conclusion false. This account of validity can be applied to any conditional statement (is it possible for the antecedent clauses all to be true and the consequent clause(s) false?). And the same account may very well enable us to say that a single statement of categorical (non-conditional) form cannot be false. Thus it follows from the account of all the possible ways the truth or falsity of a complex sentence may vary with the truth or falsity of its smallest component sentences (the account embodied in the truth table technique) that anything which has a form expressing the Principle of Non-Contradiction or the Law of Excluded Middle cannot be false.

So, if we ask, 'What is it in virtue of which such a statement is true?' or 'How is it that we can know such a truth?' these questions should be referred to the account of validity on which the claim to truth rests. This does not mean that answering it will be straightforward and unproblematic. The account of possibility on which the account of validity rests may give rise to all sorts of problems. But the question will at least have been referred to the place where those problems take shape.

Logical possibility and logical analysis

Logic is not the only discipline which explores what is possible and what is not possible. Chemistry, for example, yields an account of whether and why it is possible for certain chemical elements to combine to form compounds. Some combinations are not possible because the structure of the atoms involved will not allow bonding. But the (natural) possibilities and impossibilities which chemistry explores are thought to be of a different order altogether from logical possibilities. Chemistry may tell us what is possible or impossible given the laws which govern the behaviour of matter in the world, but it does not show us that there could not have been quite different laws, and hence quite different possible compounds. When a logician declares that 'it is not possible for the premises of this argument to be true and the conclusion false', the notion of impossibility is supposed to be unconditional, not relative to any facts about the natural world, which for all we know could be or could have been otherwise.

What hold have we on a notion of unconditional impossibility? In the section on theories of deductive ability above we took it that a person could validly infer a conclusion from a set of statements s/he had already accepted, if denying that conclusion would involve that person in a contradiction. This was to appeal implicitly to the principle that for a person to accept a set of statements which could possibly be true, the statements must not involve a contradiction. In this case to avoid a contradiction the person in question must either embrace the conclusion or reject something s/he has hitherto accepted.

This principle has not always been accepted without dispute. Followers of the Presocratic philosopher Heraclitus appear to have held that the natural world could embody contradictions, so that beliefs which contradicted one another could all be true. (In modern times some of the followers of Hegel also appear to have held this doctrine.) Aristotle found himself constrained to argue against Heracliteans and others on behalf of a form of the principle that contradictions cannot be true. His argument involved challenging his opponents to 'signify something', that is, he was in effect arguing that contradictions destroy the significance of what is said. This way of conducting the debate suggests how logicians can hope to fasten on to a notion of impossibility which is unconditional, namely by recognising that avoiding (at least explicit) contradictions is a condition of any significant discourse or thought whatever.

Because the principle of non-contradiction thus provides a hold on the required notion of unconditional impossibility, contradictions are said to be 'logically impossible'. And because there is no principle of equal power for determining what is unconditionally impossible, it is common to treat the corresponding notion, 'free from contradiction', as defining what is 'logically possible'. If a set of statements embodying a contradiction cannot all be true, then one way of ensuring that a set of statements does not embody a contradiction is (actually) to find a situation in which they are all true. (This is the principle that actuality proves possibility.) One needs, however, to be more wary of the principle that *imagining* a situation in which a set of statements is all true proves that the statements are free from contradiction and hence describe a logical possibility. It is certainly difficult to imagine something one knows to involve a contradiction, e.g. a round square, but is easy enough to imagine something (e.g. having a general way of constructing with straightedge and compasses a square equal in area to a given circle) which only careful and disciplined thinking can show to involve a contradiction.

Although it is possible to identify sets of statements which are clearly inconsistent and possible to circumscribe the meanings of words so as to ensure that a set of statements is consistent, there is no formal or mechanical way of determining whether a given set of statements does or does not embody a contradiction. If, for example, a set of statements can be assigned a form which allows a truth table test to be performed, it will be clear that the statements are inconsistent if there is no assignment of truth-values to the smallest constituent sentences which makes all of the statements true. But it is possible for a contradiction to elude this or any other formal test, if the set of statements is not assigned a form which allows the contradiction to appear.

To illustrate with a simple example: someone who is bankrupt is not solvent, but as long as the incompatibility of these two terms is not represented formally, no formal test will reveal the contradiction involved in calling a bankrupt person solvent. If we represent 'Fred is bankrupt' by P and 'Fred is solvent' by Q, there is nothing formally contradictory in the conjunction 'P and Q', unless somehow it is made explicit that if P then not Q. In other words, a test of the consistency of a set of statements or the validity of an argument depends on how adequately the connections between concepts have been represented. The task of making explicit all the important connections between concepts is called providing a 'logical analysis' of the statements in question.

A logical analysis would have to reveal the relations of incompatibility between concepts such as that between being bankrupt and being solvent. It would have to take account of when a single word or phrase was used with different senses on different occasions. For example, 'illuminated' may be applied to manuscripts in virtue of light falling on them or the calligraphic technique used in them; there may be no contradiction – only a serious infelicity of expression – in saying that certain illuminated manuscripts were not illuminated. Relations of inclusion, as well as relations of sameness or difference in meaning, might be relevant to whether a set of statements involves a contradiction. Primates are included among the mammals, but unless this fact is represented, denying that something which is true of all mammals is true of primates will not obviously involve a contradiction.

Other more complicated features of language may need to be taken into account in an exercise in logical analysis. Using some words in conjunction with each other appreciably affects their logical behaviour. A working mother works and has children, but an expectant mother, although looking forward to something, need not have children (need not be a mother). Many of the terms which need to be treated with care are forms of relational expressions. Small elephants are *small* compared with other elephants, but still *big* compared with the largest mouse. Different relational expressions have different logical properties, which may need to be taken into account. If someone is my cousin, I am that person's cousin. If someone is my parent, I am not that person's parent.

Logicians do not have any well-established techniques for representing some of these more complicated features of the concepts we use in everyday speech, such as the behaviour of what are known as 'attributive adjectives', like 'small' and 'expectant' in the examples above. This is one of several areas which are counted as fields of research by logicians who work close to natural language rather than concerning themselves with problems which belong to pure mathematics.

Analytic truths and necessary truths

It is clear that logical analysis of some kind or other is an unavoidable part of applying a logical theory to actual arguments and pieces of discourse. It is also an idea around which in this century a whole philosophic tradition, known as 'analytic philosophy', has grown up. Although a twentieth-century phenomenon, the idea that our thought or discourse needs to be subjected to 'analysis' (not unlike that which a chemist might perform to determine the composition of some compound) has roots in previous centuries. Kant spoke of the truth of certain statements as 'analytic', meaning that their truth was in effect logical; the contradictions involved in their negations would be revealed by displaying the logical composition of the concepts which they contained.

A simple example would be the statement that a vixen is female. This statement is true in virtue of the fact that the concept *vixen* is that of a female fox. To deny that a vixen is female is to deny that a female fox is female, which is to contradict something contained in the concept *vixen*. In a similar way, 'A vixen suckles her young' is an analytic truth, for *female fox* is the analysis of the concept *vixen*, *mammal* is part of the concept *fox* and *the female suckles its young* is part of the concept *mammal*. By contrast, in 'A vixen does not hibernate in winter' or 'A vixen has a litter of six to eight pups,' something is added to what is already contained in the concept *vixen*. Kant called such statements 'synthetic truths'.

Working as he did within an Aristotelian logical framework, Kant found it difficult to see when a statement involving relational concepts was self-contradictory, and hence when the negations of such statements could be regarded as analytic. Because so much of mathematics depends on relational concepts, it appeared to Kant that many of the truths of arithmetic and geometry were 'synthetic' in his sense. This doctrine was important to his philosophy since it seemed clear that such truths were *a priori*, not based on experience – for experience could not establish their universality and necessity – yet at the same time they were not analytic. The question of how some truths could be both synthetic and *a priori* was, for Kant, the central question of philosophy (see Chapter 6).

To Frege, writing nearly a century later, it seemed that Kant must be wrong about arithmetic. (Frege never challenged Kant's view of the truths of geometry.) Arithmetic struck Frege as having a feature which it shared with logic, viz. that its truths depend in no way on the subject-matter which they might involve; logic and arithmetic are both what later came to be called 'topic-neutral'. Since Frege had a way of representing the logical structure of general statements involving relational expressions (cf. section on theories of deductive validity above), he had at his disposal ways of showing statements to be logical truths which Kant had not envisaged. Frege set out to show rigorously that arithmetical truths were analytic in the sense of being provable by appeal to definitions and logical laws alone.

Frege's attempt to show that the truths of arithmetic were analytic very nearly succeeded, but in his development he made use of a principle which came to be known as the (unrestricted) comprehension axiom and which, when used in conjunction with definitions involving relational concepts (in particular the relation between a class and one of its members), led to unavoidable contradictions. This was noticed by Bertrand Russell, who communicated to Frege his famous 'paradox' involving the class of all classes which are not members of themselves: this class cannot be, nor can it fail to be, a member of itself without yielding a contradiction.

Russell was himself profoundly sympathetic to what Frege was trying to achieve, and even when Frege had given up trying to repair the damage which 'Russell's paradox' did to his system, Russell tried to carry out Frege's programme. Russell saw in Frege's work the promise of nothing less than the reduction of the whole of mathematics to logic. In other words, the truths of mathematics would be shown to be truths of logic. This was somewhat more ambitious than Frege had been. (He had concerned himself only with 'arithmetic', which he took to include fractions and irrational numbers.) But in spite of undeniable ingenuity Russell did not succeed in carrying out the original aim of using only principles which were clearly logical. He had to assume among other things that there was an infinite number of things in the physical world, which is not self-evidently true, let alone something whose denial clearly involves a contradiction.

Russell's work in the foundations of mathematics nevertheless proved to be an inspiration for further, more wide-ranging developments. After his major contributions to mathematical logic had been completed, Russell carried on developing ideas which had grown out of the application of the new logical techniques to scientific and everyday discourse. His primary motivation became that of justifying a form of empiricism not unlike that to be found in the work of the eighteenth-century philosopher David Hume, according to which the meaning of every significant term is grounded in immediate experience and any necessary truths are the product of the logical principles which structure our thought or discourse.

Russell's work was taken up by the 'logical positivists', who saw in an empiricism equipped with more powerful techniques of logical analysis a way of combating what they regarded as empty and pretentious doctrines of all kinds from the philosophy of Heidegger to the dogmas of morals and religion. They specifically rejected the framework of Kant's philosophy, proclaiming there were no synthetic *a priori* statements. Any statement which is necessary (a mark of being *a priori*, according to

Kant) would be revealed by analysis to be an analytic truth, true in virtue of the meanings of the words involved.

In other words, all necessary statements are like 'a vixen is female'; when one has subtracted the information about how words are used (we use 'vixen' to designate a female fox) no necessary statement conveys more information than does a sentence of the form 'Something which is F and G is F.' Statements which in this way say nothing because they simply repeat what is already said are called 'tautologies' and another way in which logical positivists proclaimed their doctrine was to say that all necessary statements are tautologies. Now this is the statement of a programme, something to be established by a great deal of hard work (of which the logicist programme for mathematics would be a crucial part). However the programme slides over into being an article of faith, too obvious to require much argument, and this suggests that there is an underlying doctrine which has a strong appeal of its own.

Conventionalism

The doctrine is known as 'conventionalism' and it answers to a powerful feeling, which many people have, that all truths which strike us as necessary are the result of *our* refusing to count anything as showing them to be false. The refusal may not have grown out of a conscious decision, but it is a matter which could, if we wanted, be decided otherwise. In this sense necessary truths are maintained as such by convention. The world (where part of what counts as 'the world' may be the structure of our minds) does not have in it any objective necessity and does not impose any necessary principles on our thought.

There immediately arises the question of how far this doctrine can be pushed. If the necessity of the statements of arithmetic (assuming the logicist reduction of arithmetic to logic can be carried out) reflects only our persistence in using words for numbers and for operations on numbers, why stop there? The validity of arguments, the truths of logic, are expressed by making crucial use of words like 'if', 'and', 'not', etc. Is not the emptiness of the very tautologies, to which necessary truths are supposed to reduce, simply the result of our using such words as we do?

A difficulty with pushing conventionalism this far is that someone who treats even the principles of logic as conventions would be in the position of having to treat any supposed consequences of adopting a convention also as matters of convention. Now the idea at the heart of the notion of convention is that anything that is conventional could be laid down by conscious decisions. But if every convention, C, depends entirely on further conventions to determine what is involved in laying down C, the thought that there could be any conventions at all in this sense becomes highly problematic. How does any decision come to have determinate con-

111

sequences, when the principles of determining those consequences await the outcome of further decisions?

Another difficulty is that it is unclear that there is any interesting sense in which the principle of non-contradiction is a matter of convention. If we were right to think that avoiding contradiction was a condition of saying anything significant, the claim that we could decide to abandon the principle of non-contradiction cannot amount to anything more than the obvious truth that we are free to give up coherent speech.

For these reasons extreme conventionalism is rare and it is much more common to find a modified form, which accepts a core of principles as objectively necessary – imposed on us by the world or by what is required for coherent thought – and claims that all other necessary truths have the status of conventions. In order to be able to maintain that the core is a body of trivial truths, tautologies, a fairly uncontentious body of logical principles is usually adopted; what is known as 'classical first order predicate logic' is a popular choice. Having such a core allows the adoption of a verbal convention to have determinate consequences, but the resources of this particular core of logical principles are not very great. It has not, for example, been possible to carry out within it the logicist programme for showing the truths of arithmetic to be logical truths.

One expedient for preserving the momentum of conventionalism is to extend the domain of what may count as falling within the scope of convention. So far we have taken it that the definitions of terms – for example that we apply 'vixen' to and only to female foxes or that we apply any word in this way – are matters of convention. There are, however, many statements which we regard as necessarily true about things such as foxes (e.g. that the same fox cannot be both in England and in Canada at the same time) which do not appear to follow from anything which looks like a definition of 'fox' in the sense of a list of criteria that would enable a person to recognise something as a fox. But on the other hand it is tempting to treat the truth of such statements as 'part of what we mean by' certain words. In that case we will have to extend our idea of what is involved in 'analysing a concept' to include claims to the effect that anyone using the concept properly will always have to assume that such and such statements are true.

This approach clearly makes the conventionalist programme easier to carry out. One no longer has to show that all truths which we regard as necessary are logical truths, which have been disguised by the meanings of the words which they involve. Instead one can simply treat an apparently necessary truth, which resists reduction to a logical truth, as a 'meaning postulate'. That is, one can treat it as a statement, which, as a result of our refusal to count anything as falsifying it, contributes something to the meanings of the terms involved. This may well strike some as trivialising the programme. (Russell in a closely related context described the method of postulation as 'having the advantages of theft over honest toil'.) But in support of meaning postulates it might be replied that conventionalism is just one of those doctrines whose truth may not strike one at first, but once its claim is understood will be seen to be trivially true.

Formalism

This version of conventionalism has a precedent in the way some mathematicians look at mathematical concepts. From the time of Euclid onward it has been clear to mathematicians that they could not rest the proof of all important theorems on definitions alone; they had to make use of axioms or postulates in addition to definitions. In recent times, with the proliferation of axiomatic systems, it has appeared to some mathematicians that what were traditionally thought of as definitions did not do all the work of making mathematical concepts determinate. Two mathematicians, who accepted the same set of definitions but assumed different axioms or postulates, could not be using the same mathematical concepts.

Thus the kind of conventionalism which allows itself to declare some statements to be true 'by convention' and hence necessarily true, has corresponding to it a view of the nature of mathematical truth, known as formalism. Many mathematicians, especially pure mathematicians, who do not want to be troubled by questions about the truth or falsity of the axioms which they assume, and hence about the statements for which they attempt to provide proofs, find one or another version of formalism attractive. One version of formalism, dubbed 'if-thenism' by Russell, takes mathematics to consist of nothing but statements to the effect that if one makes certain assumptions certain consequences follow (logically). This allows one to brush aside questions about the truths of mathematics; what you learn from a mathematician is what follows if you agree (adopt a convention) to hold certain statements true. This account, however, does not explain why we think of mathematics as having a distinct subject-matter. Any body of statements, about law, the theatre or agriculture, can be investigated in this way, i.e. by asking, 'What consequences follow if you assume the following ...?'

Another related view of the nature of the truths of mathematics, which calls itself 'formalism', avoids this all-embracing answer to the question about the subject-matter of mathematics. This is the view, advanced by the mathematician Haskell B. Curry, that mathematics is the 'science of formal systems'. A formal system is an abstract structure which could (although it need not) be interpreted as a deductively structured body of statements of some branch of science. Such a system is defined according to Curry by a set of conventions: conventions establish what the objects (called the 'terms') of the theory are, how terms combine to form 'elementary propositions' and which of these 'elementary propositions' are 'true'.

Curry's suggestion arose from the discovery that it

113

was possible to take the statements of an axiomatised mathematical theory and study the structure which they formed with the tools of mathematics. Mathematical theories had only recently become objects of mathematical study, but Curry's proposal amounted to the claim that the deductive structures formed by the statements of a mathematical theory are in fact the only real objects of mathematical study. This proposal restricts the domain of mathematics too much, just as 'if-thenism' entails a domain for mathematics which is too wide. Pure mathematics has long studied abstract structures, which are quite unlike those which arise from the deductive arrangement of sentences. There is nothing problematic about such structures which is not also problematic about the structure exhibited by formal systems. It is extravagant to claim that when a mathematician is concerned with, say, the abstract structure of the points on a line, the only genuine mathematical object involved is the deductive structure of the statements which s/he makes when saying how the points on a line stand to one another.

Another doctrine which called itself 'formalism' was advanced by the mathematician David Hilbert early in this century. Developments which had taken place in mathematics had left mathematicians with a sense of crisis. On the one hand were very ambitious theories regarding the concept of infinity and the fruits of exploring what happens when different axioms are assumed to be true. On the other hand, a family of contradictions (of which 'Russell's paradox' was but one) had emerged from quite unexpected quarters. Hilbert was sensitive to the taunts of a number of conservative mathematicians (known generically as 'constructivists') to the effect that the more ambitious branches of the new mathematics consisted of wild speculation unworthy of the attention of serious mathematicians.

Hilbert defended the new ventures into infinitistic mathematics, which made use in effect of the 'method of postulation', but recognised that there was a legitimate concern over the consistency of the resulting theories and he outlined techniques by which the axiom systems, which involved infinite terms and operations, could be shown to be consistent without appeal to the concepts, theorems or procedures which they employed and hence were under suspicion. 'Hilbert's programme', as it became known, posed very precise mathematical tasks, for which there were unambiguous criteria, by which to determine whether they had been carried out. What was not anticipated, however, was a proof that the most important of these tasks could not be carried out.

Hilbert took as primitive truths (his 'core' – see 'Conventionalism' above) not only the truths of logic, but those of finite ('recursive' or 'constructive') arithmetic. The first step in the programme would be to show that the axioms of ordinary (non-finite) arithmetic could be proved consistent using only procedures and principles from this 'core'. In 1931, however, Kurt Gödel proved that any formal system restricted to this core but powerful enough to *express* the axioms of arithmetic would, *if it were consistent*, have in it undecidable sentences, sentences which could neither be shown to be theorems nor have their negations shown to be theorems. This result was in itself startling enough, but Gödel's argument was contrived in such a way that it became clear that if one had a proof of the consistency of the system, one would also have (1) a proof that a certain statement, G, could not be proved, *and* (2) a proof of statement G. It followed that no consistency proof of ordinary arithmetic using only finite procedures was possible.

Hilbert's programme may have had to be wound up, but his formalist outlook remained popular among many working mathematicians. Formalists claim that their conventionalist attitude has a liberating effect on pure mathematics; a mathematician feels free to enquire wherever the results hold some prospect of being interesting or attractive. Important applications do arise from such pure intellectual activity: physicists have on occasion found that the mathematical tools which they need have already been prepared by pure mathematicians working in this way. But formalism as a philosophical account of the nature of mathematical truth still faces the question of how it is that mathematics is such a powerful tool for the formulation of physical theories and for the study of mathematical activity itself.

It is possible to hold that mathematics contributes nothing of any factual content to physical theories, that it is merely a way which we find convenient for organising our knowledge. Indeed anyone who is imbued with the spirit of conventionalism should be prepared to maintain this position. But it remains to be shown that our scientific knowledge could be stripped of its mathematical clothes and not lose layers of skin and other vital organs. A recent attempt by Hartry Field to do this for Newton's theory of gravitation had not only to use what many regard as an unsatisfactorily powerful ('higher order') logic, but had to treat space-time points, which are arguably mathematical abstractions, as concrete physical objects – all this to do (as the title of his book said) 'science without numbers'.

The attack on the analytic/synthetic distinction

We have noted two ways of elaborating a conventionalist position. One treats matters of convention as confined to the definitions of terms used in statements, the other also treats the truth of certain statements as established by convention. The plausibility of both positions rests on the assumption that the truth or falsity of every statement depends upon two readily separable factors, the way the world is and the way we use words. This assumption was challenged by, among others, W. V. Quine in the early 1950s. Quine saw this as the common root of what he called 'two dogmas of empiricism'. The two dogmas clearly constituted the sort of empiricism which gives rise to the first kind of conventionalism. They were (1) the belief in a sharp distinction between truths which are analytic and truths which are synthetic, and (2) 'reductionism', the belief that each meaningful statement is equivalent (and hence reducible to) a complex built by logical operations out of terms referring to immediate experience.

Quine's attack on the first dogma rested on the complaint that the analytic/synthetic distinction was unclear and could not be made clear by concepts which were not in equal need of clarification. The strategy struck some of the dogma's defenders as unfair. Every time a clarification would be advanced, it seemed that Quine would only add the terms in which the clarification was made to his list of obscure notions. This, at any rate, is what happened in his article to the concepts of meaning, synonymy, necessity and semantical rules. But the considerable influence which Quine's article exerted did not arise from the strength of his argument, rather from the dissatisfaction with the first kind of conventionalism, which had grown up among those of an empiricist outlook.

Quine, however, was doing more than attacking the foundations of the first (definitions of terms) kind of conventionalism; he was pointing out the instability of the second (truths of certain statements) kind of conventionalism. Calling something a matter of convention is supposed to mark that matter as non-factual; how we treat it, what we say about it, is not supposed to be constrained by how the world is. It may be a convention that we choose to regard certain statements as true come what may, but it is a fact about the world that when we do so, we have anything which helps us to manage our affairs more effectively. It may be a matter of convention that we use a concept of material body which excludes that body's occupying discontinuous and widely separated regions of space, or a concept of mass-energy which includes the principle of its quantitative conservation, but it is the way the world is that allows us to achieve anything by doing so.

It follows that elements of (what is susceptible to) decision and elements of description (true or false in virtue of the way the world is) may be inextricably bound up in what appears to be the necessary truth of some statement. That such elements of the truth of a statement ('a linguistic component and a factual component') could be extricated was the root assumption, which Quine called into question.

It is true, as some of Quine's critics point out, that cases which are neither fish nor fowl do not prove that there is nothing which is determinately fish (or determinately fowl); there may, for all Quine has said, be clear cases of analytic truths and clear cases of synthetic truths. But Quine seemed motivated to preserve the spirit of conventionalism and to give it a new embodiment. He maintained that no statement was purely analytic, immune from revision under the impact of experience, and any statement which appeared to be synthetic could, by suitable adjustment elsewhere, be preserved from falsification. In Quine's view we had all the freedom conventionalism claimed for us, and more, because our statements do not face experience (to be shown to be true or false) one by one, but *as a whole*. Whether any statement should be regarded as true or false depends in an important way on what other statements we regard as true and no body of experience determines a unique assignment of the values 'true' and 'false' to the sentences of any language.

Quine's holist version of conventionalism was on first emerging an extreme variety; not even the laws of logic, it seemed, were immune from revision. It suffered consequently from problems similar to those of the extreme conventionalism discussed above. Quine spoke of our system of beliefs (the statements we hold true) as needing adjustments under the impact of experience and capable of being adjusted in order to preserve the truth of any individual statement we chose. But adjustments made in one place have consequences for what other statements can be held true; and whether it would be coherent to include all the (logical) principles which govern this distribution, within the doctrine that nothing is immune to revision, is still debated. Quine, however, subsequently moved to a less extreme position, holding in effect that the valid forms of first-order predicate logic are immune from revision.

The topic-neutrality of logic

While extreme conventionalism is problematic, moderate versions also face a problem, viz. where to draw the line between principles of logic (or whatever is to be treated as absolutely necessary) and truths which, if treated as necessary, are done so subject to our changing our minds about how to converse about the world and the affairs which concern us. The line, it has been noted, is commonly drawn at a body of principles known as first-order predicate logic. These principles include that of non-contradiction, but also other principles not reducible to that of non-contradiction. Challenges to drawing the line here are usually assumed to come from people who want to employ more powerful forms of logic. However, many of these more powerful forms of logic are thought to involve metaphysical commitments to abstract entities such as *redness* and *goodness*, but a core of principles which are absolutely necessary should not include any which rest on prior questions of (especially metaphysical) fact. (Classical) first-order predicate logic, it is argued, involves only principles which are minimally informative (indeed tautologous) and topic-neutral, and hence represent nothing but what is required for coherent discourse about anything. They can be this only if they rest on no prior questions of fact.

But it is possible to challenge this line from another direction, to argue in effect that first-order predicate logic contains principles which involve a metaphysical commitment and are not topic-neutral. The challenge comes from yet another view of the nature of mathematics and it falls both upon a supposed logical truth, the Law of Excluded Middle (viz. every statement or its negation is true), and an assumption made in many semantic approaches to validity, the Principle of Bivalence (see Chapter 11, pp. 228–9), that every statement is either true or false.

Talk of truth, as we noted in 'The truths of logic' above, invites the question 'True in virtue of what?' The logicist's answer to this question in the case of mathematics is 'the laws of logic'; the formalist's answer is 'convention'. A third view is that mathematical statements are true in virtue of a special non–physical realm which pure mathematicians explore by exercising a form of rational intuition. This view, which is known as 'realism' or 'Platonism', has as many adherents among working mathematicians as formalism, but as a philosophic account it fails to explain why one mathematician never accepts the word of another on some report of his rational intuition without a proof, and it is open to the accusation that it is simply an inappropriate projection on to mathematics of what we think of as our relation to the physical world via our senses.

Formalism is one way to oppose realism; another, which does not involve treating the truths of mathematics as conventional, is intuitionism. Intuitionists hold that far from the objects of mathematics existing outside the mathematician's mind waiting to be discovered, they are rather the products of certain operations performed by the human mind, such as the operation of continuing a series of numbers by adding one more. The implications of taking this view seriously, intuitionists insist, are that there are inference principles which many mathematicians are prepared to apply in the proofs of theorems which are invalid and consequently some theorems which are widely accepted are unsound.

If mathematics is the product of mental constructions, to establish anything properly mathematical requires actually performing the operations or reasoning about the possibility of performing them. It is irrelevant to reason about any procedure which cannot be carried out (such as the completion of an infinite task, which by definition is something which cannot be completed) and consequently any proof which rests on the supposed result of such a procedure is not acceptable as a mathematical proof. Mathematics based on Platonist assumptions will reason that the question 'Is there a number with property P?' has an answer either 'yes' or 'no', but intuitionists insist that a 'yes' requires showing how to construct the number in finitely many steps, and a 'no' requires showing that the existence of such a number would involve a contradiction. Unless one illegitimately assumes that numbers exist independently of human mental activity, there is no reason to think that the description of every number that cannot be constructed must involve a contradiction. It follows that when reasoning about numbers one cannot take it for granted that a statement 'There is a number with the property P' is either true or false, and because the Law of Excluded Middle rests on this, its validity cannot be assumed and used in mathematical proofs.

Intuitionists went on from this critique to redevelop number theory and the foundations of the calculus along lines quite unlike

118

those which mathematicians had followed for some considerable time. They also rejected standard semantic accounts of validity (such as that at the heart of the truth table method) and developed a body of logical principles which they regarded as appropriate to mathematical reasoning. If they have a case, then the assumption that classical first-order predicate logic is topic-neutral is far from beyond question; is it not appropriate when reasoning mathematically. Classical logic, moreover, embodies an assumption which, however innocent it may be on most occasions, raises a question of fact: is the subject-matter, about which we are reasoning, a domain of objects which exists independently of our thought?

The influence of mathematics, both on the development of logical techniques and on the terms in which the applicability of logic is discussed, has been one of the most remarkable features of the development of philosophical interest in logic during the past century. Sometimes this gives this branch of philosophy a dry and forbidding appearance. In fact some of the most interesting questions about the relationship between humans and the things which they try to understand and control (themselves and the natural world) have been given new, powerful and illuminating forms by these developments. The issues are by no means settled and by no means incapable of further clarification and development.

Bibliography

There are many introductory textbooks on formal logic. One which has gone through many editions since it first appeared in 1953 is Irving M. Copi, *Introduction to symbolic logic*, 6th edn (Collier Macmillan, London, 1982). For a textbook which concentrates on a natural deduction approach to validity and explains and illustrates the notion of a completeness proof see E.J. Lemmon, *Beginning logic* (Nelson, London, 1965). Semantic tableaux are introduced in Wilfred Hodges, *Logic* (Penguin Books, Harmondsworth, 1977).

For a survey of different approaches to the tasks of logical theory, see Susan Haack, *Philosophy of logics* (Cambridge University Press, Cambridge, 1978).

The standard history of logic in English is William and Martha Kneale, *The development of logic* (Clarendon Press, Oxford, 1962).

Peirce is an excellent source on the relationship between logic and scientific reasoning. A good collection of his writings from that standpoint is Justus Buchler (ed.), *Philosophical writings of Peirce* (Dover, New York, 1955).

Frege's pioneering work in logic is best represented in *Gottlob Frege: conceptual notation and related articles*, trans. and ed. Terrell Ward Bynum (Clarendon Press, Oxford, 1972). Frege's programme for showing the truths of arithmetic to be analytic is outlined in Gottlob Frege, *The foundations of arithmetic*, trans. J.L. Austin (Basil Blackwell, Oxford, 1959).

Russell's major contributions to mathematical logic formed part of a three-volume work which he wrote in collaboration with A.N. Whitehead, *Principia mathematica*, 2nd edn (Cambridge University Press, Cambridge, 1927), but a little book written while Russell was in prison for his pacifist activities, *Introduction to mathematical philosophy* (Allen and Unwin, London, 1919), still offers one of the most accessible introductions to this period in the development of logic and the philosophy of mathematics.

An excellent discussion of conventionalism, which pays particular attention to the plausibility of applying it to what we say about the structure of space, is to be found in Graham Nerlich, *The shape of space* (Cambridge University Press, Cambridge, 1976). There is also a penetrating article by Quine, 'Truth by convention', written in 1935 and reprinted in his book *The ways of paradox and other essays* (Random House, New York, 1966).

For a lively and accessible discussion of Gödel's theorem and its implications, see Douglas R. Hofstadter, *Gödel, Escher, Bach: an eternal golden braid* (Harvester, Hassocks, 1979). Harty Field's work is to be found in *Science without numbers* (Basil Blackwell, Oxford, 1980).

A collection edited by Paul Benacerraf and Hilary Putnam, *Philosophy of mathematics, selected readings* (Basil Blackwell, Oxford, 1964) contains much important source material, including articles by Hilbert, Curry, Gödel (on Platonism and on Russell's work) and the articles by Quine mentioned above and below.

Quine's 'Two dogmas of empiricism' is to be found not only in Benacerraf and Putnam but also in Quine's book, *From a logical point of view* (Harvard University Press, Cambridge, Massachusetts, 1953). Quine's mature position is set out in *Word and object* (MIT Press, Cambridge, Massachusetts, 1960) and in *Ontological relativity and other essays* (Columbia University Press, New York, 1969).

Defenders of one or the other dogma include H.P. Grice and P.F. Strawson, 'In defense of a dogma', *Philosophical Review*, vol. 65 (1956). Hilary Putnam has discussed Quine's doctrines in, among other places, 'The analytic and the synthetic', which is to be found in Putnam's *Mind, language and reality, Philosophical papers, Volume 2* (Cambridge University Press, Cambridge, 1975). The first volume of Putnam's *Philosophical papers, Mathematics, matter and method* (Cambridge University Press, Cambridge, 1975) contains several valuable papers on mathematical truth and on formalism.

Benacerraf and Putnam contains a number of selections representing intuitionism. The person who has contributed most to understanding the wider implications of that approach to the philosophy of mathematics is Michael Dummett. See in particular his *Elements of intuitionism* (Oxford University Press, Oxford, 1977), esp. Ch. 1, and *Truth and other enigmas* (Duckworth, London, 1978), Chs. 1, 10, 11, 13 and 14.

J.E.T.

Part B: Theory of Knowledge

Introduction

Now that problems about meaning and truth have been discussed, we can turn to philosophical problems about knowledge. Such problems are the concern of a branch of philosophy that is commonly termed 'the theory of knowledge' or 'epistemology', and it is appropriate that this part of the encyclopaedia should be entitled 'Theory of Knowledge'. But, as often, there is disagreement among philosophers about the exact way in which this term should be taken, and in this introduction to Part B I must make clear just what the issues are which will be covered here.

It will be helpful to begin by referring to a distinction which philosophers draw between three kinds of knowledge. The first of these, which may be called 'propositional knowledge', is the knowledge *that* something or other is the case. The second, which may be called 'practical knowledge', is the knowledge possessed by someone who knows *how* to do something or other. Finally, there is what may be called 'object knowledge', one's knowledge of persons, places and things. Our concern here – and indeed the concern of what is commonly called 'theory of knowledge' – is with propositional knowledge, i.e. with knowledge *that*.

Philosophers ask what it is to have propositional knowledge of any kind; what is the difference between knowing that something or other is the case, and merely having a belief – even a true belief – to this effect. Some philosophers, of whom Descartes is perhaps the most important in modern times, have argued that to have knowledge is to be in a certain kind of specially privileged mental state, and that the philosopher's task is to specify just what this state is. However, this approach – often called 'psychologism' – is now widely held to have been mistaken. The philosopher's concern, it is now argued, is not with states of mind, but with matters that may broadly be called logical. Philosophers now commonly say that if one is to know that such and such (call it '*p*') is the case, then four

123

conditions must be satisfied: one must *believe* that *p*, one must be *certain* that *p*, *p* must be *true*, and one must have *adequate reasons* for believing that *p*. This important standard account of knowledge is discussed in Chapter 6, and some of the difficulties which it faces are examined.

There would be general agreement that the topic just mentioned belongs to the theory of knowledge; however, when we go further, disagreements surface. The arguments of Chapter 6 are carried on at a high level of generality and concern knowledge of any kind. However, philosophical problems about knowledge are not restricted to such generalities, for specific kinds of knowledge pose their own problems. As a first step to identifying the further problems to be considered in this part, it will be helpful to draw a distinction between our knowledge of what may be called the 'external world' and of what may be called the 'inner world'. Knowledge of the external world is knowledge of publicly observable things and events; knowledge of the inner world is our knowledge of our own feelings, thoughts and intentions. (Some philosophers object to this distinction between an inner and an outer world; they say that it suggests, wrongly, that there is an absolute distinction between our knowledge of publicly observable things and our knowledge of our mental states and acts. No suggestion of this sort is made here; the term 'inner world' is used simply as a convenient expression for that of which the human mind is aware when it scrutinises itself, together with the activities of self-scrutiny themselves.) Now, there is no objection in principle to taking the term 'theory of knowledge' in such a wide sense that it covers knowledge of both the external and the inner worlds. In fact, some philosophers do take the term in this way; the objection to this procedure is not that it is illogical, but that it makes the field of the theory of knowledge awkwardly large. For this reason, questions about our knowledge of the inner world will be regarded here (as many regard them) as belonging to a separate branch of philosophy, the philosophy of mind. They will be discussed in Part D.

Let us, then, now turn to problems that concern our knowledge of the external world. Most of us think that we know a lot about the world around us, in the sense that we claim to know that material things do exist, and to know a lot about their nature. I might claim to know, for example, that there is a typewriter in front of me at the moment. Asked to justify this claim, I might say, 'I see the typewriter; I feel its keys; I hear its clatter as I type – and others could see and feel and hear what I do.' In short, I would refer to the sensory experiences that I, and others, have or could have. But do such experiences justify one in making such claims? The problem of whether they do is a recognised part of what is commonly called 'the theory of knowledge', and is discussed here in Chapter 7. A philosopher's view about our knowledge of things that is derived through our senses is sometimes called his theory of the external world, so this chapter is entitled 'Knowledge of the External World'.

We not only claim to know how things are now, or what events are occurring at present; we also claim to know how things have been, or what events have occurred. Some of these claims – such as people's claims to know what the earth was like millions of years ago – are based on the sciences, and the justification of these claims will rest on the justifiability of the claim that the relevant sciences give us knowledge. Such claims will be investigated later in this part. Other claims to have knowledge of the past are based on testimony, in the sense of records made by human beings; claims of this sort are the concern of the philosopher of history (cf. Part F, Chapter 35). However, many of our claims to know the past are based on the memory, without any appeal either to the sciences or to testimony. Suppose, for example, that I am asked to justify my claim that I bought my typewriter in a certain shop. I might appeal to testimony, in the shape of a receipt; but I might just say, 'I remember doing so.' The question of whether our claims to remember the past are justified – whether, that is, our memory really provides us with *knowledge* – is generally regarded as part of the theory of knowledge, and is discussed in Chapter 8.

The knowledge of the external world discussed in Chapters 7 and 8 has concerned particular things and events – for example, my perceptual knowledge that there is a typewriter in front of me, or my memory knowledge that I bought it in a certain shop. But we also claim to know the truth of *universal* propositions; propositions that state that all individuals of a certain kind have such and such properties. Many of these propositions belong to logic or mathematics, and there is no need to add anything here to what has already been said about these in Chapter 5. However, there are universal propositions of another sort, which raise special problems. Suppose that I claim to know not just that all the sugar that any of us has actually come across dissolves in water, but that *all* sugar dissolves in water. What could justify such a claim? What makes this a problem is that one seems in a way to be going beyond the evidence; one starts from knowledge about *some* sugar, and moves from this to an assertion about *all* sugar – past, present or future, observed or unobserved. When one argues in this way, one is said to be arguing 'inductively'; the problem of whether this sort of argument can be justified is termed 'the problem of induction'. One way of tackling the problem is to limit one's claims. One withdraws the claim to know that, for example, all sugar dissolves in water, and says only that it is *probable* that it does. But this still leaves problems. For what is meant by saying that something is probable, and what justifies us in saying that it is? The two problems of induction and probability are discussed together in Chapter 9.

The claims to knowledge discussed in Chapters 7 to 9 concern claims that may be made by any human being, whatever his or her talents or education may be. But there are also claims to knowledge that are made by, or on behalf of, human beings of a special sort – people with special gifts, special training, and often using special equipment. These are the people we call 'scientists'. Questions about the nature of scientific knowledge, and about the nature of science itself, are commonly regarded as belonging to a branch of philosophy termed 'the philosophy of science'. I do not wish to challenge this; I would argue only that these questions are sufficiently close to those already discussed in this part to be counted as belonging to a wider area of philosophy, the theory of knowledge. What, then, are these questions? Scientists often assert universal propositions of the kind discussed in Chapter 9; for example, they say such things as 'To every action, there is an equal and opposite reaction.' Many scientists and philosophers have thought that such universal propositions are based on induction. Some would say, then, that in considering induction we have already been considering a problem that belongs to the philosophy of science. I said that 'some would say' this; some would not. Karl Popper has argued that the problem of induction does not affect the sciences, because scientists do not argue inductively. That is to say, they do not first observe that S is P in a number of cases, and then generalise from this to reach the conclusion that every S is P. Rather, they start with hypotheses, and then try to falsify them; a scientific law is a hypothesis which has resisted all attempts to falsify it. These ideas, though by no means universally accepted, have exercised great influence in twentieth-century philosophy of science, and for that reason Chapter 10 is devoted to them.

But the philosophy of science is by no means exclusively concerned with the problem of induction, and with whether it can (as Popper suggests) be bypassed. The philosopher of science also asks whether the scientist tries to describe the world as it really is, or whether scientific theories are mere devices for predicting observations. Again, the philosopher asks whether scientists are simply concerned with a knowledge of facts, or whether they are also concerned to understand and to explain; and, if the latter, what scientific explanation consists in. These problems are discussed in Chapter 11, which concludes the account of the theory of knowledge.

G.H.R.P.

6 | The Analysis of Knowledge

T. Sorell

The theory of knowledge is really two theories: one that explains what knowledge is, another that answers the question whether we have any. The first theory aims at defining or analysing the concept of factual knowledge – knowledge *that* something is so as against knowledge *of* people or places or knowledge *how* to do a thing. In the process of analysis or definition connections are exhibited between the concept of knowledge and those of belief, truth and justification. The second theory is a response to philosophical scepticism – abstractly grounded doubt about the possibility of reasonable belief, knowledge and science. The attempt to answer the sceptic lies at the centre of the theory of knowledge, and for a long time it was thought to occupy the entire field. A separate analytical part of the subject started to be recognised in Britain and America only from the 1940s, when Anglo-American philosophy as a whole was conceived to be guided by a method or methods of analysis. The attention that has since been lavished on this part of the subject, however, has probably gone beyond anything envisaged by the early enthusiasts for the analytical approach.

The analysis of knowledge

Analysis used to be thought of, naturally enough, as a brief but necessary preliminary to the main business of interpreting and responding to the challenge of scepticism. In A.J. Ayer's *The problem of knowledge* (1956),[1] for example, the analysis of knowledge occupies only a few sections of the first chapter; the remaining four-fifths of the book is devoted to the main kinds of philosophical doubt. Roderick Chisholm's *Theory of knowledge*,[2] published a decade after Ayer's book, unfolds in a similar way: first a little over a dozen pages on definitional matters, then a formulation and application over many

127

chapters of rules of evidence capable of meeting a sceptic's standards. No general book about knowledge written today could deal quite so briskly with the analytical or definitional side of the subject. It has taken on a life of its own in the last twenty years, mainly in articles in the professional journals.

The articles stretch back to a paper by the American philosopher Edmund L. Gettier in the English journal *Analysis* for 1963.[3] Entitled 'Is justified true belief knowledge?', Gettier's paper takes up a philosophically attractive analysis of factual knowledge – a statement of necessary and sufficient conditions for knowing that – and shows by counter-example that it is inadequate.

Gettier's counter-examples

The question any analysis of knowledge starts from is a simple one: 'What makes it true to say, in the ordinary sense of "know", that a person knows a fact?' For example, what makes it true to say that a particular individual knows that Edinburgh is north of London? One thing that makes it true is easily stated. For it to be known that Edinburgh is north of London, it has got to be a fact, it has got to be true, that Edinburgh is north of London. If it were false that Edinburgh is north of London, then though it could be *said* that someone knew Edinburgh was north of London, it could not be said truly, and what is at issue is what makes it said truly. Truth in things known, then, is one condition of factual knowledge. What else is required? A plausible but not incontestable thing to say is that if someone knows a fact he has got to believe it. Philosophers who deny this are obliged to explain away the oddity of attributing knowledge of a fact to someone and then adding that he does *not* believe it.

The two conditions – that things known be both true and believed – are not sufficient for knowledge even if they are necessary. An example commonly used to establish this point is that of the lucky punter. Someone has a hunch and so believes that a certain horse will win a race. The horse does win. The punter did not know it would win – he only had a lucky hunch. Still, he believed that it would win and his belief was true. So true belief is not enough for knowledge. If the punter had had more than a hunch, if his belief had been founded on good reasons, for example reasons to do with the good form of the winning horse relative to that of the rest of the field, the inclination to deny that he knew would be much weaker. Perhaps, then, it is the possession of good reasons that elevates a true belief to the status of knowledge. Perhaps justified true belief is knowledge.

That is a reasonable conjecture, but it is overturned by Gettier's counter-examples. They show that it is possible to believe a truth, have good reasons for believing it, and yet *still* end up being right in the way the punter is – accidentally or by good luck. In one of the examples a man called Smith is in competition with Jones for a job. Smith and Jones are the only people in contention. Smith believes that the man who will get the job has ten coins in his pocket, and he is right. But does Smith know that the successful applicant has ten coins in his pocket? Consider his evidence. He has just been told by the man doing the hiring that his rival Jones is going to get the job, and Smith has counted ten and only ten coins in Jones' pocket. This is what makes him believe that the one to be appointed has ten coins in his pocket. To everyone's surprise, however, it is Smith who gets the job, and as it happens Smith unwittingly has ten coins in his pocket. So it is true that the man who will get the job has ten coins in his pocket, Smith believes that truth, and believes it for reasons one would normally classify as good. For all that, Smith does not know who will get the job: all his evidence was to do with Jones and it is Smith himself who is appointed.

Gettier constructs this counter-example with two assumptions about justification in mind. The first is that someone can be justified in believing a falsehood. The second is that justification is preserved in valid reasoning: if you are justified in believing a proposition, then you are justified in believing whatever you deduce from the proposition in accordance with the laws of formal logic. Are these assumptions acceptable? It is hard to deny that there is such a thing as reasonable error, and that is all Gettier's first assumption amounts to. The other assumption, about justification being preserved in valid reasoning, is harder to assess, but it is pretty clear how it works in the Smith and Jones example. Smith takes the (false) testimony that Jones will be hired, puts that together with the incidental information that Jones has ten coins in his pocket, and deduces that the man who will get the job has ten coins in his pocket. The deduction is perfectly valid and starts from a belief that is justified in the way permitted by Gettier's first assumption. But the truth Smith deduces is believed correctly by good luck. Taking Gettier's assumptions together, we have a kind of explanation of the failure of justified true belief to amount in general to knowledge: justified belief can be false and in a piece of reasoning false justified belief can support conclusions that are only true by coincidence.

In assessing Gettier's counter-examples one has to weigh the plausibility of saying that knowledge is justified true belief against the plausibility of his two assumptions. Are the assumptions more plausible than the justified true belief analysis or vice versa? Should one reject the assumptions and retain the analysis, or scrap the analysis and save the assumptions? Most philosophers seem to be prepared to alter, if not abandon, the analysis. What they do is to keep the truth and belief conditions of knowledge and redefine the adequate justification or good reasons condition so that it escapes the difficulties posed by Gettier's examples. An early application of this strategy involved defining the kind of justification knowledge requires as justification that neither supports nor itself involves falsehoods. This disposes at once of the counter-examples in Gettier's paper. But the quick solution has proved not to be a lasting one. Further counter-examples have been devised, and, in response to them, further revisions of the justified true belief analysis. Successive revisions have unfailingly fallen prey to yet more counter-examples. Indeed, an acceptable statement of necessary and sufficient conditions has yet to be devised. Nevertheless, the failed proposals are not without interest: like the counter-examples themselves, they can tell us things we did not know before about knowledge.

After Gettier

Because of the profusion of suggested analyses after Gettier it is desirable to have a simple way of classifying different proposals and their difficulties. I shall distinguish between conservative reformulations of the justified true belief analysis and others which depart more boldly from tradition. By 'conservative reformulation' I mean an analysis which conserves conditions concerning belief, truth and justification, but which restricts the relevant sense of justification, so that adequate justification comes by definition to rule out the newer counter-examples. Less conservative is the strategy of adding to the belief, truth and justification conditions some further condition specified in terms of some new concept. Least conservative of all are analyses in which some conditions of knowledge entirely supplant some of the old. Among non-conservative proposals are the so-called reliability analysis,[4] the causal theory[5] and more recent proposals exploiting properties of counterfactual conditions.[6]

Conservative reformulations. These include the conclusive-reasons analysis[7] and statements of necessary and sufficient conditions in terms of undefeated justification.[8] According to the first of these two accounts, subjects in Gettier examples have inconclusive reasons for belief: inconclusive in the sense that the reasons would be true even in a situation where the belief they supported was not true. According to the second sort of analysis, subjects in Gettier examples have reasons for a given belief, but there is further information that would make it unreasonable to hold the belief and that defeats the justification the subject actually has for believing what he does.

Accounts like these, which keep alive a version of the justified true belief analysis, enjoy the considerable strengths of the traditional account. One of these is its applicability on both sides of the divide between mathematical and non-mathematical, or, more generally, *a priori* and *a posteriori* knowledge – knowledge independent of and knowledge based on experience. Knowledge of the truth of a mathematical theorem and knowledge of a metaphysical certainty are both easily accommodated, the latter if self-evidence is counted the limiting case of justified belief, the former if reasons for believing the theorem are identified with the reasoning that goes into proving it. Again, the analysis can accommodate moral knowledge – if moral knowledge is true judgement about what ought to be done based on sound reasoning to or from moral principles. It was partly out of an interest in moral knowledge, in the kind of knowledge that entitles someone to command, that Plato's Socrates gets Theaetetus to articulate the justified true belief analysis in the dialogue *Theaetetus*.[9] When Plato rejects the analysis, it is not on the ground that it throws no light on moral knowledge. Rather, it is rejected because of difficulties with its counterparts of a condition of adequate justification.

The traditional analysis has weaknesses as well as strengths. To begin with, it over-intellectualises knowledge. For the very reasons it is excellently suited to saying what knowledge of an axiom or a theorem might consist in, it is ill suited to knowledge that might be called pre-propositional, such as a baby's knowledge that its mother is there. Differently, the analysis seems to deny that a subject knows in cases where he lacks reasons but the *source* of his true belief seems to make it count as knowledge. There may be all sorts of reasons for believing that Schubert's Ninth Symphony is called 'The Great C Major', but a subject can be ignorant of the reasons and still have knowledge – if he has a correct belief about the name of the symphony and his belief results from reading an authoritative musical encyclopaedia or even an accurate blurb on a record sleeve. Finally, the justified true belief analysis often conflates or threatens to conflate having reasons with being able to state them. A version of this conflation is evident in Plato's *Theaetetus*, where the thought that knowledge is true belief plus an account is enlarged on by saying[10] that a knower must be able to differentiate in words between the subject-matter of his true belief and other things. The conflation also crops up in quite recent writing,[11] and it reinforces the tendency throughout all but the most up-to-date literature to confine knowledge to creatures gifted with speech and intellect over and above sensory powers.

Conclusive-reasons and defeasibility analyses are vulnerable to criticism of the traditional account and to others besides. One problem arises from what the conclusive-reasons analysis implies is essential to knowing the fact that *p*, namely the impossibility of being mistaken concerning *p* given conclusive reasons for the belief that *p*. The requirement that one's reasons guarantee the truth of one's belief makes sense when what is in question is mathematical knowledge, but it is too strong for knowledge in general. In some cases reasons are conclusive in the sense that they make it very difficult to explain how the belief founded on them could be false. But conclusive reasons along these lines fall short of reasons that guarantee truth. Unless a conclusive-reasons analysis makes room for the sort of reasons just described it will not encompass enough of what we actually recognise as knowledge; but if the weaker reasons *are* allowed the analysis will have abandoned the idea of strictly conclusive reasons.

Defeasibility analyses depend on a gap between the

reasons a subject actually has for a true belief and the totality of evidence, including misleading evidence, relevant to the true belief. Such analyses hold that a true belief amounts to knowledge if no addition to the subject's evidence from the balance of the total evidence would weaken the subject's justification or reasons for believing. This rules out not only Gettier's counter-examples but also many of their successors. Yet the analysis faces many difficulties.[12] I shall mention only two. First, it makes *any* further evidence that would weaken justification sufficient for taking away knowledge. Thus misleading evidence in Outer Mongolia against a true belief I form in London can keep me from having knowledge, even if I never go near Outer Mongolia and the misleading evidence is forever confined there. Second, and more generally, the defeasibilist approach misses what can be called the 'actualism' of our intuitions about knowledge. When we have to decide whether someone knows in a real or invented case, our intuitions are more sensitive to actual influences on the subject and the subject's belief than to what would happen if further evidence were brought into play. By concentrating on would-be effects the defeasibilist analysis distinguishes knowledge from non-knowledge in cases where our intuitions, being actualist, give out. This suggests that its underlying idea – that if one knows, further evidence should not make one change one's mind – is not really central to our concept of knowledge.

Less conservative analyses: externalism. Defeasibilist and conclusive-reasons analyses can be interpreted as attempts at rehabilitating the account criticised by Gettier. They hold that to know something is to be justified in or to have good reasons for believing it, and they lay down conditions for distinguishing the relevant kind of justification from the sort that invites counter-examples. Other proposals break cleanly with the justified true belief analysis, at any rate in the case of empirical knowledge. Alvin Goldman's causal analysis[13] is a case in point. It equates empirical knowledge with appropriately caused true belief and it defines 'appropriately caused' for a number of different types of belief. Goldman's leading idea is simple enough: a true belief that p amounts to knowledge if the fact that p is the cause of the true belief, and there is the right sort of causal chain connecting the fact that p to the belief. The analysis breaks down in the case of true general beliefs, such as the belief that cigarettes contain carcinogens. The general fact that cigarettes contain carcinogens cannot cause the true belief that cigarettes contain carcinogens, for *all* cigarettes are implicated in the general fact, including cigarettes to be manufactured in the distant future. Consider a cigarette to be made twenty years hence. How can it contribute causally to my belief here and now that all cigarettes contain carcinogens? A deeper problem with Goldman's analysis is that it is proposed only for empirical or *a posteriori* knowledge. He thinks the justified true belief analysis is adequate for *a priori* knowledge. But this only makes urgent the question of what these two kinds of knowledge have in common. Does 'know' have two different senses corresponding to the two sides of the *a priori/a posteriori* distinction, or, as is more likely, does it have only one sense which Goldman fails to capture?

An analysis sometimes associated with Goldman's identifies knowledge with true belief arrived at by reliable means.[14] The reliability analysis tends to collapse into a causal or conclusive-reasons analysis when an attempt is made to give a precise sense to 'reliable means'. Finally, there is Nozick's recently proposed conditional theory,[15] according to which knowledge that p requires not only the true belief that p, but also fulfilment of two further conditions: that if p were not true the subject would not believe p, and that if p were true the subject *would* believe that p. This improves on Goldman's theory by accommodating general, inferential *a posteriori* knowledge and by unifying *a priori* and *a posteriori* knowledge. It improves on reliability theories by being more definite than they are. But it, too, has been shown to be open to counter-examples.[16]

The causal, reliability and conditional analyses are sometimes grouped together as, on the one hand, 'externalist' analyses, and, on the other hand, specimens of a fresh, naturalistic approach in epistemology. According to an externalist theory the difference between having knowledge and having a true belief depends on an external relation between a belief and an extra-mental state, a relation that can hold whether or not the believer is aware that it does. For example, according to Goldman's causal analysis a true belief is knowledge if it is appropriately caused by the fact that makes it true. Appropriate causation is a matter of a belief's fitting into a particular kind of causal chain. A belief may fit such a chain without the believer's even thinking of his belief as caused. The externalist approach also allows for knowledge of propositions that the subject lacks conscious reasons for, and knowledge of propositions that do not seem evident to the subject. Knowledge is depicted as an ordinary by-product of an organism's waking life in a standard environment. It is a picture of knowledge that contrasts strongly with more traditional ones, notably that given by Descartes.[17] According to Descartes, knowledge in the strict sense is the possession of a non-natural soul rather than an organism, and it is acquired by applying an extremely exacting method of controlled assent. According to an externalist analysis knowledge can accumulate independently of method, *and* independently of our will. It is a natural outcome of interactions between a subject and the wider world, explicable in the same way as other natural effects.

Analysis and scepticism
How, if at all, is the attempt to formulate a correct analysis of knowledge related to the traditionally more central task of responding to scepticism? It is sometimes thought that the two parts of the theory of knowledge are con-

nected by way of the Gettier examples, which give reasons for responding sympathetically to scepticism. Scepticism is to the effect that we don't know anything, and the moral of the Gettier examples may be that conditions of factual knowledge are extremely restrictive and the scope for factual knowledge correspondingly small.[18] This way of connecting scepticism with the analysis of knowledge turns out to be misconceived, however. The reason is that scepticism calls into question our ability to form reasonable beliefs just as much as our possession of knowledge; the Gettier examples take for granted our ability to form reasonable beliefs.

A second proposal about the connection between the two parts of the theory of knowledge can be stated without reference to the Gettier examples. This proposal may be stated as follows:

The analysis of knowledge specifies what must be the case if an attribution of factual knowledge is true; in particular, it lays down a requirement of justification of one kind or another; scepticism in its most general form is the suspicion that this requirement is never properly met; scepticism in more specific forms is the suspicion that the justification requirement is never properly met in the case of beliefs about the external world, the past, other minds and the like.

This gives a clear connection between the analysis of knowledge and scepticism but it too seems to miss the mark. It implies that scepticism is a problem about justification inasmuch as justification is a condition of *knowledge*. Conceptually and historically this seems to be a misrepresentation: scepticism is not so much a problem about knowledge as about *belief* or *judgement*. Classical sceptical arguments are to the effect that wherever possible we should suspend judgement and refrain from forming beliefs.

The reasons why we should suspend judgement where it is possible to do so are briefly stated. When we make judgements or form beliefs we always represent propositions as true. We represent as fulfilled the conditions under which a proposition is true. And now, for a vast range of propositions, the conditions which obtain and do not obtain if they are true far outrun the conditions we have reasons to think are fulfilled. To take a simple example, I believe that Edmund Gettier wrote that famous paper in *Analysis* for 1963. One of the truth-conditions of my belief is that there is such a person as Edmund Gettier. Another condition of the truth of my belief is that that person and no one else wrote the paper that appeared in *Analysis*. Suppose that there is no such person as Edmund Gettier and that some committee of people wrote the paper that appeared in *Analysis*. These are possibilities I am unable to rule out on the basis of my background information. And yet when I believe that Gettier wrote that paper I represent those possibilities as ruled out, for I represent it as true that Gettier wrote that paper, and when I represent a proposition as true I thereby represent a lot of possibilities – all of the falsity conditions of a proposition – as unfulfilled. The

134

content of my belief commits me to all sorts of things my reasons for belief do not establish. So there is a sense in which my reasons do not entitle me to represent as true that Gettier wrote the paper, a sense in which it is dogmatic of me to represent that as true. The same conclusion holds for countless other beliefs. Better, then, not to represent as true in those cases. Better to adopt a more non-committal attitude, such as suspense of judgement or belief.

Answering the sceptic: the a priori

Do there turn out to be, contrary to the sceptic, beliefs we *are* entitled to hold? One of the most famous and influential of the attempts to show that there are such beliefs can be found in Descartes' *Meditations on first philosophy*. Descartes tries to overcome the formidable problem of not begging the question against the sceptic by experimentally turning sceptical himself and trying to throw doubt on all of his beliefs. The more extravagant of these hypotheses, according to which all his thoughts were produced by a deceiving demon, were supposed to compromise Descartes' belief in the reality of an external world, his belief in the reality of mathematical things, his belief in the past, in time, in motion, in his own embodiment. Far-reaching as it was, the doubt induced by the demon hypothesis was not total: conditions for limited certainty were actually written into the terms of the demon hypothesis itself. For it was a condition of being deceived by a demon that there was a medium of deception, namely thought, and if thought, some subject to do the thinking, some 'I' to be deceived. Thus the first of the truths Descartes was certain of was 'I am thinking, therefore I am.' This not even the most sweeping sceptical hypothesis could make him disbelieve. From it other truths were able to be deduced, sufficiently many, Descartes argued, to allow one to conduct mathematical physics, mechanics, medicine and morals.

'I am thinking, therefore I am' was a truth that Descartes discovered independently of all experience, independently, too, of all reasoning. In Descartes' terminology it was 'intuited': impossible to be grasped without being found evident. It was also inborn in the mind. Other propositions Descartes put in the same category as 'I am thinking, therefore I am,' notably 'I exist; so God exists,' are harder to accept as the highly evident truths he claimed they were. In recent writing it has become a question whether any proposition can credibly play the role Descartes had in mind for the two just mentioned. Such propositions were supposed to provide foundations for knowledge by being proof against refutation by experience. Hilary Putnam[19] has gone so far as to throw doubt on the whole category of the *a priori* – knowledge independent and prior to experience – on the strength of the way the truths of geometry and logic have had to be revised to agree with quantum physics. Partly as a result of second thoughts like Putnam's many theorists of knowledge and philosophers of science have broken with the Cartesian method of proving the possibility of science in the face of scepticism.

Where they confront scepticism at all, they tend not to confront it in the global form considered by Descartes. Instead, they take up specific forms – scepticism about the external world, about the past, about induction and other minds (see below, Chapters 7, 8, 9 and 17). Again, while most philosophers agree with Descartes that there are limits to doubt, they deny that the limits are revealed by reflection on the deceiving demon possibility, for they hold that this itself pushes doubt beyond its limits. According to them, doubt is possible only up to the point where it puts into question either the general facts or the conventions that are necessary for the concepts that doubt would be expressed in.[20]

Notes

(An author's name followed by a number in square brackets refers to the book or article which has that number in the bibliography.)

1. Ayer [3].
2. Chisholm [4].
3. E. Gettier, 'Is justified true belief knowledge?' *Analysis*, vol. 23 (1963), pp. 121–3. Included in Phillips Griffiths [5].
4. Armstrong [1].
5. A. Goldman, 'A causal theory of knowing', *Journal of Philosophy*, vol. 64 (1967), pp. 355–72.
6. Nozick [2].
7. F. Dretske, 'Conclusive reasons', *Australasian Journal of Philosophy*, vol. 49 (1971), pp. 1–22.
8. K. Lehrer and T. Paxson, 'Knowledge: undefeated justified true belief', *Journal of Philosophy*, vol. 66 (1969), pp. 225–37.
9. Plato [6], 201 c–d.
10. Ibid., 208c–209d.
11. R.J. Ackerman, *Belief and knowledge* (Anchor Books, New York, 1972), p. 74.
12. T. Sorell, 'Harman's Paradox', *Mind*, vol. 90 (1981), pp. 557–75.
13. Cf. note 5 above.
14. Cf. note 4 above.
15. Cf. note 6 above.
16. R. Shope, 'Cognitive abilities, conditionals and knowledge', *Journal of Philosophy*, vol. 81 (1984), pp. 29–48.
17. See Descartes [7], vol. II.
18. G. Pappas and M. Swain (eds), *Essays on knowledge and justification* (Cornell University Press, Ithaca, New York, 1978), p. 36.
19. Putnam [8].
20. L. Wittgenstein, *On certainty* (Basil Blackwell, Oxford, 1969).

Bibliography

Modern attempts to analyse knowledge confront two demands. On the one hand is the demand that what we count as knowledge be true, together with the conviction that beliefs are true (or false) in virtue of something apart from human thought. On the other hand there is the demand (arising perhaps from the older rationalist tradition, which focused on understanding) that a person with knowledge have some right to his (true) belief which is based on reasons, if it is to count as knowledge. In the nineteenth century it was common to modify the first of these demands by defining truth in some way which made it an ideal property of thought. F.H. Bradley, *Appearance and reality* (Swan Sonnenschein, London, 1893), defined truth as the object of thinking in which what is predicated is 'harmonious, and removes inconsistency and with it unrest' (p. 165). C.S. Peirce (1871) defined truth in terms of the final opinion to which human opinions are 'gravitating' under the pressure of scientific inquiry. See *C.S. Peirce: selected writings*, ed. Philip P. Wiener (Dover, New York, 1966), pp. 81–3.

Twentieth-century philosophers have been reluctant to follow in this idealist direction and have often tried instead to loosen the hold of the second demand.

[1] D.M. Armstrong, *Belief, truth and knowledge* (Cambridge University Press, Cambridge, 1974), analyses knowledge in terms of the reliability of belief.

[2] Robert Nozick, *Philosophical explanations* (Oxford University Press, Oxford, 1981), defines knowledge in terms of whether a person's beliefs *would* conform to the facts ('track the truth').

Two attempts to combine the two demands are

[3] A.J. Ayer, *The problem of knowledge* (Penguin Books, Harmondsworth, 1956), p. 35, and

[4] Roderick Chisholm, *Theory of knowledge* (Prentice-Hall, Englewood Cliffs, 1966), p. 23.

Gettier specifically mentioned the analyses of Ayer and Chisholm as the kind of account which his arguments were designed to call into question. Gettier's article is reprinted in

[5] A. Phillips Griffiths (ed.), *Knowledge and belief* (Oxford University Press, Oxford, 1967). This collection of articles includes a number which consider the concept of belief. The analysis of this notion obviously has a crucial bearing on the analysis of the concept of knowledge. For a book which brings the discussion of post-Gettier analyses of knowledge virtually up to date, see R. Shope, *The analysis of knowing* (Princeton University Press, Princeton, 1983).

Another approach to knowledge attempts to analyse it as a purely natural phenomenon. One recent essay in this vein is W.V. Quine's 'Epistemology naturalized', which appears in Quine's *Ontological relativity* (Columbia University Press, New York, 1969), pp. 69–90. As Quine acknowledged elsewhere in this book, his intellectual antecedent in this outlook was John Dewey; for Dewey's analysis of knowledge as the outcome of (competent) inquiry see *Logic, the theory of inquiry* (Henry Holt, New York, 1939).

The assumption that the central focus of a philosopher's concern should be with knowledge *that something is so* rather than with (acquaintance) knowledge *of* e.g. people or places, or knowledge of *how to do something*, is peculiar to the recent history of philosophy (particularly that written in English). Plato sharply distinguishes knowledge (*episteme*) from opinion, belief or judgement (*doxa*), but he moved from knowledge to practical skills (*technai*) or to acquaintance (*gnosis*) without suggesting the subject had been changed. See Plato's *Republic*, trans. Desmond Lee (Penguin Books, Harmondsworth, 1974), 477ab, 533b.

The sort of acquaintance which Plato had in mind was probably that which arises through long and thoughtful association with the object in question. In this century Bertrand Russell built a theory of knowledge on a notion which he called 'acquaintance', but which could be achieved at the very first experience of the object. See his 'Knowledge by acquaintance and knowledge by description' in *Mysticism and logic* (Allen and Unwin, London, 1917), or the chapter with that title in *The problems of philosophy* (Oxford University Press, Oxford, 1959). More recently Gilbert Ryle in *The concept of mind* (Hutchinson, London, 1949) suggested that much of the obscurity which surrounds the concept of knowledge could be clarified, if philosophers would study what is involved in knowing-how. When Plato subjected the claim that knowledge is true belief plus an account (*logos*) to examination in the

[6] *Theaetetus*, trans. John McDowell (Clarendon Press, Oxford, 1973), 201 *ad fin.*, it is notable that the list of interpretations of 'account' which he tries is rather short and fails to include suggestions, which he tried out in dialogues written in the same period, during which it is thought he wrote the *Theaetetus*. In an early dialogue, *The Meno*, trans. W.K.C. Guthrie (Penguin Books, Harmondsworth, 1956), where Plato distinguishes true belief from knowledge by the ability to give some kind of account, he speaks of the ability to work out the reasons why. This may be read as 'reasons why a belief should be held', but a tradition grew up of looking upon the most significant cognitive achievement as the grasp of the 'reasons why the thing (correctly) believed should be the case'. If we referred to the latter as 'understanding', philosophers in this tradition can, from Aristotle onward, be said to have offered analyses of what understanding is rather than what (mere) knowledge is.

Plato urged men to acquire knowledge (or understanding) in order to have a proper foundation for action in the (political) world. The ancient sceptics, many of whom were members of Plato's Academy in the centuries which followed his death, called into question the possibility of having either understanding or well-reasoned beliefs. They did so in order to undermine the basis of action and they employed a strategy which tried to balance equally good reasons against every belief which seemed supported by good reasons. The goal was ethical: to live in a state of freedom from disturbance, *ataraxia*. For an excellent discussion of this see M.F. Burnyeat, 'Can the sceptic live his scepticism?' in M. Schofield, M.F. Burnyeat and J. Barnes (eds), *Doubt and dogmatism* (Clarendon Press, Oxford, 1980). For a history of the revival of the sceptical tradition in the sixteenth and seventeenth centuries see Richard Popkin, *The history of scepticism from Erasmus to Spinoza* (University of California Press, Berkeley, 1979). For an account of scepticism from the perspective of contemporary analytic philosophy see Barry Stroud, *The significance of philosophical scepticism* (Oxford University Press, Oxford, 1984).

In several respects Descartes marks a watershed in the way philosophers have approached the analysis of knowledge. For the first time appearances came to be regarded as objects of knowledge, i.e. one could attain knowledge without going beyond one's subjective states. The assumption that one's own states of mind are intrinsically less problematic than the existence of the natural world is also a distinctive modern development which begins with Descartes. Some of this is touched on in the article by Burnyeat cited above; a more thorough discussion will be found in his 'Idealism and Greek philosophy: what Descartes saw and Berkeley missed' in Godfrey Vesey (ed.), *Idealism: past and present*, Royal Institute of Philosophy Lectures 13 (Harvester, Hassocks, 1980).

Descartes' *Meditations on first philosophy* (1641) was, among other things, an attempt to provide a foundation for a criterion of truth (and hence knowledge) based on the intrinsic character of our thoughts or ideas, specifically on their clarity and distinctness. See Descartes' third meditation in

[7] *The philosophical writings of Descartes*, trans. J. Cottingham, R. Stoothoff and D. Murdoch (2 vols, Cambridge University Press, Cambridge, 1985), vol. II. Locke, the first of the British empiricists, analysed knowledge (took it to consist in) 'the perception of the connexion and agreement, or disagreement and repugnancy of any of our ideas'. See his *An essay concerning human understanding* (1690) (Dent, London, 1961), Book VI, Ch. 1, para. 2. Both Locke and Descartes rendered severely problematic the natural requirement that for a thought to amount to knowledge, it must answer to something outside itself. In Locke's successors the modern form of sceptical doubts gradually emerged with clarity. Berkeley avoided scepticism by dropping the (to him) incoherent assumption that our ideas answer to a material world which lies outside the thought of any and every mind. See George Berkeley, *Philosophical works* (Dent, London, 1975), pp. 63ff. Hume attacked the basis of Berkeley's hope that we could discover through experience the laws which God had ordained our ideas of sense should follow. To *know* even that the sun will rise tomorrow, Hume argued, involves an anticipation of experience, which goes beyond any foundation we can possibly find *in* experience. See Hume's *A treatise of human nature* (Collins, London, 1962), vol. I.

It was thus that the problem of how one can have knowledge which is prior to experience (*a priori* knowledge) came to be seen by Kant as crucial. His solution (see [2]) was to insist that unless the mind organised experience according to certain principles (such as the assumption that every event has a cause), we cannot raise our sense-impressions to a level where we can be said to be (self) conscious of them. We are in other words entitled to claim *a priori* knowledge because its foundation lies in conditions which make our (self) consciousness possible. Subsequent empiricist philosophers, particularly in the first part of this century, argued that Kant was wrong to think that there was any non-trivial *a priori* knowledge. The programme of reducing mathematical truths to truths of logic (see Chapter 5) formed an important part of their strategy. When this programme stalled, empiricist philosophers gave up resisting the need to *treat* some non-trivial truths as *a priori* and instead resisted the claim that there were any truths which had to be treated once and for all as *a priori*. Science and mathematics alike need to make such assumptions, but they are at best 'provisionally *a priori*'. Thus

[8] Hilary Putnam, *Philosophical papers* (3 vols, Cambridge University Press, Cambridge, 1975), vol. I, p. xiii. For an introduction to this topic from the perspective of contemporary analytic philosophy, Jonathan Dancy, *Introduction to contemporary epistemology* (Basil Blackwell, Oxford, 1985), Ch. 14.

J.E.T.

7 | Knowledge of the External World

Frank Jackson

The problem as traditionally conceived

How do people in Australia know what is happening in America? For instance, how did Australians know that President Reagan had been re-elected? Not directly, for Reagan's re-election occurred thousands of kilometres away from Australia. Rather, what happened was that Reagan's re-election had certain causal consequences, including the transmission from America to Australia of signals which manifested themselves in Australia as sounds over radios, headlines in newspapers, and images on television sets. Australians then inferred from these various manifestations that Reagan had been re-elected. Typically, the inference was quite automatic. Australians did not go around saying something like 'Today's newspaper has a headline reading "Reagan re-elected"; usually headlines like these are accurate; therefore, very probably Reagan has been re-elected.' But had they been challenged to justify their belief that Reagan had been re-elected, they would have said something like this. The justification of their belief, what made it knowledge, lies in the reasonableness of these kinds of inferences, whatever the facts about their conscious psychological processes may have been.

This way of looking at matters seems to be generally applicable to the question of how knowledge of what is happening in regions spatio-temporally remote from us is possible. We argue from happenings near to us, via hypotheses about what probably causes them, to how things are in regions distant from us. It is a style of argument often tagged 'argument from the best explanation'. I know something about what is happening in some nearby region, perhaps the barometer is dropping; I take the most likely explanation of this to be a drop in local air pressure which in turn is caused by an approaching rain depression, and so go on to infer that rain is approaching.

But how do I know that the barometer is dropping?

140

The barometer must be doing something to me. If it has no effect on me at all – because, say, it is on the other side of a screen which stops the light rays from it reaching me – I cannot know that it is dropping. To know that the barometer is dropping, I must *respond* to its dropping. Thus, some effect of the barometer's dropping on me is required. But not any old effect. It must be a noticeable effect. A radio turned very low, too low to hear, nevertheless will vibrate to some minute extent parts of my body, but I will not know that it is on. Clearly, what is needed in order to know that the barometer is dropping, that the radio is on, and generally about what is going on around us, is that there be effects on us including most particularly *perceptual experiences*. We must see, hear, feel, taste or smell something. What we know about what is going on around us goes back ultimately to our perceptual experiences.

The following picture emerges. We know about what is happening around us, about the external world, because of what it does to us, especially because of the perceptual experiences it produces in us. These experiences constitute our fundamental ground and justification for our beliefs about the external world in the sense that, when all is said and done, what justifies our belief in an external world is that it best explains the course of our perceptual experience. We infer from experiences to the existence and nature of things around us by virtue of the latter being the best explanation of the former. Associated with this picture is the realist conception of the external world as existing and having a nature genuinely independent of us. For how else could it properly *causally explain* the course of experience in us? Genuine explanation proceeds by appeal to what is independent.

The traditional conception of the nature and source of our knowledge of the external world is now before you, at least in broad outline. It is a conception which has dominated philosophising about the subject from the Greeks to the present day. Contributions on the subject define themselves by whether they are endorsements, amendments or repudiations of it. The remainder of this chapter will be concerned, first, with filling out some of the details of, and describing some of the variations on, the traditional conception, and, secondly, with the challenge of scepticism and attempts to meet this challenge, some of which hold to the essentials of the traditional conception, and some of which involve more or less radical repudiations of the traditional conception of our problem.

The given in perceptual experience

We have seen that our knowledge of the external world has traditionally been conceived to be the result of inferring from the nature of perceptual experience via hypotheses about causal connections between experiences and objects, to external existents. How should we characterise the relevant perceptual experiences, the starting points for our inferences?

I am listening to the radio, I hear a news bulletin which includes the announcement that President Reagan has been re-elected. How might I characterise the auditory experience which leads me to the knowledge that Reagan has been re-elected? Normally, I would utter some such sentence as 'I hear that Reagan has been re-elected.' This is obviously a perfectly acceptable characterisation of my auditory experience for everyday purposes, but arguably not for our purposes here. We are seeking an understanding of the basic sources of what we know about the world around us. Now 'hear that' has what is called 'success grammar', to say that you hear that so-and-so is to commit yourself to it being the case that so-and-so. If so-and-so is not the case, you cannot, logically cannot, hear that so-and-so; at most you can *seem* to hear that so-and-so. (Provided that 'hear that' is indeed being used to characterise an auditory experience. There is another use of 'hear that' in which it serves to report what is being put about.) A similar point applies to a whole range of expressions in English, including 'see that' and 'remember that'. I cannot remember that Mary was at the party if she was not, though I may seem to remember or mistakenly think that I remember that she was there. Accordingly, if I characterise my experience as hearing that Reagan has been re-elected, it is easy to see how to go from the experience to the belief that Reagan has been re-elected. Too easy; my very way of characterising the experience presupposes that he has been re-elected. I have merely relocated our problem from that of how to pass from experience to object, to that of how to justify that way of characterising the experience.

The same point can be made about visual perceptual experiences. I know that there is a ripe tomato on my desk because of certain visual experiences I am now having, but to characterise them as seeing that there is a ripe romato on my desk is to sidestep rather than address the question of explaining my knowledge. After all, my doubt about it really being a tomato and not a persimmon or a wax imitation would equally be a doubt about whether I was seeing that there is a ripe tomato rather than seeing a persimmon or a wax imitation which I wrongly took to be a tomato.

It seems then that, for our purposes anyway, we need a way of characterising perceptual experiences which does not in and of itself presuppose facts about the external world. We need, that is, a way of characterising experience which captures its intrinsic, current, essential character, or, as it has often been put, we need a way of characterising the *given* in perception, that which perception in and of itself without explicit or implicit appeal to collateral information about external reality yields. It is the given in perception which constitutes the fundamental ground for what we know about the external world, according to the traditional conception of our problem.

Sense-data

One approach to the search for a way of characterising the given in perception is to take statements like our earlier 'I see that there is a ripe tomato on my desk,' and add qualifications which remove what we might call their 'external' implications, ending up with something like 'I seem now to see that there is a ripe tomato on what seems to be my desk' or 'I am now having ripe-tomato-on-desk-like visual experiences.'

There is, however, a more plausible and historically more important approach to characterising the given in perception. Suppose you are asked to describe in as non-committal a way as possible what you are seeing when you see a ripe tomato on your desk. It is very natural to proffer some such description as 'I seem to see a red, round shape against a brown, flat background.' This description is neutral between the hypotheses that what you are seeing is in fact a ripe tomato, that it is a persimmon, that it is a wax imitation, that it is an unusually realistic after-image, and so on. It seems to capture the intrinsic nature of your visual perceptual experience without pre-supposing anything about the external reality you take the experience to be evidence for; it thus seems an excellent candidate to be what is given in visual perception.

Statements like 'I seem to see a red, round shape' and 'There looks to be a red, round shape in front of me' are called *statements about visual sense-data*. And the coloured shapes the statements are putatively about are known as *visual sense-data*. Visual sense-data, then, are the coloured shapes we typically take to be the surfaces of external objects. Similarly, there are auditory, tactile, olfactory, etc. sense-data. Thus a certain auditory experience which you take to be a car backfiring might be described neutrally as the hearing of a sudden, loud sound of brief duration. The car backfiring is the external event which you are aware of, and know you are aware of, by having a certain auditory sense-datum, the sudden, loud sound.

Two very different attitudes are possible towards sense-data. The historically dominant attitude regards them as really existing. It regards sense-datum sentences like 'I seem to see (sense) a red elliptical shape to the left of a green square one' as really being about the coloured shapes they appear to be about, just as 'I have a car' really is about my car. The latter sentence cannot be true unless there is, really is, a car which I have; similarly, according to the view which posits sense-data as really existing, the sense-datum sentence cannot be true unless there are, really are, red and green shapes which I sense.

However, the currently favoured attitude towards sense-data holds that the right analogy is with a sentence like 'I have a limp.' Despite its grammatical similarity to 'I have a car,' it is not really about limps in the way the latter is about cars, because its truth does not require that there is, really is, a limp which I have. All that is necessary is that I limp. Similarly,

'I have a bad limp' really says that I limp badly. Thus the currently favoured attitude is sometimes referred to as the Adverbial Theory of Sensory Experience, and its protagonists insist that 'I sense a red elliptical shape' should, if logical perspicuity rather than syntactical propriety is our goal, be written 'I sense red–elliptical–shapely.'

The great advantage of the Adverbial Theory is that it obviates the need to pursue the traditional question as to whether sense-data are mental or physical. It is clear that sensing a red shape is a mental event because it is a conscious perceptual experience. But is the shape sensed mental or physical? The initially appealing answer is that it is physical. When you look at a tomato and, as a result, sense a red shape, the obvious view to take is that the red shape is the facing surface of the tomato, and so is a (two-dimensional) physical existent. But there are difficulties for this initially attractive response. Suppose you press your eyeball lightly with your finger, then the red shape will move. The tomato's surface does not move, of course; how then can the red shape be the tomato's surface? Again, science's account of the tomato's surface is that it is made up of sub-microscopic, fast moving, widely separated, colourless particles. How can *this* be the densely red shape? It seems, thus, that sense-data are not the physical surfaces we normally suppose that we see when we look around us, but are rather mental entities (akin in ontological status to after-images) which stand between us and external reality. This is the notorious 'veil of perception' doctrine particularly associated with John Locke. Indeed, Locke used the explicitly mentalistic term 'ideas' for what were subsequently called 'sense-data'. But if adverbial-ists are right, we need not pursue such matters. To ask whether the red shape in particular and sense-data in general are mental or physical is as misguided as asking whether limps (or the Cheshire cat's smile) are mental or physical.

The great disadvantage of the Adverbial Theory is the semantic obscurity of its elaborate adverbial constructions, which are, after all, the heart of the theory. Fortunately, we do not need to pursue this difficult issue. For our primary concern here is with sense-datum statements *qua* putative foundations of our knowledge of external reality; and the question of whether these *statements* play this epistemological role cuts across the metaphysical question of whether we should include what they are putatively about, sense-data, in our inventory of what exists. To say that my reasons for believing that there is a tomato before me ultimately go back to my sensing a red, round sense-datum is not to take a stand one way or the other on whether there exists a red, round sense-datum which I sense or whether it is merely that I am sensing red–round–ly. The traditional conception of our problem sees knowledge of sense-datum statements like 'I sense a red round shape' as the foundations of our knowledge of the external world, whether or not the currently popular view that such statements are translatable adverbially so as to avoid ontological commitment to sense-data is correct.

144

Incorrigibility

The final feature of the traditional conception of the problem of our knowledge of the external world that needs mentioning is the view that we cannot, logically cannot, be mistaken about the given in perception. If we succeed in properly characterising the current, essential, intrinsic nature of our perceptual experience, perhaps in the sense-datum terminology just discussed, we end up with statements we cannot be wrong about. It is impossible that we believe them yet they be false.

Clearly, if I say that I am seeing a ripe tomato, I can be wrong. Perhaps the tomato is a new variety which turns red well before ripening, perhaps I am seeing a very tomato-like persimmon, or perhaps I am seeing a clever wax imitation. In all these cases, and similar ones, it is obvious that subsequent events might prove my initial claim wrong and show that what I am in fact seeing is a wax imitation or whatever. For instance, I may try to eat it. But it is arguable that if I say that I *seem* to see or sense a red, round shape, nothing can subsequently show me to have been mistaken, provided this is interpreted as a report of current perceptual experience, a sense-datum report, and nothing more. Of course, if my report is interpreted as saying that I am sensing something *physical* which is red and round, I may be mistaken in it. A physical object which is neither red nor round can look red and round due to the nature of the circumstances in which it is viewed – in red light, through a distorting lens, or whatever. But if my report is really restricted to the nature of my experience, to how things *look* to be whether they are as they look to be or not, that is, to sense-data, the claim is that it cannot be wrong, or in the traditional terminology, the report is *incorrigible*, and the given in perception is incorrigibly known.

This alleged incorrigibility of the perceptually given has been seen as making it particularly suitable to be the foundation of our knowledge of the external world. Most things we claim to know rest on or derive from other things we claim to know. I know that Reagan was re-elected because the radio said so; I know that the radio said so because the relevant broadcast was audible and in English; and so on. The thought has been that we can halt this 'regress of reasons' at the perceptually given by virtue of the fact that there is no need to justify beliefs which are incorrigible; for how can beliefs that cannot be mistaken be in need of justification? However, it has more recently been recognised that a weaker property than being incorrigible may suffice to halt the regress.

We can distinguish *grounded* from *intuitive* beliefs as follows. A grounded belief is only justified inasmuch as it rests on some other justified belief. An example would be my belief that Reagan was re-elected. An intuitive belief is one which may be justified merely because it is had. Its justification does not derive from outside itself. Possible examples are my belief that I am not in pain; and sense-datum reports. Clearly, I am justified in my beliefs that I am not in pain and that I am sensing a red shape, but it is hard to specify *other* beliefs from which my justification derives. True, I know that I am not being whipped, being stuck with pins or whatever, but this knowledge is not what makes my belief that I am not in pain justified. It may be what makes my belief that I will remain pain free for the rest of the day justified, but it is not what makes my belief that I am not *now* in pain justified. It is plausible that if there are any incorrigible beliefs, then they must be intuitive. A belief that cannot be mistaken needs no external justification. But it may be that there are intuitive beliefs which are not incorrigible, indeed there may be intuitive beliefs even if, contrary to tradition, there are no incorrigible beliefs at all (bar here irrelevant examples like the belief that 2+2=4 or the belief that if there is something, there is something). Indeed, it may be that the very beliefs, or ones like them, which have been held to be incorrigible are in fact not incorrigible at all; they are fallible but intuitive, and that is enough to make them suitable as foundations for our knowledge of the external world.

The recent interest in such *fallibilist* foundationalist theories of our knowledge of the external world, as opposed to the classical variety (associated particularly with Descartes) which insists on infallible foundations, derive from widespread doubts about whether reports of current mental states are incorrigible. To say that I am not in pain, or do have an itch, is clearly to make a knowledge claim of substance and importance (particularly to me). How can *substantial claims*, as opposed to tautologies like that if *p*, then *p*, be logically immune from doubt? Moreover, isn't declaring a sensation to be an itch or a sense-datum to be red (or a sensing to be red-ly) classifying it, linking it to other experiences in a principled way that we learn when we learn descriptive language? How can these claims be incorrigible, why not say instead that they are fallible but self-justifying? The cost is to admit that the justified may be on occasion false; but that is a cost that must be paid anyway, for no one thinks that *every* justified belief is a true belief.

The sceptical challenge to tradition

We have just commented on one variant, the fallibilist variant, to the traditional treatment of our problem, but many philosophers have argued for a more or less radical rethinking of the terms in which our problem has been posed. Indeed, many have argued that the traditional conception of how we have knowledge of an external world is a total misconception.

The principal impetus for attacks on the traditional approach has been the conviction that it leads straight to scepticism. It is an approach which destroys what it is supposed to be approaching; for if it is right, we know nothing about the external world.

The case for the view that posing the question of how we know about the external world in more or less traditional terms leads straight to the sceptical conclusion (that we do *not* know about the external world) can be developed in a number of ways. I will develop it in a way which, in its essentials, goes back to Descartes, though I will put it in a modern scientific setting.

The traditional conception of our problem identifies three separate elements: (i) perceptual experiences, beliefs, conscious states and, generally speaking, what we might call mental contents, things that happen 'in the mind' (which, if certain versions of materialism are true, will be things that happen in the brain, but that is another story); (ii) external objects, things outside of and independent of the mind; and (iii) causal and so empirical, contingent connections between what happens outside the mind, the external happenings, and the mental contents, the experiences, beliefs and so on.

Now consider what happens when an object, say, yet again, a ripe tomato, acts on me to cause me to have the perceptual experience of sensing a red shape, which in turn leads me to believe that there is a tomato in front of me. The tomato will act on my senses to produce certain changes in my brain, which will be the immediate causes of my experiences and beliefs (be these states of the brain or not). Accordingly, if a brain scientist could *exactly duplicate* the relevant changes in my brain, I would have exactly the same experiences as those caused by the tomato. It would be with me exactly as if I were seeing the tomato; just as, if there were perfect aircraft simulators, it would be with trainee pilots exactly as if they were really flying. By extension, if a brain scientist exactly duplicated *every* input that is now going into my brain, my experiences would be exactly as they now are, and I could not tell the difference. Indeed, suppose that I were a 'brain in a vat', a brain floating in a suitable fluid in a vat with complicated machines feeding into my brain *exactly* what my body with its sense organs stimulated by the environment is now feeding in, then I could not tell the difference. My experiences and beliefs would be exactly as they now are. How then do I know that I am not a brain in a vat?

Many philosophers, from Berkeley onwards, are convinced that this kind of sceptical challenge is quite unanswerable within anything like the traditional conception of our problem. Indeed, Berkeley offered essentially this argument, minus the scientific trimmings, against Locke's version of the traditional approach to our problem. But first I will look at two less far-reaching attempts to reply to the sceptical argument.

The first, epitomised by A.J. Ayer in *The problem of knowledge*, is that the sceptic is up to his old trick of showing (successfully) that mistake is *logically possible*, and then speaking as if he has shown that it is *probable* or *as likely as not* or, even, *inevitable*. However, the challenge presented by the brain in the vat argument is not merely that it is logically possible that we are brains in vats; it is that, compatible with the total course of my experience, there are two (in fact, there are indefinitely many, but let us keep it simple) hypotheses, one has the external world much as we take it to be, including ripe tomatoes, around me, the other has a manipulative brain scientist with his machines around me. As both hypotheses are compatible with all my experiences, my perceptual experiences *in themselves* can provide no reason for preferring one to the other. How then can I justify my preference for the one over the other? Faith, intuition? Descartes in effect responded to this challenge by giving an *a priori* argument for a perfect God, and then arguing that such a God would not permit widespread deception, but this is not a particularly appealing reply. In any case, the point of the sceptical challenge is not merely that we may be wrong, but that it is so hard to give any convincing reason for supposing that we are right. It is sometimes objected that the sceptic makes it *too* hard to give the demanded reason. If someone thinks that what I take to be a tomato is a wax imitation, we can settle the matter by collecting further perceptual experiences – taste one, for instance. It is logically possible to collect experiences which discriminate between the two positions (whether or not we bother to). But no experiences discriminate between the brain in a vat explanation and the more usual explanation of the total course of my experience. Both, *ex hypothesi*, accommodate every experience. Hence, it is objected, the sceptic makes his challenge *logically* unanswerable. No possible experience turns the trick. This is a strange sort of *objection*. If the sceptic's challenge is logically unanswerable, then it is *ipso facto* unanswerable.

A second reply to the sceptic derives, in its essentials, from G.E. Moore. An argument to some conclusion is convincing, establishes its conclusion, inasmuch as it is valid *and* proceeds from *agreed premisses*. Someone who denies Q is rightly not going to be convinced by my arguing 'P, therefore Q' if she is unconvinced of my premiss P. She will be entitled to respond to my argument by arguing back, 'Not Q, therefore, not P.' Here she would be using the fact that an argument from P to Q is valid if and only if the argument from not Q to not P is also valid.

This suggests that we could not possibly have a convincing argument to conclusions such as that we are brains in vats, that there is no external world (of the usually supposed kind), or that I do not have a hand (Moore's own example). For there is nothing more certain than that we are not brains in vats, that there is an external world, or that I have a hand, from which arguments against these certainties could be launched. Any sceptical argument to the conclusion that we are brains in vats must proceed from premisses less certain than that we are not, and so may be faulted precisely on this point.

This reply does, indeed, refute any sceptic foolish enough to hold that we are brains in vats. But the wise sceptic is agnostic on the question. He holds that we have no reason to think that we are not, or that we are, brains in vats. The sceptic, of course, is not agnostic on the question of whether *it is certain that* we are not brains in vats. He holds that it is not certain. Accordingly, he can fairly be challenged to produce something more certain from which to argue that it is not certain. But it seems he can do this. Our certainty *derives* from the nature of our perceptual experiences and our general beliefs. Were our experiences a total jumble, or were it the case that brains in vats were a commonplace in our society along perhaps with associated mirth at their absurd conviction that they are not brains in vats (a situation often described with convincing detail in science fiction), we might well *not* be certain that we ourselves are not brains in vats. Thus the sceptic can argue that we must concede that our certainty that we are not brains in vats derives from the view that the best explanation for the course of our experience as it in fact is lies in the hypothesis of an external world much as we normally suppose it to be. But now we have stepped on to the sceptic's ground. He denies precisely that this explanation is any better, or any worse, than the brain in a vat one.

Radical repudiations of tradition

The vulnerability of the traditional conception of our problem to sceptical attack arises, of course, from the way it separates out perceptual experiences, what is in the mind, from the physical world, what is outside the mind, seeing a merely causal connecton between what is 'inside' and what is 'outside'. Accordingly, the obvious counter to scepticism is to bring experiences and objects closer together, to close the gap between them which figures so prominently in the traditional conception of our problem. One way to do this is to bring objects into the mind, to deny that they are external; the other way is to take experiences out into the world, to deny that they are essentially inner.

Idealism and phenomenalism

The obvious way to bring objects 'into the mind' is to construe them as being collections of perceptual experiences. This is precisely what George Berkeley did, and as he called perceptual experiences (and, in fact, mental states in general) *ideas*, his doctrine is often called *idealism*. According to idealism, the table I am now writing on is not something existing independently of experiences and minds which causes experiences such as my perception of it. Rather, the table is nothing more than a collection of experiences, including my perception 'of' it, your perception 'of' it, God's perception 'of' it in Berkeley's theistic version of idealism, and so on and so forth. Tables and stones are not *external* in any literal sense.

Idealism is typically contrasted with realist theories which hold – as does 'common sense' – that tables *et al.* exist and have a nature independently of us and our experience of them. Realism comes in many varieties, the most commonly made distinction being between *direct realism* (or *naive realism*, to its enemies) and *representative realism* or *representationalism*, particularly associated with John Locke. Sometimes the distinction is drawn in terms of the status of sense-data: according to direct realism, sense-data are surfaces of objects, while according to representationalism, sense-data are mental. Take the red, round shape I am visually aware of when I look at our ubiquitous tomato: according to direct realism, it is the facing surface of the tomato, while according to representationalism, it is a mental item caused in us by the tomato. At other times (particularly recently, with the doubts about sense-data) the distinction is drawn in terms of how much perceptual experience mirrors external reality: according to direct realism, the external world is more or less as we experience it, while according to representationalism, the world as-we-experience-it with continuous, densely coloured, solid objects is very different from the world as it really is – that is, as physics says it is, a cloud of tiny, fast-moving, colourless, widely separated particles and wave-packets.

There are two major problems with idealism. The first concerns the extent to which it is properly speaking a non-sceptical position. Idealists hold that tables, and objects in general, are nothing over and above collections of experiences, and they represent themselves as being in a particularly strong position to reply to the sceptic by virtue of not holding that objects are things 'lying behind' experiences, only to be reached by dangerously speculative reasoning. But how is this a non-sceptical position? We use terms like 'table' to name objects that exist independently of us and which cause certain things, including perhaps our use of the very word 'table'; or at least that is what we think we use such terms for, and shouldn't we know? It is our language, after all. If this is right, the idealist's declaration that tables are nothing more than collections of ideas is tantamount to declaring that there are no tables, no real ones. We now know that witches were nothing more than wrongly suspected women, and that *is* scepticism about witches. It would be completely wrong-headed to respond that witches were nothing more than wrongly suspected women, there were wrongly suspected women, therefore there were, contrary to modern scepticism about witches, witches. Consequently, if idealism is to be more than a particular version of scepticism, it must be allied with a repudiation of common-sense views about the meanings of the terms for the objects we take to be around us. Idealists avoid scepticism only inasmuch as they have to hand an appropriate theory about the meaning of statements about objects.

This theory is known as *phenomenalism* (or, in an alternative terminology, as *linguistic phenomenalism*; with *ontological phenomenalism* used for the theory we have called *idealism*). According to phenomenalism, statements about objects can be translated into statements about how things seem. Although the two are sometimes confused, idealism should be seen as a thesis in ontology concerning what there is, phenomenalism as a thesis in the philosophy of language concerning the meanings of

150

statements about objects; the two combined giving a genuinely non-realist, non-sceptical doctrine about the world. Phenomenalism is, however, very hard to believe. It is obvious that 'There is a table in the room' does not mean 'There seems to me to be a table in the room.' I may be under an illusion, so that there seems to be one when there is not; or else it may simply be that I am not in the room; or perhaps I am in the room, but am looking in the wrong direction. Nor does it mean 'There seems to someone to be a table in the room.' It may be that no one is in the room, or that everyone in the room is looking in the wrong direction.

The usual response (which goes back to J.S. Mill) to these sorts of objections has been to propose that statements about objects should be translated not in the terms of actual experiences, the way things actually seem to someone, but in terms of possible experiences, the way things would seem to someone were they to do certain things in certain circumstances. Roughly speaking, in the spirit of giving the general idea, 'There is a table in the room' would be translated as 'Were someone with senses-in-good-order to have in-the-room-looking-in-the-right-direction-with-the-light-on-and-eyes-open experiences, they would have table-in-the-room experiences.' Many questions of detail might be, and have been, raised against such analyses. For instance, does 'the right direction' just mean the direction of the table, so that circularity threatens? But there is an objection of principle. The move from actual to possible experiences has a disastrous consequence. As we saw, phenomenalism's role with respect to idealism is to lay to rest the demon of scepticism. This is hardly being achieved by an analysis of a simple categorical statement by a highly complex, *highly doubtable* subjunctive about possibilities. Idealists criticise realists for extravagant speculations about the causes of our ideas, but speculations about highly complex subjunctives are, at best, at least as extravagant. Moreover, what would be the case typically rests on what is the case. It is true that I *would* cut myself with that knife were I careless, because the knife *is* sharp. It is true that the glass *would* break were it dropped, because it *has* a certain molecular structure. Now suppose that there is no one in the next room. What then can the idealist say is the case in virtue of which it would be the case, say, that were someone to go into the room, they would have table-like experiences? It seems that idealists must swallow 'bare' possibilities.

The second major problem with idealism is that it is incompatible with the very line of thought that led to it. Realists argue that the best explanation for the nature of our experiences is that they are caused by an external, independently existing world of tables, planets, electrons and so on, and that this is why it is rational to believe in such an external world. Idealists object that this best-explanation style of argument for realism is too speculative. There are many possible explanations for the course of sensory experience. The commonsensical one that realists favour is only one among

151

many, and idealists object that realists cannot rationally defend their preference for it. But if this is right, idealists themselves exhibit an irrational
preference. For idealists, as much as realists, take a stance on the explanation
of perceptual experience. They hold that there is no explanation. (Unless they
appeal to God, as did Berkeley, in which case they are really realists, though
of a theistic variety.) Experiences for them are examples of continuous,
miraculous creation. But to say that there is no explanation (as opposed to
saying that there is, but we do not know what it is) is to stick one's neck out
just as much as to say that there is and it is of such and such a sort. Idealism is
epistemologically no better off than realism.

The challenge to the traditional conception of experience

Idealism seeks to bring objects 'inside' the mind. A more recent strategy takes
experiences 'into' the world. Traditionally, experience has been seen as
having a purely contingent, indeed causal, connection with external reality.
As we saw at the very beginning, experiences can be, and often are, characterised in a way which entails or presupposes something about external reality.
If I characterise an experience as seeing that a tomato is in front of me, I
presuppose that a tomato is in front of me. Similarly, if I characterise a smell
as the aroma of coffee, I presuppose that it is of the kind typically caused by
coffee (be it in fact caused by coffee on this occasion or not). But it has
traditionally been assumed, as we did earlier, that such characterisations of
experience are inessential and extrinsic. Experiences have special essential,
intrinsic qualities which give them their experienced character, this character
determining what it is like to experience them, and which constitutes the
fundamental basis for our knowledge of external reality. It is these qualities
which in the traditional conception are assumed to have a purely contingent,
causal connection with external reality.

The most recently influential attack on the problem
of our knowledge of external reality denies exactly this assumption. The basic
point at issue can be illustrated with the aroma example. The traditional
assumption (of Locke, Berkeley, Hume, Descartes, Russell *et al.*) is that the
aroma of coffee has a characteristic experiential property, call it C, it being
entirely contingent that C is coffee's aroma. Of course, the statement 'The
aroma of coffee is typically caused by coffee' is necessarily true, but it is no
sort of necessary truth that C is typically caused by coffee. C, for instance,
might have been caused by roses, in which case it would have been *called* 'the
aroma of roses', but it would nevertheless have *been* the very same quality we
actually call 'the aroma of coffee'.

It is exactly this which is now widely denied. The
considerations marshalled in support of this denial are varied, subtle, complex, highly controversial, and involve issues in the philosophy of language
and of mind outside the scope of this chapter. But their general thrust is

encapsulated in the challenge to make sense of my introduction of the term 'C' in the previous paragraph.

It is clear that I did not mean 'C' to abbreviate 'the aroma of coffee', for I intended that C might not be the aroma of coffee. Rather, 'C' was introduced as a private name of a directly experienced quality. But, so the challenge runs, what sense can we make of a *private* name? Language is essentially public. It is of its very nature a shared activity of a community, and naming is a relationship between words and the world which obtains in virtue of this communal nature. After all, we teach the meaning of words by teaching children the right way to use them for the things around us. Indeed, the only way to teach 'C''s meaning is by putting coffee under people's noses and saying 'That is C.' But what can that be but teaching someone that 'C' is short for 'the aroma of coffee'?

This style of attack on 'C' as a name of a private, ineffable quality derives from considerations in the philosophy of language due originally to Wittgenstein in the *Philosophical investigations*. It is bolstered by considerations in the philosophy of mind which have come to prominence in recent discussions of *materialism*. If 'C' names a privately given quality, my use of 'C' must be caused by that quality. I must be *responding* to that quality in calling it 'C'; and this is certainly what I seem to myself to be doing. But what causes the uttering of words like 'I will call it C'? The best theory we have is that it is most immediately states of the brain produced by the coffee's action on my senses which cause the contractions of my vocal chords and lungs that result in such utterances. And it is implausible that states of the brain have privately accessible properties; and, even if they do, it is their more ordinary, public properties which are responsible for the movements of my bodily organs. To believe otherwise is to fly in the face of the whole direction of neuro-physiological research into the operations of the brain.

How exactly does the modern attack on the traditional attitude to perceptual experience help meet scepticism? The challenge of the brain-in-a-vat argument is not that we might be brains in a vat. It is that we might be brains in a vat *yet have exactly the same perceptual experiences we in fact have.* But if the nature of perceptual experience is constituted in part at least by relationships to what is around us, this is nonsense. In supposing that our experiences are exactly the *same* yet everything around us is totally *different*, we contradict ourselves. For instance, suppose I am now experiencing the aroma of coffee; could I be having the very same experience were I now, and had I always been, a brain in a vat? Not according to the modern attack; for, in order for it to be the same experience, it must be caused by coffee, or at least be of the kind typically caused by coffee, and *that* it *cannot* be if I have always been a brain in a vat, or at least it cannot be if most of us are brains in a vat.

A similar point can be made about belief, and is less controversial in this case. Unlike smells, tastes, bodily sensations and sensory states in general, beliefs do not have a characteristic feel. Whatever may be true for the aroma of coffee or the hurtfulness of pain, beliefs do not have introspectible properties which make them the kind of beliefs they are. The belief that snow is white is not the belief that snow is white rather than, say, the belief that grass is green because of how it feels. (Pains but not beliefs have 'raw feels'.) Accordingly, to put it very generally, what makes a belief the belief that snow is white must be its typical causal relations, notably to snow, whiteness, and to behaviour, including especially the production of sentences about snow. Therefore, no brain in a vat could believe that snow is white, for no brain in a vat has a state which bears these causal relations to its surroundings. Or at least a brain in a vat can only believe that snow is white by virtue of being in the same kind of state which in most others has the right causal relations to snow, sentences and so on, so that, at worst, brains in vats are in a minority. They cannot be in a majority. Unfortunately, there is a 'second-order' sceptical response to this appealing attempt to lay brains in vats to rest. Suppose we accept the view that in order for something to be a belief of mine about snow, it must at least sometimes actually be caused by snow doing something to me, perhaps via sentences in books or the reports of others (I need not have actually seen or touched snow obviously). Nevertheless, it would be too quick for me to argue that I cannot be a brain in a vat because I have beliefs about snow, including that snow is white, and no brain in a vat has beliefs about snow because its states are produced by brain scientists manipulating inputs, not by snow and the like. For how do I know that I have beliefs about snow? I certainly believe that I do, but if such beliefs must be caused by snow, even if indirectly, could I not believe that I have beliefs about snow when in fact I do not? In order to lay brains in vats to rest by appeal to these sorts of considerations, we need a theory of beliefs about beliefs and, more generally, of second-order mental states.

Nevertheless, we have made this much headway with our problem. As long as the problem is viewed as how we can pass from mysterious, private, *sui generis* properties of experience to the existence and nature of an external world, it is surely insoluble. No appeal to the realist's favourite best-explanation argument can help. True, it is incredible that perceptual experience is an example of continuous, miraculous creation. Some explanation of it is required. But, so long as experience is treated as *sui generis*, how can we rationally discriminate between explanations? How can one be designated the best? The most we could achieve would be a Kantian position with an independent external world with an in principle unknowable nature. (Immanuel Kant reserved a special term, *noumena*, for external objects as they are in themselves, and held that noumena are *in principle* unknowable and unintelligible.) But once experience is endowed with some more normal properties (though perhaps not only such, raw feels do seem special), of a kind with those we attribute to the rest of nature, our problem becomes closer to being a (very) special case of inferring from the nature of one region of space-time to another region of space-time. And such inferences are amenable to best-explanation type arguments (given a solution to the problem of induction, of course; see Chapter 9).

Bibliography

Prior to Descartes (e.g. in the ancient sceptical tradition) questions about the nature and source of our knowledge about the 'external world' were questions about whether there was any knowledge (or justified belief) *at all*. This was because truth was taken to apply only to (and hence there could be knowledge only of) a real objective world (as distinct from mere appearances). Subjective experience was not a source of truth or knowledge. See M.F. Burnyeat, 'Idealism and Greek philosophy: what Descartes saw and Berkeley missed' in Godfrey Vesey (ed.), *Idealism: past and present*, Royal Institute of Philosophy Lectures 13 (Harvester, Hassocks, 1980). For a thorough and illuminating discussion of the continuity between ancient and modern discussions of the problems arising from our perception of the world around us, see Burnyeat's 'Conflicting appearances' in *Proceedings of the British Academy*, vol. 65 (1979), pp. 79–111.

Gilbert Ryle called attention to the way we speak about perceiving (e.g. the character of 'success' or 'achievement' verbs) in *The concept of mind* (Hutchinson, London, 1949). How we are best advised to speak of the 'given' (the *'datum'*) in perception was the topic of intense debate, particularly in the middle decades of this century. For a very useful collection of essays, which were products of this debate, see Robert K. Swartz, *Perceiving, sensing and knowing* (Doubleday, New York, 1965). For a discussion of the adverbial approach to this question, see Roderick Chisholm, *Theory of knowledge* (Prentice-Hall, Englewood Cliffs, 1966), pp. 95–102.

In the collection edited by Swartz is an article by Roderick Firth, 'Sense data and the percept theory', which contrasts the assumption that what is given in sensation is something like a colour or smell (something the experience of which does not entail the existence of other experiences) with the claim that what we are given in perception is the experience of physical objects incorporating (logically) elements which can only be supplied by memory and anticipation. The former are what the term 'sense-data' is usually applied to, while the latter are known as 'percepts'. A theory of this sort (but which does not use the word 'percept') is developed in G.E.M. Anscombe's 'The intentionality of perception: a grammatical feature' in her *Metaphysics and the philosophy of mind, Collected papers, Volume II* (Basil Blackwell, Oxford, 1981).

A percept theory was held by the late nineteenth-century American philosopher, C.S. Peirce, who was able to combine the doctrine that our perceptual judgements yield infallible knowledge of the nature of our percepts with the denial that our perceptual judgements are incorrigible. For every percept is an assertion about reality which may turn out to be false. See Christopher Hookway, *Peirce* (Routledge and Kegan Paul, London, 1985), Ch. 5. A twentieth-century denial of the incorrigibility of the perceptual foundations of knowledge can be found in D.M. Armstrong, *Belief, truth and knowledge* (Cambridge University Press, Cambridge, 1973).

Descartes' posing of the problem of a world external to his thought, as well as his appeal to a benevolent God to underwrite his knowledge of that world, may be found in his 'Meditations on first philosophy'; see *The philosophical writings of Descartes*, trans. J. Cottingham, R. Stoothoff and D. Murdoch (2 vols, Cambridge University Press, Cambridge, 1985), vol. II. Descartes' most famous sceptical challenge was his hypothesis that all his beliefs were the product of an evil genius, who had the power to deceive Descartes into thinking there was a world external to his mind. The claim that this most sceptical challenge is *too* unanswerable to need answering is developed in a lively fashion by O.K. Bouwsma, 'Descartes' evil genius' in his *Collected philosophical papers* (Nebraska University Press, Lincoln, Nebraska, 1965). The more prosaic response of G.E. Moore to the challenge will be found in his 'Proof of an external world' in *Philosophical papers* (Allen and Unwin, London, 1959).

Updating Descartes' hypothesis by retelling it as a science fiction horror story about brains in vats is a device used by Hilary Putnam in *Reason, truth and history* (Cambridge University Press, Cambridge, 1981). It is Putnam who advances arguments to the effect that brains in vats could not believe that snow is white because they would not stand in the appropriate causal relations to snow and white things. Considering the predicament of brains in vats has more than philosophical implications, or so argues (philosopher) Jerry A. Fodor. In virtue of the logic of the phenomena they study, cognitive scientists are in Fodor's view barred from studying the relations between cognitive states and the world. See 'Methodological solipsism considered as a research strategy in cognitive psychology' in Fodor's *Representations* (Harvester, Hassocks, 1981).

Although Locke is traditionally thought of as a representative realist, some recent scholars have contended that Locke does not treat ideas as things which stand between us and external things. For his abridged edition of Locke's *Essay concerning human understanding* (Collins, London, 1964), A.D. Woozley wrote an introduction calling the traditional interpretation into question. The question of interpretation is further discussed in articles by Douglas Greenlee, Gunnar Asplin and H.E. Matthews in I.C. Tipton (ed.), *Locke and human understanding* (Oxford University Press, Oxford, 1977).

Whatever is the correct understanding of Locke, Berkeley took him for a representative realist. Berkeley's criticisms of Locke, as well as the development of his own immaterialist (theistic) realism may be found in *Berkeley's philosophical works* (Everyman, London, 1975). For the impact which Berkeley made when linguistic phenomenalism was at its height, see G.J. Warnock, *Berkeley* (Penguin Books, Harmondsworth, 1953). David Hume did not invoke God to sustain the notion of an objective world independent of our experience of it, as Berkeley did. In his *Treatise of human nature* (Collins, London, 1962), Book I, Part IV, Hume tried to explain how a succession of interrupted perceptions could give rise to the idea of the continued existence of bodies. He concluded from his account that we have no rational foundation for the idea.

Kant's response to Hume was to insist that an objective order (including continually existing bodies) in experience is a necessary condition of self-conscious awareness of what is experienced. This led Kant to a curious double perspective on the problem of the external world. Within experience Kant maintained what he called 'empirical realism'; see his 'Refutation of [*'material'*] idealism' in *The critique of pure reason*, trans. Norman Kemp Smith (Macmillan, London, 1929), B274–279. On the other hand, from a 'transcendental' perspective, the order in experience is the product of our mental activity and Kant also claimed to be a 'transcendental idealist'. This double perspective was underpinned by the distinction between 'noumena' and 'phenomena', (on which see A235/B294–A261/B315).

156

Post-Kantian philosophers discarded the unknowable thing-in-itself (noumenon) and advanced various forms of objective idealism. These idealisms were quite unlike anything Berkeley or Hume envisaged, but they held out the same hope that Berkeley had held out, viz. that the problem of scepticism about the external world could be preempted. The objective idealists regarded their position as superior to Berkeley's in that they had a more sophisticated notion of truth. For a sensitive reconstruction of their general line of argument by someone who is otherwise unsympathetic to idealism, see Simon Blackburn, *Spreading the word* (Oxford University Press, Oxford, 1983), Chs. 6 and 7.

The nineteenth century was not entirely a history of responses to Kant. Mill remained in the tradition of Locke and Berkeley. Mill's definition of matter as a 'Permanent possibility of sensation' was given in his *An examination of Sir William Hamilton's philosophy* (1865) (Longman Green, London, 1889), p. 233. In his earlier *System of logic* (1843) (Longman Green, London, 1879), however, Mill seemed committed to a representative realism; see Book I, Ch. 3, 7–8. There was also the physicist and philosopher Ernst Mach, who in his *Analysis of sensations*, trans. C.M. Williams (Dover, New York, 1959), p. 46, acknowledged that his starting point was not essentially different from Hume's.

After being educated in a Hegelian atmosphere at Cambridge, Russell revolted against idealism and returned to the tradition of Hume and Mill; a tradition to which he brought a great deal of logical sophistication as a result of his work on the foundations of mathematics. See his *Our knowledge of the external world* (Allen and Unwin, London, 1915). Russell's approach provided the inspiration for linguistic phenomenalism, which was developed by A.J. Ayer in *The foundations of empirical knowledge* (Macmillan, London, 1964). See also 'Phenomenalism' in *Philosophical essays* (Macmillan, London, 1954), and *The problem of knowledge* (Penguin Books, Harmondsworth, 1956).

The unsophisticated person's feelings about phenomenalism were given a sophisticated expression by Isaiah Berlin in 'Empirical propositions and hypothetical statements', which may be found reprinted in Swartz (ed.), mentioned above, or in Berlin's *Concepts and categories* (Oxford University Press, Oxford, 1980). Ayer's approach was attacked (as much by ridicule as by refutation) by J.L. Austin in *Sense and sensibilia* (Oxford University Press, Oxford, 1962).

A (philosophic as opposed to unreflective) form of direct realism was advanced early in this century by a group of American philosophers who styled themselves 'New Realists'; see E.B. Holt, R.B. Parry *et al.*, *The New Realism* (Macmillan, New York, 1912). A more recent development of direct realism can be found in D.M. Armstrong, *Perception and the physical world* (Routledge and Kegan Paul, London, 1961).

Prior to the impact of Wittgenstein, a philosopher who insisted on taking experience out of the mind and into the world (locating it in the interaction between organism and the environment) was John Dewey. (Dewey was one of those identified by Firth as subscribing to a percept theory; see above.) Dewey's approach may be encountered in *Experience and nature* (Open Court, La Salle, Illinois, 1929). The argument, against the possibility of naming a private ineffable quality, to be found in Wittgenstein's *Philosophical investigations* (Basil Blackwell, Oxford, 1953), touched off a debate which may be sampled by consulting the pro-Wittgensteinian, Norman Malcolm, 'Wittgenstein's philosophical investigations' in *Knowledge and certainty:*

essays and lectures (Cornell University Press, Ithaca, New York, 1963) and the anti-Wittgensteinian, A.J. Ayer, 'Can there be a private language?' in *The concept of a person* (Macmillan, London, 1963).

J.E.T.

8 | *Memory Knowledge*

Carl Ginet

One knows facts about the past in several different ways. I know this morning that it rained during the night by inferring this from the wetness I see outdoors when I wake up. I know that there were torrential downpours in the Carolinas yesterday by seeing a statement to this effect in the newspaper. I know that it rained hard in Ithaca last Friday afternoon because I remember that it did. These three ways in which I may know a fact about the past – by inference from its effects, by the testimony of others, and by remembering it – are importantly different. Each deserves substantial discussion. In this chapter we will be concerned only with knowing by remembering, with memory knowledge.

It is natural to associate remembering with knowledge of the past. What one remembers is, of course, the past, isn't it? And to remember something is to know it, isn't it? Well, as a matter of fact, the answer to both these questions is: not always.

The verb 'remember', like the verb 'know', takes several different sorts of objects. It takes propositional (factive, 'that') clauses: 'I remember that we ate in an Italian restaurant our first evening in New York,' 'I remember that 12×12 is 144,' 'I remember that Fuengirola is west of Malaga.' It takes 'wh–' clauses: 'I remember where we were last July Fourth,' 'Of course I remember what all these English words mean: I am a native speaker!' It takes 'how to' phrases: 'I remember how to tie a bowline knot,' 'I remember how to ride a bicycle.' It takes denoters of people, places and objects: 'I remember you,' 'I remember Tintagel,' 'I remember the Crystal Palace.' It takes denoters of events: 'I remember the bombing of Pearl Harbor.' This last class of memory objects – the class of events – is always restricted to things in the past, indeed to ones that the rememberer herself was aware of, directly or indirectly, at the time of their occurrence. I can remember the bombing of Pearl Harbor – I heard the radio announcements and saw the headlines on the day it happened – but it cannot be right to say of me that I remember the Battle of Trafalgar, no matter how many facts about it I may remember.[1]

The examples for the other classes of memory objects make clear that they are not restricted to events in or facts about the past. And some illustrate how extremely important memory knowledge is. The vastly greater part of what one now knows one knows because one remembers it. Other ways in which one can now know something, by now experiencing it or now learning or inferring it or now finding it self-evident, can account for very little of what one now knows.

It can sometimes be true to say of someone that she remembers something even when she fails to know it. For example, if a person comes up with the telephone number in her childhood home when asked what it was, we can say that she still remembers it. But if she is also very uncertain that her memory of the number is correct, it would not be right to say that she *knows* that it was the number.

So why should remembering, as such, be thought of as a way of knowing *the past*, or as a *way of knowing* the past? When the question is put that way, then perhaps the answer is: it should not. But there is a conceptual link between knowledge of the past and remembering that justifies associating the two. A remembered thing must be either something that the rememberer experienced in the past or else something that the rememberer came to know in the past (or both). To say that I remember that $12 \times 12 = 144$, or how to tie a bowline, is to imply that I came to know this in the past. To say that I remember you is to imply that I had some acquaintance with you, or came to know some facts about you, in the past. To say that I remember the bombing of Pearl Harbor is to imply that I witnessed that past event, directly or indirectly. Hence, although remembering a thing is not *ipso facto* to have knowledge of the past, if I *know that I remember* it then I thereby have some knowledge of my past: if the thing I remember is not a past experience of mine then what I know about my past is that I had the experience of coming to know the thing. If I remember experiencing (perceiving, doing) a certain thing, then the remembered experience must be a past experience. The most direct way that I can know my past experience is by remembering it. I cannot know my past experience in the same immediate way as I know my present experience. It is not so obvious where the line between present and past experience comes, though it is obvious that it cannot be a very sharp line. Change is part of present experience. I see the light change from off to on. It is not the case that I know of the change only by remembering seeing the light off while I presently see it on – as it is the case, for example, that my most direct way of knowing of the change from cloudless to completely overcast sky must involve my remembering seeing the sky cloudless while presently seeing it overcast. I see the light turn on as

160

immediately as I see anything. So present experience covers more than an instant. But how much more? All that we can say about this *a priori* is that a particular moment of a subject's experience is no longer part of her present experience when it becomes sensible to say that she remembers it and conceivable that she should have forgotten it. (This puts the duration of present experience I would say, somewhere between one second and one minute.)

For the rest of our discussion we will focus attention on remembering that ... (factual memory) and knowing that ... because one remembers it (factual memory knowledge). It is arguable that memory of facts is the fundamental kind of memory to which remembering how and remembering people, places, objects and events are reducible: to attribute to someone any of these other sorts of remembering is to say that the subject remembers certain sorts of facts about the thing in question (and perhaps also, in the case of people, places or events, that she remembers them from the time of her acquaintance with the thing). But we shall not go into this question here.[2]

We will consider first what it is to remember that ... and then what it is to know that ... because one remembers it.

Factual memory

Remembering a fact can be analysed into three components: (1) a current cognitive attitude of the subject towards the remembered fact, (2) a past experience of the subject relating to the remembered fact, and (3) a connection between (1) and (2) that makes it right to say that the subject remembers the fact from that past experience.

The current cognition

Suppose that, for some proposition p, our subject S came to know that p at some past time. Then it is the case now either that S still remembers that p or that S no longer remembers that p. The difference lies in some state that S now possesses in the first case but lacks in the second case. Normally this state will be a belief or an inclination to believe that p. Such a state is a multi-faceted *disposition* to act or react or experience, in various suitable circumstances, in various ways that manifest belief that p. Acts and reactions manifesting belief may be either mental or overt. Thus I manifest my belief that X's home telephone number is ... when I say to myself 'in my mind' that it is ... just before dialling it, or when I simply dial that number (intending thereby to ring X's home telephone) without any preparatory mental rehearsal. I also manifest it when, after having tried unsuccessfully to recall the number, I have the experience of its 'popping into my head' while I am thinking about other things.

161

The present cognitive state in remembering is normally one of belief or inclination to belief, but it need not always be. If S came to know that p and as a result it now seems to S that she remembers that p, then S does remember that p, even if someone has in the meantime convinced her that it is false that p. I seem to remember that it was here that we turned off to get to X but my companion persuades me that it wasn't. If later my memory impression proves to have been correct, I can correctly claim to have remembered that the turnoff was there. It is also possible for a person to manifest that she remembers the answer to some question by, as she thinks, just guessing at the answer, when it no longer even seems to her that she remembers it or ever knew it.[3] Even if she has no inclination to believe that her answer is correct, it will be right to say that in giving it she shows that she still remembers the correct answer if her giving it is explained by the fact that she previously came to know it. But a disposition to give at least this sort of evidence of still remembering must now be there in the subject if it is to be the case that she does still remember.

Even in cases where the current cognition in remembering is belief, this state need not always manifest itself when it is relevant. It would be too simple to say that a belief that p is the disposition to act as if p were true in all circumstances where the truth of p is relevant to one's choice of action. For one can temporarily fail to think of, forget, the fact that p, even when it is relevant. Not all circumstances where the fact that p is relevant, not all promptings of one's memory with regard to that fact, will succeed in reminding one that p, in making one's belief that p active. What sorts of factors determine what sorts of promptings would succeed in activating a given belief is a question for cognitive psychology.[4] Of course, if no sort of prompting or stimulus would activate a belief that p then one no longer has that belief: one no longer remembers that p. Short of that extreme there are many degrees of remembering, many degrees of lapse in memory, many degrees of ease of access to what one remembers. It seems right to say that for practical purposes one has completely forgotten that p, if one would not be prompted by the direct query 'Is it the case that p?' to think that one does seem to remember (at least dimly) that p and one would not be more inclined to pick p than some contrary proposition when trying to give at least a guess as to the answer to a question whose answer is p. Thus for ordinary purposes it may be right to say that S just no longer remembers that p even if some extraordinary memory therapy or electrical stimulus to the brain would cause S to think that it seems to her that she remembers that p (would indeed cause her to remember that p).

The sort of act or mental event that manifests that S does remember that p need not be an act or experience of remembering that p. There need not happen anything that it would be appropriate to report by saying, 'And then S remembered that p,' using 'remember' in its 'occurrent' rather than its dispositional sense. It would be appropriate to speak of occurrent remembering, for example, in a case where it suddenly occurs to S while driving home that she intended to get groceries on the way home, or in a case where S has been trying to call to mind the name of someone she knows and then succeeds in doing so. And when S is engaged in running over in her mind or recounting what happened in a certain episode in her past experience – for example, what she did in the softball game she played last week – she could be said to be then remembering that episode. Such occurrent remembering may involve mentally imaging, usually visualising, the past experience, but it need not. S might be a poor imager and do such recalling by means of verbal descriptions or other sorts of representations.

An occurrent remembering typically does involve the occurrence of some sort of mental or overt representation of the fact(s) or experience(s) remembered, either in images or in conventional symbols. But, contrary to what some philosophers have thought,[5] it need not always do so. My remembering that I put my glasses in my jacket pocket (climaxing a period of trying to remember where they are) might consist entirely in this: my eye lights on my jacket and I go towards it saying, 'There!' In the context my 'There!' means 'I put my glasses there.' That is what I would say if I were asked what I meant. But from this it does not follow that there occurred a representation of the fact that I put my glasses there. Such a representation would have to include something representing my glasses, something representing my jacket, something representing me, and something representing my action of putting, all suitably related. But no such complex representation has actually occurred, overtly or in my mind.

So the sort of dispositions that can play the role of the present cognitive state in remembering that *p* are a most varied lot. They vary both with respect to the sorts of circumstances in which they would manifest themselves and with respect to the sorts of occurrences that would count as their manifestations.

The past experience

Such a present cognitive state counts as *remembering* that *p* if, and only if, it is connected in the right sort of way to the right sort of past experience of the subject. The right sort of past experience is one that has a suitable relation to the remembered fact, that *p*. There are just two possibilities: (a) the experience was one in which S came to know that *p*; (b) the fact that S had the experience is the fact that *p*: the proposition *p* is of the form 'S V-ed', ascribing to S a certain sort of past experience (action, perception, thought, emotion, etc.).

You might be inclined to think that we do not need to consider (b) separately, that we can do with just (a), S's coming to know that *p*. For, you might think, whenever (b) holds (a) also holds: if 'S V-ed' reports an experience of S's that she now remembers, then S must have

163

known that she was V-ing at the time of the experience: S could not later
remember having the experience of V-ing unless she knew at the time that she
was having it. This is, however, not the case. At the time of her V-ing S
might have lacked concepts or information that it was necessary to possess in
order to know that she was V-ing. For example, a very young child who has
so far acquired very little language might watch with fascination the inflation
and ascension of a huge, colourful hot-air balloon but be unable to understand the proposition that she is seeing the inflation and ascension of a huge,
colourful hot-air balloon and therefore be unable to believe or know that she
sees this. It is compatible with this that she should later, after acquiring
the necessary concepts, remember this past experience and remember *that* she
saw the inflation and ascension of a huge, colourful hot-air balloon. In such a
case her first knowledge that she had this experience would be by remembering that she did.[6]

The memory connection

For S to remember that *p*, it is necessary that S had a past experience suitably
related to the fact that *p* (related to it in at least one of the ways (a) and (b) just
discussed) and it is necessary that S have a present cognition of an appropriate
sort (a belief or inclination to believe or to guess, or a memory impression,
that *p*). But, of course, something further is necessary. The present cognitive
state must be *connected* to the past experience in the right sort of way, in a sort
of way that makes it right to say that S remembers that *p* from that past
experience. Suppose that I have just now been caused to believe that
$13 \times 27 = 351$ by someone's just now telling me that the calculator she holds in
her hand shows that result, and suppose that, were it not for that stimulus, I
would now have no idea what 13×27 equals. Then, even if I did have a past
experience of coming to know that fact, my present, newly acquired belief is
not a remembering of the fact from that or any other past experience and,
therefore, not a remembering of that fact at all.

What is the sort of connection to past experience
needed for remembering? It is a widely accepted hypothesis that a state or
process in the subject's brain makes the connection in all actual cases of remembering: S's past experience produced a state or process in S's brain that has
gone on continuously until the present when it causes (or is an essential factor
in causing) the manifestations by S of her cognition that *p*. But this hypothesis does not give us the account of the memory connection that we seek here.
If true, it is only a contingent truth. But we seek a philosophical account, not
an empirical one. We seek a condition necessary and sufficient for the memory
connection that is so just in virtue of the very concept of memory. We want
an account that could be recognised as correct even by those who are quite
ignorant of the dependence of mental functions on the brain (as some ancient
thinkers were) as long as they have the concept of remembering.

It seems to me that what we all know about the memory connection, just in virtue of having the concept of it, is this: given that S has a present cognition that p and had a past experience suitably related to the fact that p, then the former is the right sort of result of the latter to qualify as S's remembering that p *unless* further special facts about the case defeat that proposition.

The only sort of special fact that could defeat it is that something else – other than the past experience – has occurred in the meantime that is sufficient to cause S's present cognition that p. Suppose that on a certain occasion two weeks ago I figured out that $29^2=841$ and that today I believe that fact. Suppose that you know both of these things about me. Then the only thing that could give you any reason to doubt that I remember that $29^2=841$ from my having calculated it two weeks ago would be your knowing that in the meantime I have figured it out again, or been told it, or been caused to believe it in some other way not derived from my previous learning of it. In general, given that S had the experience of coming to know that p (or had the experience attributed to her by p) and then later has a cognition that p, then only two alternatives are possible: either S remembers that p from the past experience or S's present cognition that p has its origin in some other intervening cause.

There is not a third alternative: that neither the past experience nor anything intervening is responsible for the present cognition and it is just coincidence that the content of the present cognition matches that of the past experience. This is not because it is inconceivable that any cognitive state should lack a cause. It is rather that our concept of remembering does not recognise any basis for denying that S's present cognition is a memory of her matching earlier experience, when there was one, except the fact that S would not have had the present cognition had not something else happened in the meantime that was sufficient to cause it. It is always out of order to say *both* that it is a coincidence that the present cognition matches the earlier experience *and* that the present cognition has no other cause. Given the matching past experience, the assertion of coincidence can be supported only by evidence of another, independent cause.

So the absence of any other explanation is by itself *sufficient* to connect the present cognition to the matching past experience in the sort of way that makes the former memory of the latter. It is, however, not necessary. I remember that I once lost control of a car on a snowy road and it spun around and skidded into the ditch. I remember it from the experience itself. In the meantime, however, I have heard other occupants of the car recount the incident in vivid detail and this latter experience would have been sufficient to cause me now to remember everything about the incident that I do even if before hearing their accounts I had completely lost my memory of the incident. What in this case is sufficient to guarantee that I nevertheless remember the experience from the experience itself? As far as I can see, it can be only this: at each time when I heard accounts sufficient to give me my present memory of the experience I then already had a memory of it: I had a cognition that I had such an experience. Had I completely lost all memory of the experience before I heard others' accounts of it, then clearly there would be no basis for saying that my present memory is from, or of, the experience itself. It would be enough to show that I did already have a memory of it if it seemed to me that I remembered it as soon as I was told about it, if the telling *reminded* me of it – I could honestly have said, 'Ah yes, I remember that' – even if a less informative prompting ('Have you ever had any scary experiences with a car?') would have failed to produce such a reaction.

Should we say, then, that S's present impression that *p* is S's remembering that *p* from a particular matching past experience if and only if throughout the intervening time S has had a suitable cognition that *p*? No. The 'if' is all right, but not the 'only if'. For it is possible, in temporary amnesia, for example, completely to lose one's memory of something for a time and then regain it, when nothing external has impinged on one in the meantime to cause one to have the requisite cognition. What we should say is this:

Given that S has a cognition that *p* and had a past matching experience (either an experience of coming to know that *p* or an experience of a sort that *p* says S had), then the former is memory-connected to the latter if, and only if, for any time since the past experience at which something impinged on S sufficient to produce in S a cognition that *p*, S then already had a cognition that *p*.

On this account of it, the memory connection does *not* entail that the causal connection between the past experience and the present cognition is *continuous*. The condition just stated could, conceivably, be satisfied even when there is no intervening continuous chain of states or events serving as the process by which the past experience causes the present cognition. On this account, we have in our concept of memory a concept of a causal connection that could, in principle, cross spatiotemporal gaps.[7] This is an interesting, even a remarkable, consequence.

Some philosophers would say that it renders the account unacceptable. C.B. Martin and Max Deutscher have written:

Once we accept the causal model for memory we must also accept the existence of some sort of trace, or structural analogue of what was experienced. Even if someone could overcome the many difficulties of various kinds surrounding the idea of action at a distance, it could not be true to say that someone was remembering an event if his past experience of that event caused him, over a temporal gap, to recount it.[8]

I am uncertain what difficulties surrounding the idea of action at a distance

Martin and Deutscher have in mind here. Perhaps one of them is that it would be hard to accommodate spatial or temporal parameters in *general laws* governing a causal connection that could cross spatiotemporal gaps of various and haphazardly determined sizes. But this difficulty arises only on the assumption that any sort of causal connection requires that there be causal laws under which its instances are subsumed, that only a law can make a causal connection. But it seems that in the concept of memory we have a counter-example to this assumption. I remember skidding out of control on a snowy road. If I were to deny that any causal laws, about brain processes or anything else, connect my past experience and my present memory impression that I had such an experience, I would go against currently well-supported theory about memory, but I would not say something logically inconsistent with my claim to remember that experience.

Martin and Deutscher go on to say:

> Furthermore, if our past experience could act directly on us now, there would no longer be any reason to suppose that we could remember only what we had experienced ourselves. If we did not hold [some sort of storage or trace account of memory], why should we not suppose that events which occurred years before we were born could cause us to recount their occurrence?

Well, why not? Is it so clear that interpersonal memory connection is not a logical possibility? In any case, one is not saved from having to admit this possibility by holding that the memory connection must be continuous. As Sydney Shoemaker has pointed out, if there is a continuous neurological connection on which memory always depends, one could imagine that this neurological process (or something essentially similar) runs from R's brain to that of another person S, connecting impressions that S has with R's earlier experience in essentially the same way that S's remembering is connected to S's own earlier experience.[9] And one might want to say in such a case, if not that S *remembers* R's experiences from the experiences themselves, at least that S does something very like this (Shoemaker uses the term 'quasi-remembers').[10]

Memory knowledge

We now have an account of what it is for a person to remember a fact. In what sort of case is remembering a fact a way of knowing it? Given that S remembers that *p*, under what further conditions does S also *know* that *p* *because* she remembers it? (Some may quibble over the suggestion that 'S knows that *p* because she remembers it' tells us how S knows that *p*. This statement, they may say, tells us nothing of how S came by the knowledge that *p*, but only that, having acquired it in some way or other, S has *retained* it. Yes, but the fact that she has retained it in memory is nevertheless a crucial

167

part of how it is that she now knows that *p*. And there are those cases, noted earlier, where S's first knowledge that *p* is memory knowledge.)

One might suppose that all we need to add to S's remembering that *p* is that the present cognition involved in S's remembering is a confident belief that *p*: S knows that *p* because S remembers that *p* if, and only if, S has a confident belief that *p* that is memory-connected to a past experience either of coming to know that *p* or of a sort that *p* says S had. But in fact more is needed.

If S now knows that *p* then it must be the case that S has justification for claiming to know that *p*. And a person (who has the concepts of justification and knowledge) should be able in principle to tell, with respect to any proposition she understands, whether or not she is now justified in claiming to know that proposition to be true.[11] This could be so only if the facts that determine whether or not she is then justified are all then immediately accessible to her. But the condition given above does not guarantee that a justification for claiming to know that *p* is immediately accessible to S.

It is obvious that, for many a proposition, including many a one attributing a certain sort of past experience to S, it is possible that S should confidently believe that proposition while having no justification for doing so. People are capable of holding completely unsupported beliefs. It is almost as obvious that S's belief that *p* could be unjustified even in the circumstance that the belief is memory connected to S's having come to know the believed fact in the past. For S may have no inkling that she formerly came to know it. S now believes that the person in the photograph she is looking at was her great-grandmother and this belief is memory-connected to her experience some time ago of learning this fact from an authoritative source. But S now has no recollection that she ever did come to know that fact. It does not seem to her that she remembers it but rather that she has just now decided to believe it on no evidence at all or on a merely impressionistic basis. Then S lacks memory justification for believing or claiming to know it (justification that S could claim by saying, 'I know that ... because I remember it'), and, unless she has access to some other justification, she no more knows this fact now than if her belief had been produced by a hypnotist (who knew its truth). In order to know that *p* because she remembers it, it must seem to S that she remembers definitely that *p*: she must have a *strong memory impression* that *p*. This is an independent requirement, for a strong memory impression that *p* does not entail belief that *p*. It might still seem to me that I definitely remember that this was the turnoff even while I am being persuaded otherwise.

A strong memory impression, however, is not the only additional condition that is needed for memory knowledge. Suppose that, besides having both a confident belief and strong memory impression that *p* that are memory-connected to a past experience of coming to know that p, S also has some good reason to think that p is false. For example, S learned from last night's newscast the fact that her school's team won yesterday's basketball game and continues loyally to believe this even after hearing a later newscast say that the opposing team won. Then, clearly, though it may be right to say that S (still) remembers that her team won, it is certainly not right to say that S now (still) *knows* that her team won.

The attribution of knowledge is defeated by the fact that there is contrary evidence in S's ken. S knows that p only if her confident belief that p is justified in light of all of her immediately accessible memory and perceptual impressions.[12] A conflict with these other impressions can render S's belief that p unjustified even when she has a strong memory impression that p. The sorts of thing that count as conflict here are many and varied. We just saw one example. A rather different (and more fanciful) example would occur if a few minutes ago what I seemed to perceive had suddenly changed from my desk in my study to a canoe on a mountain lake, so that I now seem to remember sitting in a canoe on a lake for the last few minutes and immediately before that, without any intervening experience, sitting at my study desk, and nothing else I seem to remember provides any basis for explaining how I could now be sitting in a canoe on a mountain lake. Here there is conflict between my memory impressions regarding the very recent past and all the others, and that conflict is reason for me to doubt the deliverances of at least one of those sets of impressions. It would be easy to think of other sorts of examples. But it would not be easy to give a general account of what counts as the relevant sort of conflict and we will not attempt it here.

By itself, a conflict with other memory or perceptual impressions is not enough to make one unjustified in believing what one seems to remember. Suppose I seem to remember that a few minutes ago I saw the dogwood tree still standing in our back yard. But suppose I also seem to remember cutting it down yesterday. Since these impressions conflict I cannot be justified in believing the deliverances of both. But I may be justified in believing the first, despite its conflict with the second, if there is much else in my memory or perception that supports the first but nothing else that supports the second: I seem to see and feel the tree now and to remember other family members commenting just now on how lovely its blossoms are. (My memory of cutting the tree down could have originated in a dream.) It seems that believing that p fails to be justified, despite seeming to remember definitely that p, if and only if the largest part of what one seems to remember that has no conflict within itself or with what one seems to perceive does conflict with the proposition that p (provided that this largest coherent part is a substantially major part).

If we add what we have now seen to be needed to the too simple condition contemplated earlier, we arrive at the following definition of memory knowledge:

S knows that *p* because she remembers it if, and only if,

(1) S has a confident belief that *p*,
(2) it seems to S that she remembers definitely that *p*,
(3) this impression is part of the coherent majority of S's currently accessible memory impressions, and
(4) this impression is memory-connected either (a) to a past experience of coming to know that *p* or (b) to a past experience of a sort that *p* says S had.

Cases of S's knowing that *p* by remembering it where (4)(a) is true – cases where her present belief that *p* is memory-connected to a past experience of coming to know that *p* – we may call cases of *retained knowledge*. We noted earlier that there are cases where a person's first knowledge that she has had experience of a certain sort is by remembering it. These will be cases of remembering that *p* where (4)(b) is true but (4)(a) is not. For there will have been the experience ascribed by *p* and the later knowledge of it but no experience of coming to know that *p*. We may call these cases of *original memory knowledge*.

There are cases of original memory knowledge that are interestingly different from the sort described earlier (p. 164). Consider, for example, my knowledge that I have not seen anyone enter my study since I came into it myself a while ago. At each moment since shortly after I came into my study I have known a fact that I could at the time have expressed in those same words. At every different moment it would have been a different fact that I could have then so expressed, because 'since I came into it' would cover a different period. Each of those facts is one that I knew *only* by remembering it. It would be most implausible to suggest that I knew it by having come to know at each moment of the relevant period that I was not then seeing anyone enter my study and then later inferring to the generalisation from my retained knowledge of all of those many facts. One might suggest that I know that I have not seen anyone enter since I came in not by simply remembering that fact, but by inference from the facts that I do not remember seeing anyone enter and that I would remember seeing this had I done so. That is indeed one way of knowing such a thing. But it seems clear that one can also know it by simply remembering it. It is not merely that I do not remember seeing anyone enter but rather that I remember that I have not seen anyone enter, and I may rightly claim to know this because I remember it even if I am doubtful whether I would remember seeing anyone enter had I done so.

It is not only negative generalisations about a period of one's past experience of which one can have original memory knowledge. Positive generalisations are knowable in this way too. I believe that my very first knowledge of the fact that I have eaten pickled beets on numerous occasions in my life must have been by simply remembering that fact, and not by inference from memories of numerous distinct occasions on which I had that experience (in fact I could not remember any particular occasion) or from the testimony of another person.

Original memory knowledge of one's past experience, particularly of generalisations about it, may be very important, especially in the early stages of acquiring knowledge of the world. A child's first knowledge that objects that look or feel or sound certain ways have certain other (unperceived) properties (for example, steaming things are hot) may be by remembering.

The principle of justification, for belief and for knowledge claims, that is implied by our definition of memory knowledge, the principle of memory justification, is this:

(M) If it seems to S that she remembers definitely that *p* and this impression is part of the coherent majority of S's memory impressions, then S is justified in believing and claiming to know that *p*.

According to (M), we are justified in believing the deliverances of all of our strong memory impressions that are part of the coherent majority of our memory impressions.

Note that the condition (M) says is sufficient to give S justification does not require S to *infer* that *p*. In particular, it does not require S to infer it from the presence of that condition plus the premiss that (M). It does not imply that S has the justification because S infers that *p* from the fact that she has the memory impression and it belongs to the coherent majority. Rather, according to (M), it is just that fact itself that justifies S, whether or not S makes an inference from it. If (M) is right, memory justification is *non-inferential* justification. This is so even if the way S originally came to know that *p* was by inference. Suppose I originally came to know that $12 \times 12 = 144$ by calculating it out. Even if I no longer remember the calculation, or even whether or not it was by calculation that I learned it, I may still know it just because I remember it, just because I remember that I did come to know it. What is now immediately accessible to me, to give me justification for belief and for thinking I know, is not the original inferential justification, which I have not retained, but just my current memory impression and its place in the coherent majority of my current impressions.

Would it be right to say that, according to (M), memory *knowledge* is non-inferential knowledge? It would, if all that one meant was that the justification for claiming to know that *p* because one remembers it is non-inferential. But one might naturally be taken to mean something more: that no inferential justification for belief that *p* ever contributed to its being the case that one knows that *p*. And that will be false in many cases of memory knowledge. My originally having had inferential justification for believing that $12 \times 12 = 144$ is an essential part of what gives me my current knowledge of that fact. My current impression and belief are memory knowledge only because they are memory-connected to that past experience of coming to know that $12 \times 12 = 144$ by inference.

Why trust memory?

It is clear that we all do accept principle (M). We all do feel entitled to confident belief, and to claim to know because we remember, when and because we are in the circumstance that (M) says gives us such entitlement; we would think it appropriate to cite that circumstance (our memory impression and the absence of contrary evidence) if pressed to say what makes us entitled. But why do we accept (M)? Or rather, why should we? What justification does (M) itself have?

      We are justified in accepting (M) if and only if we are justified in accepting that

(M*) all of the beliefs that would be justified by (M), or almost all of them, would be true: the condition (M) lays down as justifying beliefs strongly correlates with truth of the beliefs.

We are justified in thinking our current memory *trustworthy* if and only if we are justified in thinking it *reliable*. Note that this does not imply that current memory *is* trustworthy only if it *is* reliable, which, as we shall see, is false.

      It is true, however, that if current memory is trustworthy – (M) is a correct principle of justification – then we are justified in believing current memory to be reliable – in believing (M*). (M) entails that I am always justified in believing true the deliverance of each of the coherent majority of my current memory impressions. This could scarcely be the case if I were not also justified in believing that all (or nearly all) such deliverances are true, that current memory is reliable. Those deliverances themselves, since they cohere, could not provide any reason to doubt this, and what other sort of reason could I have? This is as it should be. The correct principles of justification should validate themselves in this way. They should be such as to justify believing that what they justify believing reliably correlates with truth. No set of justification principles could be the right set if it could defeat itself by permitting a faithful follower justifiably to believe that their justifications in her present case do not reliably correlate with truth or that she lacks good reason to think they do.

      But the justification for believing (M*) we here seek cannot appeal in this way to (M) as given. We want a justification for believing (M*) that also gives us justification for accepting (M). How can we have such a justification? Empirically? By accumulating evidence that the coherent majority of a person's strong memory impressions never or seldom misleads to any significant extent? Undoubtedly we have a great deal of such evidence. But this can give us only a question-begging justification for accepting (M*) and (M). For as long as (M*) and (M) are in question it is also in question whether we are justified in our (memory) beliefs that we have empirical evidence for (M*). To take it that we have accumulated evidence of the reliability of memory is already to trust memory.

It is indeed the case that if memory is not trustworthy – (M) is false – then one can have no, or scarcely any, justified beliefs. Memory justification will be fundamental in any interestingly rich structure of knowledge or justified belief. If one is justified in believing much of anything then one is justified in believing one's memory to be reliable. This is an important observation and one might be inclined to think that it justifies our trust in memory. But actually it does not provide a good argument for the reliability and trustworthiness of memory. The other premiss that the argument would require is that one does in fact have a rich structure of justified belief. But anyone inclined to question (M) will also be inclined to question that premiss. If we have to assume that, then we might as well assume (M).

Could (M*) be demonstrated *a priori* as a logically or conceptually necessary truth? No, because (M*) is not a necessary truth. There are possible worlds where it is false. In a famous passage, Russell says:

> It is not logically necessary to the existence of a memory-belief that ... the past should have existed at all. There is no logical impossibility in the hypothesis that the world sprang into existence five minutes ago, exactly as it then was, with a population that 'remembered' a wholly unreal past. There is no logically necessary connection between events at different times; therefore nothing that is happening now or will happen in the future can disprove the hypothesis that the world began five minutes ago. [13]

We need not imagine a world so different from ours as Russell does in order to imagine one where (M*) is false. Consider a world that began when ours did and is otherwise much like ours except that in it there is created a person who, from her beginning, has adult human form and competence and a rich store of memories of a non-existent past. During the early part of this person's existence, (M*) would be false of her. Her memory impressions would be a very unreliable guide to the facts, especially about her past. Given (M), the trustworthiness of current memory, she herself could have no good reason to suspect this, at least for quite a while, until such time as the coherent majority of her current memory impressions support that conclusion about her early life. But others could know it at her beginning. (Russell intended his imagined world to be such that no one ever has any reason to believe of herself or anyone (the truth) that (M*) is, or was, false of them.)

Some philosophers have maintained that (M*) (or something close to it) is conceptually necessary. Norman Malcolm has argued [14] that a person's ability to express beliefs or make assertions about the past (which ability is entailed by the person's having memory beliefs or memory impressions) entails that the statements the person makes about the past are mainly true. Sydney Shoemaker has argued in a similar way[15] that it is necessary that a person's memory beliefs are generally true and that his sincere memory statements are generally true. There is a sound and important idea behind their arguments, but it does not support the conclusion that (M*) is a necessary truth.

This sound idea is this: an acceptable scheme for interpreting a person's linguistic acts – a scheme for determining what any of them means – must yield the result that a significant part (not necessarily most) of those interpreted as expressing assertions must express true assertions. For it is clear that only if that is so is there any basis for saying that the interpretation is correct, for construing the person as intending in those acts to make those statements. This idea can be generalised to a condition on any scheme for interpreting a person's mental and bodily behaviour that purports to determine which of the person's acts express propositions and what those propositions are. Any such scheme is acceptable only if it yields the result that a significant part of the propositions that, over her lifetime, the person expresses, or is disposed to express, are true. That result must be included in any set of facts that is to give us reason for judging the scheme of interpretation to be correct.

This is very vague – we have not said how big a part is a significant part or which sorts of parts (such as expressions of assent to the propositions in question) may be more significant than others – but it gives enough of the idea to enable us to see that, whatever more precise working out of the principle is correct, it can be satisfied by a person of whom (M*) is false, of whom it is false that most of the coherent majority of her current memory impressions deliver truths. The specially created person we imagined a few paragraphs back had at her beginning, according to our hypothesis, a full range of memory beliefs about her past life, and, we supposed, these beliefs cohered with everything else she currently seemed to remember and to perceive. Yet, by our hypothesis, none of these memory beliefs were true, for at that time she had no past life at all. How then could any of her acts near her beginning express beliefs about the past? What could show that she intended some of those acts to refer to the past, or that utterances she was disposed to make would have been so intended? Imagine that the utterances she made or was disposed to make were ostensibly in English. What would show that they actually were in English and that those that referred to the past when interpreted as English were so intended? Well, there could be much else that she utters or is disposed to utter at her beginning that, when interpreted as English, expresses truths – say, general truths about how the world works or necessary truths of mathematics. And after she accumulates some past experience, the ostensibly English utterances she makes then might, interpreted as English, express true memory beliefs about it; if so, this would be evidence supporting our hypothesis as to how she meant her earliest utterances. It is clear, I think, that there could be all that is needed, in the way of truth in a significant part of the beliefs our interpretation attributes to her, to confirm our interpretation. (Other sorts of facts could help to confirm the interpretation, such as the fact that her behaviour is rational given the beliefs and desires the interpretation attributes to her.) Yet, if you had said of her at her beginning that, of the memory impressions she then had, nearly all that are in the coherent majority are true, you would have been wrong: she was then a counter-example to (M*).

So no reason for saying that (M*) is a necessary truth is to be found along those lines. Nor can I see any other prospects for a successful argument to that conclusion.

But if (M*) is neither a necessary truth nor one for which we can muster empirical evidence without begging the question, how can (M) be justified? How can we be entitled to be guided by that principle in forming our beliefs and regarding them as justified? How can it be rational to trust memory? The only remaining answer I see (short of giving up and saying that (M) is not rationally acceptable) is to say that it is self-evident that memory is to be trusted. We take current memory to be reliable because we would find it virtually impossible not to do so. (M*) has a compelling appeal. No contrary hypothesis, such as that one has just been created with a rich store of largely false memory beliefs, is even in the running, practically, outside the philosopher's study, when it comes to what we rely on in our everyday cognitive conduct. Our relying on (M*), as far as I can see, has no further, deeper rationale: we just trust memory and we have no more ultimate principle that provides our reason for doing so. Our reasons for liking what we like, in matters of belief as in other matters, have to end somewhere.

Some philosophers – for example Richard Brandt – suggest that what makes (M*) acceptable is that it offers the best explanation of our memory impressions being what they are: there is no explanation for our seeming to remember what we do that is as good as the explanation that we do remember it (at least the major coherent part of it).[16] This claim is impossible to assess without some criteria for what makes one explanation better than another. I suspect that any reasonable looking criteria that yield this claim will appeal to the prior acceptability of the trustworthiness and reliability of memory, either in order to back the claim that the explanation is better supported by evidence than its rivals or by saying in effect that what makes it better is that it preserves the reliability of memory (a feature that is indeed very desirable). But the deeper problem with this suggestion is that we have been given no reason for thinking that, even if there are plausible criteria by which some contrary, logically coherent hypothesis explains our memory impressions as well as the hypothesis that memory is reliable, this would make us unjustified in preferring the latter hypothesis. There is

175

lacking any persuasive argument that the trustworthiness of memory *depends* on whether or not its reliability is the best explanation of our memory impressions in some sense of 'best explanation' that is independent of the trustworthiness of memory.

If we must point to something that justifies our accepting the proposition that memory is reliable, let us just point to the compelling and brute appeal of this proposition. To refrain generally from believing the deliverances of the coherent majority of one's strong memory impressions would be too intolerably frustrating to be borne and impossible in practice. To refrain even once would be no mean feat. This is our nature, for which we are not responsible and which we can do nothing about. One needs a very strong motive to resist the inclination to believe what one seems to remember definitely is so. We find such a motive in conflicting deliverance from other memory impressions, but we do not find it in the mere logical possibility that all of our coherent memory impressions are false. That moves us not at all. Why should it? We trust memory. If asked why we should, we should answer: why not?[17]

Notes

(An author's name followed by a number in square brackets refers to the book or article which has that number in the bibliography.)

1. This claim is not intended to cover cases of ellipsis, as in: 'What battles did you learn about today?' 'Let me think ... I remember [that we learned about] the Battle of Trafalgar.'

2. For a discussion of this question see Ginet [2], pp. 6–9.

3. As Colin Radford has pointed out, in 'Knowledge – by examples', *Analysis*, vol. 27 (1966), pp. 1–11.

4. For a philosopher's discussion of some of these factors, and of the relevance to inferential justification of belief of the fact that one does not always actively remember what one knows when it is relevant, see Goldman [6], pp. 199–226.

5. See, for example, Martin and Deutscher [12], pp. 161–96.

6. Norman Malcolm suggests that remembering *p* is knowing that *p* because one previously knew that *p* (Malcolm [9], pp. 187–240). This is an appealingly neat analysis, but we have now seen that it is too simple, with respect to both the present and the past states involved in remembering.

7. Bertrand Russell took this possibility seriously and dubbed causal connection with this feature 'mnemic causation' (Russell [5], pp. 157–87).

8. Martin and Deutscher [12], pp. 161–96.

9. Shoemaker [16], pp. 269–85.

10. Shoemaker (ibid.) argues in a different way for the necessity of continuity in the memory connection. He takes it that the memory connection does not presuppose the identity of the persons connected but can be the main element in an informative criterion for the identity of a later with an earlier person. He tries, I believe unsuccessfully, to show that a satisfactory memory criterion of personal identity must take the

memory connection to be continuous. For discussion of his argument see Ginet [2], pp. 169–71.

11. Some 'causal theories of knowledge' that have been put forward conflict with the intuitions expressed in these last two sentences. On some of these theories, a belief is knowledge if it is caused in the right sort of way by the fact believed, whether or not the belief is justified at the time; see, e.g., Goldman [13], pp. 355–72. On some, a belief is justified if it has been caused by a sort of process that reliably produces true beliefs, whether or not any justifying condition is immediately accessible to the believer; see, e.g., Alvin Goldman, 'What is justified belief?' in G. Pappas (ed.), *Justification and knowledge* (Reidel, Dordrecht, 1979), pp. 1–23.

12. The term 'immediately accessible' deserves more explanation than I can give it here. Things that clearly are immediately accessible to S include those of her beliefs that are currently active ('in mind') and also those that would easily come to mind were she to ask herself what she knows that is relevant. Things that clearly are *not* immediately accessible are beliefs or memory impressions that would be brought to mind only by a great deal of rumination or extraordinary prompting. The divide within the immediately accessible between the active and the inactive is important. We find it worth while sometimes to note that a person's belief was justified relative to what she thought of at the time even though it was not justified relative to all that she then knew and should have taken account of. For then the person is innocent of a kind of blatant fault in rationality that she would have been guilty of had her belief failed to be justified even relative to what she had in mind at the time. She is guilty instead only of a kind of negligence or irresponsibility in forming her beliefs.

13. Russell [5], pp. 159–60.

14. Malcolm [9], pp. 195–8.

15. Shoemaker [14], pp. 201, 230, 235.

16. Brandt, 'The epistemological status of memory beliefs', *Philosophical Review*, vol. 64 (1955), pp. 78–95.

17. Parts of this chapter are adapted from material in Ginet [2], Chs. 7 and 8.

Bibliography

A good introduction to the philosophical problems of memory and the past is

[1] D. Locke, *Memory* (Macmillan, London, 1971).

For further reading on the topics raised in the chapter, the reader should turn to

[2] C. Ginet, *Knowledge, perception, and memory* (Reidel, Dordrecht, 1975).

The chapters on memory in the following four books are also particularly useful:

[3] A.J. Ayer, *The problem of knowledge* (Penguin Books, Harmondsworth, 1956)

[4] D.J. O'Connor and B. Carr, *Introduction to the theory of knowledge* (University of Minnesota Press, Minneapolis, 1982)

[5] B. Russell, *The analysis of mind* (Macmillan, London, 1921) and

[6] A. Goldman, *Epistemology and cognition* (Harvard University Press, Cambridge, Massachusetts, 1986), Ch. 9, 'Memory'.

One of the greatest influences on recent discussions of philosophy of mind has been Ludwig Wittgenstein. His best known work is

[7] L. Wittgenstein, *Philosophical investigations* (Basil Blackwell, Oxford, 1953). It is Wittgenstein's whole approach which has been influential, but he does discuss

memory and the past in the course of his so-called 'Private language argument', §§ 241–304, and, particularly, §§ 258–272.

For illuminating comments on Wittgenstein's treatment of memory, see

[8] J. Bennett, *Kant's analytic* (Cambridge University Press, Cambridge, 1966), Ch. 14, pp. 204–14.

Two writers deeply influenced by Wittgenstein who have written on the subject are Norman Malcolm and Elizabeth Anscombe. The first Malcolm reference contains an interesting discussion of Bertrand Russell's hypothesis that the world might have been created five minutes ago.

[9] N. Malcolm, *Knowledge and certainty* (Prentice-Hall, Englewood Cliffs, 1963), which includes Malcolm's 'Three lectures on memory'.

[10] N. Malcolm, *Memory and mind* (Cornell University Press, New York, 1977)

Miss Elizabeth Anscombe's subtle article, 'Memory and the concept of the past', is to be found in

[11] M. Black (ed.), *Philosophical analysis* (Cornell University Press, Ithaca, New York, 1950).

The idea that memory is essentially a causal concept is expounded by

[12] C.B. Martin and M. Deutscher in 'Remembering', *Philosophical Review*, vol. 75 (1966). The idea is further discussed in

[13] A. Goldman, 'A causal theory of knowing', *The Journal of Philosophy*, vol. 64 (1967).

Sydney Shoemaker's interesting and important views on memory and personal identity have been modified over the years. They are to be found in

[14] S. Shoemaker, *Self-knowledge and self-identity* (Cornell University Press, New York, 1963)

[15] P. Edwards (ed.), *The encyclopaedia of philosophy* (Macmillan, London, 1967), vol. V, entry for 'Memory'

[16] 'Persons and their pasts', *American Philosophical Quarterly*, vol. 7 (1970), and

[17] S. Shoemaker, *Identity, cause, and mind* (Cambridge University Press, Cambridge, 1984).

What would it be like not to have memory? Some notion might be gained from the (apparently) true amnesiac case discussed by the neurologist O. Sacks in his fascinating book

[18] O. Sacks, *The man who mistook his wife for a hat* (Duckworth, London, 1985), which also contains much other fascinating material for philosophers to ponder upon.

This bibliography has been prepared with the assistance of the author of the chapter, Professor Carl Ginet.

M.A.P.

9 | Induction and Probability[1]

Donald A. Gillies

Historical background to the problem

The notion of induction goes back to Aristotle. Induction, or inductive inference, is supposed to be a process whereby knowledge of generalisations or predictions is obtained from observational data (the results of observations or experiments). To take the philosophers' standard example, from the observation of a large number of black ravens, it is sometimes claimed that we can infer by induction, or inductively, either the generalisation that all ravens are black or the prediction that the next raven we meet will be black. Some philosophers, notably Popper, have maintained that induction is a myth, but the majority do allow that there is such a process.

While the concept of induction goes back to ancient Greek times, the idea of linking induction with probability (in the mathematical sense) is comparatively modern. It appears first in the second half of the eighteenth century, and emerges quite naturally from some intellectual developments of the preceding hundred or so years. The first of these developments was the appearance of the mathematical calculus of probability – a branch of mathematics unknown to the ancient world. The calculus of probability traditionally, and with some justice, is said to originate in a correspondence in the year 1654 between Fermat and Pascal, about a dicing problem, which had been posed to Pascal by the aristocratic gambler, M. le Chevalier de Méré.[2] The new field of probability attracted many Western European mathematicians during the next hundred years, and, by 1756, when the third edition of De Moivre's *Doctrine of chances* was published, a considerable body of mathematical theory about probability had come into existence.

The same period (*c.* 1650–*c.* 1750) saw the creation and triumph of Newtonian physics. Newton himself did not contribute significantly to probability, but he did claim that his mathematical science had been inferred inductively from observation. Indeed Rule IV of his rules of reasoning runs as follows:

> In experimental philosophy we are to look upon propositions inferred by general induction from phenomena as accurately or very nearly true, notwithstanding any contrary hypotheses that may be imagined, till such time as other phenomena occur, by which they may either be made more accurate, or liable to exceptions.[3]

Newton adds, as a comment: 'This rule we must follow, that the argument of induction may not be evaded by hypotheses.'[4]

Newtonian physics was accepted as correct by the mathematical and scientific community, but its foundations were subjected to criticism by philosophers of the British empiricist school. Berkeley attacked the calculus, while, more seriously still, Hume's problem of induction cast doubt on the validity of the inductive inferences which were supposed to underpin Newton's system. Hume's essential point is simple, and now very familiar. It can be put like this. No matter how many black ravens we see, we can never deduce logically from this observational data either that all ravens are black, or even that the next raven we meet will be black. It always remains logically possible that the very next raven we see will be white, or green, or some curious combination of colours. Indeed just such an experience befell Captain Cook. Before his voyage to Australia, every swan observed by a European had been white. Yet, so the story goes, Captain Cook saw a black swan swimming in Botany Bay. Hume concluded from his argument that inductive inferences could not be given a rational foundation, and were based on some kind of animal instinct.

Hume's views became increasingly well known following the publication in 1748 of his *Enquiry concerning human understanding*, and they raised an awkward problem for the scientific and mathematical community. If Hume were right, then the admired edifice of Newtonian science rested on a foundation no stronger than animal instinct. However, one of the latest developments in mathematics itself appeared to offer a way out of the difficulty. Could not the new mathematical calculus of probability be used to explicate inductive inference, and provide a rational answer to Hume's scepticism about induction? On this approach it would not be possible to say that finite evidence rendered a generalisation or prediction *certain*, but finite evidence might, nonetheless, make such things *probable*. Moreover this probability might increase, with increasing evidence, according to the rules of the mathematical calculus of probability.

The first attempt to deal with induction in this way was made by two British Nonconformist clergymen: Thomas Bayes (1702–61) and Richard Price (1723–91). Bayes was reluctant to publish his results during his lifetime, and they were communicated in 1763, after his death, to the Royal Society by his friend Price. The view that inductive inference can be explicated by means of the mathematical theory of probability is accordingly known as *Bayesianism*. The contribution of Price should not be forgotten, however. He wrote an introductory letter, and an appendix to Bayes' paper; and, while Bayes supplied most of the mathematical results, Price discusses the general philosophical issues concerned with induction. As Hacking says: 'The inductive reasoning that Price had in mind was intended as a deliberate and conscious response to Hume.'[5] Bayesianism was subsequently taken up and developed in France – particularly by Laplace – and Bayesianism has indeed remained a powerful current within probability theory right down to the present day. I will next try to formulate the Bayesian and anti-Bayesian positions in more modern terms.

Both sides in the controversy can agree that, in science and everyday life, we use the notion of evidence (e) *confirming* or *corroborating* a hypothesis (h) or a prediction (a). We shall use the term 'confirmation' and 'corroboration' as synonyms, and write the degree of confirmation (or corroboration) of h given e as $C(h, e)$. Strictly speaking, the evidence e will be in addition to some background knowledge b. So we ought really to write $C(h, e \& b)$. b will sometimes be omitted for ease of writing, but it should not be forgotten. Now, as Hume says: 'A wise man ... proportions his belief to the evidence.'[6] We can thus assume that $C(h, e \& b)$ represents the degree to which it is reasonable to believe in h for a man who has evidence e and background knowledge b. Of course we are not here assuming that $C(h, e \& b)$ is exactly measurable, or that all 'rational' men would produce similar estimates as to its value.

The Bayesian thesis can now be formulated as the claim that $C(h, e)$ satisfies the standard axiom of the mathematical calculus of probability, or that, in symbols:

$$C(h, e) = P(h, e) \tag{1}$$

The view can, equivalently, be formulated as the claim that confirmation is a probability function.

Many confusions have arisen from conflating confirmation (or corroboration) on the one hand with *support* on the other. The difference is this. $C(h, e \& b)$ stands for the total confirmation given to h by both e and b. Degree of support $S(h, e, b)$ is a 3-place function,[7] and represents the contribution made to the total confirmation by the individual item of evidence e against a background b. From the way we have defined support, it is clear that it should have the following additive property:

$$S(h, e_1 \& e_2, b) = S(h, e_1, e_2 \& b) + S(h, e_2, b) \tag{2}$$

It also seems to me that the following holds:

181

$$C(h, e \& b) = S(h, e, b) + C(h, b) \tag{3}$$

For a Bayesian, we have from (1) and (3) that

$$S(h, e, b) = P(h, e \& b) - P(h, b) \tag{4}$$

$P(h, b)$ is known as the *prior probability* – prior that is to acquiring the evidence e, but still conditional on some background knowledge b. $P(h, e \& b)$ is known as the *posterior probability*. The effect of evidence, e, for a Bayesian is to change the initial belief represented by the prior probability $P(h, b)$ to a new belief represented by the posterior probability $P(h, e \& b)$. This change from prior to posterior probability is known as *Bayesian conditionalisation*, since the prior probability $P(h, b)$ is conditionalised by the evidence e to yield the posterior probability $P(h, e \& b)$. Bayesian conditionalisation is a procedure of crucial importance for the Bayesians, and it will be discussed in more detail later (pp. 190ff).

Having formulated the main features of Bayesianism, let us next examine its plausibility. At first Bayesianism may seem obviously true, since, in ordinary language, confirmation and probability are used almost as synonyms: 'e renders h probable' seems to mean virtually the same as 'e confirms h'. But the Bayesian thesis of equation (1), i.e. $C(h, e) = P(h, e)$, contains claims of too substantial a character to be established by an appeal to ordinary language, for, in equation (1), probability is not meant in the vague sense of ordinary language, but in the precise sense of the mathematical calculus of probability. Moreover it is far from clear that the notion of confirmation as used in science or ordinary life satisfies the usual axioms of probability. After all, mathematical probability was developed from the study of games of chance and other random phenomena. Why should it be the appropriate instrument for weighing evidence? Bayesianism can thus be seen as a research programme – the programme of attempting to explicate confirmation using the mathematical calculus of probability.

My own sympathies are with the anti-Bayesian position, and, for the rest of this chapter, I shall indicate some of the ways in which Bayesianism has been developed by philosophers of science in the twentieth century, and some of the difficulties to which it has led. Whether these difficulties can be resolved or not is something which the reader should be able to judge for himself or herself. My own view is that the Bayesian programme has not succeeded, but that, in the course of pursuing it, many interesting, important and surprising results have emerged. This situation is actually characteristic of many precisely defined programmes in philosophy. Although Frege's logicist programme for reducing arithmetic to logic did not succeed, many important results emerged in the course of pursuing it. This analogy is more than an analogy, since there is even an inner connection between the Bayesian and the logicist programmes. A Bayesian who adopts the logical interpretation of probability (to be considered in the next section) is virtually committed to a logicist view of arithmetic. The development of the mathematical calculus of probability clearly involves a great deal of number theory. So if mathematical probability is to be considered as part of logic, some kind of logicist interpretation must be given to arithmetic.

The logical interpretation of probability

As we have already remarked, the mathematical calculus of probability developed from the study of games of chance, and other random phenomena such as birth–death processes. If this calculus is to be applied to induction and confirmation, as the Bayesian wishes, it is necessary that it should be given an *epistemological* interpretation – that is to say an interpretation in which probability is identified with degree of knowledge, or degree of belief, or degree of rational belief, or something of that kind. There have been two major attempts to interpret probability in this way: namely (i) the *logical* and (ii) the *subjective* interpretation. We shall consider these in turn, but our attitude to the two attempted interpretations will be different. We shall argue that the attempt to interpret probability in a logical sense has been a failure, and that there is really no such thing as a logical interpretation of the mathematical theory of probability. The subjectivists, so we shall argue, have, however, succeeded in giving an interpretation of the probability calculus, but probability in the subjective sense cannot be identified with confirmation so that the Bayesians' equation (1), i.e. $C(h, e) = P(h, e)$, fails to hold for subjective probability. Although subjective probability does not, in our view, provide a satisfactory account of confirmation theory, it may nonetheless provide an adequate foundation for decision theory.

The logical interpretation of probability was, as far as the twentieth century is concerned, first developed in the Cambridge of Russell and Moore. W.E. Johnson gave lectures on the subject which were attended by Keynes and Jeffreys, who both went on to develop their own views of the matter. Wittgenstein in 1921 gave a logical interpretation of probability.[8] Jean Nicod, a French student of Russell's, also made contributions to the subject. Later on the logical interpretation was adopted by Carnap, who was influenced not only by Russell and the early Wittgenstein, but also by Frege, whose lectures he attended. Most of these writers were consciously attempting to extend the Frege–Russell logicist view of number to probability. Towards the end of his life, however, Carnap moved somewhat in the direction of the subjective interpretation of probability. In what follows, I shall consider mainly Keynes' account, but the criticisms will be sufficiently general to apply just as much to Jeffreys or Carnap.

To expound the logical interpretation of probability, let us return to the philosophers' favourite example, and take l = All ravens are black, and e = the several thousand ravens observed so far have all been black.

183

Now *l* does not follow logically from *e*, that is *e* does not *entail l*, according to ordinary deductive logic. This was Hume's point. Could we not, however, extend deductive logic with its notion of entailment to an inductive or probability logic with a notion of partial entailment? If this were possible, we could say that, although *e* does not entail *l*, it *partially entails l* to degree *p*, where *p* is the probability of *l* given *e* ($P(l, e)$). As Keynes puts it:

> We are claiming, in fact, to cognise correctly a logical connection between one set of propositions which we call our evidence and which we suppose ourselves to know, and another set which we call our conclusions, and to which we attach more or less weight according to the grounds supplied by the first ... It is not straining the use of words to speak of this as the relation of probability.[9]

Keynes also characterises probability as *degree of rational belief*:

> Let our premises consist of any set of propositions *h*, and our conclusion consist of any set of propositions *a*, then, if a knowledge of *h* justifies a rational belief in *a* of degree α, we say that there is a *probability-relation* of degree α between *a* and *h*.[10]

It is important that we are dealing here with *rational belief*, and not with belief in general, for as Keynes says:

> The Theory of Probability is logical ... because it is concerned with the degree of belief which it is *rational* to entertain in given conditions, and not merely with the actual beliefs of particular individuals, which may or may not be rational.[11]

As we shall see, this is the point which differentiates the logical from the subjective view of probability.

        The question which now arises is the following: 'How do we obtain knowledge about these logical relations of probability, and, in particular, how are the axioms of probability theory to be established from this point of view?' On the general problem of knowledge Keynes adopted a Russellian position. Russell held that some of our knowledge is obtained directly or 'by acquaintance'. His views on what we could know in this way varied but the set always included our immediate sense-perceptions. The rest of our knowledge is 'knowledge by description' and is ultimately based on 'knowledge by acquaintance'. In analysing the relations between the two sorts of knowledge, Russell thought that his theory of descriptions could play an important role. In Russellian vein Keynes writes: 'About our own existence, our own sense-data, some logical ideas, and some logical relations, it is usually agreed that we have direct knowledge.'[12] In particular we get to know certain probability relations by direct acquaintance, for, in the case of some propositions at least, Keynes thinks that 'We pass from a knowledge of the proposition *a* to a knowledge about the proposition *b* by perceiving a logical relation between them. With this logical relation we have direct acquaintance.'[13] Though he does admit that 'some men – indeed it is obviously the case – may have a greater power of logical intuition than others'.[14]

Perhaps the most basic objection to the logical relation theory consists in querying whether there are such things as partial entailments. Some logicians have exercised their logical intuition to the full, but have been unable to apprehend any such things as partial entailments.[15] But let us suppose, for the sake of argument, that some people, perhaps those with very great powers of logical intuition, really can perceive degrees of partial entailment. What confidence should be placed in the intuitions of such individuals? And do such intuitions establish that degrees of partial entailment satisfy the usual axioms of probability?

To judge the reliability of logical intuition, let us see how it fared in the case of deductive inference, which is surely less problematic than inductive. Frege, one of the greatest logicians of all time, was led by his logical intuition to support the so-called Axiom of Comprehension, from which Russell's paradox follows in a few lines. Moreover he had companions in this error as distinguished as Dedekind and Peano. Hilbert and Brouwer were two of the great mathematicians of the twentieth century. Yet Hilbert's logical intuition informed him that the Law of Excluded Middle was valid in mathematics, and Brouwer's that it was not valid there. All this indicates that logical intuition is not to be greatly trusted in the deductive case, and so hardly at all as regards inductive inferences.

Moreover, is so-called logical intuition anything more than a psychological illusion caused by familiarity? Perhaps it is only as a result of studying the mathematical theory of probability for several years that the axioms come to seem intuitively obvious. Maybe the basic principles of Aristotle's philosophy seemed intuitively obvious to scholars in the Middle Ages. I conclude that logical intuition is not adequate to establish either that degrees of partial entailment exist, or that they obey the usual axioms of probability. Moreover, the situation becomes worse for the logical interpretation of probability in the light of the considerations to be given in the next section.

Paradoxes of the Principle of Indifference

The first axiom of the mathematical calculus of probability states that probabilities are real numbers p such that $0 \leqslant p \leqslant 1$. It seems to me therefore that a concept can be considered as a possible interpretation of this calculus only if it is measurable in at least some situations. But then the question arises: 'Are degrees of partial entailment measurable, and, if so, how?'

Keynes does not think that the degrees of partial entailment can be measured in all circumstances.[16] However he does think that they are measurable in some cases, and is indeed very clear about the nature of such cases, for he writes: 'In order that numerical measurement may be possible, we must be given a number of *equally* probable alternatives.'[17] So in order to get numerical probabilities we have to be able to judge that a certain number of cases are equally probable and to enable us to make this judgement we need a certain *a priori* principle. This *a priori* principle is called by Keynes the *Principle of Indifference*. The name is original to him but the principle itself, he says, was introduced by James Bernoulli under the name of the *Principle of Non-Sufficient Reason*. Keynes gives the following preliminary statement of the principle:

> The Principle of Indifference asserts that if there is no *known* reason for predicating of our subject one rather than another of several alternatives, then relatively to such knowledge the assertions of each of these alternatives have an *equal* probability.[18]

The trouble with the Principle of Indifference is that it leads us at once into a number of grave contradictions. These contradictions were discovered by a number of authors, notably by Bertrand and Borel. It is greatly to Keynes' credit that, although he advocates the Principle of Indifference, he gives the best statement in the literature of the objections to it.[19] I will confine myself to stating one of the paradoxes, so chosen as to be a good illustration of how the paradoxes arise in general.

This paradox could be called the wine–water paradox. Suppose we have a mixture of wine and water and we know that at most there is three times as much of one as of the other, but we know nothing more about the mixture. We have

$$\tfrac{1}{3} \leq \text{wine/water} \leq 3 \tag{5}$$

and by the Principle of Indifference the ratio wine/water has a uniform probability density in the interval $(\tfrac{1}{3}, 3)$, therefore

$$\text{prob (wine/water} \leq 2) = (2 - \tfrac{1}{3})/(3 - \tfrac{1}{3}) = \tfrac{5}{8} \tag{6}$$

But also

$$\tfrac{1}{3} \leq \text{water/wine} \leq 3 \tag{7}$$

and by the Principle of Indifference the ratio water/wine has a uniform probability density in the interval $(\tfrac{1}{3}, 3)$, therefore

$$\text{prob (water/wine} \geq \tfrac{1}{2}) = (3 - \tfrac{1}{2})/(3 - \tfrac{1}{3}) = \tfrac{15}{16} \tag{8}$$

But the events 'wine/water ≤ 2' and 'water/wine $\geq \tfrac{1}{2}$' are the same and the Principle of Indifference has given them different probabilities.

Generalising from this example, we can see that the Principle of Indifference will lead to contradictions whenever we are dealing with a continuous parameter θ about which all that is known is that it lies in an interval (a, b).

Let us now turn to Keynes' attempted resolution of these difficulties. He believes we can avoid them if we apply the Principle of Indifference only to those cases where the alternatives are finite in number and 'indivisible':

> Let the alternatives, the equiprobability of which we seek to establish by the Principle of Indifference, be $\phi(a_1)$, $\phi(a_2)$ ... $\phi(a_r)$, and let the evidence be h. Then it is a necessary condition for the application of the principle, that these should be, relatively to the evidence, *indivisible* alternatives of the form $\phi(x)$.[20]

The trouble is that this excludes at a stroke all cases in which we are dealing with a continuous parameter θ about which nothing is known except that it lies in some interval (a, b). In all such cases we have, instead of a finite, a potentially infinite number of alternatives obtained by taking sub-intervals of shorter and shorter length, and these alternatives, far from being indivisible, can always be further divided. Moreover the continuous parameter case is the one most commonly met with in scientific practice. Whatever the area of investigation, it is normal to introduce explanatory hypotheses which depend on a finite number of continuous parameters: $\theta_1, \theta_2, \ldots, \theta_n$, say. Thus Keynes solves the paradoxes of the Principle of Indifference only by rendering the logical theory of probability quite unsuitable for use with most scientific hypotheses.

The arguments of the present and previous section lead me to the conclusion that a satisfactory logical interpretation of the usual calculus of probability cannot be given. Such an interpretation would have to be based on logical intuition, and logical intuition hardly suffices to show that degrees of partial entailment exist – still less that they satisfy the standard axioms of mathematical probability. Moreover only a quantity which is measurable in at least some cases can be considered as a possible interpretation of the probability calculus. Now degrees of partial entailment can be measured only by using the Principle of Indifference, and the Principle of Indifference leads immediately to contradictions in a wide class of cases which actually includes those cases most commonly found in scientific investigation. The suggested solutions to the paradoxes of the Principle of Indifference do not appear to be at all adequate. For all these reasons, I deny the possibility of a logical interpretation of the calculus of probability.

The subjective interpretation of probability

If the arguments of the two preceding sections are correct, and there is no such thing as a logical interpretation of the probability calculus, this is by no means fatal to Bayesianism, since another epistemological interpretation of probability has been developed – namely the subjective. This view of probability was introduced independently by Ramsey in England and De Finetti in Italy. Ramsey wrote only one paper on the subject, completed in 1926 just before his early death. De Finetti wrote several different accounts and developed the subjective view over a number of years. As far as the present chapter is concerned, we will base our account of De Finetti's work on his 1937 article.[21]

According to the logical view of probability, all rational people given the same evidence, e, will have the same degree of rational belief in a prediction a, say. The subjective theory drops this consensus assumption. Different subjects A, B, C, ..., although they are all rational, and all share the same evidence e, may nonetheless have different degrees of belief in a. To develop their theory, the subjectivists have to show first how to measure such degrees of belief, and then that the degrees of belief, as thus measured, satisfy the axioms of probability. In fact they succeed in carrying out both these tasks.

Let us first consider the question of measuring degrees of belief. Outside science fiction, there exists no electronic apparatus which we can attach to A's head and which will register on a dial his or her belief in a given proposition. The subjectivists propose a rather simpler method of measuring A's belief. We simply force A to bet, and take the rate at which A will bet as a measure of A's belief. As Ramsey puts it: 'The old-established way of measuring a person's belief is to propose a bet, and see what are the lowest odds which he will accept. This method I regard as fundamentally sound.'[22]

Let us try to make this idea more precise.[23] Let us consider an individual A and an investigator B. B wants to measure A's belief concerning an event E. E may be a past as well as a future event. B wishes to find out the strength of A's belief that E has occurred or will occur, that is, for short, A's belief in E. To do this B forces A to bet with him under the following conditions. A first chooses the (so-called) *betting quotient q*, and B then chooses the stake S such that A gives B qS in exchange for S if E occurs (or has occurred), where S may be positive or negative, but is small in magnitude. If A has to bet under these circumstances, A's betting quotient q can be taken, so it is claimed, as a measure of A's belief in E. Let me next make a few comments on the betting situation here introduced.

The first point to note is that B can choose S to be either positive or negative. This means that A, when deciding on his or her betting quotient q, does not know whether the bet is to be in favour of E's occurring (or having occurred) (S positive), or against E's occurring (or having occurred) (S negative). In this state of ignorance A has no choice but to make q correspond to his or her real beliefs. If A knew that S would be positive, then it would be rational for A to choose q as low as possible regardless of his or her beliefs, and, similarly, in the case of S negative, to choose q as high as possible.

The next point is interesting because it is one on which Ramsey's account differs from that of De Finetti (at least in his 1937 article). De Finetti takes the stakes S to be in money, but Ramsey regards this as inadequate, and suggests that they should be made in units of value or utility. I prefer the approach using money since the difficulty about the diminishing marginal utility of money can easily be overcome by specifying that the stakes S be small *in relation to the size of A's income*. We do not wish to ruin the unfortunate A, who, it will be remembered, is being forced to bet. This is quite compatible with making the stakes large enough for A to take the bet seriously, and not to consider the matter a mere trifle. Using money stakes satisfying these conditions, we have a betting procedure which (i) could be (and indeed has been) actually carried out in practice, and (ii) can be reasonably taken as providing an approximate measure of A's belief in E.

Having obtained a way of measuring belief, let us pass on to the next question of whether these measures of belief, i.e. betting quotients, satisfy the standard axioms of probability. To investigate this problem, we must introduce the concept of *coherence*, which is defined as follows. If A is betting on events E_1, ..., E_n, his or her betting quotients q_1, ..., q_n are said to be *coherent* if B cannot choose stakes S_1, ..., S_n such that B wins whatever happens. If B is able to choose the stakes, so that he or she gains money in all cases, then B is said to have made *Dutch Book* against A. So A's betting quotients are said to be coherent, if there is no possibility of a Dutch Book being made against A.

Now every reasonable person would surely wish to avoid having a Dutch Book made against them, and would therefore wish to choose coherent betting quotients. Coherence can be seen as a kind of rationality constraint, but it is very far from turning the subjective theory into the logical theory. Coherence still permits a wide range of choice of betting quotients. It does not narrow things down to a single rational degree of belief. What is remarkable, however, is that the condition of coherence enables the ordinary axioms of probability to be established on the subjective approach. This result is contained in what is now known as the *Ramsey–De Finetti theorem*, and which may be stated as follows: a set of betting quotients q_1, ..., q_n is coherent if and only if it satisfies the standard axioms of the probability calculus. This way of obtaining the axioms of probability is known (for obvious reasons) as the *Dutch Book argument*.[24]

As I shall be criticising the subjective theory later on, it seems now appropriate to say something in its praise, since the subjective theory overcomes in a remarkably ingenious fashion the difficulties of the logical view. To begin with the theory provides a simple and practical method of measuring beliefs in certain cases. This method does not use the Principle of Indifference, and, as Ramsey remarks: 'To be able to turn the Principle of Indifference out of formal logic is a great advantage.'[25] While the axioms of probability can, on the logical view, be obtained only by a quite unsatisfactory appeal to logical intuition, these axioms follow, in the subjective theory, by a subtle and rigorous argument from the eminently plausible condition of coherence. So although I deny the existence of a valid logical interpretation of probability, there seems to me no doubt that there is a subjective interpretation of the calculus in terms of coherent betting quotients.

But, granted the existence of subjective probabilities, can they be used to explicate the notion of confirmation or corroboration? Can we in the crucial Bayesian equation (1), i.e. $C(h,e)=P(h,e)$, substitute a subjective probability for P on the right-hand side? My own view is that we cannot and that the real use of subjective probability lies not in the analysis of confirmation, but in providing a foundation for the theory of decision-making under uncertainty. I shall argue for this thesis in the remainder of the chapter.

Bayesian conditionalisation and Hacking

We earlier described, as part of the Bayesian position, the view that confirmation changes by the process of *Bayesian conditionalisation*. Suppose the initial confirmation of h (relative to background knowledge b) is given by the prior probability $P(h,b)$. If evidence e is then collected, the confirmation becomes the posterior probability $P(h, e \& b)$. This change from $P(h,b)$ to $P(h, e \& b)$ is known as Bayesian conditionalisation. The point here is that the posterior probability can, in principle at least, be calculated using Bayes' theorem, a simple form of which can, ignoring the background knowledge b, be stated thus:

$$P(h,e) = \frac{P(e,h)P(h)}{P(e)} \tag{9}$$

Within the subjective theory, we can define conditional probabilities quite easily. $q(h,e)$ is the rate at which A bets on h, given that the bet is called off and the stakes returned, if e does not occur. Since, by the Ramsey–De Finetti theorem, the axioms of probability are satisfied, we have Bayes' theorem (9), and so it would seem that the whole machinery of Bayesian conditionalisation·applies. However, there is a difficulty which we shall call the *Hacking problem*, since it was first clearly formulated by Hacking.[26]

To see the problem, let us consider the following case. At time t, before evidence e has been collected, A makes bets on h and on h given e. We will denote A's betting quotients by $q_t(h)$ and $q_t(h, e)$ where the subscript t indicates that the bets are made at time t. At a later time u ($>t$), e is known to be the case, and indeed e is the only extra information A has acquired since t. A now bets on h with betting quotient $q_u(h)$. A has changed his or her belief according to Bayesian conditionalisation provided he or she sets

$$q_u(h) = q_t(h, e) \tag{10}$$

(10) is called by Hacking the *dynamic assumption*, and Hacking's point is that the condition of coherence in no way forces A to satisfy the dynamic assumption. If A makes a series of bets at time t, then coherence requires that his or her betting quotients ($q_t, q'_t, q''_t, \ldots$ say) satisfy the axioms of probability. However, coherence, as so far developed, applies only to betting quotients chosen at a particular time t. It does not relate such betting quotients to betting quotients chosen at another time u. As Hacking himself puts it:

> And neither the Dutch book argument, nor any other in the personalist arsenal of proofs of the probability axioms, entails the dynamic assumption. Not one entails Bayesianism. So the personalist requires the dynamic assumption in order to be Bayesian. It is true that in consistency a personalist could abandon the Bayesian model of learning from experience. Salt could lose its savour. [Here Hacking uses the alternative terminology 'personal/personalist' instead of 'subjective/subjectivist'.][27]

The dynamic assumption (10), like the basic Bayesian equation (1), i.e. $C(h, e) = P(h, e)$, is something which appears obviously correct at first sight, but less plausible on further reflection. Let us first consider why the assumption may at first seem to be clearly true. At t, A has chosen a conditional betting quotient $q_t(h, e)$. Between t and u, A has learnt that e is true, but nothing further. Surely his or her betting quotient on h should now be $q_t(h, e)$.

The fallacy in this line of thought is, in my view, the following. In order to work out his or her betting quotients at time t, A must make some kind of theoretical analysis of the situation with which he or she is dealing. Without such an analysis it would be humanly impossible to calculate betting quotients. Yet between t and u, in the light of further thought and the further particular results which have appeared, A may well decide that his or her original theoretical analysis was wrong, and prefer a new analysis, which may not even have occurred to him or her at t, and which may give betting quotients of quite a different character from his or her original ones.

Let us take an example to illustrate this. If A is asked

to bet on some random process $\mathcal{P}$, it would be quite reasonable to assume at first that $\mathcal{P}$ consists of independent events, and to calculate his or her betting quotients accordingly. This amounts, within the subjective theory, to making the assumption of *exchangeability*, that is the assumption that the order of the events is of no significance. The observation of a few hundred results of $\mathcal{P}$ may, however, convince A that order is relevant after all, that the sequence exhibits dependencies and after-effects. At this stage, if asked to bet again, A might want to abandon the assumption of exchangeability, and use quite a different schema for calculating his or her betting quotients. But these new betting quotients will not then be obtained from the old ones by Bayesian conditionalisation (the dynamic assumption).

It is in situations like this that the Popperian schema of conjectures and refutations seems to me much superior to the Bayesian. On the Popperian account, A can start with any conjecture about the process $\mathcal{P}$ which he or she likes, but the initial conjecture T (say that $\mathcal{P}$ consists of independent events) is in no way sacrosanct. At any stage A can replace T by another conjecture T' (say that $\mathcal{P}$ has some mathematically specified form of dependency) if T' agrees better with observation. These considerations lead to a methodological argument against Bayesianism. A Bayesian will inevitably base his or her initial betting quotients on some theoretical scheme (S say). If he or she is a strict Bayesian, the initial betting quotients will be changed only by Bayesian conditionalisation (the dynamic assumption), and hence the theoretical scheme S will remain implicitly accepted. However, scientific progress might well occur faster by criticising S and perhaps replacing it by some new and better theoretical scheme S'. By tacitly ruling out such a possibility, Bayesianism could well act as a brake on scientific advance.

It might be objected that changes in the underlying theoretical scheme occur only in 'revolutionary' science, and not in 'normal' science. This is not the case, however, as many instances from everyday science demonstrate. For example, I have described in an earlier publication[28] a down-to-earth investigation by Neyman of the larvae in an experimental field. Neyman first assumed that the larvae were randomly distributed, but, when this did not agree with observation, he introduced a new hypothesis involving the clumping of the larvae.

Do universal laws have probability zero?

Let us next examine an argument against Bayesianism due to Popper. This hinges on the important question of what probability should be assigned to universal laws, that is to laws of the form $(\forall x) F(x)$, where the quantifier ranges over a potentially infinite set of objects. A simple example of such a law would be: 'All ravens are black.'

Now Popper claims that the prior probability $P(l)$

say of such a law l is always zero. By Bayes' theorem (equation (9)), we have

$$P(l,e) = \frac{P(e,l)P(l)}{P(e)} \qquad (11)$$

Therefore, since

$$P(l) = 0 \qquad (12)$$

it follows that, for any e,

$$P(l,e) = 0 \qquad (13)$$

So, for a Bayesian,

$$C(l,e) = 0, \text{ for any } e \qquad (14)$$

That is to say, universal laws will always have zero confirmation, no matter what evidence there is in their favour. This Popper regards as absurd. He takes it as obvious that universal laws, which occur everywhere in science, can receive positive confirmation, and so rejects the Bayesian assumption that $C(h,e)=P(h,e)$ (equation (1)). This is how Popper himself puts the matter:

> *we may learn from experience more and more about universal laws without ever increasing their probability;* ... we may test and corroborate some of them better and better, thereby increasing their *degree of corroboration* without altering their *probability* whose value remains zero.[29]

It will be seen that this argument depends crucially on the claim (equation (12)) that $P(l)=0$ for any universal law l. Popper, who accepts the logical interpretation of probability, has a series of arguments designed to establish $P(l)=0$ from this point of view. Since we reject the logical interpretation, it will be more apposite for us to ask whether $P(l)=0$ holds for subjective probability.

As a matter of fact the introduction of subjective probability greatly simplifies the problem, since it is almost immediately obvious, without elaborate argumentation, that, on the subjective view, $P(l)=0$ for any universal law l. Take, for example, l = All ravens are black, and suppose A is forced to bet on whether l is true. A can never win the bet, since it can never be established with certainty that all ravens are black. However, A might lose the bet if a non–black raven happens to be observed. Thus the only reasonable betting quotient is $q(l)=0$, which indeed can be considered as a kind of refusal to bet.[30]

Let us now consider what the Bayesians might say in

reply to this argument. There are basically two possible ways out of the difficulty. The first approach was originally suggested by Carnap, but worked out in much greater detail by Hesse.[31] I shall therefore call it the Carnap–Hesse thesis, and shall discuss it in detail in the next section. A few preliminary observations and explanations are in order here.

Carnap fully accepted that $P(l)=0$ for any universal law l. Indeed he derived this result within his system of inductive logic, before it was advocated by Popper. However, Carnap did not see this result as showing that confirmation is not the same as probability. He saw nothing paradoxical in holding that universal laws have zero confirmation, because, so he argued, what we need when we use science is not the confirmation of a general law, but the confirmation of the next few instances of the law. Thus an engineer, according to Carnap, is not interested in whether the laws of mechanics are universally true throughout all space and time. He merely wants to be sure that they will hold in the next few instances where he applies them, to the next few bridges that he builds, for example. This is, in effect, a revival of Mill's idea that science proceeds directly from particulars to particulars, rather than from particulars to general laws and back to particulars again.

It is interesting to note here that both Carnap and Hesse base their approach to probability to some extent on the subjectivist's betting quotients. Already in 1950, Carnap speaks of his probability$_1$ (his logical notion of probability) as 'a fair betting quotient'.[32] In 1964, Carnap derives the axioms of probability from coherence and the Ramsey–De Finetti theorem.[33] Similarly Hesse in her book[34] obtains the axioms of probability using the Dutch Book argument.

I shall call this approach of Hesse and the later Carnap a 'topping-up' version of the logical interpretation of probability. The idea is to start with purely subjective degrees of belief. We then add one rationality constraint (coherence) to obtain the axioms of probability. However, if this can be 'topped up' by further rationality constraints derived from logical or inductive intuition, we might get closer to a single rational degree of belief. I myself am rather sceptical about the possibility of 'topping up' much beyond coherence. But the point I want to make here is that those who accept this 'topping-up' approach to probability are committed to accepting $P(l)=0$ for any universal law l, regardless of how much or how little topping up they accept. Once the betting quotient approach is accepted as a starting point, the argument for $P(l)=0$ given earlier in this section goes through whatever rationality constraints are added at a later stage. It is significant that Ramsey anticipates the Carnap–Hesse thesis in the following passage:

We can discuss whether past experience gives a high probability to the sun's rising tomorrow without bothering about what probability it gives to the sun's rising each morning for evermore ... it is true that we can agree that inductive generalisations need have no finite probability, but particular expectations entertained on inductive grounds undoubtedly do have a high numerical probability in the minds of all of us. We all are more certain that the sun will rise tomorrow than that I shall not throw 12 with two dice first time, i.e. we have a belief of higher degree than 35/36 in it. If induction ever needs a logical justification it is in connection with the probability of an event like this.[35]

Because of my emphasis on the subjective approach to probability, it seems to me that adopting the Carnap–Hesse thesis is the Bayesian's most hopeful approach to the problem of zero probability of universal laws. I shall consider the problems to which the Carnap–Hesse thesis leads in the next section. I will, however, close the present section by considering the second approach to the problem which consists in denying that $P(l)=0$ for all universal laws l. From what we have said so far, it follows that this option is available only for those who adopt neither the subjective theory of probability, nor even a logical interpretation of probability of the 'topping-up' variety, but who go for a logical interpretation of probability of the more traditional, Keynesian type.

Jeffreys is an example of an author who adopted this approach, and gave a method for assigning non-zero probabilities to universal laws.[36] Hintikka has shown that Carnap's formal system of inductive logic can be modified so as to allow non-zero probabilities to universal generalisations.[37] Niiniluoto gives a good account of this approach, which he himself has helped to develop,[38] and this point of view is also defended by Mondadori.[39]

Against these authors, Popper, who adopts a logical interpretation of probability of the traditional kind, argues that the probability (in this sense) of universal laws must be zero.[40] These arguments of Popper's have been criticised in detail by Howson,[41] who concludes that they have no compelling force. The discussion is certainly an intricate one. I am inclined to agree with Howson, since, formally at least, it is possible to introduce probability measures for which $P(l)\neq0$. But can such measures really claim to be logical interpretations of probability? This I doubt, since I doubt the existence of a logical interpretation of probability of the traditional, as opposed to 'topping-up', variety. Howson shares this scepticism for he writes: 'The utility of granting the existence of "logical probability" thus seems highly questionable.'[42]

The Carnap–Hesse thesis

We have already briefly summarised the Carnap–Hesse thesis. Let us now examine it in more detail. Carnap shows that within his Bayesian confirmation theory $C(l,e)=0$ for any universal law l and finite evidence e, and he then remarks: 'The latter result may seem surprising; it seems not in accord with the fact that scientists often say of a law that it is "well-confirmed".'[43] Carnap then goes on to explain that, when scientists speak loosely of a law being 'well-confirmed', they really mean that the next few instances of the law are well confirmed. So for Carnap the arguments of his probabilistic confirmation function should be not universal laws, but particular instances of those laws.

Nonetheless Carnap thinks that it is expedient to state universal laws, partly because these laws can be considered as a shorthand for the next few instances, and partly because they have a heuristic value for discovering predictions. As Carnap puts it, they 'serve as efficient instruments for finding those highly confirmed singular predictions which are needed in practical life'.[44] But although universal laws have a heuristic importance, they are, for Carnap, eliminable from science, *qua* finished product.

This view of universal laws as dispensable is very sharply attacked by Popper.[45] Far from being dispensable, universal laws are, for Popper, among the most important and interesting of all scientific statements. As he says:

> My criticism of the verifiability criterion has always been this: against the intention of its defenders, *it did not exclude obvious metaphysical statements; but it did exclude the most important and interesting of all scientific statements*, that is to say, the scientific theories, *the universal laws* of nature.[46]

Indeed Popper sees Carnap's probabilistic confirmation theory as having essentially the same defects as the older verifiability criterion. As he says with heavy irony, 'Carnap ... explains that natural laws are not really needed in science, and that we can dispense with them. (Verificationism made them meaningless. Confirmationism merely makes them unnecessary: this is the gain which the weakening of the verifiability criterion achieves.)'[47]

Hesse largely agrees with Carnap, as we have so far expounded him, but she adds an important point, which can, in a sense, be taken as a reply to Popper's strictures concerning the indispensability of theories. Hesse does not of course reintroduce theories – that would destroy the whole conception of scientific inference as being 'from particulars to particulars'. She does, however, introduce a surrogate for theories, and this is *analogy*. As she puts it:

> The proposal does not devalue theories. It rather reinterprets theories as expressions of the analogies between their instances, in virtue of which analogical inferences can be made to other finite sets of instances. Thus the proposal is not instrumentalist, for the analogy relations are real and sometimes recognisable relations between things without which such analogical inference would not be justified.[48]

and again:

We are no longer concerned with a dubious inductive inference from e_1 up to t and down to e_2 but with a direct *analogical* inference from e_1 to e_2. And t does not provide the upper level of a deductive structure, but rather extracts the essence from e_1 and e_2, that is to say it reveals in these laws the relevant analogies in virtue of which we pass from one to the other inductively.[49]

Hesse's notion of analogy can be explained by contrasting the way in which some theoretical advance, e.g. Newton's introduction of universal gravitation, might be described on her account, and on that of Popper. Popper would say that Newton introduced a general theory of gravitation which explained (and corrected) a number of observed phenomena: the fall of an apple, the motion of the moon round the earth, the motion of the planets round the sun, etc. Hesse would say that Newton's achievement was to *perceive the analogy* between these various observed phenomena. Hesse develops the view of theory as analogy in Chapter 9 of her book, and gives a detailed discussion of Maxwell's work from this point of view in Chapter 11. As she points out, Maxwell himself made use of the concept of physical analogy.[50]

This concludes my account of the Carnap–Hesse thesis, and I shall now proceed to criticisms, for I agree with Popper that general theories and universal laws are an essential part of science, and I do not believe that they can be dispensed with, or adequately replaced by analogies between particulars. My arguments against the Carnap–Hesse thesis are two in number.

The first concerns the claim that we can regard universal laws as a shorthand for a finite number of their instances. The trouble here is that it is very hard to decide exactly what finite number is to replace the universal law, and this introduces an intolerable vagueness. Consider Carnap's engineer, for example. Is he concerned only about the bridge which he is at present constructing, or is he considering the next few bridges as well? If the latter, is he worried about the next six bridges, but not about bridge number seven? It is clearly very difficult to draw a line here, but this must be done if the Carnap–Hesse thesis is to be taken seriously.

On this point, Hesse speaks of 'finite domains, where the domains are left unstated but assumed large enough for whatever scientific purpose is currently in question'.[51] However, apart from the vagueness, there is another problem here. If the domains are taken to be large, it follows by the same betting argument that the probability of the finitised law becomes, although not zero, yet very small. Thus the advantage of the Carnap–Hesse thesis in securing high probabilities is lost.

My second argument against the Carnap–Hesse theories concerns cases where predictions are made which are based not on observable generalisations such as 'All ravens are black' but on high-level theories such as those of modern theoretical physics. In many such cases, the scientists concerned have great confidence in what they predict, but this confidence is inexplicable unless the theories they use to make the prediction are regarded as well confirmed by observational data.

Putnam gives a particularly striking example of this situation.[52] Putnam, like Popper, argues against Carnap that theories are indispensable, and, for this purpose, considers the first test of an atomic bomb. This is how Putnam himself puts the matter:

> prior to the first large scale nuclear explosion various directly and indirectly relevant observations had been made. Let all these be expressed in a single sentence in the observation vocabulary, e. Let h be the prediction that, when the two subcritical masses of uranium 235 are 'slammed together' to produce a single super-critical mass, there will be an explosion. It may be formulated without the theoretical expression 'uranium 235', namely as a statement that when two particular 'rocks' are quickly 'slammed together' there will be 'a big bang'. Then h is also in the observation vocabulary. Clearly, good inductive judges, given e, did in fact expect h. And they were right.[53]

Now an important point to notice here, as Putnam goes on to point out, is that there is no direct inductive evidence for the prediction h, as there is when we predict that the next observed raven will be black on the basis of ravens observed in the past to be black. Before the first test of an atomic bomb two subcritical masses of uranium 235 had never been slammed together to produce a single super-critical mass. Indeed such masses of uranium 235 as had been slammed together had not, because of their size, produced an explosion. Thus the direct inductive evidence might have been taken as supporting a non-explosion rather than an explosion. Yet the scientists concerned all predicted an explosion, and they could have done this only by taking what Carnap calls 'the roundabout way through the law', or rather, in this case through the relevant theories.[54] Putnam makes the point as follows:

> I believe that we should all want to say that even the most 'ideal inductive judge' could not have predicted h on the basis of e unless someone suggested the relevant theories. The theories (in particular, quantum mechanics) are what connect the various facts in e (e.g. the fact that one gets badly burned if he remains near one of the 'rocks') with h. Certainly it appears implausible to say that there is a *rule* whereby one can go from the observational facts (if one only had them all written out) to the observational prediction without any 'detour' into the realm of theory.[55]

Putnam seems to me quite right here. The most reasonable description of this case appears to be along the following lines. In the period 1895–1945, a number of theories about the nucleus and subatomic particles were developed, and corroborated by a considerable variety of evidence. The prediction of a nuclear explosion was made on the basis of these theories, and it was believed because these theories were well confirmed, even though no explosion of that kind had occurred before. This analysis involves giving up the Carnap–Hesse thesis.

Conclusion

In this chapter, I have distinguished two problems (cf. pp. 183, 190), namely

(1) *the confirmation problem* – to assess the confirmation which evidence gives to a theory, law or prediction, and

(2) *the decision problem* – how to choose an appropriate course of action under conditions of uncertainty.

I have argued for the anti-Bayesian thesis that existing epistemological interpretations of probability do not provide an adequate solution to the confirmation problem. Let me conclude on a rather more positive note, however, by arguing that the subjective theory of probability does seem to me to provide a reasonable foundation for the theory of decisions.

Suppose an individual A is choosing between a number of courses of action $C_1, \ldots, C_n$ say. Suppose the situation is one of uncertainty so that a particular course of action C_i has a number of possible outcomes $O_{i_1}, \ldots O_{i_m}$ and A does not know which of these will occur if he or she adopts C_i. In deciding whether to adopt C_i, A has to consider the probabilities $p_{i_1} \ldots p_{i_m}$ say of the various outcomes, and the gains or losses which the outcomes will produce. Now it seems to me that the probabilities here can reasonably be explicated as A's betting quotients in the manner of the subjective theory. The difficulties which arise from identifying confirmation with probability do not arise in the present case. Each outcome is a singular event. So we do not have the problem of assigning probabilities to universal laws. If A makes a decision at time t, and then another decision at a later time u, there is no reason why A's probabilities at t should be connected in any particular way with A's probabilities at u. Thus Hacking's problem about the change of belief by Bayesian conditionalisation does not arise.

Of course this model of action is an idealisation, but it does not seem to me entirely inaccurate since, after all, life is something of a gamble, or, as Ramsey puts it: 'all our lives we are in a sense betting. Whenever we go to the station we are betting that a train will really run, and if we had not a sufficient degree of belief in this we should decline the bet and stay at home.'[56]

The confirmation problem and the decision problem, though different, have nonetheless some connection. In deciding on a course of action, we may have to take account of predictions made on the basis of theories. In such a case, as the Putnam example of the first test of an atomic bomb indicates, we should make our betting quotients high or low depending on whether the relevant theories are well or badly confirmed. As a matter of fact the scientists on the atomic bomb project did actually lay bets as to what would be the magnitude of the first nuclear explosion. This suggested relation between confirmation and subjective probability is in accordance with what could be called the Mondadori addendum. Mondadori quotes Bishop Butler's maxim: 'to us probability is the very guide of life',[57] but makes the following significant addendum: 'scientific theories are to us the very guide of probability'.[58]

Notes

(An author's name followed by a number in square brackets refers to the book or article which has that number in the bibliography.)

    1. In preparing this chapter I have been greatly helped by lengthy discussions with Mary Hesse, Colin Howson and Marco Mondadori. Particularly because our views differ (as will become clear in what follows), I have found these conversations very helpful for formulating my own position.

    2. For a translation of the correspondence and details about it, see David [4].

    3. Newton [1], p. 400.

    4. Ibid.

    5. Hacking [3], p. 76.

    6. Hume [2], Section 87, p. 110.

    7. The importance of support (or *weight of evidence*, as he calls it) and the fact that it is a 3-place function is rightly stressed by Good (cf. his *Good thinking. The foundations of probability and its applications* (University of Minnesota Press, Minneapolis, 1983), Ch. 15, para. 4, pp. 159–60). I am grateful to I.J. Good for persuading me in correspondence that support is a 3-place function.

    8. Wittgenstein [8], Sections 5.15–5.156.

    9. Keynes [7], pp. 5–6.

   10. Ibid., p. 4.

   11. Ibid.

   12. Ibid., p. 14.

   13. Ibid., p. 13.

   14. Ibid., p. 18.

   15. See, for example, F.P. Ramsey, 'Truth and probability' in Kyburg and Smokler [11], pp. 65–6.

   16. Keynes [7], pp. 20–40.

   17. Ibid., p. 41.

   18. Ibid., p. 42.

   19. Ibid., Ch. 4, pp. 41–64.

   20. Ibid., p. 60.

   21. B. De Finetti, 'Foresight: its logical laws, its subjective sources' in Kyburg and Smokler [11], pp. 93–158.

   22. Ramsey, 'Truth and probability' in Kyburg and Smokler [11], p. 73.

   23. In doing so, we shall largely follow De Finetti, 'Foresight' in Kyburg and Smokler [11], pp. 102–3.

   24. For De Finetti's original proof of the theorem, see ibid., pp. 102–10. Some

interesting developments are to be found in A. Shimony, 'Coherence and the axioms of confirmation', *Journal of Symbolic Logic*, vol. 20 (1955), pp. 1–28.

25. Ramsey, 'Truth and probability' in Kyburg and Smokler [11], p. 85.

26. Hacking [12], paras. 2 and 3, pp. 313–16.

27. Ibid., p. 316.

28. D.A. Gillies, 'A falsifying rule for probability statements', *British Journal for the Philosophy of Science*, vol. 22 (1971), pp. 246–50.

29. Popper [6], Appendix *viii, p. 383.

30. This point is strongly emphasised by L.J. Cohen in *The implications of induction* (Methuen, London, 1970), Ch. 4, pp. 129–30.

31. Hesse [5].

32. Carnap [10], Ch. IV, para. 41 B, pp. 165–7.

33. R. Carnap, 'Inductive logic and inductive intuition' in I. Lakatos (ed.), *The problem of inductive logic* (North-Holland, Amsterdam, 1964), p. 261.

34. Hesse [5], Ch. 5, p. 107.

35. Ramsey, 'Truth and probability' in Kyburg and Smokler [11], pp. 81–2.

36. Jeffreys [9], Ch. 1, Section 1.0, pp. 1–8, and Section 1.62, pp. 43–50.

37. J. Hintikka, 'Towards a theory of inductive generalisation' in Y. Bar-Hillel (ed.), *Proceedings of the 1964 International Congress for Logic, Methodology, and Philosophy of Science* (North-Holland, Amsterdam, 1965), pp. 274–88.

38. I. Niiniluoto, 'Inductive logic as a methodological research programme', *Scientia* (1983), pp. 77–100.

39. M. Mondadori, 'The probability of "Laws of nature": a case for Hintikka's inductive logic', *Statistica*, vol. 38 (1978), pp. 517–36.

40. Popper [6], Appendices *vii and *viii, pp. 363–86.

41. C. Howson, 'Must the logical probability of laws be zero?' *British Journal for the Philosophy of Science*, vol. 24 (1973), pp. 153–82.

42. Ibid., p. 162.

43. Carnap [10], Appendix, Section 110, p. 571.

44. Ibid., p. 575.

45. Popper [13], Ch. 11, pp. 253–98.

46. Ibid., p. 281.

47. Ibid., p. 282.

48. Hesse [5], p. 194.

49. Ibid., p. 212.

50. Ibid., p. 261.

51. Ibid., p. 194.

52. Putnam [14], Ch. 17, pp. 287–9.

53. Ibid., pp. 287–8.

54. Carnap [10], p. 574.

55. Putnam [14], pp. 288–9.

56. Ramsey, 'Truth and probability' in Kyburg and Smokler [11], p. 81.

57. Mondadori, 'A case for Hintikka's inductive logic', p. 534.

58. There are a few important interesting topics, connected with probability and induction, which I have not had the space to discuss in the present chapter. Some of these, with references to the literature, are briefly discussed in the bibliography. In addition, mention should be made of a new argument against Bayesianism which Popper and Miller put forward in their article, 'A proof of the impossibility of

inductive probability', *Nature*, 302 (1983), pp. 687–8. This has already generated considerable discussion. My own contribution, with references to the literature to date, is: 'In defence of the Popper–Miller argument', *Philosophy of Science*, vol. 53 (1986), pp. 110–13.

Bibliography

The reason it is difficult to relate what Aristotle says about induction (*epagoge*) to modern discussions is that he locates the process primarily in the *communication of understanding* (teaching) and in *persuasion* (rhetoric) rather than in the justification of belief. See *Aristotle's posterior analytics*, trans. Jonathan Barnes (Clarendon Press, Oxford, 1975), Book I, Ch. 1. Ch. 19 of Book II contains Aristotle's most extended discussion of *epagoge*.

Newton's 'rules of reasoning in philosophy' occur in his

[1] *Principia mathematica* (1686), trans. Andrew Motte (1729), revised by Florian Cajori (University of California Press, Berkeley, 1934).

The more significant conclusions which Newton was prepared to base on 'general induction' went well beyond simple empirical generalisations of the 'all ravens are black' type. For a brief account of the reasoning, by which Newton reached some of his conclusions from phenomena, see N.R. Hanson, *Patterns of discovery* (Cambridge University Press, Cambridge, 1958), Ch. 5.

Hume did not attack induction under that name, but argued against the possibility of establishing by reason a necessary connection between events. See

[2] *An enquiry concerning human understanding* (1748), ed. L.A. Selby-Bigge (Clarendon Press, Oxford, 1963), Section 7.

It was nevertheless as a result of Hume's arguments that philosophers came to feel that a justification of induction was called for. In the nineteenth century J.S. Mill offered an inductive justification of induction in his *System of logic* (1843) (Longman Green, London, 1879), Book III, Chs. 3–5; and C.S. Peirce argued, on the basis of a radical departure from Hume's nominalistic metaphysics, that induction is a self-correcting procedure, in e.g. 'Hume on miracles and laws of nature' in Philip P. Wiener (ed.), *Charles S. Peirce: selected writings* (Dover, New York, 1966). More recently it has been contended that Hume's arguments involve too narrow a notion of rationality; for example, P.F. Strawson, *Introduction to logical theory* (Methuen, London, 1952), Ch. 9, and Paul Edwards, 'Russell's doubts about induction', which is reprinted in Richard Swinburne (ed.), *The justification of induction* (Oxford University Press, Oxford, 1974). Swinburne's book also contains discussions of a number of other strategies for justifying induction such as the 'pragmatic' and the 'predictionist'.

The history of the approach to the problem of induction using the notion of probability is told in

[3] Ian Hacking, *The emergence of probability* (Cambridge University Press, Cambridge, 1975). For the correspondence between Fermat and Pascal leading to the birth of the calculus of probability see

[4] F.N. David, *Games, gods and gambling* (Griffin, London, 1962).

Thomas Bayes' 'An essay towards solving a problem in the doctrine of chances', together with the letter and appendix by Richard Price (1763), is reprinted in E.S. Pearson and M.G. Kendall (eds), *Studies in the history of statistics and probability* (Griffin, London, 1970), pp. 134–53.

The importance of background beliefs and assumptions in assessing the validity of an inductive inference was brought out in a famous paradox devised by Nelson Goodman and described in his *Fact, fiction and forecast*, 3rd edn (Bobbs-Merrill, Indianapolis, 1973). If we define 'grue' as 'the property of being green up to the beginning of 1996 and blue thereafter' all our inductive evidence for the proposition that 'all emeralds are green' is also evidence for the proposition that 'all emeralds are grue'. Why then do we not expect emeralds to appear blue at the beginning of 1996? Goodman's answer was in effect that one of our background assumptions is that 'green' is a 'projectible' property but 'grue' is not. For the connection between Goodman's arguments and the Bayesian strategy see Hilary Putnam, *Reason, truth and history* (Cambridge University Press, Cambridge, 1981), Ch. 8. For a useful discussion of the 'grue paradox' and the literature which it generated see

[5] Mary Hesse, *The structure of scientific inference* (Macmillan, London, 1974), Ch. 3.
Karl Popper in

[6] *The logic of scientific discovery* (1934), 6th revised impression of English translation (Hutchinson, London, 1972), pp. 251–82, clearly formulates the anti-Bayesian thesis that corroboration does not obey the axioms of probability, and he has continued to argue for this view in many subsequent publications. Several other philosophers belong to the anti-Bayesian camp, though their views on confirmation are not necessarily the same as Popper's, or each other's. Among those who may be mentioned are L.J. Cohen, *The probable and the provable* (Oxford University Press, Oxford, 1977), C. Glymour, *Theory and evidence* (Princeton University Press, Princeton, 1980) and I. Levi, *Decisions and revisions* (Cambridge University Press, Cambridge, 1984).

The development of the logical interpretation discussed in this chapter is that of

[7] J.M. Keynes, *A treatise on probability* (Macmillan, London, 1963). The Russellian position on knowledge on which Keynes relies will be found in Russell's *Mysticism and logic* (Allen and Unwin, London, 1917), Ch. 10. Other important works committed to or developing a logical interpretation include

[8] Ludwig Wittgenstein, *Tractatus logico-philosophicus* (1921), trans. D.F. Pears and B.F. McGuinness (Routledge and Kegan Paul, London, 1963), Jean Nicod, *Foundations of geometry and induction*, trans. Philip P. Wiener (Routledge and Kegan Paul, London, 1930),

[9] H. Jeffreys, *Theory of probability* (1939) (Oxford University Press, Oxford, 1963), and two works by Rudolph Carnap:

[10] *Logical foundations of probability* (1950) (University of Chicago Press, Chicago, 1963) and *The continuum of inductive methods* (University of Chicago Press, Chicago, 1952).

In addition to the difficulties mentioned in the chapter, the logical interpretation suffers from the expectation that evidence for a proposition, P, should be evidence for any proposition logically equivalent to P. In the light of this assumption Carl Hempel, in *Aspects of scientific explanation* (The Free Press, New York, 1965), Ch. 1, urged the following paradox against Nicod's formulation of the logical interpretation: 'All ravens are black' is logically equivalent to 'all non-black things are not ravens,' but a white shoe is evidence which supports the second proposition, yet it would seem very strange to cite a white shoe as evidence in support of the first proposition, that all ravens are black. The book by Hesse mentioned above also contains a discussion of, and references to the literature about, this 'raven paradox'. See [5], pp. 155–62.

F.P. Ramsey's one paper devoted to the subjective interpretation, his (1926) 'Truth and probability', appears in F.P. Ramsey, *The foundations of mathematics and other logical essays*, ed. R.B. Braithwaite (Routledge and Kegan Paul, London, 1931). The account of B. de Finetti's work given in the chapter is based on his (1937) 'Foresight: its logical laws, its subjective sources'. Both of these papers are printed in

[11] H.E. Kyburg and H.E. Smokler (eds), *Studies in subjective probability* (John Wiley, New York, 1964). Hacking's problem is set out in

[12] I. Hacking, 'Slightly more realistic personal probability', *Philosophy of Science*, vol. 34 (1967), pp. 311–25.

Carnap's views that universal laws and theories are dispensable are rebutted, respectively, by Karl Popper in

[13] *Conjectures and refutations* (Routledge and Kegan Paul, London, 1963), Ch. 11, and

[14] Hilary Putnam, ' "Degree of confirmation" and inductive logic' in *Mathematics, matter and method, philosophical papers, Volume I* (3 vols, Cambridge University Press, Cambridge, 1975), Ch. 17. Both of these papers originally appeared in P.A. Schilpp (ed.), *Rudolph Carnap* (Library of Living Philosophers, Open Court, La Salle, Illinois, 1963).

This chapter concentrates on what are called 'epistemological' interpretations of probability. For the rival, 'frequency' or 'propensity' interpretations see Richard von Mises, *Probability, statistics and truth* (Allen and Unwin, London, 1951), Popper [6], Ch. 8 or Popper's *Realism and the aim of science, Postscript to the logic of scientific discovery*, ed. W.W. Bartley III (Hutchinson, London, 1983), Part II. A detailed propensity-type analysis of scientific probability is given in D.A. Gillies, *An objective theory of probability* (Methuen, London, 1973).

J.E.T.

10 | Science as Conjecture and Refutation

T.E. Burke

Induction, i.e. inference based on many observations, is a myth. It is neither a psychological fact, nor a fact of ordinary life, nor one of scientific procedure.[1]

In this, as in many similar passages, Sir Karl Popper takes a characteristically short way with the time-honoured philosophical problem of induction. Despite the weight of opinion to the contrary, he has consistently held that inductive inference plays no essential part either in our systematic science or in our unsystematic everyday knowledge of the world about us, and hence that neither of these needs a solution to the problem of induction for its justification. His defence of this thesis, and his development of an alternative non-inductivist account of science and of human knowledge in general, are Popper's most original and influential contributions to philosophy. It is with these, and the critical reactions they have stimulated, that we are concerned in the present chapter.

Popper accepts, from the outset, that David Hume was perfectly right when he pointed out, in his *Treatise on human nature* originally published in 1739, that inductive inference is logically invalid. As a matter of elementary logic, there can be no valid argument to prove, regarding any given class of things that *'those instances, of which we have had no experience, resemble those, of which we have had experience'*[2] – or, in other words, to prove that all x's are y's from the premiss that all hitherto observed x's have been y's. Even if all the crows we have ever seen have been black, we still do not have logically sufficient grounds for claiming that all crows are black; it remains a possibility that there are some, still unobserved, which are not. We cannot get rid of this possibility merely by granting ourselves a licence to ignore it, i.e. by claiming, as some philosophers have done, that induction is a distinctive form of reasoning in which, whatever may be true of other forms, such inferences are permissible. And if we try to give them logical respectability by means of another well-worn device, the doctrine of the uniformity of nature, then – apart from the difficulty of stating the doctrine in a way that does justice to both the continuity and the change which are alike manifest in nature – there is the seemingly insoluble problem of showing, without relying on induction, that the doctrine is actually true. Any defence of induction on these lines appears doomed to circularity.

But if Hume is right, there are embarrassing consequences for science – at any rate if we assume that (i) the method of science is essentially empirical, a process of discovery through systematic observation, and (ii) it is one of the central tasks of science to establish the truth of generalisations, i.e. statements of the form 'All x's are y's.' At first sight such assumptions may well seem obvious and unexceptional, but, according to Hume, such a task *cannot*, logically, be performed by such a method. All the scientist's observations are perforce of particular x's – particular occurrences of some natural phenomenon, particular samples of a metal or an acid, or whatever it may be – rather than the whole class of x's. And hence (except in rare cases where membership of the class is so restricted that we can complete a 'perfect induction' by checking every possible x) such observations can never give us logically sufficient grounds for generalising about all x's. It follows that any claim to have established by observation the truth of an unrestricted generalisation rests on an elementary logical fallacy.

No doubt we find it hard to accept, or even to take seriously, the idea that the attempts of science to discover the general principles that govern the workings of nature are attempts to achieve the logically impossible. We are accustomed to think of science as a paradigm example of rational activity; and while religion, say, may be permitted irrational leaps of faith, science surely cannot. And, given the unquestionable successes of science in so many fields, aspersions on its rationality – no matter how plausible the arguments behind them – are liable to be dismissed as carping or frivolous, or as examples of the misguided ingenuity to which philosophy is notoriously prone. Yet Hume's criticism of induction cannot simply be ignored. If we will not permit it to discredit our science or constitute a reason for abandoning it, then it obliges us to revise our ideas about what science actually does. For, if it is indeed impossible to establish the truth of unrestricted generalisations by empirical means, and if we are unwilling to allow that our science undertakes the impossible, we have no choice but to abandon the view that it is the function of science to establish such truths by such means – and to seek some alternative account of what its function is.

Popper's first serious studies in philosophy (from which emerged, in 1934, his classic *Logik der Forschung*, translated as *The logic of scientific discovery*) were devoted to these two interconnected problems, induction and the demarcation of science from non-science. The stimulus to tackle them came not just from Hume and other philosophers critical of induction, but from contemporary developments in science, and what purported to be science, as well. Popper describes vividly how the problems first presented themselves to him during his student days in Vienna after the First World War, when

> the air was full of revolutionary slogans and ideas, and new and often wild theories. Among the theories that interested me, Einstein's theory of relativity was no doubt by far the most important. Three others were Marx's theory of history, Freud's psycho-analysis and Alfred Adler's so-called individual psychology.[3]

The important thing about Einstein's theory, in this context, was not so much that it introduced something new and exciting into the field of physics, but rather that, in so doing, it showed a need for radical revision of what for generations had been treated as the standard example of scientific certainty, i.e. Newtonian physics. Here was a veritable shaking of the foundations. If Newtonian physics had successfully been called in question, no part of science could be regarded as beyond the reach of criticism and reform. We can readily imagine how such an event in the actual history of science had a much more powerful impact than any purely theoretical argument, however valid, about the logical insufficiency of scientific evidence. And as a result Popper's starting point, in the philosophy of science, was crucially different from that of his predecessors in the field. For example, the great eighteenth-century German thinker, Immanuel Kant, in his *Critique of pure reason*, had also wrestled with the problem of how, despite Hume, science might be possible. But, as Popper points out, Kant, like virtually everyone else of his time and for long afterwards, took it for granted that Newton *had* established general truths about nature. The question was how, given the limitations of the empirical method, he had managed to do it. Popper obviously could no longer share this assumption; he had to start by raising a still more fundamental question about what Newton, and other scientists, had accomplished, what the status of their theories actually was.

As we have just noted, if Newton was manifestly not infallible, this was no better reason to suppose that Einstein or anyone else was infallible either. In some important instances, Einstein's theory proved more successful than Newton's in explaining and predicting natural phenomena; and hence it could, quite properly, be hailed as scientific progress. But there was no means of knowing in advance how it would stand up to all the further tests it might meet, and hence no grounds for claiming that *now*, at long last, the truth about nature had been revealed. (Einstein himself certainly made no such claim.) Like any other scientific theory, whatever its provenance or its successes, it remained permanently at risk. Drawing on the biological concept of evolution, Popper suggests that, like animal species, theories are engaged in an endless struggle for survival. A species may survive and flourish (like the dinosaurs) over a long span of time; but nonetheless, if it fails to come to terms with some change in climate or environment, it perishes and gives place to some more adaptable species. In the same way, any theory, even though it is for a long time successful and unchallenged in its field, may fail to account for some new range of experimental data (perhaps brought to light by an improved technology). If so, it passes inevitably into the history or palaeontology of science, to be replaced by some theory better fitted to cope with the new situation.

But it is precisely this inherent vulnerability that Popper – making, if we like, a virtue of necessity – came to see as the strength rather than the weakness of science. This indeed he declares to be its distinctive merit – that it is prepared to live dangerously, to commit itself to specific predictions as to just what will happen under specific circumstances. The more specific the predictions – the more that is prohibited or ruled out and hence the more chances taken of being wrong – then, by and large, the better the science. Granted we can never *prove* that any of it is true (though of course some of it may well be true). But our consolation is that it can be tested, and, if it fails the test, then at least we know what is false and, more importantly, what is in need of amendment. And thus Popper draws his famous line of demarcation between science and non-science:

A theory which is not refutable by any conceivable event is non-scientific ... *the criterion of the scientific status of a theory is its falsifiability, or refutability, or testability*.[4]

Of the four theories mentioned in our earlier question, only Einstein's, according to Popper, satisfies this criterion of science. The others are so constructed that *no* conceivable event can refute them. (In the case of Marxism, Popper allows that this holds only of its debased or 'vulgar' versions. The original teaching of Marx himself *did* yield specific predictions – about how industrial societies would develop, for example, or how revolutions would occur – and hence qualified as science. But, Popper adds, since events have already refuted these predictions, it must be counted as outdated and discredited science.[5]) To many, no doubt, this limitless adaptability is an attraction. It is undeniably satisfying to have a theory which can accommodate and account for any event whatsoever, like the ('vulgar') Marxist who, as Popper says, 'cannot open a newspaper without finding on every page confirming evidence of his interpretation of history', or the Freudian or Adlerian to whom all examples of human behaviour, however diverse, are equally comprehensible in terms of his overall theory. But, to Popper, such adaptability is precisely what destroys a theory's claim to be part of science, properly so called.

As Popper was, of course, well aware, the exponents of such theories *did* claim that they were parts of science, that they were the results of carrying the methods of science – and hence its discipline and objectivity – to an extent never previously accomplished, into the realms of human society and the human psyche; and that they had thus, in principle, the same status and the same authority as physics or astronomy. And their very considerable influence rested largely on the widespread acceptance of this claim. Thus, for example, Marxism presents itself, not as a Utopian vision of a classless society, or a call in the name of justice for the creation of one, but as a statement of the results of an objective analysis of the dynamics of social development. It predicts a revolution essentially as astronomy predicts an eclipse – as something which, given the structure of the present situation and the forces acting therein, will happen whether anyone wants it so or not. And hence the only rational response is to prepare for what we recognise as unavoidable.

When we think of the implications of accepting such conclusions, we can readily understand why Popper saw reasons, a lot stronger and more pressing than any merely academic interest, for tackling the questions of whether these theories were indeed scientific – and what would follow about their status and authority if they were. Genuine philosophical problems, he tells us, are always rooted in urgent problems outside philosophy; and by this criterion, his own first major problems are unquestionably genuine. Obviously, he is not trying to resolve some merely verbal wrangle over whether or not Marxism or psychoanalysis has a right – according to customary or accepted usage – to the title of science. Rather his purpose is to draw attention to what seems to him an all-important distinction between two kinds of theorising – in brief, the kind in which we are under the discipline of fitting our theories to the facts of experience, and the kind in which we are licensed, in effect, to fit the facts to our theories. That the one should be called 'science' and the other 'non-science' is a relatively unimportant matter of convention; we are free to adopt other terms if we wish. What matters is not the terminology but the distinction itself – and the question of which of our theories falls on either side of it. Non-science, of course, need not always be nonsense, or without value. But whatever its functions within the economy of human thinking, they are certainly very different from those of science; and Popper's primary concern is that the two should not be confused.

Theories, then, that belong to science properly so called, no matter how many tests they pass, are never established truths. They remain permanently *conjectures*. At first sight, this seems a strange term to apply, not merely to tentative ideas on the fringes of research, but to the basic principles taught to first-year students as well. But its purpose is to remind us that these are *all* potential objects of criticism and correction, that the status of being a basic principle can never be more than provisional. How conjectures are arrived at in the first instance – whether they are suggested by a single observation, or by an accumulation of many, or by an inexplicable flash of inspiration, or whatever – is of minor importance. According to Popper it is an error to seek, as many thinkers of the past have done, some infallible source of truth, whether in sense-experience, reason or anything else. Rather we should realise that there are many sources of conjecture, or possible truth, but that none of these is or ever could be infallible; and that what matters is that our conjectures, whatever their origins, should be faithfully tested against experience.

There has always, in every human society, been a wealth of ideas about the world and its workings, ideas arrived at in a great variety of ways. And the primary task of science, in Popper's view, is not to add to the number of such ideas, but rather to act as an iconoclast among them. Its value lies in its exposure of their weak points, the points at which they fail to account for the facts of experience. In so doing, of course, as we have already noted, it stimulates, and directs the search for, new and better ideas. And hence we may reasonably ask it for progress, even though not for finality. Science, in brief, advances from an initial conjecture, through the refutation thereof, to a better conjecture, and then perhaps through a further refutation to a still better one ... and so on, in an open-ended sequence of self-criticisms and self-corrections.

What we call our 'science' or 'scientific knowledge', at any point in history, can only be that set of conjectures which have been extensively tested and thus far survived the tests. And since membership of the set is constantly changing, today's scientific knowledge is always in danger of becoming tomorrow's error, or, more likely, tomorrow's half-truth or rough approximation. We have, of course, no means of knowing what parts of it will suffer this fate or what will replace them; as in other fields of interest, if we knew where we were going we should be there already. Given the prestige of science and the extent of our reliance on its findings, this may well be a somewhat disquieting account of it. It implies, for example, that a doctor, in diagnosing our ailments and prescribing a cure, can do no more than give us the benefit of those conjectures in the field of medical science that have not thus far been refuted. Very likely his predecessor of, say, fifty years ago would have said something different and his successor of fifty years hence will say something different again. Yet it has to be admitted that Popper's thesis accords well with a great deal of the history of science and its applications. As he puts it, with disarming simplicity, he is doing little more than elaborating the old saying that *we learn by our mistakes*, which, though trite, is manifestly true of much of the development of science, and of human knowledge in general.

It should now be apparent how Popper makes good the claim with which we started, i.e. that we have no need of induction and hence no need to worry about its inherent defect. To establish the truth of a conjecture (when it takes the form of an unrestricted generalisation), we should indeed have to rely on an inductive inference. To refute it we do not;

210

and the refutation, unlike the inductive inference, involves no logical fallacy. Again, it is a matter of elementary logic. The discovery that many x's are y's is not logically sufficient to establish the truth of all x's are y's; the discovery that even one x is not a y *is* logically sufficient to establish its falsity. One genuine sighting of a white crow is enough to disprove the generalisation that all crows are black. So science, thus understood, is *not* attempting the logically impossible or, worse, claiming to have achieved it. And the long-standing preoccupation of philosophers of science with the problem of induction proves to be merely the result of a misunderstanding about the nature of science; once this has been clarified, the problem need trouble them no longer.

There can be no doubt about the extent of Popper's influence – almost certainly greater than that of any other individual – in determining the preoccupations and problems of recent philosophy of science. Responses to his work have, indeed, often been critical; while acknowledging the brilliance of his insight into the nature of scientific inquiry, many of his successors in the field have gone on to argue that it is in various respects incomplete or one-sided and in need of amendment. But it is, of course, in itself an indication of his stature that they should feel constrained to explain why they disagree with him, and to identify their own positions by contrasting them with his.

Let us look, then, at some of the more important of these criticisms. To begin with, doubts have been expressed, for example by Sir Alfred Ayer,[6] about whether induction can really be eliminated from scientific inquiry as completely as Popper claims it can. Why should we discard a theory on the grounds that it has failed a certain test in the past, unless we treat this as evidence that it will fail the same test in the future – which is surely an inductive inference? That the same test always yields the same result is, we may grant, not an inductive generalistion but an analytic truth, since in this context 'the same' can only mean 'the same in all relevant respects' and our only criterion of relevance is making a difference to the result. We should simply never allow anything to count as the same test yielding different results at different times. But that tests, the same as those carried out in the past, can be repeated in the future, that the same sets of conditions can be realised again, is *not* analytically true. And yet we commonly treat our science, not simply as a historical record of how theories have fared in past experimental tests, but as a guide to what we may expect in the future (and hence as a useful instrument for finding our way about in the world and, to some extent, controlling it). And in so doing, it would seem, we are implicitly relying on an inductive argument from past to future.

Popper replies uncompromisingly that if a theory has failed a relevant test at any time this alone is enough to show that it is false and should be discarded. No pragmatic considerations about future utility are involved.[7] He is indeed prepared to allow that

> it is perfectly reasonable to *act* on the assumption that it [the future] will, in many respects, be like the past, and that well-tested laws will continue to hold (since we have no better assumptions to act upon).[8]

But there is an important distinction to be drawn between claiming that *S* has been established as true (where *S* is some statement) and merely acting on the assumption that *S*. If we find that *x*'s invariably have been *y*'s in the past and argue from this to the truth of the generalisation that *x*'s are *always y*'s, then no doubt we are guilty of induction. But if, having found that *x*'s invariably have been *y*'s in the past, we merely propose, or resolve, to act on the assumption that they will be so in the future also, then we are not. Our intellectual consciences remain clear.

Nonetheless, such a proposal can scarcely be an entirely arbitrary one. We surely have some reason for making it. Popper himself in the passage just quoted calls it 'perfectly reasonable' and implies that this is the best that we can do. But what makes it reasonable, or more reasonable than any alternative, other than our awareness of what has happened in the past? In the same passage Popper goes on to warn us that 'to judge from past experience and from general scientific knowledge' the future will also, in important respects, be *un*like the past, and will have some surprises in store for us. This is no doubt true enough, but again, if we do indeed judge from past experience and from general scientific knowledge (i.e. knowledge of what conjectures have thus far been tested and remained unrefuted) then whatever the content of our judgement, are we not falling back on inductive inference? And it is hard to see how we can avoid doing so. For if we cannot use the past as evidence for what we will find, or are likely to find in the future, then it is no more reasonable to act on one assumption than on another; we have no grounds for making anything more than an arbitrary choice between them. It is harder than Popper seems prepared to admit to eliminate induction from science, and from our everyday knowledge of the world, and still account for the role they play in our lives.

To come now to Popper's other major problem, the demarcation of science from non-science. A variety of questions have been raised about whether, or to what extent, the concept of falsifiability can perform the key function that Popper assigns to it. As we have already noted, Popper is not primarily concerned to expound the correct, convention-sanctioned use of the term 'science', but nonetheless he has not chosen it at random. Clearly he believes that most of what we should ordinarily call science is also science in his sense, and this indeed is what gives interest and importance to his proposed criterion of scientific status. But, as Professor William Kneale has pointed out,[9] there is a class of statements, quite central to science, which can in principle be *verified but not falsified* by observation, i.e. unrestricted existential statements. An unrestricted existential statement is one which asserts, without limitation to any region of space or time, that something with certain specific properties exists. And, as another simple point of logic, while the discovery of something which has these properties is sufficient to verify such a statement, no amount of failure to discover anything which has them is sufficient to falsify it. We may simply never have looked in the right place at the right time.

Science is as much concerned to discover the content of nature, the wealth and variety of its furnishings, as it is to discover the form of nature, the general principles governing its operations. And hence the unrestricted existential statements which characteristically record discoveries of the first kind are as important in scientific discourse as the unrestricted generalisations which record discoveries of the second kind. Philosophers, who tend to be more interested in the unifying factors than in the diversity of nature (and hence to find theoretical physics the most congenial of the sciences), are always liable to focus too exclusively on the general principles, and to over-simplify their picture of science as a result. And, according to Kneale, this is what Popper, in his attempted demarcation of science from non-science, has done.

In addition, we should note that many of our commonplace remarks about our surroundings – like 'There are six apple trees in the garden' or 'It has rained every day this week' – are certainly falsifiable; but since they are not intended to contribute to any systematic programme of research, it is surely eccentric, to say the least, to call them scientific statements. Thus, it would appear, for a statement to belong to science, in our ordinary uneccentric sense of the term, it is neither necessary nor sufficient that it should be falsifiable. For, as we have just seen, there are some unfalsifiable statements which belong to science in this sense, and some falsifiable ones which do not. The value of Popper's distinction between the falsifiable and the unfalsifiable need not be called in question; but what *is* questionable is whether, without being at least seriously misleading, we can equate this with the distinction between science and non-science.

Let us concentrate, however, on the kind of situation with which Popper is primarily concerned, that in which a scientific theory (in the form of an unrestricted generalisation) is confronted by an unfavourable experimental result. *Must* the scientist respond by treating the theory as falsified, and discarding it? Is it always, as it were, the theory that is on trial, and the experimental result the judgement of the highest court, against which there is no appeal? The answer, evidently, has to be 'No.' The scientist must, of course, take account of the discrepancy in some way; he cannot merely ignore it. But several different courses of action are always, in principle, open to him; and discarding the theory is only one of these.

213

To begin with, he may look for the fault in the conduct of the experiment, rather than in the theory it is designed to test. And not only among learners in the school or college laboratory, but in much more advanced research as well, a slip on the part of the experimenter may well be regarded as a lot more likely than a flaw in the theory he is testing, especially if that theory has already got substantial successes to its credit. And, apart from the possibility of such slips, it has to be noted that testing a scientific theory is rarely as straightforward as the 'All crows are black' kind of example may suggest, i.e. just a matter of keeping our eyes open and reporting honestly what we see. Much more often a great deal of pre-existing science goes into devising the experiments, constructing the apparatus and interpreting the results. (Think, for example, of popular science programmes on television, where we are presented with pictures of indeterminate scratches on ancient rocks, or amorphous blobs and streaks revealed in X-ray photographs, or under the microscope. We have to rely on the expert, i.e. the person with the requisite background information, to tell us what they 'show'. For without that information, they convey virtually nothing to us.) And the flaw which is creating our problem may be anywhere in this body of pre-existing science which the experimenter takes for granted.

Further, it is often difficult even to identify the theory itself without relating it to its scientific background. Suppose, for example, someone asks us what Einstein's famous theory of relativity is about, but confesses to having no knowledge whatsoever of physics. We should be at a loss to know what to tell him. Original though the theory is, it still perforce makes extensive use of ideas which we can understand only if we are familiar with their roles in other parts of science. Hence we cannot hope to offer our enquirer any brief formulation which will be intelligible *in vacuo*; indeed nothing short of an entire book (like one of the many layman's introductions to relativity) is likely to be adequate. And a theory is bound up with its scientific background in other ways as well. Thus, when we speak of its experimentally testable consequences, we almost always mean, strictly, consequences derived from the theory *in conjunction with* a set of supplementary facts. (Einstein's often-quoted prediction, confirmed in 1919, about what would be observed during an eclipse of the sun, required not only his own distinctive theory but a considerable variety of astronomical data as well.) So, once more, if we have to seek a source of error there are indefinitely many places in which it might be found.

We may appreciate then why some thinkers (notably the French physicist and philosopher Pierre Duhem, at the turn of the century, and the modern American philosopher Willard Quine) have adopted what is sometimes called a *holistic* conception of science. Briefly, this is the view that our ideas about nature form an essentially interrelated structure, like an organic body, the parts of which cannot function in isolation from each other. As a result, they face the tests of observation collectively rather than individually, and, for any conflict or discrepancy, there are always alternative explanations logically possible.

Popper is prepared to grant that there is at least a measure of truth in this.

> It has to be admitted that we can often test only a large chunk of a theoretical system, and sometimes perhaps only the whole system, and that, in these cases, it is sheer guesswork which of its ingredients should be held responsible for any falsification.[10]

He points out that, in one respect at any rate, such holism accords very well with his own account of scientific theories as always and unavoidably conjectural. He, also, refuses to divide the totality of our theories into those already established as true and hence above suspicion, and those still on trial; they are all, in principle, possible suspects and all permanently on trial. Nonetheless, Popper argues, holism characteristically exaggerates this element of interrelatedness, and the difficulty of detaching any part of a system from the whole. It is often quite feasible to do so. When we set up an experiment to decide between two rival theories on a given issue, the background information may well be essentially the same for both. So, even though it may be correct enough to say that we are deciding between whole systems rather than specific theories, the systems differ only in respect of the two theories in question; and hence, if the one fails our test and the other survives, the reason is not far to seek. To take an analogy, our state of health may well be determined by our whole mode of life rather than by any specific element within it. But if each time we change that mode of life in respect, say, of some item of diet but nothing else, we suffer a sudden onset of illness, which disappears when we reverse the change, we can have little difficulty in identifying the offending element. There may indeed be situations where we are reduced to 'sheer guesswork', but it is unwarranted to suppose that it must *always* be so.

There are other ways, however, in which we may illustrate the range of choices available to the scientist, when theory and experimental findings come into conflict. To take a simple, and doubtless somewhat far-fetched, example: suppose we throw some heavy object, say a large book, from the window. All that we know of gravitation leads us to expect that it will crash to the ground. But suppose that, instead of doing so, it remains floating in the air, or flies upwards. Are we obliged thereupon to abandon our belief in the principle of gravitation? Obviously not; our quite rational, and much more likely, reaction would be to suppose that gravity was functioning as normal, but that some other force, perhaps some powerful updraught, was counteracting it in this particular location. Even if we failed to trace the source of this counteraction, or explain how it operated, this need not demonstrate anything more than our own limitations as researchers. If the phenomenon were repeatable (and other explanations in terms of optical illusions or conjuring tricks were ruled out) we can imagine our flying books becoming quite a celebrated scientific puzzle on which a succession of researchers tried their wits. And it might baffle them over an indefinite period of time without posing any threat to our gravitational theory. We should simply assume that there *had* to be some counteracting agency, which probably someone some day would be clever enough to identify, and keep our faith in gravitation unimpaired.

From the actual history of science, it is not difficult to draw more serious, but constantly similar, examples of theories that have lived indefinitely with apparent exceptions and anomalies. Indeed, Professor Paul Feyerabend has claimed that '*not a single theory ever agrees with all the known facts in its domain*'.[11] He cites as examples Copernicus' heliocentric view of the solar system, Newton's theories of gravitation and of colour, and Einstein's special theory of relativity. All of these were faced at the outset with facts apparently inconsistent with them, and had to wait for long periods before the discrepancies were satisfactorily explained. As the scientific community has generally recognised, it is asking too much of any wide-ranging theory that it should be able immediately to cope with all the relevant experimental data. But this need not prevent it from surviving and being accepted by competent scientists as a basis for further research.

In an influential criticism of Popper's thesis that a good scientific theory is a prohibition, *forbidding* something to happen, Imre Lakatos argues that '*exactly the most admired scientific theories simply fail to forbid any observable state of affairs*'.[12] The reason is that such theories characteristically contain, implicitly at least, what Lakatos calls a *ceteris paribus* clause. They do not say, without qualification, 'If conditions a, b and c are realised then x will happen,' but rather 'If conditions a, b and c are realised, *and no counteracting conditions are present*, then x will happen.' Thus, in our example, gravitational theory does not categorically forbid flying books; it only tells us that, without some force to counteract gravity, books do not fly; and, if they do, then the theory requires us to seek, or at least to postulate, some appropriate counteracting force.

Lakatos himself uses the example (based presumably on the actual discovery of the planet Neptune) of a Newtonian scientist who, on the basis of Newton's mechanics and gravitational theory, together with the relevant astronomical data, calculates the orbital path of a given planet. Its observed path, however, differs from the calculated path. But even though the scientist accepts the accuracy of the observations, there is still no question of his abandoning allegiance to Newton. There are always auxiliary hypotheses which can be introduced to explain the discrepancy – like, for example, the one that proved successful in the case of Neptune, that of a hitherto undiscovered planet, further out from the sun, the gravitational pull of which was the missing factor in the original calculations. Even if observation fails to detect any such planet, the possibility of finding some other, more successful, auxiliary hypothesis remains open. At no point is the observational evidence ever logically sufficient to rule out this possibility and hence require him (if he is to avoid irrationality) to abandon the original theory. Hence, according to Lakatos, even the most rigorous theories in natural science have, in principle, the kind of immunity from refutation which Popper condemned in Marxism and psychoanalysis – and so the Popperian distinction between science and non-science breaks down.

Nonetheless, while it may be possible to shore up any theory indefinitely, in the face of any amount of unfavourable evidence, it is obvious that an indiscriminate use of auxiliary hypotheses would have the effect of trivialising our science. The Neptune hypothesis had the merit of being testable, independently of the discrepancy it was designed to explain, and in the event, of course, it led to an important astronomical discovery. But it would be a very different situation if, say, we were reduced to postulating mysterious 'forces' or 'powers', which manifest themselves solely by producing the phenomena which we find otherwise inexplicable. These would be on a level with the ghosts or spirits of the primitive animist; and it is evident that if we allowed ourselves to 'explain' awkward phenomena by such postulates, we could 'explain' anything whatsoever, and all our 'explanations' would be equally worthless. A theory which drives us to any such desperate expedients, even if still logically viable, is manifestly one which the serious scientist as such has to discard or reform.

At what point we decide to abandon shoring-up operations, and opt for something more radical, may depend on any of a number of factors. For example, when a theory is so well attested and has such wide explanatory powers as gravitation, we have obvious incentives to grant ourselves considerable latitude over both the time allowed for finding acceptable explanations of anomalies, and over what we count as acceptable. (If no other explanation were forthcoming, we might even be prepared to suppose a poltergeist responsible for our flying books, rather than sacrifice the theory of gravitation to them.) Another major consideration is whether we have any *alternative* to the theory in question. Popper notes that ordinarily, before we falsify a hypothesis, we have another one up our sleeves. Lakatos insists that we must have one; without it our duty as scientists is to refuse to accept the purported falsification and seek some shoring-up, or rescuing, hypothesis. His reason is, in brief, that we cannot carry on research without a theory of some sort to direct our efforts. If we approach our subject-matter with an entirely open mind, with no preconceptions about its elements or structure, there is nothing to tell us what to focus on, what to look for, or what questions to ask. (We may recall here Popper's anecdote about how he brought this point home to a class of physics students in Vienna by telling them gravely at the beginning of a lecture, 'Observe and write down what you have observed.' And, of course, since they had not been told what to observe, or why, they were at a loss. Observation, as Popper says, is

217

essentially selective, and, given no principle of selection, they literally could not observe.[13]) So, if our research is to continue, we can abandon one theory only to explore the potentialities of another. In the absence of a feasible alternative to a given theory we have no option but to soldier on with it, and solve our problems as best we can in ways consistent with it. For example, whatever problems the geocentric theory of the solar system created for medieval astronomers, however complicated the patterns of cycles and epicycles they were constrained to postulate, there was simply nothing else for it – until someone discovered, or rediscovered, the feasibility of a heliocentric theory.

Indeed, in the absence of such an alternative, there was no reason why the medieval astronomers should even think of themselves as holding a geocentric theory, or have any use for the word 'geocentric'. And hence, whatever difficulties they encountered, they would not think of them as constituting problems for, or potential refutations of, the geocentric theory. With the advantage of hindsight and long familiarity with an alternative, *we* can see them, readily enough, as holding such a theory and getting into sundry difficulties in consequence. And we may understandably be inclined to wonder how a theory beset by such difficulties survived for so long – and to regard those who first adopted *our* alternative as intellectual heroes, those who resisted it as reactionaries and obscurantists. But it is worth while to make the effort of historical imagination required to appreciate how the situation would appear to an astronomer educated *within* a tradition which took geocentrism entirely for granted. For him, as we have seen, it would be very difficult even to identify the theory, to say nothing of criticising or refuting it. And, even when an alternative was presented to him, to adopt it was a very radical move indeed, nothing less than forsaking the whole tradition of astronomy within which he had learnt his subject, in order to assist in the creation of a new one. And since the potentialities of this were largely unknown, it was very much a leap into the darkness.

The nature, and the effects, of such radical shifts of standpoint are explored by Thomas Kuhn in *The structure of scientific revolutions*. Here he draws a basic distinction between what he terms the 'normal' and the 'revolutionary' elements in the development of science. Normal science is 'research firmly based upon one or more past scientific achievements that some particular scientific community acknowledges for a time as supplying the foundations for its further practice'.[14] The outstanding achievements of the past function as 'paradigms' or models for subsequent research. A common paradigm, or set of paradigms, is what identifies a particular tradition of research, binds a scientific community together, and furnishes a basis for mutual understanding and co-operation. The alternatives just mentioned, of Ptolemaic and Copernican astronomy, are obvious examples of traditions determined by such paradigms; so also are Aristotelian and Newtonian mechanics.

Normal science, as the name implies, covers by far the greater part of scientific activity. And in normal science, Kuhn argues, current theory, i.e. the set of paradigms determining the practice of a scientific community, is *not* being tested, and is *not* even in principle a target for criticism.

> On the contrary, when engaged with a normal research problem, the scientist must *premise* current theory as the rules of his game. His object is to solve a puzzle, preferably one at which others have failed, and current theory is required to define that puzzle, and to guarantee that, given sufficient brilliance, it can be solved.[15]

Again, it is the framework of theory we bring to our task that orders the field of research for us, divides it into the problematic and the unproblematic, the puzzling and the expected, what needs explaining and what can be used to explain it. So if we discard the framework or call it in question, the problems and the means of tackling them are alike obliterated.

It does not follow, however, that such frameworks, or paradigms, are immutable. They can be altered, or replaced, but only by what Kuhn calls 'extraordinary' moves, quite outside the scope of normal scientific activity. These are the 'scientific revolutions' of his title, the radical shifts of standpoint which transform our whole conception of a given field of inquiry, and generate a whole new tradition of research. Revolutions of this kind, or at any rate successful revolutions, are rare events in the history of science. And to most professional scientists the idea of leading such a revolution would doubtless seem almost as strange, and remote from normal activity, as that of founding a new religion would to a priest or a theologian.

If we are not professional scientists, however, and can only approach the subject from the outside, as readers of popular expositions and histories of science, these extraordinary elements in science are likely to be the familiar ones. We know something of the achievements of Galileo and Newton, Darwin and Einstein, but very little of the comparatively unspectacular and routine work carried on within the research traditions that stem from these achievements. In consequence, our picture of science in general gets seriously distorted. We think of it as characterised by bold and successful challenges to fundamental and widely accepted ideas about nature, rather than by patient, piecemeal endeavours to solve specific problems within the framework of such ideas, which is what Kuhn says it *nearly* always is. And Popper, despite his considerable first-hand acquaintance with science, was also, Kuhn suggests, guilty of thus treating the exceptional in science as though it were the norm.

Popper's answer[16] is that Kuhn exaggerates and over-dramatises his contrast between the normal and the revolutionary. He grants that there may be differences in degree of conservatism or radicalism between different phases in the history of science; it has 'quieter and less quiet, less and more revolutionary periods'. No doubt many professional scientists find they can work happily enough within an accepted framework; or they are reluctant to take the risk of challenging it. (A failed revolutionary genius is, after all, merely a crank, and forfeits the right to be taken seriously by his colleagues.) And it is quite in accordance with Popper's own conception of science that a body of theories should be *provisionally* taken for granted and used as a basis for research. But, once again, Popper bars any suggestion that such immunity from criticism can be anything more than provisional, or that scientists, in the pursuit of their normal professional activities, *have* to treat any theories, however widely accepted or fundamental to a tradition of research, as sacrosanct. The whole spirit of science, as Popper understands it – and not just science in its rare revolutionary upheavals – requires that everything is, in principle at least, permanently open to question.

Nonetheless, while we may appreciate Popper's reasons for insisting that nothing in science should be beyond criticism, the question remains about how, or from which standpoint, Kuhn's paradigms can be criticised. How should we compare one with another or discover which is better? The problems which arise in a given field of inquiry, and the ways in which we tackle them, are, as we have seen, determined at least in essential part by the paradigms with which we start. If so, then there are no problems independent of, or neutral between, paradigms such that we could ask, regarding two alternative paradigms, which provides the more effective means of solving them; neither is there any neutral set of observational findings such that we could ask which paradigm accords the better with them.

We can understand then why Kuhn and others should think of different paradigms as *incommensurable*. There is an obvious sense, of course, in which scientists who adopt different paradigms, or change from one to another, are still concerned with the same world, or the same aspect of it. Our Ptolemaic and Copernican astronomers, however radical their differences, are, after all, talking about the same sun and the same planets. But the differences between the questions they are trying to answer, the things they are looking for and the interpretation they put on what they find create, at the least, a powerful barrier to communication between them. Kuhn considers seriously, though he does not accept it without qualification, the extreme thesis that 'though the world does not change with a change of paradigm, the scientist afterwards works in a different world'.[17] He himself suggests that the change is like looking at familiar objects through inverting lenses, with the resultant difficulty in relating our present view of them to our earlier view. Another analogy might be the way in which a religious conversion transforms the convert's view and evaluation of the world, perhaps to the extent that he is willing to claim, at least figuratively, that 'all things have been made new'. Neither a religious conversion nor a paradigm shift is likely, of course, to occur altogether *in vacuo*; there are doubtless things that bring it about in a particular situation, perhaps intractable problems within our present position and the promise of release offered by a new one. But whatever prompts such a move, we can never be rationally compelled to make it on the grounds that independent evidence upholds one religious creed or scientific paradigm and refutes another.

But again, Popper objects that Kuhn is overstating his case. The differences to which he points are real enough, but they do not suffice to show that the various scientific paradigms, or the bodies of theory developed from them, are incommensurable in any strict sense. Our Copernican astronomer, for example, despite all his differences from his Ptolemaic predecessor, is still able, surely, to grasp what the Ptolemaic position was, to understand why it was adopted, what difficulties it created and how its exponents tried to cope with these. And even though he cannot prove that his own position is the right, or the only tenable, position, there are clearly ways in which he might argue rationally for its advantages. He might point out, for example, that it yields a more comprehensive and consistent account of the solar system, that it requires fewer *ad hoc* hypotheses or implausibilities, that it creates fewer insoluble puzzles, or that it offers simpler and more successful methods of prediction. Since astronomers of both schools are not only concerned with the same subject-matter, but are, at least in some measure, attempting to do the same things, i.e. to find a consistent pattern among past observations and to predict future observations, they have enough in common to make comparison possible and to provide some rational ground for preference.

It is not possible here to do more than outline some of the major issues between Popper and his critics; we certainly cannot hope to resolve them. But looking back on the arguments between Popper and, in particular, Feyerabend, Lakatos and Kuhn, we may notice, in conclusion, the recurrent tension between two basic ideas about science, both undoubtedly sound enough in themselves – the idea that the scientist is a man under authority, a devoted servant of fact, and the idea that his task is essentially creative, providing endless scope for imagination and inventiveness. The two, of course, are not ultimately incompatible; the problem is to find the right balance between them, a conception of science that does justice to both. Roughly speaking, we may say that Popper has placed his emphasis on the first of these two ideas, in his insistence that all our theories, whatever roles we assign to them, must, in the end, be judged before the tribunal of observed fact. His critics, on the other hand, while not denigrating this respect for fact, have been primarily concerned to point out how much, inevitably, is left to the judgement of the scientist, how many alternatives are open and how many decisions have to be taken, even in the most disciplined scientific research.

To the critics, Popper is in danger of oversimplifying and distorting our picture of what science is actually like. To Popper the critics are in danger of straying towards a relativism which would permit different schools of thought to develop different, and mutually inconsistent, views of the world, and all be equally right – or even towards an Orwellian situation in which the truth is simply whatever some authority says it is. The issue raised by the debate between them is, very briefly, this: to what extent can we claim that science is determined by what is 'out there', in a world independent of ourselves, to be discovered; and to what extent is it determined by our own activity as scientists? And this clearly is a key question in the whole philosophy of science. The various ideas we have considered in the foregoing are certainly indispensable contributions towards an answer to it, even if none of them in itself constitutes a complete answer.

Notes

(An author's name followed by a number in square brackets refers to the book or article which has that number in the bibliography.)

1. Popper [1], p. 53.
2. David Hume, *A treatise of human nature* (Penguin Classics, Penguin Books, Harmondsworth, 1985), p. 137. Italics in original.
3. Popper [1], p. 34.
4. Ibid., pp. 36, 37.
5. Ibid., p. 37. Also *The open society and its enemies*, 4th edn (2 vols, Routledge and Kegan Paul, London, 1962), vol. II, pp. 108, 109.
6. Schilpp [2], vol. II, p. 686.
7. Ibid., vol. II, p. 1110.
8. Popper [1], p. 56.
9. Schilpp [2], vol. I, p. 206.
10. Popper [1], p. 239.
11. Paul Feyerabend, 'Against method' in *Minnesota studies in the philosophy of science* (University of Minnesota Press, Minneapolis, 1970), p. 36. Italics in original.
12. Lakatos [7], p. 16. Italics in original.
13. Popper [1], p. 46.
14. Kuhn [5], p. 10.
15. Schilpp [2], vol. II, p. 801.
16. Ibid., p. 1145.
17. Kuhn [5], pp. 121, 122.

Bibliography

Popper's classic *Logik der Forschung* (1934) was first published in English in 1959 as *The logic of scientific discovery* (Hutchinson, London). At that time Popper intended to set out in a postscript how his views had developed in the intervening 25 years. This postscript grew until it became too large to be included and was promised as a separate book. This however did not emerge until 1983, and then as three books, edited by W.W. Bartley III, *Realism and the aim of science*, *Quantum theory and the schism in physics* and *The open universe* (Hutchinson, London). But the best entry to Popper's philosophy is

[1] *Conjectures and refutations* (Routledge and Kegan Paul, London, 1963), which is a collection of essays and lectures. Popper's best treatment of the problem of induction will be found in his *Objective knowledge, an evolutionary approach* (Oxford University Press, Oxford, 1972), Ch. 1.

Many aspects of Popper's philosophy are discussed in the book (in two volumes) devoted to him in the series 'The Library of Living Philosophers':

[2] Paul Arthur Schilpp (ed.), *The philosophy of Karl Popper* (Open Court, La Salle, Illinois, 1974). This contains an intellectual autobiography by Popper, which was published separately as a book, *Unended quest* (Fontana/Collins, London, 1974). The Schilpp volume contains the critical views of A.J. Ayer, William Kneale and T.S. Kuhn referred to in this chapter. Among the other contributors special mention may be made of Hilary Putnam's 'The "corroboration" of theories' (which is also printed in [6]) for its support for the claim that Popper's account of science over-simplifies and distorts the character of scientific theories.

The contribution to [2] by T.S. Kuhn, 'Logic of discovery or psychology of research', occurs in two other books, which are rich sources. The first,

[3] Imre Lakatos and Alan Musgrave (eds), *Criticism and the growth of knowledge* (Cambridge University Press, Cambridge, 1970) consists (in addition to Kuhn's treatment of Popper) of discussion papers read at an International Colloquium where the impact of Kuhn's ideas was discussed by, among others, Popper and partisans of his approach. The second is Kuhn's book

[4] *The essential tension* (University of Chicago Press, Chicago, 1977), a collection of essays, some of which balance and clarify what Kuhn claims in his most widely known work,

[5] *The structure of scientific revolutions* (University of Chicago Press, Chicago, 1962, 2nd edn, 1970). Professionally Kuhn is a historian of science and an appreciation of his philosophic outlook needs some familiarity with his work in this area. Many of the essays in [4] will provide this, as will Kuhn's early work *The Copernican revolution* (Harvard University Press, Cambridge, Massachusetts, 1957) or his more recent *Black-body theory and the quantum discontinuity 1894–1912* (Clarendon Press, Oxford, 1978).

As is explained in a recent introductory text to the philosophy of science, Ian Hacking, *Representing and intervening* (Cambridge University Press, Cambridge, 1983), Kuhn's work, in particular [5], caused something of a *coup d'état* among the issues which govern the discussion of philosophers of science; what had hitherto exercised these professionals fell from significance and what had been taken for granted became issues. But Popper figured as a leading representative of one party both before and after the *coup*. For a flavour of those who stood in opposition to Popper over such questions as verification *v.* falsification and induction *v.* deduction prior to the *coup*, two books from different decades may be consulted: R.B. Braithwaite, *Scientific explanation* (Cambridge University Press, Cambridge, 1953) and Ernest Nagel, *The structure of science* (Routledge and Kegan Paul, London, 1961). A useful collection which gives the flavour of the philosophy of science after Kuhn is

[6] Ian Hacking (ed.), *Scientific revolutions* (Oxford University Press, Oxford, 1981).

One of Popper's close associates, Imre Lakatos, had started, shortly before his death in 1974, to develop the general Popperian outlook in his own distinctive manner, a manner which in some respects resembled Kuhn's. Lakatos' lengthy contribution to [3], 'Falsification and the methodology of scientific research programmes', forms the backbone of

[7] *The methodology of scientific research programmes*, ed. John Worral and Gregory Currie (Cambridge University Press, Cambridge, 1978), the first of two volumes of Lakatos' collected papers. Another shorter paper in [7], which represents Lakatos' approach, 'History of science and its rational reconstructions', also appears in [6] together with a penetrating appreciation by Hacking of where Lakatos' philosophy was leading.

P.K. Feyerabend, who for a short while was a colleague of both Popper and Lakatos, also struck out in his own distinctive direction. In a series of articles and then in a book *Against method* (New Left Books, London, 1975) he articulated what he called 'theoretical anarchism': the only methodological principle that does not stand in the way of progress is the principle that *'anything goes'*. This means that one scientific theory cannot be preferred on rational grounds to another and in *Science in a free society* (New Left Books, London, 1978) Feyerabend drew the conclusion that public money should not be used to support one scientific research enterprise in preference to another. There should rather be a separation of science and state similar to that between church and state enshrined in the US constitution. Feyerabend's arguments, like Kuhn's, draw extensively on the history of science. Feyerabend's use of history can be sampled in *Against method* or in the two volumes of his *Philosophical papers* (Cambridge University Press, Cambridge, 1981).

Feyerabend's outspoken attack on what had been taken as the 'rationality of science', and Kuhn's more subtle questioning of our understanding of that rationality, have provoked a number of philosophers to argue on behalf of the traditional idea that science could and should aspire to objective knowledge of the natural world. One such defence from a position which is not strongly falsificationist but otherwise not far from Popper's is W.H. Newton-Smith, *The rationality of science* (Routledge and Kegan Paul, London, 1981).

Pierre Duhem's philosophy of science is available in English in *The aim and structure of physical theory*, trans. Philip P. Wiener (Princeton University Press, Princeton, 1954). W.V. Quine exerted most of his direct influence in the fields of mathematical logic and philosophy of language, but his indirect influence on the philosophy of science has been enormous. The most striking and adventurous statement of the 'holistic' conception of science occurs in Quine's 'Two dogmas of empiricism', in his *From a logical point of view* (Harvard University Press, Cambridge, Massachusetts, 1953). For a discussion of the implication of this conception see Mary Hesse, *The structure of scientific inference* (Macmillan, London, 1974), Ch. 1.

J.E.T.

11 | Science and the World

Mary Tiles

Galileo was convinced that the earth moves. Its motion, although not apparent to the senses and although contrary to centuries of traditional common sense, was a consequence of Copernicus' theory about the structure of the universe and the motion of the heavenly bodies. Copernicus placed the sun, rather than the earth, at the centre of the universe. All the planets, including the earth, circle the sun. The appearance of night and day on the earth is not a consequence of the sun's movement around the earth but of the earth's rotation on its own axis. Cardinal Bellarmine, as representative of the authority of the Catholic Church, responsible for the calculation of calendars and the occurrence of Holy Days, was eager to adopt any model of the motions of the heavenly bodies that was less complex and more accurate in its predictions than the Ptolemaic system then in use. The Copernican system promised, at least initially, to be an improvement. But, just as the Ptolemaic system before it, it would be just a device, a mathematical model invented by astronomers to make it possible to reproduce and hence to predict the observed sequence of relative positions of the heavenly bodies. It was Galileo's insistence that an astronomical model be treated as a physical theory, as giving an account of the actual motions and mechanisms of motion of the heavenly bodies, not his advocacy of the Copernican system as such, which brought him into conflict with a church theologically committed to an earth-centred view of the universe.

This familiar story illustrates contrasting attitudes towards science. Galileo (the advocate of the realist view of scientific theories) confronts Bellarmine (the advocate of an instrumentalist view). The realist sees science as aiming to tell the literal truth about the world: science aims at knowledge of how the world really is. The instrumentalist sees science as aiming to provide useful aids to thought about the everyday world, thought which is in turn directed towards organising and improving our lives within this world. From this point of view a good scientific theory is one which makes it possible to make accurate predictions as easily as possible: the actual nature of the means employed is not too important.

When the story of Galileo's confrontation with Bellarmine is told it is usually Galileo who is presented as the hero. He apparently not only backed the right theory but also the right attitude towards theories. From the late seventeenth century onward realism has been the dominant view of scientific theories; it is part of the prevailing public image of science. However, the overthrow of classical Newtonian mechanics by relativity theory and by quantum mechanics early in this century reopened debates about the status of scientific theories. Quantum mechanics in particular has given new life to instrumentalism, for here there is a well-developed mathematical formalism which is predictively very successful but which resists interpretation in terms of any immediately available concepts. Some cases can be handled by thinking in terms of particles, others by thinking in terms of waves, but neither interpretation can be consistently used across the whole range of situations to which the mathematical formalism has been successfully applied. It is therefore not at all clear how this theory could be treated as a literal description of the world, for it seems not to carry with it any coherently conceptualisable picture of the fundamental constituents of matter. The price of realism here is high, namely, adoption of a radically new view of the nature of physical reality, something which would require introducing ways of thinking alien to the dominant traditions of Western thought. Although some have been prepared to explore this avenue (for example David Bohm[1]), the more frequently adopted attitudes are non-realist and often instrumentalist. Quantum theory has thus been, and remains, a focus for debate in the philosophy of science. It is a quite crucial test case for those advocating a realist view of scientific theories.

Much recent philosophic discussion of the relation between science and the world has taken the form of debating the opposition between realism and instrumentalism. However, questions about this relation arise in a rather different form as questions which are increasingly forced on scientists as they look for ways of funding expensive research. These are questions concerning the relation between fundamental, 'pure' scientific research and technological advance. Is the function of science principally that of securing technological developments? Can these be attained without fundamental research, or is increasingly expensive support for fundamental research in pure science a price which has to be paid for continued technological progress in the longer term? These are questions not just of the relation between scientific theories and the natural world, but also of the relation between academic science and the wider world of commerce, politics, industry, agriculture and the environment.

However, philosophic discussions, particularly as

226

carried on by those who see themselves as philosophers of science, rarely extend to a consideration of the relation between science and technology. This is in part because the whole conception of the scientific enterprise which arose from what is often called the scientific revolution of the seventeenth century, and which still feeds the public image of science, places obstacles in the way of any such extension. The relation between modern science, the new experimental philosophy, and the world was, in its seventeenth-century origins, and continues to be, highly ambiguous and problematic. The new science was to be abstract and mathematical, but also experimental; it was to yield both enlightenment and mastery of nature; it was to strive for an objective, purely intellectual, value-free view of the world in order to improve the lot of mankind by rendering technological innovations possible. The tension between the realist's view of the goal of science (objectively true, pure theoretical knowledge) and the instrumentalist's view (that science is not pursued as an end in itself but purely as a means to increased ability to predict and control nature) is inherent in the collection of features which are seen as distinguishing modern (genuine) science from its (pre-scientific) predecessors. But this also means that science and technology are not clearly separated: technology is seen as part of science, as applied science (think for example of the nature of the exhibits in a science museum), with the result that there is no space within which to raise questions about, and hence to discuss the relation between, science and technology.

Realisms and anti-realisms

Much recent philosophical literature has been concerned to discuss the opposition between realism and anti-realism, in various fields. However, these terms have come to be used in a bewildering variety of ways. In particular, debates in the theory of meaning have frequently seemed to run along quite different lines to those in the philosophy of science. This is confusing given that philosophers of science themselves often become embroiled in questions about the meaning of scientific terms. In order to try to avoid further confusion it is necessary to distinguish and relate the various realist–anti-realist positions. Once this schematic structure is in place it will be possible to place these debates in a wider historical perspective of discussions concerning the nature and place of science and its relation to technology.

Realism and anti-realism in the theory of meaning

It is best to begin with the theory of meaning because disputes here have the character of global disputes.[2] They concern the way in which language functions in the expression of knowledge in any area and thus affect the course of more local debates about the way in which language is functioning in a given area such as scientific theorising or making moral judgements.

Fundamental debates in the theory of meaning arose (in the work of Frege and Russell) out of a concern to explain how language functions as a vehicle for expressing objective (scientific) knowledge. The notion of meaning which thus forms their primary focus, and which concerns us here, is that of cognitive content, the meaning of an indicative sentence used, or capable of being used, to make a statement – the sort of linguistic unit which it is appropriate to assess for truth or falsity. The principal issue, that which divides realists from anti-realists in the theory of meaning, is whether the notions of truth and falsity can be taken for granted, taken as primitive notions in terms of which meaning is to be explicated (realist), or whether these notions themselves are seen to stand in need of explication in the light of an account of meaning which rests on some notion other than truth, such as that of justified assertion (anti-realist). Since the overall concern of both parties here is with truths as expressions of objective knowledge, another way of putting the issue is whether the notion of objective knowledge can be taken for granted or whether an account of what constitutes objective knowledge is to be derived from an account of the meaning, or representational function, of those linguistic items which are deemed capable of expressing it and of the standards by reference to which such claims are assessed.

Adapting the terminology of Dummett,[3] realism in the theory of meaning will here be referred to as 'global realism'. The global realist characteristically maintains that to give the meaning of an indicative sentence is to give its truth-conditions and, moreover, that every such meaningful sentence is determinately true or false (Principle of Bivalence) even if we might never be able to determine which is the case. Whether a statement is true or false cannot, if it is to be an expression of objective knowledge, depend on whether we know that what it says is or is not the case. Objective truth or falsity must depend solely on whether what is said to be the case is indeed the case: i.e. truth or falsity is an objective property of linguistic representations of the world and is thus dependent solely on whether their truth-conditions are or are not satisfied.

There are thus two components to global realism: (i) belief in the independent existence of the world about which we talk and of which we seek knowledge, and (ii) the view that objective knowledge of this world requires possession of correct representations of it, where it is the world itself which provides the standard of what constitutes correctness. Correctness is thus a matter of the relation between representation and the world; something which can be discussed independently of how it may be possible to determine correctness or incorrectness, truth or falsity. Representations are in themselves correct or incorrect in virture of their relation to what they represent and irrespective of whether or how this may be humanly determined (hence the Principle of Bivalence). Thus global realism is a general view concerning the nature of knowledge, the nature and function of representations, and of the world and our relation to it as potential possessors of knowledge and users of representations. On this view the world (object of knowledge) is held to be strictly independent both of language and of the nature of the knowledge seeker (subject of knowledge). Global realists go on to argue amongst themselves about what there is; whether there are minds as well as matter, whether there are numbers or electrons, etc.

The non-realist in the theory of meaning (the global anti-realist) does not deny the existence of everything but his own mental states; he merely refuses to subscribe to the Principle of Bivalence and rejects accounts of meaning based on truth-conditions. This is because he denies the possibility of knowledge which is objective in the realist's sense. He argues that any conception of the world and anything we say about it will be said from a particular perspective within it. We are part of the world and can only know it from some perspective within it. Knowledge can therefore never be wholly independent of the knowledge seeker and his activities. Those seeking knowledge of a given kind are responsible for setting standards of correctness and incorrectness via their interactions with the rest of the world.

The contrast between these two positions can again be illustrated by reference to the problems which quantum mechanics poses. We tend to assume that things in the world have, at any given time, a determinate position and a determinate momentum, whether or not we know this, by observation and measurement, and that our observation does not affect the truth or falsity of any statement concerning position or momentum, i.e. the statement has a truth-value, and the same one, whether we have confirmed this by measurement or not. This is in conformity with global realism. But Heisenberg's Indeterminacy Principle ($\Delta p \cdot \Delta q \geq h$, where h is Planck's constant) entails (i) that a particle cannot simultaneously have a precise position and momentum, and (ii) that the result of measuring position, and hence giving it a fairly precise value, will be to deprive momentum of any precise value. This situation is often interpreted as showing that one can no longer assume that the observer and the situation observed are mutually independent. The result of measurement is objective, but it depends on the sort of measurement and on its being made; one cannot say that the particle has either a definite position or a definite momentum if no measurement is made.

The anti-realist's point is that the content of a claim to knowledge cannot be wholly divorced from the sort of evidence that would be counted as justifying it. What makes knowledge objective is not relation to a wholly independent reality, but the sort of critical standards applied in assessing evidence. From this perspective realists are criticised for their lack of objectivity.

> Objectivity consists in so fully realizing the countless intrusions of the self in everyday thought and the countless illusions which result ... Realism, on the

contrary, consists in ignoring the existence of self and thence regarding one's own perspective as immediately objective and absolute. Realism is thus an anthropocentric illusion.[4]

This sort of view has influenced conceptions of scientific knowledge via Kuhn's book, *The structure of scientific revolutions*,[5] and the many discussions stimulated by it.

Realisms and anti-realisms in the philosophy of science

Realism with respect to scientific theories has already been taken to be the view that the aim of scientific theorising is knowledge, and was contrasted with the instrumentalist view that the aim is merely to construct more efficient instruments of prediction and control. Clearly the question of whether scientific theories in general, or a given type of scientific theory in particular does, or could, constitute a body of knowledge will be addressed rather differently depending on whether the background view of language, knowledge and meaning is that of global realism or global anti-realism. Most debates within analytic philosophy of science have occurred against the background of global realism. But the transition from global realism to a realism about scientific theories is far from automatic.

The form of scientific knowledge. This is primarily because the goal of science has, from its Greek origins to the present day, never been conceived merely as a matter of possessing correct factual knowledge. There are additional requirements made on the form which scientific knowledge should take. Knowledge of a motley collection of disconnected facts of the sort that might stand one in good stead in a general knowledge competition does not constitute scientific knowledge which is required to be organised, theoretical knowledge. If scientific theories are to be treated by the global realist as expressions of knowledge then he must distinguish between scientific and non-scientific knowledge. Non-scientific knowledge is at best incomplete knowledge because it includes no representation of the structure of the world, of the underlying principles in virtue of which facts are interconnected and related. If scientific theories express knowledge, then the requirements placed on the form that scientific theories should take must reflect a form of organisation presumed to be present in the world. The realist about scientific theories is thus going, at the very least, to be committed to belief in a structured world and to very general claims about the nature of that structure, claims which have to be co-ordinated with his account of the form that scientific theories themselves should, ideally, take.

But what, more exactly, is the function of scientific theories supposed to be, why do we want them? The answer which would have been given by Aristotle, and which would still be given by scientific realists, is that scientific theories serve as the basis for providing explanations, and hence for an understanding, of what goes on in the natural world. But scientific realists are not all agreed about what scientific explanation consists in. Linked to this is a disagreement about what actually constitutes a scientific theory, i.e. which of the statements that scientists make can be counted as expressions of knowledge and thus as strictly theoretical claims.

There are three basic options for the global realist confronted with a scientific theory T, such as quantum mechanics: he can treat it as a body of statements about the behaviour of sub-atomic 'particles' (scientific realism), as a body of statements about the world of experience (empirical realism), or as a mere calculus facilitating prediction and control of the world of experience (instrumentalism). The scientific realist will take T to consist of a set of sentences which are true or false in virtue of the nature of the micro-world of sub-atomic phenomena. The empirical realist will take T to consist of a set of sentences which are true or false in virtue of the nature of the world of possible experience. The difference between the two will be reflected in the kind of truth-conditions assigned to the sentences of T. The instrumentalist denies that the sentences of T are expressions of knowledge; there is thus no need to assign truth-conditions and T may be treated either as a formal calculating device or as a convenient fiction.

Scientific realism. If a theory T is a candidate for being a body of knowledge then it must be possible to assign truth-conditions to the sentences in which it is expressed, truth-conditions which give their factual (cognitive) content. Moreover, T will not even be a starter as a scientific theory if the truth-conditions assigned are such that in order for all of T's sentences to be true the world would have to contain things which we already firmly believe it does not contain (for example, a theory referring to astral influences is unlikely to be taken seriously by twentieth-century scientists). In such conditions we would already judge the sentences false.

But scientific theorising frequently involves postulating the existence of things which are not directly observable and physical magnitudes which are not directly measurable (electrons, genes, mass, charge) together with principles specifying their causal properties. These postulates are made in an attempt to explain and understand phenomena already observed, i.e. observed phenomena are presumed to have been caused by the action of the unobserved, physically more fundamental entities and properties. On a realist view of scientific theories, the terms used in them (theoretical terms) should refer to things which actually exist even if they are not directly observable.[6]

Newton's theory of gravitation, for example, involves the supposition that each material body contains a determinate quantity of matter – its mass. This quantity is not directly measurable; it is measurable only via its effects, effects which are themselves stated as part of the Newtonian theory. Mass enters into the second law of motion – force= mass × acceleration – and into the principle of gravitational attraction, which asserts that between any two material bodies there will be an attractive force which is directly proportional to their masses and inversely proportional to the distance between them ($G \propto m_1 m_2 / r^2$). Differences in mass will thus be detectable using a beam balance, and via the different forces required to accelerate (or decelerate) things. Conversely, difference in mass is used to explain why it is that some things are more difficult to accelerate and decelerate than others.

According to the scientific realist, the aim of fundamental theoretical research is to discover and describe the inner mechanisms productive of the phenomena we observe. He is thus committed to the view that everyday objects are really complexes of physically more fundamental entities whose action on our sense organs and instruments is responsible for the character of our observations and measurements.

Yet in *Principia* Newton claims only to be giving a mathematical theory of gravitation; he specifically denies that he is giving an account of the *causes* of gravitational phenomena.[7] His claim is that the principle of gravitational attraction gives a *mathematical* formula for determining the magnitude of the force acting between any two material bodies and that this single formula suffices for reproducing both the motion of the planets round the sun and for the motion of projectiles near the surface of the earth. But he leaves open the question of how the presence of this force – the apparent action of two spatially separated bodies on each other – is to be explained. He does not assert that action at a distance takes place. An attractive force between heavenly bodies was reminiscent of astrological influences and the occult powers which the Cartesian mechanism banished as scientifically disreputable. Newton, in proposing his theory, thus backs off from full realism at this point. Gravitational attraction is not proposed as an ultimately explanatory causal principle, but as a mathematical, descriptively unifying principle, which itself stands in need of explanation.

This distinction between what may be a descriptively correct universal principle, such as that of gravitational attraction, and an explanatory causal principle is not one which would be universally recognised. It is only the proponents of the strongest form of scientific realism (causal realism) who would accept it; those who, like Harré and Popper, believe in the existence of causal powers, fundamental causal properties embedded in the nature of the basic constituents of the physical universe which are responsible for structuring and ordering the course of events (nature). To put it crudely, this would be to say that it is because the sun and the planets have the power to attract one another in a certain way (i.e. in accordance with Newton's principle) that they behave as they do – forming the relatively stable structure which we know as the solar system with its characteristic pattern of relative motions.

However, those who subscribe to a Humean view of causality would not accept that the world *can* contain causal powers (see Mackie[8] for arguments to this effect). No true theory can therefore assert their existence and science cannot in this strongest sense hope to reveal inner mechanisms because ultimately there are none; there is nothing generating or producing the course of events, there is simply a structured sequence of events. The world, at any moment, can consist only of objects possessing occurrent properties (ones which entail nothing as to their future behaviour) and is in its totality the spatially related and temporally ordered sequence of such states.[9] From this point of view science does indeed aim at knowledge, does aim to discover the internal structures of observable physical objects and does aim to explain the observed behaviour of such objects on the basis of their internal structure, but the sense of explanation is weakened to accord with the Humean account of causality. On Hume's account, to say that event *A* caused event *B* is, and can only be, to say that all *A*-type events are, as a matter of fact, followed by *B*-type events. Scientific explanation, searching for the causes of an observed event *B*, can thus only consist in discovering what sort of event or complex of events *B* really was (what actually happened)[10] and finding antecedent events which can be linked to *B* as redescribed by the application of general principles, so that *B*'s following on from what went before can be seen as an instance of a general pattern of successions. Newton's *Principia* presentation of gravitational attraction is here taken as a paradigm of what science should be aiming for; Newton was mistaken if he thought that there was any scientific task which he had left undone.

We thus have two competing versions of scientific realism. Within the framework of global realism this opposition will appear in the form of disagreement over the sort of truth-conditions to be assigned to the claims of a scientific theory, or even over the claims which are thought to be properly part of the theory. To say that a scientific theory *T* can be equated with a set of sentences covers up the problem of how this is to be done. Often it is assumed that these sentences will have already been assigned a logical form (i.e. that *T* has been written in a formal logical language), but to do this one will already have to have made some decisions about the nature of the truth-conditions of *T*, decisions about what *T* is or can be saying. The causal realist will want to treat talk of force, energy and power as part of the theory because it is something which can be literally true, whereas the matter realist will not, but will want to say that such talk should ultimately be reducible to statements asserting the existence of particular kinds of states of matter in the context of certain kinds of regularities in the sequence of events and/or states. In the absence of such reductions their use is an expression of ignorance, of the incompleteness of our knowledge.

This is in part why there have been such lengthy arguments about the attribution of truth-conditions to causal statements and to statements where a dispositional property, such as brittleness, is attributed to an object. The problem for the causal realist is that in such arguments the dice are loaded against him. The demand for truth-conditions is one which predisposes one to look at the world in a way which excludes causal powers, production, processes, activity, etc. If required to give the truth-conditions of 'This plastic is brittle' one might respond by saying that this means that it can be snapped easily, will not bend without breaking, etc. But this is to characterise how the plastic will behave under certain conditions, not to give a condition, applicable now, which defines the condition or state of brittleness. Talk of truth-conditions has an inbuilt bias towards thinking in terms of states and successions of states. It is therefore hardly surprising that it is the weakened form of scientific realism (matter realism) which has been most frequently adopted and most discussed.

Problems for matter realism. But in this form scientific realism raises several problems, ones which make non-realist positions seem attractive. These have to do with the relation between theory and experience. Indeed problems concerning the relation between science and the world tend to be transformed into those of the relation between theory and experience. These problems are of two kinds, ontological and epistemological.

The first is that to which Eddington refers in the following famous passage:

> I have settled down to the task of writing these lectures and have drawn up my chairs to my two tables. Two tables! Yes; there are duplicates of every object about me – two tables, two chairs, two pens . . .
> One of them . . . is a commonplace object of that environment which I call the world . . . It has extension: it is comparatively permanent; it is coloured; above all it is substantial . . . Table No. 2 is my scientific table . . . It does not belong to the world previously mentioned – that world which spontaneously appears around me when I open my eyes . . . It is part of a world which in much more devious ways has forced itself on my attention. My scientific table is mostly emptiness. Sparsely scattered in that emptiness are numerous electric charges rushing about with great speed; but their combined bulk amounts to less than a billionth of the bulk of the table itself.[11]

The matter realist seems forced into Eddington's double vision whilst at the same time being obliged to say that in fact only one of these tables, the scientific table, is real. For on his account, if we are to give 'causal' explanations applicable to things appearing in the world of experience we have to be able to redescribe what is experienced in theoretical terms, the sort of terms in which our scientific (causal) laws are formulated. For scientific theories to be a source of explanations of what is observed, what is observed must be redescribable using the language of that theory and hence as something to which the theory applies (planets must be described as material bodies and assigned a mass). This is because if the only thing a scientific

234

theory can ultimately do is yield laws descriptive of actual states and their sequence, an explanation of the occurrence of an individual state can amount only to redescription which makes the particular case an instance of a wider pattern. To cite Eddington again:

> Notwithstanding its strange construction it (my scientific table) turns out to be an entirely efficient table. It supports my writing paper as satisfactorily as table No. 1; for when I lay the paper on it the little electric particles with their headlong speed keep on hitting the underside, so that the paper is maintained in shuttlecock fashion at a nearly steady level. If I lean on this table I shall not go through; or, to be strictly accurate, the chance of my scientific elbow going through my scientific table is so excessively small that it can be neglected in practical life. Reviewing their properties one by one, there seems to be nothing to choose between the two tables for ordinary purposes; but when abnormal circumstances befall, then my scientific table shows to advantage. If the house catches fire my scientific table will dissolve quite naturally into scientific smoke, whereas my familiar table undergoes a metamorphosis of its substantial nature which I can only regard as miraculous.[12]

This sort of explanation cannot work between levels of description to show how the little electric particles are productive of the sort of relatively stable complex structure which is a table. This would not fit the analysis of cause in terms of the regular succession of one type of event/state upon another, *distinct* event/state, for the table in one sense *is* its material constituents, and the reductionist takes this as a logical 'is' of identity. But it may also be read causally – the cell owes its being to its chemical constituents and their action – by the causal realist who is therefore not forced to choose between worlds in the same way.

The world of the matter realist is thus that of the most fundamental physical theories of matter. Any scientific theory, if it is to express knowledge of the world, must be talking about this world and thus in principle its statements should have truth-conditions expressible as conditions on this world. Any biological principles, for example, ought to be restatable as correct chemical principles, or be re-expressed in such a way as to be deducible from chemical principles, which in turn should be reducible to physical principles. The matter realist is thus led to a reductionist view of all scientific theories other than the fundamental theories of matter. This is a form of non-realism about these as scientific theories. Their theoretical entities and the kinds of properties with which they deal are not treated as part of the real world, any more than observed colours, tastes or smells. But it is still realist in the sense that these theories are seen as able to express knowledge about the world – their statements are objectively true or false, but what they say about the world can only be determined once they have been translated into the language of fundamental physical theory. The most frequently cited example of this sort of reduction is that of thermodynamics to dynamics via the equation of heat with the motion of molecules, and the identification of the temperature of a gas sample with the mean kinetic energy of its molecules.

However, Eddington, for one, was unwilling to give up his everyday table. And there is reason for being unwilling to go down the realist reductionist road, given that there are also epistemological problems to be faced at the end of it. Do we have any reason for supposing current fundamental physical theory to be (a) correct in what it says or (b) truly fundamental? In the absence of assurance on these points we would be in the position not merely of not knowing whether what we say about the world is true, but even of not knowing exactly what it is that we are saying about it, for we would not know, for example, what the real (the scientific) table is like. Moreover, if we follow Hume's arguments, we find that we can never be in a position of knowing the correctness of any causal claim. Such claims amount to making universal statements, statements about the total sequence of events/states. But we can only observe these one by one as they occur. If these claims can have only descriptive force, i.e. if they are only contingent statements about how the totality of events/states happens to be but might not have been and there can be no further explanation of why they are this way by reference to the way the sequence is produced, then there is no evidence available to us which will logically justify them. This is, of course, the problem of induction in the form it takes in Hume. For the scientific realist there is the additional problem of how experience can furnish evidence of the existence of theoretical entities (entities which are not directly observable).

Empirical realism. So far as evidence goes it would seem that we are confined to the world of experience. It is this which prompts non-realist accounts of the nature and function of scientific theories, i.e. accounts which treat the world of experience as the real world and do not allow that science can yield knowledge of a reality underlying that world. Even if there is some independent physical reality of which the experienced world is a mere appearance, we can have no knowledge about it. Non-realist accounts of science, which still work within the framework of global realism (hence the term empirical, as opposed to scientific, realism), thus start by turning the tables on the scientific realist; in order to be capable of expressing objective knowledge the sentences of a scientific theory must have truth-conditions which are conditions on the world of experience. The non-realist need not deny that science aims at knowledge, but he characteristically will deny the existence of theoretical entities, entities which are not directly observable.

But what is, or can be meant by the world of experience as an object of scientific knowledge? If it were simply the sequence of sensory experiences of an individual, then since each individual (assuming, perhaps rashly, that there are others) is acquainted with a different sequence of experiences, each inhabits his own world and there is no public world to be talked about, known or investigated in any way by science. The whole idea of scientific knowledge as objective, publicly accessible knowledge starts from a presumption that there is a single world experienced by everyone. So what is, or can be, the objective content in each person's experience, given that their qualitative character is not something which can be made public? What, in other words, can constitute the evidential base for science, and what sort of experiental knowledge could be objective knowledge, knowledge of the world experienced?

Eddington succinctly summarises the view which was widely held in the first part of this century. It is that measurement provides the observational base for science and that in measurement there is a triple correspondence between

(a) a mental image, which is in our minds and not in the external world;
(b) some kind of counterpart in the external world, which is of an inscrutable nature;
(c) a set of pointer readings, which exact science can study and connect with other pointer readings.[13]

Measurements can be publicly agreed upon because the standards in measurement are publicly set and measurement itself is a matter of the comparison of one thing with another. It thus depends on the relation between experienced items, not on the intrinsic characteristics of the way they are experienced. Objective knowledge, then, is knowledge of the structure of the world of experience (or in Russell's terms, the world of sense-data). The observational base for theories concerning the more general aspects of this structure lies in measurement, in taking instrument readings. The knowledge is expressed mathematically and the structure attributed to the world is reflected in the formal logical or mathematical structure of scientific theories. Talk of models, of mechanisms, etc. may be important as part of the heuristics of science, for developing ideas and getting them across, but it is not an integral part of any scientific theory. The function of scientific theory is thus to describe the structural organisation of measurable physical magnitudes. The factual content of a theory is determined by seeing what implications it has for the results of measurements.

In this context the strongest requirement of a scientific theory would be that it should be possible to assign each of its sentences truth-conditions expressed as conditions on the world of possible experience, i.e. to treat it as making determinate statements about this world by requiring its statements to be reducible to purely empirical statements. This was the programme inspired indirectly by Mach, more directly by Russell and pursued by Carnap.[14] The actual form of theoretical statements, the use of terms purporting to refer to theoretical entities, is treated instrumentally. Theoretical entities are logical fictions employed for the sake of convenience in expression but talk of which should be reducible to statements in which no reference is made to them. The empirical content is contained in the structure attributed to the world of sense-data, in statements concerning the values of physical magnitudes and their interrelations.

For example, $G \propto m_1 m_2 / r^2$ can be assigned an empirical content only if empirical methods of determining the various magnitudes have been specified (different detailed formulations of this requirement emerged as, for example, operationalism and verificationism). But mass is not a directly measurable magnitude, and the specification of the empirical significance of sentences involving it is not trivial. Moreover, any methods of determining the relative masses of two bodies will presuppose either the correctness of Newton's gravitational principle or his laws of motion, or both, or the correctness of special or general relativity theory. The accounts will differ if the background theory is different. Theory functions to say what the possible methods of mass comparison are by linking mass to more directly observable magnitudes. But if mass is then *defined* as that which is compared (measured) by the methods suggested by Newtonian theory, the effect will be to make the theoretical principles used to arrive at the account of empirical significance true by definition. Defined in this way mass can only be Newtonian mass, and principles originally thought to be making contingent, factual claims about the world, by means of conventions governing the use of logical fictions, come to be represented as being true by definition, mere verbal truths. This was not the position the empirical realist originally wished to defend.

Instrumentalism. The full reductionist approach pursued by the logical positivists thus runs into two closely related difficulties: (i) that of drawing the distinction between analytic and synthetic truths, and (ii) the difficulty of separating out a pure observational language for science, one which is independent of theory.[15] Given empirical procedures are interpreted as measurements of mass only in the light of theoretical principles which thus determine the way in which empirical definitions of mass are given. Again the example of 'mass' illustrates the way in which empirical meaning cannot be assigned to theoretical statements one by one. One cannot assign empirical significance to '$G \propto m_1 m_2 / r^2$' in isolation from Newton's laws of motion. Such a statement depends for its meaning on its theoretical context. This was stressed by Duhem, from whom Quine took his starting point:

the proper aim of physical theory is the schematic representation by means of mathematical symbols of the laws established by the experimenter; any theory one of whose consequences is in plain contradiction with an observed law should be mercilessly rejected. But it is not possible to compare an isolated consequence of theory with an isolated experimental law. The two systems must be taken in their integrity: the entire system of theoretical representations on the one hand, and the entire system of observed data on the other. As such they are to be compared to each other and their resemblance judged.[16]

But a clear separation between Duhem's two systems, of theory and of observationally established experimental laws, has been shown by the work of Quine, Kuhn, Feyerabend and others not to be possible.

These difficulties, and particularly the difficulty of finding any really neutral observational base for science, one which can be recorded in pure factual statements without any dependence on theory for their interpretation, have been seen as foreclosing the option of seeing scientific theories as aiming at objective knowledge of a world of experience without treating them as postulating the existence of theoretical entities. The choice is between full scientific realism and denying that scientific theories aim at knowledge – some form of instrumentalism.

Arguments based on the problems of separating out a pure objective factual base for science, arguments to the effect that all observation is theory-laden, lead most naturally to a questioning of the possibility of objective knowledge in the sense which underlies global realism. All our statements about the world are a product of interpretation in the light of an already held system of beliefs, a conceptual scheme. Scientific theorising is continuous with the wider process of world-making, which is also that of myth-making and whose function is to enable us to cope with (i.e. increase our chances of survival in) the environment in which we find ourselves (Quine and, more radically, Feyerabend). Such a fictionalist position takes a very wide view of what belongs to a scientific theory. It really sees no boundaries to scientific theory and any other descriptive discourse. But it is possible to take a much narrower, formalist view of theory – scientific theories consist simply of mathematically formulated principles and deductions. Such calculi are denied any meaning, any cognitive content. The point of developing them is purely to have more efficient ways of reasoning about, predicting and hence controlling the world.

What should be noted is that such instrumentalisms still presume that there is an external world to be coped with. The instrumentalist position is still defined by reference to the framework of global realism. The sort of knowledge it denies to science is that linked to global realism and on this ground it denies science any cognitive function. The conception of what would constitute scientific knowledge, were it possible, is not challenged.

Science and pre-science

A curious feature of the above sketch mapping of options is that it could have been given as part of a discussion of pre-seventeenth-century science. Many of the moves would have been familiar, albeit in a slightly different form, to Scholastic philosophers. It is as if the so-called scientific revolution had no impact on the conception of scientific knowledge and hence made no alteration in the basic configuration of views of how science might or should relate to the world.

Aristotelian realism

This can be illustrated by looking briefly at the Aristotelian conception of science. The Aristotelian position is that of causal realism in a form which came to be opposed by nominalism. As Aristotle explained it, scientific knowledge should serve as the basis for providing explanations (demonstrations of causes) of why or how something is the case by starting from accounts of the essences or natures of the things involved. This view of what constitutes the goal of scientific knowledge is derived from mathematics done in the style of Euclidean geometry where the properties of geometrical figures are proved by appeal to definitions, axioms and postulates. A geometrically adequate definition of, for example, a triangle is one which will distinguish triangles from all other geometrical figures (gives necessary and sufficient conditions for being a triangle) and will serve as the basis for deducing the geometrical properties of triangles. A geometrical proof based on such a definition shows why, given that a plane figure is a triangle, given what it is to be a plane figure, a triangle, an angle and a right angle, the sum of the internal angles of the triangle *must* be equal to two right angles. This second requirement on definition is far from trivial and can be satisfied only in the light of the means used for providing proofs. A definition which is adequate for Euclid is not adequate or appropriate in co-ordinate geometry.

A similar scientific knowledge of the natural world where things are constantly changing would have to focus on natural objects *qua* changeable. To be able to understand and explain change requires a knowledge of the relevant causes, reasons or principles of change. Physics, the science of change and the changeable, thus seeks knowledge of the essences or natures of natural things which, since it must serve as a basis for the explanation of change, must be knowledge of principles of change, i.e. of characteristic powers, potentialities and tendencies to action.

It follows from this account that the disciplines which Aristotle recognises and calls mathematical, namely astronomy, optics and harmonics, will not serve as a basis for giving the causes of the phenomena they study, for they do not yield demonstrations starting from accounts of physical natures. They describe the structure of the relationships between certain physical magnitudes ignoring the specific physical natures of the primary substances in which these magnitudes inhere. The most they can do is to provide mathematical models which 'save the phenomena' and which can thus be used for the purposes of prediction. It is this distinction that, as mentioned above, is still to be found in Newton's *Principia*, where the theory of gravitation is presented as being purely mathematical, not an account of causes. Orthodox Aristotelian realism in other words required a non-realist, frequently instrumentalist attitude towards mathematical astronomy. Bellarmine thus represented Aristotelian orthodoxy, not an instrumentalist attitude towards science in general, but only towards astronomy and the other mathematical arts. Galileo was not merely advocating a realist position but a non-Aristotelian realism.

According to Aristotle, demonstrations linking accounts of essence to the fact to be explained should, ideally, take the form of a sequence of valid syllogisms. The simplest form would be

S's are *M*, *M*'s are *P*, therefore *S*'s are *P*.

(Wines are products of fermentation. Products of fermentation contain alcohol. Therefore wines contain alcohol.) Here *M*, the middle term, is thought of as the cause linking *S* and *P*.

The impression conveyed by Aristotle's *Posterior analytics* is that in a fully adequate understanding the causal order of the natural world would be represented by the logical order amongst terms supplied with adequate definitions (definitions embodying knowledge of natures or essences). In taking this ideal as the goal of science it is presumed that there is a causal order in the world and that it is such that it can be mapped with the means available in Aristotelian logic. This logic deals with general terms, such as man, horse, tree, gold and their possible relations. The world is thus also presumed to have a structure representable by appropriately defined general terms, i.e. it is presumed that the things in the world do, in their own right, fall into classes (natural kinds or species) with all things of the same kind sharing the same nature (form or essence) but differing in their matter. Scientific knowledge requires discovery both of how to discern the boundaries of these natural kinds, or species (an accurate classificatory system), and accounts of what it is to be a thing of a given kind.

Again, this is no trivial matter, as the history of biology or chemistry would illustrate. In chemistry we find examples which come close to the Aristotelian ideal of accounts of essence, with chemical substances defined by formulae giving their chemical composition and chemical elements defined by giving their atomic number (modern discussions of natural kinds, inspired by the work of Kripke, focus on such examples). For us water is H_2O, whereas for Aristotle it was an element, a simple substance defined as being cold and moist. The difference between these two ways of giving an account of what water is point to an incompleteness in the purely logically articulated account of the goal of scientific knowledge. Just as in geometry what counts as an adequate definition cannot be specified independently of the method of proof in play, so too accounts of the nature of a substance will be assessed by reference to a background of causal principles which determine what counts as an explanation.

In his *Posterior analytics* Aristotle seems to misrepresent not only the geometry of his day but also his own physics. Geometrical demonstrations do not fall fully into the syllogistic pattern; constructions are performed, and appeal is made to axioms and postulates as well as to definitions. The definitions yield demonstrations only in the context of axioms and postulates; the geometrical properties of a triangle do not follow from its definitions by pure logic alone (as the existence of non-Euclidean triangles shows). Similarly in the physical case there is a background of general principles concerning change (motion) and its causes (to be found in Aristotle's *Physics*) such as that every change has a cause, that all change takes time, and that all action and hence all change is a result of the interaction of contrary qualities of which one is an active power and the other a corresponding passive power. Moreover, contrary qualities can only belong to things which have an underlying similarity; only that which could be hot can be cold, and vice versa. Heat is an active power and cold the corresponding passive one. That which is hot acts on that which is cold, making it less cold. Moist and dry are similarly opposed. The characterisation of water as cold and moist is thus, within an Aristotelian framework, an indication of its fundamental causal properties. Aristotelian physics postulates not only a structure of natural kinds (a structure which can be mapped by logical relations between substantial terms) but also a causal structure amongst qualities (linked to the logical notion of contraries) governed by general principles concerning action changes and causes. It is this causal structure which determines what form accounts of essence should take. Twentieth-century accounts of the natures of chemical substances are similarly justified by reference to a complex background of theory concerning the basic composition of matter and basic modes of action and interaction.

Nominalism

Nominalists, from whatever period, reject the claim that there are natural kinds. Instead they hold that general terms are, and can only be, names which men attach to things; the world is a world of individuals, or particulars, between some of which there may be qualitative similarities, but which do not naturally fall into kinds or species. It follows that a nominalist will see the goals of Aristotelian science as misconceived: science of this form cannot yield objective knowledge of the world, only a knowledge of the way we use words. But there were, and are, a variety of nominalist positions.[17]

There were those who, like Ockham, saw our use of general terms as a reflection not of the nature of the world, but of the nature of our own minds. This is very much Hume's position and a modern form was advocated by Quine.[18] Quine gives an evolutionary account – those

242

classifications persist and are thought of as natural which fit a human being for survival (people making different classifications do not survive). It follows that creatures whose needs are different would develop different classificatory schemes. In this way, through our classifications we do express a form of knowledge of the world, but this is a species dependent, or even culture relative, view of it. It is a view which reflects our needs and interests rather than the world as it is in itself. Divisions into kinds are necessary for us; kinds are necessary fictions.

From one point of view this is a form of instrumentalism – the adoption of a particular classification is explained by reference to the function it performs; for example, it helps us to get around in the world. Yet in a stricter sense this is naturalism rather than instrumentalism, since it suggests that the whole process of adoption of classificatory schemes is an unconscious, unreflective process – they are not developed by us as instruments.

However nominalists such as Hobbes and Locke saw the development of general terms and classificatory schemes very much in instrumental terms. Each person may invent his own, and the aim must be to develop a system that is most useful for the purposes at hand. The meanings of general terms may thus be established by convention.

Nominalism could be associated with a general sceptical rejection of the claim that any sort of knowledge of the world in itself or any understanding of its causes was to be gained by human beings using their own faculties. However it was equally associated with the shifting conceptions of science which constituted the scientific revolution. The new mechanistic science and accompanying mechanistic conceptions of the world required rejection not only of Aristotelian metaphysics but also of the Aristotelian conception of the primary goal of science as knowledge of the essences or natures of things.

The new science

The two features which, as mentioned at the beginning of the chapter, are seen as marking the birth of a new conception of science are (i) emphasis on the quantitative, on mathematically formulated principles, and (ii) emphasis on experiment. It is true (as Kuhn shows[19]) that science exhibiting both characteristics simultaneously, i.e. science living up to the seventeenth-century conception of what it ought to be, did not really exist until the mid-nineteenth century, but science has since then increasingly conformed to this pattern.

We have already mentioned that even in Aristotelian science there are general physical principles concerning change and its causes which form the background against which the search for essences is conducted. But discovery of these principles is not, for the Aristotelian, part of

243

the goal of science. Rather they are presumed to be self-evident and knowable *a priori*, prior to any empirical investigation. Aristotelian science was empirical to the extent that discoveries of natural groupings and of the natures and causes of things were to be, and could only be, furthered by observation. But the causal principles forming the framework for this investigation were set *a priori* (as metaphysical principles). It is for this reason that Francis Bacon criticised Aristotelian science – for going straight from observation to first principles. Bacon insisted that no general principles could be known *a priori* but must all be deduced by a procedure of successive generalisation from experimental investigations and observations.

Bacon thus effects a reversal of emphasis. The goal of science is to *discover* the most general causal principles structuring the world. Only once these are known can full accounts of the natures (forms) of things be given. Bacon was not, in any normal understanding of the term, a mechanist, but his reversal of emphasis happens to coincide with that required by those advocating a mathematically expressed science of mechanics. For mechanics deals with principles of motion and its causes, which are common to all manner of material objects. It therefore similarly places emphasis on general causal principles and treats these as yet to be discovered.

This revised conception of the goal of science is intimately connected with advocacy of the new experimental methods of achieving scientific knowledge. What the discussion so far has failed to give any recognition to is the question of what it means for science to be experimental. This does not just mean paying attention to observations, or even just endeavouring to test theories by reference to observation. This was done by astronomers from before the time of Ptolemy, yet these were in no sense experimental theories. They were concerned with making accurate predictions; if the predictions were not right the theory (model) was not serving its function and needed some sort of modification. Aristotelian science, in seeking knowledge of the natures of things falling into natural kinds, had similarly to be non-interventionist (natural history); it could only learn from observation of naturally occurring things and from their natural course of development. Only this would reveal innate tendencies and powers. Artefacts and artificially contrived situations, being unnatural, did not contribute to an understanding of nature.

It is important to recognise the extent to which modern science has departed from this ideal of understanding nature as it is in and by itself (following its natural course). It is based on the assumption that it is only by disrupting and intervening in the world that an understanding of the forces determining the natural order can be obtained. The point which Bacon insisted upon in urging experimental science was that the route to scientific knowledge, the sort of knowledge that would lead to increased power over nature by yielding increased ability to introduce new technology, could not be through a mere passive observation of nature taking its natural course, however detailed or accurate this observation might be, but in addition required intervention, the setting up of contrived conditions, designing and making instruments and contriving apparatus for conducting experiments. Nature was to be put on the rack and made to yield answers to the questions the scientist wanted answered. (Hacking uses a slogan which captures the spirit of experimental science: 'Don't just peer, interfere!'[20])

The need for experimental science thus arises out of the sort of understanding sought. This is explicitly required to be an understanding which will serve as a basis for influencing the course of nature, for preventing or mitigating natural disasters, for developing new improved plant and animal strains, etc. That is, its aim is to seek out underlying causal principles, which it presumes to be present and which it sees as responsible for naturally occurring phenomena, but also as manipulable, making it possible to divert the course of nature. It is in part because of the practical orientation that the principles sought are required to have a quantitative form. In practice precision is important, different orders of precision being required for different tasks. Mere qualitative principles are not enough even for the cook, still less for the apothecary. Quantities need to be specified if a reliable product is to result.

It is clear, then, that early advocates of experimental/mathematical science proposed both a new relation between science and the world and correspondingly a new conception of scientific knowledge, the goal of science. Science was no longer to be the product of speculative contemplation on nature observed from a distance (from an external viewpoint), but was to be derived from reflection on practical involvement with and intervention in the world, aimed at increasing the effectiveness of that intervention by rational, analytic dissection of problems and strategies for their solution. The world studied by the high-energy physicist in his particle accelerator is a world which is of his own making, albeit ultimately out of materials supplied to him. It is therefore not independent of his knowledge, his beliefs or his practical abilities.

Global realism is linked to the conception of knowledge appropriate to science as speculative contemplation based on passive observation (recording facts, literal truths), not to experimental, technological science. Discussion of the relation between fundamental research science, which is itself experimental and technological, and industrially orientated technology thus requires a framework based on a different conception of knowledge.

Notes

(An author's name followed by a number in square brackets refers to the book or article which has that number in the bibliography.)

1. See Bohm [1].

2. A more detailed discussion of these issues can be found in Chs. 2 and 3.

3. M. Dummett, 'The reality of the past' in [2], p. 367.

4. J. Piaget, *The child's conception of the world* (Littlefield, Adams, Totowa, New Jersey, 1972).

5. T. Kuhn, *The structure of scientific revolutions*, 2nd edn (University of Chicago Press, Chicago, 1970).

6. H. Putnam, 'What is realism?' *Proceedings of the Aristotelian Society* (1975–6), pp. 177–94. An extended version of this article appears in [3], Part I, Lectures ii and iii.

7. I. Newton *Principia*, trans. and ed. A. Motte (2 vols, University of California Press, Berkeley and Los Angeles, 1934).

8. See Mackie [5].

9. This is not strictly speaking Hume's position, although he sometimes talks as if it were. Strictly speaking all events are for Hume mental events. The sequence of events constituting the world is then the sequence of perceptual states of an individual. For a further discussion of Hume on causation see Ch. 14.

10. Hume himself would deny even this role to scientific explanation. His position is much closer to that of empirical realism, discussed below.

11. See Eddington [4], pp. xi–xii.

12. Ibid., p. xii.

13. Ibid., p. 254.

14. See Carnap [6].

15. See W.V. Quine, 'Two dogmas of empiricism' in his *From a logical point of view* (Harper and Row, New York, 1963), pp. 20–46.

16. See Duhem [7], p. 220.

17. See Goodman [9] for one twentieth-century example.

18. See Quine [8].

19. See Kuhn [10].

20. See Hacking [11].

Bibliography

For an account of the conflict between Galileo and the Church see *The sleepwalkers*, by Arthur Koestler (Penguin Books, Harmondsworth, 1964).

Niels Bohr represents an anti-realist approach to quantum mechanics. His account of his debate with Einstein, who held out for a realist interpretation, may be found in 'Discussion with Einstein on epistemological problems in atomic physics' in P.A. Schilpp (ed.), *Albert Einstein: philosopher scientist* (2 vols, Open Court, La Salle, Illinois, 1949), vol. I, pp. 199–242. A variety of realist responses to quantum mechanics ranging from orthodox to heterodox are: Karl Popper, *Quantum theory and the schism in physics*, ed. W.W. Bartley III (Hutchinson, London, 1982); P.K. Feyerabend, *Realism, rationalism and scientific method* (Cambridge University Press, Cambridge, 1981), Chs. 11 and 16;

[1] David Bohm, *Wholeness and the implicate order* (Routledge and Kegan Paul, London, 1980).

The difference between global realism and global anti-realism is explored in papers collected in

[2] Michael Dummett, *Truth and other enigmas* (Duckworth, London, 1978). Hilary

Putnam in the course of considering how a realist attitude towards scientific theories should be articulated moved from an orthodox realism to a position he called 'internal realism'. Crucial in this development is Putnam's

[3] *Meaning and the moral sciences* (Routledge and Kegan Paul, London, 1978).

It is important when considering the metaphysical issues surrounding scientific knowledge that one appreciate a distinction, regarded by many as important, between factual knowledge (well-supported true belief) and scientific understanding. Aristotle linked the possession of *episteme* (Latin: *scientia*) with the ability to explain. See *Metaphysics*, A1, trans. W.D. Ross (Clarendon Press, Oxford, 1908). Demonstrations (such as those later compiled in Euclid's *Elements*) were for Aristotle a way of setting out *why* something is the case. This established a long tradition in Western philosophy of regarding the ability to relate in a systematic way the reasons for phenomena as 'science' or genuine knowledge of the phenomena. Thus Spinoza emphasised the difference between knowing something as a rule of thumb (by 'inconstant experience' or 'hearsay') and knowing it via a demonstration such as that found in Euclid. See *The works of Spinoza*, trans. R.H.M. Elwes (2 vols, Dover, New York, 1951), vol. II, p. 113 (and cf. p. 8). The German philosopher Christian Wolff, a follower of Leibniz, distinguished 'bare knowledge of fact' (which he called 'historical knowledge') from possessing the reasons of the fact so it is understood why something of the sort should occur. See *Preliminary discourse on philosophy in general*, trans. Richard J. Blackwell (Bobbs-Merrill, Indianapolis, 1963), p. 5. In this Wolff was followed by Kant, who made the same distinction in the same terms in *The critique of pure reason*, trans. Norman Kemp-Smith (Macmillan, London, 1929), A836/B864.

If the descriptions of objects (relating their colours, degrees of solidity, ways they interact with other things, etc.) which are ordinarily regarded as constituting factual knowledge are contrasted with the descriptions given by a scientist who is interested in explaining why they look and behave in the ways they do, it is tempting to ask which is the correct, true or real description. The classic statement of this puzzle is the discussion of the two tables in

[4] A.S. Eddington, *The nature of the physical world* (Cambridge University Press, Cambridge, 1929). Gilbert Ryle in *Dilemmas* (Cambridge University Press, Cambridge, 1954), Ch. 5, argues that we should not regard ourselves as forced to choose because the different accounts do not compete with one another.

For recent examples of causal realism see R. Harré and E.H. Madden, *Causal powers* (Basil Blackwell, Oxford, 1975) and Karl R. Popper, *Realism and the aim of science*, ed. W.W. Bartley III (Hutchinson, London, 1983), Part II, Ch. 3. John Mackie argues that such a position is untenable in, among other places,

[5] *Truth, probability and paradox* (Clarendon Press, Oxford, 1973), Ch. 4.

An example of a matter realist is J.J.C. Smart, *Philosophy and scientific realism* (Routledge and Kegan Paul, London, 1963). Two examples of empirical realism are Bertrand Russell, *The analysis of matter* (Allen and Unwin, London, 1927) and

[6] Rudolph Carnap, *The logical structure of the world and pseudoproblems in philosophy*, trans. Rolf A. George (University of California Press, Berkeley, 1967). The difficulties for empirical realism which revolve around the (lack of a) distinction between theory and observation are discussed in Mary Hesse, *The structure of scientific inference* (Macmillan, London, 1974), Ch. 1.

A recent example of an instrumentalist approach is Bas C. van Fraassen, *The scientific image* (Clarendon Press, Oxford, 1980). The first person to style his philosophy 'instrumentalism' was John Dewey (see e.g. *Experience and nature* (Open Court, La Salle, Illinois, 1929)), but rather than treating theories as not embodying knowledge because they are mere instruments for predicting and controlling experience, Dewey regarded instrumental function as the touchstone of knowledge. The result constituted a thoroughgoing anti-realism.

The importance of the Aristotelian distinction between mathematical and physical branches of *episteme* is discussed in Stephen Gaukroger, *Explanatory structures* (Harvester, Hassocks, 1978). The French physicist and philosopher of science, Pierre Duhem, held that all proper scientific theories are in this sense 'mathematical'; science should not seek causes or (what was closely connected in the Aristotelian conception of a physical theory) essences. See

[7] *The aim and structure of physical theory*, trans. Philip P. Wiener (Princeton University Press, Princeton, 1954). The recent fashion for a form of essentialism, one embracing at least natural kinds, was begun by Saul Kripke, notably in work which came to be published in *Naming and necessity* (Basil Blackwell, Oxford, 1980). Another important contributer was Hilary Putnam; see the papers collected in *Mind, language and reality, Philosophical Papers, Volume 2* (3 vols, Cambridge University Press, Cambridge, 1975).

Hostility to natural kinds is particularly prominent in philosophers who identify themselves as nominalists. See for example

[8] W.V. Quine, 'Natural kinds' in *Ontological relativity and other essays* (Columbia University Press, New York, 1969), pp. 114–38. Another and in some ways more radical form of contemporary nominalism will be found in

[9] Nelson Goodman, *The structure of appearance*, 3rd edn (Reidel, Dordrecht, 1977). The best brief history of the nominalist tradition from the Middle Ages to the seventeenth century is to be found in E.C. Moore *et al.* (eds), *Writings of Charles S. Peirce* (8 vols, Indiana University Press, Bloomington, Indiana, 1984), vol. II, pp. 462–87.

To consider the question of whether the experimental movement in modern science transforms the old metaphysical issues, it is important to understand the development of this movement. For this there is no better brief treatment than that to be found in

[10] T.S. Kuhn, 'Mathematical versus experimental traditions in the development of physical science' in *The essential tension* (University of Chicago Press, Chicago, 1977), pp. 31–65. Among the philosophers who have urged that taking proper account of the role of experiment and technology in science should alter our approach to these metaphysical issues are John Dewey, *The quest for certainty* (Minton Balch, New York, 1929), Ch. 4, Gaston Bachelard, *The new scientific spirit*, trans. Arthur Goldhammer (Beacon Press, Boston, 1984) and

[11] Ian Hacking, *Representing and intervening* (Cambridge University Press, Cambridge, 1983).

J.E.T.

Part C: Metaphysics

Introduction

At the end of the Introduction to Part B, I implied a distinction between knowledge and understanding, when I asked whether scientists are simply concerned to acquire a knowledge of facts, or whether they also try to understand. This distinction, I believe, would be generally understood and accepted; one sees quite well what the poet Louis MacNeice meant when he said of his Oxford teachers that they had 'knowledge without understanding'. But many major philosophers – Plato, Spinoza and Hegel among them – would have said that this is a misuse of the term 'knowledge'. They would have said that if there is to be real knowledge (or, as Spinoza would have said, knowledge of the highest kind) then there must also be full understanding, the ability to give explanations that are completely satisfying to the intellect. Knowledge of this kind has been the goal of that branch of philosophy which is traditionally termed 'metaphysics'. I say 'traditionally termed', because in recent years the term 'metaphysics' has been used in a somewhat different sense; however, my first concern here is with metaphysics of the older, traditional sort.

There have been many different metaphysical theories, but it is safe to say that the knowledge claimed by the traditional metaphysician has four main features. (a) It concerns what exists. (b) It is *a priori* in character; that is, it does not have sense-experience as its basis. Before going further, one must note that if knowledge is to be metaphysical, it must have both these features. We know through our senses a great deal about things that exist, but this is not metaphysical knowledge. Again, we have *a priori* knowledge of the truths of mathematics, but this is not knowledge of what *exists*. Pythagoras' theorem would still be true, and known to be true, even if there were no right-angled triangles of the kind that it presupposes. (c) Such knowledge is systematic, in that to understand things is to place them

251

within a system. (d) Such knowledge often involves the radical modification of many familiar concepts and assumptions – for example, some metaphysicians would argue that the physical things which we experience are not strictly speaking real. (It is no mere coincidence that a celebrated work of nineteenth-century metaphysics, written by the English Hegelian F.H. Bradley, has the title *Appearance and reality*.)

At this point, a critic may object that this encyclopaedia is meant to be a survey of the present state of philosophy, and that metaphysics of the kind just described is a thing of the past. Powerful arguments have been brought against the very possibility of such metaphysics – by Hume and Kant in the eighteenth century, and by the logical positivists in the twentieth – and the validity of these criticisms is widely accepted. To this one may reply that by no means all modern philosophers accept the validity of the criticisms just mentioned. Again, even if these criticisms are valid, arguments which some declare dead show no inclination to lie down, and one therefore needs to have the equipment with which to meet them.

There is still another reason for considering the ideas of the traditional metaphysicians in a survey of modern philosophical thought. As I said earlier in this introduction, the term 'metaphysics' is now given a sense different from that which it previously had, and in this new sense metaphysics is beyond doubt a live concern. Instead of trying to establish, by *a priori* argument, necessary truths about the nature of existence, modern metaphysicians attempt to construct what may, in a broad sense, be called a kind of logic of reality. That is, they try to provide a systematic account of the basic concepts which we use when thinking about the world, such as 'individual' and 'cause'. Such a study is differentiated from traditional metaphysics by the title 'descriptive metaphysics'. The reasons for which it has been given this name can be stated in the following way. It is called 'metaphysics' because it is an inquiry of a fundamental kind, concerning the general structure of our thought about the world. The adjective 'descriptive' marks two ways in which this inquiry is opposed to other branches of philosophy. First, descriptive metaphysics is distinguished from those sorts of traditional metaphysics which require us to modify many of our familiar concepts and assumptions; types of metaphysical theory which the descriptive metaphysician calls 'revisionary'. Second, the adjective 'descriptive' seems to be tacitly contrasted with 'explanatory'. I said that traditional metaphysics seeks knowledge, in the sense of a full understanding of what there is, i.e. the ability to provide satisfying explanations of it. Descriptive metaphysics takes a different view; for understanding, it substitutes description. However, despite the differences between descriptive and traditional metaphysics, it can be argued that the problems that face the modern descriptive metaphysician can often be seen most clearly when they are placed in the context of traditional metaphysics, and this provides a further reason for considering both descriptive and traditional metaphysics in this part of the encyclopaedia.

Chapter 12, the first of the chapters that make up Part C, is concerned with the concept of substance. This is important for the traditional metaphysician, who would say that if one is to have an adequate understanding of what there is, one must have correct ideas about substance. Philosophers have said of substance (a) that it is the ultimate subject of predicates, in the sense of that to which predicates can be ascribed, but is not itself a predicate of anything else; (b) that it must have genuine unity; (c) that it must not depend on anything else for its existence; (d) that it must remain the same through qualitative change; and (e) that it has an essence, which must be known if the substance is to be known properly. These five features are not emphasised equally by all metaphysicians; however, when a metaphysician speaks of 'substance' he may be taken to be speaking of something which has most, if not all, of these features. Traditional metaphysicians tried to discover truths about substance by means of *a priori* reasoning; for example, some tried to show that there can only be one substance; others, that substances must be immaterial. Such attempts have now largely ceased, and indeed the term 'substance' has fallen into disuse among philosophers. Nevertheless, Chapter 12 will show that some of the problems discussed by traditional metaphysicians under this head are still alive. Philosophers still ask such questions as 'What are the basic features of what exists?' and 'Granted that individual things persist over time, what gives an individual its unity? That is, what makes it one and the same?' Finally, philosophers have come to take the notion of essence seriously again, and they ask whether essences really belong to things.

I have spoken of the way in which traditional metaphysicians see a connection between knowledge and explanation. To explain something is often to say what its cause is, and it is not therefore surprising that questions about causation should be regarded as belonging to metaphysics. The concept of cause has a long history in philosophy, going back at least as far as Aristotle, whose term *aitia* was rendered by the medievals as *causa*. In Aristotle, the term *aitia* has a wide scope, and includes the material of which a thing is made, and the form or structure which it has. When modern philosophers discuss causation, however, they usually have in mind one or other of the two remaining types of *aitia* recognised by Aristotle. These are what are traditionally called the 'efficient cause' and the 'final cause'. One uses the concept of an efficient cause when one says, for example, 'This billiard ball moved because another billiard ball hit it'; one uses the concept of a final cause when one says, 'He hit the ball at this angle because he wanted to make a cannon.' One would now tend to say that the first of these is an explanation in physical terms, and the second an explanation in teleological terms; and the problems raised by such explanations are still discussed.

One problem is this. I have just spoken of two sorts

of causation, efficient and final. But are there really two sorts? When we say that someone acts with a certain purpose or intention, are we not saying something that could be expressed better in the terms of the natural sciences? This problem is discussed in Chapter 13; Chapter 14 is concerned with another problem about causality. Here, the problem is not about the possibility of translating one set of causal terms into another set; rather, it concerns the very justifiability of what people say about causes. We often claim to know that one event is the cause of another; indeed, we might well go further, and say that *every* event has some cause or causes. But do we know this? The problem has close ties with the problem of induction, which has been discussed in Chapter 9. But it also has features which are peculiar to it, in that the answer to it depends in part on the way in which causation is viewed. Are we to accept the view that things have causal powers, or is talk about causation really talk about regular succession? The latter view has had powerful advocates, from the time of Hume onwards; but, as Chapter 14 shows, the former view is not without its modern defenders.

Metaphysics has for many centuries had close links with theology, for reasons that are easily seen. Philosophers asked what is the ultimate substance, and what is the first cause of everything, and came up with the same answer, 'God' – though what they meant by that term was by no means always the same as what the average believer in God meant by it. There are many philosophical arguments for the existence of God; there are also arguments against the supposition that God exists, and both sides of the controversy are discussed in Chapter 15. The last chapter of Part C concerns space, time and motion. These concepts are of great importance to the natural sciences, and for this reason many philosophers would regard them as belonging to the philosophy of science. Their presence here within the context of a discussion of metaphysics has two reasons. First, there is no doubt that the concepts of space and time form an important part of the conceptual scheme with which all of us – non-scientists as well as scientists – approach the world. The topic, therefore, belongs to descriptive metaphysics; but it also belongs to revisionary metaphysics, in that some philosophers have been led to argue that space, time and motion are unreal.

G.H.R.P.

12 | Substance

E.J. Lowe

'Substance' is one of those philosophical terms of art that have entered the vernacular, undergoing quite considerable changes of sense in the process while yet retaining something of its original meanings. I speak here of meanings advisedly, for the history of metaphysics reveals that even as a philosophical term of art 'substance' has always been multiply ambiguous, even though its diverse philosophical senses are intimately inter-related. But while I think it would be true to say that the notion of substance has in this century been *philosophically* more unfashionable (at least until very recently) than ever before in its long history, in ordinary speech we still very readily talk of chemical *substances* (like sodium chloride and carbon monox-ide), describe various objects as being *substantial* (like a stone or a tree) and others as being *in*substantial (like a rainbow or a shadow), and classify certain nouns as being *substantives* (like 'man', 'sun' and 'water'). And each of these familiar non-philosophical uses of 'substance' and its cognates can be traced to specific philosophical doctrines concerning substance. Moreover, even though philosophers now fight somewhat shy of the *word* 'substance', many of the philosophical concerns which motivated its technical use in earlier times are as alive as ever under the guise of different terminology. So a philosophical interest in substance is by no means doomed to be a purely historical one. All the same, an understanding of the philosophical usage of the term 'substance' undoubtedly requires, perhaps more than in the case of any other philosophical term, a more than superficial knowledge of its history. That history begins of course with the Greeks, and above all with Aristotle: indeed, almost everything that has subsequently been said about substance finds at least a germ in something said by Aristotle.

In an apparently early work, the *Categories*, Aristotle distinguishes between *primary* and *secondary* substances.[1] The Greek word he

255

uses, *ousia*, derives from the Greek verb 'to be', and its English translation as 'substance' comes to us via its Latin translation as *substantia*. This in turn is derived from the preposition *sub* ('under') and the verb *stare* ('stand'). However, etymology is a very uncertain guide to meaning, so that it would be misleading to say – as some, such as Locke, have indeed been tempted to say[2] – that 'substance' in any sense *means* that which 'stands under' (or 'supports') a thing's qualities or properties. We shall see in due course that a number of spurious problems have arisen from this too literal reading of etymology.

By a *primary* substance Aristotle seems to mean, quite simply, a *concrete individual thing*, such as a particular man or a particular tree. By the *secondary* substances he means the various *kinds* – species and genera – to which such concrete individuals belong: such as the species *man* or the genus *animal*. It is noteworthy that a good many of Aristotle's examples are, like these, biological – reflecting his own particular scientific interests – and of course biology is a field in which taxonomic divisions into species and genera spring especially readily to mind.[3] However, it should be emphasised that what Aristotle understands by 'species' and 'genus' is not quite what modern biologists would mean by these terms.

One of the things which apparently motivates Aristotle's classification of *both* concrete individuals *and* their various kinds as 'substances' (though he does this only in the *Categories*) is his perception of certain parallels between the *grammar* of proper names and that of kind terms; parallels which obtain not only in Greek but also in other Indo-European languages, including English. In particular, both proper names and kind terms can figure as the *grammatical subjects* of sentences – we may say 'Socrates is rational,' but equally we may say, 'Man is rational.' However, Aristotle considers that proper names and kind terms also differ in their grammar in that the latter, but not the former, can also figure *predicatively* in sentences. Thus, just as we may predicate rationality of Socrates by saying 'Socrates is rational,' so we may predicate humanity of him by saying 'Socrates *is a man*'; but we cannot, supposedly, likewise predicate Socrateity (as it were) of an individual, for to say 'That man *is Socrates*' is only to assert an *identity*. This, it seems, is partly what leads Aristotle to call concrete individuals the *primary* substances; though at bottom his primary/secondary distinction is intended to be an ontological rather than merely a grammatical one, the suggestion being that concrete individuals constitute in some sense the ground of all real existence. (For Aristotle, species and genera do not exist *over and above* the individuals that instantiate them, unlike Plato's 'Forms'.)

This ontological primacy of concrete individuals is also taken by Aristotle to underlie the distinction between a primary substance and the various *qualities* and *properties* that may be predicated of it. Crudely, such qualities and properties only 'exist' precisely inasmuch as they are qualities and properties *of* particular concrete individuals which exist: colour, weight, size and motion cannot exist, as it were, free-floating and unattached. Spelling out this supposed one-way ontological dependency between substances and qualities in a clear and precise fashion is, however, no easy matter, despite its intuitive appeal. For while it seemingly makes no sense to speak of a *quality* which is not the quality of some *thing*, equally it makes no sense to speak of some *thing* which is not a thing with some *qualities*. (Moreover, a further complication which I have so far glossed over is that properties may be predicated of other properties, even if ultimately the hierarchy of predication must terminate in a substance: thus brightness may be predicated of a particular shade of red.)

In the *Categories* Aristotle makes several further observations concerning substance which have often been re-echoed in the history of the subject, most importantly that (primary) substances are *subject to change without loss of identity*. As he puts it, contrary qualities (such as hot and cold) may be predicated of one and the same concrete individual provided they are predicated of it at different times.[4] Hence the notion of substance has come to be closely associated with that of *persistence*, an aspect of the notion that Kant was subsequently to emphasise. Of course, in saying that substances may change without loss of identity Aristotle is not contending that they are *eternal* and *indestructible* (though later philosophers, notably Spinoza, were to develop this view). Rather, he is committed to recognising two quite different kinds of change: *qualitative* change – as when a poker changes from being red and hot to being cold and grey – and *substantial* change, which involves the coming-into-existence or ceasing-to-be of a particular concrete individual (as when the poker was made or when it is later destroyed).

In his apparently later and more mature work the *Metaphysics* (Books Z and H), Aristotle elaborates and develops his views on substance in a number of important ways, introducing additional terminology which has loomed large in subsequent debate: in particular, he there dwells at length on the distinction between *matter* and *form*, and invokes also the notion of *essence*. It becomes clear that for Aristotle (primary) substances are distinctive in being *made of something*, that of which they are made being their 'matter' and the way in which they are made of it being their 'form': thus human beings are 'made' of flesh and blood and bones organised in such-and-such a way so as to sustain characteristically human life, and a bronze statue is 'made' of a quantity of bronze fashioned into such-and-such a shape. At the same time it becomes still clearer that for Aristotle substances have – partly *because* of their being 'enmattered' – a special sort of ontological primacy or independence: they are for him in some sense *self-subsistent* entities, not immediately and continuously dependent for their existence on anything else (or, at least, not in the way that, say, a shadow is dependent for its continued existence on the tree which casts it and the sun which provides the light). This is again an aspect of the notion of substance that some later writers have developed to an extreme not envisaged by Aristotle, who by no means intended to suggest that substances are perfectly immune to causal interactions with their environment. (Here I am thinking especially of Spinoza and Leibniz.) However, while Aristotle does not want to deny that substances are capable of generation and destruction, there is in his later work the suggestion that their ultimate *matter* is in some sense ungenerable and indestructible, and that substances can be created only out of other substances.[5] In this suggestion it is not unreasonable to see the germ of the modern scientific principle of the *conservation of mass* (or more accurately – from the viewpoint of relativistic physics – the principle of the conservation of *energy*).

The notion of *essence*, discussed at length in *Metaphysics* Z, and later to figure quite centrally in both medieval and seventeenth-century accounts of substance, is not explained altogether perspicuously by Aristotle: but it is clear enough that there is supposed to be an intimate connection between the fact that substances are conceived of as persisting through qualitative changes and the notion that the properties of substances divide into the *essential* and the *accidental*. (This idea is developed also in Aristotle's important treatise *De generatione et corruptione*.[6]) The *essential* properties of a substance (collectively constituting its *essence*) are those which, by its very nature, it cannot cease to have without thereby ceasing to be (so that their loss or gain involves a *substantial* change); loss or gain of accidents in a substance, on the other hand, constitutes only qualitative change. In due course we shall see that the notion of essence, albeit in a form considerably removed from its Aristotelian origins, has enjoyed a remarkable revival recently in the work of modern logicians and philosophers, after a period of contemptuous neglect.

One other important Aristotelian contribution to the notion of substance – an aspect which, again, was much later to be emphasised and developed by certain philosophers such as Leibniz – is the idea that substances are in some special way *units* or *simples*. In Aristotle's case, at least, this is not really to deny that substances may have *parts* which are themselves 'substantial' – thus a finger is a part of a man; but Aristotle, it seems, wants to say that a single substance is never just an *aggregate* or *compound* of distinct substances, and to the extent that its parts are 'substantial' they are only *potentially*, not *actually*, distinct substances.[7] What apparently 'unites' the parts of a single substance is its 'form'. (Aristotle's distinction between the potential and the actual, developed in *Metaphysics* θ, is in fact intimately related to his distinction between matter and form.)

To sum up what has necessarily been an extremely cursory outline of Aristotle's contribution to the history of the notion of substance: substances, for Aristotle – and here I refer to 'primary' substances – are (i) self-subsistent entities which are (ii) impredicable subjects of predication (or bearers of qualities), (iii) capable of persistence through qualitative change, and (iv) in a special way unitary or simple.

In the hands of the medieval scholastic philosophers,

Aristotle's conception of substance was subtly yet radically modified to suit the metaphysical presuppositions of Christian theology. Thus in St Thomas Aquinas' *De ente et essentia* ('On being and essence') we find substances divided into three distinct categories: divine, spiritual and material. For Aquinas there is of course necessarily only one divine substance, God, 'whose essence is his very existence'[8] – by which Aquinas means that God is a *necessary* being, in whose very nature it is to exist. This appears to put something of a strain on the Aristotelian notion of essence since, as I said earlier, it seems that on the Aristotelian conception the essential properties of a substance are those which it cannot cease to have without thereby ceasing to be: but if (somewhat controversially) a substance's *existing* is taken to be one of its properties, then by this account existence will be an 'essential' property of *every* substance, since of course a substance cannot cease to have existence without thereby ceasing to be. What this suggests, though, is that Aquinas may be operating with a slightly different conception of essence. For him, as indeed for Aristotle, 'essence is that which is signified by the definition of a thing'.[9] But what this now seems to be taken to imply is that a substance's essential properties are those which, 'by definition', it *could not possibly have failed to have*; and, clearly, if a substance is only a contingent (non-necessary) being, it is *not* the case that it could not possibly have failed to have existence. It is, incidentally, somewhat doubtful whether Aristotle, or the ancient Greeks in general, really thought much in terms of this 'subjunctive' notion of possibility – the notion of what *might have been*, as opposed to what *can be*. There is, accordingly, some ambiguity in the very notion of a 'necessary' being; for many scholastic theologians this would indeed appear to be the notion of a being which could not possibly have failed to exist – a notion which has no reference to *time*, as befits a 'Platonic' conception of God's eternity as timeless. But there is also what may be called an 'Aristotelian' notion of necessary existence according to which a necessary being is one which always has and always will exist, because it is ungenerable and inde-structible, i.e. cannot have been *brought into* existence and cannot *go out of* existence.[10] Here we need perhaps to be reminded that scholastic metaphysics involved a subtle, and at times not wholly consistent, blend of Aristotelian and neo-Platonist elements.

Aquinas' second category of substances, created spiritual (or 'intellectual') substances, is supposed to include the angels, while his third category, created material substances, includes all things animal, vegetable and mineral. Man is a special case, a kind of hybrid, because he possesses a soul united with an animal body. The human soul, being a spiritual substance, is capable of disembodied existence, although Aquinas insists that the identity of any particular human soul is logically tied to that of the particular body to which it was originally united. This is because he believes that 'matter is the principle of individuation'.[11] That is to say, for Aquinas, one can distinguish only a plurality of different individual substances of the same species either in the case of material substances or in the case of those spiritual substances (like the human soul) that are individually distinguishable by virtue of their one-to-one relationship with an individual material substance (like the human body). Accordingly, Aquinas explicitly holds that there cannot be a plurality of different individual angels of the same species: in their case, individual and specific differences coincide. Of course, though, Aquinas' very conception of *immaterial* intellectual substances is far removed from the views of Aristotle, who for the most part seems to assume that all substances are material and to take a wholly naturalistic view of man as a being ontologically on the same level as the rest of animal creation. For Aristotle, the human soul is merely the 'form' of the human body, and as such by no means a distinct substance in its own right.[12]

Very arguably, the seventeenth century saw the finest flowering of the metaphysics of substance, only too soon to wither under the onslaught of empiricist critiques. Descartes, despite his often apparently dismissive attitude towards both Aristotle and the Scholastics, in fact accepted unquestioningly many aspects of the medieval theology of substance, particularly as regards divine and spiritual substances. What he was more especially opposed to were Aristotelian and Scholastic conceptions of physical science, and this did indeed involve him in a radical revision of the notion of *material* substance. Descartes retains the Scholastic conception of the unique divine substance existing by its very essence and of the plurality of created intellectual substances both angelic and human (as indeed he was under strong pressure to do in a highly theocentric age), but he rejects the notion of a plurality of material substances – not merely in opposition to Scholastic physics, but also in opposition to the contemporary revitalisation of atomist doctrines. For Descartes, the entire material universe is a single substance, and what we call different bodies (whether animate or inanimate) are neither substances in their own right (as Aristotle and the Scholastics held) nor composed of distinct individual substantial particles (as the atomists held). Rather, bodies are for Descartes just 'modes' of the one material substance: in other words, to say that such-and-such a body is located in a certain place is, on this view, ultimately just to say that the one material substance which constitutes the physical universe as a whole is locally *modified* or *qualified* in such-and-such a way. Descartes has by no means abandoned the substance/quality distinction of Aristotle, but has merely come to consider that many terms which for the Aristotelian denote substances – like 'horse' and 'tree' and 'rock' – strictly speaking denote only qualities. One of the things that Descartes does however abandon along with the Aristotelian-cum-Scholastic conception of material substance is the notion that distinguishing material things by species and genera, each with their own peculiar essences (or 'substantial forms'), has any genuine explanatory role to play in physical science. For Descartes, all material things share the *same* essence, which is just *extension* (the property of being extended in space). This alone is the inalienable mark of the material or physical, and all explanation in the physical sciences is, for Descartes, to be couched in terms of the *modes of extension* (motion and rest, size and shape, and so on). In this respect, however, Descartes was fully in agreement with the corpuscularian or atomist scientists, who were equally contemptuous of the scholastic doctrine of 'substantial forms'.

It would be wrong to give the impression that Descartes left wholly unscathed the Scholastic conception of intellectual or spiritual substances. Most importantly, just as Descartes held that all material things share the same essence (extension), so he considered that all created or finite spiritual substances (to distinguish these from the uncreated and infinite substance God) share the same essence, which is *thought* or *consciousness*. According to Descartes, different human minds or souls are indeed different substances (unlike different human bodies), but are all alike in being essentially *thinking* substances, though of course the *modes* of thought ('ideas') will differ in different minds. It is in his philosophy of mind that Descartes' unquestioning acceptance of at least one central element of the Aristotelian conception of substance comes most obviously to the fore: the notion of a substance as a subject of predication which is not in turn predicable of anything else. For it is this idea which leads him to advance unhesitatingly from the indubitable occurrence of *thoughts* to the indubitable existence of a *thinker* of those thoughts, as immortalised in the dictum *Cogito ergo sum*. The underlying idea is indeed made quite explicit in a number of Descartes' writings, as when he asserts that 'we know by the natural light that a real attribute cannot belong to nothing'.[13] Even so, it is also clear that Descartes endorses other elements of the Aristotelian conception of substance, notably the idea that substances are self-subsistent entities. Indeed, in the *Principles of philosophy* he writes that 'by *substance* we can understand nothing other than a thing which exists in such a way as to depend on no other thing for its existence',[14] and goes on to imply that in a sense only God satisfies this definition absolutely – a thought which Spinoza was soon to develop to its logical conclusion.

Descartes' attempt to retain the Scholastic tripartite division of substances (divine, spiritual and material) in conjunction with a new paradigm of explanation in the physical sciences (explanation in terms of extension and its modes) inevitably gave rise to intolerable tensions at the interface between mind and matter. According to the new paradigm, the 'real' or 'scientific' properties of material things are those they possess purely by virtue of being extended – size, shape, motion and so on – and changes in these properties are to be explained causally in terms of antecedent changes in similar 'real' material properties (as when motion in one billiard ball gives rise to motion in another), such explanations being grounded in certain very general physical laws – principally in laws affirming the *conservation* of certain physical quantities. Descartes himself believed that in all physical transactions 'quantity of motion' is conserved – a principle similar to, but importantly different from, the modern scientific law of the conservation of momentum. The problem for Descartes was now to explain how the immaterial mind could act upon the material body and in turn be acted upon by it, consistently with the new paradigm of physical explanation.[15] He himself believed that the mind could 'direct' certain subtle fluids in the brain (the so-called 'animal spirits') without violating his conservation principle, though as it turned out his principle was incorrect and such 'direction' is not consistent with modern conservation laws. But even at the time Descartes' suggestion seemed to be *ad hoc* and mysterious, invoking as it did a *kind* of causation for physical changes ('mental' causation) radically different from that advanced by the new paradigm.

Descartes' near contemporary, Spinoza, attempted to resolve this problem in a particularly dramatic way. In Spinoza's metaphysics the notion of substance literally achieves its apotheosis. Adopting in its strictest form the notion of substance as that which exists independently of anything else, Spinoza contends that only *one* substance can exist, 'God or Nature' ('Deus sive Natura'), and all finite beings are merely its modes. Thus, just as Descartes rejected the Scholastics' plurality of material substances in favour of a single material substance, so Spinoza, while endorsing this, also rejects Descartes' plurality of finite spiritual substances in favour of a plurality of modes of a single thinking substance. More audaciously still, he *identifies* the single material substance with the single thinking substance and both with the single divine substance whose essence is existence. Descartes had adhered, without any very clear logical motivation, to a doctrine that each kind of substance must possess exactly one 'principal attribute' – *thought* in the case of mental substance and *extension* in the case of physical substance. Spinoza, on the contrary, believes that *all* such 'attributes' (and he strongly suggests that there must be infinitely many of them besides thought and extension) must belong to the one infinite substance, which is the ground of all being. At the same time, Spinoza wants like Descartes to endorse the new paradigm of explanation in the physical sciences, and accordingly holds that all explanation is an attribute-relative affair. That is to say, physical changes are to be explained wholly in physical terms (wholly in terms of modes of extension) and mental changes are to be explained wholly in mental terms (wholly in terms of modes of thought). This excludes as nonsensical Descartes' approach to the mind–body problem. Even so, it is very much open to debate precisely what Spinoza's own solution to the problem is supposed to be – whether he is offering some form of mind–body *identity* theory or some species of *parallelism*. The issue turns to a large extent on the question of precisely how Spinoza understands the logical relationships between the key notions of *substance*, *attribute* and *mode*. Minds and bodies are, for Spinoza, modes of the one substance; but they are also, respectively, modes *of thought* and modes *of extension*. But thought and extension are *distinct* attributes, so that one might assume that their modes, equally, are distinct and so non-identical; which suggests parallelism. However, everything depends here on what is understood by calling a body a *mode of extension* (or a mind a *mode of thought*): if all that is meant is that a body is a mode of substance *as conceived under the attribute of extension*, then indeed body and mind may be strictly and literally identical, since by this account 'X's body' and 'X's mind' are just different ways of referring to one and the same mode of substance.

Whichever is the 'correct' interpretation of Spinoza's views on this matter (if indeed he was clear about it in his own mind), each is fraught with difficulty. The parallelist interpretation leaves it quite obscure as to *why* the correspondences between mental and physical should obtain. The identity interpretation provides no clear criterion for deciding *which* particular modes of extension are identical with *which* particular modes of thought. On the latter interpretation, the modern theory of mind which comes closest to Spinoza's is Donald Davidson's so-called 'anomalous monism'; but his theory explicitly allows that mental and physical events may be identified by the sameness of their *causes* and *effects*, even though he rules out the possibility of psychophysical *explanation* in terms of psychophysical laws.[16] Spinoza, however, makes no such distinction between causation and explanation, nor could one easily be grafted on to his theory given his rationalist epistemology.

A more fundamental objection to Spinoza's substance-monism is that it is, to say the least, questionable whether a notion of substance seriously deserving the name can sustain the doctrine that there is necessarily only *one* substance. Aristotle himself argued in the *Metaphysics* that 'it is not possible that either unity or being should be a single genus of things',[17] the implication being that there must of necessity be a *plurality* of different kinds of substances, not all subsumable under a single genus, 'Being' or 'The One'. And whatever one makes of Aristotle's argument, it certainly seems clear that Spinoza's monism is secured only at the expense of departing so radically from the original Aristotelian conception of substance that he and Aristotle can scarcely be said to be talking about the same thing.

No account of the history of the notion of substance can afford to omit mention of Leibniz, the third of the great triumvirate of seventeenth-century rationalist metaphysicians. Though Leibniz' philosophy is no less innovatory than Spinoza's, it seems true to say that in his conception of substance he departed somewhat less radically from the Aristotelian and scholastic roots of the notion (and indeed he was in general at pains to counter what he felt to be the unjust contempt in which the Scholastics were held by his contemporaries). Two aspects in particular of Aristotle's doctrine are emphasised and developed by Leibniz: the connection between substance and subject–predicate grammar, and the idea that substances are in a special sense simple or unitary. On the latter point, he even came eventually to replace the term 'substance' by 'monad' (meaning a unit). For Leibniz, monads are never mere aggregates or compounds, and this led him to believe that, in a sense, all true substances are spiritual (soul-like) rather than material – because whatever is material is extended and so compounded of parts. On the former point, Leibniz went so far as to maintain that for every substance there is a 'complete' concept which contains within it the concept of everything that may be truly predicated of that substance (though, of course, there being infinitely many such true predications, no finite human mind can be expected to grasp such a complete concept in its entirety). The further ramifications of these Leibnizian doctrines need not concern us here, apart from one: Leibniz' principle of the *identity of indiscernibles*, according to which those substances are identical which have the same complete concept, that is, of which the same things may be truly predicated. An interesting implication of this that is drawn out by Leibniz himself is that 'what St. Thomas [Aquinas] assures us on this point of angels or intelligences (that with them every individual is a lowest species) is true of all substances';[18] though, of course, as we saw earlier, Aquinas believed this for a quite different reason, connected with his view that matter is the principle of individuation. We shall later have occasion to mention again Leibniz' principle when we come to discuss the modern notion of a 'criterion of identity'.

I remarked earlier that the rationalist conceptions of substance were soon to suffer the onslaught of empiricist criticisms. These criticisms were increasingly severe, ultimately culminating in Hume's total rejection of the idea of substance, both material and spiritual (and indeed divine). Already in Locke we find an ambivalent attitude towards the notion of *material* substance. For Locke as an empiricist, the fundamental difficulty with this notion lies in explaining how we come to have such a concept (or 'idea') given that all ideas originally enter the mind through sense-experience and that all we ever experience are the *qualities* or *properties* of material things (their shape, texture, colour and so forth). Descartes, who apparently accepted the latter point, was happy to assert that 'we can ... easily come to know a substance by one of its attributes, in virtue of the common notion that nothingness possesses no attributes, that is to say, no properties or qualities'.[19] But then he was insistent that the mind is plentifully furnished with *innate* ideas, of which the 'common notion' which he mentions provides an instance. In short, Descartes denies that the idea of material substance is entirely acquired by sense-experience. Locke however eschews the doctrine of innate ideas as thoroughly obscurantist, and is accordingly reduced to affirming that

> if any one will examine himself concerning his *Notion of pure Substance in general*, he will find he has no other *Idea* of it at all, but only a supposition of he knows not what support of such Qualities, which are capable of producing simple *Ideas* in us.[20]

Nonetheless, Locke was evidently loath to abandon the notion of material substance as wholly vacuous or meaningless, because of the central role it ostensibly played in the theories of the great 'corpuscularian' scientists of his day (men like Boyle and Newton), whose work he very much admired.

In his support of atomism, Locke was of course again at odds with Descartes: though he was at one with him in rejecting the 'substantial forms' of the Scholastics, agreeing that all genuine explanation in the physical sciences must ultimately be in *mechanical* terms. Where Locke *did* however agree with the Scholastics as against Descartes was in acknowledging the existence of a *plurality* of material substances, ranked in species and genera. A man, a tree and a rock are all, for Locke, genuine examples of particular or individual material substances (despite, indeed, their composite nature, being made up of arrangements of material atoms). At the same time, Locke was thoroughly scathing in his attack on Scholastic notions of *how* individual material substances come to be ranked into species and genera. For the Scholastics two or more individuals belong to the same species or genus by virtue of sharing the same 'substantial form'; but Locke dismisses all talk of such 'forms' as obscurantist nonsense. As he sees it, '*General and Universal, belong not to the real existence of Things; but are the Inventions and Creatures of the Understanding*'[21] – and, he goes on to explain,

> That then which general Words signify, is a sort of Things; and each of them does that, by being a sign of an abstract *Idea* in the mind, to which *Idea*, as Things existing are found to agree, so they come to be ranked under that name.[22]

Here it is necessary to say something of Locke's distinction between 'nominal' essences and 'real' essences. Nominal essence, for Locke, is a notion bound up with the way in which we rank individuals into sorts (species and genera), and indeed for him a nominal essence just *is* an abstract general idea signified by some general term like 'horse' or 'man'. Accordingly, to say that an individual has some property 'essentially' in this sense – for instance, that Socrates is essentially rational – is just to say that that individual has been classified by us as belonging to a sort or species which includes the property in question in its definition (e.g. the sort or species *man*); as such, talk of essence in this sense is purely verbal or semantic and can make no informative contribution to scientific explanation. And Locke castigates the Scholastics for thinking otherwise. At the same time, however, Locke holds that there is *another* sense of 'essence' in which a knowledge of the essences of material substances would indeed constitute scientific knowledge *par excellence*. In this sense, the so-called 'real' essences of material substances are the 'real, but unknown Constitution of their insensible Parts, from which flow those sensible Qualities, which serve us to distinguish them one from another'[23] – in other words, their underlying atomic structure. (Locke is, for the most part, very sceptical about the possibility of our *ever* coming to know such real essences; a scepticism that was no doubt warranted given the primitive state of the chemistry of his day.) It is worth emphasising that according to Locke we do not, cannot, and should not even wish to rank things into species and genera by reference to their 'real' essences: all classification must, for him, be based on the *observable* qualities and properties of things, and is ultimately largely just a matter of human convention, reflecting human interests and convenience.

One problem which arises for the interpretation of Locke's views on substance is the question of how, precisely, he understood the relationship between what he calls 'pure substance in general' – or 'substratum', as he also calls it – and real essence. Both substratum and real essence seemingly are, by Locke's account, empirically unknowable, and both are apparently given a role to play in explaining the unification of certain observable qualities or properties in an individual material object. These parallels might tempt one to suppose that Locke either did, or at least would have done well to, identify the two notions, seeing the latter as in some sense the 'scientific' version of the former, 'common-sense' idea. But this will not really do, because the role which substratum is called upon to play is one which, if it can play it at all, it is required to play even at the level of the insensible individual material atoms which contribute to the real essence of an observable material object. These very atoms have qualities or properties, albeit insensible ones, but obviously no 'real essence' in the special sense Locke has explained (since they are by definition uncompounded); and for Locke the role of substratum is to provide something 'substantial' in which a number of qualities or properties may 'inhere', so as to be the qualities or properties of a single individual 'thing' – whether that 'thing' be an observable macroscopic object like a rock or an insensible microscopic object like an atom. Clearly, one thing that underlies this Lockean notion of substratum is that aspect of the original Aristotelian conception of substance which centred on the idea of substance as a subject of predication which is not itself predicable of anything; but mixed in with this in a not entirely intelligible way is the notion of 'prime matter' – the supposedly basic but in principle indescribable and hence unknowable 'stuff' of physical reality, i.e. whatever it is that constitutes the difference between material objects and empty space. (Descartes, of course, was in a position to deny that *anything* constitutes this supposed difference, denying as he did the doctrine of atoms and the void in favour of the view that the physical universe is a plenum.)

It was this notion of matter that Berkeley, writing shortly after Locke, was so concerned to repudiate as quite meaningless and useless, taking considerable pains to argue that the achievements of Newtonian science neither warranted its acceptance nor were threatened by its abandonment. Not that Berkeley rejected the concept of substance as such, only the idea of *material* substance; he fully retained the notion of *spiritual* or *thinking* substances, both in the form of finite human minds or souls and in the form of the infinite mind of God. To the extent, however, that the conception of material substance that Berkeley was most explicitly attacking was the Lockean notion of material 'substratum', his arguments, forceful and impressive though they are, tend rather to show that this Lockean notion is a *mis*conception than that no intelligible conception of material substance is possible. Certainly, the success of these negative arguments cannot lend the sort of support Berkeley imagined it could to his much less impressive positive arguments in favour of *idealism* – the view that natural objects only exist as ideas in the minds of finite spirits and God, as encapsulated in the dictum *Esse est percipi* ('To be is to be perceived'). Nonetheless, Berkeley had done enough to shake philosophical confidence in talk of material substance, and it is unsurprising that these doubts soon spread to the notion of mental or spiritual substance, most notably in the work of Hume. In Hume's *Treatise of human nature* a memorable passage appears in which he writes:

> For my part, when I enter most inteimately into what I call *myself*, I always stumble on some particular perception or other, of heat or cold, light or shade, love or hatred, pain or pleasure. I never can catch *myself* at any time without a perception, and never can observe any thing but the perception.[24]

Hume is here effectively raising against the notion of soul-substance the very same empiricist objection that Berkeley raised against the notion of material substratum: namely, that all that introspection discloses to us are various mental *qualities* or *affections*, not the supposed spiritual 'stuff' in which they allegedly 'inhere' – and hence that on an empiricist account of meaning we must dismiss as literally meaningless all talk of such a 'substance'. Once again, however, it is less clear that Hume's argument is damning for the very conception of an intellectual or mental substance than for a particular – somewhat naive – model of the soul.

We come at last to Kant. It would of course be wrong to say that the history of substance *ends* with Kant, though I am prepared to venture an opinion that he was the last of the great philosophers to make a genuinely novel contribution to the problem of substance as traditionally conceived (the extreme monisms advanced later by Hegel and Bradley, while distinctive, were in considerable measure foreshadowed by Spinoza). As we shall shortly see, many of the philosophical concerns which philosophers in the past addressed in terms of 'substance' are still very much alive today; but the disparate elements which, as we have discovered, were formerly amalgamated under this general rubric now tend to receive separate treatment. The concept of substance has to some extent fragmented, reflecting perhaps the piecemeal approach of modern analytic philosophy in contrast with the system-building aspirations of the great metaphysicians of the past. (I do not say that this is necessarily 'a good thing'.)

Kant seems to have seen himself in some measure as

providing a synthesis of what was best in the 'rationalist' and 'empiricist' traditions – and though no doubt these labels somewhat distort the picture of intellectual history, enough of truth is captured in this remark to make its saying worth while. Although Kant rejected the rationalist doctrine of innate ideas as obscurantist, neither did he accept the empiricist doctrine that everything the mind can ever know or conceive it must acquire from experience. For Kant, there are certain very fundamental notions (the so-called 'categories') which, while they can only receive application in the field of experience, cannot be acquired *from* experience because the very possibility of experience presupposes their applicability. (Kant uses the term 'category' as a deliberate re-echoing of Aristotle, though their philosophies are about as far removed as any can be imagined.) The notion of 'substance' is, according to Kant, just such a notion. Now, the aspect of the original Aristotelian conception of substance which Kant most emphasises is the idea of substance as *that which perists in time through qualitative change*. Without attempting to recapitulate Kant's profound and complex arguments, we may perhaps say without undue distortion that, on his view, we are only able to (as we must) represent our experiences as belonging to a single unified time-order insofar as we can interpret them as being experiences of objects which *persist* through the qualitative changes which we observe in them – in short, as being experiences of *substances*. Hence Kant believes he can simultaneously deny *both* that we have an innate idea of substance *and* that we acquire such an idea from experience, while nonetheless maintaining that the notion of substance is empirically meaningful. But however much we may admire the profundity of Kant's arguments and gain genuine insight from them, we can only see him as presenting a solution to the extent that we are prepared to recognise that he was faced with a genuine problem – and this in turn depends on how seriously we view the empiricist critique of substance. Very arguably – as I have already suggested – that critique was misconceived from the outset, directed as it was against a hopelessly naive model of the relationship between substance and quality: the 'inherence' model.

Although the *term* 'substance' is not much in vogue amongst modern analytic philosophers, two recognisably 'substantial' themes have in particular exercised their attention in recent years: one is a cluster of problems involving questions of identity and individuation, and the other concerns the semantics of so-called natural kind terms. Nor are these themes treated independently, though maybe the intimacy of their interconnection is still not quite sufficiently appreciated by some modern writers. Perhaps the best way to approach modern debate on these matters, which will also serve to highlight the intimacy of the connection of which I speak, is through the notion of a *criterion of identity*.

In his important book *Reference and generality*, P.T. Geach has rightly emphasised a distinction amongst general terms between those that are and those that are not 'substantival'. And for Geach the mark of a substantival general term is precisely that it has associated with its use – as indeed a component of its very meaning – a criterion of identity for instances falling under it. A *criterion* of identity is, in Geach's own words, 'that in accordance with which we [may] judge whether identity holds' for individuals characterisable by some general term.[25] For instance, 'man' and 'gold' are substantival general terms – or, as I prefer to call them, *sortal* terms (an expression apparently coined by Locke[26]) – because there are, at least in principle, ways of determining whether, if *x* and *y* are men or portions of gold, they are the *same* man or the *same* gold. But a general term like 'red thing' is not a sortal term because no such criterion exists in its case. A sufficient, but not necessary, condition for a general term's being a sortal is that there should exist some principle for *counting* or *enumerating* individual instances falling under it. Thus there are ways of counting the number of *men* or *tables* or *books* in a given room, but no way of counting the number of *red things* there are; and this is not because there *is* such a number but one beyond our powers of determining (as in the case of the number of *atoms* in the room), but because it does not even make sense to speak of such a number. (Suppose, for example, that the room contained a red kitchen table; then that, it might be urged, is clearly *one* red thing – but what about its red top and its red legs, or the red knob on one of its red drawers? Are *these* to be counted as different 'red things' in the room *in addition to* the red table itself? And what about, say, the red paint covering one of the table's legs: is *that* also to count as a distinct 'red thing' in its own right? It rapidly becomes clear that there is no principled way of deciding these matters, until we are told what *sorts* of red things we are supposed to be counting.) 'Man', 'table' and 'book' are accordingly commonly called by grammarians *count nouns*. But, as I say, the countability of its instances is not a necessary condition for a general term's being a sortal, since so-called *mass nouns* like 'gold' and 'water' have criteria of identity associated with their use despite the fact that it makes no sense to ask *how many* instances of gold or water exist in a certain place. (Significantly, though, it *does* make sense to ask *how much* gold or water exists in a given place.) It is important, incidentally – as we shall shortly more clearly see – to realise that *different* sortal terms may well have *different* criteria of identity associated with their use.

The bearing of these remarks on some of our earlier, historical findings should be fairly obvious. If we were to ask what it is that sortal terms denote, a plausible answer would seem to be that they denote what Aristotle in the *Categories* called *secondary substances* – that is, species and genera: in other words, *sorts* or *kinds*. Correspondingly, what Aristotle called *primary substances* we may refer to as the *individuals* or *particulars* instantiating such sorts or kinds. But an important point to appreciate here is that the notions of *individual* (or particular) and *sort* (or kind) are, very arguably, interdependent and mutually irreducible. Individuals are only recognisable as individuals *of a sort*, while sorts are only intelligible as sorts *of individuals*.

When I say that individuals are only recognisable as individuals *of a sort*, I am challenging a notion that has wreaked much havoc in the history of philosophy: the notion of a 'bare particular'. This is the bogus notion of something that is individual or particular *per se*, quite independently of its falling under any specifiable sortal distinction. In short, it is the purported idea of a mere individual 'thing'. The reason why this is a bogus notion is implicit in some of the observations I have already made. The point, in a nutshell, is that the noun 'thing' – though superficially a count noun in that it admits of a plural form, 'things' – has no *criterion of identity* associated with it, and consequently cannot be used unambiguously to pick out some identifiable individual either as an object of knowledge or as an object of reference. Thus, if I point my finger in the direction of my desk and say, 'That *thing* is brown,' I shall by no means have expressed a proposition with determinate meaning, because I shall have left it quite indeterminate what *sort* of thing I am supposedly referring to – a desk, a portion of wood, a surface, or what not (all of which sorts of things carry different criteria of identity). Locke, incidentally, was one philosopher who was evidently beguiled by the notion of bare particulars; otherwise he would not so confidently have asserted that 'All Things, that exist, [are] Particulars,'[27] and (as we have seen) that '*General and Universal*, belong not to the real existence of Things; but *are the Inventions and Creatures of the Understanding*'.[28] Realism with regard to individuals simply is not compatible with such extreme conventionalism with regard to sorts or kinds; we cannot, with Locke, suppose that the mind somehow constructs certain 'abstract general ideas' from its experience of concrete particulars, by reference to which ideas all of its classification of such particulars proceeds – for particulars cannot be *experienced* at all save as particulars *of some sort*.

The other side of the coin is that sorts, equally, are not intelligible in abstraction from the individuals which instantiate them. A doctrine of Platonic 'Forms' as the referents of sortal terms is untenable for reasons which Aristotle himself made plain long ago. But to go further into this issue would involve us too deeply for present purposes in the 'problem of universals'.

I pointed out earlier that different sorts of things may very well carry different criteria of identity. The criterion we apply to judge whether or not a certain *body or quantity of water* encountered on one occasion is *the same* as a body or quantity of water encountered on a previous occasion is clearly different from the criterion we apply to judge whether or not a certain *river* encountered on one occasion is *the same* as a river encountered on a previous occasion. As the water in a river flows down to the sea it is replaced by more and different water, but the river remains the same. Hence a river is by no means to be *identified* with the water which, at any given time, 'constitutes' it – a point which has been developed more generally and in some detail by David Wiggins in his influential book *Sameness and substance*.[29]

(Locke was perhaps the first philosopher to recognise explicitly the sortal-relativity of criteria of identity, exploiting it extensively in his discussion of personal identity in the *Essay*, where he makes much of the apparent fact that the sortal terms 'man' and 'person' carry different criteria of identity.) Another point that is perhaps worth emphasising here is that Leibniz' principle of the 'identity of indiscernibles', which we encountered earlier, even if it is true, can by no means serve as a *criterion* of identity in our sense precisely because it is not a sortally-relativised principle. It is not a principle which we would in practice ever be able to *apply* in order to establish an identity between individuals encountered on different occasions or in different ways.

One thing that emerges from the example of the water and the river just mentioned is that different sorts of things may have different *persistence-conditions*, which are determined precisely by their criteria of identity. (Thus a body or quantity of water ceases to exist if all or part of it undergoes molecular dissociation into its constituent oxygen and hydrogen; but a river may continue to exist even if it has temporarily run dry.) An individual x of a sort ϕ, existing at a time t_1, *still exists* at a later time t_2 just in case there exists at t_2 a unique individual y of a sort ψ such that, according to the common criterion of identity governing the sorts ϕ and ψ, x may be identified with y. Observe that we should be prepared to allow that an individual *may* be able to change from being an individual of a sort ϕ to being one of the different sort ψ – otherwise we would be unable to countenance the phenomenon of *metamorphosis*, such as occurs when a caterpillar changes into a butterfly. But a logical restraint on any such transformation is that ϕ and ψ should share the same criterion of identity; that indeed is why Lot's wife cannot literally have 'become' a pillar of salt, if by this it is suggested that she *continued to exist* under this new form. These considerations, of course, in large measure lend support to the Aristotelian distinction between 'qualitative' and 'substantial' change, and consequently also to the correlative Aristotelian distinction between 'essence' and 'accident'. (We shall however shortly see that another notion of essence more closely related to Locke's notion of 'real' essence has recently considerably exercised philosophers and logicians.)

While on the subject of *persistence*, I should mention that not all modern philosophers would wholeheartedly endorse the neo-Aristotelian picture that I have just been sketching. There is in particular a school of thought – of which the influential American logician W.V. Quine is perhaps the foremost exponent[30] – according to which all our common-sense talk of persistent objects (or 'continuants') undergoing qualitative change without loss of identity would be replaced in a more 'scientific' description of reality by talk in terms of continuous temporal sequences of instantaneous or momentary objects ('events'). On this view, for instance, what we call a *river* is in fact a *process in time*, a four-dimensional 'spacetime worm' whose temporal parts are the momentary three-dimensional 'time-slices' of that 'worm' – a view of reality which obviously derives its inspiration from the work of twentieth-century physicists like Einstein and Minkowski. I must confess that I have grave doubts about the ultimate coherence of this view of things, suspecting that what superficial intelligibility it possesses is parasitic upon our prior grasp of the very neo-Aristotelian or 'common-sense' conception which it seeks to challenge. Some of my doubts on this score stem from the work of P.F. Strawson, particularly as developed in his well-known book *Individuals*, in which he argues (along fundamentally Kantian lines) for the position that material objects (conceived as what I have just termed 'continuants') necessarily constitute what he calls 'basic' particulars in our conceptual scheme.[31]

From questions of identity and individuation I turn now more directly to questions concerning the semantics of natural kind terms. Not *all* sortal terms, of course, are natural kind terms – in particular, terms denoting *artifactual* kinds like 'table' and 'house' are not. Examples of sortal terms that *are* natural kind terms would be: 'man', 'tiger', 'oak', 'gold' and 'water'. The study of the semantics of such terms is quite simply the investigation of what they mean and how they get their meaning. Now, one thing that such investigation has highlighted in recent years is that there are certain parallels, hitherto rather neglected, between the semantics of natural kind terms and the semantics of *proper names* – names like 'Aristotle', 'Venus' and 'London'. At one time it was thought – for instance by Bertrand Russell – that practically all proper names were in effect shorthand expressions for certain complex *descriptions* – thus 'Aristotle' might be shorthand for something like 'the pupil of Plato and tutor of Alexander the Great, born in Stagira in 384 BC and author of the *Metaphysics* ...' (The precise description might well differ for different users of the name 'Aristotle'; moreover, insofar as the description involves *other* proper names, like 'Plato' and 'Stagira', these too would ultimately have to be replaced by further descriptions – a process whose completion without circularity may well seem doubtfully possible.) This so-called 'descriptive' theory of proper names has however been very forcefully attacked of late, particularly in the work of the eminent American logician Saul Kripke.[32] According to Kripke, proper names are what he calls 'rigid designators'. What this means, in effect, is that a proper name (unlike a description) does not ever change its reference – refer to something different – when one uses it in entertaining counterfactual (contrary-to-fact) suppositions. Thus, even if all I knew about Aristotle was that he was the author of the *Metaphysics*, I could still quite intelligibly wonder what might have happened if *Aristotle* had not written the *Metaphysics*, i.e. if the author of the *Metaphysics* had not been Aristotle – which strongly suggests that I could not be using 'Aristotle' just to *mean* 'the author of the *Metaphysics*', because that would seem to imply that what I was wondering was what might have happened if *Aristotle had not been Aristotle* (which is doubtfully coherent). The point then is that in entertaining the counterfactual supposition that the author of the *Metaphysics* was not Aristotle, I automatically envisage that the description 'the author of the *Metaphysics*' changes its reference but that the proper name 'Aristotle' does not.

Now, what Kripke and certain other philosophers, like Hilary Putnam,[33] have gone on to argue is that natural kind terms like 'tiger', 'water' and 'gold' are similarly rigid designators, and consequently not equivalent to complex descriptive terms. This presents a direct challenge to Locke's views about 'nominal essence' mentioned earlier. For Locke, as we saw, the nominal essence of a species or kind like *gold* is just an 'abstract general idea' which includes the ideas of a number of observable properties that we take to be the 'defining characteristics' of gold – such as shiny yellow colour, high density, malleability, ductility, solubility in aqua regia, and so forth (again the precise list may vary somewhat from speaker to speaker). But on the Kripke–Putnam account none of these properties belongs to gold purely in virture of the very *meaning* of the word 'gold' – in the way, say, that any man correctly characterisable as a *bachelor* must be unmarried by virtue of the very meaning of the word 'bachelor'. For, once again, we can, it seems, quite intelligibly entertain counterfactual suppositions in which gold is *not* shiny, yellow, dense, malleable and so on. This however raises the question of how a natural kind term like 'gold' *does* get its meaning, given that it does not get it in the way that Locke suggests (namely, by being assigned a 'nominal essence'). Putnam's answer runs very roughly as follows: in characterising something as being a specimen of *gold* we mean that it is a sample of the *same sort of substance* as paradigm specimens of gold – where a 'paradigm' specimen of gold is one that relevant experts on the subject (in this case, chemists or perhaps jewellers) would call 'gold'. Moreover, two specimens are on this view specimens of the same sort of substance (are 'consubstantial') just in case they have – in Lockean terminology – the same 'real essence', i.e. in the case of gold the same internal atomic structure (which of course is something that, we now take it, the relevant experts can determine). Thus we see that the Kripke–Putnam view suggests, in direct opposition to Locke, that we not only *should* but *do* (or at least attempt to) classify things by reference to their 'real' essences. Of course, Locke did not believe that the real essences of substances were empirically discoverable – a scepticism perhaps warranted in his day – but that is not in fact what fundamentally determines the difference of opinion between him and Putnam; for Locke considered that even if real essences *were* to become known to scientists, laymen would *and should* in practice continue to classify substances according to their superficial sensible qualities. But history has apparently proved Locke wrong: we *do* defer to the opinion of 'experts' on the question of whether or not something is 'really' a specimen of gold, even where their knowledge rests on techniques beyond our ability to apply for ourselves. What is perhaps more surprising about Putnam's position, however, is that it implies that people at least *intended* to classify naturally occurring kinds of substances like gold and water by their internal 'real essences' even in the days before such real essences *were* empirically discoverable. (Interestingly enough, Locke himself thought that people often had such an *intention*, but that this was just a confusion on their part which could not possibly be reflected in their actual practice of classification.[34])

As we have had ample occasion to see, the term 'essence' is multiply ambiguous even in the hands of philosophers. Thus there is (1) the 'Aristotelian' sense according to which the *essential* properties of an individual substance are those which it cannot lose without thereby ceasing to exist.[35] Then there is (2) the Lockean notion of the 'real' essence of a substance, which Locke understands to be its internal microstructure or atomic constitution, ideally serving to explain scientifically its gross observable properties. Also there is (3) a notion of essence which we first encountered in our discussion of Aquinas, according to which the essential properties of an individual substance are those which, by its very nature, it could not possibly have failed to have – a conception of essence which also seems to be implicit in Descartes' position (and which, as we shall shortly see, has been revived in modern debate). And finally there is (4) Locke's somewhat questionable notion of a 'nominal essence', which he equates with an 'abstract general idea' of the supposed set of observable defining characteristics of a given sort or kind of substance. (It is true, incidentally, that both Aquinas and Locke tie the notion of *essence* to that of *definition* – though in Locke's case, of course, only the notion of 'nominal' essence – but it is important to realise that they had very different conceptions of the role of definition. Aquinas, we may safely say, supposes that definitions may be correct or incorrect, and that a correct definition will be one that precisely captures the real nature of the thing defined; but for Locke definitions are purely verbal, a matter of stipulation in which there can be no question of right or wrong, provided at least that we avoid equivocation.)

With so many senses of 'essence' abounding, it should not be surprising if philosophers sometimes conflate or confuse two or more of them. Just such a conflation may, I suspect, be present in the work of Kripke and Putnam – namely, a conflation between 'essence' in sense (2) and 'essence' in sense (3). For it is certainly clear that Kripke and Putnam suppose that the 'essences' of naturally occurring kinds of substance – which they identify as being their internal, scientifically discoverable constitutions – are features of them which they could not possibly have failed to possess. For instance, on the Kripke–Putnam view, it is part of the 'essence' of water that it is composed of atoms of hydrogen and oxygen in the ratio of two to one, because physical science has revealed empirically that the liquid we call 'water' has this internal constitution; but they also wish to urge that, given that water *in fact* has this internal constitution, it could not possibly have failed to have it, and hence that we cannot genuinely entertain the counterfactual supposition that *water* might not have been H_2O – though indeed we can readily entertain the counterfactual supposition that there might have been a substance with all the familiar observable characteristics of water (and perhaps even *called* 'water') but having a different chemical composition, say XYZ. Such a substance could not, however, have been *water*, the very same substance that we actually refer to by that name – or so Kripke and Putnam contend. But it is far from clear that *this* sort of essentialist claim follows from the previous 'Lockean' claim that water is 'essentially' H_2O – not even if we additionally accept that a natural kind term like 'water' is a so-called 'rigid designator'.[36] In other words, it is not clear that water could not possibly have had a different 'real essence' from the one it actually has, i.e. that water's essence$_2$ is essential$_3$ to it.

To conclude: we have certainly seen that modern analytic philosophers are still very much concerned with many of the issues that have traditionally been associated with the notion of substance, though it is perhaps symptomatic of modern philosophy that of the great metaphysicians of the past who principally contributed to the history of the notion it is Aristotle and Locke whose work is most influential in modern debate – symptomatic because they, like most modern metaphysicians, grounded their philosophies to a considerable extent on the twin pillars of 'common sense' (as reflected in ordinary linguistic usage) and the scientific theory and practice of their time. Revisionary metaphysics in the grand style of Spinoza and Leibniz is, for better or worse, out of vogue today, and with it the radical conceptions of substance which they advanced.

Notes

(An author's name followed by a number in square brackets refers to the book or article which has that number in the bibliography.)

1. Aristotle, *Categories*, 2a.
2. Locke [20], Book II, Ch. 23, Section 2.
3. See further Montgomery Furth's illuminating paper, 'Transtemporal stability in Aristotelian substances', *Journal of Philosophy*, vol. 75, no. 11 (1978).
4. Aristotle, *Categories*, 4a.
5. Aristotle [2], 1034b.
6. Aristotle, *De generatione et corruptione*, 317a, for example.
7. Aristotle [2], 1039a.
8. Aquinas [6], Ch. 6.
9. Ibid., Ch. 2.
10. See, e.g., Aristotle, *De generatione et corruptione*, 337b, 338a, and *De caelo*, Book I.
11. Aquinas, *Summa theologica*, 1a, xxix, 3–4.
12. See Aristotle, *De anima*.
13. René Descartes, *Second set of replies*, Definition V.
14. Descartes, *Principles of philosophy*, I, 51.
15. See further R.S. Woolhouse, 'Leibniz's reaction to Cartesian interaction', *Proceedings of the Aristotelian Society*, vol. 86 (new series) (1985/6).

16. See Donald Davidson, 'Mental events' in his *Essays on actions and events* (Oxford University Press, Oxford, 1980).

17. Aristotle [2], 998b.

18. Leibniz [16], Section 9.

19. Descartes, *Principles of philosophy*, I, 52.

20. Locke [20], II, 23, 2.

21. Ibid., III, 3, 11.

22. Ibid., III, 3, 12.

23. Ibid., III, 3, 17.

24. Hume [25], Book I, Part IV, Section 6.

25. P.T. Geach, *Reference and generality*, 3rd edn (Cornell University Press, Ithaca, 1980), p. 64.

26. See Locke [20], III, 3, 15.

27. Ibid., III, 3, 1.

28. Ibid., III, 3, 11.

29. Wiggins [33].

30. See, e.g., W.V. Quine, 'Identity, ostension and hypostasis' in Quine [32].

31. Strawson [30].

32. See Kripke [34].

33. See Hilary Putnam, 'The meaning of "meaning"' in his *Mind, language and reality, Philosophical Papers, Volume 2* (Cambridge University Press, Cambridge, 1975).

34. See further J.L. Mackie, 'Locke's anticipation of Kripke', *Analysis*, vol. 34, no. 6 (1974).

35. See further Baruch Brody, *Identity and essence* (Princeton University Press, Princeton, 1980), pp. 71ff.

36. For further criticism of the Kripke–Putnam view along these lines, see Nathan Salmon, *Reference and essence* (Basil Blackwell, Oxford, 1982).

Bibliography

Despite its central role in many major philosophical systems, there is a dearth of general introductory studies of the concept of substance, of the sort that we can readily find for, say, the concepts of space and time, or the concept of God. However, we might usefully take as our starting point R.G. Collingwood's stimulating and lucidly written work

[1] *The idea of nature* (Oxford University Press, Oxford, 1945; paperback, 1964).

Apart from this, we have little option but to go back to the classic texts in which the concept of substance has been used and developed. These, it must be admitted, are not always very readily accessible, or very readily comprehensible to the reader without some background knowledge of philosophy. Nevertheless, the selection listed below, together with some of the commentaries and critical expositions mentioned along with them, should – given a little perseverance – provide the means of enlarging usefully on the points made in the foregoing chapter.

Translations of all the writings of Aristotle referred to in the chapter can be found in the twelve volumes of *The works of Aristotle translated into English*, ed. J.A. Smith and W.D. Ross (published by Oxford University Press between 1912 and 1952). The best known is the

[2] *Metaphysics* (various translations, for example by W.D. Ross in vol. VIII of the above-mentioned Oxford translation). See especially books Z and H.

Aristotle's ideas on substance have been discussed by many commentators; for example

[3] J.L. Ackrill, *Aristotle the philosopher* (Oxford University Press, Oxford, 1981)

[4] J. Barnes, *Aristotle* (Oxford University Press, Oxford, 1982)

[5] A. Edel, *Aristotle and his philosophy* (Croom Helm, London, 1982), especially Ch. 8.

The treatise *De ente et essentia* by St Thomas Aquinas has been translated as

[6] *On being and essence*, trans. R.P. Goodwin (Bobbs-Merrill, Indianapolis, 1965).

There is a wealth of learned commentary, but we may perhaps best start with

[7] F.C. Copleston, *Aquinas* (Penguin Books, Harmondsworth, 1955) and

[8] A. Kenny, *Aquinas* (Oxford University Press, Oxford, 1980).

Turning now to the treatment of substance by the major European thinkers of the seventeenth and eighteenth centuries, we should notice

[9] R. Descartes, *Discourse on method, Meditations* and *Principles of philosophy*, first published in 1637, 1641 and 1646 respectively; there are many editions and translations, for example by E. Anscombe and P.T. Geach, *Descartes: philosophical writings* (Nelson, London, 1954), and, more recently, by J. Cottingham, R. Stoothoff and D. Murdoch, *Philosophical writings of Descartes* (2 vols, Cambridge University Press, Cambridge, 1984–5).

[10] A.B. Gibson, *The philosophy of Descartes* (Methuen, London, 1932)

[11] B. Williams, *Descartes; the project of pure enquiry* (Penguin Books, Harmondsworth, 1978)

[12] A. Kenny, *Descartes* (Random House, New York, 1968)

[13] B. de Spinoza, *Ethics* (first published 1677, various editions and translations, including that of S. Shirley, *The ethics and selected letters*, Hackett, Indianapolis, 1982), especially Part I

[14] S. Hampshire, *Spinoza* (Penguin Books, Harmondsworth, 1951)

[15] J. Bennett, *A study of Spinoza's Ethics* (Cambridge University Press, Cambridge, 1984)

[16] G.W. Leibniz, *Discourse on metaphysics* (written 1685–6, first published 1846, trans. P.G. Lucas and L. Grint, Manchester University Press, Manchester, 1955) and, also by Leibniz,

[17] *The monadology* (first published 1714, trans. M. Morris and G.H.R. Parkinson in *Leibniz: philosophical writings* (Dent, London, 1973)) (See pp. 173–94)

[18] R.L. Saw, *Leibniz* (Penguin Books, Harmondsworth, 1954)

[19] G.H.R. Parkinson, *Logic and reality in Leibniz's metaphysics* (Oxford University Press, Oxford, 1965, reissued by Garland Books, New York, 1985)

[20] J. Locke, *Essay on the human understanding* (first published 1690, many editions, for example Everyman's Library, 2 vols, Dent, London, 1961) (see especially Book II, Ch. 23)

[21] R.I. Aaron, *John Locke* (Oxford University Press, Oxford, 1955)

[22] J.L. Mackie, *Problems from Locke* (Oxford University Press, Oxford, 1976)

[23] G. Berkeley, *Philosophical works* (many editions, for example, Dent, London, 1975)

[24] J.O. Urmson, *Berkeley* (Oxford University Press, Oxford, 1982)

[25] D. Hume, *Treatise on human nature* (first published 1739–40, many editions

including Penguin Classics, Penguin Books, Harmondsworth, 1985); see especially Book I, Part I, Section 6

[26] D.C.G. MacNabb, *David Hume* (Basil Blackwell, Oxford, 1966)

[27] B. Stroud, *Hume* (Routledge and Kegan Paul, London, 1977)

[28] I. Kant, *Critique of pure reason* (first published 1781, 2nd edition 1787, various editions and translations, of which the best is that of N.K. Smith, Macmillan, London, 1929). See especially the section entitled 'Analytic of principles', Ch. 3, Section 3, iii

[29] H.J. Paton, *Kant's metaphysic of experience* (2 vols, Allen and Unwin, London, 1936), especially vol. II, Ch. 42

[30] P.F. Strawson, *The bounds of sense* (Methuen, London, 1966).

Among the more recent works, mentioned towards the end of the chapter, which are concerned with problems closely related to those of the classic philosophies of substance, even if they make comparatively little use of the term, we may notice, in particular, P.F. Strawson's careful and systematic analysis of the problems of identification in

[31] *Individuals* (Methuen, London, 1959). Also

[32] W.V. Quine, *From a logical point of view* (Harvard University Press, Cambridge, Massachusetts, 1961)

[33] D. Wiggins, *Sameness and substance* (Basil Blackwell, Oxford, 1980) and

[34] S. Kripke, *Naming and necessity* (Basil Blackwell, Oxford, 1980).

T.E.B.

13 | Different Types of Causation

G.H.R. Parkinson

I

In the Introduction to this part of the encyclopaedia, metaphysics was introduced by way of the idea (p. 251) that genuine knowledge involves the ability to explain. Chapter 12 explored those explanations that involve the concept, or the concepts, of substance; this chapter will be concerned with explanations that involve the notion of a cause. Our chief concern here will be with the analysis of the concept of cause, and in particular with the question of whether there is just one concept of cause. In the next chapter, questions of analysis will be replaced by questions of justification. The question there will be whether we are justified in our claims to have *knowledge* about causes and, if we are justified, what justifies us.

I have used the words 'explain' and 'explanation'; it is important to realise that these words have several senses. One may, for example, ask someone to explain the sense of a difficult passage from a book. Here, one is asking for an elucidation, for a paraphrase which is clearer than the original passage. Or one may ask someone to explain the workings of the internal combustion engine, where what one wants is a systematic exposition of the workings of this type of engine. Finally one may, for example, ask someone to explain the origins of the Second World War. Here one is asking for something which is not requested in the other two cases; one is asking for an answer to the question 'Why?' Our concern in this chapter is with explanations of the last kind.

We can ask the question 'Why?' about both events and states of affairs; that is, we can ask (for example) why someone blinked, and we can also ask why he is short-sighted. Answering such questions, we shall say, 'He blinked because ...' or 'He is short-sighted because ...' It may seem to be a short step from this to saying that, in such cases, we are stating

279

the cause, or at any rate a cause, of something. Our concern will be to find out when this is true, and when it is not. Further, when it is true – that is, when we do state a cause – we shall want to find out what it is to talk about a cause, and whether we always use the word in the same way.

II

As is often the case in a philosophical inquiry, it will be helpful to look first at what some of the great philosophers of the past have said. We will begin with Aristotle; for his account of what came to be known as 'the four causes' provided a framework for later discussions of the concept of cause, and is still worth consideration in its own right. Aristotle recognised four senses of the term *aitia* (plural, *aitiai*), a word which medieval scholars rendered as *causa*, as a result of which we speak of the Aristotelian 'four causes'. Aristotle's exposition of the four causes is to be found in his *Physics*, Book II, Ch. 3, where it is at once made clear that the context of the discussion is knowledge and explanation. We do not think that we know something, Aristotle says, until we have grasped the 'Why?' of it. Now, there are four different ways of explaining, four different ways of answering the question 'Why?'

(1) Suppose that someone asks, 'Why is this statue heavy?' and suppose that the answer is 'Because it is bronze.' Here, we are answering the question 'Why?' by stating the material – Aristotle would say the 'matter' (*hulē*) – out of which something is formed, and which remains a constituent of the thing. The point of the last phrase is that the bronze does not vanish when the statue comes into being; the statue is a *bronze* statue. In traditional terms, the answer to the question would be called a statement of the 'material cause'.

(2) Suppose that someone asks, 'Why do these two notes, produced by a vibrating string, form the interval of an octave?' Long before Aristotle, the Greeks knew of the connection between the musical intervals and mathematical ratios. In the present case, the answer would be 'Because when the higher note is produced, the vibrating string is half the length of that which vibrates when the lower note is produced.' A mathematical ratio is an example of what Aristotle calls 'form', and what is stated here is commonly called the 'formal cause' of the octave. The Aristotelian concept of form is a complex one, but as it is discussed in detail in Chapter 20 it is sufficient to say here that for Aristotle the 'form' of a thing is usually not its shape, which can be discerned by the senses, but is rather that which makes it intelligible, and is grasped by the intellect.[1]

(3) Suppose that someone asks, 'Why did Plato act in the way that he did?' The answer may be 'Because Socrates advised him to do it.'[2] Or, to take another example given by Aristotle, suppose that someone asks, 'Why did the Persians attack Athens in 490 BC?', then the answer may be 'Because the Athenians had raided Sardis.' In these cases, we are stating

the causes of certain events; we may also, says Aristotle, say that a father is a cause of his child. In general, 'What makes something is a cause of what is made, and what changes something is a cause of what is changed.' A cause of this kind is commonly referred to as an 'efficient cause', from the Latin *causa efficiens*, the point of the adjective being that the cause is that which brings something about.

(4) Suppose, finally, that we ask, 'Why is this man taking a walk?' Here, the answer may be 'For the sake of his health.' In replying in this way, Aristotle says, one has stated the 'end' (*telos*) of the person's activity – understanding by 'end', that at which the activity is aimed. As the Greek word *telos* was translated by the Latin word *finis*, what is stated here as an answer to the question 'Why?' has come to be called a 'final cause'. In the example, that which has a final cause is something that is done, but Aristotle notes that things which are made may also be said to have a final cause – e.g. surgical instruments are means to the end of health.

This account of the 'four causes' does succeed in distinguishing a number of ways in which the question 'Why?' can be answered. Whether the account contains just four such ways and no more, and whether there are ways of answering the question 'Why?' that are not recognised in the account are questions that will concern us shortly. The immediate question is whether all these '*aitiai*' are what we would now call 'causes'. The answer is surely that they are not. We would not say that the statue's being bronze is the cause of its being heavy, nor would we say that the ratio of two to one is the cause of the octave. For these reasons, material and formal causes do not figure in modern discussions of causality. This is not to say that they are without philosophical interest, but discussion of them belongs to the theory of substance rather than to the theory of causality. With respect to 'efficient causes', the position is different. We would readily count as causes the examples of 'efficient causation' given above; that is, we would agree that it is proper to say (for example) that an Athenian attack on a Persian city was a cause of a Persian attack on Athens. Clearly, then, a discussion of various types of causality must take into account what are traditionally called 'efficient causes'.

But what of 'final causes'? Superficially, it might seem that they are no more relevant to our inquiry than 'material causes' and 'formal causes'; we would be unlikely to say, for example, that future health is the cause of a person's taking a walk. However, discussions of the ends of people's activities, and indeed of ends in general, have long been linked with discussions of efficient causality. The question that is at issue in such discussions is whether action that is aimed at an end can be explained exclusively in terms of efficient causes. Such discussions are in effect about the scope of explanations in terms of efficient causes, and they therefore have a place in this chapter.

III

Let us, for the moment, leave Aristotle's account behind (we shall return to it later) and consider in greater detail the ways in which we use the word 'cause'. I say 'ways' rather than 'way'; for there is good reason to believe that the word is used in several senses. I will begin with the account of the concept of cause that was given by Hume. I am not concerned here with Hume's examination of the *justifiability* of our use of this concept; that is the concern of the next chapter. Rather, I am concerned with Hume's account of what it is to talk about a cause. This account has been very influential, and raises a number of important issues in an exceptionally clear way.

In his *Treatise of human nature* (1739) Hume argues that the relation between cause and effect has three criteria.[3]

(1) *Spatio-temporal contiguity.* Hume remarks that 'Nothing can operate in a time or place which is ever so little removed from those of its existence.' He adds that 'Though distant objects may sometimes seem productive of each other, they are commonly found upon examination to be link'd by a chain of causes, which are contiguous among themselves, and to the distant objects.' All this may seem uncontroversial. Let us suppose that we have a long straight row of dominoes, which stand on end and which are so arranged that when the first one in the row is knocked down the last one eventually falls. One would say that the fall of the first domino causes the fall of the last one, even though the two dominoes are some distance apart and the fall of the last one does not follow immediately upon the fall of the first. This is because they are 'link'd by a chain of causes'. We shall see later, however (Section V), that there is causation of a kind in which such a linkage does not hold.[4]

(2) *Temporal priority of the cause.* If *A* is to be the cause of *B*, then *A* must precede *B* in time. This, says Hume, is 'liable to some controversy', in that some people argue that cause and effect can be contemporary. Suppose, for example, that a metal ball lies on a cushion and, as we would say, makes a hollow in it; in this case, the cause and the effect are contemporary. Hume stated blandly that 'The affair is of no great importance.' Perhaps he meant (as J.S. Mill was to say later[5]) that all that matters is not that the cause should precede the effect, but that the effect should not precede the cause.[6] But this leaves us with a problem. For let us suppose that in certain cases the cause and the effect are simultaneous; how, in such cases, are we to tell which is the effect and which the cause? Kant (from whom the example of the ball on the cushion is taken) offered a solution. He said that in such cases we use further knowledge to determine the cause. We know, he says, that 'If I lay the ball on the cushion, a hollow follows upon the previous flat smooth shape; but if (for any reason) there previously exists a hollow in the cushion, a leaden ball does not follow upon it.'[7]

(3) *Necessary connection between cause and effect.* Hume

is emphatic that, besides the two features mentioned so far, there is another criterion of causality. Features (1) and (2) do not, by themselves, enable one to distinguish between 'post hoc' and 'propter hoc' – 'after this' and 'because of this'. As Hume puts it, 'An object may be contiguous and prior to another, without being consider'd as its cause.' For A to be the cause of B there must, says Hume, also be a *necessary connection* between the two; or, as he says in another work, it must be true to say that 'If the first object had not been, the second never had existed.'[8] In sum, if A is to be the cause of B, then not only must A and B be spatiotemporally contiguous, and not only must A precede B (or at any rate, not follow it); A and B must be necessarily connected. Most of Hume's inquiry into causality is aimed at answering the question 'With what justification, if any, do we assert the existence of a necessary connection between cause and effect?' This is not our concern here; however, in the course of looking for an answer Hume has important things to say about the nature of causal necessity, and of causality in general. He points out that it is important to distinguish between causal necessity and logical necessity. Some of Hume's predecessors, of whom Spinoza is the most famous, had argued that to say that A is the cause of B is to say that B follows logically from A. Hume argued powerfully against this view. Suppose, he said, that the effect did follow logically from the cause. Then we could not, without self-contradiction, suppose the existence of the cause and the non–existence of its effect. But no such contradiction is involved, so we must seek the nature of causal necessity elsewhere.[9]

In his search, Hume drew attention to another feature of the cause–effect relation which he believed to throw light on the nature of causal necessity. He pointed out that, if object A is declared to be the cause of object B, then it will also be the case that objects like A and like B have been in *constant conjunction*. 'We say, for instance, that the vibration of this string is the cause of this particular sound. What do we mean by that affirmation?' An important part of what we mean, Hume replies, is that 'This vibration is followed by this sound, and that all similar vibrations have been followed by similar sounds.'[10] This left Hume with the problem of the relation between constant conjunction of this sort, and the concept of causal necessity. His answer (stated very roughly) was that the constant conjunction of objects like A and B makes us *expect* B when A happens. This is to say that we feel a kind of mental tug; this tug is projected by us on to nature, and so we are led to assert that, since A has happened, B *must* happen. Most modern philosophers would reject Hume's account as too 'psychologistic', but many of them would say that Hume was right in so far as he linked the concept of cause and effect with a readiness to assert certain universal propositions. They would say, however, that he was wrong in restricting such universal proposi-tions to assertions about the past (e.g. 'All similar vibrations *have been followed* by similar sounds'). He did this in order to explain how an expectation might be generated; what he should have done was to state that when one says that a certain vibration causes a certain sound, then one *implies that* the universal proposition 'All similar vibrations are, have been or will be followed by similar sounds' is true.

Can Hume's account of the concept of cause, so modified, be accepted? In his *System of logic* (1st edn, 1843) John Stuart Mill offered an analysis of causation which owed much to Hume's account, but differed from it in two respects.

(1) I have already mentioned the fact that, even when *A*-type objects regularly precede *B*-type objects, we do not always say that there is a causal connection between them. Night is followed regularly by day, but we do not say that the night causes the day. Hume would have said that this is because we do not regard them as necessarily connected; Mill offered a different explanation. He argued that we believe, not that night will be followed by day under all imaginable circumstances, but only that it will do so *provided that* the sun rises above the horizon.[11] So Mill argued that, for something to be an effect, it must not merely be invariably consequent; it must also be *unconditionally* consequent.

(2) The second difference between Hume and Mill involves the important distinction between a condition and a cause. Hume tended to speak of *one* object as followed by another. But, as Mill pointed out, 'It is seldom, if ever, between a consequent and a single antecedent that this invariable sequence subsists. It is usually between a consequent and the sum of several antecedents,' and he adds that 'In such cases it is very common to single out one only of the antecedents under the denomination of Cause, calling the others mere conditions.'[12] By a 'condition' here Mill means what is more accurately called a 'necessary condition' – namely, that without which the consequent would not have occurred or existed, but which is not of itself sufficient to bring about the consequent. For example, the presence of oxygen in the atmosphere is necessary if there is to be a flame; but since the presence of oxygen is not of itself sufficient to produce a flame, we usually[13] say that its presence is merely a necessary condition of the flame, not its cause.

Mill goes on to say that it is inaccurate to regard the cause as just one of the antecedents, the others being mere conditions. The cause, he says, is the *sum* of all its antecedents, the sum total of its conditions. It is true that one of the conditions may, 'in common parlance', be spoken of as if it were the entire cause; but this would be incorrect 'in scientific discourse'. Various responses have been made to Mill's view; of these, the most radical is that put forward by Bertrand Russell in his paper 'On the notion of cause' (1912).[14] Far from agreeing that Mill has elucidated the scientific use of the term 'cause', Russell argued that the term has no use in science; the concept of causal law, he said, 'is a relic of a bygone age'. Briefly, Russell's thesis was that in modern physics (which he clearly regarded as the paradigm of science) the notion of a cause as a kind of entity has disappeared, and has been replaced by the notion of functional relations.[15] The physicist's aim is to find laws which make it possible, from any given state of a system, to deduce its state at any other time. It is true that explanations in physics *apply to* objects which last through time; but any state of such objects is explained, not by reference to what precedes it in time, but by deduction from certain general laws. It is now over seventy years since Russell proclaimed the imminent death of the concept of cause, and it has to be said that the patient has been a long time dying. Causal concepts, it has been pointed out in a recent book, are 'constantly being used in our attempts to understand perception, knowledge and memory, and to clarify our thought about action, responsibility, legal claims, purpose, and teleology'.[16]

The philosophy of causality, then, still has a subject-matter; but is what Mill says about causation to be accepted? In an important study of the concept of cause, R.G. Collingwood argued that Mill's account can be accepted, but with one major reservation.[17] Mill was wrong, says Collingwood, in supposing that he had expounded the only concept of cause that had claims to intellectual respectability. What he had described was the way in which the natural sciences, such as physics and chemistry, would talk about the cause of an event or state of affairs.[18] Such a concept of cause, Collingwood said, may be called the concept that is used in 'theoretical natural science'. But there are two other concepts of causation which are equally legitimate.

IV

I mentioned earlier that Mill regarded a cause (in the scientific sense of the term) as the sum total of its necessary conditions. It follows, Collingwood argues, that in this sense of the word 'cause' there is a one–one relation between cause and effect. If the cause happens or exists, the effect must happen or exist; and if the effect happens or exists, so must the cause.[19] But, says Collingwood, such a one–one relation between cause and effect does not always hold. This can be seen by considering again the distinction between cause and condition. According to Mill, when we select one condition out of a set of conditions, and call it the cause, we do so in an arbitrary way. Collingwood replies that this is not so. Rather (and this introduces another sense of the word 'cause') the cause of the event or situation is something that is under our control, and by means of which we can control that which is caused. In this sense of the word 'cause', says Collingwood, 'The cause of an event is the handle, so to speak, by which human beings can manipulate it.' More precisely, a cause (in this sense of the term) is 'An event or state of things which it is in our power to produce or prevent, and by producing or preventing which we can produce or prevent that whose cause it is said to be.'[20] It is in this sense that we say, for example, that the cause of malaria is the bite of a mosquito, or that the cause of a car's stopping is a loose high-tension lead. Now it may often happen that different people, with their different skills or interests, will produce different answers to the question 'How is one to produce or prevent *X*?' For example, the cause of one and the same car accident may be said to be cornering too fast, or a defect in the surface of the road, or faulty brakes, or a fault in the design of a car. This 'relativity of causes', as Collingwood calls it, means that in this sense of the word 'cause' the relation between cause and effect is not (as Mill implied) one–one, but is many–one.

Collingwood says that this is the sense of 'cause' that is recognised by what he calls the 'practical natural sciences', as opposed to the sense that is recognised by the theoretical natural sciences. This use of terms could mislead, in that it might give the impression that (say) physicists and chemists, whose work belongs to the theoretical sciences, merely observe and theorise about their observations. This is certainly not so, as Collingwood recognised. The theoretical sciences, he noted, do provide solutions for practical problems and can be applied to them.[21] When they are used in this way, they may be called 'applied' sciences of nature. But they are still to be distinguished from the practical natural sciences; for their applicability to practical problems is, so to speak, something added to their essential nature, which is the search for theoretical truth. In the case of the practical sciences of nature, on the other hand, their utility is their essence. One may wonder whether Collingwood was right to distinguish between the various natural sciences in this way. A defender of the pragmatic theory of truth might say that even the practitioners of the theoretical natural sciences seek what is useful.[22] Leaving this aside, however, one has to note that Collingwood's attempt to find examples of the practical natural sciences led him into paradox. He argued that medicine is a practical science, and went on to say that if someone claimed to have discovered the cause of cancer, but then said that the cause was something that could not be produced or prevented at will, he would be misusing the word 'cause'.[23] I said that this is a paradox, by which I meant that it is contrary to accepted opinions. It is surely common for doctors to say that (for example) they have discovered the virus that causes a certain disease, but that they are not yet in a position to cure the disease.

Perhaps the way out of the difficulty is to say that what we call 'the science of medicine' is a hybrid – part applied science, and part practical science. At any rate, there seems no good reason to doubt that Collingwood has drawn attention to one sense of the word 'cause', a sense which differs from that recognised by Mill. It has, indeed, been argued that the sense just discussed is the basic sense of the term 'cause'. In his *Explanation and understanding*, G.H. von Wright states that '*p* is a cause relative to *q*, and *q* an effect relative to *p*, if and only if by doing *p* we could bring about *q* or by suppressing *p* we could remove *q* or prevent it from happening'.[24] It may seem that there are obvious counter-instances to such a view. For example, the eruption of Vesuvius was the cause of the destruction of Pompeii; but human beings cannot make volcanoes erupt, or prevent them from erupting. This objection does not affect Collingwood, for whom the sense of the word 'cause' that has just been discussed is only one sense among several; von Wright, however, has to find an answer to it. His reply is that the eruption of a volcano and the destruction of a city are both very complex events, and that within each of these there can be distinguished a vast number of events between which there hold causal connections of the kind recognised by him.[25] For example, the collapse of a particular house in Pompeii is an instance of the causal law that the roof of a house will collapse under a certain load – and such a collapse is something that we can produce or prevent. But this reply is far from convincing. In explaining the collapse of that particular roof, we are not just saying that the roof collapsed under a heavy weight; we are saying that it collapsed under the weight of *volcanic ash*, and that the presence of the ash on the roof was the effect of something that human beings cannot produce or prevent – namely, the eruption of a volcano.

V

We have spoken so far of what Collingwood calls causation in the natural sciences, both theoretical and practical. We turn now to the third of the senses of the word 'cause' that he recognises. To introduce this sense, it will be helpful to look again at Aristotelian doctrine – namely, at the examples given in Section II of what came to be called 'efficient causality'. Two of them are of particular interest: the man who gives another advice, and in so doing gets him to act in a certain way, and the Persian attack on Athens in 490 BC, which was caused by a previous Athenian raid on Sardis, a Persian city. These examples have some distinctive features.

(1) They involve not inanimate objects but human beings – and human beings behaving in a way which is distinctively human. In the first example, one human being says something meaningful to another; the other understands what is said to him, and may or may not decide to act on what is said. In the second example, certain human beings are angered by an attack on their territory, decide to retaliate, and send off a punitive expedition. In sum, the two examples involve references to saying what is meaningful, to understanding and deciding, and to punishment – all of which are distinctive of human beings.

(2) In such cases, cause and effect need not be spatiotemporally contiguous. Sardis is a long way from Athens, and the Persian attack on Athens came several years after the Athenian attack on Sardis. In this case, it is not at all plausible to say that we have to fill in the gap between the two events by 'a chain of causes, which are contiguous among themselves', as Hume would argue.

Collingwood argued that we have here a separate sense of the word 'cause', to be placed alongside the two already recognised.

287

Causality of this kind, in which that which is caused is 'the free and deliberate act of a conscious and responsible agent', is the concern of the historian, and Collingwood therefore proposed to call this sense of the word 'cause' the 'historical' sense. However, this term seems unduly narrow. Philosophers of law have pointed out that lawyers, too, are concerned with causality of this kind, a kind which involves 'interpersonal transactions'. For this reason, it seems better not to use Collingwood's term, but to speak instead of 'person to person causality'.[26]

Another feature of person to person causality is of great interest. The concept of causality discussed by Mill, and the concept that belongs to the 'practical sciences', have an important feature in common. In each case, universal laws are involved; in each case, if someone says that *A* causes *B*, he is committed to the assertion that *A*-type things always precede *B*-type things. Some philosophers would argue, however, that such laws are not presupposed in person to person causality.[27] They would say, for example, that we would not understand the Persian attack on Athens any better if we knew that whenever one state attacks a city belonging to another, the second state will (unless one or other of a large number of conditions holds) retaliate.[28] Perhaps such laws might be found; but in explaining events in terms of person to person causality one does not presuppose that they can be found.

The notion of person to person causality involves (though it is not the same as) the fourth of the traditional Aristotelian four causes – 'final causality'. A person who (say) is persuaded by his doctor to undergo a risky operation does not act just because a doctor said certain things to him; he acts *in order to* recover his health. The Persians did not attack Athens just because the Athenians had previously attacked their territory; they attacked Athens *in order to* avenge themselves. For the rest of this chapter, we shall be concerned with the notion of 'in order to', i.e. with the notion of *purpose*.

VI

When Aristotle explained the fourth of the ways in which the question 'Why?' can be answered, he gave as an example a man who is taking a walk in order that he may be healthy. It was mentioned in Section II that explanations of this kind have been said to involve 'final causes', after the Latin word *finis*. Today, however, the term 'final cause' has largely fallen into disuse. Perhaps this is because the term suggests that we are here dealing with a kind of causality which is different from efficient causality – but this is something which has to be proved, and in fact many philosophers would reject such a view. But whatever the reason may be, instead of speaking of 'final causes' modern philosophers prefer to speak of 'teleological explanation', from the Greek word for 'end', *telos*. They also tend to use the related word 'teleology' when they want a general term to refer to the events or states of affairs of which such explanations are offered.[29]

As Aristotle pointed out, it is not only activities (such as walking) which are thought to have an end or purpose; we also say that certain *things* have an end. For example, the end or purpose of a surgical saw is to cut bone, and ultimately lead to the patient's recovery. The ends that are involved in both cases may be called *conscious* ends. By this I mean that the ends in question are those of agents who can say why they are acting as they do, or for what purpose certain things have been made. (Of course, the surgical saw does not know its end; but the surgeon and the instrument-maker do.) Later, we shall look at other ends; for the moment, though, let us concentrate on conscious ends.

Explanation in terms of such ends (and indeed of all ends) has a feature which distinguishes it from the types of explanation considered in Sections III to V. It is not clear from Aristotle's example whether the man who is taking a walk is doing so in order to restore his health, or in order to remain in a healthy condition. In either case, though, what is said to explain the man's activity is something that does not yet exist, and indeed may never exist. For even if the exercise does not in fact lead to the man's health, we would still explain his activity by saying 'He took a walk for the sake of his health.' It is easy to see how this differs from the examples of causal explanation so far considered. In them, that which explains an event or state of affairs is prior in time to that which it explains – or at any rate (cf. Section III) does not follow it. Again, that which explains an event or state of affairs in these cases is something that exists or has existed.

What one may call this forward-looking nature of teleological explanation has been found puzzling. To remove this puzzlement, many philosophers have tried to rephrase explanations in terms of conscious ends in such a way that the term 'end' disappears, and one speaks only in terms of the kind of causes recognised by the natural sciences. It may seem, on the face of it, that this can easily be done. For it seems plausible to say that the man in Aristotle's example had a certain desire – the desire to be healthy – and that this desire caused him to walk. This desire precedes the taking of the walk, and is certainly something that exists or existed; for even if the walk does not result in health, the desire to be healthy was there. However, this is over-simplified. The desire alone is not enough to lead to the action; for someone may desire to be healthy, but not take a walk. It is therefore necessary to complicate the account, and say that what caused the walk to be taken was the desire to be healthy, together with the *belief* that walking will lead to health. In talking of causes here, we do not seem to be using the word 'cause' in any new sense; rather, we are using it in the sense that was discussed by Hume and Mill, and considered above in Section III.

All this brings us face to face with fundamental problems: namely, what it is to talk about desire, belief and deliberate action in general. These problems belong to the philosophy of mind, and as such they are discussed in other chapters. (See especially Chapter 19, 'Behaviourism', and Chapter 21, 'The Will'.) Here, I shall confine myself to just one topic, which concerns an important distinction between the ways in which we explain both human actions and beliefs. The distinction can be conveyed by means of an example. Suppose that a British civil servant hands over state secrets to the agents of a Communist government. If one asks why he did this, one might receive answers of radically different kinds. One might be told (say) that the civil servant believes that capitalist society is corrupt, and that any action which helps to bring about its destruction is justified. It is worth noting that this explanation has to do with justification; it offers reasons (not necessarily good reasons, but reasons all the same) for what a person did. However, the same action might be explained in quite a different way, as (say) resulting from the administration of a certain drug, which made the civil servant vulnerable to certain sorts of suggestion. In this case, the explanation states the *cause* of the act, not its reason. One could also seek an explanation, not of the act of betrayal, but of the civil servant's belief that capitalist society is corrupt. Here again, one has to distinguish between reasons and causes. In all this, I have assumed that readers will recognise the distinction when it is presented to them in the form of a concrete case. If one needs general criteria by which to distinguish between the reasons and the causes of actions and beliefs, it is sufficient to note that reasons may be good or bad, convincing or unconvincing; but we cannot say this of causes.[30]

Some philosophers may object that the distinction just drawn has been shown to be non-existent by Donald Davidson, who argued in an important article published in 1963 that reasons *are* causes.[31] Davidson's analysis of our example would probably be as follows. The civil servant, he would say, has a 'pro attitude'[32] towards actions that advance Communist ideals, and also believes that handing over secrets to a certain Communist power will bring these ideals nearer to fruition. Attitude and belief together cause him to act as he does. In response to such an analysis, one might reply that there is a great difference between an act that is brought about in this way, and a corresponding act that is brought about by the injection of a drug. It is this difference that is expressed by the distinction between reasons and causes.[33]

VII

The last section was concerned with conscious ends – that is, the ends of agents who are aware of them, in the sense that they are able to state them either to themselves or to others. But the notion of teleological explanation is not restricted to such ends. We speak of the purposive activity of the predator which stalks its prey; some people speak of the purposive behaviour of other living things, such as trees or plants. Aristotle, for example, argued that if one is to understand the growth of any kind of living thing, one must see that growth as a process which is directed towards an end.[34] It has also been claimed that one may speak of the purposive activity of certain machines, such as the auto-pilot which governs the flight of an aeroplane, or a missile which follows its target whatever evasive action the target may take.

I have spoken above of 'purposive' behaviour. Many modern philosophers, however, prefer to speak of 'goal-directed' behaviour, perhaps because the word 'purposive' suggests behaviour directed towards what I have called 'conscious ends'. It must be stressed that 'goal-directed behaviour' is a wide term, which includes the behaviour of agents who have conscious ends. If we need a special term to refer just to their behaviour, we can speak of 'goal-intended behaviour'. The topic which now concerns us, then, can be expressed as follows. We have to consider the idea that teleological explanation is not confined to goal-intended behaviour; such explanations can also be given of the goal-directed behaviour of agents which are not conscious of their ends.[35]

In this context, it is important to note a distinction that is commonly drawn between 'external' and 'internal' teleology.[36] As an example of external teleology, we may consider a tool of any kind. One speaks of the purpose of a tool; but in order to explain that purpose we have as it were to go outside the tool, considered just as an object, and consider the purposes of the people who fashioned it and who used it. In speaking of a tool, of course, we are speaking of something made by human skill for human purposes; however, many people have thought that external teleology is also manifested by natural objects. Such objects are seen as having been created by a purposive deity, or at any rate by a God-like being, such as the *demiourgos* or 'maker' of whom Plato speaks in his *Timaeus*. Teleological explanations of this kind must be distinguished from those which involve 'internal teleology'. In such cases, the goal-directed behaviour of (say) plants or animals is explained without reference to the purposes of some agent which is external to them. For example, the goal-directed behaviour of the hungry lion is explained by reference to the goal *of the lion*. These two sorts of teleology are not necessarily inconsistent with each other; it is not self-contradictory to speak of a deity who created the world to fulfil his own ends, and in pursuit of those ends created beings which manifest internal teleology. (Leibniz is a famous exponent of this view.) But it is important to bear in mind that the two concepts are distinct. Aristotle, for example, gave great weight to the concept of internal teleology, but did not think that the world is the work of a purposive being.[37]

So far, I have spoken exclusively of ends, purposes or goals; but the notion of teleological explanation is also linked with the idea of *function*. To grasp this notion, it is helpful to begin by thinking again about tools. Early in Section VI, I said that the purpose of a surgical saw is to cut bone, and so lead to the recovery of the patient. It could also be said that the

291

function of the saw is to cut bone, in that this is the way in which it contributes to the patient's recovery. But it is not only tools that are regarded as having functions; one says, for example, that the function of the heart is to circulate blood. In saying this, one need not imply that the heart was designed to do this; neither, however, is one saying that the heart just *does* this. Rather, one is saying that the heart contributes to the goal of the human organism as a whole, whatever that goal may be. The notion of a function, then, is subordinate to that of an end or goal, and as such it will not receive further treatment in this chapter.[38]

VIII

I shall not attempt to discuss here the question of whether natural objects can be explained in terms of external teleology. That topic belongs to philosophical theology, and is discussed in its due place in Chapter 15. However, there is much that needs to be said here about internal teleology. The question which concerns us was posed at the end of Section II, and it is this: does one have to recognise teleological explanation as explanation of a special kind, or can one give an account of it exclusively in causal terms, understanding the term 'cause' as it is understood in the natural sciences? Modern philosophers have made a number of contributions to the solution of this problem, and their contributions – made over a period of some fifty years – constitute a kind of debate, in which one philosopher responds to another.

      We may regard the debate as beginning with the account of the concept of purpose which Bertrand Russell gave in his book *The analysis of mind* (1921).[39] In this account, Russell is careful to avoid calling in special entities in order to explain purposive activities. Instead, he presents teleological explanation as fitting the activity to be explained into a pattern of observable behaviour.[40] Russell considers the case of a hungry animal, and asks what it is to say that the animal 'desires' food. He first considers the notion of hunger, and says that to call an animal 'hungry' is to talk about its behaviour. A hungry animal is restless; it goes to places where food is to be found, and as soon as it is near enough to the food for its sense-organs to be affected, it goes to the food and proceeds to eat. Then, if the quantity of food has been sufficient, its pattern of activity changes; it may perhaps lie down and go to sleep. Generalising from this, Russell argues that what we call 'desire' in an animal is always displayed in a characteristic cycle of actions, which Russell calls a 'behaviour-cycle'. By this he means 'a series of voluntary or reflex movements of an animal, tending to cause a certain result, and continuing until that result is caused, unless they are interrupted by death, accident, or some new behaviour-cycle'. He is now able to explain what is meant by calling the animal's behaviour 'purposive'. The 'purpose' of a behaviour-cycle is 'the result which brings it to an end, namely by a condition of temporary quiescence'.

Russell has here called attention to two types of goal-directed activity, which are now usually called 'searching' and 'aiming'.[41] Searching is an activity which goes on when the object sought is not present to the seeker's senses; aiming is an activity which goes on when the seeker has found out where the object is. To these we have to add a third type of goal-directed behaviour, known as 'keeping'. Here, the goal of the agent is to keep a certain state of affairs constant. For example, if the body's temperature becomes higher than normal, then the skin sweats until the normal temperature is restored. For Russell, this would be another example of a behaviour-cycle which ends in 'a condition of temporary quiescence'.

What Russell has said may be allowed to be true of goal-directed behaviour; the trouble is, it is true of much else as well. Criticising Russell in his book *Scientific explanation* (1953), R.B. Braithwaite pointed out that what Russell has said is true of the explosion of a bomb; it is also true of a pendulum which is set swinging and gradually comes to rest. Braithwaite offered a different account of goal-directed behaviour which, he claimed, applied not only to animals, but also to mechanisms such as thermostats and target-seeking missiles. Russell, Braithwaite said, was right to a certain extent. It is indeed true that a teleological explanation postulates a causal chain between what we want to explain (e.g. the behaviour of a hungry animal) and the goal of activity (e.g. food). But Russell failed to note that such causal chains, such 'behaviour-cycles' as he called them, exhibit an important feature. This feature Braithwaite called 'plasticity'. By this he meant the fact that goal-directed activity displays persistence towards the goal under a variety of conditions. One may mention again the way in which the body maintains a constant temperature, despite changes in the temperature of the surrounding atmosphere; or one may instance the way in which an auto-pilot controls an aeroplane in such a way that it maintains its course despite (for example) changes in the direction of the wind.

Like Russell, Braithwaite tries to remove any mystery that may attach to goal-directed behaviour. In effect, he is saying that all such behaviour can be explained in terms of the concept of cause that is used in the natural sciences; for Braithwaite, there is no difference in principle between the behaviour of a target-seeking missile and a hunting animal. However, there is a serious weakness in Braithwaite's account. Like Russell, Braithwaite has called attention to an important feature of goal-directed behaviour; such behaviour does display plasticity. But, like Russell, he has offered an account which covers too much. It has been pointed out that it follows from what Braithwaite has said that death is the goal of every living thing.[42] For living things certainly display plasticity in respect of the behaviour that is terminated by death; that is, they approach death in a great variety of ways and under a great variety of conditions. Clearly, more is needed if one is to pin down the exact nature of goal-directed activity.

Several philosophers (first Charles Taylor, then

Jonathan Bennett and Larry Wright)[43] have expressed views which are in broad agreement about the defects of Braithwaite's account, and about what must be done to correct them. They agree that more needs to be said about the nature of the causal chains that lead to a goal. To say that such chains display plasticity is not enough; it must also be said that, if an event is to be counted as goal-directed, it must be capable of being brought under a law. More exactly, it must be capable of being brought under a law which states what is *necessary and sufficient* for the achievement of the goal. To simplify exposition, I will concentrate on the account given by Jonathan Bennett.[44] Let us consider again the case of a hungry animal – say, a polar bear which kills a seal. The bear, we would say, acts with a purpose; its behaviour is 'goal-directed'. How is such behaviour to be explained? Bennett replies that we explain it by bringing it under a law – namely, the law that any healthy adult polar bear which has a low level of blood sugar will do anything it can which is necessary and sufficient for its getting a protein meal. In this case, the bear can obtain a protein meal only by killing a certain seal; therefore the bear kills the seal.

By his analysis of teleological explanation, Bennett hopes to escape the objection brought against Braithwaite's account – namely, that death is the goal of all living things. This, says Bennett, does not follow from his account; for most of the things that an organism does are *not* necessary and sufficient for its subsequent death. However, Bennett's account can be shown to lead to an equally unacceptable conclusion. Let us consider a case which concerns what is necessary and sufficient, not for death of absolutely any kind, but for death from a specific disease. Let us suppose that there exists a kind of fungus which is rather like the truffle, and which is attractive to all pigs. Let us also suppose that (unlike the truffle) the fungus causes a fatal disease in the pigs who eat it. Let us suppose, too, that this disease is caused only by a fungus of this type. From this we can construct the law that any pig which roots up a fungus of this kind will do what is necessary and sufficient for its dying of this disease – that is, it will eat the fungus. Yet it would be highly paradoxical to say that the goal of a pig which eats the fungus is the disease which will kill it.

How, then, is this objection to be met? The weakness of the thesis criticised is that it is too liberal. It allows anything to be the goal (G) of anything which is of nature R (e.g. is a pig with a fondness for certain fungi), provided that anything which is of nature R will do whatever is necessary and sufficient for its becoming or remaining G. Against this, Andrew Woodfield has argued that we need to be more specific about the nature of goals; in particular, we need to recognise that there are certain natural ends.[45] In the case of the pig in our example, the natural end of the pig would be pleasure; to this one may add, as a related natural end, the avoidance of pain. The natural end of the polar bear instanced by Bennett would be survival, and to these ends we may add that of the reproduction of the species.

Let us now go further. To say that E is a natural end of X is to say that E regards X as good. E may not be *really* good for X, but it is at any rate to be counted as what Aristotle called an 'apparent good'. (Incidentally, Aristotle regarded pleasure as an apparent good – which it clearly is in the case of the pig in our example.) From all this it emerges that the concept of good plays a vital part in teleological explanation.[46]

What, then, can we conclude about the relation between teleological explanation and the concept of cause that is used in the natural sciences? If the analysis just offered is correct, then we have to say that the concept of such causation is an element in teleological explanation, but that something else is required. Teleological explanation requires both a causal and an evaluative element.[47] To give an explanation of such a kind, we have to identify an effect – actual or envisaged – of some cause; but we also have to say that this effect is good from some point of view.[48]

Notes

(An author's name followed by a number in square brackets refers to the book or article which has that number in the bibliography.)

1. Cf. Ackrill [2], pp. 32–3.

2. This version of the word *bouleusas* is that given by the translators of the Oxford Aristotle (Oxford, 1930). Some modern scholars translate the passage as 'The man who has deliberated is a cause [of his actions]' (Ackrill [2], p. 37; cf. Barnes [3], p. 52). However, our concern here is not just with the historical Aristotle, but also with what one may call the Aristotelian tradition. In this connection, it is worth noting that the very influential medieval philosopher Thomas Aquinas took the term to mean 'advised' in his commentary on a parallel passage from Aristotle's *Metaphysics*, Book V, Ch. 2. See Aquinas, *Selected writings*, ed. M.C. D'Arcy (Dent, London, 1939), p. 157.

The example of the raid on Sardis comes from Aristotle, *Posterior analytics*, II, 11, 94a37–b1.

3. Hume [4], Book I, Part III, Section 2 (pp. 75–8).

4. Bertrand Russell has produced an argument (Russell [7], pp. 134–5) to show that cause and effect are *never* temporally contiguous. The argument, which is based on the view that no two instants are contiguous, has not won general acceptance: see Mackie [11], pp. 144–5, and A.J. Ayer, *Russell and Moore: the analytical heritage* (Macmillan, London, 1971), pp. 113–15.

5. Hume [4], p. 76; Mill [6], Book III, Ch. 5, Section 7.

6. The question whether 'backward causation' is possible has been energetically debated in recent years. The debate began with a symposium between M. Dummett and A.G.N. Flew, 'Can an effect precede its cause?' *Proceedings of the Aristotelian Society*, supp. vol. 28 (1954), pp. 27–62. For a short bibliography of the controversy, see Mackie [11], p. 162 n. 2.

7. Kant, *Critique of pure reason*, 2nd edn (B), pp. 247–9. J.L. Mackie ([11], pp. 178–85) has offered a different solution, involving the idea of 'fixity'. Past and present states of affairs and events are 'fixed', in the sense that they are unalterable; however,

at least some future ones are still to be fixed, i.e. are still undecided. Mackie argues that if at any time *A* is fixed while *B* is still unfixed, *B* cannot be causally prior to *A*, since at this time things might be so decided that *B* does not occur. For a criticism of this view, see A.J. Ayer, *Freedom and morality* (Clarendon Press, Oxford, 1984), pp. 56–8.

8. Hume [5], Section VII, Part II, para. 60 (p. 76).

9. Hume [4], pp. 79–80. An introductory account of Spinoza's theory of causality is given in Parkinson [15], p. 25; for a more advanced account, see Bennett [16], pp. 29–32.

10. Hume [5], para. 60, p. 77. See also Hume [4], p. 87.

11. Mill [6], II.5.6.

12. Mill [6], III.5.3.

13. 'Usually', because in exceptional circumstances we might say that it is the cause. See Hart and Honoré [9], p. 33.

14. See Russell [7].

15. Russell has in mind here the sense in which the term 'function' is used in mathematics: that is, 'a correlation between two variable numbers, called respectively the argument and the value of the function, such that whatever value be assigned to the "argument of the function" the "value of the function" is definitely (i.e. uniquely) determined' (A.N. Whitehead, *An introduction to mathematics* (Oxford University Press, Oxford, 12th impression, 1948), pp. 107–8). This sense of the term 'function' has of course to be distinguished from what is meant when it is said that the function of the hacksaw is to cut metal. On this, see Section VII below.

16. Mackie [11], p. 154. Cf. Nagel, quoted in von Wright [10], p. 36.

17. Collingwood [8], pp. 285–337.

18. Ibid., p. 287.

19. Ibid., p. 285. It may seem strange, given this one–one relation, that Mill should also believe in a plurality of causes, i.e. in a possible many–one relation between cause and effect. (See Mill [6], Book III, Ch. 10). In such cases, however, the effects involved are of some generality. This particular person's death, Mill would say, has just one cause; but if we ask, 'What is the cause of death?', the answer must involve many causes.

20. Collingwood [8], pp. 296–7; see also pp. 299, 304, 313 n. 1. For Mill's view about the 'capricious manner' in which we select a cause from among the conditions, see Mill [6], III.5.3.

21. Collingwood [8], p. 298.

22. See Ch. 4, pp. 87–9.

23. Collingwood [8], p. 301.

24. Von Wright [10], p. 70. Von Wright notes the kinship between his view and Collingwood's notion of the cause as 'handle'; he also refers to an article by D. Gasking, 'Causation and recipes', *Mind*, vol. 64 (1955), pp. 479–87.

25. Ibid., p. 70.

26. See Collingwood [8], pp. 285–6; Hart and Honoré [9], pp. 10, 48ff. For the term 'person to person causality' see J. Hospers, *Introduction to philosophical analysis*, 2nd edn (Routledge, London, 1969), pp. 297–8.

27. E.g. Hart and Honoré [9], pp. 48–53.

28. E.g. the attacked state must not be too weak to retaliate; or it must not believe that it is always wrong to repay violence with violence.

29. Standard dictionaries often define teleology as a kind of doctrine or theory, a

definition which is suggested by the suffix '-logy'. But we find philosophers saying such things as 'Consider two extreme theses about teleology' (Woodfield [25], p. 2), where 'teleology' refers to a feature that things display, not to theories about it.

30. See, e.g., A.R. White, in the Introduction to A.R. White (ed.), *The philosophy of action* (Oxford University Press, Oxford, 1968), p. 17. On the relevance of this distinction for the philosophy of religion, see J.C.A. Gaskin, *The quest for eternity* (Penguin Books, Harmondsworth, 1984), pp. 25–36.

31. Donald Davidson, 'Actions, reasons and causes': first published in 1963, and reprinted in Davidson, *Actions and events* (Clarendon Press, Oxford, 1980), pp. 3–19; also in White, *The philosophy of action*, pp. 79–94.

32. On this term, see P.H. Nowell Smith, *Ethics* (Penguin Books, Harmondsworth, 1954), pp. 111–16.

33. It should be added that Davidson himself may not want to deny the distinction just drawn. His account of reasons as causes has a different target – namely the thesis, defended by followers of Wittgenstein, that we have to distinguish between human *actions* (which cannot be explained in causal terms) and *events* (which can). For recent discussions of Davidson's views about reasons and causes, see E. LePore and M. McLaughlin (eds), *Actions and events: perspectives on the philosophy of Donald Davidson* (Basil Blackwell, Oxford, 1985), especially the Introduction and Chs. 1, 2, 8, 9 and 20.

34. Aristotle [12], Ch. 1, Section 9, 641b11ff.

35. Some scientists argue that the term 'teleology' should be applied only to agents who have conscious ends; the goal-directed behaviour of other agents should be distinguished by the use of a special term, 'teleonomy'. (On this term, see also Ch. 24, 'Teleological Theories of Morality', note 1). Philosophers, however, retain the word 'teleology' in its wide sense, probably because this brings out something that is shared by all explanations of goal-directed activity. This is that in all such cases one is explaining what a thing does by reference to a future state that it will, or may, attain.

36. The distinction goes back at least as far as Kant, who distinguished between 'extrinsic' and 'intrinsic' finality (Kant [18], pp. 13, 15, 26, 86). See also C.D. Broad, *The mind and its place in nature* (Routledge, London, 1925), p. 83.

37. See Aristotle [12], pp. 94–8. Plato's *Timaeus* is perhaps best read in the translation by Desmond Lee, in Plato: *Timaeus and Critias* (Penguin Books, Harmondsworth, 1971). For Leibniz' views on teleology, see Broad [17].

38. For more detailed discussions of this topic, see Nagel [21], pp. 425–8; Bennett [23], pp. 78–80; Woodfield [25], pp. 107–40.

39. Russell, *The analysis of mind* (Allen and Unwin, London, 1921). See especially pp. 62–5.

40. Russell's chief target here is the idea that a desire is a mental cause, but his criticisms also apply to the concept of such supposed entities as 'entelechies'. These were postulated by the philosopher–scientist Hans Driesch (1867–1941) as the non-spatial factors which guide the development of an organism.

41. The names were introduced by G. Sommerhoff, *Analytical biology* (Oxford University Press, Oxford, 1950). Cf. Woodfield [25], pp. 55–6, 161.

42. Bennett [23], p. 45.

43. Taylor [22], Bennett [23], Wright [24].

44. Bennett [23]; see especially pp. 39–40, 45.

45. See Woodfield [25], especially Chs. 7–12.

46. Cf. Aristotle [1], 195a24–6: 'that for the sake of which' means that which is the best and is the end of the things that lead up to it. On pleasure as an apparent good, see Aristotle [13], Ch. 6, 700b30; cf. his *Eudemian ethics*, VII, 2, 1235b25–9. On pleasure and the avoidance of pain as natural ends, cf. Woodfield [25], pp. 129–30.

47. Woodfield [25], p. 206.

48. I am grateful to my colleague Dr T.E. Burke for his helpful comments on an earlier draft of this chapter.

Bibliography

A. The Aristotelian 'four causes'

Aristotle's most detailed exposition of the 'four causes' is given in his *Physics*, Book II, Ch. 3. The best edition for the student is

[1] Aristotle, *Physics I and II*, trans. and with notes by W. Charlton (Clarendon Press, Oxford, 1983).

Useful introductions to Aristotle's views about explanation are given by

[2] J.L. Ackrill, *Aristotle the philosopher* (Oxford University Press, Oxford, 1981), pp. 36–45 and

[3] Jonathan Barnes, *Aristotle* (Oxford University Press, Oxford, 1982), pp. 51–7.

B. Hume and Mill on causality

[4] Hume, *A treatise of human nature* (1739). The best edition is that by L.A. Selby-Bigge; 2nd edn, revised by P.H. Nidditch (Oxford University Press, Oxford, 1978). See especially Book I, Part III, Section 2.

[5] Hume, *Enquiries concerning human understanding and concerning the principles of morals* (1777 edn), edited by L.A. Selby-Bigge, 3rd edn, revised by P.H. Nidditch (Oxford University Press, Oxford, 1975). See especially Section VII, Part II, para. 60.

[6] J.S. Mill, *A system of logic* (Longmans Green, London; 1st edn, 1843). The last edition to be published in Mill's lifetime was the 8th (1872); this edition is still available. See especially Book III, Ch. 5.

C. One type of causality, or several?

Mention should be made first of Russell's radical view that the concept of cause is 'a relic of a bygone age', doomed to disappear eventually from the natural sciences. Russell expounds this view in his paper 'On the notion of cause'. This was first published in the *Proceedings of the Aristotelian Society*, vol. 13 (1912–13), pp. 1–25, but it is more readily accessible in

[7] Bertrand Russell, *Mysticism and logic* (first published in 1918; paperback edition, Allen and Unwin, London, 1963, pp. 132–51).

Collingwood's distinction between three types of causality is expounded by him with typical force and lucidity in

[8] R.G. Collingwood, *An essay on metaphysics* (Clarendon Press, Oxford, 1940), pp. 285–337.

A more recent account of different senses of the word 'cause', which owes something to Collingwood, is

[9] H.L.A. Hart and A.M. Honoré, *Causation in the law* (Clarendon Press, Oxford, 1st edn, 1959; 2nd edn, 1985), pp. 8–57. This has been rightly described as 'One of the best studies that have been made of ordinary causal concepts' (Mackie [11], p. 117). A more technical account of causal explanation is to be found in

[10] G.H. von Wright, *Explanation and understanding* (Routledge, London, 1971), pp. 34–82.

Still more difficult is an important study

[11] J.L. Mackie, *The cement of the universe. A study of causation* (Clarendon Press, Oxford, 1st edn, 1974; 2nd edn, 1980). Mackie argues that 'We do not need to recognise a radical plurality of causal concepts' (2nd edn, p. xiii).

D. Teleological explanation

Aristotle's views about teleology in nature are most fully stated in his *De partibus animalium*, Book I, Ch. 1. This is best studied in

[12] Aristotle, *De partibus animalium I* and *De generatione animalium I*, trans. and with notes by D.M. Balme (Clarendon Press, Oxford, 1972); see especially pp. 93–8 of the notes.

Helpful introductory accounts of Aristotle's theory of teleology are to be found in Ackrill [2], pp. 51–4, and Barnes [3], pp. 73–7. A more advanced account is contained in

[13] Aristotle, *De motu animalium*, ed. and trans. Martha Craven Nussbaum (Princeton University Press, Princeton, 1978). See especially pp. 59–99.

Aristotle's views on teleology came under severe attack in the seventeenth century; it was thought that they obstructed not only an understanding of living things, but of the physical world in general. One of the most scathing attacks on traditional views about teleology is contained in the Appendix to Part I of Spinoza's *Ethics* (1677). There are several translations of this work, of which one may mention

[14] Spinoza, *The Ethics and selected letters*, trans. S. Shirley (Hackett, Indianapolis, 1982).

An introductory account of Spinoza's views about teleology, which presupposes little previous knowledge of philosophy on the part of the reader, is contained in

[15] G.H.R. Parkinson, *Spinoza* (Open University Press, Milton Keynes, 1983), pp. 53–8.

The more advanced student should consult

[16] Jonathan Bennett, *A study of Spinoza's 'Ethics'* (Cambridge University Press, Cambridge, 1984), pp. 213–30.

Whereas Spinoza argued that purposive activity is to be explained in terms of efficient causality alone, his younger contemporary Leibniz (1646–1716) argued that final and efficient causality can be reconciled. His view was that final causality governs the real world, which consists of immaterial substances; material things, which are an appearance of these immaterial substances, have to be explained in terms of efficient causes alone. A useful introduction to Leibniz' views about efficient and final causation is provided by

[17] C.D. Broad, *Leibniz: an introduction* (Cambridge University Press, Cambridge, 1975), pp. 163–9.

The next major contribution to the study of teleological explanation was provided by Kant, in his *Critique of teleological judgement* (1790). Like Leibniz, Kant argued that efficient and final causality can be reconciled; however, he did not regard the one as concerned with appearance and the other with reality. For Kant, efficient and final causality are (very roughly speaking) different and equally legitimate ways of organising our perceptions. The *Critique of teleological judgement* forms the second part of Kant's *Critique of judgement*, of which the standard English translation is

[18] Immanuel Kant, *The critique of judgement*, trans. J.C. Meredith (Clarendon Press, Oxford, 1928).

Helpful comment on Kant's account of teleological explanation will be found in

[19] S. Körner, *Kant* (Penguin Books, Harmondsworth, 1955), pp. 196–217.

Important recent studies of teleology include

[20] R.B. Braithwaite, *Scientific explanation* (Cambridge University Press, Cambridge, 1953), pp. 322–36.

[21] Ernest Nagel, *The structure of science* (Routledge, London, 1961), pp. 401–28.

[22] Charles Taylor, *The explanation of behaviour* (Routledge, London, 1964), pp. 3–24.

[23] Jonathan Bennett, *Linguistic behaviour* (Cambridge University Press, Cambridge, 1976), pp. 36–81.

[24] Larry Wright, *Teleological explanations: an etiological analysis of goals and functions* (University of California Press, Berkeley, 1976).

Both Bennett and Wright develop and refine upon the views of Taylor [22].

[25] Andrew Woodfield, *Teleology* (Cambridge University Press, Cambridge, 1976). An acute and comprehensive account; however, the beginner may find it difficult.

See also von Wright [10], pp. 83–131, and Mackie [11], pp. 270–96.

G.H.R.P.

14 | Our Knowledge of Causality

Rom Harré

The attack on generative causality

The complex of 'causes' Aristotle thought necessary as the material of complete explanations involved two items which have traditionally excited the hostility of positivists. These were the final and the efficient cause. Final cause has found a safe haven, divided between human intentions and the positive and negative feedback of system theory. Efficient cause or agency has still to be as permanently saved. An irony of the story of the attacks on the legitimacy of the concept of agency is that while positivist philosophers have denigrated the idea in the name of a no-nonsense 'scientific' philosophy, physics, the noblest science of them all, makes essential use of agentive concepts. Who were the Humean targets in the eighteenth century? – physicists and philosophers of physics!

To understand the inwardness of the rise of the regularity account of causal concepts one must look quite closely at the way 'dynamic' philosophy, which finally flowered in the pages of Faraday and Maxwell, emerged from the critique of the *whole* Newtonian scheme – in which the metaphysics and the science of mechanics were justified.

Knowledge of powers

Just as the problem of real essences is set by Locke in immemorial terms – 'Reason calls for hypotheses about real essences but Experience cannot supply them' – so he set the corresponding problem for causal powers in a similar immemorial form. He saw that the powers of a material being to change the sensible qualities of other bodies are a topic of central importance for our inquiries into nature – but he doubted 'whether our Knowledge reaches much further than our experience'. Knowledge of observable properties would not

301

help, since we could not infer 'that they are in any subject by the connexion with any of those ideas which to us mark its essence'. And since we cannot discover the 'texture and motion of parts' which are the ways of operating of the powers of bodies, 'it is in but a very few cases we can be able to perceive their dependence or repugnance to any of those ideas that make our complex one of that sort of thing'.[1]

But it is worth noticing that nowhere does Locke cast any doubt on the propriety of speaking of powers as qualities of material beings even though our experience can only be of their effects. That had to await the Humean attack. Indeed Locke sets out the experiential conditions for knowledge of powers in his *Essay*.[2] Such knowledge is derived from the experience of change and the concomitances of change, from the experiences of like changes associated with like agents. Within the general category of powers we distinguish active powers 'able to make a change' and passive powers 'able to receive a change'.

The scene is now set for the great debate, since I believe it was Locke's views above all which seeded the epistemological controversies of the eighteenth century.

Locke's 'nescience', his view that knowledge of real essences was impossible, derived from the incompatibility of his realist conception of what a completed science would be like and his sensationalist epistemology. I shall explore several different reactions to the Lockean position, to illustrate the diversity of early eighteenth-century views about knowledge of causation.

Reactions can be classified according to whether the issue of powers or the problem of essences was the central topic of concern. The theological position is very clear. The source of the active powers of people (to think) and of things (to gravitate, cohere, etc.) had to be the Divine Being, at peril of the darkest irreligion. This theme runs from Ditton[3] to Beattie.[4] To those who wrote early in the century the most alarming form of secular dynamism was that which explained the active powers of people in terms of the active powers of matter. As Ditton says, 'Let him [the Lockean sceptic] begin with making *Matter and Motion think*; and he shall end with making the *Gospel an Imposture*.'[5] As we shall see, towards the end of the century the argument broadened and the evident powers of material beings were being cited as the best possible evidence for the existence of God, since powerless matter could not be responsible for the powers of material things.[6] The arguments concerning the limits of scientific knowledge were intimately intertwined with the theological debates concerning the source or origin of powers.

Epistemologically glossed, the most common form of the argument runs:

(1) We know that people and things have active powers.

(2) The source of these powers cannot be matter, which is essentially passive.

(3) The source must be external to the material system and is none other than God.

The founding of nescience on the empirical impossibility of knowing real essences was challenged quite early in the century. A very detailed study of the theological literature of the period would be required to confirm the choice. G. Bowles' work[7] is a valuable beginning.

Lee's *Antiscepticism*[8] takes its start from the issue of whether matter can think. It is clear that if we can 'let Matter have what Figure, Bulk, Motion or Position of its Parts that can be imagined, it can no more perceive or be conscious of its own Actions or Motions than a Stone can rise from the ground of its own accord'.[9]

But suppose Locke were right and matter had an unknown essence in which the power to think might be materially grounded? This worry could be removed at a stroke if 'our Senses be right', i.e. give us knowledge as good as intuitive and demonstrative knowledge, and if essences were perceptible in clusters of sensible qualities. But everyone means by 'Genus, Species and Essences', so declares Lee, no more than 'Names of more or fewer Qualities or Properties by which things agree or differ from each other'.[10] So our sensory knowledge is science just in Locke's sense.

Sensationalism appeared both as a support for theology (relieving us of perhaps even thinking matter) and as a support for scepticism (God as an active but hidden being is in no better case than matter). Gravity became the focus of the discussion. It seemed to be an ineliminable real power attesting to a universal natural activity. Could it be assimilated to theology and claimed as a support for religion?

The powers of matter

So central did the problem of the explanation of gravity become in the controversies about knowledge of powers that we might well speak of the theologising of the concept of a gravitational power. The connection between the implications of powers for theology and nescience is made very clear by Samuel Clarke. As he says:

> For we see and feel, and observe daily in ourselves and others, such Powers and Operations and Perception, as undeniably evince themselves either to be Properties of Immaterial Substances: or else it will follow that Matter is something of whose innermost Substance and Essential Powers we have altogether as little Idea as we have of Immaterial Beings; and then how are Immaterial Substances more impossible than Material?[11]

And then follows later in the work the oft-repeated argument that gravity depends on an immaterial substance:

> Even the very first and most universal Principle of Gravitation itself in all inanimate matters, since it is ever Proportional, not at all to the *Surfaces* of Bodies or of their Particles in any possible Superstition, but entirely to the *Solid Content* of Bodies, 'tis evident it cannot be caused by matter acting upon the *Surfaces* of Matter, which is all It can do; but must be caused by something which continually penetrates its *Solid Substance*.

But this argument can be made to cut both ways. On the other hand Whiston concludes 'that this gravity is an entirely Immechanical Power, and beyond the Abilities of all material Agents whatsoever',[12] elaborating the argument somewhat to include the point that its effect is proportional to solid content and not to surface. Whiston also notes that gravity is independent of state of motion and acts at a distance. From this it follows that

> it's not, strictly speaking, any Power belonging to a Body or Matter at all ... but is a Power of a Superior Agent, ever moving all Bodies after such a manner, as if every Body did Attract, and were Attracted by every other Body in the Universe.

Since this power has been demonstrated to be immechanical and beyond the abilities of all material agents, ' 'tis certain that the Author of this Power is an Immaterial or Spiritual Being, present in, and penetrating the whole Universe'.[13] So gravity serves as a defence of the existence of God. Indeed, it is a premiss from which the existence of God seems certainly to follow according to this line of argument.

However, by 1762, while accepting the premisses, Jones can draw the opposite conclusion:

> From these and many other experiments open to common observation it must appear to every unprejudiced philosopher that nature is furnished with a mechanical cause whose activity is not confined to the surface of the bodies, but extends to their constituent parts, that is to their quantity of solid matter.[14]

This leads Jones to argue in Hutchinsonian style:

> Shall we allow that God governs the world by a subordinate agency and mechanism in some cases, where that agency appears to us; and deny it in others, merely because we have lost sight of it, or because it would count against us?[15]

Robert Greene's massive anti-Lockean work appeared in Cambridge in 1727.[16] So far as I can discover it caused little stir. Yet to a student of the epistemological developments of the eighteenth century it is a work of importance.

Greene opens his attack on opponents of dynamism

with a pointed statement of the deep-lying incoherence in the Newtonian system.

> So that if we compare the original hypothesis of this philosophy with the Conclusions of it, the one seems to be little less than a confutation of the other. Matter is supposed to be entirely passive. The sum of all the mathematical reasoning upon that hypothesis is, that if it has in every part of it a Force of Gravitation, that is, that it is entirely Active, and if such a conclusion is not a contradiction to such a Hypothesis, I cannot tell what is.[17]

His solution was to abolish the passive materialism of the atomic hypothesis. Like Boscovich and Kant (and later Faraday) he proposes a system of forces, the balance between attraction and repulsion producing the material world as we experience it. A solid body, for instance, is a closed surface at which the nett force is repulsive. 'From a various Mixture of a greater or less proportion of these forces, all the qualities of bodies arise.'

Scientific knowledge on this view must be of forces and their mixtures. It must be formulated for a world 'on the other side', so to speak, of sensations, which are no more than effects. With such a programme the epistemology must be hypothetico-deductive. 'If I can produce', says Greene,

> those actions and forces, which will not only solve all the phenomena of matter which we are acquainted with by our sensations from it, but even those which may possibly arrive to other animals or a distinct nature and species from us, I hope I shall have given a full account, not only of the essence of matter, but of its Real and Essential properties.[18]

And this, in tedious detail, he proceeds to do. The thoroughgoing dynamism of Greene's *Principles* poses an interesting (and as far as I know unsolved) historical question. How far did the continental dynamists in the traditions of Leibniz, such as Boscovich and Kant, know anything of the British 'native tradition' exemplified, say, by Greene? For the abolition of Lockean primary qualities in favour of a balance of forces is so similar to Kant's treatment fifty years later that one wonders whether Kant perhaps had some acquaintance with Greene's philosophy. Standard works on Kant's intellectual sources make no reference to Greene as among the authors with whose works he was acquainted.

According to Greene, the sources and the forces required for the dissolution of primary qualities are either those forces themselves or the direct activity of God. The former will not do as an ultimate explanation since, according to Greene, whatever exists of itself will have a necessary principle of its existence. This sets the limit to our knowledge. 'The furthest the human mind can reach in philosophy' is to catalogue the variety of expansive and contractive forces. And this is to catalogue the variety of 'the substratum or essence of matter', since that can only be 'Action or Force'. Does this contradict Locke's limits of knowledge? It is not entirely clear that it does. Locke's epistemological difficulties derived from the impossibility of discovering in sensory experience any simple ideas of those qualities of the inner constitution of bodies on which their powers depended. But that supposes that the powers of bodies depend on some kind of texture of atomic bodies. By denying the necessity for that grounding and basing matter directly on powers or forces Greene abolishes Locke's limits by abolishing the further region. We can neither reach nor fail to reach that which does not exist. Towards the end of the century dynamism became a more and more popular solution to Locke's problem.

J. Michell (1724–93) is famous for the 'Mathematical Bridge' over the Cam. Later, translated to a country living, he brooded on philosophy, conversed with his neighbours and friends, but wrote nothing. Most of what we know of Michell's theory comes from Priestley, upon whom he exerted a considerable and lasting influence.[19]

Priestley's account of Michell's path to the conception of matter as active power runs as follows:

> This scheme of the *immateriality of matter*, as it may be called, or rather, the *mutual penetration of matter*, first occurred to Mr. Michell on reading Baxter *On the Immateriality of the Soul*. He found that the author's idea of matter was that it consisted as it were of bricks, cemented together by an immaterial mortar.[20]

Carrying this argument through, it seems that the need for an impenetrable and basic matter simply disappears. The form of the argument is close to that adopted by Greene. By comparison of hypotheses the force theory triumphs over the theory of material substance, and since observable effects are more readily and uniformly accounted for by postulating fields of force, reason and experience conspire to support the dynamicist point of view.

But the underlying causal powers and forces cannot be perceived. The final apotheosis of the Lockean theory of sensory ideas ran straight into the developing field theory, for Hume's theory of knowledge seemed to wipe out forces as mere reflections of psychological phenomena.

The field theory, whose epistemology troubled the philosophers and theologians of this period, is not usually credited to Greene but to the independent discoveries of John Michell and Roger Joseph Boscovich. Joseph Priestley, for example, couples their names when discussing the activity of matter.

Though the field theories of Michell and Greene were perhaps exceptional in being very fully developed, many people of the period held to some sort of force theory of matter, often inconsistently coupled with a vaguely substantialist basis. Preference for forces over substances accounts for one curious incident of the time: Stephen Hales' rejection of John Mayow's 'discovery' of 'oxygen'. Hales, like many chemists and physiologists, had performed experiments on the breathability of air, and knew of the reduction in volume occasioned by a plant or animal using air. Mayow had explained the phenomenon, late in the seventeenth century, as the result of the fixing of a material substance – nitro-aerius vapour, a substance which made up one-fifth of the bulk of the air – by breathing creatures. Hales rejected this view, arguing instead that by breathing the air in and out the creature reduced its elasticity, the force which held the air expanded out to a certain volume. A reduction in the elasticity would lead to a shrinkage in bulk of the original air. Hales had arrived at fields too soon.

To complete my case for the historical importance of British dynamical doctrine, and to show how deeply providential assumptions were ingrained in the epistemology, I now turn to an exegis of Hume's philosophical writings to demonstrate the importance of the eighteenth-century interest in the sources of activity, both natural and human. Only against that background, I argue, can the direction of Hume's investigation of the limits of human knowledge of causation be understood.

The Humean enigma

Hall has demonstrated how little philosophical interest was aroused, until relatively recently, by Hume's sceptical arguments. The bibliographical evidence seems conclusive on this issue.[21] And yet Hume was a considerable figure in his own time, directly influential on many important authors. In a recent essay Jessop has raised in an interesting form the historical problem of the interpretation of Hume's philosophy. Following Kemp Smith, Jessop argues that Hume saw himself primarily as a moral philosopher, and perhaps even as something of a moraliser.[22] His scepticism is directed not so much against particular doctrines as such, but against the uncritical reliance on reason in human affairs.

If indeed the central issue of concern in intellectual circles in eighteenth-century Britain was the extent of our knowledge of powers and activity, then it is hardly surprising that the analysis of causal relations should figure largely in Hume's works.[23] He does not seem to have doubted that material beings, animate and inanimate, had powers, but he claims to be unable to see how human beings could have any knowledge of powers in themselves. To summarise the well-known argument: the idea of causal connection involves four root ideas – contiguity of the idea of the cause and the idea of the effect; succession of these ideas; the production of the one by the other; and their necessary connection. To discover the status or real meaning of these ideas, one looks for the corresponding impressions. Contiguity and succession of ideas do indeed seem to be associated with contiguity and succession of impressions. But Hume can find no impression corresponding to the idea of production. The analysis of the idea of necessary connection is his *tour de force*, since he claims to show that there is a corresponding impression, but at bottom it is the psychological effect produced by repeated contiguities and succession of like pairs of impressions. In consequence it is not an idea corresponding to a real relation between things or events. Since, according to Hume, 'the terms of *efficacy, agency, power, force, energy, necessity, connection* and *productive* quality are all nearly synonymous', the same treatment will do for them all.[24]

By linking meaning to experience, the content of ideas to their original impressions, Hume abolished all ideas that purport to refer beyond experience. Science, as the totality of causal principles, can be no more than the record of repeated concomitances of impressions.

But I am convinced that the theological motivation of discussions of the extent of human knowledge was as potent at the end of the century as it was at the beginning. Priestley's discussion goes to the heart of Hume's argument. It turns upon the principle that relates an idea to one and only one impression as its original. Priestley simply points out that no reason is given for this arbitrary restriction. As soon as one enquires as to how the idea of a power is acquired one sees that it is correlated with a set of impressions, which taken together yield the idea. Following Locke, whom he quotes and discusses extensively, Priestley boldly offers a field theory of matter, quite within the tradition of Greene, Michell, Boscovich and Kant.

Priestley's argument follows the standard pattern of eighteenth-century analysis of matter. He shows how primary qualities, just like secondary qualities, can be accounted for in terms of a theory of paired forces.

> [R]*esistance*, on which alone our opinion concerning the solidity or impenetrability of matter is founded, is never occasioned by *solid matter*, but by something of a very different nature, viz. a *power of repulsion* always acting at a real but assignable distance from what we call the body itself.[25]

> No such figured thing can exist unless the parts of which it consists have a mutual attraction, so as either to keep contiguous to, or to preserve a certain distance from each other.[26]

But Priestley was a Socinian. Mind is material and man is active. He needs no immaterial soul to endow him with his capacities, since matter, it is now securely established, is an active being. Theological consequences turn the discussion back to Baxter's troubled spiritual universalism.

Baxter had supposed that the need to analyse matter as power requires that 'we make that Deity himself to *do* and *be* every thing'.[27] Priestley's theological conclusion is Unitarian in every sense.

> If I be asked how, upon this hypothesis, *matter* differs from *spirit*, if there be nothing in matter that is properly solid or impenetrable, I answer, that it no way concerns me, or true philosophy, to maintain that there is any such difference between them as has hitherto been supposed.

If we take Beattie as typical of reactions to Hume's sceptical views within the Scottish Enlightenment, it is clear that the know-ability of agency is indeed the prime topic of concern. Beattie locates the origin of scepticism in the arguments (but not, of course, the intentions) of Descartes.

His successors [Locke, Berkeley and Hume], the further they advance in his systems, become more and more sceptical, and at length their reader is told, to his infinite pleasure and emolument, that the understanding, acting alone, does entirely subvert itself and leaves not the lowest degree of evidence in any proposition.[28]

The crux of the matter is perception; and the point at issue is knowledge of power or energy, that is of causation, and of the self. Beattie points out that the doctrine that impressions and ideas have an essential identity, differing only in strength (the basis of Hume's sceptical argument), depends upon a confusion between three distinct uses of percep-tion words: for the thing perceived, for the power or faculty of perceiving, and for the impression or impulse conveyed to the mind. The idea of a thing lacks many of the qualities of the thing – but the senses present, *in their own style*, the way things really are. So, for instance, perspective is not an illusion, but how things look if they are really at different distances.[29]

The powers of things to produce effects are per-ceived in the activity we experience. Contrary to Hume's thesis, that constant conjunction is the only empirical element in causality, Beattie argues that, although it may be necessary, it is certainly not a sufficient condition for identifying causation. We need to experience also the acting of one thing on another, in short the manifestation of its power. Would Hume's sceptical attack on an empirical referent for the impressions of causal agency (power, efficiency, etc.) have been so influential without Mill's revival of the regular-ity theory? Perhaps such speculation is idle, but Mill's brisk account of the regularity theory stands historically between Hume's psychological reduc-tionism and the explosion of positivism that marked the birth and propaga-tion of Vienna Circle thought.

Mill's exposition is worth quoting at some length since it encapsulates the main epistemological and metaphysical aspects of the anti-generative position. His first point concerns the paramount importance of 'order of succession'.

Of all truths relating to phenomena, the most valuable to us are those which relate to the order of their succession. On a knowledge of these is founded every reasonable anticipation of future facts, and whatever power we possess of influenc-ing those facts to our advantage. Even the laws of geometry are chiefly of practical importance to us as being a portion of the premises from which the order of the succession of phenomena may be inferred. Inasmuch as the motion of bodies, the action of forces, and the propagation of influences of all sorts, take place in certain lines and over definite spaces, the properties of those lines and spaces are an important part of the laws to which those phenomena are themselves subject.[30]

The positivistic rejection of unobservable entities includes those which would be the generators of orderly successions. Mill's argument for the thesis that generative causes are unobservable runs as follows:

> I premise then, that when in the course of this enquiry I speak of the cause of any phenomenon, I do not mean a cause which is not itself a phenomenon; I make no research into the ultimate or ontological cause of anything. To adopt a distinction familiar in the writings of the Scotch metaphysicians, and especially of Reid, the causes with which I concern myself are not efficient, but physical causes. They are causes in that sense alone in which one physical fact is said to be the cause of another. Of the efficient causes of phenomena, or whether any such causes exist at all, I am not called upon to give an opinion. The notion of causation is deemed by the schools of metaphysics most in vogue at the present moment to imply a mysterious and most powerful tie, such as cannot, or at least does not, exist between any physical fact and that other physical fact on which it is invariably consequent, and which is popularly termed its cause: and thence is deduced the supposed necessity of ascending higher into the essences and inherent constitution of things, to find the true cause, the cause which is not only followed by, but actually produces, the effect. No such necessity exists for the purposes of the present enquiry.[31]

And, of course, science deals only with the observable.

> The only notion of a cause which the theory of induction requires is such a notion as can be gained from experience. The Law of Causation, the recognition of which is the main pillar of inductive science, is but the familiar truth that invariability of succession is found by observation to obtain between every fact in nature and some other fact which has preceded it, independently of all considerations respecting the ultimate mode of production of phenomena.

The basic structure of the regularity theory

Having sketched the history of anti-generative ideas I have now to outline the regularity theory in its 'received' form. The common tenets of the theory need to be picked out, so that, so to say, they can be 'picked off' one by one.

I take the 'regularity theory' to be the doctrine that the empirical content of a statement of causal relation is no more than a statement that events, states, etc. of the type of the cause are regularly precedent to events, states, etc. of the type of the effect. The experience of the manifestation of the productive power of potent things in causal production and the apparent necessity of their effects are alleged to be psychological phenomena, produced by experiencing the regularity of the concomitance. In more recent versions than those of Hume, the theory is expressed in terms of the necessary and sufficient conditions for the coming to be of an effect, but that the effect is produced by the obtaining of these conditions is held to be wholly contingent, since ultimately unconnected to the cause.

The theory has two central tenets:

(1) Empirically the content of the statement of causal relations is exhausted by an actual or hypothetical regularity between independent entities.

(2) The necessity ordinarily attributed to causal production is an illusion, variously accounted for.

In consequence, causes and effects are held to be absolutely independent in fact, and consequently they must be held to be so in concept too.

Epistemic atomism and the direct perception of causation

Everything depends for the regularity theorist on the assumption that there are no empirically discernible connections between events. For, if there were, the anti-theoretical arguments that mark the bias of regularity theorists would be ineffective against a generative theory. 'You think you experience a causal activity,' says Hume, 'but that idea is an indirect effect of a psychological phenomenon, not of a physical process.' Mill echoes this sentiment, without the argument. But what is the argument? It amounts to the doctrine of epistemic atomism.

In pursuing his path to the conclusion that the empirical content of a causal statement is exhausted by the co-occurrence of events of a certain type, the regularity theorist must get rid of the alleged experience of causal connection. One of his methods is to argue from the conceptual independence of the predicates by which we describe a cause from those by which we describe its usual effect (supposedly established by the no-contradiction argument) to the actual independence of our experiences of cause and effect, and sometimes even to the actual independence of cause and of effect in the realm of nature. This argument is usually backed up by the assertion that when we examine our experience of causal production we fail to find an empirical source for our idea that cause and effect are connected, and *a fortiori* that they are necessarily connected. If our experience were indeed to consist of atomic impressions, each independent of the last, it would certainly follow that there could be no impression of the connections of one atom of experience with another.

Later I shall show that the common-sense assumption that the productive action of causal powers can be and indeed is very commonly perceived is perfectly defensible. At this point I want to look critically only at the general theory of epistemic atomism, adherence to which has been a common accompaniment of belief in the regularity theory.

In common with many pervasive epistemological

theories, epistemic atomism is a loose conjunction of atomistic theories in the three realms of psychology, epistemology and ontology. In a full-scale phenomenalist version of the theory the atoms of experience are held to be experienced sensory elements which are both the ultimate components of perception as well as of the world-as-experienced. I shall, following Gibson, argue for the falsity of any atomistic psychological theory of perception.[32] It will turn out that the fundamental unit revealed in the psychological study of perception, the sensory invariant, is of the same character as the generalised thing, the fundamental unit of a realist ontology.

Gibson has shown that there is insufficient information in the sensory elements of a static perceptual situation to explain the perceptual experience we actually have. In one series of investigations he showed that in order to generate our actual perception we must be actively modifying the sensory elements, for what we actually perceive is a function of the invariants that are maintained through considerable changes in the character of the field of sensations. For example, it is easy to tell a soft hemisphere from a hard when the finger actively presses upon them, but impossible when, with the same pressure, they are pressed upon it.

In another series he established that some of the character of our perceptions derives from invariants in neural impulse patterns from sources in joints and other locations, of which we are never aware. The totality of the information encapsulated in the perception of which this is true includes some information for which there could be no sense-data. *A fortiori* an analysis of a description of that information could never be expressed in conjunctions of sense-datum statements because there would be much non-sensory material in that information.

The idea then that perception can be exhaustively accounted for in terms of sensation and its organisation is factually false. It follows that the philosophical theory that maintains that the content of perceptual descriptions, for example material object statements, can be exhaustively expressed in a conjunction of sensory statements must correspondingly be rejected.

Things and other invariants through change are ineliminable fundamental elements of experience. But these invariants are structurally complex in both space and time. There are no atoms of experience, neither coexisting qualities, nor successive events. They are internally related as the qualities of an invariant thing, and the events in a process involving powerful particulars, potent things invariant in the course of the changes marked by the occurrence of the events. Thus the psychological grounding of epistemic atomism is illusory. I shall show that the independence of empirical predicates, the sibling theory in philosophical logic to the epistemic atomism of such as Hume, has no grounding in philosophy since a rational theory of the interrelations of the empirical predicates can be provided.

The Humean does not deny that we have a phenomenologically irreducible experience of the action of causal powers; he only denies that this experience corresponds to any physical reality. The second part of his argument is to show why one mistakenly thinks one's irreducible experience points to physical reality, and it is to this end that Hume introduces his associationist explanation in terms of custom and its projection on to objects and events. Contemporary Humeans add other projection explanations. The argument which gives ontological status to causal powers in general also applies to the everyday situations where we talk about the waves eating away the shore, the axe splitting the wood, and the avalanche destroying the countryside, and hence that it is possible for one to perceive processes in which the agencies of causal power manifest directly. The direct experience of the activity of causal power is its own warrant, and we are not required to infer, by some hazardous reasoning, the existence of agents at work from the effects their working produces. The justification of our so treating this kind of experience consists in providing an analysis of 'cause' which allows us to accept the experience at face value. In order for the direct-perception doctrine to be really appealing, we need to show that it can be so formulated as to avoid the numerous pitfalls that have engulfed previous advocates of it in metaphysical and epistemic disaster.

Of course, the perception of causation is not like the perception of colour. A potent entity does not wear its causal powers like a ripe apple wears its redness. The model for the perception of causation is the perception of motion. A moving thing is perceptually distinct from a motionless thing and yet takes on no new quality. The perception of its motion is a genuine perception. Its motion is not inferred from observation of its successive occupants of different relative positions. An iron ball depressing a velvet cushion is qualitatively no more than an iron ball, yet we see it pushing upon and reshaping a cushion. As Michotte puts it:

> It is therefore quite out of the question to regard the causal aspect of the Launching Effect as due to an 'act of interpretation' on our part, or to suppose that, under the influence of past experience ... we ourselves invest certain basic impressions of movement with a 'meaning'. On the contrary, there is actual *perception* of causality, in the same sense that there is perception of shapes, movement and so on. These expressions are logically similar.[33]

Not only are we not confined to volitional contexts for our experiences of the action of causal power, we discover them at work less easily and quickly there than in physical contexts. According to Sterling Lamprecht,

> Instead of going from the psychological facts of volition to the physical thrusts of things (so that belief in causality would be a kind of lingering animistic interpretation of the material world), we begin with the experience of causality in bodily

thrusts and only later extend the notion to our own mental life (and the degree to which such extension is legitimate is still to some philosophers an open question).[34]

Indeed, the idea of causality first arises not even from an awareness of things bumping, banging and pushing on the child, but from his awareness of things banging, bumping and clashing among themselves. Only gradually does he learn to isolate his own body for special attention, learns its prowess and various kinds of skill, and eventually arrives at an understanding of his own mental powers and the efficacy of his will.

Such a theory of the external origin of the notion of 'causal power in action' receives strong support from the experimental findings of Michotte. As a result of his experiments he claims that 'we can exclude categorically any attempt aimed at reducing this impression (of causal activity) to a "projection" of our own power into things'.[35] Out of much that is of interest in his work the most significant discovery for our purposes is his finding that the experience of purely mechanical causality (that is, the causal action in which one moving object causes another object to move) external to the perceiver is primary. Moreover, he shows, contrary to Hume, that habit and expectation are not necessary conditions of the perception of mechanical causation.

The experiments are classically simple in form. The subject is presented with a slot, at the left-hand end of which is a red rectangle (A) and in the middle of which is a similar sized black rectangle (B). A is made to move towards B at about 30 cm/sec, and when it reaches B, either A stops and B moves on at about 10 cm/sec (the Launching Effect) or they both move on together (the Entraining Effect). 'The result of this experiment is perfectly clear,' says Michotte. 'The observers see object A bump into object B, and send it off (or "*launch*" it), *shove it forward, set it in motion, give it a push*. The impression is clear; it is the blow given by A *which makes B go*, which *produces* B's movement.'[36]

By varying the conditions such as relative speeds, and whether the two rectangles actually seemed to make contact, Michotte was able to distinguish mere concomitance (segregation of the motions) from causality. The phenomenal aspect of the interaction of A and B which is perceived as causal activity he calls 'ampliation of the motion'. If the conditions which produce 'ampliation' are not met, the causality is not perceived, but 'triggering' instead; that is, 'the movement of the passive object "B" was not *produced* by the movement of A, the active object, nor by the blow which it dealt, but that none the less, it *clearly depended* on it in some way not exactly specified'. As might be expected, one's mental attitude to the experiment influences in some degree what one perceives, but only if the usual conditions for the perception of causality are not met. 'The adoption by the observer of an analytical attitude can prevent the formation of a causal impression and bring about the complete segregation of the movements. In the case of the

Launching Effect this occurs very readily if the objective conditions for integration are not very favourable, e.g. if the movements are not in the same direction or if there is no hierarchy of speeds.'[37]

Michotte was able to show that the conditions under which causation was seen were quite independent of whether there was actually any causal relation between the one object and the other. This conclusion serves to emphasise our point that whether we can finally justify our claim that a certain sequence of happenings is a case of causal production and is of natural necessitation in all cases other than fundamental interactions depends upon whether we can uncover the causal mechanisms at work in the production. Since this is discovered *a posteriori* we may be mistaken in supposing that what looked like causal production really was.

It might be objected that Michotte's psychological findings are interesting but irrelevant to the logical and philosophical issues we are discussing. In one sense this objection is well taken. Michotte's experimental findings no more than the ordinary experiences of the action of causal powers even begin to refute the philosophical aspects of the Humean claim. The Humean does not deny that we have certain experiences but claims that, given certain epistemic realities, it is impossible to accept them at face value. To refute him, it is necessary to provide a counter philosophical analysis, to show that such experience can be taken at face value. But Hume's associationistic explanations of why we mistakenly think we directly experience the action of causal powers are factual in nature, and here Michotte has clearly shown him to be wrong.

The in-principle/no-contradiction argument

Even if a regularity theorist were to concede that there were grounds for accepting that people could have impressions of causal activity, this concession falls short of admitting any necessity into natural productions. It has been claimed for nearly two centuries, by the anti-generativists, that in principle there is no contradiction in conjoining a description of a causally potent entity, state of affairs, event, etc. with a negation of a description of its usual effect. To quote my colleague Edward Madden, it is not contradictory to say Shadrack, Meshak and Abednego went into a fiery furnace and were *not* consumed, indeed it was once even supposed to be true.

But the point of the tale is that they ought to have been. A divine (that is cosmically external) intervention suspended the ordinary processes of combustion, so that they were not consumed. It was not that they benefited by a random fluctuation nor was it by accident that they escaped unhurt. But of what does the ordinary necessity consist? This takes me to the issue of what tie there is which binds causes and effect into a union of such strength that the one necessitates the other. My solution is based on the claim that in real cases of causation there are either powerful particulars, natural agents, acting directly, like gravitational fields, or there are causal mechanisms, incorporating potent entities, such as the human immune system incorporating T-cells actively scavenging among the invaders. It is when causal relations are decontextualised, abstracted from the concrete reality in which they occur, and taken merely as relations among events, that scepticism can begin to take root.

The apodeictic modality appears in many varieties of necessity. All it means to say that something must happen, must be so, and so on, is that in that context there *is* no alternative to the matter in question. Our inability to imagine an alternative is at best a practical test for whether alternatives exist, but hardly constitutes the meaning of the claim to necessity. Claims that such and such is necessary are not only relative to context but of course relative to our knowledge of that context. Enrichment of knowledge may lead to changes in our willingness to ascribe an apodeictic modality. In so far as causation is a form of natural necessity, we must find out, in each case, not only if there is a real connection between events, but also whether, in the given context, any other outcome would be possible, that is lies within the scope of the productive power of the mechanism.

Varieties of generative causality

In setting out a theory of generative causality it is necessary to give an account of the ontological tie that binds causes to effects – the means by which causes are actually efficacious. This needs to be specified with the greatest care.

We must avoid at the outset the reification of an abstract term. The notion of causal power should not be conceived as an undefined descriptive predicate that refers to an ontological tie that binds objects and events together. The exercise of causal power is not a force or power that has some existence of its own but refers to *forceful objects at work*. There are not both things and causality in nature, but causally active things. In Sterling Lamprecht's words,

> Causality is a name for a certain quality of events, it is not a name for the agency behind the events. The agency is there, to be sure: it is the lava flow, the medicine, the light rays, the mechanic's muscles, the tossing waves. There is no other 'force', there is no other cause, than just these specific things. But these things are *forceful*: they operate; they produce. And they are forceful and operate and produce in that specific way we call necessary. Causality names that kind of necessary operation.[38]

The exercise of causal power or efficacy is nothing in *general*; it is precisely the relationship of production between specific and potent objects and the events discovered by the experiments of science and revealed in the experiences of daily life that they produce. And it is with the concept of powerful things and integrated structures of powerful things that we devise an ontological tie when it is required, that is, for the connection of

316

efficient causes with their effects, the very connection Hume denied to be empirically identifiable. The concept of such a connection is the concept of generative mechanism.

In his exasperation at those philosophers who attempt to reify the concept of causal power, William James exclaims, 'If there is anything hiding in the background, it ought not to be called causal agency, but should get itself another name.'[39]

What, in the background, are causal mechanisms? There are persistent and evolving structures of real beings whose successive states appear as causes and effects, and there are causal agents, the kinds of things whose nature it is to be efficacious. The latter are the basis of the efficacy of the former. They are such as electrically charged bodies and gravitational potentials. It is to their variety that I turn now.

Causal mechanisms. The next step in recommending a realist theory of causality will be to give an account of the nature of causal mechanisms and how we can come to know them, not only as themselves existents, but as generative.

In general we can compare a causal connection to a machine-system, known or assumed, such that the event or state which is the cause activates the machine-system which then operates in such a way as to produce or generate the event of state which is the effect. Productive causality occurs when the beginning and end states of the causal system are of the same physical type, and genetic causality occurs when the beginning and end states are of different physical type. It is not to be supposed that the expression 'machine-system' refers only to Newtonian push–pull mechanisms, since, for example, a magnetic field constitutes a machine-system in this sense, that is the generator exists before, during and after the pair of the events that are the cause and its effect.

The actual usage of 'produces' and 'generates' does not quite fit the distinction between productive and genetic causality, since we sometimes use 'produces' for genetic causality. For instance, 'Prolonged exposure to unfiltered sunlight produces an inflammation in the epidermis' is clearly a case of genetic causation.

Hume's attack on the claim that in the assertion of the holding of the causal relation we refer to a real connection between the events which are the terms of the relation runs, in summary, as follows:

> After he [an observer] has observed several instances of this nature [i.e. conjunction of event-pairs] he then pronounces them to be connected. What alteration has happened to give rise to this new idea of *connection*? Nothing but that he now *feels* these events to be connected in his imagination, and can readily foretell the existence of the one from the appearance of the other.[40]

That is to say we have not learned any new empirical fact other than the conjunction of the 'event-pairs', upon which we base the pronouncement that the events are causally connected. All we have is a new feeling about them derived from a new habit of mind, that of expecting the one on the occurrence of the other.

A 'cause', then, is simply 'an object, followed by another, and where all objects similar to the first are followed by objects similar to the second';[41] and, though Hume disjoins this condition, 'if the first object had not been, the second never had existed'. To see why this will not do we need to examine Hume's illustrative example. 'The vibration of this string is the cause of this particular sound' is to be understood, following the above explication, as

> that this vibration is followed by this sound, and that all similar vibrations have been followed by similar sounds: Or, that this vibration is followed by this sound, and that upon the appearance of one the mind anticipates the senses, and forms immediately an idea of the other.

This, Hume contends, must be the correct analysis since we can form no idea of the connection between the vibration and the sound. But the theory and experiments of sonic physics and neurophysiology give us a very good idea of a great deal of the connection between the vibration and the sound. We all know nowadays of the train of pressures in the air, the operation of the eardrum, the cochlea and so on, and we now know something of the train of electrochemical happenings between the inner ear and that part of the brain identified as the seat of audition. Furthermore what we mean by 'the vibration causes the sound' involves implicit reference to the intervening mechanism which links the vibration in the string to the sound we hear. The vibration of the string stimulates a mechanism, which then acts in such a way that we are stimulated and hear a sound. What we mean by 'X causes Y' is that X generates (or produces) Y, not that X is followed by Y.

A word we commonly use for causal relation is 'makes'. For instance to ask 'What makes the wheels go round?' is to ask a question to which a causal answer is demanded. Suppose we give the answer 'Explosions in the cylinders'. When the gears are in neutral there can be explosions in the cylinders while the wheels are stationary, and there can be revolving wheels, coasting downhill, with the engine switched off. We do secure the conviction that there is a causal relation by describing the mechanism of pistons, connecting rods, crankshaft, gearbox and final drive that *connects* explosions in the cylinders with the movement of the wheels. In fact, since explosions in the cylinders neither invariably accompany motion of the wheels nor are they always absent when the wheels are stationary, to say that the explosions cause the wheels to go round cannot mean that explosions are the necessary and sufficient conditions for the wheels to go round.

Why, then, has Hume's analysis so often secured

conviction? The answer, I believe, is that it correctly describes a test for causation; that is, it lays down one of the sets of criteria the satisfaction of which entitles us to assert the relational predicate '... causes ...' of two events X and Y, or two classes of events of the type of X and of the type of Y. If 'X causes Y' means 'X generates or produces Y', then it follows that a test for whether X and Y are related in this way will be to see whether whenever X occurs, Y follows, and whenever X is absent Y is absent. The motoring example shows that failure always to satisfy this test is not an adequate reason, given a mechanism linking cause and effect in a generative or productive way, for denying the causal connection. Similarly it is not difficult to find cases, for instance astronomical conjunctions, where certain events always occur together, and in the absence of one the other does not, as a matter of fact, occur; that is where the necessity and sufficiency criterion is satisfied in the highest degree. But we would still be most reluctant, and rightly, to say that a causal relation holds. If this is the case, even though we may say that the conjunctions we observe are the visible appearances of quite different trains of happening, 'X causes Y' cannot mean 'X and Y are invariably conjoined.'

We also routinely distinguish those conditions that are background from those which are causally efficacious. But if we adopt the necessary and sufficient conditions view of causality it is not easy to see our title to make these moves. Adopting the production/generation view it is plain why these necessary conditions are not part of the cause of the explosion. That they hold ensures that the appropriate generative mechanism to produce an explosion on ignition is present. By distinguishing between those conditions necessary for there to be the appropriate generators present and the event or state which activates this mechanism to produce or generate the effect we can distinguish the cause more or less uniquely. By searching out the necessary and sufficient conditions for an event we will get too much, either because we can be driven to include the whole state of the universe just prior to the appropriate moment or everything that is regularly contemporaneous. If anything in either set of conditions had been different it is at least on the cards that the event would not have occurred just as it did.

Causal agents. A certain degree of plausibility can be given to the constant conjunction analysis of the causal relation by concentrating on a special case of causality which is found in all the sciences. There are event sequences which we would be prepared to call 'causal' but which are not connected by an underlying link which we suppose to produce or generate the effect.

In every science there are certain interactions between the items in its ontology that are basic in the sense of being interactions in terms of which all other interactions are, in principle, explicable. Newtonian mechanics, for instance, contains two such interactions, impact and gravity. These relations are specified very exactly by the laws of impact and by the law of gravitation. The causes of all motions are impact and gravity. We say that one body, colliding with another, causes the second body to move; that the sun and the moon cause the tides. But we cannot supply an account of the links between bodies which explains what happens on impact, or why the sun and earth exert a mutual attraction; we can only describe impacts and gravitational systems. However, the 'cannot' in 'cannot supply an account of' finds its way into the discussion, not because of some feature of the causal relation in general, but in virtue of the place these particular causal relations have in the logical structure of Newtonian mechanics. If they are the basic interactions then, *a fortiori*, interactions more basic, into which they can be analysed and thus explained, cannot be found in Newtonian mechanics. This is shown by the fact that by giving a different formulation to mechanics we can supply the link that is absent in Newton's version. In a mechanics based upon the transfer of energy the link between impacting bodies, in virtue of which the first causes the second to move, is provided by the now basic mechanism of the transfer of energy. The laws of impact are then not just descriptive of what happens in collisions, but can be reinterpreted as laws governing the transference of energy; that is they now describe the causal link in virtue of which the first body generates (since energy and not motion is transferred) motion in the second. Newton himself, dissatisfied with two basic interactions, suggested that the cause of gravity be looked for in some contact-like interaction between the ether and material bodies.

One of the criteria for the assertion of the causal relation is satisfied, namely constant conjunction of cause and effect, but this is not to say that even in the basic interactions this is what '... causes ...' means. We use '... cause ...' of the basic interactions not just because, in some other theory either alternative or more basic, the genetic or productive mechanism could be supplied, but because in these processes we find the pure activity of elementary agents. Hume's theory is a confusion between the criteria for asserting that a causal relation obtains and the meaning of that assertion.

Humean reductions of causality have sometimes been defended as follows: the vibration–sound example is only apparently defeated by the supplying of the connection between vibration and heard sound. All that has been done is to shift the causal problem back a step from the relation between the vibration and the sound to the relations between the components of the intervening mechanism; and to these Hume's sceptical doubts of discovering connectivity still apply. The answer to this objection can be found by applying the idea sketched in the last paragraph more generally. When we begin to investigate some phenomenon of nature we know by constant conjunction that it is likely that a causal relation is present. To supply this causal relation we describe a mechanism which is such that, on the occurrence of events of the type of the cause, it produces or generates events of the type of the effect. Let us call the cause event 'a', the effect event '*b*' and the mechanism '*M*'. Now the mechanism *M* consists of certain components which interact according to laws, and we find or propose conjunctions of phenomena, say p, q and r, within *M*, which account for the way in which when it is stimulated by *a*-type events it produces or generates *b*-type events. Causal relations between these are grounded by describing other mechanisms, $M'_1, M'_2, \ldots$, which are such that p stimulates M'_2 and so on until r is produced or generated; and a produces or is identical with p, and r produces or is identical with b. To such questions as 'How does p produce or generate 1?' we answer by describing yet more mechanisms $M''_1, M''_2 \ldots$, until we come to a pair of components in a mechanism which are related by the basic interactions of the science we are using. Any scientific inquiry with which the reader is familiar can provide instances of this procedure; e.g. physics supplies the mechanisms for chemical phenomena, chemistry for many physiological phenomena, etc., etc. Far from discovered constant conjunctions being the discovery of a causal relation, they are taken as the signs of a causal relation, which is supplied by describing the mechanisms which account for the constant conjunction. Compare 'Why did he faint?'; Ans_1 'The room was overheated, and overheated rooms make people faint' with 'Why did the overheating make him faint?'; Ans_2 'Lack of carbon dioxide in his blood automatically restricted the blood supply to his head'; Ans_3 'The molecules composing the walls of capillary blood vessels shorten in the absence of carbon dioxide,' and so on through Ans_4, Ans_5, etc. until the resources of physiology, chemistry and physics are exhausted. To give Ans_1 is to supply the framework for a causal account which answers 2, 3, 4 . . . progressively fill in. At the base level are beings whose natures are their causal powers. The final step will be to try to give a convincing account of causal agency.

I shall develop the concept of agency in two steps. In the first I shall assume the notion of active tendency as an undefined, but intuitively given, root idea and use it to identify two action schemata, one of which represents the exercise of agency. The second step will be to analyse the notion of active tendency as far as possible. I will introduce these concepts in contexts drawn from the physical sciences. This should serve to dispel any idea that physical sciences do not centrally use power and tendency concepts and should make clear there is nothing unscientific about their use.

I shall speak of a particular thing as a patient if, unless it receives an external stimulus, it remains quiescent, unchanging, neither manifesting a new property itself nor producing a change in anything else. The schema for action of a patient is:

Being + Stimulus → Action

Patients are such that some stimuli produce an effect only in the patient itself. Liabilities (passive dispositions), realised by a particular category of stimulus, are tendencies for the patient to acquire some state or attribute. A particular being is an agent if it fulfils the schema:

Being—Restraint→Action

A patient must be stimulated to act; agents need only be released. An agent can act upon itself but also upon other beings.

To complete the account, the concept of 'states of readiness' must be added. In preparing to set off a race the starter creates a state of readiness in the runners with his 'Get set.' The subsequent 'Go' can be thought of as a releaser. A spring must first be wound or compressed before it can be released into action. These distinctions are fully worked out in the physics of energy, with the concepts of 'strain', 'potential energy', 'virtual acceleration' and so on. At some stages of their careers many agents are patients; then, by acquiring tendencies and powers whose realisation requires the removal of a restraint, such as countervailing and inhibiting force, they become agents.

To develop the above schemata one needs to distinguish between those agents whose tendencies to action are self-maintained by virtue of permanent intrinsic properties, and those which derive their tendencies from some surrounding medium or structured ensemble of other beings. In physical sciences the former category is exemplified by acids, which have a tendency to react with bases because they have, among their constituents, and definitive of their intrinsic natures, electrically active hydrogen ions. The latter category is exemplified in the physics of material bodies which acquire their tendency to accelerate by virtue of being located in a gravitational field which is the product of a structured ensemble of other massive bodies.

Inaction may have three different explanations. The being is a patient and has not been stimulated; the being is a potential agent at the patient stage and has not yet acquired a tendency, though it is not blocked; the being is an agent with an appropriate tendency, but it is blocked from acting, from realising that tendency. In a psychology of the will, inaction is a central phenomenon of interest.

In general, the dispositions or tendencies of agents are to produce effects in beings other than themselves which we might call 'powers', while liabilities involve changes or effects in the being that is the patient. I shall speak of the exercise of a tendency as an influence. On the definitions proposed above, a being considered as a patient necessarily cannot act upon another being, that is, exercise an influence upon or over others. Of course, the patient may become an agent later in its career.

A person is a perfect agent relative to some category of action when both the tendency to act and the release of that tendency are in the power of that person. Reactions in the face of danger are often explicated in terms of this schema. We use the idea of someone 'screwing themselves up'

322

to act. Henry V's admonitions to his troops before the attack on the walls of Calais is an example of the practical use of that schema. Being persuaded to see themselves as 'tigers' provides the soldiers with the beliefs necessary to create a readiness to attack.

Agency is less than perfect in two cases. Sometimes a certain tendency may be externally engendered, for example by a gravitational potential inducing a tendency to acceleration in a body which can be detected as weight. It may sometimes be the effect of 'internal' automatised processes emerging as a probabilistic effect, for instance radioactive decay. We also use these schemata in psychology. Sometimes a tendency can be controlled by an actor but the conditions for its blockage or release cannot. For instance a person may be very ready to work but whether this tendency can be realised in action depends on circumstances outside the actor's control.

We make use of the former subschema in assigning responsibility in the criminal courts. Psychological hypotheses are debated as to whether or not some tendency, manifested by the defendant in unacceptable conduct, is a permanent disposition; that is, whether the actor has or has not the power to control that tendency even when the conditions for its release obtain. We often use the latter in assigning moral praise or blame in everyday life. 'He would have liked to help but the opportunity never presented itself,' etc. Finally, a being is to be regarded as completely passive if both its tendencies to act and the conditions for their release or blockage are outside its control. For instance, if immunity to disease is biologically based and infection is an environmental hazard, a being is wholly passive in falling ill. In cultures where disease is drawn into the moral order, such as Christian Science, the pure passivity schema must be denied to the sick.

To complete the analysis two further steps are required. The autonomy of an agent has to be differentiated from the internal determinism of a pseudo-agent whose action only appears to be self-caused because the causal process which produces it is confined within the envelope (usually the physical envelope) of the being concerned.

Can the idea of open regressive hierarchies of dispositions, tendencies and powers save agency from reduction to a complex form of internal determinism? We can approach the problem by noticing that the regress structure for much of the preparation for human action is not made up of a simple disposition but is a more complex ranking of practical syllogisms in a multi-nested means–end structure. That such structures exist in the physical world has been well established empirically by the work of chemists and physicists.

There seem to be good grounds in the physical sciences for the belief that these are natural agents. We have a model for the empirical reality of such beings in the observable powers of many things of our common world. Contrary to Hume and his later followers we do have knowledge of causation that is more than mere regularity.[42]

Notes

(An author's name followed by a number in square brackets refers to the book or article which has that number in the bibliography.)

1. Locke [1], Book IV, Ch. 3, para. 16.
2. Ibid., Book II, Ch. 21, para. 1.
3. H. Ditton, *A discourse concerning the resurrection of Jesus Christ*, Appendix (London, 1712).
4. J. Beattie, *An essay on the nature and immutability of truth in opposition to sophistry and scepticism* (Edinburgh, 1770).
5. Ditton, *Discourse*, p. 474.
6. Bracken [9].
7. G. Bowles, 'The place of Newtonian explanation in popular thought', unpublished DPhil thesis, University of Oxford, 1977.
8. H. Lee, *Antiscepticism* (London, 1702).
9. Ibid., pp. 247–8.
10. Ibid., p. 251.
11. S. Clarke, *A demonstration of the being and attributes of God* (London, 1716), p. 83.
12. H. Whiston, *Astronomical principles of religion, natural and revealed* (London, 1717), p. 45.
13. Ibid., p. 89.
14. W. Jones, *An essay on the first principles of natural philosophy* (Oxford, 1762), pp. 26–7.
15. Ibid., pp. 30–1.
16. R. Greene, *The principles of the philosophy of the expansive and contractive forces* (Cambridge, 1727).
17. Ibid., p. 30.
18. Ibid., p. 286.
19. J.T. Rutt (ed.), *Life and correspondence of J. Priestley* (London, 1831).
20. A. Geikie, *Memoir of John Michell* (Cambridge, 1918). (Andrew Baxter's *An enquiry into the nature of the human soul* was first published in London, *c.* 1733.)
21. R. Hall, *Fifty years of Hume scholarship* (Edinburgh University Press, Edinburgh, 1978).
22. T.E. Jessop, 'The misunderstood Hume' in W.B. Todd (ed.), *Hume and the Enlightenment* (Edinburgh University Press, Edinburgh, 1974).
23. D.G.C. MacNabb, *Introduction to a treatise of human nature, I* (Clarendon Press, Oxford, 1962).
24. Hume [10], Book I, Part III, Section 14.
25. J. Priestley, *Disquisitions relating to matter and spirit* (London, 1777), p. 4.
26. Ibid., p. 5.
27. Ibid., p. 9.
28. Beattie, *Essay on the nature and immutability of truth*, p. 141.
29. T. Reid, *Essays on the intellectual powers of man* (Edinburgh, 1785).
30. Mill [17], Book III, Ch. 5, Section 1.
31. Ibid., Book III, Ch. 5, Section 2.
32. J.J. Gibson, *The senses considered as perceptual systems* (Allen and Unwin, London, 1968).
33. Michotte [23], p. 19.

34. S. Lamprecht, *The metaphysics of naturalism* (Appleton-Century-Crofts, New York, 1967), pp. 136–7.

35. Michotte [23], p. 19.

36. Ibid., p. 20.

37. Ibid., p. 256.

38. Lamprecht, *The metaphysics of naturalism*, p. 73.

39. William James, *Some problems of philosophy* (Longmans Green, New York, 1916), p. 123.

40. Hume [11], Section VII, Part 2, para. 59.

41. Ibid.

42. The material of this article draws on three earlier publications: R. Harré, 'Knowledge' in Rousseau and Porter [16], Ch. 1; R. Harré, 'Concepts and criteria', *Mind*, vol. 73 (1964), pp. 353–63, and Harré and Madden [27].

Bibliography

For further reading on the topics raised in this chapter, clearly we must start with some of the classsic works of the British empiricist school of thought, written in the late seventeenth and early eighteenth centuries. To begin with

[1] J. Locke, *Essay concerning human understanding* (first published 1690, many editions, including Everyman's Library, 2 vols, Dent, London, 1961, and Oxford University Press, Oxford, 1975, with several reprints). See especially Book II, Chs. 21 and 26. The most useful critical commentary, for the student, is probably still

[2] R.I. Aaron, *John Locke* (Oxford University Press, Oxford, 1937, 2nd edn, 1955). See also

[3] J. Gibson, *Locke's theory of knowledge* (Cambridge University Press, Cambridge, 1951),

[4] D.J. O'Connor, *John Locke* (Penguin Books, Harmondsworth, 1952) and

[5] J. W. Yolton, *Locke and the compass of human understanding* (Cambridge University Press, Cambridge, 1970).

[6] G. Berkeley, *Principles of human knowledge* (first published 1710, many editions, including *A new theory of vision*, etc., Everyman's Library, Dent, London, 1910, with various reprints, and vol. II of *The works of George Berkeley*, ed. A.A. Luce and T.E. Jessop, Nelson, London, 1949). See, for example, Part I, Section 25ff and Section 54ff.

[7] G.D. Hicks, *Berkeley* (Benn, London, 1932).

[8] G.J. Warnock, *Berkeley* (Penguin Books, Harmondsworth, 1953).

[9] H.M. Bracken, *The early reception of Berkeley's immaterialism, 1710–33* (Nijhoff, The Hague, 1959).

[10] D. Hume, *A treatise on human nature* (first published 1739–40, many editions, including that of L.A. Selby-Bigge, Oxford University Press, Oxford, 1888, with various reprints, and Penguin Books, Harmondsworth, 1985). Especially Book I, Part III; and, also by Hume,

[11] *An enquiry concerning human understanding* (first published 1748, various editions, including that of L.A. Selby-Bigge, Oxford University Press, Oxford, 1893, with various reprints). Especially Section 7. There has been much commentary on Hume's conception of causality. See, for example,

[12] D.G.C. MacNabb, *David Hume* (Basil Blackwell, Oxford, 1951, 2nd edn, 1966), especially Part I, Ch. 4.

[13] B. Stroud, *Hume* (Routledge and Kegan Paul, London, 1977), especially Chs. 3 and 4, and

[14] R.J. Fogelin, *Hume's skepticism in the Treatise of human nature* (Routledge and Kegan Paul, London, 1985), especially Ch. 4.

The works mentioned in this chapter, by various eighteenth-century writers who reacted critically to Locke, Berkeley and Hume, writers like Beattie, Clarke, etc. are unfortunately, for the most part, now difficult to find, even in university libraries. But some further account of them may be sought in various histories of ideas. One that is commendably lucid is

[15] F.C. Copleston, *A history of philosophy, Vol. V: Hobbes to Hume* (Burns, Oates and Washbourne, London, 1959). And, even more directly relevant to the content of this chapter, there is

[16] G.S. Rousseau and R. Porter (eds), *The ferment of knowledge* (Cambridge University Press, Cambridge, 1980).

Moving forward a century from Hume, we come to another important contribution to the discussion of causality and causal laws in the work of J.S. Mill,

[17] *A system of logic* (first published 1843, various editions, for example vols. VII and VIII of *Collected works of John Stuart Mill* (University of Toronto Press, Toronto, and Routledge and Kegan Paul, London, 1973)), Book III, Ch. 5. For commentary, see

[18] K. Britton, *John Stuart Mill* (Penguin Books, Harmondsworth, 1953, and Dover Publications, New York, 1969), or

[19] R.P. Anschutz, *The philosophy of J.S. Mill* (Oxford University Press, Oxford, 1953).

From many twentieth-century studies which take up, and develop, the issues raised in these classic texts, we may pick out

[20] B. Russell, 'On the notion of a cause', *Proceedings of the Aristotelian Society*, vol. 13 (1912–13), reprinted in *Mysticism and logic* (Longmans Green, New York, 1918) and, also by Russell,

[21] *Our knowledge of the external world* (Allen and Unwin, London, 1914), Ch. 8.

Also, an intriguing and lucidly written, if somewhat individual, approach to the subject can be found in

[22] R.G. Collingwood, *An essay on metaphysics* (Oxford University Press, Oxford, 1940, various reprints), Part III, C.

On the interesting question of whether we can directly perceive causal, as well as merely spatiotemporal relations, we should notice

[23] A. Michotte, *The perception of causality* (first published 1946, English translation by T.R. and E. Miles, Methuen, London, 1963) and, on a similar topic,

[24] A.N. Whitehead, *Symbolism: its meaning and effect* (Cambridge University Press, Cambridge, 1927, various reprints), Ch. 2.

It is also worth while to look at

[25] E.H. Madden (ed.), *The structure of scientific thought* (Riverside Press, Cambridge, Massachusetts, 1969), Section 4; and two important studies fairly recently published,

[26] J.L. Mackie, *The cement of the universe* (Oxford University Press, Oxford, 1974) and

[27] R. Harré and E.H. Madden, *Causal powers: a theory of natural necessity* (Basil Blackwell, Oxford, 1975).

T.E.B.

15 | Philosophy and the Existence of God

J.C.A. Gaskin

The historical connections

Thought about the nature and existence of divine beings is part of the Greek origins of philosophy. From its beginnings such philosophical thought is clearly distinguishable from religious revelations of the Judaic sort, from acts of worship and from declarations of belief. Thus in the late sixth century BC Xenophanes, one of the earliest poet-philosophers, remarks (critically) that if animals could draw with hands or create works of art 'horses would draw pictures of gods like horses, and oxen of gods like oxen'. Less than a century later the sophist Critias (*c.* 480–*c.* 400 BC) is suggesting that belief in gods is a socially useful fiction invented by clever men to set a watch over what is done in private: a watch that will be more effective than any possible guardianship by the state. A little later (*c.* 385 BC) the Greek general Xenophon represents Socrates (*Memorabilia*, I, iv, 4–8) as producing a nearly perfect version of what 22 centuries later came to be known as the – lately fashionable – teleological argument for the existence of a god; and in the following 60 years first Plato (*c.* 428–348 BC) and then Aristotle (384–322 BC) produced important and highly influential arguments about the nature and existence of the god(s).

    In later antiquity the concern of philosophy with critical thought about the god(s) continued unabated. Thus, for examples, a celebrated discussion about the nature of the gods (between an Epicurean, a Stoic and an Academic or Sceptic) is to be found in the dialogue *De natura deorum* by Cicero (106–43 BC), and an even more celebrated account of the atomist or Epicurean philosophy survives in Lucretius' great didactic poem *De rerum natura* (*c.* 54 BC): the only complete and thoroughgoing philosophical exposition of atheism (despite its nominal retention of gods) which has come down to us from ancient literature. A century later we find Seneca (4 BC–65 AD), among other Stoics, confidently reiterating the conventional *arguments* that there is a god, and then moving on to a spirited and eloquent defence of the view that the god still loves those whom he 'hardens, reviews and disciplines' despite their suffering (see the essay 'De providentia').

In the second century AD the arguments for and against the existence of god(s) still appear on a more or less equal footing in the anthology of scepticism by Sextus Empiricus (see in particular Book I of the work known as *Against the physicists*). But with the emergence of Christian monotheism as a serious intellectual force in the second century, and its final triumph over classical paganism and non-Christian philosophies in the late fifth and early sixth centuries, many of the possibilities of a *free* inquiry concerning the nature and existence of god(s) disappeared. The Christian (and by the seventh century the Muslim as well) was no longer living in a world of multiple religious and philosophical possibilities, but in a world of his own making in which the complete mundane revelation of the one true God had already been received: a revelation which *excluded* the truth of contrary revelations or incompatible philosophies, and which made atheism intolerably *impious* as well as matter of fact false.

As soon as Christianity achieved temporal power under the Emperor Constantine it turned upon other religions and unsympathetic philosophies, and even upon variations of its own doctrines, with an ideological ferocity unparalleled in any previous epoch of the Western world. Literature critical of the new religion was physically destroyed (e.g. copies of the powerful work *Against the Christians* by Porphyry were burnt in 448) and the non-Christian schools of ancient philosophy were closed in 529. Henceforth the aid that religion sought from philosophy was restricted to (a) the articulation, ordering and understanding of what was already believed; and (b) the assimilation into the Christian (and later the Islamic) tradition of such arguments from Greek philosophical monotheism as were of use to the new religions. In time, (a) resulted in many of the Scholastic sophistications of Christian theology, while (b) resulted in the incorporation within that theology of *reasons* for believing in the existence of God.

The reasons for belief in God are beginning to appear in Christianity as early as St Paul (Romans I, 20). By the time St Augustine (354–430) wrote *De libero arbitrio*, an adaptation of one of them – drawn from Plato's views about the existence of an ideal world – occupied an important place (III, 14–39) in what he had to say. As a result of the argument he concludes: 'God exists and is the truest and fullest being. This I suppose we hold with undoubting faith. Now we attain it with a certain, if tenuous, form of knowledge.' Nine hundred years later a similar conclusion was given its definitive form by St Thomas Aquinas (*c.* 1225–74) in his canonical work *Summa theologiae*. In Part I, Question II, he concludes: 'The truths about God which St. Paul says we can know by our own natural powers of reasoning – that God exists, for example – are not numbered among the articles of faith, but are presupposed to them.' He then sets out the seminal 'five ways in which it is possible to prove [note *proof* is Aquinas' intention] that there is a God'.

Reasoning of the sort exemplified by the Five Ways became part of the received teaching of the Roman Church, but the under-pinning of faith in God with reasons for accepting that there is a God is not the monopoly of medieval Catholicism. At least one of the arguments (the Kalām cosmological argument) was for several centuries accepted by Muslim theologians; others figure prominently in the writings of the Jewish philosopher Maimonides (1135–1204), who provides the source for Aquinas' First and Third Ways, and later many of the arguments appear as a part of traditional Anglicanism. They also spill over into other Christian denominations and reappear in recent centuries in semi-popular thought and secular philosophy in much the same form as they originally appeared in Graeco-Roman literature. The most thorough philosophical critique of the arguments is in David Hume's *Dialogues concerning natural religion* published in 1779, although sceptical criticism was beginning to emerge almost two centuries earlier. In recent years they have again been sub-jected to much critical attention as well as to at least one substantial attempt at rehabilitation.[1]

The historical connections between philosophy and the existence of god(s) have thus gone through three phases: a period of relatively open speculation ending between 350 and 450 AD; a long period during which discussion is confined by the requirements of the all-pervasive religious dogmas of Christian and Islamic theism; and a period of critical scepticism mainly directed at, and an intellectual reaction against, Christian theism. This last period began in the seventeenth cen-tury and has not yet ended.

Theism is belief in the one and only eternal God who created and sustains all things, who remains active within the creation and has an awareness of, and care for, mankind as a special part of that creation. It is contrasted with *deism* which is belief in a god (usually regarded as a single god) not otherwise known by revelation (i.e. by means of informa-tion revealed by god's messenger or intermediary on earth) who set the materials of the universe in orderly motion, or caused the universe as a whole to exist and be as it is, and thereafter either left everything alone or at least 'takes no care of man'.

Because the importance of the deistic/theistic distinc-tion is so considerable, when I refer to God in the theistic sense I shall use a capital 'G' or speak of 'the theistic God'. When God is given any of the specific characteristics which associate the deity with a particular theistic religion, I shall use a qualifying phrase such as 'the Christian God'. When a god (or gods) is referred to in the deistic sense, or indeterminately, I shall refer to 'god' without the capital letter.

The arguments

One of the earliest surviving catalogues of arguments for the existence of a god or gods is given by Sextus Empiricus thus:

> Those, then, who maintain that gods exist attempt to establish their thesis by four modes, arguing, firstly, from the universal agreement of mankind; secondly from the orderly arrangement of the universe; thirdly from the absurd consequences of the denial of the existence of deity; fourthly and lastly, by undermining the opposing arguments. (*Against the physicists*, I, 60)

In a more famous division (erroneously supposed to originate with Kant in the eighteenth century but in substance two thousand years older) Aristotle remarks that 'the conception of gods arose among mankind from two originating causes, namely from celestial phenomena and from events which concern the soul'.[2] In what follows I examine six arguments. They are selected on account of their persistence, influence or interest. The third and fourth arguments are the arguments from celestial phenomena and orderly arrangement; while the fifth and sixth concern the soul.

From general consent

The observation which gave rise to this argument in the Graeco-Roman world must have been that wherever men were discovered, however civilised or remote and barbarous they might be, they had gods. Thus Sextus remarks:

> Arguing from the universal conception, they say that practically all men, both Greeks and barbarians, believe in the existence of the Divine, and because of this they agree in sacrificing and praying and in setting up shrines for the Gods; and some do it in one way, some in another, as though all of them in common believed in the existence of some Divinity, but did not possess the same preconception regarding its nature. But if this preconception [of some Divinity] had been false, they would not all have argued in this way; therefore gods exist. (*Against the physicists*, I, 61)

It is notable that Cicero in reporting the argument in *De natura deorum* makes the Epicurean and the Stoic agree concerning it, though they disagree about almost everything else. Thus the Epicurean argues

> For belief in the gods ... rests on the unanimous and abiding consent of mankind; their existence is therefore a necessary understanding, since we possess an instinctive or rather an innate concept of them. But a belief which all men share by nature must necessarily be true; therefore it must be admitted that the gods exist.[3]

The badly named argument from general consent does not take the simplistic (and obviously invalid) form of arguing that what almost everyone agrees about must be true. Instead it asserts that the fact of almost universal consent to the existence of *some* sort of divinity means that we have an 'innate concept' or 'preconception' of the divine; and that the presence of this concept can *only* be accounted for by (a) the real existence of something divine that we almost all experience which corresponds to and hence helps us form the concept of itself, or (b) the real activity of something which causally implants a concept of itself so that the concept is there innately. (The former would mean that most people *have experience of* the divine; the latter that an awareness of the divine is part of us like a sexual instinct. The former leads to the argument from direct experience, see 'From direct experience of the divine', pp. 342–3, below. The latter is the argument from general consent.)

The first and obvious criticism is that worship of gods is not absolutely universal, and such universality as there might appear to be covers excessive diversity. David Hume, in *The natural history of religion*, a work on the origins of religious belief first published in 1757, makes the point judiciously in his Introduction:

> The belief of invisible, intelligent power has ... perhaps been [neither] so universal as to admit of no exception, nor has it been, in any degree, uniform in the ideas, which it has suggested ... It would appear, therefore, that this preconception springs not from an original instinct or primary impression of nature.

And the successful and prevalent atheistical philosophies of the present day – scientific and political – seem to indicate that Cicero's Stoic was wrong (in the long run) in supposing that the concept of deity would become more deeply rooted with *every* succeeding generation. In short, the alleged fact upon which the argument is based is suspect.

But secondly, even if we grant that belief in deity is indeed widely dispersed among mankind, this does not *have* to be accounted for in terms of either (a) or (b) above. A number of accounts of religion are now available which seek to explain its origins, persistence and prevalence in terms of social, tribal, psychological or other natural causes; and because these causes are thought to be very general in operation, the very general occurrence of their effect, religion, is thereby explained. Thus, for example, Hume identifies the cause of religious belief with fear of the unknown and apparently capricious natural influences upon which so much of human life depends and Marx, Feuerbach, Freud and many others all suggest causes for the phenomenon of religion. It is not necessary to hold that any of these 'natural histories' is precisely correct. The point is that they exist, and provide explanations for the prevalence of religion.

So the question remains: causes of belief apart, are there also arguments for supposing that a god or God exists apart from the psychological or natural influences operating to produce the belief?

From what God is: the ontological argument

If we follow Sextus' catalogue quoted above, this argument (originated by Anselm of Canterbury, 1033–1109) would come under his heading of argument 'from the absurd consequences of the denial of the existence of deity'; for in effect it tries to make the denial of God's existence into a contradiction and so into an absurdity.

The main thesis of the ontological argument (from *ontos*, a form of the Greek word for 'being') is a reversal of Sextus' common-sense claim that 'it is possible for a thing to be conceived and not exist'.[4] Anselm's rejoinder is in effect: this is true in general, but not in the unique case of God, the conception of whom *includes* existence. Anselm's argument is difficult to shorten from its expression in Chapters 2 and 3 of his brief work the *Proslogion*, but in his own words the main steps are as follows:

> Our belief is that God is a being than which no greater can be conceived ... Now certainly that than which no greater can be conceived cannot *merely* be in the understanding, because if it were *only* in the understanding, then it could further be conceived to exist in reality as well; but then it would be a greater thing. *Therefore* something undoubtedly exists than which no greater can be conceived, and it exists both in the understanding and in reality.

Anselm makes it abundantly clear that what he is saying is intended as an elucidation of what is already believed: in his own famous aphorism 'I do not seek to understand so that I may believe; but I believe so that I may understand.' Nevertheless his argument has always attracted the critical attention of philosophers and theologians as if it contained an *a priori* proof of God's existence.

Among those who have, with various adjustments, accepted the argument, Descartes (1591–1650) and Leibniz (1646–1716) are notable in the seventeenth century: Norman Malcolm, Charles Hartshorne and Alvin Plantinga in the second half of the twentieth century.[5] Its critics conspicuously include Aquinas, Hume, Kant, Bertrand Russell and most twentieth-century analytic philosophers.[6]

Descartes' argument in *Meditations* V is sometimes crudely paraphrased 'God is all perfections. Existence is a perfection. There-fore God exists.' But in his own words the resemblance to Anselm's argument is more apparent, for they both share the fundamental insight that in the case of God alone, his essence (the characteristics a thing has to have to be the thing it is) includes his existence: 'from the fact that I cannot conceive God without existence, it follows that existence is inseparable from him, and hence that he really exists; not that my thought can bring this to pass ... but that the necessity of the existence of God determines me to think in this way'.

Leibniz is in broad agreement with Descartes, but adds that an additional premiss is needed, namely that the idea of a supremely perfect being is *possible*. He argues that this premiss is allowable, and hence that such an idea will include the perfection of existence: 'And so it follows that this supremely perfect being exists.'[7]

The impatience which many people feel with this argument derives from the common-sense preconception that you cannot guarantee the real existence of something by the way in which you define it: verbal definitions don't create reality.[8] Outline philosophical objections are:

(1) Both Hume and Kant argue (in slightly different ways) that existence is *not* another characteristic of something along with, say, its colour, weight, location, intelligence, liveliness or moral qualities. To describe (or define) something, however strange the thing, is categorically different from saying the thing exists. To say the thing exists is to say that the descriptions *fit* something in reality, or are *exemplified* by something in reality; it is not to add to or alter the description in some way. In other words, existence is not a property that could possibly be part of the character of anything, even of God.

(2) The ontological argument implies, but disregards, a distinction between *necessary existence* and *real* (or *matter of fact*) *existence*. It attributes to God some species of necessary existence and then improperly takes this to imply God's real existence. But, it is argued, *either* 'necessary' is an altogether illegitimate notion to couple with 'existence' (since 'necessary' only describes *propositions* of the sort '$2+2=4$' or 'not both p and not p'), *or* 'necessary existence' means something like 'always has existed and always must exist'. The ontological argument, so the criticism continues, attributes the special characteristic 'necessary existence' to God, and then uses this to assert that there really exists some entity which has the special characteristic. What it should conclude is that *if* God really exists *then* he has the special characteristic of necessary existence. But this is an explication of what believers believe, not a proof that what they believe is real.

(3) Anselm's first critic, Gaunilo, pointed out that an argument of exactly the same form could prove the real existence of the most perfect anything-you-could-conceive. Thus: think of the most perfect island. Now if the island you are thinking of exists only in your understanding, then it is not the most perfect island because the island you are thinking of would be more perfect if it existed in reality as well as in your understanding. Therefore the most perfect island exists in reality *and* in your understanding, and so on for the most perfect wife, car, cake, garden, etc. Anselm's cogent reply is that God is a special case which makes him the only entity to which the argument properly applies.

The ontological argument has provoked an immense amount of thought about the logic of existence, and the difference between real existence and whatever is to be meant by 'necessary existence'. Even as a contribution to theology it contains an important insight. If I already believe in God, then I could not believe anything to be greater, and I would also believe that my God always has and always must exist. If he really exists, then he necessarily exists. But does he really exist? That is the unresolved substantial question.

From what exists: cosmological arguments

There is some dispute about what precisely constitutes the (or a) cosmological argument. The reason for this is that a *family* of arguments exists in connection with certain cosmic questions, and almost any member of the family could be identified as *the* cosmological argument (from *kosmos,* meaning 'ordered universe'). The cosmic questions are: (1) What is the originating cause of motion and/or change in the universe? (2) Is the universe eternal or must it have had a beginning? (3) Why or how is it that there is anything at all?

It is clear that rational speculation about these questions need not be and has not been confined to answers which presume or seek to establish the existence of a god. For example, what Aristotle said about (1) had, at source, very little direct bearing on any belief in the existence of god, and what modern cosmology has to say about (2) is non-committal about such a belief. Nevertheless the cosmic questions have attracted a variety of arguments which seem to point to an entity satisfying *some* of the characteristics we attribute to God: in particular that of being 'creator of heaven and earth'. The arguments are different inasmuch as a refutation of one of them may leave the others untouched. They are similar in that all are in some way focused upon the origin of the cosmos. They are clustered inasmuch as they are attached to one or other of the three questions.

Source of change arguments. In the *Laws*, Plato's warning 'I fear that the argument may seem singular' and his references to 'my unfamiliar argument' suggest that he thought it had no forebears, and indeed what he produced was the first cosmological argument as far as we can now discern.[9] His argument concerns the origin of motion (or 'change' since the concepts are commonly interchangeable in Greek philosophy). It is as follows:

> How can a thing which is moved by another ever be the beginning of change? . . .
> But when the self-moved changes other, and that again other, and thus thousands upons tens of thousands of bodies are set in motion, must not the beginning of all this motion be the change of the self-moving principle? . . . Then we must say that self-motion being the origin of all motions . . . it is the eldest and mightiest principle of change.

It is here that many later versions of the argument end. Thus Aquinas' First Way simply concludes that an unmoved mover (*not* Plato's self-moved mover) is what all men call God. But Plato goes further. He gives a *reason* for identifying the self-moving mover (or movers) as a god (or gods). The reason is that self-movement, the autonomous initiation of movement, is uniquely characteristic of things that live, i.e. that have a soul (psyche):

> If we were to see this power existing in any earthy, watery, or fiery substance, simple or compound, ... we should call such a self-moving power life ... [by definition] 'soul' means 'the motion which can move itself'. Hence ... soul is the first origin and moving power of all that is, or has become, or will be ... [and thus] all things are full of gods. (*Laws*, X, 895–9, Jowett's translation)

By contrast with Plato's, Aristotle's argument (*Physics*, VIII, 106; *Metaphysics*, XII) is of enormous complexity, and a paraphrase gives no more than a poor indication of his conclusions shorn of the reasoning that supports them. He differs from Plato in arguing (a) that motion is eternal (there is no beginning of movement), (b) that living things do not really initiate movement but are moved by their environment and by their internal parts, (c) that self-moved movers themselves owe their movement to some 'ultimate and universal source that does not move at all': 'We have shown that motion must be eternal and can never cease; so there must be some prime mover, whether singular or plural, that is eternal and not itself movable.' For economy of explanation Aristotle concludes (in the *Physics*) that there is only one unmoved mover: a mover which is both infinite, since 'a finite mover cannot cause a motion during unlimited time', and without dimension, since all dimensioned things are of finite magnitude and cannot produce the infinite magnitudes which motion and change display.

An example of a medieval version of the Aristotelian argument is to be found in Aquinas' Second Way: there must be a prime cause ('God') since if there were not, there would be no intermediate causes, and hence no effects now.

Note: (a) it is Aristotle's argument to an unmoved mover, not Plato's argument to a self-moved mover, that is generally followed. The reason for this is the Christian demand that God should be immutable, i.e. should not be subject to change in any way. (b) Source of change arguments may be formulated by reference to a regress of movements, or changes, or causes, without a fundamental alteration to the structure of the arguments. (c) Some source of change arguments refer to a first *temporal* entity which is unmoved, uncaused or unchanged. However, the majority of sophisticated medieval arguments refer to a *metaphysically* prime entity which is the unmoved mover (etc.) of the whole series of events, whether the series had a beginning or not.

If the argument is to a first (temporal) entity in the series of movements, causes or changes, then the standard objection is that nothing compels one to concede that there must be a first unmoved mover (etc.). It is possible that for *every* link in the chain of physical movements (etc.) there is a preceding link which accounts for the link under investigation. Under this possibility there will *always* be a change to explain a change, a motion to produce a motion, and so on *provided* that the notion of an infinite regress of events makes sense. If it is supposed not to make sense, then the question must be asked: what is it about the supposed beginning, the unmoved mover, which makes it nonsense to ask about *its* cause of movement?

But Aristotle occasionally hints at what is often made explicit in his medieval and more recent successors: that the unmoved mover (etc.) exists not as a finite, dimensioned, or located *part* of the universe (or as a first temporal cause among other temporal causes) but as another order of being which sustains the universe as a whole somewhat as I might sustain a game of tennis while actually playing it. But, it is often objected, this metaphysical cause of all that exists is not in any sense accessible by means of an argument which starts with actual movements or causal sequences in the physical world. Explanation of such movements (etc.) always consists in relating them to something else which happened *in* the physical world, and the final outcome of such explanations is always some general cause or origin (near or remote, depending on our state of knowledge) *in* the universe, at which point we can say, 'That's the way the world is.' The nub of this objection is that Aristotelian-type *argument* can never take us beyond the universe with its internal workings (however remote and general we find them to be). It requires a special and now largely abandoned Aristotelian/ Scholastic metaphysic of reality, not cautious reasoning from the way things are, to reach that which is not a physical part of the universe itself.

This objection is so fundamental that it is often distinguished with the name given to it by Bayle and Hume – 'Stratonician (or Stratonian) Atheism'. The term derives from Strato of Lampsacus, a successor of Aristotle's, who died about 269 BC. He argued that intelligent purposes are not apparent in nature, and that the most fundamental natural features discoverable in the world are the *ultimate* explanations: explanation is within the world, not from outside the world.

Kalām or temporal regress argument. Literally *kalām* means 'speech' – in the present usage the speech of Islamic theologians and philosophers who developed a certain species of cosmological argument (originally from the writings of one Philoponus, a sixth-century Christian from Alexandria who was concerned to prove that the universe was created a finite time ago). The history of Islamic philosophy is comparatively little known to modern European philosophy. Its contribution to cosmological argument is put thus by W.L. Craig:

The central issue ... was whether the temporal series of past events could be actually infinite. Proponents of the *kalām* argument contended that it could not and that the universe therefore had an absolute beginning; but since the universe could not have sprung into existence uncaused out of nothing, there must exist a Creator of the universe, or God.[10]

The question then is – what *reason* can be given for holding that the temporal series of past events could not be actually infinite? Arguments are supplied by both Philoponus and al-Kindi (*c*. 800–*c*. 870). The full ramifications of the discussion are of enormous complexity and may be followed in Craig's book, pages 65–140, but Philoponus' main thesis, which forms the core of the *kalām* argument, is that:

> If the universe were eternal, the generation of any object in the sublunar world would be preceded by an infinite series of generations. But an infinite cannot be traversed. Therefore, if the universe were eternal, none of the objects presently existing in the sublunar world could ever have been generated.[11]

The thesis was adopted (with variations) by the Arabian al-Kindi, by the Jewish philosopher Saadia (882–942), and by Bonaventure (*c*. 1217–1274) among others. At the present time philosophically valuable discussion of the argument depends upon comparatively recent mathematical distinctions between actual and potential infinites. It will be noted that even if the outcome of these discussions were to show that the notion of an actual infinity of past events is incoherent, this would not prove the existence of a creating god. It would only show that the universe is not infinitely old (as the current 'Big Bang' theory of cosmology seems to agree). What actually began it would be entirely indeterminate. The beginning could even be, indeed as a beginning might *have* to be, from nothing.

Contingency and sufficient reason arguments. Irrespective of whether the universe is eternal as Aristotle argued, or began a finite time ago as the *kalām* argument would have it, the universe of bits and pieces in space *exists*. From this fact two lines of reasoning lead back. One starts from the existence of the contingent things that compose the universe and argues to a necessarily existent being that causes the contingent things to exist. The other employs the principle that nothing takes place without a sufficient reason and from this reaches an entity which contains within itself the sufficient reason for its own existence. The former argument is the argument from contingency. It can be exhumed from some of the Arabic writings of Ibn Sina (i.e. Avicenna, 980–1037). It occurs in a fully developed form as the third proof of God's existence in the *Guide for the perplexed* by the influential Jewish philosopher Maimonides (1134–1204) and is borrowed from him by Aquinas to form the Third Way. From then on it is almost conventional theistic wisdom. The latter argument is Leibniz' cosmological argument.

The general form of the argument from contingency is as follows. The things that compose the universe are contingent existences in the sense that 'we find them springing up and dying away' (Aquinas). They need not exist, and at some time have not existed or will not exist. But not *everything* can be like this; otherwise there would have been a time in the past when there was nothing, and from nothing, nothing would have come. Therefore there must be an entity which necessarily exists which caused the things to exist that need not have existed. And this entity is God.

Although still defended by Thomistic philosophers (followers of Aquinas) there are a lot of difficulties with this argument.

It *is* possible that everything that exists is and has been a contingent existence. Contingent things cause other contingent things, and the overlapping this implies could have gone on forever. A reply is to concede that the 'horizontal' regress of contingent things could be infinite but is, as a whole, held in being by a 'vertical' cause which is some necessarily existent being.[12] Hume's response to thinking of this sort is seminal:

> Did I show you the particular causes of each individual in a collection of twenty particles of matter, I should think it very unreasonable, should you afterwards ask me, what was the cause of the whole twenty. This is sufficiently explained in explaining the cause of the parts.[13]

'Our reasonings', says Leibniz in a famous cosmological argument which has some affinity with the argument from contingency, 'are based on two great principles', one of which is the Principle of Sufficient Reason:

> by virtue of which we consider that no fact can be real or existing and no proposition can be true unless there is a sufficient reason, why it should be thus and not otherwise, even though in most cases these reasons cannot be known to us. ('The monadology')

> This principle having been laid down, the first question we are entitled to ask will be *Why is there something rather than nothing?* ... And although the present motion which is in matter arises from the one before it, and this in turn from the one before that, we are no further on however far we go; for the same question always remains. Thus the sufficient reason, which needs no further reason, must be outside this series of contingent things, and must lie in a substance which is the cause of this series, or which is a being that bears the reason of its existence within itself; otherwise we should still not have a sufficient reason with which we could stop. And this final reason of things is called *God*. ('Principles of nature and grace founded on reason')[14]

Leibniz' argument is impressive. It establishes that in the last resort explanation of the existence of the physical universe cannot come from within it – 'however far we go ... the same question remains'. What it does not establish is that an explanation *must* therefore come from outside. There may be *no* explanation of the sort Leibniz seeks. I say this because it is arguable that the Principle of Sufficient Reason terminates with the last available physical explanation (Stratonian atheism again!). If it does *not* terminate there, but extends to a further explanation beyond the physical, then one may ask, why does the principle not apply to *that* explanation – god or whatever we are to call it? The only possible answer seems to be because the principle holds only within the physical universe. But if it holds only within the physical universe, then it cannot be used to insist upon an explanation *of* the physical universe by an 'outside', or metaphysically different, order of being.[15]

From order and purpose: the design argument

The design argument is so old, and so fundamental a part of human thought, that in its earliest representations it is not clear whether we are dealing with a direct observation or with an inference of some sort. Thus the Psalmist writes, 'When I look at thy heavens, the works of thy fingers, the moon and the stars which thou hast established; what is man that thou art mindful of him?' (Psalm 8); and in Plato there is a persisting uncertainty whether, in looking at the heavens, one is actually looking at gods or at their evident handiwork.

It is about 385 BC, in Xenophon's *Memorabilia* (I, iv, 6–7), that a species of the design argument is first recorded *as an argument*. After observing the useful adaptation of particular organs in living creatures, he reports Socrates as saying 'With such signs of forethought in these arrangements, can you doubt whether they are the work of chance or design?' And again, having remarked the sexual adaptation of living creatures for the purposes of procreation, he concludes: 'Undoubtedly these too look like the contrivances of one who deliberately willed the existence of living creatures.' This is the earliest known version of what was eventually designated the teleological argument (from *telos*, meaning 'end' or 'goal'). It appears in numerous subsequent writings, including Aquinas' Fifth Way, most eighteenth-century attempts to establish that a god exists, almost *ad nauseam* in Paley's popular *Natural theology* (1802), and in some twentieth-century works.[16]

A significantly different argument is reported by Cicero in *De natura deorum*, II, 35. Having observed the regular movements of the world, 'controlled by fixed system and unchanging uniformity', the natural inference must be to 'a ruler and governor, the architect, as it were, of this mighty and monumental structure'. This is the argument that the *fact* of natural order is better explained by reference to an intelligent agent than by reference to an evolution from chaos – the presumed 'natural' condition of the universe. The argument has no widely agreed name. I suggest, on the Greek pattern of the other classical arguments, that it could be called the nomological argument (from *nomos*, meaning 'law' or 'law governed order'). It too appears in numerous ancient, a few medieval and many post-Newtonian writings (see note 16).

Both design arguments are empirical in depending for their data upon the way things are found to be. Both are arguments by analogy. They note (often tacitly) that the order and/or purposes apparent in humanly originated contrivances are derived from the activity of intelligent agents. From this they conclude that the similarity to these contrivances of the order and/or purposes discernible in natural objects justifies the inference to a similarly intelligent origin: at the very least, as Hume puts it in his celebrated critique of the argument (see note 16), 'the cause or causes of order in the universe probably bear some remote analogy to human intelligence'.

The teleological argument, in a version suggested by Aquinas' Fifth Way, is as follows:

> We see that things which lack knowledge, such as natural objects, act for an end ... Now whatever lacks knowledge cannot move towards an end, unless it be directed by some being endowed with knowledge and intelligence ... Therefore some intelligent being exists by whom all natural things are directed to their end; and this being we call God.

Aquinas is writing against a background assumption (absorbed into medieval Scholasticism from an interpretation of Aristotle) that *all* natural objects and processes move to an end. This assumption is difficult for us to understand, let alone accept. We can perhaps recapture the feel of it in the words of Dante's *Divine comedy*, I, 103–14:

> All things whatsoever observe a mutual order, and this is the form that makes the universe to be like God ... In the order of which I speak all things incline ... towards their source; wherefore they move to diverse parts over the great sea of being, and each one with instinct given it to bear it on.

But teleological descriptions now survive only in certain biological sciences (notably zoology). It is, moreover, a debated point whether *any* biological process that 'lacks knowledge' *needs* to be described as 'moving towards an end'. Nevertheless the teleological argument can be restated by means of the more modest assumptions set out by J.S. Mill in *Three essays on religion* (1873):

> Certain qualities, it is alleged, are found to be characteristic of such things as are made by an intelligent mind for a purpose. The order of Nature, or some consider-able parts of it, exhibit these qualities in a remarkable degree. We are entitled, from this great similarity in the effects, to infer similarity in the cause.

The trouble here is that when the 'certain qualities' are focused exclusively

340

upon *purposive contrivances* or *purposes to be served* (in the manner of the teleological argument), the whole enterprise is vulnerable to a possibility first outlined by Hume (*Dialogues*, Part I) and enormously reinforced by Darwin's theory of evolution by natural selection (1859). Namely, what we see as purposes to achieve an end may be merely the conditions which must be satisfied before the 'end' can exist at all. Thus, for example, the ozone layer in the atmosphere could be seen as one of the very delicately contrived designs which are *intended* by an intelligent agent to further life. Equally well, the ozone layer could be seen as an outcome of natural processes which have merely *happened upon* a condition in whose absence life would not have occurred. But what still remains unexplained is the existence of these natural processes themselves, the 'fixed and unchanging uniformities' which Cicero mentions, and which form the basis of the nomological argument.

The nomological argument. If, in Mill's statement of the design argument, 'law governed regularity', or 'unchanging uniformity' is substituted for 'certain qualities', then the nomological argument results. It is at first encounter an impressive argument, and even after thorough critical analysis seems to retain, as Hume and Mill and so many others have found, some persuasive force, though perhaps more as a feeling about how things are than as an argument. It argues that the only explanation of natural order available to us, *other* than the unsatisfactory process of referring the natural order to a larger-scale natural order of the same kind, is to be found in the activity of intelligent agents. We know, as it were from the inside, how the order apparent in, for example, an orrery (a clockwork model of the planetary system) is arrived at. Its order is inexplicable (like the order in nature) unless reference is made to the intelligent agent who designed it. This being so, the ultimate explanation for the regularities it models can likewise only be intelligence. Cicero (*De natura deorum*, II, 35) puts the matter vividly:

> They think more highly of the achievement of Archimedes in making a model of the revolutions of the firmament than of nature in creating them, although the perfection of the original shows a craftsmanship many times as great as does the counterfeit.

In very brief compass the standard (mostly Humeian) difficulties are: (1) Those objects (orreries, watches, etc.) whose order is known to proceed from intelligent design, and natural objects (solar systems, apples, atomic structures, etc.) where it is not so known, are too vastly dissimilar to suggest similar causes. (2) The analogy is further weakened by the fact that intelligence-originated order makes use of and is subject to physical laws while naturally originated order *is* physical laws. Thus the nomological argument depends upon comparing the result of *using* physical laws with the very different act of *creating* physical laws. (3) Order in the natural world is not a separable feature of what exists which needs explanation; it *is* what exists. As Hume puts it, there is 'an eternal, inherent principle of order to the world' (*Dialogues*, Part VI).[17] (4) Order in the natural world is not a surprising or improbable alternative to the chaos which might have existed. There is *no* alternative to the given order by comparison with which the existent order is 'improbable'. Hence no intelligent agent needs to be postulated to explain why the natural world is not a chaos. (5) Even if accepted, the nomological argument would establish too little for theistic purposes. More than one intelligent designer could be involved (as in most human artifacts). The designer(s) might be dead. They may be, indeed from the apparent moral neutrality of things they *are*, disinterested, i.e. they take no care of man: and so on.

From direct experience of the divine

We are not here presented with another argument in the sense in which we have so far been looking at arguments, but at certain constructions which are often put upon elusive, usually completely private, but apparently widely spread human experiences ('events that concern the soul', as Aristotle put it). The experiences are of what is claimed to be, and is undoubtedly felt as, some sort of encounter with the divine. The encounter may be visual, auditory, the overwhelming feeling of the presence of a divine person, or the sense of the merging of one's individual being into some mystic or cosmic other: and there are many more possibilities.[18] Almost all cultures report 'religious experiences' of this sort (to put a conventional label on a rather heterogeneous species). Ancient culture took them as so normal as to be scarcely worth mentioning. Official Roman Christianity has accepted them with some critical reluctance since their content can be both powerfully influential and heretical. The Age of Reason viewed such uncheckable private illumination with acute suspicion. But when first Hume, and then Kant, inflicted so much damage on the claim that conventional religious beliefs are reasonable, there came to be an increasing tendency, particularly among Protestant theologians, to rely upon religious experience as the existential ground for belief in God (or possibly god). The question is – are religious experiences such as should give those that have them (or others) assurance of the real existence of their apparent object?

The question would not be asked in any ordinary context of meeting somebody, or becoming acquainted with something, because the person or thing would normally be accessible to others. But this is not usually so with the religious experience, however important and reliable it is felt to be. In this respect it is more like a dream. So the question is thrust upon us – what do these experiences (given that they occur) *signify*? There are two answers. Either (i) they signify that there is some sort of actual divine entity existing independently of the experiencer to which the experience gives privileged access, or (ii) they signify nothing more than something about the cultural, physical or psychological condition of the person having the experience. Any brief discussion of these rather bald alternatives will cause irritation and disappointment to those to whom such experiences are dear. They must therefore read on elsewhere[19] to follow the subtle and uncertain way that may lie between the alternatives just stated.

Some of the considerations which can be offered in favour of the first alternative are: the wide distribution of such reported experiences; the vitality and power of such experiences and the importance that the experiencer continues to attach to them long afterwards (unlike the drug or sleep experience); the occurrence of such experiences among ordinary people not subject to special privations or peculiar influences; the enduring public consequences of such experiences (think of St Paul on the Damascus road, or Constantine on the road to Rome to claim the Empire); the ability of individuals to communicate with others who have had similar experiences and to identify with them a common object of the experience (sometimes a very precise one: more often an object of awe or fear or love imprecise and hidden).

The second alternative is supported by: the impenetrable privacy of the experience from other persons present at the time – a characteristic more in keeping with a dream than with special access to some independently existing entity; the fact that the experience comes as, and is reported as, what the subject *expects* to encounter (the Roman Catholic encounters the Blessed Virgin, not Asclepius); the way in which the experience is often related to periods in a person's life when privation, prayer, fasting, spiritual conflict or emotional crises are operative conditions and may therefore be causes; the vagueness and diversity of what is encountered. (So that William James has some justice in concluding 'The only thing that it unequivocably testifies to is that we can experience union with *something* larger than ourselves and in that union find our greatest peace.'[20])

It can of course be argued that *if* we already have reasons to believe that a certain religion is true, and *if* that religion includes the possibility that the object of devotion may selectively reveal itself in what is called religious experience, then such experience, when it takes place, is further corroboration of the truth of the religion. But in the absence of such initial reasons, religious experience is probably too fraught with ambiguities, special pleading and alternative explanations to assure any doubter of the real existence of its object.

From the nature of morality and other arguments

It is often suggested in a rather vague way that there is something about morality which requires the existence of a god. Organised as an argument, the suggestion comes in several forms.

Immanuel Kant (1724–1804) argued in the *Critique of practical reason* (1788) Part I, Book II, Chs. 2–5, that 'it is morally necessary to assume the existence of God'. This is because the *summum bonum*, the highest good, must include both moral excellence and happiness. Manifestly the two do not regularly go together in this life. Therefore, since we ought to aim for the highest good, and what we ought to aim for has to be possible, morality presupposes that there is a being (God) whose will is able to bring about the exact harmony of happiness and moral excellence, and that a state (an after life) exists in which this is brought about.

The usual objection to this argument is that what we ought to aim at does not have to be possible (my striving for a perfect garden does not entail the possibility of an actually perfect garden). But a more general criticism is that there are accounts of morality, which are not blatantly absurd, that do not rely upon Kant's presuppositions – utilitarianism, for example, advocates maximising happiness in this life rather than arriving at a *summum bonum* in the next.

A commoner version of the argument from morality holds that moral laws are *commands* from a law giver which override all human laws or instructions, and such commands can only come from something like God. But again it has to be shown that moral laws *are* transcendent commands rather than human conventions. Moreover they have to be the commands of such a being as we suppose God is. Another argument is to say that God gives an indispensable *authority* to moral laws. But such authority does not have to come from a theistic God, nor from any real god. The authority could be just the consent of the majority of mankind that certain rules must be observed (for whatever reason). The irritation of the Emperor Julian with Christian claims to have either special news about what is moral or special authority about the enforcement of morals is worth recalling as one of the last protests of a secular, pre-Christian, view of morality. Having listed the ten commandments he exclaims:

> Now except for the command 'Thou shalt not worship other gods,' and 'Remember the sabbath day,' what nation is there, I ask in the name of the gods what nation is there which does not think that it ought to keep the other commandments? So much so that penalties have been ordained against those who transgress them.[21]

The *argument from conscience* has some affinity with arguments from morality. It was not invented by, but is associated with, Joseph Butler (1692–1752) and, more particularly, Cardinal Newman (1801–90).[22] It is that conscience is an authoritative voice within each of us whose sanction and cause we can recognise to be a powerful, intelligent, external, ever-watchful being: in short, God. The standard objection was expressed by John Locke (1632–1704) almost before the point was argued. In the *Essay concerning human understanding* (1690), I, iii, 7, he points out that no moral rules can be drawn from conscience since contrary rules would result from different individual consciences. More importantly, 'education, company, and customs of the country' will set conscience to work. The same point (since Freud a commonplace) is put succinctly by J.L. Mackie: 'It is overwhelmingly plausible to see [conscience] as an introjection into each individual of demands that come from other people.'[23]

There is an argument from *degrees of perfection* which echoes some of Kant's remarks about the reality of a *summum bonum*. It derives ultimately from Plato and is enshrined in Aquinas' Fourth Way.[24] It holds that the graduation in the degrees of a quality (heat or goodness, for examples) implies that there must exist something which both exemplifies the superlative of the quality and causes lesser degrees of itself in other things. This centre of perfection is God. The argument is now very unconvincing. It is just not true that our placing something in a scale of some quality implies the existence of a top of that scale which is the absolute 'mostest' of the quality in question. Because Jim is more drunk than Jack it does not follow that someone else must be as drunk as it is possible to be.

There are other arguments for the existence of a god of gods. Many are trivial. Few are influential. Three should perhaps be noted. They are:

The argument from miracles. If miracles (defined as a divine agent intervening in the course of nature) occur, then a god must exist. The philosophical discussion of miracles is extensive but the crucial points are that it can be questioned whether a miracle in the defined sense has ever happened; and if it has, how we would ever distinguish it from an indication that our knowledge of the laws of nature was imperfect.[25]

The argument from consciousness. In the *Essay*, IV, x, 10, Locke contends that matter, of and in itself, can never *think*. In *The existence of God*, Ch. 9, Richard Swinburne points out that we cannot give any account of how material structures could think or be conscious. Hume on the other hand observes that for aught we know the little agitation of the brain we call thought could arise spontaneously in matter as one of its configurations. The inference Locke and Swinburne seek to draw is the existence of a special cause of thought over and above material things. The inference suggested by Hume is that consciousness is just a complex formation of matter. The arguments are long and subtle and must be followed elsewhere.[26]

Berkeley's argument. In George Berkeley's (1685–1753) *Principles of human knowledge* (1710) and *Three dialogues between Hylas and Philonous* (1713) there is an argument for the existence of God which is both extraordinary and all-embracing. It holds that since the existence of any *thing* consists in its being perceived, and since things do not have intermittent existence (i.e. existing only when we perceive them) there must be an all-perceiving and ever-perceiving mind (God) in whom we live and move and have our being. Hume remarked of Berkeley's arguments that 'they admit of no answer and produce no conviction' and that is precisely the difficulty here. In order to accept the conclusion you have to be *convinced* by (not merely unable to refute) the metaphysics, and the metaphysics carry less conviction to most people than the conclusion they seek to establish – the existence of God.[27]

Useful evidence for useless conclusions

At the beginning of Book X of the *Laws*, Plato points out that anyone who deliberately does an impious thing must have supposed either (1) that the gods do not exist, or (2) that they take no care of man, or (3) that they are easily appeased and turned aside from their purposes by sacrifices and prayers.

It is the second of these possibilities which has always caused concern and confusion. It *seems* to be a position which is distinct from atheism, and yet it is a position which is alien to almost all forms of religion. Thus the writer of the Epistle to the Hebrews explicitly rejects it: 'He that cometh to God must believe that he exists and he is a rewarder of them that diligently seek him' (XI, 6) and the Epicureans were regularly accused of atheism on precisely the grounds that the inactive spirits they called gods *took no care of man*. (Contrast the Stoic view 'that the world is governed by them and that they care for the fortunes of mankind', *De natura deorum*, II, 3).

In modern terminology the distinction Plato makes between the three species of impiety can be expressed thus: (1) is *atheism*; (2) is *deism* (to be contrasted with its religiously acceptable alternative *theism*); (3) is either a type of *superstition* (if you take Plato's view that wheedling the gods is offensive and absurd) or a type of *devotion* (if you take the common Christian view that God is susceptible to prayer, sacrifice, etc. in the personal approach).

The identification of (2) as a position which is unacceptable (whether to Greek polytheism or Christian monotheism) is important for any assessment of the value to religion of the arguments for the existence of a god. It is almost always assumed that the conclusion of the arguments can be identified with the God or gods worshipped (thus Aquinas concludes each of the Five Ways with a variant of the refrain 'and this all men call God'). But this assumption is over-hasty. There is a strong case for saying that the cosmological arguments and the design argument, even if sound, merely establish that there is something other than the universe itself from which the universe originates – at best a deistic conclusion where the 'god' takes no care of man.

The gap between what the most interesting of the arguments might establish and what theistic religions need to establish is evident within theistic religion itself. Thus the creator god (of Genesis, Psalms, 2 Maccabees VII, 28, etc.) could all too easily be identified with a deistic god. The personal god who hears prayers and instructs his messengers could all too easily be identified with an invisible but powerful spirit of the earth on the rejected Greek pagan model. But for theistic religion to hold good the creator god and the personal god *have to be identical*, and it is this identity which all but eludes the evidence of the arguments or the ingenuity of theologians.

Arguments against the existence of God

Unthinking agnosticism is common wisdom; reasoned atheism is vaguely bad taste. Yet it is atheism, not agnosticism, which is supported by two powerful arguments which have to be set against whatever force the arguments for the existence of god(s) might have.

(1) In its moderate form the first is what so disturbed Plato: the deistic conclusion that there are god(s) but they have no care of man. In its more acute form it appears in Judaeo-Christian history as the *problem of evil*. Thus the writer of the book of Ecclesiastes is wearied by the unjust fact 'that the race is not to the swift, nor the battle to the strong, nor bread to the wise ... but time and chance happen to them all'. For the devout Jew this awful appearance of divine injustice cannot be explained, but it can sometimes (as at the end of the book of Job) be absorbed into the mystery of Jehovah. In Isaiah this absorption is majestic and all-encompassing: 'I form the light, and create darkness; I make peace and create evil: I the Lord do all these things.' But Cicero's urbane Sceptic is less acquiescent and more critical: 'The fact really is that your character and past life make no difference whatsoever as regards your fortune good or bad.' And since this is so, everything religious collapses:

> for just as a household or a state appears to lack all rational system and order if in it there are no rewards for right conduct and no punishment for transgression, so there is no such thing at all as the divine governance of the world if that governance makes no distinction between the good and the wicked.[28]

The Stoic reply – that the good man is unharmed by evil fortune – does little to justify the ways of god to man; and for the Christian, with his much higher expectation of God, and his much more developed account of God's nature, the problem comes through in an even more acute and sometimes agonising form.

The Christian (and the Muslim is not much different) holds that God is a spirit (a body-less person) who is omnipotent (can do anything it is logically possible to do), omniscient (knows all that it is logically possible to know), and is perfectly good. This last attribute gives difficulty:[29] both from traditional Christian usages of the 'Our Father', 'Loving Father' type, and from the demand to have a God which is worthy of worship, it seems to be needful to say and mean that God is good in *some* minimal sense which relates the word 'good' to its normal human usage. And a minimal requirement for such usage must surely be that whatever sort of person goodness is ascribed to, the person must *not* be one who wilfully inflicts, or lets happen, suffering to other people which he could prevent. But this is exactly what seems to happen continuously in the world governed by the Christian God. It is not merely that robbers sometimes prosper and good men are occasionally cast down, but that there appears to be wholesale *random* suffering. Hume expresses the resultant problem with memorable succinctness: 'Epicurus's old questions are yet unanswered. Is he willing to prevent evil, but not able? Then he is impotent. Is he able, but not willing? Then he is malevolent. Is he both able and willing? Whence then evil?'[30]

There are, of course, a vast number of apologetic attempts to reconcile the evident facts of the world with the alleged goodness of God.[31] But at the end of such apologetic or critical discussions the position always seems to be: if you already devoutly believe in something like a Christian God, then with great ingenuity and after lengthy and sometimes contorted argument (J.S. Mill calls it 'the revolting spectacle of a jesuitical defence of moral enormities') you may be able to *reconcile* the facts of an amoral world with your belief. On the other hand if you start with an unprejudiced view of the world of human events, you will never *infer* the existence of an all-powerful God who is also good, and to whom life, and human life in particular, is of concern.

The conclusions from the problem of evil are thus: *either* you excuse yourself into theistic belief despite the appearances; *or* you admit that the appearances are inconsistent with the existence of such a God as Christians believe in. With the latter alternative the outcome must either be atheism: there is no god at all; or (if the design argument or cosmological argument are in some respects sound) deism: the non-religious acknowledgement that some power created or started all things but, in Hume's words, 'has no more regard to good above ill than to heat above cold' and hence is of no religious concern to us.

(2) A second argument for atheism derives from the serious difficulties in trying to make coherent the notion of God (or *any* god) as a body-less, omniscient, omnipotent person.

The worry is often thought to be very recent, but this is not so. For example Cicero's Epicurean remarks 'mind naked and simple, without any material adjunct to serve as an organ of sensation, seems to elude the capacity of our understanding',[32] and Sextus reports the argument that the concept of an unlimited god is curiously at variance with that of a living god.[33]

The crux of the matter is to be found not only in critical philosophy but in the common-sense feeling that we could not understand a person to be something that loves, forgives, commands, etc.

but has no location or body. The philosophical analogue of this common-sense feeling is to argue that such a person is impossible. Why is it impossible? Because to be a person is to have certain characteristics, among which are: location of feelings and thoughts with respect to other persons and things; a point of view of other things; a body by means of which the person can both carry out those activities which he/she or it can directly achieve without the mediation of anything else (basic acts) and which identifies the person from the viewpoint of others and possibly even from his/her or its own point of view. But in all theistic accounts, God is body-less and this nullifies the rest of what it is to be a person. Therefore it is nonsense to speak of God creating, loving us, sending his son or instructing his prophet since all these (and most other activities ascribed to God) are attributes of *persons*.

Philosophical discussion of this argument has at present reached no decisive conclusion.[34] But it should be noted that *if* the notion of a body-less person is incoherent, then a decisive objection to *all* theistic belief will have been established.

Proofs, probabilities and faith

If it is agreed that each of the arguments for the existence of God is flawed as a deductive proof, it may still be felt that as a whole they give some sort of probability to theism. But as Antony Flew vigorously points out, an accumulation of failed proofs proves nothing:

> A failed proof cannot serve as a pointer to anything, save perhaps to the weakness of those who have accepted it. Nor, for the same reason, can it be put to work along with other throwouts as a part of an accumulation of evidences. If one leaky bucket will not hold water that is no reason to think that ten can.[35]

On the other hand it can be argued that what we have left is not an accumulation of failed proofs, but an accumulation of evidence upon which failed proofs have been constructed. Thus in *The existence of god* (see especially Chapters 5 and 14) Richard Swinburne argues that the effect of the evidence is to give (or fail to give) some probability to the theistic theory over and above its prior probability. Now the prior probability of any theory depends upon its scope (the data it fits and the data it predicts) and its simplicity (the economy of entities and operations it involves). In the case of theism the predictive scope is low. But, argues Swinburne, theism is very simple. So its prior probability is a bit, but not much, above zero. On the other hand phenomena of the sort appealed to in the arguments – the existence of the universe, its conformity to order, the existence of living things with consciousness, an environment favourable to life, experience of what we take to be the divine, and so on – are all such as we would have more reason to expect if there is a God and less reason to expect if there is no God.

349

Moreover, although the prior probability of theism is low, the prior probability of there being a universe such as ours and no God is even lower: 'if there is to exist anything, it is far more likely to be something with the simplicity of God than something like the universe with all its characteristics crying out for explanation without there being God to explain it' (p. 288). Thus, given that the prior probability of God as the explanation of it all is higher than the prior probability of a brute fact universe without explanation, the phenomena appealed to in the arguments add some sort of probability to the (prior) probability of the theistic theory, despite the invalidity of each argument considered in isolation. The net effect is to make theism more probable than not.

Swinburne's argument that multiple patches probably make a bucket is, however, subject to difficulties. (a) His claims about the prior probability of theism are questionable, e.g. many find the notion of a person or will creating all things *more* improbable than the irreducible fact of the existence of all things. (b) If simplicity is important, then deism is simpler than theism since it dissolves the problem of evil. (c) Swinburne's account of the relation between evidence and probability is debatable. (d) The 'additional' probability supplied by some of the phenomena will, on some accounts, be *nil*, while the 'negative' probability of the problem of evil may well be on a larger scale than Swinburne allows.[36]

It will have been observed that the word 'argument' used in relation to the existence of a god has a very wide application. It can refer to attempts at decisive demonstrations (deductive proofs of the sort that Aquinas and Descartes among others appear to have intended), to compelling conclusions from observations on the model of scientific inference (the design argument as expounded by someone like Paley), or to the direct evidence of the sort appealed to in religious experience. 'Argument' can also indicate little more than clues and evidence of the sort that occur in a detective story whose end is a probability or consistent suspicion rather than a solution.

But whether the arguments are presented as valid proofs or (at the other extreme) as evidence for a weak probability, there is a question about their place in the religions, notably Christianity, they have been used to support.

One view is that the essence of religious faith is absolute and freely given trust in God. But *proof* that God exists would reduce the free acceptance of faith to the level of an unavoidable prudential concern with the indisputably true. To which the Thomist might reply: the proofs give us assurance that something exists having *some* of the attributes of God. Faith is still required concerning many of God's attributes and concerning most of his activities on earth. Moreover, the closer the arguments get to being treated as weak probabilities (as they now tend to be regarded), the greater the demands for faith.

A second view is that the arguments are important to

religion in the sense that without them what is believed will be arbitrary. Unless there is *some* reason to accept the fundamental assertion that there is a god, there can be no more reason to believe in the theistic God than to believe in the most esoteric religious absurdity or in no god at all. To which the fideistic Christian (Tertullian or Kierkegaard perhaps) may reply: there is positive religious merit in believing contrary to the evidence and we must trust in the grace of God to keep us from error. The overwhelming weight of Christian tradition has, however, not taken this view.

The existence and nature of god(s) is one of the oldest, most abiding and most extensive concerns of philosophy and this concern is not exhausted. The cosmological and design arguments, the nature of religious experience, the balance of probabilities between theism and atheism, the coherence of the notion of a person both body-less and universal remain lively issues. On the other hand concern with the meaning of religious language – so very evident in the middle decades of the present century – has waned, and the results of recent investigations are now largely absorbed into our general understanding of the philosophy of religion.[37]

Notes

(An author's name followed by a number in square brackets refers to the book or article which has that number in the bibliography.)

1. Swinburne [6], [7] and [8].

2. Quoted by Sextus Empiricus, from a lost work of Aristotle's, in Sextus' *Against the physicists*, I, 20.

3. Cicero [19], I, 44; see also II, 5 and III, 8–10. The passage quoted, together with most of the other quotations from classical sources, is based upon translations in the invaluable Loeb Classical Library published by Harvard and Heinemann.

4. Sextus Empiricus, *Against the physicists*, I, 49; see also Hume [25], Section 12, Part III.

5. See Descartes [23], Meditation V; Leibniz, *New essays on human understanding* (1765), Book IV, Ch. 10; Malcolm, 'Anselm's ontological arguments' in *The Philosophical Review* (1960); Hartshorne, *The logic of perfection* (La Salle, Illinois, 1962), Ch. 2 *et al.*; Plantinga, *The nature of necessity* (Oxford, 1974), Ch. 4 *et al.*

6. Hick and McGill [14] is a useful compendium of primary and secondary sources.

7. Leibniz, *New essays on human understanding*, Book IV, Ch. 10.

8. Aquinas, *Summa theologiae*, 1a.2, i, expresses the common-sense criticism with typical precision and firmness.

9. A possible exception is Plato's own earlier work, the *Phaedrus*, 235 c–e, where he argues that the self-moving (at the beginning of motion) is immortal and is a living soul. But for our purposes the passage in the *Laws* can stand by itself as Plato's most careful and mature expression of the argument.

10. L.W. Craig, *The Kalām cosmological argument* (London, 1979), Preface. At the date of writing Craig's book is not only the most recent work on this less than well-known subject; it is also the best philosophical discussion.

11. From an article by H.A. Davidson, quoted by Craig, *The Kalām cosmological argument*, p. 9.

12. Copleston [21], p. 118.

13. Hume [26], Part IX.

14. The most useful short collection of Leibniz' works is in the Everyman's Library, translated by M. Morris, entitled *Leibniz: philosophical writings* (London, 1934). The passages cited are on p. 8 and p. 26 respectively.

15. For further development of these points see Gaskin [5], pp. 56–68. For a good discussion of all the main issues see W.L. Rowe, *The cosmological argument* (Princeton, 1975).

16. Two classic statements of the teleological argument are in Bernard Nieuwentyl's massive *True uses of the contemplation of the universe*, published in Amsterdam in 1715 (London, 1719) and William Paley's *Natural theology*, or *Evidences of the existence and attributes of the deity collected from the appearances of nature* (1802). The nomological argument appears frequently, but is generally stated more briefly. It puts in an influential appearance in the 'General scholium' to the second edition of Newton's *Principia mathematica* (1713) and in many of Newton's expositors, e.g. in Colin Maclaurin's *An account of Isaac Newton's discoveries* (1748). Both arguments are subjected to devastating criticism by David Hume [25], Section 11, and throughout [26]. It is a curious commentary upon the intellectual receptiveness of intelligent men that Hume's radical criticisms were much less damaging than the largely incidental criticisms implied by Darwin's *Origin of species* (1859). One of the first signs of attempted rehabilitation of the design argument can be found in L.J. Henderson's *The fitness of the environment* (New York, 1913). Another followed in F.R. Tennant's *Philosophical theology* (2 vols, Cambridge, 1928 and 1930). More recently see R.E.D. Clark, *The universe – plan or accident* (Philadelphia, 1961) and, at a much more sophisticated philosophical level, Plantinga [9] and Swinburne [7], Ch. 8. A reply to the latter is to be found in Mackie [10], Ch. 8.

17. Davies [4], p. 50, observes '[order] is the form taken by the universe as existing; it is what we are referring to when we talk about the universe'.

18. See, for example, the classic work by William James [18], and, more recently, D. Hay's somewhat dreary investigations in *Exploring inner space* (Harmondsworth, 1982).

19. For the concepts used in religious experience see *The idea of the holy* by Rudolf Otto (1917). Recent philosophical discussions can be found in R. Hepburn, *Christianity and paradox* (London, 1958), Chs. 3 and 4; P. Donovan, *Interpreting religious experience* (London, 1979); Swinburne [7], Ch. 13; G. Gutting, *Religious belief and religious skepticism* (London, 1982), Ch. 5; Mackie [10], Ch. 10; Gaskin [5], Ch. 4; and Davies [4], Ch. 3.

20. James [18], 'Postscript'.

21. *Against the Galilaeans*, 152D.

22. Joseph Butler gives a very well-known account of conscience as a moral force in *Fifteen sermons preached at the Rolls Chapel* (1726); Newman employs a similar account in *A grammar of assent* (1870), Ch. 5, to relate conscience to an external being, namely God. But Newman's most vivid account is in his earlier work *Discourses addressed to mixed congregations* (1849), Discourse 5.

23. Mackie [10], p. 105.

24. For an excellent discussion (whose existence must excuse my own cavalier

treatment of this argument), see Kenny [22], Ch. 5.

25. See for the basic discussion Hume [25], Section 10; A. Flew, *Hume's philosophy of belief* (London, 1961), Ch. 8; Gaskin [28], Ch. 7; R. Swinburne, *The concept of miracle* (London, 1970).

26. In Locke and Swinburne as specified in the text, but also in Mackie [10], Ch. 7.

27. Berkeley as specified. See also G.J. Warnock, *Berkeley* (Harmondsworth, 1953); E.A. Sillem, *George Berkeley and the proofs for the existence of God* (London, 1957).

28. Cicero [19], III, 37 and III, 35.

29. For a succinct discussion see Davies [4], pp. 216–29.

30. Hume [26], Part X.

31. Seneca's *De providentia* is a fine piece of pre-Christian writing on the subject, and Hume [26], Parts X and XI, is an important critical discussion. For recent surveys see John Hick, *Evil and the God of love* (London, 1966) and H.J. McCloskey, *God and evil* (The Hague, 1974).

32. Cicero [19], II, 11. Note this remark in conjunction with Cicero's very modern sounding description of god in *Tusculan disputations*, I, 27.

33. Sextus Empiricus, *Against the physicists*, I, 148.

34. See, for instance, A. MacIntyre, 'A note on immortality', *Mind* (1955); Flew [11], Ch. 2; T. Penelhum, *Survival and disembodied existence* (London, 1970), particularly the last chapter; H. Oppenheimer, *Incarnation and immanence* (London, 1973), Ch. 2; Swinburne [6].

35. Flew [11], pp. 62f.

36. For a succinct criticism of Swinburne see Mackie [10], pp. 251–3.

37. The literature is far too extensive to list but major contributions include Antony Flew's much anthologised essay 'Theology and falsification' in, for example, B. Mitchell (ed.), *The philosophy of religion* (Oxford, 1971); F. Ferre, *Language, logic and God* (London, 1970); Plantinga [9]; Swinburne [6] and Kai Nielsen, *An introduction to the philosophy of religion* (New York, 1983).

Bibliography

There are many introductory volumes on natural theology and the philosophy of religion which provide expansions and elaborations of the arguments outlined in the foregoing chapter. Commendably succinct and lucid discussions may be found in, for example:

[1] A.E. Taylor, *Does God exist?* (Collins, London, 1945).

[2] J. Hick, *Arguments for the existence of God* (Macmillan, London, 1970).

[3] B. Davies, *An introduction to the philosophy of religion* (Oxford University Press, Oxford, 1982) and, by the same author,

[4] *Thinking about God* (Geoffrey Chapman, London, 1985).

[5] J.C.A. Gaskin, *The quest for eternity* (Penguin Books, Harmondsworth, 1984).

At a somewhat more advanced philosophical level, there are painstaking and sympathetic studies of the nature of theism, and the evidence for it, in three works by R.G. Swinburne:

[6] *The coherence of theism* (Oxford University Press, Oxford, 1977).

[7] *The existence of God* (Oxford University Press, Oxford, 1979).

[8] *Faith and reason* (Oxford University Press, Oxford, 1981) and also

[9] A. Plantinga, *God and other minds* (Cornell University Press, Ithaca, 1967), especially Part I; and, for a more critical look at theism, including replies to some of Swinburne's arguments,

[10] J.L. Mackie, *The miracle of theism* (Oxford University Press, Oxford, 1982). Vigorous statements of the case against theism can be found in

[11] A. Flew, *God and philosophy* (Hutchinson, London, 1966), reissued under the title *God: a critical enquiry* (2nd edn, Open Court, La Salle, Illinois, 1984) and, by the same author,

[12] *The presumption of atheism* (Elek-Pemberton, London, 1976). Among works focusing on specific arguments, useful reference may be made to

[13] J. Barnes, *The ontological argument* (Macmillan, London, 1972) and, on the same subject,

[14] J. Hick and A.C. McGill (eds), *The many-faced argument* (Macmillan, London, 1968).

[15] T. McPherson, *The argument from design* (Macmillan, London, 1972).

[16] P. Donovan, *Interpreting religious experience* (Sheldon Press, London, 1979) and, an earlier treatment of the same topic,

[17] S. Hook (ed.), *Religious experience and truth* (New York University Press, New York, 1961). Also, as a rich source of examples of, and observations on, religious experience,

[18] W. James, *The varieties of religious experience* (Longmans Green, New York, 1902).

The statements of the arguments for the existence of God given in older philosophical texts may well present some difficulties to the reader who has no systematic training in philosophy. Doubtless they often use archaic terms and concepts, or are hard to appreciate fully in abstraction from the total metaphysical systems of which they form parts. On the other hand, they are also often formulated with a terseness and succinctness which modern writers – aware of the criticisms which the original arguments have provoked, and the criticisms of criticisms, etc. – find hard to emulate. It is useful to examine at least some of these classical sources (perhaps with some assistance from modern commentaries); for example

[19] Cicero, *The nature of the gods* (various editions and translations, including that of H.C.P. McGregor and J.M. Ross (Penguin Books, Harmondsworth, 1972)).

[20] St Thomas Aquinas, *Summa theologica*, trans. Fathers of the English Dominican Province (Burns, Oates and Washburn, London, 1920), especially Part I(a), 2, 3 and, for explication and comments,

[21] F. Copleston, *Aquinas* (Penguin Books, Harmondsworth, 1955) and

[22] A. Kenny, *The five ways* (Routledge and Kegan Paul, London, 1969).

[23] R. Descartes, *Meditations* (many editions and translations, for example E. Anscombe and P.T. Geach, *Descartes: philosophical writings* (Nelson, London, 1954), and, more recently, J. Cottingham, R. Stoothoff and D. Murdoch, *Philosophical writings of Descartes* (2 vols, Cambridge University Press, Cambridge, 1984–5), especially Meditations III and V.

[24] A. Kenny, *Descartes* (Random House, New York, 1968), especially Ch. 6; and two classic statements of religious scepticism:

[25] D. Hume, *Enquiry concerning the human understanding* (first published 1748, ed. L.H. Selby-Bigge, Oxford University Press, Oxford, 1902, and by C.W. Hendel, Liberal Arts Press, New York, 1955), Section 10, and, also by Hume,

354

[26] *Dialogues concerning natural religion* (first published 1779, ed. N.K. Smith, Oxford University Press, Oxford, 1935); and for comments on these, see Flew [11] and

[27] T. Penelhum, *Hume* (Macmillan, London, 1975), especially Ch. 8.

[28] J.C.A. Gaskin, *Hume's philosophy of religion* (Macmillan, London, 1978).

Also, despite his formidable reputation for obscurity, it is worth while to look at Kant's criticisms of other arguments for the existence of God, and his statement of his own, in

[29] *The critique of pure reason* (first published 1781, 2nd edn, 1787, various translations, for example by N.K. Smith, Macmillan, London, 1929), especially the section entitled 'Transcendental dialectic', Book II, Ch. 3, and

[30] *The critique of practical reason* (first published 1788, trans. T.K. Abbott, Longmans Green, London, 1873, reprinted 1959), Part I, Book II, Ch. 2, especially Section 5. Guidance may be sought from a variety of commentaries, perhaps the most readily accessible being

[31] S. Körner, *Kant* (Penguin Books, Harmondsworth, 1955).

T.E.B.

16 | Space, Time and Motion

J.J.C. Smart

Space, time and space-time

Since the advent of the special and general theories of relativity it has become scientific orthodoxy that there are no such things as space and time taken separately, but only a unitary space-time. As Hermann Minkowski put it in 1908: 'Henceforth space by itself and time by itself are doomed to fade away into mere shadows, and only a kind of union of the two will preserve an independent reality.'[1] So the topic of space and time is more properly the topic of one thing: space-time. Furthermore the concept of motion becomes a geometrical one in the space-time theory, and so the whole topic of the present chapter is indeed a unitary one. It must be said, however, that there have been influential philosophers, for example A.N. Prior and P.T. Geach, who prefer to retain the common-sense notion of separate space and time, regarding the Minkowski space-time geometry as merely a convenient mathematical instrument for predicting phenomena describable in the common-sense way. Commonly such philosophers believe that time has some intrinsic flow or passage that cannot be captured in a geometrical representation.

It is not clear, however, that the pre-relativistic concept of space and time is not at bottom a space-time one. The theory of relativity certainly makes the belief in space-time more appealing, but even pre-relativistically we can (and perhaps must) think of the world four-dimensionally. Consider a brick. This has height, breadth and length, and also endures through time. Does not this in itself imply that the brick is a four-dimensional object? Of course an object's spatial dimensions and other properties may vary from time to time, but four-dimensionally we can talk of 'temporal stages' or instantaneous 'time-slices' of the object. Thus in the common-sense language of time and change we can say that a boy was taller

356

when he was ten years old than he was when he was five: four-dimensionally we can say that a ten-year time-slice is taller than a five-year time-slice. It is not clear that the latter statement does not give just what we mean by the former one, and so it is not clear that the common-sense way of looking at things is not a space-time one.

Whether or not the common-sense picture of the world is itself at bottom a space-time one, the special and general theories of relativity have made this way of looking at the world imperative. The general theory of relativity is essentially concerned with giving an explanation of gravitation in terms of space-time geometry. The special theory is much simpler and is concerned with reconciling mechanics with the theory of electromagnetism. Newtonian mechanics and Maxwell's electromagnetic theory do not fit very well together. Which of the two should be modified? Einstein chose to modify Newtonian mechanics and leave electromagnetic theory intact. The modified mechanics has been very well tested in all sorts of ways: for example one could not make a cyclotron without using Einstein's mechanics. The difference between the old and the new mechanics becomes practically important only when high velocities (comparable to the velocity of light) are involved.

If we were to measure the velocity of a rod moving endwise at high velocity, we should observe the rod to be contracted or shorter in length. This is the so-called Lorentz contraction. An observer on the rod would observe a rod at rest with respect to us to be contracted too. So the contraction is not intrinsic but relative to a frame of reference, which roughly speaking can be thought of as a set of rectangular axes in space. Thus the above-mentioned rod is moving with respect to a set of axes in which we are at rest, but is at rest with respect to a set of axes moving as it does.

There is a temporal analogue of the Lorentz contraction. Thus a clock (or any other periodic process) that is moving with high velocity relative to us will be observed to run slow, though observers on axes moving at the same velocity as the clock will observe it to tick at the usual rate. And these observers will observe *our* clocks to run slow relative to theirs. This is the so-called time dilation.

A simple analogy may give an idea of how time dilation can be a purely geometrical affair. Consider two roads that branch out from a certain point. One goes due north and the other north-west. Suppose that one traveller goes a certain direction north on the first road. A second traveller who is on the north-west road has to go further to get as far north as the first traveller. (Symmetrically, the first traveller has to go further north on his road to go as far *north-west* as the second one.) Time dilation is much like this. A clock can be thought of four-dimensionally as lying along a line in space-time (the 'world line' of the clock). The world line of a clock moving with respect to the first one will be at an angle to the latter's world line. The time direction for each clock will be along the world line of each clock. So in relation to the first clock the time elapsed while the first beats one second will be *less*, much as the northing three miles along the north-west road will take *more* than three north-west miles. The difference between the two cases (the *more* and the *less*) depends on the peculiar geometry of space-time, which was due to Minkowski. Minkowski explained the Lorentz contraction, time dilation, and the relativity of simultaneity in Einstein's theory in a purely geometrical way, which has since been the accepted way of developing relativity theory. Simultaneity is relative in much the same way as 'as much north' and 'as much north-west' differ from one another in the example of the intersecting roads. Events that are simultaneous in one frame are not simultaneous in a second frame moving relatively to the first one.

World lines of physical particles lie in 'time-like' directions in space-time. What this means is as follows. Consider all the possible light rays through a certain point. In space-time these lie along the surface of the double (forwards and backwards) cone whose vertex is at that point. Lines within a light cone lie in 'time-like' directions. Those that pass through the vertex but are otherwise outside the cone lie in 'space-like' directions.

The peculiarity of Minkowski's geometry is that it is a certain sort of non-Euclidean one in time-like directions but is Euclidean in space-like directions. And in time-like directions two sides of a triangle are not longer but are *shorter* than the third side. This accounts for the difference between the 'less' and the 'more' of the previous paragraph.

Consider two twins, Peter and Paul. Paul shoots off in a rocket to a distant star and returns to Peter and finds that he is younger than his brother. This is explained geometrically by the fact that Paul's world line is a bent one in Minkowski space – it lies along two lines of a triangle, while Peter's lies on the third side. Paul's time-dilation or relative youth is explained by the fact that in the geometry two of the sides of such a triangle are less than the third side. It has sometimes been thought that as Paul would see Peter receding from and then returning to him, Peter should be younger than Paul. This would be a paradox because both cannot be younger than the other. However there is no such symmetry, since in Minkowski space Peter's world line is straight and Paul's is bent. This is connected with the fact that rocket motors would be needed to decelerate and then accelerate Paul to turn him round at the distant star, whereas Peter experiences no such forces. In Minkowski's space-time bodies not acted on by a force lie four-dimensionally along straight lines.

Readers familiar with co-ordinate geometry will recall the way in which curves are expressed by algebraic equations which depend on the co-ordinate axes chosen. If you rotate the axes the equations are suitably changed. Minkowski explained the kinematical phenomena of special relativity, such as the Lorentz contraction and time dilation, as well as the mathematical transformations characteristic of the theory (the so-called Lorentz transformations) as merely a matter of rotation of axes in space-time. You can slice a sausage in many ways. If you slice at an angle you get an elliptical slice that is in one direction 'longer' than a circular slice. If you slice a space-time object at an angle you get a *shorter* slice – this explains the Lorentz contraction. There is no real contraction, any more than if you were to slice a sausage you would actually stretch it crossways.

The space-time world picture enables us to give a very simple account of change and motion. Thus two bodies are at rest with respect to one another in an inertial system if their world lines in Minkowski space are parallel to one another. Two bodies are moving with uniform velocity relative to one another in an inertial system if their world lines are at an angle to one another. A body is accelerated with respect to an inertial system if its world line is curved in Minkowski space. Again let *ABC* be the world line of a traffic light that changes from red to green at *B*, being red throughout *AB* and green throughout *BC*. The change from red to green is just the dissimilarity in colour of *AB* from *AC*.

Time flow

The sort of account of change that has been given above could be given for space too: we may say, for example, that a road becomes steeper, or that a curtain's colour changes from top to bottom. Many philosophers, however, hold that there is something special about time, that it is 'transitory' or 'dynamic', as opposed to what they regard as the 'static' space-time Minkowski world. The latter they regard as a 'block universe' in which nothing ever happens or changes. In reply we should say that it is as absurd to say that the space-time universe is 'static' as to say that it is 'dynamic'. It neither stays the same nor changes. Change or staying the same of space-time would have to be change or staying the same with respect to a hyper-time, and then if 'dynamism' were required of the hyper-time we would have to postulate a hyper-hyper-time, and so on *ad infinitum*. Unless, that is, we are willing to agree with the account of change or staying the same of four-dimensional objects already advocated: namely in terms of the difference or similarity of different temporal stages or time-slices of an object.

An obvious objection to the notion of time flow and to a correlative notion of our 'advance through time' is to ask 'How fast does it flow?' or 'How fast do we advance through time?' The answer (perhaps) of 'One second per second' hardly seems illuminating. (Does a ruler extend at the rate of one centimetre per centimetre?) Ordinary flow or advance is rate of change with respect to time of something *else*, spatial distance. It is thought that time flows like a river, bears its sons away, and so on. All this is part of common sense, and yet on inspection the flow, if it exists, seems ineffable. Consider the flow of a river. In the Minkowski world this is a matter of the relative inclination to one another of the world lines of drops of river water to the world lines of particles of soil on the bank. The flow of time could not be so represented. Of course not all talk of the flow of time has this irredeemable obscurity. Isaac Newton said that 'Absolute, true, and mathematical time, of itself, and from its own nature, flows equally without relation to anything external.'[2] We can take Newton simply to be postulating an ideal standard of time relative to which the laws of mechanics are correct. Time standards, such as that of the apparent rotation of stars round the earth, need to be corrected by a method of successive approximation, to allow for irregularities due to such factors as the non-constancy of the angular velocity of the earth round the sun, irregularities due to variations in the speed of rotation of the earth and so on. Such an ideal time standard can be sought without reference to any 'flow' of time. Nor do we need to talk of a change in events in respect of putative properties of pastness, presentness and futurity.

Talk of change in respect of such putative properties was exploited by J.McT.E. McTaggart in his celebrated argument for the unreality of time.[3] The putative properties of pastness, presentness and futurity belong to what he called 'the A-series'. When we order events in terms of earlier and later we have the 'B-series'. (McTaggart's terminology is a bit misleading, because he is really talking about two equivalent ways of ordering the *same* series of events.) McTaggart thought that since time involves change the B-series is not properly temporal: if a B-series event is later than another B-series event it is always so. A defender of the space-time world picture (or B-theorist) will of course reply that McTaggart has mis-understood the nature of change, which involves ordinary properties. He or she will argue that the words 'past', 'present' and 'future' are indexical: their reference depends on the time of their utterance. 'Event E is future' said (or written down) at time t_1 is not inconsistent with 'E is *past*' said at a later time t_2. McTaggart's argument for the unreality of time essentially depends on ignoring this fact, but I shall not attempt to argue for this now. The details of his argument have given rise to a vast secondary literature. For present purposes it is merely necessary to note that this sort of sup-posed A-change, of which even an instantaneous event can partake, is central to the notion of time flow or passage. As against this we could use as a slogan '*Things* change, *events* happen.'

The semantics for 'past', 'present' and 'future', and for tenses of verbs can be given in a tenseless locution.[4] Thus 'E is past' is true at t if and only if E *occurs* earlier than t. 'Occurs' here is in the tenseless present, which I indicate by italics. It is neutral as to its temporal relation to its own utterance. (Compare the tenseless present in 'Two plus two *equals* four,' in which time reference is not even in question.) The indexicality of 'past', 'present' and 'future', like that of 'you', 'me', 'here', 'there', implies that these expressions do not stand for properties. Some philosophers, such as W.V. Quine, have held that indexical expressions are not needed in a language adequate to express theoretical science and metaphysics. This does not imply, of course, that indexicals are not needed in daily life. A person hurrying to a twelve o'clock appointment may be interested to be told 'It is *now* ten minutes to twelve.' He or she can relate this to the time he or she hears the utterance in question and knows that he or she has ten minutes in hand. No non-indexical sentence will do the job for him. Indexicals are sometimes said to be necessary for theoretical purposes too: to specify the origins of co-ordinate system for space-time geometry. However the origin could in fact be specified by a sufficiently complex descriptive phrase. Of course if the universe were completely symmetrical, with an exactly similar person to you making an exactly similar utterance to your utterance, in relation to exactly similar surroundings, no non-indexical descriptive phrase could single out a unique origin of co-ordinates. However if the universe were as symmetrical as that, it would not matter which of two symmetrically situated origins were chosen. General scientific sentences would have the same truth-values.

If we do need indexicals, we could get by with one indexical alone, namely 'this utterance'. Thus 'here' is 'near this utterance', 'you' is 'the person addressed in this utterance', and so on, and pertinently for present purposes 'E is past' could be replaced by 'E is earlier than this utterance,' and analogously with 'future', and with 'present' or 'now'. Now if we make these replacements the temptation to regard A-series change as real change may be reduced. There is no one utterance relative to which an event is said to be first earlier and then later.

A trouble for the A-theorist arises from the relativity of simultaneity in the special theory of relativity. In ordinary life 'now' has a clear enough use because we are not concerned with communicating with persons moving at high velocity relative to us. Perhaps if in the future very fast space ships communicate with one another a convention might be adopted that 'now' refers to simultaneity in the frame of reference at which the person making the utterance is at rest. So each space ship would use 'now' to refer to simultaneity in its own rest frame.

The B-theorist may find it easy enough to convince himself or herself that talk of the flow or passage of time, of advance through time, or of absolute becoming is nonsense and born of some sort of illusion. It is harder to suggest a good explanation of such an illusion. Confusion about indexicals does not seem to be the complete explanation. A tentative suggestion that I should like to make is that we confuse the flow of information through our short-term memories with a flow of time itself.[5]

The direction of time

This leads us to a consideration of the so-called direction of time. If the flow of time made sense, the direction of its flow would give a direction, but if we reject the notion of time flow we are led to scientifically more illuminating explanations. Rather than talking of the direction of time itself it is better to talk of the temporal asymmetry of the universe. Evidence of such temporal asymmetry are all around us. A brick falls to the ground where it is stopped. We never see the energy in the ground causing a brick to be projected upwards. Milk mixes with coffee, but we never see white coffee separating out into black coffee surmounted by a layer of milk. We know about the dinosaurs from the fossil evidence, but we could have no such evidence of future forms of life. Footprints are traces of earlier perambulations but there is never the same direct evidence of future perambulations. We can have a magnetic tape record of yesterday's football commentary, but we never have one of tomorrow's. Similarly we have memory traces in the brain of past events, not of future ones. Whence this great asymmetry?

The case of the milky coffee is one simply of increase of entropy (measure of disorder). The reverse process is physically possible (the milk molecules and coffee molecules might by chance separate out from one another) but it is immensely improbable, to such an extent that we should not believe our eyes if we observed such a phenomenon. Similarly with the falling brick: the kinetic energy of the falling brick gets transformed into disordered energy imparted to the molecules and atoms of the ground. It is improbable in the extreme that the molecules in the ground should accidentally conspire to kick the brick upwards all at the same moment. (Part of the energy of the falling brick would be dissipated as heat radiation, and the reverse process would also involve the physically possible but most improbable arrival of photons in exact reverse of the original radiation of photons.)

The case of traces (footprints, magnetic tapes, memory traces, fossils) is more complicated than those of the brick and the coffee. Here we have a local decrease of entropy, though at the expense of overall *increase* of entropy in a wider system. Consider the footprint in the sand. At first the sand particles are pretty well randomly situated below the surface of the beach. When someone walks on the beach, the particles get compressed. Above this compressed volume there is a hollow volume with only air in it. The case is analogous to most of the molecules in a container getting into one half of it. There is a decrease of entropy (an increase of order). The second law of thermodynamics is not violated, because there is a net increase of entropy within a wider system, which includes the walker's body, in which the energy needed in walking comes from the breaking down of highly ordered molecules. We cannot say that the entropy of the footprint is less than that of the beach, since entropy depends on mass, but let us say that the relative entropy of the part containing the footprint is decreased: it is less than what would antecedently have been expected. Such a system as that constituted by a footprint or a magnetic tape recording was called by Hans Reichenbach[6] 'a branch system'. Other examples of branch systems are some of the things already mentioned: memory traces in the brain, magnetic tape recordings, fossils, and in general all those things from which we can directly infer the past (i.e. without retrodicting on the basis of laws of nature plus boundary conditions, just as we predict the future). Branch systems thus have very much to do with the fact that we remember earlier events, not future ones, and so with our common-sense conceptions about time.

Why do branch systems all (or perhaps nearly all) point the same way in time? This is a matter of cosmic thermodynamics, which is an obscure subject, but speaking loosely, the branch systems by definition have entropy curves below that of the rising entropy curve of the surrounding universe.

Statistical mechanics, using probabilistic assumptions together with fundamental laws of nature, has explained the practical success of the second law of thermodynamics, while nevertheless showing that it is not strictly true. Violations of the second law are physically possible, but in most cases almost inconceivably unlikely. It is physically possible that all the air molecules in this room should congregate in the far half of it, thus suffocating me in a vacuum. Such an occurrence is so unlikely that it might not happen if my room lasted even as long as the whole previous history of the universe, but it is not ruled out by what we regard now as the fundamental laws of physics. These fundamental laws are, near enough, time symmetric. Thus the laws of classical or relativistic mechanics remain invariant if we substitute '$-t$' for 't'. So also with Maxwell's electromagnetic equations and Schrödinger's equation in quantum mechanics. And so on. There is a recondite exception to do with the decay of the $K°$ meson. The laws of nature are now believed to be not quite symmetrical with respect to charge reversal (particles into their anti-particles), reflection (reversal of parity) and time reversal, when each of these is taken separately, but are believed to be invariant under simultaneous reversal of all three (CPT reversal). However, the difference between CPT symmetry and T symmetry does not show up except in recondite cases, and so it is unlikely that failure of T symmetry accounts for the gross temporal asymmetries we see in the cosmos generally.

It should be noted that there are two other sorts of temporal asymmetries besides the thermodynamically based ones that have just been discussed. (1) There is the fact that electromagnetic waves emerge from a source, whereas we do not observe spherical waves contracting from infinity to a sink (i.e. the opposite of a source – when an atom radiates energy it is a source and when it absorbs energy it is a sink). (2) There is the expansion of the universe. Galaxies are all receding from one another just as dots on a rubber balloon would recede (with velocity of recession proportional to their distances apart) as the balloon was blown further up. I shall not try to discuss whether these two asymmetries could be related to the asymmetries in respect of 'branch systems' and so on. It is the latter that seem most important for understanding the nature of memory traces and the like, and so of the way we experience temporal facts.

Let us play with the idea that at the big bang, at the

beginning of the universe as we know it, things evolved in two opposite temporal directions, so that a similar cosmic era evolved in the direction of negative time and the temporal direction of entropy increase, branch systems, propagation of spherical waves, and the recession of galaxies from one another was opposite to that in our own cosmic era. People in this cosmic era would have memories of later events, not of earlier ones (according to our time direction) though of course they would use *their* words for 'earlier' and 'later' oppositely to us. Time for them would seem to flow in the negative time direction, oppositely to the way it seems to flow for us. This consideration of course fits in very well with the idea that the flow or passage of time is an illusion. Some philosophers have tried to describe a time-reversed era as an odd one in which everything would look like a film run in reverse. They forget that they must reverse *everything* including memory traces and the direction of branch systems generally. If *everything* were reversed everything would seem exactly the same as it is in our unreversed world. It was remarked earlier that it is better to talk not of the direction of time but of the temporal asymmetry of the universe. Our supposition of a time-reversed era suggests that it might be best of all to be more cautious and talk of the temporal asymmetry of our cosmic era.

Certainly we do have differing attitudes to the future and past respectively. A.N. Prior, an A-theorist, drew attention to the following sort of case.[7] We go to the dentist for some painful treatment. Afterwards we say, 'Thank goodness that's over.' As Prior has remarked, we are not thanking goodness that the visit to the dentist is prior to our utterance. Why, he asks, should we thank goodness for *that*? Still, the B-theorist can reply that we are thanking goodness that the visit to the dentist is earlier than the time of our utterance, so that there is no need for us to make plans about it, steel ourselves to feel pain, and so on. It is in this way that our differing attitudes to past and future connect with the temporal asymmetry of the universe (or cosmic era). It is not surprising that evolution and natural selection have seen to it that we concern ourselves with the future, because we need to plan and make decisions. It is the future that we can affect, not the past. (It seems plausible that this causal asymmetry is of a piece with the asymmetry about traces, since these depend on the direction of information processing when we make decisions.) This solicitude for the future is so ingrained that it can carry over to cases in which decisions cannot affect the relevant future occurrences. (Consider a prisoner awaiting execution. His apprehension is not conducive to his survival, but it is a carry over from dispositions to fear that are conducive to survival.) At any rate, this is the sort of way in which the B-theorist will try to answer the A-theorist.

It was remarked earlier that special conventions would be needed for the use of 'now' as signalled between persons moving with respect to one another with velocities comparable to that of light. Outside science fiction the problem does not arise for us. Jeremy Butterfield[8] has recently drawn attention to the fact that the time lag in observation (including the reaction time of the observer) is usually smaller than the times during which objects change their salient and easily observable properties. (There is an obvious evolutionary explanation for this.) He argues that this explains the fact that nearly all languages indicate time but not space by means of verbal inflexions such as tenses. Because of the relative rapidity of oral communication people can share a 'now' in a way in which they cannot to the same extent share a 'here'. (Actually, the rapidity of oral communication is not great, if we take units so that the velocity of light is unity, thus removing an arbitrary constant from the expressions of the Lorentz transformations. Nevertheless, it is still rapid compared with the rate at which objects change most of their salient properties.) Butterfield also suggests that this phenomenon also explains why many people think of only the present as real.

        Some A-theorists think of the future as unreal. This may partly arise for verificationist reasons (confusing the knowability of a thing with its reality), but also because of considerations of free will and of fatalism. Thus it may be said that we can change the future but not the past. In reply, the B-theorist may say that this depends on a confusion. Suppose that I am deciding whether to take a left fork on a road or to take a right fork. I take the left fork. Have I changed the future? No – taking the left fork *was* the future. Of course one need not expect to convince the committed A-theorist, who will deny that anything *was* the future until after it has become present. Thus Peter Geach holds, in the Aristotelian tradition, that the future 'consists of certain actual trends and tendencies in the present that have not yet been fulfilled'.[9] (It is indeed hard to produce knock-down arguments in philosophy.) All this is independent of the question of whether my decision was determined or not. To say that an event is determined by an earlier state of the universe is simply to say that its occurrence follows from the earlier state of the universe together with causal or other laws of nature. The question of whether or not an event is determined is a different question from that of whether it is determinate. In an indeterministic universe events can still be determinate.

        Nor does the space-time view imply fatalism. The fatalist says that something will happen in the future, no matter what we do. The B-theorist need not (and indeed will not) accept this. He or she will agree that our decisions are necessary conditions (parts of causal chains) for events at another part of space-time. He or she can (and will) agree that our decisions are important.

Absolute and relational theories

What is space-time anyway? Is it something absolute or can it be reduced to relations between physical objects or events? In pre-relativity days the same question was asked about space and time taken separately, and since most of

365

the same issues arise, in discussing earlier philosophers and scientists I shall often put the question in terms of space or time, rather than space-time.

According to Descartes the essence of matter was extension, just as the essence of mind was thought. Descartes did have a problem, in fact, about distinguishing matter from empty space, since he believed that space was Euclidean and so homogeneous and isotropic. If he had the concept of a space of variable curvature, as in modern differential geometry (which forms the basis of the general theory of relativity) he might perhaps have been able to solve the problem, at least to his own satisfaction, by identifying matter with regions of special curvature of space.

Leibniz, by contrast, held that space merely consisted in relations between (themselves non-spatial or unextended) 'monads'. (Leibniz therefore avoids an uneasiness that some may possibly feel about the relational theory, if the things that are related are themselves supposed to be spatial.) Isaac Newton believed in absolute space and time, and a classic controversy is preserved in the Leibniz–Clarke correspondence, Clarke defending the Newtonian view.[10]

Newton's concept of space was closely connected with that of an inertial system of axes relative to which a body not acted on by a force moves with uniform speed in a straight line. (There may not in fact be such bodies, but an inertial system can be determined to any desired degree of approximation by using the third law of motion.) However if S is an inertial system and another such system S' is moving with uniform velocity relative to S, then S' is also an inertial system. So Newton's idea must have been that only one such system is at rest in absolute space. Newtonian mechanics is invariant with respect to uniform velocities. In contrast, accelerations are absolute, and since the particles that constitute a rotating rigid body accelerate towards the centre of rotation, a system that rotates relative to an inertial system is not itself inertial. This consideration led Newton to propose as an argument for absolute space his well-known case of the rotating bucket.

Suppose that a bucket is filled with water and is hanging from a twisted rope and is held steady so that the surface of the water is flat. The bucket is now let go and rotates rapidly as the rope untwists. At first the water itself does not rotate and its surface continues to be flat, but due to viscosity it gradually acquires the same angular velocity of rotation as the bucket has. The surface of the water has now become curved. This shows that the curvature of the surface is not due to motion relative to the bucket. It must therefore, thought Newton, be due to rotation relative to absolute space. The Austrian physicist and philosopher Ernst Mach, defending a relational theory of space, remarked that though the water was not rotating relative to the bucket, it was rotating relative to the fixed stars. According to Newton, the surface of the water in the bucket would become curved even though the bucket and its contents were the only material objects in the universe. Mach held that Newton had no warrant for asserting this, since we do not know what the laws of nature would be in a universe containing only a single bucket of water. Mach took the view that the curvature of the surface of the water depends on a relation to 'the mass of the earth and the other celestial bodies'.[11] He said that we have no warrant for saying how things would turn out if the sides of the bucket were increased in mass so that they were several miles thick. According to Mach, an inertial frame of reference was not to be defined as one at rest or in motion with respect to absolute space, but was to be determined by the general distribution of matter in the universe. This has been referred to by cosmologists as Mach's principle, and it is still controversial as to whether or not inertia can be accounted for by the matter and energy (which in the theory of relativity are unified as mass-energy) in the universe.

Immanuel Kant, in his short treatise 'Concerning the ultimate foundation of the differentiation of regions in space' (1768), had an argument from the handedness of asymmetrical objects. Consider a left hand and a right hand. Each is the mirror image of the other, and there is no set of continuous motions in three-dimensional space that will take one into the other. The left hand and the right hand are 'enantiomorphs'. Yet Kant thought that even if a hand were the only thing in space, it would have to be either a left hand or a right hand. Now all the relations between the parts of a left hand correspond exactly to relations between parts of a right hand. So the difference cannot lie in such relations. He therefore thought that the relation that made it (say) a left hand rather than a right hand must lie in a relation to absolute space.[12] (In his later critical philosophy he offered a different and more obscure explanation in terms of his theory of the 'transcendental ideality of space and time', so that the difference between a left hand and a right hand could be captured only by intuition.)

Graham Nerlich has neatly modified Kant's original argument.[13] We know of geometrical spaces that are different in their topology from ordinary Euclidean space. For example the surface of a sphere is a finite but unbounded space. That of a torus is also finite but unbounded but it cannot be continuously deformed into the surface of a sphere. We can conceive of spaces with three or more dimensions which are analogues of the surface of a sphere or a torus. The topological properties are deeper properties of a space than are its metrical ones. Thus the surface of a cricket ball, which is spherical, and a rugby football, which is roughly ellipsoidal, are topologically the same. Now consider another sort of topological property which is exhibited by a so-called Möbius strip. You make a Möbius strip by taking a rectangular strip of paper and twisting it through 180° and then joining the ends. Such a surface has only one side. (Another two-dimensional surface with this property is the so-called Klein bottle, which is a better example because it has no edges. But I here content myself with the more easily described Möbius strip.) A Möbius strip has only one side. Think of the paper as infinitely thin, a true surface, and with an infinitely thin asymmetrical letter such as 'B' on it, as well as a mirror image of the 'B'. You could slide the mirror image along the Möbius strip to coincide with the original 'B'. The 'B' and its mirror image are not enantiomorphs in a space like that of the Möbius strip. Yet if you had joined the ends of the strip together *without* the 180° twist, the 'B' and its mirror image would have been enantiomorphs. This illustrates the fact that whether something is an enantiomorph or not depends on the global topological properties of the space in which it exists. Nerlich sees in this the deeper lesson of Kant's example. He modifies Kant's example by replacing his assumption that a hand must be determinately left or right by the assumption that it must be determinately an enantiomorph or a homomorph, and this depends on the global topology of the space it is in. (Similarly it depends on dimensionality. A 'B' and its mirror image are homomorphic in three-dimensional Euclidean space. A hand is homomorphic in four dimensions.) Moreover, examples could be devised and the argument modified to take account of the theory of relativity, so as to suggest an absolute theory not of space but of *space-time*.[14]

Of course since the special theory of relativity it has become clear that lengths and periods of time are relative to frames of reference, and this has misled some philosophers into thinking that the theory of relativity supports a relational theory. However, recall the example of slicing a sausage. The ability to get either circular or elliptical slices does not support a relational theory of sausages, or even, in a sense, of the sausage slices themselves. Similarly, special relativity is perfectly compatible with an absolute theory of *space-time*. In space-time, invariance reasserts itself – the interval between events in space-time is invariant with respect to frame of reference. With respect to the general theory of relativity, an absolute theory of space-time seems rather natural. Einstein's theory predicted a structure of space-time even in the absence of matter. Even if theorists succeed in defending Mach's principle by showing that all the structure of space-time could be *accounted for* by the distribution of mass-energy in the universe, it will still be an open question as to whether an analytic *reduction* of the concept of space-time to those of matter and energy and their relations would be possible.

The general theory of relativity explains gravitation geometrically. The space-time of general relativity is one of variable curvature. Curvature can be defined intrinsically – one need not visualise it as occurring in a space of higher dimension, as one normally visualises the curvature of the surface of a sphere. For example on the surface of a sphere the circumference of a circle will not be equal to 2π times its radius, as is the case on a Euclidean plane. In space-time the analogue of a straight line is called a *geodesic*. A time-like geodesic is not the shortest distance (or interval) between two points but is the greatest. This can be seen from the minus signs in the expression for the metric. This should be evident from the discussion of Minkowski space given earlier, though of course the space-time metric of general relativity is more complicated, because of the variable curvature. Then in general relativity gravitation is explained by the idea that the world line of a freely falling particle is a geodesic. For example if space-time were flat the world line of the earth in its elliptical motion round the sun would be a helix, but because of the variable curvature it is a geodesic. It can be seen that this idea has some analogy to Newton's first law of motion, that a body not acted on by a force travels in a straight line, and it gives a very appealing account of gravitational force, which in a sense it explains away. Einstein spent much effort in trying to develop a unified field theory which would also explain electromagnetic force in a similarly geometrical way. In recent times 'grand unified theories' are being developed. These attempt to explain not only the electromagnetic force but also the weak and strong interaction forces. These theories are not completely geometrical but postulate gauge fields that ascribe a non-geometrical property to each point of space-time. Nevertheless they are equally congenial to an absolute theory of space-time. Attempts to unify the above three forces with the theory of gravitation (theories of 'supergravity') are currently under investigation. More recent theories of 'supergravity' aim to unify gravity and the other three forces in a purely geometrical way.

Objections to believing in space-time as an entity have stemmed from a positivist philosophy (characteristic of Mach) according to which all theoretical concepts must be defined in terms of observational ones (or else be regarded merely instrumentally as useful dodges for making predictions). More recent philosophy has exposed the limitations of this theory of meaning. We do not directly observe electrons or neutrons, but postulate them hypothetico-deductively. Why should we not do the same with space-time points? Even so, many philosophers who accept this criticism of positivism nevertheless regard space-time points as suspect because their principle of individuation seems obscure. Thus the issue between absolute and relational theories is still controversial.

Some philosophers have developed relational theories of time or of space-time in which the fundamental relation is the causal one. Others think that causality is more obscure than the geometrical notions it is meant to elucidate.

Space-time apparently has four dimensions – three space-like and one time-like. And so on the macroscopic level it certainly has. The recent theories of supergravity have postulated eleven dimensions, but the extra seven dimensions are extremely small-scale things. Consider a long thin tube in three-dimensional space. Macroscopically we can think of this tube as a line, but in fact it is a two-dimensional surface. Each 'point' on the line viewed macroscopically is really a circle in three-dimensional space. In this example intuition is easy because we visualise a three-dimensional space in which the two-dimensional space is embedded. Mathematically this intuition can be dropped because n-dimensional spaces can be defined 'from within' without the necessity for supposing an $(n+1)$-dimensional embedding space. Similarly in the 11-dimensional space-time of supergravity each point of four-dimensional space-time is really a minute but unbounded seven-dimensional space (much as the surface of a sphere is finite but unbounded). One can think of space-time as a foam-like structure. Such a theory is believed to provide hope for the complete geometrisation of fundamental physics.[15]

Continuity, discreteness and Żeno's paradoxes

Questions of continuity and discreteness of course arose in the fifth century BC with the celebrated paradoxes of Zeno of Elea. The solution of many of his paradoxes requires mathematical insights not available in ancient times. Thus consider Zeno's paradox of extension. Space is made up of infinitely many unextended points. How can even infinitely many such zeros add up to make the non-zero extensions of line segments or areas or volumes? Modern measure theory provides the answer.[16] According to this theory, points, or even denumerably infinite sets of them, have measure zero. To get a set of points of greater measure we need a set with the cardinality of the real numbers. As Georg Cantor had shown, though the rational numbers can be put in one–one correspondence with the integers, and though the points of an n-dimensional space can be put in one–one correspondence with the points on a line, there are more real numbers, or points on a line, than there are integers or rational numbers. Cantor's theory does not allow us to define dimension, because there are no more points in an $(n+1)$-dimensional space than there are in a 1-dimensional space or line segment. However, modern topology provides a theory of dimension which generalises our ordinary observation that in Euclidean space a point divides a line, a line divides an area, and an area divides a volume. Thus the set of rational points on a line is of zero dimension since not even a point is needed to divide it into two parts. The theory can deal with spaces whose dimensionality can vary locally from point to point.

Zeno's paradox of Achilles and the Tortoise will be more familiar to many readers. To catch the tortoise Achilles at point P_0 needs to go to the tortoise's position P_1. But when he gets there the tortoise is further on, at P_2. And so on. How does Achilles catch the tortoise? To catch the tortoise Achilles has to traverse infinitely many line segments. Aristotle saw that the time taken to catch the tortoise is a series of ever diminishing intervals, but uneasiness can persist if it is thought that Achilles has to do infinitely many acts. The trouble is that we think that an act must take at least some minimum time. That is so with what we ordinarily call 'acts', but it does not, on usual assumptions of continuity, apply to traversings of line segments. The situation is more easily grasped by reference to Zeno's paradox of the race course. To go a mile you have to go half way, then three-quarters of the way, then seven-eighths of the way, and so on. If you keep going in the same direction and have passed *all* the points 1/2, 3/4, 7/8, 15/16 ... you *ipso facto* have reached the point 1. Similarly, it might be asked, as in one part of Zeno's paradox of the dichotomy, how you get started, because you have to pass the points ... 1/16, 1/8, 1/4, 1/2, 1. The supposed contradiction may arise through both (falsely) believing that there is a first point you have to pass and also (truly) that there is no first point. A similar sort of fallacious argument was put forward by Kant in his first antinomy when he argued that the world could not have had a beginning in time. (He also had an argument that the world could not have lasted for an infinite time, because at any moment an infinity would have elapsed. This uneasiness about an infinite past, which is not felt about an infinite future, seems to be connected with confusion about the 'flow' of time.) It is instructive to look at the paradoxes of Achilles and the Tortoise and of the race course by thinking of velocities as relative inclinations of tangents to world lines in space-time. The feeling of possible paradox is much harder to recapture.

Zeno's argument concerning rows of moving bodies, sometimes called the paradox of the stadium, will not be discussed here. This paradox is concerned to deny that space could be discrete, with shortest intervals. In his paradox of the flying arrow, he argued against the possibility of motion, since at any instant the flying arrow is within a definite part of space, whereas, if it were moving, it would, he thought, have to occupy a space larger than itself. According to modern theories the speed of the arrow has to be defined as the limit of decreasing quotients of distance traversed by time taken to traverse these distances. So motion is not something an arrow could have if it existed for only a single instant. This is very obvious if one looks at the space-time picture – a point in space-time could not have an inclination to a line in space-time. However, there is also a non-standard way of looking at the matter. When the calculus was first developed by Newton and Leibniz, a velocity was thought of as the quotient of one infinitesimal by another. For this reason the calculus was criticised by Berkeley in his work *The analyst* as being contradictory, though useful. Berkeley rightly argued that the notion of an infinitesimal as being both of no magnitude and yet of some magnitude was absurd. The calculus (more properly the branch of mathematics called analysis, which deals with infinite sets of numbers and sets of these) was put on a sound basis by Cauchy, Dedekind and others in the nineteenth century, so that no appeal to infinitesimals was needed. However in recent times the mathematician Abraham Robinson has developed non-standard analysis, in which he has used the resources of modern logic and model theory to make the theory of infinitesimals respectable. This might be of help to those who wish to revive the notion of motion as definable without mentioning finite segments of space and time.

It should be evident that the topic of this chapter is

371

one in which philosophy, mathematics and physics are inextricably connected with one another.

Notes

(An author's name followed by a number in square brackets refers to the book or article which has that number in the bibliography.)

1. H. Minkowski, 'Space and time' in Albert Einstein *et al.*, *The principle of relativity* (Dover, New York, 1923).

2. Isaac Newton, *Mathematical principles of natural philosophy and his system of the world* (Florian Cajori edition, University of California Press, Berkeley, California, 1934), Scholium to the Definitions.

3. McTaggart [14], [13], Ch. 33. For a sympathetic account of McTaggart's argument, see Peter Geach, *Truth, love, and immortality* (Hutchinson, London, 1979), Ch. 7.

4. As by Donald Davidson, *Inquiries into truth and interpretation* (Clarendon Press, Oxford, 1984), Essay 4.

5. See J.J.C. Smart, 'Time and becoming' in Peter Van Inwagen (ed.), *Time and cause* (Reidel, Dordrecht, 1980), pp. 3–15, especially pp. 13–14.

6. Reichenbach [24].

7. See A.N. Prior, *Papers in logic and ethics* (Duckworth, London, 1976), Ch. 8, especially p. 84, and George N. Schlesinger, *Aspects of time* (Hackett, Indianapolis, 1980), pp. 34–8.

8. Jeremy Butterfield, 'Seeing the present', *Mind*, 93 (1984), pp. 161–76.

9. See P.T. Geach, *Providence and evil* (Cambridge University Press, Cambridge, 1977), pp. 52–3. Thus he finds the B-theory argument in the text above as unconvincing and even derisory.

10. See Alexander [25].

11. Ernst Mach, *The science of mechanics*, 6th English edn (Open Court, La Salle, Illinois, 1960), p. 284.

12. In *Selected pre-critical writings and correspondence with Beck*, translated and introduced by G.B. Kerferd and D.E. Walford, with a contribution by P.G. Lucas (Manchester University Press, Manchester, 1968).

13. Graham Nerlich, *The shape of space* (Cambridge University Press, Cambridge, 1976), Ch. 2.

14. For this see Chris Mortensen and Graham Nerlich, 'Spacetime and handedness', *Ratio*, 25 (1983), pp. 1–13.

15. On grand unified theories and theories of supergravity see P.C.W. Davies, *Superforce* (Heinemann, London, 1984).

16. See Grünbaum [28], p. 89.

Bibliography

For lucid and attractively written introductions to the topics of this chapter, it is still hard to improve on the writings of Sir Arthur Eddington, even though they date from sixty or seventy years ago, and some of their underlying philosophical ideas are no longer generally accepted. See, for example, his

[1] *Space, time and gravitation* (Cambridge University Press, Cambridge, 1920, reissued by Harper, New York, 1959) or

[2] *The nature of the physical world* (Cambridge University Press, Cambridge, 1928, with various reprints).

There are also some useful edited collections of readings drawn from some of the classic analyses of the problems raised by the concepts of space and time; for example

[3] J.J.C. Smart (ed.), *Problems of space and time* (Macmillan, New York, 1964).

[4] R.M. Gale (ed.), *The philosophy of time* (Anchor Books, New York, 1967, and Macmillan, London, 1968).

[5] M. Čapek (ed.), *The concepts of space and time* (vol. XXII of Boston Studies in the Philosophy of Science, Reidel, Dordrecht, 1976). Also

[6] M. Jammer, *Concepts of space* (Harper, New York, 1960) is a valuable historical study; and good introductions to the whole field of discussion, as well as arguments in defence of particular standpoints, are to be found in

[7] G. Nerlich, *The shape of space* (Cambridge University Press, Cambridge, 1976) and

[8] D.H. Mellor, *Real time* (Cambridge University Press, Cambridge, 1980) which derives from a series of broadcast talks and is commendably clear.

From among many other, perhaps rather more demanding works, written from differing standpoints, we may notice

[9] H. Reichenbach, *The philosophy of space and time* (Dover Publications, New York, 1958).

[10] A. Grünbaum, *Philosophical problems of space and time* (first published 1963, new, enlarged edition, vol. XII in Boston Studies in the Philosophy of Science, Reidel, Dordrecht, 1973) – a somewhat formidable but very comprehensive work.

[11] R. Swinburne, *Space and time* (Macmillan, London, 1968), and

[12] J.R. Lucas, *A treatise on time and space* (Macmillan, London, 1973).

McTaggart's argument for the unreality of time is set out in his

[13] *The nature of existence*, vol. II, ed. C.D. Broad (2 vols, Cambridge University Press, Cambridge, 1921 and 1927), Ch. 33, and his

[14] *Philosophical studies*, ed. S.V. Keeling (Arnold, London, 1934), Ch. 5.

For critical commentary see, for example,

[15] C.D. Broad, *Examination of McTaggart's philosophy* (2 vols, Cambridge University Press, Cambridge, 1933 and 1938), vol. II, and also, for a more sympathetic treatment,

[16] P.T. Geach, *Truth, love and immortality* (Hutchinson, London, 1979).

Regarding rival theories of the relations of past, present and future, and the role of tenses in language, we should notice an influential work by W.V. Quine,

[17] *Word and object* (MIT Press, Cambridge, Massachusetts, 1960); also

[18] W. Sellars, *Time and the world order*, Minnesota Studies in the Philosophy of Science, ed. H. Feigl and G. Maxwell (University of Minnesota Press, Minneapolis, 1962), pp. 527–616, which attempts to develop the different theories through a kind of dialectical interaction.

[19] R.M. Gale, *The language of time* (Routledge and Kegan Paul, London, 1968), and

[20] L.N. Oaklander, *Temporal relations and temporal becoming, a defence of a Russellian*

theory of time (University Press of America, Lanham, Maryland, 1984). This refers us back to (among other writings of Bertrand Russell) a paper entitled

[21] 'On the experience of time', *Monist*, vol. 25 (1915), pp. 212–33.

We should notice also, in this connection, another excellent paper of much later date,

[22] J. Butterfield, 'Seeing the present', *Mind*, vol. 93 (1984), pp. 161–76.

On the question of the 'Direction of time', the best discussions available are probably those of Grünbaum, in [10] above, and, for those with a modicum of mathematical knowledge,

[23] P.C.W. Davies, *Physics of time asymmetry* (Surrey University Press, Guildford, 1974). Also, an earlier exploration of the same topic:

[24] H. Reichenbach, *The direction of time* (University of California Press, Berkeley, 1956).

On the issue between absolute and relative ideas of space and time, in addition to discussions in the general works mentioned above, we may note some modern editions of classic contributions to the debate. For example,

[25] H.G. Alexander (ed.), *The Leibniz–Clarke correspondence, together with extracts from Newton's Principia and Optics* (Manchester University Press, Manchester, 1956).

[26] I. Kant, *Selected pre-critical writings and correspondence with Beck*, trans. and introduced by G.B. Kerferd and D.E. Walford, with a contribution by P.G. Lucas (Manchester University Press, Manchester, 1968).

[27] E. Mach, *The science of mechanics* (first published 1883, English trans. by T. McCormack, 6th edn, Open Court, La Salle, Illinois, 1960).

Finally, regarding the perennially interesting paradoxes of Zeno, and similar problems, there are useful analyses of these in

[28] A. Grünbaum, *Modern science and Zeno's paradoxes* (Wesleyan University Press, Middletown, Connecticut, 1967).

[29] W.C. Salmon (ed.), *Zeno's paradoxes* (Bobbs-Merrill, Indianapolis, 1970) and

[30] W.C. Salmon, *Space, time and motion* (Dickenson, Encino, California, 1975).

This bibliography is largely based on suggestions kindly provided by the author.

T.E.B.

Part D: Philosophy of Mind

Introduction

Parts B and C have covered branches of philosophy that are concerned primarily with our knowledge of the external world. We now turn to what is often called 'the inner world'. In using this term in the Introduction to Part B, I said that I would take it to mean that of which the human mind is aware when it scrutinises itself, together with the activities of self-scrutiny themselves. In other words, to talk of the inner world is (for example) to talk of acts of perception, reasoning, introspection, imagination, memory and will; it is also to talk of such states as intelligence, sensitivity, ambition and determination. All these are the concern of that branch of philosophy which is called 'the philosophy of mind'. But in what precise way is it concerned with them?

Some philosophers draw a sharp distinction between the philosophy of mind and the science of psychology. Psychologists, they would say, are concerned with the making of empirical inquiries into the nature of mind; their methods are those of observation and experiment. Philosophers, on the other hand, are concerned with the language that we use when we talk about mental acts and states. Such philosophers are apt to say that they are concerned, for example, with *what it is to say that* someone is thinking, or that someone is intelligent. It should be stressed that such linguistic inquiries are not always undertaken simply for the sake of clarification. It was pointed out in the first chapter that some philosophers see philosophical analysis as, in essence, the solution of puzzles. Those who belong to this school of thought would say that the task of the philosophy of mind is to sort out the problems that arise when one way of talking about human beings (for example, in physico–chemical terms) seems to clash with other ways of talking, and above all with our unsophisticated ways of talking about mental acts and states.

Such is the view of the philosophy of mind taken by some philosophers – roughly speaking, those who work within a broadly Wittgensteinian conception of philosophy (cf. Chapter 1, pp. 7–11). However, other philosophers take a different view of the philosophy of mind. They say that, although the philosopher works at a conceptual level, his work cannot be sharply separated from the processes of scientific and empirical inquiry. Those who take this view see themselves as engaged in a wide-ranging enterprise (often called 'cognitive science') which draws on the results of psychology, neurophysiology and (more recently) computer science, in order to construct an intelligible account of the human mind and its workings.

The first three chapters of Part D (Chapters 17 to 19) are devoted to philosophical problems about the relations between mind and body. Although I have drawn a distinction between the external world and the inner world, only a few philosophers (and probably no 'plain men') would want to maintain that the two worlds have no effect on each other. Our bodies belong to the external world, and the relations between our bodies and our minds are thought to be, to say the least, close. But just how are minds and bodies related? Philosophers have produced many theories in answer to this question. In classifying them, I have distinguished between those theories which are 'reductionist' and those which are 'non-reductionist'. In philosophy, the term 'reduction' has more than one sense (cf. Chapter 18, pp. 403–4). However, one may say that what is central to the notion of reduction is the idea of being able to replace sentences which are (or seem to be) about entities of one kind by sentences about entities of another kind. Not only is such replacement held to involve no loss of truth, but it is also claimed that the replacing sentences are in some way superior to those replaced. All this is very general; I must now specify more exactly how I use the term 'reductionist' when I classify theories of mind–matter relations. To put the matter in a few words: I take a 'reductionist' theory to be a 'nothing but' theory. In political theory, for example, a reductionist theory of the state would be one which says that talk about states is nothing but talk about the individuals who constitute them. Now, when I speak of a reductionist theory of mind–matter relations, I shall refer to the view that talk about minds is, in some way or other, nothing but talk about matter. (I should add that there have been reductionist theories which argued in the other direction, saying that talk about matter is reducible to talk about mind. But such 'idealist' theories have few adherents at present.) A 'non-reductionist' theory of mind–matter relations is, as may be expected, one which is incompatible with reductionist theories. However, there is a complication to be noted here. Although a non-reductionist theory (as I understand the term) denies that our language about minds can be reduced to our language about matter, it need not deny that the two languages are different ways of talking about something more fundamental. It is for this reason that I count as 'non-reductionist' the theory known as 'neutral monism', which asserts that to talk of 'minds' and 'bodies' is to group in different ways entities no one of which is either material or mental. Non-reductionist theories will be discussed first, in Chapter 17. The reason for giving them priority is that one non-reductionist theory, dualism of a kind that is ascribed to Descartes, has had great historical influence, and some of the important reductionist theories of this century (for example, that defended by Gilbert Ryle) have been advanced as answers to dualism. Reductionist theories will be discussed in Chapters 18 and 19, the second of these being devoted to a view which has been much discussed in this century – the theory, or group of theories, known as 'behaviourism'.

The distinction between reductionist and non-reductionist theories of the mind serves to mark out some familiar battle-lines in philosophy. Recently, however, a new theory has been propounded, whose supporters argue that it bypasses the old disputes. This is the theory known as 'functionalism'. The theory is much influenced by recent developments in computer science, and can most easily be explained in terms of the language of that science. The functionalist tells us not to worry about the way in which the 'hardware' of the thinking and percipient being is constructed; rather, we are to concentrate on the 'software', the information-processing aspect. We should ask ourselves what kind of organisational principles – what 'program' – must govern the human system if it is to process various inputs effectively and produce appropriate outputs. Because functionalism straddles, as it were, the battle-lines between reductionism and non-reductionism, it finds a place here both in Chapter 17, which discusses non-reductionist theories, and Chapter 18, which discusses some reductionist theories.

In Chapter 20 we move from questions about the relations between mind and body to questions about personal identity. For example, one finds it natural to say such things as 'I am thinking about philosophical problems today' and also 'I was thinking about such problems yesterday.' But what is it to say that the same 'I' is involved? Some philosophers (of whom Locke is the classical example) have seen personal identity as lying in a certain sort of relation between thoughts. Others see personal identity as bodily identity; still others see it, more specifically, as brain-identity. All these solutions have their difficulties, and these are discussed in Chapter 20.

Books on the philosophy of mind often include, quite justifiably, accounts of perception and of memory. These topics have already been discussed in Chapters 7 and 8, and need no separate treatment in this part of the encyclopaedia. However, there is another subject belonging to the philosophy of mind which has not yet been discussed. This is a topic which is not only important in its own right, but which also provides a link between the philosophy of mind and moral philosophy, to which the next part of the encyclopaedia is devoted. The topic in question is the nature of the will. Human beings are not just contemplative; we do not just observe and think about reality, as if we were merely spectators in a theatre; we also *do* things, in the sense that we act both on the environment and on ourselves. Many of the things that we do have a distinctive feature, which we indicate by saying that the acts in question are *voluntary* acts. Such acts have been, and still are, often thought of as the work of a special faculty called 'the will', and the concept of such a faculty is explored in Chapter 21. Another important problem about the will concerns not so much the way in which the term 'will' is to be understood, as something that we say about the will and its acts. We are apt to say that an act is voluntary when it is one that we were not compelled to do; when, in other words, we could have done otherwise. For many centuries, philosophers have debated whether this is so; these debates have been regarded as being about the question, 'Is the will free?' This has been a problem for the theologian, in that God's foreknowledge and predestination seem to leave no room for his creatures to act freely. In modern times the debate has taken a different form, in that the main threat to freedom now seems to be posed by the natural sciences. For if it is possible for the scientist to find necessary laws that govern all human actions, then how can we ever do anything other than what we actually do? These problems, and answers that have been offered to them, are discussed in Chapter 22.

G.H.R.P.

17 | Mind and Body: Non-reductionist Theories

A.R. Lacey

One of the main branches of metaphysics is ontology, literally 'the study of what there is'. Most philosophers have held that there are many things, and even those who deny this – monists of an extreme kind – have had to allow that there appear to be many things. But how many? Or to make the question just a little easier, how many kinds of things? Well, there are cabbages and kings, memory and muchness, colours and sounds, letters and words, numbers, theories, laws, duties, societies, days of the week, and the American Constitution, to go no further. How can we make sense of such a chaos? One way would be this. First we follow Aristotle in distinguishing substances, where this means things that can exist in their own right, from other things, which can't. Colours can exist only because there are coloured objects, and memory only because there are animals, or possibly angels, so we shall not include colours and memory in our list. Then we might bring in time and space to help us. Things that exist in time, cabbages and kings, for instance, seem to be about as different as they could be from things which don't, like the number ten, or beauty. The most obvious difference is that these latter things are immune to change, in the radical sense that it is nonsense to talk of them changing, not just that they are particularly tough and resistant, even permanently resistant. Then we might divide the things that exist in time into those that occupy space and those that either don't or do so only derivatively, by being associated with something that does. There seems to be one obvious candidate for being something that endures through time but does not directly occupy space, namely minds.

This scheme is not free from difficulties. It is less neat and tidy than it looks, as we can see when we need to distinguish between directly and indirectly occupying space. And we might wonder what to do with squares and triangles – not piazzas and musical instruments, but the kind

381

geometers talk about: in a way they are spatial, but one can hardly ask where in space they are. Even worse is the position of God, if He is both a mind and timeless – but that problem belongs to another chapter. Finally, are there things that are spatial but not temporal? Perhaps our geometrical things? But, as we have just seen, they are not exactly 'in space' – not in real space. Points might seem to qualify. But points in real space surely endure throughout time.

However, the scheme or something like it has been quite important historically. The German logician G. Frege (1848–1925), in 'The thought: a logical inquiry',[1] divided things into three kinds, the material, the spiritual, and what he called simply the 'third realm', which included things like numbers and properties and propositions – things which are plainly timeless as well as non-spatial.

For Frege the three realms were ontologically on a level, but the third realm owes its origins to Plato, for whom it was very much the first realm, containing his 'Forms' or 'Ideas' ('Idea' is a transliteration of a Greek word, which did not have the mental connotations of the modern 'idea'). Plato contrasted his Forms mainly with material objects. Just how much reality he allowed to these is controversial, but he said rather less about the remaining class, minds or souls. They can change and so are in time, which the Forms may not be (*Timaeus*, 37c–8b), but at one point (*Phaedo*, 78bff) he explicitly bases an argument for the immortality of the soul on the claim that the soul is more 'akin' to the Forms than to ordinary objects; his main ground for this is that the soul 'knows' the Forms, while material objects are known by the senses.

With Descartes it is rather the third realm that gets comparatively neglected, while he contrasts his two kinds of substance, material substance, which is distinguished by being extended in space, and spiritual substances, or souls, which are distinguished by being things that 'think'. Aristotle took more seriously than Plato the problem of saying just how the soul is related to the body, but it is from Descartes that modern discussions of the 'mind–body problem' mainly take their origin.

Before going on, a word about souls and minds. 'Mind' sounds more intellectual than 'soul', which suggests rather certain theological doctrines or something emotional ('soulful', 'heart and soul'). But 'soul' is the stock translation for the Greek *psyche* and also for the French *âme* and Latin *anima* as they occur in Descartes, etc. For Christianity souls are higher in the scale of things than minds, in so far as they differ: it is the spiritual and not the intellectual part of one that is most important and most likely to survive death. For the Greeks on the other hand mind or reason (*nous* in Greek) is the highest part of the soul: for Aristotle only *nous* has any chance of being immortal, while even plants have *psyche*. For the Greeks, and often for the seventeenth century, 'soul' is the general word for what is contrasted with the body, but in modern discussions 'mind' has become rather broader than the Greek *nous*, and we usually talk now of the 'mind–body problem' for what the Greeks would call, if they called it anything, the 'soul–body problem'.[2] But I will use whichever comes most naturally in the context.

In this chapter we are concerned with the first two items of my original list of three, and in particular with the second. We are not concerned with the 'third realm', and only with the first, the material world, as a foil for discussing the second, the mind.

But is the mind a second or separate item at all? The view that it is, and that in human beings at any rate, if not in other animals, there are two things, a mind and a body, is known as dualism. This is clearly a non-reductionist view,[3] since if there really are two things neither of them is being reduced to the other. One reductionist view would say that minds are somehow to be reduced to, or analysed in terms of, bodies, or that mental phenomena are to be analysed in terms of physical phenomena. The opposite reductionist view would say that bodies or physical phenomena are to be analysed in terms of minds or mental phenomena. But these views are not quite symmetrical, since the sort of bodies one might try to reduce minds to are only some among bodies – human or perhaps animal bodies, and not material objects in general, most of which are irrelevant. But a view that reduced bodies to minds would hardly stop at animal bodies; it would apply to all material objects, for it would seem absurdly arbitrary to say that kings, but not cabbages, were a totally different sort of thing from what they appeared to be, although they both equally register on weighing machines. No one, so far as I know, has ever held such a view, and the more general view that reduces all physical phenomena to minds or mental phenomena, in particular to ideas, is called idealism and really belongs to general metaphysics rather than to philosophy of mind. The parallel metaphysical version of the first reductionist view would be one that reduced all spirits, disembodied angels as well as human minds, to matter or material phenomena. This is materialism, and it is indeed a general metaphysical doctrine, saying that there are no denizens of the second of our three realms. But since the existence of disembodied spirits is, to say the least, less obvious than that of presumably non-mental things like cabbages, there is less urge to separate materialism as a general metaphysical doctrine from materialism as a theory in the philosophy of mind (which belongs in the next chapter).

There are other non-reductionist views, as we shall see, but dualism has been popular at least since Plato, so let us start with it.

I say 'since Plato' because I am thinking of philosophers. But in a way dualism is far older than Plato. Way back in Homer's *Odyssey*, almost the earliest European literature, Odysseus goes down to Hades and meets the ghosts or spirits of the dead. One could go even further back. The earliest known book, I believe, is the Egyptian Book of the Dead, written about 4000 BC, and that too, as its name suggests, envisages some sort of survival of death. In fact the idea that a person is, or at least can be, something distinct from his body and capable of living independently of it, even if in a rather shadowy and half-hearted way, evidently has a great intuitive appeal, perhaps encouraged by the phenomenon of dreaming.

What distinguishes philosophical dualism from these popular beliefs is that the soul becomes something fundamentally different in kind from the body. In popular myths, etc., the soul is simply a duplicate of the person, perhaps rather small, frail and wraithlike, but recognisable to his friends if they happen to meet him. In Plato all this is quite changed – or at least is well on the way to radically changing. I said earlier that Plato paid more attention to contrasting the material and abstract realms than to discussing the status of the soul. But though he never succeeded very well in integrating the soul into his favourite dualism, he left no doubt that the soul was meant to be something quite different from the body – something that existed in time but had no extension in space. It could enter into bodies, one after another, but was only really at home when it was disembodied, when it somehow managed to enter as a rather alien guest into the timeless (if it was so) world of Forms. But Plato, like Aristotle, never quite managed to link the rational soul or intellect with that part of the soul which is more obviously connected with the body. The *Phaedo*, a relatively early work which portrays Socrates in his death cell, is explicitly devoted to proving that the soul is immortal. At one point (94b–5a) Socrates (the main speaker) is challenged by a view that the soul is merely a fitting together or 'harmony' of parts of the body. The way Socrates rejects this is by saying the soul opposes the body, pulling it towards abstention when there is hunger or thirst in the body, warning and admonishing the body, and addressing the various passions as one entity might address a different entity. What is strange about this is that the bodily desires, like hunger, are treated as though they were bodily phenomena; yet surely desires, however much they may *refer* to the body, are themselves psychological phenomena, and must belong in the soul, if the soul is distinct from the body. A desire, one would think, can no more belong in my body than in the chair I am sitting on. In a later dialogue, the *Philebus* (35cd) Plato agrees. Thirst, he says, is not a bodily thing, but belongs to the soul, because it draws us towards the opposite of the (parched) state of the body, and does so because of our memory of that opposite state. Whatever we may think of this last point, it is now thirst, not just the soul, that draws us, and it doesn't oppose the body but draws *us* (the rest of the soul?) towards an opposite state of the body, i.e. towards a state of affairs where the body is in an opposite (unparched) state.

Plato, however, treats these subjects rather episodically and *en passant*. It is with Descartes that dualism first gets a sustained philosophical treatment. This may seem surprising at first, for were not the intervening centuries the hey-day of Christianity, with its fundamental emphasis on the soul's immortality? Yes, but for Catholic Christianity, in the Middle Ages as today, immortality involves having a body, be it one's original body or a new one. This certainly raises problems, but they concern topics like personal identity rather than this philosophical dualism, which insists that the soul or mind is a separate non-material substance which could exist independently of any body, whether or not it ever does.

For Descartes then (at least on the commonest interpretation) the soul, and indeed the self or person, is a spiritual substance which inhabits a body. His main reason for holding this is bound up with the basic method of his philosophy, which is to start from something he can take to be absolutely certain and move outwards from there, taking to be true what he can 'clearly and distinctly' see to be so. What he does start from is his famous *Cogito*: 'I think, therefore I am.' But what am I? Well, a being that thinks, whatever else it does. I can, at a pinch, doubt that I have a body, for might I not be dreaming, so that the body I seem to be aware of would be as unreal as everything else around me? But I cannot doubt that I think, because doubting is itself a mode of thinking: I doubt, therefore I am. The merits of the argument have been much disputed. But our real concern now is the position Descartes offers us, however he got there.

At first I suppose dualism sounds quite attractive. After all I *am* very different from the chair I am sitting on, and the main difference is that I am conscious. My body, like the chair, is extended; but I can listen to some music, or plan my next holiday, or work at a mathematical problem, without these activities having anything to do with how big I am or what shape I am. No doubt I need a brain to do such things – but that is simply what the scientists tell me, not something intrinsically obvious from the situation itself. I only know at second hand that I have a brain at all. Consciousness is what distinguishes men and animals from anything else, and I don't need to be extended to be conscious, so I don't need a body.

I think this argument does appeal to some deep intuition in us; but it has its difficulties. For one thing have I not selected my examples rather carefully? Do I not need to be extended to feel a pain in my foot, and at least to be located to view a landscape? For I must view it from a certain viewpoint; to view it from no viewpoint would be quite unlike any experience we actually do have, even if the idea is intelligible.

Yes, it may be said, but it is a mere contingency that I have these latter experiences at all. No doubt they complicate things, but the essence of consciousness is sufficiently given by experiences of the former kind. However, we might counterattack here. How can I plan my next holiday unless I at least know what it is like to go on a holiday, and that is a physical enough undertaking? And my mathematical problem had better not be in geometry, for how could I know about geometry if I had no conception of space, and what conception of space could I have if I had had no spatial experience? Some philosophers (Bergson, for instance) have said that any discrete plurality at all, even of the kind which underlies arithmetic, is ultimately spatial in nature. Also much thought involves language, and so symbols, and would I not need a body at least to produce symbols if not to understand them?

I will not claim that no experience could be had by an unextended and unlocated mind. The musical example raises some interesting questions about whether we can make sense of the idea of a purely auditory world (see P.F. Strawson, *Individuals*).[4] But we do have bodies in fact, and without them not only would our experience be vastly impoverished but much of it would be quite different in nature. Supposing for instance that we could get over the difficulty about needing a viewpoint in imagining things, how without a body would we distinguish between merely imagining something and actually perceiving it? (Not by saying the former is voluntary – it often isn't.) Could a spirit be even *located* in space (and so perhaps acquire spatial concepts) without being solid enough to join in physical causal sequences?

Not all of these objections would rule out disembodied existence altogether. As Strawson has pointed out,[5] it is easier to make sense of a spirit *becoming* disembodied after having been embodied than to make sense of one that had never been embodied at all; the former spirit could at least have acquired a suitable set of concepts. But the point is that any experience remotely like our own does involve having a body.

The next question then is: what is it for either a mind or a person to 'have' a body? How are the mind and the body related, and is the person identical with the mind, or is it somehow identical with both the mind and the body together? If you play tennis, does your mind play tennis? Or your body? Or both? Does your mind use your body to play tennis, as you might use a horse to play polo? For that matter, do *you* use your body to play tennis – and your mind to do mathematics perhaps? Certainly you can use yo. arm to hold the racket, and we do talk, though only half seriously I think, of 'using your brain'. Again I weigh nine stone or so, but my mind doesn't, nor does it use my body to do so, nor do so 'with' my body, and neither do I.

In most of the last paragraph I have been appealing to linguistic intuitions, to our feeling that it sounds absurd to say certain things. This can be a useful weapon, but it can also be a dangerous one, and we mustn't let ourselves be bamboozled by it when we shouldn't. Some remarks, like 'Tuesday is blue' or 'I stay asleep more quickly than most people,' sound absurd because we have no idea how they could be true or false, unless taken in metaphorical or poetic senses. They embody what G. Ryle (cf. Chapter 19, pp. 430–9) called 'category mistakes', since they try to force together ideas in categories that just don't go together. But other remarks sound absurd because we would never have occasion to make them, or because they would carry misleading suggestions, like 'I believe there is some air in this room' (I do indeed – but why choose a phrase that suggests doubt?), or 'I have not stopped beating my wife' (well, I never started, so how could I?).

The oddness of 'My mind uses my body to play tennis' may suggest then that it is radically false or meaningless, but it doesn't prove it. We must know why it sounds odd. A dualist might say the oddness is of the second kind mentioned above: what else could his mind use, so why bother to say it? Indeed he might go further. A user, it seems plausible to say, must be distinct from what is used; so 'He used himself as a decoy to draw the enemy's fire' *must* mean 'His mind used his body . . .', or at the very least 'He, being more than his body, used his body, as one might use one's arm, . . .'

But instead of asking further just how distinct user and used must be, let us ask how connected they must be. If the mind is so totally different from the body as to have nothing in common with it, how can it use it at all, or affect it in any other way? And if the mind does have something in common with the body after all, then what?

The whole spirit of dualism is to insist that mind is totally different in nature from body, however intimately they might somehow be linked. Descartes himself was well aware of this problem, if only because one of his correspondents, Princess Elizabeth of Bohemia, left him in no doubt about it. But he has left us (as he left her) in considerable doubt about what his answer to it is. Article 34 of Part I of his treatise *The passions of the soul* bears the promising title 'How the soul and body act on one another'. But what it actually tells us is how the pineal gland, a part of the brain which the soul uses as a sort of steering-wheel-cum-dashboard, transmits to the rest of the body the effects the soul has on itself, and how it receives from the rest of the body the effects which it passes on to the soul. Perhaps the soul just 'reads off' these latter effects, as a driver reads information from the dashboard (though with neither eyes nor light to help the process). But the driver pushes the steering-wheel; how does the soul do that? Writing to the Princess on 21 May 1643, Descartes suggests we should look at the soul and its work of affecting the body in the way people have looked on gravity, which they seem to find intelligible, though only because they confusedly attribute to it the sort of power they should attribute to soul. The Princess replied that to explain an obscure phenomenon by another which was not only equally obscure but which the explainer thought was illusory anyway was not all that enlightening, and Descartes in effect agreed.[6]

But did Descartes give in too quickly? Neither he nor the Princess could read the fundamental attack that Hume was to make a century later on the whole idea that causation could be anything more, at least to our knowledge, than regular concomitance. Perhaps then we should not expect to find any link between mind and body, but should simply accept that there are mental events (notably acts of willing) and physical events, and if they occur together in a regular enough sequence, that is all we can mean by saying that the former cause the latter.

Unfortunately, though, apart from other difficulties with Hume's view, this is just not how we experience the interaction of mind and body. When I raise my arm I don't first will it to rise and then, lo and behold!, observe it rising, as though I were practising telekinesis on a distant dinner plate. I raise my arm, I don't cause it to rise.

Descartes realised this, and always had done. He rejected the steering-wheel model as explicitly as a seventeenth-century writer could when, in the sixth Meditation, he said (just half-way through), 'I am not only lodged in my body as a pilot in a vessel [or, as he might have added if he had read G. Ryle,[7] as a ghost in a machine], but ... I am very closely united to it, and so to speak so intermingled with it that I seem to compose with it one whole.' Similarly in Article 30 of Part I of *The passions of the soul* he insists that the soul 'is really joined to the whole body' and does not exist 'in any one of its parts to the exclusion of the others'. He then adds that it nevertheless 'functions more particularly' in the pineal gland (Article 31). What he has in mind is that when, for example, my foot is damaged I don't just observe the damage, as a pilot observes a leak in his vessel, I feel it, and what is more I feel the pain as being in the foot – though the phantom limb phenomenon then convinces him that the pain cannot really be in the foot, or in any other spatial location: it is 'in' (in another sense) the mind. It is for this sort of reason that he went on to tell the Princess in the second of the above letters that we know the soul by intellect, the body by intellect plus imagination, but the union of the two by the senses, i.e. we simply experience it, and that is really as far as we can get.

Descartes then is well aware that a mind cannot be in a body as a man is in his clothes, and that dualism must be more complex than that. In fact a recent writer has even claimed that in a way Descartes is a trialist rather than a dualist. He has only two substances, soul and body, but they have between them three attributes or aspects: extension, thought and sensation. The writer[8] concludes that this introduction of sensation as a third attribute, which does not require a third substance to be its bearer, represents a step, though no more, towards the realisation that *what* has the various features or aspects that make up a human being must be a single thing, not two or three different things inexplicably united.[9]

There are other views that a dualist can take about how mind relates to body. He can say they don't really interact at all. Mental events cause other mental events and physical events other physical events (psychophysical parallelism), or else no events cause other events at all, but God uses each event as it arises as the occasion for Him to cause the next event in what appears to us as a causal sequence (occasionalism, associated especially with N. Malebranche (1638–1715)). A variant of occasionalism is Leibniz' view that every 'monad' (a kind of atom, but spiritual in nature) has a built-in program which unfolds automatically without being affected by any other monad, though there is a 'pre-established harmony' whereby God arranges that all these unfoldings fit together into a coherent universe. The last two of these doctrines (those of Malebranche and Leibniz) are general metaphysical doctrines going beyond the mind–body problem, but all three arise from certain views on what causation must involve;[10] and for all three the fact that mental and physical events occur in a coherent connection with each other is simply attributed to God. It is this last feature that makes all these views alien to contemporary opinion. No doubt God could play this role, but to appeal to Him in this way as an explanatory hypothesis is surely a counsel of despair; one could explain anything by just saying, 'Well, God decided it should be so.' It also leaves untouched the problem of the unity of a person. Finally, and for completeness, let me mention a more modern view called epiphenomenalism (a name that also has application outside the philosophy of mind). This says that physical events may cause mental events, but mental events cause neither physical events nor each other. This view is non-reductionist, in that it doesn't deny the reality of mental events, but it certainly reduces their importance. The main objections to it are its implausibility (if a pin-prick causes a pain in me, surely the pain equally causes me to jump?) and its ignoring of the coherence of mental series of events: if a proposition p logically entails another, q, and I see this and therefore deduce q from p, which I already believe, is it not remarkable that the brain-state which causes my belief in p should happen to be followed by just that brain-state which causes my belief in q, my appreciation of the logical connection between p and q being completely irrelevant? It won't help to add a third brain-state, which causes my appreciation of the connection, because we still want to know why this one and the one causing my belief in p are followed by the one causing my belief in q. Why should purely physical causal connections be so closely paralleled by logical connections, which seem entirely different? The main motive for epiphenomenalism is the apparent success of neurophysiology, which seems to promise a complete science of brain-states without bringing in shadowy things like mental events. There are real problems here, with repercussions elsewhere. But one quick point is this: the 'promise' of neurophysiology is very far indeed from being fulfilled, and if ever a set of general laws governing human behaviour is achieved, there is no reason to think the terms it will employ will be ones we should now regard as 'physical' as against 'mental'; they are just as likely to be of some category totally unknown to us yet.

So far we have considered two problems for the dualist: how are the two things supposed to interact, and how can we account for our feeling that a human being is a single thing? Let us mention one more problem: how do we know of each other's existence? There is a problem about how we can know of the existence of anything outside ourselves. But that belongs to another chapter (Chapter 7), so let us allow that we straightforwardly perceive chairs and tables, and human bodies, as common sense assumes. But if I am, or even just include, a mind that is unextended and has no material properties, how do you come to know about this mind? You certainly cannot perceive it. Do you intuit it by a special magical insight? Even if you do, to the astonishment of common sense, how do you connect what you intuit with my body as you perceive it? How do you distinguish my mind from anyone else's?

The commonest traditional answer for the dualist to take is that you infer the existence of my mind, and of its or my particular mental states, such as being in pain or having an experience of red, i.e. my sense-data. You infer this from what you observe of my body, and on the basis of what happens in your own case. This solution to the 'other minds problem', relying on argument by analogy, may be the dualist's best bet, but it can also be appealed to by those who are not dualists, or not two-substance dualists, but who think a person is a single entity with two radically different kinds of properties, ordinary observable physical ones, like moving its limbs or issuing sounds from its vocal chords, and unobservable psychological ones, like feeling a pain or desiring to order a hamburger. You know what it's like to have your toe stamped on, or to utter the words 'I'll have a hamburger, please' when you're in a café, not acting in a play, etc., and so you assume that that's what it's like for me when I am visibly or audibly in those conditions.

The argument is a very tempting one, for how else, it might seem, could we find out about other people and their experiences? It is also in part a sound argument. We do try to 'put ourselves in other people's shoes', and often gain insights by doing so; and we say things to our children like 'You don't like being hit, so why do you think your little sister does?' The trouble comes when we try to use the argument to explain *all* our knowledge of other people, including our knowledge of their very existence. If we all start, as the argument suggests, knowing only of our own experiences, and getting our concepts of experience, pain, consciousness, etc. from our own case, how do we get the idea that they even *could* apply outside our own case? How could you think that perhaps there are pains that are not your pains unless you already have a concept of yourself as one person or being among others? Even if you don't yet know of any others, how do you get to the possibility that there might be others, starting *from* your own case? Furthermore, if you ask how you know that others have *pains*, etc. (i.e. using the word 'pain') the question arises what you can mean by it, and so *what* is the question you are asking. This raises the private language question, which has been dealt with in another chapter (cf. Chapter 7, p. 153).

But what is the alternative? How *do* we know about other people? In detail who can say? But the point is that however we acquire our concepts of a person and of experiences, etc., we acquire them as essentially public concepts that we can from the start apply both to ourselves and to others as we come across them. It is experience that tells us which bits of our environment constitute persons and which don't, and here no doubt analogy plays some part along with other things. There seems no reason to doubt that a child spends as much time learning that certain things are not alive as learning that they are. Would a baby Crusoe, growing up in isolation on his desert island, attribute life to other things despite never seeing anything 'like' himself? Well, why shouldn't he treat as alive the branch, say, that 'obstinately' refuses to break when he tries to snap it off? Do we really think in fact that babies (and animals?) learn about other people by analogy? Does a baby have to see its parents gurgling and screaming and sucking at the breast before it realises that they are alive? (And about that boy who was hitting his sister: surely we are reminding him, not teaching him.)

All the views we have seen so far have been dualist, at least in the sense that they treat mental and physical phenomena as being of radically different kinds. Most of them also treat mind and body as separate substances. Epiphenomenalism in particular is not committed to doing this, though it has to give some account of what makes certain mental phenomena go together and belong to one person, whether or not they have any causal effects. Other views explicitly repudiate two-substance dualism. They may reduce mind to body or vice versa, views which belong in the next chapter, or they may take some other line.

Perhaps the most thoroughgoing attempt to do justice to both mind and matter by putting them on equal terms is one due mainly to William James and Bertrand Russell, though others have held it too, and known as 'neutral monism'. On this view there is only one substance, i.e. one basic stuff or kind of substance, which can be called neutral stuff, and which underlies and accounts for the whole of the natural world as well as all mental phenomena.

In 1904 James published an article called 'Does "consciousness" exist?', which in 1912 became the first chapter of his *Essays in radical empiricism*,[11] followed by a second chapter called 'A world of pure experience' developing the view further. Russell developed the view more elaborately in his *The analysis of mind*,[12] explicitly basing himself on James, and it is with Russell that the general notion of a neutral stuff comes in, for James makes experiences the basic entities from which everything is composed, but insists that there is no *general* stuff of which experiences are made – they are made 'of just what appears, of space, of intensity, of flatness, brownness, heaviness, or what not'.[13] 'Experience' is simply a generic term covering experiences of these various things. James realises that people will object that this implies there can be a 'red, hard or heavy thought',[14] but he accepts this, defending it simply by saying that thoughts and things do have much in common, for they are in time and have parts and can be added and arranged and compared.[15] Hotness in fact does belong to our idea of fire as well as in fire, but 'Mental fire is what won't burn real sticks,' and may or may not be put out by mental water[16] (i.e. if we imagine water thrown on fire we can imagine the fire going out or not, as we please). These experiences can be grouped in different ways, according to different relations that hold between them. One relation is that of being known, and we think of our consciousness as knowing experiences. But James insists that consciousness is not a substance that stands over against experiences and knows them; it is a relation between (some) experiences, and is itself an experience (i.e. each instance of it is).[17] When experiences are grouped like this they form 'the inner history of a person',[18] or what Russell would call a 'biography'.[19] When experiences are grouped according to such relations as those of always burning or always quenching (in the cases of fire and combustibles and water) we have 'an impersonal "objective" world, either spatial or temporal, or else merely logical or mathematical, or otherwise "ideal"'.[20] We distinguish the mental and the physical by their effects in practice. Russell introduces, to help distinguish the mental, the notion of 'mnemic causation', which occurs when 'the effect resulting from a stimulus to an organism differs according to the past history of the organism, without our being able actually to detect any relevant difference in its present structure'[21] ('mnemic' comes from a Greek word meaning 'memory').

Russell develops the theory in ways I cannot discuss here; for a summary see his last chapter. But how much of it can we accept? The most obvious objection, I suppose, is that the 'neutral stuff' seems to be given a job it hardly has the strength to perform. To unite things as disparate as conscious experiences and material objects in this way just seems to require too violent a wrench for the result to be able to stand up and be contemplated. Idealism says that matter is somehow illusory and materialism (at least in its extreme form) says the same about conscious experiences, but at least they take their stands on something familiar, conscious experiences and material objects respectively. Neutral monism seems to get the worst of both worlds, asking us to accept that *both* our familiar starting points are illusory, or at least are not what they seem, and that what they are is not something at least familiar in itself but something quite strange. What is the justification for calling this thing experiences, especially when these dissolve, as for James, into space, intensity, flatness, and other such disparate terms? And can we really be so happy about a red, hard, heavy thought? One thing James has in mind[22] is that an adequate mental picture of something extended must itself somehow embody extension. But does it follow that it must 'have all the extension of the object itself', as he puts it? One canot refute James by asking rhetorically if his image of the sun is itself 800,000 miles across, for he would simply say 'Yes' – if the image is adequate. But is one's image of a tennis-ball, however adequate, four inches across? How would one measure it to find out? Is one debarred in principle from having adequate images of things larger than one's own brain? Or must adequate images of them somehow extend outside one's head?

James, as we saw, objects to the idea of consciousness as something over against experiences. Russell takes a similar line when he considers the view, deriving from F. Brentano (1838–1917) and A. Meinong (1853–1920), that a perception or thought involves an act, a content (roughly, something in the mind) and an object (something outside the mind). Content and object raise some problems which I must pass by.[23] But

Russell thinks the act (of seeing or thinking, etc.) is 'unnecessary and ficti-tious'.[24] Roughly, what happens when I see a horse is that that bit of neutral stuff which when grouped with certain other bits in certain relations consti-tutes a horse, or part of one, is now grouped with certain other bits in certain other relations and constitutes an experience of seeing a horse. For Russell as for James there is no separate and independent element in the situation which can be called consciousness.

It is interesting to compare this with a famous article, published a year before James' original article first appeared, by G.E. Moore ('The refutation of idealism'[25] (1903)). Moore's target was idealism with its slogan that 'to be is to be perceived', the dominant philosophy in Britain when he wrote, but one neither James nor Russell had much sympathy for. But he insists that in experience object and subject must be distinguished,[26] and that in every sensation there are two distinct terms, consciousness and its object[27] – the very points James and Russell were to deny. It is true – and somewhat confusing – that Moore makes his opponents insist that both object and consciousness exist; but all they mean, he thinks, is that we must distinguish *what* is experienced from the fact *that* there is experience.[28] They do not do justice to the fact that consciousness must always be consciousness *of* something, and they treat an awareness of blue as though it were the same thing as a blue awareness, which it isn't.[29] James and Russell are not idealists, because Russell's 'neutral stuff' and James' 'experiences' (despite the name) are supposed to be as removed from being psychological as they are from being physical, and do not depend for their existence on being perceived. But they hold the view of awareness that Moore castigates as lying at the roots of idealism.

Neutral monism postulates a single stuff, any bit of which can enter into relations of two different kinds with other bits and counts as physical or mental according as it does so. It is an all-embracing theory, applying to everything in the universe, physical objects and events on the one hand and mental states and their contents on the other. There is another view that looks rather similar to this, in that it treats the physical and the mental as different aspects of the same thing, and is often called the double aspect view. One difference is that it is less all-embracing. It does not postulate a single stuff for everything, but leaves ordinary physical objects as they are and applies itself only to mental events and those physical events (roughly, ones in the brain or central nervous system) that seem most closely associated with the mental. It says that these are two aspects of a single set of events. This fact that it leaves the material world as it is, without leaving any mental world 'as it is', may seem to compromise its neutrality and put it on the materialist side of the fence, and indeed it, or one form of it, is often re-garded as an ancestor of the reductionist materialism now known as the iden-tity theory, which saw light in Australia in the 1950s. But it itself would claim to be non-reductionist in that it treats the two aspects as one the same level.

The double aspect theory is often attributed to Spinoza, but the interpretation of Spinoza is complex and controversial.[30] A more recent version is associated especially with D.M. MacKay, who uses the notion of complementarity.[31] Historically this notion arose in physics, where Niels Bohr used it to deal with certain problems about the analysis of light in terms of waves and particles, but MacKay claims that the notion is a logical one, which is needed to deal with many cases and is not limited to a particular theory in physics.

The general idea is that two descriptions of an event or phenomenon are complementary if each is exhaustive from its own point of view but each necessarily leaves out some aspect that the other puts in. An example is the descriptions of a transparent object as seen from opposite sides. Each description will mention all parts of the object but a certain part may be to the left of another in one description and to the right of it in the other: neither description leaves anything out in its own terms but they necessarily say different things; they each leave out an aspect of the thing. The descriptions, however, may be on different logical levels, as in MacKay's example[32] of a flashing lights advertisement, where an engineer would give an exhaustive description of it in terms of the electrical set-up, without mentioning the message, while an advertiser would do vice versa. These are on different levels because any message so displayed will require an electrical set-up, but not every electrical set-up will display a message.

Applying this to the mind, we shall say that certain events take place which can be described in one language as a set of brain events and in another language as a train of thought. Neurophysiologists do not mention desires or perceptions and novelists do not mention alpha rhythms or synaptic discharges, but each can give an account which is complete in its own terms, and each is describing the same set of events.

How well does the theory account for the unity of the person? The theory in itself does not say anything about substances, but we might expect it to say, speaking rather loosely, that descriptions of the brain and corresponding descriptions of 'the mind' are complementary descriptions of 'the same thing'. But what thing? We know roughly what counts as one brain – we have ordinary spatiotemporal criteria for identifying brains. But how do we know when we have the 'corresponding' mind? MacKay, who wants among other things to defend the Christian doctrine of an afterlife, allows that a body must be involved, but not necessarily the same body. Using the analogy of the message, this time in chalk, he says we could rub it out, but

> if tomorrow we, the originators, want to express the same message again, here or elsewhere, we have no difficulty in doing so. It is not necessary for us to use the original chalk, or even to use chalk at all. What matters is the arrangement of the chalk in which the message was embodied.[33]

But what counts as 'the message'? Apparently something general, not something located at a particular time and place. But on this view how would we distinguish a mind from another exactly similar to it? Minds would be like characters. One can have one's brother's character – not another character exactly like it, but the same character, for characters are general. But people are not characters, in this sense.

The double aspect theorist, who is not committed to an afterlife anyway, might deal with this by relying more on the body – the individual body – though at some cost to his mind–body neutrality. But we can repeat now a point we made against epiphenomenalism: how come that the causal story in the brain-language and the rational story in the mind-language fit so snugly and coherently together? The message analogy can be misleading here. The engineer's story and the advertiser's story fit together and are each coherent – but only because the engineer himself has a mind and arranged the initial conditions of the electrical phenomena so that they should indeed correspond in structure to the message.

One further objection I have space only to mention: it is not obvious that the mental story *can* be told without referring to external objects (those the mind in question is thinking about) which the neurophysiologist's story would certainly not refer to. The American philosopher Hilary Putnam recently expressed the point with the slogan '"Meanings" just ain't in the *head*.'

Another attempt to compromise between body–soul dualism and the abandoning of souls altogether is to postulate a third kind of thing, called persons, in a special sense.[34] Strawson distinguishes two kinds of properties, or predicates, as he calls them (rather loosely: predicates are really linguistic things), M-predicates and P-predicates. M-predicates are those which can apply to non-conscious material bodies, like 'weighing ten stone'. P-predicates imply the possession of consciousness, whether or not they also involve having a body, as 'smiling' does while 'thinking' doesn't. Smiling may not be a state of consciousness, but only conscious beings can smile. P-predicates can be applied only to persons, while M-predicates can be applied to both persons and other things, and persons can be defined as just those things which can have both M-predicates and P-predicates. For Strawson persons are logically primitive, i.e. we must not think of them as either embodied souls or besouled bodies, because unless we already understood the notion of a person we could not understand that of a soul. We would not know how to distinguish one soul from another, since we would have experience of at most one (our own) – but in that case we could not have any conception of a soul at all, not even our own, since for Strawson we cannot understand what it is to be a thing of a certain kind unless we know how to distinguish one thing of that kind from another. He does, however, allow that once we do know what a person is we can think of a person as *becoming* disembodied, i.e. as shedding all its M-predicates and those P-predicates, like smiling, which involve reference to a body – but the person must have started off having such predicates in order to gain an identity for itself; there can be disembodied survival of death, but no permanently disembodied spirits.

I will mention two objections to Strawson's view. First, how is a person related to his body?[35] Each of them can have the M-predicate 'weighs ten stone' but there aren't two things there that weigh ten stone. Perhaps the persons is *composed of* his body, as his body is composed of flesh and bones which also weigh ten stone but without leading to any paradox. But what would he be composed of if he survived his death? Nothing? One might blunt this argument by denying that survival is possible, but Strawson claims one can at least imagine surviving. Second, how easy is it to distinguish M-predicates and P-predicates?[36] Strawson appeals to consciousness, but that is itself an unclear notion.[37] (Consciousness is something the Greeks did *not* have a word for.) Perhaps I have special access to my own P-predicates? You can know as easily as I can whether I weigh ten stone, but only I can know whether I am in pain – or anyway I have a way of knowing which is not open to you. But I have a similar privileged way of knowing the M-predicate that my arm is raised (I just 'know' it is, without looking). On the other hand I may often be no better able than you to classify rightly the emotional state I am in, which is presumably a P-predicate.[38]

There is one more theory I should mention, though it leads us rather away from the non-reductionist area we have so far confined ourselves to. To put it in a crude slogan, this is the view that the mind, or that any given mental phenomenon, is what it does, or is to be defined in terms of how it functions. The view is therefore called functionalism. A leading exponent of it is S. Shoemaker, who, in his volume of essays *Identity, cause, and mind*,[39] defines it as 'the view that mental states are definable in terms of their causal relations to sensory inputs, behavioral outputs, and other mental states'. Similarly, C. McGinn says:[40] 'We are to define mental properties in terms of their typical patterns of cause and effect, including their characteristic stimuli, their interactions with other mental states, and their characteristic effects in behaviour.'[41]

This appeal to causation is well within the tradition of the last few decades, where appeal to causation has been revitalised by the return to respectability of causal necessity after a period in the doldrums induced by Hume's scepticism over two centuries ago. (Shoemaker even adopts the still rather daring view that 'causal necessity is just a species of logical necessity', admitting that this is 'radically at odds with Humean views about causality'.[42]

Functionalism has various advantages. It explains our feeling that though mental phenomena ought to be closely tied to what goes on in the brain or central nervous system, precisely *what* goes on there is in one sense irrelevant, for though we may think that, say, a desire has a physiological basis, and we could not desire if we had no physiology, if the physiologists came up, as they well might, with a radically new view about what did happen in our brains when we desired something, this would not make us think we had to alter our concept of what a desire is; and similarly if it were suddenly discovered that the Japanese had a quite different evolutionary history from the rest of us (as I believe some of them claimed when they first heard about Darwin), and that quite different physiological things happened inside them when they desired things, provided their apparent desires were caused by roughly the same situations (the smell of cooking some time after their last meal, say) and had roughly the same effects (entry into the relevant restaurant, perhaps). This is sometimes summed up by saying functionalism explains the variable realisability of mental states.

This suggests that functionalism is not straightforward materialism.[43] But taken by itself my last (and grossly over-simplified) example would suggest behaviourism, and indeed Shoemaker in the passage I quoted from above describes functionalism as 'what many regard as the most respectable descendant of behaviourism'.[44] Functionalism in fact does seem to fall rather on the materialist or physicalist side of the fence, at any rate if taken in what Shoemaker calls its strong sense.[45] This says that the definition of a given mental state, e.g. a desire to eat, may refer to other mental states if these are among the causes or effects of the first (e.g. this desire may cause a desire to enter a restaurant, given the presence of certain beliefs, such as that a restaurant is nearby and one has some money but no food at home); but these other mental states must themselves be analysable by similar definitions, in such a way that eventually all mental or psychological terms are eliminated;[46] if they cannot all be eliminated we have only weak functionalism. Only strong functionalism, incidentally, would have any hope of explaining how mind might *emerge* in a material universe.

Functionalism seems at its best with things like desires and beliefs. But can it capture the inner content of experience, e.g. (to borrow a phrase from T. Nagel)[47] 'what it is like' to see something red? Can functionalism distinguish the ordinary mental state of seeing something red from the surely different state of reacting in every way as though one had seen something red, and doing so with one's eyes open in the presence of a red object, etc., but without having any actual experience? Can it distinguish an ordinary human from a cleverly fashioned robot or a zombie? The word 'quale' (plural: 'qualia'; 'quale' is related to 'quality' as 'quantum' is to 'quantity') is used to express the ineffable psychological something, as opposed to a scientific definition using wave-lengths etc., that a word like 'red' means to us, and the above problem is known as that of 'absent qualia' (though 'the absence of qualia' would be a better name for it). A related problem, known as that of 'inverted qualia', is this: can functionalism cater for the possibility that I might have the experience of seeing red in just those circumstances where you have the experience of seeing what I, if I saw it, should call green, and vice versa? Though we both agree in *calling* blood red and grass green, perhaps when I see blood I have the experience you would call, if you had it, seeing green, and the divergence between us is undetectable in anything we say or do, and so undetectable by functionalist definitions. Whether either possibility is really coherent is controversial. (Shoemaker thinks the first is not but the second in principle is, and modifies his functionalism accordingly.)

As McGinn says,[48] we withdraw our hand from something hot *because* we are in pain, not *as part of* being so. Nevertheless, as he says elsewhere,[49] functionalism, unlike behaviourism, 'offers a conceptual, not an ontological, reduction of the mental'. It does not try to eliminate mental entities, but only the need for special mental terms to describe them. It does not say that qualia do not exist but that they cannot exist without manifesting themselves in the cause/effect sequences in our lives, where these include other mental items, such as desires, beliefs, judgements, etc. To this extent (though the comparison needs further discussion) it is more like saying water is really H2O than saying mermaids are really manatees. Mermaids sit on rocks combing their hair and enticing sailors, which manatees don't. But H_2O does everything water does. It is to this extent that functionalism is reductionist. But there we must leave it.[50]

Notes

(An author's name followed by a number in square brackets refers to the book or article which has that number in the bibliography.)

1. *Mind*, vol. 65, no. 259 (1956). Originally written in 1918–19.
2. See further Delahunty [12], Ch. 6, Section 6.
3. Introduction to this part, pp. 378–9.
4. Strawson [14], Ch. 2, discussed by G. Evans in his contribution to Z. van Straaten (ed.), *Philosophical subjects* (Clarendon Press, Oxford, 1980).
5. Strawson [14], Ch. 3; see below.
6. Letter to Elizabeth, 28 June 1643; for the whole discussion see G.E.M. Anscombe and P.T. Geach (eds), *Descartes: philosophical writings* (Nelson, London, 1954), pp. 274–82.
7. Ryle [7], Ch. 1.
8. J. Cottingham, 'Cartesian trialism', *Mind*, vol. 94, no. 374 (1985).
9. For a further interpretation of Descartes see B. Smart, 'How can persons be ascribed M-predicates?' *Mind*, vol. 86, no. 341 (1977).
10. For some discussion of this see D. Radner, 'Is there a problem of Cartesian interaction?' *Journal of the History of Philosophy*, vol. 23, no. 1 (1985), and discussion in ibid., no. 2.
11. James [9].
12. Russell [10].
13. James [9], p. 27.
14. Ibid., p. 28.
15. Ibid., p. 29.
16. Ibid., p. 33.

17. Ibid., p. 25.

18. Ibid., p. 16.

19. Russell [10], pp. 127, 295–6.

20. James [9], p. 16.

21. Russell [10], p. 86.

22. As James [9], p. 30, shows.

23. See Russell [10], especially pp. 18ff.

24. Ibid., p. 17.

25. G.E. Moore, 'The refutation of idealism', *Mind*, vol. 12, no. 48 (1903).

26. Ibid., p. 442.

27. Ibid., p. 444.

28. Ibid., p. 446–7.

29. Ibid., p. 447–51.

30. See Delahunty [12], Ch. 6.

31. See, e.g., MacKay's papers in *Proceedings of the Aristotelian Society*, suppl. vols 26 (1952) and 32 (1958), and in *Mind*, vol. 66, no. 263 (1957), his pamphlet *Freedom of action in a mechanistic universe* (Cambridge University Press, Cambridge, 1967), and his book *The clockwork image* (Inter-Varsity Press, London, 1974).

32. MacKay [13], pp. 36–8, 91.

33. Ibid., pp. 74–5.

34. Strawson [14], Ch. 3.

35. Cf. Williams [15], Ch. 4, and also Smart, 'How can persons be ascribed M-predicates?', though I have altered the argument.

36. Cf. T. Forrest, 'P-predicates' in Stroll [16].

37. See K. Wilkes, 'Is consciousness important?' *British Journal for the Philosophy of Science*, vol. 35, no. 3 (1984).

38. Forrest discusses and rejects another suggestion, too complex to discuss here.

39. Shoemaker [17], p. 337 (cf. p. 111).

40. McGinn [19], p. 33.

41. See in general ibid., pp. 33–6 and McGinn [18], pp. 33 n. 13 and 141–5, as well as his article 'Functionalism and phenomenalism: a critical note', *Australasian Journal of Philosophy*, vol. 58, no. 1 (1980). McGinn is critical of functionalism, but the beginner may find the first two of these three references rather easier than Shoemaker, where the main chapters relevant are 5, 8, 9, 12, 14, 15.

42. Shoemaker [17], pp. 222, 231.

43. But see Shoemaker [17], p. 266.

44. Ibid., p. 337.

45. Ibid., pp. 263–4, 310–11.

46. Ibid., pp. 200–1.

47. T. Nagel, *Mortal questions* (Cambridge University Press, Cambridge, 1979), Ch. 12.

48. McGinn [19], p. 35.

49. McGinn, 'Functionalism and phenomenalism', p. 36.

50. A further account of functionalism, discussed in the context of reductionism, will be found in the next chapter.

Bibliography

For Plato's views on the soul, see *Republic*, Books IV and IX (many translations exist) and also sections 245 to 256 of

[1] R. Hackforth (tr.), *Plato's Phaedrus* (Bobbs-Merrill, New York, 1952).

Discussion of Plato's views in the *Phaedo* may be found in

[2] D. Gallop (tr.), *Plato: Phaedo* (Clarendon Press, Oxford, 1975).

The main source for Aristotle's account of the *psyche* is his *De anima*, the most important portions of which are translated with commentary in

[3] D.W. Hamlyn (tr. and ed.), *Aristotle De anima Books II and III* (Clarendon Press, Oxford, 1968).

Aristotle's views are critically examined in the first four chapters of

[4] J. Barnes, M. Schofield and R. Sorabji (eds), *Articles on Aristotle* (4 vols, Duckworth, London, 1979), vol. IV.

A stimulating discussion of Descartes' views on the mind occurs in Ch. 10 of

[5] B. Williams, *Descartes* (Penguin Books, Harmondsworth, 1978).

Several aspects of Descartes' mind (including the 'trialistic' line of thought referred to above) are discussed in Ch. 5 of

[6] J. Cottingham, *Descartes* (Basil Blackwell, Oxford, 1986).

Ryle's celebrated critique of the Cartesian approach may be found in

[7] G. Ryle, *The concept of mind* (Penguin Books, Harmondsworth, 1949).

Some of the problems of mind–body interaction are examined in Ch. 30 of

[8] G.N.A. Vesey (ed.), *Body and mind* (Allen and Unwin, London, 1964).

The thesis of 'neutral monism' is advanced in the first chapter of

[9] William James, *Essays in radical empiricism* (Longmans, London, 1912) and more elaborately in

[10] Bertrand Russell, *The analysis of mind* (Allen and Unwin, London, 1921).

A classic text often regarded as the inspiration behind the so-called 'double aspect' theory is Part II of Spinoza's *Ethics*, translated in

[11] E. Curley, *The collected works of Spinoza* (Princeton University Press, Princeton, 1985), and discussed in Ch. 6 of

[12] R.J. Delahunty, *Spinoza* (Routledge, London, 1985), while a more recent exponent is

[13] D.M. MacKay, *The clockwork image* (Inter-Varsity Press, London, 1974).

The 'Strawsonian compromise' may be found in

[14] P.F. Strawson, *Individuals* (Methuen, London, 1959), which is criticised in Ch. 4 of

[15] B. Williams, *Problems of the self* (Cambridge University Press, London, 1973) and in T. Forrest's 'P predicates', printed in

[16] A. Stroll (ed.), *Epistemology* (Harper and Row, London, 1967).

A leading exponent of the functionalist view is

[17] S. Shoemaker, *Identity, cause, and mind* (Cambridge University Press, Cambridge, 1984).

Functionalism is also clearly expounded and criticised in

[18] C. McGinn, *The subjective view* (Oxford University Press, Oxford, 1983), or on a more introductory level in

[19] C. McGinn, *The character of mind* (Oxford University Press, Oxford, 1982).

A useful introduction to many of the topics discussed in this chapter is

[20] K. Campbell, *Body and mind* (Notre Dame Press, Notre Dame, Indiana, 1980).

See also the Introduction to

[21] J. Glover, *The philosophy of mind* (Oxford University Press, Oxford, 1976), and
another useful collection is

[22] S. Hook (ed.), *Dimensions of mind* (Collier-Macmillan, London, 1961).

J.G.C.

18 | *Mind and Body: Some Forms of Reductionism*

K.V. Wilkes

Introduction

Anyone coming new to the mind–body problem finds it a conceptual mess. Key terms are used by different writers in different senses, so it is difficult to disentangle the various areas of agreement and disagreement. What is the scope of 'mind', and 'mental'? What is 'a' mental, or 'a' physical, event? What is this relation called 'reduction'?

My view is that 'the problem' is to a considerable extent produced by muddles – a problem to be dissolved rather than solved. But dissolving it takes us not only up unpromising culs-de-sac, but also through philosophically scenic stretches of debate.

This chapter has two main parts. In the first, I sketch some of the most popular approaches to the mind–body problem (called by neuroscientists the brain–mind problem). By no means all the currently fashionable arguments will be discussed; the detailed bibliography at the end of the chapter should allow the reader to follow up what interests him further. In the second part, after explaining where I think that all of them go wrong, I shall describe what I take to be the most profitable current theory – noting, however, where it is vulnerable to objections.

Before starting out, though, two bits of ground-clearing. Some comment is needed on the difference between *type* relations and *token* relations; and a preliminary note on the general notion of 'reduction'.

Types and tokens

All things (entities, states, processes) fall under several categories. This is: (a)

402

my brother; (b) a man; (c) a Briton; (d) a father; (e) someone wanted by the police; (f) a jewel thief; (g) an exile in Spain; (h) an armed man ... and so on. Anything can be picked out by dozens of descriptions.

Some pairs of these descriptions may pick out classes of things which correlate in a *type–type* way. Some such correlations are one–one, e.g. 'all men are sons'. Others are one–many, e.g. 'all siblings are male *or* female' – one type correlates here with two types. Others again are many–one, e.g. 'jewel thieves are men wanted by the police' – but so are other criminal types. Some type-correlations will be tight and exceptionless, like 'all men are sons'; others rougher, like 'all explorers are brave individuals': perhaps not quite all are.

Some of the descriptions under which an object falls, however, will correlate with each other only in a *token–token* way. For example: when I say that my brother is the man holding a gun, I evidently do not want to suggest by this that all my brothers are men holding guns, nor that all men holding guns are brothers of mine. It is just this brother, now, who is one and the same as the armed individual.

This distinction is crucially important to understanding the mind–body relationship: it is the distinction between those who hold, and those who deny, that *laws* relate mental to physical phenomena. There is a world of difference between those who want to say, for example, that one day we shall find that all 'thoughts that one needs more toothpaste' correlate, type–type, with 'brain processes of type *B*'; and those who argue that my thought at noon on Tuesday that I need more toothpaste correlates with *some* brain process of mine then, but that my same belief a month later, or your belief at noon on Tuesday that you were running out of toothpaste, might correlate with wildly different brain-states.

So much for the type–token distinction, at least for the time being.

Reductions

'Reduction' is primarily a relation between *theories*, not between *things*. That is, when we talk of the reduction of entities, states or processes, saying for example that light waves have been reduced to electromagnetic waves, this means that the theory of optics has been reduced to the theory of electromagnetic radiation in such a way that we can identify light with electromagnetic radiation.

What I shall call 'smooth' reductions are, generally, *explanatory*: a theory is said to reduce to another when – roughly speaking – both it, and its predictive and explanatory success, are explained in terms of the new theory. Typically, successful reductions of this kind display a predominance of type–type correlations (laws) between the referents of reduced and reducing theories. The smoother the reduction, the more and

403

the tighter will be such type correlations between old and new. Physical optics, for example, reduced smoothly; not only its successes, but also its theoretical posits and laws, received a deeper and richer understanding in electromagnetic theory.

At the other end of the scale are 'rough' or 'eliminative' reductions; 'eliminative', in the sense that the reducing theory 'explains away' the entities of the theory being reduced. Take for example the reduction of phlogiston theory to oxygen theory. 'Phlogiston' was not related type–type to anything in oxygen theory. Nonetheless, what phlogiston purported to explain is explained better, and in different ways, by oxygen theory. The reduction strongly implied that there was no such thing as phlogiston. Such eliminative ('rough') reductions *displace*, rather than explain, the reduced theory – the new theory explains better what the old theory explained, and explains more besides; but does not necessarily do so by explaining the displaced theory itself, its entities and processes.

Thus reductions have varying implications for the *ontology* of the reduced theories. Smooth reductions are generally non-eliminative, because the reducing theory typically gives a deeper and more penetrating description of the entities and properties of the reduced theory. Example: the reduction of classical thermodynamics by statistical mechanics; properties such as pressure, volume and temperature are not denied by this reduction, but rather underpinned and confirmed. Rough reductions, though, tempt one to deny the existence of the phenomena postulated by the displaced theories. So ontological questions are variously affected by the type of reduction in question, depending on whether the reduction is eliminative or non-eliminative, 'smoother' or 'rougher'.

I shall not go into details about types of scientific reduction, which will be discussed elsewhere in this volume. Here I want to emphasise (a) that reduction holds between theories; (b) that 'smooth' reductions tend to explain, and 'rough' reductions to reject, the reduced theory; so that (c) reductions have variable *ontological* and *explanatory* implications. All these three points will recur throughout our examination of reductions between mind and brain.

Some current mind–body theories

'Nothing but' theories

A position with several variants can be encapsulated in a 'nothing-but' formula: mental phenomena are 'nothing but' physical states or processes (or vice versa). Talk about phenomena of kind K is just another, perhaps a misleading, way of talking about phenomena of kind J. Thus 'nothing but' theories deny dualism – all are *ontologically monistic*. (Some such theories are misleadingly called 'identity theories'. This is misleading because the

404

'nothing but' relation is not that of *identity* – simply because it is not, as identity is, symmetric. However, since there is in the literature a loose use in which 'identity' just means 'monism', the reader can consider this section to cover many of the so-called 'identity theories' on the market. It is also relevant to theories that claim that the mental 'supervenes' on the physical.)

Versions may vary in the following respects:

(1) A thesis no longer fashionable, which I shall not examine further, reduces physical to mental: e.g. physical things and processes are nothing but sets of (actual or possible) sense-experiences. Nowadays the direction of the relation tends to go the other way, asserting that mental phenomena are nothing but physical phenomena, and it is these theses I shall discuss.

(2) Sometimes the scope of the thesis is restricted: only certain kinds of mental phenomena, particularly sensations such as pains, are said to be 'nothing but' states of the brain. Others, though, generalise the thesis to cover all mental phenomena.

(3) Finally, to some, 'nothing but' theories are *eliminative* reductions: the phenomena to which mental terms purport to refer don't really exist. But others hold non-eliminative positions; and yet others again deny that the 'nothing but' relation is a matter of theory *reduction* (in the sense outlined in the previous section) at all.

To order all this diversity, let us distinguish between some 'moderate', and some 'revisionary', versions.

Moderate versions have ontological, but not necessarily explanatory, implications. Just as tables are nothing but swarms of molecules (token–token), or water is nothing but H_2O (type–type), so pains or thoughts are nothing but 'C-fibre firings', or sets of cerebral processes (to some via type, to others via token, correlations). The 'nothing but' assertions concerning tables and water do not encourage the inference that tables and water don't exist – instead, they say what they really are. Analogously, the 'nothing but' assertions regarding pains or thoughts affirm, rather than deny, their reality. Moreover, talk of tables, water, pains, beliefs etc., is built into our conceptual practices; even if we could forswear talk of tables *in principle*, it would be monstrously inconvenient to do so; thus 'table talk' and 'pain talk' will not be *eliminated* by the 'nothing but' claim of the moderates.

Now on the one hand, the assertion 'tables are nothing but swarms of molecules' does not *explain* or *reduce* tables. For two reasons: first, 'table' is not a term in any *theory*, so there is no theoretical reduction here; and second, token–token relations rarely explain the left-hand *relatum* in a 'nothing but' formula. (Anyway, what would count as 'explaining tables'?) On the other hand, though, the claim 'water is nothing but H_2O' does explain water. Water belongs to a low-level theory; it is a 'natural kind', and amenable to systematic, reductive explanation; here we get a 'smooth' reduction to H_2O. Moderate theorists must therefore be asked: (a) do they claim that our vocabulary of mental terms constitutes a *theory*? (b) do they expect to find type–type relations between mental and physical phenomena? Those who answer 'Yes' to both are those who think that the 'nothing but' relation is both ontological *and* explanatory. Those who deny both will see it as merely ontological. And those who say 'Yes' to (a) and 'No' to (b) are getting close to some 'revisionary' position.

Let us therefore consider these *revisionary* theorists, who are genuine reductionists. They agree with the moderates that mental talk is built into the language as we now have it. They assert that our common-sense conceptual framework is a 'theory'. But they urge on us the desirability of switching to talk in neuroscientific terms. This, they claim, will be more perspicuous and accurate than the old mentalese terminology; we should learn to drop the shallow and woolly mental terms and opt instead for the shiny conceptual framework of an ideal (future) neurophysiology. This would constitute a change – perhaps a major change – in our conceptual scheme, but one which, with discipline and the advancement of science, we could learn to absorb. An appropriate analogy might be with an assertion like 'witches are nothing but neurotic women'; this permits the inference 'so, there are really no witches', and recommends talk of neurosis rather than witchcraft. Revisionary theories thus tend to deny that mental phenomena, as described in the old mental terminology, really exist; they are instead misdescribed brain-states; once we drop the old terminology, the question 'Do beliefs really exist?' will cease to arise.

Revisionary theories are reductive; and we can ask how smooth or rough the reduction is expected to be. If it is smooth, we should find a high proportion of type–type 'nothing but' correlations between the referents of the old mental terms and those of the new. Otherwise, wouldn't it be difficult to learn to make the transitions from old to new vocabulary? However, some radical proponents of the revisionary thesis expect a considerably rougher reduction, precisely because they regard the 'theory' of common-sense psychology to be a poor, shallow and largely false one. So they hope for a reduction that *displaces*, rather than *explains*, the old mental schema. Put another way, terms such as 'pain', 'belief' etc., are crude, vague; they classify the phenomena in shallow or unhelpful ways; although some of them *may* correlate neatly with the new categories of the neurosciences, many will not, and we should just *drop* them and learn the new language.

There is one major objection to this radical revisionary approach, though. If there are few type–type correlations (even rough ones) between the new terms and the old, in what sense are we explaining the *same* phenomena that we did before? We deploy our mental vocabulary to explain purposive behaviour, and most descriptions of behaviour are infused by mental terminology. We classify behaviour, in large part, by the goals, intentions, purposes, hopes, fears, beliefs etc., that we ascribe to the agent. How can physical statements which *reject* such categories characterise, still less explain, purposive, intentional action?

This objection is important, but underestimates the radical nature of the revisionary thesis. Just as mental talk is to be displaced by neuroscientific talk, so, analogously, our descriptions of behaviour (permeated by these mentalistic overtones and dependent on mental and intentional terminology) would be displaced by a new theory. Just as talk in terms of beliefs, pains, desires is vague, shallow, superficial, so are our everyday classifications of behaviour. We should shift to a new scheme, both to describe the behaviour to be explained, and to supply the explanatory terminology.

This is perhaps not as impossible as it sounds. Consider the two different ways for persuading people to switch from Fahrenheit to Celsius. One is brutal: Fahrenheit is simply abandoned, temperatures suddenly given in Celsius. It is as if there were no correlations between the two scales. The second is gentle: there is a lengthy overlap period in which both temperatures are given, in the hope that people will learn to think – *by* exploiting the type–type correlations – in Celsius as well as Fahrenheit. (The brutal method, incidentally, is markedly more successful.) The switch envisaged by the radically revisionary theorist would be like the 'brutal' method for learning the Celsius scale: or like someone learning a language from scratch.

Such a radical position, because it is so Utopian, is evidently well nigh impossible to assess; we have little idea of what these new concepts and categories would be, nor the extent of the shift required to redescribe our purposive behaviour. Fortunately we shall find, later, quite different arguments that make this theory look at best only plausible in a very limited domain.

Functionalist theories

'Functionalism' is currently the most popular general approach to the mind–brain relation. But it comes in many forms, and it would be tedious to go into details of all of them.[1] I shall therefore describe very broadly what almost all versions have in common, and sketch some of the implications that have been drawn from the enterprise.

Functionalism can be seen as arising out of the failure of classical behaviourism. Behaviourism (discussed in detail in the next chapter) can, roughly, be characterised as treating the organism like a black box, the behaviour (output) of which is explained and predicted as a function of the input and the state of the system.

Behaviourism, despite ingenious and sophisticated modifications to its basic thesis, fails as a general theory. It explains much; but equally, much escapes it. (The reason seems to me clear: *a priori* it is

407

exceedingly improbable that so dramatically simple a theory – simple even when elaborated almost out of recognition – could be expected to account for the staggering complexity of the human organism.)

Functionalism can be seen as 'reiterated behaviour-ism'. It opens up the black box – to put inside it a postulated *system* of smaller black boxes. Each of these is treated just like the behaviourist's big black box: one does not go inside them, but explains their output in terms of the state they are in and the input they receive. Each box is an abstractly characterised function that transforms input into output; the input may be a stimulus from outside, or the output of another box in the network. Pictorially, we can think of it in terms of a flow-chart diagram, with boxes (functions) connected by arrows, and the whole network, the system as a whole, receiving input from outside and giving as output certain kinds of behaviour as a complex product of several internal functions.

A very simple example will illustrate the general point. Consider a car factory. One worker-unit (one black box) takes as its input, say, sheet metal. It moulds these sheets to produce car-body shells as output. They in turn become part of the input for an assembly unit/box, which will receive input also from other units/boxes (for instance, the windscreen-manufacturing unit) and perhaps from the 'external world' too, in the form of nuts and bolts manufactured elsewhere. Another unit may have the function of inspecting the components, and may from time to time introduce a feedback loop – returning faulty body-shells, say, to the mould-ing unit for remodelling.

It may be helpful to give a simple example from psychology. Sokolov, in order to explain habituation in the rat, stipulates as input some sensory stimulus – a noise, say. He postulates a 'classifier' function, which operates on this sensory input, and passes the 'classified' output to three further hypothesised functions: the 'expectancy generator', 'comparator' and 'amplifier'. (It does not at this stage matter at all that the reader may not understand the nature of the functions performed by these 'black boxes'.) The output of the expectancy generator is a second source of input for the comparator; the comparator's output is a second source of input for the amplifier. The amplifier's output triggers (or suppresses) the orienting reflex of the rat to the noise. Figure 18.1 expresses it diagrammatically.

What this last example shows is that we have here a *mini-theory*; confronted with some behaviour needing explanation, we *pos-tulate* an internal mechanism, the operations of which would serve to explain it. The mechanism hypothesised consists of abstractly characterised, causally related internal operations, the joint performance of which could bring about the behaviour to be explained.

Habituation behaviour in Sokolov's rats may appear somewhat distant from human mental functioning. The model, though, is easily adapted to more exciting mental phenomena; one simply gives the

Figure 18.1

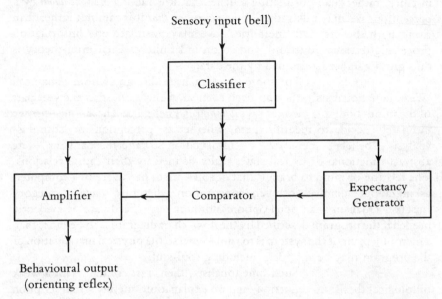

Sensory input (bell)

Classifier

Amplifier   Comparator   Expectancy Generator

Behavioural output
(orienting reflex)

boxes labels like 'belief', 'desire', 'perception', 'memory', 'analysis', or what you will. They are *abstract, functional* states, characterised solely in terms of their causal relationships to each other, to input, and to output. Human purposive behaviour is then explained in terms of how this hypothesised system of states takes the organism from sensory input to behaviour. Because functionalism insists upon a *network* of mental states, it insists upon 'the holism of the mental' – upon the way in which mental states operate together to explain behaviour.

A simple illustration may help. Suppose Angelo sees rain (sensory input). He picks up his umbrella (behavioural output). This is explained by a postulated set of states which, although essentially only abstract functions, we might label in the following way: belief that it is raining, brought about by the perception; desire to stay dry; desire to go outside; and some assumed stored information-states concerning the function of umbrellas, the wetness of rain, and so forth. Different internal states may change the behaviour; e.g. a memory that his umbrella has holes, the desire to feel rain on his head, or the belief that he has a cold coming.

So far so good; but equally, so vague. What is outlined above is indeed the bones of the functionalist approach; but so far forth, it is just too easy. *Any* system of more than rudimentary complexity can be functionally characterised. A mousetrap, a washing machine; a banking system, a rat; a factory, a computer, a human being. Moreover, and most

409

important: why prefer any one flow-chart diagram to another? Clearly numerous incompatible mini-theories could explain Angelo's behaviour. For instance, rather than postulating a belief that it is raining *brought about by* a perception, we may talk rather of *the perception that* it is raining; rather than citing both 'beliefs' and 'memories', we may postulate one 'information processing/retrieval function'; and so on indefinitely. Each mini-theory is thus grossly underdetermined by the data.

For some functionalists, though (whom I shall call 'Weak Functionalists'), the approach even so vaguely outlined answers part of the mind–body problem: it says *what mental states are*. These – *however* we ultimately decide to identify them, whether as 'perception' or 'stimulus-analysis', 'beliefs', 'memories' or 'information storage mechanisms' – are abstract functional or logical states, fully defined by their causal relations. The relation of mind to brain is that of software to hardware in a computer; asking about 'identity', or even 'constitution', therefore makes a category mistake. Dualism is an open option: although *some* 'hardware' is evidently needed if the program described by the flow-chart diagram is to be more than a mere blueprint (if the system is to run) – even so the physical instantiation of the program may be anything, including soul-stuff.

Such functionalists, then, rest content with a weak ontological thesis: no reduction, and no explanation, merely a redescription of the nature of the mental. Weak though it is, though, it runs into immediate trouble even on its own terms. The outstanding problems come with 'sentient' phenomena such as pain and perception. Pain, it appears, cannot be regarded as an abstract function operating on input to generate output; as well as that, it *hurts*. Perception is a way of discriminating colours; but we feel there is more to it than that. A machine sensitive to different light waves may discriminate red from yellow, and hence its 'perception' may play precisely the same causal role in a system of states as does ours; but we (we think) *experience* colours as well. Functionalism, in short, seems silent on the *experiential* properties of the mental. We shall return to these problems; at present I merely flag them and move on. As will emerge soon, there are deeper framework errors even in the 'weak' functionalism as so described.

One more, highly popular and prevalent, version of functionalism needs brief examination. An appropriate label might be 'the new dualism'. Its proponents are impressed by the fact (noted above) that systems of wildly differing physical kinds can instantiate functionalist flow-charts or programs. We saw that factories, washing machines, rats, computers – all could be described by such programs. If so, then any such system of sufficient complexity could, at least in principle, instantiate a program for intelligent cognitive behaviour. In other words, mental states are 'multiply realisable'; for us humans, the hardware is the brain's 'wetware'; for computers, it is silicon chips and electromagnetic pulses; but – to cite just some of the examples in the literature – the same program might be instantiated by the banking system of Bolivia, the population of China (one man per nerve cell), troupes of performing fleas, or unimaginable Martian plasma.

The new dualists, therefore, scorn any kind of reduction. To reduce mental states to states of the brain would be, they say 'parochial' and 'chauvinist'. Such reductions would only draw attention *away* from what is truly interesting, the psychological generalisations that hold whatever the hardware realisations may be. Just as it would be a waste of time to try to reduce economic theory to physical theory (societies can trade in coins, notes, gold bars, stocks and shares, work, cattle, corn, wampum or slaves), so it is of only marginal interest to note what it is that supplies, in any given case, the physical realisation of mental phenomena. Functionalist types (mental states) correlate with *so many* different hardware types that the reductive/explanatory force of type-correlations dissolves. Such correlations are for practical purposes as unhelpful as sets of token–token relations. Psychology, then, is and should be 'autonomous': independent of neuroscience. It is admitted that all functionalist types are realised in *some* hardware; and since most believe that any hardware realisation will be physical (i.e. few take seriously a 'soul-stuff'), the 'new dualism' is not ontologically dualist. But it insists on a radical cleavage between psychological and neuroscientific research, and denies that the latter contributes much to the former; and it is this radical cleavage that licenses the label 'new *dualism*'.

The new dualists, though, have few examples of intelligence outside the (higher) animal kingdom; performing fleas and the population of China have not yet been persuaded to instantiate an interesting flow-chart, and extraterrestrial intelligences remain resolutely in the realm of science fantasy. But they have the computer. So it is no accident that the computer, displaying 'artificial intelligence', dominates this theory. More interestingly, there is some hope that by means of the computer a *principled* way of characterising the postulated mental functions can be found – and this, as we have seen, is urgently needed to get round the 'underdetermination' threat: that numerous rival and incompatible theories can compete to explain the behaviour in question. If we accept that a computer can do some of the things that we can do, then we can attempt to write computer programs that obey our (conjectural) theory of our mental capacity. In so far as, and to the extent that, such simulations are successful, then there is at least *some* reason to believe that the machine's program is close to our 'program', that the description given in the program might supply us with the concepts whereby to identify our mental states.

Like all forms of functionalism, the new dualism falls foul of the objection from pains and visual experience. It also conflicts with the well nigh irresistible intuition that the structure of the brain must have *some* – considerable – bearing upon the nature of the mental states it underpins. A third source of unease is best expressed by an analogy. Artificial diamonds are not really diamonds. What licenses the assertion

411

that artificial intelligence (or seeing, thinking) is indeed *really intelligence* (seeing, thinking)? After all, the main reason why we think that artificial diamonds are not diamonds is because of their different microstructure. If the analogy held (does it?), artificial intelligence, having a different microstructure (different hardware realisation) from human intelligence, might not truly be 'intelligence'.

I shall not yet develop or discuss these sources of unease because I am about to introduce arguments suggesting that *none* of the theories sketched so far can possibly work. So I proceed to the second main section of this chapter; the bibliography should point the reader towards the prolific literature attacking and defending various functionalist positions.

Framework problems

I call this section 'Framework problems', because it raises objections to the premises upon which all of the approaches to the mind–body problem mentioned above have tacitly or explicitly assumed. With a different – and better – set of premises, a more plausible dissolution of 'the' problem can be envisaged. The chief source of objections stems from the characterisation of 'mental' and 'physical'.

'Mental' and 'physical'

So far we have assumed that we know what 'mental states (events, processes)' and 'physical events (states, processes)' are. But this dichotomy needs considerable examination.

The mental. Descartes characterised the furniture of the mind in terms, broadly, of consciousness: what we are incorrigible about, what is immediately present to us. Thoughts that run through the head; pains, mental images.

This obviously will not do; well before Freud[2] we were familiar with the need to ascribe to others mental states of which they are not conscious. It is easy to be self-deceived, for example, and to fail to realise one's jealousy; we know about subliminal perception; beliefs are dispositional states, so just as we say of sugar that it is soluble, so we can say of a sleeping man that he believes something – indeed, most beliefs are infrequently present to consciousness, yet it seems true that we have them nonetheless. We need not labour this point, because it is now adequately accepted. (Nonetheless, as we shall see, it will be the 'Cartesian' subclass of mental phenomena that ultimately constitutes the greatest difficulty for mind–body materialism.)

Brentano characterised the mental in terms of intensionality[3] or, more simply, 'aboutness'. Mental states are characteristically 'about' things or states of affairs; the things may not exist and the states of

412

affairs may not obtain, but the mental has them as its content.

This characterisation allows us to include as mental much that the Cartesian description excluded: non-conscious or tacit beliefs, for example, unacknowledged prejudices, and so forth. But it seems both to exclude, and to include, too much. Exclusion: what of pains? Having a pain seems not to be a state that is 'about' anything. And what of 'feeling sleepy'? Over-inclusiveness: those working on the brain, or with computers, constantly talk, and need to talk, about brain-states or machine-states handling 'information' – a thoroughly intensional notion. But do computers, or brain regions, have mental states? For example: in Sokolov's account of habituation we read that one role of the hippocampus is to 'compare incoming with expected stimuli'. (The hippocampus is assigned the 'comparator' function in the flow-chart illustrated above on p. 409.) 'Comparing' and 'expecting' are alike laden with intensionality; yet we are, or might be, reluctant to ascribe mental states to the hippocampus. Consider too what happens when a psychologist sets out to explain perception. Typically he breaks down 'seeing' into subordinate tasks or functions: the information-transmission tasks of retina and optic nerve; of the primary visual cortex, responding to colour contrasts, texture gradients, line alignments, and so forth; of the secondary visual cortex, putting together into a Gestalt the information selected by the primary cortex; of the posterior temporal-parietal junction, assisting in verbal recognition of elements of the visual scene. Quite often 'macro' functions like seeing, hearing, learning, remembering and so forth are thus explained, by breaking them down into sub-functions; but the sub-functions are themselves often identified in intensional ('mental') terms. In brief, *there seems to be no single 'level' of description at which, and only at which, 'mental' terminology applies.*

Mention of Sokolov, and more generally of the explanation of mental functioning by dissecting capacities into subordinate contributory capacities, introduces another ambiguity. The common-sense psychology we all use to describe and explain behaviour – citing, for instance, 'believing' or 'recalling' – what relation does this bear to the conceptual apparatus of the computer programmer or the neuropsychologist, who may talk rather of 'information processing/retrieval'? When we 'compare' or 'expect' things, how does this relate to the way the hippocampus apparently 'compares' incoming with 'expected' stimuli? We shall return to this difficulty; it evidently connects with the question, noted above, whether our common-sense conceptual apparatus can be described as 'a theory'. (*Scientific* psychology, clearly, does hope to produce a genuine theory.) For the moment, let us from now on reserve 'mental' for the everyday vocabulary of the man in the street, and 'psychological' for the vocabulary used by scientists in white coats and laboratories – leaving open the possibility that there may be a large overlap.

Another complicating factor now intrudes. Obvi-

413

ously, the mental (or psychological) is not homogeneous. What we put into 'the mind' and call 'mental' or 'psychological' may be as diverse as: events like the pain of a pinprick; long-term states such as the belief that p; short-term states like attention to a lecturer; characteristics like honesty or intelligence; reasoning processes like mental arithmetic; capacities like visual acuity or perfect pitch. This is a *very* diverse collection, even neglecting the hippocampus' 'expectation' or the computer's 'information retrieval'; and what, if anything, they all have in common, such that all can be called 'mental' or 'psychological', is wholly obscure. Already we have seen the effects of this heterogeneity, when noting that some 'nothing but' theorists (wisely) restricted their theses to sensation-type mental phenomena, leaving open the question of whether beliefs or desires might succumb to the same treatment. Look too at Davidson's *a priori* argument for an identity between mental and physical;[4] this relies on an intensional characterisation of mental phenomena, and may not work well for 'Cartesian' mental phenomena like pains; but Kripke's *a priori* argument against identity[5] concerns 'Cartesian' mental phenomena, such as pains, and may work poorly for 'Brentano' mental phenomena, such as beliefs.

We have no clear and principled way as yet, then, for picking out what it is for something to be mental. Examination of the issue can be deepened if we turn to the other half of the traditional divide, to the physical.

The physical. This at first sight seems easy: the physical is whatever the physical scientist says it is. For us, this means that the physical is whatever the physiologist says it is: cells, synapses, axons, dendrites.

But this is short-sighted. Why stop at cells – why not go lower, to molecular interactions, to atoms even? Conversely, why not go higher – to cell-columns, to patterns or spiking frequencies of cell-firing, to large cerebral masses such as the fornix, the amygdala, the occipital lobe, the left hemisphere? These are surely 'physical', if anything is; and it is a brute fact that scientists (whether we call them neurophysiologists, neuropsychologists or neurobiologists is here unimportant) talk about, examine, describe and explain all levels of the brain – from molecules in the cell nucleus up to the cerebral hemispheres. Moral: *there is no such thing as 'a' brain-state*: such levels of description are not 'given'. We must always discover the level at which the neuroscientist is operating; and he may be operating at several levels simultaneously.

Worse: as we have seen, neuroscientists talk not only about the *things* (cell nuclei, dendrites, the splenium, the left hemisphere), but also, and obviously, they need to talk about their functions, about what they *do*: cells fire, cell-columns transmit information and collate, compare, process incoming stimuli from other cell-columns; a massively complex organ

414

like the left hemisphere exercises capacities like controlling speech production. Much of this terminology looks thoroughly 'mental', or at least 'psychological'. When we read in neuropsychological textbooks that (for example) 'the septal-hippocampal system *sends a signal* via the fornix to *the decision centre* in the medial hypothalamus', then any distinction between 'mental' and 'physical' terminology, between 'functional/psychological' and 'structural/physiological' levels of description, has evidently dropped out.

In sum, the assumption upon which the mind–body problem rests – that there is an intuitively clear dichotomy between 'mental' and 'physical', 'a' mental and 'a' physical level – looks shaky. The manifest fact is that there are multiple 'levels' at which we can describe the mind *and* the brain, the mental *and* the physical, even though we are as yet a long way from identifying these 'levels'; and the terminology appropriate to characterise, say, the tasks of the hippocampus or of a computer seem not unambiguously 'mental' or 'physical'.

Implications

We are now in a position to see how many of the philosophical theories outlined above have invented, or misidentified, 'the' mind–body problem. The main mistakes seem to be these:

(1) Whether we have type or token relationships between mental/psychological and physical will depend essentially on the level of description we choose to describe either *relatum*. 'Same temperature' in two different gases is type correlated with 'same mean kinetic energy'. But only token correlations hold between the temperature of each gas and the (lower) level of atomic description. Analogously, when you and I both recite a poem we know well, there will be *some* level of description at which our brains are 'doing the same thing' – in other words, the language centres and the motor cortex, among hosts of other regions, are activated in similar kinds of ways (whereas our visual systems might be relatively quiescent). Yet at the level of individual cell-firings in our two brains, the patterns and the connections will be unique to each of us. Thus any assumption that one day the neurosciences will discover that there are type relationships *rather than* token ones, or vice versa, needs careful specification.

(2) Many of the arguments for and against the theories outlined in the previous section vastly over-simplify the issue, by assuming that 'the mental' and 'the physical' are somehow 'given'. So we find, for example, people debating whether 'pains are C-fibre firings'. Let us accept for the sake of argument that the 'mental' *relatum* here is indeed 'given', at least by intuition – by the thought that we all know what pain is! The same, however, fails for the 'physical' side. 'C-fibre firing' has been treated by philosophers like a joker card: substituting for 'whatever it is that neurophysiologists ultimately conclude to be the neural basis of pain'. (It has

415

to be such a joker, incidentally: pain *is not* C-fibre firing. C-fibre firing is normally – not always – an early member in the multiple series of parallel and sequential processes that go to realise pain; it is neither necessary nor sufficient for pain perception.) But it is mistaken to appeal to 'a' brain state that is (or is not) what pain is; there is no privileged description of 'whatever neurophysiologists ultimately conclude to be the neural basis of pain'. We must first find out what levels of description are intended. To repeat: there is no such thing, apart from a specific context and level of description, as 'a' brain state. What we want to say about monism and/or reductionism must vary radically, therefore, according to the levels of description chosen.

(3) All the theories discussed so far commit the error that I shall call 'the macro–micro jump'. This error wrongly presupposes that there is 'a' (macro) mental level, and 'a' (micro) physical level, such that we can, or should, ignore the ontological and explanatory relevance of 'middle' stages and instead debate a single macro-to-micro relationship; so that we can argue (as, for instance, Kripke[6] argues) against the identification of pains with 'C-fibre firing'; or so that we can say, with the new dualists, that 'the hardware' is irrelevant to explaining 'the software'.

The 'macro–micro jump' is both ontologically and explanatorily indefensible. Ontologically: as we have seen, 'macro' phenomena might *be* 'micro' phenomena by either type, or token, correlations. But whether we have type correlations, or only token ones, typically depends on the distance between the two. Explanatorily: explanation, note, is not necessarily transitive. That is, if we explain *As* by *Bs*, and *Bs* by *Cs*, it does not always follow that *As* are explained by *Cs*. 'Explanation' is a *pragmatic* notion – its job is to remove puzzlement. The *B*-description of gas temperature (mean kinetic energy) removes puzzlement about the sameness of temperature (the *A*-description), as the *C*-description (atomic properties) does not. Once we acknowledge the plurality of (psychological, neuro-psychological and physical) levels of description, note that there are no favoured or privileged 'brain-state descriptions', and accept that the cerebral processes (at macro,,, medium, and micro levels) that constitute some mental phenomenon will involve parallel and sequential processes in many regions of the brain, then the whole notion of 'a' brain-state, and hence the debates centring around identity, explanation or 'hardware realisation' start to look simple-minded. (So of course does the new dualists' alleged parallel with the undesirability of 'reducing' economic to physical theories: that is a beautiful illustration of the 'macro–micro jump'.)

(4) Most of the arguments in the literature take for granted that we know what 'the mental/psychological' is. As we now see, we do not. Moreover, the heterogeneity of mental/psychological phenomena make it *a priori* highly unlikely that there will be *one* theory that accounts for the relationship between 'all of them' and states of the brain. Perhaps the relationship will vary according to the mental/psychological phenomena in

question – perhaps we should expect as untidy a solution to 'the' mind–body problem as the mental is itself untidy. For instance: on empirical grounds it seems far more plausible to suppose that there will be *some* level of neuro-scientific description specifying cerebral processes which correlate type–type with certain kinds of pain – pinpricks, perhaps – than that there will be such descriptions available to pick out 'thoughts that I need toothpaste'.

(5) The distinction drawn above between 'mental' (the common-sense conceptual apparatus) and 'psychological' (the scientist's vocabulary) has considerable repercussions for all explanatory reductions. For such reductions hold only between *theories*. It is the theory of analytic chemistry that is being reduced to quantum chemistry, of molecular genetics to transmission genetics. No scientist wants to 'reduce' all the categories of everyday language – to reduce tables, carpets, ashtrays – to atomic physics. The very idea is absurd, and the reason simple: these are not terms of a theory. We have no laws concerning tables or carpets, because they are not natural kinds; hence no laws serve to group or 'explain' them; hence there are no laws to enter into explanatory reduction with the laws of a deeper theory. Scientific psychology evidently aims to develop a theory. Does common-sense psychology constitute one?

Our common-sense psychological vocabulary is but part of our everyday vocabulary more generally. If, then, we are searching for explanatory reductions between, say, 'beliefs that one needs more tooth-paste' and states or processes in the brain, there is need for hefty argument to support the idea that common-sense psychology, unlike any other part of our everyday conceptual framework, *is* genuinely a 'theory' of a kind that can fit into, and be explained by, laws at a deeper level; that 'beliefs that one needs toothpaste' are like tigers – amenable to systematic study *per se* – rather than like chairs, which are not. Scientific psychology seeks laws and regularities, searching for categories that *are* held together and explained by underlying laws. Some of the categories of common-sense psychology (for instance, perhaps, pains; capacities like seeing, hearing, tasting and so forth; some of the emotions; and others besides) will be 'natural kind' capacities and hence will also fall under scientific psychology. Similarly, our everyday terms 'gold' or 'tiger' single out natural kinds. But since common sense has no particular interest in natural kinds *as such*, it is extremely improbable that *all* the terms it deploys pick out phenomena which it profits science to study; after all, common sense talks of tables and gaskets as well as tigers and gold. Scientific psychology, though, *is* interested in natural kinds as such, seeking to explain in law-like fashion the pervasive and fundamental natural-kind capacities and traits of the organism. Thus it is rather a scientific psychology, not the rich and riotous chaos of common-sense psychology, for which explanatory reductions are appropriate.

417

Best solution: structural-functional analysis

I call this 'structural-functionalism' ('SF analysis' for short) to avoid confusion with the functionalisms described above. I shall state it very briefly, then explain and defend it.

SF analysis, like functionalism, reiterates the behaviourists' methodology: it too opens up the 'black box' and postulates interlocking systems of black boxes. But there are two differences from functionalism: (a) the boxes are characterised functionally *or* structurally; (b) each of these 'boxes' can in turn be opened up and subjected to an SF analysis, and so on without any fixed limit. It *begs the mind–body problem in advance*, by affirming that one test of any psychological theory is whether it is such that the brain can realise it, and of a neuroscientific theory, whether it serves to explain mental functioning.

Now for elaboration and defence.

(1) SF analysis applies to the scientific–psychological, not the common sense–mental. It proffers a form of reduction, and reductions hold between *theories*. (But as we shall see, most of 'the mental' will prove to take care of itself.)

(2) We saw earlier that there was no interesting or clear distinction between 'structures' and 'functions', and that there were functions and structures at all levels of description, from 'macro' to 'micro'. Thus it matters not at all whether the 'boxes' in the SF analyst's flow–chart are structurally, or functionally, characterised. (It may often be more convenient to 'talk functionally' – e.g. when we are not sure which structure(s), if any, perform the function, or when the function is complex, needing to be explained in terms of subordinate functions and structures widely scattered through the brain. Conversely, we may know of a structure such as the amygdala that it performs *some* functions relevant to memory storage, but may not know which; then 'structure talk' may be more convenient.) Few mistakes have been as misleading as the assumption by some functionalists that psychology handles 'functions/software' and neuroscientists 'structures/hardware'; to study 'human vision' is, among other things, to study 'the human visual system'.

(3) The spectrum of 'levels' (psychological and physical) of organisation in the brain shows why the (functionalists') idea of opening up the 'black box' which is the organism, and postulating internal systems of smaller black boxes, is a method that cries out to be reiterated *ad libitum*. But now, noting that the 'boxes' can be characterised functionally *or* structurally, we can see our task as both explaining functions, and analysing structures. Given, for instance, that the hippocampus has the comparator-function in Sokolov's theory, we can go on to discover by what functions and structures that organ can be capable of comparing incoming with expected stimuli – how the 'hippocampus/comparator box' is organised.

418

(4) We also saw that there is no interesting or clear distinction between 'psychological' and 'physical' terms. There was much unclassifiability 'in the middle'; neuroscientists persistently use intensional terminology. SF analysis thus debunks the old dichotomy: 'psychological' just means 'terms typically used at the macro/psychological level'; 'neuro-psychological' and 'neurophysiological', 'terms typically used by neuro-psychologists and neurophysiologists'. 'The' psychological/physical distinction is thus given the place it deserves: one of pragmatic convenience, no more. This helps show how 'the' problem is begged at the outset.

(5) SF analysis aims for a *smooth* (non-eliminative and explanatory) reduction from psychology to neuroscience. This for a simple reason: we do not as yet *have* a general psychological theory to reduce, nor do we have more than scrappy mini-theories in neuroscience; to repeat, we have not yet identified and characterised most of the 'levels' we need, whether in psychology, neuropsychology or neurophysiology. Poor, inadequate or false theories reduce roughly – are 'displaced' by the reducing theory. But we are attempting to develop 'good' psychological and neuroscientific theories alike. Thus theories of all levels will evolve together: psychology seeking for *explananda* which smoothly reduce to lower-level theories, the neurosciences seeking for *explanantia* which underlie and underpin the claims made at upper levels. We see then that *the description and characterisation of what is to be explained is constrained by the nature of the candidate explanations for the phenomena*. The fundamental and pervasive psychological capacities of the human mind are identified and grouped, in part, by what deeper study reveals to be systematically bound together. Researches 'from above', 'middle-both-ways' and 'from below' inspire and enlighten each other; the 'top down' work hints at what lower-level research might be looking for, while 'bottom up' research suggests what sorts of 'higher' functions cerebral systems might be thought to perform.

So the goal of reductionism becomes a many-pronged and co-evolutionary enterprise: *not* a matter of starting at one 'fixed' end of a kind of vertical Channel Tunnel, at the 'psychological' end (France?), and tunnelling downwards – postulating functions, sub-functions, sub-sub-functions, and hoping one day to meet those tunnelling upwards from a 'fixed' 'neurophysiological' end (Britain?), who start from mini-structures like cells and mini-processes like synapses. In the scientific study of the mind/brain, there are and must be those working at all levels of analysis.

One example, although hundreds could be provided, will serve to establish the *necessity* of such a coevolutionary enterprise. Consider the psychologist studying perception. He is trying to identify the subordinate functions involved in, say, recognition; maybe by producing a convincing flow-chart diagram that purports to explain this capacity. Now: of the utmost relevance to his task is the work done by those studying 'the next level down' – studying injuries caused by strokes, tumours, lesions to parts of the visual system: those studying the hardware and its capacities at a relatively macro level. (Already we see the hardware, the 'structures', entering in.) For such research reveals *unexpectedly* significant facts about how the visual system must be organised, by showing the peculiar ways in which it breaks down. For instance: visual recognition can be unimpaired *except* for face-recognition (a condition called prosopagnosia) – thus indicating that this may be a relatively independent sub-function within recognition more generally. How could one have guessed at this, without seeing how the *human* brain can occasionally fail? Again: recognition may be unimpaired but for the recognition of letters, words (*not* necessarily numbers) and seen colours (a condition called pure alexia): that is a brute fact which cries out for, *and can be explained by*, deeper SF analysis – in terms of damage to part of the visual cortex and part of the corpus callosum, the splenium[7] – and which the psychologist cannot, or at least should not, overlook if he wants enlightenment about how perception is organised.

(6) What now of 'multiple realisability'? SF analysis concedes *variable* realisability. We should expect that psychological states will be explained (at the next level down) by somewhat different black-box diagrams in human, chimpanzee and rat; and *those* mini-theories are in turn likely to vary in the explanation given for them. By reiterating this variability in the descent down the levels of analysis, and *if we insist on making 'the macro–micro jump' mistake*, we will inevitably find all 'macro' phenomena multiply realised by micro processes. But so it would be with any science. Sameness of temperature in two gases has the same 'realisation' in mean kinetic energy, different 'realisations' at the atomic level. 'Multiple' realisability only looks significant if we make the mistake of jumping from macro to micro, leapfrogging over the intermediate levels; and that leads as rapidly to confusion in physics as it does in psychology.

Moreover, if the 'next-level' explanation were *radically* different, then – since *explananda* are in part defined and grouped by their *explanantia* – how do we know that we have 'the same phenomenon' at all? Consider the problem mentioned earlier: is artificial intelligence (seeing, hearing) *really* intelligence (seeing, hearing)? Now it is possible that we have 'the same *explananda*' even when we have drastically different *explanantia*, as temperature theory again illustrates: 'temperature' in plasmas cannot be explained, as it is in gases, by molecular movement – simply because plasmas are not composed of molecules at all. But psychology is unlike the theory of temperature; here we are still searching for the appropriate (macro) categories whereby to classify intelligent behaviour, and so when confronted with what *looks* like 'the same' capacity in animals and computers, a great deal of empirical *and conceptual* work is required if we are to call them genuinely 'the same'. We emphatically cannot assume that they will prove to be.[8]

(7) The much-trumpeted 'computer analogy' serves to support this methodology. Far too much has, I think, been claimed for

'artificial intelligence'. Nonetheless, the computer illustrates a simple hierarchy of levels, showing how, in systems much cruder than the brain, 'lower' levels explain, group and realise capacities at 'higher' levels. We are compelled to talk of expert systems, or chess-playing computers, in intensional ('mental') terms; they 'intend' to capture the bishop, 'infer' that plant P has disease D. We can explain the 'intending', and 'inferring' by describing the programs underlying these capacities, and then the lower-level programs which underlie the various functions employed by the top-level program ... and so on down. In computers, the abilities – albeit characterised in psychological terms – of chess-playing systems are not problematic: we know (because we have created them) how it can come about that a mechanism (which at the machine-code level merely produces strings of 0s and 1s) can beat national-class chess-players. To understand fully how such computers operate, we need more than a grasp of the machine code. We need to grasp the assembly language, the translation of higher-level languages into the assembly language, and the translation of 'user friendly' languages such as PASCAL or FORTRAN into the languages intermediate between them and the assembly language.

The simple computer is, of course, too simple to serve as more than a crude analogy. When we come to consider human psychological capacity and the brain, we as yet have little idea what, or where, the appropriate 'levels' are. But the fact remains that the computer can show us how a purely physical system can *unproblematically* produce behaviour that requires description in psychological terms; it shows us how a non-eliminative explanatory reduction can take care of the bulk of the mind–body problem.

Limitations and objections

SF analysis seems to me to dissolve three-quarters of the mind–body problem. It dissolves rather than solves it, by denying that the problem arises. By assuming that the brain is responsible for psychological capacity, it strives to *explain* how it manages it. The SF theory, sketched so broadly above, aims for a non-eliminative explanatory reduction. The *ontological* question has dropped out – it is no more interesting, or important, than the parallel question would be about the program-states specified by a PASCAL program.

It should not by now be surprising, though, to find that SF analysis as so far sketched will not do everything. This is unsurprising, because we have insisted on the manifest *heterogeneity* of the mental; and have argued that the *explananda* and *explanantia* of a scientific psychology will not necessarily overlap more than partially with those of common-sense psychology. This concluding section, then, will attempt to describe and discuss what SF analysis may fail to explain.

First objection: sentience

Functionalism generally, and SF analysis too, face the common objection that even if cognitive capacity is explained, they cannot cope with the 'Cartesian' mental – with consciousness, qualia, pains; that they fail, in Nagel's deservedly famous phrase,[9] to explain 'what it is like to be' a sentient agent. It seems to the intuition of many that the fullest possible explanation of, say, the processes of perception would not come near explaining the *experience* of colour. Put another way, an organism could perhaps realise (at every level) the SF analysis of seeing red objects, responding selectively to red and only red things, discriminating between red and orange things, etc., and yet have no *experience* (sense–datum, quale) of redness. Blindsight[10] serves to bolster this thought experiment. 'Blindsighted' people can discriminate objects, shapes and colours in their visual field, while (because of specific damage to the visual system) being unaware that they are visually sensing anything. This problem goes by the name of the 'absent qualia' objection. Alternatively, two systems might indeed have visual experiences; but their colour spectra might be inverted with respect to each other. Suppose that two organisms, S_1 and S_2, look in broad daylight at a bright red object. S_1 has a quale Q_1, S_2 has a quale Q_2; but were S_1 to experience Q_2, it would call what it saw 'green', and conversely. Nothing, however, in the SF analysis could – it is argued – describe or predict this elusive aspect of subjective experience. This problem is termed the 'inverted spectrum' objection.

The chief difficulty in coping with such challenges is – as the more honest and intelligent among its proponents admit – the indefiniteness of the charge. It is no longer possible just to object that 'consciousness' is left out of the physicalist picture, when there is no theoretically sound account of just what 'consciousness' is. Nor does it help to object that qualia are ignored; for this only invites the reply that the objection cannot be clearly and seriously met unless some clear and serious specification of these 'qualia' is provided. (It is interesting, and by no means irrelevant, to note that in ancient Greece there were no terms that translate as 'consciousness' or 'qualia/sense–data/sensory experiences'; yet Aristotle produced an SF account of psychological capacity that is essentially far more modern than most contemporary accounts.) Nevertheless, the intuition may remain that a blurry finger has been placed on a blurry area of concern *somewhere*.

Much of the difficulty may yet be tractable. Dennett has delivered sketches of SF theory (he does not use this label, but his theory fits my characterisation neatly) that attempt to show how consciousness in general, and pain perception in particular, might succumb to SF analysis. He has also argued that the postulate of qualia is suspect – that the problem allegedly posed by 'absent qualia' and the 'inverted spectrum' is an unreal one. To *part* of Nagel's challenge one can answer that any objective account of course ignores any 'element of subjectivity': just as the maps you buy in bookshops don't say where you are, so the (notional) complete physicalistic description of your psychological and physiological make-up won't say 'this is you', or 'this is what it is like to be you'; but in either case one could use the map, or the description, to discover where one is, or *that* this description is of someone tone-deaf, or depressed, or red–green colour blind – and this, to my mind, is one interpretation of subjectivity, of 'what it is like to be' such an individual.

Perhaps intuition yet insists that something is still omitted. That is a pervasive worry, which provokes two thoughts. First, every effort must be made to say precisely and accurately just what *is* indeed omitted (and the defender of SF analysis should not anyway expect one theory to explain everything, as we have seen: 'the mental' is too heterogeneous). Second, suppose that a clear and specific account of some 'subjective experiences' – qualia, for instance – has been provided. Then, so far as we now know, it may well be that such phenomena can in fact be identified with some level of description of brain activity: perhaps the spiking frequency of neurons, or the pattern properties of neural excitation. We do not yet know whether this is so; but we certainly do not know that it is *not* so. Such an identification (which may be 'strict' identity, or a 'nothing but' relation) will certainly be surprising, counterintuitive and unfamiliar. But so are many accepted identities in other scientific domains. Consider, for example, the identification of matter with energy. The informed layman accepts *that* matter is indeed energy. Probably he does not quite understand how, nor why, it is – this is not something that fits common-sense intuition. The physicist understands the identification, and can explain it to those capable of mastering physical theory. So might it be with something like sensory qualia. If 'the experience of blue' is identified with a specific spiking frequency of a neural net, most of us will not understand what this involves, lacking the necessary neurophysiological background. But such failure of comprehension would not prevent the claim from (possibly) being true.

The moral of this is that the 'consciousness' objection to mind–brain reductionism awaits a clearer specification; and that it yet has to be shown that once this specification is provided, the challenge cannot in principle be met.

Common-sense psychology

The account offered above explicitly invites the next objection. SF analysis claims to explain the phenomena picked out by scientific psychology. But, as we have seen, common-sense psychology may not invariably (or indeed often) talk of the same things as does the science; so since SF analysis purports to describe a relation between scientific theories, it has little to say about the phenomena picked out by common-sense psychology.

The answer to this objection, though, is not hard to supply. There will be no explanatory, type–type, reductions between most of the phenomena singled out by common-sense psychology and by neuro-science; for precisely the same reasons that there are no such reductions for ashtrays, carpets, police uniforms – and, generally, other familiar elements of everyday vocabuary. Every ashtray, though, is token–token constituted by *some* micro-physical complex. Analogously, then, if one accepts that there are such mental phenomena as, say, 'my thought yesterday that I need more toothpaste', this will be in fact realised (token–token) by a particular set of events (at some level of description) in assorted regions of the brain. No explanatory reductions are available, if what we are discussing are not 'natural kind' phenomena. But there is clear *ontological* reduction: such thoughts *are* (again, at some level of description) realised by, constituted by, the same as, sets of neurophysiological processes.

There is another answer of a quite different sort: to claim that many of our mental ascriptions do not, despite appearances, purport to refer to 'real', 'existing' mental states and processes. In short, much (not all) of our common-sense conceptual apparatus may be *instrumentalistic*. Beliefs, thoughts etc., are ascribed because by their help we render behaviour intelligible, not because we are committed to the claim – which is in any case somewhat perplexing and confusing – that they are all 'really there'. We do not think that the expression 'doing it for your sake' commits us to sakes; so, analogously, we may not in fact be committed to 'mental images' just because we talk about them, or to 'a thought that there is another step', just because the ascription of that thought serves to explain someone's stumble. This view, though (which I myself endorse), needs fuller description and defence than I have time to give it here.[11]

Notes

(An author's name followed by a number in square brackets refers to the book or article with that number in the bibliography.)

1. For another account of functionalism, seen in the context of non-reductionist theories, see Ch. 17, pp. 396–8.

2. See L.L. Whyte, *The unconscious before Freud* (Basic Books, New York, 1960).

3. The reader innocent of what 'intensionality' is will find it clearly explained in R. Chisholm, *Perceiving* (Cornell University Press, Ithaca, 1957), Ch. 11.

4. D. Davidson, 'Mental events' in Davidson [5].

5. S. Kripke, 'Identity and necessity' in M. Munitz (ed.), *Identity and individuation* (New York University Press, New York, 1971); 'Naming and necessity' in D. Davidson and G. Harman (eds), *Semantics and natural language* (Reidel, Dordrecht, 1972), pp. 334–42.

6. Kripke, 'Identity and necessity'.

7. For description of prosopagnosia and pure alexia see: (a) D.F. Benson and N. Geschwind (eds), *Handbook of clinical neurology* (North-Holland, Amsterdam, 1969), reprinted more accessibly in N. Geschwind, *Selected papers on language and the brain*, Boston Studies in the Philosophy of Science, vol. XVI (Reidel, Dordrecht, 1974); (b)

A.L. Benton, 'Visuoperceptive, visuospatial and visuoconstructive disorders' in K.M. Heilman and E. Valenstein (eds), *Clinical neuropsychology* (Oxford University Press, Oxford, 1979).

8. One overriding reason why 'artificial' intelligence looks to be as yet far from 'real' intelligence comes with the so-called 'frame problem'. Unfortunately there is no space to discuss it here; but a *very* clear discussion of the problem is provided by D. Dennett, 'Cognitive wheels: the frame problem of artificial intelligence' in Hookway [15].

9. T. Nagel, 'What is it like to be a bat?' in Nagel [19], pp. 165–80.

10. For discussion of blindsight see L. Weiskrantz, E.K. Warrington, M.D. Sanders and J. Marshall, 'Visual capacity in the hemianopic field following a restricted occipital ablation', *Brain*, vol. 97 (1974), pp. 709–28; also L. Weiskrantz, 'Varieties of residual experience', *Quarterly Journal of Experimental Psychology,* vol. 32 (1980), pp. 365–86.

11. Instrumentalism is defended by D. Dennett, 'Three kinds of intentional psychology' in R. Healey (ed.), *Reduction, time and reality* (Cambridge University Press, Cambridge, 1981); D. Dennett, 'Making sense of ourselves', *Philosophical Topics*, vol. 12 (1981), pp. 63–81; K.V. Wilkes, 'Nemo psychologus nisi physiologus', *Inquiry* (forthcoming).

Bibliography

An introductory discussion of various kinds of reductionism may be found in

[1] P.M. Churchland, *Matter and consciousness* (MIT Press, Cambridge, Massachusetts, 1984).

Early ground-breaking articles arguing that mental states are 'nothing but' brain processes include U.T. Place's 'Is consciousness a brain process?' (1956) and J.J.C. Smart's 'Sensations and brain processes' (1962); these and other influential papers are collected in

[2] J. O'Connor (ed.), *Modern materialism: readings on mind–body identity* (Harcourt, Brace and World, New York, 1969).

More recent material may be found in another valuable collection of essays on this topic:

[3] N. Block (ed.), *Readings in the philosophy of psychology* (Methuen, London, 1980).

For a clear, up-to-date discussion of varieties of reductionism, see

[4] C.A. Hooker, 'Towards a general theory of reduction', Parts I–III, *Dialogue*, 20 (1981), pp. 38–60, 201–35, 496–592.

An *a priori* argument for the 'identity thesis' appears in Ch. 11 of

[5] D. Davidson, *Actions and events* (Clarendon Press, Oxford, 1980); and a celebrated *a priori* argument against the thesis is in the final part of

[6] S. Kripke, *Naming and necessity* (Basil Blackwell, Oxford, revised 1980).

For a radical version of the 'nothing but' thesis, see Part I of

[7] R. Rorty, *Philosophy and the mirror of nature* (Basil Blackwell, Oxford, 1980).

From the vast literature on functionalism, one of the most readable works is

[8] D. Dennett, *Brainstorms* (Harvester, Hassocks, 1978).

See also the chapter entitled 'The mental life of some machines' in

[9] H. Putnam, *Mind, language and reality, Philosophical Papers, Vol. 2* (Cambridge University Press, Cambridge, 1985).

A sophisticated defence of functionalism may be found in

[10] S. Shoemaker, *Identity, cause, and mind* (Cambridge University Press, Cambridge, 1984).

A much discussed argument against functionalism is J. Searle's 'Minds, brains and programs', to be found in

[11] D. Dennett and D. Hofstadter, *The mind's I* (Penguin Books, Harmondsworth, 1978).

The new dualism (as well as other topics in this chapter) is discussed in

[12] J. Fodor, *Representations* (Harvester, Hassocks, 1981) and in

[13] S. Stich, *From folk psychology to cognitive science* (MIT Press, Cambridge, Massachusetts, 1983).

The influential computer analogy is examined in

[14] K. Gunderson, *Mentality and machines*, 2nd edn (University of Minnesota Press, Minneapolis, 1985).

See also

[15] C. Hookway (ed.), *Minds, machines and evolution* (Cambridge University Press, Cambridge, 1985) and

[16] H.L. Dreyfus, *What computers can't do: the limits of artificial intelligence* (Harper and Row, New York, 1979).

Among works emphasising the differences between common sense and science are the brilliant but neglected

[17] L. Mandler and W. Kessen, *The language of psychology* (John Wiley, New York, 1959) and

[18] J. Russell, *Explaining mental life* (Macmillan, London, 1984).

The puzzles posed for reductionism by the phenomena of sentience, consciousness and qualia are discussed in Shoemaker [10] and Gunderson [14]; the most influential article is T. Nagel's 'What is it like to be a bat', reprinted in

[19] T. Nagel, *Mortal questions* (Cambridge University Press, Cambridge, 1979).

For the structural-functional approach see

[20] A. Clarke, *Psychological models and neural mechanisms* (Clarendon Press, Oxford, 1980).

Grateful acknowledgement is made to Dr Wilkes for her comprehensive and detailed suggestions concerning this bibliography.

J.G.C

19 | *Behaviourism*

Geoffrey Madell

Behaviourism is a form of materialism, but one which it is not always easy to distinguish from other varieties of materialism. It is easy to say that its central tenet is that the mind is somehow reducible to behaviour, but it soon becomes apparent that there is major disagreement on what is to count as behaviour. Some behaviourists argue that psychological states are nothing more than physical processes within the body; others have held that it is the behaviour *of* the body to which psychological states should be reduced, rather than to whatever may go on within the body. It is the former position which is difficult to distinguish from other forms of materialism. It looks, in fact, to be indistinguishable from the materialism of an identity theorist such as J.J.C. Smart.

A further difference among behaviourists is evident in the nature of their fundamental concerns. Some see their central concern as scientific, while others see theirs as philosophical. Behaviourism as a movement in contemporary thought began with the work of J.B. Watson, whose concern was to establish psychology as a science. If science is to be truly objective, he argued, scientists must be able to observe the same objects and events. States of consciousness, as the dualist thinks of them, are intrisically private, and cannot for this reason feature in an objective science. Watson felt that only if psychology can be reduced to physics can it have any claims to scientific objectivity. Philosophical behaviourists, on the other hand, have shared this concern with objectivity, but it is the ordinary person's right to say that he knows what other people are thinking and feeling, rather than the scientist's concern with the status of psychology, which is the centre of their interest. To this end, they argue that our ordinary language gives no support to the Cartesian view of mental states as logically private, and they also argue that such a view of mental states is in any case logically absurd.

427

Although the term 'behaviourism' has thus been used to cover quite a multitude of positions, it is possible to isolate a distinctive concern with behaviour in the sense of the behaviour of the body rather than within the body, and to detect two different motives for this concern, one being the question of the status of psychology as a science, and the other being the question of the nature of our ordinary understanding of mental states and of the language which we use in talking of such states. We may term the former school of thought 'scientific behaviourism' and the latter 'philosophical behaviourism', though it should be made clear that there can be no hard and fast line between interests which are scientific and those which are philosophical.

Scientific behaviourism

Scientific behaviourists essentially claim that the concern of psychology is the prediction of behaviour. What the scientist should be working to discover, then, are laws which relate behaviour to other publicly observable states of affairs, which enable us to see behaviour as the result of some impact on the organism (animal or human being) of some observable circumstance. But how, we may ask, does the basic position lead to the view that it is behaviour of the body rather than the behaviour of anything within the body which should be at the centre of our concern? Why should the nature of inner processes be excluded from the scene, particularly as, we may feel, it is the nature of such inner processes which may immediately determine the direction of subsequent behaviour?

The leading proponent of the view that such inner processes are to be excluded from consideration is B.F. Skinner, whose position is often described as 'radical behaviourism', but the precise nature of his opposition to the positing or investigation of inner states is not easy to determine. We might initially suppose that it is just the objection to their intrinsic privacy, and indeed he does appear to be objecting to the Cartesian view of inner experiences as essentially private. However, he appears also, and more insistently, to be objecting to the positing of inner states to explain behaviour, whatever these inner states may be, whether they are thought of as logically private on the Cartesian model, or whether they are thought of as physical states whose nature we might eventually investigate. Why should this be?

Part of the reason seems to be that he feels that reference to such inner states must always prove redundant. A theory in psychology, as in any branch of science, is successful only to the extent to which it relates antecedent conditions to subsequent behaviour. But if this is the case, then we can pass straight from the antecedent conditions to the subsequent behaviour without reference to theoretical inner states. However, if this is Skinner's main reason, it has to be said that it is without any foundation at all. To accept it would be to claim that theoretical postulates must never play any part in scientific explanation, an extraordinary dogma which would have prevented the development of atomic theory, to choose just one example, since there is no question that the atom entered science as just such a theoretical postulate. Science could not advance if it did not infer the existence of mediating events and processes. In the case of psychology, it is difficult to understand why any materialist should object to inferring the existence of inner physical mechanisms as the immediate determinants of behaviour, particularly as such a materialist will expect that these inner mechanisms will some day be described by neurophysiology.

There is, however, another strand in Skinner's thinking on this issue. He often objects to the positing of specifically mental states to explain behaviour on the grounds that such explanations turn out to be empty. They are on a par with explaining why opium puts people to sleep by citing its *virtus dormitiva*, or sleep-producing power. In this vein, Skinner complains of the ease with which each mental process is discovered to have just the properties needed to account for the behaviour it is meant to explain: a professor turns up in the wrong classroom because his *mind* is *absent*. If he repeats himself, it is because he has an *idée fixe*. A man eats because he is hungry, or plays the piano well because of his musical ability; and so on.

But it really cannot be claimed that explanation in terms of psychological states and properties is characteristically empty in this way. On the contrary, to posit some inner psychological state will typically make the prediction of behaviour far simpler and more effective than would be possible otherwise. This is true even in the case of computers; it is far easier to explain and predict the behaviour of a chess-playing computer by thinking of it as if it had powers of logical thought rather than by keeping a record of every move the computer makes and attempting to correlate particular sorts of moves with particular sorts of antecedent conditions, a procedure which is likely to get the investigator nowhere at all unless he knows about the internal state of the computer. Just as obvious is the fact that the prediction of human behaviour is far easier if one can ascribe to the subject some inner mental state: he wants x, or is indignant that p. Indeed, without our understanding of such inner states, the behavioural items which we group together and see as various manifestations of the same mental state would appear as a randomly selected bunch of events and processes, having no pattern or unity at all. Skinner's attempt to explain verbal behaviour without recourse to inner states bears startling witness to this, as Chomsky has shown. There is every reason to believe that the fact that a grasp of inner psychological states is necessary if any significant pattern at all is to be discerned in human behaviour will tell against every form of behaviourism which denies or ignores such states, as we shall see in the next section.

Scientific behaviourists, then, unite in rejecting the dualist's conception of states of consciousness as intrinsically private, for, it is claimed, such private states cannot feature in an objective science. Some who have called themselves behaviourists have argued that such inner states should be reduced to physical states, and only the accident of the label they have given themselves may prevent one from seeing that this is indistinguishable from one of the varieties of materialism which were considered in the previous chapter. The distinctive behaviourist doctrine requires the denial of inner events, or at least their dismissal as irrelevant. It seems fairly evident that the radical behaviourism of Skinner provides no reason for such a posture. Our task now will be to see whether philosophical behaviourism can make such a denial any more plausible.

Philosophical behaviourism

While the scientific behaviourism represented by Skinner is concerned with the prospects for a scientific investigation of human behaviour, the concern of certain philosophers who are often termed 'philosophical behaviourists' looks to be quite different. Scientific behaviourism deems reference to states which are supposed to be inner and private to be scientifically useless. Philosophical behaviourism, on the other hand, regards the whole idea of mental states as intrinsically private to their owners, states of which each of us is incorrigibly aware in his own case, as logically absurd. Gilbert Ryle, in his celebrated book *The concept of mind*, argues that the Cartesian conception of the mind as essentially private makes it absolutely impossible to know of the existence of any mind but one's own. But he also argues that the whole Cartesian idea of consciousness is intrinsically absurd; for if I am necessarily conscious of my mental states as they occur, then, since being conscious of something is itself a mental state, I must be conscious of my consciousness of the original state, and conscious of *that* consciousness, and so on *ad infinitum*. Wittgenstein, in an enormously influential passage in his *Philosophical investigations*, has generally been taken to have argued that the supposed status of mental states as logically private to their owners would make it impossible to refer to them in a language we all understand, a language which is governed by rules, as anything deemed to be a language must be. What assurance could I have that the logically private state I call 'pain' is anything like the state anyone else refers to by this term? How, indeed, can I have any assurance that even in my own case I always succeed in recognising pain whenever it occurs as the same sort of sensation as those I have called pains in my past experience? My impression is that I do have the same sort of sensation, but this impression is, in the nature of the case, something which cannot be checked to establish whether it is correct. At one point Wittgenstein asks us to get rid of the idea of the logically private inner state by supposing that it is in fact always changing, but that one fails to notice this.

What, then, is the correct view of the nature of mind, according to these thinkers? There are, as we shall see, certain difficulties in giving a straightforward answer to this question, but there is no doubt that Ryle much of the time appears to be arguing for something like the following position. References to supposed inner states can always be eliminated, and, in fact, it is a misconception to suppose that our ordinary talk about minds gives any credence to the Cartesian view of mind. Essentially, when we ascribe a mental state to someone, what we are doing is not to infer the existence of some ghostly inner state on the basis of our observation of the subject's behaviour, but to characterise and assess just the observable behaviour of the subject. Thus, to describe someone as 'vain' is not to infer to some inner ghostly state of vanity, but implicitly to assert that a certain pattern can be discerned in the subject's behaviour. It is to say that the subject takes whatever opportunity presents itself to show himself in the best possible light, that he is often to be found admiring himself in a mirror, and so on.

There is one qualification of considerable importance to be made. Mental terms, Ryle argues, are not names for private inner states, but terms we use to characterise the agent's behaviour, but it is important to realise that very often what we are doing is implicitly to predict how a man *would* behave in certain circumstances rather than to characterise his actual behaviour. There may, Ryle points out, be no discernible difference between the behaviour of the soldier who hits the bullseye through luck and one who hits it through the exercise of skill. However, in saying of the latter that his behaviour was an exercise of skill we are not inferring to something going on behind his behaviour; what we are doing is to imply that he can be expected to hit the bullseye not only on this occasion but on many other occasions. We imply that this single achievement is part of a pattern of achievement which has been evident in the past and which can be expected to continue. When we describe glass as brittle, Ryle says, we are saying, in effect, not that it here and now breaks, but that it would break when subject to stress, that it can be expected to break in those circumstances. In much the same way, to describe someone as skilful, rational, obsequious or rash is to ascribe a behavioural *disposition* to him, to say something about how that person may be expected to behave in certain circumstances.

Ryle, then, repeatedly denies that talk about minds is talk about a realm of intrinsically private states and processes. 'It is being maintained throughout this book', he says

> that when we characterise people by mental predicates, we are not making untestable inferences to any ghostly processes occurring in streams of consciousness which we are debarred from visiting: we are describing the ways in which these people conduct parts of their predominantly public behaviour. (p. 51)

He rejects what he calls the Two-Worlds view, the view that there exist two kinds of stuff, the physical and the immaterial, and contemptuously charac-

431

terises the Cartesian view of persons as involving the doctrine of the Ghost in the Machine. What replaces this discredited view, for Ryle, is what appears to be the view that, to put it in its most extreme form, talk about minds can always be translated without remainder into talk about actual or potential behaviour of physical processes within it.

One clear implication of such a position is that if talk about minds is always talk about behaviour, then we must reject the view that we have any special access to our own mental states. And, indeed, Ryle is only too happy to reject this view, since it is just the view that, while we have a direct and infallible access to what is going on in our own minds, we can only infer to what is going on in the minds of other people which leads to the classical problem of other minds: if I can have no direct access to the minds of others, if minds are logically private to each individual, how can I have any assurance that minds other than my own exist? Ryle, then, rejects the position that we have a 'privileged access' to the contents of our own minds. 'The sorts of things that I can find out about myself', he says, 'are the same as the sorts of things that I can find out about other people, and the methods of finding them out are much the same' (p. 155). We may, however, feel that we do have a direct access to our own mental states, and that only such direct access could possibly explain how it is that we seem able to report on our wants, likes and dislikes, moods and emotions without waiting to observe our own behaviour. Ryle's answer to this point is that when we express our state of mind in such utterances as 'I want,' 'I hope,' 'I dislike,' 'I am depressed,' 'I feel hungry' and 'I wonder,' we are not making reports on what we find our inner feelings to be. What we are doing is to manifest our feelings. His position seems to be that a state like depression can be understood as the disposition to behave in the way which is characteristic of depression, and that this way will include the tendency to come out with utterances like 'I am depressed.' It would be quite wrong, then, to suppose that these cases show that we have a special access to our own mental states, a mode of access denied to others.

Another apparent difficulty for the thesis of philosophical behaviourism which Ryle attempts to deal with is presented by the fact that the behaviour of one who merely pretends to have a certain emotion may be indistinguishable from one who genuinely has such an emotion. Since this is so, the temptation to say that the real difference must lie in the presence in the one case of the inner state of feeling and its absence in the other looks irresistible. In fact, Ryle argues, the difference is a behavioural one. Although there may be in fact no detectable difference between the respective reactions of one who has and one who pretends to have a certain emotion, we would expect there to be a difference in certain crucial situations. For example, we would expect that a man who genuinely feels deep remorse for some injury inflicted on someone to be ready to make the sort of recompense which will cost him a great deal, whereas we would not expect this of someone whose remorse is merely sham.

The flaws in philosophical behaviourism

The thesis of philosophical behaviourism certainly gives us a remarkably simple account of the nature of mind, and one which might appear to solve all the problems about the relation between mind and body in one move. There is no doubt that Ryle demonstrates over and over again in relation to many particular examples that talk about this or that mental state, which might appear at first sight to involve reference to intrinsically private states and processes, ought to be construed as essentially talk about behaviour. Nevertheless, there are a number of absolutely fundamental objections to the thesis which might appear to rule it out of court altogether.

First, Ryle's claim that there is no essential difference between the way we find out about ourselves and the way we find out about other people, a claim which is absolutely central to the overall thesis, must surely be judged quite unsubstantiated. It cannot be correct to suggest that first-person utterances like 'I want' and 'I am hungry' can always be treated as if they were not reports at all, and thus as not even indicating that the subject has a special access to his own mental states which is denied to others. Such utterances can very often only be construed as reports. We need only to put any of these utterances into the past tense to see this. Clearly, in the past tense these assertions cannot be manifestations, or 'avowals' of one's mental state, but straight reports of what one felt in the past. It is also absolutely clear that what one reports is how one felt, rather than how one behaved. Equally clearly, one does know, in a way in which others cannot, what one is at this moment doing or thinking. Indeed, Ryle's assertion that such self-knowledge involves a readiness to tell oneself or the world what one would have done had one not been prevented seems to grant just this point.

It is, indeed, not simply that one knows what one is doing in a way which others cannot, but it is also the case that one knows immediately whether the behaviour one is producing is something one is doing rather than mere reaction, an action rather than something which is happening to one. This immediate knowledge of oneself as an agent is something which it is very difficult to make sense of within the framework of behaviourism. The Cartesian view of the nature of the difference between action and mere movement is that an item of behaviour is an action if it is brought about by an act of will, or a volition. Ryle condemns this account on the grounds that it leads to an infinite regress: if what makes anything voluntary is its being brought about by a volition, then the volition itself would have to be voluntary, and would in its turn require a prior volition, and so on *ad infinitum*. This argument can certainly be questioned on the grounds that it is not at all clear that it is proper to describe volition itself as either voluntary or involuntary, but whether the infinite regress argument is sound or not, an obligation lies on those who reject the idea of volition to give an account, both of the difference between action and mere movement, and of the agent's immediate knowledge of his own agency. It cannot be said that Ryle meets either of these requirements.

One particular way in which the failure to sustain the thesis that there is no essential difference between self-knowledge and knowledge of others shows itself is in Ryle's attempt to distinguish between genuine emotion and fake emotion. The difference for Ryle, to remind ourselves, is a behavioural one, a matter of the differences in behaviour which would be shown in a conceivable crucial situation. The trouble with this is that it clearly implies that not even the subject could know whether he was feigning or not until such a situation arose and he was able to note his reaction to it. The truth is that the subject will generally know what his state of mind is, whether he genuinely has a certain emotion or is merely feigning it, and he will know this prior to any related behaviour and in a way in which no one else can. There are, of course, plenty of cases where the subject's own state of mind will be opaque to him, but, however many of these cases there are, they remain a minority, even if a significant one. The fact is, and it is a fact of fundamental importance, that Ryle does not succeed in bridging the gulf between knowledge of ourselves and knowledge of others.

In being thus aware of our mental states, we are often aware of them as the causes of our behaviour. Emotion, it seems clear, is often such a cause. A sensation such as pain, equally clearly, is another. This, in itself, presents a major difficulty for Ryle's thesis, since it is not compatible with the view that to ascribe a mental state to anyone, including oneself, is just to ascribe some sort of behavioural disposition to him. To admit that our mental states are often the inner causes of our behaviour clearly precludes the possibility of identifying mental states with behavioural dispositions. It is also to underline the fact, once again, that the knowledge we have of our own mental states is fundamentally different from the knowledge we have of the mental states of others.

There is another absolutely fundamental objection to behaviourism which is a little more difficult to spell out, but it is a point which is fundamental not only to the assessment of behaviourism, but also of any version of materialism. The objection is this: if we look at all the various possible behavioural manifestations of any mental state, it ought to strike one that, strictly as so many items of behaviour, they will seem an oddly assorted and apparently arbitrarily selected bunch of items. We only have to think of the various ways in which such mental states as pride or anger can be manifested to see this. If we consider the behavioural manifestations as such, there is no pattern of behaviour or movement which is common to them all, and no reason why, strictly as physical processes and events, they should be classified together at all. The only thing which gives sense to such classification is our experience of such states as that of pride and anger. Once we have understood this, it becomes clear that we cannot offer an analysis of mental states in terms of behavioural dispositions, since we need awareness of the underlying mental states in order to recognise that the behavioural items which constitute the various manifestations of any mental state do indeed belong together. It is no good replying, as the behaviourist may be inclined to, that pride, for example, essentially involves a certain *judgement*, the judgement that the object of one's pride redounds to one's credit, and that once we are clear about this we can understand what unites all those items we take to be behavioural manifestations of pride. The reason why this reply is unacceptable is that making a judgement is itself a mental operation, and, moreover, one which can itself be manifested in all sorts of ways. I can make some particular judgement in writing, in speech, in range of different languages, in Morse code, and so on. Once again, the only way to understand how all these different sorts of items belong together is to grasp the underlying experience itself, in this case the thought itself. What we cannot do is to begin with a collection of behavioural items and somehow grasp that they belong together without any reference to mental states or experiences which may underlie that behaviour. Still less can we imbue some selection of physical events with meaning, and regard them as constituting a token of some judgement or statement, without reference to the underlying reality of consciousness and thought which is the only thing which could allow us to see any significance in such a collection of items. This point is of major importance in the assessment of all forms of materialism, but there is reason to claim that it is a conclusive objection to behaviourism.

The impossibility of analysing mental states as behavioural dispositions is in fact evident even with regard to those mental states which might appear to be most amenable to such an analysis. We might suppose that to desire something, for example, is to be prone to act in a certain way, a way which is directed towards a certain end, the achievement of that which one desires. But a little thought must show that we cannot simply identify desire with the proneness to act in a way which is directed towards some particular end-state, for to do so will let in all sorts of behaviour which we are quite certain has nothing whatever to do with desire as such. One is tired at the end of the day because of the activities one has engaged in during the day, but it is very unlikely that one engaged in these activities because one desires to be tired. Smoke from a cigarette will rise to the ceiling, avoiding obstacles in its way, but it would be extraordinary to suggest that it desires to reach the ceiling. Moreover, a further problem will be that it is not at all clear how we are to pick out that stage in any physical process which is to count as the goal or end-state. Faced with the flux of physical reality, what will determine for us what is to count as an end-state in such a process? If we think that end-states are recognisable as stages of quiescence, as the ceasing of activity, we are likely to be seriously misled. For, while it would be wrong in most cases to suggest that the purpose one hoped to achieve by engaging in the activities of the day was the terminus of sleep, it may very well be the case that the purpose of one's getting a good night's sleep is to be fit for the activities of the next day.

Behaviourism, then, cannot make sense of our conscious experience. It is forced to deny that we are immediately aware of our own experiences in a way in which no one else can be, and in doing just this it flies in the face of what is evidently given. But in doing this, also, it deprives itself of any way of interpreting behaviour, of being able to offer a psychological interpretation of patterns of behaviour. And the reason for this is that such behaviour can only be seen as a pattern at all if we presuppose what behaviourism is denying, the fact of inner, conscious experience. It is not only that the denial of inner experience, and the attempt to put self-knowledge on the same footing as knowledge of others, means that we have to interpret our own behaviour if we are to know what our own states of mind are; it is also that, having denied the reality of inner experience, the behaviourist has deprived himself of any way of interpreting behaviour psychologically at all. Where our experiences should be, the behaviourist simply leaves a hole, and in consequence he has nothing he can bring to human behaviour which would enable him to interpret it.

A more particular failure is presented by Ryle's attempt to deal with the imagination. Ryle feels that he has to avoid any suggestion that imagining or visualising is a matter of having a mental image, for mental images are clearly the sort of Cartesian item which Ryle must expel from our view of the mind. His positive suggestion is that imagining is a species of pretending, but it seems clear that this cannot be right, if only because it is a feature of our experience that a vivid mental image may simply occur without any decision to engage in a sort of make-believe. In fact Ryle subsequently made it known that he felt his treatment of imagination to be unsatisfactory, but did not see how to improve it.

It has sometimes been said that Ryle makes the fundamental mistake of confusing the question of what it means to say that someone is in a certain mental state with the quite different question of how we verify that he is in that state. These are quite separate matters, it is claimed. It makes perfect sense to suppose that some being may be in pain even though he has no way of showing this, and there would in consequence be no way of verifying that he is in pain. As an objection to behaviourism, this seems telling, but there is a less extreme way of construing the relation between mental state and behaviour than that claimed by philosophical behaviourism, one which Ryle often appears to be arguing for, and which would preclude anything like a complete separation of meaning from verification. This thesis has played a central role in recent discussions of the relation between mind and body, and it is to an examination of it that we now turn.

Is Ryle a behaviourist?

Ryle is generally taken to be the leading proponent of philosophical behaviourism, and certainly much of *The concept of mind* seems to be devoted to arguing for the thesis that mental concepts are to be analysed behaviouristically. However, there are many passages in Ryle's book which are impossible to reconcile with a strict behaviourist thesis, and these passages are so numerous and important that they give rise to the question of whether, at least for part of the time, Ryle is in fact arguing for a thesis quite different from that of behaviourism. Ryle tells us, for example, that 'much of our ordinary thinking is conducted in internal monologue or silent soliloquy'; and in the same chapter he talks of 'mental arithmetic', and of 'silent argumentation', which, he says, has 'the practical advantages of being relatively speedy, socially undisturbing and secret'. Later in the same chapter he says that 'if you do not divulge the contents of your silent soliloquies and other imaginings, I have no other sure way of finding out what you have been saying or picturing to yourself'. Moreover, he explicitly denies that words like 'ready', 'on guard', 'careful' and 'resolute' can be given a purely dispositional analysis. They are, he says 'semi-dispositional, semi-episodic words' (p. 47). He goes on: 'They do not signify the concomitant occurrence of extra but internal operations, nor mere capacities and tendencies to perform further operations if the need for them arises, but something between the two.'

What can we make of passages like these? In order to understand them, we must remind ourselves of what Ryle sees to be the greatest objection to dualism. The Cartesian conception of mind as immaterial and, more importantly, logically private to each individual makes it impossible, Ryle claims, for anyone to know what anyone else is thinking or feeling. To suppose that mental terms denote intrinsically private states is to make it impossible to know that any such term is ever properly applied to anyone else. If this is the central problem, then one can overcome it by showing that there is nothing about the meaning of mental terms which implies that what they denote is something *essentially* private. But if this is the central point, it does not imply that the very notion of private states and events is a nonsense; all that is implied is that what makes a mental state the particular mental state it is has nothing whatever to do with whether it is realised privately or publicly. Ryle says, for example, that

> [I]t makes no important difference whether we think of the reasoner as arguing to himself or arguing aloud, pleading, perhaps, before an imagined court or pleading before a real court. The criteria by which his arguments are to be adjudged as cogent, clear, relevant and well organised are the same for silent as for declaimed or written ratiocinations.

What makes anything a process or thought, then, is independent of whether it is private or public. 'Thinking' does not mean 'taking place in private'.

If this is what Ryle means to establish, there are a number of points to be made about the enterprise. First, there is no doubt that it is incompatible with the radical behaviourist thesis for which Ryle argues elsewhere in his book. The thesis that mental states are not essentially private

437

does not, for example, require the treatment of the difference between genuine and fake emotion which Ryle develops. States of emotion will not be essentially private, though they may be kept private for the purposes of 'shamming', as Ryle calls it. There is no need, on the modified thesis we are now examining, to argue that the difference between the genuine and the 'sham' case is purely behavioural. The judgement must be that Ryle does not have a unified thesis in *The concept of mind*. Second, the thesis that mental states are not essentially private raises certain fundamental questions. Is it the very same thing which was made public but might have been kept private? What leads us to say this, rather than as the dualist would, that the mental state as such is private, though it may be manifested in behaviour? I shall pursue this question in more detail below.

A final question which arises is: what is the nature of the inner events which Ryle seems ready to allow? Are they to be construed as physical states and processes? If they are, then Ryle's view looks to be indistinguishable from physicalism. If inner mental states are taken to be, or to be realised as, physical processes, then the position is what has been called 'central state materialism', which is thus termed precisely to underline the fact that it regards as crucial what behaviourism seems to deny: the reality of inner experiences. However, Ryle appears quite explicitly to reject such a view. Materialists see no objection to regarding human beings as a sort of sophisticated machine, but Ryle rejects the view that when we have expelled the Ghost from the Machine, what we are left with is just a machine.

In fact, the nature of inner experiences is left entirely unclear by Ryle. In particular, the question of the relation of such experiences to the physical body is left unexamined. A striking fact about Ryle's treatment of this whole question is that, while the apparent absurdity of causal interaction between the material and the immaterial is singled out in the first chapter as one of the central objections to dualism, it is never mentioned again. What takes the centre of the stage is the other difficulty Ryle singles out for special attention, the alleged impossibility of knowing what anyone else is thinking or feeling if minds are logically private to each individual.

It is a clearly related concern which underlies the views of Wittgenstein on reference to mental states, and also those of P.F. Strawson, in his book *Individuals*. For both, it is not only the fact that the claimed logical privacy of the mental would make knowledge of the minds of others impossible, but also that such privacy would make it impossible to have a notion of experience, and of a subject of experiences, at all. Both thinkers lay great weight on the notion of *criteria* for the application of mental concepts; that is, on the need to see the obtaining of certain public states of affairs, certain patterns of behaviour, as settling the question of whether some particular mental state is properly ascribed to someone, and settling it in a way which would make it senseless to raise the general doubt as to whether anyone else ever really has that experience, even though they exhibit the

438

right sort of behaviour. Strawson claims that the very possibility of ascribing mental states at all, both to oneself and to others, depends on our accepting that there are criteria for the ascription of such states, and on our taking it that these criteria are 'logically adequate'; that is, that they do rule out the sort of general doubt about whether mental states are ever correctly ascribed to anyone.

It looks as if we have moved a long way from behaviourism as such. Strawson is certainly not a behaviourist, and has criticised Ryle for his behaviourist leanings. Wittgenstein also appears to dismiss the criticism that his position is behaviourist. Nevertheless, it can be doubted whether these positions succeed in avoiding behaviourism. The question turns on whether the idea that bodily behaviour serves as the criterion for the ascription of mental states can be sustained without espousing a behaviourist position. The notion of criteria has been widely debated over the last thirty years, and it is easy to see why. When it is claimed that, for example, the manifestation of pain behaviour is a criterion for the presence of pain, it is not being claimed that it is logically impossible for pain behaviour to occur without pain. On the contrary, it is freely admitted that, for all sorts of reasons, there may be cases where just this happens. What is being claimed is that *in general* the presence of pain behaviour is to be taken as settling the question of whether someone is in pain. But that makes the connection between the state of affairs described in the criterion and the state of affairs to which it applies a curious one. They cannot be identical, since it is possible for the one to obtain while the other does not. But if they are distinct, then it is not at all clear that the position can be distinguished from the dualism it is meant to replace. The view appears to be that, while experiences are not to be identified with their outward expressions, they are not merely contingently or causally connected with them either.

The central doubt about this suggestion is simply whether there can be the sort of mid-way position indicated between the claim that *A* entails *B* on the one hand and the claim that *A* is merely contingently connected to *B* on the other. David Hume taught that where we have two things which are distinct we cannot suppose that they are logically connected. It can be safely assumed that he would not have countenanced the suggestion that the connection between *A* and *B* can be less than a tight logical one, but rather more than a merely contingent one. If this doubt is sustained, then the conclusion is that the only way to avoid a view which argues for the essential privacy of the mental is to adopt some variety of materialism. The strict behaviourist thesis is such a position. The fundamental objection to it centres on its denial of inner experience. To admit the reality of inner experiences without at the same time committing oneself to the view that such experiences are essentially private is, it might seem, to espouse some other variety of materialism.

Bibliography

Among the most influential examples of scientific behaviourism are

[1] J.B. Watson, *Psychology from the standpoint of a behaviourist* (Lippincot, Philadelphia, 1919) and

[2] B.F. Skinner, *Science and human behaviour* (Macmillan, London, 1953).

Skinner presents a vivid and accessible statement of his views in

[3] B.F. Skinner, *Freedom and dignity* (Penguin Books, Harmondsworth, 1971).

The classic statement of philosophical behaviourism (though the author repudiates the label 'behaviourist') is

[4] G. Ryle, *The concept of mind* (Penguin Books, Harmondsworth, 1963; first published 1949).

A useful collection of critical essays on Ryle is

[5] O.P. Wood and G. Pitcher (eds), *Ryle* (Macmillan, London, 1970). See also Ch. 3 of

[6] O. Hanfling, *Body and mind* (Open University, Milton Keynes, 1980).

Some powerful arguments against the behaviourist approach are examined in Ch. 5 of

[7] D.M. Armstrong, *A materialist theory of the mind* (Routledge, London, 1968).

Wittgenstein's views concerning mental states may be found in

[8] L. Wittgenstein, *Philosophical investigations* (Philosophische Untersuchungen), trans. G.E.M. Anscombe (Basil Blackwell, Oxford, 1958; first published 1953) and a clear exposition of his position occurs in Ch. 10 of

[9] A. Kenny, *Wittgenstein* (Penguin Books, Harmondsworth, 1973).

A stimulating essay on the mind written from a Wittgensteinian standpoint is

[10] N. Malcolm, *Problems of mind* (Allen and Unwin, London, 1972).

Strawson's views are set out in

[11] P.F. Strawson, *Individuals* (Methuen, London, 1959).

See also the essay entitled 'Self, mind and body' in

[12] P.F. Strawson, *Freedom and resentment and other essays* (Methuen, London, 1974).

Some of the problems faced by behaviourists are discussed in Chs. 2 and 3 of

[13] A. Kenny, *Action, emotion and will* (Routledge, London, 1963).

See also

[14] D. Locke, *Myself and others: a study in our knowledge of minds* (Oxford University Press, Oxford, 1968) and

[15] J. Wisdom, *Other minds* (Basil Blackwell, Oxford, 1965).

A number of interesting essays influenced by the behaviourist outlook are gathered in

[16] D.F. Gustafson (ed.), *Essays in philosophical psychology* (Macmillan, London, 1967).

An excellent general introduction to some of the issues raised in this chapter is

[17] J.A. Fodor, *Psychological explanation* (Random House, New York, 1968).

For the status of behaviourism in recent cognitive science, see the entry 'behaviourism' in the index of

[18] D. Dennett, *Brainstorms* (Harvester, Hassocks, 1978).

Finally, a stimulating discussion which links behaviourism to wider issues in theory of knowledge and theory of meaning may be found in Chs. 1 and 2 of

[19] R. Rorty, *Philosophy and the mirror of nature* (Basil Blackwell, Oxford, 1980).

J.G.C.

20 | Problems of Personal Identity

A.J. Lyon

The central question

What is it to remain one and the same person over a period of time? Everyone changes during his or her lifetime. Occasionally we meet someone after an interval of years and are amazed to be told it is the same person as the one we knew earlier. Or one can look at a photograph of one's past self and ask with puzzlement in what sense one is the same person as the person in the picture. Perhaps I can remember doing some of the things done by that small boy, but I am greatly changed, physically and mentally: in what sense is that a photograph of *me*? Sometimes one might feel: *that* person no longer exists; *I* exist *now*, so it's not that I *am* that person, merely that I *used to be* him. And what difference does that make to anything, here and now? Furthermore, might it conceivably turn out that I'm mistaken, that the person I think I remember being, who apparently went under the same name, was not me, but somebody else? Such feelings are exacerbated when we consider cases of gross psychological disturbance, personality changes, multiple personalities, or the alarming and distressing stories of novelists such as Kafka or Max Frisch. And yet we do ordinarily think and talk of people as remaining the same person through change. Does this mean that there is something that *doesn't* change while body, character and memories alter, something we might call the soul, and that *that* is what a person essentially is?

If we are immaterial souls, then perhaps we might survive our bodily death. But lacking a clear idea of what a soul *is*, we cannot yet be sure that it can exist apart from a body; perhaps bodily resurrection is required for an afterlife. Early beliefs about spirits seem to imply they are invisible yet physical things, like air, or wind. We can fairly easily imagine such an entity being physically transported from place to place, or from body to body, or taking on a new physical form in the manner of the ancient gods, who themselves sometimes chose to become invisible, while always being in some specifiable *place*. With Plato the picture changes, and in such a way that we no longer *have* a picture – or rather, if we do have, then any such picture is necessarily misleading, being only a crutch for the ignorant and unintelligent. According to Plato the soul is a transcendental entity which perhaps dwelt 'in the realm' of Forms before our birth and which might 'return' there after death, to a place which is yet no place, no *region*. The soul is invisible, not in the way that air is, but in the way that numbers and ideal geometrical figures are. The latter alleged entities, discussed by the Pythagoreans, presented Plato with a ready-made model for his concept of the non-physical entities, the Forms, which he claimed are the archetypes mirrored by each well-formed class of material entity we find on earth. Much later, Descartes was to argue that the mind is an immaterial substance, without spatial dimensions and indeed nowhere in space, although this led him into notorious difficulties about how mind and matter might interact. Descartes' view that we are minds, interacting with our bodies in some mysterious way, was swallowed wholesale by John Locke and the other most famous British empiricists, Berkeley and Hume. Locke was indeed one of the first philosophers to discuss the question of personal identity in sophisticated detail. He argued that to remain the same soul, to remain the same person, and to remain the same man (or woman) were three quite different things, since a soul, a person and a man are three different things. To introduce this idea it is helpful first to explain Aristotle's views on Form and Matter.

What makes something the thing it is?

Aristotle pointed out that to specify what any particular object is, we need to state both what it is made of (its 'matter'), and what *kind* of thing it is (its 'form'). *This* is an earthenware jug, *that* is a bronze statue of Apollo; a bronze jug, or an earthenware statue, would be different objects. Kinds come in hierarchies: jugs are a kind of utensil, statues of Apollo are a kind of statue. In the physical world there are jugs, statues, etc.: what each of these groups has in common is, as Aristotle's teacher Plato pointed out, not itself one of the (earthly) jugs or statues, but the having of a certain *property*, or *eidos* (translated Idea, Universal or *Form*). Aristotle distinguished different sorts of Forms – properties, relations and kinds. He discussed in great detail Plato's views firstly that Forms are more real than the particulars that 'instantiate' them, and secondly that Forms exist transcendentally and independently of their having any instantiations (i.e. examples). In his middle period, Aristotle argued (i) that universals are less real than particulars – he called them 'secondary (kinds of) substances' – and (ii) that they cannot exist uninstantiated – e.g. the Dodo exists if and only if there are dodos – which is the common-sense view. Although *less* real than particulars they are nevertheless real: being a jug is quite a different *thing* from being a statue. In the case of jugs and statues the Form is just the shape (what we can still in modern English call the 'form'). But in other cases it is not; for example, being a king or being bad-tempered are nothing (much) to do with having a particular shape.

We could take this bronze statue, melt it down, and make a bronze jug. We would then have a different object, because the same matter would have ('instantiate') a different Form. So after this process there would not remain in existence one and the same statue, for the statue would no longer exist: but there would remain one and the same portion of bronze (that we bought from the foundry, for example). Thus if we point towards something and ask what it is for that thing to remain the same object through time, we need to interpret the question as being about the object considered as an *example* of something or other, i.e. as being of some *kind*. Often, it is obvious what kind is in question. Suppose I give you a silver figurine which you find hideous, and I ask some years later whether you still have my present. You should not reply 'Yes' if you have melted it down and stored the silver in the bank: obviously, I didn't mean 'Have you the same silver?' but 'Have you the same figurine?' – it was *qua* silver figure, not simply *qua* silver that I gave you the present. So we can learn from Aristotle that thinking about or pointing at an object and asking 'Has it *remained the same* as it was at some time in the past?' or, for example, 'Is this the same object as I saw last year?' demands a further specification, namely 'Object of what kind?' For it can be the same mass of silver, but not the same figurine, or the same present. More obviously, if I have a tadpole in April that turns into a frog by June, I have kept one and the same *animal*, but I have kept neither the same tadpole nor the same frog, for I didn't start with a frog and I didn't end with a tadpole.[1]

These Aristotelian ideas can be used in response to Heracleitus' claim that one cannot step into the same river twice because the water is always changing, and so the river cannot remain the *same*. The answer to this is that one steps into a *different* mass of water but the *same* river. To remain the same river it *has* to have new water in it. For consider the alternative; if the water *didn't* change then it wouldn't be a river at all, but a long stretch of stagnant water, and hence it *couldn't* remain the same *river*. The moral to be drawn is that something's remaining the same X is not only compatible with its changing in certain respects so that it is no longer the same Y, but that it may actually *require* there to be such a change, for otherwise it would not be an X at all. In other cases change may be permissible but not mandatory. In some cases the normal process of change may be so slow as to be unnoticeable, and we may become puzzled whether we are still faced with 'the same X' either when there has been unusually rapid change, or when there has been the normal slow change over a long period so that we finish up with a greatly altered object – particularly if we have not remained acquainted with the object during the intervening period. We should expect such problems to arise as much for persons as for anything else:

we might wonder whether it is *really* still Jane either after rapid personality change *or* after slow personality change over a long period.

Locke on mental connectedness

The Aristotelian thought that a thing is what it is on account of its matter and form, and hence that remaining the same *thing* depends on the kind of thing we are talking about, was used by John Locke (1632–1704) in distinguishing between a 'man' (or woman), a 'person', and a 'soul'. Locke pointed out that if these three words correspond to three different ideas (conceptions), then to remain the same man, the same person and the same soul are three different things.[2]

Locke approached the problem of personal identity by considering the idea of transmigration of souls. According to this theory, which is attributed to the Pythagoreans, and before them to other religious sects, after we die our souls can inhabit other human beings, or even animals, but we are unable, at least under normal circumstances, to remember our previous incarnations. Locke had taken over Descartes' dualistic conception of mind and body as two quite separate entities. The mind consists of a series of thoughts, feelings, desires, hopes, wishes, etc. 'inhering in' an immaterial substance or *substratum*. According to Locke, we can have only an utterly vague idea of what this substratum is like. This is because he held that every idea is built up from previous experience, and since the substratum is that which *has* all experiences, it can have no clear conception of itself. Locke asked what would follow if his own immaterial substratum or bearer of experiences were in fact one and the same as that which inhabited the body of Socrates. Would this make him the same person as Socrates, even though he could remember nothing of Socrates' life? Locke argued, surely correctly, that it would not, any more than he would now be Socrates reborn if he now consisted of exactly the same particles as previously constituted Socrates – which after all is possible, if unlikely! Compare: the very same particles of bronze can be first a jug and then a statue; this doesn't mean that the statue and the jug are one and the same jug or one and the same statue, only that they are made out of one and the same matter. Or again: when the water in a river flows into the sea, the river isn't in the sea; it is where it previously was but with new water. Similarly, we replace the particles in our bodies without gaining new bodies; what we get, unfortunately, are older ones.

So what is it that provides the continuity between the present me and my past self? The answer, according to Locke, is that I can remember doing various things in the past, and having various experiences, which other people can't remember. So I would have *been* Socrates in a previous incarnation only if I could now remember a good deal of Socrates' past life in the way in which Socrates could remember *his* past life, and in which I can remember mine. This could conceivably happen, but it seems (likely)

444

that it never in fact does, i.e. reincarnation does not as a matter of fact occur.

So Locke argued that to remain the same *man* (or woman) is to keep the same body (but of course with renewed material), to remain the same *person* is to keep the same mind, with its ability to remember its past, while to remain the same immaterial substratum is for something pretty much incomprehensible and unverifiable to happen, but which is in any event of no conceivable interest to anyone – for what would it matter if I gained a new substratum every 24 hours, when neither I nor anyone else would notice the difference? So to have an interesting theory of the soul surviving is to have an interesting theory of the mind surviving – or a goodly part thereof – whether or not this requires survival of the body as well.

There are several difficulties with Locke's theory.

Objection 1: Keeping the same body

Suppose I think I remember being Socrates, in the way that madmen claim to remember being Napoleon. Bernard Williams has persuasively argued that I (A.L.) logically *couldn't* be Socrates reborn, whatever were to happen in the world.[3] Williams' argument is a version of the objection put forward by the eighteenth-century Scottish philosopher Thomas Reid, and it runs as follows.

If A.L. logically might become Socrates reborn by taking on (by whatever means) Socrates' mental characteristics and memory-data, then somebody else, B.M., logically might do the same at the same time. Then if this would make A.L. the same person as Socrates, B.M. would also be the same person as Socrates, and so A.L. would be the same person as B.M., which is impossible, since *ex hypothesi* they are different people. This argument is sometimes expressed by saying that, in an alleged case of 'double reincarnation', if A.L. would be 'identical with' Socrates then B.M. would also be 'identical with' Socrates, and since identity is a transitive relation, A.L. would be identical with B.M., which is impossible, since they are not identical but different. So, since two people cannot now be identical with Socrates, we should conclude that neither can one living person be identical with a past (dead?) person: otherwise, A.L. might be identical with Socrates until something happened to B.M., when A.L. would stop being (identical with) Socrates, which is ridiculous. So to remain the same person logically requires retaining the same body; this is logically necessary but not logically sufficient.

There are several possible responses to this argument, but one thing it may show is how misleading it can be to express the question of what it is to remain the same person over time in terms of Locke's phrase: what is personal *identity*? This point was discussed by Hume; for now let us note that perhaps the correct description would be that both A.L. and B.M. *used to be* Socrates, while if A.L. but nobody else mysteriously took on the relevant Socratic characteristics, then this would mean not that A.L. is now ('identical with' – a redundant phrase) Socrates, but that he is now 'Socrates reborn', or that he *used to be* Socrates. So there is *perhaps* a possibility that one, two, or even more people could in the past have been Socrates, and Williams' objection is arguably not quite so convincing as it looks at first sight.

Objection 2: Forgetting one's past

There are obviously many parts of my past life that as a matter of fact (i.e. contingently) I cannot remember, but this doesn't mean that I wasn't then the same person as I am now. Locke bravely but absurdly took the line that I'm *not* the same person, but in fact his theory as it stands is not merely incorrect but leads to a contradiction, which was realised by Berkeley and then vividly portrayed by Thomas Reid.[4]

Suppose an elderly general can remember capturing an enemy's standard while a young officer, and the officer could at that time remember being flogged while a schoolboy, but the general can no longer remember being so flogged. Then, according to Locke, the general would be the same person as the officer, and the officer would be the same person as the schoolboy, and so by transitivity the general would be the same person as the boy; but also, by Locke's direct memory criterion, he wouldn't be the same person, which is a contradiction.

Perhaps this difficulty can be overcome in a way suggested by Leibniz and discussed in detail in this century by C.D. Broad and by Derek Parfit.[5] The general G is the same person as the boy B either if G can remember doing and experiencing (exactly) what B did and experienced, or G can remember doing and experiencing exactly what was done and experienced at some intermediate stage by O(fficer), who can in turn ... But here there looms at least the appearance of a potential infinite regress, for surely there is no end to the possible number of 'middle bonds of consciousness', in Leibniz' phrase. There is however an even worse problem for those who, from Locke to Parfit, wish to explain personal identity in terms of some kind of 'mental connectedness'. Surely there are periods of a person's life the consciousness of which he never does and as a matter of fact never can recall at *any* later period whatsoever. Leibniz claimed that 'the testimony of others could fill in the gap in my recollection'. But *what* would others be remembering? Not my experiences, for that is logically impossible. They would remember *me* doing and experiencing various things, but what they would be remembering would be me as a physical body in various circumstances, not me 'as a mind', whatever that might mean. So this brings us back to the body. Of course they would remember me *as a person*: this however surely underlines the thought that people aren't minds, but physical organisms *having* minds. If this is so, then we might suppose that to remain the same person would be to retain the same body *and* the same mind, whatever these two things might come to.

Objection 3: Presupposition and circularity

Butler famously objected to Locke's view by saying that 'consciousness of personal identity *presupposes* and thus cannot *constitute* personal identity'.[6] In fact the same point was made by the man referred to by Sir William Hamilton as Locke's earliest critic, John Sergeant, who wrote that 'a man must be the same, ere he can know or be conscious that he is the same'.[7] Thomas Reid also put the objection neatly and forcefully when he said it was absurd 'to say that my remembrance that I did such a thing, or my consciousness, *makes* me the person who did it'.[8] Reid claimed this shows he is some 'extra' 'indivisible thing [which] thinks, and deliberates, ... and acts'.[9]

Perhaps Reid's conclusion is in some sense correct: but this doesn't entail that he is an immaterial substratum – for apart from the (Cartesian) problem of how two quite different kinds of substance, the mental and the physical, could affect each other, it seems most odd to believe that an immaterial substratum can *act*, even if one can somehow believe that it *thinks*. Perhaps what it shows is that Reid (and of course everyone else) is not a consciousness or mind, or an immaterial substance having consciousness, but an organism, that is, a physical being which, because of its material constitution and structure, has mental attributes such as consciousness. (Presumably this would have been Aristotle's view had he had our concept of mind.) Of course this entity is not, in Reid's phrase, an 'indivisible thing' except in the sense that if you cut it up in a horrific enough way, then the person will die.

The belief that I am not just my consciousness or my memories or indeed the totality of my mental attributes can surely be correct, while being compatible with my consciousness being in many ways the most important thing about me. All this is also compatible with the logical truth that only *I* logically can remember (myself) experiencing in the past what only I experienced.

Sydney Shoemaker, and following him Derek Parfit, have neatly avoided the circularity or presupposition objection to the theory that consciousness of one's past (i.e. of one's *own* past!) constitutes personal identity by introducing the concepts of 'quasi-memory' and 'quasi-intention'.[10] One q-remembers a past experience if one seems to remember it, *someone* had that experience, and one's apparent memory is causally dependent in the 'right' (specifiable) sort of way on the past occurrence of that experience. So memories constitute a sub-class of q-memories, and having q-memories of Socrates' experiences neither entails nor presupposes that one was Socrates. Using the concept of q-memory still leaves us however with the central problem: if someone q-remembers Socrates' experiences (i.e. he has Socrates' 'memory-data'), are we to conclude that he is Socrates reborn, or is this impossible on the grounds explained in Objection 1, which suggested that perhaps retaining the same body is logically necessary for personal identity? Or would it in some circumstances be Socrates reborn and in others not? If so, what is the difference that makes the difference?

Hume and 'fictitious identity'

David Hume (1711–76) developed two of Locke's doctrines to their most radical but logical conclusions.[11] The first doctrine was that we are minds, and so to remain the same person is to remain the same mind. The second doctrine was that the criteria for 'remaining the same' depend on the type of entity with which we are dealing.

Hume radicalised the first doctrine by asserting that there is no *bearer* of the contents of the mind – no 'immaterial substratum' as claimed by Locke. Although some have claimed to be aware of such a subject of experience, or 'self', something which remains identically the same through time, Hume declared that he personally was not aware of any such thing. He further suggested that if his readers were honestly to reflect upon their so-called 'self-awareness' they would find that they were not aware of such a 'self' either: whenever one 'looks into one's mind' one always comes across some kind of thought or feeling or experience; one does not (and could not) also come across or experience something *having* that experience.

So Hume is left with the view that the person, or mind, is a collection of 'perceptions' *sans* bearer, which he likens to the ever-changing scenes and actors in a theatre, except that the mental perceptions do not take place *in* an unchanging material building. When I have no perceptions, as in sound sleep, I 'may truly be said not to exist'.[12] It is tempting to remark that when a philosopher says that something may 'truly be said' one can be certain that it is not said truly. Surely I exist while asleep because my body exists, still retaining my mind as what Aristotle called a 'first actuality'. What this means is that while asleep I retain a certain disposition, or ability, to do various things, just as I may truly be said to know various things that I am not currently aware of, or indeed have *never* specifically thought of: for example I know that the sun is more than 758,931 miles from the earth even though I have never before contemplated that fact.

When I die I shall no longer exist unless my mind can survive bodily death. A dead body is not a person, which accords with Aristotle's view that having a mind is being alive in a certain very complex way. This is surely right: what has various thoughts and experiences is neither an immaterial substratum (Locke), nor nothing at all (Hume), but a living body. If I throw myself out of a window, I do not throw just my 'self' out, and I cannot leave my 'self' (myself?) behind, gazing down at the falling body. When I use the words 'I' and 'myself', I use them to refer to the very same thing as others refer to by 'Ardon Lyon', something that both has experiences and can be seen and pinched by you (and by *me*). We can give a meaning to the words 'self', 'innermost self', 'ego', 'id', etc., but these are not *me*: they are parts of me, no doubt more important parts than certain bits of my body.

Having argued that a person is just a bundle or collection of perceptions, Hume had to ascertain what it is that makes them one bundle; since they do not 'inhere' in a single substance, it must be a relationship between them that makes them one. He concluded that the perceptions of, say, David, are more closely causally related and similar to each other than they are to those of, say, Edwina, whose perceptions again are related by similarity (through memory) and direct, immediate causality. It is probable that any such account must lead either to infinite regress or to circularity, but in any event, if we accept the common-sense view that perceptions are had by organisms, then there is no problem about what 'binds together' floating perceptions; for they are not floating. David's perceptions are whatever perceptions are had by David, and Edwina's whatever are had by Edwina, however similar or dissimilar, causally related or unrelated they may be. But Hume's erroneous account does lead him to make the important pronouncement that, since the alleged simple, unchanging 'self' or 'bearer' of perceptions is a 'fiction', it follows that the mind, or person – he uses the two terms interchangeably – has 'properly no *simplicity* in it at one time, nor *identity* in different';[13] so 'the identity which we ascribe to the mind of man . . . [just as] to vegetable and animal bodies . . . is only a fictitious one'.[14]

For something to remain identical through time it has to remain, according to Hume, 'invariable and uninterrupted' through that period. Because the contents of our minds continue in a more or less constant flow, we *say* that we keep the same mind – remain the same person – through time. But Hume says this is an 'error', an error that leads us confusedly to think that there must be a 'something' that remains invariable. This, according to Hume, is one reason for our erroneous belief in an unchanging immaterial substratum, a soul 'substance', a Cartesian ego, a 'self'. Another reason is our initial tendency, until checked by philosophical criticism, to believe that ideas, thoughts, feelings and perceptions cannot exist 'on their own', but must be entities had by or 'inhering in' something. I have suggested, *pace* Hume, that this latter belief may be correct, but that nevertheless our ideas etc. may be had by physical organisms, not immaterial substances.

Now is it a 'confusion and mistake' to think that people retain their identity through time, whether persons are minds, bodies, or both? Only, surely, if we 'attribute identity, in an improper sense' (Hume's words) to an object through time. But when we say that we are faced with the same object as we saw yesterday, we would not normally *mean* 'the same object, which has remained *identically* the same, through time', if this latter phrase is taken to mean 'has remained identically, exactly the same, without any change whatsoever'. Hume speaks of our idea of 'identity or sameness' as though these were one and the same idea. But we don't normally ask whether an object is identical with one we saw yesterday: we ask simply whether it is the same object or a different one. Hume goes on to describe very accurately some of the various circumstances in which we pronounce an object the same object over a period of time even though some things about it have changed, pointing out, as did Locke, that the kinds of change consistent with an object's being called the 'same' object depend on the kind of object we are considering. But he still writes, part of the time, as though this were some kind of error, even though it is said 'without breach of the propriety of language'![15]

Hume distinguished some of the ways of remaining the same through change which had earlier been illuminatingly, if not always accurately, described by Locke.

(1) The amount of a physical object that can be removed or changed before we 'pronounce' an object no longer the 'same' depends on the *proportion* changed. Removing a few inches would destroy a sand-castle but not a mountain or a planet – although Hume says that in all these cases such alteration 'absolutely destroys the identity of the whole, *strictly speaking*'.[16]

(2) The more gradual the change, the more inclined we are to pronounce an object the same.

(3) When the parts serve a 'common end or purpose', a great number of parts may be changed while we still consider the thing to have remained the same object, for example, the same ship.

(4) This is particularly so when the parts are organically related to the whole, as in plants and animals.

(5) When objects are 'in their nature changeable', for example rivers, a lot can (indeed must!) change while the object remains the same *object*.

It is remarkable that not even the last example led Hume to withdraw his assertion that we are always in some kind of error when we say that something has remained the same through change. For without withdrawing this charge, he simply forgets it when writing that change 'hinders not the river from continuing the same during several ages', and that such things are said 'without breach of the propriety of language'. An important observation should be made here. Suppose we *did* absurdly mean by 'remaining the same through time' remaining identically the same, unchanged. Then we would almost never be able truthfully to assert that we had seen the same object twice; so the concept would be almost useless. Secondly, and perhaps worse, we would have no means of expressing the useful *contrast*, the *difference* between for example coming across what we call the *same* object again as opposed to coming across a *different* object – unless we also reintroduced just the concepts we now have. That is precisely why we have them.

Although Hume was very muddled about this, it is important to hold on to his distinction between 'remaining the same *X*' and 'remaining identical', in one sense of this phrase, since failure to do so has, arguably, led to a good deal of confusion. For remaining the same can be a matter of degree, whereas 'being identical with' something cannot – at least in accordance with one use of this phrase. For the only thing that is, in the

450

strictest possible sense, identical with something is the thing itself; and one should hardly expect something to be more or less identical with *itself*! Admittedly, Hume again forgot that he was supposedly talking not about identity but about the allegedly confused and erroneous 'remaining the same' when he wrote, perfectly correctly, that the latter may 'diminish by insensible degrees'. When it does, he says, we have 'no just standard by which we can decide any dispute' about whether a thing has or has not remained the same, and such disputes are alleged to be merely 'verbal' or 'grammatical' except when they give rise to *further* mistaken beliefs, for example about an unknowable substratum. Such remarks have been echoed and re-echoed in twentieth-century philosophical debate, with disastrous consequences.

Personal identity and bodily identity

Since the topic under discussion is still nearly always referred to as the problem of personal *identity*, it will be convenient to retain this terminology except where it is actively misleading. As explained briefly in 'Locke on mental connectedness', p. 445, Bernard Williams at one time argued that bodily identity is a necessary condition of personal identity. He repeated a version of Reid's allegation, which can be put in the following form. If bodily identity were not necessary, then since two people, George and Harry, logically might q-remember being Guy Fawkes, this would suffice for their both *being* Guy Fawkes ('come to life again'), which is impossible. Why is this impossible? Allegedly because identity is a one–one and transitive relation: that is, one thing cannot be identical with many, or many with one; and if $A = B$ and $B = C$, then $A = C$. So if George and Harry were both identical with Guy Fawkes then they would be identical with each other, which is impossible. The conclusion must be that neither is identical with Guy Fawkes, and that being mentally connected with Guy Fawkes (roughly in the way in which each of us is normally mentally connected with our past selves) may be necessary but is not sufficient for being Guy Fawkes. Since both would lack G.F.'s body, neither would be G.F.; it seems that having the same body as G.F. is necessary for being G.F. This indeed is encapsulated in the Christian doctrine that bodily resurrection is required for an afterlife in heaven. This is embarrassing, since it seems not to occur.

Doubt can be thrown on this version of Williams' argument in at least two ways. The first is that perhaps the imaginary example shows that remaining the same person is not an example of the so-called 'identity' relation. A second move, independent of this, is suggested by a case originally described by Sydney Shoemaker. Surgeons can currently carry out heart transplants, kidney transplants, etc. Suppose in the future they were able to carry out brain transplants. Suppose further that they exchanged Brown's and Robinson's brains, where before the operation Brown is lying in hospital bed B and Robinson is lying in bed R. Then the person who woke up in bed B would believe himself to be Robinson with an incomprehensibly changed body (i.e. Brown's), and vice versa. This seems to show that retaining the same living brain is all that is necessary for remaining the same person – part of the body is required, but not all of it. A version of Williams' argument against possible duplication seems to be compatible with the story so far; neither George nor Harry would have Guy Fawkes' brain, and so it seems that neither would be Guy Fawkes.

Several problems remain. First, it isn't obvious that the person in bed B with Brown's body would be Robinson, even though he has Robinson's memory-data and believes himself to be Robinson. His character doesn't depend *only* on his brain-state. Suppose that before the operation Robinson was a sensitive violinist and Brown a champion boxer. How could we have a sensitive violinist with a boxer's physique? Such problems could of course be multiplied indefinitely. It has been replied to this that the brain-transplant argument certainly works with an imagined brain swap between identical twins. The two people would 'take over each other's bodies', and so keeping the same living brain is all that is required for personal identity, not keeping the same body. This still leaves open the question whether the person, say in bed B, call him 'Brownson', would be Brown, or Robinson, or neither. Would Brown and Robinson simply have *died*? And would two new people have been born?

Most contemporary philosophers probably now agree that retaining the same body is not logically required for remaining the same person; at *most* one needs to retain the same brain. We shall later see reasons for denying even this.

Bernard Williams has produced another, extraordinarily convincing argument designed to show that bodily continuity, and not psychological continuity, is required for personal identity.[17] To make his argument most vivid it is best to consider oneself as the subject who is to undergo various changes, during or after which *somebody* has great pleasure or great pain, and we are to ask ourselves: 'Will that person be *me*, so that I have something to anticipate, joyfully or fearfully for *myself* as opposed to someone else?' A version of the argument would be as follows.

Suppose a callous neurosurgeon is about to operate on my brain, while I am conscious and in great pain. He tells me not to worry, because soon after the operation begins he will make me lose all my memories up to that moment. That doesn't console me now, and it wouldn't console me in the middle of the operation: I shall be an amnesiac in excruciating agony, an agony so great I might well not notice my amnesia. The surgeon tells me that after that he will give me apparent memories of Napoleon's life, and then so alter my brain that I take on Napoleon's character: again, I might not notice this at the time, because the changes will be purely dispositional, not conscious. So I shall end up with all of Napoleon's character and apparent memories, having suffered a lot of pain. If a surgeon could do this to me, it doesn't look as though he would have killed me and replaced me by someone else. At the end of the surgery I shall be deluded, insane, and in agony; I won't be *dead*, even if this would be preferable. For at what stage did I die, and when did somebody else (Napoleon Mark II?) come into existence? At death I shall lose consciousness, whereas in this story I never lose consciousness, so it must continue to be *me* who goes on experiencing the agony, not somebody else.

If in the future scientists could alter the states of people's brains with a 'brain-state transfer' device, so that they took on the *physical configurations* requisite for having the mental characteristics of G.F., then why should having the physical brain be required? Answer: because otherwise we could have the logical impossibility of two *different* people being the same person, so the actual brain is required. But this answer will not do. We know that individual memories are not highly specifically located in the brain, but have their physical instantiation over wide areas. (Even if this were false, it would be a purely contingent matter, irrelevant to the logical point to be made.) We also know that large areas of the part of the brain housing memories can be damaged, apparently without impairment of memory – indeed this provides evidence of non-localisation of memory. Then the relevant parts of the brain might be split in two and transplanted into two different bodies, both of whom would have the mental characteristics and memory-data of an original, say Oswald. If it is retorted that to remain as Oswald one has to retain at least half of Oswald's brain, and so two people couldn't both be Oswald, then the reply is that this is an *ad hoc* and unbelievable suggestion, designed simply to disallow the possibility of two people being one. Could it seriously be maintained that if Oswald lost just under half of his brain in an accident he could still be Oswald, whereas if he lost a couple more brain cells he would suddenly be Oswald no longer, but ... who? A newborn person?

Some philosophers argue that a consideration of such imaginary puzzle cases tells us nothing about what it is to remain the same person; since such cases do not in fact occur, we have no idea how people would describe them if they did – we would just have to wait and see. But this is a counsel of despair, and in any event is surely wrong. Ever since the time of Plato, philosophers have discussed questions about what-it-is-to-be-X; about the nature of Beauty, Justice, Truth, Goodness, etc. They attempt to give necessary and sufficient conditions for being X in order to understand the concept X – the meaning of the term 'X'. This can *only* be done by considering possible cases as well as actual ones, for as Aristotle pointed out, if all Xs are in fact Y and all Ys are in fact X, it doesn't follow that to be X is to be Y. Perhaps all creatures with hearts are creatures with lungs and vice versa: it doesn't follow that to have a heart is to have lungs.

Now there cannot conceivably be a sound argument to show it is impossible to judge what ought properly to be said about imaginary cases. For if we *do* wait and see what happens when they in fact turn up, if they ever do, then what will then be said about them either will be in accordance with our current concepts or it will not, and in the latter case either our concepts will have changed or there will be an *error*. So there is no reason why we should not judge such cases now just as well as later. Even if it really were true that in accordance with our current concepts there is no right answer to such puzzle cases, then that too ought to be ascertainable *now*. Furthermore, we want to be able to make judgements about possible cases because some people believe, while others deny, that these possible cases are actual. Some people believe in transmigration of souls, in life after death, or that soon there will be machines that can think and feel and which will be, *properly speaking*, inorganic *people*, while others deny these claims, saying that they are, when understood aright, incoherent because self-contradictory. These disagreements obviously have practical consequences, so it is important to reach the right answers.

      One mistake that has often vitiated the search for what-it-is-to-be-X has been and continues to be the belief that to find necessary and sufficient conditions for X is to find features each of which must be either necessary or sufficient for being X. Suppose however that to be X is to be either A and B, or B and C, or C and A. Then it is necessary and sufficient for being X that a thing be either A and B, or B and C, or C and A, without any one of A, B or C being either necessary or sufficient for being X. Thus keeping the same body (or the same brain) may be neither necessary nor sufficient for remaining the same person even though it is *relevant*, i.e. counts towards the truth of 'Here is the same person as O.'[18]

      Perhaps what the imaginary puzzle cases about brain transplants, split brains, etc. show is that to remain the same person can be a matter of degree; that what we would have in the imaginary case of Robinson's brain in Brown's very different body would be a person who would be more Robinson than Brown, but somewhat Brownian.[19] Would Robinson before the operation have something good or bad to look forward to, and would Brown? If a consideration of such puzzle cases can bring to our attention that in imaginary cases remaining the same person can sometimes be a matter of degree, perhaps we should conclude that in actual cases remaining the same person can be a matter of degree, if somewhat less so. For isn't it true that we are more or less the people we used to be, more so over short periods of time, less so over long ones? We are not the least averse to making such judgements about countries and constitutions, ships and socks, restaurants and rivers. So why not about people? What indeed could be meant by claiming that a grown man is *identical* with the little boy he used to be when a child?

Personal identity and mental continuity

An enormous variety of fascinating work on personal identity has been produced over the past thirty years by philosophers in the analytical tradition. Probably the most original, influential and controversial has been that of Derek Parfit, starting with his 1971 article 'Personal identity' and culminating in his book *Reasons and persons*, published in 1984. Parfit follows Locke in arguing that some version of mental connectedness and continuity is necessary and sufficient for personal identity.[20] This leads to a myriad of so-called 'puzzle cases' which Parfit discusses in detail.

Replication

Imagine that in the future we can travel to distant planets. Even with improved space travel facilities, it will be a lengthy journey. Scientists perfect a quicker system, suggested by science fiction. A machine is invented which scans every cell in a person's body and beams fully detailed information at the speed of light (or hopefully even faster!) to the desired planet, for example Mars. Scientists there can reconstitute a replica of your body out of suitable organic matter. You step into the scanner on earth, and press a green button. You are made unconscious, and as the information reaches Mars, your earthly body is destroyed and you wake up on Mars. Before your first 'journey' you might feel exceedingly nervous, wondering whether it will really be *you* who wakes up on Mars, as opposed to somebody else, a mere Replica. Won't the destruction of your body be the destruction of *you*? Doesn't pressing the green button bring *death*? But your wife reassures you with a teasing smile; after all, she has made the journey back and forth several times with no ill effects, whereas space ships are a hazardous and expensive form of transport, wasting years of your life even if you are fortunate enough not to be blown to smithereens by a malfunction *en route*. You swallow hard, and press the green button.

Scientists later find they don't need to destroy your earthly body. This has the added advantage that when you wake up on earth you can talk to yourself on Mars. Or perhaps you would be on Mars and could talk to yourself on earth. But now this is ridiculous: you cannot be both on earth and on Mars at the same time. There would be two people, and you cannot be both of them. So the person on Mars wouldn't be you; it would be your Replica, who would merely believe he was you, rather as an insane person can believe he is Napoleon. But if keeping your earthly body intact would ensure that the person on Mars isn't you, how could destroying it mean that it was you? How could what happens on earth make any difference to who the person on Mars actually *is*? This seems once again to show that retaining the same body, or perhaps the same brain, is logically necessary for remaining the same person. But we have already seen difficulties with this view, namely from considering what happens if we transplant split brains, or if we consider the difference between replacing a smaller part of a brain compared with a greater part.

Division

Suppose you are in a car crash with your identical twin. Your body gets completely smashed up, while your twin suffers irreparable brain damage. Your brain is successfully transplanted into your twin's body. Who survives? You do, in your twin's body. 'Receiving a new skull and a new body is just the limiting case of receiving a new heart, new lungs, new arms, and so on.'[21] The survivor would think he was you, and would hardly notice his slightly changed body. Your twin would not survive because nobody would survive believing he was your twin and with your twin's character and memories.

People have survived with half their brain destroyed or put out of action following a stroke. So as a matter of fact you need only half a brain (at most) to survive. (The destroyed half could be replaced by new brain-matter, so long as it was in the physical state requisite for continuation of your mental characteristics: so could the other half, which shows that retaining the same brain is only contingently, not logically, required for remaining the same person – c.f. the space 'travel' described in 'Replication' above.) It follows that if only half of your brain were transplanted to your twin after the car crash, then even in that case you would still survive with your twin's body.

Suppose now that you are one of identical triplets. One half of your brain is put into one brother's body and the other half into the other brother's body. There would then, if all goes well, be mental connectedness and continuity between you before the operation and two people thereafter. So it seems that you would survive as two people. But how can this be? You cannot be both, since they would be two different people. So you would be neither, since there can be no possible reason why you should be the one rather than the other. But this seems absurd. If one transplant had been a failure and the person had died before regaining consciousness, apparently you would have survived with the body of the other. 'How could a double success be a failure?'[22]

John Perry, and following him David Lewis, have tried to deal with the problem of division, or 'fission', by introducing the two concepts of 'person-stages', entities that exist *at* a certain time, and 'temporally extended continuant persons', which seem to be thought of as spatiotemporal 'worms'.[23] Apparently a person is to be thought of as a continuant, not a stage. This seems somewhat odd, because it would mean that we never see people, only temporal slices of them. In any event, Lewis argues that in a case of division, what we have even *before* division occurs is two (or more) continuants (i.e. people?), which seem in all ways like one. Parfit has responded, surely reasonably, that whether we have before us (part of?) one continuant or two can hardly depend on what is going to happen in the future.[24] As one might put it – how can the future affect the past, and particularly in a way that makes no difference, detectable or undetectable, to

456

the present? There are also other difficulties with Perry's and Lewis' complex and ingenious suggestions.

Robert Nozick has argued that the one who survives is the one with the greatest continuity with what went before, while everyone else comes nowhere, or at least hardly anywhere. 'To be something later is to be its closest continuer.'[25] But this is odd: a survivor might say, 'I am not A.L. although I seem to myself to be so; and if only that chap over there hadn't survived, then I *would* be A.L.' How can this be? If he were to murder him, would he *become* A.L.? And what if there are two 'survivors' symmetrically placed with respect to the original? Does this mean that neither is a survivor? Once more; how can two successes be a failure?

Suppose it is claimed that these cases show there is more to personal identity than either bodily continuity or mental continuity or both; that there is a 'me', a 'self', which either survives 'in' a particular body or it doesn't. This view has recently been revived by Geoffrey Madell and by Richard Swinburne.[26] But as Locke argued in considering transmigration of souls, and before these puzzle cases were invented, why should the whereabouts of such an entity make any difference? Perhaps in the replication case on Mars the alleged invisible bearer of the mind flew to Mars with the information stream, leaving the person on earth otherwise unchanged and completely unaware that he has lost his 'bearer'. Why should that mean he has turned into someone else?

Perhaps even to suggest that souls might move around in space, whether with or without bodies, is to talk of souls in a crudely literal way. If someone says that on earth the individual soul can leave the body, but this is not a spatial leaving, how are we to understand such a claim? Perhaps by analogy with assertions such as the following: while staying in the same room she had left him, never to return. This means her thoughts, desires, and emotions were *directed* elsewhere (or nowhere); perhaps also she imagined herself elsewhere. She (her body) was in the room, but she (her mind) was 'elsewhere' or 'nowhere'. But body and mind are two aspects, or perhaps 'parts' of a person: it doesn't *follow* from such talk that there can be a mind without a body, even if it is true that there can. Suppose heaven or hell are non-spatial regions – even though it is difficult to understand such a claim – and when on death the soul 'leaves the body' this is a non-spatial leaving. Still, if a person were such a soul then the person would have to be where the soul was, and vice versa. How could a *person* be nowhere, unless this is a way of saying that he no longer exists?

If a 'disembodied soul' is a logical impossibility, then not even God could have 'disembodied souls' 'in' His heaven. Saying this is not denying His omnipotence, any more than saying that He cannot create a circle with the same area as a square. 'Something which is logically impossible' is nothing at all, actual or possible, so there is *nothing* that God cannot create. He can create *anything*, but a so-called 'disembodied soul' would, so the argument suggests, not be anything at all. One thing God could easily do, however, is create replicas, as in the Mars story. *If* your Replica would be you, then *pace* St Thomas Aquinas, you would not need resurrection of your body in order to survive bodily death. There are however still peculiar difficulties with such a 'heaven'. How 'old' should your new body be? If we all get replicated in delightful youth but with the wisdom of maturity, may we still not fall in love with our grandparents or our children? Perhaps God solves such difficulties by multiple replication!

Fusion and immortality

Just as a person logically might divide (fission), so two people logically might combine (fusion). Who would the resulting person be? Would fusion be death, or survival in a new form? There could be many fissions, as in a branching tree, or many fusions, or a combination of both. What we would then have, according to Parfit, would be successive 'selves'. Similarly, there could be imaginary beings with everlasting bodies, who do not reproduce, and whose minds gradually change until after a while they have no direct and individuating (distinctive) mental relationships with the earlier mind: again, there would be successive 'selves'.

Parfit argues that 'the logic of identity' shows, for example, that 'I do not survive My Division [;] the two resulting people are two of my future selves. And they are as close to me as I am to myself tomorrow.'[27] He claims this shows that 'what matters in survival' is not identity, but something else, namely mental continuity and connectedness. But this is weird. What I want to know is whether *I* survive, not whether *something* (or someone *else*) does, although of course that question might interest me as well. If mental connectedness and continuity are 'what matters', then to *whom* do they matter? Furthermore, Parfit started off with the view that these factors were logically necessary and sufficient for personal identity; now it turns out that they are necessary and sufficient for something else, without our being told what this something else is.

Parfit also claims, in varying places, that in some puzzle cases the question whether the resultant person would be me 'has no answer', or that 'we could call this person me, or call him someone else ... neither of these descriptions could be a factual mistake'.[28] This mirrors Hume's claim that since a 'transition may diminish by insensible degrees, we have no just standard by which we can decide any dispute concerning the time when they acquire or lose a title to the name of identity. All [such] disputes ... are merely verbal.'[29]

We should remember that the 'identity' Hume is here talking about is, according to him, strictly speaking not identity at all, but something else, namely remaining what we call 'the same' something or other. David Lewis writes that 'Identity certainly cannot be a matter of

458

degree ... [but] personal identity may be a matter of degree because person-hood is a matter of degree, even though identity is not.'[30] This shows what Lewis says it shows, namely that so-called 'personal identity' is not an example of *identity*, if we understand by 'identity' the logical relation that Lewis (and Hume, Williams, Parfit and others) take it to be, according to which each thing, including of course a so-called 'continuant', is (necessarily) identical with *itself* and with nothing else. Remaining the same (something) through time has sometimes been labelled 'diachronic identity', but since this, which includes 'personal identity', is arguably not an example of 'logi-cal' identity, then we need some further argument to show that it has the formal characteristics that 'logical' identity has, namely that it is one–one and transitive. The puzzle cases may indeed show that it does not have these characteristics, in which case to call the relationship diachronic *identity* is liable only to mislead, instead of clarifying the situation.

Was Hume right that when there has been a gradual transition, any disagreements about whether we are faced by the same X are merely 'verbal' or 'grammatical', except where they embody disputes about the existence of some further entity? Although in some cases nothing much hangs on whether we have before us the same X as we had previously – for example the same stone – in other cases it does. If the person before us is the same person as Amanda then she has Amanda's rights and duties, and if not then not. This is difficult to reconcile with Parfit's view that in some cases there would be 'no right answer' to the question whether it is Amanda, or that we can 'say what we like'.

A fertilised egg is not a person. A four-year-old child is. A foetus is something in between. The change is gradual, and there is no *point* at which the one becomes the other. *Stipulating* an arbitrary cut-off point would produce conceptual change which would actually lead us to *misunder-stand* the actual. Differing entities have differing rights and duties, and gradual change in the one produces gradual change in the other. Only by appreciating that rights and duties can be a matter of degree can we clearly appreciate what ought to be in respect of a continuum of cases.

Something can stop being the same X either because it becomes, gradually or suddenly, a non-X, or because it remains an X while losing the individuating features it had, while taking on those of another X. Parfit quotes approvingly some passages from Proust, and, more movingly, from Solzhenitsyn: 'A new, unfamiliar person would walk in bearing the name of her husband, and she would see that the man, her beloved, for whom she had shut herself up to wait for fourteen years, no longer existed.'[31] Parfit says of such talk that it can be 'taken too literally'. But talk by Parfit and others of personal *identity* can encourage its not being taken literally enough.

In the passage quoted opposite (p. 458), Parfit wrote that 'I do not survive My Division [; but] the two resulting people ... are as close to me as I am to myself tomorrow.' Instead of concentrating on the first half of this sentence, it may be illuminating to concentrate on the second. Perhaps every day we wake up we should say, 'It's more or less *me* again!' This might bring home to us, among other things, that after Division, both resulting people could be more or less me. One lesson to be learned from these imaginary cases is that remaining the same person *is* a matter of degree. Appreciating this might perhaps encourage Parfit's anti-egotistical morality even more strongly than his current creative but rather misleading account of so-called 'personal identity'.[32]

Notes

(An author's name followed by a number in square brackets refers to the book or article which has that number in the bibliography.)

1. See Peter Geach, 'Identity', *Review of Metaphysics*, 21 (1967), pp. 3–12. This idea, sometimes called the 'relative identity thesis', has found little favour among modern philosophers: for an opposing account see, for example, Wiggins [12] and *Sameness and substance* (Oxford University Press, Oxford, 1980).

2. Locke [2], Book II, Ch. 27.

3. Bernard Williams, 'Personal identity and individuation', *Proceedings of the Aristotelian Society*, 57 (1956–7), pp. 229–52. Reprinted in Williams [7].

4. Thomas Reid, *Essays on the intellectual powers of man*, ed. and intro. Baruch Brody (MIT Press, Cambridge, Massachusetts, 1969), Essay III, Ch. 6.

5. G.W. Leibniz, *New essays on human understanding*, trans. and ed. Peter Remnant and Jonathan Bennett (Cambridge University Press, Cambridge, 1981), Book II, Ch. 27, §9.

6. Joseph Butler, 'Of personal identity', *The works of Bishop Butler*, ed. J.H. Bernard (2 vols, Macmillan, London, 1900), vol. II. Reprinted in J. Perry (ed.), *Personal identity* (University of California Press, Berkeley, 1975).

7. Quoted by Hamilton in a footnote to his edition of Reid's *Philosophical works*, now re-edited and introduced by Harry M. Bracken (2 vols, Georg Olms Verlagsbuchhandlung, Hildesheim, 1967), vol. I, Essay 3, Ch. 4, p. 351.

8. Ibid., vol. I, Essay 3, Ch. 6, p. 352.

9. Ibid., vol. I, Essay 3, Ch. 4, p. 345.

10. Sydney Shoemaker, 'Persons and their pasts', *American Philosophical Quarterly*, 7 (1970), pp. 269–85.

11. David Hume, *A treatise of human nature*, ed. A.D. Lindsay (2 vols, Everyman's Library, J.M. Dent, London, 1911), vol. I, Book I, Part IV, Ch. 6.

12. Ibid., p. 239.

13. Ibid., p. 240.

14. Ibid., p. 245; wording slightly transposed.

15. Ibid., p. 244.

16. Ibid., p. 242; italics added to the original text.

17. Bernard Williams, 'The self and the future', *Philosophical Review*, 79 (1970). Reprinted in Williams [7].

18. See E.J. Borowski, 'Identity and personal identity', *Mind*, 85 (1976), pp. 481–502.

19. See Ardon Lyon, 'On remaining the same person', *Philosophy*, 55 (1980), pp. 167–82.

20. Parfit [9], p. 202.

21. Ibid., p. 253.

22. Ibid., p. 256.

23. John Perry, 'Can the self divide?' *Journal of Philosophy*, 69 (1972), pp. 463–88. David Lewis, 'Survival and identity' in Amélie Rorty (ed.), *The identities of persons* (University of California Press, Berkeley, 1976), pp. 17–40.

24. Derek Parfit, 'Lewis, Perry, and what matters', in Rorty, *Identities of persons*, p. 96.

25. Nozick [11], p. 33.

26. Madell [14]. Richard Swinburne, 'Personal identity', *Proceedings of the Aristotelian Society*, 74 (1973–4), pp. 231–48, and in Sydney Shoemaker and Richard Swinburne, *Personal identity* (Basil Blackwell, Oxford, 1984).

27. Parfit [9], p. 302.

28. Ibid., pp. 283–4.

29. Hume, *Treatise*, p. 248.

30. Lewis, 'Survival and identity', p. 32.

31. Quoted in Parfit [9], p. 305.

32. The author, general editor and publishers are grateful to Messrs George Allen and Unwin for their permission to use some material in Chapter 20 which partially overlaps the contents of a chapter on personal identity to appear in Ardon Lyon's *Philosophy from absolute zero*.

Bibliography

Aristotle's writings on form and matter are in *Metaphysics*, Book VII, and *De anima*, Books II and III. A good introduction to his work is

[1] J.L. Ackrill, *Aristotle the philosopher* (Oxford University Press, Oxford, 1981).

Locke's treatment of the topic of personal identity is in Book II, Ch. 27 of

[2] J. Locke, *An essay concerning human understanding* (1690), ed. P. Nidditch (Clarendon Press, Oxford, 1975).

The relevant passages, together with useful readings, may be found in

[3] J. Perry (ed.), *Personal identity* (University of California Press, Berkeley, 1975).

Locke's views are discussed and criticised in A. Flew's paper 'Locke and the problem of personal identity', reprinted in

[4] C.B. Martin and D.M. Armstrong, *Locke and Berkeley* (Macmillan, London, 1968).

For Reid's critique of Locke, see

[5] T. Reid, *Essays on the intellectual powers of man* (1785), Essay 3, Ch. 6, reprinted in Perry [3].

Hume's celebrated treatment of the subject is in

[6] D. Hume, *A treatise of human nature* (1739–40), Book I, Part IV, Ch. 6, ed. L.A. Selby-Bigge (Oxford University Press, Oxford, 1975).

Bernard Williams' influential paper 'The self and the future' is reprinted in

[7] B. Williams, *Problems of the self* (Cambridge University Press, Cambridge, 1973).

461

This paper, together with Parfit's ingenious essay 'Personal identity', may also be found in the following useful collection:

[8] J. Glover, *The philosophy of mind* (Oxford University Press, Oxford, 1976).

Parfit's views are developed more fully in his lengthy book

[9] D. Parfit, *Reasons and persons* (Oxford University Press, Oxford, 1984).

Sidney Shoemaker's important but difficult paper 'Persons and their pasts' is reprinted in

[10] S. Shoemaker, *Identity, cause, and mind* (Cambridge University Press, Cambridge, 1984), while Nozick's highly readable essay appears in his book

[11] R. Nozick, *Philosophical explanations* (Harvard University Press, Cambridge, Massachusetts, 1981).

See also

[12] D. Wiggins, *Identity and spatio-temporal continuity* (Oxford University Press, Oxford, 1967), esp. Part IV.

Other useful essays on the topics of 'division' and personal survival appear in

[13] R.A. Rorty (ed.), *The identities of persons* (University of California Press, Berkeley, 1976).

The notion of a 'self' that is independent of bodily or mental continuity is developed in

[14] G. Madell, *The identity of the self* (Edinburgh University Press, Edinburgh, 1981).

See also R. Swinburne's paper 'Personal identity', reprinted in

[15] S. Shoemaker and R. Swinburne, *Personal identity* (Basil Blackwell, Oxford, 1984).

On the notion of the unity of consciousness, see T. Nagel's paper 'Brain bisection and the unity of consciousness', reprinted in

[16] T. Nagel, *Mortal questions* (Cambridge University Press, Cambridge, 1971).

And for some of the physiological background see

[17] J.C. Eccles (ed.), *Brain and conscious experience* (Springer, Berlin, 1966).

Some of the moral issues arising out of the problem of personal identity are discussed in

[18] M. Tooley, *Abortion and infanticide* (Oxford University Press, Oxford, 1983).

Useful discussions of some of the issues raised in this chapter may be found in

[19] G. Vesey, *Personal identity* (Macmillan, London, 1974) and

[20] H.W. Noonan, *Objects and identity* (Martinus Nijhoff, The Hague, 1980).

J.G.C.

21 | The Will

Hans Oberdiek

Throughout Western philosophy will has played a central, indeed crucial, role in discussions of fundamental issues arising in metaphysics, theology, ethics, epistemology and psychology.

Nowhere is this more evident than in the centuries-old controversy over the freedom of the will. If all our thoughts, feelings and actions are causally determined by heredity and environment, some argue, then our will cannot be free. Choice must then be illusory, which precludes even the possibility of voluntary behaviour. And if we never act voluntarily, the argument concludes, moral responsibility must be a cruel illusion. Others question the tacit assumption underlying the controversy, contending that the will is neither free nor unfree because it is not the kind of thing which could be either. Yet the controversy remains far from settled, and diverse conceptions of the will, its acts and its relation to reason and desire fuel the debate.

It would be a mistake, however, to think that diverse conceptions of the will figure only in that debate, for it features prominently in a wide range of other philosophical concerns. Philosophers and psychologists eager to explain human action and to distinguish it from machine behaviour find it necessary to use notions closely bound up with the will. How does one control an urge to sneeze at a concert during a pianissimo passage? 'By an act of will power', one feels inclined to say. Or how can we distinguish an accountant adding up a column of numbers from a computer, which certainly seems to be doing the same thing – only better? Those wishing to draw a distinction – and not all do – contend that only humans can do computations because only they can create and use symbols which stand for different arithmetical operations, a feat accomplished by the intellect working through the will.

463

As we shall see, philosophers also employ the will to distinguish between intentional and unintentional action, a grave matter in many criminal law cases: did the accused wilfully or accidentally fire the deadly gun? To a large extent, findings of moral and legal guilt – as well as degree of punishment – turn on judgements of intentionality. Indeed, intentionality becomes central in those theories of the will which wish to avoid the Scylla of dualism and the Charybdis of materialism. But more of this later.

These issues barely touch the concerns occupying thinkers for centuries. But their centrality illustrates just how important the notion of the will has been, and continues to be, in coming to grips with them. As we examine the historical development of the notion more closely, we shall see more clearly its pivotal role in philosophy.

Philosophy yields few general truths. Two truths *about* philosophy, however, seem certain. First, everything a philosopher says about a key concept must be understood, at least initially, as it relates to the particular philosophical problems he addresses. Second, like nations, key philosophical terms carry scars of long forgotten metaphysical, religious and moral controversies. These truths apply with special emphasis to 'will', a short word with a long history.

We must not assume, for instance, that 'will' means the same for everyone who uses it. 'Will', moreover, is an English word. This needs stating only because we can forget that foreign words, especially those in ancient Greek and Latin, sometimes have distinctive connotations and denotations. To forget this can lead to distortion, misunderstanding and failure to appreciate subtle but far-reaching philosophical implications of the views in which these terms are embedded.

Plato (428–348 BC) provides a case in point. In *The republic*, where he introduces his famous tripartite division of the soul, Plato never even uses the Greek word usually translated as 'will'. The traditional translation of *to thumoeides* is 'spirit' or 'spirited element'. Later he refers to spirit as 'the victory-loving or honour-loving part' (*to philonikon, to philotimon*) of the *psyche*, or 'soul'. Still, despite troublesome problems of translation, scholars rightly see Plato as offering, for the first time in Western philosophy, materials and suggestive metaphors out of which modern notions of the will evolved.

According to Plato, one part of our soul searches for truth and loves wisdom; it stands in sharp contrast with our appetitive nature, which can desire almost any object imaginable. This, along with its insatiable nature, makes appetite an obvious threat to reason and harmony among various parts of the soul. Indeed, reason and appetite engage in a no-holds-barred, endless war for domination raging ceaselessly within us until we die, unless we can somehow master our powerful desires and emotions. Fortunately, reason sometimes succeeds in enlisting the spirited element on its behalf and succeeds in harmonising elements in the soul. Plato, speaking through Socrates, provides a vivid example. It seems that Leontius, a man of breeding, came on corpses of executed criminals. He passionately desired to look at them, yet simultaneously felt angry at himself, turning away in disgust. After fighting himself for some time, even covering his eyes, desire overcame him. Then with bulging eyes, Socrates tells us, Leontius ran up to the corpses crying, 'Look for yourselves, ... you evil things, get your fill of the beautiful sight!' The story, Socrates concludes, shows that the spirited element sometimes wars with desire – and does not always win! We can recognise ourselves in Leontius easily if painfully. And Socrates' elaboration rings true, too:

> we often see this elsewhere, when his appetites are forcing a man to act contrary to reason, and he rails at himself and is angry with that within himself which is compelling him to do so; of the two civic factions at odds, as it were, the spirited part becomes the ally of reason. I do not think that you can say that when reason has decided that it must not be opposed, you have ever perceived the spirited part associating itself with the appetites, either in yourself or in anyone else.[1]

As Plato understands it, then, the spirited element, or will, involves anger and other emotions, but necessarily involves reason and reasoning as well, for spirit only motivates those open to certain kinds of reasons. Leontius feels shame not because the desired object does not promise pleasure; just the reverse! Leontius feels bad because, by giving in to his base desires, he betrays his reason, the 'higher' or better part of his soul. Plato uses this example to show that spirit differs from both appetite and reason, yet appears to have more in common with the latter, not only because they are natural allies, but because spirit, or will, can be educated by reason: Leontius can learn from his weakness and, through reflection, realise that giving in to base desires betrays both his ideals and sense of self-worth. His deep sense of shame, in short, can lead to reform so that, on other occasions, reason and spirit together can triumph. This example, and Socrates' elaboration, suggests why later philosophers found in Plato a rich and suggestive source for their own reflections on the nature of the will.

Aristotle (384–322 BC), Plato's most distinguished pupil, makes far greater contributions to our understanding of will, though here, as always, we must be wary of reading too much subsequent history into his writings. Aristotle uses a variety of terms to designate the motivation that transforms thought into action; in particular, those we translate as 'wish', 'purpose' and 'choice'. In his *Nicomachean ethics*, Aristotle introduces a distinction between self-controlled activity (*to hekousion*) and uncontrolled activity (*to akousion*). Interestingly, Latin commentators often translate *hekousion* as *voluntarium*, thus suggesting that Aristotle provides us with a theory of volition or will. Further evidence bolsters that suggestion, for he does say that choice (*proairesis*) falls under the concept of self-controlled activity, and both choice and self-control suggest the will to moderns. So do *boulesis* (wishing an end irrespective of whether it can be attained) and *boule* (deliberation about possible means to an end terminating in a judgement).

But we should hesitate before assuming that Aristotle provides us with anything like a full-blown notion of will. Indeed, he finds it impossible to say whether choice belongs primarily to reason or appetite, concluding with the suggestive, laconic remark that 'choice is either intelligence motivated by desire or desire operating through thought, and it is as a combination of these two that man is a starting point in action'.[2] That Aristotle appears to be of more than one mind on the subject should surprise no one, for Aristotle, as Plato, lacked the philosophical motivation and conceptual tools to develop a distinct conception of the will, at least as it came to be understood in modern philosophy.

But here we must enter another *caveat*. If by the will we mean what many subsequent philosophers mean, then clearly Aristotle lacks a theory of the will, for he does not have a story compatible with modern accounts which declare will to be a phenomenon of subjective, introspective consciousness, a mental event causing voluntary behaviour. As will be seen presently, however, many distinguished contemporary philosophers reject this modern view in favour of an account much closer to Aristotle's. Asserting either that Aristotle does or does not have a theory of the will, then, will almost certainly beg the most fundamental questions at issue. Far better to say that, if the will be understood in one way, then Aristotle lacks a theory of the will; if understood in another way, he has one – and makes a significant contribution to its development.

Self-controlled action, as Aristotle explains it, serves as an important forerunner to our own notion of 'voluntariness'; its inclusiveness, however, rules it out as an equivalent notion. For in Aristotle's account, self-controlled (or voluntary) actions are those where an agent, acting with the appropriate degree of knowledge and without compulsion, seeks an end because of some kind of desire (*orexis*) originating within him. For example, if someone desires to strike an enemy and he does not act under compulsion, then Aristotle would say that he acted voluntarily, and so would we. But if we accept Aristotle's account, then animals can also act voluntarily, as the same applies to them. On recognising a postman, for instance, a dog can be moved to chase and bite him, yet we would not wish to endow any dog with a will – nor hold him morally responsible for his harmful attack.

Aristotle supplements his view of self-controlled activity with a particular account of deliberation which succeeds in distinguishing human from animal behaviour, and thus provides another clue to an adequate account of the will. In Book VI of the *Nicomachean ethics*, Aristotle says:

> Choice (*proairesis*) is the starting point of action: it is the source of motion but not the end for the sake of which we act [i.e. the final cause]. The starting point of

choice, however, is desire and reasoning directed toward some end. That is why there cannot be choice either without intelligence and thought or without some moral characteristic; for good and bad action in human conduct are not possible without thought and character. Now thought alone moves nothing; only thought which is directed to some end and concerned with action can do so ... Only the goal of action is an end in the unqualified sense: for the good life is an end, and desire is directed toward this. Therefore, choice is either intelligence motivated by desire or desire operating through thought.[3]

Aristotle offers here the important insight that our capacity to originate action by choice defines us as humans and distinguishes us from animals. Yet an important puzzle remains: why should we regard moral character as inextricably bound up with choice?

The answer appears to be that Aristotle thinks he needs somewhere to stop and anchor an otherwise interminable chain of means–end reasoning. And he finds that anchor in the notion of moral character expressed in a carefully worked-out plan of life. It follows that only those actions are chosen which comprise part of that overall plan of life. But if self-control does not capture our sense of 'voluntary' because of its inclusiveness, surely choice fails because of its restrictiveness: we make numerous choices which do not form part of any overall plan of life.

If we find inadequacies in Aristotle's account because it does not fit our own intuitions regarding voluntary action, we should not assume that it failed in what it set out to do: namely, to elucidate the ancient Greek's notion. Moreover, even from our own vantage point, we can see how Aristotle helped shape our present understanding of will, and why we can still learn from him.

Aristotle's contribution can be seen by reconsidering just one example, that of Leontius: we know, or think we know, what reason demands yet often fail to obey its dictates. Plato has Socrates say that it would be strange if, when someone possesses knowledge, something else could overpower reason and drag it about like a slave.[4] Indeed, he argues surprisingly that no one ever acts contrary to what is best except through ignorance.

Aristotle finds Plato's theory at variance with observed facts – or at least apparent facts. So Aristotle struggles with and against Plato's account, devoting an entire book of the *Nicomachean ethics* to moral weakness (*akrasia*) and related subjects. His painstaking and incisive analysis leads him into a thicket of difficult moral, epistemological and psychological issues which remain to this day. For instance, Aristotle distinguishes the morally weak from the self-indulgent: because the self-indulgent pursues excess by choice and feels no regret, he is worse than the morally weak because his behaviour is incorrigible. He also distinguishes the self-controlled from the morally strong: because the latter obeys reason by not giving in to his base appetites, he deserves praise, but not as much as the self-controlled man, who finds no pleasure in base appetites.

Aristotle would describe Leontius as morally weak, not self-indulgent: he tried, after all, to fight his base desires and feels regret at having given in to them. His failure, of course, deserves blame. Had his fight succeeded, Aristotle would describe Leontius as morally strong, not self-controlled, as he would still have found pleasure in the disgusting sight. Because of moral weakness, then, Leontius deserves blame; yet because he is not self-indulgent, his choices can be educated. He can even hope to become a self-controlled man who need not resist temptation because he would no longer derive pleasure from disgusting sights.

In developing these distinctions, Aristotle requires and provides an account of voluntariness and practical reasoning. Both have proven especially relevant to current discussions of practical reason. Few philosophers deny, or even wish to deny, the theoretical employment of reason. That is, that reason can and must be used to establish the truth or falsity, or at least the credibility, of statements relating to simple matters of fact, scientific laws, mathematical theorems and predictions. Characteristically, however, such statements do not, by themselves, move us to action. Even those statements which relate directly to our own situation do not move us, many believe, unless they are conjoined with present desires. One may know it to be true, for example, that drinking this glass of arsenic will cause one to die, but that truth remains 'theoretical' unless one desires to avoid death. But, the argument continues, desires in and of themselves are neither reasonable nor unreasonable. So the question naturally arises of whether reason can be both 'practical' or 'action-guiding' and 'theoretical'. To put the question more sharply, can reason play a substantial role in producing its own motivation – or must it always wait on a-rational desire?

Aristotle's conception of *phronesis*, or 'practical wisdom', offers the first recognition of and answer to the question, an answer many contemporary philosophers still find plausible, though needing further development and refinement. By rejecting Plato's tripartite division of the soul, he avoids balkanising the faculties. That is, Aristotle has no antecedent commitment to seeing the question as one of reason versus desire since he regards reason as a co-producer of desires.

If one has cultivated proper habits of action and deliberation, Aristotle thinks, one can look over one's past actions and the actions of others to determine, through reason, how to live. This reflection helps produce in one a desire to live such a life. Given one's particular situation, one discerns which means can or must be used to achieve that life, and, again, reason helps produce desires for those means. Supposing that these desires through habituation, training and reflection knead the ends of life into our character, then reason will have played an essential role in moving us to action, showing that it can be practical.

We can see why Aristotle found *akrasia*, or 'weakness of will', so puzzling, at least in someone of sound character. For if one has satisfactorily integrated rational desire into one's character, why does he ever do what he claims to know he should not do? Briefly, the answer is that the weak-willed person has not developed a fully integrated character: one recognises what one should do, but that knowledge is not fully integrated into one's character. And this should surprise no one, of course, for the notion of 'a fully integrated character' can only be an ideal. Knowledge or reason, then, is not dragged about by the passions when one manifests weakness of will.

Thomas Aquinas (1225–74) extends and alters Aristotle's thought within a medieval Christian tradition in a way which brings it closer to our own understanding of the will. Following 'the Philosopher', as he typically refers to Aristotle, Aquinas also thinks of the will as 'rational desire'. Importantly, however, the will refers only to those desires determined by reason, not by sense. Given Aquinas' view that sense alone fixes the desires of animals, it follows that they lack will, and thus cannot act voluntarily.

This contrast suggests that Aquinas grasps an essential element of the modern notion of will Aristotle overlooks: intention. The Latin word *intentio* refers to the rational direction of an action to some end, the intention with which one does something. A man may punch a policeman with the intention of escaping arrest: one's envisaged escape provides a reason for action. But although a dog may bite a postman without external compulsion (because the action originates with his desires) no intention accompanies his attack: the dog bites merely because the sight of the postman triggers an attack. Consequently, excluding divine creatures, only humans possess a will – and only they may be held morally responsible for their conduct.

Aquinas avoids the twin weaknesses detected in Aristotle by his introduction of the concept of *intentio*. We need not ascribe a will to a dog simply because his actions originate within him as a consequence of sense; nor withhold it from a human simply because one's chosen action may not have been part of an overall life-plan. The gain achieved, however, comes at a price. Because of its connection with thought, Aquinas believes that rational deliberation must take time. This seems plausible in some cases, as when we jump because a sharp noise startles us: no thought, no time, no rational deliberation. Now, what about the man who attacked the policeman? Did he necessarily deliberate before striking, thus engaging in some time-consuming thinking? It would seem unlikely, yet unless he did so, Aquinas would maintain that his behaviour was neither intentional nor voluntary. But surely we would not wish to relieve him of responsibility because of this.

Many contemporary philosophers regard Aristotle and Aquinas as substantially correct in arguing that the human will is rational appetite, where that is understood as an ability to have reasons and to act from them. Some of these same philosophers, however, balk at Aquinas' particular account of practical reasoning, which seems to require a bit of conscious, time-consuming thought. They especially lament that seventeenth- and eighteenth-century philosophers often picked up this aspect of his thought while ignoring other, more cogent aspects.

Blinks and winks differ; but how? In both, after all, one's eyelid momentarily closes as a consequence of neural impulses causing certain tiny muscles to contract. Even though neither we nor any present physiologist can distinguish between the two sets of neural impulses, we easily tell blinks from winks. One difference, perhaps the difference, is that winks but not blinks are subject to voluntary control. And what holds for such simple behaviour seems to hold as well for more complicated bodily movements. Our (relative) helplessness when pushed into a pool contrasts so sharply with our (relative) control when we dive into one that we demand an explanation. A theory involving 'volitions' promises not only to distinguish involuntary from voluntary behaviour, but to explain how voluntary actions occur and what counts as an action.

Theories of volition can be traced to Aquinas and beyond, but they received fresh treatment in the seminal work of René Descartes (1596–1650). In his *Meditations* (1641) Descartes argues that a person consists of two fundamentally different and distinct kinds of 'stuff': mind and body. Mind (or consciousness) thinks, judges, imagines and wills; body (or matter) takes up space and, unlike mind, operates according to mechanistic laws. Somehow, in a way Descartes never makes clear even to his own satisfaction, mind and body form a 'substantial union' called a person.

'Will', or its Latin equivalent, names an especially important faculty of mind for Descartes. If God is no deceiver, he wonders, why and how can man err? He answers by arguing that we freely (but wrongly) allow our virtually unlimited will to outrun our limited intellect, thus rushing headlong into one false belief after another. This entails that false beliefs spring from a defect in character: namely, our reckless disregard for the limits of our intellect. So freedom and responsibility for Descartes, as well as virtue and vice, reside in the will.

Descartes also employs the notion of the will to explain how what one thinks can cause one's body to move. Imagine someone weighing the advantages and disadvantages of preparing thoroughly for an examination as opposed to visiting friends. At some point in the deliberations we can suppose that the student makes a decision: she closes her books, gets up from her chair, turns off the lights, and leaves the room. On Descartes' view, the student, after deliberating on what to do, exercises her will, commands herself to move, and her body obediently follows orders. Volitions are mental orders of just this sort, acts of willing to do or to forbear. Because Descartes so sharply differentiates mind from body, just how volitions influence the body must inevitably remain mysterious. He creates a chasm so wide and deep that no 'mental thrust' or volition appears able to leap from one side to the other.

Many of Descartes' contemporaries and successors wrestle with the inadequacies of his dualism of mind and body. Some appeal to the miraculous intervention of God to explain how what occurs in one's mind can be followed by bodily movements. Nicholas Malebranche (1638–1715) holds such a view, known as occasionalism. When I wish to hail a friend, I will to do so. But my volition does not cause even the smallest muscle in my arm to move. God takes my (mental) act of will, my volition, as the occasion for He Himself to move my arm. Although we can be said to be the natural cause of such movements, natural causes are not true causes, for they are only occasional causes requiring the power of God's will to make them effective.

Thomas Hobbes (1588–1679) avoids this desperate move, but for a price not everyone would wish to pay: he eliminates mind as distinct and separate from body. For Hobbes, only bodies in motion exist; consequently, all mental activities must be understood as various modes of bodily action. Voluntary motions such as walking or speaking, he maintains, depend initially on the imagination, or 'decaying sense'. That is, before the student closes her books for the evening she imagines herself continuing to prepare for her examination and joining her friends; these 'imagings' create in her body small motions, or 'endeavours'. Those endeavours caused by decaying sense or imagination pushing her towards visiting her friends Hobbes calls 'appetites' or 'desires'; those endeavours pushing her away from visiting her friends he calls 'aversions'. Now deliberation for Hobbes amounts to nothing more than a tiny war of desires and aversions, a war that continues until one side gains the upper hand. This would seem to eliminate will altogether, and in an important sense it does. Will, Hobbes declares, is simply the last appetite in deliberating, that desire or aversion finally nudging us to act in this way or that.[5]

To say, as Hobbes does, that every voluntary act proceeds from the will means only that every bodily movement other than digestion, reactive blinks and the like occurs as a causal consequence of some set of physically colliding bodily desires and aversions. In short, Hobbes effectively dethrones the will from its exalted status as executor of the mind's commands and relegates it to nothing more than a (dispensable) name for whatever desire or aversion finally puts one's body in motion.

Nearly every major philosopher since Descartes and Hobbes says something about how volitions cause our bodies to move and help us distinguish voluntary from involuntary behaviour. One reason driving British philosophers of the seventeenth and eighteenth centuries to their own special understanding of the will stems from their common rejection of faculty psychology. John Locke's (1632–1704) influential attack convinced many that a person's mind could not be divided into various distinct parts, or faculties, as the ancients and medievals seemed to do:

the ordinary way of speaking is that the understanding and will are two faculties of

471

the mind; a word proper enough, if it be used, as all words should be, so as not to breed any confusion in men's thoughts by being supposed (as I suspect it has been) to stand for some real beings in the soul, that performed those actions of understanding and volition ... I suspect, I say, that this way of speaking of faculties has misled many into a confused notion of so many distinct agents in us ... which has been no small occasion of wrangling, obscurity, and uncertainty in questions relating to them.[6]

But what is the will if not a faculty? It is, Locke argues, a power; namely a simple, original and unanalysable idea arising through reflection on change. '[W]hatever change is observed,' he writes, 'the mind must collect a power somewhere, able to make that change, as well as a possibility in the thing itself to receive it.'[7] Despite the necessity to presuppose an active power of will, Locke admits that we cannot comprehend how our minds move or stop our bodies merely by thought alone.

George Berkeley (1685–1753) develops one strand in Locke's account when he says: 'A spirit is one simple, undivided, active being – as it perceives ideas it is called the understanding, and as it produces or otherwise operates about them it is called the will.'[8] Unlike Descartes, or Plato before him, Berkeley stresses the unity of spirit, so that the will simply names a way in which spirit acts.

Jonathan Edwards (1703–58), certainly the greatest American philosopher until the late nineteenth century, developed Locke's view of the will even further, showing that understanding of the good, taken in a wide sense, does not stand opposed to the will, but becomes one with it. 'By "determining the will",' Edwards states, 'must be intended, causing that the act of the will or choice should be thus, and not otherwise: and the will is said to be determined, when ... its choice is direct to, and fixed upon a particular object.'[9] Motive determines the will; indeed, Edwards argues, the strongest motive always triumphs. But what can act as a motive?

whatever is perceived or apprehended by an intelligent and voluntary agent, which has the nature and influence of a motive to volition or choice, is considered or viewed as good ... And therefore it must be true, in some sense, that the will always is as the greatest apparent good is.[10]

Here Edwards raises, and tries to solve, a problem that troubled both Plato and Aristotle, and continues to perplex philosophers: does anyone ever voluntarily choose any course of action which he does not, at the time of choice, think good? We have seen that Aristotle disputed Plato's negative answer, but many, like Edwards, continue to find it tempting. Hobbes, too, believes that the strongest motive always triumphs, though he and Edwards differ interestingly. For Hobbes, appetites and aversions push and pull one mechanistically towards a certain course of action, and the will is simply the last push. For Edwards, on the other hand, apparent good draws us towards it like a powerful magnet draws iron filings. We see something as good, and then inexorably try to make it real. Not everyone, obviously, considers the same things as good; consequently, many people mistakenly will that which is, in point of fact, evil. Why cannot everyone see that certain things are evil? With unmistakable brilliance and originality, Edwards answers by developing a Calvinistic doctrine of predestination now out of favour. But if few care for his solution, none can deny the problem.

Edwards' younger Scottish contemporary, David Hume (1711–76), radically extends Locke's empiricism by claiming that volitions are felt, indefinable internal impressions, arising from passions, accompanying every voluntary act. Yet he offers no argument of how volitions cause actions, and for good reason. The world, Hume thinks, consists of nothing but a series of separate and distinct events, essentially unconnected. In such a world, volitions have little chance of explaining anything, for they have little or no place in explaining, say, how a shy person musters courage to engage someone in conversation. 'Will' just names that feeling a shy person has when greeting another, a feeling over and above the idea that he would like to speak and distinct from other feelings, such as apprehension.

Contrary to Aristotle, Hume adamantly denies that reason, at least by itself, can move anyone to act – or restrain one from acting contrary to one's passions. He offers a simple and persuasive argument for this far-reaching conclusion: reason can only discover truth and falsehood; but passions, appetites and desires are neither true nor false; therefore, passions cannot be contrary to reason. Sometimes a passion may be based on a false judgement, as when we become angry because we falsely believe that someone has slandered us, but the feeling itself is neither reasonable nor unreasonable. It may also appear that reason and passions conflict, but this, too, is a mistake. What we take for such conflicts are really nothing more than a clash between certain calm emotions and more violent passions.

'Reason', Hume says, 'is wholly inactive, and can never be the source of so active a principle of conscience, or a sense of morals.'[11] Indeed, 'Reason is, and ought only to be, the slave of the passions.'[12] Despite these astonishing claims, Hume does think reason makes some contribution in practical matters. First, reason can aid one in selecting means to satisfy desires or express passion pointing out the consequences of one's selection. When we feel aggrieved, for example, reason might lead us to see that, however immediately satisfying retaliation might be, recourse to legal remedies may be better for us on the whole. Second, reason can inform us which objects are appropriate objects of our desires. However thirsty one may be at sea, for instance, reason will inform us that salt water will not satisfy us.

These minor concessions to reason should not obscure Hume's central claim that reason cannot be practical. It follows, of course, that one never suffers from weakness of will, either. Seeming cases of weakness of will are no more than mistaken beliefs about what one really desires. Leontius, Hume would argue, really did desire to look on the corpses more than anything else at the time, or he would not have done so. Leontius willed to do what he did in the sense that the strong feeling he had moved him to do so. His so willing was neither rational nor irrational.

John Stuart Mill (1806–73) describes the will in terms reminiscent of Hume, to whom he owes so much: namely, as that moment in a series of associations of ideas terminating in an action. We experience volitions, or acts of the will, as occurring just before we act, but, Mill argues, we do not experience any causal efficacy, or force, between the volition and the act which follows. Given what they make of it, Hume and Mill might have been better off jettisoning the notion of the will altogether, but apparently the notion was too deeply rooted in language and thought to allow it.

In moving from Descartes to Mill, then, the will shrinks in importance. Indeed, it virtually becomes a vestigial organ: while once central to a sound understanding of mind, the will comes to be regarded either as the last appetite in deliberation (Hobbes), the greatest apprehension of apparent good (Locke and Edwards), or little more than a vague, causally impotent feeling accompanying action (Hume and Mill).

This highly selective history of the place of the will in Western philosophical thought cannot be brought to a close without a brief consideration of the views of the great German philosopher Immanuel Kant, who was attracted by rationalism but shaken by Humean empiricism – and scepticism. Like Aristotle and Aquinas, Kant perceives the will as connected with reason, but he goes far beyond them in making the connection tighter. Yet, unlike Locke or Edwards, Kant does not believe that we automatically will our apparent good. Only when determined by reason do our choices constitute the will. In defining 'will' as 'practical reason', Kant characterises it as the ability to act for and from reasons. Because of this ability, the will can ignore claims made on it by desires derived from sensuous impulses, and respond to the demands of reason itself, expressed in the forms of rational imperatives, moral and otherwise. Kant stresses, however, that one often falls prey to impulses, desires and even one's apparent good, though one could always resist. Actions chosen because reason requires them, he argues, demonstrate our freedom:

> Human choice is such that, while it can be affected by impulses, it cannot be determined by them ... Freedom of choice is this independence from sensuous impulse in the determination of choice. This is the negative concept of freedom. The positive concept of freedom is that of the power of pure reason to be of itself practical.[13]

Here we see, neither for the first nor the last time in Western thought, the close connection philosophers discern between the will and freedom. As noted earlier, a common, though perhaps not the most perspicuous, way of posing the ancient problem of freedom versus determinism is to ask, 'Is there freedom of the will?' It still awaits an adequate answer. We also see in Kant many other issues that have arisen concerning the will: its causal connection with action, its assigned task of serving as a bridge between reason and desire, and its special role in explaining how reason can be practical as well as theoretical; that is, how reason can move us to action.

This takes on particular importance, especially when contrasted with those, such as Hobbes and Hume, who believe that desires alone can move one to action. According to them, every human act may be explained as the causal outcome of one's desires and beliefs at the time of action. Recall our deliberating student: she left her studies for the evening because her desire to do so, accompanied by her beliefs about various outcomes, outweighed any contrary desires. On this view, desires are to be understood as causal determinants of action, no different in kind from the causal determinants which move other objects.

By way of contrast, Kant thinks of desires as motives for, not causal determinants of, action. Alan Donagan makes the point nicely:

> Motives ... are not forces of which actions are resultants but rather considerations in view of which an agent acts ... A motive is not a causal determinant of action, but rather ... a circumstance because of which a man may take action.[14]

This way of conceiving the relation between motives, desires and reason permits Kant to argue plausibly that reason can be practical – that is, move one to action – through the will, where the will manifests itself in action as freely choosing to embody some considerations instead of others.

Despite the imaginative power and originality of Kant's alternative, many find it less plausible than the view it challenges. Certainly the triumph of empiricism did much to tip the scales against both Kant's analysis as well as those older analyses which attributed causal power to the will. Still, partisans of Aristotle, Kant and Hume concerning practical reason and weakness of will can be found on the pages of any philosophy book or article even tangentially connected to those topics. Perhaps no more pressing question arises in contemporary moral epistemology than which of these three views comes closest to the truth; each has its champions, none has yet been declared victor.

Renewed interest in the will emerged in the late nineteenth century as a result of the pioneering work of the philosopher-psychologist William James. His monumental two-volume *Psychology*, published in 1890, altered the course of psychology and continues to influence philosophical discussions of mental functions and acts, including will and volition. Trained as a physician and familiar with physiological psychology, James opens his treatise dramatically: 'Psychology is the Science of Mental Life, both of its phenomena and their conditions.'[15]

Although this definition may sound old-fashioned today, it must have sounded revolutionary in 1890. For psychologists now concern themselves less with the 'mental life' than with discovering causal laws, or at least correlations, explaining why sons rebel against their fathers, why we never forget how to ride a bicycle, or how we learn our native tongue. Many psychologists, especially in America, think of psychology as embracing the behaviour of primates, wolves and even insects, asking, for example, why moths fatally seek flames. Others believe that we can learn about aggression and love in humans by studying the behaviour of monkeys; still others, such as B.F. Skinner (b. 1904) and his disciples, express no interest in what, if anything, goes on in (alleged) 'minds' of either pigeons or humans: only operant, or instrumental, conditioning matters in developing a satisfactory science of psychology.

In his own day, however, James' definition revolutionised psychology for two important reasons. Because it demands that mental life be understood scientifically, James took psychology away from the armchair speculations of philosophers. At the same time, because it concentrates on mental life, he rescued psychology (if only for a time) from reductivists, like Hobbes, who think that life can be explained by, and reduced to, purely material states and processes.

James' psychology rested on experience, but experience understood in a way fundamentally different from that offered by empiricists, who tend to think of it as something one undergoes, something that *happens* to someone. Locke's striking image of consciousness as initially a *tabula rasa*, or 'blank slate', supinely accepting the imprint of sensations, captures the essential passivity of experience. James' rejection of empiricism stems from a radically different philosophical orientation: he sees humans as knowers and doers, not as passive recipients of external sensations. We learn by doing and in learning we do, so that knowledge and action relate to each other directly and reciprocally. Consequently, experience reveals itself as dynamic, interactive, self-correcting and systematic.

Introspection lies at the heart of William James' psychology. Unlike some of his empiricist predecessors, however, James does not think that introspection can serve as a method of inquiry; it nevertheless does yield the data of psychology. That is, introspection cannot be used, as Hume in particular does, to establish the truth of certain hypotheses; it can only be used to supply data for scientific investigation. James' decision to treat introspective phenomena as natural events in a natural setting, functioning in an environment they help create, means that a psychologist must attend to his own inner, personal and essentially private awareness of mental states and acts. 'It seems to me', James writes, 'as if the elementary psychic fact were not *thought* or *this thought*, but *my thought*, every thought being owned.'[16]

Like so many late nineteenth-century thinkers, James embraces the central tenets of Darwinian evolutionary theory. At the same time, he sees that intelligent behaviour is more than merely adaptive. It involves intention, interest, emotion and, above all, deliberation. The latter, in turn, depends on attention; that is, singling out clearly and vividly items in one's perceptual field, possible courses of action, and potential obstacles to be overcome. Deliberation typically, though not inevitably, results in a decision to do or to forbear. In one authentic kind of decision, especially relevant to the will, one possesses all relevant evidence: no additional reasons can tip the balance this way or that. Yet unlike Buridan's ass (who allegedly starved to death because he could not choose between two bales of hay equidistant from him), we find ourselves choosing. Given that neither reason nor desire pushes one, how can this be explained?

James contends that we choose through a wilful act of our own, an act we feel as effort, as a 'slow dead heave of the will'. When we find ourselves in situations like that of Buridan's ass, we keep alternatives steadily in view and realise that we shall lose in choosing one over others.

> The essential achievement of the will, in short, when it is most 'voluntary' is to ATTEND to a difficult object and hold it fast before the mind. The so-doing is the fiat: and it is a mere physiological incident that when the object is thus attended to, immediate motor consequences should ensue. A resolve, whose contemplated motor consequences are not to ensue until some possibly far distant future condition shall have been fulfilled, involves all the psychic elements of a motor fiat except the word *now*; and it is the same with many of our purely theoretic beliefs.[17]

Notice that James attempts to distance himself from any appeal to faculty psychology in talking about the will. Indeed, he explicitly rejects the tempting notion that consciousness is some kind of thing having 'faculties', such as will, at all. Consciousness (including acts of will, thoughts, beliefs and perceptions) just refers to different functions of experience.

James replaces faculty psychology by a simple, but empirically complex and rich, mechanism for associating motor response to attention. When we deliberate whether to do this or that we find ourselves attending to remembered affections connected with similar choices in the past, conflicting and perhaps irreconcilable tugs, a sense of how our lives may look if we do this or that, and so on. In short, we actively construct our experience and our future. In arriving at a decision or making a choice, then, Hobbes was mistaken: the will is not simply the last appetite or aversion adhering to action. We organise and systematise our diverse perceptions, aspirations, emotions and beliefs through deliberation into a choice.

James' account of consciousness and will provides him with a way of showing that actions can at least sometimes be voluntary: namely, just those actions which must be performed attentively and which, in doing, we experience a feeling of resolve, effort or fiat, as when we rise to defend an unpopular cause. James regards such acts of will as paradigmatically free, and his contribution in this regard continues its appeal, though we shall not pursue it further here. And James' insistence that we must attend to introspectively known feelings of resolve and effort found philosophical reinforcement abroad.

It would be a mistake to think that James merely substitutes hazy phenomenological descriptions of willing for Hobbes' reductivist, mechanistic story. His own positive account, to take just one example, distinguishes objects of will from objects of belief by noting the manner of attending to each. Objects of will crucially depend for their existence on our being able to effect a change in nature; objects of belief, on the other hand, do not involve our interposition. Yet however eagerly or reluctantly, we consent to both. In belief we concede, whether we will or no, the truth of, say, the Pythagorean theorem or that our enemy approaches. In willing, on the other hand, we consent to make something real, say our effort to understand the Pythagorean theorem or to defend ourselves.

Some beliefs, however, can and should involve interposition. In his provocative essay, 'The will to believe' (1896), James argues that we have a right to believe either disjunct of an alternative that is simultaneously living, forced and momentous:

> Our passional nature not only lawfully may, but must, decide an option between propositions, whenever it is a genuine option that cannot by its nature be decided on intellectual grounds; for to say, under such circumstances, 'Do not decide, but leave the question open,' is itself a passional decision, – just like deciding yes or no, – and is attended with the same risk of losing the truth.[18]

Although beliefs sometimes come about as a consequence of our will to believe, James carefully spells out those which we do and those which we do not have a right to believe. For instance, not everything that may be proposed to our belief ('hypotheses') may be living, forced or momentous. A living option for one person, James explains, may be thoroughly dead for another. Probably no one today, for example, finds Zoroastrianism a living hypothesis, and not everyone finds Christianity, Islam or Judaism living, either. Further, few matters are so momentous or forced that we have a right to will ourselves to believe one way or another. In particular, James thinks that we should withhold belief concerning scientific questions until evidence decides them. On some matters, however, 'faith in a fact can help create the fact', and only an 'insane logic' would prohibit us from the right to believe.[19] He has in mind those moral and religious questions which, for us, are living, forced and momentous. To suspend belief on these, James contends, would be irrational, if to do so 'would absolutely prevent me from acknowledging certain kinds of truth if those kinds of truth were really there'.[20]

James' position has never had many philosophical champions, though it cannot fairly be assessed without seeing it as part of his general pragmatism and his special notion of 'truth' as 'workable'. The point here is simply that James' notion of will leads him to conclude that believing itself can be an action which we can will to make real.

Towards the end of the nineteenth century, Sigmund Freud (1856–1940) began his own revolution in psychology, a revolution that has yet to play itself out. His interest in what came to be known as depth psychology grew out of his diagnosis and treatment of deeply disturbed patients, which led him to develop a theory of human nature bearing affinities to Plato's tripartite division of the soul.

In Freud's theory, the structure of our psyche consists of an id, ego and superego. These – along with companion notions of the unconscious, repression, sublimation and libido – provide the basic framework of his understanding of both normal and abnormal behaviour. Although he has no distinct notion of will, it seems that ego does much of the work will does in older views. Social pressures and requirements felt within us since infancy coalesce as the superego: as our conscience, it provides us with a steady supply of prohibitions and guilt. From the id, on the other hand, flows libido, which is primarily sexual. According to Freud, we often, for reasons we need not explore, direct our sexual energy towards objects the superego forbids. He believes, for example, that little boys have sexual designs on their mothers and thus wish to murder their fathers, whom they see as rivals. The ego, the centre of rationality and effectiveness in the world, finds itself under pressure, trapped in the middle.

When one fails to work out such conscious conflicts satisfactorily, the pressures can become so great that the superego and ego conspire by repressing the forbidden desires, driving them into the unconscious, where they continue to exercise their influence on our conscious lives. Repression, it must be emphasised, is perfectly normal: on Freud's view, every mentally healthy man successfully repressed a desire to murder his father! Indeed, creativity finds its roots in sublimating forbidden desires. Sometimes, unfortunately, repression and consequent sublimation fail to work themselves out satisfactorily, and then the consequences can be ugly, for one can become neurotic or psychotic, exhibiting behaviour both bizarre and destructive.

Through psychoanalysis, Freud argues, at least some unfortunates can regain their mental health. With the help of an analyst, a person probes his unconscious, trying to recall the moment and the circumstances when his fragile ego failed to cope, and forbidden desires were driven underground to find their own creative, or destructive, outlet. By bringing the content of one's disturbing desires to the surface, Freud believes, one can strive to integrate them into consciousness in such a way that they no longer interfere with normal, effective action by a strong ego.

Freud's theory of mind generates puzzles and problems. For instance, Freud never made up his mind whether the apparatus of id, ego and superego should be taken as model, metaphor or reality. And if the latter, whether they constitute topographical locations of the brain or mental faculties. Fortunately, we can ignore these and related puzzles. We can even set aside, if not altogether ignore, the general question of the plausibility of the theory taken as an entirety.

What we cannot ignore, however, are questions Freud makes us face regarding freedom, intentionality, motivation and voluntariness. For if any theory remotely like his can be defended, and candidates abound, then the complacent assumption that one always knows what one is about cannot be sustained. The source of thought and action can be located within the person easily enough, but what if the person has neither knowledge nor control over his thoughts and actions? What if an adult man does not know why he says venomous things to his father or despises women or puts himself in self-destructive situations – and cannot seem to help himself from doing so? He certainly seems to act deliberately, intentionally and on purpose. Further, no one prevents him from doing what he does, so he seems to be acting freely. Yet if he cannot explain why he says or does as he says or does – or gives completely inappropriate answers – or cannot stop himself from persisting in conduct he detests, to what extent is he free, self-controlled or acting voluntarily? It would seem that one can be held accountable for what is done knowingly and freely, but to what extent can one be held responsible for being the kind of person one has become through no conscious fault of one's own? If many philosophers and psychologists no longer think Freud answered these questions satisfactorily, few deny that he made us aware of problems yet to be adequately resolved.

Behavioural psychologists of the twentieth century have almost uniformly dispensed with any talk of the will and attendant notions. Partly this may be traced to the unfruitfulness of research programmes based on such notions, though that in itself may raise questions about the very possibility of producing a science of the mental life. Other influences should not be ignored, in particular the general rejection of introspection in psychology and certain reductivist philosophical and scientific movements, such as behaviourism and materialism.

This brief excursion into the history of the concept of the will in Western thought reveals common patterns amidst deep and persistent divergences. Nearly everyone thinks of the will as occupying conceptual space between reason and desire, for example, and as providing a crucial bridge between thought and action. Differences quickly emerge, however, once we descend from this highly abstract level of agreement, for little else unites all who have seriously reflected on the nature, scope and objects of the will. Indeed, philosophers find themselves at loggerheads on a variety of broad and narrow issues.

Still, despite divisions that run deep, philosophers since the seventeenth century do seem to fall naturally into two broad classes: those who have an 'introverted' conception of the will and those who have an 'extroverted' conception.[21] The former understand volitions as many understand pains: that is, as momentary, discrete episodes occurring in one's private consciousness known introspectively through careful attention. Descartes, Hume and James exemplify this way of understanding the will. 'Extroverts', on the other hand, start with the behaviour of people. They seek behavioural criteria that anyone can apply to distinguish voluntary from involuntary actions and that do not depend on any privileged access of those whose actions they are. Although differing on many other matters, Aristotle and Hobbes exemplify this approach.

The introvert view requires a metaphysics and epistemology many contemporary philosophers find indefensible. 'Consciousness' composed of 'stuff' radically different in nature from our brains and central nervous system runs counter to the physiological materialism of our present era; knowledge of states of consciousness gained through introspection runs counter to the psychological behaviourism of our era, too. Contemporary philosophers have led the attack on the introvert view, none more effectively than Gilbert Ryle (1900–76) in his influential *The concept of mind* (1949).

In chapter after chapter, Ryle relentlessly ridicules the views of those who accept what he contemptuously refers to as 'the Cartesian myth of the ghost in the machine'. This dogma, he argues, is not merely an assemblage of particular mistakes. It is one big mistake and a mistake of a special kind: namely, a category mistake. It represents the facts of mental life as if they belonged to one logical type or category when they actually belong to another.[22]

It would be a category mistake, for instance, were one even to wonder whether headaches were purple, since only observable objects can be coloured, and headaches do not belong to that logical type or category. Of course, no one makes this particular category mistake, but Ryle argues that many people, especially philosophers, make mistakes just as silly. In particular, many persist in thinking of the will as if it were a bodily organ, perhaps like the liver, and volitions as if they were similar to pains.

In so far as the Cartesian myth incorporates the will and volitions, Ryle demolishes it in a series of striking arguments. We cannot speak of the will and volitions as we can speak of other activities, he says, though nonetheless the theory suggests we should if acts of will are indeed like acts of charity, contrition or courage:

No one, save to endorse the theory, ever describes his own conduct, or that of his acquaintances, in the recommended idioms. No one ever says such things as that at 10 a.m. he was occupied in willing this or that, or that he performed five quick and easy volitions and two slow and difficult volitions between midday and lunch-time.[23]

Although clever, this argument has more persuasive force than logical rigour, for the argument succeeds only if expressions in ordinary English set the limits of philosophy, a highly contestable claim. Ryle's other arguments cannot be met so easily.

First, neither indirect nor direct evidence can be adduced for the volitional theory. If volitions are private items in one's consciousness, then others can only infer their presence by observing behaviour. But because blinks and winks have the same physiological triggers (namely, neural impulses), we can never know whether someone's eyelid movement resulted from an act of will. Yet if we have no indirect evidence of what goes on in our consciousness, neither do we have any direct evidence, even in our own case. Introspection simply never reveals the moment when an alleged volition causes one to wink. Knowledge of the connection between the alleged volition and the wink, moreover, remains forever mysterious, as even such partisans of the theory as James must admit, for we have no evidence whatever that it occurs. Worse, the very link between volition and wink remains shrouded in mystery, for 'Minds, as the legend describes them, live on a floor of existence defined as being outside the causal system to which bodies belong.'[24] In short, if volitions are mental, then – because the mental consists of 'stuff' radically different from the physical – how can mental volitions cause physical movements? How can my mental act of will cause me to wink my eye?

Second, Ryle argues that introverts find themselves faced with an embarrassing infinite regress problem. Introverts postulate volitions in part to distinguish voluntary winks from involuntary blinks. That is, volitions alone make actions voluntary. So what of volitions themselves? Are they voluntary or involuntary acts of mind? Clearly either answer leads to absurdities.[25] For if involuntary, then it would seem that any action arising from an involuntary cause must itself be involuntary; if voluntary, on the other hand, then surely they must in turn proceed from yet prior volitions, and so on *ad infinitum*. Ludwig Wittgenstein (1889–1951), who strongly influenced Ryle and others of his generation, makes a similar point: 'I can't will willing; that is, it makes no sense to speak of willing willing. "Willing" is not the name of an action; and so not the name of any voluntary action either.'[26]

Ryle's devastating criticisms of the introverts' position may leave one with a distinct feeling of unease. For whatever flaws may plague analyses of the will propounded by introverts, their concern to distinguish voluntary from involuntary conduct cannot be lightly dismissed. Nor does Ryle. But as many other philosophers, introverts as well as extroverts, have clarified such notions as voluntary, intentional and free, we need not concentrate on Ryle's views alone.

If voluntary acts are not best understood as caused by a volition, this does not mean that such acts are either uncaused or nonexistent. Rather than follow the moderns in trying to develop a theory of conscious volitions arising from acts of will, we might do better to return to Aristotle and Aquinas. On this view, voluntary acts originate with an agent and are done knowingly or wittingly.[27] When what someone does simply actualises one's bodily, sensory, imaginative or emotional powers, one's acts are neither voluntary nor involuntary; for example, seeing the words on this page, tasting the sweetness of a ripe cherry, or feeling angry when insulted. For in such cases, the doer is not an agent.

These distinctions do not always accord with everyday English. Ordinarily, for instance, we think that a gunman who threatens us by saying, 'Your money or your life' leaves us with no choice; we say we hand over our purse involuntarily. Given the technical meaning proposed, however, our giving the money is voluntary, for the action originates within us as agents (in the sense of being under our control) and we do so knowingly.

Nevertheless, we can capture what we wish to say without abandoning the technical meaning by distinguishing between free and unfree voluntary acts: the latter are those where we find ourselves faced with unreasonable incentives to act in some way. Coerced acts, in short, are voluntary but unfree. In the gunman situation we act unfreely though voluntarily, as the gunman's incentives are clearly unreasonable because coercive. If a grocer tells you that he will not let you have his potatoes unless you give him the posted price, on the other hand, you pay him freely as well as voluntarily – even though you might prefer not to pay him at all.[28]

Of course, not all cases can be disposed of so easily. The notion of unreasonable incentives, after all, necessarily involves principles and standards of evaluation which may be in dispute or have unclear implications. If someone steals to support a gripping drug addiction, does one do so freely? Suppose, instead, that one steals to support a political cause dear to his heart; does one do so freely? Or consider the following. In most advanced industrial nations, workers can withhold their labour from this or that employer, but unless they accept some employment or other, they face extreme poverty; if someone accepts a miserable wage for work one finds repugnant and demeaning to feed his family, has he freely joined the workforce?

These questions are properly evaluative; they cannot and should not be settled by conceptual fiat. Careful consideration must be given to moral, social and political reasons, as well as standards of conduct which prevail in a given community or institution. Politicians and soldiers, for example, may have to live up to higher standards than ordinary citizens before they can plead that their actions, though voluntary, were unfree.

Voluntary acts on this account can include mental acts, such as adding numbers in one's head or fantasising what it would be like to score the winning goal in the World Cup. Perhaps this explains why it is said that 'Whosoever looketh on a woman to lust after her hath committed adultery with her already in his heart' (Matthew 5, 28). While we may wish to dispute the degree of culpability, if any, attached to unrealised lust, we need not deny that it usually counts as voluntary, for it usually originates within one as agent and is knowingly done (whether one lusts freely is a nice question!). Mental acts are not always voluntary, however, in which case they cannot be free, either. As you read these next few sentences, try not to imagine a seal balancing a ball on its nose! You will probably fail. No doubt attention can be redirected after a moment or two, but, at least for an instant, you cannot help imagine a seal, braced upright on its haunches, balancing a ball.

Some voluntary acts, though fully conscious, are unintentional. That is, one does not do them on purpose, and they can be inhibited with effort; yawning or fantasising, for example. Intentional acts, on the other hand, differ from other voluntary acts in virtue of one's state of mind regarding the results and consequences of one's acts. To clarify this, we need to distinguish between one's purposes and intentions. J.L. Austin (1911–60) draws the distinction well: 'I act for or on (a) purpose, I achieve it; I act with the intention, I carry it out, I realize it.'[29] A purpose, in short, consists in a state of affairs that comprises an end to which a plan of action is directed; e.g. understanding the principles of modern physics or winning an election. An intention, on the other hand, is a resolve to act in such a way that one's plan will become a reality.

Descriptions under which an act is voluntary are not always descriptions under which they are intentional, as the following story, drawn from Austin, makes clear. A particular creditor foresees that by exacting repayment of a debt, he will ruin his debtor, which he has no desire to do. Because he himself will suffer greatly without the money, he nevertheless calls in the debt, ruining the debtor. Although the creditor's act of calling in the debt must be described as voluntary, intentional and free, it is not intentional under the description of 'ruining the debtor', for his debtor's ruin formed no part of his plan. Jeremy Bentham (1748–1832) and some other legal thinkers call this 'oblique' or 'indirect intention', but it would seem better not to regard the act as intentional at all under that description. This does not mean, of course, that the creditor bears no moral (or legal) responsibility for his conduct under that description, for one's responsibilities often extend to what one foresees but does not intend.

Enough has been said to sketch the outlines of a

paradigmatically intentional, voluntary and free human act. It will be one where the agent desires to do something, does it knowingly and intentionally, and without coercive constraints. Further, he will act to achieve some purpose, immediate or remote, knowing that his act will have many unintended consequences, only some of which may be welcome.

Even this, however, raises difficulties. Suppose a publican intentionally, voluntarily and freely pours the friendly stranger a whisky. Unbeknownst to the publican, however, the man whom he serves is a plainclothes detective on duty. Now English law forbids publicans from selling alcohol to any police officer while on duty. Has the publican served the officer voluntarily? The publican has a legal problem. We have a philosophical problem: if the publican serves the man voluntarily, it seems that he must have served the officer voluntarily, for the stranger and the officer are one and the same.

We can avoid the problem by treating the predicable '... is voluntary' as an intensional function. Unlike extensional predicables, whose truth does not change when we substitute equivalent designations, the sense of intensional functions is given by the relation a mind has to its objects. For example, '... is a bachelor' is extensional: we can replace it by '... is an unmarried adult man' without loss of truth. On the other hand, act-descriptions must be understood intensionally; such sentences as 'The publican served a friendly stranger' or 'The son tried to humiliate his father' do not yield the same truth-value if we substitute other designations of the same act. In particular, '... is voluntary' or 'Bloggs voluntarily did ...' must be understood as signifying intensional functions. This permits us to say that, despite the endless true descriptions of any act, an agent acts voluntarily only when the act-description is one which the agent is aware describes his act. Following this analysis, we can then say that the publican voluntarily served the friendly stranger, but did not voluntarily serve a police officer, even though the stranger and the officer are the same.

We can go further. What are we to say of someone who, thinking that he has a stag in his sights, shoots and kills his enemy? Clearly, he intentionally fires his rifle, and we can suppose he does so freely and so voluntarily. But just as clearly, he does not voluntarily kill his enemy, even though he may wish his enemy dead. He has, in fact, killed his enemy accidentally. We can truly say of the man that he shot and killed his enemy only because there is some true description of what he did which makes his behaviour voluntary; in this case, one true description (there will be many) is 'Aiming and shooting a rifle at what he took to be a stag'.

These considerations have wide-ranging implications for determining legal and moral responsibility, but they cannot be explored here.[30] What does need further elaboration, however, concerns the relation between the words 'intensional' and 'intentional'. Roughly and briefly, the disinction is this: (intensional' and 'extensional' refer to a semantic distinction having to do with the sense of a sentence or statement. 'Intentional', on the other hand, refers to what one's thought or action is about. In so far as we talk about the mind and will, intentions reflect the other-directedness of thinking and willing. In this account, mental phenomena are either *about* something, such as a belief that certain words would insult one's host, or directed *at* something, such as insulting someone. The publican and the killer act intentionally, though only under certain descriptions, because only under certain descriptions are their efforts and actions about anything they would recognise as their own. We can therefore follow Ryle in refusing to characterise the mental by innerness, by privacy or by being made of some non-physical 'stuff' without falling into Hobbesian reductionism.

Our sketch of a paradigmatically voluntary act would seem to settle the great controversy over the freedom of the will in favour of freedom as opposed to determinism. Yet we cannot forget the puzzles Freud bequeaths to us. Can we, for instance, act intentionally yet involuntarily? It would seem so. Consider again the man who lashes out at his father to hurt him, but who seems unaware that he does so and yet cannot seem to stop himself. His act seems at once involuntary – or at least non-voluntary – and yet intentional: he acts on (an unconscious) purpose and achieves his immediate aim.

Examples such as this make it clear that nothing said here dissolves the problem of freedom and determinism. Indeed, determinists and their opponents alike could embrace the analysis offered above, yet continue to disagree. For although we have touched on some issues dividing them, profound metaphysical, psychological and scientific issues yet remain.

Notes

(An author's name followed by a number in square brackets refers to the book or article which has that number in the bibliography.)

1. Plato, *The republic*, trans. G.M.A. Grube (Hackett, Indianapolis, 1974), 440b.
2. Aristotle, *Nicomachean ethics*, trans. Martin Ostwald (Bobbs-Merrill, New York, 1962), 1139b.
3. Aristotle, ibid., 1139a–1139b.
4. Plato, *The Protagoras*, 352c.
5. Thomas Hobbes, *Leviathan*, Part I, Ch. 6.
6. John Locke, *An essay concerning human understanding* (1690), Book II, Ch. 21, Section 6.
7. Ibid., Section 4.
8. George Berkeley, *Principles of human knowledge*, p. 27, in *The works of George Berkeley*, ed. A.C. Fraser (4 vols, Oxford University Press, Oxford, 1901), vol. II.
9. Jonathan Edwards, *Freedom of the will* (1754), Part I, Section 2.
10. Ibid.
11. David Hume, *Treatise of human nature*, Book II, Part III, Section 3.

12. Ibid., Section 1.

13. Immanuel Kant, *Metaphysics of morals*, Part II: 'The doctrine of virtue', Introduction, Section 1 (Ak. 212–13), trans. Mary J. Gregor, pp. 9–10.

14. Donagan [14], pp. 116–17.

15. William James, *Principles of psychology* (2 vols, Henry Holt, New York, 1890), vol. I, p. 1.

16. Ibid., p. 226.

17. William James, 'Does consciousness exist?' *Journal of Philosophy, Psychology and Scientific Methods*, vol. 1, no. 18 (1 September 1904).

18. James [10], p. 11.

19. Ibid., p. 25.

20. Ibid., p. 28.

21. Cf. Kenny [13], Ch. 2.

22. Gilbert Ryle, *The concept of mind* (Hutchinson, London, 1949), p. 16.

23. Ibid., p. 64.

24. Ibid., p. 66.

25. Ibid., p. 67.

26. Ludwig Wittgenstein, *Philosophical investigations*, Part I, Section 613.

27. Cf. Thomas Aquinas, *Summa theologiae*, I–II, 6, 3 and 1; also, cf. Aristotle, *Nicomachean ethics*, 1111a 22–5.

28. Hans Oberdiek, 'The role of sanctions and coercion in understanding law and legal systems', *The American Journal of Jurisprudence* (1973), pp. 71–94.

29. J.L. Austin, 'Three ways of spilling ink', *Philosophical Review*, 75 (1966), p. 439.

30. Donagan [14], Ch. 4.

Bibliography

Plato's account of the parts of the soul is discussed in Chapter 5 of

[1] J. Annas, *An introduction to Plato's republic* (Clarendon Press, Oxford, 1981).

For Aristotle's views on desire, action and voluntariness, see

[2] A. Kenny, *Aristotle's theory of the will* (Duckworth, London, 1979) and Ch. 6, 7, 8, 12 and 14 of

[3] A. Rorty (ed.), *Essays on Aristotle's ethics* (University of California Press, Los Angeles, 1986).

For Aquinas' account of intention, see Ch. 5 of

[4] F.C. Copleston, *Aquinas* (Penguin Books, Harmondsworth, 1955).

For a discussion of Descartes' notion of the will, see Chapter 4 of

[5] B. Williams, *Descartes* (Penguin Books, Harmondsworth, 1978) and Ch. 6 of

[6] J. Cottingham, *Descartes* (Basil Blackwell, Oxford, 1986).

A stimulating work that includes discussion of Hume's account of reason and the will is

[7] R. Bambrough, *Moral scepticism and moral knowledge* (Routledge, London, 1979).

See also Chapter 7 of

[8] B. Stroud, *Hume* (Routledge, London, 1977).

For an introduction to Kant's theory of the will, see Chapter 11 of

[9] R. Walker, *Kant* (Routledge, London, 1978).

Apart from William James' classic *The principles of psychology* (see note 5 above), readers should consult

[10] W. James, *The will to believe and other essays on popular philosophy* (Dover, New York, 1956).

Freud's views on the working of the mind are examined and criticised in

[11] R. Wollheim (ed.), *Freud* (Doubleday, New York, 1974).

Ryle's position receives detailed analysis in the following collection of essays:

[12] O. Wood and G. Pitcher (eds), *Ryle* (Macmillan, London, 1970).

Useful discussions of many of the issues raised in this chapter occur in

[13] A. Kenny, *Will, freedom and power* (Basil Blackwell, Oxford, 1975) and

[14] A. Donagan, *The theory of morality* (University of Chicago Press, Chicago, 1978).

The problem of 'weakness of will' or *akrasia* receives detailed attention in

[15] G.W. Mortimore (ed.), *Weakness of will* (Macmillan, London, 1971).

The will in relation to the concept of human action and the theory of responsibility is a major theme of two valuable collections of essays:

[16] A.R. White (ed.), *The philosophy of action* (Oxford University Press, Oxford, 1968) and

[17] T. Honderich (ed.), *Essays on freedom of action* (Routledge, London, 1973).

The relation between belief and will is examined by H.H. Price in Chapter 4 of

[18] S. Hampshire (ed.), *Philosophy of mind* (Harper and Row, New York, 1966).

A sophisticated and influential collection of papers on the themes of willing, intending and acting may be found in Part I of

[19] D. Davidson, *Action and events* (Clarendon Press, Oxford, 1980).

Finally, for a stimulating and accessible introduction to some of the problems associated with human action and freedom, see Chs. 4 and 6 of

[20] J. Searle, *Minds, brains and science* (BBC Publications, London, 1984).

Grateful acknowledgement is made to Professor Oberdiek for helpful suggestions concerning this bibliography.

J.G.C.

22 | Freedom of the Will

Ian Tipton

Sir, (said he,) we *know* our will is free, and *there's* an end on't.

A melancholy thought

Dr Johnson's dismissal of the so-called 'problem' of the freedom of the will is hardly sophisticated, but it reflects a not uncommon reaction to the equally common thought that there are considerations that threaten our belief in our status as free and responsible agents. Boswell for one was worried, and he raised the issue on a number of occasions.[1] In a letter written in 1781, for example, he noted that he had been 'troubled by a recurrence of the perplexing question of Liberty and Necessity'. Johnson again chided him for his 'affection of distress'.

The exchanges between Johnson and Boswell are interesting only because they are not unusual. Debates on this topic are perennial, and though they will not always take just the same form in every period, quite similar moves will be made, and doubtless similar mistakes too. The two men can therefore serve quite well to introduce a question that continues to exercise us. We shall start by looking at their standpoints.

As we shall see, there is more than one line of thought that has been taken to suggest that everything that happens was in fact *bound* to happen. But Boswell's route involved theological reflections. He was disturbed by the thought that if God is omniscient (as the orthodox believe) He must know, for example, just what Boswell will do at every stage in his history. But that is puzzling. For if God knows (and always knew) everything we will do, it seems that the future must be 'fixed'; and that notion seems to Boswell to undermine 'moral government', and our belief that we are free agents. After all, that belief seems to rest on the notion that the future is *open*, and that (often) what happens next may be one thing, or something quite different. A 'fixed' future does not allow for that.

Now clearly this line of thought will not trouble

non-believers; and it is also true that theists may think that there is a flaw in Boswell's reasoning. (We shall indicate a possible flaw later; and non-believers can be assured that there are other routes to a 'fixed' future.) For the moment, however, it is enough to note that Boswell's concern was at least understandable. We can then turn to Johnson's response which, though it looks like a bare assertion that we are free, in fact rested on an appeal to *experience*, together with the claim that no *argument* could undermine that. As he put it on one occasion, 'You are surer that you are free, than you are of prescience; you are surer that you can lift up your finger or not as you please, than you are of any conclusion from a deduction of reasoning.' For Johnson, there is no real issue. As he put it to Boswell, it really didn't matter if he could not answer arguments purporting to show that he lacked freedom (any more than it would matter if he could not answer arguments purporting to prove that he was blind). For he is well aware that there are many things that he is able to do, or to refrain from doing. And to know that *is* to know that he is free.

Johnson's standpoint

Johnson's thinking on this issue is not profound, and some have judged it worthless on the ground that, though Johnson has a strong *feeling* that he is free, that proves nothing if others (who have been swayed by arguments) may feel as strongly that they lack freedom. The question remains, which feeling is correct? I want to attempt only a limited defence of Johnson, and I shall make three points. The first tackles the criticism directly.

It seems likely, then, that what Johnson is relying on here is not a feeling that he has but which others lack, but something he can suppose all but the most unfortunate know: the fact that they can, for example, move a finger if they wish. And surely this is something Boswell *is* aware of. Perhaps it is just possible that he might cease to believe it, and slump inert rather than 'waste time' in even trying to act; but that is not his position. The simple experiment of *doing* it will show him that should he choose to go for a walk he can, and for Johnson this is what freedom is. It is as if Boswell has stared freedom in the face, but then failed to recognise it.

For the second point we look at an ordinary situation in which, we'll suppose, strict parents demand that their daughter does not see a certain boy and where, moreover, they can enforce the ban. So this will be one area of her life in which she might say (though it would be a pompous way of putting it), 'I wish I were a free agent in this matter.' Here we know what the girl wishes. She wishes to be able to do what *she* wants, to go out with her chosen boy. So we can suppose now that her parents relent, advising her perhaps that they think she would be unwise to see him, but conceding that she must do as she sees fit. Depression is likely to turn to delight, until a friend tells her that her feeling of freedom is an illusion.

But why should anyone do that? Well, it might be to warn her that her parents are only testing her to see if she will respect the advice. The truth is that, if she looks like disregarding it, the old restrictions will be reimposed. In *that* case, clearly, her belief that she was truly free would indeed be an illusion, though she could test this by setting out to see the boy (not by consulting any 'feeling'). If she finds that her parents allow it, the issue is settled. So suppose, instead, that the point of warning her that she is not free is quite different, and that the thought is that certain theoretical considerations suggest that the future is 'fixed'. That, I think, might leave her unworried. And the reason is simple. Whatever the arguments may be, they seem unlikely to touch what *she* meant by being 'free'.

For the third point we can relate the idea that has just emerged to a specific argument. We should bear Johnson's stance in mind as we read it, though we now jump forward two centuries. The argument, which is associated with the name of Antony Flew (writing in 1955), has been outlined as follows:

> There are various words and phrases we use in ascribing free action to people: besides the obvious 'acted freely' and 'did it of his own free will', there are such phrases as 'could have been otherwise', 'had a choice about what she did', 'had alternatives', and 'could have helped doing what he did'. We learn these phrases by watching people apply them in concrete situations in everyday life, just as we learn, for example, colour words. These concrete situations serve as *paradigms* for the application of these words: the words mean *things of that sort*. Therefore they must apply to something; they must apply at least to the paradigmatic objects or situations. Careful investigation, philosophical or scientific, of these situations may indeed yield information about what freedom of choice really consists in, but it cannot show us that there is no such thing as freedom of choice. This is strictly parallel to the following proposition: careful investigation, philosophical or scientific, may show us what colour really consists in, but it cannot show us that there is no such thing as colour.

This style of argument – from 'the paradigm case' – was popular some years ago, though it had its critics too.[2]

Of course the approach here is not the same as Johnson's. It differs in that, where Johnson is impatient with what he calls 'theory', there is a hint that we might learn something from scientific or philosophical investigations; and also because, while Johnson stresses the agent's awareness of his own freedom, the argument points to knowledge that people in general are free. And of course the argument focuses on language; Johnson does not. The claim is that it is because we learn the meaning of the key expressions by applying them in ordinary situations that it must be absurd to deny that they have application. These differences are not insignificant. But it remains the case that both Johnson and the proponent of the paradigm case argument hold that the knowledge that we act freely is basic, in that it cannot be undermined by theories of any sort. They could both use the case of the girl who is allowed to date her boy. Johnson would hold that she discovers her own freedom when she finds that she can do as she wills. And Flew has it that the words 'acted freely' get their very meaning through application to such cases. To that extent, they are close.[3]

Genuine problems?

When one eavesdrops on Boswell and Johnson one sees that, from Johnson's point of view, Boswell is at fault for failing to grasp that clearly people *are* often able to act as they will; while, for Boswell, it is Johnson who ignores the *real* worry, which is that theoretical considerations do seem to point to a 'fixed' future. The thought is not that we don't sometimes go out with the partner of our choice, or move a finger at will, but that our acting as we do does not show that the future is genuinely open. If it was always certain that the agent would deliberate and choose as he does, how can it be true that, as I put it earlier, 'what happens next may be one thing, or something quite different'? That remains a disturbing question.

Anyone who has followed the continuing debates on this issue will agree that it has not been finally resolved, and that the different approaches of Johnson and Boswell live on, with some stressing that (within obvious limits) we are able to do as we wish, and others seeing this point as somehow trivial, and not doing justice to our notion that the future is, as William James put it in a lecture in 1884, 'ambiguous'.[4] When James leaves the Harvard lecture hall he can walk home via either of two routes. So what does James mean when he calls this an 'ambiguous' choice?

It means that both Divinity Avenue and Oxford Street are called; but that only one, and that one *either* one, shall be chosen. Now, I ask you seriously to suppose that this ambiguity of my choice is real; and then to make the impossible hypothesis that the choice is made twice over, and each time falls on a different street. In other words, imagine that I first walk through Divinity Avenue, and then imagine that the powers governing the universe annihilate ten minutes of time with all that it contained, and set me back at the door of this hall just as I was before the choice was made. Imagine then that, everything else being the same, I now make a different choice and traverse Oxford Street. You, as passive spectators, look on and see two alternative universes – one of them with me walking through Divinity Avenue in it, the other with the same me walking through Oxford Street. Now, if you are determinists you believe one of these universes to have been from eternity impossible.

Here, James says, we have a very important issue. For example, he claims, only the believer in an ambiguous future can make real sense of the notion of *regret*. For if I regret that something happened (James instances a murder), I hold that it ought not to have happened; that 'something else ought to be in its stead'. But that implies that something else might have happened, and this, James says, is just what the determinist denies. For determinism is the doctrine that whatever happens is inevitable, given the past state of the world. And if that is right, whatever happens (including the murder) 'had to come at its preappointed hour'.[5]

Against this background James sees many defences of human freedom as constituting 'a quagmire of evasion', for freedom has been variously defined. If, for example, we define it as 'acting without external constraint', then of course it does follow that 'sometimes we are free and sometimes we are not'. But that, James insists, simply fails to touch the substantial problem, which concerns 'an issue of fact and not of words'. James even advises that we need to drop the word 'freedom' if we are to make progress on the issue that should matter to us, which is whether determinism is true.

Foreknowledge and logical determinism

So far we have met with only one argument that has been thought to threaten freedom, or what James prefers to call belief in an 'ambiguous' future, and that was the argument from God's omniscience. In the sixth century, Boethius put the problem like this:

> [I]f God beholdeth all things and cannot be deceived, that must of necessity follow which His providence foreseeth to be to come. Wherefore, if from eternity he doth not only foreknow the deeds of men, but also their counsels and wills, there can be no free-will.[6]

This argument had already been examined, by St Augustine for example, and it has been discussed since, but I shall say little on it. One reason for that is that the argument will not trouble non-believers; but another is that theists may take comfort from the notion that God's ways are avowedly mysterious. Our inability to reconcile His knowledge with our freedom can thus be seen as a consequence of an inevitable failure to comprehend God, or (if that is too obscurantist) of an anthropomorphic view of Him. Certainly, the claim that God knows things in advance does not tell us *how* He knows, so it would be rash to assume that His knowledge means that everything is causally determined. And it has seemed to some (including Augustine and Boethius) that the apparent problem disappears if we see that only finite beings are *in* time. If from God's standpoint everything is eternally *present*, it is only from our limited viewpoint that He seems to know things 'in advance'.

There is, however, a third reason for not dwelling on God, and that is that, for Boswell at least, reflection on God's omniscience is troubling only because it leads him to two thoughts. The first is that whatever happens in the future was always certain to happen. (And as Boswell puts it to Johnson, 'If it be certain you are to go home to-night, you *must* go home.') And the second, it seems, is that the world must be ordered in a way that allows for God's knowledge. It is in that spirit that he talks of human life as being 'machinery' (though, because of God's power, he also talks of events as being 'planned and directed' by God). We shall find, however, that these worries can be generated without reference to God.

Our main concern will be with views about how the world is ordered, so I shall be brief on an argument that holds that purely *logical* considerations are sufficient to show that whatever happens was indeed bound to occur. Thus, the argument goes, at the present time one of the propositions 'Tipton will phone his mother tomorrow' and 'Tipton will not phone his mother tomorrow' must be true. (That follows if we accept the Law or Principle of Bivalence, i.e. the principle that any proposition is either true or false, together with the principle that if a proposition is false then its negation is true.) This, however, raises the thought that if it is the proposition that I shall phone that is already true, there can, even now, be no possibility other than my phoning, so (as Boswell would put it) I 'must' phone; while if that proposition is false and its negation true, it is my not phoning that must even now be 'fixed'.

If I deal briskly with this argument, that is not because it is easy to handle (it has exercised logicians since Aristotle), but in part because it is not one that is likely to convince us that the future is not 'ambiguous' (that seems too substantial a conclusion to follow from any principle of logic); and also because it would not in fact commit us to the view that events are *causally* determined. Beyond that, I can only note that there is more agreement among philosophers that the argument is fallacious than on what the error is. Some, however, would sacrifice the Principle of Bivalence as applied to propositions concerning what are known as 'future contingents', holding these to be neither true nor false, but 'indeterminate'. Others will allow that if I do indeed phone my mother tomorrow, a consequence will be that the proposition that I would phone must indeed count as having been true. That, they will argue, gets things the right way round. The mistake is to conclude that it was already 'fixed' that I would phone. If I decide not to phone, the proposition that I would phone will simply count as having been false.[7]

Physical determinism

The most worrying problems arise when we consider the apparent implications of a view of the world around us, or the notion that everything that happens in it is the outcome of causal regularities of the sort that concern the scientist, and ultimately the physicist. We assume, to take a simple example, that if there is an explosion there must have been an antecedent state of affairs – a build-up of gas perhaps, and a spark – to account for it, and that given the initial conditions, that outcome was inevitable. Were they to be *exactly* duplicated, there would again be an explosion. That will strike most people as obvious, as may the grander claim that for *any* event in nature, were we to have full knowledge of the initial conditions, plus a complete grasp of the operative causal laws, the event should be predictable, at least in principle. In practice, of course, accurate predictions may be beyond us. The relevant factors will usually be extremely complex. Our fallibility in practice does not, however, affect the basic assumption about what should be possible *if* we had the background knowledge.

As thus presented, this thinking may seem reassuring rather than worrying, for it would surely be very disturbing to think that our best predictions concerning what I described as 'the world around us' were vulnerable to a genuinely 'ambiguous' future in James' sense. The problem arises only when we dispense with the comforting phrase 'the world around us', and appreciate that we evolved within that world, and should be included among the various things and beings that make up the rich variety that *constitutes* nature. Against that background, it is hard to see how the workings of *our* bodies (including our brains), and the events in *our* lives, can be exempted from the view of the world that sees it as a causally ordered system.

Writing early in the nineteenth century, the mathematician Pierre Laplace was clearly encouraged by his understanding of physics when he wrote:

> We ought . . . to regard the present state of the universe as the effect of its anterior state and as the cause of the one which is to follow. Given for one instant an intelligence which could comprehend all the forces by which nature is animated and the respective situation of the beings who compose it – an intelligence sufficiently vast to submit these data to analysis – it would embrace in the same formula the movements of the greatest bodies of the universe and those of the lightest atom; for it, nothing would be uncertain and the future, as the past, would be present to its eyes.[8]

In fact, no scientist could write that now. Laplace's physics was broadly Newtonian, but it is accepted in quantum mechanics that in the case of particles there are *random* movements. That is sufficient to undermine Laplace's view of what a great intellect could know; for it entails that the notion that *everything* behaves in a law-like way is false. Indeed, earlier this century some took comfort from this, arguing that the recognition of indeterminacy at this level could give new life to the view that our choices are 'free'. But that was an illusion. It cannot be concluded from particle physics that ordinary (macroscopic) objects can be expected to behave in other than a regular way; and that is enough to generate the worry brought out in this section. Further, the acceptance of randomness at *any* level should be of no comfort to anyone who is concerned with a freedom that will allow for responsibility. From that point of view, the thought that the fullest account of my behaviour would involve reference to *chance* movements can be no more satisfying than the view that it would involve atoms moving in a law-like way. Random movements are not something *I* control.

Allowing for the mental

Since its development in the seventeenth century, it has been modern science rather than theology that has dominated debates on free will. But it is worth noting now that a more general thought about causality can disturb us. Thus we can simply consider the notion that nothing happens without a cause. For if I reach out my arm and get a book, we will suppose that there must be a cause of the event. And *wherever* we look for it (to a brain-state, or to a mental state such as its occurring to me that I need the book to check a reference) we will assume that there is a cause of that, and indeed a series of causes that must, inevitably, extend well beyond factors which were within my control. The notion that the causal chain must extend to areas which are causally related to the agent's choices but not determined by him can itself cast doubt on free will.

The argument as thus presented may seem too abstract to carry conviction. A direct appeal to the view that human beings are part of the world as understood by physics seems more powerful than a vague reference to a 'causal chain' of an unspecified sort. But it is worth exploring further, if only to take account of the naturally occurring thought that it must be a mistake to concentrate on physics, given that the *mental* states which are so bound up with human behaviour are not open to scientific study anyway. A firm articulation of that position can be found in Descartes' doctrine that the mind is 'entirely distinct from the body', and thus from the *material* world that concerns science;[9] but we needn't go that far (or be at all clear how mental states relate to physical states) to feel that any account of our behaviour that does not mention thoughts and desires, for example, omits reference to what makes us human, and perhaps to what makes us free.

Any suggestion that our behaviour springs from mental states and that physical states are irrelevant should in fact leave us uneasy. For clearly there is a relationship between brain-states in particular and the mental; and it has indeed been argued that mental states *are* brain-states, or that they are causally inefficacious 'epiphenomena'. That thought must be borne in mind, but it is considered in another chapter. Here we will simply accept that the explanations we normally offer of human actions are given in terms that do not derive from science. The girl we considered earlier, for example, goes with her boy because she *wants* to; and she can go some way towards explaining *why* she wants to in terms of his qualities and the effect he has on her. We will not expect her to give a full account of all the factors, some of which she may be unaware of. But even if we suppose that there might be a full account, and that it would be causal, that may not seem disturbing. After all, it would rest firmly on facts about her as a person, not on 'cold' facts about the movement of particles. From the girl's point of view, clearly, it is not the 'cold' facts that count.

To some, however, this has seemed only superficially comforting, for the quest for explanations can proceed. We can ask, for example, why it is that being a good dancer counts with *this* girl; why *she* enjoys the boy's conversation (others might find it boring); and why *she* glows in his presence. And, as the search for explanations proceeds, we will soon find ourselves mentioning things she did not choose. Even if we refer vaguely to her and the boy's 'chemistry', or to how she was brought up, we are appealing to things that from her point of view were fortuitous, even though they in turn may be explicable in terms of factors that she did not control.

Normally we don't press explanations of this sort very far. Each of us will acknowledge the importance of factors that are fortuitous in the sense indicated, as I do when I note that I probably would not be a philosopher had it not been for 'chance' events, including that, when faced with a row of advisers, I happened to be directed to one who liked the subject, of which I had then scarcely heard. But to the extent that we do look for explanations at this level they are rarely, if ever, complete. In explaining the *sort* of person an individual is we may, if he is delinquent perhaps, point to uncaring parents, to the unemployment situation, to his low IQ, and so on. And the account may be impressive. Even so, any suggestion that it was complete would be vulnerable to the fact that a very similar boy with a very similar background might turn out quite differently. Ted could be stealing a car while his twin is mowing a pensioner's lawn. That too calls for explanation.

Note, though, that here we have only a 'very similar' boy and background, together with an explanation of the first boy's character that is far from complete. So we might ponder the following question. If we can suppose a twin world where a baby with an *identical* make-up to mine is born into an *identical* environment, and we suppose that up to a given point the 'fortuitous' factors in my life are exactly paralleled in his, is it conceivable that at some stage, with our histories the same to that point and the same choice facing us, I should choose one way, my twin another? If we think it is not, that will be because the divergence would seem inexplicable, and that thought is puzzling. But if it is not conceivable, then it seems that both our future histories should be accountable for solely in terms of our inheritance and 'fortuitous' facts. Nor does it matter that there is no twin world. My position will remain just as it was.

Libertarianism

Clearly a form of determinism that gives prominence to our psychology will be rather different from one resting on natural science,[10] and it follows that a philosopher who describes himself as a 'determinist' and leaves it there is not telling us very much. That said, many philosophers do accept that *some* form of determinism is true. In this section, however, we will consider a claim that determinism is simply false.

This was the view taken by William James. It will be recalled that he asked us to suppose that he walks down one street, and then that the clock is turned back so that the situation is *exactly* the same as obtained just before the original choice. This thought-experiment serves the same function as the twin worlds of my last section, and James sees that the determinist will recoil from the suggestion that he might choose differently. Indeed he sees why the determinist recoils. If there were a divergence, we would be left with something inexplicable, or 'chance'. '[A]nd chance', James imagines determinists saying, 'is something the notion of which no sane mind can for an instant tolerate in the world. What is it, they ask, but barefaced crazy unreason, the negation of intelligibility and law?' It is on *that* basis that the determinist reacts as he does; but James responds differently. There is a clear sense in which different outcomes *are* conceivable. We must just accept 'chance'.

James does not claim to *prove* that determinism is false. What he does ask is that we should concede that it could be, and then accept the contrary doctrine (usually known as 'libertarianism') on the basis that only it can give validity to our view of ourselves as moral agents, and in particular to the notion of regret. I shall not comment directly on this claim here, but there are three points that should be made.

The first is that James is right to point out that the standard arguments for determinism do not *prove* it true, any more than James *proves* it false. What they do is to indicate the cost of rejecting it (just as James tries to show the cost of accepting it). And the second point is that James does hold that there is a price to be paid for accepting *his* world. Thus:

> The indeterminism I defend . . . represents that world as vulnerable, and liable to be injured by certain of its parts [human beings] if they act wrong. And it represents their acting wrong as a matter of possibility or accident, neither inevitable nor yet to be infallibly warded off. In all this, it is a theory devoid either of transparency or of stability. It gives us a pluralistic, restless universe, in which no single point of view can ever take in the whole scene; and to a mind possessed of the love of unity at any cost, it will, no doubt, remain for ever unacceptable.

A friend, James notes, had told him that 'the thought of my universe made him sick, like the sight of the horrible motion of a mass of maggots in their carrion bed'. To which James answers that if his world is 'repugnant and irrational in a certain way', it is because it offends 'the native absolutism of my intellect'. Determinism, he adds, is 'irrational in a deeper way', for it 'violates my sense of moral reality through and through'. But this brings me to my third point on James.

It is that it is far from clear that James' desire to give prominence to his sense of 'moral reality' is served by the universe he describes. For it is difficult to see how a world in which choices arise through 'accident' fits with our view that we can be praised or blamed for them. In short, 'chance' choices seem no more likely to give us what we want than the random movement of particles. After all, if it might have been no more than 'accident' that I choose A while you choose B, it would seem to be just *luck* that I made the 'right' choice. I can hardly criticise you for choosing B if 'chance' might have reversed our choices.

The compatibility thesis

The idea that has just emerged may strike us as bewildering. For initially one fears that determinism cannot allow for what we may be tempted to describe as 'genuine' freedom. (How can I be properly held to account for choices resulting from factors I did not control?) But now it seems that a blunt rejection of determinism does no better. (How can I be accountable for 'chance'?) Thus, neither a 'fixed' future nor an 'ambiguous' one *seems* to give us what we want. That, though, might suggest the following thought.

If both determinism and indeterminism seem to rule out what we thought of as 'genuine' freedom, and 'genuine' responsibility too, is it so clear that we can understand these notions, or want them to have application? On the face of it, we end up needing neither determinism nor its denial to be true, and that is not possible. We do know, however, that determinism is compatible with freedom in *one* sense (the sense that mattered to the girl we met earlier), so maybe that should satisfy us. If that is the *only* sort of freedom we can either understand or aspire to, we need not bemoan the incompatibility of determinism with something else: a so-called 'genuine' freedom that ultimately we cannot comprehend.

The view that determinism is compatible with freedom as properly understood has a long history. Consider for example the following pronouncement from Thomas Hobbes, writing in the seventeenth century:

> *Liberty*, and *necessity* are consistent: as in the water, that hath not only *liberty*, but a *necessity* of descending by the channel; so likewise in the actions which men voluntarily do: which, because they proceed from their will, proceed from *liberty*; and yet, because every act of man's will, and every desire, and inclination proceedeth from some cause . . . proceed from *necessity*.[11]

Writing in the eighteenth century, David Hume was similarly optimistic, arguing indeed that 'all men have ever agreed in the doctrine both of necessity and of liberty, according to any reasonable sense, which can be put on these terms'.[12] Asking himself 'what is meant by liberty, when applied to voluntary actions?' Hume answers:

We cannot surely mean that actions have so little connexion with motives, inclinations, and circumstances, that one does not follow with a certain degree of uniformity from the other, and that one affords no inference by which we can conclude the existence of the other. For these are plain and acknowledged matters of fact. By liberty, then, we can only mean *a power of acting or not acting, according to the determinations of the will*; that is, if we choose to remain at rest, we may; if we choose to move, we also may. Now this hypothetical liberty is universally allowed to belong to every one who is not a prisoner and in chains.

Liberty, Hume concludes, should be opposed, not to 'necessity' but to 'constraint'. The only alternative is to put one's faith in 'chance', which (Hume thinks) is 'universally allowed to have no existence'.

In our century, A.J. Ayer is just one philosopher who has argued (in a 1946 paper) that 'it is not . . . causality that freedom is to be contrasted with, but constraint', and (very much in the spirit of Hume) that 'from the fact that my action is causally determined . . . it does not necessarily follow that I am not free'.[13] So this doctrine, known as 'compatibilism', has to be taken seriously. Indeed, it has been suggested that '90% of philosophers in the analytic tradition today are compatibilists'.

Causality and constraint

The fact that most philosophers are compatibilists does not mean that there is now little scope for debate. For, even if as many as 90 per cent of philosophers do take *broadly* the same line, the debates within that group are as important as the measure of agreement; and the dissenters cannot be dismissed as not counting.[14] In this section, however, I must continue to paint with a broad brush. We need to see what it is that makes *some* form of compatibilism attractive to many philosophers. I shall make just four points.

The first is that there clearly is an important distinction between cases where men's actions 'proceed from their will', as Hobbes put it, and those where we are prevented from acting, or forced to act *against* our will. And the second is that this distinction is relevant to many of the judgements we actually make when using words such as 'acted freely', including those where praise or blame is at stake. The cashier who is forced to hand money to an armed robber is under constraint, so he will not normally be blamed; but if he gives the money to an accomplice, perhaps under cover of a mock robbery, he will be held to account once the facts emerge. Normally, an explanation in terms of his character will not serve to exonerate him, however we think his character was formed. So it is constraint or its absence that normally counts with us, and the compatibilist is right about that.

The third point connects with the first two, for the fact is that, far from doing justice to the distinction just outlined, those who have worried about determinism have often simply blurred it. Boswell for example does that when he urges that if the future is 'fixed' we are bound by 'chains', even if the chains are 'covered by leather', and we are unaware of them. And Isaiah Berlin has used a similar metaphor, holding that determinism 'represents the universe as a prison', though with 'chains . . . decked with flowers'.[15] Against this, the compatibilist replies that the metaphors cheat. For *real* prisons constrain, and they exist to prevent prisoners doing much that they would wish to do; while *real* chains prevent voluntary movement even more. Chains 'decked with flowers' have that effect too of course, but that is why it is misleading to say that determinism involves them. 'Prisoners' who can go where they will really aren't prisoners at all.

This point could be developed, for the literature is full of misleading language of this sort, and it is certainly true that if, as one philosopher has put it, we do not 'feed the bugbears', determinism loses much of its menace. Resisting talk of 'prisons' and 'chains' turns out to be just a start,[16] and many traps are more subtle than, for example, Boswell's fear that we may be 'machinery'. Against this one, however, the compatibilist simply insists on the *differences* between us and, say, clocks. Once it is accepted that ordinary machines do not reason and deliberate, and that explanations of what they do never involve serious reference to their *wants* or *desires*, it ceases to be clear why we should mind being 'machines' of our special sort, or, indeed that the description is appropriate at all. We certainly aren't *robots*, and if the compatibilist is right, it is the differences that make us free.

Finally, there is a fourth point, and it concerns the lurking fear that lies behind Boswell's assumption that if a 'fixed' future involves Johnson's going home, then he 'must' go home. Putting it another way, the fear – and it has been very common indeed – is that determinism seems to entail that no person ever *could* have done anything other than what he in fact does. The question is, is this correct?

Against Boswell, it seems that there is clearly a sense in which it is false, in that the word 'must' suggests that Johnson will be *made* to go; and (unless Boswell plans to force him home) that presumably will not happen. But this point can serve to introduce an influential suggestion G.E. Moore made about the word 'could'.[17] For, as Moore pointed out, even if we accept that determinism does entail that 'in *one* sense of the word "could", nothing ever *could* have happened, except what did happen', this does not show that we do not act freely unless we agree that it is *that* sense that freedom requires. But this, Moore stressed, was far from obviously the case. It seemed clear to him that 'when we say that we *could* have done a thing which we did not do, we *often* mean merely that we *should* have done it, *if* we had chosen'. Nor was it obvious that 'this may not be *all* that we usually mean and understand by the assertion that we have Free Will'.

Developments

Clearly it is important to distinguish between causality and constraint, even though a fully worked out statement of compatibilism will say more on the notion of 'constraint' and related concepts. Hume for example stressed *external* constraints, but, as is often pointed out, there may be inner compulsions too. Again, if you frog-march me down the road I cannot help but go, but if I act at gun-point I have *some* sort of choice, though it would be odd to say that I acted freely. This in fact confirms the link between the freedom that concerns us and moral responsibility. It is therefore necessary to attend to the way in which that notion of freedom differs from, for example, an animal's freedom to roam where it will. There are many issues that will not be tackled here. We must just be clear that many philosophers do hold that, when all the concepts are correctly understood, determinism is seen to be compatible, not simply with *a* notion of freedom, but with the freedom that is ordinarily and properly thought to belong to us as moral beings.

Of the minority who dissent, there must be few who would describe themselves as 'hard' determinists,[18] and none who would write as Mark Twain did:

> Man is not to blame for what he is. He didn't make himself. He has no control over himself. All the control is vested in his temperament – which he did not create – and in the circumstances which hedge him round from the cradle to the grave and which he did not devise . . . He is as purely a piece of automatic mechanism as is a watch, and can no more dictate or influence his actions than can the watch. He is a subject for pity, not blame – and not contempt. He is flung head over heels into this world without ever a chance to decline.[19]

Even if there is something right about that, there is too much wrong. Man is *not* like a watch (which we would never pity); and, as the compatibilist will insist, the talk of 'control' clearly raises another bugbear. On the other hand, *of course* I did not choose to be born, or to be born into a certain environment; nor did I choose my temperament. But these are things I could not expect to have chosen. Indeed, much of the appeal of compatibilism lies in the fact that 'hard' determinists so often seem to be hankering after something nobody could coherently wish for. The notion that my freedom would require that I should, for example, have been able to choose the circumstances of my birth seems just too absurd to contemplate.

For all that, debates continue, and, to repeat, the claim that most philosophers are in *broad* agreement leaves much unsaid. There are, for example, some who doubt whether determinism is an intelligible doctrine; others who hold that freedom *requires* determinism; and yet others who hold that the truth or falsity of determinism is irrelevant to freedom. In general, those who examine the literature will become acutely aware of the complexity of many underlying issues; of the sophistication of the contributions; and of the points on which there is still no agreement. They will also find able philosophers conceding that there is indeed a tension between determinism and *something* that appears to matter to us. And this requires comment.

Doubts about freedom

The defence of Dr Johnson's avowal of our freedom offered earlier in this chapter was a limited one, for the truth is that Johnson was not at all clear what to do with what he calls 'theory'. Thus we can find him leaning towards compatibilism. (God's knowing with certainty what we will do is, he argues, no more threat to our freedom than a friend's less impressive ability to predict our choices.) More often, perhaps, he is inclined to ignore 'theory'. However, when he concedes on one occasion that 'All theory is against the freedom of the will; all experience for it', he reveals that there is a tension *within* his thought, even though he insists that one tendency should be resisted. We found a similar tension in William James, though in his case this lay in a conflict between 'the native absolutism of my intellect' and his sense of 'moral reality'.

    The compatibilist should of course hold that there is no tension, but he may himself feel some unease if only because the notion that something is at stake has been so persistent. Boswell's feeling that Johnson's avowal of freedom is point-missing continues to strike a chord, as does James' desire for an 'ambiguous' future and, even, Twain's assertion that 'man is not to blame for what he is'. We can eschew talk of 'prisons' and 'chains', and yet still feel that if there is *some* sense in which, as Moore put it, 'nothing ever *could* have happened, except what did happen', that remains disturbing.

    It would beg the question against the compatibilist simply to assert that if this feeling persists in some minds it must be justified. But it remains true that even those who have seen the attraction of compatibilism can find it compelling. Thus, for example, A.J. Ayer's 1946 paper provides a vigorous defence of compatibilism, but his later contributions strike a less confident note. For example: 'If, as seems likely, our ordinary notion of responsibility involves the conception of the will as something self-propelling, it may very well not withstand critical scrutiny.'[20] To others, the conviction remains that to safeguard the notion of responsibility we do require not just that, had I chosen to go for a walk instead of typing this, nothing and no one would have prevented me, but that, all things being as they were, it might have turned out that I made that choice.[21] The notion may be that my decisions should be, as John Hospers has put it, *'self-caused'* in a sense that requires precisely that they are *not* 'the inevitable consequence of antecedent conditions';[22] and even if this turns out to be hankering after the unintelligible (and that remains a disputed question), this does not strike everyone as a comforting thought. *If* it is true that our ordinary notion may 'not withstand critical scrutiny', we may need to modify or reject it. And that would be quite a concession to those who have found determinism worrying. The pleasing notion that determinism is compatible with freedom as 'ordinarily' understood may have to give way to doubt whether the 'ordinary' notion stands up.

Persons and things

With this thought before us, it should not seem surprising that debates among philosophers continue and that various options remain open, not in the sense that all are equally plausible, but in the sense that many are still canvassed. No final resolution of the question should be expected here. Instead, I conclude this chapter by looking at the issue of what is at stake from another angle.

One way of bringing out that there is something at stake would be to return to the lines of thought developed in 'Physical determinism' and the following section and consider whether, if *either* were accepted by a being (we can say 'God'), it would not strike us as *unfair* were he to consign those who had lived 'badly' to eternal punishment and 'reward' others. But while that approach may be persuasive, it has disadvantages.[23] We really need to grasp the nettle and ask what difference it would make if *we* accepted either line of thought. We need not suppose that accurate *predictions* of behaviour should be possible, either in principle or in practice. We need only suppose that we come to accept (minimally) that if I am making a 'bad' choice, you a 'good' one, that is ultimately down to factors we did not control.

On the face of it this might have an effect. For even now, if a friend is petty, I find that I sometimes reflect on facts that partly explain it (perhaps just that he was an only child), and that this does mitigate my censure. If it does not prevent my criticising him at all, this is at least in part because I know that not all only children turn out as he has, and I judge that, by now, he should have overcome any tendency to pettiness. If I come to accept even the minimal thesis just mentioned, however, I will have gone beyond accepting that environmental influences have some effect on character, and will have a commitment that seems strong enough to put me under pressure not simply to moderate my censure, but to excuse entirely. And this is an intuition others share. It underlies the recurrent thought that a sense of accountability is threatened, and perhaps more besides, including a range of what P.F. Strawson has called 'reactive attitudes': resentment, for example, gratitude and esteem.[24] In a deep sense, losing these might mean ceasing to regard ourselves as *persons*, and taking what Strawson calls an 'objective' stance. And that would be a very radical shift.

This does suggest that there is something to concern

us, though it is interesting to note that Strawson's own view is that the apparent threat is illusory. And his account rests on the consideration that the shift in our attitudes would be so very radical. For one thing, Strawson says, though it is perhaps 'not absolutely inconceivable' that our reactive attitudes might decay, he is 'strongly inclined to think that it is, for us as we are, practically inconceivable'; but, for another, if we could imagine that we did have a choice, it would still not be *rational* for us to abandon them. Strawson's case for this claim is not easy to summarise without risk of distortion. But we get the flavour of it if we see that the shift would involve us *as people* making the choice from a standpoint external both to our ordinary view of ourselves, and to what the thesis of determinism may seem to require. Strawson's point is that there is no such external standpoint, so our choice could only be a practical one. '[W]e could', he suggests, 'choose rationally only in the light of an assessment of the gains and losses to human life . . . and the truth or falsity of a general thesis of determinism would not bear on the rationality of *this* choice.'

Strawson thus presents us with a form of compatibilism. He does not claim that determinism is true (professing to find the doctrine obscure), but he does insist that *if* we accepted it (and 'of course, though darkling, one has some inkling – some notion of what sort of thing is being talked about'), this could not affect our ordinary standpoint. His position is reminiscent of William James to the extent that both stress the importance to us of a viewpoint that has been supposed to be threatened. It differs from that of James in that, while James held that we could defend the viewpoint only by rejecting determinism, Strawson disdains the 'panicky metaphysics of libertarianism'. If Strawson is right, it is the very importance of the 'threatened' view that makes it immune from threat.

A firm evaluation of Strawson's position would be out of place here, but it would be equally wrong to end this chapter by suggesting that any contributor to the debate has obviously had the last word. So it must be stressed that Strawson's contribution remains controversial. It can be questioned for example whether a general acceptance of determinism might not indeed lead to a weakening of our reactive attitudes. As Ted Honderich puts it, 'The answer that it might do so seems as arguable as a denial.'[25] And Ayer, in a reply to Strawson,[26] confesses that, though he accepts that there is a sense in which it would not be rational to treat ourselves as *things*, he cannot ignore 'another sense of "rational" in which the rationality of an attitude is measured not by the probable consequences of adopting it but by the standing of the beliefs which enter into it'. For Ayer, there remains an 'intellectual discomfort', and misgivings about the concept of desert.

This feeling of 'intellectual discomfort' is one that has permeated discussions of the free will problem through the ages, and though many would still argue that it is misplaced or inappropriate, it remains the case that it persists in the minds of many who concede that the problem concerns two perhaps irreconcilable standpoints, *neither* of which we seem able to abandon. John Searle, for example, captures one element of Strawson's case when he holds that 'Our conception of ourselves as free agents is *fundamental* to our overall self-conception' (my emphasis). But, giving weight to the case that can be made for physical determinism, he confesses:

> [I]deally, I would like to be able to keep both my commonsense conceptions and my scientific beliefs . . . But when it comes to the question of freedom and determinism, I am – like a lot of other philosophers – unable to reconcile the two.[27]

Searle, then, agrees that we *cannot* give up our belief in free will, but he holds that there is a problem in that we will not give up the scientific conception either. So, in Searle's view, 'the problem is likely to stay with us'. And though for him and many others it is a clash between physics and the view of ourselves to which 'our own experience inclines us' that generates the problem, it seems significant that Thomas Nagel can come to a similar conclusion, though he starts from a consideration of the extent to which the actions for which we hold people responsible are 'disturbingly subject to luck'.[28] For Nagel, like Strawson, it is an 'internal view' of ourselves and our fellows that is essential to our conception of ourselves as agents, and the conflict is with an 'external' evaluation under which 'The area of genuine agency, and therefore of legitimate moral judgement, seems to shrink . . . to an extensionless point.' Where Searle talks of a 'conundrum', Nagel leaves us with a sense of what he calls 'paradox' which he takes to be embedded within the concept of responsibility itself.

But that may be the right note on which to end this chapter, for even if Searle and Nagel for example are too pessimistic and the apparent tensions are, after all, illusory, there is no disguising the fact that the issue of free will remains a live one, and that it is far from clear that agreement on it is close. Perhaps the most we can say with confidence is that proponents of various different responses are likely to avoid at least the grosser confusions that have permeated arguments in the past, and that rigorous attention to the many points of detail is making the options clearer. It may also be true that we are closer to understanding what the basic problem really is. Eventually, this may lead to an agreed solution. It cannot be ruled out, however, that an adequate understanding of the problem may only confirm us in something close to Boswell's unease.

Notes

(An author's name followed by a number in square brackets refers to the book or article which has that number in the bibliography.)

1. Quotations from Johnson and Boswell are taken from Boswell's *Life of Johnson*, ed. G.B. Hill, revised by L.F. Powell (Clarendon Press, Oxford, 1934–50). The

relevant exchanges are in vol. II, pp. 82 and 104, vol. III, pp. 290–1, vol. IV, pp. 71 and 328–9, and vol. V, p. 117.

2. The outline offered above is in fact that given by one critic, Peter van Inwagen, in Inwagen [3], p. 107, though it is based on Flew's 'Divine omnipotence and human freedom' in Flew and MacIntyre [1]. Earlier critics of the argument included John Watkins, in 'Farewell to the paradigm-case argument', *Analysis*, vol. 18, no. 2 (1957); and Gellner [2], pp. 30ff. In his Introduction to Flew (ed.), *Essays in conceptual analysis* (Macmillan, London, 1956), Flew himself conceded that there were 'limitations' to this form of argument, which he and others who had used it had sometimes failed to see.

3. It is in this spirit that Gellner describes Flew's argument as 'the *Dr Johnson-plus*' approach, noting that the 'plus' comes with 'a theory of meaning, and a theory of philosophy' (Gellner [2], p. 32). Flew himself refers to a romance when he argues: 'A paradigm case of acting freely, of being free to choose, would be the marriage of two normal young people, when there was no question of the parties "having to get married", and no social or parental pressure on either of them' (Flew [1], p. 149).

4. All quotations from James in this chapter come from 'The dilemma of determinism', which is included in James' *The will to believe* (Longmans Green, New York, 1897).

5. 'Determinism' in fact comes in a variety of forms, and it is variously defined even by philosophers who clearly have much the same thing in mind. Thus for one philosopher it will be the thesis that 'for everything that ever happens there are conditions such that, given them, nothing else could happen'; for another it is 'the proposition that every event has a cause, implying that each event is predictable, given the previous conditions and the laws of nature'; for another it may be that 'every state of affairs can be explained in terms of an *earlier* state of affairs', and so on. Here I can only note that the formulations are not equivalent, and that there is more agreement on the view that a form of determinism is true than on how the truth should be stated.

6. Boethius' examination of this argument is in *The consolation of philosophy*, Book V.

7. The argument considered here is often called 'fatalism', but it must be distinguished from the fatalism that goes further and claims that nothing I do will affect what is fated to happen. That is certainly false. Even if we accepted that it may already be a fact that I will lose my wallet, it doesn't follow that I will lose it even if I am careful with it. For if I do lose my wallet through carelessness, then the argument that 'proves' the loss was inevitable must 'prove' that the carelessness was inevitable too.

8. This frequently quoted passage comes from Laplace's *A philosophical essay on probabilities*, Ch. 2.

9. Descartes, *Discourse on the method*, Part IV.

10. Whether the position considered in the last section should count as a form of 'determinism' will depend on how we define the term. If we define it (as I did above) as the doctrine that 'whatever happens is inevitable, given the past state of the world', it seems that it might. But it is weaker than what is often described as 'psychological determinism', which requires there to be discoverable causal laws covering mental events in just the way that causal laws are taken to cover physical events.

11. From Hobbes [9], Ch. 21.

12. The quotation comes from Hume [10], Section 8.

13. Ayer's 'Freedom and necessity', first published in 1946, is included in Ayer [11].

Later reprintings include that in Watson [19].

14. The estimate was in fact given in an appreciative review (by Storrs McCall) of Peter van Inwagen's *An essay on free will*. Inwagen mounts an impressive case *against* compatibilism and then argues (perhaps less persuasively) that determinism is false and that freedom is secure. There is an interesting echo of James in his assertion that '[I]f the reality of moral responsibility entails the existence of free will, then, I would suggest, we have a perfectly good, in fact an unsurpassingly good, reason for believing in free will. For surely we cannot doubt the reality of moral responsibility?' (Inwagen [3], p. 206).

15. Isaiah Berlin, *Four essays on liberty* (Oxford University Press, Oxford, 1969), p. 106.

16. The talk of 'bugbears' derives from Ch. 1 – 'Please don't feed the bugbears' – of Dennett [18]. But many have insisted that there are bugbears. Ayer, for example, argues in his 1946 paper that 'the use of the very word "determinism" is in some degree misleading', as is 'the use, in this context, of the word "necessity" and even of the word "cause" '. Ayer notes that we incline to an 'uncritical use of a concept of force which is derived from primitive experiences of pushing and striking', and that we 'tend to form an imaginative picture of an unhappy effect trying vainly to escape from the clutches of an overmastering cause'.

17. Moore [12], Ch. 6. Moore's claim concerning the analysis of 'could' has been much discussed, notably by J.L. Austin in his 'Ifs and cans', which is included in Austin [13].

18. The terms 'hard' and 'soft' determinism were coined by William James. A 'soft' determinist is a compatibilist, and a 'hard' determinist is an incompatibilist who believes, in addition, that determinism is true. It is of course possible to be an incompatibilist and yet not a hard determinist if one maintains, as James did, that determinism is false, or if one has come to no decision on that issue.

19. The quotation comes from Twain's 'Reflections on religion', written in 1906 but first published, in *The Hudson Review*, in 1963.

20. A.J. Ayer, *The central questions of philosophy* (Weidenfeld and Nicolson, London, 1973), p. 43.

21. Moore's claim that his sense of 'could' is the one relevant to ascriptions of freedom was in fact put forward quite hesitantly, for he conceded that he could 'find no conclusive argument' either way. Others have continued to insist that more than what Hume termed 'hypothetical liberty' is certainly required if our judgements are to have their present point. Berlin, for example, notes: '[I]f I were convinced that although acts of choice, dispositional characteristics, etc., did affect what occurred, yet were themselves wholly determined by factors not within the individual's control (including his own motives and springs of action) . . . the concept of worth and desert, as these terms are now used, would become empty for me' (*Four essays on liberty*, p. 64n).

22. John Hospers, *An introduction to philosophical analysis*, 2nd edn (Routledge and Kegan Paul, London, 1967), p. 345. Hospers' contribution here ends on a pessimistic note. If we cannot find some way of clarifying the 'strange' concept of a self-originating decision, we may, he thinks, be faced with a view that is 'palatable but unintelligible', and alternatives that he holds are 'intelligible but unpalatable'.

23. The main disadvantages are that one might at any rate have doubts about the justification of *eternal* punishment, and that one can get bogged down in theological

questions that are largely irrelevant to the point at issue. In fact, the 'being' introduced here need not be the God of any particular religion; and we need no more suppose that he exists than Laplace had to suppose that of his hypothetical 'intelligence'.

24. P.F. Strawson, 'Freedom and resentment', originally delivered as a British Academy Lecture in 1962, and reprinted in Strawson [15] and in Watson [19].

25. Ted Honderich's examination of Strawson's position is in his *Punishment: the supposed justifications* (Penguin Books, Harmondsworth, 1971), pp. 130–7. Honderich concludes, '[I]t is mistaken to think that *if* determinism is true there are no logical consequences in terms of reactive attitudes. There *is* the consequence that they are, in their present form, out of place.'

26. A.J. Ayer, 'Free-will and rationality' in Zak Van Straaten (ed.), *Philosophical subjects* (Clarendon Press, Oxford, 1980).

27. John Searle, 'The freedom of the will', the sixth of his 1984 Reith Lectures, delivered and published under the title *Minds, brain and science* (BBC, London, 1984).

28. Thomas Nagel's 'Moral luck' is included in Nagel [16] and reprinted in Watson [19].

Bibliography

The 'paradigm case' argument is put forward in Flew's 'Divine omnipotence and human freedom', printed in

[1] A. Flew and A. MacIntyre (eds), *New essays in philosophical theology* (SCM Press, London, 1955).

The argument is criticised by Ernest Gellner in

[2] E. Gellner, *Words and things* (Victor Gollancz, London, 1959) and more recently in

[3] P. van Inwagen, *An essay on free will* (Clarendon Press, Oxford, 1983), which includes useful discussions of many of the issues raised in this chapter.

A clear exposition of various kinds of determinism may be found in Ch. 2 of

[4] J. Glover, *Responsibility* (Routledge, London, 1970).

See also Parts I and II of

[5] S. Hook (ed.), *Determinism and freedom in the age of modern science* (Collier-Macmillan, New York, 1961).

The contrast between physical and psychological determinism is discussed in Sections 15 and 16 of

[6] J. Lucas, *The freedom of the will* (Clarendon Press, Oxford, 1970).

A clear introductory presentation of the indeterminist/libertarian case occurs in Ch. 3 of

[7] C.S. Lewis, *Miracles* (Collins, London, 1947).

See also Part 4, Ch. 1 of

[8] J.-P. Sartre, *Being and nothingness*, trans. H. Barnes (Methuen, London, 1957).

For the compatibilist position see Ch. 21 of

[9] T. Hobbes, *Leviathan* (1651), ed. M. Oakeshott (Basil Blackwell, Oxford, repr. 1960) and Section 8 of

[10] D. Hume, *An enquiry concerning human understanding* (1748), ed. L.A. Selby-Bigge (Oxford University Press, Oxford, 1975).

An influential modern statement of compatibilism is A.J. Ayer's 'Freedom and necessity' in

[11] A.J. Ayer, *Philosophical essays* (Macmillan, London, 1954).

Moore's analysis of 'could' occurs in Ch. 6 of

[12] G.E. Moore, *Ethics* (Oxford University Press, London, 1912) and is discussed at length in Austin's 'Ifs and cans', to be found in

[13] J.L. Austin, *Philosophical papers* (Clarendon Press, Oxford, 1961).

See also Ch. 7 of

[14] M.R. Ayers, *The refutation of determinism* (Methuen, London, 1968).

Strawson's notion of 'reactive attitudes' appears in his paper 'Freedom and resentment', reprinted in Ch. 1 of

[15] P.F. Strawson, *Freedom and resentment and other essays* (Methuen, London, 1974).

The contrast between 'external' and 'internal' conceptions of ourselves is developed in the concluding chapters of

[16] T. Nagel, *Mortal questions* (Cambridge University Press, Cambridge, 1979).

See also Ch. 6 of

[17] J. Searle, *Minds, brains and science* (BBC, London, 1984).

A recent stimulating essay on the problems of free will is

[18] D. Dennett, *Elbow room* (Clarendon Press, Oxford, 1984).

Finally, four of the more useful of the many collections of papers published on these topics are

[19] G. Watson (ed.), *Free will* (Oxford University Press, Oxford, 1982)

[20] B. Berofsky (ed.), *Free will and determinism* (Harper and Row, New York, 1966)

[21] K. Lehrer (ed.), *Freedom and determinism* (Random House, New York, 1966) and

[22] T. Honderich (ed.), *Essays on freedom of action* (Routledge, London, 1973).

J.G.C.

Part E: Moral Philosophy

Introduction

The last two chapters of Part D discussed the questions of what it is to choose or decide, and in what sense choices and decisions can be called 'free'. Moral philosophy, which forms the topic of the following part of the encyclopaedia, is also concerned with people making decisions; it is concerned with people's decisions that such and such is the *right* course of action, or is what *ought* to be done, or is one that will lead to something that is *good*. People who make such decisions (or who recommend others to make them, or who comment approvingly or disapprovingly on such decisions) are said to make 'value judgements', and moral philosophy is concerned with value judgements of a certain kind. I say 'of a certain kind'; for not all value judgements are its concern. Contrast the following two groups of assertions:

(I) 'I ought to use a chisel for that job,' 'The right thing for me to do would be to use a chisel,' 'By using so-and-so's chisels, I will do a good job.'
(II) 'I ought to return that loan,' 'It would be right for me to return that loan,' 'By returning that loan, I will contribute to the general good.'

In each of the six cases, I am making a value judgement; yet there is a clear difference between the subject-matter of the two groups, which we normally mark by saying that the judgements which form the second group, and only they, are *moral* judgements.

Now that we have roughly isolated moral judgements from other value judgements, we can ask what the moral philosopher does about moral judgements. Faced with the assertions contained in group (II), one might ask, 'Is what they say to be accepted? Is it, for example, really right to return this loan? Again, is it right to return a loan in all circumstances?' But one might ask questions of a different sort. Abstracting from

513

questions about what is really obligatory, or right, or good, one might ask, '*What is it* to say that something is obligatory, or right, or good?' Questions of the latter kind are said to be the concern of moral philosophy; more precisely, they are said to be the concern of 'meta-ethics'. Many philosophers argue that moral philosophy is meta-ethics, and no more; that, in other words, philosophers as such are not concerned with what is really right, or good, or one's duty. I say, 'as such'. As a person (say) involved in commercial transactions, or as a member of a family, or of a church, or of a trade union, a philosopher will have views about such matters. But *as a philosopher* he or she is neutral about such issues. There is, however, another view about the nature of moral philosophy. But before I describe this, there is more to be said about meta-ethics.

Meta-ethical theories can be divided into two main groups, according to the answer that they give to the question 'Are moral judgements *objective*?' To say that a moral judgement is objective is to say that its rightness or wrongness is independent of the personal preferences and inclinations of any individual or group of individuals. The opposing schools of philosophical thought on this issue could be called 'objectivist' and 'subjectivist'. These terms, however, give no clue to the way in which objectivity and subjectivity are understood in the context of moral judgements, and it is more helpful to describe the opposing schools as 'cognitivist' and 'non-cognitivist'. The cognitivist school of thought holds that whatever is morally good or right is a matter of *knowledge* and, in particular, that it can be recognised by the reason. The non-cognitivist may allow the reason a role in moral judgement, but will argue that this role is the subordinate one of finding means to ends that reason itself does not determine.

I said that some philosophers argue that moral philosophy is meta-ethics, and no more. But there are those who think that there is more to moral philosophy – namely, something which is called 'normative ethics'. What this is can be understood by way of a further consideration of cognitive theories of ethics. Since cognitive theorists say that moral judgements are the work of reason, and since reason is by its nature systematic, it is not surprising that they should also say that their philosophy provides a system which gives guidance as to what is morally right or good. Such philosophies are said to enter the realm of 'normative ethics'. It is worth noting that philosophers who belong to this school of thought do not deny the legitimacy, or the importance, of meta-ethics. Their objection is only to the view that meta-ethics is all that there is to moral philosophy, and that the philosopher as such is therefore morally neutral.

The distinction between cognitive and non-cognitive theories of ethics will provide a framework for Part E. Chapter 23 forms a kind of prologue. It discusses in detail that of which this introduction can give only the barest sketch – namely, the nature of moral philosophy, and the distinction between meta-ethics and normative ethics. Chapters 24 and 25 deal with moral theories of a cognitive type. The first of these discusses 'teleological' theories of morality, which are based on a distinctive view of human nature – namely, that we are beings which have, and strive for, an end. The theory has a long history, which goes back to the ancient Greeks, and is still a topic of serious discussion. Chapter 25 deals with the relations between morality and universal law. Here, the dominant figure is an eighteenth-century philosopher, Immanuel Kant. Kant's moral philosophy, and in particular his theory of a 'kingdom of ends', has teleological aspects. However, his main contribution to moral philosophy is his idea that reason is not a mere servant, but is a legislator; further, that this legislative character is manifested in laws that are universally binding.

Kant believed that in considering the morality of an act we should pay no attention to its consequences, but should consider only the nature of the rule that the agent follows. In this respect his views differ sharply from those of the theory known as utilitarianism, which, in one form or another, has been dominant in British moral philosophy in both the nineteenth and twentieth centuries. This theory, which is discussed in Chapter 26, does not belong exclusively either to the cognitivist or the non-cognitivist camp. Put crudely, the theory states that the moral goodness or badness of an act is to be judged in terms of its consequences – that is, in terms of whether it helps or hinders the achievement of some ultimate good. Views about the nature of this ultimate good have varied. For the classical utilitarians of the nineteenth century, such as Bentham and John Stuart Mill, the ultimate good was happiness; modern utilitarians see the ultimate good as definable in terms of the agent's interests, or of the enlargement of the scope of human choice. However, what matters for the purposes of our classification of moral theories is the answer that utilitarians give to the question 'What entitles us to say that such and such *is* the ultimate good? Do we *know* this, or have our assertions about the ultimate good some other, non-cognitive basis?' Mill's answer to the question was notoriously obscure, but he seems to have thought that the nature of the ultimate good is a matter of knowledge, although no rigorous proof of its nature can be given. Other philosophers, such as G.E. Moore, have argued that ultimate ends are known by a kind of non-sensuous intuition. But the contemporary utilitarian, asked to justify his views about the ultimate good, is apt to talk about 'ultimate attitudes and feelings'.

This brings us to non-cognitive theories of morality, the main forms of which are discussed in Chapter 27. Some philosophers have argued that moral judgements, so far from being cognitive, are simply expressions of feelings. This view, known as 'the emotive theory of ethics', has been given its most subtle form by C.L. Stevenson. He sees moral judgements as expressions of feeling which also have the function of getting people to feel differently, to adopt new attitudes. Stevenson's views had most influence in the 1940s and 1950s; at the present time, the most influential non-cognitive theory is the 'prescriptive theory', which may be regarded as an amendment to the emotive theory. As its name suggests, the basic idea of the prescriptive theory is that the function of a moral judgement is to prescribe, not to describe; in linguistic terms, the function of moral language is imperatival rather than indicative. The most important prescriptive theory is that of R.M. Hare. Hare argues that although moral judgements are not purely descriptive, they share with descriptive judgements a feature which he calls 'universalizability'. That is, if we judge that anything (call it 'S') has some attribute (call it 'P'), we are committed to saying that anything which is like S in relevant respects also has the attribute P. From this formal account of the nature of moral judgements, Hare goes on to develop a kind of utilitarianism.

Our discussion of moral philosophy closes in Chapter 28 with an account of some of the moral aspects of what has been called (following Nietzsche) 'the death of God'. The title of this chapter could mislead. Those philosophers who are its chief concern – Nietzsche, Heidegger and Sartre – are by no means the only moral philosophers whose moral philosophy is atheistic. But whereas most of those philosophers who are atheistic see the collapse of belief in God as irrelevant to morality, the philosophers who are the concern of Chapter 28 see man as in a way the heir to God, or at any rate to a role that God once played. They stress in various ways not the cognitive or the emotive, but the creative aspects of morality, and it is no coincidence that two of them – Nietzsche and Sartre – are important figures in the literary history of their respective countries.

G.H.R.P.

23 | The Nature of Moral Philosophy

Richard Lindley

Introduction

The nature of moral philosophy is itself philosophically controversial in a way in which the natures of other areas of philosophy are not. Other branches of philosophy, such as philosophy of science, are concerned with a definition and evaluation of assumptions made by specialist practitioners. Scientists produce and test scientific theories, whilst philosophers of science ask, 'What is a scientific theory?' and 'Can the truth of scientific theories be established?' (see Chapter 9). The substantive theories of science are often called by philosophers 'first-order theories', whereas the philosophical theories about the *nature* of science are called 'second-order'. Much philosophy is undoubtedly a second-order activity. It is therefore tempting to suppose that moral philosophy must be essentially second-order, the attempt to define and evaluate the assumptions made by ... whom? Unlike, say, physics, there is no established science of morality with its own community of specialists. We all face moral problems directly, and cannot just leave their resolution to the experts. Indeed there is no agreed methodology for solving moral problems. Hence it has fallen to philosophers to address substantive moral questions about what would constitute a good life, what are our moral obligations, and how we should resolve moral dilemmas.

For these reasons there is something to be said for dividing moral philosophy into two parts – meta-ethics and normative ethics. Whereas the latter is primarily concerned with how people ought to conduct their lives, the former addresses questions such as 'Are there any objective truths of morality?' and 'What is it that distinguishes *moral* reasons for action from other justifications?' For most of the twentieth century, until the late 1960s, the prevalent view among philosophers in the English-speaking tradition was that moral philosophy is, like philosophy of science, really just a second-order activity. First-order ethics, which was referred to disparagingly by these purists as 'moralising', should be left to moralisers, who would include among their ranks clergy, doctors, schoolteachers and politicians, but certainly not philosophers in their professional capacity. According to this view the philosopher as such has no views about the content of moral judgements. Since the 1960s, perhaps in large part because of the moral crisis which befell American society in the wake of the Vietnam War, there has been a resurgence of interest in normative ethics. The result is that much work is now being done by philosophers in both branches of moral philosophy.

Part One: Meta-ethics

The meaning of moral terms

There was a period, starting roughly from the end of the First World War, when meta-ethics was thought of as being essentially about the *meaning* of moral concepts such as 'good', 'ought' and 'right'. Interpreted in this way meta-ethics may be regarded as a branch of the philosophy of language. The role of the moral philosopher as meta-ethicist is to give a correct logical analysis of moral concepts. Although such a linguistic or logical analysis of moral concepts is undoubtedly a crucial part of an inquiry into the nature of morality, the questions which *define* meta-ethics are about moral truth: what is moral truth, and how, if at all, may it be discovered? People who ask these questions wish (misguidedly or not) to discover whether there really is such a thing as moral truth, and not simply what we mean by 'moral truth'.

Nevertheless, those who are interested in the question of whether there are any substantive moral truths cannot avoid questions about the meaning of moral terms. To pursue such an inquiry it is necessary, after all, to know what we are trying to talk about. One of the most influential books on the subject of the meaning of moral concepts is G.E. Moore's *Principia ethica*.[1] In this work Moore criticised those who sought to define 'goodness' in terms of some 'natural' quality. The naturalists believed that moral properties could be discerned in a way similar to less controversial properties which are properly the subject of science, that goodness was a natural property in the sense that hardness is a natural property. For example, one popular definition of 'goodness' was 'that which maximises pleasure' (see Chapter 26 for a discussion of utilitarianism). If goodness were such a natural property, then first-order ethics would simply be a branch of applied psychology and sociology. All that would be necessary to discover what ways of life or forms of government are good would be to ascertain what would maximise pleasure. Moore argued against the naturalists that if 'goodness' meant, for example, 'that which maximises pleasure', then it would be absurd to ask whether the maximisation of pleasure was good. Because such a question is obviously not absurd (and would not be absurd were any 'natural' property offered instead of pleasure maximisation), such attempted analyses are mistaken. Moore believed that the attempt to define moral concepts in terms of a 'natural' property rests on a failure to distinguish the question 'What is goodness?' from the quite different question 'What things are good?' He called this kind of attempt to establish naturalism 'the naturalistic fallacy', and much has been written on the subject since.

Moore thought he had established that goodness was a 'non-natural', simple, unanalysable concept. He did not doubt that there really are such properties as goodness and badness, but he believed they could be apprehended by a faculty of 'intuition', intuitions being a special kind of moral observation or non-inferential judgement. On Moore's view people could tell just by consulting their intuitions what was good and bad, but they could and need offer no further analysis of goodness and badness.

Moorean intuitionism about 'good' ran into two major difficulties, and no longer enjoys the popularity it once attracted. The first, and most easily appreciated, difficulty is that intuitions conflict. People do not universally agree in their judgements about what is good, let alone in those about right conduct. If people's intuitions differ, then how are disputes between them to be resolved? It is implausible to suggest they should be resolved simply by direct appeal to intuition (since intuitions conflict), and if a higher court is to be the arbiter between conflicting intuitions, then at best individual intuitions are just a rough and ready guide to what is good and right. In fact, it seems most likely that people's moral intuitions are in large part the product of their own particular socialisation process. Their acceptability is no greater than that of the societies that produced them, and they cannot be appealed to as infallible guides to the good (see discussion of Hare in Chapters 26 and 27).

The other criticism of Moorean intuitionism comes out of logical positivism and its verification criterion of factual meaning (see Chapter 2). According to the positivists all cognitively meaningful statements are either analytic (true or false in virtue of meanings alone) or empirical (verifiable in principle by sensory observation). But what of the supposed judgements of morality? On Moore's view judgements of value, such as 'The promotion of happiness is good' are not analytic (this is the whole point of his critique of naturalism). On the other hand, they are not obviously subject to empirical verification either, since intuition provides the sole validation for moral judgements, and, as we have claimed, intuitions may conflict.

Ethical judgements thus appear to fail the test of the verification criterion of meaning and, according to logical positivism, lack cognitive meaning (fail to make any assertion). Hence A.J. Ayer[2] claimed that the function of ethical terms used in moral judgements is purely emotive. The sentence 'Stealing money is wrong' is neither true nor false, since it is in principle unverifiable. To say such a thing is equivalent to saying 'Stealing money!!' in a particular tone of voice, chosen to express moral disapproval.

This view of moral judgements, known as 'the emotive theory of ethics', or simply 'emotivism', was developed most systematically by C.L. Stevenson,[3] who espoused the psychological theory of meaning (see Chapter 2). He developed a sophisticated account of the way in which ethical judgements are used to influence people's attitudes (see Chapter 27). Although moral judgements are used to express approval or disapproval, and to try to persuade people to adopt certain attitudes or behave in certain ways, they are not, according to Stevenson, without cognitive content. Moral judgements, like ordinary judgements about matters of fact, have a descriptive meaning; they are certainly about a particular subject-matter. However, unlike the latter, they are said to have, in addition, a special kind of emotive meaning, and it is the possession of this emotive meaning which distinguishes moral judgements from simple statements of fact.

This sort of emotivism is vulnerable to the charge that it fails properly to distinguish between *moral* judgements and other expressions of emotion and attempts to persuade. Another difficulty with emotivism is that it appears to misrepresent the nature of moral disagreement. On this theory, if I tell a friend: 'It would be wrong to swindle the shopkeeper' and someone else tells her: 'It would be all right to swindle him,' it seems we are not contradicting each other, since I am in effect saying 'I don't like (approve of) swindling the shopkeeper,' whereas the other person is saying that he (the other person) doesn't dislike (disapprove of) it. Yet we do appear to be disagreeing about something substantial, and we certainly could anticipate a reasoned discussion on the subject. In order for our judgements truly to be about the *morality* of swindling the shopkeeper, our attitudes of approval and disapproval must be supported by a certain kind of reason. This realisation led to the development by R.M. Hare (see Chapter 27) of the meta-ethical theory known as 'universal prescriptivism'. Universal prescriptivism shares with emotivism a rejection of both naturalism and Moorean intuitionism.

Prescriptivism is the view that moral judgements essentially *prescribe* courses of conduct, in other words that it is part of the *meaning* of moral judgements that they tell people how they ought to behave. On this view, if someone sincerely said, 'I know that it would be wrong to swindle the shopkeeper, but I don't see any reason why I shouldn't, and I have no scruples about swindling him,' this would show that the speaker had misunderstood the logic of moral discourse. Prescriptivism is therefore consistent with emotivism, in so far as for an emotivist to make a moral judgement is to express an attitude towards a type of conduct, and attitudes are, in the relevant sense, action-guiding.

Universalism is the view that moral judgements are universalisable. Descriptive judgements such as 'This is red' are universalisable in the sense that a person who sincerely says of an object, 'This is red' is committed (on pain of inconsistency) also to the proposition 'Everything like this in the relevant respects is red.' For example, it would betray a linguistic confusion for someone to say the following of two cups: 'The first cup is red, but the other one is not red, even though the two are similar in respect of the property in virtue of which I called the first one red.' The claim that descriptive judgements are universalisable in this sense is entirely trivial. Hare derives universalism from the claim that moral judgements do have descriptive meaning. If a judgement has descriptive meaning, then it is inconsistent to assent to the judgement on one occasion, whilst dissenting from it on another in the absence of any relevant difference between the two occasions.

The combination of universalism and prescriptivism yields the following analysis of moral discourse. Naturalism is correct in its assertion that moral judgements have descriptive meaning, but it is wrong to claim that the descriptive exhausts their meaning. Emotivism is correct in its claim that moral judgements are not just attempts to state matters of fact, but wrong in its failure to recognise that moral judgements are universalisable. So if someone sincerely says, 'It would be wrong to swindle the shop-keeper' he commits himself (should the issue arise) not to swindle the shop-keeper. Furthermore, he is also committed to the view that any conduct which, in relevant respects is like the swindling of the shopkeeper, is wrong and to be avoided.

Universal prescriptivism is a good example of linguistic philosophy at its most ambitious. Although it is put forward as a purely logical analysis of the meaning of ethical discourse, its acceptance has consequences for first-order moral argument. If the protagonists to a moral dispute are logically committed to prescribing universally their moral judgements, then in principle many disputes should have a rational solution, even if there are no ultimate substantive moral truths of the sort required by intuitionism and naturalism.

Universal prescriptivism arose in the heyday of linguistic philosophy (an approach to philosophy which aims to solve philosophical problems by logical analysis of the concepts believed to give rise to the problems). Linguistic philosophy has been especially helpful in showing how much philosophical confusion has been caused by people using the same word to mean different things. However, in recent years the focus of meta-ethics has moved away from questions about the *meaning* of moral discourse, since attention to the meaning of moral concepts has revealed that they are too flexible and fertile for a purely conceptual analysis to produce a lot of concrete results. Furthermore, there is nothing sacrosanct about the moral language we use and the presuppositions which accompany it. For example, even if it is true that the linguistic rules governing the use of moral notions such as 'ought' and 'good' commit (morally or logically?) their users universally to prescribe certain courses of action, there still remain the questions of whether there are substantive moral truths which transcend human conventions, and whether anyone has a reason to act with a non-instrumental concern for other people irrespective of her goals in life. For linguistic conventions can and do change, and as new discoveries are made, it can emerge that whole ways of thinking have rested on a mistake.

The nature of moral truth

To a young child the sun appears to be a small object, smaller, for example, than a football. However, the truth is that the sun is many times larger than the earth. It appears that the sun goes round the earth, but for several centuries it has been known that this appearance is deceptive. It is relatively uncontroversial to speak of pre-Copernican conceptions of the movement of heavenly bodies as being (understandably) mistaken. Scientific inquiry seeks to go beyond the *appearance* of things to discover what they are really like. Appearances can be deceptive because they are appearances of a world which exists independently of people's perceptions.

Beliefs about the natural world arise out of a confrontation between human consciousness and a world which exists independently of human cognition. But what about moral beliefs? Is there an independent moral reality which, in analogous fashion, is the subject-matter of moral beliefs? Those who believe there is such a reality are called 'moral realists' or 'cognitivists', whilst their opponents are referred to as 'anti-realists' or 'non-cognitivists'. The controversy between cognitivism and non-cognitivism remains the central question of meta-ethics, reappearing throughout the history of the subject in different guises. Each position has its own plausibility. Hence the controversy.

What is the worst atrocity of human history? Many would say the extermination of six million Jews by the Nazis during the 1930s and 1940s. Belief that it was wrong, indeed monstrous, to perpetrate the holocaust is so widespread that outside philosophical circles it would probably be bizarre to ask: 'Was it *really* wrong for the Nazis to exterminate the Jews?' And yet there is evidence that at least some Nazis sincerely believed that their actions were not merely morally permissible, but actually *required* by morality.

What are we to say of the racist moral beliefs of sincere Nazis? In so far as these beliefs derive from false factual beliefs, for example biological beliefs about the necessity for species survival of so-called 'racial purity', they are false in a philosophically uncontroversial way. Such a Nazi would have a mistaken belief about scientific reality. But what about those who just detest Jews, not even on supposedly scientific grounds? Would it be wrong for such a person, or such a culture, if there were one, to kill Jews? The common view is that, irrespective of the racist's hatred of Jews, it would be totally unacceptable for him to kill other innocent human beings.

If he disagreed, he would just be mistaken – not necessarily about scientific matters of fact concerning the natural world – but about morality. This plausible view surely presupposes the truth of cognitivism. It seems hard to imagine how a person can take his own moral views seriously without being a cognitivist.

On the other hand, non-cognitivism also has an immediate appeal. Different communities have different customs. For example, in some cultures it is thought quite wrong for a couple to marry unless their marriage has been arranged for them by senior relatives, whereas non-arranged marriages are thought perfectly acceptable in others. Suppose someone asked, 'Are non-arranged marriages immoral? A tempting answer is to say that they are disapproved of and forbidden in some cultures (for example among Pakistani Muslims), whereas they are acceptable in others (for example in secular European cultures). If the questioner persisted by saying: 'I know that, but are such marriages *really* immoral?', it would be reasonable to deny the presupposition behind the question. There is no distinctively moral fact of the matter beyond the empirical fact that the practice is accepted within some cultures, forbidden in others. This is borne out by the apparent fact that two people might agree about the nature and consequences of arranged marriages, and yet disagree about the morality of the practice.

Cultural diversity of moral attitudes has especially interested social anthropologists, who have been impressed by the viability of societies which seem to be based on moral principles very different from those prevalent in the West. Anthropologists and sociologists are also quick to point to the fact that the moral beliefs of individuals are, to a large extent, shaped by those who hold power in the society in which they live. Different societies have different moralities which have evolved to solve problems which may be specific to the society in question. It is tempting to conclude from these observations of widespread diversity that any belief in a culturally transcendent true morality is an illusion.

Such observations, interesting though they are, do not, however, establish the truth of non-cognitivism, nor even cultural relativism (the version of cognitivism according to which although there are substantive moral truths, these are all just relative to particular cultures, not universally true). The question of the origin of a belief or set of beliefs is different from that of its truth. It may be irrational to accept the evidence of hearsay, but some beliefs arrived at in this way do turn out to be true. Sociological findings should make us critical of our own moral intuitions, since they reveal that intuitions may well simply reflect cultural prejudice rather than rational assessment. But sociology cannot provide an answer to the philosophical question of the nature of moral truth.

Another route to non-cognitivism is via the principle of parsimony, which is widely accepted within philosophy of science.

According to this principle, we should posit the existence of entities only if the supposition that they exist provides the best explanation for our observations. Thus, it is not irrational for scientists to posit the existence of electrons, even though they are unobservable, since the supposition that they do exist offers the best explanation of what is observed in a cloud chamber. On the other hand, it is irrational to suppose that this room is populated with 'quonks' (a quonk being defined as a totally unobservable kind of elephant, with no discernible effects on the world). Supposing that there are quonks in the room does nothing to explain anybody's observations. Without such a principle of parsimony there would be no limit to the sorts of entity over whose existence we should have to suspend judgement.

Let us now consider a moral 'observation' (using an example of Gilbert Harman).[4] You watch a group of adolescents pouring petrol over a cat and setting fire to it. Immediately you judge that this is morally wrong (outrageous even). Such immediate (non-inferential) judgements are called 'observations'. How are you to explain why you make this observation (or any other moral observation)? The best explanation would refer to your, perhaps natural, abhorrence of pain being inflicted on a helpless creature, and also to the process of your socialisation, the fact that such behaviour is roundly condemned in our society. Unlike the case of electrons, there is no need to posit the existence of real (though unobservable) moral values, which explain why people make the moral observations they do. On this view, to suppose that there is a world of moral reality which transcends human conventions and sentiments is no more rational than to suppose that the room is populated with quonks. If moral entities are part of the furniture of the world, they must be very strange objects indeed.

A cognitivist could reply to this challenge by denying that cognitivism requires the existence of such shadowy entities. Cognitivism does not require one to believe that moral statements really refer to moral entities, but rather that the way the world is makes some moral statements true and others false. The most important substantive moral questions concern how people should behave. The cognitivist needs to claim only that there is a morally correct way for people to behave which transcends their particular aspirations and inclinations.

The Categorical Imperative

Regarded in this way, the debate between cognitivist and non-cognitivist is really about the nature of reasons for action. Suppose someone says to you, 'You ought to go to the medieval archaeology class at the community college.' It would be perfectly reasonable to reject the statement on the grounds that you are not especially interested in medieval archaeology, and that there are preferable ways to spend your Tuesday evenings. The original statement is an imperative (since in it the speaker is telling you how to act), but there is no reason why someone should be bound by it, unless she has an interest in medieval archaeology. The force of the imperative is dependent on possession by the person to whom it applies of a particular end. Such recommendations for conduct have been called 'hypothetical imperatives' since Kant (1724–1804), who coined the phrase.[5]

Whilst non-cognitivists typically believe that all reasons for action (including moral reasons) derive from hypothetical imperatives, cognitivists maintain that there are conducting–guiding principles which are not hypothetical in the above sense. Suppose someone says to you, 'You ought not to swindle the shopkeeper.' If this were just a hypothetical imperative, an adequate answer would be 'I don't see why I shouldn't, since I could probably get away with it, and anyway I don't particularly like the shopkeeper.' But this answer scarcely seems adequate to most people. One is inclined to say that you ought not to swindle the shopkeeper whether or not you care about him, and whether or not you could get away with it. Similarly, it is thought that people ought on the whole not to hurt one another, and, where practicable, ought to help one another. These prescriptions are not thought to depend on particular projects, preferences or cultural mores, but apply to all of us, even if we feel very little for our fellow people. Such imperatives are referred to as 'categorical imperatives', since their power is thought not to be dependent on the existence of contingent or hypothetical desires or projects.

According to this Kantian conception of morality and rationality all rational creatures are bound by a supreme principle of rationality, a categorical imperative in the strongest sense. This principle states that everyone should act only on principles which she or he can will to be a universal law (for a full discussion of hypothetical and categorical imperatives, and the idea of universal law, see Chapter 25).

For Kant moral philosophy is supposed to show why it is *necessary* to posit a categorical imperative in order to make sense of taken-for-granted assumptions about human behaviour (especially concerning our ability to exercise autonomy). It is also meant to show how it is *possible* that there can be a categorical imperative, to answer the question 'How can there be reasons which apply to all people, independently of their particular concerns, inclinations and projects?' There is still considerable controversy over this latter question. Non-cognitivists maintain that the very idea of a categorical imperative in the sense outlined above is confused.

Modern non-cognitivism owes a great deal to the Scottish philosopher David Hume (1711–76). Hume argued that the idea of motivation by rationality alone is absurd since, in the absence of a relevant desire, coming to believe a proposition is incapable of motivating an action. He maintained that reasons for action (including moral reasons) are all relative to the current desires of their possessors. Furthermore, he claimed that it does not make sense to call desires intrinsically irrational. In a famous passage he wrote:

> 'Tis not contrary to reason to prefer the destruction of the whole world to the scratching of my finger. 'Tis not contrary to reason for me to chuse my total ruin, to prevent the least uneasiness of a ... person wholly unknown to me. 'Tis as little contrary to reason for me to prefer even my own acknowledg'd lesser good to my greater, and have a more ardent affection for the former than the latter.[6]

Hume believed that rationality was the mental faculty which enabled us to arrive at true beliefs. For a belief to be true is for it to be a correct representation of the world. But desires and passions are not representations of anything, and therefore cannot be true or false, and therefore are strictly speaking neither rational nor irrational.

If substantive morality is supposed to tell us how we ought to behave, there is, on the Humean view, no uniquely rational morality, since there are no ultimate action-guiding truths for reason to discern. Suppose I realise that if I throw the hand grenade into the shopping precinct this will kill dozens of people. Does the realisation give me a (moral) reason not to do so? According to the Humean it does so only if I have a reason not to kill dozens of people. If I were a terrorist the realisation that the grenade would kill dozens of people might actually give me a good reason to hurl it.

On this version of non-cognitivism the point of moral argument is not to persuade one's adversary of the truth of one's own moral convictions. Rather, it is to show the connection between certain courses of conduct and the adversary's own fundamental desires and projects. It is possible to have such a rational argument about appropriate means to achieve given ends, but not over the legitimacy of ultimate ends.

If choice of ultimate end is up to the individual agent, it may be thought miraculous that there is any moral consensus at all. If there are no categorical imperatives, why are people (sometimes and to a certain degree) prepared to sacrifice their own immediate gratification for the good of others? This question takes us into the realm of moral psychology, which has been a focus for much recent work in meta-ethics.

Belief and motivation (moral psychology)

What is the relationship between coming to believe a proposition and being motivated to act in a certain way? According to the empiricist, non-cognitivist view associated with Hume, but extending to the present through, amongst others, Ayer, Stevenson and Hare, the picture is as follows.

Rational deliberation is motivationally effective because it shows the deliberator that a particular course of action either promotes or detracts from a pre-existing goal. Coming to believe a proposition is in itself motivationally inert. Therefore, it would be possible for two people each to have a correct perception of the facts of a given situation, and yet, without error on either side, to be motivated to act in diametrically opposed ways. For beliefs about the facts of a situation fall within the domain of *cognition* and cognitions may be mistaken, whereas motivational drive is provided by *conation*, which can neither be true nor false.

This view is, of course, consistent with the recognition that beliefs affect conduct. However, on this model, the way that coming to believe a proposition may affect a person's conduct is by pointing out how a possible action or strategy would promote or subvert her pre-existing goals. It should further be pointed out that this model allows for deliberation about goals or ends. This is because people's ends form a hierarchy. Someone might have as an end becoming a Member of Parliament. The discovery that the power of backbench MPs is severely limited may lead her to abandon this goal. But, the non-cognitivist Humean would argue, this would only be because she realised that her more fundamental goal (say to be significantly instrumental in promoting education) could not be well served by becoming a Member of Parliament. There could be someone else who realised the same sad truth about Parliament, but still maintained her goal: for she wanted to enter Parliament to satisfy other ambitions.

What about moral beliefs? It does appear that coming to believe it is wrong to swindle the shopkeeper *would* provide someone with a motivation to refrain from swindling him. There are two strategies which a non-cognitivist could employ here to answer this apparent objection to her theory. She could say that in order for the recognition that a course of action is morally wrong, to motivate someone not to engage in it, she would already have to have a desire not to act immorally. Alternatively she could say that a person's moral beliefs are themselves the product of her non-rational fundamental preferences. In both cases the model of deciding what to do is dualistic. First there is the business of getting straight about the facts. Then there is the matter of applying one's knowledge to a set of non-rational desires.

This model is challenged by modern cognitivists, who maintain that beliefs and desires are equally subject to critical evaluation. They claim that judgements about how one ought to behave are no less correct or incorrect than judgements about what one ought to believe.

Reconsider the case of the children who set fire to the cat. Suppose you tell them that they ought to stop what they are doing. They are unmoved, and just ask, 'Why?' You tell them that what they are doing is cruel. Assuming that the hooligans were prepared to continue the conversation, they might either deny that what they were doing was cruel, or else say something like 'So what, why shouldn't we be cruel?'

In such a case the cognitivist would claim that it is true, in the same way as uncontroversial 'matters of fact' are true, that the children should not set fire to the cat, because such behaviour is cruel (cruelty being something to avoid on moral grounds). If the children fail to realise this, then they have just not perceived the situation correctly. Perhaps they do not realise the degree to which cats suffer pain, or perhaps they fail to recognise their own personal roles in what is going on. Anyone who *really* understood what cruelty was would realise both that the conduct was cruel, and that the recognition that an action is cruel in itself provides a reason for preventing it from taking place.

The action-guiding reasons for not setting fire to the cat do not stem from the individual's personal preferences or goals. Even if he felt like doing it, the realisation that igniting the cat was cruel should provide a person with a sufficient reason not to do it. Someone who failed to realise that he should not ignite the cat would be suffering from a failure of cognition. It would be, to use an analogy of the contemporary cognitivist John McDowell,[7] similar to a listener dismissing jazz as a mere welter of unco-ordinated noise (whilst in reality it has a recognisable structure). Unlike the traditional Kantian version of cognitivism, the new moral realism does not rely on the claim that there are moral requirements deriving from rationality alone, which bind all rational creatures. The failure to detect and respond appropriately to moral requirements could equally be a failure of perception as a failure of rationality. To see things aright morally requires a particular kind of sensitivity, rather than a rejection of all sentiment in favour of pure rationality.

Non-cognitivists, of course, deny that there is such a thing as seeing things aright morally. They still maintain that in so far as an action's being regarded as cruel provides a direct reason for avoiding it, there is no fact of the matter concerning whether it is cruel. On the other hand, in so far as 'cruel' has an 'objective' descriptive meaning, the recognition that an action would be cruel provides no direct reason for preventing it. They insist that two people could equally realise that an action is cruel, and yet be rationally motivated in entirely different directions by their realisations. Consider, for example, the Marquis de Sade. If someone were to tell him he ought to refrain from humiliating a victim because such conduct was cruel, he could reply that he was perfectly well aware that it was cruel, and that it was precisely for this reason that he was doing it. Perhaps de Sade had a *heightened* awareness of the true nature of cruelty. He is thought to be so evil because he deliberately behaved cruelly, knowing very well exactly what he was doing. A non-cognitivist would argue that it is arbitrary to accuse him of a failure properly to appreciate the situations he was in. Rather, they would claim, he had a different pattern of desires from most of us, which means that, for him, there was no direct reason to avoid cruelty.

The controversy between cognitivist and non-cognitivist was at the heart of disputes among eighteenth-century moral philosophers, perhaps because they were very concerned with the problem of how moral motivation was possible at all, and also because the scientific revolution generated a concern with all kinds of knowledge claim. The controversy shows no signs of dying out today. Meta-ethics, although appearing at first sight to be rather a narrow subject, really draws on work from many branches of philosophy, including metaphysics, philosophy of language and philosophy of mind. For these reasons it is understandable that there has been a tendency among academic moral philosophers to concentrate on meta-ethics to the relative exclusion of normative ethics. Furthermore, it used to be thought that philosophers, in their professional capacity, had nothing to say about practical moral issues. Whereas positivist non-cognitivists believed there was simply nothing to discuss, since substantive moral judgements were thought just to reflect non-rational attractions and aversions, traditional cognitivists believed either that substantive moral questions should be decided by sociology and psychology, or by direct appeal to moral intuition. This traditional aversion of philosophers to normative ethics is now being challenged.

Part Two: Normative ethics

Normative ethics has staged a dramatic revival since the late 1960s in the English-speaking philosophical world. During the Vietnam War large numbers of hitherto law-abiding United States citizens disobeyed the law by refusing to be drafted into the army. They professed moral grounds for their action, based on the view that the war against the Vietcong was unjust. Many of these same people also recognised that in a democratic society people should obey the law, even if they disagreed with it. The clash of these deep-seated principles ('Don't fight an unjust war' and 'Don't disobey the laws passed by a democratically elected government') presented opponents of the war with a serious moral dilemma. How should such a dilemma be resolved? It was difficult even to begin to answer this question, and it clearly could not be answered technically, say through psychology, sociology or formal logic. Traditionally philosophy has had a pioneering role, in that it has sought answers to questions about whose solution there is no agreed methodology. Modern normative ethics is centrally concerned with the resolution of moral dilemmas.

The levels of normative ethics

What is the relation between normative ethics and meta-ethics? For cognitivists the distinction is analogous to that between philosophy of science and the everyday practice of scientists. Both are inquiries into truth, the former providing at the most abstract level criteria for the acceptability of first-order propositions and principles. For non-cognitivists the distinction is more radical; although they *do* believe there are truths or facts of the matter about the nature of moral thinking, they deny that there are any substantive *moral* truths. Thus for them normative ethics is not an inquiry into truth. Nevertheless, few non-cognitivists would claim that anything goes in normative ethics, and that one view is as acceptable as any other.

There are different levels of normative ethics, ranging from straightforward practical questions about what to do in a concrete moral dilemma to the attempt to justify grand over-arching *theories* of right conduct such as utilitarianism.

Suppose you are a doctor who is being consulted by a 13-year-old girl wanting a prescription for oral contraceptives. You are a friend of her parents and realise that they would very much disapprove of her being given the pill. Indeed you think she would be better off avoiding a sexual relationship until she was 16. But she is determined to go ahead with it, and really wants the pill. What should you do? Anyone who attempts to solve such a dilemma is engaged in first-level normative ethics. Because moral dilemmas are so pervasive whether or not one is interested in ethical *theory*, it is hard to escape normative ethics of the first level. This activity requires a person to consider and evaluate the relative strengths of competing reasons. Very often, once the reasons have been articulated, it may be obvious what one ought to do. For example, in the above case, if you discovered that the girl would commit suicide if her parents tried to prevent her from having a sexual relationship with her boyfriend, it might make it clear that you should not tell the parents. However, gaining a clearer understanding of what is going on in a particular situation cannot resolve all dilemmas. For this reason it is necessary to seek moral *principles*.

Suppose, in the example, that the girl would not commit suicide if her parents tried to interfere, but would probably run away from home. The fact that the child would run away from home if her parents tried to restrict her sexual freedom might well constitute a strong reason for you, the doctor, to give her a prescription without parental knowledge. However, you may feel that your friendship for the parents would be seriously compromised if you kept your knowledge of their daughter's request from them, and this may give you a strong reason for informing the parents. So far you may just have (conflicting) gut reactions (intuitions). But gut reactions may themselves be the product of factors which are irrelevant to the rights and wrongs of the case in point. Why should you want the girl not to run away from home? Why should you want not to compromise your friendship with her parents? In order to answer such questions it is necessary to appeal to moral *principles*. For example, perhaps you should not want the girl to run away because this would restrict her freedom in the long run and *'One ought to promote people's long-term freedom.'* On the other hand, perhaps you should tell the parents because *'One ought not to keep important secrets from one's friends.*' The italicised sentences state moral principles, and many principles may be at stake in a concrete situation. Principles of this sort offer general rules for determining what considerations should count as moral reasons for action.

The second and third levels of normative ethics consist of the attempt to arrive at a *principled* guide to conduct. In other words, their aim is to provide a normative ethical *theory*.

Although one *may* derive principles of conduct through rational reflection, it is almost inevitable that by the time a person begins to do moral philosophy she will have a set of principles of the sort mentioned above (general rules such as 'Don't tell lies,' 'Be loyal to your friends,' and so on). We acquire them in childhood – mainly from parents, peers and teachers. One function of having these principles is to enable practical decisions to be made in particular situations, without having to engage in a detailed analysis of the situation. Undoubtedly it is useful to have such principles, but on their own they are unsatisfactory guides to conduct, even if they survive rational scrutiny; for they may conflict with one another.

Suppose you have promised your son that you will buy him a hi-fi for Christmas, but shortly before the festive season you realise that if you buy it for him, you will be unable to send money to a disaster emergency appeal about which you have just heard. What should you do? There is likely to be a conflict here, because most people accept the following principles: 'Keep your promises' and 'Make sure you do your best for your children.' On the other hand, most of us would accept principles of benevolence such as 'Strive to minimise distress' and 'It is more important to save lives than to give people luxury goods.' These two sets of principles pull in opposite directions, so in the example it is impossible to avoid violating at least one of the principles. The resolution of such conflicts between principles is the task for the third level of normative ethics. This, perhaps, is where most work needs to be done.

Although people with quite different meta-ethical theories may share the same normative principles, it is clear that at this point one's meta-ethical theory may have a bearing on how one is to engage in third-level normative ethics. For example, a universal prescriptivist judges competing moral principles by applying the universalisability test to them. According to Professor Hare, this approach leads to a justification of a form of preference utilitarianism (the view according to which actions are right in so far as they maximise the satisfaction of preferences). On the other hand, an intuitionist would have to consult her intuitions directly, and be bound by what they told her, whereas an emotivist would have to discover which courses of conduct she would approve. It is, it should be stressed, entirely possible for an emotivist or an intuitionist, or indeed a traditional naturalist, to be a utilitarian, or to reject utilitarianism.

Although intuitionism and emotivism do rely on

531

appeal to intuitions and attitudes, even for them there is more to third-level normative thinking than simply reading off the answers by a simple introspection. The attempt to theorise itself requires an acceptance of the fundamental logical principle of consistency. The common goal of normative ethical theory in this sense is to produce a principle or principles which will both explain the appeal of the principles endorsed by second-level normative thinking, and to provide a guide to consistent action. This means that there are close analogies between normative ethical theory and natural science, even for those who are realists about science, whilst remaining non-cognitivists about ethics. Whereas scientists in a laboratory may perform actual physical experiments, most creative normative moral philosophy takes the form of thought experiments.

Thought experiments in normative ethics

Laboratory experiments are, of necessity, artificial. They seek to isolate variables in order to determine the cause or causes of the phenomenon under examination. Such experiments are necessary because the ordinary world outside the laboratory is too complex and confusing to yield the appropriate kind of determinate answers. Laboratory tests often entail the study of phenomena which are similar in all relevant respects but one. By closely regarding the differences which the addition or subtraction of one element can make in the laboratory, it is possible for scientists to ascertain the causes of events in the complex outside world.

By analogy, real life is far too complex for the direct evaluation of normative principles. In many situations different moral principles are consistent with each other, and may prescribe the same actions (for example, honesty does not usually conflict with benevolence). In order to test the relative strengths of these principles it is necessary to think of examples where they do conflict with each other, and no other principles are relevant. These situations hardly ever, if at all, occur in ordinary life. Hence the need for thought experiments.

These experiments often proceed by the traditional method of logical reasoning dating from Euclid known as *reductio ad absurdum* – they aim to show that a favoured principle has absurd consequences – or at least consequences which even one's opponent would find unacceptable. It is important to realise that this style of conducting moral argument is neutral between cognitivism and non-cognitivism. To illustrate how thought experiments work in normative ethics, consider the following problem.

The main reason why some acts are wrong is that they harm other people. It is commonly supposed that if an act has imperceptible effects on other people, it cannot be wrong because it has those effects. For none of those affected by the act would notice any difference. Harms which are imperceptible in this way (such as stealing a grain of sand from someone's private beach) are the product of what are sometimes called 'sub-threshold actions'. Is the principle of common-sense morality, according to which sub-threshold harms may be ignored, as plausible as it seems? If the principle has absurd consequences it should be abandoned. This ingenious thought experiment of Jonathan Glover isolates the principle and shows its absurdity.

> Suppose a village contains 100 unarmed tribesmen eating their lunch. 100 hungry armed bandits descend on the village and each bandit at gun-point takes one tribesman's lunch and eats it. The bandits then go off, each one having done a discriminable amount of harm to a single tribesman. Next week, the bandits are tempted to do the same thing again, but are troubled by new-found doubts about the morality of such a raid. Their doubts are put to rest by one of their number (who believes in the principle under examination). They then raid the village, tie up the tribesmen, and look at their lunch. As expected, each bowl of food contains 100 baked beans. The pleasure derived from one bean is below the discrimination threshold. Instead of each bandit eating a single plateful as last week, each takes one bean from each plate. They leave after eating all the beans, pleased to have done no harm, as each has done no more than sub-threshold harm to each person.[8]

Anyone who accepts the plausible-sounding common-sense principle that sub-threshold harms can be ignored would have to agree that in their second raid the bandits' thefts harmed nobody. And this is a conclusion which even those inclined to accept the principle would find absurd.

The case of the baked beans makes plausible a principle called by Glover 'the principle of divisibility', which states that

> in cases where harm is a matter of degree, sub-threshold actions are wrong to the extent that they cause harm, and where a hundred acts like mine are necessary to cause a detectable difference I have caused 1/100 of that detectable harm.

This principle has great significance, particularly for our thought about the enormous problems of world poverty, where purported defences by individuals of their neglect of the starving often may require a rejection of the principle of divisibility.

The problems of making normative ethics practical

The systematic questioning of moral principles by thought experiments is likely to reveal that the enquirer's action-guiding principles are mutually inconsistent. For example, if one accepts the principle of divisibility, it is difficult to resist the conclusion that neglect of the starving (by individuals as well as by governments) is very seriously wrong (perhaps worse than robbing a bank). What is one to do, when faced by such a result?

It should be remembered that within science,

although theoretically a theory or hypothesis is falsified by a single counter-example, in practice the discovery of an apparent counter-example is not decisive. When an inconsistency is discovered at least one of the inconsistent beliefs should be abandoned, but it may not be obvious which. Within moral philosophy there is an analogous problem. A moral principle is theoretically refuted by a single counter-example. However, when a principle, or even a moral theory, produces a counter-intuitive result, it may not be clear whether the principle should be abandoned, or the intuition discounted. Much normative ethics consists of a play between individual intuitions, principles and theories. The state where, after deliberation, intuitions and principles do not seriously conflict has been called by John Rawls 'reflective equilibrium'.[9] If a moral theory is acceptable, espousing it should not be inconsistent with reflective equilibrium. And the reflective equilibrium criterion provides a practicable guide for those who seek to theorise about ethics.

A potentially devastating difficulty for the normative ethicist is that the principles one is forced to accept by the criterion of reflective equilibrium may be radically at odds with one's whole way of life. If it is worse knowingly to fail to prevent avoidable starvation (except to prevent something of comparable awfulness) than it is to rob a bank, then the conduct of nearly all relatively affluent people who do little to fight world starvation is worse than that of bank robbers.

Moral theory, in its attempt to eliminate bias, to free itself from arbitrary principles, seems to lose sight of the fact that human beings are not purely rational creatures. The moral theories which abstract reflection produces appear to ignore important psychological and sociological facts about human beings – especially the fact that we need particular relationships and commitments in order to thrive. The purely objective theories of abstract moral philosophy are irrelevant if they have no practical implications for people's conduct.

Nowhere is this thought to be a problem more than with utilitarianism (see Chapter 26). According to classical utilitarianism it is wrong deliberately to act in any way which fails to maximise utility, each person's interests being accorded an equal weight. Utilitarianism appears to be the paradigm of a rational ethical theory, since it advocates conduct which produces optimal results, and it requires the elimination of arbitrary distinctions between the interests of individuals. However, utilitarianism is arguably too exacting a morality. For example, according to it, if a father were confronted with a burning building full of children, where it was possible for him either to save his own child or to save several strangers' children, it would almost certainly be wrong for him to rescue his own. It has been objected, for example by Bernard Williams,[10] that any philosophy which requires people to be prepared to abandon their own children is at best absurdly unrealistic, and at worst downright inhuman. Human beings have specific commitments and relationships which give them projects without which their lives would be hollow and meaningless. As such projects cannot be justified from the neutral perspective of abstract moral philosophy, so much the worse for that perspective.

To incorporate these observations within ethical theory it is necessary to distinguish different parts of normative moral theory. Derek Parfit has distinguished five such parts.[11]

First there is a need to establish an *Ideal Act Theory*. Such a theory would tell us what we should *all* ideally do if we knew that we should succeed in acting in accordance with the theory. Because we realise that we and others are fallible, it is necessary to develop a *Practical Act Theory*. This is a theory which tells *each* of us what to do, given that (we know that) some of us will act wrongly, and that we cannot be certain of the effects of our acts.

Furthermore, a normative moral theory should not concern itself exclusively with *acts*. If someone became an act utilitarian, and resolved to base all her decisions about what to do on a calculation of what would maximise overall utility, she would apparently have to deny herself close special relationships, and the chance to develop passionate interests in any non-utilitarian pursuit. How could a human being make herself prepared to sacrifice her children, except by denying herself the capacity for natural parental concern? If such concerns do not develop in a parent, it is likely that the parent will be psychologically unable to respond appropriately to the needs of other people. It is therefore most likely that the denial of such *motives* would, overall, fail to maximise utility. Therefore, the substantive goal of utilitarianism might be best promoted by people adopting non-utilitarian motives. Consequently, there is a need for motive theories. Just as there are ideal and practical act theories, so there are two kinds of motive theory. *Ideal Motive Theory* tells us what motives we should all ideally have, given our uncertainty about the effects of our actions, and given the fact that the motives we adopt will affect more than just the acts we perform. A *Practical Motive Theory* tells us what motives we should each have, given the special factors taken into account by the Ideal Motive Theory, and in addition the fact that some of us will act wrongly.

Practical Act and Motive Theories, although ultimately grounded on neutral, abstract principles, are able to take into account specific facts about human nature and society. Of course, although moral philosophy has a crucial role to play in the derivation and justification of such theories, this task could not be accomplished by philosophy alone, but requires empirical information from psychology and sociology. These parts of moral theory are all about how we ought to conduct ourselves. However, there is a final set of moral questions which is not *directly* about our conduct at all. A moment's reflection shows that nobody (except perhaps a few saintly people) is likely to live a perfectly moral life. We all do wrong sometimes. Given the fact that people do act wrongly, a question arises about what our attitude should be to various sorts of misconduct. Hence there is a need for a *Reaction Theory*.

A Reaction Theory, according to Parfit, should tell us which are the acts for which we ought to be blamed and should feel remorse. Such a theory should take account of the fact that when we feel remorse or blame each other, this may affect subsequent actions, and have other effects. For example, it may be very wrong for relatively affluent individuals to neglect the starving. However, the effect of engendering remorse in them for their neglect could be counter-productive in terms of the goal of alleviating suffering. If we felt remorseful for all our misconduct this could make life seem not worth living, and could result in a widespread demoralisation, or cynicism about any conduct which showed concern for others.

There is also a strong case for extending our Reaction Theory to include positive as well as negative attitudes. Which are the acts for which we should be praised, and feel satisfied? A more ambitious theory would attempt to work out principles for deciding on degrees of praiseworthiness and blameworthiness.

Finally, a Reaction Theory could usefully include principles for assessing motives or characters. Affluent people who deliberately neglect the starving are probably instrumental in more pain, suffering and death than would be a relatively poor, sadistic murderer. The latter is likely to be regarded as beyond the moral pale, whereas the former are likely to be accepted. What are the principles on which such a distinction should be made?

The future of moral philosophy

Several fields of inquiry which used to come under the heading 'philosophy' are now studied by specialists who work within more or less well-defined methodologies. For example, there was a time when what is now called 'astronomy' was a branch of philosophy. As techniques for studying the heavens improved, normal astronomy became less speculative, and a new science evolved. Philosophy no longer occupies the central stage of the natural sciences, but has a different role in regard to scientific understanding, through the philosophy of science. Philosophy of science asks questions about the nature of science itself, and philosophical inquiry connects directly only with the more speculative pursuits of scientists on the frontiers of their subject. Should we expect a similar future for moral philosophy?

The more purely philosophical part of moral philosophy – meta-ethics – has certainly been regarded as a legitimate subject of philosophical inquiry since the time of Socrates, and there is no reason to suppose this is about to change. The future of normative ethics is less certain.

Within the last twenty years philosophers have certainly overcome their shyness about speaking on matters of public concern. Indeed philosophers now sit on ethical committees determining public policy – on issues as diverse as pornography, surrogate motherhood, *in vitro* fertilisation and euthanasia.

Thinking about these moral problems is speculative, and as yet there is no agreed methodology for solving them. Normative ethics is certainly not yet ready to become a special science to be hived off from philosophy in the manner of astronomy, physics, psychology and linguistics. The main threat to philosophers engaging in normative ethics comes from an entirely different direction – scepticism.

There are different levels of scepticism about normative ethics. At the most superficial level there is a scepticism about whether philosophers are better equipped than anyone else to grapple with ethical questions of public concern. Although there is some force in this complaint (doctors and nurses are likely to know more about what it is like to suffer from terminal illness than are philosophers in their professional capacity), a training in philosophical analysis can be helpful in making important distinctions and in articulating the principles upon which difficult decisions have to be made.

A second level of scepticism is about whether there can be any plausible *general* ethical theory which is also specific enough to be of any use to practical decision-making. If fundamental moral values conflict, the goal of a unified moral theory may be misguided, and there may be no substantial role in ethics for the kind of abstract reasoning distinctive of philosophy. This type of scepticism may be defused to a considerable extent by distinguishing the different parts of normative moral theory. Even if there is no completely general practical theory of moral conduct for all people at all times, there can still be better and worse answers to the specific moral problems which confront particular societies at particular times.

The deepest scepticism arises out of doubts about the very possibility of knowledge of moral truth. This kind of nihilism seems to render normative ethics impossible, or at best a trivial pursuit. To answer this cognitivists need to resist the charge of dogmatism, whereas non-cognitivists need to establish that rational moral argument does not depend on the existence of a knowable moral reality. It should be borne in mind that in so far as radical scepticism threatens normative ethics, it also poses a challenge to any rational decision-making. This is one reason why meta-ethics has an importance which extends well beyond academic philosophy.[12]

Notes

(An author's name followed by a number in square brackets refers to the book or article which has that number in the bibliography.)
1. Moore [6].
2. Ayer [8], Ch. 6.
3. Stevenson [10].
4. Harman [12].
5. Kant [15].
6. D. Hume, *A treatise of human nature* (first published 1739). Quotation from Selby-Bigge edition (Oxford University Press, Oxford, 1968), p. 416.
7. J. McDowell, 'Are moral requirements hypothetical imperatives?' *Proceedings of the Aristotelian Society*, Supplement (1978).
8. Glover [23], pp. 178f.
9. J. Rawls, *A theory of justice* (Oxford University Press, Oxford, 1972).
10. B. Williams, 'Against utilitarianism' in J.J.C. Smart and B. Williams, *Utilitarianism: for and against* (Cambridge University Press, Cambridge, 1973).
11. D. Parfit, *Reasons and persons* (Oxford University Press, Oxford, 1984), p. 99.
12. The author would like to thank John Baker, Roger Fellows, Anthony O'Hear, Derek Parfit and G.H.R. Parkinson for their helpful comments on an earlier draft of this chapter.

Bibliography

Introductory

[1] J. Hospers, *Human conduct, an introduction to the problems of ethics* (Rupert Hart Davies, London, 1963) is a useful comprehensive introduction to moral philosophy, with extensive reading lists, and

[2] J.L. Mackie, *Ethics: inventing right and wrong* (Penguin Books, Harmondsworth, 1977) is also an excellent introduction.

[3] R. Norman, *The moral philosophers* (Oxford University Press, Oxford, 1983) relates the work of important moral philosophers in the past to modern concerns.

[4] G.J. Warnock, *Contemporary moral philosophy* (Macmillan, London, 1967) is a clear and brief introduction to twentieth-century moral philosophy up to the date of publication, and

[5] G.J. Warnock, *The object of morality* (Methuen, London, 1971) urbanely expresses dissatisfaction with the direction of recent moral philosophy.

Meta-ethics

It was G.E. Moore who coined the expression the 'Naturalistic Fallacy' in

[6] G.E. Moore, *Principia ethica* (Cambridge University Press, Cambridge, 1903).

The most forceful opponent more recently of naturalism has been Richard Hare, in a number of works, starting with

[7] R.M. Hare, *The language of morals* (Clarendon Press, Oxford, 1952). For further details of Hare's prescriptivism, see Chapter 27.

Among other works which might be classified as meta-ethical are

[8] A.J. Ayer, *Language, truth and logic* (Victor Gollancz, London, 1936), whose treatment of ethics was brief but influential,

[9] P.H. Nowell-Smith, *Ethics* (Penguin Books, Harmondsworth, 1954) and

[10] C.L. Stevenson, *Ethics and language* (Yale University Press, New Haven, 1944), in which Stevenson expounds emotivism (see Chapter 27).

Moral truth

The importance of seeing moral beliefs, and moral philosophies, in their historical and social contexts, is stressed by

[11] A.C. MacIntyre, *A short history of ethics* (Macmillan, New York, 1966).

Moral relativism is discussed by Gilbert Harman in

[12] G. Harman, *The nature of morality* (Oxford University Press, Oxford, 1977), and in his paper 'Moral relativism defended', *Philosophical Review*, 84 (1975), reprinted in

[13] M. Krausz and J.W. Meiland (eds), *Relativism, cognitive and moral* (University of Notre Dame Press, Notre Dame, Indiana, 1982), which is a useful collection in general.

Bernard Williams discusses what he calls 'vulgar relativism' in

[14] B.A.O. Williams, *Morality: an introduction to ethics* (Cambridge University Press, Cambridge, 1976), which is brief and to the point.

The Categorical Imperative

Kant's exposition of the Categorical Imperative is to be found in 'The groundwork of the metaphysic of morals', the most readily accessible version of which is

[15] I. Kant, *The moral law*, trans. H.J. Paton (Hutchinson, London, 1948).

Useful discussions of Kant's Categorical Imperative are:

[16] H.J. Paton, *The Categorical Imperative* (University of Chicago Press, Chicago, 1948) and

[17] T.C. Williams, *The concept of the Categorical Imperative* (Oxford University Press, Oxford, 1968).

[18] M.G. Singer, *Generalization in ethics* (Eyre and Spottiswoode, London, 1963) is a fascinating discussion of some of the problems of application of the Categorical Imperative, and the notions of generalisation and universalisability.

[19] B.A.O. Williams, *Ethics and the limits of philosophy* (Fontana/Collins, London, 1985) includes an interesting critique of the Kantian approach.

[20] P. Foot, *Virtues and vices* (Basil Blackwell, Oxford, 1978) discusses categorical imperatives in a number of essays.

Moral psychology

Moral philosophers have become much more interested in psychology recently, especially the psychology of emotion. See the essays by B.A.O. Williams, 'Morality and the emotions', and by R. Scruton, 'Attitudes, beliefs and reasons', both in

[21] J.P. Casey, *Morality and moral reasoning* (Methuen, London, 1971).

Mrs P. Foot discusses the relationship between moral philosophy and psychology in [20], as does

[22] I. Murdoch, *The sovereignty of good* (Routledge and Kegan Paul, London, 1970).

Practical ethics

Interesting examples of normative ethics in action are provided by

[23] J. Glover, *Causing death and saving lives* (Penguin Books, Harmondsworth, 1977), who, with exceptional clarity, discusses the issues, such as abortion, contraception, euthanasia and war, suggested by his title; and

[24] P. Singer, *Practical ethics* (Cambridge University Press, Cambridge, 1979), who, with a great sense of conviction, discusses some of the same issues, as well as racism, animal rights, and our attitudes towards poverty and starvation.

[25] S. Bok, *Lying: moral choice in public and private life* (Harvester, Hassocks, 1978) is a model of clarity and good sense.

M.A.P

24 | *Teleological Theories of Morality*

Mary Midgley

Introduction

What is teleology? First, the word. It means 'reasoning or explaining from purpose' (Greek *telos*, purpose or end). We do this most simply and obviously when we answer questions about what something is by explaining what it is for. Thus, suppose that the thing were a strangely shaped red blob in a shop window, or a stone picked up off the Downs: there are at least three sorts of way in which someone might answer the question 'What is it?'

(1) *Material explanation.* Polyurethane foam/Slightly impure silica.
(2) *Causal or mechanical explanation.* Processed in the Dreamglow Factory as follows . . ./Hardened from chalk by concretionary action.
(3) *Teleological explanation.* A new type of armchair/A Neolithic knife.

These different kinds of explanation are all legitimate and do not compete with each other. This is worth saying at once, because during the last three centuries, with the rise of modern physics, an idea has grown up that the first two kinds, when combined into a scientific method, give us all that we can possibly need. All other kinds would then be in some sense 'reduced' to them and eventually vanish.[1]

      This hope was understandable in the glowing dawn of physical science, but it is a most obscure one. It is, however, part of a very interesting range of doubts and queries about how widely teleological explanation can be used. What is its proper function, or range of functions? This last question is itself a teleological one, as are some others we shall meet which do not at first seem to have that form.

      Starting from the obvious, straightforward kind, however, how far can this kind of thinking extend? It can certainly do much

541

more than answer the question what a thing is. It can explain a good deal about its qualities. For instance, the odd shape of a chair or knife may be fully explained once we know the use it was meant for. And though human artefacts like these supply the simplest examples, they are not the only ones. It also works for the parts of living things –

> Why has not man a microscopic eye?
> For this plain reason; man is not a fly.[2]

Aristotle, grasping the importance of this sort of reason, used the Greek word *organon*, tool, for these working parts. The concept is still central for our biology. Knowing the function of the heart, the liver or the tree's bark is the key to all other understanding of their structure and behaviour. Without this idea, biology proper cannot start. This way of thinking is so useful that biologists, having once taken it up, have unhesitatingly used the whole vocabulary of purposeful human action here. They speak constantly of mechanisms, devices, workmanship, systems, design, adaptation, resources, difficulties, success and failure, without any sense of using a metaphor or of raising any awkward questions.[3]

     All the same, we must repeat that in the case of living things there is actually no literal human designer, no present, visible work-man with a purpose. And even if we think of God as the Creator, it cannot be right to imagine him on the model of a human workman, solving particular limited problems with the material that happens to be at hand. He does not decide to put in the liver in the same way that those who invented cars decided to put in carburetors, to deal with a particular problem. His role is quite different. Can it then be right to use the concept of purpose, or of something analogous to purpose, at all when we are talking about natural objects?

     The anti-teleological thinkers already mentioned have taken alarm at this point and called for the fire engines. They think all such uses must be superstitious or 'anthropomorphic', and resist them in a wholesale and highly puritanical manner. They often add (like other puritans) that they know we shall not actually obey their veto, but that through sustained efforts the human race may in the end become less child-ish. Making this great renunciation of teleology, it will in the end be guided only by 'science'.

     The idea of science here is an odd one, since biology absolutely needs teleological thinking. But in general, ways of thinking which work cannot be jettisoned like this unless substitutes which actually work better have been found. The project of finding substitutes in physical science for all our other ways of thinking – logical, historical, legal, symbolic, linguistic, etc. as well as teleological – has never come to anything. Nor will it do to damn a way of thinking merely because people have in the past misused it. Teleological thinking certainly has been grossly misused, notably when people have credited Providence with arranging plagues or earthquakes to rid them of their enemies, or with designing bananas entirely for their convenience. But this cannot discredit its proper uses.

What then are those uses? Beyond individual human purposes, there are two areas of thought where it is specially useful. One, internal to human life, is that where we ask about the meaning or purpose of life generally. The other, which is wider, concerns the study of living things. Besides the concepts already mentioned, we need to speak of organisms, adaptation, selection, nature, law, function (especially evolutionary function), development and evolution itself. Since Darwin, this set of terms has of course gained a wider use and a new justification, whose rules are still obscure. In both these realms, we shall need both to look for legitimate uses and to watch out for limits, remembering that no pattern of thought can be used everywhere. And it will also be worth our while to look out for connections between the two areas – for ways in which evolution and the meaning of human life may throw light on each other.

This discussion will deal chiefly with the first area – the one which more directly affects ethics, though we shall come back to the biological one briefly at the end. In beginning now on the topic of 'the purpose of life', it seems best to start from familiar uses of that notion made by its traditional exponents, and to move outwards towards the doubts and difficulties.

Aristotle and the purpose of life

It is quite natural to use teleological thinking about moral questions – to try to resolve them by looking for the general purpose of life. There is nothing pretentious or gratuitously theoretical about asking such a vast question. People are led to vast questions when their lives are torn by conflict, because they need a wider framework in which to reconcile values and standards which have begun to clash. They want to resolve those conflicts, not by a mere brute confrontation of emotional forces, but by somehow working out a priority system which will suit their nature as a whole. This is true both of individual conflicts and of the larger ones which distract communities. European moral philosophy was born out of such a clash of values, when hard times hit Athens and Socrates began to work on the questions people around him were asking – such as 'What is justice really?' and 'Can it be worth our while to practise it?'[4] The vast questions can of course be put in other ways, without mentioning purpose. One can ask for a central *law* of life – a question more congenial to the Jews or the Romans than to the Greeks. This question was later asked with great effect by Kant. Or one can ask for the *meaning* of life in a different sense from that of purpose, seeking for a non-terrestrial reality, something which lies behind life as we know it and supplies its sense.

Aristotle, however, asked about purpose, and he did

not do so in a vacuum, but in considered reaction to the questions and answers of his teacher Plato. Plato had asked for the meaning of life in both the senses just mentioned. He wanted to find its purpose by seeking for the spiritual reality which lay behind it. This search took him far into constructive metaphysics, leading him to posit a world of Forms or ideal entities as the ground and explanation of the world we know.[5]

Aristotle eventually rejected this approach, opting for a much more economical, unpretentious, earthly way of approaching moral problems. He is humanistic – not in the sense of being anti-religious, since he still thinks that God exists and should be worshipped[6] – but in the sense of relying on the human race and treating it as containing in itself the materials to deal with its own problems. I have chosen to look at his discussion before that of Plato and at much greater length, both because it really is simpler and because it is closer to our official present-day attitudes. Indeed, Aristotle's relation to Plato has something in common with the relation between Enlightenment thinking – which is still the official intellectual creed of the West – and Christianity. If we want to understand the point of the more ambitious, metaphysically bold kind of ethics, it is probably best to look first at the problems which the apparently simpler, more cautious kind encounters.

Aristotle begins his main book on ethics thus –

> Every art and every enquiry, and similarly every action and pursuit, is thought to aim at some good, and for that reason the good has rightly been declared to be *that at which all things aim* ... Now as there are many actions, arts and sciences, their ends also are many; the end of the medical art is health, that of shipbuilding a vessel; that of strategy, victory; that of economics, wealth ... In all of these, *the ends of the master-arts are to be preferred to all the subordinate ones* ... If then there is some end of the things we do, which we desire for its own sake (everything else being desired for the sake of this) and if we do not choose everything for the sake of something else (for at that rate the process would go on for ever and our desire would be empty and vain) clearly this must be the good and the chief good.
>
> Will not the knowledge of it, then, have a great influence on life? Shall we not, like archers who have a mark to aim at, be more likely to hit upon what is right? (italics mine)[7]

The question is startling; does it really make sense? Aristotle plainly thought that it did, and that we had to face it. He says elsewhere:

> Everyone who has the power to live according to his own choice ... should set up for himself some object for the good life to aim at, whether honour or reputation or wealth or culture, by reference to which he will do all that he does, since *not to have one's life organized in view of some end is a sign of great folly.*[8]

He is assuming that his question has an answer; that such a single central

544

purpose does exist. Critics have rightly pointed out that it might not. 'There is an illicit transition from "all chains must stop somewhere" to "there is somewhere where all chains must stop".'[9] This is an important objection, because we need to do justice to the immense complexity of human aims and motives. But it need not be fatal to Aristotle's unifying enterprise. If we want to avoid frustrating ourselves, it may still be vital for us to make an effort to bring our many aims into some kind of intelligible relation – to give them some priority system – even if the work can never be completed. The idea of a single, all-connecting aim can still function as an ideal limit, even though we do not think of it like the North Pole as something we might actually locate and reach.

Dominant and inclusive aims

The examples which Aristotle and other people give, however, may make us uneasy, because they tend to seem somewhat narrow. They raise a very important question about the relation between the Chief Good we are look-ing for and the other, lesser goods. Is it to be a dominant or an inclusive aim?[10] A dominant aim would be a single element in life, to which everything else must give way. An inclusive aim would be a comprehensive pattern of life, a way of ordering the whole, a principle determining priorities among all other aims. An example of a dominant aim alone would be the miser's passion for gold. An example of the inclusive aim alone would be a devotion to balance, leading somebody to limit every individual element in his life which threatened to interfere with any other. Both these examples are slightly odd, because normally the two things go together. Dominant and inclusive aim must fit each other. One cannot (for instance) be a first-rate musician within a framework of careful balance between all one's interests. But choosing a dominant aim does not at once settle the question of what the general pattern of life shall be. People are not capable of complete specialisa-tion, and even the most single-minded have the problem of disposing of the rest of their life. Dramatic, reductive claims like Nietzsche's 'Man should be trained for war and woman for the recreation of the warrior; all else is folly'[11] are implausibly narrow. This is true too of most descriptions of Paradise, including that which sees it as eternal rest. Overworked people like this last proposal, but a week in hospital is usually enough to discredit it. Aristotle was surely right to suggest rather that we rest and amuse ourselves in order to be refreshed for the occupations which we really think worth while – not just the other way round.[12]

Obviously, the reductive claims have a point. They are usually correctives, drastic compensations for a faulty emphasis in con-temporary culture. But however badly they may be needed, they do not seem to describe a state of life we could actually aim at. Is it possible to describe or conceive such a state?[13]

It may well be that all attempts to do so are limited by the difficulty just mentioned – by being intended as correctives against local evils. Certainly none of them can be universal, because there is no detached, final viewpoint from which to settle this matter once and for all. But this kind of relativity affects all human speculation. Every enquirer starts somewhere. This does not mean that no theory can be taken seriously; merely that we must continually check one point of view against another.

The notion of happiness

Aristotle's proposals are a useful example here. His inclusive aim, which occupies much of his book, is *eudaimonia*, which means a good or blessed destiny and can be roughly translated as 'happiness'. This name (he remarks) is too general to tell us much. The question is what kind of life it really makes sense to consider as a happy one. It is interesting to see how far his different standpoint distances his final conclusions about this from those which the utilitarians reached using the rather similar English word 'happiness'. For Bentham, happiness meant pleasure, which was a fairly standard commodity, and the problem was to distribute it skilfully among those present, so as to maximise the sum of it available. This is essentially an administrative and political enterprise, a way of dealing with the wants of *others*. It tends to look at human affairs from a certain distance, and largely from above.

By contrast, Aristotle's ethical writings scarcely touch on political questions of this kind. He stands inside, at the point of view of an individual who is by no means sure what he really wants, and who seriously asks himself that question in order to find a way of life. At this angle (as he points out) pleasure is not a very useful guide. To choose a life is indeed to choose one's pleasures, and the idea of those pleasures can certainly be an inducement to make a particular choice. But what we choose is primarily the life itself, with its characteristic activities. 'No-one would choose to live with the intellect of a child throughout his life, however much he were to be pleased at the things that children are pleased at.'[14] This seems to be true, and it is a very telling point against hedonism. It shows the limitations of pleasure as a universal aim. Aldous Huxley's *Brave new world* – which might well have been written to illustrate this remark of Aristotle's – displays a Benthamite Utopia whose main difficulty is people's constant tendency to want other things besides pleasure. A great deal of strenuous conditioning from the benevolent despots is necessary to keep this artificially narrowed hedonistic way of life on the rails.

By contrast, says Aristotle, the real end is always an activity. And the chief end – the supreme activity – must be something final, something which is not wanted as a means to anything else. In this way he eliminates not only external instruments like wealth and honour (as the utilitarians did too), but also mere static internal states. We are what we do. True happiness, then, must consist in full activity, the complete and suitable deployment of one's faculties. 'Honour, pleasure, reason and every virtue we choose indeed for themselves (for if nothing resulted from them we should still choose each of them) but we choose them also for the sake of happiness.'[15]

This shift from viewing happiness as the *end* – to which other goods are means – to viewing it as the *whole* – of which they are parts – is very important. It abandons the strict 'consequentialist' or pay-off pattern where means have no value in themselves and the valued end is always something later in time; usually but not always pleasure.[16] Bentham was a strict consequentialist, and for his limited political purposes this narrow stance worked fairly well – though, as *Brave new world* shows, even at a political level it can have grave moral implications. It calls for a deliberate, surgical narrowing of demands, so that adequate pleasure may always follow effort. Aristotle, by contrast, says that though pleasure is indeed important, it is not the whole aim. Pleasure for him is (the sense of) *'unimpeded* activity'.[17] People with a wider, more ambitious spread of activities will certainly be likely to encounter more impediments than others. But since the activity itself is the aim, theirs will still be a better bargain.

This emphasis on the whole, and the full activity of the whole, may well strike many of us as an important moral insight. It blocks the one-sided demands of those theorists – including hedonists – who allow us only one ideal, as well as avoiding the unthinking narrowness of many traditional moral systems. It is a good suggestion for an inclusive aim. And Aristotle makes it still more inclusive by a remarkable approach to time. Happiness, he says, must belong to a complete life. It is not the kind of property which can be ascribed to mere phases or moments, nor is it a word which you could properly use of a child or an animal.[18] This is not true of the English word 'happy', but it is of *eudaimon*. The point however is of course much more than a linguistic one. Aristotle's central question is the one which is faced by somebody who is trying to *choose a life*. And a life is chosen as a whole.

Consequential reasoning therefore drops into the background. Ends in Aristotle's sense need not be later events or even events at all. Very telling examples of this time-free aiming can be found in the performing arts. The point of a performance of *The Marriage of Figaro* is not something reached at the last curtain, still less at the applause that follows or at the rave reviews next day. Nor are the earlier scenes just means to the effects in the later ones, nor the earlier notes in a particular song to the reward paid out at the end. There is no moment of pay-off at all. The value belongs to the whole. And there is surely much to be said for looking at human life in the same sort of way – at least if we want to avoid the gratuitously desolating idea that everything in it is (as Schopenhauer suggested[19]) only a means to death. The various parts of our lives contribute to the whole just as the parts of a musical work do. Such works are not just quarries for collections of *Operatic Highlights* or *Vocal Gems*, nor are our lives merely facilities for the production and consumption of some standard product called pleasure.

Relations between moral views

Aristotle's inclusiveness can therefore be seen as correcting a serious weakness in consequentialism. This brings up an important wider point about the relation between different moral views. These are often seen as competitors – rivals for a single position of authority. This pattern can look plausible because those who put them forward do often dispute with each other, and do sometimes make competing claims. Thus, Hume described his topic as a dispute 'concerning the general foundation of Morals, whether they be derived from Reason or Sentiment'[20] and came down as a partisan of sentiment. Similarly, Mill begins his *Utilitarianism* somewhat crossly, by complaining that 'the question concerning the *summum bonum*, or, what is the same thing, concerning the foundation of morality' has been around too long unsolved, and proposes to settle it at once with the simple and obvious utilitarian answer. But in truth the great moral philosophers are never just offering rival answers to the same question. They face different questions, and their relation is rather one of a division of provinces. Typically, the central insights for which each of them is most valuable light up different aspects of life. For instance, people in hard and terrible situations have their own special conceptual problems, as well as practical ones. Some moral views have been built up specially to cope with these – for instance Stoicism. And the later philosophers who have most closely followed the Stoic tradition, such as Kant and Spinoza, are perhaps at their best for such situations. In the less harsh phases of life, different ways of thinking are needed. The theories we have been considering here seem to be more suited for these milder climates. Both Aristotle and the utilitarians address situations where there is quite a lot of free choice available. What is needed then is guidance in choosing among various goods, rather than the strength to understand and resist irremovable evil. The question then is indeed more often 'What is our real aim?' than 'What law must we obey?'

Even in this distinct field, however, there is room for them to use quite different approaches. Accordingly, what Mill saw as a single question with several competing answers divides up into a family of questions, all still of great importance. 'End' or 'purpose' is a much more versatile term than it seemed at first. This means that the whole notion of teleological reasoning covers a number of forms. Mill's mistake, however, is not just a fault. It was a fault in him not to be more clearly aware that his questions were more complex than Bentham's, but not a fault to ask those questions. Their specialness does, however, vitiate the large claims to supremacy – to having won a single contest – with which he opens his book.

There is no such thing as a single, all-purpose 'foundation of morals', any more than there is a 'foundation of science'. No one element in morality precedes and explains and dominates all the rest. Nor is there any reason why it should. In different situations different elements need to be emphasised, and different relations between them traced. Much of this is a matter of correcting bias, not of once-for-all discovery. And it is also often important to emphasise the unity of the whole. Aristotle's approach to his question about the 'chief good' or central purpose of life helps this emphasis. But in some degree his sense of the importance of being fair and comprehensive is shared by all great moral philosophers, and is indeed what makes them great. Even those like Plato and Nietzsche who finally reach fairly extreme conclusions do not entirely neglect the moral insights against which they struggle. And most are much more many-sided than this.

It is worth remarking here that the common division of moral philosophers into 'teleologists' and 'deontologists' is far too crude. Every serious investigator must take notice of both purpose and duty; the difference is one of emphasis. For instance Kant, known as the supreme deontologist, devoted the third of his great trilogy of critiques (*The critique of judgment*) to teleology and related matters, and, even at an obvious level, his view that rational beings are ends in themselves and form part of a Kingdom of Ends is a powerful piece of teleology at the heart of his analysis of duty.[21] And Aristotle, often taken to have ignored duty, takes its importance for granted in many places, most notably in his discussions of responsibility and excuses,[22] since the idea of being excused would hardly arise if one had not a duty in the first place. Yet of course it is true that he did lay most of his stress on purpose, and that – as we have just seen – this purpose largely appears as a general shape which life ought to take, an inclusive aim.

The primacy of reason

There remains, however, the question of the many possible dominant aims. If Aristotle could say nothing about them, his proposal would remain a rather general formula. It would certainly direct people to avoid narrow, inactive and fanatical options, but it would still be silent about a wide range of choices.

Aristotle does not leave things in this suspense. He declares a clear dominant aim with as much conviction as his inclusive one, though at less length. This aim is knowledge and understanding of the world, reached through philosophical contemplation. The contemplative life is, he says, an even better one than the life of full and vigorous outside activity – say, in politics – which much of his book would have suggested that he had in mind. Why so? He answers:

Firstly, this activity is the best (since not only is reason the best thing in us, but the objects of reason are the best of knowable objects); and, secondly, it is the most continuous, since we can contemplate the truth more continuously than we can *do* anything. And ... the activity of philosophic wisdom is admittedly the pleasantest of virtuous activities... and it is to be expected that those who know will pass their time more pleasantly than those who enquire. And the self-sufficiency that is spoken of must belong most to the contemplative activity.[23]

These arguments – which are essentially the same ones that Plato had used – may satisfy people who are already intellectuals. But have they the kind of force which would be needed to make people of different tastes and interests change their lives? Indeed, could any sort of arguments have that kind of force?

Facts and values

A question arises here which may have begun to bother us already. Is the whole inquiry about what we actually do aim at, or what we ought to aim at? Its claim on our attention seems to depend on its being the first, but increasingly it begins to look like the second. If it tells us correctly what we do aim at, then its authority springs from our existing desire. It is a 'hypothetical imperative', having force because 'he who wills the end wills the means also'.[24] But if it misrepresents our existing desires, then reasons must be separately given why we should begin to aim at something which we do not at present want.

Aristotle has already conceded that many people do in fact unthinkingly aim chiefly at pleasure, honour or wealth. Many, too, are lopsided in their aiming and do not try to satisfy their nature as a whole. Many are practising consequentialists, beavering away at worthless activities in order to collapse in contented inactivity in the future. Many take no special pleasure in thought. He needs to convince all these people that, if they reflected, they would realise that they are going in the wrong direction for happiness. But suppose that mere spontaneous reflection does not make them think this? Can he supply reasons which will show why it ought to do so? Can he – to use current terminology – make what has so far looked like a purely descriptive enterprise also do the work of a prescriptive or emotive one?[25]

Before going into his particular difficulties, we need to look at the general question of what work it is possible and proper for moral thinking to attempt. In the middle decades of this century, 'anti-naturalist' philosophers drew a sharp and radical distinction between descriptive discourse – which tells us how things are – and prescriptive or emotive discourse, which tells us how to act. These were not just distinguished but considered to be wholly separate activities, with no logical or intelligible connection between them. Description belonged essentially to science, which was value-neutral. Prescriptions arose from value-judgements which

550

had a quite different source, flowing entirely from our feelings or our arbitrary free choice. In principle, any moral judgement could be combined with any belief about the facts. Moral views which seemed to be necessary and appropriate responses to particular facts about the world were really only connected with it by the brainwashing effect of culture, or by an entirely free choice. Thus, if we approve of a heroic rescue and disapprove of a gratuitous murder, we can perfectly well reverse these reactions without producing any rational or conceptual anomaly. None of the reasons which we give for such judgements is any better or worse than any other. In fact, they are not really reasons at all, but just considerations which happen to move people.[26] Accordingly the work of moral philosophy is, in general, to make this fact/value division clear, and, in particular cases, to police it, forbidding all inference from facts to values. Making this kind of inference was called committing the 'naturalistic fallacy'.

This intensely sceptical view needs to be understood as a revulsion against certain over-confident, dogmatic moral systems which (in varying ways and degrees) claimed to prove moral judgements from scientifically established facts. This kind of dogmatism looked increasingly hollow in a rapidly changing world and against an ever-widening back-ground of knowledge of other cultures. The revulsion, however, was so wide and extreme as to blur all differences between appropriate and inappropriate moral arguments. But such arguments are in fact needed even more in a rapidly changing world than they are in a static one, because moral beliefs are then more often called in question, and choice can no longer be guided by simple moves like 'this is right because our fathers did it'. This particular example (which may be called the ancestral argument) is weak, not just because it makes an inference from fact to value, but because the fact in question cannot do the work it is invoked for. But this does not show that no fact could do that kind of work. For instance, suppose that someone asks why either art or science is important, and particularly why they should find any place in education? Among the answers which might be given today, there would certainly be at least some which would take the form 'these things should be done *because human beings have capacities which can only – or best – be deployed in these activities'*. But this highly Aristotelian consideration is a fact. Or is it a range of facts? Or is it that and something else as well?

Once we begin to look at more plausible candidates like this, we see that there is not one simple vast logical gulf between facts and values. The class of 'facts' itself is indeed not at all a simple or distinct one.[27] The case is rather this. Whenever a difficulty is reached in a serious moral argument, the name 'facts' is easily given to the earlier part of the argument, the parts which are being accepted as correct. The difficult part – the dark area ahead for which thought is needed – appears for the moment as a void, impenetrable to reasoning, crossable only by a blind leap of a faith. This impression of the uselessness of moral reasoning is strengthened if only a very simple kind of reasoning is actually attempted. And from Hume's time on, this was done. Philosophers wrote as if any argument for a moral position would take the form of a deductive proof from a single factual premiss. This would of course be quite inadequate for any but the simplest of disagreements. Serious disagreements always arise between quite wide-ranging attitudes and lifestyles. They therefore involve a great number of premisses, many of which will normally not yet have been stated, and often not even recognised, by those concerned.

For instance, in the change from a society policed by revenge to one with law-courts, a huge mass of presuppositions must surface and be examined by people who have managed not to reflect about them before.[28] They will concern both facts and values, and they will fall on both sides of the argument. The work of resolving the disagreement is done by making these premisses articulate and intelligible, and then seeing how they can best be fitted together afresh, with different priorities among them. This work does not have to be done separately for facts and for values, since – although it is indeed often useful to distinguish roughly between these two aspects – people's factual view of the world and their value-judgements about it normally vary together. People describe the world in a way that reflects their value-systems, and alter their priorities about value when they are confronted with quite new facts. Of course they often make these connections badly, just as they may do with any other set of conceptual connections which they need. But this is clearly a *fault*. Coherence between one's factual beliefs and one's value system is as badly needed as coherence in any other area of thought. Making this coherence possible has been the traditional work of moral philosophy.

The backgrounds of moral judgement

The need for this work becomes clear if we notice how implausible is the idea that a moral judgement could be made, arbitrarily and 'freely', in a vacuum, without presupposing any particular conceptual background. Such a judgement, though it might be recited like a lesson, would be unintelligible. If, for example, somebody declares that it is terribly wrong to tread on the lines of the paving-stones, or that the only proper goal of human endeavour is to play the trumpet,[29] they will simply be asked to explain what they mean. Before we can even disagree – let alone agree – with a moral view, we need to grasp the general attitude from which it flows. If we are to see it as a serious judgement, rather than just a fancy or an obsession, we need to know what is supposed to be wrong or right about doing the things in question. And the qualities which are wrong or right about it have to be ones which fit into the general context of human life. It will be no good merely saying that something is wrong because it happens on Tuesdays, or is done in Liverpool.

What then are appropriate qualities for explaining

552

approval or disapproval? Further examples where they do seem to be present might arise if somebody said that it is wrong to keep your child in total solitude, or to stop it playing, or to punish it when it laughs. Or again, in the claim which Socrates made at his trial, that 'an unexamined life is unlivable to man'.[30] If we accept – as a fact – that these situations really would frustrate central human faculties, this does seem to provide so clear an explanation of what is wrong with them that anybody who simply waved it aside as irrelevant would himself have a lot of explaining to do. Any set of beings which has free choice must – if it is to act – possess in common a range of options so plainly bad that anyone who does not see what is wrong with them must be asked, 'Well, what would you consider bad if not *this*?' Answers can sometimes be given. And if they work well enough the priorities among the accepted bad things may be altered. But to establish such a change, reference to the remaining group of accepted bad things will be needed. (Thus, to establish euthanasia as justified, it will be necessary to point out that some other evils can at times be graver than death, and to show how we can act to avoid those evils without licensing murder in general.) But it is hard to see how this group of accepted bad things could ever be assembled except by observing general facts about the capacities and vulnerabilities of the beings who make up the group. A change in these facts would alter the values. If human beings became physically invulnerable, there would be nothing against battering them; if they lost their problems or their power of thought, Socrates' claim would cease to hold.

Human nature and human function

This is Aristotle's typical form of argument. It is 'naturalistic' not only (1) in the wide sense of the phrase 'naturalistic fallacy' – that is, in having factual premisses. It also is so in (2) the stricter, commoner and probably more useful sense of that word, that is, in relying on facts about nature – in this case, human nature. And it is so too in a third sense (3) of not invoking the supernatural. The argument from the possession of certain capacities to the value of using them is direct. It does not depend on accepting as binding the intentions of a Creator who has put them there.[31] It says nothing for or against the existence of such a Creator, but proceeds simply from the existence in the world of a being with certain given natural needs. That being's quest for a hierarchy of aims is then seen as an inquiry into those needs and the relation between them. It is an attempt to find out which needs are deepest and most central. Aristotle's biological approach gives him confidence to ask, in what may seem startling terms, what man is essentially *for*. What is his function?[32] Aristotle's word *ergon*, or 'work', is actually rather more general than our 'function', and may make this idea more plausible than has sometimes been thought. It is surely true that a living creature can have work or activity which is fit for it, which constitutes part of its prospering, and without which it can get neither satisfaction nor its full development. Thus, horses must run, and must do so with other horses, if they are not to be incomplete and damaged specimens of their kind. To say this is not to express some arbitrary value-judgement imposed by human beings out of their unaccountable prejudices, but simply to do zoology. Its meaning is quite unlike that of the demands imposed at dog shows for dachshunds to have impractically long backs.

The notion of a human condition

How far is the case with human beings different? Of course, since Aristotle's day, and especially during the last century, we have become much more aware of the vast variety and mutability of human cultures. We know that demands which have been seen as universal human needs have repeatedly turned out to be merely local habits. So striking is this fact that many influential thinkers have concluded that there is no such thing as human nature at all. On this view, human babies come into the world entirely plastic, infinitely adaptable to any cultural pattern which may be stamped on them – 'blank paper at birth'.[33] This idea received great force from political considerations, because the idea of a fixed human nature was often used by oppressors to resist all kinds of reform. In the heat of battle, therefore, the blank paper view looked plausible. But on calmer consideration it is not easy to make sense of it. Even for the reforming purposes for which it has been most treasured, consideration of the natural needs of human beings must (as we have just seen) frequently be used. And the dramatic overstatement that the 'blank paper' analogy involves becomes clear if we look (as we easily can) at the striking similarities between unrelated cultures, instead of only at their differences. There is also something extraordinary in the idea of the infinite adaptability of babies, if we consider the great difficulties which parents everywhere find in moulding their children to the pattern which their culture requires. People are in fact satisfied with a very rough conformity to cultural demands from the next generation, and often do not even get that.

Besides these obvious but neglected facts, however, blank paper theorists themselves commonly continue to make use of the idea of *the human* in their own thought. Thus Marx, when he spoke of the industrial working class as being *dehumanised*, did not only mean that they were ill fed and ill housed, but that they were being denied the proper use of their faculties. Had they been blank paper, this would have meant nothing. Again, if we call the life portrayed in *Brave new world* an inhuman one, we imply that its inhabitants had a certain definite nature which was being distorted by their conditioning, even though they themselves had no idea that there was anything wrong with their society. Writers who distrust the notion of *human nature* because of its past misuses, but still want to make points of this kind, usually now fall back on 'human condition', or similar terms, to

554

refer to a set of conditions inevitably belonging to human life, yet somehow independent of innate causes in the human genome. This idea has a clear enough use when it refers to outside physical conditions such as heat and cold, neighbouring species, crops and weather. It seems to become much more obscure when it refers to matters involving human responses, such as our emotional capacities and vulnerabilities. This obscurity, however, may not matter too much for the present argument. If the 'human condition' is taken to be something universal and unavoidable, even though non-genetic, arguments of the Aristotelian kind are still relevant. For instance, such theorists do not deny the need for children to play and laugh, even though they may refuse to admit any innate causes for it.

The search for the true self

Thus, in spite of all intervening changes, there is still a wide range of cases today where we quite properly use Aristotle's basic form of argument from characteristically human needs. The problem about such arguments does not seem to be that they are unusable because of a 'naturalistic fallacy'. It is rather that there are so many of them, and it is hard to arbitrate between them. How *much* should children play in proportion to the other things they do? And how do we weigh Socrates' quite proper demand for an examined life against the need for free action and spontaneity?

As the long history of moral conflict now makes clear to us, the idea of a *single* human function is mistaken. Human beings are not like tack-hammers or pruning knives, any more than they are like pieces of blank paper. Their natural needs do not converge inevitably and harmoniously to a single pre-set aim. Instead, the needs tend to conflict, and the various ways of life which different cultures and individuals devise are varying attempts to harmonise them, always imperfect ones. When this imperfection becomes specially glaring, people look behind their traditional morality to find a principle by which to amend it. At such times, it is natural to use the notion that at a deeper level our needs do converge towards a central aim, deeper than others. This is often expressed by expanding the notion of personal identity, and saying that each person's real or true self – underlying the everyday one – has an aim desire of a different order, and of higher authority than any with which it may conflict. That is the aim of the whole person.

This notion of the real or true self cannot be fitted neatly into either the category of fact or that of value. It combines elements of both. This ambivalence can be held to show *either* that the notion itself is illicit, *or* – as I have been arguing here – that those categories are inadequate and misleading. The notion seems entitled to respect on account of its usefulness. It is one we often use in real life to help us in resolving difficult moral conflicts – 'What do I really want?' It has also played a central part in the psychoanalytic tradition, especially in the Jungian concept of 'integration of the personality' as the condition of psychic health. The meaning of words like 'real' and 'true' here is certainly complex, and needs metaphysical attention. But then there has never been any reason to expect problems about the human self to be metaphysically simple.

Apart from these metaphysical questions, a strong moral attack on the whole notion of the true self as an integrating agent has recently been mounted by philosophers who resist the very aim of integration, and insist that human desires should always be treated as an irreducible plurality. Their case is partly a political one, against the imposition by society of a narrow pattern of aims on individuals. But it is also directed, more deeply, against any insistence by individuals themselves on establishing an inner hierarchy among their aims (as Aristotle advised).[34] In both cases, the critics are clearly right to insist on the need for respect for all elements present, and to say that integration ought not to be premature. Yet, if life is to go on, integration of some sort will certainly be needed. Each of us has only one life to lead, and must also lead it in some particular society or other. Sitting on all fences will not help us to do justice to the richness of our nature. Both inner and outer conflicts have to be resolved somehow, or action will be paralysed.

True selves and their neighbours

The question how far we should attempt integration, and how far we should rather try to make room for every impulse, both in individual life and in society, is itself a moral question. Moral theories can guide us in making such decisions, but they cannot settle them simply on formal grounds. As we have seen in Aristotle's case, a moral theory cannot move far towards the second alternative without becoming a mere unhelpful catalogue of existing desires. To find ideas which will help us by directing our choices more clearly, we must move the other way – beneath the chaotic surface of the existing conflict-ridden self towards an authoritative centre within it capable of helping it to change itself. Anarchists and immoralists as much as conventional moralists need this dynamic if they are to make changes. The journey is inwards, so it does not necessarily infringe on individual autonomy. Commonly, however, it does lead to the recognition of certain outside entities as having a standing and authority which should affect our choice. The true self, in short, usually turns out not to be a solitary, but part of something larger. At that level, each of us exists in a context – in society, which can be conceived in most varied ways, in the Kingdom of God or the Kingdom of Ends, in the class struggle, in the evolutionary process, in the love of God and of our neighbour, in dependence on the Form of the Good, in some enterprise such as art or scientific inquiry or perhaps the production of the Nietzschean Superman.

Every serious moral position seems to involve some

metaphysical view of this kind about what the human self or soul essentially is and what world it properly inhabits. Even individualistic views like existentialism or the social contract model, whose purpose is to isolate the self, need a suitable metaphysical world-picture in order to do it. Emotional attitudes like approval and disapproval, which have sometimes been treated as the sole stuff of morality, would make little sense without some world-picture, some metaphysical background of this kind. They also require a characteristic view of the facts. These three elements need to fit together, and also to be tolerably coherent with the pattern of action. When a morality changes, all these aspects need to change together. What happens is not that new factual beliefs first appear and new moral precepts are then logically derived from them. (This was the stereotyped, somewhat unreal idea of 'naturalism' which the anti-naturalist philosophers attacked.) Nor is it that value-judgements are changed on their own, regardless of facts, whether by the will, by the feelings, or by direct perception – as these philosophers in their various ways claimed. What changes is a whole complex of beliefs and attitudes, extending – if the morality is a real one – to the actions which express them. Some sort of coherence is needed right across this highly confusing field. It never amounts to a complete logical system. But then we do not get that over the whole field of factual beliefs either. Scepticism which extends beyond noticing the difficulties and limitations of this process and claims that the whole enterprise is so faulty as to be useless is itself confused, arbitrary and mistaken.

Part of our difficulty about this today stems from the fact that our tradition has now accumulated many different maps of this vast and awkward area. Naturally, they vary, and their divergence is now itself a prime source of scepticism. I have suggested that we should look on this divergence primarily as a division of labour rather than as a competition, which some map-maker will win. If, instead of playing them off against each other on small issues, we consider each of their maps as a whole, with its own characteristic emphases and selections, each will illuminate a different aspect of life – which is quite large enough to have room for all these elements.

To illustrate this relation, I end with brief thumbnail sketches of three very different further moral stances which are yet all teleological. They may be seen as raying outward from that of Aristotle, each choosing one of the central themes which he tried to hold together in a somewhat unstable balance.

Divergent teleological perspectives

Plato

First comes Plato's view – the logical consequence of embracing fully Aristotle's Dominant Aim, the exaltation of the intellect. For Plato, the human soul appears as radically divided. The lower part attaches itself to the body. The upper part is spiritual, intellectual and akin to the eternal Forms. The two parts are necessarily in conflict. In the *Republic*, where their drama is most fully deployed, the central question is 'Does it profit us to be just?' Sternly rejecting the consolations of a cheap morality, Plato points out that in ordinary terms it can totally fail to profit us. The just man may end up crucified while the unjust man reigns as king. Yet still (says Plato) we can ask what it shall profit a man if he shall gain the whole world and lose his soul.[35] The unjust man is ruined in his deepest self, in the centre of his being. And at that level, the just man is saved. The unjust man really has made a worse bargain. And this is not only because of retribution after death. Plato does indeed go on to expound reincarnation, and to explain that it will reward and punish. But he insists that the central point of his argument still holds independently of this.

Here the desires and satisfactions of the 'true self' diverge remarkably from those which the everyday self commonly professes. Plato's position approaches that of those later Greek philosophers who said that the just man is happy on the rack. Ideas like this can sound like mere hypocrisy or idle paradox. But since Plato clearly struggles to this position out of the real bitterness of moral conflict, he conveys instead what is surely an essential moral insight – namely, that moral demands must not be seen as external to the agent. If there is no sense in which we *want* to do what we ought, then our morality is merely social and conventional. This was the point that Socrates made in his famous paradox that 'nobody does wrong willingly'.[36] Vicious people, however apparently contented, are really deceiving themselves. They exist in a state of self-destructive blindness, steadily losing the capacities which are their most precious possession, the 'eye of the soul'.[37] It is another central insight of Plato and Socrates to accord this peculiar respect to the intellectual and contemplative faculties, and to place them at the core of our being. For these philosophers – and for Aristotle too – contemplation of the highest truths was the central experience of life, the true *telos* which gave all the rest its meaning. This thought has a special interest today, when the immense prestige of intellectual attainment still survives, but the metaphysic which gave it its full sense is often dismissed as irrelevant. If one does not believe the world one studies to be divine – as these philosophers did – why is science so important?

Hegel

Plato's view of the True Self is (in this-worldly terms) rather a narrow and exclusive one, cutting it off from a great deal of its normal context, including the rest of the personality. At the opposite extreme stands Hegel, for whom wholeness is all. Taking up Aristotle's idea of self-development and self-realisation as the core of the moral enterprise, Hegel refused as firmly as Aristotle did to accept the division of the self into a mariner to be saved and a disposable ship to be sunk. He treated all conflicts dynamically as cases of dialectic – clashes of incomplete truths which will be united later in an inclusive synthesis. Hegel proposed that the world was not – as nearly all Europeans till the eighteenth century had believed – essentially unchanging. Its history was a steady, gradual, unfinished dialectical progress. In fact, it was itself a vast Mind or Spirit within which new pairs of opposing ideas were continually appearing and being resolved. Plato's sharp opposition between intellectual Reality and unintelligible, barely real Matter was itself resolved for Hegel by treating Matter as merely an incomplete expression of Mind or Spirit. (In this metaphysical idealism, though not in its belief in progress, Hegel's position approaches that of Buddhism.) Throughout Hegel's cosmos, things have varying degrees of reality, and the more real is always the more valuable. Items are less real in so far as they are limited and cut off from their context. To become more real is to become more closely integrated into it – therefore more fully intelligible. The only completely real thing is therefore the totality itself, the Absolute, to which everything else is relative. Individual beings find their fulfilment in extending their lives so as to identify with the whole as fully as possible. Since the Absolute is itself moving forward – as it were, thinking its way towards ever greater harmony and unity – its goal is the true goal of all individual striving.[38]

The key move giving rise to this formidable system is the Aristotelian resolve to respond to inner conflict by attempting reconciliation, rather than by the ascetic rejection of one warring motive or another. It is the opposite of the Platonic spirit that says, 'If thine eye offend thee, cast it out.'[39] Hegel makes the project of reconciliation look more plausible by expanding both the time-scale and the social unit within which it is to take place far beyond Aristotle's. Harmonies which individuals cannot achieve in their own lives may still be possible for whole communities with a long span of history before them. And in so far as the individuals feel that their own lives are continuous at the deepest level with this context of communal life, they should then – on this way of thinking – feel that their essential selves are realised.

Plainly, this last idea is an alarming one. There is a stark gap between communities as they might be – into which an individual could pour all his or her efforts with a confident assurance that they would reach the proper goals – and the societies people actually live in. Hegelian ideas have in fact often been used politically to justify unbalanced insistence on corporate solidarity, and sometimes to support outright iniquity. All the same, this variant of Aristotle's approach has a point. If we are to ask what an individual really does want – as opposed to casual and passing and uncriticised wantings – it is not clear that we do right to assume, as Aristotle did, that his whole aim must be something for himself. People are profoundly social beings. Appallingly though they often treat each other, they often do directly desire one another's good. Psychological egoism is an error.[40] And they certainly often throw themselves into communal projects which will last much longer than their own lifetime, and find deep satisfaction in them. In good Hegelian thought, the dialectic between the demands of individual autonomy and those of communal solidarity is recognised as an extremely serious one, not to be fudged away by any premature synthesis.[41] All dialectic, in fact, is viewed there as a demanding enterprise. Its historical dimension means that, at any particular time, it is never possible to see far ahead in the task; truths which will be reached tomorrow may be fearfully hard to grasp for those who search for them today. Both sides, therefore, must always be given due weight.

The Hegelian idea of a genuinely progressing world has remained extremely powerful, and it gives an extra dimension to teleological thinking. The idea of a human function gains a clearer sense when there is any larger entity within which human lives find their meaning. At a modest everyday level, we do find some fulfilment in serving the group around us. And the larger and more comprehensive the aims of this group itself become, the richer does that meaning grow. If it is added that the process of which our lives form part is so vast that the goal itself is always evolving, this thought adds awe and excitement, though it increases mystery.

It may well be that some suprapersonal context of this kind – some sense of belonging to a corporate project – is an essential condition of all practical thought. But the project can take many forms. Very ambitious, all-embracing forms of it like those of Hegel and Marx are impressive because they seem to combine intellectual with moral authority. But in fact they can and should be criticised from both these angles. All such vast views of history are selective both in their reading of past facts and in their choice of goals for the future. Their moral approach shapes their view of the facts as much as the facts shape their moral conclusions. Understanding of history can indeed help us enormously in deciding how to spend our lives. But it never does so in the simple form 'Since *x* has happened, *y* will follow, and we must *therefore* work to produce it.' Commandments cannot be imposed on us as following simply from historical or scientific reasonings and predictions. They need moral choices as well.

Evolution

This point is particularly important when we come to consider the last of these teleological options – evolutionary thinking.

The word *evolution* was brought into use not by Darwin, but by Herbert Spencer, as a name for a process of continuous linear improvement in the admirable qualities of organisms. It culminated so far in man, but was expected to go on indefinitely, exalting him to hitherto unknown spiritual heights. This is an entirely different notion from the Darwinian one which became officially accepted as the basis of biology, in which different life forms are seen as raying out from a single centre to fill various ecological niches. Darwinian thinking makes no particular predictions about future development, sees no single direction as central, and indulges in no comparative value-judgements about the various kinds of organism. For it, *Homo sapiens* is just one element in the pattern, not at all the whole point of the evolutionary process.

Because the first conception has been so attractive, especially to people losing faith in the consolations of Christianity, these two ideas have become chronically confused, and the imputed authority of 'science' has been extended from the second to the first. Hence arises 'evolutionary ethics', in which the fixed direction of evolution is taken to supply us with a moral guide.[42] The attempt to use it in this way has naturally proved even more difficult than the Hegelian and Marxist attempts to get similar guidance from the direction of history. The time-scale is even more unsuitable, the selection of facts even more arbitrary. Ideas of what evolution demands next are idle. They can only add a specious air of scientific standing to moral judgements arrived at on other grounds.[43]

This approach is so obviously faulty that academic thought today more or less unanimously rejects it. Yet the imaginative pull of evolutionary thinking remains very strong. In a world as changeable and confusing as ours, the general Hegelian idea that a reliable upward process exists is a very welcome one, and the thought that we can use it to guide our footsteps is a central part of its attraction. The deep respect currently felt for the physical sciences makes it seem highly suitable that this idea should have biological backing. Unluckily it does not, however, actually have that backing at all. This 'evolutionary' form of teleology must be seen frankly as an independent philosophical system. It is quite as extravagant metaphysically as Plato's or that of the Buddhists. It is not supported by modern science, but only by faith. It belongs among the religions.[44]

It is unfortunate that this crude approach has distracted attention from a much more modest and helpful aspect of evolutionary thinking, namely the careful pursuit of such questions as: What ways of life are we best adapted for? What are we fit for? As we have seen, noisy and tendentious answers to these questions in the past have brought discredit on the whole inquiry. Yet the questions remain and constantly confront us even more urgently than they did Aristotle, because we are engulfed in so much change. Answers to them are confidently given, as much by those who reject biological evidence as by those who accept it. Yet these questions certainly have a biological aspect, as well as − not instead of − their historical, anthropological, psychological and sociological aspects. Human bodies are not just accidental vehicles for human minds, ships in which they happen to travel. They shape our whole consciousness through our immensely complex nervous systems. These really did evolve, and unquestionably do fit us better to live in some ways than in others. The great fund of knowledge which, since Aristotle's time, we have acquired about them, and about the many possible ways of human life, is not just a destructive factor depriving us of his confidence in a single 'human function'. It is also a rich source of further guidance. The kind of teleological thinking which asks what lives we are naturally best fitted or adapted for is quite legitimate. It can often warn us of our dangers. We would do well to make more use of it.

Notes

An author's name followed by a number in square brackets refers to the book or article which has that number in the bibliography.

1. The ideas out of which this program has arisen are well expounded by B.F. Skinner [8] and Jacques Monod [9]. Monod goes so far as to invent a word 'teleonomy' for the few teleological ideas which he thinks legitimate in biology, on the model of 'astronomy' and 'astrology'. This is needless. The word teleology is a wide one, covering both proper and improper ways of reasoning from purpose.

2. Pope, *Essay on man*, Epistle 1, 1.393.

3. For the importance of such metaphors for an understanding of the theory of evolution, see Gillian Beer, *Darwin's plots* (Routledge and Kegan Paul, London, 1983).

4. The central questions of Plato's *Republic*. The second and deeper one is introduced at the opening of Book II and answered in Book IX, 579–90.

5. See for instance his *Phaedo*, 78–80, and *Republic*, Book VII, 514–19 – the famous Allegory of the Cave.

6. For Aristotle's idea of God, the impersonal Unmoved Mover that moves all other things by being the object of their desire, see his *Metaphysics*, book Λ (or XI), Ch. 7.

7. *Nicomachean ethics*, I.1.

8. *Eudemian ethics*, I.2.

9. G.E.M. Anscombe, *On intention* (Basil Blackwell, Oxford, 1957), §21.

10. W.F.R. Hardie, 'The final good in Aristotle's ethics', *Philosophy*, vol. 40 (1965), pp. 277–95. Reprinted in J.M.E. Moravcsik (ed.), *Aristotle: a collection of critical essays* (Macmillan, London, 1968), pp. 297–322.

11. *Thus spake Zarathustra*, Part I, Section 'Of womenkind, old and young'.

12. *Nicomachean ethics* (*EN* henceforward), Book X, Ch. 6.

13. A very astute analysis of the difficulties in deciding just what sort of 'ideal state' one is talking about may be found in Moore [11], at the opening of Ch. 6 on 'The ideal'.

14. *EN*, Book X, Ch. 3. Compare Mill's remark that 'it is better to be a human being dissatisfied than a pig satisfied, better to be Socrates dissatisfied than a fool satisfied' (*Utilitarianism*, Ch. 2, Everyman edn, p. 9) – one of many places where Mill broke through his Benthamite framework to a position much nearer to Aristotle's.

15. *EN*, Book I, Ch. 7.

16. G.E. Moore, for instance, insisted that these valued consequences were good states of mind – chiefly aesthetic and affectional. See the last chapter of Moore [11].

17. *EN*, Book VII, Ch. 13.

18. *EN*, Book I, Ch. 9.

19. Cited by Freud in arguing for his hypothesis of a death wish, in *Beyond the pleasure principle* in *Complete psychological works* (Hogarth Press and Institute of Psycho-Analysis, London, 1966), vol. XVIII, p. 49.

20. David Hume, *Enquiry concerning the principles of morals*, Section 1, §134.

21. See the *Groundwork of the metaphysic of morals*, trans. H.J. Paton under the title *The moral law* (Hutchinson University Library, London, 1948), p. 90 – 'The formula of the end in itself'.

22. *EN*, Book III, Chs. 1–5 and Book VII, Chs. 1–9.

23. *EN*, Book X, Ch. 7. In case Aristotle's confidence about the pleasures involved seems surprising, it is worth remarking that full-time intellectual inquiry was in his time a fairly new pursuit, still viewed as somewhat odd, and there were therefore no reluctant students or career academics. Those who did it were there because they wanted to be. Moreover Aristotle's *Ethics*, like most of his writings which have survived, are the notes for his lectures to these highly motivated students. So he was referring – as far as they were concerned – to the facts of their own experience.

24. See Kant, *The moral law*, Ch. 2, section on classification of imperatives (Paton translation, pp. 78–83).

25. Several distinct modern views must be somewhat hastily grouped together here. After the original move of detaching moral judgement from all supporting reasons (the 'intuitionism' of G.E. Moore in *Principia ethica*) there followed two proposals – first that moral judgement was really a matter of feeling ('emotivism') and then that it was the issuing of universalisable commands ('prescriptivism'). All three positions used Moore's language of 'anti-naturalism' and were predominantly destructive of traditional ways of supporting morality by relating it to considerations drawn from the rest of life, though prescriptivism did allow argument *within* morals, from universal to particular moral judgements. For details, see Ch. 27.

26. A position clearly spelt out in, e.g., C.L. Stevenson's analysis of the concept of relevance – 'To be relevant, any belief . . . must be one that is *likely* to lead one side or the other to have a different attitude, and so reconcile disagreement in attitude', *Facts and values* (Yale University Press, New Haven, 1963), p. 4, italics mine. Compare R.M. Hare's example of the 'fanatical trumpeter' who sees no reason ever to do anything but play the trumpet (R.M. Hare, *Freedom and reason*, Ch. 7, p. 112). I have discussed these views more fully in my *Beast and man* (Harvester, Hassocks, 1979), Ch. 9, and in several papers in my *Heart and mind* (Harvester, Hassocks, 1981). I also have, forthcoming in *Philosophy*, an analysis of the wider meaning of this whole movement, called 'The flight from blame and the fear of judgment'.

27. See G.E.M. Anscombe, 'Brute facts', *Analysis*, 19 (1958) and an extremely rich and thorough development of the point in Julius Kovesi's *Moral notions* (Routledge and Kegan Paul, London, 1967), especially in the first chapter, 'Between good and yellow'.

28. This is the topic of Aeschylus' *Oresteia* trilogy.

29. See Philippa Foot, 'When is a principle a moral principle?' *Proceedings of the Aristotelian Society*, supp. vol. (1954) and (for the trumpeter) Hare, *Freedom and reason*, Ch. 7, p. 112.

30. See Plato, *Apology of Socrates*, 38A.

31. A point well made by Bishop Butler, who notes that conscience has the same authority for unbelievers as it has for believers, since 'your obligation to obey this law is its being the law of your nature' (see his Sermon 3, Section 5, Sermon 2, Section 8).

32. See *EN*, Book 1, Ch. 7, and Book X, Ch. 5.

33. 'White paper receives any characters' – John Locke, *Essay concerning human understanding*, Book I, Ch. 3, Section 2. Locke was chiefly denying that we are born knowing true propositions, but the point has been widely generalised into a denial that we have any innate tendencies at all. I have discussed its meaning, and its influence on various modern prophets, in *Beast and man*, centrally in Ch. 3.

34. See Peter Strawson, 'Social morality and individual ideal', *Philosophy*, vol. 36 (1961), reprinted in his *Freedom and resentment* (Methuen, London, 1974). Bernard Williams has taken the matter deeper, especially in relation to inner conflict, in his paper 'Moral luck', originally in *Proceedings of the Aristotelian Society*, vol. 50 (1976) and reprinted in his collected papers, also called *Moral luck* (Williams [18]). I have tried to answer their extremely interesting contentions in Midgley [19], Ch. 2.

35. St Matthew's Gospel XVI, 26. Plato's conclusion in Book IX of the *Republic* is essentially similar.

36. See Plato, *Protagoras*, 352.

37. Plato, *Republic*, 519.

38. See bibliography under 'Hegel'.

39. Thus in Plato's *Symposium* the prophetess Diotima (who is there his mouthpiece) rejects Aristophanes' suggestion that love is essentially 'the desire and pursuit of the whole', insisting rather that 'men are quite willing to have their feet or their hands amputated if they believe those parts of themselves to be diseased' and that the real object of desire is not what is one's own, but what is good (*Symposium*, 205E).

40. Butler's arguments for this seem fairly conclusive. See especially his Sermon 11, *On the love of our neighbour*, and two tremendous footnotes against Hobbes – one at Sermon I, Section 6, and one at Sermon 5, Section 1.

41. See, for instance, *Ethical studies* by F.H. Bradley (Oxford University Press, Oxford, 1876).

42. Spencer's version of this was well criticised by G.E. Moore [11], Ch. 2, pp. 46–58. Other versions, and the history of the project, are discussed by A.G.N. Flew [30]. A striking statement of a version still popular today can be found in C.H. Waddington's *Science and ethics* (Allen and Unwin, London, 1942).

43. For instance this –

An existence which is essentially evolutionary is itself the justification for an evolution towards a more comprehensive existence; a society implies a direction of development into a society which could include the earlier stage, as, to take an exaggerated example, *American culture can include that of the Red Indian but not vice versa*. (Waddington, *Science and ethics*, p. 17, italics mine)

Waddington was convinced that his moral views were timelessly scientific, yet their dependence on passing fashions is now obvious. Compare his book *The scientific attitude* (Penguin Books, West Drayton, Middlesex, 1941), p. 63, on modern architecture as scientific.

44. I have argued this view, and tried to distinguish the various forms and roots of the notion, in Midgley [31].

Bibliography

Teleology

One of the classic works on teleology is Kant's *Critique of teleological judgement*, first published in 1790, contained in

[1] I. Kant, *The critique of judgement*, trans. J.C. Meredith (Oxford University Press, Oxford, 1928)

[2] A. Woodfield, *Teleology* (Cambridge University Press, Cambridge, 1976) is a useful introduction and survey: it has a good bibliography.

An excellent example of the employment of the notion of teleological explanation in biology is provided by

[3] G. Sommerhoff, *Analytical biology* (Oxford University Press, Oxford, 1950).

[4] R. Trigg, *The shaping of man: philosophical aspects of sociobiology* (Basil Blackwell, Oxford, 1982) and

[5] M. Ruse, *Sociobiology: sense or nonsense?* (Kluwer Boston, Hingham, Massachusetts, 1979) are also relevant.

Useful philosophical discussions of teleological explanation can be found in

[6] C. Taylor, *The explanation of behaviour* (Routledge and Kegan Paul, London, 1964) and

[7] J. Bennett, *Linguistic behaviour* (Cambridge University Press, Cambridge, 1976), the second chapter of which is a thought-provoking treatment of the concept. See also the bibliography to Ch. 13.

The idea that all types of explanation can be reduced to one, physical, type of explanation is put forward in

[8] B.F. Skinner, *Beyond freedom and dignity* (Penguin Books, Harmondsworth, 1973), and discussed by

[9] J. Monod, *Chance and necessity*, trans. A. Wainhouse (Collins/Fount, London, 1977).

For a discussion of the distinction between teleological and deontological ethics, see

[10] W.K. Frankena, *Ethics* (Prentice-Hall, Englewood Cliffs, 1963).

G.E. Moore's utilitarianism is expounded in

[11] G.E. Moore, *Principia ethica* (Cambridge University Press, Cambridge, 1903) in which also the famous 'naturalistic fallacy' is explained and denounced.

Aristotle

Aristotle's *Nicomachean ethics* can be found in a variety of editions: for example,

[12] Aristotle, *Nichomachean ethics*, trans. W.D. Ross (World's Classics, Oxford University Press, Oxford, 1954).

For discussion of them,

[13] A. Kenny, *Aristotle's theory of the will* (Duckworth, London, 1979) is interesting, and

[14] A. Rorty (ed.), *Essays on Aristotle's ethics* (University of California Press, Berkeley, 1980) and

[15] J.M.E. Moravcsik (ed.), *Aristotle: a collection of critical essays* (Macmillan, London, 1968) are also helpful.

On the notion of happiness in Greek ethics and in general,

[16] J.C.B. Gosling and C.C.W. Taylor, *The Greeks on pleasure* (Clarendon Press, Oxford, 1982) is very interesting.

Morality and the self

The relationship between the notions of the individual, the self and morality have been explored in a variety of articles and books by Bernard Williams. Some of the articles are collected together in

[17] B.A.O. Williams, *Problems of the self* (Cambridge University Press, Cambridge, 1973) and in

[18] B.A.O. Williams, *Moral luck* (Cambridge University Press, Cambridge, 1981).

[19] M. Midgley, *Wickedness* (Routledge and Kegan Paul, London, 1984) attempts to answer Williams. In his later book,

[20] B.A.O. Williams, *Ethics and the limits of philosophy* (Fontana/Collins, London, 1985), as well as discussing Aristotle's teleology, questions many of the fundamental presuppositions of modern moral philosophy.

Plato

The first clear distinction of teleological reasoning from mechanical reasoning is to be found in

[21] Plato, *Phaedo*, trans. Hugh Tredennick, in *The last days of Socrates* (Penguin Books, Harmondsworth, 1954), Sections 97c–99d.

The relation of teleology to the tripartite soul is expounded in

[22] Plato, *Symposium*, trans. Walter Hamilton (Penguin Books, Harmondsworth, 1952), Sections 202a–212c, and in

[23] Plato, *Phaedrus*, trans. Walter Hamilton (Penguin, Harmondsworth, 1973), Sections 246a–250d.

The tripartite division of the soul is expounded in

[24] Plato, *The republic*, trans. H.D.P. Lee (Penguin, Harmondsworth, 1955), in Part V, pp. 174–98.

For a discussion of Plato,

[25] J. Annas, *An introduction to Plato's republic* (Clarendon Press, Oxford, 1981) is one of the best guides, and

[26] J.C.B. Gosling, *Plato* (Routledge and Kegan Paul, London, 1973) is also a good introduction.

Hegel

For a helpful introduction to the moral philosophy of Hegel and his British followers, see

[27] W.H. Walsh, *Hegelian ethics* (Macmillan, London, 1969).

A clear and concise study of Hegel's political philosophy, emphasising the part played in it by the notion of a community, is

[28] R. Plant, *Hegel* (Allen and Unwin, London, 1973).

[29] C. Taylor, *Hegel* (Cambridge University Press, Cambridge, 1975) gives a

comprehensive and thoughtful survey of the entire Hegelian system. The key ideas of the system are well presented in Ch. 3 of the work, entitled 'Self-positing spirit' (pp. 76–124).

Evolution

Discussions of evolutionary ethics can be found in Moore [11], and in
[30] A.G.N. Flew, *Evolutionary ethics* (Macmillan, London, 1967) and in
[31] M. Midgley, *Evolution as a religion* (Methuen, London, 1985).
The notions of moral progress and Utopia are thoroughly discussed in
[32] J. Passmore, *The perfectibility of man* (Duckworth, London, 1970).

This bibliography has been prepared with the assistance of the author of the chapter, Mary Midgley.

M.A.P.

25 | Morality and Universal Law

Marcus G. Singer

The idea of morality as somehow involving universal law has been in existence a long time. It reached its fruition and received classic expression in the philosophy of Immanuel Kant, but it did not originate with Kant. And although there are immense differences between utilitarianism (and teleological ethical theories generally) and the Kantian theory, as J.S. Mill observed, they agree in regarding 'the morality of an individual action [as] not a question of direct perception, but of the application of a law to an individual case'.[1]

Perhaps the earliest law or principle of this kind is the Golden Rule: 'Do unto others as you would have others do unto you.' This principle traces back to Confucius and perhaps beyond, and in one form or another is a constituent in every known culture and religion. In its earliest incarnations it may not have been meant to be applicable beyond the limits of the tribe or clan, but it was at least meant to be applied universally within those limits or within the limits of a given class, such as adult males. Part of the progress of morality has been the gradual extending of the moral community to include greater and greater numbers of beings within the community of persons who are to be both protected and governed by moral ideals. But despite its widespread dissemination, there are various problems with the interpretation and formulation of the Golden Rule, and it has not received general acceptance by philosophers as a principle capable of precisely determining the confines of right and wrong, nor indeed has it even been much discussed in philosophy. Nonetheless it was taken by Hobbes as providing in an easily understood formula the sum and substance of the laws of nature, 'intelligible', Hobbes said, 'even to the meanest capacity ... Do not that to another, which thou wouldest not have done to thy self.'[2] Now Hobbes was a teleological moralist, though not a utilitarian. Yet Mill, certainly a utilitarian, claimed that 'In the golden rule of Jesus of Nazareth we read the complete spirit of the ethics of utility. To do as you would be done by, and to love your neighbour as yourself, constitute the complete perfection of utilitarian morality.'[3] As between one's own happiness and that of others, says Mill, utilitarianism requires everyone 'to be as strictly impartial as a disinterested and benevolent spectator'. It is this ideal of impartiality, fairness, equity, justice, that the Golden Rule is taken to embody, and this is what is seen as a moral law of complete universality. Thus Samuel Clarke, a deontological moralist of the early eighteenth century, held that there was a fundamental and self-evident 'Rule of Equity': 'Whatever I judge reasonable or unreasonable that another should do for me, that by the same judgement I declare reasonable or unreasonable that I should in the like case do for him,' and Henry Sidgwick claimed that this is the Golden Rule 'precisely stated'.[4] Whether it is or not it is nonetheless manifest that this statement presupposes that there is an essential connection between morality and universal law.

The idea of a connection between morality and universal law is also an essential feature of the natural law tradition, which holds that morality is not arbitrary or conventional but belongs somehow to the order of the universe, either through the intervention of the deity or through other means.[5] The laws of nature, understood thus, represent how things really and essentially are, and thus how society and human conduct ought to be determined if human beings are to be able to achieve the minimal aim of survival or something better.

Thus we see the terms of our topic connected in many otherwise quite dissimilar traditions. But the connection between morality and universal law is most pronounced in the philosophy of Kant, and to Kant we now turn.

The good will and the moral law

The primary work for understanding Kant's key moral ideas is his *Grundlegung zur Metaphysik der Sitten* (1785), variously translated as *Groundwork* (or *Fundamental principles*) *of the metaphysics of morals* (or *ethics*),[6] and this is the work to be relied on primarily here. But Kant developed his moral theory in many other writings; it actually developed through time, and in its various ramifications is extraordinarily complex. (Some of these other writings are *Critique of practical reason* (1788); *Critique of judgment* (1790); *Religion within the limits of reason alone* (1793); *Metaphysics of morals* (1797); and *Anthropology from a pragmatic standpoint* (1798); his posthumous *Lectures on ethics* were first published in 1924.)

An insight of uncommon penetration is embodied in the following observation:

The concept of law is fundamental to the whole body of Kantian thought, theoretic as well as practical. Not only is Kant's ethics decidedly legalistic – its supreme principle is expressed in terms of universal legislation – but his basic conception of nature is that of a system of laws not far removed from the Stoic identification of the natural and the rational ... There are doubtless differences between the laws of external motion applicable to the sensory world and the moral law within us. But both in essence emphasize abstract and invariant uniformities. Kant's moral world is an idealized celestial mechanics in which all conduct is governed by absolute rule or regularity.[7]

It will be well to keep this in mind in contemplating the account to follow.

The *Groundwork* opens with the striking statement: 'It is impossible to conceive anything at all in the world, or even out of it, which can be taken as good without qualification, except a good will' (*Gr.* 393). Kant is not saying that only a good will is good as an end, but rather that only a good will is good unconditionally. He allows for all sorts of things to be good and desirable even as ends. For instance, he lists intelligence, wit, judgement, courage, resolution, power, wealth, honour, and even happiness as good, but claims that none of these things is good if unaccompanied by a good will, and that therefore none of them is good without qualification. By a *good will* Kant means the settled determination to do one's moral duty. Another word for this is 'character'; it can also be understood as conscientiousness. A 'rational and impartial spectator', Kant says, 'can never feel approval in contemplating the uninterrupted prosperity of a being graced by no touch of a pure and good will'. In other words, our rational and impartial judgement, manifested in the image of a rational and impartial spectator, can never approve of an evil person enjoying happiness, because an evil person does not *deserve* it. A good will is the indispensable condition of being *worthy* of being happy, though as the world is it is not in fact an indispensable condition of being happy.

Kant's opening statement can be elucidated further as implying: (1) only a good will is necessarily good; (2) it is inconceivable for a good will not to be good; (3) only a good will or what manifests one can be *morally* good.

By a good will, then, Kant means moral character, the condition of determining one's actions always on the principle that they are morally right or in accordance with duty. To do what is right because it is right is to act *from duty*, and this is to be distinguished from acting merely *in accordance with duty*. It is not that acting in accordance with duty is wrong, and it is not that acting in accordance with duty is bad. But acting in accordance with duty has no *moral* value. Kant herewith introduced a new conception to the moral scene, that of moral worth as distinct from moral rightness. Whether an action has moral worth depends on its motive. Consequently Kant's first proposition says that nothing is morally good except a good will and actions or persons manifesting a good will. If you do something that is right for fear of being punished or disapproved of or merely out of habit, although what you have done is right, you have not done it because it is right, and therefore your action, although it may have value of other kinds, has no *moral* value.

Kant conceives of moral action as taking place under special conditions, that of tension or conflict between inclination, to which as human beings we are all subject, and duty. If we were perfectly rational, as we conceive God to be, we would *always* act in accordance with reason. But as imperfectly rational beings we sometimes – and some of us somewhat more often – act on inclination contrary to reason and what duty requires. The operative principle is: what a perfectly rational being would do, out of necessity, is what an imperfectly rational being, therefore a human being, *ought* to do; for Kant the concept of an 'ought', or of duty, applies only to beings who are imperfectly rational and thus free to act contrary to reason.

Kant tells us that a good will – conscientiousness or moral character – is not good because of what it brings about or accomplishes, but is rather good in itself. And he argues that nature's purpose in supplying us with reason is not to enable us to be happy – since instinct would be better for that purpose – but to generate a good will, which is the only thing of unconditional and therefore supreme moral value. Kant is not actually making happiness take a back seat. He thinks happiness plays an essential role in human motivation and action. But he is trying to determine what that role is. For him, as distinct from teleological or utilitarian or hedonistic thinkers, happiness is not our ultimate end or the highest good. The goodness of happiness is always conditional on its being accompanied by a good will, on its being *deserved*. Hence Kant's view is not one that accords priority to the satisfaction of desire or inclination, but rather one that accords priority to what is morally right. For Kant the supreme good is the good will; the *highest* good is a state of affairs in which those with a good will are happy; and a state of affairs in which those with a bad will are happy or those with a good will are unhappy is one of evil, to be changed for a better state.

It is Kant's view, then, that an action has moral worth only if it is in accordance with duty, that is, right (or sincerely and conscientiously believed to be right), and is done for that reason alone. Hence whether an action has moral worth depends on the maxim on which it is done.

In Kant's view, every human action is purposive, that is, done for some purpose. Hence every action is undertaken on some principle or maxim. An agent's maxim (which the agent need not consciously formulate) is like a self-imposed rule, and specifies what one proposes to do under what circumstances and for that purpose. Every maxim has the general form 'If I am in circumstances C and wish to attain P, I will do D': and it is as though one is acting on the general maxim or rule 'Whenever I am in C and wish to attain P I will do D.' The moral question then is not whether the agent can act on the maxim, but whether the agent ought or has a moral right to. This is the question whether the maxim is in accord with the moral law. If one's maxim is in accord with the moral law, and one acts on it for that reason alone, then, and only then, does one's maxim, and one's action, have moral worth.

The moral law is the principle on which a good will (or a person with a good will) acts. Whereas a maxim is a subjective principle, a principle on which a person actually does act, the law is an objective principle, a principle on which a person ought to act. This objective principle, the moral law, Kant calls the 'Categorical Imperative', and to understand what this means we first have to understand what Kant means by imperatives in general.

An imperative is a 'command to will', expressed by an 'ought'. It is a command of reason to a will that does not of necessity act in accordance with reason. Thus 'oughts', or imperatives, are not applicable to a perfectly rational being or to a holy will but only to imperfectly rational beings, who are capable of having or developing a good will and are also capable of evil and irrationality. The moral law thus expresses the principle on which a perfectly rational being necessarily acts, and therefore the principle on which an imperfectly rational being ought to act. Kant says, 'Everything in nature works according to laws. Only a rational being has the power to act *in accordance with his idea* of laws – that is, in accordance with principles – and only so has he a *will*' (*Gr.* 412). It is on this basis that a rational being can be self-determining, that is, capable of determining his own conduct or acting in accordance *with his idea* of a law. And a law, on Kant's conception, is of necessity universal, applying to everything within its range.

It is here that we can see how the conception of universal law is necessarily connected with the conception of a good will, for it is already part of the conception of a will. For to have a will is to have the power to act in accordance with one's *idea* of a *law*, and to have a good will is persistently to exercise the power to act in accordance with the moral law because it is the moral law, so that the idea of the law is what determines one's action.

Kant connects the idea of a good will with the idea of universal law in this way. An action done from duty 'has to set aside altogether the influence of inclination, and along with inclination every object of the will', that is to say, set aside as determining motives of the will; so that there is, Kant says, 'nothing left able to determine the will except objectively the *law* and subjectively pure reverence [respect] for this practical law, and therefore the maxim of obeying this law even to the detriment of all my inclinations'. Whereas the maxims Kant was talking about earlier, which are involved in all action, are material maxims, since they involve reference to some object or purpose, the maxim Kant is referring to here is the 'formal maxim' of doing one's duty because it is one's duty. Thus, Kant continues, 'the moral worth of an action does not depend on the result expected from it', that is, on the agent's purpose or object or goal, whether it is achieved or not. The *moral* worth of an action depends on the agent's motive or intention, the formal maxim of doing one's duty simply because it is one's duty. Consequently, Kant says, 'nothing but *the idea of the law in itself ... so far as it, and not an expected result, is the ground determining the will* – can constitute that pre-eminent good which we call moral, a good which is already present in the person acting on this idea and should not be awaited merely from the result' (*Gr*. 401).

It is important to notice that a maxim is not an imperative or a directive, and contains no element of 'ought'. Maxims rest on inclinations, and it is because we, as imperfectly rational beings, can form and act on maxims that can be contrary to our interests or contrary to reason that imperatives apply to us. Imperatives are or have the force of commands, claiming to be commands of reason, stating what *ought* (or ought not) to be done. Kant distinguishes between hypothetical and categorical imperatives. A hypothetical imperative tells one how one ought to act in order to achieve certain ends, and makes no judgement about the value of those ends. It takes the form '*If* you want to achieve *that*, then you *ought* to do *this*,' and rests on the law of nature that the doing of *this* is necessary, as means, to the achieving of *that*, as end. If one gives up the purpose, then one escapes from the imperative. The imperative is hypothetical in being conditional on the agent's purpose. Hypothetical imperatives are rules or judgements of prudence, specifying what one ought to do or avoid in order to achieve some arbitrary or contingent end, or what one ought to do in order to be happy. But happiness, on Kant's view, although something that every human being certainly aims at, by a necessity of nature – since in the concept of happiness we have a summing up of the satisfaction of all inclinations – is also at the same time incurably indefinite, since no one can ever say definitely and with certainty what will make him happy. We often want things which, on attaining them, make us unhappy. Consequently, whether a hypothetical imperative relates to an arbitrary or variable or dependent end, or whether it relates to the necessary end of happiness, it cannot be a basis for *moral* laws, which must hold universally and of necessity. Moral imperatives, therefore, must not rest on any end that is either capable of being given up or is indefinite. Kant describes this by saying that they must be categorical. Consequently a categorical imperative tells one what one must do in order to be moral, or what is morally required.

The general principle for all hypothetical imperatives is 'Who wills the end, wills (so far as he is rational) also the means which are indispensably necessary and in his power' (*Gr*. 417). If you wish to lose weight, and this is not a mere idle wish but something you will as an end, then, if you recognise that in order to lose weight you have to cut down on the amount you eat, then if you are rational you will cut down the amount you eat, and it can be said that you ought to. In this situation, the imperative 'You ought to cut down on the amount you eat' is a hypothetical imperative, a requirement of prudence, and you can escape from it by giving up the end. But you cannot retain the end and rationally escape its requirements.

The general principle for all categorical imperatives is more complicated, and Kant finds it necessary to state it in several forms. What Kant calls the Categorical Imperative is the general principle of all categorical imperatives, that is to say, of all injunctions about what ought (or ought not) morally to be done. It is the form in which Kant understands and elucidates the moral law.

Kant says that 'if I conceive a *categorical* imperative, I know at once what it contains'. For besides the law this imperative contains only the necessity (that is, the duty) that our maxim should conform to this law, and the law itself contains no condition to limit it. Consequently, Kant maintains, there is nothing to which our maxim has to conform except the *universality of law as such*, 'and it is this conformity alone that the imperative ... asserts to be necessary' (*Gr.* 420–1). Therefore the Categorical Imperative states: 'Act only on those maxims that you can at the same time will to be universal laws.' Alternatively, 'Act as if the maxim of your action were to become through your will a *universal law of nature.*' That is to say, supposing it were an invariable law of nature that every time you acted on a maxim it became a universal law of nature that henceforth you and everyone in such circumstances with such a purpose would have to act on that maxim – so that this became an unalterable feature of the world – would you be willing so to act? To be willing so to act is to will one's maxim to be a universal law, and Kant is maintaining that where you could not be willing to act on such a maxim, the maxim is wrong.

Kant now applies this principle of universality to four examples, chosen to illustrate the various kinds of duties, determined by two principles of division: duties to oneself and duties to others, and perfect and imperfect duties. The former distinction should be self-explanatory, the latter will be explained in due course. At any rate, these kinds are, in order of illustration, perfect duties to oneself, perfect duties to others, imperfect duties to oneself, imperfect duties to others.

The first example involves someone who is tired of life as a result of a series of misfortunes, and contemplates suicide. Kant claims that the maxim of such a person – it will be my principle to end my life if its continuation threatens more pain that it promises pleasure – cannot be willed to be a universal law, and is therefore opposed to the supreme principle of all duty (*Gr.* 442). This is meant to illustrate a perfect duty to oneself.

The second example involves someone who is in a difficult situation that he can get out of only by borrowing money, even though he 'knows that he will not be able to pay it back', and is inclined to promise to pay it back regardless in order to get over the present difficulty.

Kant argues that here also the maxim cannot be willed to be a universal law, since it cannot even be conceived of as one.

> For the universality of a law that every one believing himself to be in need may make any promise he pleases with the intention not to keep it would make promising, and the very purpose of promising, itself impossible, since no one would believe he was being promised anything, but would laugh at utterances of this kind as empty shams. (*Gr.* 422; cf. 403)

If this reasoning is sound it would show dishonest promising to be morally wrong, and the principle can be applied also to promise-breaking and to lying generally.

The third example involves the case of someone who is 'in comfortable circumstances' but 'prefers to give himself up to pleasure rather than to bother about ... improving his fortunate natural aptitudes'. Kant says that one's maxim of neglecting one's natural gifts, though it agrees with one's 'tendency to indulgence', does not agree with duty. For although such a system of nature (meaning a world with such a law of nature in it) could exist, one cannot possibly *will* that this should become a universal law of nature. 'For as a rational being he necessarily wills that all his powers should be developed, since they serve him, and are given him, for all sorts of possible ends.'

The fourth example involves someone who is 'himself flourishing' and sees no reason why he should help anyone else who is in need of help and 'whom he could easily help'. Again, Kant claims that such a system of nature is possible but that it is impossible to will that such a principle should be a universal law of nature. 'For a will which decided in this way would be at variance with itself, since many a situation might arise in which the man needed love and sympathy from others, and in which, by such a law of nature sprung from his own will, he would rob himself of all hope of the help he wants for himself' (*Gr.* 423). Kant concludes that we therefore have a duty to help others who are in need of help.

In all these cases there is operative a 'general canon for all moral judgment of action': we must *be able to will* our maxim to be a universal law. 'Some actions are so constituted that their maxim cannot even be conceived as a universal law of nature without contradiction.' In other cases there is not 'this inner impossibility, but it is still impossible to will that their maxim should be raised to the universality of a law of nature, because such a will would contradict itself ... The first kind of action is opposed to' perfect duty, the second to imperfect. Kant observes:

> If we now attend to ourselves whenever we transgress a duty, we find that we in fact do not will that our maxim should become a universal law – since this is impossible for us – but rather that its opposite should remain a law universally: we only take the liberty of making an *exception* to it for ourselves (or even just for this once) ...

575

Consequently if we weighed it all up from one and the same point of view – that of reason – we should find a contradiction in our own will, the contradiction that a certain principle should be objectively necessary as a universal law and yet subjectively should not hold universally but should admit exceptions ...

'This procedure', Kant continues, though it cannot be justified 'in our own impartial judgment', nonetheless proves 'that we in fact recognize the validity of the categorical imperative and ... merely permit ourselves a few exceptions' (*Gr.* 424).

It seems to be admitted on all sides that Kant's argument against suicide is singularly weak, since it is not impossible for a system of nature to subsist in which everyone who is suffering from some painful and incurable disease committed suicide; since not everyone is so suffering, this would not lead to universal suicide nor would it be self-defeating. But there is no hint in Kant's discussion of the idea, which has been attributed to him by certain rather careless commentators, that no one should commit suicide since if everyone did there would be no one left to do so. Kant was taking it for granted without argument that it is a duty to preserve one's life, even under conditions of great adversity. Whether his principle shows this to be the case is another matter, and if it does not, this is not, as some commentators have supposed, an argument against his principle, but only an argument that Kant himself misapplied it and that its application is not such an easy and obvious matter as Kant supposed it to be.

The examples that seem best to support Kant's claim are the second and fourth. In the second example, Kant is arguing that one who is inclined to tell a lie for his own temporary advantage is acting on a maxim he could not be willing to have everyone act on, since he is claiming for himself a privilege he would not and could not be willing to grant to others. And Kant claims that the institution of promising could not exist if as a matter of course and as a general rule people did not intend to keep their promises when they make them, any more than it could exist if promises were generally broken. This is consistent with some promises being lies when made, and some promises being broken. But if promises were generally to be made falsely or to be broken, one could no longer make an honest promise, since the devices available for the making of promises would lose their plausibility and their meaning. If Kant is right on this, then he has established the wrongness of false promising and promise-breaking and lying in general, and has unearthed a general principle of considerable power.

The fourth example is a bit more complex. What Kant is relying on here is the undoubted fact that no human being can be self-sufficient or certain that a situation would never arise in which he would not have need of the help of others. Imagine someone with as much money as he needs or more, so that he is not in need of financial help from anyone.

Nonetheless, though he may never be in need of financial help, he may some time be in need of help of some other kind. He may, for instance, be in danger of drowning and not be able to swim, or be trapped in a plane wreck or a burning building and need the help of others to escape. If he had willed his maxim – 'When I am not in need of help myself I will not help anyone who is' – to be a universal law of nature, he would have deprived himself of all possibility of the help he now needs. Thus, Kant says, he cannot will that maxim to be a universal law without contradicting himself. If this argument is sound, however, it would not follow that everyone has on all occasions of life the duty to help others and to spend one's life in the full-fledged service of others. The duty is imperfect. This means that it is relatively indeterminate. If one cannot will one's maxim, of not helping others who are in need of help as long as one is not in need of help oneself, to be a universal law, then it is a moral duty to help others who are in need of help. But this rule does not determine whom to help, to what extent, in what way, how much, and at what cost. It is up to the agent to decide, curiously enough on the basis of inclination. With a perfect or determinate duty, there is no such indeterminacy or latitude for the agent to decide. No one has the discretion to decide whom to lie to, to what extent, in what way.

The third example, which claims to establish the duty of developing one's talents, is also an example of a duty (if it is a duty) that is imperfect in the sense of being relatively indeterminate. For everyone has many talents and no one can develop all of them, at least equally. Thus it would be up to the agent to decide which talents to develop, to what extent, at what cost, and by what means. What is established by reason, on Kant's view, is the duty to develop one's talents. Reason alone cannot decide these other questions, though they must be answered for the rule to be put into practice.

It is clear from these examples that Kant's ethics, the ethics of universal law, is not as remote from everyday life as is suggested by the austere language in which it is expressed and the comments of numerous commentators. But we should note that the Categorical Imperative, the formula for the moral law, is not a premiss from which particular duties or general rules of duty are to be deduced. Such more particular moral judgements are 'derived' from the Categorical Imperative only in the sense that the Categorical Imperative serves as a test of the moral acceptability of maxims. If a maxim can be willed to be a universal law, then it is morally all right (permissible) to act on it; if it cannot, then it is contrary to duty to act on it and morally obligatory to act on its contrary.

It has sometimes been alleged, as for instance by Hegel and some of his followers, that Kant's Categorical Imperative is without content, and that from a principle without content no principle with content can be derived. But this rests on a misunderstanding. The Categorical Imperative, in the form of the Principle of Universality, is meant to provide a test for the morality of maxims and of actions involving those maxims. The content enters through the maxims. Without some maxim to begin with, that is, without some inclination to do something in certain circumstances to achieve some purpose, there is nothing to test. With a maxim, there is something to test. And if the Formula of Universality can serve as a test of the morality of maxims, it has all the content it needs.

A more difficult criticism is that it is often difficult to be certain what the maxim is and how it should be formulated. Some critics have thought this provides some insuperable difficulty for the Categorical Imperative as a moral test. But there is no sense in imagining someone with no vestige of a good will trying so to formulate a maxim as to be an exception to some general rule that would apply to others. Even aside from whether such a procedure can be made to work – something that has not itself been established – this overlooks that for Kant the Categorical Imperative is the principle on which a good will acts, and someone with a good will would not be looking for verbal formulas for escaping from moral requirements.

We must now notice the other formulations Kant provides of the Categorical Imperative. The second main principle, the principle of humanity or personality, says: 'Act in such a way that you always treat humanity, whether in your own person or in the person of any other, never simply as a means, but always at the same time as an end' (*Gr.* 429). The ground for this principle is that rational beings, and therefore human beings, exist as *ends in themselves*, 'not merely as means for arbitrary use by this or that will'. 'Rational beings', says Kant, 'are called *persons* because their nature ... marks them off as ends in themselves,' that is, as beings who have the right to be consulted about actions affecting them and their interests and who have the right not to be treated in certain ways without their consent. And Kant tries to show how in each of the four examples action on the maxim involved would involve treating humanity, whether in one's own person or in the person of another, merely as a means. For instance,

> the man who has a mind to make a false promise to others ... is intending to make use of another man *merely as a means* to an end he does not share. For the man whom I seek to use for my own purposes by such a promise cannot possibly agree to my way of behaving to him, and so cannot himself share the end of the action. (*Gr. 429*)

To treat someone merely as a means is to treat that person merely as a means to an end that person cannot share, to treat that person in a way in which no person can rationally consent to be treated. In a case where one is being treated as mere means it is contrary to reason to consent to such a mode of treatment, even though one can *in fact* give one's consent to that mode of treatment. Examples of practices that violate this principle are provided by slavery, exploitation, kidnapping, holding someone as a hostage, or punishing someone who is not guilty merely to provide an example for others. It is to be noted that this principle does not prohibit treating people as means; it does not prohibit making use of peoples' services. It prohibits treating them as *mere* means, as mere tools or utensils. For that is not to treat them as persons, who have ends of their own, and whose ends are as much entitled to respect as anyone else's.

> A violator of the rights of man intends to use the person of others merely as a means without taking into consideration that, as rational beings, they ought always at the same time to be rated as ends – that is, only as beings who must themselves be able to share in the end of the very same action. (*Gr.* 430)

The ground of this principle is that this is the way every one of us necessarily conceives of our own existence and consequently we must recognise that this is the way other rational beings conceive of their own existence (*Gr.* 429). The upshot is that human beings have an absolute value – a *dignity* – that is beyond price, and are not articles to be bought and sold (*Gr.* 434). The ground of the dignity – the absolute value – of human and of all rational nature is *autonomy* (*Gr.* 436), and this leads to other formulations of the supreme principle.

Autonomy, as Kant conceives it, is not just the capacity to govern one's own conduct, but the capacity to govern one's own conduct by laws that one lays down for oneself. All rational beings are rightly subject only to laws that they give themselves – that is, can rationally consent to – and are at the same time universal. So everyone at the same time is subject to the same laws, which they both give to themselves and also legislate universally. For Kant, autonomy is the supreme condition of morality for it is the paramount condition of being self-governing, and the laws that any one person lays down for himself are the same as the laws that all others lay down for themselves. They are thus universal in two senses: each can will his maxims to be universal laws, and all universally can will the same maxims universally as laws. Thus the principle of autonomy: so act that your will can at the same time regard itself as giving universal law through its maxims (*Gr.* 434). This in turn leads to the concept and the principle of the kingdom of ends: we ought each of us so to act as to be able to regard ourselves as both subjects and law-givers in a kingdom of ends.

By a 'kingdom' Kant means 'a systematic union of different beings under common laws' (*Gr.* 433). 'Now', he says,

> since laws determine ends as regards their universal validity, we shall be able – if we abstract from the personal differences between rational beings, and also from all the content of their private ends – to conceive a whole of all ends in systematic conjunction (a whole both of rational beings as ends in themselves and also of the personal ends which each may set before himself); that is, we shall be able to conceive a kingdom of ends which is possible in accordance with the above principles. (*Gr.* 433)

These common laws are laws we can consent to – since they are of our own making, in the sense that we can rationally consent to them – and also ones to which our wills, subject to practical reason, are subject. We thus in the end bind ourselves by laws which are universal in being the same as the laws everyone else binds themselves by. And thus, for Kant, the prescribing of laws for oneself that are identical, because universal, with the laws everyone prescribes for themselves is what morality consists in. 'Morality', he says, 'consists in the relation of all action to the making of laws whereby alone a kingdom of ends is possible' (*Gr.* 434).

> Morality consists ... in the reference of all action to the legislation which alone can render a kingdom of ends possible. This legislation must be capable of existing in every rational being, and of emanating from his will, so that the principle of this will is never to act on any maxim which could not without contradiction be also a universal law, and accordingly always so to act *that the will could at the same time regard itself as giving in its maxims universal laws*.[8]

Kant recognises that a kingdom of ends 'is admittedly only an ideal' (*Gr.* 433). This ideal, however, provides the theoretical and moral basis of democracy or any system of self-government, and its validity as an ideal is not lessened by its being 'only an ideal'. As Kant observes:

> a kingdom of ends would actually come into existence through maxims which the categorical imperative prescribes as a rule for all rational beings, *if these maxims were universally followed*. Yet even if a rational being were himself to follow such a maxim strictly, he cannot count on everybody else being faithful to it on this ground, nor can he be confident that the kingdom of nature and its purposive order will work in harmony with him, as a fitting member, towards a kingdom of ends made possible by himself ... But in spite of this the law 'Act on the maxims of a member who makes universal laws for a merely possible kingdom of ends' remains in full force, since its command is categorical. (*Gr.* 438–9)

It is at this point that a number of later writers, otherwise sympathetic to Kantian basic ideas, part company from Kant. For what one ought to do under conditions of perfect and universal compliance is not necessarily what one ought to do under conditions of imperfect and far from universal compliance, the conditions of the actual world. Kant has managed to state a problem, but his easy solution is not so easily accepted. For if one knows that others are not going to comply this alters the circumstances one is in, and consequently alters one's maxims. Two actions otherwise identical can be significantly different if performed under different circumstances.

For Kant, the opposite of autonomy is heteronomy. Being subject to laws that do not come from oneself or from reason is heteronomy, and contrary to morality. Heteronomy of the will – the determination of the will by factors outside it, such as desires, inclinations, fears, or threats – he regarded as the source of all spurious principles of morality (*Gr.* 441), and this would include all teleological or utilitarian accounts. There have been many attempts since Kant, however, to combine some account of utilitarian theory with universalisability elements in Kant. Although Kant would regard this as a heteronomous unworkable and indeed corrupting hodgepodge, such attempts go on, and they are tribute to the fact that, despite great difficulties with the theory, Kant seems to have singled out some factors essential to morality. Where current writers differ is in determining what these are.

On Kant's view, 'The three modes of presenting the principle of morality ... are at bottom only so many formulae of the very same law, and each of itself involves the other two' (*Gr.* 436), so that they differ only in emphasis and in what they bring nearer to intuition. Although he regards 'autonomy of the will as the supreme principle (condition) of morality' (*Gr.* 440), Kant nonetheless ends up saying:

> It is ... better if in moral *judgment* we proceed always in accordance with the strictest method and take as our basis the universal formula of the categorical imperative: *'Act on the maxim which can at the same time be made a universal law.'* (*Gr.* 436–7)

And this brings us back to our opening topic of morality and universal law.

Universalisability and the Principle of Justice

Although it first appeared two hundred years ago, Kant's moral philosophy is in essential respects still contemporary. The language may be a bit stilted and the talk about the metaphysics of morals is now out of fashion, has been replaced by talk about the logic of morals, but this deals with much the same thing. There have been many commentaries, critiques and defences, and formulations of similar though not identical principles have been influential and widely discussed in recent decades. Some of these later developments, which involve attempts at linking morality with universal law, require mention here.

A term that came into vogue in the 1920s in connection with Kant's principle of universality is 'universalisability'. A maxim came to be called *universalisable* if it could be willed to be a universal law; otherwise not. So this term merely provided a short way of speaking of whether or not a maxim satisfies the general canon of moral judgement, and in this use it is a moral or normative notion. But it has gone through several permutations since.

In his masterful treatise *The methods of ethics* (1874) Sidgwick tried to establish utilitarianism on an intuitionistic and partly Kantian basis. His argument in essence was that the principle of utility can be deduced from certain abstract principles that when clearly stated and understood can be seen to be self-evident. One of these he called the Principle of Justice: 'Whatever action any of us judges to be right for himself he implicitly judges to be right for all similar persons in similar circumstances.' Or, as we may otherwise put it:

> if a kind of action that is right (or wrong) for me is not right (or wrong) for some one else, it must be on the ground of some difference between the two cases, other than the fact that I and he are different persons.[9]

Sidgwick takes this principle to be the core of truth, necessary truth, involved in both the Categorical Imperative and the Golden Rule. Now more recent writers have come to call *this* principle, often stated in the form 'What is right (or wrong, obligatory, etc.) for one person must be right (or wrong, obligatory, etc.) for every relevantly similar person in relevantly similar circumstances,' the principle or thesis of Universalisability. And this principle has by some come to be thought of not as a principle for determining the moral acceptability of actions, but rather as a principle for distinguishing the moral from the non-moral (as distinct from the immoral). Thus, on this conception, someone who claims that I ought to do something but is not prepared to universalise this to the claim that everyone relevantly similar ought to do the same thing, is not making a moral judgement but a judgement or a claim of some other kind. Universalisability thus came to be thought of as not about morality but as about the *language* of morals.

This is the way the idea of universalisability first appeared (1955) in the thinking of R.M. Hare. But Hare's thesis about universalisability was developed in his book *Freedom and reason (FR)* into the basis of a complex and ingenious form of utilitarianism. Hare claims to have found a way of combining a theory based on Kantian ideas (universalisability) with utilitarian reference to satisfaction of interests (*FR* 34, 124), even though Kant himself rules out such a combination as heteronomous and impossible. In Hare's first book, *The language of morals*, although the term 'universalisability' does not itself appear, the germ of it is presented in discussions of *supervenience* and *consequential properties*.[10]

Supervenience is a notion first introduced by G.E. Moore in his discussion of intrinsic value. Moore observed that whether something is good or bad depends solely on what other properties it has, and if two things are alike in all essential respects or in their 'intrinsic nature' then if one is good the other must be also.[11] The value properties (good, bad) and by extension the moral properties (right, ought, duty) of something thus depend solely on its intrinsic nature, and are said to *supervene* on these essential or intrinsic properties. Alternatively, whether something is good or bad is totally a consequence of the other properties it has; hence goodness is said to be a consequential or 'toti-resultant' attribute.[12] Now in *Freedom and reason* Hare introduced 'universalisability', on the basis of his earlier account of supervenience, as a linguistic or logical thesis, and as a feature that moral judgements, in particular ought-judgements, share with descriptive statements in virtue of having descriptive meaning (*FR* 37, 10). This is not to say that for Hare moral judgements are descriptive. On the contrary, it is an essential part of his view that moral judgements are prescriptive. (Compare Ch. 27, pp. 622–5.) But they are also universalisable, and they have this characteristic because they have descriptive meaning, since they contain general terms governed by meaning rules. 'If I call a thing red, I am committed to calling anything else like it red. And if I call a thing a good *X*, I am committed to calling any *X* like it good' (*FR* 15).

This thesis, that moral judgements are both prescriptive and universalisable (*FR* 16–18), is put to powerful use. By itself, claims Hare, it is only a logical thesis about the meanings of the moral words.

> If a person says 'I ought to act in a certain way, but nobody else ought to act in that way in relevantly similar circumstances', then, on my thesis, he is abusing the word 'ought'; he is implicitly contradicting himself. (*FR* 32)

Nonetheless Hare discovers that the thesis, ostensibly morally neutral, does have a powerful use in moral argument, by the route of what he calls 'golden-rule arguments', leading ultimately to a form of utilitarianism.

The Golden Rule asks us to consider, 'How would you like it if you were to be treated in the same way you are treating or proposing to treat someone else?' Hare transforms this question to eliminate what he takes to be the objectionable reference to hypothetical circumstances encapsulated in 'How *would* you like it, *if* ...' Faced with such a question, someone who is (say) victimising another might reply, 'Well, of course, if anybody did this to me I should resent it ... but this has absolutely no bearing on the validity of the moral opinion which I am now expressing' (*FR* 108). To involve such a person in a contradiction, says Hare, 'we have to show that he *now* holds an opinion about the hypothetical case which is inconsistent with his opinion about the actual case'. The point is that because of someone's aversion to something's being done to him in the hypothetical case,

> he cannot accept the singular *prescription* that in the hypothetical case it should be done to him; and this, because of the logic of 'ought', precludes him from accepting the moral judgement that he ought to do likewise to another in the actual case. (*FR* 108–9)

This procedure is then generalised beyond the two-person case.

> When I have been the round of all the affected parties, what can I possibly do except advocate that course which will, taken all in all, least frustrate the desires which I have imagined myself having? But this ... is to maximize satisfactions. (*FR* 23)

And this, as is readily apparent, is a form of utilitarianism, which seems thus derivable from the purely formal consideration of universalisability. But whether this apparent derivation of utilitarianism from universalisability is valid, as Hare maintains, or involves sleight-of-hand, as his critics contend, is not a question for us to deal with here.

In a book entitled *Generalization in ethics* the present writer attempted to show how Sidgwick's Principle of Justice – renamed the 'Generalisation Principle' – is fundamental in being involved in all moral reasoning and all genuine moral judgement, and how it can be defended against such objections as that it is trivial, mere tautology, inapplicable, or merely linguistic with no moral implications.[13] It was argued that the generalisation principle is presupposed both in the Categorical Imperative and also in a form of argument much like it, christened the 'Generalisation Argument': if everyone did that it would be terrible, so no one has the right to do that. That the generalisation principle is presupposed in the Categorical Imperative was used to show how the impossibility of willing a maxim to be a universal law shows the maxim and the action involving it to be wrong: one who acts on a non-universalisable maxim is claiming for himself a privilege he would not and could not be willing to extend to others, without showing how there is a difference in his situation relevant to and sufficient to justify this claim. Whether the generalisation argument is sound and also validly deducible from the generalisation principle and a principle of consequences is a matter that has generated both perplexity and controversy.

A more recent work attempting to establish *a priori* a supreme principle of morality, also based on the principle of universalisability, complete and sufficient to answer all moral questions, is Alan Gewirth's *Reason and morality*.[14] From an analysis of the fundamental conditions of agency, which claims that all actions are both voluntary and purposive, and from a careful analysis of universalisability as a logical condition on moral principles, Gewirth derives as the supreme principle of morality the 'Principle of Generic Consistency': 'Act in accord with the generic rights of your recipients as well as yourself.' Gewirth regards this principle as logically necessary, in the sense that it would be self-contradictory either to deny it or to violate it (*RM* 135), and also materially or categorially necessary (as Kant would put it, categorical), in that the obligations it imposes cannot be evaded by any shifting of inclinations, interests, or ideals. This is perhaps the most significant recent development stemming from Kant's linking of morality with universal law and the Kantian idea that the fundamental principle of morality must be *a priori*, claims supported by Gewirth with respect to the principle of generic consistency with a wealth of argument. The obvious relation between this principle and the Golden Rule has also been explored by Gewirth; the gist of his view is that the Principle of Generic Consistency is the Golden Rule rationalised, and that the Golden Rule is sound only if interpreted in the light of this principle. Kant, curiously, did not himself attach any importance to the Golden Rule, thought it trivial and incomplete, but he also did not devote any considerable discussion to it (it is mentioned only in a note at *Gr.* 430). If Gewirth and some others are right, there is a closer connection between the Golden Rule and the principle implicit in the Categorical Imperative than Kant had allowed for.[15]

There have been a number of other significant developments on this topic, but reference to them can be compressed merely by mentioning a recently published collection of essays on universalisability, *Morality and universality*.[16] This book contains essays on Kantian universalisability, Hareian universalisability, consequentialist universalisability, utilitarian generalisation, the variety of universalisability theses, and the relations between universalisability and consistency. It also contains a useful introduction and bibliography and should facilitate the route of anyone who wants to pursue the subject further. Interconnections and difficulties that have only been hinted at here come in for illuminating discussion from various points of view, and it is thus a useful compendium on a subject that is growing rapidly in significance and volume. What remains is to establish the connection between universalisability in ethics, on the one hand, and the principle of precedent and the 'rule of the case' in law, on the other.[17] Once that connection is traced out, as would have to be done in another essay, we should have a further connection between morality and universal law.

Notes

(An author's name followed by a number in square brackets refers to the book or article which has that number in the bibliography.)

1. Mill [17], p. 2.
2. Thomas Hobbes, *Leviathan* (1651), Part I, Ch. 15, para. 35 (Everyman edn, Dent, London, 1978), p. 82. A list of discussions of the Golden Rule may be found appended to the article 'Golden Rule' in Edwards [1], vol. III, pp. 365–7. Other more recent discussions of moment are: Reiner [2], pp. 271–93; Hans-Ulrich Hoche, 'The Golden Rule: new aspects of an old moral principle' in [3], vol. I, pp. 69–90; and Alan Gewirth, 'The Golden Rule rationalized' in [4], pp. 133–47.
3. Mill [17], Ch. 2, para. 18, p. 16.
4. Sidgwick [18], pp. 384–5. Clarke's Rule of Equity was stated as reported by Sidgwick; the original can be found in Clarke's *Discourse upon natural religion* (1706), in L.A. Selby-Bigge (ed.), *British moralists* (Clarendon Press, Oxford, 1897), vol. II, pp. 23–4.
5. W.R. Sorley, *A history of English philosophy* (Cambridge University Press, Cambridge, 1920), p. 157. Good discussions of natural law, from differing points of view, may be found in: d'Entreves [5]; Finnis [6]; Fuller [7]; Hart [8]. See also Morris R. Cohen, 'Jus naturale redivivum', *Philosophical Review*, vol. 25 (1916), reprinted in Cohen [9], Bk. III, Ch. 4.
6. This will be cited for the most part in the translation by H.J. Paton (occasionally modified by the present writer) in a book entitled *The moral law* (Hutchinson,

London, 1948), and will be cited in parentheses as '*Gr*'; the page numbers given are those of the Prussian Academy edition of Kant's works, which appear in the margins of Paton's translation. Occasionally the translation used will be the one by T.K. Abbott, in his work entitled *Kant's theory of ethics,* 6th edn (Longmans, London, 1909). Another translation of note is by L.W. Beck, which first appeared in his collection *Kant's Critique of practical reason and other writings in moral philosophy* (Chicago University Press, Chicago, 1949), and both Beck and Paton are drawn on occasionally for interpretation.

7. Morris R. Cohen, 'A critique of Kant's philosophy of law' in *The heritage of Kant,* ed. G. Whitney and D. Bowers (Princeton University Press, Princeton, 1939), p. 279; reprinted in Cohen's *Reason and law* (Free Press, Glencoe, 1950), p. 105.

8. *Gr.* 424; in Abbott (cf. note 6), Ch. 2, para. 65, p. 52

9. Sidgwick [18], p. 379; cf. pp. 208–9 and xvi–xxi.

10. Hare [29], [30], [31] and *Moral thinking* (Clarendon Press, Oxford, 1981). This last work contains a list of Hare's writings. See also 'Ethical theory and utilitarianism' in *Contemporary British philosophy*, Series 4, ed. H.D. Lewis (Allen and Unwin, London, 1976), pp. 113–31. W.D. Hudson, *Modern moral philosophy* (Macmillan, London, and Anchor Books, Garden City, 1970) contains a lucid account of Hare's view.

11. G.E. Moore, 'The conception of intrinsic value', *Philosophical studies* (Routledge and Kegan Paul, London, 1922), pp. 257, 260–1, 265, 269. An illuminating account is R.L. Holmes, 'Descriptivism, supervenience, and universalizability', *Journal of Philosophy*, 63, 3 March 1966, pp. 113–19, esp. 114–15.

12. W.D. Ross introduced these terms in *The right and the good* (Clarendon Press, Oxford, 1930), pp. 120–3.

13. Singer [33].

14. Gewirth [34]; a list of Gewirth's writings on this subject and of discussions of them appears on pp. 367–8. A collection of essays on Gewirth's views is *Gewirth's ethical rationalism*, ed. E. Regis Jr. (Chicago University Press, Chicago, 1984). Gewirth's essay on the Golden Rule is cited in note 2.

15. A penetrating discussion is by Martin Scott-Taggart, 'Recent work on the philosophy of Kant', *American Philosophical Quarterly*, vol. 3 (1966), at pp. 198–200; cf. also pp. 194–8.

16. Nelson T. Potter and Mark Timmons (eds), *Morality and universality: essays on ethical universalizability* (Reidel, Dordrecht and Boston, 1985).

17. Very little if anything has yet been written on this matter, but the interested reader will find illumination as well as stimulation in A.W.B. Simpson, 'The *ratio decidendi* of a case and the doctrine of binding precedent', *Oxford essays in jurisprudence*, ed. A.G. Guest (Oxford University Press, Oxford, 1961), pp. 148–75; and in Rupert Cross, *Precedent in English law* (Clarendon Press, Oxford, 1961).

Bibliography

The Golden Rule

A list of discussions of the Golden Rule may be found appended to the article 'Golden Rule' in

[1] P. Edwards (ed.), *The encyclopedia of philosophy* (Collier-Macmillan, New York and London, 1967), vol. III, pp. 365–7.

Other more recent discussions of moment are

[2] H. Reiner, *Duty and inclination* (Nijhoff, The Hague and Boston, 1983), particularly pp. 271–93, 'The Golden Rule and natural law'.

[3] Hans-Ulrich Hoche, 'The Golden Rule: new aspects of an old moral principle' in *Contemporary German philosophy* (Pennsylvania State University Press, College Park, Pennsylvania, 1982), vol. I, pp. 69–90, and

[4] Alan Gewirth, 'The Golden Rule rationalized' in *Midwest studies in philosophy*, vol. III (1978), pp. 133–47.

Natural law

Good discussions of natural law, from differing points of view, may be found in

[5] A.P. d'Entreves, *Natural law*, 2nd edn (Hutchinson, London, 1964)

[6] J. Finnis, *Natural law and natural rights* (Oxford University Press, Oxford, 1980)

[7] L.L. Fuller, *The morality of law* (Yale University Press, New Haven and London, 1964) and

[8] H.L.A. Hart, *The concept of law* (Clarendon Press, Oxford, 1961).

See also Morris R. Cohen, 'Jus naturale redivivum', *Philosophical Review*, vol. 25 (1916), reprinted in

[9] M.R. Cohen, *Reason and nature* (Kegan Paul, London, 1931), Book III, Ch. 4.

Kant

The best introduction to Kant's ethics is

[10] H.J. Paton, *The Categorical Imperative* (Chicago University Press, Chicago, 1948).

Kant's own writings on moral philosophy are best approached by means of his *Groundwork of the metaphysic of morals*, the most accessible translation of which is available as

[11] I. Kant, *The moral law*, trans. H.J. Paton (Hutchinson, London, 1948). This work also contains useful commentary and notes.

Kant's examples in the above work have been much discussed, for instance, in

[12] J. Harrison, 'Kant's examples of the first formulation of the Categorical Imperative', *The Philosophical Quarterly*, vol. 7 (January 1957).

[13] J. Kemp, 'Kant's examples of the Categorical Imperative', *The Philosophical Quarterly*, vol. 8 (January 1958) and

[14] J. Harrison, 'The Categorical Imperative', *The Philosophical Quarterly*, vol. 8 (October 1958).

These three articles are collected together in

[15] R.P. Wolff (ed.), *Kant: a collection of critical essays* (Macmillan, London, 1968), which contains other interesting contributions.

[16] L.W. Beck, *A commentary on Kant's Critique of practical reason* (University of Chicago Press, Chicago, 1960) is an exceptionally lucid book on an often far from lucid text.

Utilitarianism

A discussion of utilitarianism, and a bibliography, can be found in Ch. 26 of the present volume.

The classic text, in which utilitarianism is explained, and defended against a variety of misunderstandings, is

[17] J.S. Mill, *Utilitarianism*, first published 1861 (Everyman edn, Dent, 1st edn, 1910).

Henry Sidgwick discusses the generalisation principle, which he calls the 'principle of justice', in

[18] H. Sidgwick, *The methods of ethics* (1st edn, 1874, 7th edn, Macmillan, London, 1906).

[19] D. Lyons, *The forms and limits of utilitarianism* (Oxford University Press, Oxford, 1965) is a detailed discussion of act and rule utilitarianism, which questions whether there is a genuine distinction at all.

Universalisability and the generalisation argument

Important contributions to the modern conception of universalisability can be found in the following:

[20] C.D. Broad, 'On the function of false hypotheses in ethics', *The International Journal of Ethics*, vol. 26 (April 1916), pp. 377–97

[21] R.F. Harrod, 'Utilitarianism revised', *Mind*, vol. 45 (April 1936), pp. 137–56.

[22] A.C. Ewing, 'What would happen if everybody acted like me?' *Philosophy*, vol. 28 (January 1953), pp. 16–29

[23] J. Harrison, 'Utilitarianism, universalisation, and our duty to be just', *Aristotelian Society Proceedings*, vol. 53 (1952–3), pp. 105–34

[24] A.K. Stout, 'But suppose everyone did the same', *The Australasian Journal of Philosophy*, vol. 32 (May 1954), pp. 1–29

[25] K. Baier, 'The point of view of morality', *The Australasian Journal of Philosophy*, vol. 32 (August 1954), pp. 104–35

[26] K. Baier, *The moral point of view: a rational basis of ethics* (Cornell University Press, Ithaca, 1958), Ch. 8

[27] E.A. Gellner, 'Ethics and logic', *Aristotelian Society Proceedings*, vol. 55 (1954–5), pp. 157–78

[28] E.A. Gellner, 'Morality and *je ne sais quoi* concepts', *Analysis*, vol. 16 (April 1956), pp. 97–103

[29] R.M. Hare, 'Universalisability', *Aristotelian Society Proceedings*, vol. 55 (1954–5), pp. 295–312.

Hare has written very extensively on the subject of universalisability: the two fullest treatments are

[30] R.M. Hare, *The language of morals* (Clarendon Press, Oxford, 1952, and Oxford University Press paperback, 1964) and

[31] R.M. Hare, *Freedom and reason* (Oxford University Press, Oxford, 1963).

A list of Hare's other writings on the topic can be found in the bibliography to Ch. 27.

[32] D.H. Monro, *Empiricism and ethics* (Cambridge University Press, Cambridge,

1967) contains, in Part III, pp. 137–234, an interesting discussion of the place of universalisability in ethics.

Other recent works covering various aspects of the subjects discussed in this chapter include:

[33] M.G. Singer, *Generalization in ethics* (Alfred A. Knopf, New York, 1961, Eyre and Spottiswoode, London, 1963).

[34] A. Gewirth, *Reason and morality* (Chicago University Press, Chicago, 1984)

[35] J. Rawls, *A theory of justice* (Oxford University Press, Oxford, 1972).

This bibliography has been compiled with the assistance of the author of the chapter.

M.A.P.

26 | *Utilitarianism*

T.L.S. Sprigge

A man may be said to be a partizan of the principle of utility, when the approbation or disapprobation he annexes to any action, or to any measure, is determined by and proportioned to the tendency which he conceives it to have to augment or diminish the happiness of the community: or in other words, to its conformity or nonconformity to the laws or dictates of utility. (*Introduction to the principles of morals and legislation* by Jeremy Bentham, 1789, Ch. 1, §9)

Bentham (1748–1832) can reasonably be regarded as *the founder of utilitarianism*, so we will start our account with him. Various thinkers before him had formulated something much the same as his principle of utility or greatest happiness principle and put it forward as the basis of ethics. He himself acknowledged Helvetius, Hutcheson and David Hume among other propounders of it. But no one before him had used the principle of utility so systematically as a fresh and fundamental basis for rethinking all moral and social matters and made of it a definite school of reformers and thinkers.

     Bentham is the outstanding figure in the background of a whole range of social, political and legal reforms which were carried out in Britain during the nineteenth century. Here, however, we are concerned with him not as a figure in history, responsible for various achievements, but with the content and value of the moral philosophy which lay behind them. This had two leading principles, a psychological thesis according to which every voluntary action is motivated by the thought that it will bring one more pleasure or less pain than any alternative, and an ethical or evaluative thesis according to which nothing is good in itself except pleasure or bad in itself except pain, and that acts are right or wrong, good or bad, according as to whether their overall tendency is to maximise pleasure and minimise pain among all those affected, or the converse. Or at least that will do as an initial formulation.

It is acceptance of the ethical and evaluative thesis that makes one a utilitarian. For Bentham this thesis ran in harness with the psychological thesis, but most subsequent utilitarians see the two as awkwardly paired. If everyone is, of psychological necessity, concerned only to maximise his own happiness (understood as a maximum of pleasure with a minimum of pain), what point is there in saying that what one ought to do is seek to maximise the universal happiness?

One reason why Bentham did not find any great clash between the two views was that he looked with little favour on the word *ought* and was therefore not primarily concerned even in his moral views with advocating a personal way of behaving. His view was that people will, in any situation, do what seems to them most likely to maximise their happiness, so that there is no point in moralists saying that they *ought* to do anything else. However, when they do act, we can try to decide whether their actions are good or bad ones, ones which are socially desirable or socially undesirable, as tending to promote or reduce the general happiness. While there is not much point in saying that those who acted badly *ought* to have acted well, there is point in deciding which sorts of actions are socially desirable and which not, and how society can best be organised to promote the former. The obvious question is: for whom is there point in this? One Benthamite answer is that there is such point for those who take personal pleasure in trying to build up a happy society. Another is that we all have some interest in society being thus organised, partly because we will stand to gain therefrom for the most part, partly because almost all of us do feel happier in a happier community and less happy in a predominantly wretched one.

But let us now consider the strictly ethical view, that is the very principle of utility. This sets out to tell us, with regard to an individual action, or a legislative enactment, whether it is right or wrong. Take two examples. (1) A son arranges for his almost senile mother to move from his home to an old person's home. Was his action good or bad? (2) Parliament enacts a law forbidding discrimination among applicants for a job on racial grounds. Was enactment of the law good or bad?

How are we supposed to go about answering such questions as 'partisans of the principle of utility'?

The essential answer is that we must consider its total tendency to promote happiness, on the one hand, and to promote unhappiness on the other, and judge which predominates. If the former does, then we say of the action

> that it is one that ought to be done, or at least that it is not one that ought not to be done; at least that it is not wrong that it should be done, that it is a right action; at least that it is not a wrong action. (*Principles*, Ch. 1, §10)

To clarify this, Bentham lists seven so-called dimen-

591

sions of pleasure and pain. These are (1) intensity; (2) duration; (3) certainty or uncertainty; (4) propinquity or remoteness; (5) fecundity; (6) purity; (7) extent.

How would these bear on the first of our questions? Well, consider intensity first. If we conceive of the least pleasant experience which is still a pleasure, then one way of quantifying intensity would be by characterising the number of times more pleasant a pleasure is at a particular moment than that. Perhaps the slightest pleasure of which I can conceive is that of sucking a boiled sweet. Then listening to Beethoven's Fifth Symphony, well performed, and when one is in the mood to enjoy it, might be – let us say (on the average, taken moment by moment) one thousand times more pleasurable. Similarly, we should evaluate pains as so many times worse than a minimal pain.

Now one of the pleasures caused by having the aged relative in a home might be that one could play the hi-fi very loudly, which all the household except the aged relative enjoyed. Let us say that the average intensity of this pleasure is 1,000 units. We now take the dimension of extent into account, by multiplying our thousand units of intensity by the number of suitably musical people in the house. If we can now form some idea of how often in the period of time in question they will enjoy that pleasure we can now multiply our figure again by the number of some suitable units of time representing the average total length of time for which each person will enjoy that pleasure on occasions which require the absence of the aged relative. Finally, suppose there is only a 3 in 4 chance of this being the result of the departure of the aged relative; then we multiply by $\frac{3}{4}$ in order to take account of the dimension of probability.

The same sort of calculation needs to be made of every pleasure and pain conceived as liable to occur as a result of the action. Then everything is added up and we get a balance in favour either of pleasure or pain, and thus an action which is either right or wrong.

A word must now be said about the dimensions which I ignored in the above 'calculation'. Purity, in Bentham's special sense, means the chance of a pleasure not leading to pains, or a pain not leading to pleasures, while the fecundity is the extent to which a pleasure breeds or leads to other pleasures or a pain to other pains. Bentham's idea is that we may know some pleasures or pain have a generally high or low degree of purity or fecundity without its being practicable on a particular occasion to specify and evaluate specifically the precise 'lots' of pleasure or pain they will produce. (If we could, they would simply come in as further pleasures and pains to be weighed in.) Thus the pleasures of heroin can be dismissed summarily as counting against, rather than for, the action of taking heroin, if we can say that it is a highly impure pleasure (liable to lead to much wretchedness later).

The most problematic of Bentham's dimensions is propinquity. It seems that he included this mainly because his theory of value was closely linked with his theory of motivation, and it is psychologically true that we are more influenced by thoughts of the more immediate than the more remote future. It seems better not to include it as a criterion of value, once it is clearly distinguished from probability.

We are not only to include pleasures and pains liable to be produced by an action in estimating its rightness or wrongness, but pleasures and pains liable to be prevented by it. Pains prevented, given a value in accordance with the same dimensions of intensity, duration, probability, extent count along with pleasures produced, in favour of an action, while pleasures prevented count along with the pains produced, against it. Many have thought it an objectionable feature of utilitarianism, in its classic formulations, that pleasure and pain are supposedly set off against each other in this simple way. The difficulties in accepting this seem particularly striking when pleasures and pains *prevented* come into account, for one might think preventing some particular suffering a good in a quite different way from that in which preventing some particular pleasure is bad. However, it has never proved an easy task to find an alternative approach. It will not do to adopt a so-called negative utilitarianism, once advocated by Karl Popper, for which all that matters is the prevention of pain, for that would seem to favour mass killing of all who feel any pain at all in their lives.

It is no real objection to Bentham that we can look for only an approximation to the truth. It would perhaps be an objection that there is no real truth there to be approximated to. There are at least two reasons for thinking this may be so. First, it appears that there may be no truth as to how many times more pleasant or painful one experience is than another. Secondly, probability judgements may not have the kind of truth they seem to need for Bentham. Moreover, there are difficulties in knowing how to relate various different sorts of probabilities, for example ones which relate to the likely truth of a judgement to ones which concern more objective statistical matters. There are, however, some indications that Bentham did not think there was some absolute truth to these matters, but that there was, so to speak, a vagueness in the very nature of these matters which, all the same, served to make some would-be precise statements more true than others, and that the element of free play here did not matter too much in practice. (For example, for most purposes it would not matter much if one pain is twice or thrice as bad as another, since either way the lesser is to be preferred.)

Sometimes Bentham, or if not Bentham then a still more perfect Benthamite, is thought of as holding a significantly different view from the one just described, according to which an action which it is right for me to do at any moment is either one which produces a greater surplus of pleasure over pain than any alternative available action (in which case it is the one right action) or produces as great a surplus as any alternative (in which case it is *a* right action), while all actions not thus right are wrong.

We may call this the *rigorist* interpretation or version of utilitarianism.

The requirement implied in this formulation that I am always morally obliged to do the best I can is accepted as reasonable by some commentators, while it is thought of as unreasonably demanding by others. Take, by way of example, a devoted nurse who is quite exceptionally sensitive to patients' needs. Her nursing activities would be right on the less rigoristic version of the Benthamite view we gave initially, for it does good by way of lessening pain and promoting pleasure and either does no harm at all, or none that is significant. However, on the second, more rigorist, view her action would turn out to be wrong, should it be true that with even more effort she could have relieved still more suffering, or caused just a little more happiness (without countervailing harm). This implication of rigorism seems a bit absurd.

It is sometimes thought that rigorism can take account of what troubles people here sufficiently by recognising that if we ask too much of ourselves we damage our power to do good by becoming worn out or embittered, as a nurse might do whose would-be heroism was taken too far. But it still remains problematic whether the utilitarian should condemn as wrong all actions which are not the very best, or at least equal best. In favour of rigorism, there is the apparent reasonableness of saying that if one fails to do all one can to promote happiness (and, in particular, to reduce suffering) one has not done the best one could do, and that must be wrong. To allow people to comfort themselves that less than the best (or equal best) is good enough is, it may be said, just a recipe for idle complacency. Against rigorism, is the sense that it is rather absurd to lump all who are not utilitarian saints with actual wrongdoers.

The debate between rigorism and our original less rigorist version of utilitarianism has a morally earnest character alien to Bentham. Still, if we try to pin him down we will find his actual formations are usually non-rigorist. As we have seen, he regards an action as right if its main tendency is to augment happiness, and wrong if its main tendency is the opposite. Undoubtedly, he would think an action the better the more it augmented happiness, but it seems that it is only wrong, for him, if it actually augments unhappiness.

However, there is one feature of his formulations which does seem to suggest the rigorist view. On the whole, he identifies the bad consequences of an action with pain caused, and the good consequences with pleasure caused. At times, however, he implies that the bad consequences of an action consist not just in pain, but also in loss of pleasure, and the good consequences of an action consist not just of pleasure, but of pain prevented (see *Principles*, Ch. 12, §15). It does seem, indeed, that he must intend something of the sort, for otherwise an action could not be counted as good simply because it prevented more pain than it caused. Thus a well-advised, but painful, piece of surgery might have to count as a wrong action

594

because what *actually* ensued (discounting the pain which would have been there without it) was more painful than pleasant, and this would be absurd. But if one is to count in as harm done by an action all the pleasure it prevented, it would seem that any action which was done when another which would have caused still more pleasure (without causing more pain) could have been done would be bad. But that amounts to rigorism.

It seems reasonable, however, to distinguish between two different types of thing which might or would have happened if the agent had not done an action. First, there are things which might or would have happened as consequences of some other action which he might have done instead. Secondly, there are things which would have occurred if he had not acted thus without being consequences of some alternative action of his. One can then say that it is only things of the second sort which count as things his action prevented, when one is calculating its good and bad effects. If this distinction can be sustained one can distinguish Bentham's criterion of rightness and wrongness from a rigorist one. It stands as the view that an action is wrong if its consequences, in terms of pain produced and pleasure prevented, outweigh its consequences in terms of pleasure produced and pain prevented, and that other actions are right, even if not the best possible.

This formulation still has an implication which one can be sure Bentham would have rejected. Suppose that the good consequences, in terms of pleasure produced and pain prevented by an act, outweigh its bad consequences, in terms of pain produced and pleasure prevented, but that a similar amount of good could have been achieved with less bad. For example, the surgeon callously made an operation more painful than it need have been, although it was still predominantly beneficial in its effects. Bentham would certainly have thought the action, taken as a whole, was wrong. He might, indeed, have said that it was only causing the extra pain that was wrong. However, if it was a whole operational procedure which was more painful than some alternative would have been, one can hardly regard causing the extra pain as a distinct action, but must regard it as a feature of the action as a whole.

I suggest that, in effect, Bentham's view was probably that a right action must not only do more good than harm, but that it must also be true that neither the particular good it does nor any other comparable good could have been achieved at less cost in terms of harm done.

That utilitarianism needs some such addition to be remotely acceptable and in the intended spirit of Bentham is beyond doubt. However, the addition is almost as problematic as it is important. Consider the dispute over fox hunting and suppose it agreed that the pleasure of men, hounds and perhaps horses outweighs the pain of the fox (and suppose that these are the only factors in question). Or consider, similarly, the cruelty of the Roman circus and suppose that there are enough happy spectators to outweigh the pain of the victims. Surely Bentham would want to say that they should have sought their pleasures in other ways which would, in fact, have been equivalent. It seems, therefore, that without returning on our tracks and urging the rigorist position (that one must always do as much good as possible), there must be some kind of requirement that one do as little harm as possible, in terms of actual pain (though not perhaps in terms of pleasure prevented) in order to achieve the amount of good one does.

This formulation still allows it to be a justifiable ground for causing pain that it will promote a 'greater' pleasure, when no equivalent pleasure can be obtained otherwise. One may well object to this, but I doubt whether one can do so on grounds which could be regarded as properly Benthamite.

I remarked above that it is often thought an objection to Benthamite utilitarianism that it combines the view that each man necessarily seeks to maximise his own happiness with the view that he ought to act so as maximise the general happiness.

A first thing to note in considering this is that Bentham urged emphatically that what makes an action right or wrong is not its motive, and that motives, as opposed to intentions, are best not distinguished into good and bad ones.

When someone does something we can ask: (1) what he actually did; (2) what he intended to do; (3) what his motive was. What he actually did was right or wrong according to the criteria we have discussed, while his intention was right or wrong according (to sum up Bentham's complex view very roughly) as to whether his action would have been right or wrong if things had turned out as he expected. His motive is the kind of pleasure for himself (or pain avoided) at which he was ultimately aiming. Bentham tries to show that on no useful classification of motives can one divide them into those which are always good or bad. Take, for example, the motive of becoming rich or winning admiration. These are neither good nor bad in themselves, they are simply normal bits of human psychology, operating more or less strongly in different people. The important thing for the legislator or social engineer is to create a society in which these motives will operate so as to generate good intentions, for, since by and large people achieve what they intend (or can be educated, without too much difficulty, to do so), producing good intentions will, in turn, commonly produce good actions, i.e. those which augment happiness. To regard motives as good or bad is idle; they are simply the raw material of human psychology with which the legislator or social engineer must deal.

But what part does the moralist, as opposed to the legislator or social engineer, play in Bentham's scheme? Curiously he comes out as another kind of social engineer who tries to show people that granted their fundamental motives (to obtain a range of pleasures and avoid a range of pains for themselves) they will do best to act rightly (in terms of the happiness of all in any way affected). But what if it is untrue that this is so? The answer

596

seems to be that here the moralist does his best to keep quiet on the matter while turning to the social engineer to modify the social situation so that 'moral goodness' becomes 'the best policy'.

It follows that much of what ordinarily counts as moral or ethical doctrine is simply absent from Bentham. People are what they are, but some acts are good, others bad, and legislators, reformers and 'moralists' should aim at organising society so that human beings as they really are find themselves in circumstances where they tend to do the former. This obviously poses the problem: what motivates the moralists, social engineers and legislators, who must be Bentham's main intended audience?

Bentham's views on this shifted. Originally he thought of his main audience as consisting in enlightened rulers who happened to have power and who, with sufficient for themselves already, sought their main further pleasure in seeking the happiness of their subjects. His mature view is of more interest to us today. It was something like this. We virtually all take some pleasure in the pleasure of others and find pain in their suffering. Where we are not dealing solely with our own affairs but forming preferences as to the general kind of society we would like to live in, the main pleasures and pain we are concerned with are precisely these pleasures and pains of sympathy. At that level, then, we do regard the social arrangements and the general customs of society from the point of view of, so to speak, benevolent part-time social engineers. Thus our views of public policy are, for the most part, those of social engineers who want actions which are right in a universalistic hedonistic sense to be promoted. If we live in a democracy which, thinking both selfishly and altruistically, is what most of us will want, we will support a structure of society for people in general which will make both them, and, when it comes to it, us, want to form good rather than bad intentions.

Though much subtler than is usually recognised, Bentham's views, even for those who sympathise with their main gist, have considerable defects. The next great utilitarian thinker was J.S. Mill (1806–73), whose father, James Mill, was a close reforming colleague of Bentham's, and who was brought up by the two of them to carry on their work. Mill attempted to improve on Bentham's utilitarianism in various ways.

Mill's initial statement of the principle of utility, or greatest happiness principle, is similar to Bentham's. The principle is that

actions are right in proportion as they tend to promote happiness, wrong as they tend to promote the reverse of happiness. By happiness is intended pleasure, and the absence of pain, by unhappiness, pain and the privation of pleasure. (*Utilitarianism*, Ch. 1)

The first apparently big difference between them is that Mill says that quality of pleasure counts as well as quantity.

597

It is quite compatible with the principle of utility to recognise the fact, that some *kinds* of pleasure are more desirable and more valuable than others. It would be absurd that while, in estimating all other things, quality is considered as well as quantity, the estimation of pleasure should be supposed to depend on quantity alone. (*Utilitarianism*, Ch. 1)

Suppose that one is choosing between two actions, both of which produce either no pain or the same amount, while one produces *more* pleasure. Bentham would say that the one which produces more pleasure is the better action, but Mill would say that it need not be, if the quality of the pleasure which is lesser in amount is sufficiently much higher. It is true that, if we take Bentham and Mill in a non-rigorist way, then each action, since it produces more good than harm, is a right action, but the better action will still be the one which promotes happiness to the greater extent, and the difference is as to whether this is a purely quantitative matter. A decision on this matter will also sometimes affect decisions as to whether actions are right or wrong, when the pleasures prevented are weighed in the balance in determining this.

Incidentally, Mill does not discuss whether pains as well as pleasures differ in quality in an ethically significant way. It seems likely he would have said they did. He might, for example (having been somewhat high-minded) have thought of the distress of a guilty conscience as worse than a quantitatively equal amount of physical pain. If so, an immense difference would arise in decisions on right and wrong between Bentham and Mill.

So it would seem, at least. Yet there is some difficulty in knowing whether Mill really meant to say anything very different from Bentham. If one takes 'amount' as referring to duration and extent (number of people affected), perhaps together with probability and proximity, Bentham certainly does not think that all that matters is amount, since this would be to forget intensity, which seems to mean simply the extent to which it is actually liked moment by moment. (It certainly does not mean any kind of degree of physical excitement.) Similarly, when Mill tries to explain how we can decide which is qualitatively the better of two pleasures, his actual answer is more or less that the higher pleasure is the one which is actually more liked by those in a position to compare them. So it may well be that there is no real difference between Mill and Bentham here.

However, Mill is usually understood as holding that there may be two pleasures, of equal duration, etc., such that one is the pleasanter, but the other the better, in virtue of its higher quality, and that it is morally more important to promote the latter than the former. Generations of philosophers, most notably F.H. Bradley and G.E. Moore, have said that this is to abandon ethical hedonism, in a way which is quite inconsistent with Mill's avowed intentions. If one experience can be better than

598

another without being pleasanter, does it not follow that there is something determining value besides pleasure? This does seem a fairly devasting criticism of such a position.

But Mill may have meant something rather different, namely that, although all pleasures are, in themselves and apart from their effects, good, and all pains, with a similar qualification, bad, they are pleasant and painful, and hence possessed of value or disvalue, in incommensurable ways. Thus in choosing between two alternative sets of pleasure one cannot necessarily decide which is preferable by an arithmetical calculation, nor could one necessarily do so even if one was omniscient.

It is crucial to Bentham's strict doctrine that if one considers two pleasures, the one is a definite number of times more pleasurable moment by moment, on the average, than the other, in terms of some possible unit of measurement. Thus the average momentary pleasure of hearing *Parsifal* on a certain occasion must be a definite number of times more or less pleasant than that of a particular episode of sucking a boiled sweet. This does seem rather ridiculous. Maybe what Mill was getting at was that one might want to say that the experience of hearing *Parsifal* was more pleasant, was a greater pleasure, but that we must describe this as its being of better quality rather than quantity, since measurement is out of the question. That this represents an advance on a strictly quantitative hedonism may be brought out by the following thought experiment.

Suppose that we identify or biological engineers construct a slug-like creature which, throughout its life, experiences a low level of pleasure consisting in an inarticulate feeling of humdrum comfort. Suppose also that it is somehow possible to place it in a space capsule in which it can survive, so far as can be seen, for ever, without any external aid. To construct this capsule is, however, immensely expensive. Suppose, next, that a catastrophe, which will wipe out life on this planet, threatens, and can only be prevented by an expenditure the same as would be needed for that capsule for the slug. A utilitarian dictator can either spend the resources he has at his disposal for developing the slug capsule or on saving life on this earth. He is a Benthamite and he reasons as follows. If I save life on this planet, it will be saved for only ten thousand years. (Let us take it that he is right in this.) If I let life on this planet die out and send the slug into space, then, since it will exist for ever, the quantity of pleasure it will enjoy will eventually outweigh all the pleasures enjoyed on this earth for ten thousand years.

This would be the only possible course for a strict Benthamite. Even if life on this planet were, for the next ten thousand years, to be pretty joyful, on the whole, the infinite number of low-level moments of slug pleasure will be more valuable. If the idea of infinite continuance is too suspect, it must remain true that there is some number of moments of slug pleasure which would outweigh any finite amount of joy on the earth, since every finite quantity is outweighed by another.

599

So perhaps Mill's claim is that the pleasurableness of life is all that matters but that this cannot always be so well promoted by increasing the quantity of low-level pleasure as by obtaining lesser amounts of high-quality pleasure. Doubtless this means the end of straight arithmetical calculation, but it may still make sense to speak of informed judgements as to which patterns of pleasurable experience form more pleasurable lives.

A final point about Mill is that he put an immense emphasis upon the value of personal freedom which is absent from Bentham. There is a modern classic, by the behaviourist psychologist B.F. Skinner, called *Walden Two*, describing an ideal community in which people have been conditioned by behavioural psychology to act in ways richly promotive of communal harmony and happiness. This is just what Bentham hoped to see done by reforms deriving from his ideas. To Mill, at least at times, any such idea was most unattractive, and personal autonomy is almost the most important goal for men. He attempted to derive his high valuation of autonomy from a purely utilitarian concern for happiness, though here again he is charged with not sticking strictly to utilitarianism.

The next major figure in the history of utilitarian ethics is the moral philosopher and economist Henry Sidgwick. His somewhat laboured *The methods of ethics*, first published in 1874, makes some substantial advances on Bentham and Mill.

One advance is the much firmer distinction between psychological hedonism and the utilitarian doctrine of right and wrong. Sidgwick rejects the former and endorses the latter. A reason for rejecting the psychological view is one that had been especially insisted on by the eighteenth-century moral philosopher and theologian Joseph Butler, namely that most pleasures occur only because the desire for something other than pleasure is satisfied, so that the very existence of these pleasures shows that people can desire things other than pleasure. (People typically get pleasure from fame because they want it; they do not typically desire fame for the pleasure it will bring.)

For Sidgwick the goal of theoretical ethics is to decide what ultimately makes conduct right or reasonable, whether the conduct be considered as right in itself, or as the means to some ultimately reasonable end (*Methods of ethics*, p. 77). He claims that in the thought of ordinary men, as also in that of philosophers who have thought systematically about ethics, there are just three main methods to which appeal is made in deciding what sort of conduct is right or reasonable. The first is *egoistic hedonism*. It is widely thought that the reasonable thing for any man to do at any moment is what presents itself after appropriate inquiry as most likely to help increase his own happiness. The second is the method he calls *intuition*, according to which we have rational insight into the rightness or wrongness of various classes of action, an insight which, since a genuine rationality cannot be a merely private possession, must be the morality of civilised common sense. The third is the *utilitarian method*, according to which the only finally satisfactory method of deciding what it is right or rational to do is that of settling what will most advance the general happiness.

An elaborate inquiry leads him to two main conclusions:

(1) The egoistic method and the utilitarian method both rest on objective truth as to what is reasonable, though on the face of it they are in irreconcilable conflict with one another;

(2) the intuitional method is only acceptable as a decision method which works by and large as a guide to utilitarian truth, and not as a genuinely alternative rational method.

Let us examine his second conclusion first. If there is a system of objective moral truths about right and wrong conduct, self-evident in the sense that they are discernible by reflective reason as valid in themselves and not merely as derivative from utilitarian considerations (or any other kind of more ultimate support, if there could be such), one would expect to find its basic elements incorporated into the morality of civilised common sense. However, the rules of common-sense morality (apart from ones which reduce directly to utilitarianism) lack the features which such self-evident truths would have, for example (1) being expressible in clear and precise terms; (2) being evidently distinguishable from propositions which represent either mere first impressions of a matter or from customs of the tribe; (3) mutual consistency. On the other hand, if one interprets them as having evolved as generally, but not universally, acceptable guides to the kind of conduct which best promotes the general happiness, clashes between which are to be resolved by an appeal to utility, they appear largely sound. It follows that the intuitional method of ethics is acceptable only as a decision method which works by and large as a guide to utilitarian truth, and not as a genuinely alternative method.

This leaves only egoism and utilitarianism standing. Sidgwick thinks that a reflective person will find himself unable to resist the conviction that each specifies a genuine directive of reason, in spite of their apparent incompatibility. Since their inconsistency was one of the reasons for rejecting any claim for such a status on behalf of the principles of common-sense morality, this is rather puzzling. I suppose he thinks that the principles of common sense purport to be a consistent system representing a single method, whereas egoism and utilitarianism represent themselves as alternatives which, at least taken individually, are satisfactory. Still, Sidgwick's position remains somewhat odd.

He thinks that the two methods would be reconciled if there were known to be a divine government of the world which ensures that performance of utilitarian duty will ultimately be in one's best personal interests. He doubts, however, whether we can reasonably assume the existence of God simply to resolve this problem in rational ethics. Anyway, as F.H. Bradley pointed out, even if there is the required divine government of the world, it offers only a *de facto* reconciliation and cannot really harmonise the principles logically.

Still, to Sidgwick it seems undeniably against reason knowingly to do what will be for one's own long-term harm (or even for one's less than maximum benefit) and also against reason knowingly to do what will be for the long-term harm of sentient life at large (or even for its less than maximal benefit). These are both things which it seems plain one *ought* not to do. Perhaps one only naturally talks of an ethical *ought* in the second case, but both are equally directives of reason.

Thus although Sidgwick has freed himself from the problem which arises in the thought of Bentham and Mill as to how the *ought* of utilitarianism is to be reconciled with their egoistic and hedonistic psychology, he has his own problem as to how it is to be reconciled with the egoistic *ought* of personal prudence. Subsequent utilitarian thinkers have usually disembarrassed themselves of any such difficulties by rejecting both sorts of egoism.

There is another matter which does still greatly puzzle utilitarian thinkers on which Sidgwick seems to have been the first to touch. Is the utilitarian goal the maximisation of total or of average welfare? Having raised the question Sidgwick settles without much ado for total welfare (see *Methods of ethics*, p. 415). This has the implication that it is better to produce a sufficiently large population with low average happiness than a smaller one with a high average happiness, since that way (with a sufficiently large population) the 'amount' of happiness will be larger. Indeed, so long as total pleasure just outweighs total pain an ever-increasing population is likely to be a more effective way of increasing happiness than making life better for each individual. It has often been contended since that this implication is absurd and that therefore the goal should be the increase of average happiness. However, this suggests that it might be a good thing to prevent anyone being born who would be less than maximally happy (on average, throughout his life) since he would be lowering the average happiness by his existence. This seems even more paradoxical.

There are quite genuine problems here as to how the utilitarian should view large-scale government policies affecting size of population. However, if our policies once allow for the possibility of the human race existing for ever or into the quite indefinite future one can take average happiness over all future time as the effective goal, even from the totalistic point of view, since the contribution to quantity of happiness from population size will anyway be maximal. Many attempts have been made to find a version of utilitarianism which avoids the oddities of either straight totalistic utilitarianism and straight average utilitarianism, but none seems to be really satisfactory.

The issue is somewhat similar to that concerning quality as opposed to quantity of pleasure. Both turn on the oddity of a purely arithmetical approach to the idea of promoting happiness. Sidgwick, it should be noted, regarded Mill's attempt to introduce quality as well as quantity of pleasure into utilitarianism as inconsistent with his hedonism: if less pleasure can be of more value than more pleasure, the extra value must be contributed by something other than pleasure. This criticism has been widely supported, but we have seen that it is hardly decisive. Surely the more pleasurable life is not necessarily the one which gains the highest marks when pleasures, evaluated in isolation, tot up to the highest figure.

Another suggestion of Sidgwick's still inspires lively debate. May it sometimes be better, from a utilitarian point of view, that people should not think as utilitarians? Perhaps it is best for the general happiness that people should believe that a certain obligation to keep promises holds independently of its effects on happiness. Sidgwick even floats the idea that the person who sees the truth of utilitarianism might, as a utilitarian, think it best to keep some aspects of his doctrine secret. Rather similar to this apparent endorsement of insincerity is the distinction he draws between qualities of character the praise of which is useful, and qualities of character which are useful themselves. Only the first is praiseworthy for the utilitarian, since praise is essentially itself an act to be judged as good or harmful. Thus we should praise only conduct which needs to be stimulated in this way, even though other (perhaps more selfish) conduct which will be done anyway is itself good or better. For Sidgwick and for some modern utilitarians (for example, J.J.C. Smart) recognition of this helps remove elements of conflict between utilitarianism and ordinary moral common sense, but for others it is a symptom of a kind of bad faith which is endemic to utilitarianism.

Finally, it is to be noted that Sidgwick holds that a kind of intuition, not capable of empirical or discursive proof, is at the root of utilitarianism, that although what we ought to do is to maximise the surplus of pleasure over pain, the concept of 'ought' cannot itself be defined in terms of pleasure. Thus although Sidgwick rejects the intuitionism which takes common-sense morality as resting upon a kind of intellectual intuition of right and wrong, he does think that utilitarianism itself rests upon such an intuition. Thus he saves himself beyond dispute from the 'naturalistic fallacy', the fallacy which, since publication of G.E. Moore's *Principia ethica* in 1903, many have thought was committed by Bentham and Mill. This is the fallacy supposedly committed by anyone who presents a moral judgement as though it were simply a clarification of the meaning of key ethical words, such as 'good', 'bad', 'right' and 'wrong'.

A chief argument given for identifying this as a fallacy is that if this was all that the words mean, the moral judgement which is being put forward would be no more than an idle tautology. Thus if calling an action 'wrong' simply means that it produces more pain than pleasure, saying that it is wrong to produce more pain than pleasure is simply saying that to do so is to produce more pain than pleasure. (This is a point already made by Sidgwick himself.) For Moore and other non-naturalist moral philosophers this shows that basic ethical truths concern unique non-natural qualities or relations and are known by a kind of intellectual intuition. Since Sidgwick's position amounts to the claim that *ought* is a non-natural relation and that we can know by a fundamental intuition that we stand in it to actions which maximise happiness, he is a non-naturalist in this sense.

Such an appeal to intuition is uncongenial to most supporters of utilitarianism. We can find the beginnings of an alternative answer to the charge of the naturalistic fallacy in Bentham who contends, in effect, that ethical words serve to pick out actions for approval or disapproval and that guidance of our approval and disapproval by the principle of utility is the only serious option on which people can be expected to agree. It is less clear how Mill would have answered the charge.

Although Moore thought that one could not define an ethical concept in terms of merely 'natural' concepts (such as effects on happiness) he did not, in fact, think that the concept of *ought* was indefinable. In his opinion the fundamental indefinable concepts of ethics are *intrinsically good* and *intrinsically bad*. To say that one ought to do something is to say that it will produce *intrinsically better* results than any alternative action (this being determined by the intrinsic good and bad in each case).

The theory of ethics which Moore elaborated upon this basis is often known as 'ideal utilitarianism'. It shares with traditional utilitarianism (understood in a rigorist way) the view that the right action is the action which will have the best results. However, for ideal utilitarianism many quite different sorts of thing can be intrinsically good (or bad). The view that all good things must have some empirically ascertainable feature in common, such as being pleasurable, is a prejudice from which we naturally shake ourselves free once we realise that 'good' does not stand for any empirically ascertainable property. In fact, according to Moore, the chief goods (that is things possessing the non-natural quality of goodness) are personal affection and the contemplation of beautiful objects. Pleasure is an element in these good things, but they are not good simply in virtue of their pleasantness, and some experiences (such as those of malice) are the worse for being pleasurable. Pleasure merely in itself is at best a very minor good, though pain, in contrast, is a considerable evil.

The practical upshot of ideal utilitarianism has a good deal in common with Mill's qualitative utilitarianism. However, they differ in their intellectual foundations. Besides, Moore held the fairly unusual opinion that states of affairs not involving sentient life at all (such as unobserved beauties in nature) could have at least a low level of intrinsic goodness, something Mill would not have allowed.

Ironically, Moore himself has been charged with

something like the naturalistic fallacy in his definition of *ought*. There is a basic divergence between teleological views of ethics for which results alone determine right and wrong, and deontological ethics for which there are duties with a degree of bindingness independent of the results of fulfilling them, and Moore supports the former by appeal to a mere verbal definition.

Moore's ideal utilitarianism stands somewhat apart from the main stream of utilitarian thinking. Let us look now very briefly at the course this main stream has taken in the last few decades. Utilitarianism has several times been pronounced dead or moribund in this century, but in fact there has been so much subtle utilitarian thinking in recent times that we cannot do more than cast a glance at some of it.

Some modern utilitarian thinkers have recognised the need to relate their utilitarianism to some so-called meta-ethical theory as to what is going on when one supports an ethical position. Most now would be disinclined to appeal to an intuition of supposed objective ethical truth, as did Sidgwick. One common view is that ethical propositions do not say something which can be either true or false in the sense of reporting or misreporting how things really are in some realm of values (though we can reasonably call them 'true' or 'false' to signal our agreement or disagreement with them). Rather, they express some 'attitude' of the speaker, such as some ultimate preference as to how we should behave or society be organised, and invite the hearer's adoption of the same attitude.

A utilitarian who holds this 'attitudinist' meta-ethical view will see utilitarianism as the expression of a fundamental attitude in favour of a certain way of reaching decisions. He will not suppose that there is any possibility of proving that the principle of utility is *true* in any strong sense, but will put it forward as a guide to life which he endorses and, as a philosopher, seeks to make precise and free of confusion. He will probably think, what is more, that there are features of human nature which make it likely that most other people who have properly understood what is at issue, and who are free from the influence of various confusions and false beliefs, will come to share the attitude it expresses. A philosopher who has advocated utilitarianism in this spirit is J.J.C. Smart.

A form of attitudinism which has been worked out with especial thoroughness is the prescriptivism of R.M. Hare. For him, the essential meaning of the key ethical terms lies in two features, universalisability and prescriptiveness. To say that they are prescriptive is to say that their role is to prescribe (which means much the same as recommend) some particular sort of conduct. Thus they cannot be true or false in a basic way, any more than a command can be. However, ethical words are also universalisable. It is linguistically unacceptable to apply them except on grounds which would always lead to further application of them in all similar cases. It follows that I am not using language properly if I say you ought to do something, unless I hold by some universal principle from which this prescription follows and all other implications of which I would be prepared to endorse, most notably those which would prescribe under certain circumstances that I do something.

When he first put forward the view he largely went along with the view of most attitudinists that understanding the meaning of ethical language had no definite implications as to what moral views one should take. But in successive writings Hare has gradually worked around to seeing the account of the very meaning of ethical language which he regards as correct as offering a kind of proof of utilitarianism.

In virtue of their universalisability I misuse the word 'ought' and related words, if I say things about what people ought to do when I do not endorse any universal rule from which it could be drawn. If, on reflection, I cannot accept any such universal rule as can be supposed to be playing this role I am misrepresenting myself in my statement about what people ought to do.

Suppose now I say that 'Arabs ought not to have jobs in British firms' and this is my universal principle. Do I really accept the implication that if I were an Arab I should not be given such a job? Do I really prescribe myself being rejected for such a job if I should be an Arab? (Hare thinks you can reasonably be asked what you prescribe for unactual cases like that of your being of another nation, sex, or perhaps even species.) Probably I will not.

Hare argues elaborately that one cannot (if one really thinks it through) accept the total set of prescriptions implied by any universal ethical rules except those which attach weight, in proportion to their strength, to the desirability of satisfying the desires which everyone affected by an action would have if they possessed proper prudence. This is because I can always ask, 'Would I still prescribe that action if it was I who had that desire?' The idea is that I do not really accept a universal rule unless an imaginative attempt to put myself in the place of everyone who could conceivably be affected in any way by actions of which it might prescribe the performance would leave me still happy with it. Only so do I accept in each case the prescription that the action would remain one which should be done if it was I rather than someone else who was in a situation to be affected by it in that way.

The upshot is a version of what is known as 'preference utilitarianism', which is often thought of as having superseded the older hedonistic utilitarianism of Bentham, Mill and Sidgwick.

For preference utilitarianism what counts in favour of an act is not that it promotes a kind of experience known as pleasure or prevents a kind of experience called pain, but that it provides people with what they would prefer to have and prevents their having what they would prefer not to have. The following are the main points supposed to favour preference over hedonistic utilitarianism.

606

(1) The fact that someone prefers X to Y, as shown in their behaviour, is empirically ascertainable in a way in which the greater intensity or duration, or even very existence, of a private feeling of pleasure or pain is not. It is also supposed that comparisons between welfare gained or lost for different people are, though still difficult, less intractably so, if what is in question are not qualities of feeling but the satisfactions of behaviourally manifested preferences. (2) Then again it is regarded as doubtful whether there really is a specific quality of pleasure, and even of pain, which covers all experiences that people either want to have or avoid, and it is thought obviously desirable that people should have experiences they want rather than those with a certain quality. (3) Even if the nature of these qualities of pleasure and pain are themselves unproblematic, it is said that what people want (or want to avoid) is not necessarily any kind of private experience, but, at least often, objective states of affairs in the public world, and it is thought no less reasonable to take account of wants of this sort than those for private experiences.

To me these supposed advantages of preference utilitarianism seem spurious.

(1) Doubtless a person's behaviour in choosing between alternatives is observable in a way in which his felt satisfaction or dissatisfaction is not. However, if preferences are understood merely as patterns of physical behaviour which tend towards certain results, then there would be no more of a moral reason for satisfying them than for assisting a computer to carry out its programme when this was something undesired by any conscious being. Only if it is taken for granted that the preference behaviour is that of a conscious subject does it, of itself, provide a reason for promoting the preferred end – it would not matter in the least if there was no conscious individual there to mind about anything. But once it is granted we have an adequate ground for interpreting their preferences as those of conscious beings, it is not clear why it should be denied that we have adequate clues as to whether they have pleasant or unpleasant experiences under various circumstances and for some judgement as to the degree of the pleasure or pain involved such as allow interpersonal comparisons.

(2) The denial that there is some one and the same quality of pleasantness and another of painfulness which mark all those experiences which it is properly thought of as desirable to promote or prevent is a more forceful objection to Benthamite utilitarianism. Preference utilitarianism is right to try to get away from this idea. It risks, however, giving the impression that what matters is not the quality of life as we each experience it in our individual consciousness, but simply what takes place in some objective world – which is surely a betrayal of the whole point of utilitarianism. Mill's qualitative utilitarianism can be understood as providing a better alternative to any view that pleasure and pain are simply some kind of uniform sensation of which we want, respectively, as much and as

little as possible. We can recognise that pleasures are of radically different kinds, some of them consisting in energetic activities as experienced from within, others in more passive conscious states, each being a specifically different form of the genus pleasure. If I sometimes like listening to music and at other times going swimming, it is not because there is some one qualitatively unvarying sensation by which I have found that they are both usually accompanied. They are both pleasures, but pleasures of quite different sorts. They are distinct species of a common genus, pleasure, rather as the different shades of colour are distinct species of a common genus, colour, without colour being some distinguishable extra quality which accompanies them. (This seems a better version of qualitative utilitarianism than the view often mooted that pleasures have nothing in common but for being objects of pursuit, which hardly does justice to the fact that the worthwhileness of pleasures lies within them. Besides, some pleasures come spontaneously and unpursued.)

(3) The third consideration supposedly favouring preference utilitarianism was that we may desire things other than experiences for ourselves. Once we reject psychological egoistic hedonism we have virtually admitted this fact. I may prefer that people should not be malicious about me behind my back, even if I am not to know of it, or be indirectly affected by it, and that certain deathbed wishes of mine be carried out without supposing I will persist to be affected by them. Moreover, I have preferences regarding the happiness of others which are not concerned with them merely as means to certain feelings for myself.

If preference utilitarianism is to go all the way with the idea that preferences always give a ground for satisfying them then we must say not just what we should aim at people in some sense *having* as much as possible of what they prefer to have but that as much as possible of what they would like to have happen should happen. One difficulty in this is that someone with very strong preferences about what happens beyond his own person seems, on this view, to acquire a power of attaching importance to something being done or not being done, even if his preferences concern matters which really have little in any ordinary sense to do with him. Indeed, this influence can extend beyond the grave, when he will not even know (let us assume) whether things are working out as he preferred.

Another variant of utilitarianism which commanded a good deal of support in fairly recent times was *rule* as opposed to *act* utilitarianism. For the traditional 'act' utilitarianism the right act is that which maximises welfare (or something of that sort, perhaps less *rigorist*) while for rule utilitarianism rules are to be regarded as morally binding because general adherence to them maximises, or would maximise, welfare, individual acts being right or wrong in virtue of their conformity to such rules. Rules are, indeed, important for act utilitarianism, too, and not only as rules of thumb, but rather as felicific habits; still, the effects on people's inclination to stick with generally felicific rules remains a consequence of the individual acts to be weighed along with all of its other consequences. For rule utilitarianism, in contrast, once a rule is shown to be felicific, it is established as something to be obeyed, unless perhaps in very special cases, and is not to be considered merely as one factor to be weighed against others. Thus, granted institution of a rule against murder is in general felicific, we should abide by it even when individual calculation of the results of a particular murder might show it to be beneficent. Rule utilitarianism is often advocated on grounds of fairness as necessary to counter the excuses of the 'free rider' who does not bother to stick to a moral rule because enough others are doing so to produce its benefits.

The usual objection to rule utilitarianism is that if the sole point of the rule is to promote happiness it seems only sensible to jettison it when more happiness is gained thereby. On the face of it, this criticism carries the day against any rule utilitarianism which is genuinely distinguishable from act utilitarianism. The issue is complicated, however, by the variety of forms which rule utilitarianism can take.

Utilitarianism, in general, has been both vigorously defended and attacked in the last few decades. I must pass over the continuing debate, already initiated by Mill in Chapter 5 of his *Utilitarianism*, as to whether utilitarianism can, so to speak, do justice to justice, a point particularly made against it by modern proponents of rights theory. For the utilitarian, what is described as a just organisation of things is seen as one particular way of maximising welfare, an account rights theorists think inadequate. We must, however, note one important line of criticism levelled against it in recent literature, one which is especially associated with Bernard Williams. Utilitarianism, he suggests, ignores the real significance which life has for mature human beings.

For each of us our lives are given sense by certain projects, whether it be that of being a certain sort of person, achieving something in such fields as the political, or cultural, or in our personal relations. For the person with these projects the forwarding of them has an importance to which utilitarianism cannot do justice, for it must regard them simply among the many preferences of which as many as possible are to be satisfied. In a sense the real utilitarian has only one project he takes seriously, the satisfaction of preferences, desires, whatever they are for, or, in the older version, the maximisation of happiness. Yet if one's life has significance for one, one cannot simply throw one's own most serious projects into the melting pot of desires and preferences along with everyone else's.

Suppose that I am committed to an ideal of conserving areas of natural beauty or variegated wildlife in my country. If I am serious, I cannot simply see the preservation of the countryside as a desire of a few people like myself, to be weighed in the balance against the desires of others for holidays abroad, when it comes to deciding on whether a new airport should be built in some place of outstanding beauty.

609

A similar objection to utilitarianism urged by Williams, Alasdair MacIntyre and others is that utilitarianism goes with a manipulative approach to human life. It is said to be the philosophy of government administrators, dangerous in their hands, corrupting when treated as the basis of private morality. Then it is also objected that utilitarian thinking, which has reached its apotheosis in modern cost/benefit analysis, regards all values as commensurable, and therefore (like the Anglo–Saxons with their system of *wergild*) thinks of every harm as something which can be compensated, reaching, it is felt, particularly repellent extremes when the value of a human life is calculated as something to be set against the goods achieved by a motorway or by economy in safety precautions at a factory.

These objections deserve to be taken seriously. However, the suspicion may be felt that the following remark of Bentham's still applies.

When a man attempts to combat the principle of utility, it is with reasons drawn, without his being aware of it, from that very principle itself. His arguments, if they prove anything, prove not that the principle is *wrong*, but that, according to the applications he supposes to be made of it, it is *misapplied*. (*Principles*, Ch. 1, §13)

Bibliography

Classical utilitarianism

The classical texts of utilitarianism are Jeremy Bentham's *Introduction to the principles of morals and legislation* (London, 1789), John Stuart Mill's *On liberty* (London, 1859) and Mill's *Utilitarianism* (London, 1861). The two Mill works complete and the first five chapters of Bentham are collected together in

[1] M. Warnock (ed.), *Utilitarianism* (Fontana/Collins, London, 1962).

[2] H. Sidgwick, *The methods of ethics* (Macmillan, London, 1874, later editions incorporate additions) is the fullest elaboration of classical utilitarianism.

[3] F.Y. Edgworth, *Mathematical psychics* (London, 1883, reprinted, London School of Economics, London, 1932) is an intriguing early attempt by an economist to treat pleasure and pain in a quantitative fashion.

[4] G.E. Moore, *Principia ethica* (Cambridge University Press, Cambridge, 1903) presents Moore's own 'ideal utilitarianism' and provides a classic critique of hedonistic utilitarianism.

Contemporary utilitarianism

Contemporary defences of various different kinds of utilitarianism can be found in

[5] J.J.C. Smart, *An outline of a system of utilitarian ethics* (1963) in [19],

[6] R.B. Edwards, *Pleasures and pains: a theory of qualitative utilitarianism* (Cornell University Press, Ithaca, 1979) and

[7] R.M. Hare, *Moral thinking* (Clarendon Press, Oxford, 1981).

Critics of utilitarianism

Works which are, or contain, strong criticisms of any kind of utilitarianism include

[8] F.H. Bradley, *Ethical studies* (Clarendon Press, Oxford, 1876) – the second edition, 1927, contained important additions,

[9] W.D. Ross, *The foundations of ethics* (Clarendon Press, Oxford, 1939) and

[10] B.A.O. Williams, *Ethics and the limits of philosophy* (Fontana/Collins, London, 1985).

Discussions of utilitarians and utilitarianism

[11] R. Harrison, *Bentham* (Routledge and Kegan Paul, London, 1983) is particularly good for understanding how Bentham saw the relation between the work of the political thinker and of the moralist.

[12] A. Ryan, *The philosophy of J.S. Mill* (Macmillan, London, 1970).

[13] A. Quinton, *Utilitarian ethics* (Macmillan, London, 1973) is a clear survey of the major works and issues.

Problems and applications

[14] D. Lyons, *The forms and limits of utilitarianism* (Oxford University Press, Oxford, 1965) is an admirable discussion of the relationship between act and rule utilitarianism, and asks if there is, in fact, any genuine distinction between them.

[15] S. Scheffler, *The rejection of consequentialism* (Clarendon Press, Oxford, 1982) bears on the contrast between a rigorist and a non-rigorist utilitarianism.

[16] D. Parfit, *Reasons and persons* (Oxford University Press, Oxford, 1984) is a richly imaginative application of an essentially utilitarian ethic to metaphysical considerations about the nature of selfhood.

A vigorous application of utilitarianism to a range of contemporary issues can be found in

[17] P. Singer, *Practical ethics* (Cambridge University Press, Cambridge, 1979), and an admirably clear and lucid treatment of abortion, euthanasia, war and other life or death issues is

[18] J.C.B. Glover, *Causing death and saving lives* (Penguin Books, Harmondsworth, 1979).

Collections

[19] J.J.C. Smart and B.A.O. Williams, *Utilitarianism: for and against* (Cambridge University Press, Cambridge, 1973) consists of [5] above, together with 'A critique of utilitarianism' by Williams

[20] M. Bayles (ed.), *Contemporary utilitarianism* (Doubleday Anchor, New York, 1968)

[21] M. Bayles (ed.), *Ethics and population* (Schenkman, Cambridge, Massachusetts, 1976)

[22] A.K. Sen and B.A.O. Williams (eds), *Utilitarianism and beyond* (Cambridge University Press, Cambridge, 1982).

Utilitarianism

The collections listed contain defences and elaborations of and attacks on utilitarianism, and are especially useful for studying the relations between act and rule utilitarianism and hedonistic and preference utilitarianism.

This bibliography has been produced in collaboration with the author of the chapter, Professor Timothy Sprigge.

M.A.P.

27 | Emotivism and Prescriptivism

Stavroula Tsinorema

Emotivism

Emotivism appeared on the scene of British moral philosophy as a reaction to ethical intuitionism. Intuitionism, as advocated by G.E. Moore, H.A. Pritchard and W.D. Ross,[1] was, like the naturalism it rejected, itself a cognitivist theory of ethics, though of a special kind. Dominated by the referential theory of meaning according to which a piece of language means what it refers to, it held that moral terms refer to moral properties, except that these are not natural ones like redness but 'non-natural', perceived not by the physical senses but through a special faculty of moral intuition. Moral judgements were thus taken to be essentially informative, like all descriptive statements, designating facts, albeit of a special, non-natural kind. The emotivists broke sharply with this basic intuitionist assumption. They were the first analytical philosophers to argue that moral judgements are not fact-stating or descriptive, at least not primarily or exclusively so. Like the intuitionists, they rejected all naturalist definitions of 'good' and recognised the existence of a logical gap between 'is' and 'ought'. But, unlike the intuitionists, they held that the logical gap does not divide two kinds of property (moral and non-moral) but separates one use to which language can be put (description) from another use (evaluation).

Emotivism embraces a number of different views. A form of it appeared first in Sweden, in the writings of Axel Hägerström (*On the truth of moral ideas*, Uppsala, 1911). Its first statement in the English-speaking world is probably that given by I.A. Richards and C.K. Ogden in their *The meaning of meaning* (Kegan Paul, London, 1923). The best-known expressions of the theory are to be found in the writings of A.J. Ayer and the American philosopher C.L. Stevenson; and it is with their versions of emotivism that we shall deal in the following pages.

A.J. Ayer

Ayer's and Stevenson's forms of emotivism are based on two different theories of meaning. In particular, Ayer takes over the logical positivists' *verificationist* theory of meaning and argues that a statement is 'literally meaningful if and only if it is either analytic or empirically verifiable'.[2] By 'literally meaningful' Ayer means 'capable of being shown to be true or false'. Analytic statements are those which can be shown to be true or false from the definitions of the words used in them, whereas empirically verifiable statements are those which can be shown to be true or fase by empirical observation. Moral judgements cannot be shown to be true or false either by empirical observation or from the meaning of the terms used in them. Ayer concludes that they are literally (i.e. cognitively) meaningless. Moral concepts, he says, are 'mere pseudo-concepts'. What he means by this is that 'the presence of an ethical symbol in a proposition adds nothing to its factual content'.[3] He compares the role of ethical terms in a sentence to the utterance of the sentence in a peculiar tone of voice or the addition of special exclamation marks. In saying, for example, 'Stealing money is wrong,' what is meant is 'Stealing money!!', where the exclamation marks show 'by a suitable convention'[4] the speaker's disapproval of stealing. The function of ethical terms is purely 'emotive': they are used 'to *express* feeling about certain objects but not to make any assertion about them'.[5] Moreover, ethical terms are also used, according to Ayer, to arouse feeling and thus stimulate action: 'We may define the meaning of various ethical words in terms both of the different feelings they are ordinarily taken to express, and also the different responses which they are calculated to provoke.'[6]

Ayer carefully distinguishes his emotivism from subjectivist theories of ethics. He stresses that in saying that moral judgements express feelings he does not mean that moral judgements are statements about feelings; if they were, they would be fact-stating and therefore capable of being true or false. 'Whereas the subjectivist holds that ethical statements actually assert the existence of certain feelings, we hold that ethical statements are expressions and excitants of feeling which do not necessarily involve any assertions.'[7]

Since moral judgements do not assert anything, Ayer concludes that it is impossible to argue about genuine questions of moral value. For, if nothing is asserted, nothing can be denied either. To the possible objection that people do in fact argue about morality, Ayer's reply is that such disputes turn out to be about either empirical facts or questions of logic. In moral arguments we attempt to win our opponent over to our way of thinking by showing to him either that he is mistaken about the facts of the case (the actual qualities of the relevant act, its probable effects, the agent's motives, etc.) or that he is not consistent in the application of his moral principles. If our opponent acknowledges all the facts and is also consistent but still disagrees with us about the moral value of the act under consideration, then 'we abandon the attempt to convince him by argument'.[8] Pure questions of value cannot, according to Ayer, be solved by argument. We accept or reject moral values 'in the light of our feelings'.[9] Moral values cannot be forced upon us by the recognition of factual or logical considerations.

Ayer's theory aims firstly to discredit the intuitionist belief in the existence of mysterious 'non-natural properties' which moral judgements were supposed to designate and secondly to show how morality, although not mysterious, as the intuitionists seemed to suppose, is not like science or logic either. Moral judgements are neither statements of (natural or non-natural) fact to be ascertained by empirical investigation or intuitive apprehension, nor logical deductions following from such statements. However, in his attempt to highlight this point Ayer falls prey to the criticism that he puts moral values beyond reason and views morality as fundamentally non-rational (see below, pp. 618–20).

C.L. Stevenson

With the decline of the verificationist theory it became clear that a sentence could be meaningful though neither analytic nor empirically verifiable. New developments in the theory of meaning had an important effect on ethical theory, as appears in Stevenson's account of moral discourse. Stevenson maintains that in order to know the meaning of a piece of language we have to know what particular *use* is made of it in discourse. Starting with this assumption, he puts foward what is called a 'causal' or 'psychological' theory of meaning, according to which the meaning of a linguistic sign is 'a dispositional property'[10] of the sign to cause or be caused by certain psychological processes, in the hearers and speakers respectively. This dispositional property of the sign constitutes its meaning 'only if it has been caused by, and would not have developed without, an elaborate process of conditioning which has attended the sign's use in communication'.[11] Stevenson distinguishes two kinds of meaning, descriptive and emotive. The former is the disposition of a sign to affect cognition (mental activities such as thinking, supposing, etc.), whereas the latter is its disposition to affect feelings or emotions or attitudes. One of the definitions he gives of emotive meaning is as follows: 'The emotive meaning of a word is the power that the word acquires, on account of its history in emotional situations, to evoke or directly express attitudes, as distinct from describing or designating them.'[12] Stevenson takes moral language to have primarily emotive meaning. Moral judgements typically express the attitudes of the speaker and may also be intended to evoke similar attitudes in the hearer. He sometimes speaks of moral judgements as expressing and evoking 'emotions' or 'feelings' but on the whole he uses the word 'attitude'.[13] He also argues that moral judgements exert a 'magnetism': 'A person who recognises X to be good must *ipso facto* acquire a stronger tendency to act in its favour than he otherwise would have had.'[14]

Stevenson emphasises two fundamental features of moral language which the intuitionists had ignored, namely its *expressive* character and its *dynamic* relation to action. His emphasis on these features marks a new departure in ethical theory. Focusing on the ordinary use of moral language,[15] he argues that the difference between moral judgements and descriptive statements consists not in the designation of different kinds of property but in the performance of different functions, the specific function of moral judgements being essentially expressive and practical.

Stevenson does not altogether deny that moral judgements can have descriptive meaning. His claim is that there is always an emotive element in their meaning which differentiates them from mere statements of fact and gives them their distinctive function in language. When a moral judgement is delivered, a distinction can be drawn between (i) what is taken to be the factual state of affairs under judgement, and (ii) the positive or negative evaluation which is passed on that state of affairs. The former is a factual *belief* about what is the case and constitutes the descriptive meaning of the judgement; the latter is an expression of a (favourable or adverse) *attitude* towards what is said to be the case and constitutes the emotive meaning of the judgement. Beliefs and attitudes in moral discourse are logically distinct. But they are causally related in that beliefs may serve to influence attitudes and thus 'cause' them to change.[16]

In the light of this distinction Stevenson differentiates two kinds of agreement or disagreement in morals: one in belief, the other in attitude. Often disagreements in attitude rest on disagreements in belief, so that settling matters of fact and securing agreement in belief may lead to agreement in attitude. But, because attitudes are logically distinct from beliefs and no belief can be said to entail any attitude, it is possible for two people to agree on the relevant facts but still disagree in their attitude towards them. Stevenson's point is that no factual or logical considerations can compel us to adopt certain attitudes rather than others. No factual statement is logically more relevant to a moral evaluation than any other factual statement. The choice of factual statements to adopt as reasons for our value judgements is itself a matter of evaluation.[17]

In order to bring out more clearly the relationship between beliefs and attitudes in morals, Stevenson offers what he calls two 'patterns of analysis' of the meaning of 'This is good,' which he regards as complementary and as applying *mutatis mutandis* to all moral judgements.

According to the first pattern of analysis, 'This is good' means 'I approve of this; do so as well.'[18] In his earlier writings he takes the clause 'I approve of this ...' to express the descriptive meaning of 'This is good', and '... do so as well' to express its emotive meaning. But in his 1963 article 'Retrospective comments'[19] he rejects what he calls the 'autobiographical', descriptive sense of 'I approve of this ...' and takes it to be nothing but a genuine expression of the speaker's approval. Thus amended, this pattern of analysis brings out very lucidly the attitude-expressing and attitude-directing character of moral discourse.

The second pattern of analysis serves to clarify the relationship between the emotive and descriptive meanings. Stevenson states it as follows: ' "This is good" has the meaning "This has qualities or relations X, Y, Z ...," except that "good" has as well a laudatory emotive meaning which permits it to express the speaker's approval, and tends to evoke the approval of the hearer.'[20] The statement 'This has qualities or relations X, Y, Z . . .' specifies those factual characteristics by virtue of which certain things are called good and thus furnishes the descriptive component of 'This is good.' Its emotive component is provided by the laudatory force of the term 'good'.

This second pattern of analysis has led Stevenson to his insightful idea of 'persuasive definitions'. Words with both emotive and descriptive meanings such as 'democracy', 'tyranny' and 'freedom' can be used in the following way: their emotive (laudatory or derogatory) meaning is retained while changes are proposed in their descriptive meaning. To use Stevenson's illustrations, a laudatory term such as 'charity' or 'love' or 'courage' can be used in order to commend a certain activity by redefining the descriptive meaning of the term so as to include this activity. 'Charity', one might say, 'in the true sense of the word, means the giving not merely of gold, but of understanding.' 'True love is the communion between minds alone.' 'Real courage is strength against public opinion.' 'Real' and 'true' in such contexts, as Stevenson rightly points out, are used with the persuasive force of 'to be accepted'.[21] The purpose of such definitions is to redirect the hearers' attitude from one thing to another by retaining the emotive [laudatory] meaning of the word and attaching it to the favoured descriptive characteristic. In the same way a derogatory term such as 'tyranny' or 'hypocrisy' can be used to discredit some activity. Persuasive definitions are used 'in an effort to secure, by this interplay between emotive and descriptive meaning, a redirection of people's attitudes'.[22] The important point about them is that they highlight the logical primacy of emotive meaning: the emotive meaning of moral judgements remains constant and by so doing it becomes an instrument for changing their descriptive meaning.

In his discussion of the methodology of moral argument, Stevenson distinguishes two main methods of procedure, the logical and the psychological. The logical way of solving disagreements calls into question the consistency of the reasons (i.e. factual beliefs) given in support of moral judgements. But this method, according to Stevenson, represents the 'exception',[23] not the rule. The rule in moral argument is that ethical judgements are supported or attacked by reasons related to them *'psychologically*, rather than logically'.[24] Within the psychological way of securing agreement Stevenson draws a distinction between 'rational' and 'nonrational' methods. The 'rational' methods test the truth and comprehensiveness of the supporting beliefs, and by changing people's beliefs in this way they may effect a change in their attitudes. The 'nonrational' methods are employed when an attempt is made to change attitudes by means other than change in beliefs, e.g. by 'the sheer, direct impact of words ... emotive meaning, rhetorical cadence, apt metaphor, stentorian, stimulating, or pleading tones of voice, dramatic gestures, care in establishing *rapport* with the hearer or audience, and so on'.[25] Both 'rational' and 'nonrational' methods aim at creating an influence. But the 'rational' methods in normative ethics, according to Stevenson, 'may lack finality',[26] in which case non-rational methods are called for as psychologically more effective in 'remoulding' people's attitudes.

The weaknesses of emotivism

The emotive theory of ethics has been subjected to a wide range of criticism. J.O. Urmson[27] has criticised Stevenson for presenting moral discourse as a matter entirely of standard-setting and never as standard-using. There is clearly a difference between these two activities. From time to time, when there is some ambiguity about the criteria for the goodness of a certain kind of thing A (wines, knives, etc.), people use 'good' in deciding what their standards will be; then they must proceed to use 'good' in accordance with the standards they have set when they say that X is a good specimen of A (a good wine, a good knife, etc.). Urmson observes that both Stevenson's patterns of analysis of 'This is good' are exclusively models of setting up standards. Both presuppose that the meaning of moral judgements is to express the speaker's own approval (and his intention to arouse similar approval in others) for *anything* he may wish to approve of. They represent the speaker in morals as always setting up standards but never actually coming round to using them. And this Urmson finds to be an inadequate account of moral discourse because (a) moral judgements are normally standard-using, and (b) there is no point in setting up a standard unless it is a preliminary to using it.

Another criticism of emotivism is that it represents moral discourse as fundamentally non-rational. Ayer and Stevenson rightly take moral judgements to be primarily expressive, but from this they fallaciously infer that rational argument about moral values themselves is not possible. When genuine matters of value are in dispute, according to Ayer, rational argument breaks down, and, according to Stevenson, non-rational psychological influence is the only means of securing agreement. The consequent charge of irrationalism concerns two main features of emotivism: (i) its assumption that moral judgements are nothing more than emotional responses or expressions of personal attitude to various states of affairs, and (ii) its contention that the distinctive function of moral discourse is to work on people's emotions and by so doing to produce a certain effect.

(1) As regards the first point, if all that the distinctive meaning of moral judgements amounts to is a mere expression of approval or disapproval, an emotional response like 'Boo' or 'Hurrah' with regard to various states of affairs, then moral judgements become indistinguishable from expressions of taste, personal preference, or even mere prejudice and caprice. And an ethical theory which is unable to distinguish moral convictions from mere personal preference, sheer prejudice or caprice undermines rather than explains morality. It may be noted in fairness to Stevenson that he does seem to have some regard to the need for a distinction between moral and non-moral expressions of preference or attitude. He says that what differentiates the two is that the attitudes expressed in moral contexts are 'marked by a special seriousness or urgency'.[28] However this criterion will not suffice. If someone said that he ought to jump up and down ten times in an hour, and expressed his approval of this practice with special seriousness and urgency, this would hardly make his point of view a moral one. In ordinary discourse, intense seriousness or urgency is not regarded as a sufficient condition for calling somebody's personal approval or recommendation a moral one. There seems to be a need for a further criterion to distinguish the moral from the non-moral cases (see below, pp. 623–4).

(2) Warnock[29] counters Stevenson's contention that the 'major use' of moral judgements is to create an influence by arguing that creating an influence is neither a sufficient nor a necessary condition of moral discourse. Discourse can create an influence without being moral, e.g. advertising, political speeches, threats; and, conversely, discourse can be moral without creating an influence. Warnock observes that if someone sets out to 'create an influence' by delivering a moral judgement, three conditions need to be fulfilled: (a) he must suppose that his hearers do not already have the attitude which his judgement is intended to promote; (b) he must want his hearers to have it; and (c) he must think it at least possible that his uttering the judgement will tend to promote the adoption of the relevant attitude. But, Warnock points out, moral judgements are often delivered without any of these conditions being fulfilled. We may utter moral judgements on occasions on which: (a) our hearers already share our attitude; (b) we can hardly be said to want our hearers to adopt the attitude, since they already do; and (c) we may not think that our judgement will change anybody's opinion, but may merely be concerned to make our attitude known to others.

Warnock goes on to say that in logic it is always possible to draw a distinction between an argument being valid and an argument producing conviction. The emotivists, he protests, leave no room for this distinction in moral discourse. Whereas in questions of factual belief they accept distinctions between good and bad evidence, mere prejudice and well-founded belief, and so on, when it comes to moral attitudes, they do not think that such distinctions can be drawn. Specifically moral 'arguments' are, in their view, judged not in terms of good or bad reasons but according to their capacity to produce the desired effects. Hence the criticism that the emotive theory represents moral discourse as fundamentally non-rational. For, if the specific function of a universe of discourse is to produce a certain psychological effect, it may achieve its purpose even without being understood. As Warnock has it, 'a dictum to be "emotively" effective, need not necessarily be understood, or even be intelligible; it will be right – for the purpose – on the sole condition that it works'.[30] Moreover, we can often achieve influence more effectively through non-rational means such as bribery or threats. Notice, however, that morally we disapprove of both these methods, no matter how effective they may be in moving people to behave in the desired ways.

Stevenson, it may be recalled, recognises the operation of 'reasons' in morals, but he conceives of their function in causal terms. Firstly he claims that it is not always necessary to have reasons in morals (non-rational psychological methods may be more effective in remoulding attitudes);[31] and secondly he argues that reasons (if and when given) support moral judgements not in the ordinary sense of the word, but 'psychologically rather than logically'.[32] By conceiving the 'reason'-giving character of moral language in causal terms and by arguing in effect that the rules of moral discourse are such that anything said in it can only be assessed as either effective or ineffective, he presents us with a view of morality not as a form of rational communication but as a form of manipulation or propaganda.

Stevenson is alert to the criticism that he assimilates morality to propaganda, and responds by saying that in morality, unlike in propaganda, the use of 'nonrational' methods is only one possibility among others.[33] However, as we have just seen, there are reasons for believing that non-rational methods (threats, etc.) should be excluded from moral argument as such. Stevenson maintains that when questions of validity of belief (requiring rational procedures) are not concerned, any decision about what methods are to be used in moral argument 'is itself a normative ethical matter', so that 'To ask "What method shall I choose?" is in effect to ask "What method *ought* I choose?" Any argument about the question will involve disagreement in attitude.'[34] But there seems to be a considerable difference between disagreement in moral attitude and disagreement about the method of moral argument. In morals, as in all kinds of rational discourse, questions of method cannot be solved by appeal to the attitudes or the motivation of the participants, but rather by appeal to the logical structure of the discourse itself.

Universal prescriptivism

Universal prescriptivism was advanced to rectify the errors of emotivism. Its leading exponent is R.M. Hare, who while endorsing the fundamental emotivist insight that moral judgements are primarily expressive rather than descriptive, decisions rather than discoveries, nevertheless seeks to demonstrate the rationality of moral thought which the emotivists had virtually ignored. Hare's ethical theory is to be found in *The language of morals* (1952), *Freedom and reason* (1963), and *Moral thinking* (1981), as well as in numerous articles.

Hare's earlier account

Moral discourse as action-guiding and reason-requiring. Hare's starting point is to accept the emotivist idea that there exists a dynamic connection between moral discourse and action. But unlike the emotivists he regards the purpose of moral judgements not as to persuade or create an influence but rather to give guidance or advice.[35] Moral judgements *tell* people what to do (advice); but they do not as such *make* them do it (persuasion). To demonstrate the difference he uses J.L. Austin's[36] distinction between three kinds of 'speech-act'. A 'locutionary' act is, according to Austin, the act of simply saying something. An 'illocutionary' act is what we are doing *in* saying something (informing, describing, commanding, advising, etc.). A 'perlocutionary' act is what we are doing *by* saying something (surprising or pleasing somebody, frightening him, etc.). Hare maintains that knowing the *il*locutionary force of an utterance, as distinct from its *per*locutionary force, is a necessary condition of knowing its meaning. E.g. 'You will open the door' may be a prediction, a threat, an order, a request, etc.; we do not know which it is until we know what the speaker intends to do *in* saying it. Hare takes it to be part of the *il*locutionary force of moral judgements that they guide action. He accuses the emotivists of blurring the illocutionary/perlocutionary distinction and thus confusing the meaning of moral judgements with their perlocutionary force. Influencing people's behaviour may be a possible effect (indeed sometimes the intended effect) of delivering moral judgements. But it is nevertheless essential to distinguish between telling someone what to do (illocution) and the possible effects of doing so (perlocution). That the meaning of a moral judgement is logically independent of whether or not we succeed in getting people to act in a certain way (i.e. its perlocutionary force) is obvious from the fact that if we were not successful that would by no means imply that our moral judgement was meaningless.

Another feature which Hare notices in moral discourse as it actually occurs is what may be called its 'reason-requiring' character. As against Stevenson, who considered the need for logically consistent reasons as the 'exception' in moral argument (see p. 617 above), Hare takes this need to be characteristic of moral discourse as such. This feature shows that the making of moral judgements is always a *rational* process. Anyone uttering a moral judgement, he points out, is expected to have a reason for doing so. If he says, 'I ought to ...' or 'You ought to ...', it is always logically legitimate to ask him for a reason and it is never logically legitimate to refuse to give one. This characteristic, not fully appreciated by the emotivists, is what differentiates moral judgements from other not altogether dissimilar judgements such as expressions of taste, feeling or personal preference. Unlike in matters of taste where one is entitled to choose between alternatives (e.g. white wine as opposed to red wine) without having to have a reason for doing so, once a certain act has been called good we can always ask, 'What is good about it?' and the answer cannot be 'Just its goodness.' Goodness, like all moral properties, is always 'supervenient'[37] upon other non-moral properties of the act or person which is called good. 'Good' and other moral terms are applied to various situations *because* they possess certain non-moral characteristics. E.g. 'Act *X* is good.' 'Why?' 'Because it is an act of helping the poor.'

Hare, like Stevenson, maintains that reasons given in support of particular moral judgements are factual statements about the objects of our moral pronouncement. But, as against Stevenson, he argues that factual statements get to be reasons for moral judgements not because they 'cause' or 'influence' people psychologically to act in the desired ways but because they offer them *justifying* grounds for doing so. Stevenson blurs a fundamental distinction between reasons and causes. The cause of an utterance is what has determined it (anger, fear, surprise, etc.); but to give a reason for it is to bring it under a rule. Moral judgements furnish reasons for action in that, unlike psychological causes, they bring various types of action under certain principles of conduct. Implicit in them are certain moral principles which ensure their moral relevance. In this way all moral reasoning is, according to Hare, in the last analysis an instantiation of a kind of practical or mixed syllogism. The major premiss is a universal principle, the minor premiss is a statement of fact, and the conclusion is a particular moral judgement. Thus the example given above has the following structure: (i) Major Premiss, 'All acts of helping the poor are good'; (ii) Minor Premiss, 'Act *X* is an act of helping the poor'; (iii) Conclusion, 'Act *X* is good.' Hare calls the moral principles which figure in the major premiss 'decisions of principle'.[38] They constitute the starting points of moral reasoning and secure the relevance of factual statements to it. We are free to accept, reject or modify such principles by testing them against particular cases and seeing whether we can accept them for ourselves and others (see below, pp. 625–6).

Prescriptivity and universalisability. Hare offers an account of the meaning of moral language mainly in terms of two logical properties, prescriptivity and universalisability. *Prescriptivity* follows from the 'action-guiding' character of moral discourse. Moral judgements are prescriptive in that they 'entail imperatives'.[39] It is because they have this distinctive property that they can guide action. What anyone is doing *in* saying that something is good or ought to be done is by implication saying

'Do it!' or 'Let me do it!' Hare justifies this point from ordinary usage. Remarks such as 'This is the right act, but don't do it!' or 'You ought to do X, but don't!' would strike us as odd, unless a further explanation was given (e.g. 'You also ought to do Y and you can't do both').

Nevertheless, Hare allows that moral judgements sometimes do not entail imperatives, and of such uses he distinguishes three kinds: the 'inverted-commas', the 'ironic' and the 'conventional' uses.[40] He argues that in such cases moral judgements are used in a non-evaluative sense. But all such uses are parasitic on the more fundamental one, namely the evaluative, in which moral judgements are prescriptive and as such entail imperatives. If someone professes to assent to a given moral judgement but does not assent to the entailed imperative, then either he has misunderstood the moral judgement (by taking it to be non-evaluative when the speaker intended it to be evaluative) or he is insincere.[41] This does not mean, of course, that sincere assent to the entailed imperative always entails acting upon it: it does so only 'if now is the occasion for performing it and it is in our (physical and *psychological*) power to do so'.[42] Cases in which we are psychologically inhibited from acting on the entailed imperative are cases of 'weakness of will'. The latter however do not, according to Hare, constitute a counterexample to prescriptivity. For the point about prescriptivity is not that people will always do X if they think X is right, but only that in saying X is right they mean to say, 'Do X!' or 'Let me do X!', even though for some physical or psychological inhibition they may be prevented from actually doing it.

The notion of prescriptivity also links moral judgements with the notion of desiring or wanting.[43] To say that moral judgements are in their fundamental (evaluative) use prescriptive is to say that they are linguistic expressions of desires. If people had no desires, it would make no difference to them what happened in the world, and so they would see no point in using prescriptive language, i.e. language which calls for one thing to happen rather than another.

Universalisability is the property according to which we are logically prohibited from saying of two acts or situations which are identical in their universal descriptive properties that one is good and the other not. This property follows on from the logical requirement that moral judgements made in various situations be made for reasons (see above, p. 621). And the notion of a reason brings with it the notion of a rule which has *universal* application. If for example someone calls an act X good *because* it possesses certain factual features, he must in consistency call any other act which shares the same features good, unless a further reason is adduced to differentiate the two cases.

However, Hare's 'universalisability thesis'[44] does not merely consist in the fact that reasons, which are by their nature universal, must be given for moral judgements. For reasons can be given for other things besides moral judgements, e.g. commands ('Hurry up!' – 'Why?' – 'Because your train is leaving in five minutes.'). The reasons given for or against moral judgements must be of a special type. Following Gellner, he calls such reasons 'U-type' as distinct from 'E-type' reasons. He defines a 'U-type' reason as 'A rule wholly devoid of any personal reference, a rule containing merely predicates (descriptions) and logical terms'.[45] Consider the following example: 'You ought to visit him.' 'Why?' 'Because you promised to do so.' This, according to Hare, is a 'U-type' valuation because implicit in the reason given is the principle 'One ought to do what one promises,' which is universal 'in the stricter sense of "universal"',[46] in that it does not contain any reference to particular individuals. Put summarily, Hare's view is that moral judgements are universalisable in the sense that they encapsulate universal principles which require that in *all* cases of a certain *kind*, not needing individual references for its determination, an action of a certain *kind* should be performed or avoided.[47]

Several criticisms have been levelled against Hare's views on prescriptivity and universalisability, to some of which we shall now attend, albeit in the most summary fashion.

Firstly, it has been objected that by considering all moral evaluations to be prescriptive Hare takes too narrow a view of the meaning of moral language. A.C. MacIntyre[48] adduces as an illustration of the non-prescriptive use of moral evaluations what he calls 'appraisals of action', i.e. principles by which we can appraise actions of ourselves and others. One may appraise actions by one set of principles and guide one's own conduct by another. The fact that we may find this morally objectionable shows, according to MacIntyre, that it is not unintelligible, as it would have to be if it was part of the meaning of 'ought' always to entail imperatives.

Similarly, G.J. Warnock objects to Hare that 'there are dozens of things which those who employ moral words may therein be doing' besides prescribing, i.e. 'advising, exhorting, imploring; commanding, condemning, deploring; resolving, confessing, undertaking; and so on, and so on'.[49] Hare's reply[50] to Warnock is that, if we examine the 'dozens of things' which Warnock lists, we will find that they are all species of one genus, namely prescribing, and, as such, they incorporate imperatives for action. It would, for example, be odd to deplore a certain action and in the same breath to tell someone to perform it.

As regards universalisability, it has been objected that it is not part of the meaning of 'ought' that all moral judgements are universalisable. MacIntyre[51] and Peter Winch[52] fasten upon cases of anguished moral conflict to argue that Hare's 'universalisability thesis' overlooks the perplexity of real-life moral situations. MacIntyre refers to the well-known example of Sartre's pupil,[53] who could not decide whether he ought to join the Free French Army in Britain or to stay in occupied France

624

and look after his aged mother. In such a case, he says, no universal prescription could help him. 'He might decide what to do without being willing to allow that anyone who chose differently was blameworthy.'[54]

To such criticisms Hare replies that they over-dramatise real-life moral situations. In real life people who have been in situations of moral conflict usually say that they did the best they could in the circumstances. And as W.D. Hudson remarks,[55] in such situations people will have to make up their own minds about what is best. But if anyone in a moral dilemma thinks that, in his own case, an agent ought to do what he thinks is best, it is part of the meaning of 'ought' that he is committed to accepting as a corollary that anyone else in a moral dilemma ought to do what he thinks is best.

Against the criticism that the 'universalisability thesis' overlooks the particularity of real-life moral situations one line of defence is Hare's distinction between *universality* and *generality*.[56] The thesis that moral judgements are universalisable does not mean that they are sweeping generalisations which ignore the complicated character of specific moral situations. 'Specific', Hare points out, is the opposite of 'general', whereas 'particular' is the opposite of 'universal'. Generality, unlike universality, admits of degrees; some moral principles are more general than others. E.g. the principle 'One ought not to tell lies' is more general than 'One ought not to tell lies to one's family' and this, in turn, is more general than 'One ought not to tell lies to one's father.' But all are equally universal, for they all require that something of a certain *kind* be done in all cases of a certain *kind*. Even if one can envisage a case in which a moral judgement is so specific that it only applies to one single act *A* because there is nothing else in the world which is like *A* in the relevant respects, the judgement that *A* is good will still be universalisable, in the sense that *if* there were anything else in the world which resembled *A* in the relevant respects, it would also have to be called good.

Moral reasoning and utilitarianism. The 'logical framework' of prescriptivity and universalisability generates, according to Hare, a system of reasoning by which we decide which moral principles to adopt. This feature of his theory differentiates it fundamentally from emotivism. For unlike Stevenson, who argues that '*any* statement about *any* matter of fact which *any* speaker considers likely to alter attitudes may be adduced as a reason for or against an ethical judgement',[57] Hare insists that the selection of reasons in morals is a rational process determined by strict rules of procedure generated by the logical properties of moral discourse.

Hare is of course aware that these properties, together with the rules of reasoning they generate, are purely formal and as such cannot by themselves generate substantial moral principles. The substance of particular moral judgements in each case is supplied by arguments which require three other 'necessary ingredients' besides 'logic': (i) an appeal to fact (made relevant by the requirement that moral judgements be supported by reasons); (ii) an appeal to inclination or interest; and (iii) an appeal to imagination.[58] These three 'ingredients' together with logic 'govern a man's moral opinion on a given matter'.[59]

Put briefly, the procedure of moral reasoning is as follows: (i) universalisability requires someone making a moral judgement to go the round imaginatively of *all* the affected parties 'giving equal weight to the interests of all', irrespective of whose interests they happen to be (for individual references are not permitted by universalisability); (ii) prescriptivity requires him to ask the question 'How much (as I imagine myself in the place of each man in turn) do I *want* to have this or avoid that?' In other words, the moral thinker is required, in deciding what principle(s) to adopt, to put on a par the interests (or inclinations) of all those who will be affected by actions which result from the adoption of the principle(s). At the end of his moral reasoning, after having realised that the rules of moral discourse commit him to treat the interests of all other affected parties as on a par with his own, he will discover whether he is really prepared to make a certain 'decision of principle'. When he realises, for example, that the logic of moral discourse does not allow him, on pain of inconsistency, to advocate the principle that all liars ought to be executed and at the same time to deny that, if he were a liar, he ought to be executed, he may not be willing to adopt it. In this respect, according to Hare, 'decisions of principle' may be compared to scientific hypotheses. Both are provisional principles which we have to test against particular cases before we finally adopt them.[60]

Hare is explicit that 'the logical character of moral language, as I have claimed it to be, is the formal foundation'[61] for utilitarianism. For universalisability, he points out, requires us in making moral judgements to take account of *all* affected parties, and prescriptivity requires us to take account of the *wants* of all affected parties; taken together, they require us to 'maximize satisfactions'.[62] The logic of moral discourse generates the 'formal component' of utilitarianism, i.e. the principle 'Everybody to count for one, nobody for more than one,' which is nothing but a restatement of the requirement that moral principles be properly universal. The substantive component of the moral judgements of a utilitarian kind is provided by 'A consideration of the substantial inclinations and interests which people *actually* have'.[63] Thus Hare arrives at utilitarianism, understood as a substantive theory of normative ethics, by combining formal and empirical theses. Given the formal properties of moral language and the facts of the world (mainly facts about what people actually desire), the 'decisions of principle' that they will be prepared to make will be ones that a utilitarian would accept.

Choice, evaluation and description. The thrust of Hare's argument seems to be that, subject to the formal constraints of prescriptivity

626

and universalisability, people are free as far as logic is concerned to choose for themselves what moral principles to adopt. This feature of his moral philosophy has been a storm-centre of criticism. His critics concentrate on two types of example: firstly 'One ought not to walk on the cracks of the pavement,' or 'One ought to clasp and unclasp hands three times an hour,'[64] etc., which, although they may fulfil the requirements of prescriptivity and universalisability as well as of Hare's three other 'necessary ingredients' (see above), seem absurd as moral principles; secondly, 'All Jews ought to be exterminated,' etc., which although again they may pass Hare's formal tests, most people would find objectionable on moral grounds.

Hare counters these criticisms by drawing a distinction between empirical and logical considerations. As regards the bizarre principles of the first type he maintains[65] that a distinction can be drawn between 'logical absurdity' and 'contingent improbability'. The oddity of such principles is not a logical one. It derives from the fact that it is 'contingently extremely unlikely' that anybody will ever adopt them as moral principles. Moral judgements, because of their prescriptivity, express desires; and the world being as it is, people normally have certain desires and not others. As a result, the moral prescription of, for example, clasping and unclasping hands would strike them as odd. But there is nothing logically impossible about making such a moral prescription. People may come to desire different things. Logic cannot determine what desires people will or will not have, and cannot therefore determine what particular things they will or will not say ought to be done.

Hare adopts a similar line of argument in dealing with the second type of principles, which he calls morally *fanatical*. If someone advocates the principle 'All Jews ought to be exterminated,' he is required by the rules of moral reasoning to give assent, having put himself imaginatively in the place of each Jew, to the imperative 'Let me, as a Jew, be exterminated.' Hare thinks it empirically impossible that anyone should have such a strong desire to see all Jews exterminated that this would outweigh his desire to survive and thus sincerely assent to the above imperative. And given the logic of 'ought', if he declines assent to the singular prescription, he cannot on pain of inconsistency give assent to the universal prescription 'All Jews ought to be exterminated' which entails it. It is a 'happy fact that most people want to live'.[66] It is, therefore, a fortunate contingent fact that (self-consistent) moral fanaticism does not occur. Nonetheless, it is, according to Hare, logically possible. It is logically possible for someone to have such a strong desire to see all Jews exterminated that it would outweigh his desire for his own survival, and thus assent sincerely to the imperative 'Let me, if a Jew, be exterminated.' In that case it is perfectly consistent for him to advocate the principle 'All Jews ought to be exterminated.' Logic alone cannot prohibit him from discarding his own interest in survival, and cannot therefore prohibit him from thinking that he ought to exterminate all Jews.

The consequence of Hare's argument is that extremely 'bizarre' or 'fanatical' principles, however empirically unlikely to be held, can logically go through as moral principles. But Hare's critics object that he has evaded a logical criticism by making an empirical point. They contend that it does not *make sense* to say that bizarre and fanatical principles can count as moral ones. They emphasise the need to introduce more restrictions into the definition of a 'moral' principle than Hare's formal conditions seem to require.[67]

Another of Hare's contentions which has been widely criticised is that it is always logically possible to separate the evaluative from the descriptive meaning of moral terms, so that no moral evaluation can be said to follow from a description by virtue of the meaning-rules of moral language. Mrs Foot[68] uses words such as 'courageous' and 'rude' to argue that this is not so. To call an act courageous, for instance, is both to describe and commend it simultaneously. In such adjectives, according to Mrs Foot, the descriptive and evaluative elements are logically tied together. The 'ought' is inseparable from the 'is'; a certain evaluation is logically deduced from a certain description. In reply to this criticism, Hare firstly points out that from the mere fact that if we use a 'secondarily evaluative word'[69] such as 'courageous', 'pretentious,' 'honest', etc., we are almost committed to the evaluation implicit in it, it does not follow that we have to use such a word to refer to a certain act or person. He takes as an example the term 'nigger', which has its descriptive meaning fixed and is also a term of contempt. Someone who is not prepared to despise people just because they are negroes will simply not use the word 'nigger' to refer to them. Secondly, Hare argues that even when a 'secondarily evaluative word' is used, it can be used in a purely descriptive sense without evaluative commitment, so that even in this case the adoption of the moral commitment is in principle separable from the adoption of the word. If S is a secondarily evaluative condemnatory adjective (e.g. 'rude') which corresponds to our accepted standards, we can always ask 'Granted that something is S ("rude"), would it be wrong?' There exist in language, beside the secondarily evaluative words, words such as 'ought', 'good', 'right', which are not tied (logically) to particular descriptions and which can be used to criticise, change or develop our more specific moral vocabulary. Hare's point is that substantial moral commitments cannot be established by appeal to the uses of words alone. What moral principles we shall adopt is not something that language alone can determine.

Another, related criticism concerns Hare's view that there is a fundamental connection between evaluation and choice.[70] Mrs Foot[71] objects that a connection with the speaker's choice is *neither* a sufficient *nor* a necessary condition of the correct use of evaluative terms such as 'good'. She deploys expressions such as 'good knife', 'good rider', 'good father' and 'good coal' to show that the criteria of the correct use of 'good' are always determined and not a matter of individual choice. A speaker's readiness to choose a rider that constantly fell off the horse's back, or a father that offered his children for sacrifice would not, according to Mrs Foot, make his use of 'good' in such contexts appropriate. (The only exception she allows occurs in cases of what she calls 'competition examples', e.g. when setting the standards of what a good spaniel will be in a dog show.)

Hare's reply consists largely[72] in urging the distinction between someone's saying '*X* is good' and his saying 'I think *X* is good.' He maintains that the speaker's readiness to choose *X* is both a sufficient and a necessary condition for saying that he *thinks* *X* good, but not for saying that *X* *is* good. If someone says, '*X* is good,' he may be merely describing *X* as falling under the standards which other people generally accept (descriptive use). But if he uses 'good' evaluatively, he is thereby purporting to express his own commendation and will be thought to be insincere if he then refrains from choosing *X* (if and when an occasion for choosing arises). This means that he does not really think what he purports to think, i.e. that *X* is good. But of course that a speaker thinks something good does not prove that it is good; other people are still at liberty to disagree with him. Hare accuses Mrs Foot of this confusion and thus of erroneously attributing to him the view that the speaker's *thinking* something good shows that it *is* good, which she then proceeds to attack.

Hare's recent account

In his recent book *Moral thinking* and in a number of recent articles Hare introduces certain developments which he sees both as constituting a rapprochement between his opponents' theories and his own universal prescriptivism and as underlining where the supremacy of his own theory lies.

The two levels of moral thinking. The major development in Hare's recent writings is his distinction between two levels of moral thinking, namely the 'intuitive' and the 'critical' levels respectively. The intuitive level is that at which most of us do nearly all of our moral thinking. It consists in the application of generally accepted principles such as truthtelling, promise-keeping, etc., which Hare describes as 'habits of mind, dispositions, intuitions, principles, rules or whatever one cares to call them, which we take as given and do not question'.[73] These 'prima facie principles' *qua* moral are universal prescriptions. They are in addition accompanied by firm dispositions and feelings to act in accordance with them, built into our character through our upbringing and moral education. 'Intuitive' principles represent the 'given' element in moral thinking. They show that to a large extent people are, as Urmson would say, standard-using rather than standard-setting.

However, Hare is alive to the fact that even a good

set of prima facie, intuitive principles may on occasion prove inadequate to guide us for the best. He lists three kinds of circumstance in which we have to ascend to what he calls the 'critical' level of moral thinking: when our moral intuitions *conflict*; when the situation confronting us is so *unusual* that our existing moral intuitions prove inadequate to guide us; and when we have to *select* which prima facie principles to use in our intuitive thinking and pass on to the succeeding generations.[74] Critical thinking is rational thinking. When we employ it, we 'listen to reason as to a father'.[75]

To illustrate the difference between intuitive and critical thinking, Hare borrows the expressions 'prole' and 'archangel' from Orwell (*1984*, 1949) and Godwin (*An enquiry concerning political justice*, 1793) respectively. Archangels are moral beings who think entirely at the critical level. Possessing superhuman knowledge and no human weaknesses, they do not need settled general principles and good dispositions to act for the best. They can do everything by reason in a moment of time. Proles, by contrast, have all human weaknesses to a high degree. Their only hope of making correct judgements is to go by the principles which they have acquired under the influence of others. Hare maintains that any human being shares the characteristics of both the archangel and the prole. We all think, in varying degrees, partly intuitively and partly critically. Intuitive thinking is highly desirable. For, given our human limitations, we need 'intuitions', 'good dispositions', firmly ingrained in our character to avoid the temptation to 'cook' our moral thinking to suit our own interests. However occasions may arise in which, as we have just seen, critical thinking is called for. Critical thinking is 'epistemologically prior'.[76] It selects the principles for use at the intuitive level and provides the vantage point from which such principles can always be reappraised.

Hare sees the distinction between the two levels of moral thinking as bringing together his own views and those of his descriptivist opponents such as Mrs Foot, while exposing what is true and what is false in the latter. He concedes that most of what they say holds good of the intuitive level, where, because of the existence of firmly established criteria of right and wrong, moral terms are used with fairly constant descriptive meanings. But he contends that moral words

> also have other properties (connected with their prescriptivity) which escape these theories ... My own more complex theory, which tries to do justice to both the descriptive and the prescriptive meanings of these words, is therefore a more adequate account of their meaning.[77]

The method of critical thinking, utilitarianism and fanaticism. When engaging in critical thinking we need to be clear about two matters, the *logic* of the moral concepts and the empirical *facts* of the case on which we are pronouncing morally. What Hare says about the constraints of 'logic' and 'the facts' in *Moral thinking* is not in any material way different from what he said about them in his earlier writings (see above, pp. 622–4). But a new note is struck when he contends that if we were to think in complete accordance with 'logic' and 'the facts', 'they would constrain so severely the moral evaluations that we can make, that in practice we would be found all to agree to the same ones'.[78] By tightening up his account of the constraints of reason in morals, he now comes to see that, if people reason within the familiar limitations imposed by the *meaning* of the moral judgements they will be making and the *non-moral facts* of the situations to which they will be applying them, they will agree to the same answers to moral questions.

The considerations which have led him to this conclusion are as follows.[79] The framework of prescriptivity and universalisability ('logic') compels the moral thinker, in deciding what he ought to do, to take into account the preferences (prescriptivity) of all those affected (universalisability) by the act under consideration. In order to appreciate fully what their preferences are, he has to identify imaginatively with these preferences. This involves contemplating the hypothetical situation in which what are actually preferences of other people would be preferences of his own, and thus acquire a hypothetical concern for their satisfaction in that hypothetical situation. Then, because of universalisability, the moral thinker finds himself constrained to turn this hypothetical concern into an actual concern for the satisfaction of these preferences. (For hypothetical similar cases are not different from the actual ones in their universal descriptive properties.) In this way, the moral thinker will have turned an *interpersonal* conflict of preferences into an *intrapersonal* one. The answer to the question of what ought to be done will be the same as in a case in which his own actual preferences conflict with one another; that is, he will prescribe the satisfaction of that preference which, being the strongest, outweighs the others, no matter whose actual preference it happens to be. It is clear, according to Hare, that everybody (including, of course, each of the other affected parties) who engages in the moral reasoning process, and does so correctly, will arrive at the *same* moral prescription about the same situation. For, after having identified himself imaginatively with all the affected parties and made their preferences his own, he will prescribe the satisfaction of the greatest (cumulative) preference. Hare is, of course, aware that in actual practice people may not always reach the same moral conclusions, for they may be clouded in their logic or mistaken about the relevant facts. But if it is assumed that we have 'perfect command' of logic and the facts, i.e. that we think like 'archangels', at the end of our critical thinking we shall all say the same thing.

As in his earlier writings Hare concedes that the moral evaluations which will be reached by the application of the method he is proposing will 'have a content identical with a certain kind of utilitarianism'.[80] For the person who is deciding within the constraints of 'logic' and 'the facts' is bound to give equal weight to the equal preferences of all the affected parties, and thus prescribe the impartial maximisation of the satisfaction of the preferences of those affected in total. It may be noted that Hare's brand of utilitarianism does not contain a principle of utility which being somehow at the top of the hierarchy constrains us to derive all our moral principles from it. In his system of reasoning there are only the logical properties of moral discourse, which taken in conjunction with the non-moral facts (mainly about what people actually prefer) generate a whole host of substantial critical principles, none of which is supreme. But his system is recognisably utilitarian in that the principles which it maintains that the logical properties of moral discourse (together with 'the facts') generate are such as the utilitarians had hoped to reach by applying their supreme principle, 'One ought to maximise preference-satisfaction impartially.'

Hare amplifies his earlier views on moral fanaticism. Firstly, unlike his earlier writings, in which his examples of fanaticism were all repellent (e.g. Nazism, sadism), he now stresses that one may be fanatical about perfectly sound moral opinions. Secondly, he now comes to see that consistent fanaticism, that which goes through as a moral point of view, is 'not after all inconsistent with utilitarianism'.[81] In *Freedom and reason* (Ch. 8) he conceived of the moral fanatic as someone who is so firmly wedded to his ideal that he lets it override his own and other people's interests and thus makes logically impeccable (even if outrageous) moral judgements which are not however utilitarian. But in *Moral thinking* he realises that the fanatic who is prepared to reason morally (i.e. the 'pure' as opposed to the 'impure' fanatic) will be faced with two alternatives: either he will find that his own preferences, which mainly stem from his ideal, are not strong enough to outweigh the preferences of all those who will be harmed by implementing it, in which case he will have to abandon his fanatical ideal; or he will find that his own preferences, stemming from his ideal, are so strong that they outbalance the preferences of all other people affected, in which case critical thinking will prescribe the satisfaction of his preferences, being the strongest. In both cases the right answer will be utilitarian: it will prescribe the satisfaction of the greatest preference considered impartially.

The scope of Hare's non-descriptivism: 'The freedom to prefer what we prefer'. Hare's moral philosophy can be seen as an attempt to show how one can be a committed *rationalist* while at the same time remaining an uncompromising *non-descriptivist*, i.e. while rejecting the view that the meaning of moral judgements, as of descriptive statements, is exhausted by their truth-conditions. He has in particular resisted that form of descriptivism known as ethical naturalism, according to which moral judgements can be validly deduced from factual statements given the meaning-rules of moral language.[82] In so far as Hare's theory is non-descriptivist, it stresses that there is an 'irreducibly *evaluative* or *prescriptive*'[83] element in moral thinking which makes it impossible to derive moral judgements from mere statements of fact. In so far as it is rationalist it stresses that there exists in morals a very precisely determined method of reasoning about which principles to adopt in various situations. In particular, he explicitly denies that his recent 'screwing up tight'[84] of his system of reasoning marks a departure from his original non-descriptivism. His theory remains, in his own submission, non-descriptivist inasmuch as it accords an essential role to freedom in moral thinking and insists that no moral evaluation can be forced upon us by the mere recognition of facts.

In his recent writings Hare restates his belief in the existence of a fundamental connection between moral judgements and human preferences, made possible by prescriptivity. This logical point is his strongest justification for saying that moral judgements are ultimately rooted in freedom. For as far as logic is concerned we are 'free to prefer what we prefer' and thus prescribe what we prescribe. Logic cannot determine any single preference on anybody's part. What it does determine is what combinations between preferences (and singular prescriptions) are possible in moral judgements. In particular, logic constrains us 'to coordinate our individual preferences into a total preference which is impartial between us'.[85] But we retain our freedom in the sense that this total preference (expressed in a universal prescription) is a function of our separate individual preferences and their respective intensities and of *nothing else*. An illustration is provided by the case of the moral fanatic who is, as we have seen, in principle free to have a *preference* for the realisation of his ideal strong enough to outweigh the preferences of all those who would be harmed through its realisation. The logical possibility of fanaticism shows that, although according to Hare's prescriptivism 'logic' and 'the facts' restrict severely the moral evaluations we can make, they ultimately leave us with 'the freedom to prefer whatever we prefer'. Moreover, our individual preferences can change; and if they change sufficiently, our moral judgements, which express these preferences, will also have to change.[86]

Another way in which freedom is preserved in moral thinking is through what Hare calls the 'escape-route'[87] of amoralism. The amoralist is a total moral abstainer. He may be acquainted with the moral words and capable of using them correctly, but only uses them in sentences beginning with the phrase 'It is not the case that ...' Although, according to Hare, there are strong prudential reasons for not opting for amoralism, for the amoralist is a man who has no universal desires at all even in cases in which his own interests are affected, it is despite its awkwardness an option left open by logic. (Of course, only consistent amoralism is logically permitted, i.e. only if one refrains from making moral judgements universally and not just when it suits one's interests.) The consistent type of amoralist can escape the conclusions of particular moral arguments because he has chosen not to make any universal prescriptions, affirmative or negative. He is a man who, on Hare's prescriptivism, can admit all the facts and also know the canons of moral thinking but still refuse the moral conclusions to which these lead. The logical possibility of this position, provided it is consistently followed, confirms that we 'remain free to prefer what we prefer' in moral thinking. For it shows that when a universal prescription or prohibition is proposed, we are free 'either to accept it if it is consistent with the other prescriptions that our preferences commit us to, or if we are an amoralist, to reject it'.[88] We are constrained to accept the moral conclusions to which 'logic' and 'the facts' take us only in so far as they are in accordance with the preferences we have.

Criticisms of Hare's recent account. One objection to Hare's account of moral thinking as conformity to 'logic' and 'the facts' is that it lands him, despite his protestation to the contrary, in the very type of theory he has always been most concerned to rebut, namely descriptivism, and in particular naturalism.[89] For, if to be a naturalist is to deduce substantial moral conclusions from statements of fact together with certain premisses about the meaning-rules of the moral words, does not Hare do precisely that? Has he not set up a system of reasoning which compels moral thinkers to go from facts by logic to substantial moral conclusions?

In *Moral thinking* Hare deals with this danger in two ways. Firstly he recalls what he has said about the logical possibility of amoralism (see above) as establishing his '*bona fides* as a non–descriptivist'.[90] For what (consistent) amoralism shows is that neither logic nor the facts can compel us to a moral prescription, unless we ourselves give assent to certain singular prescriptions – and this will depend on what preferences we have.

Secondly, he refers to the nature of the substantial premisses involved. These premisses, he says, which are mainly about people's preferences (or aversions), do not state neutral facts but contain a prescriptive element.[91] When moral reasoning requires us to go the round of all the affected parties and identify imaginatively with each of them, this does *not* mean that we should describe certain facts (about their preferences) but that we should *give assent to* certain (singular) prescriptions. Hare relates this with a certain view of personal identity. The word 'I', he says, 'is not wholly a descriptive word but in part prescriptive'.[92] When I identify with somebody else, as moral thinking requires, I identify with his preferences and thus acquire a concern for the satisfaction of these preferences. Given the prescriptive sense of 'I', I can pass from a *fact* about what I would be prescribing, were I that person, to a *prescription* without illegitimately bridging the gap between 'is' and 'ought'. And then, Hare adds, it is perfectly consistent with universal prescriptivism to infer moral conclusions from such (singular) prescriptions.

A basic step in Hare's method is that by which in so far as I fully represent to myself the preferences of the other affected parties, I myself have preferences now regarding what should happen to me, were I in their situation with their preferences (see above, pp. 626–7). But it has been objected that although it is trivially true that if I were in somebody else's place with his preferences, I would prefer what he prefers, it does not follow from this that I should *now* prefer what he prefers. Hare's critics[93] adduce various examples. A reformed heroin addict, an ex-alcoholic and a dentist may be said to know in the fullest sense what it is to have an overwhelming preference for heroin, alcohol or the absence of drilling, but nevertheless firmly prefer now that, were they in the position of a heroin addict, an alcoholic or a reluctant dental patient, their preference for heroin, etc., should be frustrated.

Hare's reply[94] is to point out that what his argument requires is that the moral thinker who fully represents to himself another's situation forms *a* preference (for what should happen to him, were he in the other's situation) which is identical to that which the other has. But this does not mean that he will have no other preferences conflicting with this. Which of his various conflicting preferences will override the others will depend in the end on the overall strength of these preferences. The reformed heroin addict, the ex-alcoholic or the dentist may acquire through imaginative identification a strong preference for heroin, etc., but let this preference be overidden by their stronger preference to be free from the menaces of heroin addiction, alcohol or tooth decay.

Another criticism concerns Hare's contention that in moral reasoning 'equal preferences count equally, whatever their content'.[95] His critics[96] object that preferences are not homogeneous as to their moral significance. A method of moral reasoning which requires us to put on a par the preferences of slaves with those of their enslavers, of victims with those of their victimisers, requires us to do what we find morally impossible. If somebody is required in his moral thinking to take account of preferences which he considers immoral, he is thereby required to disregard moral considerations in the very process of making a moral decision.

Hare's reply is in effect that this puts the cart before the horse. For, if someone starts his moral thinking by insisting on the priority of some preferences as being morally more worthy than others, he has begged the question. The only way *critical* thinking can perform its function without becoming viciously circular is to consult the preferences of all those affected in proportion to their strength, regardless of their content.[97]

On such grounds, then, Hare seeks to defend his recent account of moral thinking against various kinds of criticism. In so doing, he insists that everything that he says in his latest writings, either by way of defence against his critics or by way of developing the implications of his account further, constitutes a reinforcement of his original form of rationalist non-descriptivism.

Notes

(An author's name followed by a number in square brackets refers to the book or article which has that number in the bibliography.)

1. G.E. Moore, *Principia ethica* (Cambridge University Press, Cambridge, 1903); H.A. Pritchard, *Moral obligation* (Clarendon Press, Oxford, published posthumously in 1949); W.D. Ross, *The right and the good* (Clarendon Press, Oxford, 1930) and *Foundations of ethics* (Clarendon Press, Oxford, 1939).

2. Ayer [1], p. 9.

3. Ibid., p. 107.

4. Ibid., p. 108.

5. Ibid., emphasis mine.

6. Ibid.

7. Ibid., pp. 109–10.

8. Ibid., p. 111.

9. Ibid., p. 112; cf. Ayer [2], pp. 17–34.

10. Stevenson [3], p. 54.

11. Ibid., p. 57.

12. Ibid., p. 33.

13. See ibid., pp. 59–60. Stevenson's failure to distinguish clearly 'emotions' (and 'feelings') from 'attitudes' has been criticised by Urmson [5], pp. 40–8.

14. C.L. Stevenson, 'The emotive meaning of ethical terms', *Mind* (1937); reprinted in Stevenson [4], p. 13.

15. Stevenson [3], p. 13.

16. Stevenson, 'The emotive conception of ethics and its cognitive implication', *The Philosophical Review* (1950); reprinted in Stevenson [4], p. 66.

17. Stevenson, 'Relativism and nonrelativism in the theory of value', *Proceedings of the American Philosophical Association* (1960–1); reprinted in Stevenson [4], p. 87; cf. also p. 89.

18. Stevenson [3], p. 81.

19. Stevenson [4], p. 210; cf. also pp. 213–14.

20. Stevenson [3], p. 207.

21. Ibid., pp. 213–14.

22. Ibid., p. 210.

23. Ibid., p. 115.

24. Ibid., p. 113, emphasis mine.

25. Ibid., p. 139.

26. Ibid.

27. Urmson [5], pp. 63–71, 77–80.

28. Stevenson [3], p. 90.

29. G.J. Warnock, 'Contemporary moral philosophy' in Hudson [6], pp. 446–51.

30. Ibid., p. 453.

31. Stevenson [3], p. 139.

32. Ibid., p. 113; cf. also p. 27.

33. Ibid., pp. 156–7; cf. also Ch. 11.

34. Ibid., p. 158.

35. R.M. Hare, 'Freedom of the will', *The Aristotelian Society*, supp. vol. 35; reprinted in Hare [12], pp. 1–12.

36. J.L. Austin, *How to do things with words* (Clarendon Press, Oxford, 1962), esp. Lecture 10; cf. Hare [10], esp. pp. 53, 100–16.

37. Hare [8] (2nd impression, Oxford University Press, Oxford, 1964), pp. 80f, 131, 145, 153f; cf. his 'Supervenience', *The Aristotelian Society*, supp. vol. 58 (1984), pp. 1–16.

38. Hare [8], Ch. 4.

39. Ibid., p. 172.

40. Ibid., pp. 124–6; cf. also pp. 167–8.

41. Ibid., pp. 171–2.

42. Ibid., p. 20, emphasis mine; cf. also Hare [9], p. 79.

43. Hare [9], pp. 70–1, 170.

44. Hare, 'Universalizability', *Proceedings of the Aristotelian Society*, 55 (1954–5); reprinted in Hare [12], pp. 13–28.

45. Ibid., p. 13. Here Hare regards only moral value-judgements as 'U-type', but in *Freedom and reason* he takes all value-judgements to be 'U-type'.

46. R.M. Hare, 'Principles', *Proceedings of the Aristotelian Society*, 73 (1972–3), p. 4.

47. Ibid., p. 5. For the further logical property of 'overridingness' see Hare [9], pp. 166–9 and Hare [15], pp. 53–62.

48. A.C. MacIntyre, 'What morality is not', *Philosophy*, 32 (1957), pp. 329–30.

49. Warnock, in Hudson [6], p. 457.

50. R.M. Hare's review of G.J. Warnock's 'Contemporary moral philosophy', *Mind*, 77 (1968), p. 438.

51. MacIntyre, 'What morality is not', pp. 325–8.

52. Peter Winch, 'The universalizability of moral judgements', *Ethics and Action* (Routledge and Kegan Paul, London, 1972), pp. 151–70.

53. Jean-Paul Sartre, *Existentialism and humanism*, trans. H.E. Barnes (Methuen, London, 1957), pp. 35–9.

54. MacIntyre, 'What morality is not', p. 328.

55. W.D. Hudson, *A century of moral philosophy* (Lutterworth, Guildford and London, 1980), pp. 138–9. For a further discussion of these criticisms see Hudson, *Modern moral philosophy*, 2nd edn (Macmillan, London, 1983), pp. 201–48.

56. Hare, 'Principles', pp. 1–4.

57. Stevenson [3], p. 114.

58. Hare [9], pp. 92–5.

59. Ibid., p. 97.

60. Ibid., pp. 91–2.

61. Ibid., p. 123.

62. Ibid.

63. Ibid., p. 118, emphasis mine.

64. See Phillipa Foot, 'When is a principle a moral principle?' *Aristotelian Society*, supp. vol. 28 (1954); 'Moral beliefs', *Proceedings of the Aristotelian Society*, 59 (1958–9); 'Moral arguments', *Mind*, 67 (1958); the last two reprinted in Foot [18]; D.J. Phillips and H.O. Mounce, 'On morality's having a point', *Philosophy*, 40 (1965), reprinted in Hudson [14].

65. Hare, 'Descriptivism', *Proceedings of the British Academy*, 49 (1963); reprinted in Hudson [14], pp. 254–7.

66. Hare [9], p. 173.

67. E.g. G.E.M. Anscombe, 'Modern moral philosophy', *Philosophy*, 33 (1958);

R.W. Beardsmore, *Moral reasoning* (Routledge and Kegan Paul, London, 1969); Stuart Hampshire, 'Morality and pessimism' in his *Public and private morality* (Cambridge University Press, Cambridge, 1978).

68. Foot, 'Moral beliefs', esp. pp. 113–19, 124, and 'Moral arguments', pp. 102–9.

69. Hare [9], pp. 25, 187–91; cf. Hare [8], pp. 121–2.

70. Hare [8], pp. 100–10.

71. Foot, 'Goodness and choice', *Aristotelian Society*, supp. vol. 35 (1961); reprinted in Foot [18], pp. 132–47.

72. Hare, in Hudson [14], pp. 252–4. For a similar criticism of Hare, but from a teleological standpoint, see Peter Geach, 'Good and evil', *Analysis*, 17 (1956). For Hare's reply, see 'Geach: good and evil', *Analysis*, 18 (1957). Both reprinted in P. Foot, *Theories of ethics* (Oxford University Press, Oxford, 1967).

73. Hare, 'Ethical theory and utilitarianism' in H.D. Lewis (ed.), *Contemporary British philosophy* (4 vols, Allen and Unwin, London, 1976), vol. IV, p. 146. The two-level view is anticipated briefly in Hare [9], pp. 42–6.

74. Ibid., p. 124.

75. Hare [15], p. 46.

76. Ibid., p. 46.

77. Ibid., p. 82.

78. Ibid., p. 6; see also Hare, 'What makes choices rational?' *Review of Metaphysics*, vol. 32, no. 4 (June 1979), pp. 633, 636.

79. Hare [15], Chs. 5, 6, 7.

80. Ibid., p. 4.

81. Ibid., p. 171.

82. See e.g. Foot [18].

83. Hare [15], p. 6.

84. Ibid., p. 218.

85. Ibid., p. 227.

86. Ibid., p. 226.

87. Ibid., p. 183.

88. Ibid., p. 219; see further Hudson, *Modern moral philosophy*, pp. 428–30.

89. See e.g. H.M. Robinson, 'Is Hare a naturalist?' *Philosophical Review*, vol. 91, no. 1 (January 1982), pp. 73–86. This paper was written before *Moral thinking* appeared.

90. Hare [15], p. 186.

91. Ibid., p. 222.

92. Ibid., p. 96.

93. Ingmar Persson, 'Hare on universal prescriptivism and utilitarianism', *Analysis*, 43 (1983), pp. 43–9; Fred Feldman, 'Hare's proof', *Philosophical Studies*, 45 (1984), pp. 269–83; G.F. Schueler, 'Some reasoning about preferences', *Ethics*, 95 (October 1984), pp. 78–80; cf. also Ayer [2], pp. 47–8; and H.M. Robinson, 'Imagination, desire and prescription', *Analysis*, 41 (January 1981), pp. 55–9.

94. Hare, 'Some reasoning about preferences: a response to essays by Persson, Feldman, and Schueler', *Ethics*, 95 (October 1984), pp. 81–5.

95. Hare [15], p. 144. Cf. the qualification in ibid., pp. 101–16, 140–4, 1980, and 'What makes choices rational', pp. 629–32.

96. See e.g. Ayer [2], pp. 48–50; R.W. Beardsmore's review of Hare's *Moral thinking* in *Times Higher Educational Supplement*, 7 May 1982.

97. Hare [15], pp. 178–9.

Bibliography

Emotivism

Ayer's brief account of moral judgements as devoid of 'literal meaning' and of moral terms as purely 'emotive' occurs in

[1] A.J. Ayer, *Language, truth and logic*, 1st edn (Victor Gollancz, London, 1936).

A recent defence of his emotivism is to be found in his lecture 'Are there objective values?', printed in

[2] A.J. Ayer, *Freedom and morality and other essays* (Clarendon Press, Oxford, 1984).

Charles Stevenson's much lengthier accounts of emotivism are

[3] C.L. Stevenson, *Ethics and language* (Yale University Press, New Haven, 1944) and

[4] C.L. Stevenson, *Facts and values* (Yale University Press, New Haven, 1963), which includes his influential 1937 article, 'The emotive meaning of ethical terms'.

[5] J.O. Urmson, *The emotive theory of ethics* (Hutchinson, London, 1968) is an excellent critical discussion.

Emotivism presents moral talk as fundamentally non-rational: a view questioned and discussed by G.J. Warnock in his essay 'Contemporary moral philosophy', printed in

[6] W.D. Hudson (ed.), *New studies in ethics* (2 vols, Macmillan, London, 1974), vol. II.

Emotivism also presupposes a view of emotions as irrational, and independent of the will, a view challenged by, for instance, Bernard Williams in 'Morality and the emotions' in

[7] J.P. Casey (ed.), *Morality and moral reasoning* (Methuen, London, 1971).

Universal prescriptivism

Richard Hare has written prolifically on moral philosophy: his views can be found, mainly, in

[8] R.M. Hare, *The language of morals* (Clarendon Press, Oxford, 1952, and Oxford University Press (paperback), Oxford, 1964)

[9] R.M. Hare, *Freedom and reason* (Oxford University Press, Oxford, 1963)

[10] R.M. Hare, *Practical inferences* (Macmillan, London, 1971)

[11] R.M. Hare, *Essays on philosophical method* (Macmillan, London, 1971)

[12] R.M. Hare, *Essays on the moral concepts* (Macmillan, London, 1972), which includes his seminal 1955 article, 'Universalizability'

[13] R.M. Hare, *Applications of moral philosophy* (Macmillan, London, 1972), in his lecture, 'Descriptivism', reprinted in

[14] W.D. Hudson (ed.), *The is–ought question* (Macmillan, London, 1969), which also contains many other relevant articles, in

[15] R.M. Hare, *Moral thinking: its levels, method and point* (Clarendon Press, Oxford, 1981), where he attempts a rapprochement with his descriptivist opponents' views in so far as he thinks they carry some weight, and in his article, 'A reductio ad absurdum of descriptivism', printed in

[16] S. Shanker (ed.), *Philosophy in Britain today* (Croom Helm, London, 1986).

For articles on Hare's philosophy, as well as his own 'Replies to critics', see the forthcoming

[17] N. Fotion and D. Seanor (eds), *Hare and critics: essays on moral thinking* (Oxford University Press, Oxford, forthcoming).

Philippa Foot has been one of Hare's most important critics in a series of articles first printed in philosophical journals: most of them are reprinted in

[18] P. Foot, *Virtues and vices* (Basil Blackwell, Oxford, 1978).

[19] D.H. Monro, *Empiricism and ethics* (Cambridge University Press, Cambridge, 1967) is an admirably clear-headed discussion of naturalism and non-naturalism.

This bibliography has been prepared with the assistance of the author of the chapter, S.F. Tsinorema.

M.A.P.

28 | Value, Authenticity and the Death of God

John Llewelyn

Friedrich Nietzsche (1844–1900)

'God is dead,' announces Nietzsche's Zarathustra, descending from the mountain to whose solitude he had climbed ten years before.[1] In the forest on the lower slopes he meets again the hermit who saw him go up, who continues to worship a transcendent God, and is quite incapable of understanding Zarathustra's news. Moving on to the nearby town, Zarathustra preaches in the market place that sin, which was once sin against a God beyond this world, is now sin against this world. It is now not with a supraterrestrial Divinity, but with the earth that we are called to keep faith, and with the overman, the *Übermensch*, who is 'the meaning of the earth'. The man who has any greatness in him is the man who answers the call to be a bridge to the overman. However, for the people in the market place also Zarathustra's message comes too soon. They are unable to grasp what this overman could be. This is because, although they may acknowledge that they have murdered God, they think they have therefore become God in His place. 'The insipid and cowardly concept "man" à la Comte and Stuart Mill, perhaps even the object of a cult – It is still the cult of Christian morality under a new name –'.[2] John Stuart Mill does indeed claim in the second chapter of *Utilitarianism* that 'in the golden rule of Jesus of Nazareth, we read the complete spirit of the ethics of utility.' And Auguste Comte's *Course of positive philosophy* envisages a cult of humanity based on a system of education that will promote a science of sociology to the point at which it takes over not only theological ways of thought, but also the metaphysical ways of thinking in which explanation by appeal to divinities gives way to explanation in terms of hypostatised abstractions. Nietzsche welcomes the refusal to

641

postulate underlying causes and subjects or souls or wills conceived as entities or faculties that act. There is no necessity to go behind the deed to an invisible doer. This is to make the mistake of believing that where there is a noun or pronoun which is the grammatical subject of a sentence there must be a metaphysical subject to which it refers. The self is no more than a fiction. The assumption that it is not is the product of a trick the weak man plays on himself so that he may believe that his weakness is something he chooses and that he is therefore entitled to some credit for freely making this choice.[3]

What Nietzsche objects to in Comte is the idea that society is made up of the enlightened and those within their care. This, Nietzsche holds, is to make the fatal error of treating the masters as shepherds. The flock exists for the sake of the masters. Hence the kind of man that Zarathustra loves is the one who sees himself not as an end, but as a means to the overman and is ready to sacrifice himself for his sake. The men Zarathustra meets in the market place have not yet learned to see themselves in this perspective. They have no greater ambition than to conform to Zarathustra's description of what Nietzsche calls the last man. The last man is the man who has provided himself with a system of education designed to minimise suffering. The morality of the flock or the herd, the slave morality, gives priority to the abolition of pain among all human beings without distinction of rank. Everyone should be motivated by pity for those who suffer. What is bad for one is bad for another and what is good for one is good for another. By the standard of the master morality, however, it is not the case that what is good for one is good for another. Universality, a criterion of morality according to both utilitarians and their Kantian critics, becomes irrelevant once the master morality is distinguished from the morality of the slave. It is only those who pity that are pitied by the masters. For their part, the masters consider great suffering to be a welcome discipline. It is suffering that fosters strength of the right sort, the sort that rates higher on their table of values than what are pre-eminent virtues for the slaves: benevolence, unselfishness, modesty, moderation, friendliness, industriousness, compassion and humility.[4] The latter virtues are the virtues of the creature. The morality of the master is the morality of the creator. The Creator is dead. Long live the creator of values, of values beyond good and evil.

Beyond the antithesis of good (*gut*) and evil (*böse*) is the antithesis of good and bad (*schlecht*). In a note in his *On the genealogy of morals* the former Professor of Philology at the University of Basel proposes a research project that would bring together philologists, philosophers, historians, physiologists and doctors of medicine to study the history of morality and to seek, in particular, an answer to the question 'What light does linguistics, and especially the study of etymology, throw on the history of the evolution of moral concepts?' One implication of the fact that Nietzsche makes this proposal is that it would be wrong to see as more than provisional sketches the contributions towards an answer to this question that Nietzsche himself makes in *On the genealogy of morals* and elsewhere. He does nevertheless lay down guidelines that would have to be followed if the programme were to be properly carried out. For example, when the various tables of values have been distinguished it would be necessary to ask what value is to be ascribed to each table of values. Here we see the difference between the possibility of a reversal, which remains within the limits of a given scale, and the possibility of a transvaluation, which substitutes one scale for another and compels us to ask 'Valuable *for what?*' What is valuable for promoting the survival of a race or the happiness of the greatest number might not be valuable for the development of a powerful elite. Unless this question is kept in mind we shall, like certain English historians of morality to whom Nietzsche refers as 'English psychologists', assume that the opposite of goodness is the egoism, ruthlessness or cruelty from which one suffers at the hands of others. In assuming this we have already forgotten that these qualities are valuable when the community is threatened from outside. Even in time of peace the community may need leaders with these qualities. The danger they then comprise for those whose table of values rates the community above the individual is met by electoral and other arrangements for ousting the leader who does not keep in mind that he is only society's servant.

However, Nietzsche maintains, it is historically inaccurate to locate the origin of the idea of good in the society whose members prize above all the values of hedonistic utilitarianism. This is incorrect whether it be said that 'good deed' and 'socially useful deed' are synonymous or whether it be said that, although these expressions are not synonymous, 'good' first acquired its meaning from being applied to useful and unegoistic behaviour. The historical inaccuracy of this genealogy is indicated by the etymological facts that *gut* was first opposed to *schlecht*, and *schlecht*, like *schlicht*, meant plain or common, rather as the English 'villain' derives from 'villein', the word for a menial servant or ignoble serf, and as the ancient Greek word for good, *agathos*, originally meant 'well born' and was contrasted with *kakos* and *deilos*, plebeian. 'Good' was the word the noble used of themselves. As for *gut*, Nietzsche speculates, does not that go back to the name Goth, and did not that mean 'like a God'? In any case, it is only the man of action, the aristocrat and the ruler who have the power and right to give things their names. The ruled are merely men of reaction and resentment. Their reactivity and resentment were demonstrated when the dominance of the lords waned and

> the Jews achieved that miracle of inversion of values thanks to which life on earth has for a couple of millennia acquired a new and dangerous fascination – their prophets fused 'rich', 'godless', 'evil', 'violent', 'sensual' into one and were the first to coin the word 'world' as a term of infamy. It is in this inversion of values (with which is involved the employment of the word for 'poor' as a synonym of 'holy' and 'friend') that the significance of the Jewish people resides: with *them* there begins the *slave revolt in morals*.[5]

With this revolt in morals the slave manifests his resentment by describing as evil the noble qualities of the masters by whom he feels himself threatened. This, Nietzsche adds, is a spiritual revenge which the priests of Israel consolidate by the most wily stroke of all: by nailing their ostensible opponent to the cross in order to spread the gospel of the common man.

Although in *Beyond good and evil* Nietzsche writes that the noble type of man is the creator of values, in *On the genealogy of morals* he allows that resentment is creative and gives birth to values. The difference is that noble creativity says 'Yes' to itself, while the creativity of slavish resentment says 'No' to something outside itself. The master morality issues from the affirmation of the good and moves as an afterthought to the idea of the bad applied to inferiors. The slave morality begins by denying that good, by calling it evil. The slavish mentality moves from the concept of evil and generates by contrast the concept of good which it applies to itself. The slave's concept of good is thus doubly negative. It is the negation of evil which is the negation, in the sense of rejection, of the values that the master calls good. From this it follows that the slave subscribes to the faith in antithetical values which, Nietzsche says, is the fundamental faith of the metaphysicians. Perhaps Hegel is one of the metaphysicians he has particularly in mind when he says this. Nietzsche's slave, like the slave of Hegel's *Phenomenology of spirit*, is preoccupied with how he is perceived by someone else and with whether he achieves recognition. This is part of what is meant in saying that the slave is reactive. Nietzsche's master, on the other hand, is indifferent to the opinion others have of him. 'He does not need to be approved of.'[6] He is himself the paradigm for his concept of what is good. Any thought he may give to the mean and despicable is entirely incidental.

It may be objected that the master is as committed as the slave to antithetical thinking, for does not the master's concept of the good depend for its content on the concept of the bad, and is not the latter its opposite? In reply to this it could be said first that although a concept depends on its opposite for its content, it can be before somebody's mind when its opposite is not. It could be replied secondly that bad is a contrary of good and that the latter admits of more than one contrary idea, somewhat as both blue and green are contraries of red. Rather as I can have the concept of red if I have that of some other colour with which it contrasts, so I can have the concept of good without my having to have that of bad. It is tempting to add that the comparison with colours is especially relevant because it brings with it a correlation between different colour qualities and different degrees of wavelength, and this fits Nietzsche's theory that the differences between tables of values are different expressions of the will to power, power being a matter of more or less in relation to power expressed elsewhere. The will to power is itself a will to difference which manifests itself in different ways. With the slave, as we have seen, it manifests itself as a negative reaction to standards set by others. With the master the standards are set by himself and are standards that set him apart. This affirmation of his own difference is not dependent on any belief about how he appears in the eyes of others. It is an affirmation of aristocracy and distinction that

> acts and grows spontaneously, it seeks its opposite only so as to affirm itself more gratefully and triumphantly – its negative concept 'low', 'common', 'bad' is only a subsequently-invented pale, contrasting image in relation to its positive basic concept ...[7]

Furthermore, the high-born feels himself to be happy without need of comparing his state with that of anyone else, whereas the low-born deceives himself into believing that he is happy. The man of resentment deceives himself because his idea of bliss is absence of pain, the passivity of Buddhist Nirvāna. He says 'No' to life. His only 'Yes' is the 'Yes' with which he embraces nihilism. But, Nietzsche argues, and his argument is directed also against Schopenhauer, this idea of bliss rests on the erroneous supposition that pleasure is the antithesis of pain. Pleasure, as the high-born know, is increase of power, and that may be a process of overcoming the pain of resistance. Pain may even be an ingredient of pleasure.[8] Once we see through the bogus antithesis of pleasure and pain we see the fallacy behind psychological hedonism, the doctrine that what man always seeks is pleasure and the avoidance of pain. We see that the desire for happiness understood as the maximum of pleasure and the minimum of pain is not a motive for action. Pleasure is a side-effect, not what one wants; 'what man wants, what every smallest part of a living organism wants, is an increase of power'.[9] Philosophers and psychologists have failed to see this because they have not distinguished, on the one hand, the displeasure of meeting a resistance which stimulates an increase of power in order to conquer it and, on the other hand, the displeasure of listlessness resulting from exhaustion. The assumption that this second kind of displeasure is the only kind is the foundation of religious and philosophical nihilism, 'Buddhism for Europeans'.

Nihilism in the writings of Nietzsche takes more than one form, and he offers more than one explanation for its existence. When understood as the belief that nothing has meaning or value it may result from an imperfect comprehension of Nietzsche's own teaching. If our conception of moral value is based on the premiss that what human beings seek ultimately is only pleasure and freedom from pain, we may be thrown into despondency when Nietzsche persuades us that this premiss rests on a confusion.

Nietzsche's teachings expose his readers to other forms of disillusionment. When Zarathustra declares that God is dead he speaks not only of the God of religion, but of the absolutes of traditional metaphysics and morals. He is denying that existence moves towards some goal. He is challenging the coherence of the thought that having its own extinction as its goal is preferable to the thought that existence has no goal at

645

all. He is rejecting the idea that man is part of a unified whole. And he is repudiating the doctrine that behind or beyond the phenomenal world in which we live lies a true noumenal world in itself.[10] However, this questioning of man's will to transcendent truth itself suggests that the antidote to the flaccid nihilism which the destruction of this idea might produce is to welcome the prospect of living dangerously in the bracing climate of the acknowledgement of the fictitious character of the classical values advocated by Platonism, Christianity, Kant, Schopenhauer and so on, inspired by the realisation that with the destruction of this ideal of transcendent truth we destroy the idea that the world in which we actually live is a world of mere appearance. We bring values down to earth. He who rejoices in this prospect is the man who has health and self-discipline to overcome both the hankering after other-worldly values and the nausea of the nihilism that threatens when that hankering is shown to be vain. He is the overman for whose coming Zarathustra bids us prepare.

The closest anticipations of this man of the future have been men such as Alcibiades, Caesar, Leonardo, Goethe and Napoleon. But such men have emerged by chance, and they have usually been objects of fear. Now they must be willed and purposefully bred.[11]

Thus the sermon Zarathustra brings down from his mount is very much a programme for action. Nietzsche himself, descending from his upland '6000 feet beyond man and time',[12] formulates a prescription that many of his readers see as his alternative to Kant's Categorical Imperative. This prescription is contained in Nietzsche's doctrine of eternal recurrence. Exactly what this doctrine amounts to remains a matter of controversy. In some places Nietzsche expounds it as though it were a theory of descriptive natural science. Regarded prescriptively, as a recipe by following which man may transcend himself, the doctrine of eternal recurrence specifies what it means in practice to face the fact that there is no source of eternal values beyond the world of passing phenomena, and that the latter make up the only reality there is. Kant's Categorical Imperative commands that we perform only those actions where a rule is followed that we could consistently will everyone to follow in relevantly similar circumstances. That imperative is addressed to man's rationality as opposed to his animal nature. Nietzsche refuses to make this sharp opposition. This is not because he rejects reason. It is because he holds that reason and passion are not antithetical but are manifestations of a single principle, namely will to power. Accepting this is a corollary of accepting that the world of sensory becoming is not a second best. Nietzsche goes as far as to assert that every passion contains a quantum of reason and that reason, far from being opposed to the passions, is 'a state of the relations between different passions and desires'.[13] Therefore when Nietzsche declares himself to be a supporter of Dionysus against the Crucified[14] he is not advocating the virtue of unbridled passion. And when he posits as fundamental what he calls will to power, he is not contrasting will and desire. Nor is some faculty of rational will as opposed to desire being addressed by the demon in Nietzsche's parable who asks us whether we are capable of longing for nothing more than that everything in our life should be repeated over and over for ever in the same order and in every least particular. What greater affirmation of life could there be than to be able to will this? 'That *everything recurs* is the closest *approximation of a world of becoming to a world of being*.'[15] What surer test of our love could there be than Nietzsche's formula?

> My formula for greatness in a human being is *amor fati*: that one wants nothing other than it is, not in the future, not in the past, not in all eternity. Not merely to endure that which happens of necessity, still less to dissemble it – all idealism is untruthfulness in the face of necessity – but to *love* it . . .[16]

Greater love hath no man than this. It is such love of necessity that separates the sheep among us from the lions, 'the blond beast'. It is his response to this challenge that decides whether, on the one hand, man continues to harbour resentment against others, to direct that resentment inward against himself in the form of festering bad conscience, to sink into the narcosis of nihilism so bereft of a sense of value that it is incapable even of rising to resentment and shame, or whether, on the other hand, man listens to Zarathustra's exhortation to see himself as a creator of value and a bridge to the overman, the man who overcomes not others but himself, the man whose mastery is authenticity, the man who is the self-excelling author of himself.

Evidently, Nietzsche's genealogy of morals is more than a programme for theoretical research. It gives rise to a programme for action. Can the same be said of the account of value given in the phenomenological ontology of Jean-Paul Sartre?

Jean-Paul Sartre (1905–80)

Sartre's subtitle for *Being and nothingness* is 'An essay in phenomenological ontology'. That would appear to forestall any expectation that it will contain precepts for behaviour. First, because phenomenology, as exemplified in the work of one of Sartre's principal mentors, Edmund Husserl, aims to be unprejudiced description, so that prescription would be by implication outside its scope. Secondly, if ontology is a study of being and what is, as the word itself implies, how can it be concerned as such with what ought to be done? This does not mean, as Sartre himself points out, that a description of a state of affairs or an assertion of a matter of fact may not have effects, whether or not the speaker intends them, on how the hearer behaves. How else could we explain Zarathustra's disappointment over the lack of response from the people in the market place to his announcement that God is dead? And it makes a practical difference in the life of the character Goetz in Sartre's play

647

The Devil and the Good Lord when he finally brings himself to believe that there is no God. No longer dependent on the judgement of God, he feels himself emancipated from the established ideals of the sinner and the saint, free to admit that he is the inventor of values and that 'man is nothing other than what he makes himself'. This is what Sartre calls the first principle of existentialism in the popular lecture published under the title *Existentialism is a humanism.* [17] But in that lecture he takes pains to distance himself from the view expressed in *The Brothers Karamazov* that everything is permitted if there is no God. Whether or not there is a God is irrelevant to Sartrian existentialism. Although this version of existentialism is atheistic, it does not see any need to spend time arguing that there is no God. Like Nietzsche, Sartre is primarily intent on exposing man's inclination to worship idols, whether they bear the name of God or the name of Man. For although Sartre's lecture states that existentialism is a humanism, the humanism here meant is not one that infers precepts for conduct from the nature of man along the lines of traditional theories of natural law. That is ruled out for two reasons. In the first place, because precepts cannot be inferred from any natural fact. In the second place, because there is no such fact as human nature. The character in *Nausea* who makes an idol of Mankind is not one that Sartre expects us to admire.

With regard to these two points, Sartre writes trenchantly in *Being and nothingness* of the 'seriousness' of everyday morality for which 'Values are sown on my path as thousands of little real demands, like the signs which order us to keep off the grass.' [18] When it is said of someone that he ought to do this or that, it is implied that there is a reason why he ought to, and it is reassuring if we can think that these reasons are written into the nature of things and are there waiting to be invoked. But what makes obligations obligatory cannot be matters of fact. The foundation of the demand that values lay upon us cannot be something that just is, cannot be being. 'Value derives its being from its exigency and not its exigency from its being.' We do not perceive this when we are absorbed in carrying out the tasks of our daily agenda. When we are engaged in these our world is one of buses-to-be-caught, letters-to-be-written and bills-to-be-paid, where this gerundive character of what requires to be done is as though it were part of its nature. Only when we draw back are we struck by the thought that the importance of paying the bill or writing the letter is in the last resort up to me. I am free to change my order of priorities. The value of a thing or an action does not belong to it in the way that roundness belongs to the stone. It most certainly does not belong to it in the way that three-sidedness belongs to the triangle. Value is not an accidental or essential attribute of the valued thing. It is not founded in what I value. It is founded rather in me. But again, not founded in my essence. The only essence I have is itself the character formed by my actions, that is to say, by my own evaluations. So my essence is not a foundation. It is the product of evaluations which I can either endorse or revise. This is what Sartre means when he says, in a formula adapted from Heidegger, existence is prior to essence. 'I have to realise the meaning of the world and of my essence; I make my decision concerning them – without justification and without excuse.' This reflective apprehension that I am the unfounded foundation of value is an experience of ethical anguish.

Ethical anguish is what its opposite, the spirit of seriousness, hopes to keep at bay by imagining values as petrified footholds within the world. Much of Sartre's work is illustration and analysis of the various stratagems we employ in the hope of escaping this consciousness of our dreadful freedom. None of these stratagems can succeed, because in adopting them to escape the thought of my freedom the thought of that freedom must be in my mind, even if not explicitly before it. Typical of these stratagems is the recourse to psychological determinism. Despite the immediate intuitive evidence of freedom, or because of it, and because the consciousness of this freedom is such a burden, the psychological determinist tries to shuffle the burden off by telling himself that every state of consciousness, including this consciousness of his freedom, is explicable by laws that are not in principle different from those that explain the behaviour of phenomena in his physical environment. He sees himself as though from the outside, as though under the gaze of the Medusa which turns everything before it to stone. Daniel in Sartre's novel *The reprieve* longs for petrifaction, to be a paederast as a stone is a stone, to be as others see him, to be a statue of himself. His counterpart in the chapter on *mauvaise foi* in *Being and nothingness* also acknowledges his homosexual behaviour, but it is behaviour of which he is ashamed. He could also acknowledge, Sartre writes, that there is more to himself than the behaviour others see. There is the free choice he makes to do whatever it is that he does. This more is also a less. It is what makes a person less than a statue in the sense that a person lacks the statue's dense solidity. To be a statue is to be something in-itself. Its way of being is to be entirely self-contained. To be a person is to be aware of not coinciding with oneself. It is, in the phrase Sartre borrows from Hegel, to be what one is not and not to be what one is. The statue is what it is, and although it endures through time, it does not exist its temporality. In saying this Sartre is following Heidegger and the etymological clue that 'exist' derives from *ekstasis*, 'standing outside'. To exist in the way that a person exists is to transcend one's own past, one's habitual dispositions, the essence one has made for oneself, hence not to be what one is and was, to be other than oneself. But one also transcends oneself towards a goal one has not reached. According to Sartre, the being that is not in-itself but for-itself, the conscious human being, is oriented towards an end. He is conscious of possibilities, even if he has no explicit awareness of these. As Sartre puts it, converting an intransitive verb into a transitive one, he exists these possibilities, he is them. Because being one's possibilities is an aspect of what it is to be a human being, Sartre says that to be a human being is to be what it is not. It is to be them in the mode of not being them, not in the mode in which a table is a table. It is actively to exist and to live them.

So the way of being of the human being is to be both towards a particular concrete future in the light of a particular concrete past and retrospectively towards a particular concrete past in the light of a particular possible future. This is what Sartre means when he says that man is a self-referring circuit of transcendence and facticity. Pro-ject is another word Sartre borrows from Heidegger to convey this idea of transcendence. And the idea of project or projection is a facet of intentionality, a concept Sartre borrows this time from Brentano and Husserl. In Sartre's analysis, however, the intentionality of all consciousness is explicated by the negativity of the Hegelian notion of being what one is not and not being what one is. The way of being of a being that is conscious of something is a way of being that is at the same time a way of not being, that is to say, a way of not being its body or its past or its concrete situation. As is implied in what we have already said, this way of not being must be distinguished from the way in which this table is not this chair. The former not-being is intrinsic to being, the latter purely external. It is precisely this distinction that is blurred by the homosexual in *Being and nothingness* when he denies that he is a homosexual, while admitting homosexual behaviour. Daniel's dream in *The reprieve* is to save himself from the embarrassment of having to answer for his actions by acquiring self-identity of the sort exemplified by a slab of stone. The character described in *Being and nothingness* attempts to achieve the same result by saying that he is not a homosexual, but, without being fully conscious that he is doing it, he construes his not being a homosexual in the way we construe the table's not being a chair. Both he and Daniel are in bad faith. They endeavour to conceal from themselves the hyphenation of their irresoluble transcendence-facticity.

Another variation of this self-induced myopia is illustrated by Sartre's frequently retold story of a girl who pretends that the amorous advances of her companion are being made as though to someone else. While wanting to enjoy the adventure of aroused desire by acknowledging it and her transcendence, she simultaneously attempts to disclaim responsibility for her response by disowning her body and treating it as impersonal, external facticity cut off from what she sees as the pure spirituality of her mind.

Sartre's literary and philosophical works contain many representations of real or imaginary persons acting roles. *Saint Genet, actor and martyr* treats of the writer Jean Genet who, when a little boy, was branded a thief. Sartre sets out to show how the imposition of such labels is a device by which we hope to localise the possibility of stealing to those we have categorised as thieves, thereby protecting ourselves from the discomfort of the thought that we too are capable of theft. Genet comes to accept this role of scapegoat and, as the phrase goes, plays it for real. But it is a role that he plays, as too does the waiter in *Being and nothingness* whose every gesture is a reading of a minutely detailed imaginary script. However, his choosing to play this role is at odds with his unconfessed aspiration to be a waiter in the manner that the tray he is carrying is a tray. Role-playing as an expression of bad faith is no less in contradiction with itself than is bad faith in its various other forms. Perhaps the most radical of Sartre's statements related to this particular form is that even a feeling or mood like sadness is the playing of a part. Sadness is an affliction, but, says Sartre, it is an affliction we inflict on ourselves, the so-called cause of our sadness being only the occasion of our behaving in those ways that are normally manifested when people are in this mood. However difficult it may be, it is always in principle possible to smile. Quite generally, argues Sartre in his *Sketch for a theory of the emotions*, emotions are a kind of magical rite in which we turn away from the difficulty of deciding what would be the rational thing to do. And to suppose one is irresistibly overwhelmed by sadness or, for that matter, by joy, is once more to give way to the seduction of bad faith. I am not overcome by an emotion in the way that a sandbank gets covered by the tide. Paradoxical though it may seem, my succumbing to a mood or an emotion is something I choose, and my choice has to be continually renewed. The non-rationality of emotion is the contradictoriness of bad faith. For choice, even when, as here, it is not reflective, presupposes a distance of negativity between the act of choosing and the object of that choice. But in this case what is chosen is a melancholy state of consciousness that must be imagined to be an entirely positive plenitude if it is to afford an escape from the responsibility of coping rationally with the emergency that is the occasion for the choice. This is therefore a practically contradictory choice, since no state of consciousness is without negativity. One of the main theses of the phenomenological ontology of *Being and nothingness* is that all consciousness is intentional, consciousness *of* something, as Husserl maintains, and that this *of* is to be explicated with the help of the notion of negativity by Hegel out of Heidegger. As Sartre says, in a sentence which shows that throughout this discussion of his phenomenology of bad faith we have still been talking about value: 'The being-in-itself of sadness perpetually haunts my consciousness [of] being sad, but it is as a value which I can not realize; it stands as a regulative meaning of my sadness, not as its constitutive modality.'[19]

In the *Cahiers pour une morale* Sartre remarks that value is revealed like the expression on a face.[20] This indicates that what he writes early in *Being and nothingness* about value cannot be properly understood in isolation from what he writes later when his account of the being for-itself of a human being is supplemented by an account of his being for-others. The chapter on concrete relations with others describes a series of ways, ranging from the sadism of the master to the masochism of the slave, in which one person is in conflict with another. There is no exit from this interpersonal conflict, according to *Being and nothingness*, because there is no way of achieving a synthesis of my consciousness of the other, which makes him my slave, and my being an object of his consciousness, which makes him my master and which leads Sartre to say in his play *No exit* that other people are my hell. Now it is the other as an object for me that makes it possible for me to have ideals. According to Sartre, I conceive my sadness in terms of sadness as I see it expressed on another's face. My sadness is a state of my consciousness that nevertheless aims to have the consistency of sadness looked at from outside, the frozen essence of sadness that one sees on the face of a statue. This ideal synthesis of being for-itself and being in-itself is what Sartre understands by value.

Value cannot be realised. Since it is supposed to be a whole combining conscious existence that implies distance from itself with the self-coincidence of material objects, its way of being can be neither existence nor being in-itself. It can only be that of ideality and of a necessarily unrealisable ideal. Employing a phrase used by Hegel to remind us that the optimism of Hegelian idealism is what Sartre is criticising here, he concludes: 'Human reality therefore is by nature an unhappy consciousness with no possibility of surpassing its unhappy state.'[21]

It will be asked why we try to realise an unrealisable ideal whose unrealisability is not all that difficult to see. Sartre's answer to this is that we close our eyes and slip into bad faith like we slip into sleep. The values of bad faith are aimed at, but not explicitly. It should be noted too that Sartre distinguishes values and ends.[22] An end or goal may be posited explicitly and also ultimately realised. A value is not focused on. It is marginal. It haunts the for-itself. In the *Cahiers* he writes that a value is familiar, the suggestion being that it is comparable with a familiar spirit or ghost. Value is familiar because it is *my* ghost. It is the ideal self that haunts each for-itself, the self that would be not only the freedom that founds the nothingness of its consciousness, but is also the foundation of its being. However, the only being that would be the foundation of its non-being as well as the foundation of its being, the only being that would be in-itself-for-itself, would be a self-caused being, *ens causa sui*, in one word: God. 'Thus the best way to conceive of the fundamental project of human reality is to say that man is the being whose project is to be God.'[23] Each man's ideal self is each man's missing God. This God is missing not because God is dead, but because God could never have been alive. Sartre's atheistic existentialism confesses an unquenchable thirst for God. The ideal of thirst itself, on Sartre's account, is not thirst's satisfaction. It is satisfaction combined with a continued desire to drink: eternal thirst.

We now have some understanding of Sartre's reasons for saying that whereas the Passion of Christ is that man may be born, the passion of man is that God may be born, and this passion is a *passion inutile*.[24] Employing an expression that gains prominence in the *Critique of dialectical reason*, Sartre brings out the self-contradictoriness of man's ideal by calling it a detotalised totality. From our survey of his philosophy so far it would appear that Sartre maintains that as well as being condemned to be free, man is condemned to the contradictoriness of bad faith. How could he not be, given that he is both facticity and transcendence? Yet, quite early in *Being and nothingness* Sartre asserts that 'These two aspects of human reality are and ought to be capable of a valid coordination.'[25] He goes on to explain that a coordination or synthesis is impossible for bad faith because bad faith 'affirms facticity as *being* transcendence and transcendence as *being* facticity'. Although in the Introduction of the same book he states that 'Being has not been given its due',[26] here he is saying that bad faith fails to give non-being its due. This is another way of saying that it does not give freedom its due. The person who is in fad faith aims to evade the anguish of being confronted with the intuitive evidence of his freedom revealed in reflection by postulating psychological determination on the weaker basis of faith. His reflection is prejudiced or, as Sartre says, accessory and impure. Pure reflection will face up to the fact that we are authors of our values. It will enable us to achieve authenticity at least from time to time. The first step towards understanding this is made when we understand that reflection is not contemplation but pro-ject. It is second-level projective reflection on the ground-level project of my immediate engagement in the world. Pure reflection is an *à faire*, a to do and to make. What it does is to keep asking a question, to keep the question open. It keeps open, for example, the question whether I love her or not, and the question whether I am cowardly or brave. It keeps such questions open in the sense that it resists the temptation to conceive dispositions as fixed states. Pure reflection remembers that what I am always remains to be seen, at least until my death. Until then I never cease to be challenged by choices. It is what I choose to do and to make of myself that comprises my courage or love. In the authenticity of pure reflection I remember that 'my Being is in question in my Being'.[27] I recognise that my projects call perpetually to be endorsed and are therefore exposed to the risk of being revised. This holds for subsidiary projects and for the fundamental project that is the framework within which they are organised and is the source of the meaning of my world.

Where bad faith is haunted by the substantial spectre of an unrealisable value, authenticity is 'haunted by the spectre of the instant'.[28] The instant is the point of crisis at which one fundamental project, like atheism, is succeeded by the choice of another fundamental project, like belief. Since this choice is the fundamental choice of a foundation, it is, as Sartre uses the term, absurd.

Whereas pure reflection is practised on myself, existential psychoanalysis is practised on others, as Sartre practises it on Genet, Flaubert and Baudelaire in extensive studies of these authors; but presumably it can also be practised on oneself when, as in Sartre's *Words*, what is being studied is one's past as though it were another person. The psychoanalysis that Sartre practises must be distinguished from the Freudian kind because it substitutes a theory of prereflectivity for the theory of the unconscious which, on Sartre's reading of Freud, lapses into the bad faith

653

of psychological determinism. Although existential psychoanalysis is based on the existential–ontological structures outlined in *Being and nothingness*, it goes beyond ontology into the interpretation of very specific biographical and historical detail.

The *Critique of dialectical reason* undertakes the ambitious task, only partially accomplished, of constructing a synthesis of pure reflection, existential psychoanalysis and the socio-historical theories of Marx. This programme is implicit in the assertion made in the *Cahiers* that pure reflection is a practical project in which I affirm solidarity with myself and with others.[29] In the project of pure reflection the ideal solidity of unrealisable value makes way for an actual, contractual solidarity with others and with myself. But the ethical question opened here in the project of pure reflection is not a question for ontology. Confirming the remarks with which we began this section of our chapter, and restating the topic with which it has been concerned, Sartre writes in the section entitled 'Ethical implications' with which *Being and nothingness* ends:

> Ontology itself can not formulate ethical precepts. It is concerned solely with what is, and we can not possibly derive imperatives from ontology's indicatives. It does, however, allow us to catch a glimpse of what sort of ethics will assume its responsibilities when confronted with a *human reality in situation.* Ontology has revealed to us, in fact, the origin and the nature of *value* ...[30]

Although the *Critique of dialectical reason* is an analytic and dialectical treatment of the pledge and other forms of engaging oneself with others, its first and only volume is subtitled 'A theory of practical ensembles'. We should not be surprised therefore if it reads more like sociology than a compendium of ethical precepts. If we are looking for ethical imperatives from Sartre, we do better to turn to his vast output of occasional articles and speeches, situating them in the wider context of his political life.

Martin Heidegger (1889–1976)

What am I? A being which is not its own foundation, which *qua* being, could be other than it is to the extent that it does not account for its being. This is that first intuition of our own contingency which Heidegger gives as the first motivation of the passage from the un-authentic to the authentic. There is restlessness, an appeal to the conscience (*Ruf des Gewissens*), a feeling of guilt. In truth Heidegger's description shows all too clearly his anxiety to establish an ontological foundation for an Ethics with which he claims not to be concerned, as also to reconcile his humanism with the religious sense of the transcendent.[31]

This passage raises the following two questions. How can Heidegger profess not to be concerned with ethics if he is concerned with conscience and guilt? And how can he profess humanism, if indeed he does, while witnessing to a religious sense of the transcendent? In this section we shall try to find answers to these questions in the second chapter of the second division of Heidegger's *Being and time*. This chapter above all is the one in which we might expect its author to be concerned with ethics. It is also a chapter, occurring half-way through the book, from which we can get a good idea of what is going on in the book as a whole. That Heidegger himself considered it a key chapter is plain from his statement in it that 'the call of conscience, existentially understood, makes known for the first time what we have hitherto merely asserted, that uncanniness pursues Dasein and is a threat to the lostness in which it has forgotten itself.'[32] Our attempt to answer the two questions raised by Sartre will take the form of a gloss on certain words of what we shall refer to as this seminal sentence.

'Dasein' is the word Sartre translates as *réalité humaine*. This translation is unfortunate in two respects. Heidegger uses the word Dasein in order to avoid the implication that *Being and time* is a contribution to anthropology, the science of man, or that it is a study of human nature in the tradition of, for example, Descartes and Locke. That tradition treats the human being as a species of thing, as a *res*, in Descartes' words, a thing which thinks, alongside other entities like trees and tables and stones, reality being the sum total of these and whatever other sorts of entity there may happen to be. It is true that Heidegger sometimes uses the word Dasein as a noun to refer to an individual human being, but he hopes his readers will not forget that it is the being of these beings that his word primarily intends, their being as expressed by the verbality of the participle *Sein*, which is a different way of being from that of trees and tables and stones. He contends that our involvement with beings of the latter kind is primarily and for the most part as wherewithal for getting on with our everyday life, the table for eating off, the tree for making a table, and the stones for building a house in which to put the piece of furniture we have made. It is only in the second place that the table presents itself to us as a material object with so-called primary qualities like rectangularity and so-called secondary qualities like colour. These traditional primary and secondary qualities come to light only when we have to take account of them in order to make good a defect of some kind or other, for instance to replace a strip of veneer or renew a leg, and we have to look around for a piece of timber of the appropriate size and grain. Then the present at-handness of things takes over from readiness to hand and we become aware of the practical context in which things (*pragmata*, as the Greek calls them) are normally handy or unhandy for achieving a particular immediate or mediated end. The structured totality in which they have this orientation depends on there being a being who is-there, a being who is (exists) its there, Dasein. Hence the instrumental value of things is not correctly interpreted as a tertiary property superimposed upon a substance already endowed with layers of primary and secondary qualities.

The way of being that Heidegger calls Dasein is misinterpreted if we suppose that it can be subsumed under the categories of readiness to hand or presence at hand. His term for the basic structures of Dasein's way of being is existentials. The matrix existential is care (*Sorge*). In Dasein's involvements with what is ready to hand care manifests itself as concern (*Besorgen*), a term Heidegger uses to cover also what we ordinarily understand by carelessness and unconcern. In its personal relationships care is solicitude (*Fürsorge*), a term that also extends over the deficient modes of cruelty, callousness and indifference. Care is the unity of existentiality, facticity and falling. Existentiality is Dasein's being thrown ahead of itself, pro-jection into its future. Facticity is its finding itself thrown into a world that is already there as a *fait accompli*. Falling is Dasein's disposition to be taken over by the world as a being present in it side by side with others. Falling manifests itself in the way one 'does' the Louvre in order to be able to report that one has seen the sights one is expected not to miss. It manifests itself in the kind of small talk that merely mouths accepted opinions. Instead of speaking in your own voice you repeat what 'they' say. The author of your words and deeds is no one in particular. Dasein has succumbed to 'the lostness in which it has forgotten itself'. Heidegger's pages on falling and the forms of inauthenticity look back to Kierkegaard and to what Nietzsche writes on the language and morality of the herd. They are pages to which Sartre is in turn indebted, as he is to what Heidegger writes about facticity and existentiality.

Whereas Dasein's falling is displayed in the peddling of platitudes, its facticity is how it is predisposed, the mood in which it finds itself. Its existentiality, on the other hand, is how Dasein understands itself in its directedness ahead, an understanding that in everyday life is primarily an understanding how to do something, not an understanding or knowing that something is the case. The conceptual knowing of facts is but one sort of understanding, and it presupposes the non-theoretical understanding of how to do what is called for, just as the factuality claimed by an assertion presupposes the facticity of the asserter's Dasein.

Each of these structures of Dasein is meshed with the others, as no one dimension of temporality makes sense on its own. Dasein's present is retentive of a past that was protentive of a future, and it is protentive of a future that will be retentive of a past. Or, as Heidegger puts it, Dasein's having been arises out of its to come, in such a way that the coming to have been of the to come releases from itself the present.[33] The difficulty we have grasping what this means is the difficulty we have preventing ourselves falling into an inauthentic grasp of temporality as the time of calendars and clocks. If we fail to get what Heidegger is struggling to convey when he writes that temporality temporalises itself, rather than that temporality is such-and-such, we fail to gather what he means by care, for 'temporality makes possible the unity of existence, facticity, and falling, and in this way constitutes primordially the totality of the structure of care.'[34] To be a being with care is to be a being who is there, and to be there, *da sein*, is to be elsewhere, at a distance from myself across the space-time of my inhabited, lived, existed, world. Dasein interprets itself as spatio-temporal ek-sistence. Hence Heidegger's generic title 'existentials' for the structures of Dasein of which the aspect of care called 'existentiality' is but one. Hence too his description of the analysis of the way of being of Dasein as existential ontology.

We now have an inkling at least of what Heidegger means when in the seminal sentence on page 277 of *Being and time* he refers to an existential understanding of the call of conscience. This will be an understanding of the kind appropriate to existential ontology where that is the study of those structures of Dasein underlying the subject-matter of, for example, a psychological investigation of the phenomena of conscience. Psychology and the other special sciences describe and explain facts. Fundamental ontology describes what makes factuality possible. It is more fundamental also than the theory of knowledge, and more fundamental than the theory of practice. It treats of what is prior to the distinction between theory and practice. It is therefore more basic than ethics.

The phenomena of conscience described in the second chapter of the second division of *Being and time* are not phenomena specific to ethics or the metaphysics of morals. They are the topic of phenomenological ontology. Why in the sentence we are interpreting does Heidegger say that the phenomenological ontological approach to the call of conscience discloses the uncanny? There is nothing obviously uncanny about the ordinary moral conscience. We are quite familiar with the idea that the voice of conscience tells us either that we are guilty of acting or failing to act in a certain way in the past or that we should take care to avoid such guilt in the future. Typically, guilt is failure to pay a debt, and debt or duty is construed according to a book-keeping model. I must keep my account straight and pay my dues. Like Nietzsche,[35] Heidegger points out that *Schulden haben* is to be in debt and *schuldig sein* is to be guilty. But while Nietzsche's genealogy maintains that the economic and commercial concept gets moralised, Heidegger's ontology maintains that the moral and legal concepts of guilt and indebtedness depend on a primordial non-economic 'Guilty!' The idea of imbalanced economy behind the moral and legal notions of guilt is implied by the contrary concept of justice whose symbol is the pair of scales on the dome of the Old Bailey. Moral and legal guilt is lack of balance established by a procedure of calculation like totting up columns of figures in a ledger. My guilty moral conscience is consciousness of the result of a reckoning made in my transactions with other people in the pursuit of my everday concerns. It has to do with solicitude (*Fürsorge*) regarding that kind of beings whose way of being is Dasein and concern (*Besorgen*) with the kind of beings whose way of being is not Dasein. It is a relationship with beings as beings. And it is a relationship in which the guilty party in some way or other falls short. His conduct with regard to the other is wanting in some respect. The other is deprived. There is something missing or amiss, as there is when a table or a hammer is not functioning as it should. According to Heidegger, it will be recalled, the malfunction of *a being*, an 'ontic' matter of fact, puts us on the way to an awareness of the existential structures of Dasein's *being*-in-the-world, a matter of ontology. Similarly, he claims, the phenomena of moral conscience and guilt, ordinarily conceived on analogy with the absence of some entity that ought to be present, like a negative balance of one pound, depends on an existential absence or nullity in the very being of Dasein. Not to see this is not to see the difference between beings of which the way of being is explicable in terms of the categories of readiness to hand and presence at hand, and the way of being whose interpretation must be in terms of existentials.

In particular, the moral phenomena of conscience and guilt are not properly grasped unless they are placed in the context of the call of the voice of ontological conscience that pronounces the verdict 'Guilty!' This is a verdict pronounced not only over the morally guilty. It is pronounced over the morally innocent as well. For, as we have observed, one of the positive existential structures of Dasein is falling. Dasein is prone to regard itself as one among other things in the world and as undistinguished from the 'they' whose opinions it merely passes on. It regards itself as *a* being, forgetting the ontic-ontological difference between beings that can be counted and accounted for and being that is beyond any reckoning. The morally innocent, if there are any, are not free from ontological guilt. ontological guilt is not something for which one can be morally censured. And the freedom in question is not the freedom of voluntary or deliberative choice. The latter is related to ontological freedom as the truth of assertions is related to primordial truth understood as the disclosure of a space in which things of its everyday world is the outcome of falling, and if falling is, as Heidegger says, an existential structure, how can Dasein be guilty, since it would appear that lostness in the 'they' self is something it cannot help? This problem arises from not distinguishing levels of freedom and responsibility. Ontological freedom is the ground of ethical freedom and choice. So ontological guilt is not something for which one can be morally censured. And the freedom in question is not the freedom of voluntary or deliberative choice. The latter is related to ontological freedom as the truth of assertions is related to primordial truth understood as the disclosure of a space in which there can be objects about which assertions can be made. To speak of primordial truth and primordial conscience or guilt is to speak of the opening or unconcealing that is prior to the distinctions between the asserted proposition and the action done, between theory and practice. The correctness and incorrectness of propositions, the rightness and wrongness of acts, presupposes what the Greeks called *alētheia*, which Heidegger reads as *a-lētheia*, unconcealing. *Alētheia* is also unforgetting, that is, becoming mindful again of what Dasein is prone to forget. It even forgets this forgetting. To call it to mind is to respond to the call of ontological conscience. Primordial conscience is the call of care (*Sorge*). And care is care of and for being. This is a call that Dasein addresses to itself, but it is as if the call originates beyond or above it. It seems to have its source beyond the self and beyond the world of Dasein's everyday concerns. That is why, in his seminal sentence, Heidegger says that the call of conscience disloses that uncanniness pursues Dasein and is a threat to the lostness in which it has forgotten. The word 'uncanniness' in this sentence translates *Unheimlichkeit*, which means literally not being at home. In its everyday existence Dasein is at home in its involvement with ready to hand or present at hand entities, accomplishing or failing to accomplish the tasks on its immediate daily agenda. As it goes about its business Dasein's moral duties make themselves known much as what calls to be done in the running of a household economy. When, however, we give ear to the 'still small voice' of ontological conscience, it is as though Dasein is disclosed to itself, to the very *Sein* of its *Da*. This voice is still in the sense of the German *still*. It is a silent call. So too is the responsible response. Here, silence speaks louder than the words that propound propositions and pass them along: communications.

All this may sound very strange. Perhaps if it does not, we have missed the central point. In either case, we have begun to answer the first of the two questions raised by Sartre with which this section of this chapter began. Heidegger's concern is with ontological conscience and guilt, with a call in responding to which we cease to be closed into our preoccupation with things conceived as no more than objects over against us or means by which to meet our biological, economic and cultural needs. We achieve, if only momentarily, the unclosedness, *Ent-schlossenheit*, of authenticity. Authenticity is not ethical virtue, but what makes ethics, ethical virtue and ethical vice possible. Hence concern with conscience and guilt as *Being and time* is concerned with them is not a direct concern with ethics as this is ordinarily understood. So much for the first question about Heidegger raised by Sartre.

Our answer to the second question about Heidegger raised by Sartre can be very brief. The voice of conscience seems to come from above and beyond us. It would therefore be natural to suppose that it comes from some transcendental being such as God. Whatever one may think about the origin of the ontic moral conscience which pronounces specific commands, the voice of ontological conscience cannot be traced back to any being, thus it cannot be traced back to any transcendent being, whether God or something or somebody else. The voice of ontological conscience, according to Heidegger, is the voice of being, not the voice of a being, however strange that may sound. And being, the concept of which medieval philosophers called a transcendental because it transcends every genus, is transcendent only in the sense that it is presupposed by all beings, including concepts, hence by the concept of divinity, and by the being, if he is a being, referred to as God. This has nothing to do with the idea suggested by Plato's *Euthyphro* that moral goodness must be prior to God if we are to say informatively that God is morally good. Heidegger is not talking about moral goodness except by implication. He is asking after the meaning of being and particularly, in *Being and time*, after the way of being that Dasein is. Strictly speaking, therefore, as we mentioned at the outset, because *Being and time* is a work of fundamental ontology, it is not a discussion about man. Thus, as Heidegger emphasises in his *Letter on humanism*, except indirectly or in an extended sense of the term, he is not professing humanism. It is no wonder that in that *Letter* he complains that he has been misunderstood by Sartre. Further evidence of that misunderstanding is Sartre's phrase 'religious sense of the transcendent', if what Sartre means here by transcendent is a transcendent being. As for the word 'religious', that has so wide and in-definite a connotation that it may not be inappropriate to attribute a religious sense to Heidegger, and we could justifiably expect him to wish to include an account of the conditions for such a sense within his fundamental ontology. Further light on this question, and on the two questions about Heidegger raised by Sartre with which we have been dealing in the present section, is cast by the response to Heidegger made in the writings of Emmanuel Levinas. A brief indication of the nature of that response will be given in the following postscript.

Postscript on Emmanuel Levinas (1906–   )

If Sartre attributes to Heidegger a sense of the transcendent or says that *Being and time* witnesses to such a sense, this is precisely what Levinas says is absent from that book. And if Nietzsche and his Zarathustra proclaim 'God is dead', Levinas appears to be proclaiming 'Long live God.'

Levinas points to several features of *Being and time* that he believes to be incompatible with recognition of transcendence. He notes, for example, that according to Heidegger care is a unifying existential. He notes also that Dasein's projects are the source of the order of its world. Furthermore, he observes, Dasein's being-in-the-world has a wholeness derived from Dasein's being towards its death; from its birth Dasein exists endingly, though I may try to draw death's sting by speaking as though death is an event that happens to someone, not in particular to me. Fourthly, Levinas points out, Heidegger holds that being-with (*Mitsein*) is a basic structure of being-there. This aspect of Heidegger's existential analytic is also criticised by Sartre, who argues, rightly or wrongly, that being-with is merely psychological, and that if it is treated as ontological it is incompat-ible with the conflictual character of all interpersonal relations. Levinas criticises Heidegger's notion of being-with because, he contends, it implies

that relations between persons are symmetrical. This, and phenomenological ontology as a whole, is a denial of the irreducible asymmetry where
You and I are face to face.

The face to face is an ethical encounter in which no
one is more responsible for you than I. You accuse me, and this accusation is
an irruption into my world from what is absolutely exterior and outside the
embrace of my projects. What Levinas says about this responsibility is not
provided for in what Heidegger says about the call of conscience. The call of
conscience in *Being and time* is the call being-there addresses to itself, sum-
moning its responsibility to being. But the vocative in which You, the
Other, address me is not the voice of being and it does not call for a response
to being. The only response can be 'Here am I.' This is the response of an
existent being to another existent ethical being, and both call and response are
beyond being and nature, *Otherwise than being or beyond essence*, as Levinas
puts it in the title of one of his books. The ethical, which is beyond nature,
metaphysical, exceeds ontology. And it transcends the totalisation Heidegger attributes to my being towards my death. The vital question at issue for
me is not my being and my death, but your life and death and you, you who
are not another I, but an absolute Other.

Levinas calls the Other the Master. It would be a
mistake to interpret this along the lines of either Nietzsche's or Hegel's
analysis of the relation of master and slave. I and the Other, according to
Levinas, are not in co-relation. We are not terms within a system, so we are
not in a relation in any ordinary sense. Further, although the Other is my
Master, he is Master in the sense of teacher, and although Levinas does say
that the Other commands my responsibility, the authority of this command
is grounded in the Other's irremediable poverty and need. I look up to the
Other, but what I look up to is his humility. And thirdly, although I more
than anyone have an indelible non-contractual obligation to serve the Other,
that does not make me his slave.

Levinas goes as far as to say that the tie which binds
me to the Other is religious, and he explains the sense in which the Other
transcends me infinitely by reminding his reader of the statement made by
Descartes in the third Meditation that God's infinity overflows the idea I have
of it. The aim of that Meditation is to demonstrate the truth of the proposition that God exists. This is the proposition that Nietzsche's Zarathustra
claims to be false. Sartre claims that its truth and falsity are irrelevant to
existentialism and that, anyway, it is incoherent. Heidegger claims that
whether this proposition is true, false or incoherent is an ontic question, a
question about what is, hence outside the scope of *Being and time*, which asks
the prior ontological question, 'What is the meaning of being?' Levinas
claims that belief in God has its root beyond both ontology and ontics, in the
face to face with the other person, in ethics, which disrupts being-in-the-
world.

661

Notes

(An author's name followed by a number in square brackets refers to the book or article which has that number in the bibliography.)

1. Nietzsche [1], Prologue, Section 2.

2. Nietzsche, *The will to power*, ed. W. Kaufman (Viking Press, New York, 1968), Section 340.

3. Nietzsche [2], I, Section 13.

4. Nietzsche, *Beyond good and evil*, trans. R.J. Hollingdale (Penguin Books, Harmondsworth, 1973), Section 260.

5. Ibid., Section 195.

6. Ibid., Section 260; *The gay science*, trans. W. Kaufman (Vintage, New York, 1974), Section 289; Nietzsche [4], Section 113.

7. Nietzsche [2], I, Section 10.

8. *The will to power*, Section 699.

9. Ibid., Section 702.

10. Ibid., Section 12; *The twilight of the idols*, trans. R.J. Hollingdale (Penguin Books, Harmondsworth, 1968): 'How the "Real World" at last became a Myth'.

11. Nietzsche, *The Antichrist*, trans. R.J. Hollingdale (Penguin Books, Harmondsworth, 1968), Section 3.

12. Nietzsche, *Ecce homo*, trans. R.J. Hollingdale (Penguin Books, Harmondsworth, 1979): 'Thus spoke Zarathustra'.

13. *The will to power*, Section 387.

14. Ibid., Section 1052.

15. Ibid., Section 617.

16. *Ecce homo*: 'Why I am so clever'.

17. Trans. P. Mairet (Methuen, London, 1948).

18. Sartre [14], p. 38.

19. Ibid., p. 61.

20. Sartre, *Cahiers pour une morale* (Gallimard, Paris, 1983), p. 261.

21. Sartre [14], p. 90.

22. *Cahiers pour une morale*, pp. 259–60.

23. Sartre [14], p. 566.

24. Ibid., p. 615.

25. Ibid., p. 56.

26. Ibid., p. xxxvi.

27. Ibid., p. 497.

28. Ibid., p. 467.

29. *Cahiers pour une morale*, pp. 495–6.

30. Sartre [14], pp. 625–6.

31. Ibid., p. 80.

32. Heidegger [20], p. 277 (marginal pagination).

33. Ibid., p. 326.

34. Ibid., p. 328.

35. Nietzsche [2], III, Sections 4, 20–1.

Bibliography

Nietzsche

Nietzsche's own writings are provocatively readable. His best known book is also perhaps his worst and probably best avoided, at any rate initially:

[1] F. Nietzsche, *Thus spoke Zarathustra*, trans. R.J. Hollingdale (Penguin Books, Harmondsworth, 1961).

More approachable are, for instance:

[2] F. Nietzsche, *On the genealogy of morals*, trans. W. Kaufmann and R.J. Hollingdale (Vintage, New York, 1969)

[3] F. Nietzsche, *The twilight of the idols* and *The Antichrist*, in a single volume, trans. R.J. Hollingdale (Penguin Books, Harmondsworth, 1968)

[4] F. Nietzsche, *Daybreak*, trans. R.J. Hollingdale (Cambridge University Press, Cambridge, 1982).

Useful selections from Nietzsche can be found in

[5] W. Kaufmann (ed.), *The portable Nietzsche* (Viking Press, New York, 1954), which contains *Zarathustra*, *Twilight of the idols*, *Antichrist* and *Nietzsche contra Wagner* complete, and much else, and

[6] G. Clive (ed.), *The philosophy of Nietzsche* (Mentor, New American Library, New York, 1965).

A useful introduction to Nietzsche is provided by

[7] R.J. Hollingdale, *Nietzsche* (ARK paperback, Routledge and Kegan Paul, 1985). This is a revised and condensed version of the hardback originally published in 1965.

A carefully sanitised defence of Nietzsche is given by the well-known

[8] W. Kaufmann, *Nietzsche: philosopher, psychologist, Antichrist* (Princeton University Press, Princeton, 1950).

A recent book, greeted as 'the most important book on Nietzsche in English', is

[9] A. Nehemas, *Nietzsche: life as literature* (Harvard University Press, Cambridge, Massachusetts, and London, 1985).

Some of the most distinguished writing on Nietzsche has been by Erich Heller, and essays by him on Nietzsche can be found in

[10] E. Heller, *The disinherited mind* (Penguin Books, Harmondsworth, 1961) and

[11] E. Heller, *In the age of prose* (Cambridge University Press, Cambridge, 1984).

Sartre and Heidegger

Sartre's views are most easily approached by his own attempt to present a brief introduction to them:

[12] J.-P. Sartre, *Existentialism and humanism*, trans. Philip Mairet (Methuen, London, 1948), which was first published in 1946 in French under the title *L'existentialisme est un humanisme*, or perhaps by means of his novels, particularly the trilogy

[13] J.-P. Sartre, *The roads to freedom*, which consists of *The age of reason*, *Reprieve*, and *Iron in the soul*, all available in Penguin.

Sartre's major philosophical work is the lengthy

[14] J.-P. Sartre, *Being and nothingness*, trans. Hazel Barnes (Methuen, London, 1969).

For writings on Sartre,

[15] M. Warnock, *The philosophy of Sartre* (Hutchinson, London, 1965) and

[16] I. Murdoch, *Sartre, romantic rationalist* (Bowes and Bowes, Cambridge, 1953, Fontana paperback, London, 1967) are short and readable.

[17] A. Manser, *Sartre, a philosophical study* (The Athlone Press, University of London, London, 1966) is a longer work, which deals with the philosophical aspects of Sartre's fiction as well as theoretical works.

Two other books by Mary Warnock relate to other topics in this chapter as well as to Sartre:

[18] M. Warnock, *Existentialist ethics* (Macmillan paperback, London, 1967) deals lucidly with Kierkegaard, Heidegger and Sartre, and is particularly useful on Sartre, and

[19] M. Warnock, *Existentialism* (Opus paperback, Oxford University Press, Oxford, 1970) covers Kierkegaard, Nietzsche, Husserl, Heidegger, Merleau-Ponty, and, at greater length, Sartre.

Heidegger's major philosophical work is

[20] M. Heidegger, *Being and time*, trans. J. Macquarrie and E. Robinson (Basil Blackwell, Oxford, 1962).

[21] M. Heidegger, *Existence and being*, trans. W. Brock (Vision Press, London, 1949), contains the essays which constituted Heidegger's main output after *Being and time* (first published in 1927).

A useful compilation of Heidegger's writings is

[22] M. Heidegger, *Basic writings*, ed. D.F. Krell (Harper and Row, New York, 1977, Routledge and Kegan Paul, London, 1978).

[23] M. Grene, *Martin Heidegger* (Bowes and Bowes, London, 1957) is a general discussion of his work.

Levinas

Levinas' works are available as follows:

[24] E. Levinas, *Existence and existents*, trans. Alphonso Lingis (Nijhoff, The Hague, 1978)

[25] E. Levinas, *Otherwise than being or beyond essence*, trans. Alphonso Lingis (Nijhoff, The Hague, 1981)

[26] E. Levinas, *Totality and infinity*, trans. Alphonso Lingis (Nijhoff, The Hague, 1969)

[27] E. Levinas, *Time and the other*, trans. Richard A. Cohen (Duquesne University Press, Pittsburgh, 1987)

Another accessible, introductory work is the dialogue:

[28] E. Levinas, *Ethics and infinity*, trans. Richard A. Cohen (Duquesne University Press, Pittsburgh, 1985).

This bibliography has been compiled with the assistance of the author of the chapter, John Llewelyn.

M.A.P.

Part F: Society, Art and Religion

Introduction

From moral philosophy it is a short step to political philosophy; from questions such as 'Why ought I to tell the truth?' or 'Is this a morally good action?' to questions such as 'Why ought I to pay the taxes that the state requires me to pay?' or again 'Is this law a good law?' As in the case of moral philosophy, one is asking questions about such concepts as those of obligation, right and good, but now one is concerned with one particular context in which these concepts function – that of the state.

It would be possible to draw, within political philosophy, a distinction which parallels that drawn in moral philosophy between meta-ethics and normative ethics. That is, one could distinguish between the political philosophy which (for example) merely analyses concepts such as those of the state, or of political obligation, and that which makes pronouncements about what *is* obligatory on the citizen, or what it is right for states to do or not to do. In fact, there is no commonly accepted pair of terms in political philosophy with which to make such a distinction. Perhaps this is because, in the course of most of its history, political philosophy has been concerned with normative quesitons. Even questions such as 'What is the state?' are not, as a rule, asked in order to clarify ordinary usage, but are asked with a view to deciding how citizens ought to behave in relation to the state.

This can be seen from Chapter 29 and 30, which are concerned with different answers to this question. The views about the nature of the state discussed in Chapter 29 support a sceptical response to the assertion that states have a moral claim to obedience. The theories discussed in that chapter assert that states are by their nature oppressive institutions; that civil law is essentially a set of commands which are in the interests of a power group of some kind. Whilst it would be foolish to underestimate the com-

667

plexity of Marxist theory, it is fair to say that the classical expression of this view of the state is to be found in Marxism, more specifically in the very influential form of it propounded by Lenin. But such a view is by no means peculiar to Marxism. In recent years, the war in Vietnam led many Americans to reassess their relations to the state, and to adopt critical attitudes to it which owed little or nothing to Marxist ideas.

Chapter 30 presents the views of those philosophers who have seen the state as an institution whose existence can be justified to its citizens. Their theories are basically of two kinds: the organic theory of the state, which argues that life outside the state would be incomplete, and the social contract theory, which sees political obligation as resting on the obligation to carry out one's side of a contract. These two theories give different answers to a question which may already have occurred to the reader. The question is this: if both moral philosophy and political philosophy are concerned with questions about what is obligatory, right and good, what reason is there for drawing a sharp distinction between them, and for treating them as separate parts of philosophy? Both theories would agree that there is a distinction; however, the organic theorist would say that the distinction is that between a part (moral philosophy) and the whole (political philosophy). Theories of social contract, on the other hand, are apt to say that morality does not depend on the state for its existence. They would say that although morality implies the existence of interpersonal relations, and hence a *society* of human beings, there is a distinction between the idea of a society and the idea of a *state*, with all the institutional apparatus that the state involves.

One important form of the social contract theory, that put forward by John Locke in the seventeenth century, links the defence of the state as an institution with the existence of certain human rights. The philosophy of rights merits a chapter to itself, and is discussed in Chapter 31. One must first note a distinction. When one speaks of 'rights' one may be speaking either of one's rights in law or one's rights as a human being – rights which the law ought to respect, and perhaps even promote. One's rights in law are the first topic of Chapter 31. Discussions of such rights are commonly regarded as forming a part of what is called 'the philosophy of law', and as this represents an alternative way of grouping some of the topics that are considered in this encyclopaedia, it may be useful to turn aside for a moment and say something about its content. I have already said that the philosophy of law deals with questions about an individual's rights in law. Another branch of the subject concerns the philosophy of punishment (discussed here in Chapter 33); for punishment is an institution which is chiefly, though not exclusively, designed to deal with violations of legal rights. The concept of punishment involves further concepts, notably those of responsibility and intention, and these topics (discussed here in Chapter 21 and 22) also form part of the philosophy of law.

The rest of Chapter 31 is concerned with the philosophy of human rights. The concept of human rights was of great importance in the seventeenth and eighteenth centuries; it is hardly necessary to mention the role that it played in the thinking of the men who drew up the constitution of the United States of America. In recent years, human rights have again become a focus of philosophical attention. For as the demands for the recognition of human rights, or at any rate the rights of large sections of humanity, have become increasingly insistent, so philosophers have paid more attention to questions about the precise nature of what is demanded, and the justifiability of such demands. Some philosophers try to justify them within the framework of an existing moral theory, such as utilitarianism; but perhaps the most influential defence offered in recent years is that offered by John Rawls, who bases his argument on the choices that people would rationally make in an 'original condition' of ignorance.

Rawls offers not only a justification of rights, but an assessment of the relative importance of rights – the right to liberty having, in his view, the greatest weight. Questions about the liberty of the individual are discussed in Chapter 32. The question here is whether there are any limits which the state ought not to transgress, in the sense that there are many activities of human beings which are simply not its concern, and which it should therefore leave them free to perform. The classical works on this issue are nineteenth-century ones – the defence of liberty made by John Stuart Mill, and the critique of Mill offered by Fitzjames Stephen. But the issues involved are by no means peculiar to the nineteenth century, and they are still the subject of intense debate.

Chapter 33 deals with the philosophy of punishment, and is the last of the chapters of the encyclopaedia which are devoted to political philosophy. Of course, it is not only states that punish; parents sometimes punish their children, and trade unions and religious communities punish rebellious members. But the harsher forms of punishment are the prerogative of the state, and it is the punishment inflicted by the state through the medium of courts of law that chiefly concerns philosophers. The basic questions are two: first, which persons are proper subjects for punishment, and second, what is the justification of punishment? The first of these has close links with the question of what exactly is involved in the concept of responsibility, whilst the second is linked with questions about the nature of punishment. The questions here are whether punishment is essentially a means of deterrence or a means of reform, or whether it involves an element of moral condemnation, which is not logically connected with either of these aims.

So far, the questions discussed in this part of the encyclopaedia are allied to those of moral philosophy; they concern problems which arise out of our use of words such as 'good', 'ought' and 'right'. We come next to questions in which problems of knowledge figure prominently, and which take up some of the discussions contained in Part B. The connecting link is the notion of a society. The state is a society of a certain kind, and societies are the fields of study of what are called the social sciences – anthropology, for example, or economics, or sociology. The main question for the philosopher is

> What exactly is meant by calling these disciplines *sciences*? Do they use methods which do not differ fundamentally from those of the natural sciences, or are their methods peculiar to themselves? If the latter, do they still deserve the title of 'science'?

Our inquiry will concentrate on sociology, which is discussed in Chapter 34.

Chapter 35 considers another form of inquiry into the activities of groups of human beings, to which the name of 'science' is only rarely (and then, controversially) given. This form of inquiry is history. The term 'philosophy of history' covers two main branches of study – which is not to suggest that there is no overlap between the two. On the one hand, the philosopher of history asks questions about what historians do. Here, one asks questions such as 'Do historians seek to discover laws? If so, how do their activities differ from those of sociologists?' Again, if there is to be something that merits the name of historical knowledge, historians must surely be capable of objectivity; but is this so? Such questions belong to what may be called the analytical philosophy of history; however, the term 'philosophy of history' is also applied to theories about the general pattern of historical change, such as those provided by Hegel and Marx. But such theories (which may be said to belong to the 'substantive' or 'speculative' philosophy of history) are not outside the range of the analytical philosopher. For one can ask of such theories whether they provide us with knowledge – whether, indeed, we can even expect knowledge of the kind that they claim to provide.

I said that one of the problems which concerns the philosopher of history is that of the objectivity of historical judgements. Problems of objectivity are at the heart of the two branches of philosophy which are discussed in the last two chapters of the encyclopaedia. Of these, Chapter 36 is concerned with aesthetics. Just as the moral philosopher is concerned with moral judgements, so the aesthetician is concerned with what may be called 'aesthetic judgements'. In these, words such as 'good' and 'bad' are used of works of art, whilst words such as 'beautiful' and 'sublime' are used both of works of art and of natural objects. Aesthetics is concerned with the meaning of such terms; it is concerned, for example, to explore the differences (and perhaps the resemblances) between 'This is a good flute' and 'This is a good flute concerto.' The problem of objectivity arises in this way. Many people would claim that to call a concerto 'good' is not just to express what they themselves feel, but is to say something which is objective; philosophers ask whether this is so.

The final chapter, Chapter 37, is concerned with the philosophy of religion. It may seem strange that, in this encyclopaedia, this topic should be separated so widely from the arguments for the existence of God. This separation, however, brings out a great difference between the topics of the two chapters. The point is that the arguments discussed in Chapter 15 are metaphysical arguments; but many philosophers who reject these arguments nevertheless believe that what religious people think and do can be rationally justified. To put this in terms of objectivity: such philosophers believe that religious utterances are not mere expressions of some feeling or attitude, but concern matters on which agreement can in principle be reached. The discussion of this issue is a crossing-point for many lines of philosophical inquiry; or, to change the metaphor, it involves references to many of the themes which we have already met. As such, the philosophy of religion is a particularly appropriate topic with which to conclude this survey of philosophy as a whole.

G.H.R.P.

29 | Political Obligation: Some Sceptical Views[1]

Graeme Duncan

The relationship between individual and state – the demands that the state can properly make on its citizens, or the legitimate expectations it may have of them, and vice versa – is clearly a central and continuing issue in political philosophy. To defend political obligation, or to justify political obedience, is just as demanding and appropriate a task as that of denying obligation or defending political disobedience: one cannot, least of all the sceptic, simply take for granted that 'the state' and its commands are legitimate.

What, indeed, is this state, that supposedly has so many claims upon us? Presented broadly, it is a territorially defined national political entity. Its rules and arrangements make it a particular kind of state, e.g. federal or unitary, liberal democratic or socialist, open or closed. In the real world, precise or ideal political types are likely to be fudged, e.g. we may find no pure examples of a liberal or a totalitarian state, or even of a unitary or a federal one. In addition, we may find that governments in power often deviate from the values, traditions or political assumptions of the state, so that there is a lot that is neither liberal nor democratic about the practice of British or American or Australian governments, and little that is egalitarian or genuinely Communist about the practice of Russian or Chinese or Czechoslovak governments. At this point the difference between government and state needs to be noted, although in the British liberal tradition the state is defined often as the political machinery of government in a community. However, there is an equally familiar and more useful interpretation, according to which government is the political authority engaged in the processes of government, whereas the state is a community or association of which people are part, to which they belong, which calls upon their loyalty and emotions, and with which they commonly identify. The dark side of incorporating affective elements into theories of the state is that these may include charismatic appeal, prejudice and narrow emotionalism, which easily support governments in making unjust demands upon citizens. But it is to the state in this deeper sense that obligation is acknowledged generally by citizens, and justified by philosophers.

The difference between the ideal relationships assumed in the theory of the state, or of particular states, and their actuality (including the actual practice of governments) is important because the philosopher or ideologist may justify our obligation to the ideal when in fact we are living in the only too real world. Our allegiance to a phantom, or an extreme and potentially morally crippling allegiance to everything the state asks, may be demanded. The political philosopher asks grand questions, and often provides grand answers. Why should we obey the law? Why should we assume that we are part of a political community, sharing in its benefits and reponsibilities? Why should we be citizens? What, precisely, does being a citizen involve? The political sociologist, the critical philosopher and the ordinary person tend to concentrate more on the actualities of political life, though these themselves require interpretation.

The question of political obligation – what obliges me to act as a citizen – is not a question of political behaviour. It is not: why are people, by and large, politically obedient? That question has various answers which are, on the face of it, empirical: people obey out of habit, convention and conformity, out of fear, ignorance and prudence, out of deep conviction or true belief. To others, their obedience may seem craven, absurd or destructive, with disobedience being justifiable if not morally compelling. At this point, accounts of political obedience and disobedience may be incorporated into normative theories. Jürgen Habermas, for example, links his account of the actual behaviour of citizens towards the state with a view of a legitimate order which would call properly on people's allegiance because they would participate fully in its arrangements. The account of the legitimation crisis of the modern state occurs alongside the image of free, participatory arrangements which would bond people deeply, rationally and voluntarily. As things are, the crisis of legitimacy of the modern state, which is essentially a decline of civic virtue, seems appropriate to him given the character of that state. The explanation of the alleged crisis of the state is its perceived lack of legitimacy – perceived by disaffected citizens as well as by Habermas – and it also is assumed that a legitimate state will be perceived as such by its citizens.[2]

The complex relationships between describing and evaluating political allegiances, and between the assumption that a certain kind of state is worthy of reflective allegiance and the agreement of the citizens that this is the case, is highlighted by the context in which this set of issues is commonly explored today. As a matter of fact, and not simply as a result of the internal contradictions of liberal democracy, the legitimacy of state commands and arrangements and, beyond these, of family, work and educational institutions has been challenged widely over the past two decades. What is at issue is not the legitimacy of this or that command, but the legitimacy of the whole framework. At the height of the Vietnam protest, two American professors of political science remarked on the way in which law and order had become the basic question of the day in advanced societies, with a crisis of legitimacy present in non-political sectors of life also. They wrote:

> This crisis of legitimacy has been visible for some time in just about all of the non-political sectors of life – family, economy, religion, education – and is now spreading rapidly into the political realm. The gigantic and seemingly impregnable organisations that surround and dominate men in the modern states is seen by more and more people to have at their centre not a vital principle of authority, but a hollow space, a moral vacuum. Increasingly, among the young and rejected, obedience is mainly a matter of lingering habit, or expedience, or necessity, but not a matter of conviction and deepest sentiment.[3]

The Vietnam War and the development of feminism (in particular) have pushed questions of political obligation to the centre of serious discussion, which serves to emphasise the practical origins and the practical bearings of what can easily appear abstract philosophical investigation. Similarly, Hobbes, Locke and Hegel had immediate political issues at least at the backs of their minds.

It is worth noting also that there is a great deal of political disobedience in advanced societies, some of which is justified by those who usually champion law and order. Thus there is not only disobedience to laws against some forms of protest, e.g. demonstrations, and refusal to fight in bad wars, but there is tax evasion and the black economy. Hugh Thomas' sad sketch of entrepreneurs losing their nerve as they are 'exhausted by problems of labour, hampered by taxation, tempted by increasingly corrupt practices, or at least tax evasion'[4] leads on to the claims that taxation exceeds its role, and that taxes need to be cut, bureaucracy reduced and state power weakened and decentralised. If this is not an incitement to the wealthy to evade their social responsibilities, it at least presents such evasion as understandable, and reminds us that questions of political obligation are going to be faced concretely and directly, and not at a distance, in relation to grand abstractions. However, the familiar and normally unprincipled evasion of civic duties is not a primary concern in the analysis of political obligation.

The familiar answers to the question of political obligation[5] – why should I in general accept and obey the law? – are as follows:

– Obligation arises because of commands issued by rational or legitimate

674

authorities, e.g. the various versions of the divine right of kings. Such answers are anti-democratic and normally pre-democratic as well.

– Obligation arises because otherwise societies would fall apart. Law-abidingness is necessary to hold society together. If society means a community of ideas or a moral entity, held together by the 'invisible bonds of common thought', then moral deviation, including a denial of one's political obligations, is likely to be seen as socially destructive. Thus Lord Devlin, in the various essays which make up *The enforcement of morals*, declares again and again how too great a relaxation of the bonds (or the bondage?), part of which is common morality, would lead to social disintegration.[6]

– Obligation arises because some kind of contract or exchange has been made, e.g. liberal contract theory, with its central notions of tacit or hypothetical consent, representing the exchange of freedom and insecurity for order and security. In the absence of a historical contractual act,[7] efforts are made to hypothesise a rational understanding or agreement, in order to establish a voluntary basis for both social union and political obligation. Freud's speculative anthropology presents us with a rational exchange by men in accepting civilisation. 'Civilized man has exchanged a portion of his possibilities of happiness for a portion of security.'[8] In ordinary discussion, one often meets a looser though structurally similar conception of exchange or of assumed obligation – that we receive benefits in the state and therefore incur duties. Apart from the problem of how, between whom and for what the imagined exchange took place, we are faced with the difficulty that the benefits received in the state vary immensely. Certainly the force of the claim must depend in large part on the responsiveness of the political order to those who find themselves in it. This has particular relevance to the liberal democratic order.

– Obligation can only arise, and only be assumed widely, where citizens are autonomous and equal, and manage their own society. This is the kind of arrangement sketched by Rousseau in *The social contract*, where the participation of equals motivated by consideration of the public good is assumed to resolve the problem of political association, that of combining freedom and association. Rousseau himself, along with most of those following in the participatory tradition, has emphasised the emotional or affective elements which underlie actual allegiances, and which must have a place within theories of reflective allegiance. People do not accept a particular order or act as citizens because they have meditated on the insights of Locke or Rawls, and come to a philosophic conclusion. Attachment to a state is not an attachment to an abstract ideal or set of values: it is to the Australian or the British or the Russian state. But while such a vision of Rousseau's has moral force, there are many difficulties in relating it to the actual world, including the shortcomings and differences of both actual and possible people and states.

Any theory of political obligation contains sets of assumptions which are combined in different ways to produce particular perspectives on the subject. Roughly, these assumptions concern legitimate and illegitimate power, social bonds and human nature, and the appropriate behaviour of individuals and groups, which is the prescription flowing from the analysis.

The account of social bonds and social order is central. The view of what bonds are needed to hold societies together, and how strong they need be, is also a view of what kind of creatures human beings – perhaps naturally – are. Clearly societies need a large amount of agreement, or at least obedience, if they are to hold together. But we disagree as to the amount and the character and sources of the necessary cohesion, largely because we disagree about human nature.

Our views of society and human nature strongly influence our assessments of states and governments, the power or the authority which makes commands in the form of laws, decrees, rules, etc. If we assume that the natural relationships between human beings are chaotic and destructive, a mêlée of rampant egoisms or unrestrained subjectivities, we are likely to justify a strong or rational sovereign to hold the parts together.[9] In that case, we are likely to burden the citizen with obligations. However, the defence of a powerful sovereign need not rest upon an articulated social theory. The divine right of kings asserts the right of properly appointed monarchs on the basis of theology, though it may also be assumed that the multitude must be controlled.

Views of the rights and obligations of the individuals who constitute society flow naturally from views of society, human nature and legitimate authority. An authority which is justified by a mandate from heaven, or by the potential chaos against which it protects its citizens, leaves little space for acceptable challenges to the law.

Taking the (historically variable) liberal democratic states as the context, it is clear that the different political theories will have distinctive positions on each of these issues, and that together these form particular views of political obligation. To the liberal democrat, a state described correctly in this way is, broadly speaking, legitimate, in that society is taken to be open, with its various elements represented adequately under a responsible government, though it may be accepted that individual conscience can override some political obligations. To the conservative, it will probably seem that the balance has been allowed to swing too far away from citizenship and duty, that conscience, dissent, individualism and self-interest are allowed too easily to tear the seamless web of society, where every tear shows and contributes to a larger process of disintegration. Connected assumptions about legitimate authority, the dangers of social conflict and individualism, and the quality of ordinary people combine to produce a strong defence of extensive and demanding political obligation. The liberal and the conservative are likely to have very different models of moral integrity – perhaps the obedient, even blindly obedient, person as against the one who follows higher laws or conscience as a sacred duty.

To the left, these conservative and liberal democratic views, if distinguishable, seem at best waffle. Whether the primary target is patriarchy or capitalism or the state, the common claim is that political arrangements endorse or confirm deeper inequalities: people are so widely different in power and other resources that they cannot be equal as citizens. Weighty and penetrating institutions and ideologies control and even deform people. Consequently these theorists do not bother engaging in the typical liberal balancing (or contractual) act between citizen obligations and citizen rights. The liberal democratic state is not worthy of allegiance because it is not and cannot be a people's state or a state of equals. Political obligation amounts to subordination to the will of others, normally minorities. Given such views, the traditional liberal discussion of political obligations appears as ideological cover, irrelevant to the life of a good society.

Although sufficient books have been written on the Marxist account of the capitalist state to suggest that it should be widely familiar, a brief recapitulation is in order, to locate its exact relevance to argument over political obligation.[10] The essential underlying claim, whether the state is presented as alienated social power, or as class instrument, or a subject to bureaucratic aggrandisement, is its separation from the genuine (or human) interests of the people. In his early writings, Marx presented the state as alienated social power, meaning that the state is an ideal and detached embodiment of human needs and powers which are not expressed in actual social life. Man's yearnings and capacities are expressed in a mythical way in constitutions and theories of the state, e.g. the rights of man. But as, in fact, most people do not enjoy the rights and the equality imputed to them, the state becomes a kind of grotesque pretence, masking the emptiness of citizenship. Alienated man cannot have the stuff of citizenship within him. The more common and familiar Marxian view of the state presents it essentially as the organs of government which are used by, or serve the purposes or interests of, the dominant class. The view can be either directly instrumental – a dominant class wielding weapons to its own perceived advantage – or more remote or structural, in the sense that government policies inevitably meet the needs of capitalism (whether or not 'the capitalists' are in government). In either case laws would be capitalist laws, whether concerned directly with economic issues, or war and peace, or civil liberties. Thus, although the precise relationship between class and state varies in different capitalist societies and at different times, the state is treated as

commonly and essentially a class state. Whether or not Marx himself moralised, such a power can have no moral claim on the people. At other points,
the state is presented as subject to almost autonomous bureaucratic expansion, in which the pores of society are clogged up, and bureaucracy – persons
and mechanisms – separates itself increasingly from the people. The implications of each of these analyses – and I will not be pursuing questions of their
empirical plausibility or internal coherence – is that the commands of the
state, surrounded as they are by mystical and ideological illumination, cannot
be given more than a prudential force: it may be better for people to obey than
to have their heads battered, or to lose future strategic opportunities. But that
is all, unless the Marxist treads the slippery path of reformism.

Marxist revisionism, which accommodates a revised
Marxist economic theory to the democratic state, resolves the issue in a quite
different way. For its starting point is the incorporation of the proletariat into
society. The alienated worker of Marx's early vision has been replaced by the
relatively comfortable and generally patriotic worker who has been tied to
society and polity by a mixture of economic improvement, control of working conditions, social provision and political rights. Given acceptance of the
basic claims of the democratic state, discussion of political obligation is likely
to approximate to the liberal democratic form.

According to a strict Marxist view, the questions of
political obligation cannot be resolved within liberal political forms because
these are class-based and alienated. In a Communist society the question does
not arise, because that society is characterised as one in which the people
voluntarily and clear-mindedly accept the common rules, of which they are
the co-authors. To earth-bound critics, problems of choice, minorities and
social order are seen as inescapable: it is assumed that not everybody will
agree, even on fundamentals, and that there will be some whose claims must
be rejected or diverted, even if they are not to be forced to be free. Of course,
replicating the illusion of liberalism, it may be assumed that the overall
bargain, or the compelling worthiness of the new society, warrants the
allegiance of all citizens to it.

The rejection of the claim that liberal democracies
deserve the moral commitment of their citizens may seem weighty, though
it will probably make us wonder whether any earthly realm could deserve
such commitment. This means doubting the possibility that any state (or
large human grouping) can constitute a community which leaves all as
free as before. But when the Marxist ceases critique and refers us to actual –
rather than imagined – societies in which the issue of political obligation
has been transcended, liberal hackles reasonably rise. Many Marxists do
not like the states which have been established and run in Marx's name.
But others do, and those states offer us the spectacle of harsh and uncompromising treatment of conscientious objectors, e.g. Jehovah's Witnesses,
and the complacent assumption that a system of law which 'represents'

proletarian or more broadly human interests will be seen as obligatory by all proper persons, to be defied only by renegades and criminals. As we shall see, a similar general objection can be brought as to liberal democracies – the state is not like that at all, and an ideological aura surrounds its laws, disguising their actual character.

The anarchist rejection of the liberal democratic state focuses directly on the complex of political institutions itself. Because the state is conceived to be such a negative and destructive force, it can never be the proper object of allegiance. If the basic function of the state and its surrounding and supporting institutions is to destroy autonomy, independence, conscience *and* sociality, then there is no ground for negotiation between people and government. Proudhon colourfully presented the harsh aspect of the anarchist view of government. To be governed is to be, 'on the pretext of the general interest, taxed, drilled, held to ransom, exploited, monopolized, extorted, squeezed, hoaxed, robbed; then at the least resistance, at the first word of complaint, to be repressed, fined, abused, annoyed, followed, bullied, beaten, disarmed, garotted, imprisoned, machine-gunned, judged, condemned, deported, flayed, sold, betrayed and finally mocked, ridiculed, insulted, dishonoured. That's government, that's its justice, that's its morality!'[11] If and only if the root of evil is destroyed can the people develop their creative and social powers, allowing the emergence of societies sustained by the voluntary and natural bonds of community. In state-dominated societies there is no moral order, merely brute power, while in societies based upon mutual aid and free agreement the problem of political obligation would dissolve, in the spontaneous harmony of voluntary agents. Yet while the starting point may be correct – that equality and individual freedom are incompatible with political authority and obligation – the concluding point lies amid the mists of imagined possibility. There is no reason for thinking that free agents would enter a condition of spontaneous harmony, where no one would feel subordinated to the laws or rules of others. Autonomy and conscience are likely to remain at odds with political authority, even if that authority is democratic and responsive.

Feminism in its various forms has also challenged the complacencies of liberal democracy in regard to political obligation. Do women occupy a place in society equal to that of men? If not, do political obligations fall equally upon them? As Marxism stressed the impossibility of political equality given the pervasive economic inequalities of capitalism, so feminism underlined how mythical the formal equality of women was, given the power and the ramifications of patriarchy (and perhaps of capitalism as well). Feminism has identified the dense private realm as the site of basic and often hidden oppression and inequality, and thereby suggests the need for fundamental change at various levels. But as things stand, the position of women cannot sustain a call for citizenship.

679

It is nonetheless a common view, within the liberal democratic tradition, that the (philosophical) problem of political obligation has been solved in the liberal democratic state – that, because of its character, citizens have a general obligation to obey its law. For this reason, the remainder of this discussion will address liberal democracy particularly. This has the added advantage that, as liberal democracy is assumed so commonly to be the institutional embodiment of political virtue, it puts a heavy burden on the sceptical questioner. It hardly needs saying that one is not obliged to obey the decrees of a tyrant, though there may be strong prudential reasons for doing so. Does the citizen, then, have a general moral obligation to obey the law in a liberal democracy? This leaves open, for the time being, whether the question is put on behalf of conscientious individuals, oppressed classes or groups, or whoever.

The political values associated most commonly with liberal democracy are freedom, choice, consent. The assumption, at least within the justificatory theory, is that citizens can choose genuinely through the normal arrangements of the state. Such theory holds, at least, that the people play some part, however indirect, in the formulation of the laws to which they submit, and that they have the opportunity to change the government and, through this and other forms of peaceful pressure, to change bad, unjust or unacceptable laws. In these typical portrayals of pluralist democracy, the evasiveness of the key terms is obvious – we slip away steadily from proximity to power. But let me at the outset hypothesise an effective and functioning democratic system, in terms of institutional arrangements and practices, or what is sometimes called the formal political level. I am not inventing a society of rational and autonomous citizens, or a genuinely participatory or self-managing society, which would avoid, though perhaps only in an act of imagination, many of the problems we face in the actual world.

Pressing towards greater definitional precision, I will take effective democracy to mean that elections are free (anyone is permitted to stand, all political views have a right to circulation), fair (a close relationship between percentage of votes and percentage of representatives in parliament or assembly), frequent (elections to be mandatory at least every three to five years) and general (all persons of an appropriate age, probably from 18 or 21 upwards, with a right to vote, with some possible exclusions, e.g. lunatics and criminals). Further requirements would include the rule of law – impartial rules applying equally to all – and civil liberties, especially freedom of the press and freedom of association. Leaving aside the large issues of what these freedoms actually amount to or, alternatively, how far rights can become powers, it is clear that liberal democratic states fall short of even this limited standard, though perhaps for good or understandable reasons. The procedures may be deficient, and laws favoured by majorities may violate the rights of others in the community. Schumpeter presents an imaginary example:

680

Let us transport outselves into a hypothetical country that, in a democratic way, practises the persecution of Christians, the burning of witches and the slaughtering of Jews. We should certainly not approve of these practices on the grounds that they had been decided on according to the rules of democratic procedure. But the crucial question is: would we approve of the democratic constitution itself that produced such results in preference to a non-democratic one that would avoid them?[12]

Leaving aside the simplistically presented choice, it seems clear that a government which is not popularly elected *could* give its citizens more liberties and better laws than *does* many a democratic one. Liberty may be enjoyed at the foot of a despot's throne, though it should be remembered that it is at the foot, and that the issue of self-government is likely to emerge no matter how good the laws or how wide the conceded liberties.[13]

The case for democratic government cannot rest primarily upon the superiority of democratic laws as far as content is concerned, as there are plenty of examples of bad democratic laws – though the general justification of democratic laws may come from the process through which they are determined. That process may in fact be deficient, as it is by definition in Schumpeter's hypothetical case, because of the destruction of minority rights along with the minorities themselves. Democracy, on my interpretation, requires much more than majority decisions. Within the boundaries of liberal democratic argument it can be admitted that many so-called liberal democratic states are not properly democratic, and that where this is the case, whatever morally compelling character obedience to its laws may have had diminishes. Grounds for scepticism about political obligation emerge, e.g. why should I be bound by laws passed by a government supported by only 38 per cent of the people, or where the Communist Party is outlawed, or where racist propaganda is banned? But the root of liberal scepticism is deeper: if the ideal standard of liberal democratic decision-making was reached, political obligations might still be questioned – theoretically and actually – because not even a true liberal democracy can represent adequately all the claims and consciences of a society. Even if decisions represented the will of the people accurately, they would not necessarily warrant our acceptance. If we were agreed about fundamentals the problem might disappear, but we are not.

The decisions made by my governors, who may not have been chosen by me, often threaten my interests and, more importantly here, may make demands upon me which I cannot accept. These are typically demands that I participate in activities of which the purpose is to kill or subdue other peoples. It is not necessary to determine whether particular governmental decisions are democratic or unavoidable, merely that they violate deeply held personal standards. Thus the gap between positive and divine or natural law is replicated, in our more secular world, in the familiar gap between law and conscience. A legitimate or legally constituted (democratic) authority may make evil or offensive commands or demands on some individuals. Meeting the procedural requirements of democracy does not remove the problem, given frequent conflicts between morally assertive individuals, determinedly autonomous and armed with conscience, and the rules, commands and practices of the state.

The Vietnam War provoked critical reactions which relate directly to the question of political obligation. The war was taken by many of its American, and other, opponents to be an imperialist war fought by a state of enormous military power against a popular if cruel nationalist movement, on behalf of a puppet government behind which its own interests sheltered. It was argued that not only did citizens have no obligation to obey the commands of the liberal democratic state for military service, but that they had a positive moral obligation to reject immoral commands. There are two points to observe here. First, this is a most familiar context for the discussion of political obligation, where an individual is required to carry out a certain duty, normally that of military or a related or alternative service, which violates that individual's conception of what is right. The appeal to a higher or more personal law has been made in every war fought by liberal democratic states. The message is simple: citizens are not bound universally by state commands because these may be illegitimate. The second point is that principled rejection of positive law is regardless of whether the commanding authority is democratic, whether in origin or in process (regular consultation with the people) or both. This may suggest that no constitution or set of political procedures could establish a general duty to obey the law.

In the extreme case, the dissenter may appeal to the Nuremberg trial, without necessarily claiming that modern liberal democracies are in any substantive way equivalent to the Nazi German polity.[14] The moral assumption underlying the German war crimes investigation was that there are certain things which the state – any state – cannot properly demand of its members, who can be condemned in terms of a higher law or morality if they do obey it. The prosecutors and judges proclaimed the moral responsibility of the individual for his own behaviour, and insisted that people could be judged and condemned for the things they did in obedience to the state. The essence of the prosecution case was that individuals do not merely have a right to reject the laws of the state where they clash with humanity or morality (even though these may hardly be unambiguous except at the extremes) but that they have a positive duty to do so, and that it is not the source but the nature of the laws that counts. Democratic states may have advantages and safeguards, but they do not remove the problem.

Liberal democratic procedures cannot offer salvation because democratic laws may impinge just as heavily and sharply on individual consciences as the laws of non-democracies. It was all very well for George Kennan to comment, regarding the moral furore over Vietnam and the draft: 'The best things the government could do, when this miserable war is over, would be to revise basically the entire system governing the relationship between the young male American and his obligation of military service.'[15] But such a revision would inevitably be too late for those currently being asked to practise what they regard as evil. A hypothetical future change of government or the law is no answer to their problem, which is immediate.

In response to the issue of conscientious objection, the liberal is likely to aim at a body of law which is 'flexible, enforceable and compassionate'.[16] Provision will probably be made for certain classes of people to be freed from specific obligations which apparently violate their consciences, though they may be punished nonetheless, or forced to carry out some alternative form of service. These, in turn, must not be excessive. The argument does not end at this point, of course. Conscience is not some impregnable and unchallengeable fortress to which we can retreat whenever the spirit moves us. Conscience may be dogmatic or base or tender or squeamish or, more to the point, may seem adopted for the purpose, not the person's own. Therefore tests of conscientiousness must be devised. Liberalism praises conscientious citizens who both challenge and perhaps refuse to obey what they regard as bad laws *and* question the still small voice within (as, for example, did Dietrich Bonhoeffer). The strident moral proclaiming of the conscience-ridden individual may be mere vanity or fear or self-seeking or moral grandiosity. Disobedience, supposedly inspired by conscience, may be inspired by a host of other things. The relevant principle is that, where individuals repudiate political obligations for reasons of conscience, the reasons must be genuine. The fact that magistrates, with interests of state in mind, often behave stupidly or maliciously in trying to destroy claims of conscience, does not affect the point. The second issue of importance to the liberal at this stage concerns the actions to be condoned in the name of conscience, e.g. the differences between refusing to pay a proportion of taxes because the state is fighting in a bad war, a refusal to serve in that or any war (when called), and perhaps accepting imprisonment, hiding away, blowing up munitions trains and armaments factories, and killing generals or those more loosely implicated in the practices of a bad society. All of us may find sabotage justifiable in certain circumstances, but such discussion goes beyond my brief.[17] Our answers will depend upon our perceptions of where we are – how bad and unchangeable the polity is, how oppressive and evil particular laws are, how democratic we are. Hence, while I would not rule out on principle sabotage or even assassination in a liberal democratic society, it would seem to be absurd and disproportionate to assassinate a Prime Minister because of an offensive parking law. It would seem less outrageous were the same done to a Minister responsible for genocide. And the dangers of nuclear power, whether or not the particular forms are supposedly peaceful, raises the issue of political disobedience sharply. Chernobyl merely confirmed the anxieties of principled opponents of nuclear development.

The immediate perception underlying liberal scepticism about political obligation in liberal democratic states is that, as a matter of fact, conscientious individuals dispute, and refuse to obey, commands of the state. The liberal is likely to claim that the honourable individual should follow conscience *and* that the state is required to recognise – though not necessarily to acquiesce in – this. Recognising a legitimate diversity of beliefs and consciences, the liberal wants simultaneously to defend citizen obligations and citizen rights, which involves at least a qualified acceptance of a right to civil disobedience. But legitimate disobedience is seen most commonly as a mere ripple on the calm of liberal equilibrium, and not as a permanent challenge at the centre of liberal society or as a sign of deeper deficiencies.

It is clear that, as I have presented it, our interpretation of the problem of political obligation is related intimately to our theory of democracy and, related to this, to precise estimates of the societies in which we live. Thus, if we are basically dubious about the claims and pretensions of liberal democracy, then we will doubt its capacity to deal with the question of political obligation. Certainly at its outer edges liberal scepticism begins to recognise that liberal democratic procedures cannot resolve the problem of political obligation because they neither presuppose nor guarantee the activity of equal and autonomous individuals. The new cry is likely to be: 'Beyond liberalism to democracy.' It seems to me that the uneasy combination of democratic institutions with pre-existing liberal arrangements and values, which we call liberal democracy, has failed to solve the problem of citizenship either in theory or in practice. It is not surprising to find many scholars arguing that political obligation cannot be given expression within the context of liberal democratic institutions, because they do not embody voluntary and equal relationships. For example, Carole Pateman concludes that a solution can be found only through 'the development of the theory and practice of participatory or self-managing democracy'.[18]

It may seem easier to start with those polities which do not deserve political obligation, rather than sketching the ideal or the idealised circumstances in which political obligation is warranted. But if we begin with such negative conditions as where individuals do not have sufficient opportunity to participate significantly in decision-making, we immediately open a can of worms. The issues are those of definitional precision and justification of a truly democratic order, and of feasibility. Thus we might agree that there is no general obligation under a tyranny, where nearly all are excluded from political life. The same point would apply under a majority tyranny, where only some are dominated. But anarchists, feminists and Marxists (and others) press further. The common point is the denial that some or many members of the polity do or can share power sufficiently, because of the patriarchal or economic or political structures, and that this deficiency – which others will see as justifiable and inescapable – removes or reduces the obligations of citizens. It may then be urged that the condition for true citizenship, a society in which all members are equally obligated, is fundamental social transformation. But what are the consequences if imperfection is part of our lot? Do the obligations of semi-citizens lapse if political and social arrangements fall short of an ideal standard? If we are not participants in a voluntary and rational social contract, do we owe nothing? Perhaps we are more obligated the more share we have: in a society of equals, obligations are equal, whereas in a society of unequals, they are also unequal.

Returning now to the familiar answers to the question of political obligation – what state has a legitimate claim on my allegiance? – my tart conclusions are as follows:

There is no obligation arising from claims to non-democratically derived legitimacy or rationality, e.g. God, or pure reason, or even social need. (People in God-governed societies may have obligations to each other, however.) This is not to deny the claims of expertise in particular areas. To the question: 'Who says?' the answer must be, in some ultimate sense, 'The people'.

There is no binding obligation arising from the fact that, if I (and many others) denied obligations to the state, then society might fall apart. What kind of entities we take societies to be, and what we think worth preserving of particular societies, is central to the question of political obligation. There are empirical issues. The extent and intensity of political obligation or of mere political obedience necessary for social cohesion may be exaggerated. Much more disobedience and freeloading may be compatible with social order than we imagine. There are normative issues. Societies may be bad societies, which shouldn't hang together, except literally. It may be that I shouldn't obey or accept obligation even if my disobedience and its repercussions are going to be socially costly. In any case, sociological generalisations about what societies require, themselves highly contentious, do not establish moral obligations, which depend upon further and different judgements. It should be added, however, that a reflective moral person would take seriously decisions about political behaviour, freeloading and possible social costs.

Obligations do not arise out of hypothetical contracts or exchanges imagined between unequals. The gist of Carole Pateman's critique of liberal democracy is the absence of any actual validation or confirmation of its ideals of voluntarism, self-assumed obligation or free moral commitment. There is no historical agreement either to form a political community or to accept a representative system as the best means of governing it.[19] There are those who explicitly deny or reject the exchange which might be envisaged for members of society, e.g. the totally self-contained hermit, making no claim on public provision (though complete withdrawal is probably impossible practically). However, we may regard persons with no love or loyalty to others as less than human. At this point we begin to move from the thin liberal theory of contract – thin because it both de-socialises and inflates common human relationships – to theories of community, loyalty and allegiance which constitute fuller theories of society and people. The egoistic individualism which is an important part of classical liberalism both emasculates real human relationships and holds them static and abstract. The hypothesised relationship between citizen and government is largely fictional, not only because it fails to answer the questions 'Who agreed?' 'How?' 'When?', but because it underrates the actual solidities and attachments of social life.

We can bring the idea of contract or exchange closer to common life, however. One often reads, in what is loosely called neo-liberal writing, that members of society have duties matching the benefits and rights which come from membership of a society. Because the state provides specific benefits to people, e.g. national defence, policing and social security benefits, something is owed in return. I find that there is a certain force to this claim, even though it sometimes seems vacuous to assert the duties of citizenship with things as they are (high unemployment levels, remote and wasteful or militaristic governments, etc.). And the general claim needs to be broken down. What is given? Is it asked for? What is owed? What is the appropriate balance? Do those who are better provided for and have a great range of choices owe more?

Do obligations arise only in social arrangements resting on voluntary commitment or free reflective allegiance? Pateman's transcendence of liberalism, which aims at fulfilling its empty promise, follows Rousseau. 'If there is to be a genuine free agreement, a valid social contract and justified political obligation, then the material conditions of social life have to be transformed, as well as political institutions and the consciousness of individuals.'[20] These new societies would be characterised by high participation and autonomy, where people's motivations and social needs coincide. They would be based on horizontal 'relationships' between citizens rather than 'vertical' relationships between each citizen and the state. They would be just and equal communities where each remains as free as before.

Yet, although we can invent rational and autonomous individuals, who would voluntarily submit themselves to good laws, which they themselves helped formulate, we cannot assume realistically that there will be agreement on fundamentals in large and complex societies. There will still be conscientious dissidents and minorities feeling hard done by, though admittedly fuller real opportunities to participate in the authorship of laws and other social forms may lead to a greater readiness to accept (temporary) defeat. The problem, at the level of ideal and reality, is the tendency to slide from the justification of an imagined state of affairs to rather doubtful real-world approximations. Hence, if liberal democracy is actually polyarchy or elitist democracy – let alone a mere front for capitalism – the philosophical argument does not run through. With the participatory ideal the case is similar. While I accept the participatory and self-managing model of society as giving a proper ground for political obligation, in the real world I may be forced to accept an improved form of liberal democracy as the best we can have, though not the best we can hope for. In that case, a more realistic and specific but less grand theory of political obligations than that of classical liberalism could be derived from arrangements which are more rather than less egalitarian, participatory, open and responsive. Then political obligation would have more to do with the actual circumstances of human beings.

Notes

(An author's name followed by a number in square brackets refers to the book or article which has that number in the bibliography.)

1. My thanks to colleagues at a seminar at the University of New England for instructive comments on my first draft, and to Neil Thornton.

2. See Habermas [12], *passim*.

3. S. Wolin and J. Schaar, *The battle of Berkeley* (New York Review, New York, 1970), p. 93.

4. H. Thomas, *An unfinished history of the world* (Hamish Hamilton, London, 1979), p. 553.

5. These are discussed, historically and in greater detail, in the following chapter.

6. Patrick Devlin, *The enforcement of morals* (Oxford University Press, Oxford, 1965), *passim*.

7. It may seem fair to claim regarding the United Kingdom, as did Admiral Hill-Wood, that 'We joined a club called Western Democracy and we've got to pay the subscription' (quoted in *The Observer*, 20 April 1986, p. 28). Yet who joined the club (all Britons? how?) and whether the subscription includes permitting American bases in Britain to be used in the attack on Libya remain moot points.

8. S. Freud, *Civilization and its discontents* (Hogarth Press, London, 1975), p. 52.

9. Hobbes is the obvious example. Hegel, in presenting the rational essence of the state, took the major enemy to be the assertion of intuition and subjectivity, e.g. the Sophists, who located what is right in

> subjective aims and opinions, in subjective feeling and particular conviction, and from them there follows the ruin of the inner ethical life and a good conscience, of love and right dealing between private persons, no less than the ruin of public order and the law of the land.

Preface to *The philosophy of right*, trans. T.M. Knox (Oxford University Press, Oxford, 1958), p. 8. The murder in 1819 of Kotzebue, suspected of being a Russian spy, by a student, revealed the danger of subjective good intentions.

10. I have elaborated my views in 'The Marxist theory of the state' in G.H.R. Parkinson (ed.), *Marx and Marxisms* (Cambridge University Press, Cambridge, 1982).

11. Quoted by Joll [2], p. 79.

12. J. Schumpeter, *Capitalism, socialism and democracy* (George Allen and Unwin, London, 1957), p. 242.

13. There are familiar democratic arguments denying that laws in a despotism could be good either procedurally (by definition) or substantively (because of the absence of necessary inputs).

14. The claim of equivalence or close to it may be made, of course. It was made by both Chomsky and Marcuse in the course of the Vietnam War.

15. G. Kennan, *Democracy and the student left* (Little Brown, Boston, 1968), p. 221.

16. The quoted words are those of the then Canadian Minister of Justice, Mr Turner, as reported in *The Australian*, 28 September 1970.

17. Apart from the appropriateness of such particular actions, in terms of the possibilities of peaceful change, the degree of wrong in government action, and the precise nature of the response, there is also the matter of public opinion, which is highly important for those engaged in the politics of conscience and social change. Violence may be both unjustified and counter-productive. For a discussion of these issues, see Chomsky's essay 'On the limits of civil disobedience' in *For reasons of state* (Fontana, London, 1973).

18. Carole Pateman, *The problem of political obligation* (John Wiley, New York, 1979), p. 1.

19. Ibid., *passim*.

20. Ibid., p. 150.

Bibliography

Anarchism

The idea that government is an evil and should be abolished has a long history. The first major exponent of philosophical anarchism was William Godwin (1756–1836: *Enquiry concerning political justice*, 1793). In the nineteenth century, the most important defenders of anarchism were Joseph Proudhon (1809–65) and Mikhail Bakunin (1814–76), who are now best known through Marx's criticisms of their views. The last of the great exponents of anarchism was Peter Kropotkin (1842–1921), who in his *Mutual aid: a factor in evolution* (1902) argued that the basic law of evolution was co-operation, not struggle.

The history of anarchism is well covered by

[1] George Woodcock, *Anarchism* (Meridian Books, Cleveland and New York, 1962) and by

[2] James Joll, *The anarchists* (Eyre and Spottiswoode, London, 1964).

A useful collection of texts is

[3] George Woodcock (ed.), *The anarchist reader* (Harvester, Hassocks, 1977).

Both Woodcock [1] and Joll [2] close their account of anarchism at the end of the Spanish Civil War in 1939; however, anarchist ideas resurfaced in the 'New Left' movement of the late 1960s. An account of anarchism and the New Left is contained in

[4] David Miller, *Anarchism* (Modern Ideologies Series, Dent, London, 1984).

Marxism and the state

The relations between Marxism and anarchism are complex. Marxists look forward to a 'withering away' of the state, and their ideal of a Communist society does not

688

seem to differ in any major respect from anarchist ideals. What differentiates Marxists is the fact that their critique of the state is placed within an elaborate theory of society and history in general; it is perhaps the lack of such a theory that Marxists have in mind when they denounce anarchism as a 'petty-bourgeois socio-political trend' (M. Rosenthal and P. Yudin (eds), *A dictionary of philosophy* (Progress Publishers, Moscow, 1967), p. 19).

Marx himself did not write a connected treatise on the state; his views on the subject have to be put together from a number of sources, of which the most important are *The eighteenth Brumaire of Louis Bonaparte* (1852), *The civil war in France* (1870) and the *Critique of the Gotha programme* (1875). A useful collection of texts, with commentary, is provided by

[5] David McLellan, *The thought of Karl Marx: an introduction* (Macmillan, London, 1971), Chs. 6 and 8.

By far the most important Marxist work on the state is

[6] Lenin, *The state and revolution* (1917). There have been many editions of this, of which one may cite

V.I. Lenin, *Collected works* (English translation), vol. XXV (Progress Publishers, Moscow, 1964).

In recent years, many scholars have discussed Marx's theory of the state; particularly helpful are

[7] Shlomo Avineri, *The social and political thought of Karl Marx* (Cambridge University Press, Cambridge, 1968)

[8] Graeme Duncan, *Marx and Mill* (Cambridge University Press, Cambridge, 1972), Parts II and IV

[9] John Plamenatz, *Karl Marx's philosophy of man* (Clarendon Press, Oxford, 1975), especially Ch. 11, 'The state as a form of alienated life'

[10] Ralph Milliband, *Marxism and politics* (Oxford University Press, Oxford, 1977)

[11] John M. Maguire, *Marx's theory of politics* (Cambridge University Press, Cambridge, 1978).

An important work by a modern Marxist referred to in the chapter is

[12] Jürgen Habermas, *Legitimation crisis* (English trans., Beacon Press, Boston, 1975). On Habermas' views, see

[13] Thomas McCarthy, *The critical theory of Jürgen Habermas* (Hutchinson, London, 1978), Ch. 5.

Feminism

The feminist critique of the state has to be seen in the context of feminist ideas in general. Two excellent philosophical books on feminism are

[14] Janet Radcliffe Richards, *The sceptical feminist* (1st edn, Routledge, London, 1980; reissued by Penguin Books, Harmondsworth)

[15] Mary Midgley and Judith Hughes, *Women's choices: philosophical problems facing feminism* (Weidenfeld and Nicolson, London, 1983).

G.H.R.P.

30 | Defenders of the State

R.A.D. Grant

The state: classical origins

The first use, in its political sense, of the actual word 'state' (*Staat, état, stato*) is generally credited to Machiavelli (1469–1527). The concept, however, was far older, dating back at least to ancient Rome. Its revival was part of that far-reaching enthusiasm for rediscovered antiquity known as the Renaissance. The ancient Greeks had an idea of the state, but it was inseparable from its physical embodiment in the independent city-state or *polis*. They recognised other patterns of social organisation, but for them the adjective 'political' literally pertained only to the city.

The *polis* represented the highest type or 'golden mean' of association. In smaller groups, such as the family and the clan, man failed to reach his full potential. In larger organisations, such as nation-states or empires, the citizen would be deprived of a voice in public affairs. (The Greeks had no notion of 'representation'.) No Greek thinker seems to have considered anything larger than the *polis* worth serious intellectual attention. Such things were associated in the Greek mind with despotism, a type of government fit only for slaves and barbarians.

Plato (428–348 BC) and the Stoics (third century onward) had imagined a purely ideal *polis*, without earthly power or institutional form, intended as a celestial yardstick by which to judge everyday politics. But the Romans seem to have been the first to detach the state from the city without thus letting it escape into the ether. *Res publica* (literally, the people's business) came to signify the ultimate object of earthly allegiance – in other words, the state. Latterly most Romans were born, lived and died hundreds or more miles from Rome itself. Yet in *res publica* they experienced a portable sense of 'home'. The Greek cities felt a vague ethnic solidarity, but nevertheless regarded their constant mutual warfare as quite normal. Rome,

690

on the other hand, bound together in a single jurisdiction and a common allegiance peoples of the greatest ethnic diversity. To Greek eyes the Roman 'state' must have seemed a puzzling abstraction. Yet without it the astonishing achievement of the Roman Empire could hardly have come to pass.

Minimal definition of the state

A watertight definition is almost impossible to arrive at, since the expression 'state' has two elements not easily disentangled. We may call them the ethical and the formal. Suppose that a Communist, a socialist, a liberal and a conservative (say) sit down to discuss the state. They might see it as respectively an instrument of class rule, a distributive agency, a guarantor of individual rights, and the voice of society. In each case, an ethical conception determines the holder's view both of the state's actual function, and of its precise scope and limits. Thus by 'the state' each means something substantially different. One reason why their disputations are usually so futile is the lack of any common ethical premiss. Nevertheless, they might agree on some minimum formal features of the state. If baffled by the following somewhat lapidary formulations, the reader should skip directly to the next section, and return to them at the end of the chapter.

(1) *Politics*. The state is the background and implicit object of politics in its literal sense, viz. the pursuit and exercise of power, influence and control in, or in relation to, government.

(2) *Government*. Government is the ordering, by superior agency, of relations between citizens *qua* citizens, in either their interests, or its own, or both. This agency may be personal (a monarch), collective (a council or assembly) or abstract (e.g. the 'rule of law'); it may be appointed, accepted or merely endured by the citizens; it may or may not be held to be themselves in a certain capacity; superior to them individually by definition, it may or may not also be thought superior to them collectively; and its superiority may consist either in power alone, or in both power and authority.

(3) *Citizenship*. Citizenship is a formal and public, not a private or intimate, relationship. An intimate, like a friend, is unique. The citizen's identity, however, consists precisely in what does *not* differentiate him from his fellow citizens. Aristotle (384–322 BC; see below) nevertheless spoke of citizenship as a 'dilute' form of friendship, the implication being that fellow citizens were at least potential intimates. Many make a distinction between 'citizen' and 'subject', but it is substantially an ethical one.

(4) *Roles, offices and institutions*. Like any institution, a state is a structure of similarly 'formal' offices (including, in a sense, that of citizen). An office is in principle separable from its holder and possesses an independent authority. For this reason some speak of law and the state as being authoritative in themselves.

691

The idea that an office is separable from its holder is meant to ensure impartiality. But this principle was also notoriously used at the Nuremberg trials to disavow the defendants' personal responsibility for their crimes. An idealist (see below) would probably say that an office must be separated only from its holder's private interest, not from his moral sense.

(5) *Sovereignty*. A state proper is sovereign; that is, the supreme temporal power, subject to none other either within or without its frontiers. The precise source of its subjects' obedience (e.g. duty, interest or fear) is irrelevant, though it may be important in assessing a state's legitimacy. Sovereignty is a matter of power, legitimacy of right. Relations between states are usually, from necessity, conducted on a basis of mutually recognised sovereignty, rather than any mutual concessions of legitimacy.

Theorists differ over precisely who or what is the actual 'sovereign'. According to one school (usually called 'positivist'), sovereignty can always in the last resort be traced to some determinate human person or persons. According to another, if those persons are consciously acting in a public capacity, and are so accepted by their subjects, the 'will of State', being common to all, loses its narrowly personal, arbitrary-sounding character. For such thinkers (e.g. the idealists), it makes perfect sense to speak with Harrington (1656) of 'an empire of laws, and not of men'.

(6) *Territory*. One orthodox distinguishing mark of a state is sovereignty over a designated territory. This will do well enough, but it does raise one or two interesting questions. What, for example, is the status of an underground movement furnished with many of the offices, and all the popular support, of a normal state (i.e. of a state minus sovereignty)? Again, what of an ecclesiastical jurisdiction? This might command more allegiance and obedience than its subjects' temporal rulers. Is it not then politically sovereign – a state minus territory – despite laying claim only to souls? (Contemporary Poland perhaps illustrates both points.)

(7) *Arbitration*. The sovereign power is by definition the final court of appeal in any dispute, whether between subjects, or between subjects and itself. In the latter case it looks as though a state must always be judge in its own cause. For this various remedies have been devised, sophisticated or sophistical according to the observer's taste. They include 'separation of powers', and various means whereby the state can be identified with its citizens, or distinguished from its agents.

Beyond the formal state: ethics and purpose

A state, let us now assume, is an organisation which satisfies all or most of these criteria: it governs, its relations with its subjects are formal rather than intimate, it has offices, institutions and frontiers, and is the arbiter (and much else) of last resort. We have enough to distinguish it from other organisations, but so far nothing to distinguish one state from another.

692

The really deep disagreements in politics are ethical. Characteristically they involve preferences for this or that 'system' seen, not as an alternative means to the same end, but rather as serving, or embodying, a rival schedule of ends. Yet 'system' is not everything. If it were, we could not distinguish benevolent despotism from tyranny, nor an armed policeman from an armed criminal. Surely *intentions* are decisive. Whether or not, as some argue, the state itself can have intentions, rulers and subjects do, and a state's distinctive character lies in how it reflects those of both; in the ends, or purposes, it is either meant to, or does in fact, serve. The most radical conflicts in real-life politics are over divergent ends; but, if not the most provocative, probably the most far-reaching division among political theories lies between those which see the state as a means to something else, and those which see it as an end in itself.

The distinction turns out itself to have ethical significance, and bears on the nature of political obligation (see Ch. 29). My reasons for acquiescing in the state's claim to my obedience will obviously vary widely, in accordance with what I take its 'purpose' or 'end' to be. If I think, for example, that the state is devised essentially for my convenience, my feelings about it, my conception of its legitimate extent, and my motives for obedience will all differ greatly from yours, for whom it merges into your country, is bound up with your own identity, and is thus suffused with moral significance. These examples, of course, do not exhaust all the possibilities.

The state as end: the organic tradition

Aristotle

For Aristotle the *polis* was the culmination of man's biological destiny. Man is the *zōon politikon*, the only animal who lives specifically in a city. He has language, which provides him with things unknown in the herd or hive, reasons and values.

Aristotle's account is certainly naturalistic. But it should be contrasted with modern biological or pseudo-biological explanations of human behaviour. For Aristotle man's essence lies in what differentiates him from other species, not in what he shares with them. Aristotle does not explain man's conscious purposes as expressions of hidden animal impulse. Rather, reason is to man what instinct is to the animals. Unlike his counterpart in Plato, Aristotle's man is not divided between his rational and his animal nature. For his animal essence consists precisely in his rationality.

Plato's *polis*, at least in his highly authoritarian *Republic*, is based in part on the need of irrational men for discipline. Aristotle's *polis*, by contrast, grows out of natural sympathy. It is the end-point, purpose or *telos* of an evolutionary process begun in the family and continued

693

in the village or clan. These earlier associations are inchoate gestures towards man's full self-realisation in the *polis*.

A thing's essential nature, says Aristotle, is its *telos* (purpose). An organic thing's *telos* is internal to itself, and present even in its embryonic stages. When its *telos* is reached it attains *autarkeia* or self-sufficiency. *Autarkeia* is essentially the state of full flourishing, of a thing's finally becoming an end in itself. Everything earlier than the *polis* falls short in this respect, except (in part) disinterested friendship, which is the true paradigm of civil and political order. States are to be judged according to their ability to satisfy man's essential nature, i.e. how far they foster friendship and related goods: virtue, moral nobility, peace, happiness and 'leisure' (activity undertaken for its own sake). All together make up the good life, and virtually define the 'good' *polis*. Like them, the good life is an end in itself.

It should be noted, first, that Aristotle's 'good' state, unlike Plato's Republic, exists in some sense here and now. For Plato, the actual state, being intrinsically imperfect, could never command the rational man's full allegiance. Secondly, Aristotle needs no extra-political criterion in order to criticise the 'bad' state. (He is thus not what the English political philosopher Michael Oakeshott would call a 'rationalist', i.e. one who thinks, like Plato, that society should conform to some abstract pattern derived from outside it.) Aristotle calls 'bad' states 'perverted', because in them man's development is in some way thwarted or turned aside. They stand condemned ultimately for making the good life impossible, being governed by will, self-interest or naked power rather than by law. They are, variously, tyrannies (states governed by the self-interest of one), oligarchies (by that of a few), and unconstitutional democracies (by that of unstable majorities).

Under lawless power every man must fend for himself or seek the protection of the strong. The prevailing moral type will thus be self-seeking, either despotic or servile. Under law, however, the citizen can, so to speak, 'afford' generosity and disinterestedness. Thus the law-governed *polis*, be it a monarchy, an aristocracy or a constitutional democracy, has a friendly, patriotic unity unknown in the 'perverted' state. All citizens, including the rulers, are equally subject to the law (and in that sense, at least, are equals). The law signifies 'reason unaffected by desire': it is practical reason, embodied in custom, culture and tradition, rather than in any abstract Platonic theorem.

Aristotle is in many ways the patron saint of philosophical conservatism. His outlook has provided the main competition to the dramatic, imaginative and often revolutionary Platonic tradition. Amongst his heirs may be listed the conservatives Burke and Hegel; St Thomas Aquinas, 'the first Whig', according to Lord Acton; the wayward radical Rousseau; the liberal British idealist T.H. Green; and even some among the strongly civic-minded early Fabian socialists. What all share, and what excludes (say) even a staunch defender of law such as F.A. Hayek from their company, is their distrust of individualism.

It is not that they necessarily depreciate the individual, but rather that they define him as constituted by his social relations, and thus see his welfare as inseparable from that of his society. Thus for the Aristotelian the 'liberal' opposition between the individual and society (and between the individual and the state) is a chimera. It is this interdependence, as it were between the parts and the whole, that (along with the evolutionary model) has caused the tradition to be dubbed 'organic'.

The goal of 'flourishing' is peculiar neither to Aristotle nor to conservatism. For Marx human *autarkeia* or perfection will lie only in 'full communism'. Unfortunately (and by contrast with Aristotle) Marx reveals almost nothing about it except that it must come. (So far he resembles St Augustine, for whom the Heavenly City takes the place of 'full communism'.) For Marx man can flourish only in a post-political world, since the state as such (even the socialist state) is defective. States governed by law are 'really' organised to suit the self-interest of a ruling class, of which law is the disguised expression.

A similar diagnosis ('justice is the interest of the stronger') was offered by the Sophists, who were criticised for it by Plato and Aristotle. Some actually found cause to celebrate. For if true, such a set-up must favour the strong and ruthless individual over the weak and compliant mass, and in that way, rather than in Aristotle's, lead to the highest human 'flourishing'. A truly law-governed state would mean the subjugation of illustriousness, distinction and joyous animal spirits to small-minded prudence and the tyranny of the average. Such a view, structurally close to Marx's, but in its unashamed egoism ethically opposed to it, is nowadays familiar from Nietzsche, a great admirer of the Sophists. Vulgarised and misinterpreted (though not as unjustly as is often claimed), this doctrine served to prop up the most brutal mediocrity among modern despotisms, National Socialism.

Plato is both more individualistic and more authoritarian than Aristotle. Only central organisation, he thinks, can direct very disparate individuals each to his own specific fulfilment. Politics, however, is at best a means. Man's highest fulfilment, to which only the enlightened can aspire, lies in no earthly, political community, but in a transcendent world of scientific truth. Hence the philosopher is finally exempted from all political loyalties. Only the cosmic order, we might say, and the individual who has made himself part of it, are truly 'self-sufficient'.

Burke

The voluminous political writings of Burke (1729–97) were all topical. He constantly emphasised that political ideas, unless generated by practice and continuously tested against it, were worthless, visionary and dangerous. Rare amongst political thinkers in being a working statesman, he had in any case no more leisure than inclination for systematic political theory. Nevertheless, he believes as firmly as Aristotle (with whom he is clearly familiar) that political society, though a human artefact, is profoundly 'natural' to man. But it is equally natural that there should be no single approved (or 'natural') model of it, since widely divergent political arrangements have satisfied men's needs and engaged their affections.

It was on this account that he attacked the French Revolutionaries' prescription of the universal Rights of Man. When he defended the American colonies against royal despotism, the Irish Catholics against Protestant discrimination, and India against Warren Hastings, he did so not in the name of abstract human rights, but rather of the right of established societies to flourish, Aristotle-fashion, in whatever way had *become* 'natural' to them. Accordingly, his definition of a free (or desirable) society was simply that 'for any practical purpose, it is what the people think so'. This did not make him a modern liberal democrat; but it made him a firm defender of parliamentary government, whereby power is always constrained by public opinion to reflect it.

For Burke, as for Aristotle, there is no real distinction between the 'good' state and society or 'culture'. The 'good' state *is* society, but in its conscious, active, political aspect. As in Aristotle, the individual has no meaning outside his culture. Thus to repress society, as the 'bad' or despotic state does, is to destroy the individual together with all that most matters to him. Burke's horrified imaginings – based, however, on his correspondence with eye-witnesses, whom he frequently chose from among his political opponents – of French life under the Jacobins and the ensuing Directory are uncannily prescient of twentieth-century totalitarianism. Severed from society, the state becomes (what anarchists and even some liberals think it) merely an external apparatus of power and control. Properly understood, and properly constituted, it is, as in Aristotle, the terminus of a widening complex of social relationships, with their implicit natural, non-contractual obligations, beginning in the family.

Burke differs substantially from Aristotle only in two additional emphases: first, that all subordinate institutions (and not merely family, tribe or clan) are part of the same process; and secondly, that patriotic sentiment or civil 'friendliness', so far from precluding it, further promotes the universal human sympathy which, despite his hatred of the rhetoric of 'rights', played so large a part in Burke's various crusades on behalf of the oppressed. 'To love the little platoon we belong to in society', he wrote, 'is the first link in the series by which we proceed to a love to our country and to mankind.' Thus such things as class, rank and office are by no means evils, but intermediate nurseries of allegiance and moral attachment. Burke's affection for subordinate institutions is shared by Aristotle and

Hegel, but emphatically not by Rousseau, who otherwise belongs in much the same camp. (For this and other reasons, and in defiance of chronology, it has been convenient to postpone consideration of Rousseau awhile.)

Hegel

The philosophy of Hegel (1770–1831) was thoroughly Aristotelian. According to his *Phenomenology of spirit* (1806), Reality (or all that exists) is – despite appearances – a single whole. It alone is truly self-sufficient. It has logical structure because thought (the idea) is actually what reality is. Human thinking apprehends it in evolutionary stages or 'moments', emerging first from unselfconscious 'unity' with it into a perception of itself and everything else as possessing objective individuality, and finally into a conscious recovery of its identity with mind or reality as a whole.

The process differs from Aristotle's in that, pending the final 'synthesis', each 'moment' both completes and (in so doing) 'negates' the one previous. Hegel called this shuttle-like advance the dialectic, and though it was of mythic centrality in his (and later in Marx's) theory of history, his attempt to identify it in the evolution of society is rather perfunctory.

Hegel's theory of the state is set out in *The philosophy of right* (1821). Like Aristotle and Burke, he begins with the family. The ascent to the state is logical rather than historical. For example, Hegel's family, being based in part on enforceable property rights, presupposes the state. The primitive 'unity' of the household consists (in Roman phrase) in *pietas*, or customary, pre-contractual trust. Recapitulated in the adult's self-aware patriotism, piety is the model of political obligation.

The next stage, corresponding to the 'moment' of individuality, is civil (or 'bourgeois') society. Roughly speaking, it signifies voluntary association under the rubric of 'interest', substantially what modern sociologists (after F. Tönnies, 1889) call *Gesellschaft*. Here family breadwinners encounter each other as economic agents competing under law. Here too the various 'estates' – the socio-economic classes, functionally conceived – negotiate their group advantage. (The chief estates are the landed interest and the enterprise and labour corporations.) But the facts of law and economic interdependence point forward to the common, disinterested, ethical life of the state proper.

Class, then, is both natural and valuable. But as in Plato and Aristotle, 'class rule' is bad. The estates are essential as the source of public opinion (the sole standard of justice), and as such are the central representative bodies in the Assembly or parliament. Hegel thinks them too partial directly to conduct policy, or to enact the legislation they introduce. These tasks fall to a third, artificial estate, the so-called 'universal' class, consisting of the civil service and the judiciary. Recruited on merit, they are supposed (like Plato's Guardians) to be free of normal class interest. They are answerable not to the Assembly, but to the constitutional monarch, who may encroach on their independence only in emergencies such as war.

To some extent Hegel's ideal state was based on Prussia, and foreshadowed Imperial Germany. Though liberals in the idealist tradition (see below) are indebted to *The philosophy of right*, few would now call it liberal. But the once-common accusation that Hegel is totalitarian is absurd. His ungrudging respect for law, opinion and spontaneous association is surely sufficient evidence to the contrary, to say nothing of his arguments in favour of tolerating cultural minorities and conscientious objectors. He even incorporates the liberal model (as civil society) into his political scheme, though regarding it as inadequate by itself.

It is true that Hegel is neither an individualist nor a pluralist. The social whole, nevertheless, still emerges out of its parts. The 'wholeness' of a totalitarian society is surely achieved by the opposite process (the Nazi *Gleichschaltung*), being arbitrarily imposed *ab extra* by a self-constituted agency that usurps the title of the 'true' state along with its (grotesquely hypertrophied) powers.

Liberal critics of the 'organic' state have usually been misled by the superficial likenesses between an organic and a mechanical system. Totalitarianism is the politics (though not the only politics) of the mechanical state. Hegel's misfortune is first to have been unscrupulously plagiarised by Fascist thinkers, and then to have fallen victim to post-war liberals curiously anxious to believe Fascism's own inflated account of its intellectual pedigree. Mussolini indeed employed the Hegelian Gentile (1875–1944) to make Fascism look respectable. But the difference from Hegel was obvious: Fascism's corporations were not *represented* at state level, but (using identical structures) were actually state-*run*.

If there is any real excuse for linking Hegel's name with totalitarianism, it is to be found in his popular lectures called *The philosophy of history* (posth., 1831). Hegel's romantic fantasy of a 'world-historical' process (and state) superior to all narrow ethical considerations unquestionably helped to liberate both Marxist and Fascist (to say nothing of National Socialist) thinking from normal moral constraints. It verges on the notion of the state as means, i.e. as the agent of some transcendent mission. It also at least *appears* to countenance an international ruthlessness that the civilised state of *The philosophy of right* could scarcely hope to survive.

Rousseau

Jean-Jacques Rousseau (1712–78) imported into the Aristotelian tradition the radically alien conception of the Social Contract (*Du contrat social*, 1762). The idea originated with the Sophists, and was central to the political thinking of the Epicureans (see below). Its first modern formulation, however – one of unsurpassed profundity and brilliance – was by Rousseau's immediate source, Hobbes (again, see below). The fundamental assumption, implicit in most subsequent liberal thought (though Hobbes himself was no liberal), is that no alleged obligations – and particularly political obligation – can truly bind except those one has voluntarily undertaken, and has therefore elected to be bound by. Thus (the argument runs) I am the author of my obligations; in honouring them I effectively obey myself; and to obey oneself, rather than some external ordinance, is to be free.

The main objection is almost as old as the original theory, and has seemed conclusive to many besides Cicero (106–43 BC). That is, that if I am free to disobey anyone, I am surely free to disobey myself. Why should my own previous commitment, unsupported, be morally more compelling than any exterior authority? What reason is there not to break inconvenient agreements if you can get away with it, unless there is some existing obligation to honour them (as specified, for example, in the Roman law principle that *pacta sunt servanda*)? In sum, though one can choose to enter an agreement, and equally 'choose' to break it, one cannot choose whether or not to be bound by it. Moral obligation is previous to choice, and lies simply in the nature of things (Cicero). And as Burke and Hegel observed, the deepest obligations, such as those between parents and children, cannot originate in choice since infants are incapable of it.

It seemed to Rousseau, as it seemed to Burke, that the legitimacy of a social order ultimately rested upon the people's consent. Contract theory at least makes this explicit. But it is also implicitly egoistic, and therefore incompatible with that Graeco-Roman patriotism, or republican 'virtue', which Rousseau agreed with both Machiavelli and his own immediate predecessor Montesquieu in admiring. (In his *Spirit of laws* of 1734, Montesquieu – also a great influence on Burke – had defined civic virtue as 'a constant preference of public to private interest', or 'moral virtue as it is directed to the public good'.) What Rousseau needed was some theory that, whilst retaining the principle of *consent*, should purge it of its intimations of egoism.

He found what he wanted substantially in Plato. For Aristotle egoism, in the shape of private or arbitrary will, was unnatural, 'perverted', and the mark of tyranny. (Our word 'idiot' derives from the Greek for 'private'.) For Plato, by contrast, it was all too natural. Yet the rational man can free himself from it by submitting to truth, which he is not at liberty to repudiate. In accepting cosmic necessity, he masters himself, achieving permanent fulfilment in the place of temporary, shallow gratification.

What Rousseau did, in effect, was to recast Plato's metaphysical dichotomy in Aristotle's more secular, political idiom. Man's superior will integrates him not with cosmic, but with social, order; not with the ideal, but with the actual *polis* (Rousseau, a Genevan, habitually thought in terms of the city-state); and its mainspring is not reason, but sympathy or sentiment. This superior will is identical in all the members of a society (what, in fact, makes them a society, and that one in particular), and is called the 'General Will'. Clearly if a society could contrive to be ruled exclusively by its General Will – that is, by each man's commitment to the common interest – it would be free. The conflict between the individual and society would be illusory, a shadow of the real internal conflict between the individual's selfish and his general will.

Rousseau's insight was riddled with paradoxes, some perhaps being the unavoidable price of profundity. It generated, if it did not elaborate, a novel penal theory in which the punished criminal implicitly obeys his own will-to-justice. It influenced both the liberal Kant and the conservative Hegel. Its constitutional implications, as Rousseau himself realised, were ambiguous. His Jacobin disciples, such as Robespierre, used Rousseau's principles to justify an extreme, unconstitutional democracy, amounting to mob tyranny, and modern critics have seen him, as they have seen Hegel, as proto-totalitarian (see, for example, J.L. Talmon's *The origins of totalitarian democracy*, 1952). And it must be admitted that for Rousseau (as his own life testified *ad nauseam*) the 'private' was virtually identical with the 'selfish'.

It is doubtful, however, whether things are so simple. The fact is that the intrinsic difficulties of his theory, and his own intellectual scruples, caused Rousseau constantly to change tack. Jacobin 'direct' democracy is certainly present in *The social contract*, but so is Rousseau's final abandonment of it. Half-realising that in any majority decision it must be impossible formally to distinguish the General Will from a temporary coincidence of selfish interests (the so-called 'Will of All'), and thus that direct democracy is an invitation to tyranny, he is inclined after all to locate the General Will in the continuity of law, rather than in a stream of plebiscites. And having originally proposed to forbid all genuine offices, and all subordinate associations, as potential rivals to the General Will (rather than, as Aristotle and Burke thought, rehearsals for it), Rousseau in the end accepts some minimal structure of offices, and even constitutional monarchy.

He comes down eventually in favour of an 'elective aristocracy' not so very different from Locke's (see below). The original contract could never have been undertaken by pre-social man (a 'stupid, limited animal'); but the idea of contract survives in the institution of regular elections. These have a twofold significance: on the one hand, the citizen body (the collective Sovereign) really does choose a government, which is obliged to it, and which it is at liberty to renew; and on the other, they symbolise the citizens' abiding commitment to their common identity in the state, a thing (the General Will, in effect) which they never positively chose. In other words, democracy is only workable against a background of 'virtue', viz. of a public-spirited will to make it work. (Whether democracy can *create* that will is very doubtful; so, at least, its fragility in newly independent states seems to suggest.) And even that is insufficient: Rousseau is well aware that democracy is not infallible, and that, ignoring the counsels of the wise, a nation may with the noblest will in the world consign itself to perdition.

British idealism

Rousseau, Hegel and the Greeks were the main sources for those nineteenth-century Oxford philosophers known as the British idealists. The leading lights were T.H. Green (1836–82), F.H. Bradley (1846–1924), and Green's pupil B. Bosanquet (1848–1923). Together they present the doctrine of the organic state in its most explicit, non-metaphorical and closely reasoned form.

Society is not a machine, designed for some ulterior purpose. It is literally an organism, differing from a natural organism in that the parts consciously belong to the whole. The whole as such actually consists of their common consciousness. Each of the idealists more or less explicitly identifies Rousseau's General Will with the individual's 'higher self' or 'real will'. The result, as in Rousseau, is not only to moralise the state, but furthermore, and especially in Bradley, to endow it with a literal, singular personality. Here idealist thinking converges with German jurisprudence (e.g. the Roman law-derived theory of corporate personality then being elaborated by Gierke), and anticipates Collingwood's later suggestion that minds sharing the same thought are *pro tanto* identical. Such ideas, on paper, have often seemed queer and repellent to the English disposition, which has nevertheless happily accepted them in practice. Much depends on how narrowly we construe the terms 'political' and 'state'.

In effect, and within an overall Hegelian framework, British idealism conflated Kant's definition of organism with his second Categorical Imperative. According to the former, in an organism 'every part is reciprocally both means and end' (*Critique of judgement*, 1790); the latter enjoins one to treat human beings 'never as means only, but always also as ends in themselves' (*Metaphysics of morals*, 1785: see Chapter 25 of the present work). Applied to the state, these maxims imply an order both liberal, in the sense of existing to promote the freedom, autonomy and self-realisation of its members, and anti-individualist, in that the members as such are indistinguishable from itself. The corollary – which Kant himself would have queried – is that society, in the name of the citizen's 'real' will, may have a duty to coerce him, not merely to protect others, but also for his own good, and the authority to determine, in defiance of his 'actual' will, where his objective good lies. Such interference – and equally non-interference when appropriate – is justified as removing hindrances to the good life, and conduces to what Berlin (with some irony) has called 'positive freedom' (see Chapter 32, note 53).

The boldness of such ideas at the time, when many liberals and conservatives could still deplore the 1870 Education Act as a monstrous encroachment upon the historic rights of John Bull and his children (e.g. to poverty and ignorance), can hardly be overstressed. That they were persuasive cannot be doubted, for they are clearly the foundations of twentieth-century 'interventionism', in which socialists, liberals and Tory paternalists still find much common ground. Doubtless this consensus has also been due to the fact that the 'objective good' appealed to is no rationalist abstraction, but something which emerges compellingly out of everyday *Sittlichkeit*, the customary, unreflective morality that Bradley and Hegel defended against the new-fangled liberal 'conscience'.

The difficulties, however, are the same as Rousseau's. We may concede that there is an authoritative General Will at large in society. But how can we know whether it, rather than some pretentious tyrannical imposture, informs the apparatus of state? Would it not be better to minimise the risk by curtailing the state's powers, even if that also curtailed its ability to do good?

The idealists have little to say about such technicalities, or about constitution generally (it is not clear now an idealist would vote). For them the citizen may have rights against the visible state, but not against the 'real' or ideal state, which is nothing else than society articulated and personified. Society is the sole source, not only of right, but of the individual too. How could a man have 'rights' against what is really himself, and his 'best self' at that (cf. Matthew Arnold's *Culture and anarchy*, 1859)?

The theory of limited politics still rests more or less where Burke left it. But it is not clear that the world is thereby any the worse, or that the incompleteness of idealist politics gave totalitarianism its chance. When Green said that 'will, not force, is the basis of the State', he meant by 'will' not what Hitler meant, but simply consent, of which idealism gave a far richer account – as it did also of the individual – than the empiricists and utilitarians who had previously held the field.

The Fabians

The thinkers of the Fabian Society (founded 1884) were interesting among socialists for many reasons, of which one deserves mention here: they had not a scrap of anarchism in their make-up. While that lent all their attitudes and pronouncements a bureaucratic drabness (many were civil servants), at the same time they believed (unlike Marx, whom they utterly repudiated) that a society meeting all three of the following conditions was both possible and desirable: it should be just, workable and *political*. In other words, whatever the state's importance as a means (of production and distribution), it was still held to be also an organ of community, and hence (what it could never be for Marx) self-sufficient, an end in itself.

702

Their arguments for socialism were impressive, but need not concern us. What is significant is that their vision, however unimaginative, was an extension of the tradition charted above. This is so even if one suspects that for some a mechanical rather than an organic model predominated, and thus that, in any choice between democracy and socialism (say for instance if people found they didn't like socialism), democracy, not socialism, would have to be sacrificed. (Sidney Webb, for example, asserted that 'the perfect and fitting development of each individual' lay in 'the filling, in the best possible way, of his humble function in the great social machine'. This is not Aristotle, but Plato, speaking from Whitehall.)

The state as means

Epicureans and Stoics

The Sophists have already been mentioned. Two other pre-Christian doctrines were also markedly individualistic. Epicureanism and Stoicism both dated from about 300 BC, and flourished for centuries. Each foreshadowed a different aspect of liberalism. The Epicurean ethic was one of prudent but not ignoble hedonism. The highest good was happiness, and the highest happiness friendship. The best government was whatever secured the citizen's private happiness: in practice, a strong monarchy. Government thus rested on a kind of contract. The resemblance to Hobbes is striking.

Stoicism's kingdom, like Christ's, was not of this world. All humanity, simply as such, belonged to an ideal World-City, or Cosmopolis (cf. Kant's 'kingdom of ends'). All being thus equally subject to the laws of reason and nature (= the moral law), all possessed certain correlative natural rights. Politics was relevant largely as a gymnasium, or testing-ground, for virtue.

Christianity

Despite its founder's maxim (just quoted), Christianity had somehow to come to terms with the world. The two central statements of specifically Christian politics are those of St Augustine (354–430) and St Thomas Aquinas (1226–74). Augustine divided the entire universe, temporal and eternal, into two sectors, one called the Earthly City and the other the City of God. Only the Elect (such Christians as will be saved) inhabit the City of God, from which their membership of earthly states need not debar them. The Earthly City is not exactly coterminous with the State, but only with that part (in pagan states, the whole) excluded from the City of God. Its members are destined to eternal damnation. Nevertheless, a Christian is subject to such of its ordinances as do not positively conflict with Christian duty. For its constraints are a discipline upon rebellious man (as is slavery), and its 'earthly

703

peace' may be valuable as a means to undistracted devotion. Augustine's view of the state is not only gloomy, but also essentially utilitarian. For man's goal, and ultimate allegiance, are not political at all (cf. Plato and Marx).

Aquinas also sees the state effectively as a means, but in no way as a punishment or a necessary evil. His outlook, like Aristotle's, is genial. The state is now not the final, but the penultimate, term in the teleological series (i.e. it is *almost* self-sufficient). Men live in society because they like it, and because it makes the good life possible. The state can at least put them in the way to salvation. (Hence virtuous pagans ignorant of the Gospel might well be saved.) If this world were all-in-all, as Aristotle thought, then the good state would indeed be the highest good. St Thomas is still the model for official Roman Catholic political doctrine. Much of that, in the last century or so, has been impressive for its wisdom, humanity and intellectual sophistication (not least by contrast with the competition).

Hobbes

Hobbes (1588–1679) was the greatest of all contract theorists (see above under 'Rousseau'). The extraordinary argumentative rigour of his *Leviathan* (1651) led him to conclusions greatly at variance with the 'proto-liberalism' (so to speak) of his original assumptions. From the axiom of egoism Hobbes derives a defence, not of liberty, but of what many would call despotism. Beneath the logic, however, one perceives Hobbes' vicarious experience of the English Civil War, which (though he was in Paris at the time) may already have forced upon him both premises and conclusions.

Chief among the former is that anarchy, or 'the war of all against all', is the greatest evil; among the latter, that absolute government is our only defence against it. By absolute government is meant undivided sovereignty, in which the subject has (and understands that he has) no right of disobedience. The sole exceptions are when the sovereign directly threatens his life, or when he can no longer protect it (in which case sovereignty is already extinct).

Hobbes favours monarchy, but claims equally to justify aristocracy and democracy so long as they can stand undivided by faction. He recommends his book to all sovereigns, and urges them to make their subjects read it. The latter, if they will not obey from duty, may at least yield to cost-benefit calculations. Self-interest is the ethical basis of the whole work.

Thus egoism – not perhaps the only human motive, but the only reliable one – supplies its own remedy. Men surrender all but one of their allegedly 'natural' rights to the sovereign in order to safeguard the most important, the right to life (without which the rest are obviously worthless). Thereafter it is up to the sovereign how many privileges he grants in return. Rights are meaningless unless they can be enjoyed; and no human good can be secured, unless the owner is prepared to do what necessity in any case constrains him to do, viz. give almost all his rights up. All enforceable rights are creatures of law, and law, of power and will. (The idea that the ruler could be subject to the law, or that 'law' itself could somehow be said to 'rule', is for Hobbes simply an abuse of language.)

Hobbes casts all these insights in the form of myth. Unlike Aristotle, Hobbes imagines a condition, the 'state of nature', logically prior to all association. There is no law, no authority, no government, and hence no security. Morally speaking, it is total liberty; there is no justice, legitimacy, or right and wrong, only force. Civil war, and international relations, afford us a glimpse of it. It is so utterly wretched that men are forced simply out of self-interest into Hobbes' celebrated 'covenant', whereby political society, and with it the possibility of other associations, is born.

The covenant has two main forms, and their plausibility is greatly disputed. Either vanquished men contract directly with their conqueror, to obey him on condition that he spare their lives, or men spontaneously contract with each other to surrender all their natural liberty (except the right to defend their lives if need be) to a third party, empowered to protect them all. The first is 'sovereignty by acquisition', and is doubtless truer to historical fact. (But since the contract is visibly extorted, it is hard to see how the subjects could ever be morally persuaded of the sovereign's right.) The second is 'sovereignty by institution'. The main problem here is that it will always be in somone's interest to have the rest surrender, and everybody knows this. Who then is going to surrender first, or (consequently) at all? There can be no contract without some previous security against non-performance, yet the only security here postdates the covenant, the whole point of the covenant being to create it.

Hobbes is frequently listed as an apologist of the organic state – the frontispiece of *Leviathan* depicts the sovereign as a gigantic regal figure made up of normal-sized people – but this seems doubtful. Hobbes makes no distinction between the individual and the General or Real Will. The original bond of society consists in no sympathy or reciprocity but merely in an aggregate self-interest. The citizen is essentially a shareholder in exactly what Burke denied the state could be, a political joint-stock company. Its dividends come not in money, but in security. However indispensable, the state is still explicitly a means. It guarantees – what should certainly not be underrated – a sort of minimum political subsistence. Thenceforward the subject can, if he wishes and his sovereign permits, fulfil himself in non-political pursuits (and they had better be non-political).

Such pursuits (though Hobbes does not say so directly) may well engage those nobler, more altruistic impulses excluded from the covenant. It is not impossible, of course, that in the ensuing association altruism may come to reinforce self-interest. The sovereign has

705

already (on Hobbes' advice) enlisted religion on his side, simply by taking charge of it himself. But so long as he continues to do his job (protecting life), there is nothing to stop him (except his *own* self-interest) either from similarly recruiting all of his subjects' private or cultural activities, or, if he prefers, from suppressing them. If his subjects rebelled (at the risk of their lives), that would show that his job would have been better interpreted as being to protect not just their lives, but also things that had become yet dearer to them (in which case altruism would have *superseded* self-interest). And if he refrained, that would show that he knew the conditions for consent to be very much more complex and numerous than Hobbes assumed.

Nevertheless, whatever his deficiencies (and they are usually the price of his virtues), Hobbes points as clearly as the organic school to a profound truth. This is that, in the last resort, authority derives not from the sovereign, still less from anything outside society, but from the subject himself, even if he is, so to speak, coerced by necessity into his act of authorisation. The undercurrent of necessity, which in part lends Hobbes' writing its tragic urgency, is what most obviously distinguishes him from other contract theorists, and what leads one to doubt whether, if he were not forced into their company by his chosen myth and his tenacious pursuit of its implications, he really belongs with them at all. The last word on Hobbes has yet to be pronounced by anyone.

Locke

For Locke (1632–1704), as for Aristotle, informal association antedates political society, and political society exists to safeguard and satisfy certain existing predilections, each supposedly the subject of a 'natural' right (see Chapter 31). Locke's state of nature – which Locke clearly thinks historical, since it recalls colonists' records of native life – is portrayed as being tolerable enough to make political association, to say nothing of the details, strictly optional. This means, by contrast with Hobbes, that the associates have the right to dissolve their compact, or change their sovereign, if either should not be to their taste. (It is well known that Locke wrote his *Second treatise of civil government* to justify the deposition of James II in the previous year, 1688.)

In the state of nature, through informal alliance, life and liberty can just about be secured. What calls the state into existence is private property, a topic on which the normally placid Locke waxes uncharacteristically warm. The protection of property, and the representation of property interests, is the distinctive purpose of the state. Property, it might be said, is really a mark of personality, since it is in 'mixing his labour' with some portion of the common holding that a man establishes a claim (Locke would say, a right) to it as his own rather than the community's. (It does not occur to Locke, as it did to the Fabians, that the community might equally detach a man's right in his labour, and thus assign his labour to the collectivity who furnish his opportunities and materials.) To allege that a man's identity is so closely bound up with property is either (as in Hegel) to reveal spiritual possibilities in material objects, or simply (as Locke's critics assert) to take a low, materialistic view of persons.

The truth may lie somewhere between; but it must be admitted that Locke's view of the state is disenchanted, instrumental and unideal. It is hard to see how people could prefer its interests to their own, since their own interests separately considered is all it exists to serve. It has no independent life, spirit or personality that might make it, for example – what most states, among them some of the least deserving or attractive, actually are to the great majority of their members – an object of loyalty or affection. It is not that Locke was ignorant of higher things than life, liberty and property. But he thought that (e.g.) religion and morality were best left to fend for themselves (cf. the Hart–Devlin controversy, Chapter 32 below). He did not reflect that it might be precisely by representing and protecting such immaterial things – which are not in any case really private, but belong to that common mental world we call society or culture – that the state engages its citizens' permanent affections.

Locke's constitutional theories are well known. They include the famous 'separation of powers' and the idea that the sovereign's power is 'fiduciary' and thus revocable (so that the real sovereign, as Rousseau later explicitly suggested, is the citizen body). They influenced both Montesquieu, and Burke, and (famously) the architects of the American Constitution, and continue to flourish, being much the most persuasive part of his thinking.

What has less often been remarked is the curious double standard in Locke's theory of consent. Full citizenship is to be accorded only to property owners (since that is the point of the 'contract'). It is they who appoint the government. The unpropertied who do not emigrate are deemed, by virtue of having remained, to have 'tacitly consented' to an authority they have no power to dismiss. But why should they accept a criterion of legitimacy that the propertied classes (who dismissed James II, and retain the right to dismiss his successors) have taught them to despise? There are enormous problems hidden here, which liberal democracy still faces.

Summary and conclusion

Some 'means-theories' of the state (as we may call them) almost amount to 'end-theories'. For Hobbes government is indispensable to any recognisably human life. The immediate end, which prompts the covenant, is security. But security – except by comparison with the alternative – is hardly an end in itself. (Though men may have to settle for it, and have no just complaint against a sovereign who, whilst providing it, permits nothing in addition:

Hobbes' logic is impeccable.) The 'real' end, as Hobbes intimates in a justly famous passage (*Leviathan*, I, 13), may be those co-operative enterprises, industry and culture, on which no one would embark without the long-term security that only government can provide. The state, therefore, will presumably partake, by association, of their end-like character. In other words, the state will seem as *necessary* as whatever society it makes possible – whether that consists in minimum physical security, or in a flourishing civilisation – whilst remaining in principle distinct.

More 'optimistic' outlooks, such as those of Locke or (see Chapter 32) Mill (1806–73), make the state much more a matter of choice, and consequently (it seems) much more instrumental. The individual can survive without it, and so (at least in Locke) can society; neither, therefore, has any intrinsic motive for allegiance, as they have in Hobbes. (Yet it is Hobbes who is always accused of cynical individualism.) The end is whatever further satisfactions the state secures to the individual or enables him to secure for himself. Locke mentions property as being one; another might be a more civilised society than anything possible in the state of nature (and thus one doubtless dependent on property). Nevertheless, both Locke and Mill are far less specific than Hobbes (for all Hobbes' egoism) about the benefits of society *qua* society, which they separate far more radically from the state.

For Mill, indeed, society poses hardly less of a threat than the state to the individual. (It might even pose more, since a major function of the state, in Mill's view, should be to protect the individual against society.) For Mill (as later for Sartre) the individual *is* his 'freedom', a condition which, though apparently devoid of any positive content, is offered as man's true *telos*. As with Marx's 'full communism', we are required to take its value on trust, and (it is hardly too much to say) to sacrifice everything to it. But it is only fair to add that the conservative's shibboleth of 'order' and the socialist's of 'equality' are equally vulnerable to the sceptic's query: 'Yes, but these are not goods in themselves, merely alleged conditions of possible goods. Which things that I positively and already know to be goods are you asking me to give up for their sake?'

Some 'organically' inclined liberals, however, are disposed to identify society specifically as the locus of value, and hence as an end in itself (certain anarchist views approximate to this). They think, though, that it will emerge undistorted only under conditions of minimum constraint, out of the 'free' choices of individuals. This implies a clear-cut separation of society and the state, and the state's banishment to society's periphery, where it is restricted to maintaining the bare conditions of spontaneous association.

An 'end-theorist' might reply to both individualist and 'organic' liberals that society needs the state to supply the positive authority, rather than the merely negative conditions, for its maintenance.

The spontaneity and individuality necessary for (social) fulfilment are in fact, like all such skills and values, acquired only through moral education. Only society, articulate in the state, can direct people to a goal which at the outset they are incapable of perceiving and thus cannot prize. The state need not, perhaps should not, undertake such education itself; but it should underwrite with its authority (and if need be, with its power) the relevant institutions, in particular family and school. Once the goal has been reached, authority either becomes superfluous and is lifted (as for example at the 'age of consent'), or, because the subject's will is one with and thus shares in it, is no longer felt as constraint. On this view, effective authority (and thus the state) is a prior condition of real freedom. For to enslave oneself to what is valueless is an illusory freedom, and society has the duty, if not to forbid the adult from doing so, at least to minimise the chance that he will ever wish to.

That would be a conservative answer. Possibly its differences with the 'organic' liberal position can finally be settled only by empirical evidence, and in any case are less important in practice than on paper. But other end-theories are doubtless possible. For example, one who (like an anarchist) saw in the state nothing but the apparatus of coercion, yet nevertheless also thought it an end in itself, would be a power-worshipper, and if frank and explicit about it, a Fascist ('dynamism', as in the Futurist movement, was another aspect of Fascism, which was all things to all men). It may make little difference in practice, but Nazis and Communists, by contrast (and if sincere), are essentially means-theorists. They see the state as deriving its all-embracing power from something, such as race or history, transcending all visible political entities – the individual, society and the state itself – and determining what form, if any, all shall take. (The same is true of theocracies, such as contemporary Iran.) It is not only liberalism that sees the state as morally subordinate, and its subordination, in the instances just given, far from limiting the state's secular power, actually increases it. Conversely, end-theories of the state are not, as liberals tirelessly allege, necessarily totalitarian. All depends on what, and how much, the term 'state' is supposed to cover. The Fascist example shows that a narrow, rather than (as one might expect) a wide, construction is quite able to deliver a state with unlimited powers.

We have seen how the state can be defended as an end in itself: as the realisation of man's social nature, and as power for its own sake. It can also be defended as a practical necessity, an aid to salvation, a spiritual discipline, a guarantor of rights, a distributional agency (if that does not also count as guaranteeing rights), and the bearer of a historic mission. Yet again, it can be defended (or attacked) as an organ of class interest. Contemporary political philosophers, whatever their particular merits and originalities in regard to other topics, have so far added little, in essence, to the spectrum of possibilities rehearsed in the present chapter.

709

Bibliography

The state as end: the organic tradition

Plato

Plato's mature political philosophy is contained (along with much else) in what is perhaps his most famous dialogue,

[1] *The republic*. There are several English translations, of which one may mention those by A.D. Lindsay (Everyman's Library, Dent, London, 1st edn, 1935) and by Desmond Lee (Penguin Books, Harmondsworth, 2nd edn, revised, 1974). A helpful guide to the work is provided by

[2] Julia Annas, *An introduction to Plato's Republic* (Clarendon Press, Oxford, 1981); see especially Chs. 1–7. Still worth reading is a book by the Victorian scholar Richard Nettleship (1846–92):

[3] R.H. Nettleship, *Lectures on Plato's Republic* (Macmillan, London, 1901).

Aristotle

[4] *The politics*. Of several English translations, one may mention the rather free version by Ernest Barker (Clarendon Press, Oxford, 1946) and the version by T.A. Sinclair (Penguin Books, Harmondsworth, 1962).

A useful introduction to Aristotle's theory of the state is provided by

[5] R.G. Mulgan, *Aristotle's political theory* (Clarendon Press, Oxford, 1977). See also

[6] A.C. Bradley, 'Aristotle's conception of the state' in Evelyn Abbott (ed.), *Hellenica* (Rivingtons, London, 1880).

Burke

Burke did not write a systematic treatise on political philosophy; the work which is richest in philosophical ideas about the state is

[7] *Reflections on the Revolution in France* (1790). There have been many editions; see, e.g., the one published in Everyman's Library (Dent, London, 1st edn, 1910). For Burke's political ideas, see e.g.

[8] David Cameron, *The social thought of Rousseau and Burke* (Weidenfeld and Nicolson, London, 1973).

Hegel

There is an excellent English translation of Hegel's *Rechtsphilosophie* (1821):

[9] *Hegel's philosophy of right*, trans. T.M. Knox (Clarendon Press, Oxford, 1942). Two helpful books on Hegel's political philosophy are

[10] Shlomo Avineri, *Hegel's theory of the modern state* (Cambridge University Press, Cambridge, 1972)

[11] Raymond Plant, *Hegel* (Allen and Unwin, London, 1973).

Defenders of the State

Rousseau

A good English translation of Rousseau's *Du contrat social* is

[12] Rousseau, *The Social Contract and Discourses*, trans. G.D.H. Cole (Everyman's Library, Dent, London, 1st edn, 1913). The totalitarian implications of Rousseau's political philosophy are explored by

[13] J.L. Talmon, *The origins of totalitarian democracy* (Secker and Warburg, London, 1952), Ch. 3. For Rousseau's political theory in general, see also Cameron [8]. For an earlier but still helpful account, see

[14] T.H. Green, *Principles of political obligation* (Longmans Green, London, 1888), Section E.

British idealism

A wide-ranging and lucid survey of the movement is provided by

[15] Anthony Quinton, 'Absolute idealism' (*Proceedings of the British Academy*, 1971); reprinted in Quinton, *Thoughts and thinkers* (Duckworth, London, 1982), pp. 186–206.

The state as means

Epicureans and Stoics

[16] T.A. Sinclair, *A history of Greek political thought* (Routledge, London, 1951), Chs. 12–14.

Christianity

Some useful selections from St Augustine's vast work, *The City of God*, are to be found in

[17] M.B. Foster, *Masters of political thought* (3 vols, Harrap, London, 1942), vol. I, pp. 196–227.

For Aquinas' political writings, see

[18] A.P. D'Entreves (ed.), Aquinas, *Select political writings*, trans. J.G. Dawson (Basil Blackwell, Oxford, 1948). See also Foster [17], pp. 238–65.

Hobbes

There have been several editions of Hobbes' masterpiece, *Leviathan* (1651). See e.g.

[19] Michael Oakeshott (ed.), Hobbes, *Leviathan* (Basil Blackwell, Oxford, 1946).

For discussions of Hobbes' views, see

[20] J.W.N. Watkins, *Hobbes' system of ideas* (Hutchinson, London, 2nd edn, revised 1973), esp. Chs 4–7

[21] Thomas A. Spragens, Jr., *The politics of motion: the world of Thomas Hobbes* (Croom Helm, London, 1973), especially Chs. 5–6

[22] Michael Oakeshott, *Hobbes on civil association* (Basil Blackwell, Oxford, 1975).

711

Locke

For Locke's political ideas, see especially

[23] *Second treatise of civil government* (1689). A useful edition for the student is J.W. Gough (ed.), John Locke, *The second treatise of civil government* (Basil Blackwell, Oxford, 1946).

For comment on Locke's political philosophy, see Chs. 14–20 of a general introduction to Locke:

[24] J.D. Mabbott, *John Locke* (Macmillan, London, 1973).

I am grateful to Dr Grant for some helpful suggestions concerning this bibliography.

G.H.R.P

31 | The Philosophy of Rights

Jeremy Waldron

Moral and political philosophers use the concept of a right to do two quite different sorts of things. Like everyone else who is interested in the law, they use it to describe certain types of *legal* arrangement: situations in which the law of the land provides a person with some liberty, opportunity or benefit. But they also use the concept of rights to express certain *moral* claims: these include claims about the legal rights that people morally ought to have; ethical claims about the way people ought to treat and deal with one another; and abstract claims about the fundamental principles of social and political organisation. Though it is important to keep these moral and legal uses apart, it is also necessary to recognise that a lot of what is said about moral rights is modelled on what jurists have said about legal rights. Accordingly, the first section of this chapter will explore the role of rights in the law, while the sections that follow will consider their wider use in moral and political philosophy.

Legal rights

We shall begin with the following very broad definition: an individual has a legal right whenever the law of the land puts her in a position of advantage. Here are some familiar examples: (i) the law gives an individual the right to free speech by not setting out any prohibitions or penalties for acts of political dissent; (ii) the law of property gives someone a right to the exclusive use of a piece of land by providing her with the option to sue for the eviction of anyone else who tries to use it; (iii) if she has loaned money to a friend, the law of contract confers on her a right to the repayment of that money; (iv) the criminal law gives a person a right not to be assaulted by prohibiting assaults and requiring officials to prevent and punish them; (v) if someone is destitute,

713

social welfare law may give her a right to subsistence by empowering administrators to make cash payments to people in her position; (vi) constitutional law may give a person a right to vote by setting up democratic procedures and perhaps also by prohibiting officials from dismantling them. As these examples indicate, the types of advantage conferred and the types of law that confer them can differ considerably under this general heading of legal rights.

There are various ways in which a law can put an individual in a position of advantage. Most legal philosophers use the following scheme of distinctions first set out by the American jurist, Wesley N. Hohfeld.[1] (1) *Rights as privileges*. The law may benefit an individual simply by remaining silent – that is by not imposing what would otherwise be an onerous duty upon her. In England, the right of free speech (no legal duty not to speak one's mind) and the privilege against self-incrimination (no duty to answer questions put by a police officer or prosecutor) fall into this category. (2) *Rights as claims*. More positively, the law may give an individual an advantage by placing somebody else – a fellow citizen or an official – under a duty. Examples (ii), (iii) and (iv) all fall into this category. (3) *Rights as powers*. The law may put an individual in a position to effect a change in the legal relations that exist between her and other people. For example, a property owner has the right to give away her property, and in so doing she has the power to alter the powers, privileges and claims of other people. (4) *Rights as immunities*. On the other hand, the law may also insulate a person from the exercise of another's powers. For example, a stranger cannot dispose of my property, and there are limits on my spouse's capacity to dissolve my marriage. In countries like the United States of America, certain claims and privileges are given immunity even from the legislative powers of Congress; for example, the privilege against self-incrimination cannot be abrogated by any law. That right, then, involves an immunity as well as a privilege.

Opinions differ as to the importance of these distinctions. Certainly, confusion has sometimes arisen from a failure to distinguish privileges from claim-rights – particularly claim-rights to certain freedoms. But it is rare to find these Hohfeldian atoms in isolation from one another. The main significance of the scheme is to indicate that the practice of rights has a complexity which is sometimes belied by the bland simplicity of expressions like 'Susan's right to £100'. A creditor's right to repayment, for example, involves not only her debtor's duty but also her own power to initiate proceedings for the enforcement of that duty, her privilege of exercising that power, her immunity against the extinction of the debt within a period of limitations, her power to waive or reduce the debt as she pleases, and so on.[2]

Philosophically, most attention has focused on what Hohfeld called claim-rights: cases in which the rights of one individual correspond to the duties of another. For example, Susan's right to the repayment of a loan corresponds to Celia's duty to repay it; Susan's right to privacy corresponds to Celia's duty to refrain from invading her household; and so on. In these cases we know exactly what advantage the right confers, because we can point to the individual or agency required by the law to confer it. But this correspondence between rights and duties raises an awkward question about the redundancy of the language of rights. We know what it is for an individual to be under a duty: roughly it is for her to be commanded to carry out some action and for some other official to be commanded to visit her with some penalty should she fail to do so. Duty, in this sense, is one of the fundamental concepts of law. Now once we have established that Celia has a duty to give something to Susan or to refrain from interfering with Susan's conduct, is anything *added* to our understanding by saying that Susan *has a right* that Celia should behave in this way?

Responses to this challenge have concentrated on what it is for a duty to be owed *to* an individual. Here there are two main traditions of thought.

(1) The Choice Theory. Choice Theorists argue that Celia's duty is owed *to* Susan just in case Susan has the power to enforce or extinguish it. So, talk of Susan's right, on this analysis, is not just talk of Celia's duty in the passive voice, but of Susan's sovereignty or dominion over Celia's position in this regard. She has a right when it is *for her* to say whether another's duty should be enforced.[3] The Choice Theory analysis works best, in law, for rights arising in tort or contract; for there, no duties will be enforced unless a plaintiff chooses actively to pursue her remedy. It works less well, however, for the rights that are thought to arise in criminal or constitutional law. Though I am commonly thought to have the right not to be wounded, and though it is commonly thought that this right corresponds to the criminal prohibition against wounding, it is not for me to say whether this duty is enforced or not. If someone wounds me, her prosecution is a matter for the public authorities. The fact that we would describe it nevertheless as *my* right and not the public prosecutor's casts some doubt on the Choice Theory analysis. In ethics and political philosophy, the model suggested by the Choice Theory is necessarily more complicated, since there is no straightforward notion of enforcement. Some philosophers argue that the essence of having a moral right is being in a moral position to *claim* or *demand* the performance of a duty by another, to complain when that duty is not carried out, and to forgive any failure to perform it.[4] An individual has a right, on this account, when her claim or her complaint or her forgiveness are deemed morally more appropriate than those of other people in relation to some duty. And, by the same token, the theory becomes less credible for cases in which rights are understood to exist without any special privilege of claiming or forgiving.

(2) The Benefit Theory. On an alternative analysis, a duty is said to be owed *to* Susan, and Susan is said to have the corresponding right, if and only if the point of imposing the duty is to confer some benefit on Susan or advance some interest of hers.[5] According to this view, duties which I can neither waive nor enforce on my own account may be thought of as corresponding to my rights if the point of imposing them on other people is the advancement of some interest of mine. Now sometimes this may be unclear. We all have duties laid down in the criminal law, to refrain from cruelty to animals. But maybe the point of these prohibitions is simply to stop people from exhibiting the vice of cruelty, rather than to protect the interests of animals. If so, these prohibitions do not correspond to any *animal rights*. The controversy about animal rights, then, is partly a matter of ascertaining the point of the laws that happen to protect the interests of animals. By itself, the mere fact that someone derives a benefit from another's duty is not sufficient to establish that she has a right; if it were, my grocer's creditors would have a right that I should pay my grocery bill. We have to enquire into the point of the imposition of the duty in question. But the controversy about animal rights is also partly a matter of how rights are to be understood. On the Choice Theory analysis, not even the fact that a duty is intended to benefit an animal is sufficient to establish that the animal has a right. For the Choice Theorist, talk of animal rights is appropriate only to the extent that it makes sense to talk of animals' exercising, enforcing and waiving the rights that are putatively attributed to them. It is easy to see how similar controversies may also arise in relation to the rights of children, foetuses, trees, landscapes and so on.

The debate between the Choice Theory and the Benefit Theory also raises some deeper issues about rights. If the essence of a right is that it may be waived or enforced by the right-bearer, then in principle any right may be signed away. Historically, defenders of political absolutism have relied on this to establish the possibility that even the most oppressive regime might be founded on the consent of its citizens. People, they say, may have waived their rights to political freedom in return for the comfort or security that absolutism guarantees. Conversely, liberal philosophers have used the thesis of the *in*alienability of certain rights to deny that possibility. Some rights, they say, are too important to be left at the mercy of the people who have them. They are better conceived as a *trust* from God than as the alienable property of His creatures.[6] Partly this is a matter of how the right-bearer is perceived and what the point of rights is taken to be. The Choice Theory connotes an image of the right-bearer as a free agent, self-determining, in full control of her own destiny, and fully responsible for the consequences of her own decisions. The function of rights is to provide a framework which enables people to determine comprehensively the course of their own lives. On the other hand, the Benefit Theory allots rights a wider role in human life. Rights are capable of protecting *any* human interest deemed sufficiently important, and not only those connected with self-determination. People need many things besides freedom; and if the importance of some of those needs can be established without reference to the conscious choice of the people in question, it may be thought appropriate to talk of rights which cannot be set aside by the right-bearer – rights which are in that sense inalienable. Now, no doubt, these deep philosophical issues lie dormant when we are talking about ordinary legal rights in tort or contract; there the issue between the Choice and Benefit Theories is largely one of technical analysis. But when we turn to the analysis of constitutional and human rights, or rights whose interpretation is a matter of political disputes, then these questions about freeedom, need and the image of the right-bearer become much more significant.

We have said that the function of a right is to confer some benefit or advantage on an individual. But even after we have established what sort of advantage is involved, there are other questions to ask. Are we to speak of a right *whenever* an individual stands to benefit from a legal determination or only when that benefit is somehow *guaranteed*, something he is *entitled* to in law? An official may have discretion to award a welfare benefit to one claimant and withhold it from another in exactly similar circumstances. Do we say that the first claimant turns out to have a right while the second does not? Or do we say that the determination is so arbitrary that neither can be said to have *rights* in the matter? Or, to take another example, a judge may award punitive damages to one plaintiff because he thinks, as a utilitarian, that the general interest requires an example to be made of the unfortunate defendant: does this count as a determination that the plaintiff has a *right* to the damages in this case? Or does it fail to be a matter of right because it is not something the plaintiff could count on in advance? The idea that the function of legal rights is to provide some sort of guarantee is an attractive one. The jurist Ronald Dworkin has argued that judicial decisions should concern themselves only with rights, understood in this sense.[7] The judge's job is not to allocate the penalties and rewards at her disposal in whatever way she thinks would advance the good of the community; instead she is to allocate them on the basis of the legal rules and principles with which the parties in front of her are already familiar. Their rights are the expectations of benefit they might reasonably hold on the basis of a prior understanding of the law. Of course, often the tenor of existing law is disputed or unclear. But even in these cases, Dworkin suggests that the job of the judge is not to legislate anew but to make her decision on the basis of the most attractive construction of the legal materials in front of her. In so doing, she respects the expectations of the litigants by engaging in the same enterprise they did when they sought to ascertain their rights. So, in a judicial context at least, rights represent not only legally conferred benefits, but benefits that are understood to be guaranteed by legal rules even when their conferral may turn out to be socially inconvenient in a particular case.

Similar ideas have been expressed about other areas in which people stand to gain or lose from official determinations. Social welfare law sometimes makes the payment of benefits discretionary, resting them on an administrator's assessment of the merits of each individual case. When people demand that benefits should be given out 'as a matter of right', they are calling for an end to this sort of discretionary decision-making and for the institution of simple and well-publicised rules to govern welfare benefits, rules which make it clear in advance when a given person is entitled to a benefit and when she is not. Those who are covered by the rules can then go to an administrator and claim their benefits in a dignified fashion as theirs by right, instead of having to make a case or plead for an official determination in their favour. Moreover, rules that confer rights in this sense allow people to plan their lives more effectively knowing in advance what they can count on and what claims of theirs they can expect officials to respond to.

These two aspects of a legal guarantee – dignity and predictability – become particularly important in the case of constitutional rights. In those countries where there are Bills of Rights, certain basic guarantees are set down to constrain not only the exercise of judicial and executive discretion, but also legislative or parliamentary decision-making. People participate in politics in the knowledge that certain basic freedoms and benefits are given, and are not at the mercy of the whims of the electorate or the fickle forces of the political market place. So they need not be so apprehensive of being silenced, expropriated, imprisoned or disenfranchised if their opponents win an election or political contest. In politics there are often losers; but losses like these are regarded as so serious that the power to inflict them should not be included among the spoils of political victory. People, then, can count on these guarantees as they go about their political business.

The mistake is often made of thinking that individual rights are a threat only to the ambitions of those who are bent on personal political aggrandisement. Only tyrants and scoundrels, it is thought, can be opposed to the idea of constitutional rights. In fact, the sorts of rights we have been talking about are often very costly to the community at large. They inhibit judges and officials from making their decisions sensitive to considerations of marginal social cost. The demand for predictability and for clear and well-known rules laid down in advance prevents administrators from taking due account of changes in circumstances – in the fiscal economy, for example, or in patterns of demand for the services they are supplying. Above all, constitutional rights stand as obstructions to the democratic will of a majority of citizens and may often prevent the people from doing what they evidently want to do, or from maintaining forms of stability or solidarity for which there is overwhelming demand. So when philosophers celebrate rights as 'trumps' over utility or as constraints on 'the tyranny of the majority', we need to remember what this means: rights prevent the community from being as prosperous as its officials think they can make it, or from doing everything it wants to do. Because it involves these costs, the business of guaranteeing rights to individuals needs a justification. That is the function of the theories of rights put forward by moral and political philosophers.

Moral rights, natural rights and human rights

Sometimes when people talk about moral rights, they mean only to indicate the moral desirability of the existence of some legal right. The claim, for example, that abortion is a woman's moral right may just be another way of expressing the moral claim that women *ought* to have a legal right to abortion.

But often talk of moral rights goes deeper than this. If it is appropriate to talk of legal rights when a rule of law secures a benefit for an individual, surely it is appropriate to talk of moral rights in cases where the point of a *moral* rule is to advance or protect some individual interest. Some philosophers – notably the English utilitarian Jeremy Bentham – have suggested that this is a misuse of the concept, and that the word 'right' should be confined to strictly legal contexts.[8] But, apart from general scepticism about moral rules (a scepticism which would also undercut the moralistic use of 'duty'), there does not seem to be any good reason for this restriction. Morality, like law, can be modelled as a normative system of duties, privileges, claims, powers and so on, and there is in principle no reason why the concept of a moral right should not have the same rigour and clarity as jurists have been able to provide for the concept of rights in positive law.

However, it may not always be easy to say when a moral rule gives rise to a moral right. Consider, for example, the rule that one must not tell lies: does this generate a moral right not to be lied to? On some accounts of the point of the rule it does not. A utilitarian will say that the rule against lying aims at the promotion of the general good through the maintenance of trust and credit in the community. Each person's duty not to lie is justified by the contribution it makes to this overall state of affairs. Since the point of imposing it is not to benefit any individual in particular, the moral duty does not correspond to any individual right, on this account. A similar conclusion can be reached in a Kantian theory of ethics. Here the point of the rule against lying is not to protect the interests of the individuals who are spoken to but to preserve the rational integrity of the agents constrained by the duty. A person who lies, Kant argued, exhibits a heteronomous will – that is, a will that cannot be thought of as governed by the pure law-like form of reason alone. She therefore abuses her faculty of reason and does less than justice to her rational nature. Since this account focuses on the nature of the agent and not on any concern for those who stand to benefit from her truth-telling, it can hardly be thought of as a duty based on concern for individual rights.[9]

So what would a *right*-based account of the rule

against lying look like? It would have to go something like this. Each person has an interest in organising her life on the basis of accurate information about the world in which she lives. The main source of this information, apart from her own senses, consists in what other people tell her. Without this information, her life may be a mess. Maybe the moral importance of her interest in having this information is such as to justify imposing a duty on other people to refrain from telling her things they know to be inaccurate. If this is the rationale for the rule against lying, then it is plausible to say that that rule gives everyone a moral *right* not to be lied to. But the possibility of giving the utilitarian or the Kantian rationale indicates that in morality as in law, the inference of a right from a rule imposing a duty is always a matter of interpretation.

A *natural* right is probably best understood as a certain type of moral right. The term 'natural' here connotes two related ideas. First there is the idea that people's conduct should be thought of as governed not only by the laws and mores of their local communities but by rules and principles that have *universal* moral validity. The authority of these rules is taken to be natural not conventional for, like the laws of nature that scientists study, they apply without exception throughout the world. In the heyday of natural rights, this law was identified with that laid down by God for all His creatures, revealed to them in the Bible or through the workings of reason. The independence of natural rights from conventional law was crucial to their use in political argument. Such rights were thought of as pre-political rights – that is, rights which men and women held prior to and independently of their political allegiances and legal obligations, and which they would continue to have held even if government and positive law had never come into existence. In this way, the concept was linked with that of *the state of nature* – the concept used by social contract theorists like John Locke to describe the human condition apart from the institution of political society.[10] In the state of nature, people have rights and duties which define their moral relations with one another: prominent among these were thought to be rights to life, liberty and property, and duties not to interfere with them. Governments were thought of as devices set up by groups of men and women for the promotion and enforcement of these rights. That was taken to be the function of the state and the only condition under which its institution was morally intelligible. Accordingly, we could say with confidence that all governments were subject to certain moral constraints. They were not themselves to interfere with or violate the rights they were instituted to protect. And the laws of a particular state could claim no moral force against these natural rights since the state had no other authority than that which arose from the terms of its institution. Any state which ignored or violated natural rights was to be overthrown and replaced just like any other functional device that had outstripped its usefulness.

The other idea involved with natural rights is that of

human nature. Though humans live in utterly different social environments, they are thought to share a common nature – common needs and capabilities, a common potential for moral action and social relationships, as well as common sensitivities, fears and vulnerabilities. (The concept of the state of nature was partly intended as a model of human life based on this common essence alone.) This idea is very controversial, being denied by those who think culture, history and level of economic development make a comprehensive difference to the predicaments humans face and the powers and susceptibilities with which they face them. But those who take it seriously believe that our common nature provides a basis for believing in certain universal rights – rights which of course transcend those guaranteed by the laws of particular societies.

The modern idea of *human* rights draws on both these strands of thought, though it is more commonly associated with the second. It is thought that the people of the world share a common moral heritage of respect for human life, toleration of cultural and religious diversity, racial and sexual equality, the dignity of labour, and political freedom and democracy. In fact, that heritage is mocked by the proliferation of various forms of oppression in the modern world. Nevertheless, faith in human rights is predicated on the idea that the opponents of oppression can appeal to a set of common moral principles which have not only universal scope but some sort of global acceptance, embodied in documents like the Universal Declaration of Human Rights. The moral pressure, such as it is, that can be brought to bear against violations of human rights is perceived to be the pressure of the world community, and not just the outrage of people who happen to hold particular moral opinions.

Still, the philosophical foundations of this confidence in human rights remain unclear. Few now accept a Divine Command view of natural law, and anyway it would be hard to deploy such a conception in defence of religious toleration and diversity. Moreover, philosophers are acutely aware of the fallacies involved in trying to infer moral standards from putative facts about human nature. These issues about the justification of human and natural rights will be taken up in 'The justification of rights', pp. 727–34.

The distinctiveness of rights

It is important to see that not all moral claims can be expressed in the language of rights. There are a number of ways in which talk of rights has been thought to differ from other forms of moral discourse.

Individualism

The first and most obvious of these is the *individualism* of the language of rights. When something is demanded as a matter of right it is always demanded as *somebody's* right; in this respect talk of rights differs from more impersonal locutions like 'It ought to be the case that ...' or 'It would be a good thing if ...' Rights pick out benefits to be secured to individuals severally or one by one. Even when they are taken to be universal, in the way that human rights are, they apply universally to individuals, and the demand is understood to be that every person should receive such and such a type of individual benefit. Moreover, to say that Susan has a moral right that Celia should do something is to imply that Susan's individual interest in the matter is important enough to justify imposing that duty on Celia. Thus even if everybody has a right not to be tortured, it must still be the case that *each person's* interest in not being tortured is *by itself* sufficient to warrant the imposition of duties on other people not to torture her. This means that the language of rights is probably inappropriate for expressing a commitment to values whose importance cannot be pinned down to individuals in this way. Examples include commitments to certain aesthetic values (the beauty of the planet quite apart from the well-being of the people who live in it) and, most importantly, communal values like fraternity and solidarity. Though the latter goods benefit men and women, they do not benefit them as individuals, and it cannot be said that their worth to any *individual* is sufficient to account for the imposition of a duty to impose them. If there are such duties, they are justified by reference to the good of people taken together as a community, not severally as individuals. They are values whose moral desirability would be distorted if we had to pin it down in terms of the worth of individual benefits and enjoyments. Of course, to say that these values cannot be expressed in the language of rights is not to denigrate them. It is simply to indicate the futility of trying to construct an exclusively *right*-based moral and political theory.

Moral priority

Secondly, it is widely believed that the language of rights connotes a certain *urgency* and that it should be reserved for considerations that are to be given priority in moral argument when moral considerations conflict. Yet few philosophers are prepared to argue that rights express moral *absolutes*. Partly this is because the rights admitted by most theories are capable of conflicting among themselves. One person's freedom of speech may threaten another's right to personal security. Or, more acutely, one person's right to be rescued may conflict with another's when the time and resources that can be devoted to saving them are scarce. In these situations we cannot say that all the rights are absolute for fear of making our theories incoherent.

There are ways of formulating rights theories so that conflicts like these can be avoided, but the price of doing so is very high. One can drop from one's theory any rights whose fulfilment is likely to require the use of scarce resources – socio-economic rights, for example, like rights to medical care or free education. That would leave only rights to liberty – rights correlative to duties of omission rather than duties positively to provide goods or services.[11] The trouble is, however, that the sentiments and convictions that inform and underpin our commitments to individual rights do not always track the availability of resources in the precise way that this move would require. When we learn that there are not enough resources to satisfy both Susan's right to medical care and Celia's, our concern does not necessarily diminish in either case. Anyway, the elimination of all rights save those requiring omissions is not by itself sufficient to remove the possibility of conflicts of rights. Someone may still face a situation in which the best way to prevent a large number of rights violations is to violate somebody's rights herself. (A police officer steals a car in order to prevent mass murder, or frames an innocent suspect in order to deter a large number of offences.) To avoid conflicts like these, rights would have to be understood as corresponding not only to duties of omission but to what have been called 'agent-relative side constraints', along lines suggested by Robert Nozick.[12] Thus Susan's right not to be killed is – so far as Celia is concerned – simply her (Celia's) duty not to kill her. It is Celia's overriding responsibility to see that she does not become a murderer, no matter what others are doing. Each person is to be concerned to see only that *her* conduct does not violate the right, and, unless she can ensure this as a matter of priority, she is not to trouble herself about the conduct of others. So the police officer in our example must not frame the innocent suspect or steal the car even if she could prevent a larger number of other people from violating rights by doing so. Now the trouble with this is that it looks increasingly unlike a *right*-based approach to the problem. The moral concern seems to be the Kantian one that each agent should keep her own hands clean rather than that the interests of all the right-bearers be protected as far as possible. The concern is with how bad it is to be a killer, rather than how bad it is to be killed.

This suggests that a credible theory of rights will be one in which there are moral conflicts. Accordingly, rights cannot be regarded as absolute. When they come into conflict with one another they may have to be weighed up and balanced in a roughly consequentialist way.[13] But rights may still have priority over moral considerations. Suppose that the suppression of dissent in a society would generate more happiness than unhappiness: a vociferous minority might suffer greatly but that would be more than outweighed by the greater contentment and complacency of the overwhelming majority of a politically apathetic population. Indeed, this greater contentment might even make up for the backwardness and stagnation of a society starved of free debate. In these circumstances, the ethical theory of utilitarianism will suggest that it is right or permissible to place a ban on political dissent. However, a theorist of rights, though not wanting to deny the force of these utilitarian considerations, might insist that the individual right of free speech matters more from a moral point of view than the greater happiness that could be secured by suppressing it. Of course, we await her argument for this proposition; but that seems to be the sort of proposition people commit themselves to when they talk about individual rights. The function of a right is to single out certain individual interests for special attention or protection in social decision-making, distinguishing them from ordinary run-of-the-mill interests and preferences. There would surely be no point in doing this if the interests that were singled out were not given greater weight than they would have been given anyway in the ordinary calculus of social utility. That calculus counts every interest and preference according to its intensity and prescribes an action calculated to produce the greatest possible balance of satisfaction over dissatisfaction in society. If there is any point at all to picking some key individual interests out of that process and giving them special attention, then it must be the case that the protection or promotion of those interests is regarded as a matter of moral importance in itself quite independently of the importance that a utilitarian would attach to it.[14]

Two notes of caution should be sounded, however. This argument does not show that rights are singled out in order to prevail over any or all considerations of utility. The argument establishes only that there would be no point to the practice if we did not expect rights to prevail over *ordinary* or at least *marginal* utilitarian calculations. The situation may be quite different in cases where massive or extraordinary amounts of utility are at stake. The other point is that this argument tells us nothing so far about what rights people have. It tells us only what it is to make the claim that such-and-such an individual has such-and-such a right. To say that Susan has a right to something is to single out some interest of Susan's as sufficiently important in itself to warrant the imposition of duties on other people in circumstances where ordinary calculations of social utility might not justify the imposition of those duties. But we need a substantial theory of human needs and the relative moral importance of human interests before we can say which aspects of human well-being are to be singled out for this exceptional treatment and which are not.

Enforceability

It is commonly believed that the language of rights should be reserved for those moral requirements which it is thought morally appropriate to enforce.[15]

There are many things people ought to do, or which it would be decent or morally desirable for them to do, but which nevertheless should not be made the subject of coercion or legal enforcement. To take a couple of extreme examples: almost everyone believes that the moral prohibition on killing should be enforced with all the coercive apparatus available to the state; and almost nobody believes that the moral requirement to show politeness to strangers in the street should be enforced with threats and penalties. In between, there is an immense no-man's-land of political dispute about how far moral standards should be embodied in the law. Should we enforce religious morality, sexual morality and the mutual respect that ought to characterise relations between members of different racial groups? Should there be laws banning abortion, homosexuality, adultery, the use of narcotics, pornography, sexist language and so on? There are many different views about how to answer questions like these. Some say that moral standards should not be enforced unless other people's *rights* are affected. But if rights are identified in turn with *enforceable* moral rules, this theory does not in itself offer any guidance about *which* moral rules to enforce. Some say that only those standards should be enforced which protect people from *harm* or interference with their *liberty*. (The latter test has the analytical attraction that it authorises an interference with freedom only in order to prevent or punish a prior interference with freedom.) But both *harm* and *liberty* are politically contested concepts. Is a person *harmed* when she is sickened or offended by another's conduct? Is her *liberty* affected if others' lifestyles establish a social environment in which her moral or religious convictions cannot be pursued? Anyway, many theorists believe that there is sometimes a justification for using state force not only to protect people from harm or coercion, but also to actively promote their interests and satisfy their needs: taxation for health, education, culture and welfare provision has exactly this character. If we admit that force may be used in pursuit of these goals, why may it not also be deployed to promote ideals of moral conduct? These issues will be found, explored in more detail, in Chapter 32.

The connection with freedom

The final claim about the distinctiveness of rights that we ought to consider concerns the connection between rights and individual freedom. Their distinctiveness, it is said, is not just a matter of the *form* of the language of rights; it has to do with the substantial values that are invoked whenever talk of rights is in the air. To talk of rights is to talk about individual freedom and the conditions that are necessary for its realisation. On this view, the paradigm rights are the traditional liberal rights to political liberties: free speech, freedom from arbitrary arrest and imprisonment, freedom of travel, and freedom of association. Rights of property and contractual rights are justified a little more indirectly on the ground that those institutions are necessary for individual freedom and that particular rights arise under them as a result of the exercise of that freedom by individuals. But, on this view, the language of rights is distorted and misused when people claim that there are rights to things like education, free medical care, guaranteed employment and basic welfare provision, without making any attempt to relate those concerns to the value of freedom.[16]

A number of the points we have already considered are connected with this view. The Choice Theory of rights locates choice, and therefore freedom, at the very heart of the practice. The view that rights correlate with duties of omission is connected with freedom because in a negative sense our freedom is constituted by other people's *omitting* to interfere with our conduct. And the view that rights are necessarily enforceable has been connected by at least one philosopher with the idea that rights are concerned with liberty: H.L.A. Hart has argued that since a right constitutes a *justification* for interfering with another's freedom, the very existence of the practice presupposes a background right to liberty in general, which is to be rebutted in the special circumstances of other rights.[17] The view about the connection with freedom, then, brings together considerations of the form and the content of rights in a complicated way. However, I want to postpone any further consideration of that view until 'The justification of rights', pp. 727–34, where we will be examining the main justifications that have been put forward for believing in a morality of rights.

Attacks on the idea of rights

It would be unwise to end this section without saying something about the reasons some philosophers have given for repudiating the idea of rights altogether. Though natural rights were appealed to historically in the foundation of the American and French republics, we should remember that the idea of the rights of man was attacked at that time by liberal utilitarians such as Jeremy Bentham, conservatives such as Edmund Burke, and socialists like Karl Marx.[18] The main themes of their attacks have continued through into the modern debate. Human rights are said to represent simplistic moral claims whose abstraction, universalism and absolutism do violence to the detailed complexity of human life. They cut across the autonomy and integrity of local customs and traditions; they are insensitive to the relativity of social and economic development; and they try to pass off as eternal values the claims that have been made on behalf of a certain type of individual at a certain phase of world history. In their substance, the rights of man are seen as egoistic claims put forward to promote the arbitrary whims and pleasures of the individual at the expense of the well-being of the society of which she is a part. In so doing, they gnaw at the very basis of social solidarity and communal responsibility.[19]

The charge of abstraction is a general indictment of liberal social theory and cannot be pursued in detail here. But the charge of egoism is one that demands an answer. It is alleged that a preoccupation with rights encourages a selfish and litigious mentality – a spirit of strident and querulous concern for one's own interests and a devaluation of those wider moral considerations that are essential for the sustenance of human society. People take their rights to be warrants for selfish or self-centred conduct and use them as reasons for resisting any call for individual sacrifice and social co-operation.

In response to this, three things can be said. First, there is nothing in the logic of rights to license the view that having a right to do something provides a reason or a justification for doing it. The function of rights is not to insulate us from moral criticism but to protect us from coercion, and people misunderstand their moral position if they take their rights as warrants for selfishness. Secondly, there is nothing in the logic of rights to require that everyone should be concerned with her own rights to the neglect of those of others. It is true that rights protect certain individual interests, the interests of particular individual selves. But this individualism is not the same as selfishness or egoism, and in the modern world the language of human rights is most commonly deployed by people who are concerned about attacks on the selves and the individual interests of *others*. Thirdly, rights need not be thought of as antagonistic to wider moral or social considerations. On the contrary, if – as we shall argue below – one of the functions of rights is to secure the conditions that make moral agency possible, then rights may be viewed as complementary to, and indeed as necessary prerequisites for, a deeper and more pervasive sense of social responsibility.

The justification of rights

If people have rights, what are they based on? We have seen that it is not sufficient to point to human nature as a justification for human rights. Facts about our nature provide no basis for any logically compelling argument about the rights that we have. If human nature is relevant at all to the justification of moral rights, it must be because the way we understand ourselves – our needs and our capacities – already involves certain values, principles and commitments which we would be reluctant to abandon and which are best articulated, wholly or partly, in terms of individual rights. At the very least, the demand for a justification is the demand to know which values, principles and commitments these are.

We should expect the values in question to be reasonably important ones. As we have seen, the rights are normally understood to have a certain priority in moral argument over utilitarian or democratic considerations that would in normal circumstances be decisive. We said, though, that rights are not moral absolutes; after all, they often conflict with one another. The possibility of this sort of conflict is another reason for examining the justification of the rights we believe in, for it is only by referring to deeper values and principles that we can get any sense of how to handle such conflicts. If Susan's right to free speech appears to conflict, say, with Celia's right to economic security, we need to be able to refer back to the respective values that underlie these rival claims in order

727

to see, first, how seriously those values are engaged in the particular case and, secondly, how much weight is to be given to each of the competing rights in these particular circumstances.

Before we look at the various theories that have been put forward, some notes of caution are in order. First, we must not expect too much of our justificatory theories in this area. If the justification of moral views is problematic anyway, then it will be problematic in the case of rights. There is no more (and no less) reason to expect the derivation of an 'ought' from an 'is', or a vindication of the idea of objective value, in the case of rights than there is in any other area of moral philosophy. Philosophers have never tired of the attempt to find knock-down arguments in favour of their moral views – arguments that are rationally irresistible. Whether any such arguments can be constructed is a matter of general controversy in meta-ethics (see Chapter 23). It is not a special problem for the philosophy of rights. Secondly, unless we are wedded to a particularly strong view about the connection between form and content in the language of rights, we need not suppose that all moral rights will have the *same* justification. The rights that are claimed nowadays are many and diverse, and they have little more in common than that they base the imposition of social and political duties on the importance of an individual interest rather than on the demands of social utility. As the interests in question vary, the account that is given of their importance may vary also. So it should not be taken as an objection to any of the theories that I am going to outline that there are some plausible claims of right that that theory cannot account for.

Utilitarianism

As we have seen, rights are commonly thought of as having priority over considerations of social utility. But it is possible nevertheless that rights themselves may rest on a utilitarian foundation. It may sometimes be dangerous from a utilitarian point of view for decisions to be taken by individuals or officials on the balance of social advantage as it appears to them at the time. In stressful cases, utilitarian calculations may be difficult, unreliable or time-consuming. In the long run, we may do better if we require people to follow rather rigid moral rules than if we permit them to take decisions in an act-utilitarian way. (This possibility is discussed in more detail in Chapter 26.) So a sophisticated utilitarian theory will have to address the question of what moral dispositions to inculcate and what moral rules agents should be required to follow. This question itself will be answered on utilitarian grounds. But the answer will be given at a very *general* level; at the level of particular cases, decisions will be taken on the basis of the rules and dispositions that have this general justification. Now some of these rules may be best thought of by those who operate them as rules intended to protect or promote certain individual interests even at the cost of apparent marginal gains in social utility. If so, it is plausible to say that these rules generate moral rights, and also that they have a utilitarian foundation.[20]

No one much doubts that a utilitarian argument is capable of establishing some such rights. But utilitarians have been much less successful in showing that these would be the rights to liberty and tolerance that liberal theorists have usually favoured. The best candidate is perhaps John Stuart Mill's argument for freedom of thought and expression in the second chapter of *On liberty*, but that argument remains very controversial indeed.[21] Furthermore, those who believe in rights are likely to remain suspicious even of this sophisticated utilitarian theory. Utilitarians – even those with a 'two-level' theory – are still ultimately committed to the view that all interests and all aspects of human benefit and advantage can be weighed together on a single scale to determine what ought to be done. But the hunch behind many theories of rights is that certain human interests are of such crucial moral importance that they should not be weighed in the balance against lesser interests at all, and that there is no number, however great, of lesser satisfactions that could possibly make up for the loss or violation of one of these interests. The priority that rights are given in moral argument reflects the fact that the importance of the interests they protect cannot be expressed quantitatively as a function of the importance of any lesser human interests. Utilitarianism seems incapable in its very nature of capturing the force of this conviction. (To say this, of course, is not to detract from the importance of the arguments that two-level utilitarians can make in favour of insulating certain decisions from act-utilitarian calculations; but it casts doubt on the utilitarians' pretension to provide a *complete* account of our moral convictions.)

Liberty

We have already come across the view that the basis of a theory of rights is a concern for human liberty. Humans are potentially free agents and the realisation of their freedom is a matter of the greatest moral importance; and the language of rights is said to be the part of moral discourse most directly concerned with this issue.

But a commitment to liberty in this general form is not enough for a theory of rights. No one believes that people have a right to liberty across the board – that is, a right to perform just any action they choose. Maybe we have a right to perform at least those actions that do not interfere with the liberty of others. But even if the circularity that threatens this definition can be avoided, the right that it defines is far too broad. For one thing, it does not leave room for rights of property (as distinct from rights of physical possession). Many of us believe that people may be wronged by others' interference with their goods even when that does not amount to an interference with their personal freedom. So property, if it is justified at all, cannot be established in any scheme dominated by a right to liberty. There is another reason why a general right to liberty is far too broad. As Ronald Dworkin has pointed out, it is widely accepted that utilitarian arguments provide satisfactory justifications in politics for overriding claims to freedom in ordinary cases: my freedom to drive along Oxford Street is quite properly restricted if this turns out to be in the interests of social utility. Since rights are supposed to prevail over considerations of utility in special cases, there cannot be a right to liberty as such if liberty yields to utility in run-of-the-mill cases.[22]

If liberty is important for a theory of rights, it is not in the crude sense that the more actions one is free to perform the better. Rather, importance is accorded to certain 'basic liberties' – the freedom to perform types of action that are thought to have some special significance for human life. Thus liberals place immeasurably greater emphasis on freedom of conscience, freedom of speech, free choice of sexual partner, and so on than on, say, freedom to drive at a certain speed or freedom to walk across a certain field. The former are upheld often at a significant social cost; the latter are abrogated whenever it is socially convenient to do so. Now the basis for this discrimination between important freedoms and run-of-the-mill freedoms cannot be inferred from a bland commitment to freedom as such. It must be based on something like the importance of certain key actions in the shaping and direction of an autonomous human life.

The other point to stress in this connection is that liberty is sometimes interpreted as implying a commitment not only to 'negative' freedom of action, but to more 'positive' ideas about the moral personality of the free man. (See the discussion in Chapter 32.) To be free is not just to be left to one's own devices to follow one's whims; it is to be capable of genuine moral deliberation, choice and responsibility. Rights, then, may be seen as the conditions that are necessary for the realisation of these capacities. But once again, in order to establish these rights, a bland commitment to freedom is not enough. One needs a full-bodied account of the conditions and prerequisites of moral agency.

Moral agency

Moral agency and the associated idea of autonomy have provided the focus of much of the most interesting recent work on moral rights. The American philosopher Alan Gewirth has argued that each of us, in our actions, makes a claim to the conditions that make human action possible – a claim which cannot then be consistently denied by any agent when it is put forward on behalf of others. Simply by acting in the world, we show what we think of the values associated with agency, and that implicit commitment provides the basis and justification for some of our most fundamental rights.[23] How convincing Gewirth's argument is depends on how seriously we take the view that people necessarily evince a claim about their agency when they act. Maybe people just *act* without implying any evaluation on the matter at all.

But there are other ways in which agency may figure in an argument for rights. Instead of deriving moral claims from action itself, we may ask what conditions need to be present before moral action becomes possible. Though it is true that individuals should act in the interests of others and of the community in which they live, the ability to do so is not something which should be taken for granted. In the modern world, altruistic action requires sensitivity, complex deliberation, insight, courage and mature responsibility. These qualities presuppose not only education in virtue but also a certain amount of freedom and social and psychological *space*, as it were, for the agents concerned. Only a few heroes are capable of thinking and acting morally under conditions of oppression and terror. For most of us, such conditions – and others like the panic of starvation or exposure – overwhelm our faculties and crowd out moral deliberation. If something like this is true, then freedom and the satisfaction of basic needs may be cited as the necessary prerequisites for morality. And they may be claimed as rights for everyone from whom moral action and social responsibility are reasonably expected.

Social contract

In 'Moral rights, natural rights and human rights', pp. 719–21, we considered the link between natural rights and the idea of the social contract. Though philosophers no longer say that society is actually based on a contract, some find it useful to model individual rights as the terms that a social contract might have had in the unlikely event that one had been negotiated. Rights, on this account, are like the guarantees that people would hold out for as a condition of accepting any of the sacrifices of social life.

But how can we be confident about what people would demand in this hypothetical scenario? One approach is to ask whether there are any terms that people are perhaps *incapable* of agreeing to. The English philosopher Thomas Hobbes argued that people must have a right of self-defence, since this is a privilege an egoist is psychologically incapable of relinquishing. He also argued that no one can be obliged by an agreement to perform the impossible, and so a putative contract not to defend oneself would always be invalid on this ground as well.[24]

A similar sort of argument has been developed recently by the American philosopher John Rawls.[25] Rawls asks us to imagine a group of people coming together to settle terms of social co-operation in circumstances where none of them knows precisely what talents, abilities and commitments she would have. He argues that people in this 'original position' would repudiate straightforward utilitarian principles for fear that these might impose impossible burdens on them – obligations to

731

make sacrifices for the general good that they would be unable to discharge. Though no one in the original position would know what her moral, religious and political commitments were, each would know that she had *some* such commitments and would know too that she was unlikely to be able to honour any commitment to abandon them in favour of some officially sanctioned morality instead. On this basis, Rawls argues that the only principles of justice capable of being accepted in the original position must include rights to moral, religious and political freedom. In the area of socio-economic rights, Rawls argues that people in the original position would similarly conclude that they could not honour any promise to accept poverty or deprivation if it turned out that lower life chances for a few were necessary to guarantee better life chances for the majority. Once again, the only set of principles capable of acceptance in the original position would have to include principles safeguarding the interests of the worst-off group in society. Roughly, Rawls argues that socio-economic inequalities should be allowed to exist only when the worst-off group would be even worse off if the inequalities in question were diminished.

Both parts of Rawls' contractarian argument are controversial. There are some moral and religious commitments that cannot be pursued individualistically but only by people acting together as a society. Now if the people in the original position think there is a possibility of finding themselves with commitments of this kind, they will view the liberal spirit of Rawlsian liberties with as much abhorrence as a conscientious individual views the confessional state. And as far as the Rawlsian principle of equality is concerned, that has been attacked by utilitarian critics who maintain that rational people *are* capable of undertaking the gamble that agreeing to utilitarian principles would involve and of honouring that agreement should the worst outcome eventuate for them.[26]

More important than these controversies, however, is the argument about the overall character of Rawls' strategy. In itself, a hypothetical contract – negotiated in thought by beings deprived of so much of the information we ordinarily rely on – has no weight in moral argument. The contract model contributes to moral justification only to the extent that it embodies deeper values that are independently persuasive. Examination of Rawls' argument reveals two main values he is relying on. First, there is the view that certain of the contingencies of human life are morally irrelevant. Our particular talents and abilities are undeserved and we cannot base any fundamental entitlements on our possession of them. And the contingencies of our present social arrangements are irrelevant to arguments about justice and right precisely because they embody values and principles which are necessarily the objects of our re-examination. Secondly, implicit in the contractarian approach is a deep and radical commitment to *equality*. The social contract embodies the idea that no set of social arrangements is right unless it is acceptable to each and all of those who are to live under it. One cannot be voted into a social contract: each person has a veto, and so each person's interests must be consulted and respected. Even if the particular arguments that Rawls bases on this premiss do not go through, that idea of equal concern and respect for all remains an attractive foundation for a theory of rights.

Equality

We turn finally, then, to equality as a basis for individual rights. It is plausible to say that a government must treat all its subjects with equal concern and respect: it must not give exclusive or privileged attention, for example, to the needs and interests of white men, as opposed to women or members of other racial groups.

But equality in this sense is a very abstract idea. Does it generate any substantial conclusions about the rights that we have? The jurist Ronald Dworkin has argued that equality can generate more concrete moral rights in three areas.[27]

First, in settling basic principles of property and economy, equality requires that people be thought of as having an equal claim to the benefits that can be derived from the resources of their society. But this is still very abstract. Must the state ensure that everyone's welfare is equally promoted by the use of resources? Or does this ideal only dictate an equal division of resources, leaving each with her own share to pursue her well-being in her own way? There are many different conceptions of economic equality, and controversy continues as to which of these is the best.

Secondly, equality may be thought to require a policy of official neutrality on questions about what makes an individual life worth living. People differ in their answers, and perhaps the only way to accord equal respect to people in the views that they hold is to allow them the moral and religious liberty to follow their convictions. Clearly this view is subject to some of the same objections as Rawls' theory. But in addition the liberal must respond to the view that there is in fact nothing inegalitarian about requiring everyone to pursue the same values if the government is convinced they are the best. If a conception of the good life is enforced because it is thought correct rather than because it is held by some group or other in society, its enforcement need involve no derogation from the principle of equal respect even for those who disagree with it.

Thirdly, Ronald Dworkin has developed an argument for political rights which sees them as correctives for a certain kind of defect that is liable to corrupt processes of utilitarian and democratic decision-making. When preferences for and against a policy are added up, it may be difficult to distinguish those which relate to the personal welfare of the person with the preference from those which relate to her view of the welfare that others ought to receive. Dworkin argues that a social calculus

733

which counts only preferences of the first type – *personal* preferences – may be a satisfactory expression of the principle of equal concern. But a calculus that also counts preferences of the second type – *external* preferences – loses its claim to that egalitarian character, for it is liable to be infected by people's anti-egalitarian preferences that some should receive greater or lesser consideration than others. According to Dworkin, the function of rights is to act as safeguards in those areas where it is antecedently likely that external preferences will be decisive in social decision-making. This argument has evoked a great deal of criticism. The distinction between personal and external preferences is a difficult one, and in any case, many utilitarians reject the view that counting external preferences undermines the egalitarianism of their approach to social choice. But at least in those areas of policy where it is clear some citizens have strong beliefs that others should be treated unequally – areas, for example, where racial or sexual prejudice is rife – straightforward utilitarianism looks morally unattractive. Its trouble is that it takes all human preferences as they are, treating each of them as worthy of satisfaction in itself no matter what its moral character. In some areas that is no doubt a laudable expression of the liberal spirit. But given that prejudice and hatred continue to exist in society, maybe some greater vigilance on behalf of equality is called for. If so, a theory of rights may be considered as one way of undertaking that vigilance.

Notes

(An author's name followed by a number in square brackets refers to the book or article which has that number in the bibliography.)

1. Wesley N. Hohfeld, *Fundamental legal conceptions, as applied in judicial reasoning* (1923), ed. W.W. Cook (Yale University Press, New Haven, Connecticut, 1964).

2. There is an excellent discussion of the complexity of rights in Wellman [7].

3. The Choice Theory is adopted in H.L.A. Hart, 'Are there any natural rights?' *Philosophical Review*, 64 (1955), pp. 175–91.

4. For example, Joel Feinberg, 'The nature and value of rights', *Journal of Value Inquiry*, 4 (1970), pp. 243–57.

5. The Benefit Theory is adopted by David Lyons, 'Rights, claimants and beneficiaries', *American Philosophical Quarterly*, 6 (1969), pp. 173–85. A version of it is also adopted by Joseph Raz, 'The nature of rights', *Mind*, 93 (1984), pp. 194–214.

6. This difference between the two views of rights is comprehensively discussed in Richard Tuck, *Natural rights theories: their origin and development* (Cambridge University Press, Cambridge, 1979).

7. Dworkin [8], Chs. 1–4. See also his more recent discussion in *Law's empire* (Harvard University Press, Cambridge, Massachusetts, 1986).

8. Jeremy Bentham, 'Anarchical fallacies' (1795) in Bhiku Parekh (ed.), *Bentham's political thought* (Barnes and Noble, New York, 1973), Ch. 20.

9. This argument is found in Immanuel Kant, *The moral law, or groundwork of the metaphysics of morals* (1785), ed. H.J. Paton (Hutchinson, London, 1948), Ch. 2, pp. 89–90.

10. See John Locke, *Two treatises of government* (1689), ed. Peter Laslett (Cambridge University Press, Cambridge, 1960), particularly the *Second treatise*.

11. This approach is urged by Maurice Cranston, 'Human rights—real and supposed' in Raphael [4], pp. 43–53.

12. Nozick [9], pp. 28–51.

13. There is an excellent discussion of this balancing in Amartya Sen, 'Rights and agency', *Philosophy and Public Affairs*, 11 (1982), pp. 3–39.

14. This argument is developed in Dworkin [8], p. 92.

15. See, for example, Hart, 'Are there any natural rights?' p. 176.

16. See Cranston in Raphael [4], p. 52.

17. Hart, 'Are there any natural rights?' p. 178.

18. Bentham, 'Anarchical fallacies'; Edmund Burke, *Reflections on the Revolution in France* (1790), ed. Conor Cruise O'Brien (Penguin Books, Harmondsworth, 1969); Karl Marx, 'On the Jewish question' (1843) in T.B. Bottomore (ed.), *Karl Marx – early writings* (C.A. Watts, London, 1963), pp. 3–40.

19. Modern critiques of the idea of rights can be found in the literature of 'the new communitarianism'. See, for example, Michael Walzer, *Spheres of justice: a defense of pluralism and equality* (Basic Books, New York, 1983); Alasdair Macintyre, *After virtue: a study in moral theory* (Duckworth, London, 1981); Michael Sandel (ed.), *Liberalism and its critics* (Basil Blackwell, Oxford, 1984); and John Charvet, 'A critique of human rights' in *Human rights: Nomos XXIII*, eds. J. Roland Pennock and John W. Chapman (New York University Press, New York, 1981).

20. See John Stuart Mill, *Utilitarianism* (1863), ed. Mary Warnock (Collins, London, 1972), especially Ch. 5. The same idea has been developed more recently in Hart [15]. There is also an excellent discussion in the essays in R.G. Frey (ed.), *Utility and rights* (Basil Blackwell, Oxford, 1985).

21. John Stuart Mill, *On liberty* (1859), ed. Gertrude Himmelfarb (Penguin Books, Harmondsworth, 1974). See also John Gray, *Mill on liberty: a defence* (Routledge and Kegan Paul, London, 1983).

22. This argument is taken from Dworkin [8], pp. 269–72.

23. Gewirth [17]. There is a full critical discussion of Gewirth's idea in Regis [18].

24. Thomas Hobbes, *Leviathan* (1651), ed. C.B. Macpherson (Penguin Books, Harmondsworth, 1981), Chs. 14 and 21. See also Hobbes, *De cive* (the English version), ed. Howard Warrender (Clarendon Press, Oxford, 1983), pp. 57–60.

25. Rawls [11].

26. For critical discussion of Rawls' theory, see Daniels [12].

27. See Ronald Dworkin, 'What is equality?' (Parts I and II), *Philosophy and Public Affairs*, 10 (1981), pp. 185–246 and 283–345; 'Liberalism' in Stuart Hampshire (ed.), *Public and private morality* (Cambridge University Press, Cambridge, 1978); Dworkin [8], pp. 231–9 and 275–8, and also 'Is there a right to pornography?' *Oxford Journal of Legal Studies*, 1 (1981), pp. 177–212.

Bibliography

Four valuable collections of papers dealing with the issues discussed in this chapter are

[1] J. Waldron (ed.), *Theories of rights* (Oxford University Press, Oxford, 1984)

[2] D. Lyons (ed.), *Human rights* (Wadsworth, Belmont, California, 1978)

[3] R. Frey (ed.), *Utility and rights* (Basil Blackwell, Oxford, 1985) and

[4] D.D. Raphael (ed.), *Political theory and the rights of man* (Macmillan, London, 1967).

An introductory account of various kinds of right may be found in

[5] J. Feinberg, *Social philosophy* (Prentice-Hall, Englewood Cliffs, 1973).

See also Ch. 8 of

[6] J. Mackie, *Ethics* (Penguin Books, Harmondsworth, 1977), while an excellent discussion of the complexity of rights occurs in

[7] C. Wellman, *A theory of rights: persons under laws* (Rowan and Allenheld, New York, 1985).

Perhaps the most influential recent work on this topic is

[8] R. Dworkin, *Taking rights seriously* (Duckworth, London, 1978).

A celebrated exposition of rights as 'agent related side constraints' occurs in

[9] R. Nozick, *Anarchy, State and Utopia* (Basil Blackwell, Oxford, 1975) and is discussed in Part II of

[10] J. Paul (ed.), *Reading Nozick* (Basil Blackwell, Oxford, 1981).

A famous version of the contractarian approach is developed in

[11] J. Rawls, *A theory of justice* (Oxford University Press, Oxford, 1971), which is critically discussed in

[12] N. Daniels (ed.), *Reading Rawls* (Basil Blackwell, Oxford, 1975).

Discussion of H.L.A. Hart's work on rights may be found in D.M. MacCormick's 'Rights in legislation' in

[13] P.S. Hacker and J. Raz (eds), *Law, morality and society* (Clarendon Press, Oxford, 1977).

See also Chs. 7 and 8 of

[14] N. MacCormick, *Legal right and social democracy* (Clarendon Press, Oxford, 1982).

A utilitarian approach is developed in

[15] R.M. Hare, *Moral thinking: its levels, method and point* (Clarendon Press, Oxford, 1981).

See also Ch. 4 of

[16] D. Lyons, *Ethics and the rule of law* (Cambridge University Press, Cambridge, 1984).

Alan Gewirth's account, centring on the notion of human agency, may be found in

[17] A. Gewirth, *Human rights: essays on justification and application* (University of Chicago Press, Chicago, 1982) and it is critically discussed in

[18] E. Regis (ed.), *Gewirth's ethical rationalism: critical essays* (University of Chicago Press, Chicago, 1984).

For rights as applied to practical issues in law and politics, see Sections 5–8 of

[19] R.M. Dworkin (ed.), *The philosophy of law* (Oxford University Press, Oxford, 1977) and Section 3 of

[20] J. Rachels (ed.), *Moral problems* (Harper and Row, New York, 1971).

Finally, the relation of rights to other concepts in ethical theory is usefully examined in Part I of

[21] D. Miller, *Social justice* (Clarendon Press, Oxford, 1976).

Grateful acknowledgement is made to Dr Waldron for some helpful suggestions concerning this bibliography.

J.G.C.

32 | The Limits of the State

C.L. Ten

J.S. Mill's 'On liberty'

In his famous essay *On liberty*, published in 1859, John Stuart Mill posed the problem of 'the nature and limits of the power which can be legitimately exercised by society over the individual'.[1] For Mill the problem was not solved with the arrival of democracy as a system in which the government was responsible to the people. Democracy conferred power not on everyone in society but on the majority of the people, and the majority might abuse this power by imposing their wishes on the rest of society. So there was a need for safeguards against 'the tyranny of the majority'.

Mill saw the tyranny of the majority as operating not merely through oppressive laws but also through the use of extra-legal penalties to impose prevailing values and practices. Popular opinion is often based on feelings unsupported by reasons, but people have taken it for granted, or have been encouraged to believe, that the majority were justified in appealing to their 'likings and dislikings' as the standard of conduct applicable to all. Even enlightened thinkers have merely tried to change these feelings rather than challenge the view that one group in society was entitled to impose its values on the rest of society. It was only in the area of religious beliefs and practices that differences were tolerated, and the principle that individuals had the right to their own religious beliefs had been acknowledged. But even here individual liberty was threatened in matters about which the majority felt strongly. For example, Mill pointed out that some people might be quite happy to extend religious toleration to believers of all kinds, but would stop short at tolerating atheists and those who did not believe in an after-life.

Mill thought that the solution to the problem he

posed was to be found in the acceptance of what he called 'one very simple principle':

> That the only purpose for which power can be rightfully exercised over any member of a civilised community, against his will, is to prevent harm to others. His own good, either physical or moral, is not a sufficient warrant. He cannot rightfully be compelled to do or forbear because it will be better for him to do so, because it will make him happier, because in the opinions of others, to do so would be wise, or even right.[2]

        Mill's principle was designed to set limits to the coercive interference with the liberty of individuals. It was not meant to rule out the use of persuasion, advice or argument in order to change people's conduct. Indeed Mill later pleaded for greater attempts to influence the conduct of others by non-coercive means. He also excluded from the scope of his principle children and 'barbarians', or people who were not capable of being influenced by 'free and equal discussion'.[3] But he believed that the principle applied to his own society and to all neighbouring societies. The excluded societies appeared to include some of the colonies. Mill's principle asserted that the prevention of harm to others was the only basis for interfering with the liberty of individuals, and it also specifically ruled out limitations on a person's conduct in order to promote his or her own good. It thus excludes the policy of paternalism such as that embodied in legislation which requires the wearing of seat-belts and of crash-helmets and which is solely motivated by the desire to protect motorists and motor-cyclists from the increased risk of harm, or from the likelihood of greater harm. Mill also ruled out interference with the conduct of individuals in order to make them conform to the dominant morality or values of society. The policy of enforcing, by means of the criminal law, society's shared morality is usually called 'legal moralism'.

        Mill's principle was directed not only against legal paternalism and legal moralism but also against the use of extra-legal social coercion for paternalistic and moralistic purposes. But much of the contemporary discussion has been confined to an account of the legitimate function of the criminal law. In this context we may state the doctrine of moderate liberalism as the view that, whereas the prevention of harm to others is always a relevant reason for interference with an individual's conduct, legal moralism and at least certain forms of paternalism fall outside the proper limits of the criminal law. A more radical liberalism shares the anti-paternalism and anti-legal moralism of moderate liberalism, but goes further to assert, with the first part of Mill's principle, that the *only* justifiable interference by the criminal law with the conduct of individuals is to prevent harm to others. Unlike radical liberalism, moderate liberalism is silent on whether some harmless conduct may properly be interfered with by the criminal law. The difference between the two doctrines is significant in the case of certain acts, like the performance of some sexual acts in public and public defecation, which many people in society find offensive, but it is difficult to show that they are harmful to others, or even to the participants themselves. In order to justify legal prohibitions on them, the radical liberal would have to assimilate acts offensive to others to harmful acts, thus treating offence as a type of harm. On the other hand, the doctrine of moderate liberalism is compatible with the legal prohibition on such offensive acts even if they do not harm others, provided that the basis of the prohibition is not paternalistic or an attempt to enforce the shared morality of society.

Mill's principle has been the centre of much debate both in his time and in our own day. His contemporary, James Fitzjames Stephen, wrote a book, *Liberty, equality and fraternity*, which attempts to refute the arguments of Mill's essay.[4] Much more recently, in 1957, the Wolfenden Committee recommended changes in the English law on prostitution and homosexuality based on its view that the function of the criminal law is 'to preserve public order and decency, to protect the citizen from what is offensive or injurious and to provide sufficient safeguards against exploitation or corruption of others'.[5] The Committee recommended that although public soliciting may be legally suppressed because it is offensive to people, prostitution itself should be legal. It also recommended that homosexual practices between consenting adults in private should not be a criminal offence. The Committee seemed to echo Millian sentiments when it claimed that 'There must remain a realm of private morality and immorality which is, in brief and crude terms, not the law's business.'[6] The most well-known criticisms of the Committee's views came from Lord Devlin, who asserted that the legal enforcement of society's shared morality was a legitimate function of the criminal law.[7] Devlin's arguments were in turn subjected to detailed critical scrutiny by H.L.A. Hart, who defended a modified Millian position.[8] The debate continues and in recent years it has focused on whether pornographic books and films should be legally prohibited.

Legal moralism

Stephen argued that it was proper that the criminal law be directed to the suppression of vice and the promotion of virtue. But he warned against the indiscriminate use of this 'most powerful and by far the roughest engine'.[9] Before an act was to be made criminal it should be capable of being defined and proved clearly, and this would, for example, rule out making ingratitude a criminal offence. The harm done by the application of the law should not be greater than the good to be achieved. Before punishing an act one should also ensure that there is an overwhelming moral majority against the act. For this reason Stephen believed that the punishment of adultery, seduction or fornication could not be justified. However these precautions do not alter the fact that 'there are acts of wickedness so gross and outrageous that, self-protection apart, they must be prevented as far as possible at any cost to the offender, and punished, if they occur, with exemplary severity'.[10]

Sometimes Stephen wrote as if the fact that the law enforced moral values, independently of any harm to others, was sufficient to show that it was right to do so. This of course begged the question against Mill, who was well aware of existing practices, and sought to change them. However there was perhaps a suggestion on Stephen's part that existing laws and institutions, which have survived the test of time, embody the wisdom of the ages.[11] But the plausibility of this view depended partly at least on whether society had developed a critical tradition of subjecting its laws and institutions to scrutiny. Stephen's emphasis on the role of the criminal law in branding 'gross acts of vice with the deepest mark of infamy',[12] and his belief that it was important to gratify 'the feeling of hatred' which grossly immoral conduct excited in 'healthily constituted minds',[13] served only to identify the dangerous passions which sustained the law and social institutions in his scheme of things. Today we are acutely aware of the dangers of racial and religious bigotry which feed precisely on the same 'elements of human nature' which Stephen regarded as so healthy. There are few things in human nature more ugly and more in need of suppression or sublimation than the fanaticism and intolerance of a group of people spurred on by the certainty of the truth of their long cherished and deep-seated beliefs.

In *Law, liberty and morality* H.L.A. Hart distinguishes between two different theses about the enforcement of society's shared morality. According to the moderate thesis the shared morality is of instrumental value and its enforcement is necessary to prevent society from disintegrating or weakening. On the other hand, the extreme thesis maintains that the enforcement of the shared morality is valuable in itself and would therefore be justified even when the punishment of those who violate that morality does not protect society from harmful effects. Hart attributes the extreme thesis to Stephen, and traces one basis for Stephen's view to a version of the retributive theory of punishment, that punishment of a wrongdoer is justified not in terms of the good effects produced, but because it is a 'fitting' return for the moral wrong done.[14] Hart argues that this theory of punishment is plausible when applied to cases where the offender's act harms his victim. Thus many people have felt the force of the claim that Nazis should be punished for intentionally inflicting suffering or death on their Jewish victims even if punishment will not produce beneficial future consequences. But where, as in the case of homosexuality between consenting adults, the act which violates a society's shared morality causes no harm to others, the application of the retributive theory seems to rest on the implausible claim that the addition of the suffering inflicted by punishment to the wrongness of the offender's act produces something which is morally good: 'two blacks make a white'.

741

Hart also identifies the denunciatory theory of punishment as another element in Stephen's extreme thesis. On this view, the function of punishment is to express moral condemnation of the offender. But, as Hart points out, moral condemnation is normally expressed verbally, and the suffering inflicted by punishment would be unnecessary.

Devlin seems to subscribe to the moderate thesis. He argues that a shared morality is essential to society's existence because a society is not just a collection of individuals but 'a community of ideas'. Shared political and moral values hold a society together, and violations of the shared morality threaten the society with disintegration. The shared morality is manifested in the attitudes of the ordinary person, 'the man in the street'. Devlin suggests that mere disapproval of a form of conduct is not sufficient for the law to act against it. However if the feelings of the man in the street reach a level of intensity marked by 'intolerance, indignation and disgust', then the limits of society's toleration have been reached and the law's enforcement of the shared morality is justified.[15]

The general idea that some shared morality is essential to the survival of society need not be, and in fact was not, disputed by Mill and other liberals. It is clear that societies cannot exist without some prohibitions against acts, like murder, assault and theft, which cause obvious harm to others. And, as Hart points out, laws against such acts would not be very effective if they were not supported by a shared moral belief about the wrongness of the acts.[16] But it is a very different matter as to whether a shared sexual morality condemning, for example, homosexuality, prostitution and pornography is necessary for society's survival. Devlin cites no evidence to support his view but relies instead on the claim that social morality is a connected whole so that violations of the shared morality in one area will eventually lead to the undermining of the rest of the social morality. But this latter claim too suffers from lack of supporting evidence, and conflicting, and apparently more plausible, views have been held by others. Thus some have argued that violations of the shared morality act as safety-valves which release in harmless ways sexual energies which would otherwise find outlets in violent crimes. Still others have held that different parts of a society's shared morality form separate compartments so that what happens in one compartment has little or no effect on what goes on elsewhere.

It is Devlin's view of social morality as a connected whole which leads him to fear the 'interregnum' between the rejection of one set of shared moral values and the adoption of a new set. He warns that changing the shared morality is not like changing a coat.[17] In the interregnum, without the cohesive force of a shared morality, society will disintegrate. But he is wrong here, for piecemeal changes in society's shared values are constantly taking place without the society collapsing. If we grant that some shared morality is necessary for the survival of society, we are still not confronted with the prospect of social dissolution, because as one part of the shared morality undergoes change, the rest of the shared morality remains to provide the bonds holding the society together. So society need not be caught with its pants completely down.

In any case it is not clear that there is a shared sexual morality in societies like our own. The Moral Majority in the United States of America does not constitute Stephen's 'overwhelming moral majority' and there is no general consensus about the correct sexual morality. Mill and others have argued that in pluralist societies it is the acceptance of the values of individual liberty and toleration, rather than the more specific beliefs of particular moral or religious groups, which provide the bonds of social union.[18] If this is true, then the liberty of individuals to participate in a range of activities not harmful to others is not only compatible with the continued survival and stability of society, but is also the only basis for such survival and stability in some societies.

Devlin's belief in the connectedness and inseparability of different parts of the shared morality also leads him to his well-known analogy between violations of the shared sexual morality and treason. Violations of the shared morality are supposed to undermine the moral foundations of society in much the same way that treason undermines its political foundations. 'The suppression of vice is as much the law's business as the suppression of subversive activities.'[19] But the analogy does not stand up to scrutiny. Democracies allow for a peaceful change of government, and a current political majority is not justified in curbing the activities of other groups just in order to prevent them from gaining power. So too, continued violations of society's shared morality may lead to a change in that morality. But those who engage in unconventional sexual activities are not trying to foist their standards of conduct on unwilling participants. What needs to be protected at the political level are those institutions, including freedom of expression, freedom of association and regular and free elections, which allow diverse political groups to participate in the political forum. In a similar manner we need to protect the freedom of minority sexual groups from suppression by the current moral majority, if they exist.

Devlin does not seem to have a very clear conception of what is involved in society's 'disintegration' when some parts of its shared morality are widely violated. Sometimes the disintegration of society is seen in terms of a loss of its physical strength and the discipline of its members brought about by 'unrestricted indulgence in vice'. Thus he believes that 'A nation of debauchees would not in 1940 have responded satisfactorily to Winston Churchill's call to blood and toil and sweat and tears.'[20] But it is incomprehensible why, if excessive indulgence in sex is physically debilitating, this effect is confined only to those who violate the shared morality and not to those whose prolific sexual activities are carried out within the institution of marriage.

Hart accuses Devlin of sometimes identifying a

society with its current shared morality. In that case, if violations of that morality lead to a change of the shared morality, society would cease to exist.[21] But in this sense the 'disintegration' of society is merely synonymous with a change in its shared morality, and does not necessarily produce chaos, widespread violence and destruction of social life, or other undesirable social consequences.

Devlin fails to show that violations of society's shared sexual morality will cause harm to society. But, on the other hand, if indeed there is harm, the legal enforcement of morality could be brought within the scope of Mill's principle since that principle permitted interference with the liberty of the individual in order to prevent harm to others. Mill has sometimes been interpreted as maintaining that interference with the individual's conduct is justified only when the conduct is morally wrong, and the criterion of moral wrongness is that there is harm to others.[22] On this interpretation Mill can be said to subscribe to the view that morality may be legally enforced, but still not to the doctrine of legal moralism which justifies the legal enforcement of the shared morality of society even when there is no harm to others. Indeed if harm to others is the criterion of moral wrongness, then the shared standards in terms of which the majority condemn conduct not harmful to others cannot really be said to be *moral* standards but matters of taste or preference. But whether or not we regard the judgements made on the harmless conduct of others as moral or non-moral judgements, the liberal view is that these judgements should not be legally enforced no matter how intense or how widely shared they may be.

Harm and morality

A further objection to Mill's principle is that the notion of harm on which it relies is morally impregnated and cannot therefore be used as a neutral basis between conflicting moral views for determining the extent of legitimate interference by the state.[23] But as it stands the objection is too general to be effective. It fails to distinguish between political morality and personal morality. Political morality, consisting of principles of justice, is needed to regulate the relationship between different groups and individuals in society. Personal morality, on the other hand, is a particular individual's or group's conception of a good or worthwhile life. Thus different religious groups have different personal moralities, and yet they might each agree that the correct political morality regulating their relationships is that centring round the mutual toleration of one another's religious practices. It may be that the principle of toleration, and the notion of harm in Mill's principle, depend ultimately on the values of a controversial political morality. But this shows only that there is a need to argue for one political morality as against rival political moralities. It does not show that one political morality is just as good as another, or that the notions of toleration and harm are impregnated with the specific and disputable values of a personal morality not shared by other personal moralities.

Unlike political moralities, several different and even incompatible personal moralities can coexist. Christians, Muslims and atheists can live together in the same society while being faithful to their respective beliefs in their own lives. But it is not possible to have conflicting political moralities, as each seeks to enforce a different set of political values. For example it is not possible to accept both a theory of justice which requires the redistribution of resources from the rich to the poor, and one which allows individuals to retain all their existing resources. In his influential book *A theory of justice*, John Rawls develops a political morality whose defence of liberty will be discussed later.

Another way of looking at the issue of what form of conduct is harmful is to ask whether there is a common core to the notion of harm which different personal moralities, except the most indefensible, in fact acknowledge, even though they might each also go in different directions beyond this core. Consider for example the notion of physical harm which centres round the notion of bodily injury. Suppose that someone says that cutting off his hands is not harmful. If this were the full story it would be quite unintelligible.[24] We begin to understand him only when, for example, he explains that he had frequently stolen in the past, and that cutting off his hands is both a way of atoning for his wrongdoings and of ensuring that he does not steal again in future. Again, he may be like the 'young and strong and lustie rogue' in the case of *Wright* (1603) who made his companion strike off his left hand so that he would be a more successful beggar.[25] In the absence of some supposed good that is to be achieved, the person himself would regard cutting off his hands as harmful. Given this fact, we see that his notion of harm, though peculiar in some respects, shares with ours the notion of bodily injury as harmful.

Consider another case. A persistent rapist is caught and begs to be castrated. He does not regard his castration as harmful, but one should not conclude that he also believes that castration is not harmful for other people with less troublesome sexual desires. Someone could only believe that castration is not harmful, independently of any good to be achieved by it, if he was unaware of the function of the sexual organs. Perhaps one day an anthropologist might report the discovery of a primitive people who regard the sexual organs as purely decorative, and who believe further that the organs are most attractive when they have been subjected to what we would regard as harmful mutilations. We would not really believe the anthropologist, although our journals and newspapers would no doubt play up his story.

There is also a common core to the notion of harm which can be extracted from the idea of survival in a human society. As Hart has pointed out in a different context, if we are concerned with '*how* men should live together, we must assume that their aim, generally speaking, is to live'.[26] Given survival as the aim, there are some very general facts about human nature and the world in which we live which make it necessary for there to be certain rules in any viable human society.

The general facts about human nature to which Hart draws attention are: (i) human vulnerability, which requires protection by rules restricting the use of violence in killing or in inflicting bodily injury; (ii) the approximate equality of persons, which makes it necessary for them to submit to rules imposing mutual forbearances; (iii) limited altruism, which makes such forbearance both necessary and possible because, unlike angels, human beings are sometimes tempted to injure others, and, unlike devils, they are not prepared to destroy their fellow human beings without regard to the cost to themselves; (iv) limited understanding and strength of will, which sometimes tempt people to seek their own immediate benefits by breaking mutually beneficial social rules, and which therefore have to be held in check by an organisation for the detection and punishment of those who violate rules. Without such a coercive organisation, those who voluntarily obey the rules would be unfairly treated relative to the malefactors, and would themselves tend to succumb to the temptation of breaking the rules.

The relevant general fact about the world in which we live is that there are limited resources for providing us with the food, clothes and shelter which we need. This fact makes it necessary for there to be rules regulating property so that for example crops can grow on land without being destroyed by indiscriminate entry. Again division of labour and co-operation among people for efficient production lead to rules governing the transfer, exchange and sale of goods.

We can develop, along the lines of Hart's illuminating discussion, a basis for showing why certain rules are necessary for the viability of social life in complex pluralist societies. This account will also provide us with a concept of harm as violations of the rules, or a weakening of the institutions necessary for the survival of society.[27]

Theoretical limits to state intervention

Mill's principle is usually interpreted as distinguishing between self-regarding conduct, which does not harm others and should never be interfered with, and other-regarding conduct, which harms others and may justifiably be interfered with. It is the notion that there is a class of self-regarding conduct which is absolutely immune from legal intervention which Devlin attacks. He asserts that 'it is not possible to set theoretical limits to the power of the State to legislate against immorality'.[28] His argument in support of this is that even though an act of 'private immorality' may be quite harmless, acts of that kind are harmful when engaged in by many. Thus he points out that while a few people being drunk in private will cause no problem, widespread drunkenness will create a serious social problem.[29] But Devlin's objection to Mill's principle rests on a misunderstanding. If it is true that widespread indulgence in a form of conduct is socially harmful, then Mill's principle will not exempt it from intervention. What is important is not whether there is any type of conduct which is always harmless, but rather whether the state's reasons for intervention are sound.[30] Thus the state is not justified in prohibiting private drunkenness simply because the majority disapprove of it, but the state would be justified in prohibiting even private drunkenness if it can be shown that it is harmful to society.

If by 'private drunkenness' we mean that the act is harmless, then of course it should always be exempt from legal intervention. But if by 'private drunkenness' we are simply referring to the fact that the act is committed in a place to which members of the public do not normally have access, then this in itself is not an absolute barrier to legal intervention. An act of murder is not private in the first sense, but it can be, and sometimes is, committed in a private place in the second sense. If a person murders his or her spouse in the privacy of their bedroom this does not mean that the act is harmless and that acts of this kind should not be legally prohibited.

The 'theoretical limit' which Mill's principle imposes on interference by the state with individual conduct is one which rules out absolutely certain kinds of reasons as irrelevant while recognising that harm to others is always a relevant reason for legal intervention. As Mill himself argues, 'No person should be punished for being drunk, but a soldier or a policeman should be punished for being drunk on duty.'[31] A similar distinction was made by Locke in his *A letter concerning toleration*, first published in 1689. He argued that one would not be justified in objecting to the killing of a calf as a sacrifice in a religious ceremony while at the same time allowing the killing of a calf for a feast. But this did not imply that the killing of calves should never be prohibited. Prohibiting the slaughter of calves would be justified in order to increase the stock of calves. He pointed out that in such a case the slaughter of calves is not prohibited for purely religious reasons but as 'a political matter'.[32] Again it is the reason for intervention which is crucial.

According to Mill both legal moralism and legal paternalism do not provide justifiable grounds for interference with the liberty of individuals. We have already discussed legal moralism and will now consider the doctrine of legal paternalism.

Legal paternalism

One argument against paternalism, which Mill and others use, is that individuals know their own interests better than others, and have a greater motivation to protect those interests. But this argument has not impressed critics. Although generally sympathetic to Mill, Hart points out that Mill held an unrealistic conception of what a normal human being was like:

> Mill, in fact, endows him with too much of the psychology of a middle-aged man whose desires are relatively fixed, not liable to be artificially stimulated by external influences; who knows what he wants and what gives him satisfaction or happiness; and who pursues these things when he can.[33]

Certainly the considerations to which Hart draws attention help to undermine an absolute anti-paternalism if this is conceived broadly as a refusal to take any action designed to prevent individuals from harming themselves or to promote their own good. But the sort of paternalism to which liberalism is opposed is narrower in scope. Mill himself thought that a public official would be justified in forcibly preventing a person from crossing an unsafe bridge if the person was unaware of the condition of the bridge.[34]

In recent discussions of the issue, a distinction has been drawn between weak and strong paternalism.[35] Weak paternalism allows intervention to prevent individuals from harming themselves only in situations in which their choices of courses of action are significantly impaired. Thus, as in Mill's example of the unsafe bridge, a person may be unaware of the undesirable consequences of a proposed course of action, and there is good reason to believe that had he been aware of them he would not proceed with the act. Choices are impaired when they are made in ignorance of relevant information, or under emotional stresses of various kinds or under undue influence by others, or when agents are mentally ill. On the other hand, a doctrine of strong paternalism justifies intervention to prevent a person from harming himself or to promote his own good even when the person's choices are totally unimpaired.

The claim that often people are not the best judges of their interests is most persuasive when their choices are impaired in some way. But the acknowledgement of this fact supports weak paternalism and not strong paternalism. When a person's choice is impaired and he decides on a course of action which is harmful to himself, restraining him protects those interests of his which, under more favourable circumstances, he would regard as paramount. The priority of interests in terms of which intervention is justified is not externally imposed, but is determined by his own settled values and preferences. So interference is justified not simply because it prevents the agent from inflicting harm on himself, but because such infliction of harm does not serve any overriding purpose which the agent recognises.

However when decisions are unimpaired, the case for saying that people are not the best judges of their own interests is very much less clear when these decisions turn out to be harmful. The harm would be foreseen as certain or likely, in which case there would be a powerful countervailing interest which dictated the harmful course of action. For example, a Jehovah's Witness, who clearly foresees that her refusal to take a blood transfusion will be fatal, has an overriding interest in remaining true to the tenets of her religious beliefs. Paternalistic interference is usually based on a failure to acknowledge or to understand the countervailing interest, or it is a camouflage for the enforcement of alien values on the Jehovah's Witness. The camouflage is transparent in other cases where interference is based on the prevention of what is called 'moral harm'. For example, attempts to justify the suppression of pornography sometimes rest on the claim that readers of pornography are to be rescued from moral harm. But moral harm turns out to be no more than having certain sexual thoughts or fantasies, or engaging in what is regarded as unacceptable conduct, like masturbation, which causes no harm to others, or even to the agents themselves.

However there remains the possibility that in some cases it can be shown that a chosen course of action is not the best even within the framework of the agent's own values. But even here it is not clear that interference is justified. There is still the fundamental interest of persons in determining for themselves the course of their own lives, of framing, developing and revising their plans of life in accordance with their preferences and values and their own assessments of situations. This interest, or something like it, has often been referred to as the interest in autonomy, and it is the basis of much opposition to strong paternalism. We want to take responsibility for our own lives even if we know that doing so will not necessarily promote our welfare to the greatest degree. This is clear enough in areas of our lives that are generally recognised as important. Thus even if it is true that forced arranged marriages are more successful and productive of greater happiness than freely choosing our spouses for ourselves, most people in the Western world would regard it as an insult if they were forced to submit to parental choices of their spouses. It would be tempting, but a mistake, to treat autonomy as an interest on the same level as our other interests; it is in fact a higher-order interest which shapes our other interests and determines which of them should take precedence over the others. It is the interest with which we identify and which gives direction and point to our lives.

It is now clear why the strong paternalist's claim that people are often not the best judges of their own interests cannot be so easily sustained. The strong paternalist ignores the claims of autonomy, or treats autonomy as an interest on par with our other interests and therefore to be outweighed by some of them. The claim that people are not the best judges of their own interests then ceases to be a purely factual claim, and becomes instead a normative claim which places less value on the interest in autonomy than is acceptable to the agent whose interests are supposed to be protected.

Sometimes when the choice of an agent involves the sacrifice of a major interest for an apparently minor one, or the taking of a very high risk of grave harm for an apparently minor benefit, one is inclined

749

to conclude that he does not have sufficient information about, or appreciation of, the effects of his conduct, or that his choice is otherwise impaired. Interference on this basis involves an appeal to weak paternalism. But if it is clear after further investigation that although his choice is odd, it is in fact an informed choice, and there is no independent basis for treating the choice as impaired, then interference would no longer be justified on weak paternalistic grounds.

Pornography and offensiveness

Much of the recent discussion of the proper function of the criminal law has concentrated on the case of pornography. In England and Wales the level of public debate was raised by the publication at the end of 1979 of the *Report of the Committee on Obscenity and Film Censorship*, chaired by the distinguished philosopher Bernard Williams.[36] Adopting a position similar to Mill's, the report maintains that the *prohibition* of the sale of pornography would be justified only if it is shown beyond reasonable doubt that pornography is harmful. But after a masterly survey of the evidence, the report concludes that the harmful effects of pornographic publications have not been proven. So the case for prohibiting such publications falls down except in cases where there is exploitation of persons under the age of sixteen or the infliction of actual physical harm on persons in the process of producing pornographic materials.

However the report argues that pornography may be *restricted* in order to prevent offence to reasonable people or to protect young people from exposure to it. These restrictions do not prevent willing consumers of pornography from having access to it. They are designed to prevent people from 'being forced or importuned' to see unwanted scenes which are offensive to them.[37] But the report adopts a fairly broad interpretation of what materials would be offensive to reasonable people. It argues that whether or not a picture is offensive depends on the context in which it is seen. A picture of a woman in underwear on the cover of a woman's fashion magazine would not offend in the way that a similar picture on the cover of a 'man's magazine' would. So the relevant restrictions are directed not just at indecent displays, or displays of materials which are intrinsically offensive, but also at displays of the indecent, or displays of materials which are offensive because they are associated with pornography. But even this broader interpretation would still allow pornography to be sold in shops which 'announced their nature but did not allow their contents to be seen from the outside'.[38]

The report defends its proposal for restrictions of some pornographic material on the ground that these restrictions are not directed at the advocacy of any opinion. It acknowledges that it would be a violation of the principles of free expression to restrict publications simply on the ground that they advocated opinions which are offensive to many. For this reason, the report confines the legitimate restrictions on pornography to pictorial pornography, and exempts works which consist only of written texts. Works of the latter kind are found not only to be less offensive but they are also much more likely to advocate opinions and to express serious artistic intent.

The general principle that the state may restrict, but not prohibit or suppress, certain activities which are offensive to reasonable people is plausible. However, the report does not fully capture the proper basis for such restrictions. It recognises that the relevant factor is that people should not be forced to witness unwanted scenes. But it goes on to make recommendations on live sex shows which go well beyond the limits of justifiable interference. It argues that 'The idea is that insofar as simulated or represented sexual activity is in question, its offensiveness will justify its merely being restricted; but as soon as it is a matter of real sexual activity, offensiveness will justify prohibition.'[39] But no one is forced to witness a show with some real or simulated sexual activity if it is discreetly advertised and performed indoors with admission by ticket. So if people are offended it can only be because the mere knowledge that such activities are going on in their society upsets them. But this is no basis for suppressing or restricting any activity.

The report also points out that live sex shows might provoke audience participation giving rise to 'public order problems'.[40] Again this is not peculiar to such shows: many other activities, like pop concerts and various sporting activities, can produce similar problems. Prohibition has not been suggested as a solution in these other cases even though sometimes the 'public order problems' are far more serious. It is reasonable to assume that very simple preventive measures, which fall far short of prohibition, will be sufficient to stop unwanted participation in the case of live sex shows.

If the relevant consideration in justifying restrictions is that people should not be forced to witness scenes which offend them, then not all offensive public acts may be restricted. In one sense a public place is any place which ordinary citizens are legally permitted to visit. But many such public places can easily be avoided and no one is forced to witness anything going on there. It is only when offensive activities are conducted in such a manner as to make it difficult for ordinary citizens to avoid witnessing them while going about their normal social life that restrictions would be justified. Thus offensive public nudity in a busy shopping centre may be restricted, but offensive public nudity on the stage of an indoor theatre or club may not be restricted.

The basis for restricting certain offensive acts does not rely on the doctrine of legal moralism. It is true that some acts are offensive because they violate the community's shared moral values, but it is not the violation of such values which itself justifies the restrictions; it is the fact that the offensive acts are forced upon unwilling witnesses. Nor is the violation of society's shared morality a necessary condition for intervention, for acts can be offensive for a variety of reasons. Loud noises and foul smells are offensive even when they are caused by activities which are otherwise very desirable.

Recently the case for the suppression of pornography has focused not on the alleged harm caused by pornography but on the undesirable intrinsic features of pornography, including its degradation of women. The availability of pornography in society is treated as a form of cultural or moral pollution, and concern for its eradication is regarded as analogous with a concern for environmental protection.[41]

Since the objection to pornography is now made independently of any of its allegedly harmful effects, the objection cannot then gain any support from the case against environmental pollution. Environmental pollution is objectionable partly at least because of its harmful effects. These effects may not be immediate, but they are cumulative and can be very damaging. On the other hand, environmental protection to preserve a natural asset of unique flora and fauna, or to prevent the destruction of a beautiful landscape, has no obvious equivalents in the case of suppressing pornography. Of course some of the public manifestations of the free circulation of pornography can be aesthetically ugly, but these manifestations only support a case for the imposition of restrictions on the sale of, and advertisements for, pornography very much along the lines discussed earlier of restricting offensive conduct.

Again, no doubt some pornography expresses attitudes towards women which are degrading in that they are regarded as sex objects to be used for the pleasure of men. But this in itself does not justify the suppression of pornography. For the claim is not that these expressions of undesirable attitudes are harmful because they produce harmful effects in the relationship between men and women (for that is a causal argument which needs empirical support), but that they are intrinsically offensive. A society committed to freedom of expression cannot censor the expression of views or attitudes simply because they are offensive, although perhaps some restrictions on the circumstances in which offensive and insulting views may be expressed may be contemplated. It is interesting to note that some of those who want to suppress pornography do not direct the same hostility towards much commercial advertising in which women are used as sexual objects to promote the sale of all sorts of products. These advertisements are far more difficult to avoid than are the offensive attitudes displayed in pornographic books. In any case both the contents of commercial advertisements and of pornographic books are symptoms of more general attitudes which censorship is unlikely to alter. But, more fundamentally, suppression of works which display intrinsically offensive attitudes will lead to the suppression of a great deal of moral, political, religious and social opinions.

752

Liberty and utility

Can the kind of freedom enunciated by Mill's principle be defended in purely utilitarian terms? Utilitarianism is the doctrine that the rightness or wrongness of actions depends entirely on the overall consequences of the actions in promoting the general welfare. In its most familiar forms, utilitarianism spells out the promotion of the general welfare either in terms of the production of happiness or of the satisfaction of desires and preferences. A right act is that which, among the available alternatives, produces the greatest balance of pleasure over pain (maximises happiness), or which maximises the satisfaction of desires. If we take Mill's principle as ruling out absolutely the doctrine of legal moralism, it would appear that the principle cannot be defended on a purely utilitarian basis. It is a matter of contingent fact, variable from one situation to another, whether or not the legal enforcement of society's shared morality as such will maximise happiness or the satisfaction of desires. For example, suppose that the moral majority in a society is overwhelming and they strongly desire to suppress homosexual acts between consenting adults in private. A utilitarian calculation might then conclude that the general welfare is best promoted by satisfying these desires.

However, it is possible for utilitarians to adopt an absolute principle like Mill's, ruling out certain reasons for interfering with individual liberty, if they think that the protected liberty is generally vital from the utilitarian point of view, and the exceptional cases, in which violations of liberty would be justified on utilitarian grounds, cannot be easily identified in practice. Consider the following analogy. Utilitarian parents, concerned with the moral education of their children, might conclude that they should inculcate in their children the acceptance of the absolute injunction to tell the truth, even though they are aware of exceptional cases in which telling the truth would not be most conducive to the general welfare. The parents do not trust their children to carry out the right utilitarian calculations under the pressures and constraints of daily life, and they believe that the best strategy for the promotion of the utilitarian end is the adoption in practice of the absolute rule. Once the rule is adopted children are debarred from making direct appeals to utilitarian considerations in deciding whether to tell the truth in a particular case. Indeed the effective implementation of the rule may require the cultivation of dispositions in children which make them treat truth-telling as desirable independently of its utilitarian contribution.

Utilitarian strategies of this kind have been quite popular in recent times,[42] and there is no doubt that from the purely formal point of view there is no inconsistency in adopting these strategies. But utilitarian calculations would have to be made in deciding whether to adopt a particular strategy in the first place. It is doubtful that those calculations would favour the adoption of liberal strategies protective of the liberty of minority groups if there is an overwhelming and stable moral majority who intensely desire the suppression of certain forms of harmless conduct. Some utilitarian reason would have to be found for discounting such illiberal desires. It has sometimes been suggested that as a matter of fact people who have experienced freedom prefer not to give it up. But the unwillingness of the majority to give up their own freedom provides no basis for the defence of the freedom of minorities, for the majority have not shown any particular tenderness towards the similar liberties of minorities. So even if the liberties of minorities are a powerful source of their happiness or the satisfaction of their desires, the happiness of minorities may still be outweighed by the intense illiberal desires of the overwhelming majority.

For the utilitarian there is also the problem of whether or not in a changing world any absolute rule can be allowed to become too entrenched. People will periodically have to be re-educated out of beliefs and attitudes which were useful in one set of circumstances but have ceased to be so in a different situation.

Rawls on the basic liberties

John Rawls' *A theory of justice* provides a non–utilitarian theory of justice in terms of two principles:

First principle. Each person is to have an equal right to the most extensive total system of equal basic liberties compatible with a similar system of liberty for all.

Second principle. Social and economic inequalities are to be arranged so that they are both:
(a) to the greatest benefit of the least advantaged, consistent with the just savings principle, and
(b) attached to offices and positions open to all under conditions of fair equality of opportunity.[43]

The first principle takes priority over the second principle when society has reached stages in its development at which all basic wants are satisfied and the basic liberties can be effectively exercised. Liberty can then be restricted only for the sake of liberty and not in order to promote increases in, for example, income and wealth. The liberties protected by the first principle are confined to the 'basic liberties' which Rawls identifies as 'freedom of thought and liberty of conscience; the political liberties and freedom of association, as well as the freedoms specified by the liberty and integrity of the person; and finally, the rights and liberties covered by the rule of law'.[44] As we shall see, these basic liberties contribute to the development and exercise of what Rawls calls the 'moral powers'.

Rawls justifies his principles of justice by showing

that they will be chosen by persons in a hypothetical state called the 'original position'. In this state, rational and mutually disinterested persons choose from behind 'a veil of ignorance' the principles which are to govern the basic institutions of their society. The veil of ignorance deprives them of knowledge about their own talents and abilities, their class interests or social positions, their conceptions of the good or their particular moral and religious views, and their psychological make-up. It does not, however, rob them of knowledge of general truths about the world or about human societies and human nature. Rawls argues that persons in the original position would prefer his principles of justice, with the priority of liberty, to rival principles such as the utilitarian principle of maximising the general welfare.

Hart has pointed out that Rawls does not provide sufficiently clear or developed grounds for the choice of the basic liberties and their priority.[45] Hart maintains that from the standpoint of the original position, a person would not only consider the advantages for him of having the basic liberties but would also take into account the disadvantages to him of the exercise of such liberties by others. If the latter outweighs the former, it would not be in his interest to choose Rawls' first principle of justice. Hart's arguments are effective against Rawls' position as presented in *A theory of justice*. In responding to Hart in his Tanner Lecture, 'The basic liberties and their priority', Rawls provides new arguments for his position.

He poses the problem as that of determining the fair terms of social co-operation on the basis of mutual respect. Persons are seen as 'capable of being normal and fully co-operating members of society over a complete life'.[46] They therefore have what Rawls calls two 'powers of moral personality' or 'moral powers'. These are: (i) the capacity for a sense of justice, which is the capacity to honour fair terms of social co-operation; and (ii) the capacity for a conception of the good, which is 'the capacity to form, to revise, and rationally to pursue' a conception of what is regarded as a worthwhile human life.[47] Rawls provides various grounds for equal liberty of conscience (and the other basic liberties).

Since persons in the original position know that different people have different conceptions of the good, and since each person does not know the content of his particular conception, each will wish to secure equal liberty of conscience in order to protect his own conception of the good. Persons do not know, for example, whether their religious views will be a majority or minority view, and they would not permit greater liberty to be granted to the dominant religion, for this means that they would suffer if it should turn out that they do not belong to the dominant religious group. A person's conception of the good is something which he takes seriously, and is therefore not to be gambled away.

The exercise and development of the capacity for a conception of the good can be regarded as a means to a person's good. This moral power allows the person to rationally pursue his good, and to revise aspects of his present way of life. Unless there is liberty of conscience, which includes the liberty to make mistakes, the social conditions necessary for the full development and exercise of the moral power will be absent.[48] Our capacity for a conception of the good can also be regarded as part of our broader conception of the good rather than just as a means to that good. We do not simply accept our conception of the good, but we also seek to understand why we have that conception and the proper grounds for it. In order to realise this broader conception of the good, we must again be allowed to make our own mistakes. Hence liberty of conscience is necessary.

The second moral power, our capacity for a sense of justice, also provides distinctive grounds for the adoption of equal liberty of conscience. The two principles of justice provide the most stable scheme of social co-operation, and this will be advantageous to everyone's conception of the good. The contribution of the first principle of equal basic liberties to social stability is based on the fact that it is unconditionally concerned with everyone's good.[49] If the principle, and its priority over the second principle of justice, is accepted, a person's basic liberties will not depend on calculations about whether those liberties produce the greatest net balance of social interests. No one's basic liberties will be sacrificed for such a gain in the balance of social interests.

Rawls enunciates his principles of justice in terms of the allocation of primary goods like the basic liberties, income and wealth. The notion of primary goods is that of goods which all rational persons are presumed to want because they are all-purpose means for achieving whatever ends one may have. According to Rawls self-respect is a very important primary good, and it is most effectively supported by the basic liberties and their priority. Self-respect refers, first, to a person's sense of his or her own value and the value of his or her major projects and plans of life, and, secondly, to the person's confidence in his or her ability to advance these plans of life. The public affirmation of equal basic liberties provides an effective social basis for self-respect because that affirmation expresses the mutual respect citizens have for each other, and their recognition of the value that each attaches to his or her own plan of life.[50]

Finally, the basic liberties and their priority promote a conception of society as what Rawls calls 'a social union of social unions' in which each citizen's conception of the good can be sustained and enlarged by participation in a more comprehensive good.[51] Rawls draws attention to von Humboldt's idea that each person can develop only one perfection of human character at a time. To try to do more is to dissipate one's limited energies in a multiplicity of directions. But we can escape one-sidedness by participating in a social union in which each person has access to 'the rich collective resources of all the others'.[52] Rawls himself illustrates the idea of social union with the example of a group of gifted musicians with the same natural talents to learn to play equally well any orchestral instrument. But since the ability to play an instrument well requires long training and practice, each person is unable to acquire a high proficiency in many instruments. However, by co-ordinating their activities they can realise the whole range of capacities. So an orchestra of these gifted musicians can be viewed as a social union.

Social unions can grow out of many types of activities in a society. The principles of justice co-ordinate and combine these many social unions into one social union of many other unions. This social union of social unions is made possible by various aspects of our nature as social beings: the complementarity of human talents; the fact that our capabilities far exceed what we can do or be in one life; and our capacity to honour fair terms of social co-operation. Rawls believes that his principles of justice, which lay down the terms of social co-operation on the basis of mutual respect, will be most effective in providing the co-ordination and combination of various social unions into one social union. In particular the public affirmation of equal basic liberties allows citizens to recognise that they have a shared public purpose and a common allegiance to fair terms of social co-operation.

Rawls distinguishes between the basic liberties, which entitle individuals to act in various ways and prohibit interference by others, and the *worth* of these liberties which is adversely affected by lack of resources.[53] Thus although the poor have the same basic liberties as the rich, these liberties are less useful to the poor than they are to the rich. Since Rawls' second principle of justice permits some citizens to have greater income and wealth than others, it gives differential value to the liberties of citizens. But Rawls points out that the second principle also maximises the primary goods to the least advantaged and thus gives greater value to their basic liberties than would be the case under some other principle. Again, although the first principle guarantees equal basic liberties rather than the equal worth of these liberties, an exception is made in the case of the political liberties whose worth must be approximately equal. This means that 'everyone has a fair opportunity to hold public office and to influence the outcome of political decisions'.[54]

Rawls' *A theory of justice* provoked unprecedented discussion. His more recent and more detailed and persuasive defence of the basic liberties and their priority will set the agenda for further debate. Like Mill's case for individual freedom, Rawls' defence belongs to the liberal tradition. Again, like Mill's case, it does not rest on a false conception of the person as an atomistic being whose liberty is needed simply to enable him or her to develop in complete or substantial independence of social influences. Rawls makes it clear that while the basic liberties protect persons from interference by others and thereby enable them to pursue their own conception of the good, these liberties form part of a broader theory of justice which allows and encourages persons to participate on fair terms, and as free and equal citizens, in a co-operative social life.

Notes

(An author's name followed by a number in square brackets refers to the book or article which has that number in the bibliography.)

1. Mill [4], p. 65.
2. Ibid., p. 73.
3. Ibid., p. 73.
4. Stephen [5].
5. Wolfenden [6], para. 13.
6. Ibid., para. 61.
7. Devlin [7], esp. Ch. 1.
8. Hart [8].
9. Stephen [5], p. 151.
10. Ibid., p. 162.
11. Ibid., p. 157.
12. Ibid., p. 162.
13. Ibid., p. 152.
14. Hart [8], p. 59.
15. Devlin [7], pp. 16–17.
16. H.L.A. Hart, 'Immorality and treason', *The Listener*, vol. 62, no. 1583 (1959), p. 163.
17. Devlin [7], p. 114.
18. See Ten [9], pp. 92–8.
19. Devlin [7], pp. 13–14.
20. Ibid., p. 111.
21. Hart [8], pp. 51–2.
22. Ibid., p. x.
23. For a recent statement of this point of view, see John Horton, 'Toleration, morality and harm' in John Horton and Susan Mendus (eds), *Aspects of toleration* (Methuen, London and New York, 1985), pp. 113–35.
24. See Philippa Foot, 'Moral beliefs' in Philippa Foot (ed.), *Theories of ethics* (Oxford University Press, London, 1967), pp. 83–100.
25. See Glanville Williams, 'Consent and public policy', *The Criminal Law Review* (1982), p. 154.
26. H.L.A. Hart, *The concept of law* (Clarendon Press, Oxford, 1961), p. 188.
27. I discuss Mill's concept of harm in Ten [9], pp. 55–61. For a more detailed account of the notion of harm, see Joel Feinberg, *The moral limits of the criminal law, vol. I: Harm to others* (Oxford University Press, New York, 1984).
28. Devlin [7], p. 12.
29. Ibid., p. 113.
30. Ten [9], pp. 40–1.
31. Mill [4], p. 138.
32. John Locke, *A letter concerning toleration* (Bobbs-Merrill, Indianapolis, 1955), pp. 39–40.
33. Hart [8], p. 33.
34. Mill [4], p. 152.
35. See Joel Feinberg, 'Legal paternalism', *Canadian Journal of Philosophy* 1 (1971), pp. 105–24; and Ten, *Mill on liberty*, pp. 109–17.

36. *Report of the Committee on Obscenity and Film Censorship* (Cmnd 7772, HMSO, London, 1979). An abridged version of the report is also available: Williams [12]. I confine my discussion to pornographic publications. The case of films is more complicated. For detailed comments on the report, see Dworkin [13] and C.L. Ten, 'Pornography, offensiveness, and the Williams Report', *Law in Context*, 1 (1983), pp. 1–14.

37. *Report of the Committee on Obscenity and Film Censorship*, para. 7.11.

38. Ibid., para. 7.14.

39. Ibid., para. 11.12.

40. Ibid., paras. 11.4 and 11.9.

41. For a clear and sympathetic exposition of this point of view, see Susan Mendus, 'Harm, offence and censorship' in Horton and Mendus, *Aspects of toleration*, pp. 99–112.

42. See Rolf E. Sartorius, *Individual conduct and social norms* (Dickenson, Encino and Belmont, 1975); and R.M. Hare, *Moral thinking* (Clarendon Press, Oxford, 1981). See also Gray [10], in which such a strategy is attributed to Mill in his defence of liberty. For a different point of view see Ten [9], esp. pp. 33–40.

43. Rawls [15], p. 302. Rawls alters the formulation of the first principle in Rawls [16], p. 5. The 'just savings principle' is a principle of justice between different generations, and it determines the amount of savings which each generation is required to accumulate for the benefit of future generations. For Rawls' discussion of this principle, see *A theory of justice*, pp. 284–93.

44. Rawls [16], p. 5.

45. Hart [17].

46. Rawls [16], p. 15.

47. Ibid., p. 16.

48. Ibid., p. 27.

49. Ibid., p. 32.

50. Ibid., p. 34.

51. Ibid., pp. 34–5.

52. Wilhelm von Humboldt, *The limits of the state*, ed. J.W. Burrow (Cambridge University Press, Cambridge, 1969), p. 17; quoted by Rawls, 'The basic liberties and their priority', p. 35.

53. In [15], pp. 201–5, Rawls briefly discusses the concept of liberty, but he does not buy into the debate about negative and positive concepts of liberty, on which see Isaiah Berlin, 'The two concepts of liberty' in Berlin [14], pp. 118–72 and also pp. xxxvii–xliii.

54. Rawls [16], p. 42.

Bibliography

When modern philosophers consider what J.S. Mill called 'the liberty of thought and discussion', they tend to treat Mill's work as central. But it is worth noting that the issues were discussed earlier, and that at least two works written in the seventeenth century are still worth the attention of the modern reader. These are:

[1] John Locke, *A letter concerning toleration* (first published in 1689). See, e.g., the edition published by Bobbs-Merrill, Indianapolis, 1955.

Another important seventeenth-century defence of liberty is contained in

[2] B. de Spinoza, *Tractatus theologico-politicus* (1670), Ch. 20. This is best read in the edition and translation by A.G. Wernham: *Benedict de Spinoza, The political works* (Clarendon Press, Oxford, 1958), pp. 226–43. See also

[3] G.H.R. Parkinson, 'Spinoza on the freedom of man and the freedom of the citizen' in Z. Pelczynski and John Gray (eds), *Conceptions of liberty in political philosophy* (Athlone Press, London, 1984), pp. 39–56. But, as mentioned earlier, the central work is

[4] J.S. Mill, *Essay on liberty* (1859). There have been many later editions, of which one may mention J.S. Mill, *Utilitarianism, liberty and representative government* (Everyman's Library, Dent, London, 1st edn, 1910).

A famous attack on Mill's essay is

[5] James Fitzjames Stephen, *Liberty, equality, fraternity* (1873). See the edition by R.J. White, Cambridge University Press, Cambridge, 1967.

The *Essay on liberty* has not just exercised philosophers, but has also played a part in the world of politics. Mill's ideas were behind

[6] The Wolfenden Report: *Report of the Committee on Homosexual Offences and Prostitution* (Cmnd 247, HMSO, London, 1957). The report of this committee (whose chairman, incidentally, had once been a teacher of philosophy in the University of Oxford) led to important changes in English law. A very different approach to law and morals was followed by an eminent lawyer,

[7] Patrick Devlin, *The enforcement of morals* (Oxford University Press, Oxford, 1965). This collection of essays, which includes a celebrated lecture, 'Morals and the criminal law' (first pub. 1959), is broadly in line with (though it does not consciously follow) the approach of Fitzjames Stephen. Both Devlin and Stephen are criticised in

[8] H.L.A. Hart, *Law, liberty and morality* (Oxford University Press, London, 1st edn, 1963).

Recent studies of Mill's defence of liberty include

[9] C.L. Ten, *Mill on liberty* (Clarendon Press, Oxford, 1980) and

[10] John Gray, *Mill on liberty: a defence* (Routledge and Kegan Paul, London, 1983).

Questions of the freedom of expression have been the concern of another official committee set up relatively recently in Great Britain. This committee reported in

[11] The Williams Report: *Report of the Committee on Obscenity and Film Censorship* (Cmnd 7772, HMSO, London, 1979). An abridged version of the report was published as

[12] Bernard Williams (ed.), *Obscenity and film censorship* (Cambridge University Press, Cambridge, 1981). The report follows the broad lines laid down by Mill, arguing that 'No conduct should be suppressed by law unless it can be shown to harm someone' (Williams [12], p. 50). A detailed critical discussion of the report is to be found in

[13] Ronald Dworkin, 'Is there a right to pornography?' *Oxford Journal of Legal Studies*, vol. I (1981), pp. 177–212. Reprinted in Ronald Dworkin, *A matter of principle* (Harvard University Press, Cambridge, Massachusetts, and London, 1985).

The twentieth century has seen the appearance of at least two important philosophical works on liberty. The first of these is

[14] Isaiah Berlin, 'Two concepts of liberty', first published in 1958; reissued in I. Berlin, *Four essays on liberty* (Oxford University Press, Oxford, 1969), pp. 118–72. The two concepts are those of negative liberty and positive liberty. The first (which

may roughly be described as 'freedom from') is the kind defended by Mill; the second is the idea that freedom means self-mastery. Berlin argues that the second concept has proved disastrous, in that it has been used to justify tyranny. For a discussion of many aspects of Berlin's views, see Pelczynski and Gray [3].

Another important defence of liberty relates it to principles of justice. This is

[15] John Rawls, *A theory of justice* (Clarendon Press, Oxford, 1972); see especially Ch. 4 (pp. 195–257). See also

[16] John Rawls, 'The basic liberties and their priority' in Sterling M. McMurrin (ed.), *The Tanner lectures on human values*, vol. III (1982) (University of Utah Press, Salt Lake City, 1982). Rawls' views are examined by

[17] H.L.A. Hart, 'Rawls on liberty and its priority', *University of Chicago Law Review*, 40 (1973), pp. 534–55. Reprinted in Norman Daniels (ed.), *Reading Rawls* (Basil Blackwell, Oxford, 1975), pp. 230–52, and in H.L.A. Hart, *Essays in jurisprudence and philosophy* (Clarendon Press, Oxford, 1983).

I am grateful to Professor Ten for many helpful suggestions concerning this bibliography.

G.H.R.P.

33 | *The Philosophy of Punishment*

John Cottingham

Introduction

Punishment is one of the oldest human institutions. It is hard to imagine a society in which penalties of some kind are not imposed on those who offend against the written or unwritten rules in terms of which that society is governed. Punishment also has a firm and long-standing place in most religions: it is believed that those who offend against God, or the gods, can expect punishment from above – either in this world or, failing that, the next.

The opposite of punishment is reward, and the practice of rewarding people for good conduct is probably as ancient and well established as that of punishing them for bad. But there is an obvious feature of punishment which seems to make its practice problematic from a philosophical point of view, in a way which is not true of rewarding: punishment is characteristically *unpleasant* for those who are punished. Admittedly some offenders may be reconciled to their punishment (the extent of this may vary from case to case). But all punishment must logically involve the *penalising* of the offender – the imposing of a sanction that is in principle unwelcome. The punished person has done to him something which, other things being equal, he would not choose to have done.

This central fact about punishment has especially worried philosophers in the utilitarian tradition. Because being punished is unpleasant, and so has a negative utility, utilitarians see it as something *prima facie* bad. On the utilitarian view, punishment can be justified, if at all, only by pointing to the future consequences of the practice for society at large (such as a reduction in the crime rate, perhaps); such consequences have to be beneficial enough to outweigh the initial negative utility caused to the person punished. Jeremy Bentham voiced this disquiet felt by utilitarians about punishment in his famous dictum 'All punishment is mischief; all punishment is in itself evil.'[1]

Notwithstanding Bentham's disquiet, it is clear that punishment is not simply a long-standing institution whereby the powerful do nasty things to their subjects. If this were so, punishment would be regarded simply as a kind of tyranny – something which we could expect to be eliminated as society becomes progressively fairer and more democratic. But from earliest times punishment has been regarded as more than simply the imposition of unpleasant penalties by rulers; punishment has always been closely associated with the ideas of law and justice. Punishment, at least in the standard cases, is not gratuitously inflicted; typically people are punished *for* something they have done. At the very least this means that a punishment is something which is imposed on an offender for a breach of a law or rule. But, beyond that, there is a widespread notion that punishment, if it is to be proper punishment and not a gratuitous exercise of power, must be *deserved*. Exactly what is involved in this notion of desert is a complex question; but many would insist, first, that the offender must have brought the punishment on himself by his own voluntary conduct, and, second, that the punishment must be in some sense 'fitting' or appropriate to the offence committed. This is not to deny that punishment is unpleasant; but the unpleasantness which it involves is (or is believed to be) justly inflicted. These two central features of punishment – its unpleasantness and its supposed connection with justice – have played a crucial role in most philosophical examinations of the subject, and they will figure importantly in much of what follows.

Two kinds of justification

The main question that has preoccupied philosophers about punishment is the question of how, if at all, it can be justified morally. Broadly speaking, this question has been approached from one or other of two quite different perspectives. On the *forward-looking*, or teleological approach, the justification of punishment is seen as lying in some future goal which it is hoped will be achieved or furthered either by a particular act of punishing or by the practice of punishing in general. Jeremy Bentham's celebrated account of punishment in his *Principles of morals and legislation* (1780) typifies this forward-looking approach;[2] but the seeds of such an outlook are found as early as Plato. In Book XI of his *Laws*, Plato observes that 'one does not punish for the sake of a past wrong, since what is done will never be undone but with a view to the future, in order that the offender and others who see the punishment will come to detest the crime'.[3] In strong contrast to this is what may be called the backward-looking or retrospective approach to punishment. An insistence on considerations such as that of desert, and the question of whether the punishment is appropriate for the offence committed, is typical of this retrospective approach; the focus of attention is not on future results of punishing, but on the particular wrong that has been done by the offender. Thus, according to Aristotle, the purpose of judicially imposed penalties is to 'rectify' past wrongs.[4] Both forward-looking and backward-looking approaches to punishment will be discussed below; but it will be convenient to begin with the backward-looking approach, and in particular with its best known manifestation, the retributive theory of punishment.

Retribution

The term 'retribution' comes from the Latin verb *retribuere* ('to pay back'), and the central idea of the retributivist is that punishment is in some sense a *payment* for crime. 'Paying back' is a familiar notion at the level of primitive revenge: if child A hits child B, B may say, 'I'll make you pay for that,' and once blow has been returned for blow, payment is considered to have been extracted. In the more formal setting of criminal punishment the same sort of metaphor is used: the criminal, it is often said, has a 'debt to pay' to society; once an offender has served his sentence, he may be said to have 'paid the price' for his crime. But although such expressions are widespread, the precise significance of the payment metaphor is by no means clear. Exactly *how* does punishment 'pay' for crime? Where payment is literally exacted, as in ordinary civil litigation, things are clear enough. Suppose I damage your property, and you sue me: if the court makes me pay you a sum in damages, then I will have quite literally paid for – i.e. covered the cost of – the damage I have done. But if we move from the sphere of civil damages to that of criminal punishment, it is far from clear how the serving of a prison sentence constitutes 'payment' for the crime committed. For, as far as the victim is concerned, his costs are in no sense 'paid back' by the imprisoning of the offender. The loss or harm he has suffered still stands. It is true that the person who caused that loss or harm is made to suffer in return; but why is the offender's suffering supposed to 'pay for' the sufferings of the victim? This is left quite unexplained.[5]

Faced with this difficulty, retributivists sometimes switch to another metaphor, that of the *balance*. Justice is traditionally depicted as holding a pair of scales: criminal wrongdoing is regarded as upsetting the balance, and the punishment, placed, as it were, in the other pan of the scales, restores the equilibrium. But once again it is hard to see how this metaphor can be cashed out in a convincing manner. How, exactly, is the punishing of the offender supposed to set the balance right? Again, as far as the victim of the crime is concerned, the harm or loss that has been suffered remains, and it is unclear how the imposition of a corresponding harm or loss on the offender (e.g. loss of liberty) is supposed to 'set things right'.

A third metaphor often used by retributivists is that of *annulment* or cancellation. The punishment of the criminal is said to 'wipe the slate clean'. Hegel, in his *Philosophie des Rechts* (1833) stated that punishment 'annuls the wrongdoing which would otherwise continue to stand'.[6] Here again one is inclined to ask *how* the imposition of a punishment is supposed to cancel out or annul the crime; what is done, as Plato remarked, cannot after all be undone. Hegel does not fully explain what he means by annulment, but his remark that the crime, if unpunished, would 'still stand' (in German 'gelten würde': literally, 'would remain in force', 'would remain valid') does give voice to a deep intuitive conviction that many people have about law-breaking, at any rate serious law-breaking. Where someone has been killed, or assaulted or robbed, we feel strongly that we cannot simply 'let it go'. We must endeavour to apprehend the offender and make him answer for his conduct – otherwise we would seem to be acquiescing in the wrong done – allowing it to 'remain valid'. Once the offender has been 'dealt with', however, we feel that we have responded appropriately to the wrong, and that 'justice has been done'.

It is worth underlining how deep, and how wide-spread, such convictions are. If nothing else, they serve to show that for many people there is something radically counter-intuitive about Bentham's claim that 'all punishment is mischief'. For retributivists, the boot is very much on the other foot: *not* to punish would be mischief – for this would involve allowing a wrong to stand. Nevertheless, it has to be said that the logic of the claim that punishment 'annuls' the crime is highly obscure. It is one thing to insist that society cannot allow crime to 'stand'; action must be taken to uphold the moral and legal order. But this does not of itself explain or justify what is done to the offender once he is apprehended. An explanation still seems required of exactly how the imposition of a penalty such as a fine or imprisonment is supposed to cancel out the wrong done.

It seems, then, that none of the metaphors examined so far (repayment, balance, annulment) can serve to provide the retributivist with a convincing justification of punishment; at best these metaphors illustrate, in different ways, the extent to which retributivist ideas are rooted in our everyday language and thought. The more closely one examines 'retribution theory', in fact, the less it seems like a *theory* in the sense of something that provides an elaborate (or even a non-elaborate) logical framework for the justification of punishment. And indeed many retributivists would accept that they do not have a theory in this sense. What they would claim to rely on, instead, is a supposedly self-evident principle or axiom: it is inherently right and proper that the guilty criminal should suffer punishment. Some retributivists formulate the principle slightly differently, but no less baldly, and assert that, quite simply, punishment is what the offender *deserves*.[7] The notion that certain things are 'inherently' good or 'intrinsically' good has been regarded as highly problematic by some moral philosophers; but others would defend it by reference to the fact that all ethical justification must stop somewhere. Not everything can be a means to an end; there must be some things (pleasure, freedom, truth) which we take to be good in themselves. In

765

the particular case of punishment, however, an appeal to 'intrinsic' goodness seems unsatisfactory; for unlike such goods as pleasure or freedom, which are universally – or nearly universally – accepted as valuable and worthwhile, punishing people is a practice whose value is, to say the least, highly controversial. To sidestep the debate over the justification of punishment by an appeal to its 'intrinsic goodness' is not a manoeuvre designed to win many converts.

As for the proposition that the guilty simply deserve to suffer punishment, there seem to be similar problems in claiming that this is a self-evident principle. Some writers have construed the proposition that the guilty just deserve to suffer punishment as follows: if a person S deliberately transgresses a rule R knowing that he risks incurring penalty P, then no further reasons can, or need to be, given for punishing him: the punishment is due for the offence and that is all there is to it. Thus in a well-known article on punishment the Oxford philosopher J.D. Mabbott remarked of his experiences as college dean charged with upholding disciplinary rules: 'they [the defaulters] had broken a rule and they knew it and I knew it; nothing more was necessary to make punishment proper'.[8] Now on one level this does accurately describe the position in which a judge (or a college dean, for that matter) is placed. If an offender is shown to deserve a given penalty in the sense that he has knowingly and voluntarily committed the offence for which penalty is prescribed, then there is a sense in which no further questions need to be asked. The judge already has a full and sufficient basis on which to pass sentence. But although all this is true, it holds good, as it were, only *within* the institution of punishment. That institution is set up in such a way that the deliberate commission of an offence with a prescribed penalty is, by definition, normally a sufficient reason for imposing the penalty. None of this, however, can help to answer the higher-level question of whether the general institution or practice of inflicting of punishment on offenders is itself justified. Facts about what are taken to be sufficient conditions for punishment within the penal system cannot provide a sufficient reason why we should punish in the first place. The upshot is that appeals to the self-evident appropriateness or deservedness of punishment, while they may accurately reflect the thinking of those who operate within the structure of penal systems, cannot do the work needed to show that the institution of punishment as such is self-justifying or self-evidently good.[9]

Punishment, rights and fair play

No adequate justification for punishment has emerged from the versions of retributivism so far examined. We may now turn to a more promising theory that is often regarded as a kind of retributivism, although it has no direct link with the classic retributivist models of repayment, balance and annulment. It does however share with the classical retributivist models the feature of being an essentially retrospective account of punishment. The focus of justification is not on some future goal, but on the past wrong that has been committed.

The central idea in the 'fair play' theory of punishment, as it may be called, is that the criminal, in failing to respect the rights of others, has taken unfair advantage of his fellow citizens. He is a 'free loader' or a 'free rider' – someone who has enjoyed the benefits of the system of law and social co-operation without being prepared to shoulder his share of its burdens. The burglar, for example, takes advantage of his fellow citizens who gain their money by honest toil; rather than playing his part in the system, the burglar gets his money by taking an unfair 'short cut' – by violating the property rights of others. It is thus only fair to the law-abiding citizens that he should be punished if caught. The situation, on this view, is somewhat similar to that which may arise in a game such as football. If team A gets an unfair advantage by fouling, it is only fair to team B that the offenders should be made to pay some penalty. The referee's duty to impose a penalty is part of his general duty to see fair play.[10]

It would perhaps be possible to formulate the fair play theory without referring to rights, but it is in terms of rights that the theory is most commonly, and most plausibly, developed. Typically the offender who is punished forfeits some (though of course not all) of his rights – for example a prison sentence involves forfeiting the right to freedom of movement. The fair play theory explains this forfeiture of rights as follows: since the offender has gained an unfair advantage by violating the rights of others, it is only fair that he should be deprived of that advantage by suffering a reciprocal curtailment of his own rights.[11]

This approach seems to constitute a clear improvement on the retributivist models discussed earlier. In place of vague and elusive metaphors, we have a justificatory framework which links punishment with the important and attractive ethical ideal of fairness. Instead of pure retribution, which has seemed to many to amount to the gratuitous and vindictive inflicting of harm for harm, we have a system of penalties involving the curtailment of rights, combined with the proposition that law-abiding citizens are entitled to expect that those who have gained unfairly by violating the rights of others should forfeit that advantage by having their own rights curtailed.

An important feature of this model is that it presupposes that the social system of mutual benefits and burdens under which we live is itself fair, or reasonably fair. To revert to the football analogy, if the rules of the game were biased so that one team was at a permanent disadvantage, then it would *not*, surely, be plausible to invoke the notion of fair play to justify the imposition of penalties. This suggests that those who support the fair play approach to punishment will not be able to treat the justification of punishment as a self-contained issue, but must be prepared to engage in general questions of political philosophy – such as the question of whether our existing social structures are fair.[12]

A second important feature of the fair play model is that it invokes the idea of *proportionality* between offence and punishment. The offender, having violated the rights of others, must suffer an appropriate or proportionate curtailment of his own rights; having gained an unfair advantage, he must incur a suitably corresponding disadvantage. These notions of proportionality or correspondence between penalty and offence have a long history in retributivist thought, typified for many by W.S. Gilbert's reference in the *Mikado* to the 'object all sublime' of letting 'the punishment fit the crime'. From time to time the notion of proportionality in punishment has attracted hostile criticism; the Old Testament maxim 'an eye for an eye, a tooth for a tooth' seems to many to typify the vengeful and merciless side of retributivism. There are also certain practical problems about proportionality. If the offender is supposed to forfeit precisely that right that he has violated in others, then how are we supposed to deal with the rapist, say, or the child molester?[13]

The answer to this last difficulty is that the principle of proportionality of punishment need not imply a commitment to the dubious notion of an exact fit between punishment and crime. Rather, one could plausibly construct a table of offences ranked in terms of the gravity of the rights violations involved, and then construct a table of corresponding penalties, where the most grave forfeitures of rights on the part of the offender were correlated with the gravest violations. There would no doubt be room for dispute about the relative gravity of particular offences and penalties; but the notion of such a table of proportionalities does not seem to be in principle absurd or impracticable. As for the charge that proportionality might lead to harsh punishments (an eye for an eye), this cuts both ways. If some relationship between gravity of offence and gravity of punishment is *not* preserved, then the door is open to all kinds of extreme and excessive penalties (such as imprisonment for parking offences), where the punishment is out of all proportion to the violation committed. The fact that the principle of proportionality rules out such excessive punishments is a strong point in its favour. Where the offence is very grave, of course, the proportionalist will be prepared to countenance grave penalties; but it is incorrect to suggest that this automatically commits him to executing murderers or mutilating mutilators. Such exact fit, as we have seen, is not required by the notions of proportionality; and in any case the proportionalist may accept that certain kinds of penalty (such as death or mutilation) should be excluded from the penal system on other grounds. (One such ground is that these penalties are irreversible: the fact that there is always a possibility of wrongful conviction seems a strong argument for outlawing punitive measures that cannot possibly be compensated for at a later date should it be found that there has been a miscarriage of justice.[14])

'Negative' retributivism

The theories discussed so far may be called 'positive' retributivist theories, in so far as they all see the fact of the criminal's having committed an offence as providing a reason why he deserves punishment. Quite separate from these positive theories is the position which is sometimes known as 'minimalist' retributivism, but which is more aptly named 'negative retributivism'. This is the view that no one should be punished *unless* he is guilty of a crime. In other words, what is proposed is not a sufficient condition (or set of conditions) for just punishment, but rather a necessary condition for just punishment. A person is justly punished only if he has committed an offence. The reason why this position counts as 'negative' rather than 'positive' is that it does not attempt to provide a positive justification of punishment. Rather, it articulates a kind of limiting principle or side-constraint: however we operate the institution of punishment, and whatever its justification may be, its application must always be restricted to those who are actually guilty.[15]

Negative retributivism, unlike the positive variety, is entirely uncontroversial and commands virtually universal acceptance. It is hard to imagine any civilised ethical system which does not lay it down as a fundamental rule of justice that guilt is a necessary precondition for the proper imposition of penal sanctions. It is important, however, not to construe this widespread support for negative retributivism as implying any sympathy for positive retributivist doctrines; and for this reason one needs to be very cautious in using the label 'retributivist' to describe the limiting principle 'only the guilty may be punished'. Two crucial points about the negative version need to be stressed in particular, if confusion is to be avoided. First, as has already been mentioned above, the negative version is quite unlike all other versions of retributivism in that it does not purport to provide a positive reason for, or justification of, punishment. Second, the principle it invokes is, as just noted, one which is widely accepted by moralists and penal theorists of all sorts and varieties. 'Never punish the innocent, only the guilty' is a fundamental principle of justice which is defended by groups as diverse as natural rights theorists on the one hand and utilitarians on the other hand. (The former may say that all are born with an inalienable natural right not to be subject to penal sanctions unless they have been properly found guilty; the latter may see it as a valuable utility-maximising rule that the state should never be allowed to punish the innocent.) Neither of these groups need have any inclination to support retributivism in any of its positive manifestations.

In the light of these very crucial differences between 'negative' and 'positive' retributivism, one may legitimately wonder whether it would not be better to devise a completely new label for the 'negative' doctrine. Unfortunately, however, the negative or minimalist position is so frequently classified in textbooks as a kind of retributivism that any attempt at relabelling would probably be doomed to failure. There is, however, one legitimate reason for regarding the maxim 'punish only the guilty' as having a genuine, if rather general, connection with retributivism proper, namely that it shares retributivism's essentially 'backward-looking' perspective. That is, it takes the primary focus in discussions of the morality of punishment to be the question 'What acts were performed in the past?' not 'What can be achieved in the future?' It is now time, however, to turn from such retrospective approaches to punishment, and take a look at forward-looking approaches which see the justification of punishment as lying in the beneficial consequences which it is taken to produce.

Reductionist theories

Those who seek to justify punishment in terms of its consequences commonly point to one very simple and straightforward result which they claim is produced by the penal system: it reduces the amount of crime committed. This, in brief, is the *reductionist* view of the justifying aim of punishment. The two principal ways in which punishing is generally supposed to reduce the crime rate are by prevention and by deterrence.

If we take *prevention* first, the idea at its crudest is that if a criminal is behind bars for a certain length of time, then at least he will not be robbing, raping or whatever during that time. He will, as they say, be 'out of circulation'. Things are not quite as simple as this, however, since it is well known that, statistically speaking, a prison sentence actually increases the chances of a criminal re-offending when released (this is known by criminologists as the problem of *recidivism*). What the advocate of prevention needs to show, then, is that a spell in prison of a given length will succeed in reducing the total overall amount of crime likely to be committed in the lifetime of a given individual. If prison sentences are lengthy enough, there seems little doubt that such a reduction will indeed be achieved. There is, however, a major problem with preventive detention. If the aim is simply to prevent the convicted criminal from committing future offences by restricting his liberty, then this would seem to justify keeping him inside for as long as he poses a threat to society. And this in turn could involve detaining him for considerably longer than the period of detention which constitutes an appropriate punishment for the crime he has actually committed. To put the point slightly differently, if considerations of justice and proportionality suggest ten years, say, as an appropriate punishment for a particular offence, there is no reason why considerations of prevention should not require additional detention for a further five, ten or even twenty years. What this shows is that, though preventive detention may be an effective weapon of crime control, it is not strictly speaking a theory of *punishment*. Rather it is a coercive technique that operates alongside, and independently of, punishment proper. Whether or not society is justified in imposing preventive detention on its citizens (or for that matter in using other preventive measures such as compulsory chemotherapy for sex offenders) is an important and complex question; but it is a different question from the question of whether society is justified in punishing.[16]

The standard reductionist theory of punishment, and perhaps the most widely supported account of how punishment is to be justified, is the *deterrence* theory. The Latin verb *deterrere* means, literally, 'to scare off', and the central idea of deterrence is that the criminal will be discouraged from committing an offence out of fear of the penal sanction he risks incurring if caught. The idea of deterrence has been widely criticised in recent years and the objection most commonly raised is that it has been shown not to work. The high rates of recidivism, even among those who have served long prison sentences, surely demonstrate, it is argued, that the threat of punishment has little or no effect.[17] This argument, for all its popularity among sociologists and criminologists, is completely invalid. The fact that convicted criminals often re-offend certainly shows that they were not deterred; but of course *any* offender, even a first-time offender, is by definition someone who was not effectively deterred by the threat of punishment. The deterrence theorist does not claim to achieve the unrealistic goal of a total elimination of crime; what he does claim is that punishing those who do offend will substantially reduce the amount of crime that would have been committed by *others*, were there no punishment for offenders. The focus of justification is not on the individual offender – who is necessarily a failure of the system – but on the population at large.[18]

But *is* the ordinary citizen deterred by the punishment received by criminals? It is sometimes said that this is doubtful: most people clearly do not on waking up each morning wonder, 'Shall I commit a crime today?' and then proceed to weigh up the risks of punishment. Rather, most ordinary citizens have a more or less unreflective habit of conforming to the law; there are large sections of the population for whom serious criminal acts such as robbing a bank would be virtually unthinkable. The conclusion drawn from this by some critics of the deterrence system is as follows: on the one hand, there are the criminals who are not deterred by threat of punishment, and on the other hand there are the honest citizens who never seriously consider crime; in neither case does deterrence have a useful role to play in reducing crime.

Although this criticism may seem plausible, it involves the serious over-simplification of dividing the population into two supposedly fixed groups – the criminals and the law-abiding. In fact, between those on one side who would be determined to continue with crime come what may, and those on the other side for whom any criminal act would be inconceivable, there is likely to be a sizeable middle group who might be tempted to offend, were it not for the penalty. The size of this middle group may of course vary from crime to crime. Most of us, fortunately, do not find murder a tempting option, but in the case of crimes like smuggling and tax evasion the risk of punishment (and its associated disadvantages such as the stigma of having a criminal record) probably play an important role for many people. Even crimes which people do not normally contemplate might in time become tempting if punishment were abolished. If, for example, there were no penalty for shoplifting, and every day we saw people loading up with free goods and getting away with it, then within weeks or months all but a few of the most austerely high-principled citizens would probably be tempted to join in the bonanza. In short, common sense overwhelmingly suggests that deterrence can and does play a vital role in protecting law and order in general.

Apart from these (largely misplaced) objections about the efficacy of deterrence, there are a number of ethical objections that the deterrence theory has to face. If deterrence is the sole rationale for punishment, the sole concern that lawmakers and judges have to address in setting up and operating the penal system, then does this not open the door to all sorts of morally dubious uses of punishment? Why not control crime by imposing really terrifying punishments such as evisceration or boiling in oil? Why not employ (as the Nazis did with considerable deterrent success in parts of occupied Europe) collective punishment – so that a whole village or a whole family is penalised for the offences of a single member? Come to that, why bother about guilt at all? Why not select innocent scapegoats, frame them with faked evidence, and organise spectacular show trials leading to savage sentences – all with a view to maximum publicity and deterrent effect? Supporters of deterrence may reply that such practices may bring the law into disrepute, and so would not be expedient methods of crime reduction in the long run; but the point remains that the notion of deterrence does not of itself lay down any limits on what we may do to an individual in order to secure the desired result of deterring others. To put the matter in Kantian terms, the individual criminal seems to be regarded entirely as a *means*: what we do to him is not governed by considerations of fairness, or by asking what would be the just punishment for this individual in this particular case; rather his penalty is simply an instrument for producing a benefit (crime reduction) for society in general.[19]

Although these criticisms are perhaps not fatal to the deterrence theory, what they do seem to show is that if the theory is to avoid violating our sense of justice, its operation needs to be constrained in certain ways. There need to be principles which restrict the ways in which we may legitimately secure the desired result of crime reduction. Two such principles seem especially important: punishment must be restricted to those found guilty of an offence by due process of law; and punishment must not be excessive in relation to the harmfulness of the offence. (These principles are ones which, as we saw above, are often stressed by retributivists; but they have a strong intuitive claim on our sense of justice quite independently of whether we believe in retribution as a positive justifying aim of punishment.) If these two restricting principles are adopted, the resulting theory might be called a 'combination' theory of punishment: deterrence provides the general aim in terms of which the penal system is justified; but the penal system is structured in terms of our two principles of justice which define the limits within which the aim of deterrence may be pursued.[20]

The issues raised in the two preceding paragraphs illustrate a tension which is familiar in many other areas of ethics: the tension between the collective goal of social utility, and the demands of individual justice. One particular issue in the theory of punishment where this tension seems especially strong is the issue of exemplary sentences. Suppose *A* vandalises a telephone box and gets a small fine or conditional discharge. Then suppose there is a spate of such offences and *B* is had up for the same offence six months later; the magistrate says, 'There has been far too much of this sort of thing lately,' and imposes the maximum sentence of six months' imprisonment. On the one hand our sense of justice or fairness seems to require that two equally guilty offenders should receive similar sentences; on the other hand the aim of deterrence suggests that if a certain type of offence becomes an increasing menace, the courts may legitimately decide to 'make an example' of a particular offender. The way out of this conflict seems to be as follows. It is for the legislature to set the maximum sentence for a given offence, bearing in mind its general harmfulness to society. The courts may then impose *less* than the maximum in any case where they believe such a course would be justified without weakening the deterrent effect of the law. (This is an example of what is sometimes called the 'principle of economic deterrence': never impose a greater penalty when a lesser will be as efficacious in deterrent terms.) Where, however, the courts decide that an example needs to be made, they may impose the maximum sentence; but the recipient – though there is a sense in which he has been unlucky in that he committed the offence at a time when it was causing public concern – cannot complain of unjust treatment, since the penalty in question was the one duly and properly authorised in advance by the legislature as a possible sentence for the offence in question.

Rehabilitation, reform and cure

One of the stated aims of the prison service is to 'rehabilitate' offenders so they may again take their place in society once they have served their sentence. It seems clear, however, that this worthy (though in many cases depressingly unfulfilled) aim is incidental to punishment proper. One of the foreseen though unintended effects of incarcerating someone for lengthy periods is that he or she may become 'institutionalised' – less able to cope with normal life in the outside world. Rehabilitation techniques are designed to counteract this and other undesirable effects of punishment; but clearly they are not part of the punishment itself, nor can they be part of the justification of punishment (though by making the effects of punishment less damaging for an individual's future prospects, they may serve to remove some of the obstacles to its justification).

Reform is rather different, since it is thought by some to be part of the purpose of, and perhaps a partial justification of, punishment. 'By suffering we learn' says the ancient Greek proverb; and there is some force to the belief that the offender will come to appreciate the error of his ways by experiencing the unpleasant shock of being subjected to punishment. This will not always be the case, as is graphically shown by the W.C. Fields joke about the condemned man who says on mounting the scaffold, 'I'll certainly learn my lesson from this!' Even in cases of imprisonment, though, where there is the opportunity for lengthy reflection on one's misdeeds, a change of attitude is by no means inevitable. The offender may simply become hardened, or determined not to be caught again. Clearly, then, punishment is not a sufficient condition (not enough in itself) to reform the offender. And equally clearly it is not a necessary condition (not an essential or indispensable requirement) for reform, since an offender may experience remorse and become convinced of the need to change his outlook without being punished (or even apprehended).

An important point to note about the concept of reform is that it does not simply imply a change in behaviour patterns. When flogging was a commonplace part of the penal system, there were no doubt offenders who were so affected by the ordeal that they were frightened of repeating their offences and risking further punishment. But what is involved in that type of case is deterrence, not reform. Reform implies a change of heart, a recognition that what one has done is bad, and a sincere resolve to amend one's life in the future. It thus involves a modification in the ethical outlook of the offender; and this in turn suggests that if we are interested in reform it would be sensible to turn to educative techniques rather than the simple imposition of penalties. With this in mind, courts in some areas have experimented with so-called 'alternative sentencing' policies, whereby for example drunken drivers are required to work in hospital accident departments, or rapists are required to confront their victims under controlled conditions so they can learn about the distress they have caused. Although such measures have something in common with punishment, in that they are sanctions which are imposed on offenders by the courts, they are perhaps better thought of as alternatives to punishment. For while punishment is essentially coercive – it invokes a penalty which is meted out to the offender whether he likes it or not – these 'reforming' techniques require the voluntary co-operation – and indeed active participation – of the offender. Reform, then, is different from punishment proper, though it is surely a legitimate and worthwhile aim of the courts and other law enforcement agencies, and may well come to play an increasing role, at least for some types of offence, as an alternative to the traditional fine or prison sentence, or as a supplementary aim of the penal system. (On the 'supplementary' approach, the courts might for example pass a reduced prison sentence on condition that the offender agrees to participate in approved procedures designed to induce reform.)

A very different approach to crime, which is sometimes confused with the reforming approach, is the *curative* approach. This is relevant to our purposes since it often goes hand in hand with a radical critique of the whole notion of punishment. Crudely, the critique goes like this: criminals are not 'wicked'; they are sick; their anti-social conduct is a manifestation of some kind of personality problem or other psychological disorder. Since punishment, it is argued, would only make matters worse, what we need to do is to scrap the practice of punishing entirely and replace it with a systematic set of measures designed to *cure*.[21]

Although it may initially sound enlightened, this approach is in fact beset with a host of philosophical confusions. Firstly, there seems to be a misconception about the concept of crime. Criminal acts do not form some simple, homogeneous group. They range from horrible acts of violence, such as murder and rape, to offences such as smuggling or smoking cannabis, which are virtually harmless as far as the rights of others are concerned; we should also not forget that political criticism of the state authorities is, in effect, treated as a crime in some countries. Given the enormously varied nature of the activities classified as 'crime', it seems wildly implausible to claim that they are all manifestations of illness. Secondly, there is a confusion about the term 'sick'. Sickness or illness typically involves some kind of defect or malfunction which impairs the mental or physical life of the patient. And the notion of a 'cure' implies that this defect or malfunction can be rectified or alleviated. But it is just false that the average bank robber has an 'illness' in this sense. Robbing banks is not an indication of some mental or physical malfunction (on the contrary, to be a good bank robber one has to be in excellent mental and physical health). What is wrong with the thief is not that he has a psychological disorder, but that he fails to respect the property rights of others; and this is a moral, not a medical, problem. (No doubt *some* criminals are mentally disturbed, just as some non-criminals are; but that is not the point. The point is that there is no sound reason for inferring illness from the fact of crime alone.[22])

Supporters of the 'curative' approach may object at this point that the comments made so far ignore the main purpose of their campaign, namely to replace the harshness, vindictiveness and impersonality of the penal system with more gentle, humane and constructive measures designed to meet the needs of the individual offender. Against this it may be objected that experiences in totalitarian countries have shown that the psychiatric treatment can be every bit as repressive and cruel as the most ruthlessly applied traditional punishment. In any case, there is an important point about individual liberty to be made here. Under the traditional penal system, what is done to an offender – though it is certainly not pleasant – is measured and determinate: in exchange for violating the rights of others he forfeits specific rights of his own (e.g. he is imprisoned for five years). 'Cure', by contrast, is open-ended and indeterminate. The authorities have an individual in their power until such time as they consider him cured; and in the meantime he may be subjected to all kinds of behaviour modification techniques (chemical, electrical, surgical) at the discretion of the doctors in charge. What this suggests is that there are important considerations, connected with the preservation of our civil liberties, why we should be reluctant to abandon the present 'fixed-penalty' system of punishment in favour of a system which in effect gives a blank cheque to the state to impose what 'treatments' it sees fit. No citizen can be sure that he will not find himself (perhaps as a result of an honest mistake or perhaps as a result of dubious or planted evidence) in the hands of the authorities; and it is an important safeguard that, while he may be condemned to languish in gaol, he can at least be sure that his brain will not be tampered with, nor his personality be changed, against his will.

Punishment and the victims of crime

The approaches to punishment so far discussed have all been primarily concerned with the criminal, or potential criminal. This is true both of backward-looking justifications such as retributivism where the purpose of punishment is to give the offender his just deserts, and of forward-looking approaches such as deterrence (where the aim of punishment is to discourage possible future offenders). The notions of rehabilitation, reform and cure also have the offender as the central focus of attention. But what of the victims of crime? Is it not the hapless victim who is – or at least should be – our primary concern when we punish?

This concluding section of our survey will examine two theories of punishment which aim to justify the practice with reference to what is owed to the victims of crime. The first may be called the *satisfaction theory*, and asserts that it is right to punish offenders because such punishment brings satisfaction or comfort to the victims of crime (and also perhaps to their family, friends, neighbours and associates). At first sight this may seem to come down to the crude gratification of the desire for revenge. Revenge, says the proverb, is sweet; and it has been suggested that institutional punishment stands to revenge as marriage stands to lust, i.e. as a socially approved vehicle for a natural and powerful emotion. But to put the matter in terms of crude revenge may be to cast an unfair light on the satisfaction theory. 'Revenge' in the ordinary connotation of that term suggests something which is, if not downright unethical, at least morally dubious; Christian teaching in particular suggests that it is wrong. There is, however, such a thing as 'righteous indignation' – the legitimate sense of grievance felt by someone who has been wronged (and by his family, friends, etc.). Further, there is no doubt that this sense of grievance will typically be assuaged when the person who caused it has been apprehended and brought to justice. The satisfaction theory, then, asserts that we punish in order to satisfy the legitimate sense of grievance felt by the victims of crime.

There are a number of problems with this notion, some practical and some ethical. Clearly, great practical problems would arise if we were supposed to calculate the amount of grievance felt by a victim, and measure this against the amount of satisfaction he felt on seeing the offender punished. The amounts in question, moreover, are likely to vary greatly from individual to individual – some people are enormously indignant if a child treads on their flower-beds, while others are forgiving even of major wrongs. It is not at all clear how one could devise a coherent sentencing policy based solely on the principle that punishment should be aimed at assuaging the sense of grievance felt by victims. But quite apart from these problems there is a more serious worry about the ethical framework of the satisfaction theory. No one would dispute the psychological facts that victims do feel indignation, and that punishment of offenders does go some way in alleviating that indignation. But these psychological facts surely cannot, in and of themselves, carry sufficient weight to justify the whole elaborate apparatus involving judges, juries, lawyers, probation officers, prison warders and so on, which our penal system requires. In view of the enormous costs of the penal system to the taxpayer, the fact that punishing offenders sometimes makes some people feel better just seems too weak, by itself, to provide a convincing justification.

This last point suggests that the satisfaction theory needs to be combined with some further theory of the justification of punishment if it is to carry weight. One common move is to say that punishment is not only satisfying to the victim but is also a just repayment to the offender for his wrongdoing; this line would take us back to the notion of retribution already discussed above. Alternatively, the satisfaction theory may be combined with a forward-looking consideration: if the victims of crime did not have some expectation of the offenders being brought to justice, they would eventually 'take the law into their own hands'. This in turn would lead to unregulated acts of revenge and counter-revenge – and in time things would degenerate to the point where one had a series of uncontrolled vendettas rather than the rule of law. Not only are vendettas socially destabilising, but they also favour the ruthless and powerful, who can take terrible revenge on their enemies, as against the weak and helpless who may have to suffer serious wrongs without any redress. This line of thought does provide a strong utilitarian justification for the penal system, namely that it prevents the unfairness and instability which would in all likelihood arise if there were no officially institutionalised punishment.

A second and quite distinct victim-centred theory of punishment is what may be called the *restitution* theory; here the justifying aim is seen as that of restoring or making good the loss suffered by the offended party. One way of approaching this notion is by reflecting on the shortcomings of traditional retribution theory. Suppose that someone has property stolen, and the thief is gaoled. Not only does this do nothing to make good the loss, but the victim is subjected to further costs, as a taxpayer, to support the penal system. Even if we add in the consideration just discussed above, namely the satisfaction produced by seeing the offender get his deserts, this may seem, from the victim's point of view, a dubious and weak compensation for what he has suffered. It is of course possible, under the present system, for the victim to sue the criminal for damages in the civil courts; and such a suit if successful might result in compensation for the loss incurred. But in the nature of things it is often very difficult to recover damages from the average criminal: he may have swiftly squandered his ill-gotten gains, or alternatively he may have managed to conceal the proceeds in a safe place.

The central idea behind the restitution theory, then, is that the aim of the penal system should be to ensure that the losses suffered by the victims of crime should be as far as possible made good by the offender.[23] Instead of being, as at present, an institution involving two parties – the state on the one hand and the criminal on the other – the criminal law would become more like the civil law, where the three parties are involved: the state, the plaintiff and the defendant. Judges would be asked to assess the damage suffered by the plaintiff – the victim; and the defendant, if convicted, would be ordered to make good that damage, plus costs. To meet the frequent problem of recovering the money from the offender, he would be required to work the debt off, in prison. There are various versions of the restitution theory at this point, but a fairly typical scenario would be that prisons should be run as profit-making institutions, with an appropriate notional wage paid to the convict-workers. The workers would not however receive their wages, but the money would be transferred to the victim each week, less a deduction for the costs of incarceration, until the debt determined by the courts was paid off.[24]

There are no doubt all sorts of practical questions that come to mind at this point, about exactly how the system envisaged would operate; but discussion here will be confined to the philosophical and in particular, ethical problems posed by this restitutional approach. Perhaps the most obvious ethical wrong is that the system seems to envisage 'one law for the rich and another for the poor': a rich offender could pay off his debt out of his own resources, while a poor one would be compelled to work it off. To make the system more fair, it might be stipulated that all offenders, irrespective of means, should be required to work off their debts; but it is by no means clear that this would be in the interest of victims – who are supposed, after all, to be the focus of attention in the restitutionary theory – since the 'working off' stipulation would mean they would have to wait much longer for their money in many cases. A somewhat different objection to the restitutionary approach is that while it might be appropriate enough in the case of offences involving property, there is something invidious in putting a price on the distress caused by such crimes as violent assault or rape. A fair reply to this is that the amount assessed by the court as appropriate restitution for such crimes is not supposed to take away the distress suffered, or 'pay off' the victim in any vulgar or straightforward sense – any more than is supposed in ordinary civil cases. Suppose a hospital bungles an operation, and a patient loses a leg. Nothing can bring the leg back, but substantial damages may nonetheless be accepted by the unfortunate patient as a public recognition of, and at least partial compensation for, the harm he has suffered. If this works in the civil arena, there seems no reason in principle why it should not be transferable to the criminal sphere.

An important philosophical question that needs to be asked about the restitutionary approach is whether the loss to be made good by the criminal should be assessed in terms of the actual distress caused, or, instead, in terms of what might be called the 'moral' harm done. The actual amount of distress caused by a rape or a burglary, say, may vary widely from case to case; but if we define moral harm in terms of the violation of the victim's rights, then whenever a particular right has been violated a certain amount of moral harm has been occasioned. In so far as the courts focused on this type of harm, they would in effect be imposing penalties in proportion to the moral gravity of the offence committed; and to this extent the restitutionary approach might end up as being closely similar, in its actual operation, to the retributive approach – except that the victim would be a direct financial beneficiary of the system.

It is this last feature – which initially seems to be an advantage of the restitutionary approach – that turns out in the end to generate the most serious objection to it. If the victim has a direct financial interest in securing the conviction of the offender, this provides a strong incentive for perjury. It would be very much in the victim's interest to get a conviction – any conviction – leading to a restitutionary payment, and this might well lead to miscarriages of justice. For similar reasons, the risks of blackmail would seem to be greatly increased under the restitutive model, since if an unscrupulous person is able to fabricate evidence against X, he may be in a 'no-lose' position: he can say to X, 'Either pay me off now, or else I will testify that you have wronged me and the courts will require you to pay me anyway.'

It is worth noting in conclusion that the restitution theory does not necessarily have to be seen as an attempt to displace other justifications of punishment. It seems possible that courts might see retribution or deterrence as the principal aims of the penal system, but might think it appropriate, at least for certain types of crime, to reduce a sentence or even suspend it entirely, on condition that the offender was prepared to do something by way of compensating his victim.[25] This would be rather different from the restitutionary model described above, since the debt would be paid off outside prison rather than inside; but in view of the increased overcrowding of prisons and the increasing costs of running them, many might be attracted by an approach which reduces pressures on the prison service while at the same time providing some measure of compensation for those wronged. In the case of minor crime in particular, sentencing the petty thief to do so many hours of household repairs or gardening work to compensate his victim may be a course of action that would commend itself to all those involved. But since such restitutive schemes involve the willing co-operation of the offender, it seems highly unlikely that they could serve to control the more ruthless or dangerous criminals.

Conclusion

It should by now be more than clear that the justification of punishment is not a matter that can be discussed within one single theoretical framework. Indeed, part of the fascination of the philosophy of punishment is that the subject can be approached from a number of quite distinct perspectives: we can take a forward-looking or a backward-looking approach; our primary concern can be social utility or individual justice; we can focus on the offender or on the victim. Some philosophers have been sceptical about whether any of the proposed justifications of punishment hold water; and some have even suggested that punishment is part of a coercive system of control that would wither away in a truly just society. Such speculation belongs in Utopia: in any remotely plausible model for how society can in fact be organised, punishment of some kind will remain an unavoidable element. Even if there were a dramatic and continuing fall in the crime rate, society would surely continue to announce penalties for serious rights violations such as killing or stealing, and would have to be prepared to impose the relevant penalties whenever such offences did occur. For the system of criminal sanctions is one way whereby society defines the limits of the permissible: it announces the fundamental ground rules, transgression of which cannot be tolerated. This 'declaratory' or 'denunciatory' function of punishment cannot by itself provide a justification for the penal system;[26] for that we must look to one or more of the theories examined above. But it is no bad thing to end our discussion by stressing the importance of the symbolic role of punishment. In tyrannical societies punishment may be a symbol of state oppression; but in a free society it is a symbol of the rule of law. The figure of Justice is traditionally depicted as being blindfolded: punishment is, or should be, meted out impartially to rich and poor, to the famous and the ordinary. The existence of an impartially organised penal system, with a scale of penalties for each offence laid down in advance by the legislature, is a sign that society is not prepared to tolerate violations of the rights of any of its citizens by anyone, no matter who they may be. In so far as the penal system involves the use of coercion, its existence is a sign that society is not perfect; but it is also a sign that, for all its imperfections, society is firmly committed to protecting the rights of its members.[27]

Notes

(An author's name followed by a number in square brackets refers to the book or article which has that number in the bibliography.)

1. Bentham [7], Ch. 13, Section 2.
2. See Bentham [7], Chs. 13–17.
3. Plato, *Laws* (*c.* 350 BC), 934.
4. Aristotle, *Nicomachean ethics* (*c.* 330 BC), 1132a.
5. The belief that suffering 'pays' for wrong finds expression in the Christian doctrine of the atonement (where the suffering of Christ is supposed to pay for the sins of the world). But the logic of this doctrine is obscure. See J. Cottingham, 'Varieties of retribution', *Philosophical Quarterly* (1979).
6. Punishment is directed towards 'das Aufheben des Verbrechens, das sonst gelten würde', G. Hegel, *Philosophie des Rechts* (1883), Part I, Section 99.
7. The notion of the 'inherent' or 'intrinsic' goodness of punishment is vigorously criticised in Honderich [5], pp. 212ff; for the notion of desert as a justification of punishment see L.H. Davis, 'They deserve to suffer', *Analaysis* (1972).
8. J.D. Mabbott, 'Punishment', *Mind* (1939); reprinted in Acton [4], p. 42.
9. For the distinction between analysis of a concept or institution and the task of moral justification, compare A. Flew, 'The justification of punishment' in Acton [4], p. 92.
10. The idea of the duty of fair play as a basis for moral obligation is developed in J. Rawls, 'Legal obligation and the duty of fair play' in S. Hook (ed.), *Law and philosophy* (University Press, New York, 1964).
11. Formulations in terms of rights may be seen in B. Bosanquet, *The philosophical theory of the state* (1899) and Ross [10]. For a more recent discussion see A.H. Goldman, 'The paradox of punishment', *Philosophy and Public Affairs* (1979) and Hodson [17], Ch. 9. That the offender does not lose *all* his rights is clear from the fact that a prison sentence does not imply the loss of basic rights such as the right to life, or the right not to be tortured.
12. Compare Honderich [5], p. 238.
13. For more on proportionality see J.G. Murphy, 'Cruel and unusual punishments' in Stewart [18], pp. 328ff.
14. For the problem of the incompensatability of the death penalty see J. Cottingham, 'Punishment and respect for persons' in Stewart [18], p. 430.
15. For the 'minimalist' position see Golding [2], p. 85, and A. Quinton, 'On punishment', *Analysis* (1954) in Acton [4], p. 58. For the term 'negative retributivism' see J.L. Mackie, *Persons and values* (Clarendon Press, Oxford, 1985), Ch. 15, and Cottingham in Stewart [18], p. 424.
16. For more on prevention see Walker [13], Ch. 5.
17. For this view see M.D.A. Freeman in Stewart [18], p. 408.
18. Another way of putting this point is to say that we should distinguish carefully between *individual* deterrence and *general* deterrence; see Hart [3], pp. 128–9.

19. For more on this objection to deterrence see Duff [6], Ch. 3.

20. For arguments pointing in the direction of a combination theory, see Hart [3], Ch. 1.

21. For an influential statement of the curative approach see Wootton [14]. For criticisms see Murphy [16], Part III.

22. See further Flew [15].

23. See G. del Vecchio, 'The struggle against crime' in Acton [4].

24. For this type of scheme see P.J. Ferrara, 'Retribution and restitution: a synthesis', *Journal of Libertarian Studies* (1982).

25. Experiments of this kind have been tried in some parts of the UK (Leeds is the best-known example) during the 1980s.

26. For the denunciatory view see Ewing [9] and Lord Denning's comments in the *Report of the Royal Commission on Capital Punishment* (HMSO, London, 1953), Section 53. The reason why the notion of denunciation does not of itself seem sufficient to generate a justification of the penal system is that there appear to be several theoretically possible ways of denouncing rights violations, apart from punishment; what needs to be shown is why society is justified in expressing its condemnation in *this* particular way.

27. For an elaboration of this approach, see Ross [10].

Bibliography ·

Brief general introductions to this subject may be found in

[1] D. Lyons, *Ethics and the rule of law* (Cambridge University Press, Cambridge, 1984), Ch. 5, and in

[2] M.P. Golding, *Philosophy of law* (Prentice-Hall, Englewood Cliffs, 1975), Chs. 4 and 5.

An enlightening collection of essays by one of the most influential authors on philosophical issues in the law is

[3] H.L.A. Hart, *Punishment and responsibility* (Oxford University Press, Oxford, 1968). See esp. Chs. 1, 7 and 9.

A useful collection of critical discussions, with a valuable introduction, is

[4] H.B. Acton (ed.), *The philosophy of punishment* (Macmillan, London, 1969).

A stimulating critique of many standard views on punishment is

[5] T. Honderich, *Punishment: the supposed justification* (London, 1969; reprinted with a new postscript, Penguin Books, Harmondsworth, 1984).

There is also much food for thought in

[6] A. Duff, *Trials and punishments* (Cambridge University Press, Cambridge, 1985).

The following classics continue to exert an important influence:

[7] J. Bentham, *An introduction to the principles of morals and legislation* (1780), which lays the foundations of the utilitarian approach to punishment;

[8] T.H. Green, *Lectures on the principles of political obligation* (1881), which provides a rights-based account;

[9] A.C. Ewing, *The morality of punishment* (1929), which provides a detailed analytic treatment of the subject and defends a 'denunciatory' view; and

[10] W.D. Ross, *The right and the good* (1930), which argues that punishment is a 'promise to the injured person and his friends and to society'.

A valuable collection of source materials ancient and modern is

[11] H. Morris (ed.), *Freedom and responsibility* (Stanford University Press, Stanford, 1961), esp. Ch. 10.

Another handy compendium of materials on philosophy of law, including punishment, is

[12] J. Feinberg and H. Gross (eds), *Philosophy of law* (Wadsworth, Belmont, California, 1980), esp. Part V.

For a useful introduction to the subject from a criminological perspective, see

[13] N. Walker, *Punishment, danger and stigma* (Basil Blackwell, Oxford, 1980).

For an influential statement of the 'curative' approach see

[14] B. Wootton, *Crime and the criminal law* (Stevens, London, 1963), and for a vigorous counterblast

[15] A. Flew, *Crime or disease?* (Macmillan, London, 1973).

Two readable books which emphasise the importance for penal theory of the Kantian principle of respect for persons are

[16] J.G. Murphy, *Retribution, justice and therapy* (Reidel, Dordrecht, 1979) and

[17] J.D. Hodson, *The ethics of legal coercion* (Reidel, Dordrecht, 1983).

Further explorations of the non-utilitarian outlook may be found in

[18] M.A. Stewart (ed.), *Law, morality and rights* (Reidel, Dordrecht, 1983).

Finally, two stimulating books on wider ethical issues, which include chapters on punishment:

[19] A. Kenny, *Free will and responsibility* (Routledge, London, 1978) and

[20] J. Glover, *Responsibility* (Routledge, London, 1970).

J.G.C.

34 | *The Philosophy of the Social Sciences*

Michael Lessnoff

Three earlier chapters (Chapters 9–11) have already dealt with problems in the philosophy of science. Why, then, should it be necessary to embark on a separate discussion of the philosophy of the *social* sciences? The answer is, simply, that the philosophical status of social science is peculiarly problematic – indeed much more fundamentally so than in the case of natural science. The scientific study of nature exists, its aims and methods are well established, its results are undeniably impressive; notwithstanding all possibly legitimate philosophical caveats, reservations and questions, there is an obvious sense in which it is clearly on the right track. No such confident statements can be made about the scientific study of society. The central philosophical problem of the social sciences, therefore, is whether its subject-matter – human social life – is or is not sufficiently similar to non-human nature to be studied and described by established natural scientific methods, or, as one might put it, whether the social sciences actually *are*, or *should be*, natural sciences. On this central question controversy has raged for centuries, and continues unabated. The present chapter will be largely a guide to that controversy in its various branches, which include the role of scientific law and of causality, the nature of explanation, the appropriateness and implications of empirical method, and the place of value-judgements. Many of these issues are, at least in part, aspects or corollaries of more general philosophical problems and so the discussions in several earlier chapters – notably Chapters 3, 7, 9–11, 13, 14, 17–19 and 21–27 – are again relevant here. But we shall also encounter a further major issue, to do with the very nature and definition of the object of study, the 'social': are social phenomena, fundamentally and essentially, nothing but the relations of individual people, or do they constitute a reality *sui generis* which is irreducibly *social*? This question of the reducibility of the social is clearly specific to the social sciences, but it is analogous to problems of reducibility that arise elsewhere in the philosophy of science, and indeed is continuous with them – for if the social is indeed reducible to the individual, might not the individual person be reducible in turn to purely physical matter (cf. Chapter 18 above)? Might not social science, then, be not only essentially similar to, but ultimately *derivable*, at least in principle, from physical science? The affirmation of both these theses about the social sciences constitutes what may be called *scientism*.

J.S. Mill's 'System of logic'

The spectacular success of natural science since the seventeenth century makes the attraction of scientism for students of society easy to understand. Especially from the nineteenth century we find numerous demands for a 'science' of society, and indeed claims to have established it, from such writers as Auguste Comte, Karl Marx and Herbert Spencer. But the clearest, most careful, subtlest and most comprehensive articulation of the scientistic position was the work of the utilitarian philosopher and economist John Stuart Mill. The argument of his classic *System of logic* (1843), in particular of its famous Book VI on the 'Logic of the moral sciences' (Mill's name for the social sciences), still repays careful study.

        Mill believed that, as he put it, 'the course of nature is uniform', that is, all the phenomena of the world conform to specific regularities, the most fundamental of which are called 'Laws of Nature'.[1] The task of science is to discover these uniformities, of which there are two kinds, uniformities of coexistence and uniformities of succession. The latter, which Mill says are the more important, are *causal* laws: a law of invariable succession relates an invariable antecedent (the cause) to an invariable consequent (the effect). The entire order of nature is, in Mill's eyes, causal: 'every fact which has a beginning' is the effect of an antecedent cause, everything happens in accordance with causal laws;[2] but for Mill (following Hume) there is nothing more in causation than invariable succession.[3]

        How does science discover the causal order of nature? The most fundamental logical operation involved, Mill says, is induction, 'the operation of discovering and proving general propositions'. Induction is the method 'by which we infer that what we know to be true in a particular case or cases, will be true in all [similar] cases'.[4] The most basic Laws of Nature (or of science) are discovered inductively, by inference from knowledge of particular cases; and this knowledge of particular cases is acquired empirically (that is, by observation) or (more precisely) experimentally, using what Mill calls the 'Method of Difference', that is, observation of the difference made by the (experimentally controlled) presence or absence of a given factor in otherwise constant conditions.[5] But Mill believed that the purely inductive or experimental method is often impossible to apply because of the complexity of interacting causes; if so, science, he says, uses the 'deductive' method. This begins from the relevant causal laws, inductively established; it then attempts to deduce from these causal laws the effect of their joint action in given combinations. But, as Mill admits, such a calculation is subject to various uncertainties, and so its results must be tested by a further step, called by Mill 'verification'. '[Deductive] conclusions must be found, on careful comparison, to accord with the results of direct observation.'[6] Uniformities thus deductively arrived at, which also accord with experience, may be considered as laws.

Mill's view of the social sciences fits entirely into this picture: there is, he says (or at least there may be, and should be) a *science* of *human* nature, just as of nature quite generally.[7] In the science of human nature, the most fundamental laws, known inductively, are the Laws of Mind, that is, laws stating causal regularities that determine states of mind in individuals, laws which are the basis of the science of psychology. Prominent among these are laws governing the association of ideas.[8] Several deductive sciences, Mill holds, are derivable from the basic Laws of Mind (just as they are, in the case of the physical sciences, from the basic laws of mechanics). One such is Ethology, the science of the formation of individual character, to be obtained by deducing the effects of the Laws of Mind in particular circumstances.[9] Another is what Mill calls the 'Social Science', or 'Sociology': 'The actions and feelings of human beings in the social state are ... entirely governed by psychological and ethological laws.'[10]

Actually, it would be more accurate to talk of social sciences in the plural; for Mill recognised two categories of social science, first a general Science of Society, and second, special or separate 'abstract' sciences dealing with particular areas of social life, in which (as is sometimes though not typically the case) human action is mainly governed by one single 'law of human nature', one single human passion or motive or desire. Thus, for example, the science of political economy is a deduction from men's 'desire of wealth' and from that desire (almost) alone.[11] Mill was careful to stress both the validity of this social science and its limitations. It is valid because, although it is not generally true that social life is ever wholly governed by the desire for wealth, it is sufficiently close to the truth in the area of economic production and distribution. Its validity, therefore, is limited to this area; and even in this area its laws are only an approximation to the truth. And there is a further limitation: the laws of political economy are valid, even in the economic sphere, only in particular 'states of society', i.e. particular societies at a particular stage of historical development, states of society where the science's assumptions both about motivation and about relevant social circumstances hold (at least approximately) true. Mill was well aware that this is far from universally the case: thus we cannot arrive, by deduction, 'at any great number of propositions which will be true in all societies without exception', because of 'the eminently modifiable nature of the social phenomena, and the multitude and variety of the circumstances by which they are modified'.[12]

Areas of social life not susceptible of treatment in the abstract, deductive manner of political economy must, according to Mill, be considered to belong to the general Science of Society. This too Mill termed deductive, but it is a different and somewhat unusual sort of deduction.[13] First, it is what Mill calls 'concrete' (as opposed to abstract) deduction, which has to reckon with not a single human motive or desire, or law of human nature, but with the interaction of a large number of them. Second, the deduction is necessarily 'inverse' because, as Mill concedes, it is strictly impossible to deduce any reliable results from the multitudinous premises involved. In this case, it is necessary to begin with the 'verification', or rather with empirical regularities discovered by observation (of the history of mankind). Their status as genuine laws should then be tested by a kind of quasi-deduction from 'the laws of human nature', that is, it must be shown that they are at least consistent with the latter, fundamental laws even if not the necessary consequence thereof. Within the general Science of Society, Mill distinguished between two kinds of laws, uniformities of coexistence (of social facts within a State of Society) and uniformities of succession (i.e. of successive States of Society).[14] Both social coexistence and social succession are thus, in Mill's view, governed by laws. He believed, also, that both 'the evidence of history and that of human nature' show that the 'predominant, and almost paramount' cause of societal change is change in the realm of ideas, specifically in knowledge and belief.[15]

Mill's belief in causal laws of human nature led him to consider again an age-old philosophical problem, that of freedom of the will. Does universal causality imply that the individual cannot genuinely determine his actions for himself? Mill denies any such implication. True, 'our actions follow from our characters, and our characters follow from our organisation, our education and our circumstances'; but among these character-determining circumstances are our own *desires* to mould our characters in a particular way. Admittedly, whether we have such desires must, once again, depend causally on antecedent circumstances; nonetheless, that we can form our own characters, *if we wish*, is for Mill sufficient for freedom of the will.[16]

In summary, Mill's scientism consists, above all, in his belief that all nature, including human nature and therefore man's social life, is governed by causal laws discoverable by induction and deduction. For all the caution and sophistication of his discussion of 'abstract' social sciences such as political economy, and for all his awareness of the limited validity of the latter's conclusions, nevertheless it is implicit in his position that, in principle, the laws of such a science must be derivable as special cases from universally applicable causal laws. Are the laws of human nature, in turn, ultimately derivable from physical laws? Mill considered this to be 'extremely probable', but not yet conclusively proved,[17] and to this extent his scientism (unlike that of Comte) is less than total. Laws of Mind, he claims, are discoverable in their own right, and are the proper basis of the moral sciences.

Some further features of Mill's particular brand of sociological scientism should be pointed out. First, it is notably *individualistic*: sociological laws are held to be deducible from Laws of Mind and of Ethology having reference to the motives, actions and characters of individuals. Second, it is unashamedly *mentalistic*: Mill shows no qualms whatever about the status of mental phenomena as objects of scientific study; indeed his fundamental laws of human nature are, precisely, Laws of Mind. What is more, it is clear from Mill's discussion of free will, of the roots of social change, and of political economy that he thinks of such mental contents as motives, desires and beliefs as causes like any others. Mill's mentalism, however, has been repudiated by later thinkers – notably the behaviourists – as 'unscientific'. Others, such as the Marxists and the French sociologist Emile Durkheim, no less scientistic than Mill, reject his individualism. Indeed, a thoroughgoing anti-individualism, such as Durkheim's, must entail rejection of mentalism in the normal sense (which is Mill's sense), since minds in the normal sense are attributes of individuals. Durkheim's anti-individualism, accordingly, goes along with a repudiation of Mill-style mentalism, the explicit grounds for which are similar to those of the behaviourists. We shall look briefly at the argument of Durkheim's *Rules of sociological method* (1893) as an alternative version – a positivist and collectivist version – of scientism.

According to Durkheim's famous dictum, the social scientist must 'consider social facts as things'.[18] By this he means that the scientist must take as his data only such phenomena as are objectively ascertainable by scientific observation; and further, that such 'things' can be grasped only 'in terms of their external qualities', perceived 'only through sense perception'. Durkheim claims that 'ideas', and the contents of consciousness generally, do not belong to this category, because they are not 'immediately given' to observation. Thus Mill was wrong, in Durkheim's view, to define political economy as those social facts resulting from the desire for wealth; since such desires are unobservable, their existence, and still more the causal efficacy attributed to them by Mill, are, says Durkheim, 'merely conjectures'.[19]

This anti-mentalism of Durkheim's quickly leads him to anti-individualism, or collectivism, for he believed that social facts 'lend themselves to objective representation in proportion as their separation from ... individual facts ... is more complete'.[20] Among such objective social facts are codes of law, social conventions, popular proverbs, social statistics – all of these are definite, objective, *social* (i.e. collective) realities which exist quite apart from individual actions and manifestations (Durkheim even claims that they 'can exist without being actually applied' by individuals).[21] From this an important conclusion about social causation follows for Durkheim, namely that social facts are not the product of the individual will; on the contrary 'they determine it from without'. To Durkheim, it is definitive of a social fact that it exerts a pressure for conformity on the individual; hence (contrary to Mill) sociology cannot be deduced from individual psychology. Social facts, Durkheim concludes, cannot be explained 'by states of the individual consciousness', but only by other social facts.[22] Durkheim does, however, agree with Mill that social facts are explicable in terms of deterministic causal laws.[23]

Wilhelm Dilthey and hermeneutics

The word *Geisteswissenschaften* was used by the German translator of J.S. Mill's *System of logic* to render Mill's term 'moral sciences'; nevertheless, it has come to connote an approach to the social sciences diametrically at odds with his, largely owing to its adoption by the philosopher and historian Wilhelm Dilthey (1833–1911).

Unlike that of Mill, Dilthey's philosophy of science is not set out in a single comprehensive book-length statement, nor was it unchanging throughout his life. However, his view of the nature of knowledge remained (in contrast to the scientistic monism of Mill and Durkheim) always dualistic, a dualism he expressed by the opposition between *Naturwissenschaften* and *Geisteswissenschaften*.[24] The social sciences, for Dilthey, belong in the latter category, in other words they are *not* (like) natural sciences. The term *Geisteswissenschaften* (usually translated as 'human studies') means literally 'sciences of mind'; and the literal translation is in some ways preferable, for it makes immediately clear Dilthey's total rejection of Durkheimian positivism. Mill, unlike Durkheim, agreed with Dilthey that the social sciences are sciences of mind, but held them to be none the less natural sciences for that; and this, for Dilthey, was his great error.[25]

The cardinal point, for Dilthey, is that the social sciences seek knowledge of the human world, that is, *our* world, which we know in a way different from our knowledge of non-human nature. That nature is essentially alien to us, and our knowledge of it, from sensory experience, is correspondingly external; as Dilthey graphically put it, our picture of nature is 'a shadow cast by a hidden reality'.[26] Natural science, then, is such a picture; lacking direct contact with ultimate physical reality, it offers knowledge that is necessarily hypothetical. It is also a schematic abstraction from experience dictated by its particular purposes – hence the scientific world-picture, that is, its subsumption of the world under highly general categories and universal necessary causal laws.[27] Dilthey's account does not intend to impugn the status of the physical sciences; on the contrary, given the nature of things, its hypothetical method is the only way to knowledge of the physical world, and its search for causal order therein has been brilliantly successful.

Nevertheless, it does not, in Dilthey's view, offer an appropriate model for the social sciences, and for several reasons. First, the human world is one that we know as it were from the inside, immediately, from 'lived experience' (*Erlebnis*), by contrast with the external experience (*Erfahrung*) that we have of the physical world. It is not an alien, mechanical world, but a world suffused with meaning and values – values which we can in principle share, and even if we do not share them, we can understand them, empathise with them. Whereas the physical scientist seeks to *explain* (*erklären*) by subsuming particulars under general laws, the practitioner of the human sciences should seek to *understand* (*verstehen*) the phenomena of the human world as the works and actions of men and women essentially like himself, the expression of *minds* essentially like his own.[28] Understanding phenomena as expressions of mind (*Geist*) is not like explaining them as the effect of causes, and the human world is not to be understood as a deterministic causal order of necessary uniformities such as natural science has constructed to describe the physical world. Rather, the workings of mind are *purposive* (unlike those of blind physical causality), *free* (at least within limits) of the trammels of necessity, and hence genuinely *creative* (whereas, Dilthey believed, physical change is simply a rearrangement of existing elements).[29]

Dilthey did not mean to ban all generalisation from the human sciences of mind; he accepted its validity in the 'systematic' human sciences such as sociology and economics – what we would call the social sciences.[30] Even there, however, the appropriate generalisations are only rough regularities and patterns, not strict universal laws: for Dilthey, unlike Mill, human freedom makes a radical difference here. The human sciences, wrote Dilthey, can discover regularities that have held in the past, but '[their] validity is historically limited: [they] can never bind or determine ... what may appear in the future'. In this sense the human sciences are historical, and 'History does not cause, it creates' – and therefore, it is unpredictable.[31] The affinities of the (systematic) social sciences lie, in Dilthey's view, not with the natural sciences, but with the human sciences in general, which in the English sense of the word are not necessarily sciences at all – such disciplines as history, linguistics, philosophy, jurisprudence, as well as the study of religion, literature, poetry and architecture.[32] All of these disciplines equally contribute to what, in Dilthey's view, is the task of all the human sciences, including the social sciences, namely to understand human life and the human mind in all their varied manifestations.

Among the human sciences, according to Dilthey, is the science of psychology; and Dilthey's view of this science makes an instructive contrast with Mill.[33] At one stage Dilthey, like Mill, considered psychology to be the fundamental human science – a view he later abandoned. But unlike Mill he never considered that it should be a natural science of causal laws modelled on mechanics – rather, it should be descriptive, analytical and comparative, seeking to discover typical psychic structures and patterns, not by the experimental methods of a natural science, but rather by the study of human history, and of writers and philosophers such as Augustine, Montaigne and Pascal whose works give insight into human character. The psychology of associationism, endorsed by Mill (see above), Dilthey repudiated on the grounds that it considers perceptions as related in terms only of physical contiguity, not *meaning*: hence it treats 'only the form of mental process ... the fundamental power of mental life falls outside its scope'.[34] For the same reason Dilthey rejected out of hand any possibility of deriving human psychology from physiology.[35]

For Dilthey, all the human studies – including both social sciences and humanities – have essentially similar subject-matter and a common characteristic method: their method is understanding (*Verstehen*), and their subject-matter is what Dilthey termed *expressions of mind*, or the mind-created world.[36] Such expressions are objictifications of mind, perceptible to the senses but not understandable in terms of pure sense-perception; understanding means grasping the relation of an expression to what it expresses, that is, seeing it as the physical expression of some mental state. 'Understanding penetrates the observable facts of human history to reach what is not accessible to the senses and yet affects external facts and expresses itself through them.'[37] Among the expressions or objectifications of mind, to be grasped by the method of understanding, are individual gestures, words and actions, as well as social institutions, customs, language, states, churches, legal systems, tools, books, works of art, and so on. Thus the apparatus of a legal system, 'law-books, judges, litigants, defendants, at a particular time and place is, first of all, the expression of a purposive system of laws', and is to be understood by going behind this apparatus to the 'intellectual system of legal imperatives' which it manifests.[38] The human studies require a special methodology because mankind (unlike other animals) has 'reached the stage in which concepts, valuations, realisation of purposes ... occur', and shape its life.[39]

Among the objective expressions of mind which are the object of the human studies, one kind was for Dilthey paradigmatic – namely language or, more specifically, its permanent form, written texts. 'In language alone human inwardness finds its complete, exhaustive and objectively comprehensible expression ... The art of understanding therefore centres on the *interpretation of written records of human existence*.'[40] The methodology of textual interpretation (*Auslegung*) – namely hermeneutics – was therefore proposed by Dilthey as the basis or model for understanding in the human sciences generally; as one modern follower of Dilthey has put it, social phenomena generally should be treated *as if* they were texts to be interpreted.[41] This view followed, no doubt, from Dilthey's conception of the mind-created world as essentially meaningful, together with the obvious fact that language is the bearer of meaning *par excellence*. Nevertheless the scope for a hermeneutic methodology for the human sciences seems more limited, the analogy between language and other 'expressions' of mind weaker than Dilthey supposed; linguistic elements do not just express but *have* a meaning, by convention, in a way that is not generally true, for example, of non-linguistic actions. Dilthey's hermeneutic methodology took him down some questionable paths.

Perhaps Dilthey's major specific application to the human sciences of his hermeneutic methodology concerns the relation of part and whole. The parts of a text have a meaningful relation to each other, so that the text is a meaningful whole, understandable in a sense that has nothing to do with the relation of cause and effect. This is connected with the so-called hermeneutic circle, the fact that in the interpretation of a problematic text the meaning of the whole depends on the meaning of the parts, yet the parts cannot be fully understood except within the context of the whole – hence adequate understanding requires what has been called a shuttling to and fro between parts and whole as focus of the investigator's attention.[42] Something similar applies, Dilthey suggests, to the systems studied by the social scientist. This suggestion seems more fruitful in some branches of social science than others. It is best suited to descriptive analysis (such as historians and anthropologists may seek) of institutions which, like texts, are indeed expressions of ideas – for example, systems of law and advanced religions. By contrast, in other areas and kinds of social science the hermeneutic analogy and the hermeneutic circle in particular seem unhelpful, especially in the realm of social *theory*. The hermeneutic methodology casts very little light – much less than Mill's scientism – on, for example, theoretical economics.

It may, indeed, be objected that Dilthey's hermeneutic methodology leads him into a position that is unduly holistic – for the analogy of the hermeneutic circle implies that nothing can be understood except as part of a larger whole. As Dilthey wrote: 'Each [expression of life] is a whole with parts and a part of a whole ... It is significant, through this double relationship, as a link in the greater whole'; likewise, 'every action, every thought, every common activity, in short, every part of [a] historical whole has its significance through its relationship to the whole of the epoch'.[43] This holism, arguably, is inherently hostile to theory in social science, or at least one kind of theory – the kind that Mill called abstract (for instance, political economy) – for abstract theory depends precisely on treating certain limited areas of social life in detachment from the rest of society.

Beyond this, Dilthey's hermeneutic methodology – or at least the way he applied it – appears to fall into equivocation as to the meaning of 'meaning'. This is exemplified by his doctrine of *Besser-*

Verstehen, that is, the notion that (in the words of a recent commentator) 'The interpreter can understand the author of a work (or agent of an action) better' than the author or agent understands himself.[44] Dilthey is explicit that the meaning of an expression is not deducible from its author's or agent's *intention*: an expression is an 'objective' and enduring phenomenon that can legitimately be understood in contexts unknown to its author. Perhaps so; but Dilthey's account seems to conflate three different senses of 'meaning'. First, there is 'meaning' in the strictly semantic sense, a sense that depends on linguistic conventions current among some relevant language-using group. Second, there is what may be called the 'historical significance' or influence of expressions (which, in the case of linguistic expressions, includes later interpretations of their meaning in the semantic sense, possibly different from their authors'). But third, there is the author's *own* meaning, which is hard to understand better than the author, since understanding here is precisely understanding of what was in the author's mind. Roughly speaking, the author's meaning corresponds to the meaning of his text to the extent that the latter's conventional meaning matches what he intended to convey (this may fail to be the case where, for example, the text is obscure or corrupt as well as for subtler reasons). In other words, the author's intention *is* crucial here, *pace* Dilthey.

In the case of actions the agent's intention is likewise crucial to understanding, since presumably that which an action expresses is, precisely, the agent's intention. More precisely, the agent's intention is crucial if we wish to understand *why* he acted as he did, as distinct from *what* action he performed. Thus, an agent might be said to have voted, if he went through certain performances conventionally defined as voting, even although he had no intention to vote (and thus did not know what he was doing). But if we want to understand (in anything like Dilthey's sense) *why* he voted as he did, we must discover whether he had some intention in voting, and if so what. This crucial distinction, between 'understanding why' and 'understanding what', tends to be effaced in Dilthey's quasi-hermeneutical focus on the 'meaning' of actions.

In summary, it seems essential to distinguish Dilthey's general methodology of *Verstehen* from his specifically hermeneutic version of it. The latter is by no means universally applicable, but the former is a valuable corrective to Mill's, and still more to Durkheim's, scientism, through its emphasis on the special character of mind, and the human world as a mind-created world. It found fruitful application in the methodology of Max Weber.

Max Weber and *Verstehen*

The methodological position of the German sociologist Max Weber (1864–1920), as set out in the opening section of his posthumously published *magnum opus*, *Wirtschaft und Gesellschaft*, can be seen as a careful and judicious blend of elements of Mill's scientism and Dilthey's conception of *Geisteswissenschaft*. Weber agrees with Dilthey that there is a radical difference between the social and natural sciences; the former 'can accomplish something that is never attainable in the natural sciences',[45] namely subjective understanding of their object, human action, whereas the objects studied by natural science cannot be so understood, but only observed, and explained in terms of causal uniformities generalised from observation. Hence – contrary to Mill – social science cannot be derived from any natural science, such as psychology.[46] But it does not follow that the concept of causation is inapplicable to the social sciences, as Weber makes clear in his celebrated definition of 'sociology' as 'a science which attempts the interpretive understanding of social action in order thereby to arrive at a causal explanation of its course and effects'.[47] In Weber's view of social science, causal explanation and interpretive understanding go hand in hand.

Weber accepted Dilthey's dictum that the object of study in the social sciences is meaningful human behaviour or action, but he departed from Dilthey in two important and connected ways. First, for Weber, the 'meaning' that is central for the social scientist is the *subjectively intended* meaning of the acting individual – in other words, the individual's motive for acting. Thus there is no question of the scientist understanding the 'meaning' of an agent's action better than the agent himself, by viewing it in some wider context. Second, Weber, unlike Dilthey, made a clear distinction between 'direct understanding' (*aktuelles Verstehen*), for example understanding the utterance of the proposition $2 \times 2 = 4$ or the action of pointing a gun at an animal, and 'explanatory understanding' (*erklärendes Verstehen*), that is, understanding a person's *motive* in so acting.[48] Weber's very use of the phrase *erklärendes Verstehen*, uniting two terms Dilthey had contrasted, marks his difference from as well as his debt to the latter. It should also be noted that Weber's interpretive methodology, unlike Dilthey's, is resolutely individualist – only individuals are bearers of subjective meaning, and while social collectivities may often legitimately be treated 'as if' they were individuals, in Weber's view their 'actions' are '*solely* the resultants and modes of organisation of individual persons'.[49] This methodological individualism assimilates Weber to Mill.

For Weber, the central task of the social sciences is, precisely, to seek explanatory understanding. Action must be, at one and the same time, understood as meaningful and causally explained. Here the concept of motive is crucial, for the motive for an action in Weber's view *both* renders it understandable (or meaningful) and is (as Mill had held) a cause of it: 'A correct causal interpretation of a concrete course of action is arrived at when the overt action and the motives have both been correctly apprehended and at the same time their relation has become meaningfully comprehensible.'[50] But social science (in contrast to history) is concerned not with particular actions as such, but with regularities of action or, as Weber puts it, typical actions – regularities which can contribute to the causal explanation of the particular actions and events that are of interest to the historian.[51] Such explanations are, Weber says, subject to a dual requirement: they must be referred to motives that make them intelligible, and there must be evidence that the imputed motives were actually causally operative in the given case. The regularities educed by social science can satisfy both requirements. If they connect phenomena in a way that is intelligible in terms of typical individual motivation, they satisfy the requirement of 'adequacy at the level of meaning'; at the same time, if they conform to 'established generalisations from experience', they provide evidence that the motives do typically operate as assumed, so that the occurrence of the *explicandum* was, given the circumstances, at least probable. This inductively grounded probability, Weber says, confers on the explanation the necessary 'causal adequacy'. (Weber's terminology here is somewhat confusing since it appears that this 'causal adequacy' is not, in his view, the only or even the best evidence conceivable for the causal efficacy of imputed motives. It is, however, the specifically *sociological* form of such evidence.) Weber is emphatic that, from a sociological point of view, neither regularity nor intelligibility is alone sufficient, but both are necessary: 'If adequacy in respect to meaning is lacking, then no matter how high the degree of uniformity and how precisely its probability can be numerically determined, it is still an incomprehensible statistical probability.' As an example of a regularity which is both intelligible and well confirmed by experience, Weber cited Gresham's Law, which states that 'bad money drives out good'.[52]

Weber's twin requirements for sociological generalisations – intelligibility and empirical evidence – are at first sight reminiscent of Mill's twofold methodology of deduction (from laws of human nature) and verification, especially in view of the fact that for Mill, as we saw, 'verification' can come first, and the deduction need not be (often cannot be) strict. However, there are also differences. There is, for example, no real analogue in Weber's methodology to Mill's 'concrete deduction', which attempts to derive the implications of several interacting kinds of motive. Instead, Weber proposed a general methodology which is more like the 'abstract deduction' limited by Mill to the 'special' social sciences. For Weber, the sociologist must seek to understand the action he studies; but, as he admits, this is easiest when action is *rational*, that is, when it takes the form of choosing appropriate means to a given end, or acting in conformity to a clear principle. Sociological theorising, in Weber's view, should take the form of constructing *ideal types*, 'purified' models of action perfectly appropriate to a given end or principle, and he cited as an example economic theory (of which Gresham's Law is a part) just as Mill cited political economy as an abstract social science.[53] Weber's ideal type methodology agrees with Mill's that such a theory cannot correspond perfectly to reality, and corresponds approximately only in certain cases. But, unlike Mill, Weber did not suppose that the limited 'abstract' theories should in principle all be derivable from fundamental psychological laws of universal validity. Rather, he saw them as fated to remain forever approximate generalisations useful for explaining concrete phenomena, not only by subsuming them (where this is possible), but equally by alerting the investigator to look for *other* factors to explain deviations from them. Weber's position on the possibilities of sociological generalisation was thus closer to Dilthey than to Mill.

One reason for this was his view of the relevance of value-judgements to the social sciences. According to Weber (here clearly influenced by the neo-Kantian philosopher Heinrich Rickert), scientific study of the historico-social world, by contrast with the natural sciences, stems from our interest in its 'cultural significance'. As Weber writes, 'the significance of cultural events presupposes a *value-orientation* towards these events. The concept of culture is a *value-concept*.'[54] We wish (in this sphere) to understand and explain that which is of interest to us in the light of our values; a 'focus of attention' which is quite different from the reduction of reality to laws. Thus, for Weber, in social science not only the selection of problems and the formation of concepts, but also generalisation and the construction of theories (such as ideal typical theories) must be guided by cultural interests and hence by evaluations. Weber concluded (here departing radically from Rickert) that there can be no definitive concepts or theories in social science, simply because judgements of value and hence of cultural significance are not definitive, but vary from one investigator to another. Put simply, different people are interested in different aspects of the socio-historical world.[55]

However, this does *not* mean that the *truth* of propositions in the social sciences is in any way relative to or dependent on value-judgements. On the contrary, Weber firmly maintained that the propositions of all science are, by definition, factual propositions subject to critical assessment in terms of universal canons of relevant evidence and logical reasoning. Science can give no knowledge of ultimate values. Social science concepts, though *reflecting* evaluative judgements of cultural significance, should not themselves *be* evaluative, nor should they blur through vagueness the crucial fact–value distinction (Weber instanced as objectionable on this score such concepts as 'adaptation' and 'progress'). In this sense, social science should be, indeed must be, value-free (*wertfrei*).[56]

Peter Winch: society, language and value

In recent years, the notion of 'meaningfulness' as central to the human (and social) sciences, which originally stemmed from the tradition of German idealism, has been developed in a new – and controversial – way by the British philosopher Peter Winch. In *The idea of a social science* (1958), Winch broadly adopts Weber's view that action has to be understood in terms of the subjectively intended 'meaning' of the agent, but in the case of 'explanatory understanding' he prefers to speak of the agent's *reason* for acting rather than his motive. The difference is not in itself material, but it leads Winch into further analysis. If a man voted Labour 'because he thought that a Labour government would be most likely to preserve industrial peace', then it necessarily follows that he possessed the *concepts* of 'a Labour government', 'industrial peace', and so on.[57] In general, any meaningful explanation must, in the reasons or purposes it attributes to agents, attribute to *them* the understanding of the relevant concepts. But the understanding of concepts is not simply a fact about an individual, for concepts belong to *language*, and language (as Winch holds, following Wittgenstein) is inherently *social*: 'the very existence of concepts depends on group life'.[58] Winch's point is that the meaning of a concept depends on *rules* governing its applicability to particular cases – rules that determine which particulars fall under 'the same' general concept – and that these rules are necessarily embodied in the actual practice of some relevant social group.[59] An agent understands a concept only if he understands how it is applied by such a group. In sum, 'meaningful' explanation turns out to depend on the understanding of meaning in the narrower linguistic sense, and understanding this meaning involves understanding certain social practices. If this is so, social science could be said to be after all hermeneutic, if not quite in Dilthey's sense – to explain actions one must know the meaning of concepts used by relevant social groups.

Winch presses his analysis further. While the explanations offered by social scientists may legitimately use concepts unknown to those whose actions they explain, still the explanatory concepts must be 'logically tied' to concepts familiar to the latter – as, for example, the economist's concept of 'liquidity preference' is tied to such businessmen's concepts as money, profit and risk.[60] More stringent conclusions are drawn by Winch in relation to social scientific *description*. Such description requires a language, but social scientists are not free to construct a scientific language in the way that natural scientists are: rather, scientific language must here follow the meanings inherent in the social life studied. This life, and the concepts embedded in it, embody rules or criteria of identity which the social scientist must respect. The sociologist of religion, for example, can decide that two acts are of the same kind – perhaps, that both are 'prayers' – only if he understands what a prayer is. But 'prayer' is a *religious* concept; hence the sociologist's concepts are given to him in advance by the form of social life that he studies. If the sociologist chose to reclassify the phenomena in some different way he would rob them of their meaning as social phenomena. 'It is not open to him arbitrarily to impose his own standards from without.'[61]

From this, Winch has drawn two controversial conclusions. First, since the meaning of legitimate sociological concepts derives from the part they play in the practice of particular social groups, *cross-cultural concepts* in the social sciences (i.e. concepts purporting to subsume phenomena occurring in different cultures) are highly suspect if not, indeed, inadmissible – whence the same must apply to 'the claim that there are sociological uniformities' across cultures. For example, the Italian sociologist Vilfredo Pareto was, according to Winch, guilty of intellectual 'philistinism' in supposing that the Christian rite of baptism belongs in the same category as pagan purification rites using lustral water – that both can be treated as manifestations of a 'vague feeling that water somehow cleanses moral as well as material pollution'. On the contrary, the true nature of baptism and of lustral rites depends on their place in, respectively, Christian and pagan social practices and ideas, which are quite different.[62]

Even more controversially, Winch has argued that no whole social practice can ever be condemned as irrational or illogical – for the concepts 'rational' and 'irrational' also derive their meaning from the practices of specific groups, in other words, standards of rationality inhere in, and are relative to, these practices:

> Criteria of logic ... arise out of, and are only intelligible in the context of, ways of living or modes of social life ... For instance, science is one such mode and religion is another; and each has criteria of intelligibility peculiar to itself. So within science or religion actions can be logical or illogical ... But we cannot say that either the practice of science itself or that of religion is either illogical or logical.[63]

Since science seeks knowledge of the (natural) world, and religion seeks knowledge of God, it might be thought that the rationality of these pursuits depends on whether the natural world, and God, objectively exist. According to Winch, such questions cannot arise: the meaning of such fundamental terms is revealed by the social practices of those who use them, not externally. In that sense, they cannot but be used correctly in these practices. Similarly, and famously, Winch has argued that witchcraft beliefs such as those (once?) held by the Azande tribesmen of the Sudan (or any other 'primitive' culture) cannot be fundamentally irrational or mistaken – for the meaning of 'witchcraft' among the Azande is given by the part the concept plays in their social practices.[64]

To this, there seems an obvious objection, namely that the belief in 'witchcraft' involves certain *causal* claims, whose truth can scarcely depend on the way of life of the Azande or anyone else. What is more, their truth has important *moral* implications (as to how the 'witches' may be treated). Winch has, in fact, moved to an extreme sociological idealism, in which not only *meaning* but *truth* depend on social practices. For him there is no such thing as an objective world independent of such practices and the conceptualisations and belief systems that develop therein. As he himself put it in a much-quoted passage, 'Reality is not what gives language sense. What is real and what is unreal shows itself *in* the sense language has.'[65] Winch's philosophy is also profoundly conservative, or at least anti-critical, in its implications – every functioning way of life is seen as self-validating, and genuine understanding of any social form *ipso facto* immunises it against one major (but misguided) type of criticism. This view contrasts starkly with Max Weber's doctrine that sociological knowledge cannot settle any evaluative question.

Critical theory

If Winch's Wittgensteinian idealism calls for an uncritical attitude to social institutions, quite the reverse is true of another school of thought that stands in the tradition of German idealism stemming from Kant and Hegel (and by which Dilthey too was influenced); namely the exponents of 'critical theory', associated with the Frankfurt Institute of Social Research (the 'Frankfurt School') after Max Horkheimer became its director in 1930. Besides Horkheimer, the major representatives of critical theory include his contemporaries Theodor Adorno and Herbert Marcuse, and Jürgen Habermas, who is now the leading spokesman of the school.

Habermas' philosophy of social science shows a clear debt to Dilthey and his distinction between *Naturwissenschaften* and *Geisteswissenschaften*, while at the same time holding it to be insufficient – insufficient in both a philosophical and a political sense. Like that of the Frankfurt School as a whole, Habermas' is a recognisably idealist philosophy, but an idealism of a somewhat unusual brand, being strongly influenced by the social and political analyses of the materialist Karl Marx, which are, so to speak, translated into philosophical and methodological terms. The fight against 'positivism' and 'scientism' in the social sciences becomes for Habermas as for his Frankfurt predecessors a form of political struggle.

Central to Habermas' argument is the doctrine that human knowledge ('science') is never a mere mirroring of reality, but is always constituted by specific interests (cf. his *Knowledge and human interests*, 1968). These knowledge-constitutive human interests guide the selection of 'truths' and govern the form in which they are presented as knowledge. Thus, the natural sciences grasp reality from a particular point of view, namely the interest of mankind in *technical control* of nature. Natural science takes the form of empirical causal laws, not just because these laws correspond to reality, but because they enable us to predict and control natural events – to use nature as means to our ends.[66] This is a view not much different from Dilthey's.[67]

Again like Dilthey, Habermas and other Frankfurt theorists see natural science, thus understood, as a misleading model for the human sciences, but not merely misleading – also deplorable in its political consequences. As Habermas has put it: 'The positivist self-understanding of the nomological sciences lends countenance to the substitution of technology for enlightened action.'[68] This seems to mean at least two things. First, nomological knowledge is so structured as to yield mastery of its object

799

(technology); and while mastery over nature may be morally unexceptionable, mastery over human beings is not: such mastery is manipulation, domination and repression. What Habermas calls the 'technocratic consciousness' seeks 'to bring society under control in the same way as nature', by means of, for example, techniques of propaganda, indoctrination, drugs and even genetic intervention, turning man from *homo faber* to *homo fabricatus*; and this serves 'a *particular class's* interest in domination'.[69] A science structured for domination must serve the interest of the dominant social class. In similar vein, Marcuse has diagnosed 'scientific management', industrial sociology, motivation research, marketing science and public opinion studies as tools of 'advanced capitalism'.[70] In addition, critical theorists object to the positivistic exclusion of value-judgements from the realm of scientific knowledge (cf. Max Weber above); this undermines critical opposition to existing structures of domination, and indeed drives all public discussion of 'the good life' out of politics, which becomes instead a matter of the 'scientific' solution of technical problems by 'experts'. The 'expertise' of social and other scientists (especially perhaps economists) has come to serve as a legitimation, and even a mask, for the exercise of power by dominant groups. In this sense, as Habermas puts it, 'technology and science . . . take on the role of an ideology'.[71]

Habermas is again close to Dilthey when he identifies a second form of knowledge (besides nomological knowledge of nature) answering to a second knowledge-constitutive human interest: the *historical-hermeneutic* sciences, which respond to and are shaped by the so-called 'practical' interest.[72] By this term Habermas means the need interacting individuals have to understand one another so that they can function effectively as social agents – a kind of knowledge structurally different from the knowledge men need to have of physical nature. For Habermas, sciences of 'interpretative understanding' are basically an extrapolation of this kind of knowledge: even when the anthropologist or historian seeks knowledge of societies or agents with whom he has (and perhaps can have) no interaction, nevertheless the understanding sought is of a type that could in principle facilitate such interaction. 'Hermeneutic enquiry discloses reality subject to a constitutive interest in the preservation and expansion of possible action-orienting mutual understanding.'[73] Clearly the historical-hermeneutic sciences are, by definition, social or at least human sciences. Nevertheless, for Habermas, in contrast to Dilthey, they too offer an inadequate model for social theory as a whole. This is because knowledge structured by the 'practical' interest is a partial and one-sided kind of knowledge: if it is knowledge of a kind that enables a social agent to function in society, it cannot go very deep, for example it cannot explain why society is as it is. Its understanding of society remains limited to society's own understanding of itself. This, perhaps, is roughly the uncritical social science endorsed by Winch – but not by Habermas.

What, then, is the proper path for social theory? Habermas does not totally reject either the nomological or the historical-hermeneutic model in this sphere, but he holds that, as soon as one becomes aware of their true nature, one must immediately realise their insufficiency. There is a place for 'systematic sciences of social action' (economics, sociology, political science) which aim at 'nomological knowledge'. But the regularities embodied in such sciences may be of two types: 'invariant regularities of social action as such', and those which express 'relations of dependence that can in principle be transformed'.[74] The latter, presumably, are relations of domination and subjection such as result from the application to society of knowledge structured by the interest in control. These regularities may appear to be a manifestation of impersonal causal necessity, but in fact they result from the exercise of social power. Thus 'they can in principle be transformed'. The belief that they are invariant laws, like laws of nature, is thus an error, and indeed an error which serves to preserve the power structures that sustain them. (Examples might be the belief that social inequality is inevitable, or that inequality of rewards is necessary for economic efficiency.) Such beliefs are called by Habermas, following Marx, ideologies.[75] There is thus, for Habermas, an intimate connection between repressive power structures and the prevalence of systematically false (or distorted) beliefs – and this is the feature of social life which is missed by 'historical-hermeneutic' science, which understands a society on its own terms, does not question its beliefs, and thus cannot explain them.

Analysis such as the above, says Habermas, stems from 'self-reflection' and constitutes what he and his Frankfurt forerunners call 'critical theory'. The unmasking of repression and distorted belief is no 'value-free' social science, but stems from a specific cognitive interest (different from either the technical or the practical), namely the interest in emancipation (or, simply, freedom).[76] To see social structures in their true colours as repressive and alterable is to *make* them alterable, when otherwise they might not be. There is here a peculiar instance of the more general sociological phenomenon of the self-fulfilling prophecy. As Habermas stresses, the alterability of social structures due to critical theory results from the self-awareness that social subjects gain from it, not from the authoritative application of technical nomological knowledge to society.

Notwithstanding this, some aspects of Habermas' analysis seem questionable, for example his understanding of 'value-free' social science and the 'emancipatory' cognitive interest. It is highly dubious whether the latter, like the technical and practical interests, represents an inherent general necessity of human life, rather than a specific ideal, however noble. And if the latter is true, emancipation is a social goal, to which it would seem reasonable to seek appropriate means. But knowledge of means–ends relations is precisely what Habermas calls technical knowledge and is, indeed, value-free, even though the end is valued and perhaps valuable (that is, it is equally true, regardless of whether one values the end or not). Habermas' argument shows only that social theory must be *guided* by values, or 'value-relevant' (*wertbeziehend*) – a view fully accepted by Max Weber, and quite compatible with his other doctrine, of value-free social science. Whatever the weaknesses overall of the positivist or scientistic position, that part of it seems still to stand unrefuted.

Notes

(An author's name followed by a number in square brackets refers to the book or article which has that number in the bibliography.)

1. Fletcher [1], pp. 57–8.
2. Ibid., p. 61.
3. Ibid., p. 96.
4. Ibid., p. 54.
5. Ibid., pp. 66–9, 71.
6. Ibid., pp. 75–9.
7. Ibid., pp. 102f.
8. Ibid., pp. 107f.
9. Ibid., pp. 117f.
10. Ibid., pp. 131f, 152.
11. Ibid., pp. 157f.
12. Ibid., p. 155.
13. Ibid., pp. 164f, 151f.
14. Ibid., pp. 169–70, 175f.
15. Ibid., p. 184.
16. Ibid., pp. 95–100.
17. Ibid., p. 109.
18. Durkheim [2], Ch. 2, esp. pp. 14, 27, 42–3.
19. Ibid., pp. 23–4.
20. Ibid., p. 44.
21. Ibid., pp. 2–3, 7–8, 30.
22. Ibid., pp. 101–10.
23. Ibid., Ch. 6.
24. Cf. Ermarth [4], pp. 94–6.
25. Rickman [3], p. 161.
26. Ibid.
27. Ermarth [4], pp. 96–100, 306–8; Rickman [3], p. 172.
28. Ermarth [4], pp. 97, 246; Rickman [3], pp. 182–6.
29. Rickman [3], pp. 172–82; Ermarth [4], pp. 306–8.
30. Ermarth [4], pp. 263–6, 293, 298–9, 304–6; Rickman [3], pp. 171, 205.
31. Ermarth [4], p. 308.
32. Rickman [3], p. 170; Ermarth [4], p. 95.
33. Ermarth [4], pp. 141–8, 169–78; Rickman [3], pp. 87f.
34. Ermarth [4], p. 148.
35. Ibid., p. 171.
36. Rickman [3], pp. 173–6, 190–4, 208, 218–21, 229–30; Ermarth [4], p. 181;

Makkrell [5], pp. 247–51.

37. Rickman [3], p. 173.
38. Ibid., p. 174.
39. Ibid., p. 173.
40. Ibid., p. 249.
41. Ibid., pp. 10, 228, 246–9, 260–1; Ermarth [4], pp. 234, 244–5, 249, 277–8; Makkrell [5], pp. 255f.
42. Rickman [3], pp. 10, 237, 259, 262.
43. Ibid., pp. 240, 198; cf. also pp. 233–8.
44. Ermarth [4], p. 276.
45. Weber [6], p. 103.
46. Ibid., p. 108.
47. Ibid., p. 88.
48. Ibid., pp. 89f, 94–5.
49. Ibid., p. 101.
50. Ibid., p. 99.
51. Ibid., p. 109.
52. Ibid., pp. 96–100, 107–8.
53. Ibid., pp. 91–2, 99–100, 109–12.
54. Weber [7], p. 76.
55. Ibid., pp. 76–81, 84.
56. Ibid., Ch. 1, p. 84.
57. Winch [8], pp. 45–7.
58. Ibid., pp. 43–4.
59. Ibid., pp. 25–33, 51–2.
60. Ibid., p. 89.
61. Ibid., pp. 86–8, 108.
62. Ibid., pp. 103–9.
63. Ibid., p. 100.
64. P. Winch, 'Understanding a primitive society' in Wilson [9], pp. 78–111.
65. Ibid., p. 82.
66. Habermas [10], pp. 191–7, 307–9.
67. Rickman [3], p. 172.
68. Habermas [10], p. 316.
69. Habermas [11], pp. 106–7, 111, 117.
70. Marcuse [12], pp. 34, 93, 121 and Ch. 6 generally.
71. Ibid., p. 123; Habermas [11], pp. 99–104.
72. Habermas [10], pp. 175–6, 192–5, 309–10.
73. Ibid., p. 310.
74. Ibid., pp. 212, 310–12.
75. Ibid., pp. 62–3, 310; Habermas [11], p. 112.
76. Habermas [10], pp. 197–8, 210–12, 287–9, 303–4, 310–12, 314–17.

Bibliography

The portions of Mill's *System of logic* which bear upon the social sciences have been combined with extracts from his *Principles of political economy* and other books, essays and letters in

[1] *John Stuart Mill: a logical critique of sociology*, ed. Ronald Fletcher (Michael Joseph, London, 1971). Representative writings by those of Mill's contemporaries, who contributed to the development of a scientific approach to society, have been gathered in the following books: *The essential Comte*, ed. Stanislav Andreski, trans. Margaret Clarke (Croom Helm, London, 1974); *Karl Marx: selected writings in sociology and social philosophy*, ed. T.B. Bottomore and M. Rubel (Penguin Books, Harmondsworth, 1963); *Herbert Spencer*, ed. Stanislav Andreski (Michael Joseph, London, 1971).

Emile Durkheim's *Suicide, a study in sociology*, trans. J.A. Spaulding and George Simpson (Routledge and Kegan Paul, London, 1952) is widely treated as a model (adequate or inadequate, depending on one's viewpoint) of what a scientific theory of a social phenomenon should be. Durkheim's own understanding of the task and methods of sociology is set out in

[2] *The rules of sociological method*, ed. George E.G. Catlin, trans. Sarah A. Solovay and John H. Mueller (The Free Press, New York, 1964). Steven Lukes, *Durkheim* (Allen Lane, The Penguin Press, London, 1973) contains a thorough account of Durkheim as a social theorist and scientific methodologist.

It is instructive to compare Durkheim's position with his American contemporary, George Herbert Mead. A self-styled 'social behaviorist', Mead was anti-individualist and anti-mentalist, but in a less severe way than was Durkheim because he accepted the possibility of new phenomena 'emerging' in nature. This left Mead free to reject the demand that social phenomena be explicable *entirely* in terms of deterministic causal laws. The best of Mead's published papers appear in *Selected writings, George Herbert Mead*, ed. Andrew J. Reck (University of Chicago Press, Chicago, 1981). Mead's lectures and unpublished papers appeared posthumously in three volumes. The one most relevant to the concerns of this chapter is *Mind, self and society*, ed. Charles W. Morris (University of Chicago Press, Chicago, 1934).

Dilthey's dualism with respect to human understanding had an early eighteenth-century forerunner in *The new science* (i.e. of what man has made) by Giambattista Vico. Vico claimed that man is better able to understand his own productions (including mathematics and social institutions) than he is able to comprehend nature. For a sample of Vico's work in English see *Vico, selected writings*, ed. and trans. Leon Pompa (Cambridge University Press, Cambridge, 1982). For valuable essays on the significance of Vico and that of another figure, Johann Gottfried Herder, who contributed to the idea that human society requires an approach quite unlike that required to understand the natural world, see Isaiah Berlin, *Vico and Herder* (Hogarth Press, London, 1976).

Dilthey's work appears in English in

[3] H.P. Rickman (ed.), *Dilthey: selected writings* (Cambridge University Press, Cambridge, 1976). For a fuller exposition of Dilthey's thought see

[4] M. Ermarth, *Wilhelm Dilthey: the critique of historical reason* (University of Chicago Press, Chicago, 1978) or

[5] R.A. Makkrell, *Dilthey: philosopher of the human studies* (Princeton University Press, Princeton, 1975).

Dilthey not only gave a clear expression to a methodological outlook which had been taking shape well before his time; he shaped subsequent thinking about correct procedure in the human sciences. A book edited by Kurt Mueller-Vollmer, *The hermeneutics reader* (Basil Blackwell, Oxford, 1986) provides a selection of translations of texts of the German tradition in hermeneutics from both before and after Dilthey, as well as a historical survey of that tradition. For an account of how 'the challenge of hermeneutics' was met by social theorists from Marx (before Dilthey) and Weber (who knew Dilthey's work) to Talcott Parsons and Martin Heidegger, see Zygmunt Bauman, *Hermeneutics and social science, approaches to understanding* (Hutchinson, London, 1978). Hans Georg Gadamer is just one example from a long list of (largely continental) philosophers who regard hermeneutic method as central to any adequate philosophy. See *Truth and method* (Sheed and Ward, London, 1975). A book by Richard Bernstein, *Beyond objectivism and relativism* (Basil Blackwell, Oxford, 1983) introduces recent developments in this tradition with special reference to Gadamer and Habermas.

A substantial portion of Weber's *Wirtschaft und Gesellschaft* appears in English in

[6] *The theory of social and economic organization*, ed. Talcott Parsons, trans. A.M. Henderson and Talcott Parsons (The Free Press, New York, 1947). Three lengthy essays by Weber on methodology, paying particular attention to the role of values and neutrality, appear in

[7] *The methodology of the social sciences*, ed. and trans. Edward A. Shils and Henry A. Finch (The Free Press, New York, 1949). A criticism of Weber's view of the role of values in social science appears in G. Myrdal, *Objectivity in social research* (Duckworth, London, 1970).

The focus of debate about the nature of the social sciences among analytical philosophers has, since its publication, been

[8] Peter Winch, *The idea of a social science* (Routledge and Kegan Paul, London, 1958). One consequence of this debate has been the way philosophers and sociologists have been drawn into a discussion of human rationality and whether this concept is culture relative. An important collection of essays taking its bearings from a selection from [8] and including a further essay by Winch is

[9] Bryan R. Wilson (ed.), *Rationality* (Basil Blackwell, Oxford, 1970). The debate continued and a collection takings its bearings from [9] and representing the state of play twelve years later is Martin Hollis and Steven Lukes (eds), *Rationality and relativism* (Basil Blackwell, Oxford, 1982).

R. Harré and P.F. Secord in *The explanation of social behaviour* (Basil Blackwell, Oxford, 1972) defend the possibility of a scientific study of man within the general conceptual framework (human beings in their social behaviour are rule-following agents) laid down in [8]. Two volumes in the *Oxford Readings in Philosophy* series contain articles which bear on [8], but also cover a wide range of other issues. These are *The philosophy of social explanation*, ed. Alan Ryan (Oxford University Press, Oxford, 1973) and *The philosophy of history*, ed. Patrick Gardiner (Oxford University Press, Oxford, 1974). Another useful collection is John O'Neill, *Modes of individualism and collectivism* (Heinemann, London, 1973). For a general introduction to these issues by a single author see Michael Lessnoff, *The structure of social science* (George Allen and Unwin, London, 1974), or Alan Ryan, *The philosophy of the social sciences* (Macmillan, London, 1970), or F.A. Hayek, *The counter-revolution of science* (Free Press, Glencoe, Illinois, 1964).

A useful collection of essays representing the confrontation between the methodological approach of the 'Frankfurt School' and Popper's view of the nature of science (see Ch. 10 above) is Theodor W. Adorno *et al.*, *The positivist dispute in German sociology*, trans. Glyn Adey and David Frisby (Heinemann, London, 1976). A number of books by Jürgen Habermas have been translated into English. See in particular

[10] *Knowledge and human interests*, trans. Jeremy J. Shapiro (Heinemann, London, 1972) and

[11] *Toward a rational society* (Heinemann, London, 1971). A position on the role of values in sociological theory similar to that held by the Frankfurt School can lead to specific criticisms of the society in which we live. See for example

[12] Herbert Marcuse, *One dimensional man* (Sphere Books, London, 1968). For a brief but penetrating critical account of the constellation of ideas advanced by the Frankfurt School see Raymond Geuss, *The idea of a critical theory: Habermas and the Frankfurt School* (Cambridge University Press, Cambridge, 1981). There is a sympathetic and readable survey of critical theory by B. Fay, *Social theory and political practice* (George Allen and Unwin, London, 1975). Critical theory is also discussed in articles (by Apel, Lessnoff and Papineau) in S.C. Brown (ed.), *Philosophical disputes in the social sciences* (Harvester, Hassocks, 1979), which also contains material relevant to [9].

Two approaches to social theory not mentioned in this chapter are 'functionalism' and 'phenomenology'. For the former see B. Malinowski, *A scientific theory of culture* (Oxford University Press, New York, 1960), A.F. Radcliffe-Brown, *Structure and function in primitive society* (Cohen and West, London, 1952) and R.K. Merton, *Social theory and social structure* (Free Press, Glencoe, Illinois, 1957). For the latter see A. Schutz, *Phenomenology of the social world* (Northwestern University Press, Evanston, Illinois, 1967).

J.E.T.

35 | *The Philosophy of History*

R.F. Atkinson

Substantive and analytical approaches

Two sorts of philosophy of history may be distinguished by reference to different applications of the term 'history'.

Historians study the past or, more narrowly, what was done or happened and how things were in the human, social, even civilised past – preliterate people, including the unlettered masses of otherwise civilised periods, being held to belong to nature rather than to history. 'History' is sometimes used to refer to the past itself, as when it is said that wars and revolutions happen in history; at other times it refers to the study of the past, the historian's treatment of his subject-matter, as when it is said that history did not become fully systematic and professional until the late eighteenth century. In the light of this distinction it may be said that *substantive* or speculative philosophers of history study history in the sense of the past, typically generalising about it in a more ambitious way than workaday historians, whereas *analytical* or critical philosophers of history study history in the sense of the study of the past, that is, they interest themselves in what historians count as evidence or explanation, in whether or not their conclusions are capable of objective truth, in whether or not it belongs to the historian's role to pass moral judgements on historical figures. Substantive philosophers of history include Kant and Hegel, Marx and Toynbee – Marx, with his conception of history as the story of class conflict, being currently the most influential. Analytical philosophers of history include Croce and Collingwood, Popper, and a number of less generally known philosophers who have made significant contributions in their particular field: Gardiner, Dray, White and Gallie, to name only a few. As would be expected, some working historians have expressed philosophical opinions about their subject too.

Substantive philosophy and analytical philosophy of history are distinct in principle and, though it is scarcely possible to practise either entirely out of relation to the other, most authors fall mainly into one of the categories. What follows is consequently arranged on this basis, beginning with the analytical.

Analytical philosophy of history

A second-order study

Philosophy of history in this sense is to be conceived, on the analogy of the philosophy of mathematics or science, as the second-order examination of a first-order discipline. Philosophers of mathematics and science do not, as such, engage in mathematics or science; their office is rather to consider the procedures, conceptions of evidence, proof, explanation, etc. of mathematicians and scientists. In the same way the analytical philosopher of history is not, except accidentally, a historian. The work of historians is his subject-matter, more particularly the conceptions of evidence, objectivity and explanation there involved. The term 'analytical' implies continuity with the generally analytical, logical and empiricist emphases which are, or at least in the middle years of this century *were*, dominant in the academic philosophy of the Anglophone world. It is nevertheless the case that such pioneering analytical philosophers of history as Croce and Collingwood were idealist in their philosophical orientation.

Although the interests of the philosopher of history are different from those of the historian, his conclusions have up to a point to be tested against the practice of historians. Not, indeed, that he is simply describing what they do: he is as much concerned with what is *possible* by way of evidence, explanation and evaluation as with what historians mainly in fact provide. Even so, he needs to try to acquire a reasonable grasp of the variety of historical writing and a sensitive awareness of developments in the subject that its practitioners feel to be important. In so far as it might be a reproach to a historian that he was content to go on producing traditional political narrative, so would it be a reproach to the philosopher of history that he confined his attention to such narrative. The philosopher cannot shirk the hard task of coming to terms with historical analysis as distinct from narrative, with the economic and social aspects of 'total' history, with the perhaps vanishing frontier between history and social science, with 'cliometrics' (the adoption of quantitative methods) etc., etc. The philosopher must beware too of distorting his findings by unduly concentrating on histories of one period, say the modern where evidential material is superabundant, as opposed to some medieval or ancient periods, where literary material is scarce. It is no less important and probably no less difficult for the philosopher of history than it is for the philosophers of mathematics and science to keep up with developments in the subjects they study.

Analytical philosophy of history has to be comparative, seeking to explore resemblances and differences between history and the natural and social sciences; and even, though this is less popular nowadays, between history and literature. History tends to be suspected of being inferior in generality and explanatory rigour to most of the sciences, though hopefully superior to fiction in its commitment to truth. Just as the philosopher must be prepared to revise his conclusions in the light of developments in history, so must he revise them as his understanding of other subjects changes. This is particularly important in connection with the social sciences. Disagreements about the relationship between history and the social sciences are as likely to reflect differences about the social sciences as about history.

Since a little illustration will outweigh any amount of generalisation, the next step is to look at certain of the topics that have figured largely in recent philosophy of history. First, the prospects of establishing truths about the past.

Truths about the past

What is in question here are such claims about single events as that Charlemagne was crowned by the Pope in 800 AD. They are not widely felt to be problematic in the way that historical generalisations and explanations are; but some consideration of them helps correct misconceptions about the possibility of historical knowledge and miscomparisons between history and the sciences.

A source of confusion is that, when a statement refers to the past, it plainly cannot be verified by direct observation, as could an otherwise similar statement referring to the present. From this it may seem to follow that historical statements can be established only indirectly on the basis of fallible memory, or of testimony, notoriously unreliable at second or third let alone twenty-second or twenty-third hand, or of evidence in the shape of documents or other remains, which bear upon the case only in virtue of hard to formulate or otherwise insecure generalisations. From all this it may appear that history hardly deserves to be dignified as a body of knowledge, for the whole of it must be corrupted if radical uncertainty attends its statements of basic fact. But, 'Radical uncertainty compared with what?' it must be asked. Is it to statements about the present? But by no means all these refer to what is literally within sight, touch or hearing, and so incontrovertibly capable of direct verification. Statements about the present situation in distant places can be established only indirectly, though they less frequently provoke sceptical doubt than do statements about the past. Maybe this is because it is thought that one could always go and check; but, since travel takes time, what is found on arrival bears upon what obtained at the time the statement was made only in virtue of generalisations about the way things change or persist through time. And, manifestly, if such regularities are reliable here, they would be equally reliable in establishing statements about the past.

Another trouble is the too rare appreciation that statements ostensibly about the present have backward and forward temporal reference.[1] What we might be thought directly to see, say, a horse winning a race or the signing of a peace treaty, will count as winning or making peace only in virtue of the occurrence of previous events which are now unwitnessable. As for forward reference, it is the case that what the onlookers saw in Dallas in 1963 was the assassination of President Kennedy only because of his subsequent death. What commonly pass for present events are rarely literally witnessable in the present moment under the descriptions normally applied to them.

The truisms rehearsed above should tend to counter such scepticism about history as derives from the thought that there is something uniquely uncertain about statements basic to it. Moreover, verification in the natural and social sciences is, at its most direct, a matter of relating hypotheses to singular statements about the past (statements reporting observations or the results of experiment). Such statements are neither more nor less establishable by literally direct observation than are those in the history books. History is by no means alone in relying on memory, testimony and evidence, as distinct from direct observation. In particular it is not, as has often been uncritically assumed, *specially* dependent upon memory. Most of the human past is anyway outside the range of living memory; and putative memories relating to the part that is accessible cannot always be accepted unchecked. It is, indeed, the case that, in checking memory by testimony and evidence, historians will have to use their memories; but then memory in this *general* way is just as much involved in the natural and social sciences too.

Many historical statements report past *actions*, which have to be understood in terms of their agents' motives, intentions and beliefs, that is, in terms of subjective or mental factors, as well as objective social conventions of their day. (Collingwood is notable for stressing this.) Here some have found new grounds for doubt, others for credence. Doubters worry that past beliefs, intentions and motives can be recovered only by shaky inferences from patchily reported overt behaviour. Indubitably there is often too little evidence available for conclusions to be reliably drawn; but this is hardly a difficulty of principle, since in other cases there is more evidence, and anyway it is often deficient with regard to the states of mind of contemporaries. The prime source of confusion, however, lies in the tendency to construe as specific to history doubt which really reflects an uncritical dualism about other minds – the assumption that minds are, so to say, hidden inside bodies, so that people have direct knowledge only of their own. This is a general philosophical position, to which alternatives are available: for example, that statements about other people's beliefs, intentions and motives are to be construed as statements about how they tend to behave (cf. Ryle's views, discussed in Ch. 19). The issue belongs to philosophy of mind and has no special bearing on history in particular. So much, then, for the doubters. Of the credulous, Collingwood holds, or notoriously writes as if he did, that history's concern with actions affords it an advantage over natural science. Historians, being themselves people, can imaginatively identify with past people, sharing their thoughts (including motives and intentions), even if not their feelings. There is something right here. Empathy and insight are possible across the centuries. A historian without them is to that extent handicapped; and an amateur with relevant experience, for example a soldier considering ancient strategy, may see things professionals miss. There is something wrong too, however: namely any implication that historians may acquire insight independently of the troublesome procedures of assembling and assessing evidence. It is certain, despite some appearances to the contrary, that Collingwood did not intend this implication, but was mainly concerned to insist that history involved 'thought', the framing and testing of imaginative hypotheses, and was not simply the compilation of chronicles ('scissors and paste').

Objectivity

Objectivity problems arise at different levels. One, just considered, is whether a singular statement about the past can in principle be known to be true. Others derive from the necessity of selectivity in description or reportage. This will be the present topic. Further issues, concerning explanation and evaluation, will be considered later.

'Objective' is a word which often causes confusion by being employed uncritically or without explanation. Two senses, at least, must be distinguished: first, something like 'correspondent with fact or reality', in which use its opposite is 'subjective'; second, 'capable of being settled by any informed or rational person', when the opposite is 'arbitrary'. It is desirable not to use 'objective' to mean 'absolute', to which the opposite is 'relative', since the best hope of explaining how a selective account can be objective is to represent it as relative to a point of view or question asked. Relativity does not then imply subjectivity, rather the reverse. Singular statements about the past are in principle objective in both the suggested senses. Selective description, however, cannot be objective in the former sense, since it involves discrimination *within* a body of truths, all of which are supposed equally correspondent with reality. It can, nevertheless, be objective in the sense of justifiable to rational people.

The widespread suspicion is that, in producing selective narrative, historians will be indulging their personal and class prejudices, their moral, political and religious attitudes. Though the past cannot change, it is remarkable that history books constantly do. How can history be objective in the relevant sense when competent historians regularly and radically disagree?

One suggestion that has been made is that disagreement simply results from the attempt to generalise, to summarise in a short space a mass of detail about, for example, the American or English civil wars. It could hardly be expected that brief summaries would capture all relevant detail nor, consequently, is it surprising that informed historians should disagree about their formulation. This should raise no serious objectivity worries, however, for disagreements could always be resolved by going into more detail (Oakeshott, Butterfield). In favour of this view is the fact that much historical discussion takes the form of testing rather general theses against the detailed facts. But, even so, it can hardly be the whole story. For, in the first place, such general theses (concerning, for example, the alleged rise of the gentry in early modern England, or the openness of the aristocracy to recruitment from below) seem to be valued as much or more for their role in structuring historical investigation and debate as for their simple truth. And, secondly, it cannot always be possible to resolve disagreement by moving down into greater detail, since the 'whole truth' manifestly can never be told. This is an impossibility of *principle*, not to be confused with the very real practical obstacles in the way of telling very much of it.

The better strategy is to accept the necessity for selection, whilst insisting that there is no offence to objectivity in different selections being equally in accord with the facts. Selections may be judged objective relative to a particular object of investigation or question asked (Popper, Walsh, Dray). Granted that we are interested, say, in the question of how ancient Athens changed from a 'closed' to an 'open' society, a certain selection from the available information becomes relevant. If the interest is rather in the development of military techniques or of dramatic literature, different selections will be appropriate. Moreover, it is evident that the vaunted, or at any rate commonly uncriticised, objectivity of the natural sciences themselves cannot derive from their being unselective. It must rather be a matter of their being selective from determinate and widely accepted points of view. Popper has emphasised this, maintaining further that the difference between science and history in this respect is that in science the points of view too are prescribed by the state of the subject itself, whereas in history they come from outside and reflect the personal commitments of individual historians. But, as Kuhn has pointed out (cf. Chapter 10), there are periods of revolutionary change in the histories of the sciences, when consensus breaks down. On the other side, moreover, there can at times be consensus within schools of historians, as to what is worth studying and in what way. It is doubtful whether Popper is right in supposing there to be a difference of kind between history and science, especially if the social sciences are included, though there are certainly large differences of degree between some of the sciences and history.

Exception is sometimes taken to representing objectivity as relative to points of view on the grounds that some events, so to say, select themselves, that is are *absolutely* important, regardless of any historian's particular interest or point of view. The most commonly cited example is the killing of the Jews in Nazi Germany. All that is here true, however, seems to be that such events are appallingly significant in relation to widely respected human values. In human terms they are undeniably important and could hardly be excluded from general histories. But it does not follow that they must loom large in specialised histories of the periods in which they occur. It is not self-evident that the Holocaust should figure in the history of the Nazi car industry. Possibly there are particular reasons why it should, but that would only reinforce the point: that it would have to figure for reasons specific to a particular line of investigation, not for its general human significance.

The line of thought being followed is that there is no loss of objectivity so long as the historian's personal commitments affect not the answers he gives, but the questions he asks and the sorts of investigation he undertakes. His personal commitments are represented as extra-historical and as such not compromising to objectivity within history. This attitude is evident too in the way that some historians, keen to defend the autonomy of history, try to narrow the scope of the subject by avoiding commitment on extra-historical matters, for example to the explanatory adequacy of the categories of Freudian psychoanalysis. Collingwood, by contrast, takes a larger view of the autonomy of history, holding that questions of *possibility* (for example, of alleged miracles) might be settled by some process of *historical* thinking, rather than by appeal to criteria borrowed from science or philosophy. This seems scarcely credible unless, absurdly, the notion of history is extended to cover all possible considerations. Collingwood does nothing to show that history, in the ordinary narrow sense, can adjudicate on philosophical questions.

It should not, of course, be *assumed* that history will remain as it is now conceived by the more conservative professional historians and their lay public, or indeed that analytical philosophy of history will be unaffected by general changes in philosophical, historical or sociological thinking. There is no knowing what changes will come about. One may believe, nonetheless, that there will remain a place for history in a narrow sense, and find some support in the further conviction that there is considerable consensus in professional standards – evidence, verification, validity – even between Marxists and non-Marxists, who are likely to be as far apart in their philosophical as in their social thinking. It may perhaps be said that they exercise the same *historical* judgement, just as it is widely recognised they exercise the same mathematical and scientific judgement, despite their wide philosophical differences. It is possible in principle that general philosophical differences might reach right down into historical judgement itself; but there is little evidence that this actually happens.

813

Explanation and causation

In addition to describing and narrating, historians are commonly credited with producing explanations, some of them causal explanations, that is, with trying to answer Why and How as well as What-questions. History's subject-matter is, however, varied and considered at different levels of generality, so it is hardly surprising that explanations of virtually every sort are found in history books. The question, consequently, has to be whether there is any type of explanation that is peculiar to or specially prominent in history. Philosophers differ over the answer. *Some*, of a generally positivistic persuasion, with a consequent tendency to see history as continuous with the sciences, tend to claim that law explanations hold pride of place in both history and science. A historical example might be the explanation of a government's loss of popularity by reference to its having increased taxation, it being implied to be universally or generally true that governments which raise taxation are disliked. *Others*, however, impressed more by difference than by similarities between history and the sciences, emphasise the explanation of the actions of historical agents by reference to their wants, beliefs, intentions, standards, in short to their *reasons*, so that this may be called the rational conception of historical explanation. Political narrative overflows with explanations of this sort. *Another* group still maintains that there is a third type of explanation, allegedly characteristic of history, whereby an event is explained by narrating its antecedents. This may accordingly be called the narrative conception of historical explanation.

Each type of view has strengths and weaknesses. It is perhaps specially clear how a *law explanation* explains. It does so by representing the event to be explained as an instance of a generalisation to the effect that events of that sort invariably or usually occur in situations of a certain kind. Weaknesses include the difficulties of formulating and justifying appropriate generalisations, and the fact that historians seem not specially concerned to formulate and justify them. *Rational explanations* too are intelligible enough, though there has been controversy whether they are reducible to law explanations by representing the agent's desires and beliefs as the causes of what he does. (Discussion of the reducibility question may be left to the philosophers of mind.) A more serious difficulty is that, although the explanation of the actions of individuals is conspicuous in history, there are many other things which cannot be so explained because they were not thought of by those caught up in them. The unforeseen and unintended consequences of actions can by no means be ignored, though in the nature of the case they are not susceptible to rational explanation proper. With *narrative explanations*, by contrast, the main doubt is whether they explain at all, or whether the conditions of relevance they must be subject to (since all narrative must be selective) can be specified without bringing in the sort of generalisations on which law explanations depend. As for *causal explanations* specifically, it

814

would be helpful if 'cause' could be restricted to use in connection with law explanations or a sub-class of them. Law and rational explanations could then be distinguished as being in terms of causes or reasons respectively. Unfortunately 'cause' and 'reason' are no more systematically differentiated in application by historians than they are in common speech. A historian's causes may very well be what have here been called reasons. Indeed, even narrating the antecedents of an event may well be called giving its causes. The distinctions which philosophical students of historical explanation have to make are not clearly presented in the terminology of the subject.

The three main views of historical explanation will be considered in turn.

The law theory (Popper, Hempel). Apparent law explanations certainly occur in history, as when, for example, the defeat of Finland in 1940 is explained by the greater size of the Russian army. There are, however, uncertainties about them. Are they to be interpreted as citing sufficient or necessary conditions? On the one hand, it is difficult or impossible to include enough to make an explanation literally sufficient – larger armies have sometimes beeen defeated. On the other, a necessary condition, strictly speaking, shows only that an event could have happened, not that it did. There is the further uncertainty whether the general statements involved are to be taken as universal (true for all cases) or merely general (true for the most part), the former being more obviously explanatory, the latter easier to establish.

The root problem is whether law explanations can ever be made complete. The remarkable thing is the extent of the *agreement* between defenders and opponents of the law theory about the facts of the situation. Nobody seems to think that law explanations, as actually offered, ever are complete. At best they need the support of an 'other things being equal' clause; and even some supporters of the view have gone so far as to admit that the most that can ever be provided is an 'explanation sketch'.[2] It looks very much as though, at best, the law theory expresses an ideal of explanation, which is rarely or never entirely realised in the general practice of historians. It is to be suspected too that the theory results more from a preconception about explanation generally than from anything specific to history. Final judgement must, however, wait upon a consideration of alternatives.

Rational explanation (Collingwood, Dray). This term is most usefully employed to refer to explanations of individuals' actions by reference to their purposes, to their desires and beliefs as to the means for satisfying them – Napoleon's and Hitler's abandonment of plans for invading Britain might be explained on these lines. They need to be distinguished, on the one side, from simple dispositional explanations, in which particular actions are explained by reference to general tendencies (resourcefulness, combativeness, etc.) in an agent's behaviour: these may be regarded as explanations in terms of quasi-laws of limited application. And on the other side they need to be distinguished from the practically committed appraisal of an agent's actions as right or wrong: this is justification or criticism rather than explanation proper, and widely thought nowadays to exceed the professional scope of the historian.

As already noted, there is disagreement whether rational explanations as here understood are indeed essentially different from law explanations. A reason for thinking they are is that they trade upon a conception of means–end rationality rather than that of what always or usually happens. But granting this, and despite their very frequent occurrence in history books, there are still great obstacles to giving rational explanations the central role in a general account of historical explanation. One is that, in addition to explaining why an individual acted as he did in the situation he was in, there is an equal or greater need to explain why his actions had sufficient importance to attract the attention of historians. This requires consideration of social structure and circumstances, which probably cannot be in principle, and certainly never are in fact, explained without remainder in terms of the means–end activity of individuals. This is so even when the prime object of interest is the action of some important individual. But, additionally, a very great deal of what historians report and try to explain is not individual human action at all. Long-term variations in plenty and poverty, inflation and deflation, boom and slump; variations in general patterns of life and the gaining of livelihood; the development of international trade, mercantile capitalism, the shift of dominant economic activity from Mediterranean to Atlantic, the Industrial Revolution – none of these is, in any significant way, susceptible to explanation in terms of individual purposes and intentions. They are nevertheless recognised as part of the subject-matter of history and, as long as this is so, rational explanation can be only part of the truth about historical explanation.

The narrative view (Oakeshott, Butterfield, Gallie) is a third conception of historical explanation, according to which it consists in narrating the antecedents of what is to be explained. Explanatory narratives will, as we have seen, have to be selective at an appropriate level of detail, and may well include some law and rational explanations, but will not consist entirely of such. Explanations have the strictly subordinate role of helping the reader to accept developments that he would otherwise find puzzling or incredible (Gallie). It is plausible to suggest that such narratives are what is mainly provided in typical histories, and that they are consequently good candidates for what is normally meant by the expression 'historical explanation' – though little turns on ordinary usage here. One may, moreover, resist allegations that mere narratives *cannot* be explanatory, on the ground that they largely reflect question-begging preferences for other sorts of explanation (usually law explanations), preferences commonly adopted without any specific consideration of history. Positively it may be argued that historical narratives are capable of achieving a species of coherence, which carries with it intelligibility and explanatory power. Unfortunately, it is by no means easy to articulate the notion of explanatory narrative. Attempts that are non-vacuous tend to be insufficiently general. For instance, the sometimes canvassed idea that narratives should be intelligible in human terms, that is about people acting in ways we can relate to our own experience, seems to fall foul of the facts that evidence may not be available to make this possible and that a great deal of what is of interest in history may not as such have registered in the consciousness of people alive at the time. The Renaissance and the Industrial Revolution, for example, are primarily historians' categories, and any unity or intelligibility they confer upon narratives cannot therefore be in the relevant sense in human terms. Of course, *some* collectives, nations, churches, classes on some definitions, will be objects of awareness to their members; but history is certainly not confined to the consideration of entities such as these.

It may be suggested that a major obstacle to explicating the idea of explanatory narrative lies in the temptation, common in all areas of philosophy, of trying to operate at too general a level. Coherence and explanatory capacity must be relative to the objective of a particular inquiry, to a particular question asked or point of view, and the variety of questions and points of view is great enough to make general treatment impossible. Detailed case studies would seem the most promising way forward. Additionally, there is an institutional factor which should not be neglected. History is to an important extent a corporate activity: there are groups and schools whose members develop conceptions of what is worth asking and how topics should be treated. The consequence is that answers, even though they do not take the shape of law or rational explanations, may still present themselves as explanatory.

A further problem for the narrative view of explanation is that it has been developed on the basis that history is essentially narrative in the literal sense of recounting actions, usually in the political arena, of past people in generally chronological order. No doubt there is a permanent place for such history; but there has in the present century unquestionably been a vast expansion of historical subject-matter to include the economic, cultural and social generally, the life of masses as well as elites; and an associated tendency to play down or abandon narration in favour of analysis of situations. Narrative histories themselves often include scene-setting chapters, in which is accommodated material that would otherwise interrupt the main story line; but there are also, of course, works – often, it seems, the most admired by professional historians – which are predominantly or exclusively analytical. For the narrative theory to attain credibility it

817

needs, therefore, to be extended (and perhaps its name appropriately changed) to fit historical analysis. No doubt analytical history is less likely to content itself with the common-sense categories of narration; but it does not seem that its tendency is towards greater generality and the provision of law explanation. The aspiration may be in some way scientific, but not in practice on the model of the pure or applied natural sciences. Historians remain typically more interested in, say, what took place between 1789 and 1815 as a unique configuration, rather than as an instance of some general concept of revolution and restoration, of which another instance may be found between 1640 and 1660 in England. Comparisons are, it is true, made between revolutions; but, it may be claimed, more with a view to shedding light on the individual case than establishing a general law, or even constructing an 'ideal type'. All allowance made for the conceptual sophistication of analytical history, its interest seems to remain in the individual, and thus to be different from the generalising interest of even the social sciences. (One must, however, beware here of uncritically assuming that all the so-called social sciences are of the generalising type. Some sorts of sociology and social anthropology arguably manifest a direction of interest akin to that of history as portrayed here.)

Levels of historical causation. Mention was made above of the considerable variety there is in the use of the word 'cause', of the way in which it is not systematically distinguished from 'reason' and ranges over the territories of the three sorts of explanation distinguished above. It should further be noted that historians readily entertain the notion that some causes are more important than others. For instance, in the much-discussed case of Britain's going to war in 1914, more weight might be given to the country's threatened loss of naval and economic supremacy to Germany than to her traditional foreign policy or the violation of Belgian neutrality. There is, too, a tendency to recognise long-term fundamental causes, which are felt to make certain developments inevitable in the long run; and there are general theories which purport to specify what such causes are. At this point substantive philosophies of history, notably Marxian historical materialism, may engage with analytical concerns.

Two, sharply contrasting, such theories will be looked at here: psychologism, in its more up-to-date form of methodological individualism, and historical materialism. Popper is a rather moderate proponent of the former, not going so far as J.S. Mill's view that ultimate explanations are to be found in individual psychology. Popper does not deny that there may be social laws irreducible to those of psychology, but nevertheless adopts the *methodological* principle of seeking to represent the 'actions' of collectives as the resultants of the actions of individuals in their *social situations*. The italicised clause is crucial. Without it the view is challenging, but false or very probably so – in few or no cases can the collective be reduced to the individual. If the clause is taken seriously, however, the view gains plausibility at the expense of significance. It is possible to explain the actions of collectives if reference is allowed to the *social* contexts in which individuals act; but this is not to explain the social *without remainder* in individual terms. It would seem that Popper inclined towards methodological individualism, partly in the interests of concreteness, and partly with a view to demystifying collectives and so undermining the associated collectivisms, which he finds morally and politically abhorrent; he was, however, then led to concede so much to the autonomy of sociology as to render his original position virtually empty.

A similar verdict has to be passed on historical materialism. It is false or very doubtful, if taken to be the thesis that economic factors, narrowly defined, are fundamental to the explanation of everything else, including all political, cultural and religious developments. It is plausible but undistinctive, if it means that broadly economic factors should be taken into account and recognised to interact with others when constructing historical explanations. In its looser form it seems to appeal to many historians; more, for instance, than does psychoanalytical theory, of which the scientific status is largely similar. This is because it reinforces historical attitudes not peculiar to Marxists. It is, for example, a barrier against superficiality in explanations: it is not individuals and their fancies that matter, but long-term economic and social change. Moreover, it underpins the truths that people and institutions change through time, that human nature itself is not the same in all periods and places, that it is shaped by social and cultural factors. There is no need to be a historical materialist to arrive at such views; but the theory's popularity derives from the fact that it is congenial to them.

Values

Opinions about the role of values in history are inevitably determined as much by general philosophical views about value-judgements as by considerations specific to history. It is, however, here necessary to concentrate on the latter, with no more said on the general question than that it should not, as it too commonly is, be simply taken for granted that value-judgements are invariably subjective or arbitrary. What will be argued here is that history is not more seriously 'compromised' than are many other subjects by the presence of value-judgements in it.

On *one side* it is often maintained that, for history to be a reputable intellectual discipline, more optimistically a science, it must be purely factual, value-neutral or value-free. By this it is normally meant that the historian's personal *life* values, as they may be called, should not be allowed to intrude. (Life values include moral, political and aesthetic commitments, as contrasted with such, say, *intellectual* values as respect for truth, evidence and validity. That intellectual values evidently figure in history distinguishes it from no other discipline.) On the *other side*, however, it may be contended that it is absurd or impossible to keep life values out of history: how could anybody innocent of moral, political or aesthetic concerns be interested in history at all? This is, in fact, a rather superficial antinomy, which begins to dissolve as soon as a distinction is drawn between value-judgements in the *subject-matter* of history and value-judgements in the historian's treatment of it. Plainly value-judgements are to be found in history's subject-matter, as they are not in that of physics, chemistry or biology. Offering a rational explanation involves referring to the value-judgements of past agents (to their ends or aims, what they thought worth going after), and changes in value standards are a staple topic in cultural history. But the appearance of value-judgements in his subject-matter is not the same as the historian making them in his own person.

Another way of making the same distinction is to hold that, whilst historians in their professional capacity must mention value-judgements, they need not as such make them – *need* not, because it would no doubt be absurd pedantry to insist that all clues to personal evaluations should be suppressed. Nor, indeed, is it an altogether easy matter to confine personal value-judgements to subject-matter. Even if, controversially, it be thought possible, on general philosophical grounds, to make a sharp distinction between value-judgements and factual statements as they are expressed in ordinary, non-technical language, it is clear that an entirely value-neutral terminology for reporting human actions is far to seek.[3] 'Murder' evaluates one way, 'execution' the other; even the hopefully neutral 'killing', by its conspicuous abstention from partisan commitment, will be perceived by those engaged as conveying a judgement on their dispute. Rigorous evaluative neutrality is an ill match for the human interests that bring many people to history. In practice historians do not try very hard to achieve it, but leave it to their readers to try to make the necessary allowances.

There has, then, to be some qualification to the thesis that a historian's personal evaluations should not appear in his professional work. Another qualification is that they may very well influence his choice of subject-matter for study – which is different, however, from influencing the study of it once chosen. The feeling that conflicts in the Middle or Far East might spark off suicidal great power conflict could well encourage the historical study of these areas. Such 'intrusion' of life values would not, however, distinguish history from the *applied* natural and social sciences generally, since in them directions of inquiry are manifestly determined by extra-scientific value-judgements.

History, like the social sciences, tries to deal impartially and objectively with topics to which it is humanly scarcely possible to remain indifferent. All the same, in no case is partisan commitment considered either a necessity or a merit. The view of the celebrated Lord Acton, that it is the prime office of the historian to pronounce moral verdicts on the great criminals of the past, nowadays seems simply absurd. Not the least among the determinants of this attitude is the influence of history itself in showing how standards of value themselves (as well as the situations in which they are appealed to) change through time, thus undermining the absolutes on which Acton's view depended. Also compromised in this way is the, at least until very recently, common substantive view that history has been on the whole *progress*, that is, change in a direction judged to be good. Simple certainties of this sort evaporate as soon as it is realised that standards of value themselves are slaves to time.

Some substantive theories

Beginnings

It was noted above that, as well as analyses of the practice of historians, the philosophy of history includes attempts to discern pattern or structure in the course of history itself. There is a great wealth of possible examples, some of them elaborate and impressive intellectual constructions which, whatever doubts have to be entertained about their cogency, deserve to be judged in the light of their detailed content. It is a loss that no more than their bare outlines can be presented here.

The great flowering of substantive philosophy of history came with the works of Herder and Kant in the late eighteenth century and of Hegel in the early nineteenth century. The somewhat neglected Vico had written rather earlier, however, and there are much remoter origins in the cyclical theories of the ancient world and in the Judaeo-Christian scheme of creation, rebellion and dispossession, redemption and salvation, echoes of which are discernible in Hegel and Marx. Substantive philosophy of history is older than analytical. The eighteenth-century views contributed to, as well as reflecting, the development and professionalising of history itself and helped bring about its consequent recognition as a distinctive and philosophically interesting intellectual enterprise.

In what follows I shall concentrate attention on Kant, Hegel, Marx and Toynbee. All have as their focus of concern something supra-individual: for Kant the human species; Hegel the nation; Marx the proletariat – allegedly the true universal class; Toynbee the civilisation, in his opinion the smallest self-subsistent unit of historical study. This direction of interest is a pointer to a typical motivation for substantive philosophy of history: the desire to compensate for the dismaying prevalence of accident and frustration in individual lives, by representing them as contributing to a larger and more satisfying development. Thus will the ways of history, if not God, be justified to man.

Kant

The above sort of motivation is very evident in Kant's *Idea for a universal history from the cosmopolitan point of view* (1784). To all appearance history is a melancholy record of human folly and vice, in which the achievements of one generation are commonly lost in the next. Nevertheless, by standing back a little, it is possible to see in history the steady development of forms of order, which are the necessary conditions of moral and intellectual progress. The first stage, the termination of the Hobbist war of all against all by the establishment of state power, has already largely been accomplished in Europe. The next step has to be the construction of an international order, in the shape of a confederation of nations, which will outlaw and prevent war between states. Such developments have and will come about, not in spite of man's selfish and anti-social motivations, but *because* of them. If altruism were the precondition of order, humanity's case would be hopeless. It is rather that man's 'unsocial sociability', aggression, competitiveness, drives people to innovate in all spheres of life. There is, of course, frequent, destructive conflict, but the very horrors of this are new motives for seeking forms of order. Kant plainly sees a providential teleology at work here, as later does Hegel with his notion of reason 'cunningly' exploiting the basest human passions for the promotion of its own ends. Kant's work in philosophy of history, though important in relation to his philosophy generally, is not entirely impressive in itself. No doubt history *could* be regarded as manifesting progress in the direction he favours, but the question is whether it *should* be, and Kant works out his scheme with too little concrete reference for there to be a convincing answer. Hegel does rather better, though his political history (as opposed to his pioneering history of philosophy, where he had first-hand competence) does not go far beyond conventional outline. Marx does better still, which is no doubt the foundation of his continuing relevance for some professional historians. It is a difficulty for all substantive philosophy of history that the growth of detailed historical knowledge has made large-scale generalisation more suspect.[4]

Hegel

In his *Lectures on the philosophy of history* (published 1837) Hegel brings to history the notions of a dialectically self-developing reason, of society as 'mental' or 'spiritual', i.e. informed by thought and not just the mechanically determined outcome of association between biological creatures, and of the progressive achievement of freedom as the theme or guiding thread. Notoriously these preoccupations (coupled perhaps with his ignorance and that of his day) led him largely to ignore the oriental world, ancient China, India and Persia, where nothing happened and only one, the despot, was free. History proper begins in ancient Greece, with a great burgeoning of human spontaneity, which is subsequently regulated and distorted by Roman law, but also widely disseminated through the Roman Empire, as later was Christianity with its antithetical individualistic and subjectivistic emphases. Graeco-Roman society was slave-based, so in it only some were free; not until the constitutional monarchies of Hegel's own day, with medieval church and empire, Renaissance and Reformation behind them, was there the institutional possibility of all being free.

Hegel's generalising sweep is not more impressive than the apparent arbitrariness of his inclusions and exclusions, and the perfunctoriness of his compassion for the casualties of history, who fall victim to 'world historical' individuals and nations. A possible line of defence, though, is to credit him with a more selective aim than that of outlining the plot of human history as a whole.[5] If his concern was rather the origins of the then contemporary European notion of freedom, then it is true that Greece and Rome, Christianity, Renaissance and Reformation, contribute in a way that Egypt, China, Islam and pre-conquest South America do not. It is doubtful, though, whether such a defence gives him all he needs. More than Kant, who fully recognised that he was bringing a point of view to history, Hegel writes as one whose theme is not one among other possibilities, but the only true and significant one. Of course he thought he had philosophical justification for this, but his general philosophy is no easier to credit than his philosophy of history. His philosophical apriorism can, however, be exaggerated. Despite lavish reference to necessary developments, and to a personified reason apparently working away according to a preconceived plan, Hegel explicitly denies that the course of history can be predicted. History is of the past. The philosophy of history likewise stops with the present day. Not, as is sometimes supposed, because he thought the present cannot be improved upon; but because there can be no history of the future. Afterwards, perhaps, we shall see that what came about had to do so; but we cannot see what is to come.

Marx

Marx is partly a disciple, partly a critic, of Hegel. He retains but does not greatly emphasise the idea that history develops dialectically: thesis, antithesis, synthesis. For Hegel there is Roman law, Christian morality, 'ethical life' or moral freedom under law; for Marx, feudalism, capitalism, the hoped-for socialist classless society. Notoriously, however, he repudiated Hegel's 'idealism'. For Marx the actors in the historical drama are real social entities, classes determined by their members' relationships to the forces of production, not socially rootless ideas. (Marx is here less than fair to Hegel, who certainly employs an unhappily idealist idiom, but who also indubitably was concerned with ideas as embodied in institutions. It is true, though, that Hegel does not anticipate Marx in holding significant social groupings to be economically based.)

Marx is seized with the truisms that people must eat before they can think, and work if they are to eat. How they have to work, the techniques or forces of production, bring into being a mode of organisation, the relations of production: serfs cultivating strips of land, partly for themselves, partly for their lords; or wage-earners in a factory. The forces and relations of production taken together constitute the economic foundation of society. On this there builds up an institutional superstructure: law, a system of property rights and class structure, a political system, educational and religious institutions. Also superstructural are 'forms of consciousness': economic, moral, political, philosophical, literary ideas – ideologies, which reflect the class structure of the society in question, in the way that, for instance, the Protestant emphasis on the individual conscience has sometimes been supposed to match the economic individualism of bourgeois society. In Marx's well-known words: 'It is not the consciousness of man that determines his being; but his social being that determines his consciousness' (*Preface to a critique of political economy*, 1859). The view is that forms of consciousness are the dependent, determined variable; the independent, determining variables being the forces of production. It is changes at this 'material' level that ultimately lead to institutional and intellectual, social and cultural change. The revolutionary violence by which social change is liable to come about is explained as the result of 'frictions', which impede the smooth working through into social structure of changes in the forces of production. The temporarily dominant class, by employing the means of coercion at its disposal (in the capitalist era the bourgeois state machinery), may be able for a time to delay social changes detrimental to it. The effect of such resistance is that pressure for change builds up to revolutionary proportions.

It is possible to exaggerate the materialistically deterministic side of the theory. There are, certainly, Marxists who deny that they are one-direction economic determinists and allow causal efficacy to superstructural factors; some going so far as to adopt a persuasive, though no longer distinctively Marxist, organicist view, according to which every element in social reality relates to and interacts with every other. For them economic determinism would be as much a distorting abstraction as Hegelian idealism. The more orthodox view, found in Engels for example, is that, whilst other factors have their importance, in the last analysis it is the economic which count. In Marx himself, it is interesting to note, there is evidence of a disposition to allow a role to human agency as a causal force. It is men who make their history, even though not exactly how they like. What comes about will be the possibly unintended resultant of what were, nevertheless, intentional human actions.

There are at least two ways of assessing historical materialism: as a purportedly scientific theory of social change; or as an interpretational perspective, which may suggest hypotheses testable by historical research, and have methodological implications for the practice of history. It is in the former shape, in which it is an example of the historicism Popper has attacked, that it is most vulnerable. Quite apart from any strength there may be in Popper's *general* criticism (for which see below), there are serious particular objections that require to be met. At the very least, for the theory to be true or probable, there would have to be correlations *between* certain techniques of production (say, crudely with *The poverty of philosophy*, 1847, the windmill and the steam mill) *and* certain socio-political superstructures (say, the feudal lord and the industrial capitalist). But, for elements to be correlated, they have first to be distinguished. For the theory to succeed it has, therefore, to be possible to draw a clear distinction between the forces and relations of production, and between the forces and relations together (the economic base) and the superstructure. It is at least doubtful whether the distinctions have yet been made with sufficient precision for the theory to be both testable and true or probable. Some Marxists would on this account not wish the theory to be considered a candidate for empirical science; though there are signs that Marx, in this respect a true son of his century, might have intended the theory in this way, and there has been at least one determined and sophisticated attempt to follow in this direction (G.A. Cohen, *Karl Marx's theory of history*, Clarendon Press, Oxford, 1978).

As an interpretational perspective the theory is more promising, suggesting hypotheses that have inspired valuable historical work, for example, about the class differences between people on different sides in the English and American civil wars. In this respect historical materialism differs from most substantive theories in actually influencing the practice of history. It has, moreover, had a more general methodological influence in encouraging the development of social and economic history, and not least in being one of the inspirations of the 'total history' of the French *Annales* school, the history of the very long term, for which political events seem merely epiphenomenal. Whatever its shortcomings as a substantive theory, Marxist historical materialism has indubitably left its mark on professional history.

Toynbee

The present sampling of substantive theories will conclude with a brief consideration of Toynbee's *A study of history*, a very large work appearing over a period of some twenty years from 1934. Toynbee's topic is not mankind generally, nor the nation or social class, but the civilisation, of which twenty or so complete specimens are recognised – Far Eastern, Hindu, Orthodox, Islamic, Contemporary Western among them – plus about half as many abortive or arrested examples. (There are some similarities with Spengler's *Decline of the West* 1918 and 1922, which treats the life cycles of cultures. Toynbee, however, has a much more impressive fund of solid historical knowledge at his disposal.) Civilisations are not held to have a fixed life cycle, though they do go through similar phases, for example times of trouble, the secession of internal proletariats, loss of creativity by elites. Civilisations are distinguished by their dynamism, having arisen from pre-existing society when a sufficiently threatening challenge evoked a creative response. Thus Egyptian civilisation originated when the challenge of drought provoked the development of irrigation and water management procedures, and the Minoan rose to the opportunity presented by the challenge of its island situation. The optimum civilisation-producing challenge has to be great enough to call forth a qualitatively new response, but not so great as to be entirely crushing.

The challenge–response schema is supposed to explain not only origins but subsequent growth, though the later challenges may be more internal than external, for instance the need for unified political institutions to match the cultural and economic unity of ancient Greece. Though there is no necessary limit to the number of challenges that can be successfully met, in fact in all civilisations except possibly our own creativity has failed and breakdown or ossification occurred. Toynbee was perhaps initially motivated by a desire to predict the future of Western civilisation, but developed a reluctance to draw pessimistic conclusions, and turned his attention to quasi-religious questions about the final purpose of mankind.

Toynbee aimed to proceed on an empirical basis, unfortunately understood in a rather crudely inductivist way, so that he saw himself as trying to establish laws from the consideration of his twenty or so specimens. This (though his actual procedure was more intuitive and less systematic) invited criticisms that there was unclarity about the criteria of identity for civilisations, that his instances were too few, and his generalisations consequently too insecure to support predictions. Such criticisms are both fair and valid but, like the author's conception of his own work, rather beside the point. Indisputably the scientific standing of Toynbee's work is very low, but that makes it no less valuable as a record of the changing visions of a remarkably informed and creative mind. Not history, of course; but more, as well as less, than it. In this it is not different in principle from the other substantive theories here considered. None is true or even probable, none at all in a shape easily testable. They are not science, which might justify prediction, but rather a species of imaginative literature, expressing and evoking reflections about human destiny and ultimate values. They belong, at their best, with the religions they somewhat mimic, certainly not with Newtonian and Einsteinian physics or Darwinian evolution.

Historical determinism

The substantive views that have been considered, with the possible exception of Kant's since it is *presented* as no more than a perspective on the past, have a deterministic or necessitarian aspect. The long-term course of events, it seems to be maintained, will be what it will be, irrespective of anything individuals can do. For Marx the revolution and the classless society will come in the end no matter what we may do to promote or prevent them; for Hegel things had to develop the way they did; all resistance, all attempts to proceed in different directions were necessarily ineffectual. There are, as has been noted, other tendencies in the views of these authors; but the determinism certainly seems to be there as well. Indeed it is a determinism apparently running into a sort of fatalism. Determinism of the physical or psychological sort, determinism at the individual level, has often been perceived as a threat to free will (though there are also well-known views to the effect that there is no genuine incompatibility, e.g. in Hume); but it does not entail that human action is ineffectual. To maintain that actions have causes is consistent with allowing that they have effects. It is in apparently questioning this latter that the specific interest of historical determinism lies.

The most obvious implication of fatalism is quietism, a refusal to engage in practical activity that can make no difference in the long run. Evidently this moral was not drawn by the revolutionary Marx, with his talk of the point of philosophy being to change the world; and his many followers have, perhaps paradoxically, been inspired to activism by the thought that history is somehow on their side. (Belief in divine providence, that God will not let his chosen people down, has had the same strange effect.) Logic apart, though, it is perhaps not really surprising that historical determinism has not inhibited political action. The pressures of the short term are insistent; the alleged necessities of the indefinitely long term can engage with them only by way of inspiration and support. It must be doubted how far historical determinism is effectively a matter of cognitive belief to the faithful: creeds have more to do with maintaining group unity than propositional truth. And, if the question of truth be raised, we have already seen there is small reason to accept any substantive historical determinism as true or probable.

Popper, however, is notable for having offered a systematic interpretation, culminating in a purported formal refutation of all *historicism*, i.e. any view to the effect that there can be large-scale, long-term predictions about the course of human society. The interpretation, though inevitably yoking together very disparate views, is valuable, not least for its distinction between historicist prophecies and the conditional, short-term predictions about human affairs that can be genuinely scientific, and so form the basis for reformatory 'social engineering' as opposed to 'Utopian' transformations, implementable if at all only by grossly coercive methods. He makes much too of a distinction between scientific laws, e.g. the law of gravitation, and *trends*, e.g. the course of biological evolution and the patterns of development allegedly discerned by substantive philosophers of history. In the universality of law, its application to *all* cases, past, present and future, lies the only basis for scientific prediction. Trends are essentially observed or inferred *facts*, calling for explanation in terms of laws, and not in themselves the basis for justified predictions.

Given so much, and in view of the intrinsic implausibility of historicist theorising, it must seem a work of supererogation to have sought a formal refutation. Popper's motivation is evident from his dedication of his *Poverty of historicism* (1957 in book form) to the memory of the countless victims of the Fascist and Communist belief in inexorable laws of Historical Destiny. The refutation requires as its premisses: that the course of history is strongly influenced by the growth of human knowledge; and that (for reasons set out in the now published *Postscript* to Popper's *Logic of scientific discovery*) we cannot rationally predict the future growth of knowledge – whence it follows that we cannot predict the course of history. This short argument is only the immediately visible fragment of a great mass of interconnected ideas, which are set out at length in Popper's many writings. He is notable among philosophers of a generally 'analytic' persuasion for the way in which he harnesses many minute and technical considerations to very general theses. Of set purposes, he exposes many particular contentions to attack; and it is hardly to be expected that he should prove invulnerable at every point. One thing, however, is certain, and Popper has done much to make it so: no historicist theory has been established as more than an interesting, perhaps dangerous, speculation. The burden of proof falls on the upholders, not the critics, of such theories.

Notes

(An author's name followed by a number in square brackets refers to the book or article which has that number in the bibliography.)

1. Danto [15], Ch. 8.
2. Hempel [8].
3. Cf. Berlin [25], pp. 91–6.
4. Dray [2], p. 61.
5. Ibid., p. 78.

Bibliography

General introductions to the philosophy of history

[1] W.H. Walsh, *An introduction to philosophy of history* (1st edn, Hutchinson, London, 1951; 3rd edn, revised, 1967)

[2] W.H. Dray, *Philosophy of history* (Prentice-Hall, Englewood Cliffs, 1964)

[3] R.F. Atkinson, *Knowledge and explanation in history: an introduction to the philosophy of history* (Macmillan, London, 1978).

Each of these works discusses both the substantive (or speculative) philosophy of history and the analytical philosophy of history. The rest of the books mentioned in the bibliography are classified under one or the other heading – though it should be stressed that the dividing line between the two is not always sharp.

Analytical philosophy of history

Two useful anthologies are

[4] W.H. Dray (ed.), *Philosophical analysis and history* (Harper & Row, New York, 1966)

[5] Patrick Gardiner (ed.), *The philosophy of history* (Oxford University Press, Oxford, 1974).

Two major problems in this area concern (a) historical objectivity and (b) the nature of historical explanation.

Historical objectivity. Besides Walsh [1], Ch. 5, and Atkinson [3], Ch. 3, see

[6] K.R. Popper, *The open society and its enemies* (1st edn, Routledge, London, 1945), Ch. 25, Sections 1–3, and

[7] W.H. Dray, *Perspectives on history* (Routledge and Kegan Paul, London, 1980), Section 2.

Historical explanation. Besides Walsh [1], Ch. 3, and Atkinson [3], Ch. 4, see

[8] C.J. Hempel, 'The function of general laws in history', *Journal of Philosophy*, 39 (1942). This is a classical exposition 'covering law theory', which is also defended by Morton White, *Foundations of historical knowledge* (Harper and Row, New York, 1965). For the view that historical explanation is 'rational explanation', in the sense of explanation by reference to the purposes and beliefs of individuals, see

[9] R.G. Collingwood, *The idea of history* (Clarendon Press, Oxford, 1946), pp. 210–17, 282–302)

[10] W.H. Dray, *Laws and explanations in history* (Clarendon Press, Oxford, 1957), Ch. 5, and

[11] R. Martin, *Historical explanation* (Cornell University Press, Ithaca, New York, 1977).

For the 'narrative' view of historical explanation, see

[12] H. Butterfield, *The Whig interpretation of history* (Bell, London, 1931), esp. Ch. 5, 'The art of the historian'

[13] W. Oakeshott, *Experience and its modes* (Cambridge University Press, Cambridge, 1933), Ch. 3, esp. pp. 126–45 (also in Dray [4], pp. 193–212)

[14] W.B. Gallie, *Philosophy and the historical understanding* (Chatto and Windus, London, 1964)

[15] A.C. Danto, *Analytical philosophy of history* (Cambridge University Press, Cambridge, 1965), Ch. 11.

[16] H. Fain, *Between philosophy and history* (Princeton University Press, Princeton, 1970).

Substantive philosophy of history

Kant. Kant's major work in this field is

[17] *Idea for a universal history from the cosmopolitan point of view* (1784). English translation in Kant, *On history* (Library of Liberal Arts, Bobbs-Merrill, Indianapolis and New York, 1963).

For Kant's views on history, see Walsh [1], pp. 122–32; Collingwood [9], pp. 93–104.

Hegel. Hegel's *Lectures on the philosophy of history* were published posthumously in 1837. Perhaps of most help to the English reader is the Introduction to the work, translated as

[18] *Lectures on the philosophy of world history. Introduction: Reason in history*, trans. H.B. Nisbet (Cambridge University Press, Cambridge, 1975).

See Walsh [1], pp. 137–54; Dray [2], Ch. 6; Collingwood [9], pp. 113–26.

For a more recent account, see a chapter from a general survey of Hegel's philosophy:

[19] Charles Taylor, *Hegel* (Cambridge University Press, Cambridge, 1975), Ch. 15. Taylor approaches Hegel by way of another important philosopher of history, Herder (1744–1803).

Marx. Marx's views on the philosophy of history are summarised in a famous and much-discussed passage from

[20] Preface to *A contribution to the critique of political economy* (1859), trans. S.W. Ryazanskaya (Lawrence and Wishart, London, 1971), pp. 20–2. There are many other editions. Another important source is

[21] Marx and Engels, *The German ideology* (1845–6), Part I, *Feuerbach*. There are again many editions of this text; see, e.g., Karl Marx and Friedrich Engels, *Collected works*, vol. V (1845–7) (Lawrence and Wishart, London, 1976), pp. 27–93.

Marx's philosophy of history has been much discussed. A savage attack is to be found in Popper [6], Chs. 13–21; a subtle and intricate defence is provided by

[22] G.A. Cohen, *Karl Marx's theory of history: a defence* (Clarendon Press, Oxford, 1978).

Toynbee. Perhaps the last of the great speculative philosophers of history is Arnold Toynbee (1889–1975). His major work is

[23] Arnold Toynbee, *A study of history* (10 vols, Clarendon Press, Oxford, 1934–54). A useful abridgement has been prepared by D.C. Somervell (2 vols, Clarendon Press, Oxford, 1946, 1957). See also Dray [2], Ch. 7.

Historical determinism. The problem of whether the course of historical events is determined by necessary laws is raised in an acute form by Hegel and Marx. A celebrated attack on historical determinism was made by Popper in

[24] K.R. Popper, *The poverty of historicism* (Routledge, London, 1957).

Another important essay on the subject is

[25] Isaiah Berlin, 'Historical inevitability' in I. Berlin, *Four essays on liberty* (Oxford University Press, Oxford, 1969), pp. 41–117.

I am grateful to Professor Atkinson for many helpful suggestions concerning this bibliography.

G.H.R.P.

36 | Aesthetics

Michael Proudfoot

The subject (Aesthetics) is very big and entirely misunderstood as far as I can see. (Wittgenstein[1])

I

It would be hard to think of a subject more neurotically self-doubting than aesthetics. Claims that the subject is dreary,[2] irrelevant, muddled and misunderstood have been a persistent theme, not only of recent, that is to say, post-war, writers, but from the very start of the subject. Alas, these claims have all too frequently been justified.

One consequence of lack of confidence in the subject has been that contributions to aesthetics in the last fifty years or so, in the English-speaking world at least have been marked by their modesty and brevity. They have characteristically been in the form of articles rather than books: and where there have been book-length contributions, they have, in the main, concentrated on some one problem or art-form. The full-scale synoptic work on aesthetics has been out of favour, as also, it must be said, has been the full-scale, grand philosophical work in general.

The word 'aesthetics', and, it might be said, the subject too,[3] were invented by the German philosopher Alexander Baumgarten, who, in his *Aesthetica*, 1750–8, used the word to apply to 'criticism of taste' considered as a science or philosophy. During the nineteenth century, the word gradually became generally accepted to refer to 'the Philosophy of Taste, the theory of the Fine Arts, the Science of the Beautiful, etc.'.[4]

Towards the end of the nineteenth century, the word 'aesthetic' came to be applied as well to particular movements in various art-forms, and especially to the movement of writers and artists associated with the slogan 'Art for art's sake'. The names of Pater, Wilde and Whistler were specially associated with this movement, adherents of

831

which, particularly Wilde, were often entitled 'aesthetes' – poked fun at by Gilbert and Sullivan in *Patience*.

It must be admitted that there is something rather forbidding in terms such as 'the philosophy of taste' and 'the science of the beautiful', as well as in the very word 'aesthetic' itself. Coleridge, in 1821, wrote, 'I wish I could find a more familiar word than aesthetic, for works of taste and criticism', and many would echo his sentiments.[5]

More recently, aesthetics has often been described as 'the philosophy of art'. This might be thought of as misleading in several ways, one of them being the presupposition that there *is* an identifiable area, with its own identifiable set of 'problems', which is *the* philosophy of art (rather than artistic activity being part of general human activity, about which a wide range of philosophical problems might arise, not exclusively connected with art).

Another way in which the description of aesthetics as the philosophy of art may mislead is that it fails to take account of our aesthetic experience of nature and natural objects – of landscapes, sunsets, flowers and faces, for example. In fact, recent aesthetics has tended to ignore such experience[6] and this neglect has affected the way in which our experience of works of art has been discussed as well, as we shall see.

Nevertheless, most aesthetic judgements, as well as most contributions to the subject, are concerned with works of art, the products of fellow human beings. This is a contingency, albeit an important one. It is certainly possible to imagine a society in which aesthetic judgement and evaluation play an important role, but primarily, or even only, in respect of nature and natural objects. There may be people in such a society who are thought of as possessing 'artistic flair', whose exercise of this flair consists entirely in drawing the attention of others to previously unnoticed aesthetically interesting objects, sights or features. There are, of course, such people in our present society.

But in our society it has certainly been true that the major concern of aesthetics has been with works of art. The experience of art is an important and profound part of many people's lives. Trying to give any sort of an account of it, especially in general terms, is a difficult task: but the sheer difficulty ought not to be used as a reason for not making the effort. It is perhaps in contrast with the profundity and intensity of our experiences of great works of art that contributions to aesthetics have seemed so unimpressive. There is an asymmetry between aesthetics and ethics here. For whereas ethics is not primarily concerned with great men, it is great works and great artists that make art supremely interesting and important. Further, bad people surely provide a far greater worry than bad works of art.

Aesthetics has been approached from two different directions. On the one hand, it has been approached by the philosopher (without necessarily having any profound interest in art) who wishes to 'plug a gap'. Having dealt with truth and goodness, he turns his attention (if he has time) to beauty. What so frequently has resulted have been philosophical works of great generality and abstractness, with very little in the way of examples or references to any actual works of art: perhaps the paradigm case here is Kant's *Critique of judgement.* One notable exception was Croce, who believed it important to consider the way of thinking involved in the creation and experience of works of art before moving on to consider other ways, such as logical, rational or conceptual thought. On the other hand, the artist, or critic, may find himself – usually because his art is innovatory – having to defend himself against hostility and philistinism, by means of general claims, manifestos or quasi-philosophical offerings.

In some periods critics have considered general and theoretical questions about art, but recently the stress among the most interesting and important critics has been on practical criticism, and the consideration of more general questions has been thought to be not so much uninteresting or unimportant, but at best irrelevant, and, at worst, pernicious. Perhaps this isn't altogether surprising, for how can an age which is uncertain about so many fundamental issues of human life hope to have an adequate aesthetic theory? Aesthetics isn't – or oughtn't to be – a *sui generis* discipline. To be clear about the place of art and aesthetic experience in the whole economy of human life, one would have to be clear about many other areas of philosophy.

When, as in some periods in the past, there have been standards more or less universally agreed on, there would have been no pressure to consider theoretical questions, to move outside criticism. The terms used wouldn't have been seen as standing in need of any general defence.[7] But when, as now, there are no universally agreed standards, there will be pressure on the critic from those who disagree with, or are uncertain about, his position, to produce a more general defence – a request difficult to comply with because the critic's case ultimately rests on the works themselves, and he will be unwilling to argue except in terms of criticism of these works.

In talking about works of art, and in particular in giving reasons for one's critical judgements, the reasons take their force from the work of art about which the judgements are made. The clarity of language is relative to the context in which it is used. There is a *necessary* imprecision in critical language. Good criticism will contain lots of quotations: perhaps this helps to explain the general poverty of musical criticism.

One of the most celebrated examples of a critic under pressure to produce a general defence of his position is provided by the exchange between the philosopher Rene Wellek and the literary critic Dr F.R. Leavis.[8] Wellek wrote, 'I could wish that you had stated your assumptions more explicitly and defended them systematically.' What Leavis had failed to do, Wellek obligingly provides.

Allow me to sketch your ideal of poetry, your 'norm' with which you measure every poet: your poetry must be serious in relation to actuality, it must have a firm grasp of the actual, of the object, it must be in relation to life, it must not be cut off from direct vulgar living, it should not be personal in the sense of indulging in personal dreams and fantasies, there should be no emotion for its own sake in it, no afflatus, no mere generous emotionality, no luxury in pain or joy.

Wellek continues in the same vein, outlining a series of 'general rules' extracted from specific critical comments in Leavis' recently published book *Revaluation*. Wellek concludes the paragraph: 'the only question I would ask you is to defend this position more abstractly and to become conscious that large ethical, philosophical, and, of course, ultimately, also aesthetic *choices* are involved'.

Leavis replied in the next issue: 'I knew I was making assumptions (even if I didn't – and shouldn't now – state them to myself quite as [Wellek] states them) and I was not less aware than I am now of what they involve.' Though it might be possible to extract some principles and 'norms' from criticism, this was only, as it were, *a posteriori*: what came first were the detailed responses to the individual works.

If I avoided such generalities, it was not out of timidity; it was because they seemed too clumsy to be of any use. I thought I had provided something better. My whole effort was to work in terms of concrete judgements and particular analyses: 'This – doesn't it? – bears such a relation to that; this kind of thing – don't you find it so? – wears better than that,' etc.

Leavis points out that his comments are all related to actual works:

I do not, again, argue in general terms that there should be 'no emotion for its own sake, no afflatus, no mere generous emotionality, no luxury in pain and joy'; but by choice, arrangement and analysis of concrete examples I give those phrases (in so far, that is, as I have achieved my purpose) a precision of meaning they couldn't have got in any other way.

It is because of the way in which criticism and aesthetics are so closely tied to particular works that aesthetics has a peculiar relationship to its own history. There are some areas of human thought which, it has been said, have no history:

There is a massive central core of human thinking which has no history – or none recorded in the histories of thought; there are categories and concepts which, in their most fundamental character, change not at all. Obviously these are not the specialities of the most refined thinking. They are the commonplaces of the least refined thinking; and are yet the most indispensable core of the conceptual equipment of the most sophisticated human beings. (P.F. Strawson[9])

834

But aesthetics is not one of these areas. Although most writings on epistemology, for example, strike us as being contemporary, this isn't so with aesthetics. The writings of aestheticians very quickly come to appear dated. Aesthetics is more like ethics in this respect:

> Some philosophers have ... written as if moral concepts were a timeless, limited, unchanging, determinate species of concept, necessarily having the same features throughout their history, so that there is a part of language waiting to be philosophically investigated which deserves the title *'the* language of morals' (with a definite article and a singular noun) ...
>
> [But] it would be a fatal mistake to write as if, in the history of moral philosophy, there had been one single task of analyzing the concept of, for example, justice, to the performance of which Plato, Hobbes, and Bentham all set themselves, and for their achievement at which they can be awarded higher or lower marks. (Alasdair MacIntyre[10])

But aesthetics is even more of a historically changing subject than MacIntyre claims ethics is. For the subject-matter of aesthetics has a history, and it doesn't only change, it also grows, for new works of art, and new art forms, are constantly being created. And these new works may change our perspective on the past as well. It isn't just that each age has to confront its own, contemporary, works of art, which previous generations, previous critics, previous aestheticians couldn't have known of, for they weren't yet created: but also that each new age has to re-confront, re-interpret, the artists and works of the past from their own standpoint. Each age re-interprets the art of the past.

It is therefore paradoxically *because* aesthetic concepts have a history that the history of aesthetics has a strictly limited relevance to the study of current problems in aesthetics. For those who wrote on aesthetics in the past were not writing about the same things that those who write on aesthetics now are concerned with.

II

We know that the tail must wag the dog, for the horse is drawn by the cart;
But the Devil whoops, as he whooped of old: 'It's clever, but is it Art?' (Rudyard Kipling, *The Conundrum of the Workshops*)

What *is* aesthetics concerned with? What *are* characteristic aesthetic problems? Given what has been said about the history of aesthetics, it is, perhaps, not surprising that it would be difficult to list a set of central problems which anyone with any pretensions to being counted as an aesthetician would have had to deal with. The problems vary from age to age. The characteristic preoccupation of twentieth-century aesthetics has been with the question 'What is Art?' And the reason for that has been the nature of twentieth-century art, which has self-consciously posed the question as a challenge.

The attempts to produce a satisfactory definition of 'work of art' have often centred upon trying to find some one feature or set of features which all works of art possess, and which constitute the essence of art. The most obvious and most ancient candidate is beauty. But it obviously won't do. Many things are beautiful which are not works of art, so beauty cannot be a sufficient condition of art. And, of course, many things which are undeniably works of art are undeniably not beautiful. This isn't because they are poor works of art and simply, as it were, *fail* to be beautiful, for beauty was not what was aimed at.

Many works of art are beautiful, and for some of these works, their beauty may well be a very important feature of them, but it is not a feature of all and only works of art: it is certainly not that which unites together the works of Ibsen, Zola, Hogarth, Berg and Beckett, for example, and which makes them works of art. Beauty is neither a necessary nor a sufficient condition for art.

It has often been remarked that the phrase 'work of art' has an evaluative meaning as well as a descriptive meaning. That is, to say that something is a work of art is often to praise it, as well as categorise it. Consider Dilys Powell on the film *Death in Venice*: 'In the past quarter of a century there have been films potentially more influential (not, of course, necessarily for the good). I can think of none which has been more truly a work of art.'[11]

So the question 'What is a work of art?' can receive a descriptive answer, or an evaluative answer. The descriptive answer will say what art is – or, more often, what it is not: for example, that it is not science, propaganda, craft or amusement.[12] The evaluative answer will say what art *ought to be*, what successful art is. Typically it will describe art as the achieving of something: the conveying of information, for instance, or the arousal of a particular kind of response, or the expression of emotion. There will therefore be two distinct ways in which something might fail to be a work of art. It might not be art because it was never intended to be: it is simply not that sort of thing, as a matchbox or a radiator are not (normally) works of art. Or it might not be a work of art because it fails to achieve what it sets out to do – it is simply too feeble an example.

Faced with the hostility that new works of art can attract, the critic who defends the innovatory artist will attempt to show how the works he is defending *are* works of art by employing both descriptive and evaluative criteria. Typically, he will try to show how the works he is concerned with relate to other, acknowledged, works of art, and also how they achieve something, how they are important or valuable (so showing both how they are art rather than non-art, and good art rather than bad art). In showing how they relate to already accepted historical works of art, he will often seize upon some quality they share with historical works: which quality will then be claimed to be definitional of art. The wise critic, as we have seen with Leavis, will reject any attempt to universalise from his comments on particular works – but not all critics have been wise.

An example of a critic generalising from his defence of an artist to making wild claims about the definition of art in general is provided by Clive Bell in writing about Cézanne and the post-Impressionists. Defending the post-Impressionists against the criticism which was heaped upon them, Bell took a feature, namely formal structure, or as he put it 'significant form', which Cézanne's paintings had in common with the accepted masterpieces of the past, and erects the feature into the essence of art: the necessary and sufficient condition for something's being a work of art. So extreme was Bell in his claims that he rejected any *other* feature apart from significant form as being simply irrelevant – for instance, the subject-matter of the painting. So he says:

> The representative element in a work of art may or may not be harmful; always it is irrelevant. For to appreciate a work of art we need bring with us nothing from life, no knowledge of its ideas and affairs, no familiarity with its emotions.[13]

Again:

> You will notice that people who cannot feel pure aesthetic emotions remember pictures by their subjects; whereas people who can, as often as not, have no idea what the subject of a picture is. They have never noticed the representative element.

Such a theory is of course clearly absurd with painters such as Hogarth or Constable, but it is equally absurd applied to Cézanne. If somebody had failed to notice that Cézanne's painting of apples *was* of apples, then he would have failed to have noticed Cézanne's painting, we might say, however much some colours in a frame may have attracted his attention. And since some people, including Bell himself, have thought that what he says applies to all works of art, it is worth adding that a theory which is absurd when applied to paintings is meaningless when applied to, for example, *David Copperfield*.

The trouble about such definitions, and there have been many others, such as that the essence of art is organic unity, or imitation, or the expression of emotion, is that when it is shown, on the one hand, that many works of art seem to lack the essential property, and on the other hand that there are many things which possess the property which are not works of art, is that the sense of the terms is extended, so that they do cover the exceptions. At the same time, the meaning of 'work of art' is stretched as well, so that it covers all the things that possess the relevant property. So both the phrase 'work of art' and its intended definition become so stretched that they cease to have any real meaning.

It has been the influence of Wittgenstein that has led

to attempts to discover the 'essence' of art having been, by and large, abandoned (even though every now and then one can still spot attempts being made). In *Philosophical investigations* he suggests that for some concepts, instead of looking for some one thing common to all instances which makes us use the same word for all of them, we should rather see that the various instances are *related* to each other in a multiplicity of ways, and it is because of these relationships that we use the same word for them all. He considers the example of games in some detail. We shouldn't think that there is something in common to all games which is what makes them games. If we '*look and see* whether there is anything common to all' we shall see 'a complicated network of similarities overlapping and criss-crossing: sometimes overall similarities, sometimes similarities of detail'.

> I can think of no better expression to characterise these similarities than 'family resemblances'; for the various resemblances between members of a family: build, features, colour of eyes, gait, temperament, etc. etc. overlap and criss-cross in the same way. – And I shall say: 'games' form a family.[14]

Now although Wittgenstein did not intend (as some have misunderstood him) the idea of family resemblances to apply to *all* words, it was quickly realised that the idea applied with particular neatness to concepts such as 'art', 'work of art' and 'aesthetic'. Professor W.E. Kennick, in his influential article 'Does traditional aesthetics rest on a mistake?'[15] (first published in *Mind*, 1958), was the first to spell out the application of Wittgenstein's idea to aesthetics. The message was further reinforced when Wittgenstein's brief *Lectures on aesthetics* were published in 1966,[16] for in them he repeatedly makes the point that in thinking about aesthetics we should not be looking just at the word 'beautiful', for example, but rather 'on the enormously complicated situation in which the aesthetic expression has a place, in which the expression itself has almost a negligible place' (p. 2).

Attempts to define art are doomed. They are made either by philosophers trying to plug gaps in their metaphysical schemes, or by critics who cannot resist the temptation to generalise. But as Hanslick, the great nineteenth-century music critic and author of the impressive essay on the aesthetics of music *Of the beautiful in music*, says, any general definition of art is in any case unlikely to be very helpful in thinking about any particular art form:

> We can't get a general metaphysical definition of art from which the aesthetic principles of any specific art can be deduced: for one thing, the works of art themselves must be the starting points; and also, each individual art can only be understood by studying its technical limits and inherent nature.[17]

Instead of attempting to produce a definition of art, it might be more useful to consider works of art in relation to what M.H.

Abrams calls 'Some co-ordinates of art criticism'.[18] Abrams says we can distinguish four major types of critical theory, according to which of four elements in the total situation of the work of art they concentrate upon. The four elements are the artist, the subject-matter, the audience and the work itself. Corresponding to each of these four elements there are critical theories, each associated with a characteristic set of critical terms. For instance, *expressive* theories see works of art as the expression of the feelings, thoughts or imagination of the artist, and will use terms such as 'sincerity' and 'spontaneity'; *mimetic* theories stress the relationship between the work of art and its subject-matter, and 'truth' and 'realism' will be characteristic critical terms; *pragmatic* or *didactic* theories stress the achievement of certain effects in an audience, and will speak of works of art as being 'moving' or 'up-lifting'; and *objective* theories claim that works of art should be judged in isolation from these other elements, by their own intrinsic qualities alone, and will speak of a work of art's structure, its unity or its balance.

The popularity recently of objective theories owes much to the fear of committing the Intentional Fallacy or the Affective Fallacy. These fallacies were the inventions of W.K. Wimsatt and Monroe C. Beardsley.[19] The intentional fallacy is that of confusing biography with criticism, of supposing that facts about a poet's life were relevant to interpreting and evaluating his poetry. It is a special case of what philosophers call the Genetic Fallacy. It is certainly true that some people are influenced in their responses to works of art by facts, or supposed facts, about the artist – facts which bear little or no relationship to what is actually *there*, in the work. But the situation is more complicated than Wimsatt and Beardsley apparently allow, as many have subsequently pointed out.[20] For we inevitably treat works of art as the products of fellow human beings, and our response to them is conditioned by our belief in the existence of an artist who intended them to be the way they are.[21] We shall look at this point in more detail shortly.

If the Intentional Fallacy is a confusion between a work of art and its causes, the Affective Fallacy is a confusion between a work of art and its effects. It is the fallacy of interpreting and evaluating a work by the psychological effects it has on people. Judging works of art by their effects seems to make them replaceable; the work itself fades out of view. However, one's responses to (most) works of art are not purely of the 'shiver down the spine' variety, for they are more complex than that. They have, we could say, the work of art as their *object* as well as their *cause*.[22] They could not have been caused by anything else. Again, we shall investigate this further shortly.

III

The distinction, already noted, between works of art and other objects of aesthetic interest, such as landscapes and flowers, raises important questions.

The crucial difference between the two categories is that the former are created, the intentional products of fellow human beings. (I shall simply ignore essentially irrelevant considerations of chimpanzees, Martians and computers). A work of art is a worked, artful product in a medium with known qualities, limits and constraints. The so-called 'fine arts' are just as much skills as other arts, such as the art of the conjuror. Art and nature may, of course, combine, as in landscape gardening, flower arranging and facial make-up. A completely rigid distinction between 'human product' and 'nature' cannot be drawn, for, ultimately, all human creations involve the rearrangement of 'nature' in some way or other.

However, the idea of a work of art being an intentional human product enables us to distinguish in our experience those elements that are relevant to our experience of an object as a work of art from those which are irrelevant. Such a distinction between the relevant and the irrelevant cannot in general be made, or cannot so easily be made, with natural objects of aesthetic interest.[23]

Consider some examples in order to make it clear what I mean. When I read a book of poetry, there will be many elements of my experience which, although they may be important for my general welfare, are irrelevant to my experience of the poems as poems: for instance, my hunger and tiredness, the acutely uncomfortable chair, the noise of the pneumatic drill in the street outside – all of these are significant, obtrusive elements of my experience, but are not part of my response to Hardy. Even with no such external distractions, there will still be irrelevant elements of experience: that is to say, irrelevant to our understanding and appreciation of Hardy. Thus, while the words, the punctuation, the rhythm, the metre are all relevant, the page numbers, the quality of the paper, the binding and the typography are not. Those features are relevant which the poet intended to constitute the poem.

Again, imagine someone who went to a concert and thought that it was the *movements* of the orchestra and conductor that were of central importance, who saw the orchestra and conductor as antagonists in some drama – perhaps seeing the conductor as representing man battling against a hostile environment. Without wishing to deny that the visual element of a musical performance can sometimes be very powerful (or that the behaviour of some conductors might positively encourage such an interpretation), we can surely say that the work of art is what the artist intended as the work, and in the case of conventional composers and concerts, this means the sound produced.

We are (as Hepburn points out) aided in distinguishing the relevant from the irrelevant in our experience of art by the conventions of different art forms. There is often a frame, or something like a frame, which marks off the work of art from its (irrelevant) surroundings. This is obviously true of paintings in galleries, but is true also of many other art forms. Our ability to distinguish between the orchestra tuning up and the start of a piece of music (which is more difficult with some pieces than others[24]) is aided by such conventions as the arrival of the conductor and his raising of the baton. In the theatre, the raising and lowering of the curtain marks the temporal limits of the play, the stage and the proscenium arch its spatial limits. Thus the man in a dinner jacket who steps in front of the curtain to announce a change of cast is not to be judged as part of the performance, and neither is the behaviour of the people in the most expensive boxes part of the play (though it may occasionally be more interesting).

The idea of the work of art as *intended*, and therefore of certain elements of our experience as being relevant and others irrelevant, is a crucial one in thinking about debates over objectivity and subjectivity and art. For while 'each of us is different', and the circumstances in which people experience a work of art will differ in countless ways, nevertheless, there will be a 'common core' of experience which most will have, and which the artist will have intended them to have. Although there will be many differences between me and the man in the next seat to me at a concert, it is likely that our experiences of the symphony will be similar in certain crucial ways. Not only will the sounds entering our ears be similar, but those of the sounds that we attend to as constituting the symphony will, assuming we are both familiar with the conventions of concerts, also be similar. We will both dismiss as irrelevant the rustle of sweet papers and the noise of the air conditioning system, for example. And further, if we are both familiar with the conventions of the musical style, with, say the Western tonal system, the sonata form, and so on, then what we make of what we hear – the *way* we hear it – will be similar too.

Knowledge (even if not explicit knowledge) of the rules and conventions of a particular style or art form provide, we could say, a common mode of understanding: a means of communication between artist and audience. The artist, via the work of art, exercises a sort of control over our experience.

The perception of works of art as intentional enables us to 'understand' them, and helps to make our experiences of them sharable and public, rather than private and undiscussable. We can illuminate this point by thinking about abstract painting. It might be asked, 'What is meant by abstract art? What is abstract contrasted with?' There are various possibilities: realistic art, or representational art, for example. But abstract art cannot be contrasted with realistic art as if the two formed an exhaustive dichotomy, for there are many paintings which are not realistic, but not abstract either. Nor, in fact, will 'representational' serve to mark off non-abstract art. For *any* visual work of art *can* be seen as representational. This is an important point. I do not mean that any visual work of art can be seen as representing some specific, named, known thing. Rather that it can be seen as representing something which *it*, the painting on the canvas, is not.

841

Here is what I mean more specifically. Imagine a painting which consists of a uniform white canvas, in the centre of which there is a large irregular patch of black paint – as if painted by a house-painter's brush with two or three large bold strokes. The painting might look like Figure 36.1. Now it is possible to see this as representational – indeed,

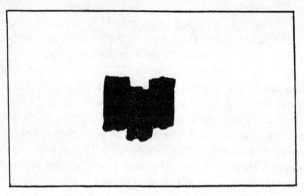

Figure 36.1

hard not to. Not, I mean, that one sees it as a face, or a building, but that one might see, for example, the black as being *on* the white, or as being in the foreground. This has nothing to do with the actual way the canvas was painted. Those who see the black on the white can 'accompany their perception with, for instance, fantasies about there being a yellow patch behind the black, or there being another black patch behind it, or there being a deep orifice behind it' (Richard Wollheim).[25]

Another example is given in Figure 36.2. It is possible to see such a squiggle as representational in a number of ways. It is difficult *not* to see it as representational in some way. Again, I do not mean that one must see it, as in the children's game of transforming squiggles or doodles into pictures, as a dog, a cyclist or a face, but rather one sees it as possessing properties different from those the actual physical drawing possesses. Thus, for instance, it is possible to see, where the lines in the squiggle meet, one line as *crossing*, that is, as going over, the other line. So one is seeing the drawing rather as if it were, or were of, a piece of string that had been dropped on the floor. By thinking of the lines as passing over or under each other one is thinking of the drawing as possessing three dimensions: as being of, say, a crazy Spaghetti Junction.

Seeing a (virtually) two-dimensional drawing as possessing three dimensions is one of the most obvious ways in which we see drawings as representations. Our habits of perception are such that we almost inevitably see some two-dimensional drawings as (representing) three-dimensional objects. It requires an almost impossible effort *not* to see them in this way (Figure 36.3).

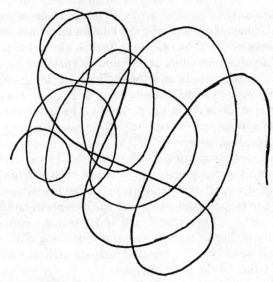

Figure 36.2

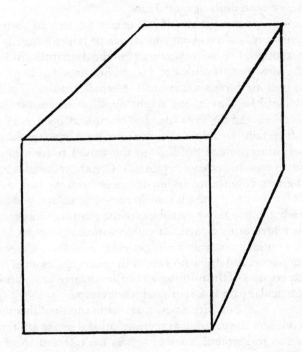

Figure 36.3

Now it is an important part of our perception of most of what is usually called 'abstract art' that it can be seen in this way as representational. Again, I stress that by this I do not mean that we have to see abstract art as being of a face, or a specific object. Rather what I am saying is that attributing depth, foreground, background to a painting by, say, Rothko or Pollock is an intrinsic part of seeing them. That is, seeing them as *paintings*, rather than seeing them as something else (something to cover a patch on the wall, for example) involves the sort of perception I have described. That is to say, the simultaneous appreciation of their existence as 'paint-on-canvas' *and* as possessing form, line, coherence, depth, etc.; that is, *as capable* of being seen as possessing these properties. In this way abstract art is like realistic art, for as Wollheim says, arguing against a 'deception theory'[26] of realism, part of the pleasure we derive from art (realistic art) comes from the simultaneous perception of a painting as paint-on-canvas and as representational.

Our ability to use and appreciate various different media for art, our ability to see something as something else, is connected with our imaginative abilities in general. It is also closely connected with our ability to invest the world with intentionality. In art we can recapture something of the astonishing imaginative power of children to invest objects with meaning, to see them as something they are not. Children become totally absorbed for hours in playing in the sand pit, or in treating a broomstick as a horse, or with dolls or model cars.

I'm not sure if it is true to say that *all* abstract art is seen as representational. What about Mondriaan or Jasper Johns? In the case of Mondriaan, though, I wonder whether even the description of a painting as, for example, consisting of vertical and horizontal lines dividing the canvas into rectangles isn't itself 'representational'. After all, the lines don't have to be seen as dividing the canvas: one might think of the canvas as already having been divided, and the lines added afterwards as borders to the rectangles of colour. Again, we might ask, do the colours have spatial relationships with each other (which differ from the spatial relationships of the portions of canvas on which they are painted)? Can the rectangles of colour, for example, be seen as lying at varying distances from the spectator?

My point is this. In non-abstract art, where one can talk fairly unambiguously about the subject of the painting, the perception of the painting as representing a particular subject-matter provides a 'mode of perceiving': in a sense, it controls our experience. And that, it seems to me, makes communication and discussion about the painting possible, for different persons' experiences of the painting will be, *in certain respects*, similar: they will all see a particular part as foreground, for example.

But with abstract art, as in my first illustration, the way in which one sees the painting as representational seems arbitrary: what one person sees as foreground, another sees as background. And so communication and discussion become difficult. And it becomes difficult to say anything about the painting or one's experience of it. One is lost in subjectivity. One has no way of deciding what the artist intended, or of deciding what is intentional in the painting and what accidental. So one has no way of distinguishing one's experience of the work of art from one's experience of what is not the work. So art dissolves, and art objects become indistinguishable from natural objects.

Somebody might say here, 'Surely music is an abstract art? How, if at all, are musical experiences sharable?' The temporal nature of music, as well as the conventions of music (such conventions, for instance, as the Western tonal system) impose upon music rules, limits, constraints which provide a framework which makes the perception of intention, and therefore understanding, possible.

Intention and understanding are not *all* that is important though: there is a danger of 'over-intellectualising' our experiences of art. In much recent musical aesthetics, there is an over-insistence on the structural nature of music. There has been a corresponding tendency to ignore the actual sensory properties of music – for example, such things as instrumentation and timbre. The sound itself is important, the 'sound-itself-at-a-time', as well as the 'sound-as-part-of-a-pattern'. It is as if, in cookery or gastronomy, one concentrated entirely on 'planning the menu', the order and combination of dishes, rather than the actual taste itself. One might enjoy a meal, but be very puzzled by being asked if one had *understood* it.

IV

We might say that for something to be a work of art, it must be available, in the sense of being *there*, capable of being experienced by someone. One way, perhaps, to put my point is to say that a work of art must be the object as well as cause of the experience that constitutes the experience of it. The experience of tasting a little cake dipped in tea, however rich, significant and complex an experience for Proust's narrator, Marcel, in *Remembrance of things past*, does not count as an experience of a work of art. We would not seek out the Paris baker who produced the petite madeleine in order to try to reduplicate for ourselves the same experiences as Marcel. His experiences were caused by the cake, only in the sense that they were triggered off by the cake.

Sometimes works of art induce a mood of dream and reverie which allows the audience to drift away, where the work of art is more like a stimulus which triggers a response than the 'focus' or object of that response. And there are some people on whom works of art have this effect, whether intended by the artist or not. Hanslick describes them well:

These enthusiasts, reclining in their seats and only half awake, suffer themselves to be rocked and lulled by the mere flow of sound... They are also the most easily satisfied part of the audience, and it is also they who tend to lower the dignity of music. For their ear the aesthetic criterion of intelligent gratification is wanting, and a good cigar, some exquisite dainty, or a warm bath yields to them the same enjoyment as a symphony.[27]

A work of art, a poem, for example, can sometimes fail to be fully available, because it is inadequate as an expression of what the artist wished to convey. There need be no lack of sincerity here. Quite the contrary: much bad poetry is perfectly sincere, just as sobs and sighs are sincere. But it is more a betrayal or evincing of emotion than true expression, for it fails to convey anything to the reader – the experience has not been transmuted and objectified.

Failure to be 'available' in this sense isn't confined to sentimental bad poetry. The last line of *The Waste Land* by T.S. Eliot is 'Shantih shantih shantih'. Turning to the notes Eliot himself conveniently provides for the poem, we find 'Shantih. Repeated as here, a formal ending to an Upanishad. "The peace which passeth understanding" is our equivalent to this word.' Now some might reflect here that it's all very well for Eliot to *tell* us that. If that's what he *meant*, why didn't he say it? And if it is rather a mouthful to finish the poem with:

The peace which passeth all understanding, The peace which passeth all understanding, The peace which passeth all understanding

then he could have written

X, X, X

and then told us in the notes at the end, 'By "X" I meant "the peace which passeth understanding".' One might just as well give up writing poetry altogether, and instead say, 'The sort of poem I have in mind expresses unendurable grief.'

Unless the reader is already familiar with Sanskrit and the Upanishads, he has to take Eliot's note on trust – a dangerous step, where Eliot's notes to *The Waste Land* are concerned, for some are positively misleading. The note, if taken seriously, is not just an aid, but is essential to the understanding of the poem. The word in the poem will not be understood without the note (except by a reader familiar with Sanskrit). Critically, a lot more could be said here, no doubt, and a variety of possible defences of Eliot's procedure here will have occurred to the reader. However, I hope that the philosophical point concerning 'availability' is clear.

An example from another art form, music, might reinforce the point. The composer Peter Maxwell Davies has written the following in a programme note on his own work *Vesalii Icones*:

In No. 8 *St Veronica wipes His face*, I have developed the idea of the reproduced photographic image on Veronica's cloth in musical terms. The opening music of the movement consists of a line of *Ecce Manus Tradentis* on the cello, accompanied by an inflated plainsong fragment, in a musical style which suggests a Victorian daguerrotype. This is immediately 'reproduced' in a modified version which suggests to me a hand-operated cylinder phonograph. The *raw material* from *Ecce Manus* is then *bent* to resemble a Schenker analysis, but instead of *stripping off* layers of music to expose a 'common' skeleton below, the 'skeleton' is heard first, and levels are added (the reference to Vesalius is obvious) – but when it would just about become clear to a perceptive ear that the analysis concerned is of the Scherzo of the fifth symphony of Beethoven, the flute twists the *Ecce Manus* fragment into a resemblance of the Scherzo of the ninth – it is a *related but false* image.[28]

What I should like to ask is: could any of this be *heard* in the music? Could anyone who had not read Maxwell Davies' programme note have grasped all this complexity of reference? I should have thought the answer obvious.

Tolstoy required a work of art to be available in a very strong sense. A work of art, for him, must be not just such that it is capable of being understood, but such that *anyone*, and in particular the peasant, could immediately appreciate it. This view famously led him to condemn all his own novels, and to hold that Beethoven's Ninth Symphony was not a good work of art because 'I am unable to imagine to myself a crowd of normal people who could understand anything of this long, confused, and artificial production, except short snatches which are lost in a sea of what is incomprehensible.'[29]

V

In any discussion of aesthetics, the question of the objectivity or subjectivity of taste inevitably arises. The discussion unfortunately often reduces to an argument between two extremes, with no room being left for any intermediate positions. On the one hand, there is the view expressed by Kant.[30] 'The judgement of taste exacts agreement from everyone; and a person who describes something as beautiful insists that everyone *ought* to ... follow suit in describing it as beautiful.' On the other hand, it is maintained that 'one man's meat is another man's poison' or 'De gustibus non disputandum est' – 'There's no disputing matters of taste.' This polarisation is too simplistic, and it has tended to prevent any serious investigation of taste from getting under way. All I can hope to do here is to offer some brief notes on the subject.

Those who speak of the subjectivity of taste sometimes present our tastes as being *a priori*, unchangeable, 'given'. However, the fact is that they change, develop, mature, as well as coarsen or disintegrate. How many times do we find people saying of some food, or drink, or work of art, or type of experience in general, 'I didn't like it at first, but now I adore it.' It is also true that argument and discussion about works of art are not only possible, but often an important part of our experience of them. And going with such discussion and argument is the possibility of our views of a work changing, being modified.

The undeniable fact that there are (now) widespread disagreements about art doesn't of itself prove that there isn't a right answer, just as the fact that there are disagreements about the suitability of various diets doesn't prove that some diets aren't better than others. The analogy can perhaps be pursued further. While there are widespread variations in diet, and one man's meat may well be another man's poison, there are some items of diet which are essential for everyone, and some things which are (and are universally recognised to be) inedible or poisonous for everyone. But with art, as with diet, there are individual differences and personal preferences. We are differently constituted, have different personalities, have had different sets of experiences. These factors will affect our aesthetic preferences, as they will affect our preferences in other areas, too: there is, *pace* Kant, a limit to the agreement we can expect from others.

With works of art, as with people, there are some we love, some we feel affection for, some we like, and some we admire. There are clear differences between these attitudes. Just as there are people who we admire without liking or wishing to emulate, so there are works of art that we are fully prepared to admit are great works of art, without our wishing to spend much time on (sometimes for personal reasons or associations). Some of those things that we like, we might describe ourselves as 'having a soft spot for', especially where we recognise that the reasons we have for liking them will not be shared by others. Such personal preferences are not necessarily irrational: it is just that others do not have the reasons we have. It is rather like a couple saying 'It's our tune' when the band starts playing the music that was being played the first time they met. There may be more complex sets of reasons than that for preferences, as well. Something can be liked (or, of course, disliked) for its associations, even simply because of long familiarity. It is not a limiting judgement on a man's taste that he is fond of the (rather undistinguished) town where he lives and was brought up, or the songs he was taught at his mother's knee. But none of this implies that taste is therefore totally subjective. We would certainly expect, for a start, that the more we have in common with someone else, both in terms of personality and shared experiences, the more likely our tastes are to be similar. And we are more likely to share our tastes, of course, with our contemporaries, rather than with people of a hundred years ago.

The word 'taste' itself can mislead, because it is also used specifically of the gustatory sense. Preferences in art are generally more complex than those involving, as it were, just a single dimension within a single sensory mode. Comparing, for instance, Beethoven and Spohr, isn't just a matter of giving each a 'lick', and saying which 'taste' is preferred, the Beethoven taste or the Spohr taste. This would be to suppose that all our experience of art was concerned with the homogeneous taste of a particular work or artist, with a sort of undifferentiated 'licking', like preferring raspberry to strawberry. It is clearly much more complex than that. Indeed, ultimately, in artistic preferences and choices as well as in other areas, moral choices may be involved. We do not, after all, say, 'Well, you enjoy embroidery as a hobby, I enjoy mugging old ladies – it's all a question of taste.'

Even where purely gustatory taste is concerned, the matter is more complicated than facile comparisons sometimes suggest, for surely there is a degree of objectivity, for there is a common experience which more than one person can share in. What I mean is this. With taste, as, for example, wine tasting shows, an extremely wide range of tastes can be differentiated, identified and reidentified. What is more, the ability to do this can, in the majority of cases, be developed and trained. What had initially seemed to be a group of identical, or very similar tastes can come to possess strongly individuating characteristics, agreed upon by different tasters. You can't hope to appreciate something if you don't understand it, and understanding requires as a minimum the ability to recognise and differentiate the thing to be understood. In art, as in other areas of expertise, we are more likely to trust the judgement of those with wide experience, and a demonstrated ability to differentiate accurately the items being judged.

We noted at the start of this chapter that each age reinterprets the art of the past: but something like this also happens within the lifetime of an individual. Our own tastes and preferences change and develop. There are certain characteristic changes of preference that occur as we grow older. These changes often consist of the rejection of some previously intensely admired works, together with the acceptance of other works previously rejected or ignored. The works may have appealed in the first place, for example, to adolescent romanticism: their later rejection may partly be due to the embarrassment of being reminded of that time in one's life. Sometimes, the same works are admired over a long period, but different aspects of them come to be admired and relished. We might have reason to be suspicious of someone whose tastes and preferences failed to change in any way throughout his life: for one thing, he would have to be immune to the impact of the new. There is something suspicious, too, about those who subsist on a very limited and one-sided aesthetic diet, even where the items comprising that diet are worthy: think for example of the 'Janeites', whose novel-reading is confined to a continuous rereading of Jane Austen's novels.

Previous generations weren't necessarily wrong in their judgements, where those judgements differ from ours, and neither are ours. For the basis of the judgements may be different in the two eras. It is sometimes asked, 'Which of today's artists will still be remembered in 100 years' time?' as if the answer to that question, 'The Test of Time', were it known, would settle critical bets about who, now, was the better artist. But it wouldn't. There are, indeed, some works which have been admired in all ages, just as some people have been universally admired throughout history. In just the same way some items of diet are essential and some best avoided. But some diets might be better suited to one particular way of life, just as a particular character may be admired only in certain circumstances.

The point I have been wishing to make is that to speak of tastes and preferences, and to recognise that individual and historical differences inevitably exist, is not to rule out any talk of 'better' or 'worse', of values. Even though works of art are difficult to evaluate because of their extreme complexity, that shouldn't deter us from the task. The task of evaluation in morality is scarcely less complex. Criticism, and aesthetics, involve a sort of arduous thinking that isn't usually asked of people, and is produced normally only by artists, and the very greatest moralists and psychologists (so often themselves novelists). In the end, questions of values are inextricably connected with our thoughts about works of art, for choices *have* to be made. In the end, we can experience only a limited amount of art. Consistent and repeated choice of the trivial or the corrupt in art will reflect something wrong with one's moral values.

VI

Recent contributions to aesthetics, then, have done little to dispel the charge of dreariness and irrelevance that has hung over the subject throughout its brief history. The familiar and the obvious are the first casualties in philosophical discussion: thus aesthetic theory often seems false to our experience of art (and sometimes the uneasy suspicion can arise that the philosopher has not *forgotten* the familiar, for he doesn't know what responding first-hand to art is like). Recently, such an inadequacy to our experience of art has been evident; a result, I believe, partly of aestheticians' preoccupation with what it is to treat something 'aesthetically', and partly from a concentration on works of art in isolation from the circumstances in which they are actually created or appreciated.

This concentration is a consequence of anti-romanticism, and a reaction to an expressive theory of art – a reaction in which the 'exposures' of the Intentional and the Affective Fallacies played their part – so that many aestheticians recently have stressed the importance of 'the work itself', and reject as irrelevant any considerations about the artist or the effect of the work on its audience. An additional factor has been that philosophy has recently been thought to be the study of various forms of linguistic activity, and the various branches of philosophy as studies of different sorts of linguistic activity. Aesthetics, therefore, is taken to be the study of critical language – criticism, that is, of works of art. Again, MacIntyre's comments[31] on recent moral philosophy apply with equal force to aesthetics:

A certain unsystematically selected class of moral concepts and judgements is made the subject of attention. From the study of these it is concluded that specifically moral discourse possesses certain characteristics. When counter-examples are adduced to show that this is not always so, these counter-examples are dismissed as irrelevant, because not examples of moral discourse; and they are shown to be nonmoral by exhibiting their lack of the necessary characteristics.

The twentieth century has seen a self-consciousness about art which has manifested itself particularly in a practical assault upon the concept of art by the creation of challenging objects. For every feature which has been put forward as being definitional of art, or important in works of art, it is virtually certain that someone has produced an object lacking that feature, with the explicit or implicit challenge, 'I dare you to say it isn't art.' One consequence of this challenge is that questions about the definition of 'art' or 'work of art' have proved virtually unanswerable, and, what is more, there seems no point in trying to produce an answer. Faced with the works of, for example, Duchamp, Cage, Carl Andre, Rothko, Gilbert and George, faced with Pop Art, Op Art, Minimalist Art, Cornelius Cardew's Scratch Orchestra, as well as all the more outrageous and well-publicised Arts Council-funded projects, the proper question is not so much 'Is it art?' but 'Is it important?' or 'Does it matter?'

The challenge of the avant garde, combined with the genuine difficulty of saying anything interesting or profound in general about such a diverse range of phenomena as works of art, has led aestheticians to retreat nervously from the large-scale exposition to the more specialised investigation of particular problems. But if there are important general things to be said about art, they will not be reached by a long study of just a small portion of the field. Not only will all arts and all periods have to be considered, but also the whole position of artistic activity within the whole economy of human life.

In fact, it was Wittgenstein, whose enormously influential but frequently misunderstood later philosophy was partly responsible for the linguistic turn of much post-war philosophy, who stressed that in our actual appreciation of art, the words we use are only part, and a small part, of an 'enormously complicated situation'. If we want to understand aesthetics, we should be looking at certain occasions and activities, not at forms of expression, and especially not at the word 'beautiful': ' "Beautiful" is an odd word to talk about because it's hardly ever used'. 'To describe what it [appreciation] consists in we would have to describe the whole environment.'[32]

What we need, then, but do not have, is the bold and adventurous attempt by a contemporary philosopher to delineate the place of art and aesthetic appreciation in human life. Such a work could be written only by someone who was not only a profound and acute philosopher, but also who was sensitive to the whole range of aesthetic experience, and who drew on his or her first-hand experiences of the arts: someone, in other words, who sees that aesthetics is a very big subject, but doesn't misunderstand it.

In 1960, Mary Warnock voiced a series of criticisms of moral philosophy which were typical of many others being made at the time.[33] She complained that 'a small and general set of concepts [had] been singled out for treatment in books about ethics'. But the words chosen do not have any particular relevance to ethics, and (echoing Wittgenstein's words) 'as for "good", I doubt whether it comes in very much except in the pages of books about moral philosophy'. This has led to 'the increasing triviality of the subject'. But she was optimistic for she thought that 'the most boring days are over', and after outlining her reasons for thinking this, she concludes her book by speculating about moral philosophers in the immediate future:

> It is impossible to predict what kinds of books they will actually write. But the examples which they contain will necessarily have to be long, complicated and realistic. I think that the days of shouting to revive the fainting man, and the days of grading apples, are over. Moral philosophy will be much more difficult, perhaps much more embarrassing, to write than it has been recently, but it will be far more interesting to read.

It must be said that these speculations have proved accurate. Aesthetics has so often lagged behind other areas in philosophy, feeling the effects of major developments in more central areas only after a long delay. Is it too much to hope, over a quarter of a century after (as she then was) Mrs Warnock's comments on moral philosophy, that the most boring days might be over for aesthetics, too?

Notes

(An author's name followed by a number in square brackets refers to the book or article which has that number in the bibliography.)

1. Wittgenstein [4], p. 1.

2. The *locus classicus* of this particular claim is J. Passmore, 'The dreariness of aesthetics', *Mind* (1948), and reprinted in Elton [12]. One of the few dissenters has been Ruth Saw, who, in her *Aesthetics: an introduction* (Macmillan, London, 1972), accuses philosophers of being 'as sheeplike as ordinary mortals' in agreeing with Passmore.

3. Stuart Hampshire, in 'Logic and appreciation', *World Review* (1952), and reprinted in Elton [12], questions whether aesthetics is a *genuine* subject: he mentions the 'alexandrianism which assumes that there are so many classified subjects waiting to be discussed'.

4. Sir William Hamilton, *Lectures on metaphysics* (1859), I, vii, p. 124. Kant, it seems, did not approve of this use of the word 'aesthetic'. Although he made a distinguished contribution to the *subject* of aesthetics in his *Critique of judgement*, he used the *word*

'aesthetic' to refer far more generally to our sensory capacities, as in the 'Transcendental aesthetic' in *The critique of pure reason*, where he discusses the *a priori* principles of all sensory knowledge.

5. S.T. Coleridge, 1821, in *Blackwood's Magazine*, 10, p. 254. Sir William Hamilton, *Lectures on metaphysics*, also objected to the word, but his alternative suggestion of 'apolaustic' has little to recommend it!

6. R.W. Hepburn has written illuminatingly on this in 'Contemporary aesthetics and the neglect of natural beauty' in Bernard Williams and Alan Montefiore (eds), *British analytical philosophy* (Routledge and Kegan Paul, London, 1966) and in 'Nature in the light of art' in Vesey [11].

7. There is a distinction between the features (in the sense of phenomenal properties) of a work of art, and its aesthetic qualities (see 'Aesthetic concepts' by F. Sibley in Barrett [10]. Within a tightly knit cultural community, it may be necessary only to point to the features. Some features have (for the members of that community) certain effects, and because they have these effects they have been picked on and erected into rules, and the effects forgotten about. When, as happens, these properties no longer have the original effects, the rules come to seem ludicrous (because the essential connection is now missing).

8. Wellek's letter appeared in *Scrutiny* (March 1937), and Leavis' reply in the June 1937 issue. The exchange has been reprinted a number of times, for example in Eric Bentley (ed.), *The importance of Scrutiny* (New York University Press, New York, 1964).

9. P.F. Strawson, *Individuals* (Methuen, London, 1959), p. 10.

10. Alasdair MacIntyre, *A short history of ethics* (Macmillan, London, 1966), p. 1. Not all philosophers would agree with either Strawson or MacIntyre.

11. Dilys Powell, *Sunday Times*, 7 March 1971.

12. Collingwood [3] provides an interesting discussion of what art is not.

13. Clive Bell, *Art* (Chatto and Windus, London, 1914).

14. Ludwig Wittgenstein, *Philosophical investigations* (Basil Blackwell, Oxford, 1963), pp. 31–2.

15. Reprinted in Barrett [10].

16. Wittgenstein [4].

17. E. Hanslick, *Of the beautiful in music*, originally published 1854, trans. Gustav Cohen (The Library of Liberal Arts, Bobbs-Merrill, Indianapolis, 1957).

18. M.H. Abrams, *The mirror and the lamp* (Oxford University Press, Oxford, 1953), p. 6. L. Lerner, in *The truth tellers* (Chatto and Windus, London, 1967), uses a similar framework to discuss theories of literary criticism.

19. 'The Intentional Fallacy' and 'The Affective Fallacy' first appeared in the *Sewanee Review*, 54 (Summer 1946), and 57 (Winter 1949). They appear as the first two chapters of Wimsatt's book, *The verbal icon* (Methuen, London, 1970).

20. The best discussions of the Intentional Fallacy are to be found in Hirsch [16] and F. Cioffi, 'Intention and interpretation in criticism', *Proceedings of the Aristotelian Society*, 64 (1963–4), reprinted in Barrett [10].

21. Anthony Savile, 'The place of intention in the concept of art', *Proceedings of the Aristotelian Society*, 69 (1968–9), reprinted in Osborne [9], makes this point.

22. J.P. Casey, *The language of criticism* (Methuen, London, 1966), pp. 30, 90, 93 and 132, while allowing the importance of one's response to a work of art, curiously denies that it is *caused* by the work. I presume Casey does not say this because of some

esoteric view of what a work of art actually is, for example that it is a purely imaginary object in the artist's mind, which could not cause the spectator's response. Casey overlooks the fact that the very same thing can be both the cause and the object (i.e. that to which my feelings are 'directed') of my response or emotion. They *needn't* be the same thing: the object of my fear need not exist (a nuclear war), though the cause must (a film perhaps). Or a drug (cause) might make me delighted with my fingernails (object). Works of art are both the causes and the objects of our responses to them – because our responses are directed towards the work, it doesn't follow they are uncaused, or uncaused by the work.

23. Hepburn, 'Contemporary aesthetics and the neglect of natural beauty'.

24. The composer Kagel has a piece which begins with the oboe playing A sharp, and the other instruments joining in randomly playing A sharp, then practising their parts. The effect is exactly that of the orchestra tuning up. The conductor then slowly comes to life and gradually starts beating time and the 'piece' proceeds. For every convention there is some artist in the twentieth century willing to exploit it. But the exploitation only makes a point because of the prior existence of the convention.

25. Richard Wollheim, 'On drawing an object' in Osborne [9], p. 140.

26. The deception theory could be stated simply (too simply) in the following terms: a painting is realistic to the extent that it deceives (or tends to deceive) the spectator into thinking he is in the presence of the objects it depicts. The most impressive advocate of the deception theory has been E.H. Gombrich in *Art and illusion* [17] and many subsequent works.

27. Hanslick, *Of the beautiful in music*, pp. 90–1.

28. P. Maxwell Davies, programme notes for 'Masterconcert five', City Hall, Glasgow, 27 February 1972.

29. Tolstoy [2].

30. Kant [1], p. 82. Kant's own view was more subtle than this small extract suggests: he draws attention to the distinction between liking and admiring, between judging something to be beautiful and finding it agreeable.

31. MacIntyre, *Short history of ethics*, p. 4.

32. Wittgenstein [4], p. 7.

33. *Ethics since 1900*, pp. 144–7, Home University Library, 1960. Many others – Miss Anscombe, W.H. Walsh, Stuart Hampshire, Bernard Williams and, as we have already seen, Alasdair MacIntyre all made similar points.

Bibliography

General works

For the reasons given in the chapter, the writings of aestheticians of the past have less relevance than the historical works of great philosophers generally have to present-day concerns. To see a great philosopher tangling with aesthetics, see

[1] I. Kant, 'Critique of aesthetic judgement' (first published 1790) in *The critique of judgement*, trans. J.C. Meredith (Oxford University Press, Oxford, 1952), though this will prove heavy going, especially to anyone unacquainted with Kant's other philosophical works.

[2] L. Tolstoy, *What is art?* (originally published 1896), trans. Aylmer Maude (The

Liberal Arts Press, Bobbs-Merrill, New York, 1960), is another, highly idiosyncratic, classic. Tolstoy's moralistic viewpoint, produced at the end of his life, leads him to reject almost all great works of art as worthless, including almost all his own writing.

For a twentieth-century classic, see the fascinating and sometimes infuriating

[3] R.G. Collingwood, *Principles of art* (Oxford University Press, Oxford, 1938).

Ludwig Wittgenstein, one of the greatest twentieth-century philosophers, wrote only briefly on aesthetics. His *Lectures on aesthetics* are fertile but brief. They can be found in

[4] L. Wittgenstein, *Lectures and conversations on aesthetics, psychology and religious belief*, ed. C. Barrett (Basil Blackwell, Oxford, 1966).

A very useful survey of the history of aesthetics, with excellent bibliographies, is provided by

[5] M.C. Beardsley, *Aesthetics from classical Greece to the present* (Macmillan, New York, 1966).

Sound general introductions to the subject are

[6] M.C. Beardsley, *Aesthetics: problems in the philosophy of criticism* (Harcourt, Brace and World, New York, 1958)

[7] A. Boyce Gibson, *Muse and thinker* (C.A. Watts, London, 1969, and Penguin Books, Harmondsworth, 1972) and

[8] J. Hospers, *Understanding the arts* (Prentice-Hall, Englewood Cliffs, 1982).

The characteristic contribution to aesthetics after the Second World War was in article form: some of the most influential of these articles have been collected in

[9] H. Osborne (ed.), *Aesthetics* (Oxford University Press, Oxford, 1972)

[10] C. Barrett (ed.), *Collected papers on aesthetics* (Basil Blackwell, Oxford, 1965)

[11] Royal Institute of Philosophy Lectures, vol. VI, 1971–2, edited and with a Foreword by G.N.A. Vesey, *Philosophy and the arts* (Macmillan, London, 1973) and

[12] W. Elton (ed.), *Aesthetics and language* (Basil Blackwell, Oxford, 1954).

Recent interesting attempts to produce more comprehensive accounts of art and aesthetic judgement are

[13] R. Scruton, *Art and imagination* (Methuen, London, 1974)

[14] R. Scruton, *The aesthetic understanding* (Methuen, London, 1983) and

[15] A. Savile, *The test of time* (Clarendon Press, Oxford, 1982).

[16] E.D. Hirsch, Jr, *Validity in interpretation* (Yale University Press, New Haven and London, 1967) is an excellent treatment of the Intentional Fallacy and related problems of interpretation.

Treatments of specific art forms

The classic exposition of the deception theory of realism in the visual arts is

[17] E. Gombrich, *Art and illusion* (Phaidon Press, London, 1960) – a theme which Gombrich has pursued in many subsequent books.

[18] N. Goodman, *The languages of art* (Oxford University Press, London, 1969) has an excellent discussion of theories of realism.

[19] R. Arnheim, *Film as art* (Faber and Faber, London, 1958) contains much of Arnheim's classic 1933 essay 'Film'.

[20] S. Cavell, *The world viewed* (Harvard University Press, London, 1971, enlarged edition 1979) isn't really a work of aesthetics: but it is a profoundly interesting book

about the cinema by a distinguished philosopher: for anyone seriously interested in film, compulsory reading.

[21] M.J. Budd, *Music and the emotions* (Routledge and Kegan Paul, London, 1985) is a densely, and acutely, argued survey of the main philosophical theories concerning the nature of music.

[22] R. Scruton, *The aesthetics of architecture* (Methuen, London, 1979) continues Scruton's theme that a proper treatment of aesthetics must crucially involve philosophy of mind and moral philosophy, and argues for objectivity of judgement.

M.A.P.

37 The Philosophy of Religion

Ronald W. Hepburn

Philosophy of religion is the philosophical examination of religious concepts, discourse and claims, and of the evidence and argument offered on their behalf. It is linked by the closest connections to the other main branches of philosophy. Thus, it connects with *moral philosophy* through attempts to ground moral obligation in the command or will of God, and through moral–religious concepts like sin, repentance, forgiveness, obedience, the 'meaning of life'. It connects with *philosophy of mind* through questions about the nature of persons, questions about immortality and resurrection as they relate to concepts of personal identity, body, mind and spirit. It has links with *theory of knowledge* – through differing accounts of the nature of knowledge, some of which make knowledge of God a possibility, while others – limiting knowledge to finite objects of experience – rule it out. It connects with *logic*, through claims, for instance, that normal rules for consistency and meaningfulness do not apply to thought and reasoning about an infinite deity. In that context paradox is to be expected and our conceptual schemes may well break down. The same is true of reports on mystical experience. Again, it connects with *philosophy of language*, on the grounds just mentioned, also because religious language has distinctive features, fusing historical, cosmological, symbolic, metaphorical, mythical and other elements, and raising complex questions of how fairly to appraise it. And it is involved with *metaphysics*: a link that to some religious people seems closest and strongest and most obvious of all, but which others deny or repudiate. How the so-called 'God of the philosophers' relates to the God of historical, revealed religion is itself a problem for (and within) the philosophy of religion. Like other 'philosophies of ...', philosophy of religion must constantly remain receptive to developments and new insights in the 'core' of philosophy – in epistemology, ontology, philosophical logic. Conversely, it should itself seek to contribute to discussion at the centre of the subject, witnessing to a range of human experience that any philosophy must reckon with in some way, where moral notions are fashioned and refashioned, and contrasted ways of seeing humanity and its cosmic setting are presented, often with great imaginative force.

The actual philosophical treatment of these various issues is of course immensely diversified. It may be metaphysically systematic, detailed and comprehensive, or analytical – whether extended or piecemeal, or phenomenological (systematically descriptive of basic forms of religious experience, such as for instance the 'sense of the holy').

There are substantial, all-important differences in the way religious objects of concern are understood, ontologically, and in the ways in which philosophers and others respond to the differences of treatment. The study and appraisal of these alternatives and responses constitutes a significant part of the philosophy of religion.

To some, religious beliefs are continuous with – and overlap with – *cosmological* beliefs: a religion is among other things a metaphysic – a set of beliefs about what ultimately exists and about the fundamental pattern of *events* (e.g. creation by God, Fall of man, redemption, final judgement). The basic objects of religious belief are *actual*, not imaginary, not intentional objects only. The atheist denies that the world, and the pattern of events, are like that: the agnostic that we have adequate grounds for the theistic claims. The issue between them is a difference over the explanatory power of a view of the world. (It is at least that, though it may be more.)

A second group passionately retains the view that the objects of religious belief, God, hereafter, etc., are actual and that they are not reducible to experiences, values, ideals of ours here and now. But it denies that they are proper subjects for metaphysical treatment: they are not metaphysical notions, and no valid conclusion can emerge from metaphysical debate about their existence or non-existence. God is known not through our arguments and observation of the world, but only through His own self-disclosure: we know Him only as He addresses and reveals Himself to us. Philosophical theology is a snare, a danger. It is liable either to bring God down to the grasp of our categories and concepts, or (if, not surprisingly, He eludes these human conceptual nets) to have a misleadingly sceptical outcome!

Thirdly, a person may see certain religious values, attitudes, behaviour and modes of integrating life as supremely and indispensably important, but may be unable to accept the arguments of theistic metaphysics or the claim that an actual God may be encountered, or may reveal Himself to us. How, if at all, can such a person avoid total religious scepticism or an incoherent position? This is not an uncommon quandary, and various proposals can be (and recently have been) made for 'radical revisions' of theological claims, revisions necessary for affirming at least some of the values, but without the support of belief in God as independent or 'objective'. These, essentially, argue that claims of the latter kind can fall away, and forms of spirituality remain. More boldly, defenders of such views have argued that they in fact achieve a 'purer' form of spirituality than does traditional theism, precisely by virtue of that severance from cosmological thinking and from ideas of deity that have, in our time, become unsupportable and incredible.

Each and all of these three views is able to call upon serious argument in its support. Philosophy of religion has great scope for rational appraisal here; decision among these options need not be unguided or arbitrary. One of the most important tasks for philosophy of religion, in this area and more generally, is the clarifying of what beliefs are presupposed in any particular religious view; and what implications flow from it for the believer – for instance, what expectations concerning the course of his life and about any conscious existence after death may he form on the basis of the view?

In attempting now to consider some contrasted ways of understanding and appraising concepts of deity and the philosophical problems these raise, we shall make use of the distinctions that have just been outlined.

Some questions about God can be understood as primarily questions about the possibility of reference to a transcendent being: others as primarily about the coherence or incoherence of the concept of God. Others again are of so general a nature as to be relevant to both these areas of inquiry.

To refer to God, to identify Him as our subject of discourse, is (if it can be done) to refer out of our experience and 'beyond' our world. It is not only in the context of the natural–religious arguments for God's existence that philosophy needs to explore the meaningfulness and the feasibility of such reference. Any attempt to achieve a metaphysical 'placing' of deity requires to make sense of the relation between God and the world. That relation will arguably be unique, in that no entities *within* the world will be related as are Creator and the creatures He calls into being from nothing, and which remain utterly dependent upon Him. That uniqueness will mean that our thought and language will be operating under severe stress when we try to speak of God and the world in relation: we shall no doubt stammer. Some philosophers will take our stammering to indicate conceptual confusion and an illusory relation, while others will take it to signify only the strenuousness that goes with a difficult and important task.

The relation of cause and effect will readily illustrate this. In relating God to the world, it is hard *not* to make central use of the relation; but it is no less hard to make sense of it and justify it in that role. The relation of cause and effect is forged by us to connect our experiences of events occurring in time, to point us towards forming rules, laws that give intelligibility to successions of experiences, provided that initial conditions are known to us. How very different must be the relation between God and world; and it is very questionable whether the cause–effect relationship can survive so drastic a shift of context without loss of meaningfulness. Nevertheless, analogies may be posited with potter and clay, author and play, etc., together with the caveat that none of these is more than suggestive. Our conception of God's nature is itself involved in our attempt to understand how He could be related to the world. An insistence on a straightforwardly causal relationship may come too near to conceiving Him as one with the cosmos – as turning the cog-wheels of the world, Himself part of the machine, and thus insufficiently transcendent: while to insist on the transcendence at all costs may leave us with a troublingly attenuated conception of the God–world relation.

A philosopher of religion may see God as the paramount *explanatory* concept. God, he may say, is the best explanation of the existence and the nature of the world. To postulate God is at once to unify and hence to simplify a great range of disparate data that otherwise have to be seen merely as *happening* to be the way they are. For some writers, the type of explanation that unifies the data and satisfies an enquirer most effectively of all is *personal* explanation, explanation in terms of the intentions and actions of a person, having both rationality and power to execute his intentions. In the case of God, both occur in highest measure. It is quite certainly tempting to unify one very diversified set of data, assembled through the work of contemporary scientists, namely the conditions necessary for the emergence and continuance of life and mind. Numerous factors, laws of nature and constants, if they were minutely different from what they are, would instantly render impossible the stabilities and the patterns of physical and chemical change necessary to the life we know. Do we best explain the form of these laws and the values given to those constants in personal theistic terms? – as having, that is, the greatest unifying power? Life would be seen as 'intended' to arise, and on that account its conditions are built into the world.

On the other hand, to serve as explanation – a critic will say – what we invoke to provide the explanation must itself be *less* problematic, less obscure than the phenomena it is invoked to explain. In particular, the concept of God surely cannot *both* be appealed to as reducing the opacity of the world to reason, *and* as more deeply mysterious than any of the objects and events that puzzle us in nature. Moreover, it does look as if the attempt to grasp and elaborate the idea of God as personal agency (and able therefore to provide such explanation) is mysterious – or highly problematic – indeed. God's intentions have to be seen as directly bringing about their effects, since God has no body.[1] He cannot, again, be thought of as occupying some region of space; and whether He is to be understood as 'sempiternal' (endlessly existent) or as 'timeless' (time-transcending) is vigorously disputed. Again, to be the *ultimate* explanation is to be the terminus of an explanatory regress: to be itself in no need of explanation, and not to generate further puzzlement and restless inquiry. That is to say, on this view the universe must be seen as a suppliant for explanation, but God must not be so seen. Once again, philosophers divide over whether this regress can not only be reasonably *continued* to the point the theist requires, but also *halted* where he needs it to stop.

A very basic question underlying these arguments and problems is what characteristics of order and intelligibility can be seen simply as the universe's *own* characteristics, aspects of its own nature, and what features, if any, cannot. Frustratingly, there can be no comparing of (a) the universe sustained and ordered by God, as the theist claims it is, and (b) the universe as it would be in the absence of that divine ordering (if it would exist at all).

Philosophy of religion is interested not only in the most general, pervasive and constant relation between God and world, but also in any more particular, 'special' episodes of divine action upon the world – i.e. the question of *miracle*. How do philosophical problems arise over the concept of miracle? Surely no philosophical legislation could rule out the possibility that the world's Creator might from time to time produce a miracle. Might He not have reason to act upon His own creation in ways that involve suspending the normal pattern of natural laws? – and this in order to reveal or teach some message about His own being, His own will for man.

The biggest philosophical problems here are probably epistemological problems, problems of assessing the evidence for claims to the miraculous. Such a claim must, in its nature, clash with the entire testimony of our regular experience of nature, both informal and systematic, scientific. We invariably confront a dilemma, sometimes (it may be) an agonisingly difficult choice, in answering the question: which should I believe – the accumulated experience of humanity about the sequences of natural events or the miracle-testimony under appraisal? Neither is infallible, but we necessarily have vastly greater weight of testimony to the non-miraculous than to the alleged miracles we are considering.[2] Indeed, it may be argued that the very possibility of our pursuing objectivity in historical studies depends upon our applying such criteria as would result in scepticism towards testimonies to miracle. In response, however, a theologian may talk of the divine preparation of a context of event and interpretative concepts whereby miraculous events may be recognised and understood as such, and scepticism in some measure mitigated. A Messiah may be anticipated: given the interpretation of Jesus as the Christ, his resurrection from the dead may become credible to believers.

On the other side again, not only contemporary scepticism may oppose the acceptance of a miracle-story. So too will certain (philosophical, metaphysical) conceptions of deity – on very different grounds. Ought not God – a *perfect* God – be conceived as fashioning his created world in such a way that it will achieve His ends by the laws (and the constants) built into it? Would not our thinking become less adequate to God if we thought of Him as having to interrupt and supersede those law-abiding processes – in miraculous interventions? Some philosophers and theologians will urge that the conception of deity that goes with the idea of miracle is in other ways too an inadequate, anthropomorphic, 'supernaturalistic' conception, closer to that of the God who walked 'in the garden in the cool of the day'[3] than to that of a transcendent Ground or Source of being.

It may also be argued that since religious values relate essentially to *inwardness*, to such attitudes as disinterested love, compassion, thankfulness, reverence, these values could not be fostered by the display of supernatural power over external nature. In a word, another philosophical–religious debate springs up from a critique of the miraculous as belonging to a now outgrown stage of religious understanding.

A further, related set of problems in the philosophy of religion arises from consideration of 'religious experience'. In our brief discussion of this topic, we shall mean by a religious experience one of the following: an episode that a subject describes as an 'encounter' with God or a god or other supernatural being; or as a vivid realisation of God's presence, action or will; as an occasion when the unity of God and the believer, or a divine unity in all things, is glimpsed or movingly grasped: more widely, an episode in which there seems to be given very directly and forcefully some sense of the ultimate nature of the world as benign or as hostile.

In considering religious claims as they relate to general philosophical and metaphysical reflection, it may be contested whether religious experience should be discussed here at all. Is there not a very sharp *contrast* between a philosophical approach to the justification of religious claims and an experiential approach? – 'I know God exists, because I encounter Him, because He has revealed Himself to me ...'

There are, however, two respects in which these approaches are continuous rather than divergent. Religious experience is relevant to reflection about reaching out from finite to infinite, from the this-worldly to the transcendent; secondly, philosophy is interested in how such experience is interpreted, in the reports of those who testify to it, often in the concepts and language of particular religions. Where there is interpretation, is there not also the possibility of *mis*-interpretation? There is certainly scope for philosophical interest and inquiry – and perhaps appraisal.

Among the claimants to revelatory experience, some may undeniably be correct. They cannot all be, since the claims have contradictory content: people have satanic experiences (the cosmos as under the sway of a malign power) as well as beatific experiences. A powerful sense of religious conviction can attach itself to highly varied contents. But that is no ground for a dogmatic and comprehensive philosophical scepticism about religious experience as such. Indeed, a philosopher may argue that theistic experiences must be taken, for fairness, at their face value, unless and until shown to be illusory. Another will urge that we have sufficient naturalistic, this-worldly, explanatory materials (anthropological, psychoanalytic . . .) to furnish an understanding of such experiences without positing any transcendent being or beings. It is fair to say that a person's readiness to cry 'Illusion!' or to accept the experience as veridical will, in significant measure, depend on his or her general philosophical-theological orientation.

Writers have argued, for instance, that basically similar 'mystical' experiences are interpreted by different subjects in a monistic or a theistic fashion: despite great difference of vocabulary and conceptual scheme, the underlying structure may remain discernible. The perceptual content, if any, in religious experience can be very closely related to the instruction that the believer has had in his particular faith. But, to complicate matters, religious experiences vary greatly in the degree of *specificity* in which they are understood or interpreted – from the high specificity of an alleged encounter with a particular god or saint, to the sense of an almost uncharacterised and uncharacterisable 'Presence that disturbs . . .'

> Whose dwelling is the light of setting suns,
> And the round ocean and the living air.[4]

Crucial though the distinction is between experience and interpretation, it cannot, in many instances, be made in any clear-cut or confident manner. An incipient interpretation can be expected immediately to modify the experience-in-the-making that it is seeking to interpret: it solemnises, shapes and possibly limits the final experience. (Unless, of course, the primary experiential elements are so powerful, so uncontainable by the subject's available concepts and framework of beliefs that he experiences them as overthrowing or exploding that framework.)

Philosophy of religion does clearly have work to do in this area. It can stand back from the complex phenomena of experience-and-interpretation (in tension, in fusion, etc.) and attempt to appraise – with caution and without arrogance – the claims that arise out of them. 'Without arrogance', because episodes of religious experience, as we have just reminded ourselves, may indicate the insufficiency of our everyday and scientific conceptual schemes – perhaps also of the conceptual scheme with which the philosopher who investigates the field intends to carry out his appraisal! Furthermore, he cannot *dismiss* a religiously believing account of experience of God on the ground that it imports interpretative concepts, thoughts, into the total experience-as-understood; for he himself is an

interpreter, even if his sources are different – Nietzsche perhaps, or Feuerbach, or Freud. In a word: the conceptual apparatus of philosophical appraisal
and metaphysical or religious or anti-religious schemes that are poised to
explain or 'explain away' religious experience – these cannot fairly be seen as
themselves beyond or above challenge: challenge that may come not least
from precisely the range of experience we are noting here. But they too, *qua*
interpreted, are never unchallengeable . . .

A further set of problems and tasks for philosophy of religion arises over the
internal coherence or intelligibility of concepts of God. These problems very
often arise because, although the component notions in concepts of God are
familiar notions (like knowledge or power), in the context of a 'perfect' being
they require extrapolation from everyday employment to a *limit*: a process
that may threaten their intelligibility.

       Omnipotence is one concept that readily develops
paradoxes. What is it to be omnipotent? Not simply to be able to do
'everything', if that includes the logically impossible as well as the possible. It
is no limitation to exclude the logically impossible, since the latter is not a
class of coherently stated tasks that God cannot perform: it is a class of failed
descriptions, *non*-tasks. Paradoxes are generated when we ask questions of
the kind: could God create something, say a heavenly body, which He could
not later reduce to fragments?[5] To say, 'No, He could not' is surely to
indicate finitude: but if we say, 'Yes, He could,' then equally there is something He cannot do. Does it mitigate or resolve this paradox if God is
considered as indeed able to terminate His own omnipotence by creating such
an object, but as under no necessity of doing so at any time? So long as he does
not act so as to frustrate his own omnipotence, omnipotent he remains.[6] No
other rival being or power can snatch it from Him.

       The existence of evil in the world can also present
itself as a problem about the coherence of the concept of God. Can we render
consistent the claims that God is all-good, all-knowing and all-powerful –
together with the facts of evil? Suffering, on the scale this planet has known it,
is argued by some to be the strongest of reasons for atheism: yet others, while
admitting it to be a 'mystery', find it insufficient to disturb faith in a God of
perfect goodness. Between these extremes are positions – of belief and of
unbelief – in which consideration is given to possible vindications of God's
goodness, theories about the necessary place of suffering in the achieving of
certain forms of moral excellence, its connections with the existence of
freedom (seen as a great good) and attempts made to mitigate at least the
conflict with the central claims of theism.

       The *'natural'* evils of pain, frustration, disablement,
the fear and the reality of death, diseases, the inhospitability of the environment, the suffering of non-human animals, together with the *'moral'* evils –
the miserable consequences of egoism, cruelty and callousness, the drive for

personal power – these have been seen in remarkably different lights. They have been taken to be the consequences of 'man's first disobedience', his 'Fall' from a prior happy state. Alternatively, we should think not of a Fall, but of a stage in man's *ascent*: his freedom is a necessary condition for personal relationships ultimately with God, while at the same time his abuse of that freedom results in many of the evils we deplore. Some see a tolerable theodicy as necessarily relying on a future life, beyond bodily death, in which the fulfilling of God's loving purpose for each individual can be brought about: here and now it may be lamentably frustrated. Religious views that deny any literal life after physical death will urge believers to see God's love in *whatever* is the case: that being the essential nature of faith. 'Though he slay me, yet will I trust in him.'[7] Philosophers will disagree over the relevance of the question: 'May we look for a justifiable *basis* for such faith?'

It is argued that many forms of moral excellence are possible only in a world where some suffering occurs. Courage, patience, endurance can be elicited by both natural and moral evil. If the world is seen as a 'vale of soul-making' (Keats), a substantial amount of evil can be reconciled with the existence of a God who attaches high value to the efforts of creatures like ourselves to bring that good result out of the evil. Soul-making is the work of freedom. In the currently popular Free Will Defence, the value of freedom is understood as sufficiently great to offset the evil produced through its abuse. Difficulties do remain in such a position, however. An opponent, if a 'compatibilist' determinist,[8] may argue that an omnipotent God could very well have chosen to create a world in which freedom of choice exists but is in fact never abused. Free acts are themselves part of the causal network of nature. Yet compatibilism has its critics, who see in it an attenuating of choice and of independence from circumstances (hereditary, environmental) over which an agent has no control.

'Soul-making' is a plausible account of how *some* evil is assimilated by *some* individuals and turned to moral good. But it cannot make sense of, for instance, the life and the suffering of a child mentally sub-normal from birth, in whose case there can be *no* soul-making through moral choice. And it is on most precarious ground in implying that enough evil becomes ingredient in overall good situations clearly to justify the divine decision to create this world. Some evils, too, suffered by the innocent are so hideous that we cannot conceive how they could be compensated for in any imagined hereafter. No 'sequel', here or hereafter, could make a morally tolerable whole of which these have been a part.

Particularly difficult for theism (among the forms of *natural* evil) is the problem of animal suffering, a problem taken with insufficient seriousness by many writers on the subject. It is, of course, easy to overestimate the intensity and the extent of animal suffering: it is free of most of the anxiety, dreadful anticipation and sense of loss that make up a substantial part of *human* misery. But it is no less easy to *under*estimate it. The extent to which living nature is a theatre of destroying and being destroyed certainly sets a *prima facie* obstacle to seeing its creator as all-loving.

For a different sort of example of philosophical difficulty over the concept of God let us ask how we should conceive of God's mode of being in relation to *time*. What would it be to have 'perfection' in this area? What are the options? (a) Since finitude in time suggests, first of all, that one's existence has a beginning and an end, to cancel finitude, for God, would be to say, He always was, He is and will always continue to be: sempiternity. (b) But there is another, and to many religious minds intriguing, possibility. Even with endless existence, the constraints and limitations of temporal experience, as we ourselves know it, would not be eliminated. There would still be '... not yet ...' and '... no longer ...', and these seem inevitably to entail *lack* – inaccessibility, limitation, confinement to the present; and the present can readily be apprehended as a vanishing knife-edge (between the moment just past and the moment about to arrive). Moreover, human time-consciousness has a measure of amplitude, caught in the phrases 'specious' or 'conscious' present, that can be more or less, richer or poorer. Why, then, should we resist extrapolating to a divine, time-transcending, synoptic mode of aware-ness, in which *all* time is present in a single 'eternal' grasp? Anything less than that could hardly be proper to the 'greatest conceivable being'. Yet that last judgement would be vigorously contested. It may be that although we ourselves do experience a range of temporal contents, from the meagre to the compressed and rich, we are deluded in supposing that the extrapolation can be thorough-going and that it is coherent. We are left with the difficult choice: do we see this inconceivability of the divine *totum simul* as signalling delusion indeed; or is it precisely the sort of inconceivability we should *expect* in thinking towards a being who is necessarily greater than can be thought – i.e. who, in transcending time (as He must), transcends also our powers of comprehension?

In the last sentence above I am alluding to a claim made by St Anselm, in Chapter 15 of his *Proslogion* (a tiny section of some four lines). It is a highly relevant claim in relation to the whole question of God's nature and ontologi-cal status. Far from being vitiated by its obscurity and mysteriousness, discourse about God *has* to be mysterious and obscure, for God must be 'something greater than can be thought'. Since it is possible to think that there exists such a being – that is, an inconceivably great being, 'then [says Anselm] if Thou are not this same being, something greater than Thou could be thought' – which is impossible. In other words: the God you *can* think cannot be the true God.

How helpful, if at all, is Anselm's argument? It can surely be legitimately used to defend a difficult theistic doctrine against premature and unfair rejection. On the other hand, it clearly cannot be used as a self-sufficient criterion for the *acceptability* of a doctrine. Together with Anselm's basic and definitional account of God, as *id quo maius cogitari nequit*('that being than whom no greater can be thought'), we have a requirement for developing our thinking about deity: if you *can* enhance your concept of God, then you *must* enhance it.[9] It is an irreducibly evaluative prescription; the inner logic of the concept of God is at least as much dependent on the *nisus* to think worthily of God as it is upon any considerations of fact.

We can see it illustrated again in the question of how God's *infinity* is to be understood. We can at the same time illustrate how we are by no means infallibly led to a single indisputable conclusion. Less developed thinking about gods sees a god as an essentially finite being, in the world and interacting with it. If a shift occurs to belief in a single God who 'created heaven and earth', He has to be seen as somehow not part of the created world, but 'over-against' it. But we do not yet have a resting place for thought: the world over-against God can be seen as limiting Him and excluding Him ... so the *nisus* to think adequately about God may thrust us on again to a different view of Him, perhaps one according to which God both transcends the world and is immanent in it; or is the 'complete realisation' of what is developed, but imperfectly, in and through the phases of the world's history.[10] Or again, arguing against traditional conceptions of God's infinity, Keith Ward claims that God's freedom and creativity can be made intelligible only if theology works with a concept of 'dynamic infinity', that involves 'potency and temporality in God'.[11]

Such explorations are obviously closely related to questions about God's 'ontological status', where again evaluative and metaphysical-explanatory aspects are closely intertwined. There is a development from finite deity, as 'in' a tree, say, or a grove, or behind the veil of the Temple – to deity as behind (screened by) all phenomena.[12] He is revealed-concealed by the created world as such. Even that conception may still be rejected, as insufficiently exalted, if it sees God (though a God of unlimited powers) as *a* being among beings. Some theologians, like Paul Tillich, wish to say that God is not a being, but being-itself, or the 'ground' or 'power' of being: only such a view would do justice to His transcendence.

With these and similar ascents from finitude and the anthropomorphic, there goes also, however, an increase in metaphysical elusiveness, and in the danger of attenuating the concept of God towards a sublime emptiness. There is a criticism of theism, implied rather than explicitly filled out, in Hume's *Dialogues concerning natural religion*, in which this danger is seen to be coupled with an opposite, or complementary, threat. The character Demea is determined to think worthily of God, and reaches what amounts to a religiously toned agnosticism in, and through, doing so. God, to him, is 'being without restriction'. Demea readily admits that to attempt to apply ideas, for instance, of mental life, to God is to make these ideas 'totally incomprehensible' in that context, so remote from the context of their normal use. He goes so far as to say, we 'cannot reach any ideas in the least corresponding to the ineffable sublimity of the divine attributes'. If these movements of thought carry the concept beyond understanding, so much the worse for our understanding: the movement must continue even so. (Compare Anselm, *Proslogion*, Chapter 15 again.) Suppose, on the other hand (turning to the other threat), we judge that intelligibility cannot be thus relinquished without our losing along with it the meaningfulness, purpose and value of religion. We decide we must keep substantially the ordinary meaning of the words we use about God, even though that compels us to retain finitude in our discourse and our thought about Him. That, in Hume's *Dialogues*, is Cleanthes' anthropomorphic way. To go that way is, however, to reduce the concept of God in a manner that a developed theism would be most reluctant to accept. The deeply rooted religious attitudes of complete trust, confidence and hope in the power and wisdom of God and, in general, His worthiness of worship seem to rely upon His infinite and unconditioned status.

The problem we have been outlining leaves a philosopher with the task of deciding whether there is any standing ground at all between these two opposite-phased movements of thought: or whether they point only towards a thoroughgoing agnosticism, reverential or simply non-religious. If religiously adequate, then incomprehensible: if comprehensible, then unacceptably anthropomorphic ... Or *is* there a way between the horns of the dilemma? Philosophy of religion must consider whether there is a reasonable prospect of developing a doctrine of *analogy* between the everyday and the religious senses of words applied to God.

It will be clear by now that philosophy of religion has many more tasks than the examining of arguments for the existence of God. Some writers, indeed, hold the view that furnishing such arguments, finding grounds for religious views of the world, is no part of its work. To them, the idea that grounds could, even in principle, be found is itself a confusion. Norman Malcolm, for instance, has argued that a 'religious viewpoint is not based on grounds or evidence'.[13] It is one thing to search for, and even perhaps to discover, evidence in support of the factual beliefs of particular religions. It is quite another thing to find any of these beliefs *religiously meaningful*. It is precisely the switch, all-important as it is, from a non-religious to a religious vision or 'world-picture', for which grounds and evidence are ineffectual and inappropriate. All useful and relevant testing and justifying take place within a 'system' – constituted, in part, by framework principles like nature's continuity and regularity. The principles that make up the system are presupposed in our testing but are not themselves tested or grounded. As with the 'language-games' that describe a way of seeing the world and a way of living in it, so it is with religious language-games in particular. '*Within* a language-game there is justification ...'; but the language-game itself is ' "groundless" '.[14] This is no cause for bewilderment: justification must come to an end. 'Religion is a form of life ... Science is another. Neither stands in need of justification.'[15]

    This account may well be right, in respect of broad religious ways of seeing, and religious attitudes. But, as its defenders realise, there are theistic-Christian and non-theistic Buddhist (and other) ways of giving religious significance to life and death. Questions of grounds, arguments and evidence cannot be prevented from arising again when we attempt to *discriminate* among the rival ways of structuring, making specific, not simply a general religious stance but the particular beliefs and interpretations and doctrines that are to fill out and articulate a religion.

    Philosophers have certainly claimed that God might be properly taken as 'basic' in our framework of beliefs (Alvin Plantinga, for one).[16] The difficulty, however, in taking God as basic to one's structure of beliefs is the complexity and challengeability of the theistic 'reading' of experience. Plantinga allows that we may still point to 'circumstances ... that call forth belief in God', circumstances that include 'guilt, gratitude, danger, a sense of God's presence'. But these and other circumstances can be read in non-theistic ways also; and the dispute over which of those ways is more appropriate cannot properly be stifled. It may be that the move to declare belief in God as not derived from evidence or attained by argument – as 'basic', that is – will make no very great difference to philosophical–religious debates ...

    One rather different position can be noticed at this point: a position distinct from theism, but certainly of both religious and philosophical interest. In writings of the 1970s and 1980s, John Leslie has called it 'Extreme Axiarchism'. In the context of the present chapter, it can be seen as one way of taking to the limit the value-component that we have already found crucial in the theistic tradition itself. The axiarchic claim is that our fundamental principle of explanation must be not a quasi-personal deity whose existence would itself remain an inexplicable brute fact, but a principle of 'creative ethical requirement' that the good, the valuable should exist. The ethical requirement of the universe is argued to be 'sufficient to produce it'.[17] Such a view would not exclude the existence also of a personal God (though critics have declared that redundant); but what is ultimate for it is much more like Plato's Form of the Good. Extreme Axiarchism is a seriously defensible current philosophical–religious position, 'revisionary' and counterintuitive though it is. It stands or falls with the possibility of an objectivist account of values. Its plausibility is dependent on a complex web of teleological considerations; some of the more arresting and controversial of which (as we noted earlier) centre on the 'delicacy' of the conditions necessary for the appearance of life. Leslie concludes that if nature's laws 'encourage life's development ... the razor edge on which this truth balances suggests that ethical requirements have a hand in it'.[18] That is not, however, the only possible explanation: the issue invites – and has begun to receive – vigorous discussion.[19]

Philosophical reflection on difficulties, tensions and paradoxes in traditional concepts of deity have also prompted revisions of doctrine within a broadly theistic perspective. A bold example of how this can happen is provided by 'process theology', the main sources of which are writings of A.N. Whitehead and Charles Hartshorne.[20] For this form of theology, process and temporality are taken as essential to the real – in God's case as well as for finites. God is not a detached, withdrawn ruler of the cosmos: He works by the agency of love rather than by constraint, and is affected by what happens in the processes of the world as well as affecting them. There is thus a changing and contingent aspect of God's nature, necessary for the responsiveness of love. This theism, in Hartshorne's version, is 'dipolar' and 'panentheistic'. In addition to the temporally changing and contingent mode of being, God possesses also an aspect of necessary, changeless existence. Panentheism claims that everything exists *in* God: it will not accept the sharp differentiating of the traditional theistic deity from His creation, nor the simple identification of God and world as in pantheism. The attempt is made to do justice to God as the biblical accounts speak of Him – a living and a loving God – while not relativising and finitising Him. Success or failure will obviously hang on how far such a theology can unify all this conceptual material into a coherent and convincing whole.

Many religious people, however, at very different times and places have felt there to be something deeply inappropriate in any sort of metaphysical treatment of the concept of God, and in attempts to reason ourselves into belief in God by philosophical argumentation. Not rational persuasion but conversion, they maintain, is the authentically religious path to belief: not through the examining of evidence and argument, but by our response to God's addressing us through His revealed Word. There is no route for reasoning from the world's mixture of good and evil, delight and suffering, to the infinites and perfections of a divine being. Metaphysics may well be daunted, but not so *faith*. We are dealing not with abstract ideas of intelligibility and ultimate explanation, but with a concrete 'personal', acting, 'wilful' and mysterious deity, to intellect a *deus absconditus*, a hidden God. To affirm a reasoned scepticism about the 'God of the philosophers', they say, is by no means to dispose of the God of revelation. More strongly, philosophical theology is a *snare*: it is liable to bring God down grotesquely to the level of our (finitising, relativising) concepts and categories; or else, if He not surprisingly eludes these conceptual nets, it mistakenly judges that He cannot exist at all.

Clearly, at the core of this view is a determination, again, to be faithful to biblical conceptions of God, which, for the vastly greater part, are anti-metaphysical in spirit and style of expression. God's independent reality, His 'objective' or absolute existence (one cannot avoid some such terms) are decisively affirmed.

These claims, however, cannot escape all critical questioning. Although the biblical writings are non-metaphysical, that does not mean that they do not raise implicitly metaphysical problems, or that questions about their own coherence and the truth or falsity of their assertions do not have metaphysical conditions and implications. And surely they do carry such implications. (To mention one example only: if speaking of a general resurrection of the dead is to be taken literally – as a coherent thought – we must be presupposing that personal identity can be understood as preserved between existence before death and existence (again) after such a resurrection.)

More fundamentally, the proponent of the anti-metaphysical view, faith-centred and revelation-centred, is telling us (in a very comprehensive judgement) – '*This* is how the world is': in proclaiming the content of the Christian revelation, he rejects (implicitly) numerous other, thinkable but incompatible, views of the world in favour of this one, the view that the God who is inaccessible to philosophical thought is indeed revealed in the life and teaching of Jesus Christ. 'He that hath seen me hath seen the Father.' How does the person who affirms this, however, know that it is true? It will not do to reply once more, 'God, through Christ, has revealed it to be so.' For the question will be repeated in the same form. Or it can be varied and elaborated: 'How do we rule out misjudgement, misinterpretation?' Again, not all our talk about God can be reworked as (non-metaphysical) talk about Jesus – though that is a tempting thought. But what then would we say about Jesus' relation with God, God to whom he prayed, and who raised him from the dead? There are presuppositions in all this: that God and the world are of such a nature as to make possible those relationships and interactions, even some kind of causal interactions. To examine and appraise the coherence of notions like these, however, is again to do philosophical analysis or metaphysics, so these cannot properly be excluded. There exists a plurality of 'revealed' religions, among which choice has to be made. How do we tell which alleged revelation to take as veridical? If there exist no criteria to guide choice, choice is completely arbitrary: if criteria do exist, what are they like? Whatever answer comes cannot fail to provide proper work for philosophical reflection and appraisal. In other words, a philosopher may justifiably resist claims that he can be concerned only with a so-called God of the philosophers, irrelevant to the genuine concerns of religion. Not even a revelation-centred theology can avoid making commitments that are a proper object of philosophical examination.

Now it is one thing to accept that, for traditional Christian thought, revealed religion as well as 'natural religion' depends on certain presuppositions of a metaphysical kind. It is quite another thing to be confident that these presuppositions are sufficiently coherent and well founded to supply the basis theistic religion needs. Some writers have taken the view that the metaphysics of traditional theism is not, in the end, defensible, but that by way of a drastic, 'radical' revision of religion, something – perhaps even the most important thing – may be saved.

The core to be saved may be seen as the life of *agape*, neighbour-love, of purity of heart, freedom from egoistic obsession, together with the evocation of attitudes of wonder, awe, reverence for life . . . With peculiar vividness, it may be argued, the Scriptures of Old and New Testaments express such a total response to existence, show it being won from more primitive religious elements, morally and politically biased and restrictive – until it is 'the world' as such that the creator-God is eventually said to love and to send His Son to redeem. The metaphysically problematic cosmological elements may be allowed to fall away; and the whole taken as an extended parable concerned essentially with the *practical*, firing the imagination as no ethic of rules and drily described virtues could do.[21]

The 'falling away' of the metaphysical and cosmological dimension can be presented not as a calamity for a religious view that cannot ultimately do without it, but as a coming to maturity of religious self-understanding, a following through of the 'inner logic' of religious notions which are only half-heartedly developed in metaphysical (or 'objective') theism. The central theme for spirituality is the internalising of the doctrines of religion, the moral assimilation of religious symbols that were *initially* presented as descriptions of external reality. Demonic powers, for instance, have long been internalised by most reflective believers. Holiness and divine reality itself can now be also internalised. God comes to be seen as a symbolic fusing or integrating of the values of spirituality. These values can be grasped, autonomously, as unconditioned in their demands: free therefore of the condition that they should be objectively embodied in an actual 'supreme being'. That is the crux of this argument; for if the autonomous recognition of spiritual values, and response to their claims, is logically independent of any *facts* – whether metaphysical or empirical-historical – then to press the case for an actual God, a historical resurrection of Jesus, and so on, is religiously *irrelevant*. It may be seen even as a *dis*service to religion, since 'an objective God cannot save'.[22] Disinterestedness, a very high spiritual value, is threatened, not secured, if we rely upon an objective or realistically conceived deity and life hereafter, that can provide the conditions for the recognition and reward of merit. Here we have, unexpectedly perhaps, a 'moral argument' not for the existence but for the *non*-existence of God so conceived: Kant's argument inverted.[23] A thoroughgoing internalisation of deity also eliminates the burden of anguished speculation over the 'problem of evil'; for that arises only if God is still conceived as an independent centre of awareness and power and (allegedly) of moral perfection.

In similar vein, the Swedish philosopher Axel

Hägerström (1868–1939) wrote, 'although the tendency to objectify God is psychologically explicable, it does not have the least religious significance'.[24] One can say to mankind:

> If the darkness in the world causes you to suffer, this is simply because you have not ignited the torch which alone can make the world light. You are waiting for the light to come from without, presenting itself to you. But such a light can only be an illusion.

It is for man himself to light it, 'and it will burn with an undiminished flame'.[25]

The intention of these accounts may be in one way anti-metaphysical, but they do afford the philosopher of religion much material for examination and appraisal. He will want to enquire how far we can take that analogy between moral autonomy and an alleged autonomy of spiritual, religious values. Such language must not be allowed to obscure the *differences* between some valued attitudes and emotions that traditionally have been seen as *responses* to God's nature (His holiness, righteousness ...) and those that are not necessarily seen in that way. The philosopher will wish to clarify the relationship between the spiritual values and the scriptural, objectivising accounts of God. He will want to enquire how far a morally and spiritually energising faith can survive the complete rejection of traditional interpretations. Hägerström's brave metaphor of the torch that we have to light ourselves – is it also pathetic in its over-optimism? Will not any 'torch' *we* can light serve only to emphasise the mindless circumambient darkness into which it has no strength to shine, or shine far? Or might one reply that the spiritual and the spatial are simply incommensurables: so that the thought of spatial minuteness has no real power to vilify the values of finite mind or spirit?

In conclusion, let us gather together a few characteristic features of philosophy of religion as a field of study. It is certainly a field in which the unexpected happens, and there occur adventures of ideas. An argument for God's existence, long thought to be refuted, is persuasively revised and revived. A 'sublime mystery' may come to be displayed as an unedifying confusion of concepts. What at one time or in one context may seem an inescapable task for reason looks at another time as an unedifying *impertinence*-of-reason. But conversely, in the midst of an analytical–critical examination of a theistic proof – even one he judges to be unsound in the end, a philosopher may find himself profoundly and religiously moved by the ideas he is confronting. Witness Kant, in his criticism of the Cosmological Argument:

> Unconditional necessity, which we so indispensably require as the last bearer of all things, is for human reason the veritable abyss. Eternity itself, in all its terrible

873

sublimity ... is far from making the same overwhelming impression on the mind ... We cannot put aside, and yet also cannot endure the thought, that a being which we represent to ourselves as supreme amongst all possible beings, should as it were say to itself, 'I am from eternity to eternity, and outside me there is nothing save what is through my will, *but whence then am I?*' All support here fails us. (*Critique of pure reason*, A613, B641)

There can be irony and pathos in philosophy of religion, and constant and powerful tensions. Religiously, God is the source and the object of intense aspiration and self-commitment: He is seen as the promise of peace, security, bliss. Yet, as the philosophical debate gives now more and then less credibility to God as a reasonable object of belief, the contrast between that promised peace and the extreme uncertainty, precariousness of rational assurance over God's existence, can be extremely poignant. Mitigating this insecurity in some measure, and mediating between theism and atheism, is the range of 'radical revisions' outlined above.

What one philosopher wrestles to make credible ('objective' theism, say) another argues to belong to an immature and outgrown stage in religious development. The central and crucial article of belief for the former is, for the latter, no more than a 'superstition'. What one philosopher sees as a path of sound argument leading to remarkable (religious) conclusions which he adopts with gratitude, another takes to be a *reductio ad absurdum*, because its conclusion is so unacceptably at odds with his experience of life or 'sense of reality'. On the other hand, it must not be suggested that a 'sense of reality' is itself necessarily something fixed and unchangeble. In the present context, religious experience and reflection upon it may certainly help to form and re-form that sense, but in conjunction with many other factors. Among them are our estimate of how vulnerable to illusion is religious experience; our knowledge that religious conviction of great intensity may be held in respect of quite irreconcilably different beliefs; and the influence upon us of the dominant philosophical styles of our day. 'Reflective equilibrium' at any time is the outcome of the 'play' of these and many other forces. Yet this metaphor carries an inappropriately *passive* implication. The philosopher of religion may see as his vocation the very *active* testing and challenging of orthodoxies, both believing and sceptical – in the knowledge that he risks disturbing, as he does so, his own fundamental convictions.

Notes

(An author's name followed by a number in square brackets refers to the book or article which has that number in the bibliography.)

1. See, e.g., Mackie [11]; Swinburne [10].
2. See David Hume, *Enquiry concerning human understanding* (1748), Section 10; also

J.C.A. Gaskin, *Hume's philosophy of religion* (Macmillan, London, 1978), Ch. 7.

3. Genesis III, 8.

4. Wordsworth, *Tintern Abbey*.

5. Cf. Swinburne [9], Ch. 9.

6. Ibid., pp. 152ff.

7. Job, XIII, 15.

8. Cf. Ch. 22.

9. Anselm, *Proslogion*, Chs. 2, 3, 4, 15.

10. Cf. Errol Harris, *Revelation through reason* (Allen and Unwin, London, 1959), Ch. 4.

11. K. Ward, *Rational theology and the creativity of God* (Basil Blackwell, Oxford, 1982), pp. 2ff.

12. Cf. Smart [8].

13. S.C. Brown (ed.), *Reason and religion* (Cornell University Press, Ithaca and London, 1977), p. 187.

14. Ibid., p. 152.

15. Ibid., p. 156.

16. C.F. Delaney (ed.), *Rationality and religious belief* (University of Notre Dame Press, Notre Dame, Indiana, 1979), pp. 7ff. Also S.M. Cahn and D. Shatz (eds), *Contemporary philosophy of religion* (Oxford University Press, New York, 1982), pp. 255–77.

17. J.L. Leslie, *Value and existence* (Basil Blackwell, Oxford, 1979), p. 1.

18. Ibid., p. 117.

19. See, e.g., Mackie [11], Ch. 13.

20. Whitehead, [26], [28]; Hartshorne [29], [30].

21. Cf. Braithwaite [22]: other radical revisers have included J.A.T. Robinson, Don Cupitt and Stewart Sutherland.

22. D. Cupitt, *Taking leave of God* (SCM Press, London, 1980), p. 126.

23. Cf. Ch. 15, pp. 343–4.

24. Axel Hägerström, *Philosophy and religion* (Allen and Unwin, London, 1964), p. 301.

25. Ibid., pp. 304ff.

Bibliography

Discussion of the philosophy of religion obviously presupposes some interest in, and knowledge of, religion itself and religious writings. In the Western world this ordinarily means at least some familiarity with the teachings of the Bible and its place in the Judaeo-Christian religious tradition. And since we are trying to uncover something about the nature of religions in general, it is well to learn as much as we can about the beliefs and practices of other traditions also. There are many useful factual and comparative studies; readable introductory surveys can be found in, for example,

[1] A.C. Bouquet, *Comparative religion*, 6th edn (Penguin Books, Harmondsworth, 1962) and

[2] G. Parrinder, *The world's living religions* (Pan Books, London, 1974).

There are many general studies in the philosophy of religion which enlarge on the various topics raised in this chapter; for example

[3] B. Davies, *Introduction to the philosophy of religion* (Oxford University Press,

Oxford, 1982). Besides this concise and compact work, see a lucid collection of essays:

[4] J. Hick, *God and the universe of faiths* (Macmillan, London, 1973). See also

[5] M.L. Diamond, *Contemporary philosophy and religious thought* (McGraw-Hill, New York, 1974). This is especially useful for its introductions to such influential figures as Kierkegaard, Rudolf Otto and Martin Buber.

[6] D. Cupitt, *The sea of faith* (BBC, London, 1984) gives a lively, if controversial, survey and assessment of the development of recent religious thought.

[7] W. Nicholls, *Systematic and philosophical theology* (Penguin Books, Harmondsworth, 1969) introduces some of the major twentieth-century theologians, like Barth, Bultmann and Tillich, while

[8] N. Smart, *Reasons and faiths* (Routledge and Kegan Paul, London, 1958) is valuable for its awareness of Eastern as well as Western traditions in religion.

On the central issues of theism, what it means to say that God exists and what reasons there are for saying so, there is, of course, a vast literature. Among fairly recent and readily accessible studies, we may note

[9] R. Swinburne, *The coherence of theism* (Clarendon Press, Oxford, 1977) and

[10] R. Swinburne, *The existence of God* (Clarendon Press, Oxford, 1979). In a more sceptical vein are

[11] J. Mackie, *The miracle of theism* (Clarendon Press, Oxford, 1982) and

[12] A. Flew, *God: a critical enquiry*, 2nd edn (Open Court, La Salle, Illinois, 1984) (a vigorous and entertainingly written statement of the case against theism).

The problem which has most persistently haunted theism, the problem of evil, is very concisely stated, along with the standard solutions and objections thereto, in

[13] J. Mackie, 'Evil and omnipotence' in B. Mitchell (ed.), *The philosophy of religion* (Oxford University Press, Oxford, 1971), pp. 92–104. An ingenious attempt to show that a solution is in principle possible is provided by

[14] A. Plantinga, 'The free will defence' (ibid., pp. 105–20).

The problem is examined at greater length in

[15] J. Hick, *Evil and the God of love* (Macmillan, London, 1966) and

[16] H.J. McCloskey, *God and evil* (Martinus Nijhoff, The Hague, 1974) and there is a well-known treatment of it from a Christian standpoint in

[17] C.S. Lewis, *The problem of pain* (Bles, London, 1940).

The tendency of many modern writers in the field to focus on the distinctive character of religious belief and discourse – and to suspect, at least, that many of the traditional problems arise from misunderstandings about these – owes its inspiration primarily, though not exclusively, to Wittgenstein, and in particular to his

[18] *Philosophical investigations*, trans. G.E.M. Anscombe, 2nd edn (Basil Blackwell, Oxford, 1958).

Wittgenstein's own direct contributions to the philosophy of religion consist of some rather fragmentary comments, mostly collected in his

[19] *Lectures and conversations on aesthetics, psychology and religious belief* (Basil Blackwell, Oxford, 1970) and

[20] *Culture and value*, trans. P. Winch (Basil Blackwell, Oxford, 1980).

The implications for religious thought of his theory of language in general, as a multiplicity of 'language-games' each with its own rules, have been carefully set out in

[21] W.D. Hudson, *Wittgenstein and religious belief* (Macmillan, London, 1975) and there are many examples of Wittgenstein's influence, in this field, one of the earliest and most notable being

[22] R.B. Braithwaite's 'An empiricist's view of the nature of religious belief' in Mitchell (ed.) [13], pp. 72–91. Besides this widely discussed paper, see

[23] D.Z. Phillips, 'Religious belief and language-games' in Mitchell (ed.) [13], pp. 121–42. See also Phillips' books, such as

[24] *The concept of prayer* (Routledge, London, 1965) or

[25] *Religion without explanation* (Basil Blackwell, Oxford, 1976).

For another important development in twentieth-century thought, what has become known as 'process theology', the primary source is, no doubt,

[26] A.N. Whitehead, *Process and reality* (Macmillan, New York, 1929, corrected edn, ed. G.D.R. Griffin and D.W. Sherborne, Free Press, New York, 1978), especially the final section. This is, however, a somewhat formidable work, and is perhaps best approached through the briefer and less technical outline of Whitehead's ideas on the organic, endlessly developing nature of reality in his

[27] *Science and the modern world* (Macmillan, New York, 1925), or his application of his ideas specifically to religion in

[28] *Religion in the making* (Macmillan, New York, 1926).

Another major influence in this field has been C. Hartshorne, in such works as

[29] *The divine relativity* (Yale University Press, New Haven, 1964) and

[30] *A natural theology for our times* (Open Court, La Salle, Illinois, 1967).

T.E.B.

Further Notes
and References

Notes
on
Contributors

R.F. ATKINSON   Professor of Philosophy at the University of Exeter since 1979; Professor at York, 1967–79; Lecturer at Keele, 1953–67. Educated Cockburn High School, Leeds, and Keble College, Oxford. Author of *Sexual morality* (Hutchinson, 1965); *Conduct: an introduction to moral philosophy* (Macmillan, 1969); *Knowledge and explanation in history* (Macmillan, 1978). Current interests: Kant and Sartre.

T.E. BURKE   Dr Burke is a Lecturer in Philosophy at the University of Reading. He is the author of *The philosophy of Popper* (Manchester, 1983). He has also published papers about the philosophies of Whitehead and Wittgenstein, and is at present writing a book about the philosophy of religion.

BRIAN CARR   Lecturer in Philosophy, University of Exeter. Author of *Bertrand Russell* (1975), *Metaphysics* (1987) and co-author (with D.J. O'Connor) of *Introduction to the theory of knowledge* (1982). Work in progress includes a monograph on *Rational belief* and (with I. Mahalingam Carr) *Sankaracarya.*

B.J. COPELAND   Jack Copeland took his doctorate in philosophy at the University of Oxford, and since then has taught at universities in Australia, Malawi, Ireland and New Zealand. He has published articles on logic and the philosophy of language in *Mind, Analysis* and other journals, and he is currently writing a book on the philosophy of artificial intelligence.

J.G. COTTINGHAM   Dr Cottingham is a Reader in Philosophy at the University of Reading. He has edited Descartes' *Conversation with Burman* (Clarendon Press, 1976) and, with R.H. Stoothoff and D. Murdoch, has published a two-volume translation of Descartes' works, *The philosophical writings of Descartes* (Cambridge University Press, 1985). Besides this, he has published *Rationalism* (Granada, 1984) and *Descartes* (Basil Blackwell, 1986), and is at present working on a book about seventeenth-century rationalism for the 'Opus' series (Oxford University Press).

GRAEME DUNCAN   Professor of Government, University of Queensland. Author of *Marx and Mill* (1973), *Critical essays in Australian politics* (1978) and editor of *Democratic theory and practice* (1983).

JOHN GASKIN   Among Professor Gaskin's publications are *Hume's philosophy of religion* (Macmillan, 1978; 2nd edn, 1987) and *The quest for eternity* (Penguin Books, 1984). His non-academic interests include gardening and writing ghost stories, a collection of which, *Tales of twilight and borderlands*, is in preparation. He is a Fellow of Trinity College, Dublin.

D.A. GILLIES   Dr Gillies was formerly a fellow of King's College, Cambridge; since 1971 he has been a Lecturer in the Philosophy of Science and Mathematics in London University. His publications include the books *An objective theory of probability* (1973) and *Frege, Dedekind and Peano on the foundations of arithmetic* (1982).

CARL GINET   Professor of Philosophy at Cornell University. He is the author of *Knowledge, perception and memory* (Reidel, 1975) and of various articles on topics in epistemology, metaphysics, philosophy of language and Wittgenstein. He is currently working on a collection of essays on action.

R.A.D. GRANT   Dr R.A.D. Grant read English at Trinity College, Cambridge, and was later Research Fellow of Trinity Hall. Currently Lecturer in English at Glasgow University, he has published in several journals, especially in *The Salisbury Review*, of which he is an Editorial Board Member. He has written a new 'History of Western political thought' for *Encyclopaedia Britannica*.

O. HANFLING   Dr Hanfling is Reader in Philosophy at the Open University. Author of *Logical positivism* (Basil Blackwell, 1981) and Open University booklets on Kant, Wittgenstein, Locke, Body and Mind, Uses and Abuses of Argument, etc. Articles published in several philosophical journals; books forthcoming on *The meaning of life* (1987) and on *The later philosophy of Wittgenstein*.

ROM HARRÉ   Fellow of Linacre College, Oxford; University Lecturer in the Philosophy of Science; Adjunct Professor of the Social and Behavioural Sciences, State University of New York at Binghamton. Publications include *Great scientific experiments* (1981), *Personal being* (1986), *Varieties of realism* (1986) and (as editor) *The physical sciences since antiquity* (1976) and *The social construction of the emotions* (1986).

R.W. HEPBURN   Professor Hepburn has held academic posts in Aberdeen, Nottingham and Edinburgh, where he is Professor of Moral Philosophy. He has published chiefly in the fields of philosophy of religion and aesthetics; also in moral philosophy and philosophy of education. *'Wonder' and other essays* (Edinburgh University Press) was published in 1984.

FRANK JACKSON   Professor Jackson has taught at Adelaide, La Trobe and Monash, and is currently Professor of Philosophy, Research School of Social Sciences, Australian National University. Author of *Perception* and articles on various topics, including philosophy of mind, conditionals, confirmation and the logic of obligation. Currently completing *Conditionals* for Basil Blackwell.

A.R. LACEY   Dr Lacey was educated at Cambridge; after two years' research in Greek philosophy at Manchester he joined the Philosophy Department of Bedford College, London, in 1954, transferring with the Department to King's College, London, in 1984. Apart from articles on ancient and modern philosophy he has published *A dictionary of philosophy* (Routledge, 1975; 2nd revised edition in press) and *Modern philosophy: an introduction* (Routledge, 1982).

MICHAEL LESSNOFF   Studied Politics and Political Economy at the Universities of Glasgow and Oxford, and is now a Reader in the Politics Department at Glasgow. His publications include *The structure of social science* (Allen and Unwin, 1974), *Social contract* (Macmillan, 1986) and journal articles on philosophy and the social sciences.

RICHARD LINDLEY   Dr Lindley is a Lecturer in Philosophy at the University of Bradford. He is a founder member of the Society for Applied Philosophy and his book *Autonomy* was published in 1986. He is currently writing (with a consultant psychiatrist) a book on the ethics of psychotherapy.

JOHN LLEWELYN   Reader in Philosophy, University of Edinburgh. He is the author of *Beyond metaphysics? The hermeneutic circle in contemporary continental philosophy* and *Derrida on the threshold of sense*. He is in the course of writing *Emmanuel Levinas and the Absolute Lord*.

JONATHAN LOWE   Dr Lowe is a Lecturer in Philosophy at the University of Durham. He has contributed to various journals on topics in philosophical logic, metaphysics and the philosophy of mind. He is currently working on a book concerning identity, individuation and the logic of sortal terms.

A.J. LYON   Ardon Lyon wrote his doctoral thesis on personal identity under John Wisdom at Cambridge. He has published articles on personal identity, the prediction paradox, criteria and meaning, causation, scientific explanation, and laws of nature. He has taught at Durham and at City University, until 1985 as chairman of its Philosophy Division.

G.C. MADELL   Dr Madell is a Lecturer in Philosophy at the University of Edinburgh. He is the author of *The identity of the self* (Edinburgh University Press, 1981), and of articles in *Mind, Philosophy, Inquiry* and *Analysis.* He is at present working on a book about contemporary materialism.

MARY MIDGLEY was formerly Senior Lecturer in Philosophy at the University of Newcastle upon Tyne. Her books include *Beast and man* (1978), *Heart and Mind* (1981), *Wickedness: a philosophical essay* (1984), *Animals and why they matter* (1984), *Evolution as a religion* (1985) and (with Judith Hughes) *Women's choices: philosophical problems facing feminism* (1983).

HANS OBERDIEK   Hans Oberdiek (PhD, University of Wisconsin), a frequent visiting lecturer at the University of Oxford, is Professor and Chairman of Philosophy at Swarthmore College. He teaches and publishes in the areas of moral philosophy, philosophy of law, political philosophy, and philosophy of mind.

G.H.R. PARKINSON   Professor of Philosophy at the University of Reading. Author of *Spinoza's theory of knowledge* (1954), *Logic and reality in Leibniz's metaphysics* (1965), *Georg Lukács* (1977) and (as editor) *Leibniz: logical papers* (1966), *The theory of meaning* (1968), *Georg Lukács: the man, his work and his ideas* (1970), *Leibniz: philosophical writings* (1973) and *Marx and Marxisms* (1982). He has also written on Hegel and on the early philosophy of Wittgenstein.

MICHAEL PROUDFOOT   Michael Proudfoot is a Lecturer in Philosophy at the University of Reading. His work includes papers on Wittgenstein and on the concept of intelligence. He is at present at work on a book about the aesthetics of music.

MARCUS G. SINGER   Professor of Philosophy at the University of Wisconsin, Madison; is the author of *Generalization in ethics* (1961) and editor of *Moral values* (1977) and *American philosophy* (1986). He was President of the American Philosophical Association, Central Division, 1985–6, and is working on a book on justification and proof in ethics.

J.J.C. SMART Before his retirement in 1985 Professor Smart was a member of the Department of Philosophy, Research School of Social Sciences, Australian National University. He is the author of *Philosophy and scientific realism* (1963), *Between science and philosophy: an introduction to the philosophy of science* (1968), *Ethics, persuasion and truth* (1984), *Essays metaphysical and moral* (1987), and (with Bernard Williams) *Utilitarianism, for and against* (1973); he has also edited *Problems of space and time* (1964).

T. SORELL Dr Sorell is a Lecturer in Philosophy at the Open University. He is the author of *Hobbes* (Routledge, 1986) and the Descartes volume in the Oxford University Press 'Past Masters' series. He has published articles in *Mind*, *Ratio* and *Kant-Studien*.

T.L.S. SPRIGGE Professor of Logic and Metaphysics at the University of Edinburgh. His publications include *Correspondence of Jeremy Bentham*, vols. I and II (Athlone Press, 1968), of which he was the editor; *Santayana: an examination of his philosophy* (Routledge, 1970); *The vindication of absolute idealism* (Edinburgh University Press, 1983); *Theories of existence* (Penguin Books, 1984). His present research is into the foundations of ethics and on William James and F.H. Bradley.

R.H. STOOTHOFF Professor Stoothoff has taught at the University of Edinburgh and at the University of Canterbury. He has contributed to several philosophical journals and is a co-translator of *The philosophical writings of Descartes* (Cambridge, 1985).

C.L. TEN Chin Liew Ten is Reader in Philosophy at Monash University, Australia. He is the author of *Mill on liberty* (1980) and a forthcoming book, *Crime, guilt and punishment*.

J.E. TILES Dr Tiles is a Lecturer in Philosophy at the University of Reading. He is the author of *Things that happen* (Aberdeen University Press, 1981) and is at present writing a book on Dewey for the series 'The Arguments of the Philosophers' (Routledge).

MARY TILES Dr Mary Tiles has held teaching positions at Balliol College, Oxford, and at the University of Cambridge where she was a temporary fellow of King's College. She is currently Secretary to the Royal Institute of Philosophy. Her publications include *Bachelard: science and objectivity* (Cambridge University Press, 1984), and she is currently working on an introduction to the philosophy of set theory for Blackwells.

IAN TIPTON Reader in Philosophy, University College of Wales, Aberystwyth. His publications include *Berkeley: the philosophy of immaterialism* (1974) and he edited *Locke on human understanding* (1977).

S.F. TSINOREMA   Stavroula F. Tsinorema teaches philosophy at the University of Ioannina, Greece. She studied philosophy at the University of Athens, and obtained her PhD from the University of Exeter. Her publications include articles on moral philosophy and the philosophy of language, and she is at present writing a book (in Greek) on Wittgenstein's later philosophy.

JEREMY WALDRON   Professor Waldron, formerly Lecturer in Political Theory at the University of Edinburgh, is now at the University of California, Berkeley. He is the editor of *Theories of rights* (1984).

KATHLEEN V. WILKES   Dr Kathy Wilkes is Fellow in Philosophy at St Hilda's College, Oxford. She is the author of *Physicalism* (1978) and *Real people* (forthcoming), and of articles in philosophy of science, philosophy of mind, ethics and ancient philosophy. Two more books, *The autonomy of psychology* and *Aristotle's absences*, are in preparation.

Glossary

This glossary covers many of the philosophical terms that are in common use, and that may be found either in this encyclopaedia or in other discussions of contemporary philosophical issues. There is no mention of terms which are of purely historical interest.

I am grateful to my colleagues, Dr T.E. Burke and Dr J.E. Tiles, for many helpful comments on an earlier draft of this glossary.—G.H.R.P.

achievement words: words which signify not just that some action has been performed, but that something has been done successfully. Contrast, e.g., 'treat' and 'cure', 'seek' and 'find'.

acquaintance and description, knowledge by: terms popularised by Bertrand Russell, who used them to describe two ways in which objects are known. According to Russell, we have *acquaintance* with anything of which we are directly aware (namely, sense-data: *q.v.*). This is to be distinguished from knowledge *by description*, which includes our knowledge of those whom we would normally call our acquaintances. In the normal sense, I would claim to be acquainted with a colleague; but according to Russell, my colleague is for me the body and mind connected with certain sense-data.

akrasia: a Greek word now commonly used to refer to weakness of will. In essence, the problem of akrasia is: how can I believe that I ought to do something, and yet not do it?

analytic philosophy: a term covering a variety of philosophical schools, which have in common the view that the primary function of philosophy is to clarify statements. Some philosophers have regarded analytic philosophy as opposed to metaphysics (*q.v.*). But some analytic philosophers, such as Bertrand Russell, have held metaphysical views.

analytic propositions: propositions which can be denied only at the expense of self-contradiction; or, which are true by virtue of the meaning of the words used in stating them. So if, for example, one means by the word 'bachelor' 'an unmarried male', then the proposition 'All bachelors are unmarried' is analytic. Propositions which are not analytic are termed 'synthetic'. So if by 'bachelor' one means 'a person who has been awarded a first university degree', then the proposition 'All bachelors are unmarried' is synthetic. For even if it were true (which it is not) it could be denied without self-contradiction.

antecedent: *see* 'conditional'.

apodeictic: *see* 'modality'.

a posteriori: *see* 'a priori'.

a priori: an *a priori* proposition is a proposition such that, in order to know its truth, one does not require sense-experience (except in so far as sense-experience is necessary for one to understand the sentence used in stating the proposition). The distinguishing marks of such a proposition are necessity and strict universality, i.e. universality such that no exceptions to it are allowed. (An example of this would be 'All bachelors are unmarried,' understanding 'bachelor' to mean 'unmarried male'.) Propositions which are not *a priori* are termed '*a posteriori*'.

assertoric: *see* 'modality'.

behaviourism: the thesis that to talk about a person's mental states or acts is to talk about that person's behaviour, or dispositions (*q.v.*) to behave.

bivalence, principle of: this states that every proposition is either true or false, i.e. that it has one, and only one, of the two truth-values (*q.v.*) 'truth' and 'falsity'. (Cf. 'excluded middle, principle of'.)

calculus: in philosophy a system of words or symbols governed by precisely stated rules, which can be applied in a mechanical way.

categorical imperative: a term introduced into moral philosophy by Kant. If one says, 'Do X, because X is good for some further end, Y' one is in effect saying, 'If you want Y, do X,' and the imperative is 'hypothetical'. If one says, 'Do X, because X is good in itself,' the imperative is 'categorical'. Kant argued that moral judgements are in effect categorical imperatives.

categorical proposition: a proposition which states that something is or is not the case, without any 'ifs'. As such, the categorical proposition is distinguished from the hypothetical proposition. (On this, *see also* 'conditional'.)

category: in the Aristotelian sense of the term, categories are *summa genera* (cf. 'genus and species'), i.e. the widest classes into which reality can be divided. Kant viewed a category as a 'concept of an object in general'; i.e. categories are what you have to think of an object – any object – as being. These senses of the term 'category' still influence philosophers, though there is now no longer any attempt to draw up complete lists of categories, of the kind to be found in Aristotle and Kant.

category mistake: a mistake which arises when a term which belongs to one category is regarded as if it belonged to another. Take, for example, 'He ran away because he was a coward.' It might be thought that cowardice caused him to run away, i.e. that the relevant category is that of cause and effect. However, it has been argued that this is a category mistake; the relevant category is that of disposition (*q.v.*) and actualisation. To say that the man ran away because he was a coward is to say that this is the sort of thing that he *would do*, having the disposition that he does.

causal theory of perception: the theory that the things that we perceive are the causes of our perceptions of them. This theory is compatible with the view that, in reality, things are very different from what we perceive them as being. (Cf. 'primary qualities'.)

central state materialism: a form of physicalism (*q.v.*).

cognitive: having to do with cognition, i.e. with knowing or perceiving. A 'cognitive theory of ethics' is one which regards ethical judgements as a kind of knowing or perceiving. A 'non-cognitive theory of ethics', such as the emotive theory (*q.v.*) or prescriptivism (*q.v.*) denies this.

coherence theory of truth: this states that truth cannot be asserted of one proposition in isolation from others; truth belongs to a *system* of propositions, i.e. a set of propositions which cohere with each other.

compatibilism: the view that, although all events are determined (cf. 'determinism'), it may still be said that human beings act freely. Also known as 'soft determinism'.

concept: philosophers now tend to regard a concept as the meaning of a word or phrase; in this sense, they speak of (e.g.) 'the concept of mind', 'the concept of moral responsibility'. Some philosophers have regarded concepts as mental entities; it is this sense that is relevant to the term 'conceptualism' (*q.v.*).

conceptualism: a theory about the nature of universals (*q.v.*). According to this theory a universal term, such as 'triangle', is not a mere word which applies to a number of particular triangles, nor does it stand for a special kind of entity, a 'universal', which exists outside the mind. It does indeed stand for an entity, but this entity exists only in the way that concepts exist.

conditional: a 'conditional' proposition is a hypothetical proposition, i.e. one which would be expressed in the form 'If p, then q'; for example, 'If this is blue, then it is coloured.' 'p' is termed the 'antecedent', 'q' the 'consequent'. 'Conditional' may also be used as a noun; in this sense it is equivalent to 'conditional proposition'.

confirmation: to 'confirm' a hypothesis is to provide evidence for it which, although it does not establish its truth, does at any rate give it some support. So, the hypothesis that all ravens are black would be confirmed by the discovery of a black raven.

confirmation, paradox of (also known as 'Hempel's paradox' and 'the raven paradox'): a paradox formulated by Carl Hempel. Suppose that we wish to confirm the hypothesis that all ravens are black. Hempel argues that the hypothesis is confirmed by the discovery of something (whatever it may be) that is not black and not a raven. The reasoning is that the propositions 'All ravens are black' and 'If something is not black, it is not a raven' are equivalent. Consequently, to observe (say) a white shirt must be regarded as confirming the hypothesis that all ravens are black – though one would normally regard the observation as quite irrelevant.

conjunction: in logic, a compound proposition which is true if, and only if, each of its component propositions is true: e.g. 'She came and she saw and she conquered.'

connotation and denotation: a term such as 'man' *denotes* the individuals for which it stands; it *connotes* the attributes which a thing must possess if it is to be properly called a man. In a sense, then, the connotation of 'man' is the *meaning* of the term 'man'. Cf. 'extension and intension'.

consequent: *see* 'conditional'.

consequentialism: in moral philosophy, the view that the goodness or badness, or the rightness or wrongness, of actions depends entirely on their consequences. Cf. 'utilitarianism'.

constative: *see* 'performative utterance'.

contingent: a 'contingent proposition' is a proposition which, if true, is not a necessary truth and, if false, is not necessarily false. Many philosophers speak also of 'contingent things'; these are things which could have been different from what they are, or indeed need not have existed at all.

contradiction, principle of: this states that a proposition cannot be both true and false. Some writers prefer to call it 'the principle of non-contradiction'.

contradictory: strictly speaking, two contradictory propositions are propositions such that they cannot both be true, and cannot both be false; that is, one and only one of the pair must be true. E.g. 'All men are rational' and 'Some men are not rational' are contradictory propositions.

contrary: strictly speaking, two contrary propositions are propositions such that they cannot both be true, but they can both be false: e.g. 'All men are rational' and 'No men are rational.' (Both can be false, in that it may be that *some men only* are rational.) In ordinary usage, 'contrary' and 'contradictory' are not always sharply distinguished.

correspondence theory of truth: a theory of the nature of truth, which states that truth consists in the agreement of a proposition with a fact. There has been much debate about the meaning of the terms 'agreement' and 'fact' in this context.

corroboration: some philosophers of science (notably Karl Popper) distinguish between 'confirmation' and 'corroboration'. They argue that it is idle to seek to confirm a hypothesis, in the sense of producing supporting evidence for it. For however much evidence of this sort one produces, the hypothesis may still turn out to be false. But the more a hypothesis stands up to attempts to *falsify* it, the more it is 'corroborated'.

cosmological argument: a term that may be used to refer to either of two arguments for the existence of God. (a) The first, better called 'the argument from the contingency of the world', has as its premiss the existence of contingent things (cf. 'contingent'). It argues that there must be a complete reason for the existence and nature of any contingent thing; but if one gives an explanation in terms of some other contingent thing, one is left asking 'Why does that thing exist, and in the way that it does?' So the complete reason for contingent things can only be a necessary being, which contains within itself the reason for its existence. This necessary being is God.

(b) The second, better called 'the first cause in argument', rests on the principle that every event or state of affairs must have a cause. Now, we know by experience that certain things exist; any such thing must have a cause, and that in turn must have another, and so on. However, the 'and so on' must have a limit, for an infinite regress of causes is impossible; therefore a first, or uncaused, cause must exist; and this cause is God.

counterfactual conditionals (also termed 'unfulfilled conditionals'): a conditional (*q.v.*) which states what *would have* been the case, if something had been the case which in fact was not. For example: 'If antibiotics had been known in the seventeenth century, Spinoza would have lived longer.'

covering law model: a thesis about the nature of explanation: namely, that if something is to be explained, it must be brought under ('covered by') some universal law which entails it (cf. 'entailment').

criterion: in standard usage, a criterion of *F* is a feature that something must have if it is to be correctly called '*F*'. For example, some philosophers have argued that verifiability is a criterion of factual significance. (Cf. 'verifiability, principle of'.) In the philosophy of Wittgenstein, the term has a different sense, in which it is opposed to 'symptom'. Symptoms are discovered by experience, but criteria are fixed by convention. But to say that *X* is a criterion of (e.g.) *Y*'s being in pain is not to say that *X* entails (*q.v.*) that *Y* is in pain; the criterial relation is weaker than that of entailment.

de dicto and **de re** (or '*in sensu composito*' and '*in sensu diviso*'): an important distinction in modal logic (see 'modality'). Take the sentence 'A man who is not writing can write.' This is false if the sentence is taken in the composite sense (*in sensu composito*; *de dicto*); for a man cannot both write and not write (cf. 'contradiction, principle of'). But if taken in the divided sense (*in sensu diviso*; *de re*) the sentence can be true, for a man who is not at present writing can write on some other occasion. The distinction is now chiefly used in discussions of what it is that can be called necessary. Some philosophers assert (and others deny) that necessity can be taken *de re*, i.e. that individuals have properties that necessarily belong to them.

deduction: a deductive argument is one in which one cannot assert the premises (*q.v.*) and deny the conclusion. Some standard dictionaries say that deduction is inference from the general to the particular. This is often, but by no means always, the case; for example, 'If *p*, then *q*; so if not *q*, then not *p*' is a deductive argument.

defeasible: a legal term adapted by philosophers. In law, 'defeasible' means 'capable of annulment'; in philosophy, the term is used to refer to concepts which are presumed to apply unless one or more of a set of defeating conditions obtains. Thus it is pointed out that we are held to be responsible for what we do, *unless* (e.g.) we act out of inadvertence, or by mistake, or to defend ourselves, or are under physical compulsion. The concept of responsibility, then, is said to be a 'defeasible' concept – to be defined through exceptions.

definiendum: in a definition, the word or group of words (or the symbol or group of symbols) which is to be defined.

definiens: in a definition, the word or group of words (or the symbol or group of symbols) which is declared to be substitutable for the definiendum. So in 'An obtuse angle is an angle which is greater than a right angle,' 'obtuse angle' is the definiendum, 'angle which is greater than a right angle' is the definiens.

definition, contextual: a definition which explains the meaning of a word or phrase through sentences in which it is used. Also known as a 'definition in use'.

definition, descriptive: a definition which states how a word or phrase is actually used, and which may therefore be correct or incorrect (cf. 'definition, stipulative'). The definitions found in dictionaries are descriptive.

definition, ostensive: to give such a definition is to explain the meaning of a word or phrase by pointing to one or more examples of it.

definition, persuasive: a term introduced by C.L. Stevenson, to refer to definitions which are meant to induce people to take up certain attitudes. The word 'true' is often used in such definitions; thus 'True freedom is total obedience to one's rulers' may be meant to induce the attitude of obedience.

definition, recursive: in such a definition, one first gives an example or examples of the class of objects to be defined, and then states a procedure for generating all other examples of the class. For example, 'positive integer' may be defined recursively as follows: '(i) 1 is a positive integer; (ii) If *n* is a positive integer, $n+1$ is a positive integer.'

definition, stipulative: sometimes called a 'prescriptive definition'. A definition which declares the speaker's or writer's intention to use a word or phrase in a certain way. For example when Humpty-Dumpty, in *Through the looking glass*, uses the word 'glory' to mean 'a nice knock-down argument', he is putting forward a stipulative definition. Such definitions cannot be true or false, but they can be assessed in other ways – e.g. they can be enlightening, obfuscatory or perverse.

denotation: *see* 'connotation and denotation'.

deontology: a name applied to any ethical theory which takes as primary the concept of duty (from the Greek *to deon*).

description, knowledge by: *see* 'acquaintance and description, knowledge by'.

descriptions, definite: a definite description is a phrase which is so used as to apply to one and only one object; e.g. 'the kitten to whom Alice is now talking'. But use of the word 'the' does not always signal a definite description: e.g. in 'The kitten begins to crawl when about 18 days old' the phrase 'the kitten' refers to the whole class of kittens.

descriptions, theory of: Bertrand Russell's attempt to show how a definite description can have meaning even when there is nothing that answers to that description. How, e.g., can one say meaningfully, 'The present King of France is bald?' Russell's strategy is to move the definite description out of the position which it occupies, i.e. that of the subject (*q.v.*) of the proposition. So, for 'The present King of France is bald' Russell would substitute, 'There is at least one individual which is at present a King of France, and there is at most one individual which is at present a King of France, and that individual is bald.'

descriptivism: the thesis that ethical terms describe something. Opposed to 'prescriptivism' (*q.v.*) and to the 'emotive theory of ethics' (*q.v.*). *See also* under 'cognitive'.

design argument: an argument for the existence of God, which starts from the premiss that the things around us are not a mere chaos, but display order of many kinds. This, it is argued, implies the existence of an intelligent agent who gave things the order that they have; and this agent must be God.

determinism: a term which covers a wide variety of views, which have in common the thesis that every event or every state of affairs is determined by certain factors, in the sense that given those factors, the event must occur or the state of affairs must hold. In the past, determinism has been thought to hold in the natural world; however, the rise of quantum physics has led to this claim being abandoned, or at any rate modified so that it is regarded as applying only to the world as studied by macro-physics. Philosophers are particularly concerned with determinism in the sphere of human action. Here, determinism is contrasted with libertarianism, understanding by this the belief that human beings have free will. An act is said to be done freely, or to be an exercise of the agent's free will, when the agent *could have done otherwise.* The determinist argues that people never could do other than what they actually do; the belief that they could (the determinist argues) springs from ignorance of the factors that determine action. However, most determinists distinguish their position from that of fatalism, which is the view that what will happen will happen, regardless of what human beings do in the hope of influencing the course of events. For 'soft' and 'hard' determinism, see respectively 'compatibilism' and 'incompatibilism'.

disjunction: a compound proposition which is false if, and only if, all its component propositions are false. The English word 'or' is sometimes used in this sense; e.g. 'Either he was drunk or he was in a rage' would not be thought false if he was both drunk and in a rage. This is often termed the 'non-exclusive' sense of 'or'; an example of the 'exclusive' sense of 'or' would be 'Either he was in London at the time of the crime or he was in Leeds,' where the speaker means to assert that one and only one of the alternatives is true.

disposition: in philosophy, to speak of a 'disposition' of X is to speak of what X will do, if ..., or what X would have done, if ... So, for example, brittleness is a disposition, in that to call something brittle is to speak of what it will do if, or would have done if, subjected to impact.

double aspect theory: a theory of the relations between mind and body. According to it, mind and body are different aspects, or expressions, of an underlying reality.

double effect, doctrine of: a distinction drawn by some theologians and philosophers between the effects of a human action. The distinction is between an effect which is intended, and an effect which is foreseen but not intended. For example, suppose that a drug is given to a man, with the intention of relieving his sufferings; suppose that it does this, but that it has the further result that the patient's death is hastened. Those who subscribe to the doctrine of double effect say that the giving of the drug is morally permissible, provided that the acceleration of death, though foreseen, was not intended. But to give the drug *in order to* hasten death would not be morally permissible.

dualism: a theory of the relation between mind and body, according to which minds and bodies are substances of radically different kinds.

emotive theory of ethics: the view that ethical terms do not describe anything; they are *expressive* of the feelings of the person who uses them, much as a swear-word may express irritation. E.g. to say, 'This is good' is to express one's feelings of approval.

empiricism: roughly, the view that all knowledge of truths of fact depends on sense-experience (from the Greek *empeiria*). Empiricists are not committed to the view that absolutely all truths are known in this way; they can allow that our knowledge of the truths of logic is of a different kind. (Cf. 'analytic propositions'.)

entailment: a term that refers to a certain kind of conditional proposition (cf. 'conditional') – namely, that in which the relation between antecedent and consequent is one of logical necessity. E.g. the proposition 'If Mrs Bardell is a widow, then Mrs Bardell has been married' is an entailment. Contrast 'If Mrs Bardell is a widow, then Mrs Bardell is happy,' which is not an entailment.

epiphenomenalism: a theory of mind–matter relations, which asserts that mental states and acts are caused by the body, but have no effect on the body or on each other. The theory is not a form of materialism – it does not say that mental states, etc. *are* the states, etc. of matter – but it does seem to reduce the mind to the status of a useless accompaniment of matter.

epistemology: the theory of knowledge (from the Greek *epistēmē*). Strictly, the branch of philosophy which considers the nature and criteria of knowledge, together with its sources, kinds and extent. But books on epistemology often discuss also the relevant topics of meaning and truth.

ethics: *see* 'meta–ethics', 'normative ethics'.

excluded middle, principle of: this states 'Either *p* or not–*p*', where '*p*' is any proposition. Related to, but to be distinguished from, the principle of bivalence (see 'bivalence, principle of').

existential import: a proposition is said to have 'existential import' if it commits one to asserting the existence of the entities to which it refers. There is a controversy as to whether universal propositions have existential import. For example, if one says, 'All cats hunt mice,' is one thereby saying that there are such things as cats? Or should one be taken as saying 'For any *x*, if *x* is a cat, then *x* hunts mice'?

extension and intension: the extension of a term is its denotation (*see* 'connotation and denotation'); the term 'intension' has more than one sense. Some philosophers distinguish between the definition of a term and its intension; thus 'having equal base-angles' would be part of the intension of the term 'isosceles triangle', since it is part of the meaning of the term though not of its definition. For other philosophers, 'intension' is the same as 'connotation'.

extensional and intentional occurrence: *see* 'opacity and transparency, referential'.

falsifiability, criterion of: for Karl Popper, what distinguishes a genuinely scientific theory from one which is pseudo-scientific is that the former can be falsified by experience, whereas the latter cannot. Some philosophers have taken falsifiability to be the criterion of any meaningful utterance, but this is not Popper's view.

force of an utterance: a theory of the use of words, developed by J.L. Austin. Austin distinguishes the *meaning* of an utterance from its *force*. For example, suppose that someone at a dinner-party says to his hostess, 'This sauce is lumpy.' This utterance has a certain meaning; but in uttering the words the speaker is also passing an adverse judgement on the sauce (the utterance has 'illocutionary force'), and the utterance may also have the effect of offending the hostess (it has 'perlocutionary force').

freedom, positive and negative: terms introduced by Isaiah Berlin to mark a distinction between that sort of freedom ('negative freedom') which one has when one is not prevented from doing what one wants to do, and that sort of freedom ('positive freedom') which lies in being one's own master.

functionalism: (a) in the philosophy of mind, a theory of the nature of mental states, which says that they are to be defined entirely in terms of the relation of cause and effect. According to the theory, a mental state is that which is (i) caused by certain characteristic physical stimuli, (ii) causes and is caused by other mental states, and (iii) causes certain characteristic behaviour. Supporters of the theory distinguish it from behaviourism (*q.v.*); some of them say that it is compatible with (though not committed to) dualism (*q.v.*).

(b) In the social sciences and their philosophy, 'functionalism' refers to the idea that in every society, each custom or belief or concept has some important task to accomplish.

genus and species: in common usage, the term 'genus' tends to be a zoological or botanical term, referring to a wide group of animals or plants, which have important characteristics in common. Sub-groups of such a group are called 'species'. In logic and philosophy the terms have a broader sense, referring to any wide group (genus) and its sub-groups (species). For example, the circle and the triangle are both species of plane figure.

Goodman's paradox: a puzzle about induction (*q.v.*) formulated by Nelson Goodman. The puzzle involves a feature of induction which may be called 'projection'. Suppose that we find that all observed things of a certain kind have a certain property – e.g. that all emeralds are green. Arguing inductively we 'project' this, saying that all emeralds, at whatever time they may be observed, are green. Goodman now asks us to consider the predicate 'grue' which applies to all things which are observed prior to the year 2000 and are green, or which are not observed prior to the year 2000 and are blue. Now, all the emeralds that we have seen so far are green; but they are also grue. So which predicate – green or grue – are we to project for the years following 2000? Why say 'All emeralds are green' rather than 'All emeralds are grue'? For both seem to have equally good inductive support.

hedonism: philosophers distinguish between (a) psychological hedonism and (b) ethical hedonism. (a) Psychological hedonism is the doctrine that each person, as a matter of fact, acts for the sake of pleasure. The pleasure in question is usually held to be the person's own, and the doctrine is then known as 'egoistic psychological hedonism'. (b) Ethical hedonism is the doctrine that each person *ought* to act for the sake of pleasure. The pleasure in question is usually held to be that of all, or at any rate of most, people, and the doctrine is then called 'universalistic ethical hedonism'.

Hempel's paradox: *see* 'confirmation, paradox of'.

hermeneutics: a term originally applied to the interpretation of texts, particularly those of Scripture. It was used as a philosophical term by Wilhelm Dilthey (1833–1911) to mark the distinguishing features of the 'human studies', as opposed to the natural sciences. Human studies rest on interpretation, and that in turn rests on understanding (*Verstehen*), a kind of imaginative reconstruction of the human activities or views that are studied.

historicism: a term which has several senses. (a) The view (held, e.g., by R.G. Collingwood) that history is the all-encompassing discipline, which absorbs philosophy itself. (b) The view that one cannot speak in non-temporal terms of the truth or falsity of a proposition; one can say only that a certain proposition is (or was) counted as true or as false by those who belong (or belonged) to a certain culture at a certain time. (c) Karl Popper understands by 'historicism' the view that the social sciences have prediction as their principal aim; further, that such predictions can be made on the basis of a knowledge of the basic laws that underlie historical development.

holism: (a) the view that propositions about wholes cannot be completely analysed into propositions about their parts; sometimes expressed by saying that the whole is more than the sum of its parts; (b) a theory of meaning or truth, according to which meaning or truth attaches only to a system as a whole, and not to any part of the system. The coherence theory of truth (*q.v.*) is a holistic theory in this sense.

holism, methodological: the view that social scientists should take social wholes as their fundamental data. It is opposed to 'methodological individualism', which argues that propositions about societies as wholes can, and if possible should, be completely translated into propositions about individuals.

hypothetical imperative: *see* 'categorical imperative'.

hypothetico-deductive method: a term that belongs to the philosophy of science, referring to a method which, it is said, scientists follow in their investigations. A hypothesis is formulated, its observable consequences are deduced, and observations or experiments are made to find out whether what, according to the hypothesis, should be observed is in fact observed.

identity of indiscernibles, principle of: this states that if x has every property that y has and y has every property that x has, then x and y are identical.

illocutionary: *see* 'force of an utterance'.

implication: a term which is often equivalent to 'conditional proposition' (*see* 'conditional'). Sometimes (especially in non-technical usage) an 'implication' is that which is implied, i.e. the consequent of a conditional proposition.

implication, material: a truth-function (*q.v.*). 'p materially implies q' is false if and only if p is true and q is false. This has the consequence that a false proposition materially implies all propositions, and a true proposition is materially implied by all propositions. 'p materially implies q' is often read as 'if p, then q'; there has been much discussion of the question whether every implication can be regarded as a material implication.

implicature, conversational: implication (*q.v.*) is a relation between propositions; so, for example, the proposition that some Yorkshiremen are stubborn implies the proposition that some who are stubborn are Yorkshiremen. But *p* 'conversationally implies' *q* if a speaker's utterance of *p* gives the audience reason to believe that the speaker thinks that *q*. Thus, 'Some Yorkshiremen are stubborn,' said by a wife in exasperation to her Yorkshire-born husband, might conversationally imply that this particular Yorkshireman is stubborn. (Note that the proposition that some Yorkshiremen are stubborn does not imply the proposition that this particular Yorkshireman is stubborn. For he might be one of those who are not stubborn.)

incompatibilism: the view that determinism (*q.v.*) is incompatible with the notions of human responsibility and freedom of choice. Also known as 'hard deerminism'. (*See also* 'compatibilism'.)

indiscernibility of identicals: *see* 'Leibniz' law'.

individualism, methodological: *see* 'holism, methodological'.

induction: a type of reasoning in which one proceeds from the proposition that (1) all observed members of a certain class have a certain property to the proposition that (2) all members of the class have this property. The 'problem of induction' is the problem of finding a justification for moves of this sort.

inference: to 'infer' *q* from *p* is to say that *q* follows from *p*; or, it is to say something of the form '*p*, therefore *q*'. A statement of this form is called an 'inference'; the term is also used to refer to that which is inferred.

instrumentalism: in the philosophy of science, the view that scientific theories are not descriptions of the real world, but are simply devices which enable scientists to make successful predictions on the basis of the data that they have.

intension: *see* 'extension and intension'.

intentionality (also 'intensionality'): words used to render the German term *Intentionalität*, used by Brentano (1838–1917) to refer to the distinguishing feature of mental states: namely, that they have an object. E.g. one desires *success*, one expects *a friend's arrival*, one thinks of *a dead acquaintance*. What is peculiar about these objects is that they may not yet exist, or may no longer exist, or may never exist or have existed.

judgement: (a) a term often used to mean the same as 'proposition' (*q.v.*); it can also mean (b) the faculty by which we affirm or deny propositions, or (c) the act of assertion or denial.

language-game: a fundamental concept in the later philosophy of Wittgenstein. Its precise nature is disputed, but the general idea seems to be that the meaningful use of language is basically a social activity, in which the use of words is guided by rules.

language, philosophy of: that branch of philosophy which is concerned with meaning, truth and with the force (*q.v.*) of utterances. To be distinguished from 'linguistic philosophy' (*q.v.*), which is wider in scope.

Leibniz' law: also known as 'the indiscernibility of identicals', this is the converse of the identity of indiscernibles (*q.v.*). It states that if x and y are identical, then x has every property that y has, and y has every property that x has.

liar paradox: Epimenides says, 'All Cretans are liars' – but Epimenides is himself a Cretan. Is what he says true or false? Attempts to solve this puzzle have involved the use of the notion of a 'metalanguage' (*q.v.*).

libertarianism: *see* 'determinism'.

linguistic philosophy: another way of referring to what is also called 'analytic philosophy' (*q.v.*); what differentiates the term is the fact that it makes explicit the concern of that philosophy with language. One may say that the idea behind linguistic philosophy is the idea that philosophical problems can be solved by means of a better understanding of the ways in which we use language.

logical constant: this is usually taken to be a symbol of a certain sort. It is *constant* in that its meaning is determinate; it is *logical* in that it helps to give a logical argument its structure. For example, if one represents symbolically the argument 'If all men are rational, some who are rational are men,' the symbols for 'if', 'all' and 'some' will be logical constants. The term is also used not for a symbol, but for the word or words it symbolises.

logical construction: *see* 'reductionism'.

logical positivism: the philosophy of the 'Vienna Circle', a group who flourished in Vienna in the 1930s. The group argued that the business of philosophy is analysis (cf. 'analytic philosophy'); metaphysical utterances were rejected as meaningless, in that they cannot be verified (cf. 'verifiability, principle of').

mention and use: contrast the sentences: (a) 'The Absolute enters into, but is itself incapable of, evolution and progress' (F.H. Bradley). (b) 'The words "The Absolute" have been the source of much philosophical dispute.' In (a) the words 'The Absolute' are *used*; in (b) they are *mentioned*.

meta-ethics: the study of the rules that govern the use of ethical terms. Unlike normative ethics (*q.v.*), meta-ethics is held not to commit one to any views about what actions are in fact good or bad, right or wrong.

metalanguage: we often comment on what is said; e.g. we say such things as 'This statement is true,' 'That command is self-defeating.' The sentences by which we make such comments are said to belong to a 'metalanguage'; the statements or commands on which they comment are said to belong to an 'object language'.

metaphysics: (a) a metaphysical theory is a theory about that which, in the last analysis, really exists; or (and this may come to the same) about that which provides the ultimate explanation of everything. The propositions that belong to such theories are *a priori* (*q.v.*) in character, in that they state what must be the case – e.g. 'There must be a first cause of everything.' (b) The term 'metaphysics' is also used to refer to accounts of the general conceptual schemes which order our experience. Metaphysics of this kind is called 'descriptive', and may stand in opposition to metaphysics of type (a). That sort of metaphysics is often 'revisionary', in that it calls on us to revise, and perhaps abandon, some of our commonly held ideas.

methodology: literally 'the theory of method'; the philosophical study of (e.g.) the methods of scientists, or of historians, or of philosophers themselves.

mind—brain identity theory: *see* 'physicalism'.

modality: propositions are distinguished in respect of 'modality' – roughly, the mode or way in which they are asserted. The traditional distinctions are into (a) assertoric, (b) problematic and (c) apodeictic propositions – i.e. assertions about what (a) is, (b) possibly is, and (c) must be the case. What has just been described is termed 'logical' modality; philosophers also recognise 'epistemic' modality (X knows that, or believes that, p), 'deontic' modality (It ought to be the case that, or, it is permitted that, p) and 'temporal' modality (It is, or was, or will be the case that p).

monism: this term often refers to the doctrine that there is one and only one substance, and that what are called 'particular things' are forms of this substance. However, some theories which are called 'monistic' are compatible with a belief in several substances, provided that these are of the same fundamental kind. For example, 'neutral monism' is the theory that minds and bodies are not substances of fundamentally different kinds; to talk of bodies and minds is to group in different ways certain basic entities (e.g. sense-data: $q.v.$) no one of which is either mental or physical.

naive realism: the view that physical objects do not in any way depend on the mind for their properties; that they really are (e.g.) coloured, remaining coloured even when not perceived.

name, logically proper: though a word such as 'Socrates' would normally be called a 'proper name', some philosophers (e.g. Bertrand Russell) would say that it is not a name in the strict sense, or, that it is not a 'logically proper name'. Their point is that a name in the strict sense ought to stand for a particular; the name 'Socrates', however, does not. Russell suggested that one might identify Socrates with the series of his experiences, and since people have many experiences simultaneously, this implies that Socrates is really a series of classes.

naturalism: in moral philosophy, any doctrine which states that ethical terms can be defined in terms of statements of fact: e.g. 'That is morally good which produces the greatest happiness of the greatest number.'

naturalistic fallacy: a term introduced into moral philosophy by G.E. Moore. Moore argued that it is fallacious to say, 'Being good means having the natural property P,' because one can grant that something has the natural property P and still ask, 'But is it good?' The term 'naturalistic fallacy' has also been used to refer to what many philosophers regard as fallacious attempts to derive moral judgements about what *ought* to be the case from statements about what *is* the case.

necessary and sufficient conditions: the necessary conditions of some event or state of affairs S are those conditions without which S would not occur or be the case. For example, it is a necessary condition of X's being a husband that X be married. But being married is not a *sufficient* condition of being a husband, since one may be married and not be a husband. A sufficient condition of being a husband would be being a married man; for from X's being a married man it follows that X is a husband.

neutral monism: *see* 'monism'.

nominalism: a theory about the nature of universal terms (*see* 'universals'). The nominalist rejects the view that universal terms, such as 'triangle', stand for entities ('universals') which either exist in reality or which have an existence as concepts. For the nominalist, universal terms are just words which are applied to a number of things.

non-contradiction, principle of: *see* 'contradiction, principle of'.

normative ethics: a branch of moral philosophy. Unlike meta-ethics (*q.v.*), which is restricted to the analysis of moral terms (such as 'right' and 'good'), normative ethics tries to provide a rational basis for judgements about what is right or good.

object language: *see* 'metalanguage'.

observation statement: a statement which records an actual or possible observation.

Ockham's razor: a maxim usually expressed in the form 'Entia non sunt multiplicanda praeter necessitatem' – 'Entities are not to be multiplied beyond what is necessary.' The maxim, which is ascribed to the medieval English philosopher William of Ockham (*c.* 1285–1318) can be illustrated by the theory of perception known as 'phenomenalism' (*q.v.*). If, as the theory states, everything that can be said about a physical thing can be said in terms of appearances, then there is no need to postulate physical things as well as appearances.

ontological argument: a term applied to certain arguments for the existence of God which have in common the fact that they take as their premiss a definition of God. (a) One form of the argument starts from a definition of God as the most perfect being; it then states that existence is a perfection, therefore the most perfect being must be thought of as existing, and must therefore exist. (b) Another form of the argument starts from the definition of God as a necessary being, i.e. a being whose essence involves existence. Now, to say that the essence of a being involves existence is to say that that being must be thought of as existing; therefore a necessary being must exist.

ontology: (a) a branch of metaphysics (*q.v.*) which is concerned with the study of pure being, i.e. being in its most abstract aspects; (b) the assumptions about what exists that underlie any conceptual scheme or theory. So a philosopher's ontology consists of the views that he holds about what there is.

opacity and transparency, referential: Leibniz' law (*q.v.*) is not universally applicable. For example, 'Cicero' and 'Tully' have the same reference (cf. 'sense and reference'), in that they are two names for the same man. But suppose that someone, X, does not know this: then it might be true (a) that Cicero is believed by X to have denounced Catiline, and (b) that Tully is believed by X not to have denounced Catiline. In other words, although Cicero and Tully are the same man, Cicero does *not* appear to have every property that Tully has, and conversely – contrary to Leibniz' law. It is usual to call '. . . is believed by X to have denounced Catiline' the 'context' of the use of the term 'Cicero'; in the case considered, the context is said to be 'referentially opaque'. In cases in which Leibniz' law is satisfied, the context is said to be 'referentially transparent'. Referential opacity and transparency are specific forms of a wider distinction between 'extensional occurrence' (which includes referential transparency) and 'intensional occurrence' (which includes referential opacity). This wider distinction covers not only singular terms such as 'Cicero' and 'Tully', but also predicates and propositions.

open texture: a word used to describe propositions which (a) do not entail (*q.v.*) a precise set of observation statements (*q.v.*) and (b) are not entailed by a precise set of observation statements. It is argued that propositions about material objects have open texture.

operationalism: a theory of the nature of scientific concepts, which states that such a concept is no more than a set of operations. E.g. the concept of length is simply the set of operations by which length is determined.

organic theory of the state: a holistic view (cf. 'holism' (a)) of the nature of the state; it compares the state to an organism, in that each is more than the sum of its parts.

paradigm: a term given a technical sense by Thomas Kuhn, and used in the philosophy of science. In this sense, a paradigm may be either (a) a whole set of beliefs or methods shared by a group of scientists or (b) concrete solutions of problems which are used as examples, and as such can serve as a basis for the solution of other scientific problems.

paradigm case argument: an argument for the truth of certain assertions, based on the fact that certain words have a clear and unequivocal application in certain (paradigm) cases. For example, we learn the meaning of the words 'free action' through their application to paradigm cases of free action – e.g. a child sharing its sweets with another, without compulsion of any kind. Now unless there really are free actions (the argument runs) the words 'free action' have no meaning; but they do have meaning, as is clear from their use in paradigm cases, therefore there are free actions.

parallelism, psycho-physical: a theory of the relations between mind and body. It asserts that mental and physical events are quite independent of each other, but that for any mental event there is a corresponding physical event, and conversely.

performative utterance: a term coined by J.L. Austin. It refers to utterances by which a speaker does not so much *say* something (these would be called 'constative utterances') as *do* something. For example, in saying 'I promise' I thereby perform the act of promising, provided that certain specifiable conditions hold – e.g. that I intend to do that which I promise to do, and believe it feasible. The term 'performative utterance' is still used, though Austin came to regard such utterances as special cases of his wider theory of illocutionary force (cf. 'force of an utterance').

perlocutionary: *see* 'force of an utterance'.

phenomenalism: a philosophical theory of perception. There are two main types of the theory, which may be termed 'ontological' and 'linguistic' respectively. The first type states that a material thing just *is* a class of actual or possible sense-data (*q.v.*). The second states that *propositions about* material things can be reduced to propositions about actual or possible sense-data.

phrastic and neustic: terms invented by R.M. Hare to clarify the logic of imperatives. Compare the sentences (1) 'You are going to open the window' and (2) 'Open the window.' Both are about the same thing, your opening the window in the immediate future. Hare argues that this fact can be brought out by recasting the sentences as: (1a) 'Your opening the window in the immediate future, yes' and (2a) 'Your opening the window in the immediate future, please.' In (1a) and (2a), the phrase preceding the comma is called the 'phrastic' (from a Greek word meaning to point out or indicate); the word following the comma is called the 'neustic' (from a Greek word meaning to nod assent).

physicalism: a term sometimes used in a wide sense to refer to every philosophical theory which asserts that all mental states and processes can be described in purely physical terms. In this sense, behaviourism (*q.v.*) is a form of physicalism. However, the term is sometimes used in a narrower sense to refer to what is also called 'the mind–brain identity theory'. This theory, unlike philosophical behaviourism, is not based on an analysis of the meaning of words. Rather, it says that mental states are physical states – more exactly, states of the brain or central nervous system – in the way in which lightning is an electrical discharge. That is, it declares that the identity of mind and brain is a matter of fact, established by (or at any rate establishable by) scientific investigation.

possible worlds: a term used in recent modal logic (cf. 'modality') and derived from Leibniz, who distinguished between the actual world that God created and possible worlds that God could have created. Some modern philosophers regard possible worlds as extra-linguistic entities; others, whilst recognising that the concept of possible worlds is a useful tool for investigating problems about possibility and necessity, deny that such worlds have a real existence.

pragmatics: *see* 'semiotics'.

pragmatism: a term which usually refers to a theory of truth, according to which a belief is true if it 'works'. (What this word means is explained by different pragmatists in different ways.) There is also a pragmatist theory of meaning, which states that the meaning of a word consists of those of its effects that have, or might have, bearings on human practice.

predicate: in a broad sense, that which is ascribed to an individual or a class. So if one says, 'This tennis-player is successful' or 'This team is successful,' one predicates success of the tennis-player or of the team. Many philosophers distinguish between predicates and relations; a predicate is ascribed to an individual or class, whereas a relation holds between individuals or classes. For example, 'London is large' would be called a subject–predicate proposition, and 'London is larger than Birmingham' would be called a relational proposition. But some philosophers would prefer to say that 'large' is a 'one-place' predicate, and 'larger than' a 'many-place' (more specifically, a 'two-place') predicate.

premiss (plural 'premises' or 'premisses'): the proposition or propositions from which the conclusion of an argument follows. The term is used, for example, to refer to the first two propositions of the three that constitute a syllogism (*q.v.*).

prescriptivism: a meta-ethical theory (cf. 'meta-ethics') which says that moral judgements are not factual propositions, but prescribe what is to be done. That is, they function as imperatives rather than as descriptions.

presupposition: suppose that someone says, 'All John's children have red hair.' Some philosophers would say that this 'presupposes' that John has children, in the sense that if he does not, the utterance is neither true nor false. Other philosophers take the view that such an utterance would be false, in that John's having children is a 'conversational implicature' of what is said (*see* 'implicature, conversational').

prima facie obligation: a term used in moral philosophy to mean an action which is morally obligatory unless overruled by a stronger obligation. For example, some would say that one has a *prima facie* obligation to tell the truth, in that truth-telling is obligatory unless overruled by a stronger obligation – e.g. the obligation to save life.

primary and secondary qualities: these terms express a distinction drawn by some philosophers between (a) the qualities which a physical object really has (its 'primary qualities') and (b) the qualities which it does not really have, but is perceived as having, and which can be scientifically explained in terms of the primary qualities (its 'secondary qualities'). Examples of primary qualities are extension and solidity; examples of secondary qualities are colour and sound.

private language: as philosophers use the term, a private language is one which is of necessity intelligible only to its user, in that the words which belong to it refer to experiences which only the user can have. Wittgensteinians argue that the idea of such a private language is incoherent. A language of this kind is to be distinguished from a language which (like that of some small children) is contingently private. By this is meant a language which refers to physical objects and which, although peculiar to the speaker, is such that others (e.g. the child's parents) can come to understand it.

privileged access: a term coined by Gilbert Ryle, referring to claims made about one's knowledge of one's own states of mind and mental acts. Such knowledge, it is claimed, is both infallible and peculiar to the knower. Not only can I not be wrong about my own mental states and acts, but I alone am in the position of being able to know for certain what they are.

problematic: *see* 'modality'.

proposition: that which is true or false; that which is believed or disbelieved, doubted or affirmed, etc. Many philosophers distinguish between a proposition and the sentence which expresses it, the point being that the same true or untrue thing (the proposition) can be expressed by the use of different sentences in the same language, and can also be expressed in different languages.

propositional attitudes: if one says that X knows, believes, hopes, fears, desires ... that such and such, one is speaking of X's 'propositional attitudes', in that what X knows, believes, etc. is a proposition.

qualia (singular 'quale'): a term used to refer to the sensible qualities that a thing presents to us, understanding this to mean the qualities which we sense it as having. So Nelson Goodman, for example, speaks of 'the colour quale presented by a (red) apple now'.

quantifier: universal propositions (propositions about *all* such and such) and particular propositions (propositions about *some* such and such) are represented in modern logic by symbols known as 'quantifiers'. The universal quantifier – i.e. (x) or $\forall x$ – may be read as 'For any x'; the existential quantifier – i.e. $(\exists x)$ – may be read as 'For some x' or 'For at least one x'. 'All cats have claws' would be read as 'For any x, if x is a cat, then x has claws'; 'Some cats are black' would be read as 'For some x, x is a cat and x is black.'

rationalism: (a) in the narrow sense, the view that we can obtain knowledge about the nature of what exists by the mere use of reason; (b) in a broad sense, 'rationalism' means a confidence in reason. In this sense, reason may be opposed either (i) to superstition, or (ii) to experience. A philosopher may be a rationalist in sense (ii) – that is, he may insist that our reason contributes in an important way to our knowledge of things – without being a rationalist in sense (a).

raven paradox: *see* 'confirmation, paradox of'.

realism: (a) in the theory of meaning, the view that universals ($q.v.$) have a real existence; (b) in the philosophy of perception, the view that the nature and existence of physical things do not depend on perception.

reductionism: a 'reductionist' view employs Ockham's razor (*q.v.*) to reduce the number of basic entities that are recognised in people's thoughts about the world. For example, a philosopher might argue that propositions about societies can be 'reduced' to propositions about the individuals who constitute them. This would be to claim that everything that can be said about societies can be said, without any loss of meaning, about individuals; in other words, that societies have no existence over and above the individuals who make them up. This thesis has also been expressed by saying that societies are 'logical constructions' out of individuals.

reference: *see* 'sense and reference'.

representative theory of perception (also termed 'representationalism' or 'representationism'): a theory which states that we do not perceive physical objects directly; we perceive them through the medium of entities that represent them, such as ideas or sense-data (*q.v.*).

rigid designator: a term introduced by Saul Kripke. A designator is 'rigid' if it designates the same object in every possible world (*q.v.*). For example, 'square of 3' is a rigid designator, since in any possible world it designates the number 9. But 'the number of the planets' is not a rigid designator; for though there are nine planets, there are possible worlds in which the number of planets is greater or less than nine. Some philosophers argue that proper names are rigid designators.

satisfaction: a sentential function (*q.v.*) such as 'x is red' is satisfied by anything that is red; e.g. this pillar box. This is to say that if the variable (*q.v.*) x is replaced by the words 'This pillar box', the resultant sentence is true.

secondary qualities: *see* 'primary and secondary qualities'.

semantics: *see* 'semiotics'.

semiotics: the theory of signs. It is commonly divided into (1) syntactics, the study of the grammar and syntax of a language; (2) semantics, the study of meaning; and (3) pragmatics, the study of the purposes and effects of language.

sense and reference: these terms render a distinction drawn by the German philosopher and logician Frege. The 'sense' (*Sinn*) of an expression is its meaning, as opposed to that which the expression names, its 'reference' (*Bedeutung*). Expressions can have different meanings, but the same reference: e.g. 'the Morning Star' does not mean the same as 'the Evening Star', but both have the same reference, the planet Venus. (Cf. 'connotation and denotation'.)

sense-data: the term 'sense-datum' (plural 'sense-data') means that of which we are immediately and infallibly aware in perception. It is also asserted that sense-data are necessarily private to the percipient; i.e. one person *cannot have* another person's sense-data.

sentential function (or 'open sentence'): an expression containing one or more free variables (cf. 'variables'). It is not so much a sentence as a framework for sentences, becoming a sentence when each variable is replaced by one of its substituends (*see* 'variable'). E.g. '*x* is white' is a sentential function, which becomes a sentence when the variable '*x*' is replaced by (e.g.) 'snow'. The term 'sentential function' has largely replaced the older term 'propositional function'.

species: *see* 'genus and species'.

speech act: an act of saying something, in the full sense of the word 'say'. A person who says to another, 'You're a scoundrel,' meaning what he says and being in a position to make the remark, performs a speech act. A parrot which has been trained to produce the corresponding sounds does not.

statement: this term is used by some philosophers instead of the word 'proposition' (*q.v.*).

subject: that about which something is said. For example, in 'This tennis-player is successful,' this tennis player (the individual) is the subject. 'Subject' is also used to mean the subject *term*, e.g. (in the sentence just quoted) the words 'This tennis-player' rather than the person.

sufficient condition: *see* 'necessary and sufficient conditions'.

supererogation: a term used in moral philosophy to refer to the doing of more than one's duty requires. Such actions are typical of the heroic individual or the saint.

syllogism: a form of deductive argument (*see* 'deduction') in which one proposition, the 'conclusion', is inferred from two other propositions, the 'premisses'. For example: 'All Greeks are rational, all Athenians are Greeks, therefore all Athenians are rational.' A syllogism has three and only three terms (*q.v.*); the subject term and the predicate term of the conclusion are called the 'minor term' and 'major term' respectively; the other term, which occurs only in the premisses, is called the 'middle term'. The forms of a valid syllogism were first studied systematically by Aristotle, and the theory of the syllogism forms a large part of what is termed 'traditional logic'.

symptom: *see* 'criterion'.

syntactics: *see* 'semiotics'.

synthetic propositions: *see* 'analytic propositions'.

tautology: in logic, a proposition which is always true, no matter what the truth-values (*q.v.*) of its constituent propositions may be. So, for example, 'Either it is raining or it is not raining' is a tautology.

teleological ethics: this term may mean (a) a view of ethics which relates moral conduct to the fulfilment of the essential nature of human beings; or (b) a view of ethics which is opposed to deontology (*q.v.*), in that it sees the moral goodness or badness of an action as lying in its consequences. *See also* 'consequentialism' and 'teleology'.

teleology: having to do with an end (Greek *telos*). A distinction may be drawn between what is termed (a) internal teleology and (b) external teleology. (a) To explain X's acts in terms of internal teleology is to explain them in terms of X's own end (which need not, in the view of some philosophers, be an end which is consciously adopted). (b) To explain X's acts in terms of external teleology is to explain them in terms of the ends of some being other than X. So, for example, one explains the working of a mechanism by saying what it is *for* – i.e. what are the purposes which it serves.

term: this word is often used to refer to any word or phrase which has a definite sense: e.g. 'scientific term', 'technical term'. In traditional logic, a term is one of the component parts of a proposition. In a subject–predicate proposition, two terms are recognised (cf. 'subject' and 'predicate'); relational propositions contain more than two terms.

theory-laden: a word or phrase is 'theory-laden' if a theory enters into its meaning. For example, the terms 'kinetic energy' and 'potential energy' are theory-laden, the theory in question forming part of the science of mechanics.

token/type ambiguity: this ambiguity arises when the same word is used to refer (1) to a class of resembling entities and (2) to an individual member of that class. For example, the word 'sentence' is ambiguous in this way. Suppose that a computer prints the same sentence 25 times on a page: how many sentences are there on the page? One could answer 'Twenty-five' (taking 'sentence' to refer to tokens) or 'One' (taking 'sentence' to refer to types).

topic neutral: consider a deductive argument, such as 'All cats hunt mice, some pets are cats, therefore some pets hunt mice.' The validity (*q.v.*) of this argument does not depend on its topic; one would not check its soundness by investigating the cat-world. Rather, its validity depends on the use made of the expressions 'all' and 'some'. Such expressions are therefore called 'topic-neutral'. Topic neutrality is a feature of the logical constants (*q.v.*).

translation, radical: translation in which the translator is assumed to have a minimum of information. He is assumed to have no dictionary of the language in question, and no bilingual dictionaries or bilingual speakers; all that he has to help him are native speakers of the language, and their behaviour. According to Quine, consideration of translations made in these circumstances shows that all translation is 'indeterminate', in that the empirical evidence brought to support the translation of one word or phrase can with equal justification be made to support another translation.

transparency: *see* 'opacity and transparency, referential'.

truth-function: a proposition is a truth function if, and only if, its truth or falsity is determined by the truth or falsity of its component propositions. For example, to say that 'p and q' is a truth function is to say that, once we can answer the questions (1) 'Is p true?' (2) 'Is q true?' we are in a position to answer the question 'Is "p and q" true?'

truth-value: as a rule, the possible 'truth-values' of a proposition are truth or falsity. Logics which recognise only these two truth-values are termed 'two-valued logics'; in 'multi-valued logics' more than two truth-values are recognised.

type: *see* 'token/type ambiguity'.

type fallacy: a term used to refer to fallacies of a kind first explored by Bertrand Russell. The fallacies spring from the supposition that one can meaningfully say that a class is, or again is not, a member of itself. Russell showed that this supposition generates contradictions. To avoid such contradictions, Russell argued, we have to recognise that although it makes sense to say that a class has or does not have individuals as members, it makes no sense to say that a class has, or does not have, itself as a member. The point of the term 'type' is that individuals are held to be of a *lower type* than a class; a 'type-fallacy' occurs when this logical hierarchy is disregarded.

unfulfilled conditionals: *see* 'counterfactual conditionals'.

uniformity of nature, principle of: this may be formulated as: whatever happens once in certain circumstances will happen again, whenever circumstances recur which are similar in all relevant respects. The principle plays a part in discussions of the problem of induction (cf. 'induction').

universalisability: a thesis about the distinguishing feature of moral judgements. It asserts that if, for example, I say that it is morally right for a certain person to perform a certain action on a certain occasion, then I must take the same view of any other action that resembles it in relevant respects. Failure to take such a view would be a mark of inconsistency on my part.

universals: it has been argued that universal terms, such as 'triangle', can have meaning only if there exist in some way entities which are called 'universals', e.g. the triangle as such, or triangularity. See also 'conceptualism', 'nominalism' and 'realism (a)'.

utilitarianism: an important ethical theory, of which there are several versions. All of these agree that the rightness or wrongness of actions has to be judged by reference to their *utility* – that is, by whether they do or do not promote the achievement of some ultimate good. Utilitarianism is therefore a form of consequentialism (*q.v.*); its distinguishing feature is the fact that it regards the ultimate good as involving a maximisation of what may broadly be called 'welfare'. Differet utilitarian theories take different views about what it is that is to be maximised. For the classical utilitarians of the late eighteenth and the nineteenth centuries, such as Bentham and J.S. Mill, the ultimate good was the greatest happiness of the greatest number. Bentham and Mill agreed that happiness was to be defined in terms of 'pleasure, and the absence of pain' (Mill), though Mill introduced a complication by recognising a difference of quality in pleasures. Modern utilitarians have put forward other views of the ultimate good, e.g. that it is to be understood in terms of a maximal satisfaction of agents' interests, or of a maximisation of the range of human choices.

Modern theorists also distinguish between 'act utilitarianism' and 'rule utilitarianism'. For the act utilitarian, the question that the moral agent has to ask is simply, 'What will be the consequences of this action?' The rule utilitarian says that the question is a different one: namely, 'What would be the result if everyone did this kind of thing?' Here, the consequences involved are not the consequences of one particular action; they are the consequences of following a universal rule.

validity: the term 'validity' applies to arguments; an argument is called 'valid' if its conclusion follows from its premises (*q.v.*). An argument is said to be 'deductively valid' if it is not possible for the premises to be true and the conclusion false. Many philosophers, indeed, wish to restrict the terms 'valid' and 'invalid' to deductive arguments. Such philosophers do not necessarily assert that there are really no arguments other than deductive arguments; but they say that non–deductive arguments (e.g. those involving induction, *q.v.*) are better called 'sound' or 'unsound' rather than 'valid' or 'invalid'.

It is important to distinguish between the validity of an argument and the truth of the proposition which is its conclusion. One can argue validly for a conclusion which is false: e.g. 'All cats hunt mice, all frogs are cats, therefore all frogs hunt mice.' But note that *if* the first two propositions (the 'premises') were true, then the conclusion would necessarily be true as well.

variable: in the sentential function (*q.v.*) '*x* is white', '*x*' is what is termed a 'variable'; it can be regarded as holding open a place into which a noun or noun phrase can meaningfully enter. An expression which can be substituted for a variable is called a 'substituend' of the variable; e.g. in the example just given, 'snow'. Snow itself (the stuff, not the word) would be called a 'value' of the variable. Variables may be either 'free' or 'bound'. In the example, '*x*' is a free variable; but if we were to say (e.g.) 'For some *x*, *x* is white,' then the '*x*' which occurs in '*x* is white' would be 'bound' by the quantifier (*q.v.*) 'For some *x*'.

verifiability, principle of: this term has two senses. (a) It can refer to a *criterion* of meaning; this states that a proposition is factually significant if, and only if, it can be verified in principle. (b) The term can also refer to a theory of the nature of meaning; this states that the meaning of a proposition *is* the method of verifying it.

Philosophy, 1600–1960: A Chronological Survey

This survey tries to place philosophy within its general cultural context by comparing its history with that of the arts and sciences. (Political history and the history of technology have been excluded, on the grounds that an attempt to include them would lead to overloading.) The survey begins when modern philosophy began, in the seventeenth century. It ends in the year 1960, as it takes roughly a generation before it becomes clear which works are of lasting importance. Ancient philosophy was excluded from the survey because of the difficulty of establishing with any precision when the works of the ancient Greek philosophers were written; medieval philosophy has been omitted because little reference is made to it in the course of the encyclopaedia.

Unless otherwise specified, the dates assigned to books or articles are the dates of publication, and the dates assigned to musical works are those of first performance. The titles of works not written in English have been translated, unless they are better known in their original form.

G.H.R.P.

Philosophy		The arts and sciences	
1600		1600	William Gilbert, *De magnete*
1605	Francis Bacon, *The advancement of learning*	1605	Cervantes, *Don Quixote*, Part I (Part II, 1615)
1610		1610	Galileo, *The sidereal messenger* (a report of his telescopic observations)

909

Philosophy		The arts and sciences	
1611		1611	'Authorised Version' of the Bible
1612	Arnauld *b.*	1612	
1616		1616	Shakespeare *d.*
1620	Francis Bacon, *Novum organum*	1620	
1623	Francis Bacon, *De augmentis scientiarum*	1623	First Folio edition of Shakespeare's plays
1626	Bacon *d.*	1626	
1628	(?) Descartes' *Regulae ad directionem ingenii* written	1628	Harvey, *Concerning the motion of the heart and blood in animals*
1632	Spinoza and Locke *b.*	1632	Galileo, *Dialogue on the two chief world systems* Rembrandt, *Dr Tulp's Anatomy Lesson*
1633		1633	Galileo condemned by the Inquisition for upholding the Copernican theory
1634		1634	Académie Française established
1637	Descartes, *Discourse on method*	1637	Milton's *Lycidas* written
1638	Malebranche *b.*	1638	Galileo, *Discourse on two new sciences*
1641	Descartes, *Meditations* (with *Objections and replies*)	1641	
1642	Hobbes, *De cive*	1642	Rembrandt, *Night Watch* Monteverdi, *L'Incoronazione di Poppea*
1644	Descartes, *Principles of philosophy*	1644	Milton, *Areopagitica*
1646	Leibniz *b.*	1646	
1650	Descartes *d.*	1650	
1651	Hobbes, *Leviathan*	1651	Harvey, *On the generation of animals*
1660		1660	Arnauld and Lancelot, *Grammaire générale et raisonée*

Philosophy		The arts and sciences	
1661		1661	Boyle, *The sceptical chymist*
1662	Arnauld and Nicole, *La logique ou l'art de penser* ('The Port Royal Logic')	1662	Royal Society founded
1665		1665	Newton discovers the differential and integral calculus Hooke, *Micrographia*
1666		1666	Académie Royale des Sciences founded Molière, *Le misanthrope*
1667		1667	Milton, *Paradise lost*
1670	Spinoza, *Tractatus theologico-politicus*	1670	Molière, *Le bourgeois gentilhomme*
1671	(Third Earl of) Shaftesbury *b.*	1671	
1674–5	Malebranche, *De la recherche de la vérité*	1674	Lully, *Alceste*
1675		1675	Leibniz discovers (independently of Newton) the differential and integral calculus
1677	Spinoza *d.* Spinoza, *Ethics*	1677	Racine, *Phèdre*
1678		1678	Huygens' *Treatise on light* written Bunyan, *The pilgrim's progress* (Part II, 1684)
1679	Hobbes *d.*	1679	
1683	Arnauld, *Des vraies et des fausses idées*	1683	
1685	Berkeley *b.*	1685	
1686	Leibniz' *Discourse on metaphysics* written	1686	
1687		1687	Newton, *Philosophiae naturalis principia mathematica*
1690	Locke, *Essay concerning human understanding* and *Two treatises of civil government*	1690	

Philosophy		The arts and sciences	
1692	Joseph Butler *b*.	1692	
1694	Hutcheson *b*.	1694	
	Arnauld *d*.		
1695	Leibniz, *New system*	1695	Bayle, *Dictionnaire historique et critique* (vol. II, 1697)
1700		1700	Berlin Academy of Sciences founded
1703–5	Leibniz' *New essays on the human understanding* written	1703	
1704	Locke *d*.	1704	Newton, *Opticks* Swift, *The battle of the books*
1709	Berkeley, *Essay towards a new theory of vision*	1709	
1710	Berkeley, *Treatise concerning the principles of human knowledge* Leibniz, *Theodicy*	1710	
1711	Hume *b*. Shaftesbury, *Characteristics*	1711	Pope, *Essay on criticism* Handel, *Rinaldo*
1712	Rousseau *b*.	1712	
1713	Berkeley, *Dialogues between Hylas and Philonous* Shaftesbury *d*.	1713	
1714	Leibniz' *Monadology* written	1714	
1715	Malebranche *d*.	1715	
1716	Leibniz *d*.	1716	
1717	Publication of correspondence between Leibniz and Clarke	1717	Watteau, *Embarquement pour Cythère*
1719		1719	Defoe, *Robinson Crusoe*
1723	Richard Price *b*.	1723	Bach, *St John Passion*
1724	Kant *b*.	1724	
1725	Hutcheson, *An inquiry into the original of our ideas of beauty and virtue*	1725	
1726	Butler, *Fifteen sermons*	1726	Swift, *Gulliver's travels*
1728		1728	Gay, *The Beggar's Opera*

Philosophy		The arts and sciences	
1729		1729	Bach, *St Matthew Passion*
1732	Berkeley, *Alciphron*	1732	
1733		1733–4	Pope, *Essay on man*
		1733–5	Hogarth, *A Rake's Progress*
1736	Butler, *The analogy of religion*	1736	
1739–40	Hume, *A treatise of human nature*	1739	
1742		1742	Handel, *Messiah*
1746	Hutcheson *d.*	1746	
1748	Hume, *Philosophical essays* (later entitled *Enquiry*) *concerning human understanding* Bentham *b.*	1748	Smollett, *Roderick Random* Montesquieu, *L'esprit des lois*
1749		1749	Fielding, *Tom Jones*
1751	Hume, *An enquiry concerning the principles of morals*	1751–76	Diderot and D'Alembert (eds), *L'encyclopédie*
1752	Butler *d.*	1752	
1753	Berkeley *d.*	1753	
1755		1755	Johnson, *Dictionary of the English language*
1756	Price, *A review of the principal questions in morals*	1756	
1759		1759	Voltaire, *Candide*
1762	Rousseau, *Social contract*	1762	Gluck, *Orfeo*
1765	Leibniz' *New essays* first published	1765	
1768		1768–71	*Encyclopaedia Britannica*, 1st edn
1770	Hegel *b.*	1770	
1771		1771	Smollett, *Humphrey Clinker*
1774		1774	Goethe, *The sorrows of young Werther*
1776	Hume *d.* Bentham, *Fragment on government*	1776	Adam Smith, *The wealth of nations*
		1776–88	Gibbon, *The decline and fall of the Roman Empire*
1778	Rousseau *d.*	1778	

	Philosophy		The arts and sciences
1779	Hume, *Dialogues concerning natural religion*	1779	
1781	Kant, *Critique of pure reason* (1st edn)	1781	
1782		1782	Mozart, *Il Seraglio*
1783	Kant, *Prolegomena to any future metaphysic*	1783	
1785	Kant, *Groundwork of the metaphysic of morals*	1785	
1786		1786	Mozart, *The Marriage of Figaro*
1788	Kant, *Critique of practical reason* Schopenhauer *b.*	1788	
1789	Bentham, *Introduction to the principles of morals and legislation*	1789	Lavoisier, *Traité élémentaire de chimie*
1790	Kant, *Critique of judgement*	1790	Burke, *Reflections on the Revolution in France*
1791	Price *d.*	1791	Mozart, *The Magic Flute* Boswell, *Life of Johnson*
1793	Kant, *Religion within the boundaries of pure reason*	1793	
1795	Schiller, *On the aesthetic education of man*	1795–6	Goethe, *Wilhelm Meister's apprenticeship*
1796		1796	Laplace, *Système du monde*
1798		1798	Wordsworth and Coleridge, *Lyrical ballads* Haydn, *The Creation*
1800		1800	Beethoven, First Symphony
1804	Kant *d.*	1804	
1805		1805	Beethoven, *Fidelio* (1st version)
1806	J.S. Mill *b.*	1806	
1807	Hegel, *Phenomenology of spirit*	1807	Beethoven, Fourth Symphony
1808		1808	Dalton, *A new system of chemical philosophy* Goethe, *Faust*, Part I
1809		1809	Goethe, *Elective affinities*

	Philosophy		**The arts and sciences**
1811		1811	Jane Austen, *Sense and sensibility*
1812	Hegel, *Science of logic* (vol. II, 1816)	1812	
1814		1814	Scott, *Waverley* Laplace, *A philosophical essay on probabilities*
1816		1816	Coleridge, *Kubla Khan*
1817	Hegel, *Encyclopaedia of the philosophical sciences* (1st edn)	1817	Ricardo, *Principles of political economy*
1819	Schopenhauer, *The world as will and representation*	1819	Byron, *Don Juan*, Cantos I and II
1821	Hegel, *Philosophy of right*	1821	Constable, *The Haywain*
1830		1830–42	Comte, *Philosophie positive*
1831	Hegel *d.*	1831	Hugo, *Notre Dame de Paris*
1832	Bentham *d.*	1832	Goethe, *Faust*, Part II
1833	Dilthey *b.*	1833	
1835		1835–6	D.F. Strauss, *The life of Jesus critically examined*
1836		1836–7	Dickens, *Pickwick papers*
1837		1837–43	Balzac, *Illusions perdues*
1838	Sidgwick *b.*	1838	
1839	C.S. Peirce *b.*	1839	
1842	William James *b.*	1842	
1843	J.S. Mill, *A system of logic*	1843	
1844	Nietzsche *b.*	1844	Turner, *Rain, Steam and Speed*
1846	F.H. Bradley *b.*	1846	Adams and Leverrier discover the planet Neptune
1847		1847	Boole, *The mathematical analysis of logic* Helmholtz, *On the conservation of force*
1848	Frege *b.*	1848	Marx and Engels, *The Communist Manifesto*
1856		1856	Flaubert, *Madame Bovary*
1859	J.S. Mill, *On liberty* Husserl *b.*	1859	Darwin, *The origin of species*
1860	Schopenhauer *d.*	1860	

Philosophy		The arts and sciences	
1861	J.S. Mill, *Utilitarianism*	1861	
1863		1863	Manet, *Déjeuner sur l'herbe*
1865		1865	Wagner, *Tristan and Isolde*
1866		1866	Dostoevsky, *Crime and punishment*
1867		1867	Marx, *Capital*, vol. I
1868		1868–9	Tolstoy, *War and peace*
1871		1871	Darwin, *The descent of man*
		1871–2	George Eliot, *Middlemarch*
1872	Bertrand Russell *b.*	1872	
1873	J.S. Mill *d.* G.E. Moore *b.*	1873	Clerk Maxwell, *A treatise on electricity and magnetism*
1874	Sidgwick, *Methods of ethics*	1874	
1875		1875–7	Tolstoy, *Anna Karenina*
1876	James, *The will to believe*	1876	Wagner's *Ring* cycle first performed at Bayreuth Brahms, First Symphony
1877	Peirce, 'The fixation of belief'	1877	Rodin, *The Bronze Age*
1878	Peirce, 'How to make our ideas clear'	1878	
1882		1882	Wagner, *Parsifal*
1883	Dilthey, *Introduction to the human studies*	1883–4	Seurat, *Bathers, Asnières*
1883–5	Nietzsche, *Thus spake Zarathustra*		
1884	Frege, *The foundations of arithmetic*	1884	
1887		1887	Hertz proves the existence of electromagnetic waves Verdi, *Otello*
1888		1888	Van Gogh, *Night Café*
1889	Wittgenstein *b.*	1889	
1891	Carnap *b.*	1891	
1892	Frege, 'On sense and reference'	1892	

Philosophy		The arts and sciences	
1894		1894	Debussy, *Prélude à l'après-midi d'un faune*
1895		1895	Röntgen discovers X-rays
1896		1896	Cézanne, *Lake Annecy*
1897		1897	Thompson discovers the electron
			Durkheim, *Suicide*
1898		1898	Rodin's *Balzac* first exhibited
1899	Heidegger *b.*	1899	
1900	Nietzsche *d.*	1900	Planck states the quantum theory
	Sidgwick *d.*		
	Ryle *b.*		Freud, *The interpretation of dreams*
1902		1902	Debussy, *Pelléas et Mélisande*
		1902–3	Rutherford and Soddy offer an explanation of radioactivity
1903	Moore, *Principia ethica*	1903	
	Moore, 'The refutation of idealism'		
1904		1904	Freud, *The psychopathology of everyday life*
			Conrad, *Nostromo*
		1904–5	Max Weber, *The Protestant ethic and the spirit of capitalism*
1905	Peirce, 'What pragmatism is'	1905	Einstein states the special theory of relativity
	Russell, 'On denoting'		Richard Strauss, *Salome*
	Sartre *b.*		
1906		1906–7	Picasso, *Les Demoiselles d'Avignon*
1907	James, *Pragmatism*	1907	
1910	William James *d.*	1910–11	First Post-Impressionist Exhibition, London
1910–13	Russell and Whitehead, *Principia mathematica*		
1911	J.L. Austin *b.*	1911	Mahler, *Das Lied von der Erde*
	Dilthey *d.*		

Philosophy		The arts and sciences	
1912		1912	Schönberg, *Pierrot Lunaire*
1913	Husserl, *Ideas for a pure phenomenology*	1913	Bohr's theory of the atom
			J.B. Watson, 'Psychology as the behaviorist views it'
			Stravinsky, *The Rite of Spring*
		1913–27	Proust, *A la recherche du temps perdu*
1914	Russell, *Our knowledge of the external world*	1914	
	C.S. Peirce *d.*		
1916		1916	Einstein states the general theory of relativity
			Saussure, *Course in general linguistics*
		1916–23	Pareto, *Mind and society*
1918	Russell, lectures on *The philosophy of logical atomism*	1918	
1919		1919	Rutherford shows that nuclear changes can be produced deliberately
1922	Wittgenstein, *Tractatus logico-philosophicus* (English translation)	1922	T.S. Eliot, *The Waste Land*
			Joyce, *Ulysses*
1924	F.H. Bradley *d.*	1924	
1925	Frege *d.*	1925	Berg, *Wozzeck*
1927	Heidegger, *Being and time*	1927	Heisenberg states the principle of indeterminacy
			Hesse, *Steppenwolf*
1928	Carnap, *Der logische Aufbau der Welt*	1928	Brecht, *The Threepenny Opera*
1929		1929	vol. I of Pavlov's *Lectures on conditioned reflexes* translated into English (vol. II, 1941)
1931		1931	Gödel, *On formally undecidable sentences*

Philosophy		The arts and sciences	
1932		1932	Chadwick discovers the neutron
1934	Popper, *Logik der Forschung* ('The logic of scientific discovery')	1934	
1936	A.J. Ayer, *Language, truth and logic*	1936	Keynes, *General theory of employment, interest and money*
1937		1937	Picasso, *Guernica* Bartók, *Music for Strings, Percussion and Celesta*
1938	Husserl d.	1938	Sartre, *Nausea*
1939	Moore, 'Proof of an external world'	1939	Joyce, *Finnegans wake* Epstein, *Adam*
1943	Sartre, *Being and nothingness*	1943	Hesse, *The glass bead game*
		1943–4	Henry Moore, *Northampton Madonna*
1945	C.L. Stevenson, *Ethics and language*	1945	Orwell, *Animal Farm*
1946	Austin, 'Other minds'	1946	
1947		1947	Thomas Mann, *Doctor Faustus*
1949	Ryle, *The concept of mind*	1949	Messiaen, *Turangalîla Symphonie*
1951	Wittgenstein d. Quine, 'Two dogmas of empiricism'	1951	Stravinsky, *The Rake's Progress*
1952	R.M. Hare, *The language of morals*	1952	
1953	Wittgenstein, *Philosophical investigations*	1953	Crick and Watson construct a molecular model of DNA
1954		1954	William Golding, *The lord of the flies*
1955		1955	Beckett, *Waiting for Godot* Boulez, *Le Marteau sans Maître*
1956	Austin, 'A plea for excuses'	1956	
1957		1957	Chomsky, *Syntactic structures*

Philosophy		The arts and sciences	
1957		1957	Pasternak, *Doctor Zhivago*
1958	G.E. Moore *d.* Isaiah Berlin, 'Two concepts of liberty'	1958	Stockhausen, *Gruppen*
1959	P.F. Strawson, *Individuals*	1959	Grass, *The tin drum*
1960	J.L. Austin *d.* Quine, *Word and object*	1960	

Index
of
Names

(Names mentioned in the notes or bibliographies are indexed only when the reference is a substantial one.)

Index
of
Subjects

(Subjects mentioned in the notes or bibliographies are indexed only when the reference is a substantial one.)